THE SHAPING OF
TWENTIETH-CENTURY AMERICA

THE SHAPING OF TWENTIETH-CENTURY AMERICA

Interpretive Essays

SECOND EDITION

Selected and with commentary by

RICHARD M. ABRAMS
LAWRENCE W. LEVINE

University of California, Berkeley

LITTLE, BROWN AND COMPANY
Boston

PREFACE

As our title indicates, this collection of essays offers insights into those twentieth-century forces that have been primarily responsible for shaping our present United States. Our criterion for selection has been significance rather than comprehensiveness. A few of the authors delve back into American history before 1900 as they attempt to explain the genesis of more recent trends and events, so that on the whole this volume treats, in the perspective of both the recent and the more distant past, the changes that have helped to make the United States a richly heterogeneous nation as well as the changes that have helped to create the problems that currently confront all Americans.

Most of the articles in this volume appeared originally in scholarly books and journals, though a few have come from the more popularly circulating magazines. "The Failure of Progressivism," by co-editor Richard M. Abrams, is published here for the first time. In addition, breaking with our practice in the first edition, we have taken a whole chapter from each of three book-length monographs and a slightly abbreviated chapter from one other book. The decision to use chapters was dictated by their individual excellence, the importance of their subject matter, and their essentially self-contained, integral qualities. We have not pieced together excerpts from books or, except in two cases, abridged the selections in any way, because we still wish to maintain the original integrity of the authors' own work.

Since the first edition of this volume was published in 1965, a number of other collections on twentieth-century America have appeared. Our collection differs from these, of course, in its emphasis. But more important, in lengthy introductions to each article, we have attempted to provide a scholarly dialogue between ourselves and the authors of the essays. Since we have chosen articles that we believe have something important to say rather than those that we necessarily agree with, we have presumed to raise questions that remain unanswered, to amplify the author's arguments, and even to take issue with them whenever we thought it necessary and appropriate. Our introductions, therefore, are an integral part of this collection and are intended to expand its coverage and to increase its educational value. We hope they make it clear to all students that scholarship is a continuing quest and that whatever the excellence and probity of these articles, there may nevertheless be serious questions left unanswered.

In suggesting supplementary reading we have not attempted to be "exhaustive." We have stressed articles and books that we thought would prove most valuable to students desiring to learn more about a subject. These in turn will lead the interested student to additional useful bibliographical items. We have placed an asterisk (*) after the titles of books that we know are available in paperback editions.

To enhance the usefulness of this collection, we have divided it into six parts. Parts II through V are chronological and require no further explanation. Many important articles, however, defy any attempt at rigid chronological classification. Articles of this nature make up Part I, "Continuing Themes in Twentieth-Century America," and can be read with profit at almost any time during a course in recent American history. Since the writing of history no less than the making of history reflects the tenor of an age, in the last part of this volume, "The Historian and the Twentieth Century," we have included two interesting and provocative reviews of recent American historiography. The structure of a course and the interests of the teachers and students involved in it should readily determine the best use of these sections.

We are indebted to Susan Sherwin for her help in preparing this collection for publication and to the scholars and publishers who have given us permission to reprint the material that makes up the body of this volume. Finally, we wish to acknowledge with thanks the helpful comments of those who were kind enough to let us know their reactions to the first edition. They are too many to name here, but they will recognize some of the products of their suggestions.

Richard M. Abrams
Lawrence W. Levine

CONTENTS

vii

PART IV
THE AGE OF PERPETUAL CRISIS: WORLD WAR II AND ITS AFTERMATH

31

THE HISTORIAN AS "RADICAL"   710

PART I

CONTINUING THEMES IN TWENTIETH-CENTURY AMERICA

1

THE FARMERS' PROBLEMS:
THE SOCIAL AND INTELLECTUAL ROOTS

The following article is a survey of the transformation of farm life and farm attitudes over the course of American history. Written by Paul H. Johnstone, Senior Agricultural Historian for the Division of Farm Population and Rural Welfare in the United States Department of Agriculture, it has remained unjustly obscure because it is printed in the little-known *Yearbook of Agriculture* for 1940. Johnstone's treatment is unusual in that it avoids sentimentalizing the American farmers' "plight." It highlights instead their painful ambivalence toward conflicting values and ideals, an ambivalence that has made American farmers among the most persistently discontented groups in our society.

The urban-rural conflict has been a continuing theme in agricultural discontent. It may well have been the dominant issue in the elections of 1896 and 1928. It is the crux of the recent controversy over reapportionment of electoral districts. The political character of the conflict, however, has undergone sharp change. As late as 1896, the rural districts were the principal source of populist "radicalism." By 1928, farmers' discontents had begun showing up increasingly in the form of an ugly authoritarian militancy, and generally the political power of the farming community had become committed to the most conservative forces in American society. According to some of the recent literature on "status politics" [see D. Bell, ed., *The Radical Right* (paperback edition, 1964); and C. Vann Woodward, "The Populist Heritage and the Intellectuals," *American Scholar*, 20 (Winter 1959–60)], farmers' behavior in the last half-century would appear to reflect status anxieties even more than specific economic grievances. [Compare Michael Rogin, *The Intellectuals and McCarthy* (1968)].

Almost from the beginning, American farmers have lived with certain contradictions that have made it difficult for them to square their ideals with their predicament. Their modern "plight" is only an aggravated form of an early condition. Long before they became a minority segment of the population, farmers complained of political impotence. Long before their industry came to represent only a fractional part of the national product, their economic needs appeared neglected. Scornful of city ways and suspicious of city people, they came to emulate urban values and to anguish over their failure to measure up to city standards of elegance and success. Almost unique

3

in Western civilization for taking pride in farming as a way of life,
American farmers have been equally distinctive for regarding their
land as well as their produce as objects of commerce.

Many observers have made a special point of the farmers' loss of
their independence and the transformation of farming from a prideful
way of life to a mean way of making a living. Occupations other than
farming were "casualties" of industrialism in this respect. [See, e.g.,
J. R. Commons, "American Shoemakers, 1648–1895," *Quarterly
Journal of Economics* (Fall 1909). R. Hofstadter, *The Age of Reform*
(1955), pp. 155–163, makes a similar point about lawyers.] But the
farming community and its partisans among reformers and intellectuals have lamented the development most persistently and with
greater political consequence. Especially in the last half-century since
agriculture has ceased to represent the major sector of the American
economy, farm spokesmen have pressed their claims for governmental
favor largely on the grounds of farming's value to society as a source
of stability and virtue. [See A. W. Griswold, *Farming and Democracy*
(1948).]

The irony is that however highly farmers may have placed self-
sufficiency among the values they cherished, most of the evidence of
agricultural history argues that American farmers, particularly those
of the midwest and west, have been among the least independent
groups in the society; and moreover, their dependency has been
largely a function of their own ambitions. They have been prey, it is
true, to the vagaries of government land policy. They have had to
draw capital from bankers hundreds of miles away. And the value
of their assets has often depended more directly upon the conditions
in France, Russia, and India than it has on their own enterprise or
lack of it. Such facts serve to emphasize their role as victims. But it
is also essential to understand how readily American farmers were
seduced from "farming as a way of life" for the greater prizes of
specialization, commerce, and speculation. As Thorstein Veblen once
cracked, the American farmer has always been "a cultivator of the
main chance as well as of the soil."

The literature on these subjects is voluminous. Among the journal
articles, the following stand out: C. F. Emerick, "An Analysis of
Agricultural Discontent in the United States," *Political Science
Quarterly*, 11 (Sept. 1896); T. Saloutos, "The Agricultural Problem
and Nineteenth-Century Industrialism," *Agricultural History*, 22 (July
1948); P. W. Gates, "The Role of the Land Speculator in Western
Development," *Pennsylvania Magazine of History and Biography*, 66
(July 1942); M. Rothstein, "America in the International Rivalry
for the British Wheat Market, 1860–1914," *Mississippi Valley His-
torical Review*, 47 (Dec. 1960); and F. A. Shannon, "The Status of
the Midwestern Farmer in 1900," *ibid.*, 37 (Dec. 1950). Mildred
Throne's "Southern Iowa Agriculture, 1833–1890: The Progress from
Subsistence to Commercial Corn-Belt Farming," *Agricultural History*,

23 (April 1949), is a case study that demonstrates, among other things, how very soon after settlement farming usually departed from the ideal of independence or self-sufficiency.

Old Ideals Versus New Ideas in Farm Life

PAUL H. JOHNSTONE

In the century and a half since the United States became a nation, our agriculture has moved all the way from the sickle to the combine, from the wooden plow drawn by a yoke of oxen to the gang plow powered by a tractor. Our population has grown during this period from 4,000,000 to about 130,000,000; and whereas about 9 out of every 10 persons lived on the farm in the days of the Revolution, today only 1 person in 4 is a farmer. Farm life and work were concerned with more than agriculture then, for the farm family supplied itself with goods provided nowadays by special industries. The family took not only food and fuel, but lumber from the land; it boiled its own sugar, made its own soap, grew its own wool, and wore its own homespun. There were then no large factories nor great financial accumulations; there were no urban and industrial masses to be fed by commercial agriculture. But in 1928 over $63,000,000,000 worth of gross assets were owned by 150 huge corporations; and in 1930 nearly 70,000,000 Americans living in towns and cities of 2,500 or larger, and many more millions in smaller towns, were dependent on the farmer for their food and clothing. A century and a half ago a rich continent of unexploited cheap land awaited the agricultural settler; today there is not enough land to go around.

The economic and technological conditions of American agriculture have in the course of a century or more been altered out of all recognition by thousands of innovations of a drastic and even revolutionary character. These changes have not taken place in a vacuum. Neither farm life, nor any other kind of life, can be divided up. It comes all in one piece and hangs together. The changes that have come to agriculture have not altered just single phases of farm life, leaving everything else untouched. On the contrary, they have profoundly influenced the very essence and character of rural living. Even philosophies and ideas of right and wrong have in some cases taken on a new shape and character. It is the purpose of this article to

Abridged from the Department of Agriculture, *Farmers in a Changing World*, *Yearbook of Agriculture*, 1940 (Washington, D.C.: U.S. Government Printing Office, 1940), pp. 111–70.

suggest how the philosophy and social substance of farm life in the United States have altered in response to the tremendous changes that have taken place during the last century in the physical and economic worlds in which we live.

The Seed of a New Growth

. . . The United States, at the very outset, developed special institutions directed in one or another way to the service and betterment of agriculture — first agricultural societies of an aristocratic nature, then agricultural societies and fair associations on a more popular level, then agricultural journalism. State boards and departments of agriculture, national agricultural organizations, a Federal Department of Agriculture, and a Nation-wide system of State agricultural colleges and experiment stations were to follow. In the present day, when such things are taken for granted, their significance is likely to be overlooked. They were in fact, however, something new under the sun. Agriculture had from the earliest times grown like Topsy. It was wholly traditionalized, conducted automatically according to customs transmitted down the centuries without change or question from father to son. Until the age in which the United States became a nation there had been very little rational and systematic effort to improve agricultural practices. . . . The idea that agriculture might be improved simply did not exist in any effective way. . . .

The existence of a growing body of institutions deliberately and directly devoted to the alteration and improvement of agriculture is therefore a fact of tremendous significance in American history. It has meant that there has been within the agricultural world itself a force constantly working to overcome traditional inertias and to direct agriculture into new paths. A stout core of customary resistance has of course remained, but the unrelenting agitation for progress has resulted in an accelerated change that is unprecedented in all previous agricultural history. The story of American agriculture during the last century and of the changes that have taken place in it in that time is to a very large extent the story of the interaction between agricultural leadership on the one hand, striving for improvements and innovations, and the inertias of folkways and informal tradition on the other hand, naturally and inevitably resistant to novelty.

Agrarianism

The tradition

The early leadership of agriculture in America planted the seed of an intellectual tradition that in essence had two parts. The first of these was the idea of progress and scientific improvement. The second was the literary agrarianism derived originally from classic antiquity. Typical of the eighteenth century, these ideas were an integral part of the rising new spirit of that age, in the world at large as well as in the world of farms and farmers.

The agrarianism of classic tradition became the political and social agrarianism of Jefferson:

> Those who labor in the earth are the chosen people of God, if ever He had a chosen people, whose breasts He has made His peculiar deposit for substantial and genuine virtue. It is the focus in which He keeps alive that sacred fire, which otherwise might escape from the face of the earth. Corruption of morals in the mass of cultivators is a phenomenon of which no age nor nation has furnished an example. It is the mark set on those, who, not looking up to heaven, to their own soil and industry, as does the husbandman, for their subsistence, depend for it on casualties and caprice of customers. Dependence begets subservience and venality, suffocates the germ of virtue, and prepares fit tools for the designs of ambition . . . generally speaking, the proportion which the aggregate of the other classes of citizens bears in any State to that of its husbandmen, is the proportion of its unsound to its healthy parts, and is a good enough barometer whereby to measure its degree of corruption.[1]

Such ideas were in close harmony with the romantic intellectual currents of the day because both were based upon assumptions of the goodness of nature, of natural man, and of simplicity of manners. And they amounted also to a philosophical elaboration of a deep but less articulate distrust of the city widely held among the masses of country people. Regardless of political party, Jeffersonian agrarianism came to be accepted as the expression of the rural social creed.

A cardinal point of the agrarian creed was the concept of the complete economic independence of the farmer. In the days when production on the farm was directed principally to the supply of home consumption needs — when all the food except occasional luxury items, when all the power and housing and fuel and most of the clothing for the farm family were produced upon the farm — the doctrine of rural independence harmonized with reality. It was the doctrine of agricultural leadership, regularly repeated by all rural spokesmen. A typical statement is this excerpt from the Union Agriculturist and Western Prairie Farmer of August 1841:

> The farmer is the most noble and independent man in society. He has ever been honored and respected from the days of Cincinnatus, the Roman farmer, to the present time. . . . He is not placed in that station which requires him ever to be seeking or courting popular favor, bowing and bowing to this or that man to gain their favor; but he looks upon the earth and the indulgent smiles of Heaven to crown his ef-

[1] United States Bureau of Agricultural Economics. *Washington, Jefferson, Lincoln and Agriculture.* (From Jefferson's Notes on Virginia.) 102 pp. 1937. [Processed.] See p. 48.

forts, resting with the fullest assurance that "seed time and harvest" shall ever continue through all coming time (3).

The second important point of the agrarian creed — agricultural fundamentalism, it has been called — was the idea that agriculture is the fundamental employment of man upon which all other economic activities were vitally dependent. This was literary doctrine, but it was also popular belief — was bound to be, perhaps, in a country where three-fourths to nine-tenths of the population lived on farms. And thus farm people generally, and most nonfarm people also, firmly believed that, as General H. K. Oliver declared in 1858 —

> . . . the whole pulse of commercial and monetary operations is affected by the healthful and unhealthful beatings of the agricultural heart; that stocks and prices in the market and on "change," rise and fall as the agricultural tide ebbs and flows; that, as come the crops, either plenteous or meagre, so darts or limps the gigantic business of the busy world. . . . (65.)

The third and most important point of the agrarian creed was the idea that agricultural life is the natural life, and, being natural, is therefore good. The ever-present corollary was that city life and urban culture are inevitably enervating and corrupt. The first part of this, concerning the inherent goodness of country life, was generally, so far as it was explicit, a literary or intellectual doctrine. The second, concerning the corruption of the city, was popular belief.

Rural-urban antagonisms

There is evidence to indicate that much of the praise of rural life expressed in popular literature was a defensive gesture against real or imagined slurs. Farm journals in those early days were constantly preoccupied with derogatory urban opinions of farm people and rural manners. Farm people were constantly advised by their leaders to be proud of themselves and of their occupation. From this repeated advice it is easy to infer a significant hypersensitiveness, for although it was regularly pointed out that urbanity of manners was superficial at best, and even an indication of shallowness of spirit, frequent exhortation was made to acquire the learning and social grace that would leave no room for such criticism. "There has . . . a certain class of individuals grown up in our land," complained the Cultivator in 1835, quoting the Genesee farmer, "who treat the cultivators of the soil as an inferior caste . . . whose utmost abilities are confined to the merit of being able to discuss a boiled potatoe and a rasher of bacon. . . ." (51.) And Joseph Brayshaw, in an address in 1841 reported by the Union Agriculturist and Western Prairie Farmer, declared that "it is really mortifying to the well-wisher to his country, to see how anxious many of the cultivators of the soil are to leave this occupation, in order to follow some other, which they think will make them gentlemen. Shame upon that gentility which depends only on dress or occupation!" (43.)

Closely associated with this common resentment against a consciousness of urban disdain was a deep dislike of many of the trappings of aristocracy and the corruptions of the city. Country people have always felt some hostility toward urban cultures. From age to age the specific objects of that hostility have varied; but in the early United States, farm people concentrated their dislike of the city upon the wealthy and aristocratic, upon "dandies" and loafers, and upon bankers, "loan sharks," "land sharks," middlemen, monopolists, and other symbols of an unwelcomed capitalism. In its first issue in June 1819, the Plough Boy in declaring its purposes heaped scorn upon "*female* as well as *male* DANDIES" and detailed its praise of the "real, unsophisticated American; a virtuous, intelligent, brave, hardy, and generous yeoman, who despises alike the trappings of *royalty* or *aristocracy*." Solon Robinson, writing in the Cultivator for May 1838, expressed the typical resentment of farmers against "the butterflies who flutter over them in British broadcloth, consuming the fruits of the sweat of their brows" (67). And in November of the same year the Cultivator repeated a common warning to farmers of the dangers in store for them in banks. In the list of "things a farmer should not do" was the following:

> A farmer should shun the doors of a bank as he would the approach of the plague or cholera; banks are for traders and men of speculation, and theirs is a business with which farmers have little to do.

Farm journals made a regular feature of the iniquities of speculators, usurers, and middlemen. There was much outright preaching against the perils of credit dealings, and short tales were told to illustrate this moral. "The Unjust Usurer — A Tale of the Prairie," printed in the Prairie Farmer in 1860 ended on the following note:

> This is no imaginative sketch, but a stern reality. It shows the danger of getting into debt, of the sure ruin that will arise from accumulating interest, and the tender mercies of land-sharks and unjust usurers.

Urban culture was considered bad not only for its possible effect upon country people; it was deemed even more disastrous in its effect upon the poor and the unfortunate within the city itself. It was regularly emphasized that in the city "vice and immorality are held up as examples for the unprovided children of unfortunate families" (50). And when a correspondent of the Prairie Farmer ventured in 1849 to praise the "luxuries," the "polished society," and the "investments" possible in the city, he was strongly rebuked for failing to see that city life "*crushes, enslaves, and ruins so many thousands of our young men, who are insensibly made the victims of dissipation, of reckless speculation, and of ultimate crime*" (8).

There was a long historical background for this rural-urban antagonism. It had been especially strong during the colonial period, except in New England. In the middle and southern colonies, the cities were settled and to a large extent governed by the representatives of European commercial houses, sent here to milk the hinterland, and by representatives of European landholders and aristocrats. The upper stratum of the colonial city population, therefore, was identified with European merchants and aristocrats rather than with the American rural settlers whom it exploited.

The farmers and the laboring classes, on the other hand, were for the most part of yeoman and peasant stock and felt akin both because of common origins and common dislike of aristocracy. They had come from a Europe where class lines were relatively rigid to a land of opportunity where they could acquire property and move up the economic ladder. But in many cases they found obstacles in the way of moving up the political and social ladders. The transplanted aristocrats, who came over as members of the ruling class, were slow to recognize the changed situation, even slower to find it desirable. Farmers tended therefore to become progressives and rebels in order to reinforce the economic opportunity of the New World with social and political opportunity as well. Out of long resentment against aristocracy and privilege, the basic belief was developed and perpetuated that virtue is the characteristic of the poor and humble. This good agrarian doctrine linked the struggling farmer with the urban laborer. But it was inconsistent with prevailing Calvinistic doctrine, which said by implication that virtue was rewarded by material blessings, and tended to link the successful farmer with the successful city dweller.

Regional differences in rural-urban relationships

In New England the proportion and importance of representatives of European aristocracy and commercial interests was very much less than in the Crown Colonies farther south, at least until Massachusetts lost her charter. Furthermore, the population distributed itself in townships, where the people lived in the town and went into the fields to farm. The community of interests within the town cut across occupational lines. There was much part-time farming and part-time manufacturing or business. Since many people were therefore part of both the rural and the urban occupational groups at the same time, the whole pattern tended to minimize both the differences and the antagonisms between those who earned a living by farming and those who earned one by trading or manufacturing. This township plan of living based on community of interests and the political democracy that developed through it fostered a sense of equality that was relatively little disturbed by class antagonisms.

In the middle Colonies, which were largely settled by the parceling out of large estates, the township plan never developed, and the county, an unwieldy social unit in those days of slow transportation, became the political unit. It was in these Colonies that the isolated farmstead which was to be the pattern on western homestead lands was first found. With isolated farmsteads rural-urban antagonism increased, because a sharp division of functions between the city and the country developed. The city seemed to exist as a parasite on the country.

In the South, where the plantation system developed side by side but in successful competition with the yeoman's subsistence homestead, the only function served by the city was as a marketing and transshipping point for the cash crops of the plantations. The city seemed only the agent of remote and somewhat parasitic commercial interests with whom the planters were often at odds. Agrarian liberalism was in the air, and the great plantation owners snatched it up as a rationalization of their own position. Thus, because it was somehow easy for the proprietors of vast estates to believe the praise of humble yeomen applied to themselves, the anomaly of a liberal gentry developed.

The democratic character of American agrarianism

The United States has never had a peasant agriculture, and farm people in this country have never had the sense of inferiority and awkward rusticity of a European peasantry. There was, undoubtedly, a certain crudity of manners that the inevitable rawness and privation of the frontier engendered. And there is, indeed, much evidence that rural people were aware of the cultural inadequacies and the lack of refinement so frequent in their very young civilization and that they resented snobbish criticisms from the city and the seaboard. But that resentment did not spring from any feeling of innate inferiority. Rather, there developed among the small freehold farmers along the frontier a spirit of lusty democracy and social equality. Aristocracies of birth and wealth were left behind in the East. Along the line of westward expansion especially, everyone was close to both poverty and wealth. Wages were generally high in proportion to the cost of becoming a proprietor. Class lines did not exist, hardships were routine, and every man's hands were calloused. The resentments of these frontier agricultural people were directed principally against the lily fingers of the idle, the posturing of aristocrats, and the devious devices of those who lived by manipulation rather than by creative labor. For themselves they knew that toil was preparation for security, and crudity the prelude to refinement. Probably no people ever built so many schools and churches on such a slender margin above the necessities of existence. Homespun was still a sign of virtue, but this did not mean that some day they would not wear silk.

There was a great deal of shifting back and forth between farming and town trades. The carpenter and the blacksmith probably had been farmers and might well become farmers again; the farmer down the road had perhaps worked for a while as a bootmaker. The traditional household practice of crafts that advancing technology was just then beginning to displace by factory industry made this possible. Few people, therefore, were ever far removed either from farming or from commerce and industry.

As settlement moved farther west into prairie lands, subsistence practices became difficult and even impossible, and farmers were forced into commercial production, with increasing dependency upon distant markets, intermediate middlemen, and transportation facilities. There was ordinarily very little local industry with which the agriculture and the farm people of a community could be economically linked and socially bound. The farmers of these regions therefore tended to identify themselves according to a vocational and economic grouping rather than by neighborhood or social classification.

Another factor that influenced the growth of attitudes and institutions in the agricultural West, where the predominant rural culture of this age was developed, was the fact that a large proportion of its pioneers and settlers were the disinherited of the older East. The rebellious suspicion felt by so many toward the East from which they had fled helped to direct hostility toward wealth and aristocracy and ease and polish, all of which long remained as symbols of the East.

THE VIRTUE OF LABOR

The famous French observer of American life, Alexis de Tocqueville, was impressed 15 years later by the fact that labor was so highly esteemed as an economic necessity that it became a social necessity and a moral virtue. There is nothing about this that seems very notable to us today, for it is a part of common American belief. But it looked new and strange to Europeans who were used to the aristocratic tradition that work is degrading.

> Among a democratic people, where there is no hereditary wealth, every man works to earn a living, or has worked, or is born of parents who have worked. The notion of labour is therefore presented to the mind on every side as the necessary, natural, and honest condition of human existence. Not only is labour not dishonourable among such a people, but it is held in honour: the prejudice is not against it, but in its favour. In the United States a wealthy man thinks that he owes it to public opinion to devote his leisure to some kind of industrial or commercial pursuit, or to public business. He would think himself in bad repute if he employed his life solely in living (70, *p. 162*).

Industry and thrift were considered cardinal virtues to a degree that was perhaps unprecedented in many previous centuries of Occidental history. There was no aristocracy on the frontier to establish ease as a social distinction, and hard, grubbing toil was generally necessary for even the barest maintenance of life.

Gain without toil was considered unnatural, and reverence for labor was heightened by religious sanction taken from the Bible. Thus the Cultivator reminded its patrons in 1836 that "the Lord God took the man and put him into the Garden of Eden, *to dress it and keep it*; and He further told him, 'in the sweat of thy face shalt thou eat bread, and thou shalt *till the ground* from whence thou art taken' " (2). The concept of the necessity and the honor of labor penetrated ideas of rearing the young, in whom the habits of industry should be inculcated from an early age. "There is no greater defect in educating children," declared the Farmer's Monthly Visitor in 1846, "than neglecting to accustom them to work. It is an evil that attaches mostly to large towns and cities" (6). Much of the literary effort of that day celebrated the honor and profit of labor. . . .

Work was work in town and country alike

Wherever the small freehold pattern prevailed, rural people tended strongly to identify themselves with all labor, whether strictly agricultural or not. The word "labor" referred to all creative work with the hands, and "laborer," though sometimes used specially to distinguish the unskilled worker from the "mechanic," was ordinarily understood to include the farmer. . . .

There is much significance in the fact that the agitation for agricultural education that developed during the 1830's included mechanical or industrial education as a matter of course. The desired establishments were frequently referred to by farmer spokesmen as "manual labor schools," to provide "industrial education"; and they were urged as a benefit to "the laboring classes," or in the interest of developing "educated labor." The frequent present-day combination of engineering and agricultural colleges is a historical vestige of this once prevailing community of interest between farmers and urban workers. . . .

There was frequently an exultant optimism in the expressions of the nobility and accomplishments of labor. Those who with their own hands carved farms from the forest and with their own eyes saw the wilderness transformed into a peaceful and productive countryside, with roads and railroads and schools and flourishing towns, could appreciate labor's accomplishments and also believe in unending improvement and progress. The eighteenth-century doctrine of progress had taken root and flourished in America as in no other country in the world. The unequaled opportunity that America offered, the rapid expansion and growth, and the rise in material living standards were so evident that what had been a new and startling idea in early eighteenth-century Europe appeared in nineteenth-century America to be an eternal truth. . . .

THE IDEA OF PROGRESS

The idea of progress was a basic element in the creed of early America, both rural and urban. It was not merely an opinion reached by calm deliberation.

It had begun, indeed, as an intellectual doctrine but soon became an unreasoned basic attitude, an assumption that the very law of nature itself compelled man and society to go on improving indefinitely. . . .

The doctrine of technological progress, from being merely the idea of a few intellectuals, rapidly became a widely accepted popular assumption. The extent to which this was true is illustrated by an incident related by de Tocqueville:

> It can hardly be believed how many facts naturally flow from the philosophical theory of the indefinite perfectibility of man, or how strong an influence it exercises even on men who, living entirely for the purposes of action and not of thought, seem to conform their actions to it, without knowing anything about it.
>
> I accost an American sailor, and I inquire why the ships of his country are built so as to last but for a short time; he answers without hesitation that the art of navigation is every day making such rapid progress, that the finest vessel would become almost useless if it lasted beyond a certain number of years. In these words, which fell accidentally and on a particular subject from a man of rude attainments, I recognize the general and systematic idea upon which a great people directs all its concerns (70, p. 34).

The United States thus accepted broadly and popularly, at an early period, the idea of indefinite technological progress. In that youthful age, the United States was in fact unusually disposed to accord at least some welcome to almost any innovation, because she was herself an innovation inclined lustily to impatience with methods and traditions that had only age and custom to recommend them. It seems probable that the readiness to accept technological novelties developed more rapidly among some urban, industrial, and commercial groups than in the more remote rural areas. But the ever-present reform element of agricultural leadership was not surpassed by any in its zeal for progress and kept up a ceaseless and impatient agitation for improvement, regularly insisting that —

> The characteristic of the present day is *reformation* and general improvement in the agricultural department — in the sciences and arts — by general diffusion of agricultural and scientific knowledge and by *"elevation* and *refinement of intellect"* (31).

RESISTANCE TO "BOOK FARMING"

Although labor-saving mechanical devices were generally welcomed and adopted relatively fast, nonmechanical technology encountered stubborn resistance. Agricultural science a century ago had in fact very little to offer aside from new machines, unless it was enthusiasm and faith, and for a long time labored under the disadvantage of the contemptuous label, "book farming." In the year the Cultivator was founded (1834), its editors received the following counsel from an early subscriber:

> I think in the *Cultivator* you ought to dwell continually on the importance of science to agriculture; I mean of all the applicable science the world has got. . . . We want to see the application of geological and chemical science to the different processes in agriculture (1).

That they needed the advice is questionable; that they followed it is certain. Book farming was advocated steadily by every agricultural journal of the day. But only a few farmers — generally the more prosperous ones — were ready to risk following the practices advocated in the name of science by agricultural societies and farm journals. For this fervent few, however, science held an appeal that was more than the lure of profit alone. . . .

BELIEF IN THE TRIUMPH OF THE GOOD

Logically essential to the doctrine of progress and to the prevalent ideas of the goodness of nature was the moral optimism of the age. This moral optimism amounted to a belief that the universe is morally ordered and that for that reason good is inherently stronger than evil and will therefore inevitably triumph. This faith had theological, philosophical, and literary foundations of great dignity and prestige. Like the idea of progress and the romantic attitudes toward nature, it developed with the intellectual element; also like them its essence was popularized during the nineteenth century. The phenomenal increase of literacy in that period accelerated to an unprecedented degree the rapidity with which intellectual traditions were transferred to the masses. Metaphysical speculation and aesthetic elaboration were distilled into the earthy slogans of the people. "Behind every cloud there's a silver lining," "Right is bound to win out in the end," "Children (or dogs) are good judges of human nature," and "A true lover of nature (or of children, or of animals, or of music, or of good books) can't be an evil man" were popular applications of the intellectualized moral optimism of Berkeley, Rousseau, and Wordsworth.

RISING LAND VALUES AND BOOMER PSYCHOLOGY

But certain folk beliefs logically similar to intellectualized ideas seem to have developed independently. Perhaps the reason for this was that widely prevailing characteristics of the age in which they evolved determined the general nature of both. A case in point is that of boomer psychology — one of the most important of all the influences that have shaped the course of American agricultural development — which very obviously grew up out of the peculiar set of circumstances in which millions of Americans lived their everyday lives. Boomer psychology, although in a logical sense merely an extension of the idea of progress, was much less the product of any intellectual vogue than of the everyday experience of a people feverishly colonizing a rich and unexploited continent in an age of unprecedented world-wide commercial expansion. . . .

From the earliest days of frontier expansion, sensational rises in land value were the repeated experience of pioneer farmers. Villages sprang up overnight and rapidly became thriving towns. Population grew, roads came in, river traffic opened up. Settlement, commercial development, and speculation increased land prices, sometimes phenomenally. Out of the experience of witnessing and being part of this expansion, the idea developed that land prices would always rise, population always increase, towns always grow larger. Farming in new regions therefore more often than not assumed a speculative nature founded upon a universal confidence in rising land values. Morris Birkbeck in 1817 described this phenomenon as follows:

> The merchant invests his profits, and the professional man his savings, in the purchase of uncultivated lands. The farmer, instead of completing the improvement of his present possessions, lays out all he can save in entering more land. In a district which is settling, this speculation is said to pay on the average, when managed with judgment, fifteen percent. Who then will submit to the toils of agriculture, further than bare necessity requires, for fifteen percent? Or who would loan his money, even at fifteen percent, when he can obtain that interest by investing it in land? (39, *p. 85.*)

De Tocqueville was among those who first noted the character that was given to American agriculture and rural life by the speculative and commercial optimism that pervaded the land. Coming from a country where land descended from father to son for generations and even centuries, he was in a position to be impressed by the impermanence that resulted from the boomer psychology and commercial enthusiasm that in agriculture was peculiar to America. His observations obviously did not apply to some parts of New England or to much of the older South where a landed aristocracy had taken root in the soil, but they were pertinent to most of the newer country.

> It seldom happens that an American farmer settles for good upon the land which he occupies: especially in the districts of the far west he brings land into tillage in order to sell it again, and not to farm it: he builds a farmhouse on the speculation, that, as the state of the country will soon be changed by the increase of population, a good price will be gotten for it (70, *p. 168*).

In some of the older regions, there was a pronounced rise in land values during the eighteenth century (38, *p. 70*). In the ante bellum South, land values were seldom consistently high, and in general rose and fell with business cycles; but settlement of new areas was there as everywhere accompanied by pronounced increases in land valuation (55, *p. 642ff.*). Benjamin Horace Hibbard's History of Agriculture in Dane County, Wisconsin indicates that in many cases there the price of land tripled or quadrupled between 1845 and 1855, and doubled again in the next 10-year period (59, *p. 195 et passim*). In Iowa the average value of an acre of improved land increased from $6.09 in 1850, to $11.91 in 1860, to $20.21 in 1870; thence it rose more slowly, to $43.31 in 1900, before booming to $96 in 1910, $134 in 1915, and $255 in 1920 (56, *p. 4*). Land booms were frequently promoted by large owners of land and land speculators from the earliest times, and by canal and railroad interests later. . . .

In the course of time it became the prevailing fashion to be "a booster, not a knocker." Such wide, unquestioning adherence was developed for the assumptions that unlimited growth and expansion and increased prosperity were the natural disposition of things, that to suggest even mildly that such might not forever be the case meant in most communities to be branded as a dangerous eccentric. This extraordinary optimism was probably necessary to the great rapidity with which the second half of the continent was settled, civilized, and tied together. But it gave to American agriculture a speculative and impermanent character that was to be the cause of many later evils. It contributed heavily to an increase in farm capitalization and debt load that could not be justified or liquidated unless the anticipated growth and expansion continued indefinitely — which turned out not to be the case.

The moral aspects of our agricultural traditions, deriving as they did from times of greater stability, implied an ideal of a permanent agriculture neither speculative nor highly commercialized. The little farm, well-tilled, highly sufficient unto itself, with no binding ties to the town and market place and untouched by the vagaries and passions of the changing world, was the assumption upon which the qualities of security, serenity, and independence were imputed to the agricultural life. This moral tradition, perpetuated in its idealized form principally by agricultural journals and writers and other farm leaders, has served by its persistence to develop a conflict in agricultural ideas because of its inconsistency with the speculative and commercial tendencies that were growing up in modern American agriculture.

THE VOGUE OF SELF-EDUCATION

The doctrine of progress meant more than confidence in technological progress alone; it meant, just as vitally, a faith in human perfectibility. Although many Americans were the disinherited of older lands, once in America they were not submissive; although they resented the trappings of wealth, the symbols of ease, and the pedantry of a learning they did not possess, they were not willing meekly to accept inferior status. They would not accept what they did not have as symbols of superiority, but they aspired to those things no less.

A significant proportion of farm people shared enthusiastically in the vogue of self-education and self-improvement that prevailed widely a century ago. This popular passion for self-education originated in New England, if it can be said to have had any geographical point of origin. . . .

Growth of farmers' clubs

In the course of time, reading and study for cultural ends — for the enrichment of life — was more and more urged for groups rather than for lone individuals. Lone study by candlelight was still suggested for those whose aim was to get ahead in the world. But for general intellectual improvement it was advised that families spend their evenings reading and discussing good books, or that they form neighborhood clubs for that purpose. During the Civil War, and especially in the years immediately following, neighborhood farmers' clubs sprang up in great numbers. The common purposes were to overcome the isolation which was, significantly, for the first time being widely regarded as a social handicap, and to cultivate the intellectual interests and capacities of rural people. Both the motives and the methods of these farmers' clubs are evident in an article describing how to organize and conduct them that was printed in both the Country Gentleman and the New England Farmer in 1871:

> The long evenings are now at hand, and the farmer, finding a little leisure after the labors of the day, looks about him for some means of pleasure and amusement wherewith to occupy the time. He will find no more profitable way to spend an occasional evening than in the meetings of a wide-awake Farmers' Club. . . . Here he can in a measure obtain that Mental Culture which is so much neglected by those who labor day after day upon their farms.
> . . . Mind needs contact with mind to rub it into activity. . . . These Farmers' Clubs then, are just what is needed to draw the farmers together, and to give them an opportunity to bring their minds in contact. . . .

It is more than mere coincidence that the growth of community farmers' clubs came in the same period with the first rapid development of the Patrons of Husbandry. The Granger movement grew out of the same common desires and aspirations and ministered to the same needs, and in many instances the formation of a local farmers' club turned out to be a preliminary to the establishment of a Grange affiliated with the national organization. Thus the impulse to enrich rural life proceeded according to the familiar sequence of individual effort first, then local group action, and finally national organization.

The vogue of self-education should not be confused with the contemporary craze for refinement. Once the worst hardships of pioneer life were overcome, or as soon as progress permitted some leisure, small-town people and many of the more prosperous farmers sought to cultivate refinement in

manners and gracious accomplishments. . . . But among most farm people
. . . the common opinion was that: "The piano and lace frame are good in
their places; and so are ribbons, frills, and tinsel, but you cannot make a dinner of the former, nor a bed blanket of the latter." . . .

THE DRIVE TO DEMOCRATIZE EDUCATION

The genuine vogue of self-education and self-improvement among farmers
and working people was in a sense only an incident of their long campaign
for enhanced educational opportunity. . . . For more than a generation,
until the passage of the Morrill Land Grant College Act of 1862, education
was the most constant and prominent political cause advocated by farmers
and their leaders.

The Lyceum movement was the first phase of the organized drive for education for farmers and working-class people. In the 1820's, agricultural spokesmen confined themselves generally to demands for State financial aid to
agricultural societies and fair associations, which were in their way devoted
to the dissemination of information concerning better farming methods. . . .
In general, the popular demand for a broadening of educational opportunities by the establishment of public schools grew out of the democratic
ideals of the people and constituted a protest against the aristocratic practices and purposes that characterized most of the private schools of that day.
. . . The inadequacy of State financing led to Federal support through the
Morrill Act of 1862. The extent to which the drive for agricultural and
mechanical education was the common purpose of both farmers and urban
working people, as well as the degree to which it was a reaction against the
aristocratic temper of the prevailing forms of higher education, is indicated
by the words of Jonathan Turner, of Illinois:

> The industrial class needs a . . . system of *liberal education* for
> their own class, and adapted to their own pursuits; to create for them
> an *Industrial Literature*, adapted to their professional wants, to raise
> up for them *teachers* and *lecturers*, for subordinate institutes, and to
> elevate them, their pursuits, and their posterity to that relative posi-
> tion in human society for which God designed them (*61, p. 69*).

It is easily observable that by the time the agitation for formal agricultural
education had grown to effective proportions it had acquired a strong tendency to emphasize practical ends and aims. Intellectual improvement for its
own sake declined in importance, and the idea of training for vocational and
professional efficiency gained in proportion.

Education as a means of personal advancement

Many forces joined from the very outset to alter slowly yet fundamentally
the ideals and motives of education and self-improvement. The ideal of in-

tellectual cultivation for its own sake began to give way to utilitarian motives almost before it was fully established. It did not, of course, completely disappear; it is present even today. Yet the very urgency of describing attractively the benefits of self-education led to claims that personal advancement up the social and economic ladder was the purpose of education.

The regularly repeated argument of advocates of education and self-improvement was that great men were once poor boys who by hard work and discipline had made themselves great. And there was repeated appeal to the established and very real idea of opportunity. Optimism, respect for industry and accomplishment, and hunger for wide esteem for the class of hard-working common men reshaped educational desires into aspiration for mundane success. . . .

Implicit in the repeated opportunity stories of poor boys who rose to greatness was the moral that the object of self-improvement was advance in rank. And in general the earthy practicality of the people tended in the long run to give emphasis to ideals that fitted the real desires of everyday life. Psychologically, there is no reason to assume that any contradiction necessarily exists between such variant motives of self-education. And historically it is a fact that they not only could but did live side by side. But what began as a vogue of self-improvement almost entirely for the sake of cultural enrichment of life rapidly became a vogue of self-improvement in order to advance in station. The former never died out, but the latter in the course of time became predominant and contributed to, as well as shared in, the success motif that has colored so much American thought and American life.

The individualistic and success philosophy that motivated much of the agitation for formal education and self-education was revealed in the answer of the Prairie Farmer to a Canadian query regarding the proud and intelligent way in which Americans articulated their opinions.

> The secret is to be found in our Common Schools, Lyceums, and the modes of conducting political canvasses. It is the natural and necessary result, of the doctrine "every man for himself" — that is, his *elevation* or depression, socially or politically, depends entirely upon his own exertions (36, *p. 100*).

Considerable significance is to be attached to the identity and accomplishments of the men who were judged to be great and who were held up as examples to the young. In the period before the Civil War, writers, philosophers, scientists, inventors, and political and military figures predominated among those named as illustrious. Among those most frequently named were Benjamin Franklin, Jeremy Bentham, Shakespeare, Ben Jonson, Linnaeus, George Washington, Robert Burns, and William Cobbett. There was a wide and varying assortment of contemporary governors, senators, and scientists and inventors who had been born poor but through extraordinary effort had made themselves famous and great. Almost never, during this early period, was a financier, industrialist, or businessman so mentioned; but there was a growing tendency to think of attainment in terms of commercial criteria, and this was, in the course of time, to alter the specific ideals of success. It is to be noted that farming was never cited as the vocation of great and illustrious men; models of success were invariably others than farmers. This is significant because farm youth were urged simultaneously to prepare for success and yet to stay on the farm and ignore the false lure and illusory rewards of the city.

Farm youth was already beginning to crowd to the growing towns and cities, thereby arousing the protest that cityward migration has immemorially excited. But among the masses of older rural people, the greatest opportunity was still believed to exist in farming, partly because of eternally expected rises in land values and prices generally, and partly because of the abundance of cheap lands and the financial ease with which one could become a free-holding farmer.

FORCES OF CHANGE: COMMERCIALIZATION, URBANIZATION, AND TECHNOLOGICAL ADVANCE

The principal alterations in the pattern of agricultural life that have come during the past century may be summarized under the titles of commercialization, urbanization, and technological advance. The forces underlying these changes were present, and in varying degrees operative, a hundred years or more ago; but their total effect upon the everyday life of rural people was by no means then what it later became. . . .

The most profound differences between rural life today and a century ago do not in any case consist intrinsically in an increased commercialization, or in a more advanced technology, or in a wider adoption of material things from the city. Many farms then sold as high a proportion of their products as do many commercial farms today. There were farms then that had as much labor-saving equipment as do many farms in this more modern mechanical age. The most profound changes in farm life — those that have had the greatest effect upon the destinies, the course of daily life, and the happiness or unhappiness of farm people — have not been the changes in material things themselves but those involved in the gradual alteration of habits, customs, institutions, and ideas that has constituted the social or cultural adaptation to material change. . . .

NEW ECONOMIC DEMANDS UPON AGRICULTURE

The extension of industrial technology, the growth of urban markets, the increase of transportation facilities, the general rise in the standard of living — all these and related things have exerted tremendous pressure upon the farmer to become a cog in a vast and infinitely complex economic machine.

Urban industry has removed from the farm one by one the industrial functions that once were performed there. The farmer who once wore homespun from his own sheep now wears denim from Oshkosh and cotton shirts from Troy. Soap making is gone; and not one of a thousand farmers who grow wheat eats his own grain. Few farmers build their own houses; and their houses are not lighted with home-made candles or tallow wicks but with kerosene or electricity. Ordinarily they do not sell or barter a variety of produce for the use of nearby townfolk; their customers are 100 or 1,000 or 3,000 miles away.

Commercialization and specialization have been the necessary complements in agriculture to the factory system and mass production in industry. In the space of 60 years, between 1869 and 1929, the annual total of manufactured products turned out by American industries grew in value from about 3⅓ billion dollars to about 70 billions. During this same period, the number of those gainfully employed in agriculture increased slowly from about 6½ to 10¼ millions, while nonagricultural employment quadrupled — from 12 to 48 millions. Vast urban accumulations grew up. In 1870 only a fifth of our people lived in places of 8,000 or more population; but in 1930 roughly half — over 60 millions — were residents of such places. And only a quarter of our people are now on the farm. All this has meant that agriculture must be commercialized, for in no other way could the urban and industrial masses be fed and clothed. It has also involved specialization, to which heavy advantages frequently accrue in production for the market. The rising standard of urban living has had the same commercializing effect as the growth of urban population. The growing demand for fresh fruits and vegetables in winter and the increasing substitution of delicacies for breadstuffs and heavier foods have tended to place a premium upon highly specialized production for special urban markets.

American agriculture was called upon, moreover, to supply a European market as well as a growing domestic demand. In the Civil War period and after, this Nation was still very young financially and industrially. There were few American manufactures with which to pay for the European goods sold in this country. It was largely American agriculture that paid this bill by vast exports of food and fiber for the crowded industrial peoples of Europe.

In the fiscal year 1850–51 total agricultural exports amounted to $146,-717,000; from this they climbed gradually to a record figure of $260,280,000 in 1859–60. Cotton was then the single item accounting for most of the total. But after the Civil War, when farm products sold abroad came more and more to include a large quantity of breadstuffs, meats, and fruits, agricultural exports climbed to $296,962,000 in 1869–70, to $694,315,000 in 1879–80, fell back to $634,856,000 in 1889–90, and climbed again to $844,-617,000 in 1899–1900. The slight rise to $869,244,000 in 1909–10 was merely a prelude to the tremendous World War expansion that skyrocketed the figure to $3,849,663,000 in 1919–20. During the 1920's, our agricultural exports regularly totaled between $1,500,000,000 and somewhat over $2,000,000,000.

The effect of the growth suggested by these figures was to increase vastly the involvement of American agriculture in a commercialized, specialized, interdependent world economy. American grain and meat production in the latter half of the nineteenth century became a cog in the international economic machine, just as tobacco production had become in the seventeenth and eighteenth centuries and cotton production in the early nineteenth. Thus the dominant American crops — tobacco and cotton, corn, pork, and wheat — became the special products of an agricultural plant geared to the needs of an international and interdependent economy of regional and national specialization.

Without this vast expansion of urban and industrial markets for farm products in both America and Europe the agricultural settlement of our grain-producing areas could neither have proceeded with the same speed nor have developed the same kind of farm economy. It would have had to depend on very limited local markets and would have been forced into diversification rather than specialization, subsistence practices rather than commercial dependency. Thus there has been an irresistible impulse toward specialization and commercialization in American agriculture that was generated by forces as remote and impersonal as population trends, the rising standard of living, and changes in the national economy not only of this but of other countries. Involuntarily, and by dint of circumstances, the farmer has lost much of his old-time independence and has found himself tied to the market, to industry, and to the city.

Self-sufficiency gives way to interdependence

. . . It was upon . . . self-sufficiency that the traditional independence of the farm family was based. Equipped by habit and skill to supply its own needs for food, shelter, and clothing, the farm family could if necessary face away from the world and live completely and even happily upon the products of its own making. But in proportion as industries were transferred from the farm and home into the shop or factory and as rural people began to acquire new tastes for urban products and luxuries their independence was lost. . . . Between 1810 and 1840 industry was rapidly removed from the home to the factory. In this period, except in the most remote frontiers, farm families largely ceased to manufacture their own textiles and clothing. Grist-mills, flour mills, and sawmills became common and grew larger as they served increasingly wide areas.

In addition to the loss of home industry, which necessitated cash outlay for products previously supplied right on the farm, new needs were developed. In the Civil War period the sewing machine, based on Howe's patent of 1846 and Singer's patent of 1851, was coming into common use on the finer textiles that were issuing in increasing quantities from the looms of manufacturing towns. At about the same time kerosene began to be used widely for better lighting, and this too increased the need for cash outlay. There were to come telephones (in 1930, 34 percent of all farms reported telephones), electricity, modern plumbing, automobiles (in 1930, 58 percent of all farmers reported automobiles). Many farm families were destined in the first third of the twentieth century to give up home butchering and baking and buy all their meat from the butcher and all their bread from the grocer or baker. Social prestige came more and more to be attached to the possession of various products that were supplied by industry and could be obtained only by cash outlay. Most of these changes and innovations have resulted in a higher standard of living, but they have also involved the surrender of economic independence.

THE INFLUENCE OF FARM BOOKKEEPING

. . . After the Civil War the drive was intensified to induce farmers to think of their farms as a business and of themselves as businessmen. This meant the keeping of books, counting of costs, and determination of farm procedures on the basis of calculated commercial profits. In this vein the Southern Cultivator and Dixie Farmer preached in 1887:

> The time has come when the farmer must be a business man as well as an agriculturist. . . . He will have to keep farm accounts, know how much he spends, what his crops cost him, and how much the profit foots up.

. . . The idea that the farm is an investment on which the farmer should expect to draw interest above and beyond the direct reward for his labor or that the farmer should make a monetary calculation of the value of his labor is an application of principles entirely harmonious with the modern commercial world of the city and industry, but it is a radical departure from the older agrarianism. The emphasis upon a paper concept of ownership, as opposed to a use concept, is obvious; and the remoteness from earlier attitudes which identified the farm as a home providing an opportunity for the production of the necessities of life by the sweat of the brow, where obstacles were natural rather than social, can hardly be exaggerated.

THE FARMER BECOMES A BUSINESSMAN

. . . Thus under the progressive slogan, "How we have all advanced," the Prairie Farmer argued in 1868:

> The old rule that a farmer should produce all that he required, and that the surplus represented his gains, is part of the past. Agriculture, like all other business, is better for its subdivisions, each one growing that which is best suited to his soil, skill, climate, and market, and with its proceeds purchase his other needs (15).

A prominent agricultural educator and leader who for a generation has been one of the most distinguished spokesmen for modern trends in farm management and progress expressed very well the new point of view in an article written for the Cornell Countryman in 1904:

> . . . Now the object of farming is not primarily to make a living, but it is to make money. To this end it is to be conducted upon the same business basis as any other producing industry. No matter what the yield, it must have been produced at a profit or the farmer is not making money; again, no matter what the profits, the fertility of the land must not be allowed to run down or the capital stock will depreciate and the business will evaporate and come to naught even under conditions of apparent success (48).

By developing along such lines American agriculture increased vastly its cash income. But on the other side of the ledger its cash outgo was also increased. By 1929 American farmers paid out annually nearly a billion dollars for feed, over a quarter billion for fertilizer, nearly a billion for labor, nearly three-quarters of a billion for implements and machinery, and nearly fifty million dollars for electricity and power to power companies, exclusive of home generating outfits.

Much of the changed character of the farmer in this age has come about as the result of a long and persistent effort to identify farming directly with business and the farmer with businessmen. Increasing emphasis was given to the merchandising aspect of farming. In an article entitled "The Farmer as a Merchant," this typical counsel was given in 1887:

> Given farms and farmers of equal productive power, the one who sells best will have the best success. The work of farming is only half done when the crop is made out of the ground; sometimes the biggest half is in making the money out of the crop. This branch of farm business needs cultivating; this (the merchant) side of the farmer needs development. Watch and study the markets, and the ways of the marketmen, and dealers in all kinds of goods, and learn the art of "selling well" (22).

When agricultural colleges began to carry their work to farmers through farmers' weeks, institutes, and so on, they too preached the ideal of the businessman. The Cornell Countryman announced in 1903 that the Farmers' Institute, held at the agricultural college there, was "a business meeting for business men. . . ." (24.)

CHANGED ATTITUDES TOWARD LABOR

One of the most significant phases of the long trend toward the identification of farmers with businessmen has been an almost complete reversal in attitudes toward labor. Whereas a century ago farmers generally identified themselves as of the working class and did not ordinarily distinguish themselves from other groups of workers, they have in the course of time acquired an employer consciousness and have developed a strong inclination to regard those who work for wages as of a different class, with other and even hostile interests.

In the period when farmers identified themselves so closely with urban labor, a significant proportion of that labor was still of the pattern of the independent craftsman who owned his tools and shop and sold his product or his services directly to the consumer. A good deal of the time he came closer to being a small businessman than a wage worker in the modern sense. Independent craftsmen of this sort had much in common with farmers that was lost when they became mere factory wage hands.

During the past century, however, urban workers have been losing both economic independence and social status; and farm people, though losing economic independence, have continued to be proprietors in a world in which proprietors are relatively less common than before. Their living standards in terms of industrial products have been rising, and the social status of the more prosperous class of farmers has been greatly improved. A very real differentiation in economic and social position has thus developed between segments of society that once were united in interests and outlook.

Rural opposition to organized industrial labor

Farmers appear never to have been in a position to sympathize generally with organized industrial labor. So long as urban workers looked like independent craftsmen, their situation could be regarded sympathetically through symbols familiar to the farmer. Thus when in 1851 a group of New England workmen banded together to start a factory of their own, there was sufficient appeal to the farmer to win enthusiastic approval from the agricultural press under the slogan, "Labor is capital" (11). But by the time trade unions of a modern character began to develop, the farmer was conscious of himself both as an employer and as a commercial proprietor and was already partly converted to the association of virtue with economic status. Therefore, in spite of his continuing antipathy to trusts and great capital accumulations, he was not prepared to look kindly upon the outlandish innovation of militant unions or the violence incidental to strikes. And labor unions appeared as a companion monster of monopoly, both of which were set to prey upon the farmer. "While labor and capital strive to adjust their differences, the farmer peaceably grows the crops to feed both," was the typical comment of the Farm Journal in 1886 (20). At times there was a readiness to believe that capital and labor acted in collusion. Thus the Orange Judd Farmer expressed the opinion in 1903 that:

> Labor and capital engaged in the manufacture of window glass have apparently united to prevent any others going into business. By this plan manufacturers expect to absolutely monopolize production and

shove up prices at will, and under these circumstances they agree to give their help an increase in wages. . . . The farmer feeds them all, and when he gets tired of being robbed by such combinations, he will strike back.

Much of the trouble came from the fact that higher pay and shorter hour agitation by labor unions sometimes offended the rural mind, which out of its own experience had acquired a deep respect for long hours of hard work for humble rewards. The enforced dependence of the urban wage worker has never been sympathetically comprehensible to the farmer with his traditions of independence and individualism. In considering industrial disputes, country people have tended to look upon work as a moral duty, to regard insistence upon conditions and terms of labor as a partial abrogation of that moral duty, and to project their own moral and nonexploitative outlook into the industrial situation. The milder form of this agrarian attitude is suggested by a statement written 30 years ago by L. H. Bailey, one of the grand old men of American agriculture:

> It is doubtful if city industrialism is developing the best type of working-men, considered from the point of view of society. I am glad of all organizations of men and women, whether working-men or not. But it seems to me that the emphasis in some of the organizations has been wrongly placed. It has too often been placed on rights rather than on duties. No person and no people ever developed by mere insistence on their rights. It is responsibility that develops them. The working-man owes responsibility to his employer and to society; and so long as the present organization of society continues he cannot be an effective member of society unless he has the interest of his employer constantly in mind (*37, pp. 139–140*).

The rural hostility toward labor unions has been so well appreciated by some agents of industrial interests that upon occasion farmer groups and representatives have been easily maneuvered into a front position of opposition to labor causes. An example of this was the case of the agitation for repeal of the Adamson eight-hour law about the time of the National Agricultural Conference in Washington in January 1922. When expenditures for the relief of urban unemployed became an issue in recent years, the cleavage between agricultural and labor interests in the rural mind was emphasized still further. Farm people, still clinging to ideals of thrift and industry, and as their own bosses conscious of the ever-present work to be done on their farms, tended to associate all unemployment with the idleness of laziness and to regard huge relief expenditures as prodigal waste.

The widening gap between proprietors and hired hands

Just as, in the course of a century, a social cleavage has developed separating farm people from urban working people, during the same period there has also been a strong tendency toward stratification within rural society, a widening gap between proprietors of farms and those who do farm work for wages. Until a half century or so ago there had not been in the North and West any widely prevailing class distinctions between operators and hired hands. The individual farm proprietor had as likely as not been a hired hand himself at one time; the rungs of the agricultural ladder were still in place, and the hired man likewise would probably be an owner in the course of time. They were social if not economic equals because what one was, the other had been or would be. Furthermore, the tendency of the freehold farmer to identify himself with the under-dog element of society endured in many applications until the collapse of the agrarian revolt in the Populist defeat of 1896. And as long as this attitude endured, the farmer could not with complete consistency separate himself from those who labored hard and honestly with their hands.

But such attitudes and the customs expressing such attitudes in everyday living were due in the course of time to change profoundly as the farmer became more and more a businessman — yet a businessman working under peculiar disadvantages.

All of the agrarian unrest of the post–Civil War period amounted in sum to a protest against the primary dislocation caused by the impact of the new commercialism and industrialism. The frequent statement that it was the farmer as well as the South that lost the Civil War contains an element of important truth. For the Civil War confirmed the protectionist policies of the industrial Northeast and left the farmer no alternative but to buy in a protected, expensive market while having to sell in a cheap world market. With this initial disadvantage, he was forced increasingly by the march of mechanization and rising land prices into ever higher capital investment; and the increasing desire that spread to every hamlet in the land for more of the new products of industrial specialization placed a multitude of new demands upon him. Both factors increased the need for cash, and owing to the farmer's economic disadvantage, both resulted in a growing rural debt load. And always the farmer labored under disadvantages that prevented him from receiving a full share either of his own increased production or of the industrial goods that the improved technology of urban industry made possible. Farm living standards rose, but they did not rise in proportion to the farmer's increased efficiency or as rapidly as those of the urban middle class whose tastes and standards were increasingly important as models for rural emulation.

The farmer was becoming a businessman, but he was doing so under a great disadvantage. The main advantages were beginning to accrue to large-scale organization, and the farmer as a lone individual had to pay tribute. Not only did he get low prices for his products, but he frequently paid excessive freight charges to get his stuff to market because others could combine where he could not. Trusts and monopolies of various kinds upon

occasion overcharged him exorbitantly. He bought stocks and bonds to secure market transportation that often failed to materialize. And when he
sought redress for grievances, he frequently was thwarted by a wall of corporation legalisms.

He became a small, individual businessman just as the economic world
began to be dominated by great and corporate businesses. He might have
tried to return to the practices and ideals of an earlier agricultural life, but
that was impossible. He was already a cog in the modern economic machine
and had to turn as the adjacent cogwheel turned him. He himself wanted
modern things; he was in debt; and there was no alternative to muddling
through.

Because he was in debt, he participated in the Greenback movement, distrusted the "hard-money" men, and yielded to the lure of 16-to-1. Because
distribution by middleman was generally devious and frequently expensive
and was always suspect to traditional agrarian ideals of directness and because he had to pay dearly for his credit, he naturally favored crop-credit
and storage schemes such as the Sub-Treasury Plan. Because of the prices
he had to pay and because he was still a consistent go-it-alone individualist,
trusts and monopolies loomed like monsters.

Although he was the under dog in the struggle against great combinations
of industry and finance, the farmer had assimilated the ideas and ideals of
opportunity and business success to the extent that he found it just as impossible to join forces with impecunious wage labor below as to sympathize
with great accumulations of capital above. And thus, after the great Populist
disappointment of 1896, he was heartened by the business revival that followed and recovered courage to face forward again on the path of the new
commercialism. It should already have been clear that farmers of the dominant group, from having been proud and rebellious under dogs, were destined, after another brief flurry or two of rebelliousness, to become essentially defenders of the state of things as they are, or even of the state of things
as they used to be.

This change in attitudes had been helped along by the increasing awareness among farmers of their own commercial proprietary interests, by the
decline of economic self-sufficiency within family units, and by the discovery
that regionally and by occupation farm proprietors had common commercial
interests generally distinct from all others. The increasing acceptance of
commercial ideals, the aspiration for higher material living standards, the
faith in economic opportunity, the conversion of the self-improvement
vogue into the success idea, and the moral optimism that believed virtue
is inevitably rewarded, all combined to foster a rebirth of the Calvinistic
notion that the Lord reveals His predilections by the bestowal of mundane
favors. Thus the way was slowly prepared for a gradual subscription to the
idea that right is the companion of wealth and station rather than of humble
poverty, that success is a reward of virtue and failure the penalty of vice.

This change did not come quickly, nor has it ever been logically complete. But in many applications, this realignment of the virtues and the vices proceeded rapidly enough to make typical by the eighties the basic sentiments suggested in the following opinions of the Ohio Practical Farmer in 1885 (19): "Here are two grand divisions of society — the honorable and useful, and the poor, the vicious and criminal." Log-cabin birth was long considered a desirable attribute of public men — from 1840 on, practically a prerequisite to Presidential aspiration — because it signified sympathy for the humble; in the course of time it was increasingly considered as proof of having risen. Democratic sentiment thus began to shift from sympathy for the lower stratum to approval of the individual who rose above it. Basic attitudes thus tended to shift from resentment at the existence of privileged social strata toward a belief that social stratification was natural and that moral qualities were somehow correlated with economic levels.

This change has been related to the changing status of the hired man. The increased flow of immigration in the middle of the nineteenth century provided an incident for the first expression of altering attitudes toward hired help. Many of the more indigent newcomers went to work as hired hands and servants, and in many cases much of the hostility toward the strange ways of foreigners was directed toward the ranks they filled. Preceding the discovery by the farmer that he had a labor problem was a period of growing complaint at the supposedly declining quality of hired men and hired girls frequently attributed to their European origin and manners. The neighbor boy and the neighbor girl who had hired out were reported to be supplanted by "a distinct caste," "an inferior class" of foreigners whose incompetence, vice, and ignorance had a "tendency to degrade labor." And the frequent warning was repeated that —

> While Cincinnatus held the plow, the cultivation of the soil was an honorable employment. But when the prisoners . . . were compelled to hold the plow, the cultivation of the earth became too degrading an employment for the Roman soldier or citizen (35).

. . . Hired labor has in fact become a very important consideration to agriculture generally and a personal concern to a substantial proportion of farmers. By 1929, according to census figures, there were over 2,600,000 farmers (nearly 42 percent of the total) who employed hired labor, paying a total cash labor bill in that year of nearly a billion dollars.

In addition to the conditions and facts that tended to place the farmer in the ranks of employers, the influence of farm journals and agricultural-reform agencies of all kinds was in the direction of making the farmer conscious of his status as a real or potential employer with interests different from those who worked on the farm for wages. By the eighties discussion of the "farm labor problem" became a frequent feature of farm journals. When the various branches of economics began to develop special applications to agriculture, farm management and agricultural economics sought to systematize and commercialize the handling of farm labor. Almost invariably the influence of the leaders, intellectuals, and educators and reformers working in agriculture was in the direction of stratifying rural society, because they emphasized making employer-employee relationships formal and contractual. . . .

In spite of farm-management preachments, relatively few hired hands ever gave or received written contracts, but the spirit prompting the advice spread slowly over the land. It became the practice of farm-management experts to classify farm help into simple groupings, with blanket advice on the over-all virtues and defects of each. Thus a textbook on farm management published in 1921 had a chapter on "Farm Labor" in which hired help was divided into several classifications: White (Irish and Swedish), Negro, Mexican, etc. In such advice as that on "Handling Hobo or Tramp Laborers" there was an unquestioning assumption of deep social stratification.

> These men should be provided with a reasonably warm, dry place to sleep, but as a rule no special housing is needed for them. They are satisfied to furnish their own bedding and sleep on a pile of hay, and to get plain food . . . if ample in quantity and well cooked.
>
> As a class they are easily disgusted with poor machinery, and if an implement continually breaks, they are likely to quit without notice. . . .
>
> These men will not stand crowding or pressing. If any attempt is made to drive them they will quit. Yet they can be held to the daily quitting time, although if over-time or extra work is attempted, a clear understanding must be had and extra money be paid. . . .
>
> Sunday work is usually taboo with the real hobo.
>
> One cannot afford to allow poker playing or gambling of any kind, or tolerate radical talk or preaching by discontented individuals (32, pp. 520–521).

Farmers in the traditional pattern of the family farm have generally been generous employers within the limits of their means. Being hard-pressed to make ends meet, they have sometimes had to pay low wages, but when farm prices boomed, as during the World War, good hired hands in the Middle West got as much as $75 to $125 a month with board and room. This fact, however, has not altered the course of the proprietor's growing feeling of separateness from those who work for him or might work for him. The hired hand has moved out of the parlor in most regions and out of the house in many. In some sections in the Middle West, where hired hands lived with the family a generation ago, they now live in town and carry their lunch to work.

This development has been partly the result of a complex of circumstances that has in effect frozen farm help into its inferior status. The old ladder from hiring out to proprietorship has been severely damaged, even working in reverse; and farm hands have in contemporary times become increasingly aware that they are farm hands permanently — not merely climbers on the first of a series of rungs that lead to farm ownership. The famous announcement of the Director of the Census in 1890 about the end of the frontier meant in effect that cheap land was gone and with it the opportunity for the poor man to become a proprietor. For as available land diminished, difficulties were multiplied by increased capital equipment costs. Commerce and industry became the sole remaining hope of the rural disinherited who wished to rise above poverty.

Farmers in general have inclined strongly toward paternalistic treatment of hired help. Although they have grown aware of caste distinctions, they have not in general inclined toward the psychology of exploitation. The attitudes of farmers toward the help they themselves hire has in general been subject to moral considerations of their own that prevent full development of exploitative motives. On this score farmers appear so far to have withstood partially the advice sometimes given by economists and farm-management experts, and they have seldom followed the examples of huge or highly industrial types of agricultural enterprises. The farmer's hostility to labor, where such hostility has really developed, has generally been directed, not against the farm labor with whom he has contact, but rather against urban labor or the urban aspects of labor. In this case, it would seem that the immemorial distrust and dislike for the city has in effect undergone some change in that the specific urban objects of that distrust and dislike have been partially changed. Whereas a century ago the American farmer was inclined to concentrate his suspicion of the city upon the wealthy and aristocratic, he now tends more to look upon the idleness of the unemployed and the tactics of industrial unions as the most prominent symbols of urban corruption. . . .

The Persistence of Some Older Ideas

In very recent times, particularly in the last decade, popular confidence that virtue is inevitably rewarded by economic success has been somewhat dissipated; but the association of economic success with moral qualities remains. A strong tendency to suspect the means whereby great wealth has been acquired still exists. But cheap land and individual opportunity to win independence by thrift and industry were facts of existence for so long that a code of social ethics evolved that, persisting into a later day, seeks to solve the problems of the metropolis and the great society in frontier terms. Thus many believe that the cure for unemployment is hard work and the remedy for technological displacement, old-fashioned moderation and thrift. Both individuals and groups think and act only in terms of their experience. When they are confronted by a situation of crucial importance that is essentially novel, a confusion develops out of which they follow ordinarily one of two general types of behavior. They may appeal to a framework of fantasy, which in the case of social or political problems means faith in some utopian dream. Or they may recur to fragments of past experience connected with established patterns of behavior and, in an effort to escape their sense of inadequacy and insecurity in the new dilemma, emotionalize the older patterns of behavior into eternal standards of right and decency.

Being more at home within the older cultural pattern, farmers and rural people have been more inclined than others to see present difficulties in the light of long-established practices and standards of value. For this reason, the startling new expedients and institutions that have developed within the urban culture to meet new situations that were primarily urban and industrial were bound to arouse a hostile rural reaction in a time of psychological crisis. Relief appropriations have been perhaps the most striking example. Although the country had been acquiring city ways, it was not prepared for such devices. And in its newer forms, the ancient antagonism of the farmer to the city has been directed principally at such innovations and in effect at that stratum of the urban population to whom the farmer once felt most akin.

Changing Ideals in Agricultural Education

. . . There has . . . consistently been a conflict in ideals of agricultural education. There has always been a group that sought to include cultural graces and social understanding with purely vocational training. This is the element that in the tradition of the Lyceum, the self-improvement vogue, farmers' clubs and debating and literary societies, the early Grange, the country-life movement, and the Chautauqua movement has sought to improve farm life not only by economic and technological improvement but also by intellectual and social enrichment. Among agricultural educators, Kenyon L. Butterfield and Liberty Hyde Bailey were perhaps the best-known advocates of this intellectual leaven. Within the institutions of agricultural education, this group was not successful in diverting the drift toward increased emphasis upon technical specialization and commercial standards. But its participation in the country-life movement, in farm-life surveys and conferences and rural uplift generally, served nevertheless to hasten the growth of rural sociology as an academic and scientific discipline (52).

It is significant that the Country Life Commission was never given the political sanction of congressional support, for the vogue of rural uplift in the early twentieth century was limited principally to educators, clergymen, and small reform groups. It had no strong popular backing and even aroused resentment among many farmers, whose opinion seems to have been that what agriculture needed was more money, and that, with that simple need granted, farmers themselves would be amply able to look out for their own uplift. Social reform in agricultural life had in effect been professionalized; it lacked deep roots in workaday rural society. In the hands of an element largely removed from immediate contact with the soil and not harassed by the same economic difficulties that beset the farmer, it occasionally appeared to the rural mind to be both urban and condescending. The Prairie Farmer in its issue of June 15, 1913, described the continuing rural uplift movement as a case of "too much yeast in the dough," and expressed typical annoyance that —

> There are well up toward a dozen organizations in Chicago that are trying to uplift the farmer. For the most part they are financed and managed by city men.

During the first quarter of the twentieth century, agricultural economics was rapidly attaining academic respectability as well as a wide reputation for being practical. Economics was, in effect, a much more perfect response than uplift to the pressing needs and concerns to which the farmer was then subject.

The Popular Acceptance of Science Applied to Agriculture

. . . During a century of what was one of the most persistent and intensive propaganda campaigns in history, the benefits of science were advertised to the rank and file of farmers; but only in the present generation has conclusive victory been attained. The intellectuals interested in agricultural progress, farm journals generally, and farm leaders and organizations, with immeasurable faith in scientific progress, have from every quarter urged farmers to adopt the latest scientific devices and methods. . . .

In spite of the ready adoption of mechanical devices by all who could afford them, farmers for generations remained generally skeptical of the heralded benefits of science in other forms. The resistance to new methods was slowly worn down, however, by the constant preaching of farm journals and other private agencies. Finally, in the years since the Smith-Lever Act of 1914 and the Smith-Hughes Act of 1917, county-agent work, secondary education in agriculture, and demonstration and extension work generally have broken the last major resistance to agricultural science. . . .

Technical progress in many fields

The period between 1864 and 1890 saw the development of the gang plow and the sulky, barbed wire, wheel and two-horse cultivators, spring-tooth and disk harrows, the hay loader and baler, the wire binder, improved reapers, the twine binder and bundle carrier, the silo, the cream separator, and the refrigerator car. By 1890, 910 companies, employing 39,580 men and having a capital aggregating $145,313,997, were engaged exclusively in the manufacture of agricultural machinery. The census estimated that on the 4,564,641 farms enumerated that year there was farm machinery worth half a billion dollars. By 1890 or 1900 most of the major mechanical improvements practicable with horses for power had been developed. With the development of the tractor a great new wave of mechanization began. The 1930 census, taken before the recent great increase of mechanization based on the rubber-tired tractor and supplementary implements, reported 3⅓ billion dollars' worth of farm machinery on about 5,600,000 farms, or nearly $600 per farm.

The technology of plants and animals has developed similarly through introductions from abroad, scientific breeding, and the control of diseases and insects.

This technological progress has resulted in an increase in agricultural wealth so vast and complex that it cannot well be estimated. The agricultural domain has been extended by new varieties of plants resistant to disease, drought, and cold. Yields have been increased. New plants have been found to supply special needs and to provide products that older plants could not. Losses from disease and pests have been greatly curtailed. Hand-labor requirements have been reduced, sometimes phenomenally, and the amount of land cultivable by a single farm family has been much increased (60). The reader will find elsewhere in this Yearbook a much fuller discussion of the nature and effects of agricultural technology (The Influence of Technical Progress on Agricultural Production, p. 509).

Technological advance has fostered specialization by increasing the need for and value of special skills. Technology has made economic specialization possible by counteracting the natural vulnerability to pests and diseases that accompanies concentration and specialization. It has increased the amount of necessary capital investment in equipment and working capital. Thus agricultural science and technology have made the farmer a much more efficient producer of agricultural supplies for the market, but they have also collaborated with other forces in the modern world to make him vitally dependent upon the working of an increasingly complex society.

The laboratory apron is rapidly becoming, for the farmer as for the rest of the world, a priestly vestment of authority. The slogans and fetishes that have accompanied the expansion of science and technology have been accepted along with sober scientific truth. If the judgment of advertisers is an indication, rural as well as city people are impressed by the vitamin content of everything from breakfast food to cold cream, and the approval of white-garbed scientists with test tubes in their hands can be a cogent recommendation of fencing, potash, hybrid corn, tooth paste, or tires for the tractor.

THE DEVELOPMENT OF PROFESSIONAL FARM LEADERSHIP

Traditionally, agriculture has been conducive to democracy. Responsible local leadership has tended to develop more freely and democratically among free-holding farmers than among most other social groupings. But in the process of adjustment to the great society, what was adequate to community organization has sometimes failed to apply on a national scale. A busy farmer may assume civic responsibilities in local matters without prejudice to his farming; but when the level of activity rises to embrace the State, the region, and the Nation, it generally becomes impossible to be both an active leader and a practicing farmer. Since agriculture has been drawn into a national economic orbit, agricultural concerns of the greatest importance have become national problems, and agricultural leadership has tended correspondingly to become national, and therefore professionalized. This professional leadership has been farm-reared; but, in becoming professionalized, it has sometimes grown urban. Farm leaders have of necessity taken urban residence, developed urban associations, become partly urban in outlook. A significant proportion of farm leaders have been farm youth who went to town, made or failed to make a fortune there, and then in later life became leaders of rural reform.

The oldest national farm organization of today — the Grange — illustrates this modern tendency toward urban and professionalized farm leadership. None of the seven founders was by occupation a farmer for more than a small portion of his life. Of the 10 masters of the National Grange (second to eleventh) of whom biographical sketches are given in the official Semi-Centennial History of the Patrons of Husbandry (34), only two could be called practicing dirt farmers. Most of the others had spent their youth on the farm, and some engaged in farming as a hobby.

Agriculture has taken its political leadership from the town, too. The great agricultural State of Iowa, for instance, had a total of 419 elected Congressmen between 1844 and 1938. Only 15 of these are identified by the Iowa Official Register as farmers; of the rest, 309 were lawyers, 35 were bankers, 22 were editors, journalists, or publishers, 34 were businessmen (merchants, manufacturers, brokers, nurserymen, grain dealers, lumbermen) and 4 were of the learned professions. Of the total of 15 elected Congressmen who were farmers, 12 were elected to office in the period 1844–90, and not one was elected during the 40 years from 1892 to 1932. The other 3 were elected between 1932 and 1938.

In the far-flung agrarian unrest of the seventies, eighties, and nineties, a substantial proportion of the agricultural leadership rose to prominence directly from the farm. There were Sockless Jerry Simpsons as well as Ignatius Donnellys. And although agricultural leadership has in the course of the last generation or two become increasingly professionalized, there has continued to be much dirt-farmer leadership in purely economic causes. Probably no movement was ever more genuinely indigenous than the farm-holiday movement of the early 1930's. But the contemporary situation is such that noneconomic organizations and causes cannot ordinarily depend upon popular support or leadership from farm people; farm problems have become increasingly technical in nature as well as national in scope, and farm people have generally been content to have others act for them, retaining only a veto power.

FARMERS AND MIDDLEMEN

The old agrarian distrust of devious business methods and devices has persisted and has sometimes led to strange contradictions as agriculture has been increasingly commercialized. Dislike of middlemen is as old as history. Medieval law and trade regulations were full of statutes and rules intended to curb the power of middlemen to influence prices. "Middlemen" has essentially the same unfavorable connotation today to many people that "regrators," "forestallers," and "engrossers" had to medieval yeomen. Historically, farmers have been the most consistent of all economic individualists. No group has been more thoroughly or consistently hostile to combination and monopoly and to all that savored of Big Business. Whatever was indirect was under suspicion. This eternal tendency to distrust the agencies of distribution and to suspect them of profiteering is the psychological basis upon which cooperatives have been built.

In the name of a war on speculation, monopoly, and middlemen's unfair profits, producer cooperatives were developed; yet producer cooperatives frequently have declared control of prices an aim. Thus during the campaign for producer cooperatives in 1920, the Prairie Farmer in its issue of September 25 printed an article entitled "Almond Growers Act Like Real Business Men; They Fix Prices and Control Their Product, and Have Run the Speculator to Cover." The article itself, like the title, emphasized the price-fixing role, and told how directors of local associations met annually to fix prices. When in 1926 the Farm Journal told "What the Big Co-op Can Do" (28), it emphasized the adjective "big," and declared that, among other things, it —

> . . . can fix, and force buyers to accept fair and uniform grades; can establish its own brands and maintain an exclusive market for them through advertising.
> . . . can afford to hire a trained sales force familiar with markets and "the tricks of the trade" . . .
> . . . can secure and furnish to members reliable figures on production and consumption or probable demand.
> . . . can block laws restricting co-operative sales methods, and keep legislative "hands off"; and secure and maintain any necessary tariff protection on its products.
> A *single farmer or a small co-op cannot do any of these things.*

In January 1925 the Pacific Rural Press told with much enthusiasm how California poultry producers' cooperatives entered the market and by manipulative buying raised the price of eggs (27). Thus the economic necessity of holding one's own in the highly commercial modern world has forced the farmer to engage as best he can in the very practices which he was once inclined to condemn as the peculiar corruptions of urban economy.

THE COUNTRY ADOPTS CITY WAYS

Rural life has for a century been throwing off the characteristics that once distinguished it so sharply from urban life. The countryside has been undergoing a process of accelerating urbanization for nearly a century. Country people in America have generally aspired to the refinements of middle-class urban culture and have achieved them when possible. Most of the deliberate efforts toward rural improvement during the nineteenth century were inspired by a desire to relieve farm life of the roughness that the frontier had imposed upon it. . . . Hostility to urban culture as such has not disappeared, although perhaps it has declined and been altered in its manifestations. The rural world has come in large measure to accept urban ideas of success, though it has continued the ancient tradition of decrying rural exodus and deploring the false lures and illusory opportunities of the city.

But in spite of everything, the younger farm people have been attracted to the city and to city traits and behavior; and they have been important agents in the extension of the urban culture to the country. Sympathetic commentators upon the exodus of rural youth have repeatedly explained the exodus in terms of the progressive, up-to-date temper of youth, and the backwardness and conservatism of age; they have urged modernizing — urbanizing — farm equipment and household furnishings as the measure necessary to keep youth on the farm. Here is an example from the Nebraska Farmer of July 1, 1885 (18):

> In most cases the trouble will be found with the farmer instead of his son. . . .
> The old man is content with some improvements on the ideas of fifty years ago. He can't see why any one should want anything better than bare floors, Windsor chairs and cowhide boots. He would as soon go to meeting without a collar as with one. . . .
> And now what's the matter with farmer's boys? They live in a new world — the father in an old one. No matter how little schooling they have had, they are better educated than he is. No matter if the father refuses to do more than subscribe to a weekly paper, his boys are fairly posted on all the daily happenings all over the world. He wants to farm after the old ideas — they after the new ones. . . .

Commercialization was only one phase of the urbanization of farm life; and it was in effect merely the means whereby farm people could obtain the products of industry that the absorption of urban culture has taught them increasingly to desire. It was generally the case that as the agricultural frontier moved westward there had to be a period of development of the primary necessities and rudimentary capital equipment. For a time the struggle to accomplish this much exhausted the means and the energies of the agricultural settlers. But when these first needs were met, they generally sought the comforts, the refinements, the labor-saving devices, and the pleasures of a less arduous life.

When farm journals first began to print fiction, shortly before the Civil War, the stories that they ran were almost without exception especially written to fit the real or imagined tastes of a rural audience. The heroes were poor young farmers, the heroines were country girls, the villians were wealthy city men; after many vicissitudes rural simplicity and virtue triumphed over urban duplicity and corruption. But by 1900 or shortly thereafter, such fiction as appeared in farm journals — those with a large national circulation were the principal purveyors — was generally the same as that appearing in any class of popular magazines. Rural people thus read fiction based on the cultural assumptions and ideals of the urban reading masses; and country readers followed willy-nilly the vagaries and shifting fads of popular urban fiction. The country has been motivated to seek some urban refinements as a defense mechanism, adopting customs of the town while continuing to decry them. . . .

The misgiving aroused in the minds of many farmers by the decline of self-sufficiency and the spread of commercialization and urban ways, backward-looking though it sometimes was, amounted to a perception of the social and economic maladjustments that the modern world was bringing to the countryside. The farmer himself, pushed one way by the impact of the new and pulled the other by the persistence of the old, sensed the cultural conflict that was frequently ignored by professional experts, who were for the most part one-sided enthusiasts. Yet the greater force has been in the direction of change, and although there have been many regretful backward glances, farmers have, in their way, adjusted themselves to their times.

Rural free delivery, farm-to-market roads, and parcel post all resulted from agitation by farm leaders strongly supported by the masses of farmers. The mail-order house came in, disseminating widely a taste for the new products of industrial civilization by attractive illustrated catalogs and making new products actually available in remote places. The influence of these catalogs is suggested by the colloquial name for them — "wishing books" — that grew up in some of the more remote regions. Late in the nineties the movement to extend telephone service to the country began; and the building of cooperative lines, sponsored or at least suggested generally by farm organizations or farm journals, gained headway. All these things brought the farmer closer to town and served in the end to extend the town into the country.

Wartime and early post-war prosperity brought an accelerated wave of urbanization to the country that reached an initial climax in a blaze of silk-shirt glory before prices fell in the autumn of 1920. But the trend toward urbanization of country living survived the slump. By the middle 1920's, automobile manufacturers were sure enough of the urbanity of the farmers who read farm journals and bought automobiles to advertise their product as "A regally luxurious motor car . . . beautifully engineered, beautifully built — and stylish as the *Rue de la Paix*." Each new convenience, every new gadget, has bound the country more closely to the town and made it more like the town. Educational effort indicated the virtues of more and still more contrivances to make life easier; and although for most farmers possession of these things was a dream rather than a hope, their existence has been driving ever higher the minimum desired living standard. Farmer visitors to Farm Home Week at Cornell in 1929 were shown a model farm home whose kitchen was described by the Cornell Countryman in the following terms (29):

> In the kitchen . . . everything was arranged to give the housewife a convenient, pleasant work room. The electrical apparatus included a refrigerator, a range, a dish washer, and a food mixer. It had that great boon to the farm woman, a complete water system. The water was heated by an electric water heater. The range was one of the kind in whose oven you put the supper and go to town for the groceries and forget about it. The clock turns the heat on and the heat is regulated so that when you come in it is all done. The central light eliminates shadow. The switch for it also had an outlet in the bottom for a flat iron. There were local lights at the sink so you would not be working in your own shadow. There was a power outlet by the table for the food mixer, toaster, or grill, and one by the refrigerator. Every farm woman who saw it probably desired a kitchen like it, so spotlessly white and convenient with all the labor saving devices that are so needed on a farm.

The ephemeral fads and fashions of the city have penetrated to many farms. Beauty columns have entered into the farm press. We find in the Idaho Farmer, April 1935:

> Hands should be soft enough to flatter the most delicate of the new fabrics. They must be carefully manicured, with none of the hot, brilliant shades of nail polish. The lighter and more delicate tones are in keeping with the spirit of freshness.
>
> Keep the tint of your fingertips friendly to the red of your lips, and check both your powder and your rouge to see that they best suit the tone of your skin in the bold light of summer.

It is certain that few farm wives have a chance to heed such "beauty hints," even if they would; but the model is there, and the advice is not all lost, especially on the younger generation.

Several farm journals have for some time sponsored winter tours by farmers; and the idea has spread that farmers should get out and see the world, to broaden their outlook and to give them a vacation, in the urban sense, from the cares of everyday life. Thus, in the syndicated colloquialisms of the Lazy Farmer, from the Idaho Farmer, 1935:

I planned to take Mirandy Jane and take a trip somewhere by train or in the car, and see some sights, nor have to go to bed of nights until we'd seen most ev'rything, nor have to rise at five, by jing. Us farm folks ought to travel more, we stay at home until we're sore at ev'rything, and raisin' hob, because we're too close to our job. It does us good to git away, when we come back some other day we're fresh in body and in mind, and if the work's a mite behind, we can pitch in and git it done, and, best of all, we've had our fun.

Loss of the Old with Acceptance of the New

It should be continually emphasized that the adoption of new things was inevitably followed, sooner or later, by the creation of new customs and new dependencies. This, in turn, involved the desertion of old ways and codes of living. This fact was in one way or another repeatedly observed, generally with regret, because the standards of value and the moral codes that constitute social adaptation to material things always outlive the things themselves. Sometimes, too, the regret was based at least partly upon a sense of social maladjustment, upon a feeling that the efficiency of an older institution had been impaired without a new one rising to take its place. Thus as long ago as 1905 one writer on rural affairs observed (68):

> Social matters are not conducted as they once were among farmers. They are following in the wake of other people, and are putting more expense and formality in entertainments than old. . . .
> . . . the "neighbor woman" has gone back on her record. The doctor and hired nurse have come to take her place. She doesn't know now the uses of sage tea and catnip, or of camomile and tansy. She can not take one of her own family through a bilious attack, or spell of colic, as the old-time mother with her garret full of herbs. . . .
> It takes more money to live now that people are not so serviceable nor so sociable. Farmers cannot afford to be sociable as sociability is conducted nowadays. . . . People want fine houses and furniture and expensive lighting and heating appurtenances; they want clipped horses and fine carriages, and they try to dress as near like the *elite* as possible and to entertain their guests as sumptuously as those do who have thrice their wealth. All this is sociability run wild — it will not endure to the end.

When, late in 1929, Farm and Fireside conducted a questionnaire survey among its subscribers to determine the extent of rural social change and of resistance to change, the editors were impressed, more than by anything else, by the evidence of rapid decline of differences between farm and city people. Interpretation of the results of this poll must be consistently qualified by recognition of the fact that the circulation of Farm and Fireside was to a disproportionate degree among the more prosperous strata of rural society and that the opinions of this group would probably not correspond to those of the majority of the whole rural population. It should also be remembered, however, that the more prosperous elements of rural society have generally been in the lead in long-time trends of change. It is this group that has generally been the first to adopt innovations that later attained wide acceptance. Although the Farm and Fireside survey showed rural opinion heavily against easy divorce and repeal of prohibition, 67 percent favored "legalizing doctors to impart birth control methods to married couples who apply jointly" — an opinion that the editors called "a most astonishing departure from old-fashioned standards." The survey also disclosed that articles dealing with "world events and modern thought" were the most popular of all with Farm and Fireside readers. One of the most significant of all was the vote on consolidated schools. It was reported that 78 percent were in favor of them. On this vote Farm and Fireside commented (30):

> Distinctly on the side of progress is the vote as to consolidated schools. They cost money, a good deal of money; they represent what old-timers call citified, new-fangled nonsense, but the countryside of America clamors for them, four votes out of five.

What may well be the earliest complete repudiation of the old agrarian social code by a spokesman for agriculture occurred, as might be expected, in a region where farming has been more industrialized and farm life less distinctly rural than in any other large section of the country. In 1915, the Pacific Rural Press reprinted a little story from a midwestern farm paper. This is the story.

> A man and a woman sat together at a theater one afternoon last week. He wore a cheap suit of clothing that fitted him poorly. Her dress was not in the latest mode. Plainly, they were from the country.
> Right behind them sat two women of the city. One of them put her lorgnette to her eyes, bent forward and looked critically at the woman in front of her. Then she settled back in her chair and said in a voice evidently intended for the woman in front to hear: "Why do some people have such awful taste as to dress as they used to before the flood?"
> The woman in front heard it and her face went red. The man with her heard it too, and he quietly laid his hand upon his companions's arm and patted it lovingly.
> A man who sat near, and had heard and seen this little tragedy, told of it afterward. "I knew the man from the country, and his wife," he said. "I know that she is his partner in running that farm. Her vegetables, butter and eggs provide an important part of their income. Now they have come to the city for an outing. To my mind they belong to the class who are really our best people, and the woman behind them with the lorgnette is just a coarse, vulgar frump" (25).

This was an almost perfect example of the stereotyped homily that had appeared thousands of times in farm journals for nearly a century in expression of the older agrarian social creed. But the Pacific Rural Press reprinted it only in order to make its modern comment:

> Of course, our Middle West contemporary has to preach upon the text this incident presents, but it needs no sermon here. In the first place, we believe our rural women are relatively better dressed than elsewhere, and therefore the incident would have no local foundation. . . . Our point is that the contrast between rural and urban women in costuming is probably less in California than anywhere else in the world. And we are of the impression also that California rural women are not infrequently outfitted to do the lorgnette act toward the urban women were they not prevented by inborn politeness. . . . (25.)

The conflict between the old and the new

. . . American agriculture has lived through a long series of cultural conflicts during the past century. There has been almost continuous conflict between folkways and folklore on the one hand and applications of scientific rationality on the other. The intellectual and reform elements in agriculture have invariably sought to hasten and to alter the direction of our cultural evolution. There was a conflict in the middle-western agricultural regions in the ante bellum period between the matter-of-fact, severely practical culture, inherited principally from New England and the Middle Atlantic States, and the idealism and optimism fostered by the intellectuals of that period. There has consistently been a conflict between the moral concept of the farmer, developed in part out of older experience but perpetuated by the literary tradition of agrarian fundamentalism, and new realities brought into being by the commercialization of agriculture. Thus the literary tradition has it that the farmer is independent and secure unto himself — which in most cases he has manifestly ceased to be; that he is remote from the ills and corruptions of the market place and unenvious of urban luxuries — which ordinarily he obviously cannot be.

This concept of the farm as a gentle haven from the world's strife is in flat contradiction to the tendencies toward commercialization, mechanization, specialization, and urbanization that are the dominant trends of modern agriculture. And yet it is a fact that this idyllic agrarian fundamentalism has been perpetuated principally by the intellectual and reform elements that have been most active in modernizing American agriculture.

Farm people themselves, genuinely devoted as they may be to country life, have not fooled themselves in this way. They have been too close to the monotony of chores, the dust of harrowing, the threat of drought and pests and disease. Yet among some professional agricultural leaders and educators there has evidently been a desire to idealize rural life in a moral and aesthetic way, and also to see agriculture principally in terms of the most prosperous group of farmers. In order to establish good examples for emulation, or because of class or economic predilections, the farmer has thus been identified with a level of ease, equipment, well-being, and prosperity far above any average for the Nation as a whole. Thus a secondary-school text in farm management, written 26 years ago by one of the most capable experts in the field, displayed as the first of many illustrations a photograph with the legend, "An American Farm Home" (*41, p. 8*). The inevitable implication was that the house shown was average or typical. Actually, however, the picture portrayed the hobby farm of a wealthy city man far out of the class of anything that could be called an average or typical farm. In another high-school text on agriculture published in 1939 is a photograph flat-footedly captioned "An airplane view of a typical farm in the North Central Region" (*42, p. 3*). This "typical" farmstead includes a white house of apparently 8 to 10 rooms; a windmill and pump house; a poultry house large enough for at least 1,000 chickens, with incubator and brooder space extra; a dairy barn large enough for 40 or more milk cows in addition to stalls for horses; hog houses to take care of a dozen or more brood sows, and shelter also for shoats; a large milkshed; and in addition one large building that looks like a machinery shed, another apparently a garage or workshop, and another that seems to be a large crib for grain storage.

Incidents of this kind would be trivial were it not that they indicate the frequent confusion of the real and the ideal in thinking about agriculture and that — much more important — they illustrate the social stratification of agricultural ideas that corresponds to the social stratification that has been developing in fact. The majority of educational, reform, and adjustment programs have tended strongly to be directed toward the benefit of a class of farmers who came nearest to corresponding to the abstract conception of the farmer suggested by such illustrations as are noted above.

Thus both the deliberate attempts to improve agriculture and rural life and the untoward, uncontrolled social forces of this age have for the most part concentrated their benefits upon the more prosperous element of the farm population. For only the more prosperous ones have been able to take full advantage of modern technology and commercialism. And while this upper economic stratum has had its living standards raised rapidly, the lower stratum has not been able to follow. As a result the cleavage between the two has grown increasingly wider. The rising proportions of tenancy and farm indebtedness, the growing population pressure in many rural regions, the dramatic migrations of the disinherited are other symptoms of the growing stratification of rural society.

Beyond a doubt the present trends are forcefully directed toward a great split in the agricultural population — the upper group, inclined to take on more and more of the traits of the urban and small-town middle class, while the lower economic stratum seems destined for wage-labor status within a society in which caste consciousness and class lines based on economic means are developing to a rigidity previously unknown among freemen in this country.

A situation has been created out of which new kinds of economic dispari-ties and social dislocations have developed. Measures conceived in tradi-tional terms, although helpful, have generally failed to achieve any substan-tial adjustment. The inadequacy of older institutions and arrangements, even as means to attain the substance of older ideals and aspirations, has become more apparent as the modern situation has intensified. As a result the boundless confidence and optimism by which the agricultural domain of this country was first settled and made productive have been increasingly qualified by bewilderment and pessimism, and the former ideal of progress is giving ground to a new ideal of security.

Literature Cited

(1) Anonymous, "Extract of a Letter to the Editors, *Cultivator* I (1834) 113–114.

(2) ———, "To the Patrons of the Cultivator" (letter), *Cultivator* II (1836) 161–162.

(3) ———, ["The Farmer"], *Union Agr. and Western Prairie Farmer* I(8) (1841) 63.

(4) ———, "The Garden," *Cultivator* IX (1842) 55–56.

(5) ———, "Manufactures at Lowell," *Farmer's Monthly Visitor* VII(1) (1845) 4.

(6) ———, "Work for Children," *Farmer's Monthly Visitor* VIII(2) (1846) 29.

(7) ———, "Indian Corn: What Is Known and What Is Wanted to Be Known About It," *Monthly Jour. Agr.* II (1847) 537–547.

(8) ———, "Poetry and Profit of City Life" (by a Lover of the Country), *Prairie Farmer* X(1) (1850) 18–19.

(9) ———, "Random Notes of a Journey East" (by an old sucker), *Prairie Farmer* X (1850) 180.

(10) ———, "Honor and Profit of Industry," *New England Farmer* III (1851) 391–392.

(11) ———, "Labor Is Capital," *New England Farmer* III (1851) 150.

(12) ———, "What Is Respectability?" *Northern Farmer* II (1853) 121.

(13) ———, "Humble Worth," *Amer. Farmers' Mag.* XII (1858) 634.

(14) ———, "Gold Mines at Home," *Prairie Farmer* (n.s. V) XXI (1860) 148.

(15) ———, "How We Have All Advanced," *Prairie Farmer* (n.s. XXI) XXXVII (1868) 17.

(16) ———, "Hired Labor," *Kans. Farmer* VII (1870) 138.

(17) ———, "Refinement Among Farmers" (Editorial comment on a letter by "An old Subscriber"), *Ohio Practical Farmer* LXVII(12) (1885) 198.

(18) ———, "Short Talk With the Boys," by M. Quad, *Nebr. Farmer* IX (1885) 205–206.

(19) ———, "What Are You Reading?" by "Rusticus," *Ohio Practical Farmer* LXVII(8) (1885) 127.

(20) ———, "Cultivation," *Farm Jour.* X (1886) 102.

(21) ———, "Study Your Business," *Farm Jour.* X(1) (1886) 8.

(22) ———, "The Farmer as a Merchant," *Farm Jour.* XI (1887) 130.

(23) ———, "How to Economize," *Ohio Practical Farmer* LXXVII (1890) 442.

(24) ———, "The Farmers' Institute" (editorial), *Cornell Countryman* I(1) (1903) 14.

(25) ———, "Two Great Things in California," *Pacific Rural Press* LXXXIX (1915) 290.

(26) ———, "The 'Divine Law' of Supply and Demand," *Ohio Farmer* CLV (1925) 280.

(27) ———, "Putting a Crowbar under the Market," *Pacific Rural Press* CIX (1925) 70.

(28) ———, "What the Big Co-Op Can Do," *Farm Jour.* L(6) (1926) 8.

(29) ———, "Rural Electricity and the Home," *Cornell Countryman* XXVI, illus. (1929) 208.

(30) ———, "The Forces of Change," *Farm and Fireside* LIV(1) (1930) 9, 32–38.

(31) A., A.E.A., "Knowledge Is Power" (letter), *Cultivator* VIII (1841) 164.

(32) Adams, R. L., *Farm Management: A Textbook for Students, Investigator, and Investor*, illus., New York and London, 1921, 671 pp.

(33) Alley, J. P., "What a Farmer Really Looks Like," *Country Gent.* LXXXVI(31) (1921) 7.

(34) Atkeson, Thomas Clark, *Semi-Centennial History of the Patrons of Husbandry*, 364 pp., illus., New York, 1916.

(35) B., "Female Help," *New England Farmer* (n.s.)IX (1857) 247–248.

(36) B., C. D., "The Canadian Excursion," *Prairie Farmer* (n.s. VI) XXII (1860) [65], 72, [81], 89, [97], 100–101.

(37) Bailey, L. H., *The Country-Life Movement in the United States*, New York (1911) 220 pp.

(38) Bidwell, Percy Wells, and John I. Falconer, *History of Agriculture in the Northern United States, 1620–1860*, Washington, D.C., 1925, 512 pp.

(39) Birkbeck, Morris, *Letters from Illinois*, Ed. 3, London (1818) 114 pp.

(40) ———, *Notes on a Journey in America, from the Coast of Virginia to the Territory of Illinois*, Ed. 4, London, 1818, 156 pp.

(41) Boss, Andrew, *Farm Management*, illus., Chicago and New York, 1914, 237 pp.

(42) ———, Harold K. Wilson, and William E. Peterson, *American Farming: Agriculture* I, illus., St. Paul, Minn., 1939, 526 pp.

(43) Brayshaw, Joseph, "Mr. Brayshaw's Address" (letter to editor, enclosing address), *Union Agr. and Western Prairie Farmer* I(8) (1841) 59–60.

(44) Carrier, Lyman, *The Beginnings of Agriculture in America*, illus., New York, 1923, 323 pp.

(45) Collin, Nicholas, "Physico-Mathemaćical [sic] Enquiries," *Amer. Phil. Soc. Trans.* III, xiii–xv.

(46) Curti, Merle, *The Learned Blacksmith: The Letters and Journals of Elihu Burritt*, New York, 1937, 241 pp.

(47) D., "Study and Labor" (letter to editor), *New England Farmer* III (1851) 210–211.

(48) Davenport, Eugene, "The Outlook for the Educated Farmer," *Cornell Countryman* I (1904) 204–205.

(49) Editor of *Farm and Fireside*, "The Editor's Letter . . . ," *Farm and Fireside* XXXIX(22) (1916) 2.

(50) G., C. J., "The Country and the City," *Prairie Farmer* X (1850) 378–379.

(51) G., W., "Query to Farmers," *Cultivator* I (1835) 189.

(52) Galpin, Charles Josiah, "The Development of the Science and Philosophy of American Rural Society," *Agr. Hist.* XII (1938) 195–208.

(53) Gilbert, A. B., "These 'Fair' Crop Prices," *Farm Jour.* L(11) (1926) 48–49.

(54) Gilbert, Z. A., "Farmers' Clubs," *New England Farmer* V(2) (1871) 81–82.

(55) Gray, Lewis Cecil, *History of Agriculture in the Southern United States to 1860*, 2v., Washington, D.C., 1933.

(56) ———, and O. G. Lloyd, "Farm Land Values in Iowa," U.S. Dept. Agr. Bul. 874, 45 pp., illus.

(57) Greeley, Horace, *What I Know of Farming: A Series of Brief and Plain Expositions of Practical Agriculture as an Art Based Upon Science*, New York, 1871, 321 pp.

(58) Grundy, Fred, "What Shall the Young Man Do?" *Farm and Fireside* XXXII(5) (1908) 3.

(59) Hibbard, Benjamin Horace, "History of Agriculture in Dane County, Wisconsin," Wis. Univ. Bul. 101, pp. [69]–214, illus. (Econ. and Polit. Sci. Ser. v. I, No. 2, pp. 67–214) 1904.

(60) Hurst, W. M. and L. M. Church, "Power and Machinery in Agriculture," U.S. Dept. Agr. Misc. Pub. 157 (1933) 38 pp., illus.

(61) James, Edmund J., "The Origin of the Land Grant Act of 1862 (The So-Called Morrill Act) and Some Account of Its Author, Jonathan B. Turner," Ill. Univ. Studies v. IV, No. 1, 139 pp., Urbana (Appendix C, The Turner Pamphlet, pp. 45–111) 1910.

(62) Kelsey, David Stone, *Kelsey's Rural Guide . . .* , Boston, 1925, 299 pp.

(63) Liebig, Justus, *Organic Chemistry in Its Applications to Agriculture and Physiology*, Ed. from the manuscript of the author, by Lyon Playfair, London (1840) 387 pp.

(64) Loehr, Rodney C., "The Influence of English Agriculture on American Agriculture," 1775–1825," *Agr. Hist.* XI (1937) 3–15.

(65) Oliver, H. K., "Extract from an Address," *Amer. Farmers' Mag.* XI(1) (1858) 22–26.

(66) Petty, Fred L., "Sugar Beets as Cash Crop," *Ill. Farmer* LXXVIII (1930) 563.

(67) Robinson, Solon, "A Proposition to Facilitate Agricultural Improvement," *Cultivator* V (1838) 60–61.

(68) Sidney, Mary, "Sociability among Farmers," *Farm. Jour.* XXIX (1905) 109.

(69) Thaer, Albert D., *The Principles of Agriculture*, Trans. by William Shaw and Cuthbert W. Johnson, London, v. I, 1844.

(70) Tocqueville, Alexis C. H. C. de, *The Republic of the United States of America, and Its Political Institutions, Reviewed and Examined*, Trans. by Henry Reeves, Esq., with preface and notes by John C. Spencer . . . , pt. 2, New York, 1849, 355 pp.

(71) True, Alfred Charles, "A History of Agricultural Education in the United States 1785–1925," U.S. Dept. Agr. Misc. Pub. 36, illus., 1929, 436 pp.

(72) True, Rodney H., "Early Days of the Albemarle Agricultural Society," *Agr. Hist. Soc. Papers* I, Washington, D.C. (1921) 243–259.

(73) Tryon, Rolla Milton, *Household Manufactures in the United States, 1640–1860: A Study in Industrial History*, Chicago, 1917, 413 pp.

(74) Willard, X. A., ["Address . . . Before the Illinois and Wisconsin Dairymen's Association], *Prairie Farmer* (n.s. 21) XXXVII (1868) 115.

(75) Williams, A., "Agriculture in California," [U.S.] Commissioner of Patents Ann. Rpt. 1851 (1852) 3–7.

2

AMERICAN ATTITUDES TOWARD THE CITY

"The city" has always been "a problem." Though the word itself derives from the Greek for "civilization," it has, through most American history at least, suggested something closer to "Sodom" or "Gomorrah." "The great city," announced progressive Senator Moses Clapp in 1914, "is a place where vice feeds upon itself like a festering sore thriving on its own rottenness. The best interests of our Republic demand the widest possible extension of our population outside the cities."

Part of "the problem" was that the city contradicted the model of self-sufficiency conjured up for the ideal American by the Jeffersonian dream. Perhaps mainly for that reason, the nation persistently declined to attempt institutional and political adjustments which the rapid ascendancy of urbanism in American life demanded. Movements for reform usually pointed to restoring the vitality of country living, even though economic imperatives and social preferences plainly pointed in the other direction. For example, twenty times as many Americans entered the cities in the last decades of the nineteenth century as left the cities for the farms. And by the beginning of the twentieth century, a decisively greater proportion of the national population growth was occurring in the cities. The growth ratio, moreover, was to increase in favor of the cities very substantially over the first three decades. By 1930, 30 percent of the population lived in cities of over 100,000. More significantly, by that year, 61 million people, or a little less than half the population, lived in 115 metropolitan areas. By 1965, 121.5 million, or almost two-thirds of all Americans were residing in metropolitan areas.

In the article reprinted below, Scott Donaldson, who teaches at the College of William and Mary, surveys the efforts of various American thinkers to improve the condition of living for American city-dwellers. It is a rare article indeed, in that it combines history with critical analyses of reform proposals both past and current.

For bibliographic guidance and excellent survey coverage, students should consult Mel Scott's *American City Planning Since 1890* (1969), and Blake McKelvey's two-volume history of the American city, *The Urbanization of America: 1860–1915* (1963), and *The Emergence of Metropolitan America, 1915–1966* (1968). Peter J. Schmitt, *Back to Nature: The Arcadian Myth in Urban America* (1969) elaborates on one of the important themes of Donaldson's article. Jane Jacobs, *The Death and Life of Great American Cities* (1967), passionately criticizes modern urban renewal programs – partly on the grounds that they usually seek to achieve a pseudo-rural environment; the book is especially useful for its subtle presentation of the vital relationship between people and place, and of the devastating human consequences that have often followed upon the obliteration of whole neighborhoods in the interest of modern housing projects. Roderick Nash, "The American Cult of the Primitive," *American Quarterly*, 18 (Fall 1966), focuses upon early twentieth-century American fears of the decline of the frontier and nature, and the growing doubts about the values of "civilization."

City and Country: Marriage Proposals

SCOTT DONALDSON

David Riesman, in his essay on "The Suburban Sadness," acknowledges that he writes as "one who loves city and country, but not the suburbs." [1] Riesman's position is not at all unusual. Most social commentators regard today's suburbs more with loathing than with love, finding them homogeneous, conformist, adjustment-oriented, conservative, dull, child centered, female dominated, anti-individualist — in a word, impossible — places to live. It was not always thus, with intellectuals.

For one thing, the American intellectual has not, until recently — until, in fact, the suburb came along as a scapegoat to replace the city — been willing to confess any affection for the city. For another, as Ebenezer Howard suggested in 1898, there was a time when the suburb was thought of as the hope of civilization, as the happy, healthy offspring of the marriage of town and country: "Town and country *must be married*, and out of this joyous union will spring a new hope, a new life, a new civilization." [2] Howard's Garden Cities represented the apotheosis of the suburban dream — places which were at once *real* communities, collections of people who would work and live together in civic and social harmony, and at the same time totally self-sufficient units, made up of discrete individuals able and willing to pursue their own private goals. Indeed, if hopes had not once been

Reprinted by permission of the University of Pennsylvania and the author from *American Quarterly*, 20 (Fall 1968), 547–66. Copyright, 1968, Trustees of the University of Pennsylvania. This article, in amended form, constitutes part of *The Suburban Myth* by Scott Donaldson (Columbia University Press, 1969).

[1] David Riesman, "The Suburban Sadness," in William M. Dobriner, ed., *The Suburban Community* (New York, 1958), p. 375.

[2] Ebenezer Howard, *Garden Cities of Tomorrow* (London, 1965), p. 48. Italics his.

so high for suburbia, it surely would not have fallen so low in critical esti-
mation at the midpoint of the twentieth century. For Howard was by no
means the only theorist to envision the suburb as the product of a happy
marriage between town and country, a union designed to resolve one of the
most troublesome paradoxes of American civilization.

The paradox is, of course, the continuing worship of rural, countrified
life in a nation where the pull of progress has created unmistakably urban
civilization. The roots of the agrarian myth stretch back to the beginnings of
western culture and the paradisiacal garden. But the most powerful expressions of the myth came with the new nation and the Enlightenment, in
the voices of such men as Hector St. John de Crèvecoeur and Thomas Jefferson. Jefferson's fondness for the farm and dislike of the city are legendary,
and Crèvecoeur located his ideal Americans on the farms of the "middle settlements," midway between sea and wilderness, where the simple cultivation
of the earth would purify them. These men expressed beliefs which have demonstrated amazing staying power. Their persistence can hardly be denied
in a land where the Supreme Court must step in to assure city and suburb
dwellers something like fair legislative representation, where farmers are
subsidized not to grow crops, where it is still expedient for a politician to
claim a rural heritage. And the beliefs persist despite their obvious lack of
relevance to reality. Men mouth agrarian sentiments, but go to the cities,
where the money is to be made. The American thinker, almost since the
first days of the Republic, has been confronted with this paradox, and as
time proceeded American thought arrived at a potential solution. It would
be the suburb which would represent the best of both worlds, which would
preserve rural values in an urbanizing world, which would enable the individual to pursue wealth while retaining the amenities of country life.

After the Civil War and owing to the development of the railroads, the
first American suburbs were developed around New York, Boston and Philadelphia. From the beginning, these suburbs were regarded as ideal places to
live, representing a rather wealthy middle landscape between crowded, unhealthy city life and the "coarse and brutal" frontier.[3] "So long as men are
forced to dwell in log huts and follow the hunter's life," Alexander Jackson
Downing wrote, "we must not be surprised at lynch law and the use of the
bowie knife. But, when smiling lawns and tasteful cottages begin to embel-
lish a country, we know that order and culture are established." [4] Downing
had in mind rural villages full of tasteful "cottages" of real elegance, like
those going up at Newport, Rhode Island.

Efforts soon began to scale down the lavish Newport cottage to the

[3] The term "middle landscape" is borrowed from Leo Marx, *The Machine in the
Garden* (New York, 1964). Marx applied the concept of the middle landscape primar-
ily to literature, not to intellectual history, but it has relevance to both disciplines.
Note, for example, its application to Crèvecoeur's "middle settlements" in J. Hector St.
John de Crèvecoeur, *Letters from an American Farmer* (London, 1926), pp. 44–45.

[4] Alexander Jackson Downing, in John Burchard and Albert Bush-Brown, *The Ar-
chitecture of America* (Boston, 1961), p. 101.

pocketbooks of the middle classes. Suburban homes and lots served as promotional bait in an 1876 *Harper's Weekly* advertisement aimed at attracting readers to "the Fourth of July Centennial Demonstration at the Third Avenue Theater." Two two-story cottages and ten $100 lots in Garden City Park, on Long Island, would be raffled off at the demonstration, the advertisement announced, as well as 100 silver watches and 388 one-dollar greenbacks.[5] Later in the same year, this magazine celebrated the joys of suburban life with a cover picture and article on "Summer in the Country." The picture, which shows a young boy and girl "walking side by side in the sweet summer fields," was designed to remind readers, "by contrast, of the sad lot of poor city children, who rarely have the opportunity to breathe the pure air of the country, and refresh their eyes with the sight of flowers and grass." [6] The "flowers and grass" make it clear that the "country" *Harper's Weekly* finds so desirable is somewhat nearer at hand than the Iowa corn fields, say. If such a stretch of country was inaccessible to most readers of the magazine, as it probably was in 1876, it still represented a popular goal. Then as now, the place to bring up children was out in the open air, far from noise and smoke. Three years later, in 1879, the radical Henry George proposed in *Progress and Poverty* that his single tax on land would have the effect of creating a sort of ideal middle landscape. Such a single tax, George maintained, would do away with wholesale speculation in real estate, and

> The destruction of speculative land values would tend to diffuse population where it is too dense and to concentrate it where it is too sparse; to substitute for the tenement house, homes surrounded by gardens, and to fully settle agricultural districts before people were driven far from neighbors to look for land. The people of the cities would thus get more of the pure air and sunshine of the country, the people of the country more of the economics and social life of the city. . . .[7]

Certainly most Americans agreed with this urban politician in an emotional preference for country over city; certainly most desired above all that union of country and city, sunshine and social life, he envisioned as a consequence of the single tax.

It remained for Ebenezer Howard, the London court reporter, to propose specific arrangements for this marriage of city and country in his influential 1898 book, *Garden Cities of Tomorrow*. Howard's proposals were welcomed on both sides of the Atlantic, and they remain today the guiding principles of so important an American critic and theorist as Lewis Mumford. Clearly, they are motivated by agrarian sentiments:

> It is well-nigh universally agreed by men of all parties, not only in England, but all over Europe and America and our colonies, that it is deeply to be deplored that the people should continue to stream into

[5] *Harper's Weekly*, XX (Apr. 8, 1876), 294.
[6] *Harper's Weekly*, XX (Sept. 5, 1876), 709.
[7] Henry George, *Progress and Poverty* (New York, 1884), p. 405.

> the already over-crowded cities, and should thus further deplete the country districts. . . .

How should we go about restoring people to the garden — "that beautiful land of ours, with its canopy of sky, the air that blows upon it, the sun that warms it, and rain and dew that moisten it — the very embodiment of Divine love for man?" [8] The restoration can be accomplished, Howard wrote, only if we reject two-valued, black and white thinking, and consider instead a third alternative.

"There are in reality not only . . . two alternatives — town life and country life — but a third alternative, in which all the advantages of the most energetic and active town life, with all the beauty and delight of the country, may be secured in perfect combination. . . ." To illustrate the point, Howard constructed the metaphor of the magnets. Each person may be regarded as a needle, attracted by magnets. Until now, he wrote, the town has had the most powerful magnet, and so it has pulled citizen-needles from the no longer all powerfully magnetic "bosom of our kindly mother earth." To remedy the situation, "nothing short of the discovery of a method of constructing magnets of yet greater power than our cities possess can be effective for redistributing the population in a spontaneous and healthy manner. . . ." Howard set about to construct this magnet "of yet greater power," the magnet which combined the best of both town and country. There was social opportunity in town, but it was balanced by a "closing out of nature"; there was beauty of nature in the country, but it was measured against "lack of society." The town-country magnet would merge the country's beauty of nature with the town's social opportunity. In economic terms, the town's magnetism resulted at least partly from the high wages paid, but rents were high in town as well. In the country, rents were low, but so were wages. In the new town-country land, however, the citizen would make high wages and pay low rents — he would have his cake and eat it, too.

What the town-country magnet boiled down to, in Howard's theory, was the Garden City, which was to be economically self-sufficient while still at peace with nature. Population would be restricted to a workable size in the Garden City, and jobs, including industrial jobs, provided for all inhabitants. But the homes would be surrounded with greenery; the presence of nature was never to be lost sight of in a pell-mell drive for the dollar. In his conception of the Garden City, Howard had constructed a new version of the middle landscape, closer to town than Crèvecoeur's. In Crèvecoeur's version, the middle settlements were located halfway between the city seaports and the wild woods; Howard had moved his middle landscape (in conception if not in fact) so that it was now placed between the city and those rural settlements which had served as Crèvecoeur's ideal. The ideal middle

[8] Howard, pp. 50–57.

landscape, in short, was coming closer and closer to suburbia. It would be more explicitly located there by intellectuals in the early decades of the twentieth century.

This movement of the middle landscape closer to the city reflected a growing awareness, already obvious in the negative features of Howard's country magnet, that rural life left something to be desired. The farm could never be subject to the vilification the muckrakers brought to bear on the American city, but the agrarian life was not milk and honey, either. The Country Life Commission appointed by President Theodore Roosevelt in 1908 reported that drudgery, barrenness and heavy drinking characterized rural regions.[9] The town boy did not have to visit Paree to pack up and leave; the question was rather, "how you gonna keep 'em down on the farm," after they've seen the farm? Young people continued to desert farming for the city, but the standard operating rhetoric of all Americans, whether they were urban or rural by birth, continued to hymn the praises and celebrate the virtues of life on the land. In their hearts, Americans knew that the good life was agrarian; but they listened to their heads, which told them to seek their future in the city.

Somewhat in the manner of Al Smith, who believed that the ills of democracy could be cured by more democracy, Teddy Roosevelt's Country Life Commission recommended a revival of rural civilization as a solution to its apparent degeneration. This revived rural life was to be different, however. In the words of the Commission chairman, Dean Liberty Hyde Bailey of the Cornell Agricultural School, it would be a "working out of the desire to make rural civilization . . . a world-motive to even up society as between country and city." [10] The scales were over-balanced in favor of the city. Something was needed to give more weight to the country's side of the contest. That something, several turn-of-the-century observers were convinced, was represented by the suburb.

Adna Weber, writing in 1900, surveyed suburban growth, then scarcely beginning, and pronounced it the happiest of social movements:

> The "rise of the suburbs" it is, which furnishes the solid basis of a hope that the evils of city life, so far as they result from overcrowding, may be in large part removed. . . . It will realize the wish and prediction of Kingsley, "a complete interpenetration of city and country, a complete fusion of their different modes of life and a combination of the advantages of both, such as no country in the world has ever seen." [11]

Court reporter Howard had located his town-country magnet in carefully planned Garden Cities of the future. Weber was more optimistic: mere dis-

[9] Carl N. Degler, *Out of Our Past* (New York and Evanston, 1959), p. 327.

[10] In A. Whitney Griswold, *Farming and Democracy* (New Haven, 1952), pp. 179–80.

[11] Adna F. Weber, *The Growth of Cities in the Nineteenth Century* (Ithaca, N.Y., 1963), p. 475.

persal of population to the suburbs, a trend already going its own merry, unplanned way, would accomplish the modern utopia.

Frederic C. Howe, in his 1905 book, *The City: The Hope of Democracy*, qualified the title's message by suggesting that suburbanization, not urbanization, represented the democratic hope of the future:

> The open fields about the city are inviting occupancy, and there the homes of the future will surely be. The city proper will not remain the permanent home of the people. Population must be dispersed. The great cities of Australia are spread out into the suburbs in a splendid way. For miles about are broad roads, with small houses, gardens, and an opportunity for touch with the freer, sweeter life which the country offers.[12]

Avowedly pro-urbanite, Howe could not resist, at least rhetorically, the charms of the countryside. These, he thought, could be made available to every man, living in "small houses" with gardens, in the suburbs of the future.

Two eminent Harvard philosophers took much the same view as Weber and Howe, though they did not advocate suburbanization by name. Josiah Royce, who deplored the excessive mobility, the homogenizing tendencies, and the "mob spirit" of city life, maintained that the individual was swallowed up by the city, and could avoid this fate only by fleeing to the provinces. In the "provinces" (what he seems to have meant by this term might be designated "rural villages") were located the small social groups in which freedom was now to be found. The individual could best exercise his individualism in a socio-economic-political community of limited size: the message, basically, of Thomas Jefferson, restated in twentieth-century terms by the leading idealist of the age. George Santayana blended a strong strain of the bucolic with his urbane philosophy. Describing his boyhood town of Avila, Spain, he "expressed his admiration of situations that he described by the phrases *rus in urbs, oppidum in agris,* or *urbs ruri,* some combination of city and country." [13] The search for the ideal middle landscape persisted along with the belief that city life was stifling to the soul. Louis Sullivan, in his *Autobiography of an Idea,* tells the sinister effects of being taken to Boston as a young lad. "As one might move a flourishing plant from the open to a dark cellar, and imprison it there, so the miasma of the big city poisoned a small boy acutely sensitive to his surroundings. He mildewed; and the leaves and buds of ambition fell from him." He would surely have run away, the architect recollects without tranquility, had it not been for his father's wise excursions with him to the suburbs, "on long walks to Roxbury,

---

[12] Frederic C. Howe, *The City: The Hope of Democracy* (New York, 1905), p. 204.

[13] Josiah Royce, *Race Questions, Provincialism and Other American Problems* (New York, 1908), pp. 97–98; George Santayana, *The Background of My Life* (New York, 1944), p. 298.

to Dorchester, even to Brookline, where the boy might see a bit of green and an opening-up of things. . . ." [14]

Perhaps the worst thing about the twentieth-century city, as such observers as Robert Park and John Dewey examined it, was its very bigness. In the urban maelstrom, the individual lost the identity that had been so assuredly his on the farm, in the village. The primary group tended to dissolve in the city, Park wrote in 1916, and people lost sight of the values of the local community in a search for excitement. "Cities," he wrote, "have been proverbially and very properly described as 'wicked.' " It is both ironic and appropriate that Park, the nation's first great urban sociologist, should have revealed a nostalgic preference for the secure values of an agrarian civilization, of the family on the farm.[15] Dewey, like Park, noted the frenetic quest for excitement in cities and suggested that it might be simply "the expression of [a] frantic search for something to fill the void caused by the loosening of the bonds which hold persons together in [an] immediate community of experience." As Morton and Lucia White point out in their valuable survey, *The Intellectual Versus the City,* Dewey and Park were both playing modern variants on an old theme of Jefferson's, "divide the counties into wards." Like Jefferson, these public philosophers of the twentieth century regarded the small local community as the fit habitation of democratic men.[16]

In 1917, John R. McMahon published a remarkable book entitled *Success in the Suburbs.* He agreed with Park and Dewey that the city failed to provide man with a healthy environment. By some mystical process, nature refused to function inside the city limits, as O. S. Morgan of Columbia's department of agriculture wrote in a foreword:

> Soil somehow has ceased here to function normally on root systems, has become dirt and dust. Tonic sunshine has ceased to function in chlorophyll bodies in the leaf, has become an unrevered model after which to pattern an enervating midnight glare.

The elect of the city, if they followed the good advice of author McMahon, would throw off this city spell. The advice was simplicity personified. Take yourself to the suburbs, he told his readers, where you can find true success. What was meant by success? Simply "an independent home establishment

---

[14] Louis Sullivan, *The Autobiography of an Idea* (New York, 1922), pp. 98–99.

[15] Robert Ezra Park, *Human Communities: The City and Human Ecology* (Glencoe, Ill., 1952), pp. 34, 140.

[16] John Dewey, *The Public and Its Problems* (New York, 1927), pp. 211, 214. See also Morton and Lucia White, *The Intellectual Versus the City* (New York, 1964), pp. 177–79. The Whites maintain that the attitude of the intellectual toward the American city underwent a change in the late nineteenth century, from an attitude of basic hostility to one of belief in the potentiality of the city, once it was reformed. But the reformers seemed almost invariably to want to change the city back into the rural village.

in a fairly countrified suburb; a household that is self-supporting as to fruits, vegetables, eggs, broilers, and such-like, produced for home use and chiefly by the efforts of the family itself. . . ." Such a successful life not only "means health and happiness"; it also means financial independence. There will be no *cash* dividends, but "in terms of edibles produced and economies effected above the cost of living in the city," suburban life "returns an annual profit on the investment of something like twenty-five percent." In the suburbs, then, a man and his family can enjoy the moral and physical benefits of contact with the soil, and they can make a pretty penny as well.[17]

McMahon's was a "how to" book, as the subtitle makes clear. To achieve *Success in the Suburbs,* one must know "How to Locate, Buy and Build; Garden and Grow Fruit; Keep Fowls and Animals." McMahon provides the answers. For him, clearly, "suburbs" seem to have little value connotation by themselves, until they are transformed into farms. But as the future site of a nation of subsistence farmers, providing economic as well as spiritual gain, the suburbs would come to represent the Jeffersonian paradise regained. This paradise is within your grasp, McMahon told his readers; simply follow my suggestions.

Every spring, he writes, "city folks yawn and have a hungry look in the eyes. They are restless and discontented, peeved and out of kilter." It is not love that troubles them, but nature: "they are bitten by the bacillicus countrycus," which "is beneficent to those who live in the country, but . . . torments those who are prisoned in offices and flats." Urbanites should divorce their city jobs and residences to form a more perfect union. Like Howard, McMahon adopts the marriage metaphor. "My argument is that all city folks who can, should marry nature and settle down with her." You don't have to be rich to escape to suburban wedlock, he counsels. All that is needed is "a snug little home in the nearby country and a piece of ground large enough to grow eggs, fruits, and vegetables."

It is amazing how the family will thrive in its new arrangement. Pale cheeks will grow rosy. Everyone will sleep like a log. Members of the family will get acquainted with one another, finding with relief that they are not "all monotonous Henry James characters" after all. There will be economic rewards as well. The family will raise its own crops for consumption, "thereby collar[ing] a string of middlemen's profits." In town, the family had lived up to its income and could save little or nothing; on the suburban farm, they "live better and are able to stow away a few hundred dollars annually without feeling it." In bestowing advice, McMahon seasons his overt agrarianism with good, hard, common, dollar sense. The first problem is to find a site, and beauty deserves some, but not final, consideration. "Scenery sticks around your habitation a long time and it is wise to pick out a brand that is pleasing and wears well," he writes. "At the same time scenery is not

17 John R. McMahon, *Success in the Suburbs* (New York and London, 1917), pp. x–xi.

edible and *butters no parsnips.*" [18] The "dollar fiend" and the philosophical agrarian come together in the same paragraph; the author speaks at once with the voice of Thomas Jefferson, and with that of Benjamin Franklin. Like Franklin, McMahon keeps his eye on the main chance; he is nothing if not practical and up-to-date. It is the availability of modern tools and materials, in fact, which has made a utopian life on the suburban farm possible. You can achieve your individualism, and be comfortable about it as well. "On a country place you can attain much of the old frontiersman's independence while having comforts and a fullness of life of which he did not dream." There is not even any real risk involved. "Farming," he acknowledges, "is a gamble; suburban gardening should be a leadpipe cinch." Marry nature and you live happily ever after; spurn her charms and you reject paradise. Attainment of health, happiness and wealth was ridiculously easy. All one had to do was to move out to the "real up-to-date suburbs, of uncrowded and unfettered Nature, [which] have become the promised land for the city man with limited means but a fair endowment of vim and enterprise. . . ." [19] The world of Thomas Jefferson was not lost. Every man could find agrarian peace and plenty, every man could achieve success on the suburban farm. A rural paradise waited for Americans, just around the corner.

Motivated by much this same kind of thinking, Franklin K. Lane, Secretary of the Interior at the end of World War I, backed legislation to return soldiers to health and prosperity on the farm. They would want "a man's life on returning, or a chance to make their way on the farm." But they would not tolerate the lack of society and the cultural barrenness unearthed by the Country Life Commission. The solution, once again, was a mixed marriage of town and country — "a new rural life with all the urban advantages." Each family should have enough land to provide for its own needs, Lane believes, but there should also be a central, John Dewey-style local "community, and that community having the telephone, and good roads, and the telegraph and the post office, and the good school, and the bank, and the good store all close together, so that the women can talk across the back fence and the man can meet his neighbors." Several soldier settlement bills designed to finance this latest version of the ideal middle landscape were introduced into Congress, but only one, appropriating $200,000 for a preliminary investigation of the public lands available for settlement, ever passed.[20]

The bills were opposed by the farm lobby, which figured there were enough of nature's noblemen already working the soil. Their position was understandable, especially when the depression of 1921 drove millions out of work and back to the land. By that time, Ralph Borsodi had moved his

[18] McMahon, pp. 16, 24, 193–94. Italics added.
[19] McMahon, pp. vii, 173, 201.
[20] Paul K. Conkin, *Tomorrow a New World* (Ithaca, N.Y., 1959), pp. 51–53.

family out to a subsistence farm, and while others tramped city streets look-ing for work, the Borsodis cut hay, gathered fruit, made gallons of cider and "began to enjoy the feeling of plenty which the city-dweller never experiences." Borsodi stressed the economic advantages of such a life, par-ticularly if the family produced only for its own consumption. His wife, he concluded, could produce a can of tomatoes "between 20 percent and 30 percent" cheaper than the Campbell Soup Company by eliminating all middlemen. This kind of saving enabled them to be secure in times of eco-nomic stress. "The farmer at one time was self-sufficient," he wrote, produc-ing his own food and clothing, building his own shelter, chopping wood for his own fuel. Borsodi's message was that those days were *not* gone forever; the farm family could still be self-sufficient.[21]

Like McMahon, Borsodi emphasized the part modern machinery played in making his "adventure in homesteading" a success. But Borsodi viewed "success" almost exclusively in economic terms. The healthfulness and vir-tue of country life he may have taken for granted; he did not make much of these beneficial effects in recounting his financial success story. For a cen-tury and more, the city had lured people with the promise of economic gain; the country suburb, its adherents now claimed, held even greater promise. An early advertisement for Waleswood, a 220-acre suburban tract outside Minneapolis, paid only token homage to the agrarian myth before hammer-ing home its selling message:

> Instead of paying 19 to 90 cents or more of hardearned money for rich milk a day from a cow for practically nothing.
> Instead of paying 19 to 90 cents or more of hardearned money for a dozen eggs only once in a while, pick up dozens of eggs every day laid for you for almost nothing by generous hens.
> Instead of buying potatoes by the peck, dig them by the bushel.
> Instead of buying dried apples or canned peaches at the store, gather all kinds of fruit from your own trees, vines and bushes.
> Instead of buying wilted vegetables once in a while, take young and crisp vegetables from your own garden.
> Instead of buying one golden egg, buy the goose that laid it for the same money.

Not only was the land fruitful and its creatures generous, but a lot pur-chased now would be a sound investment for the future. Quite accurately, prospective buyers were reminded that "as the city grows, the value of your property grows. Opportunity knocks but once at every man's door. This is your call." [22] Jefferson would hardly have recognized his agrarian utopia. Base motives threatened to sully the virgin land.

[21] Ralph Borsodi, *Flight from the City: The Story of a New Way to Family Security* (New York, 1933), pp. 1–19.
[22] Newspaper advertisement, undated, in files of Bloomington Historical Society, Bloomington, Minn.

Most intellectuals, however, remained faithful to the Jeffersonian ideal. Twelve famous Southerners, for example, took their famous stand for agrarianism in 1930. The South, they wrote, could — and must — throw off the yoke of industrialism and restore men to cultivation of the soil, "the best and most sensitive of vocations." In a joint opening statement, John Crowe Ransom, Robert Penn Warren, Andrew Nelson Lytle, Allen Tate and the others agreed that to "think that this cannot be done is pusillanimous. And if the whole community, section, race, or age thinks it cannot be done, then it has simply lost its political genius and doomed itself to impotence." Lytle himself took a stand against emphasis on the economic advantages of rural life. Do not industrialize the farm, he advised; ignore those modern tools and methods urged on you by such preachers of the gospel of success as McMahon and Borsodi. "A farm is not a place to grow wealthy; it is a place to grow corn." [23]

The American public generally, despite the dollar appeal of "how to" books and advertisements about generous hens, and despite the inspiring rhetoric of the agrarian ideal, continued to flock to the cities. Then, in the 1920s, suburbanization became a demographic process of real magnitude for the first time. Compared to the flight from the cities after World War II, the exodus of the 1920s represented only a minor trend. And few who migrated to the suburbs were industrious enough to "succeed," in McMahon's agrarian terms. There was nothing particularly visionary about these new suburbs; they were built to make money for developers, not to conform to anyone's idea of the perfect community. Still, the high hopes inherent in Howard's conception of the town-country magnet and in McMahon's successful suburb-farm refused to fade. In 1925, H. Paul Douglass concluded that a "crowded world must be either suburban or savage." [24] If they had their way, the planners would make sure that it turned out suburban. Clarence Stein and Henry Wright, under the financial sponsorship of Alexander Bing, started plans in 1927 for Radburn, New Jersey, before the greenbelt towns of the New Deal the nation's closest approximation of a Garden City. Other experiments were to follow.

The melodrama of American thought persisted, well into the twentieth century, in assigning the role of villain to the city slicker. Confronted with his scheming, legalistic ways, the poor farm girl faced Hobson's choice: either sign over the beloved farm or face a fate worse than death. It was the most natural thing in the world, of course, for the American intellectual of the 1920s and 1930s to regard the city with a jaundiced eye; urbanization was steadily destroying the agrarian ideal. In desperation, he turned to the suburbs as the hope of the future, just as the New Deal planners did. When that hope, too, came crashing to earth; when the suburbs turned out to be

[23] Twelve Southerners, *I'll Take My Stand* (New York, 1930), in *City and Country in America*, ed. David R. Weimer (New York, 1962), pp. 121–22.
[24] Harlan Paul Douglass, *The Suburban Trend* (New York, 1925), p. 327.

more citified than countrified, the intellectual of the 1950s relieved his frustrations with a spate of embittered attacks on suburbia, which had replaced the city as the villain in the rural-urban melodrama. In the mid-50s it was almost inconceivable to imagine that the suburb, in the dim days before World War II, had been regarded as the *hero* of the piece, the one who would rescue the farmer's daughter from the clutches of the city villain, and carry her off to a vine-covered cottage halfway between city and country. The record of New Deal legislation, however, makes it unmistakably clear that this was the case.

One of the more interesting and ambitious New Deal programs involved the construction of new communities. The 100 communities begun by the federal government in the 1930s, historian Paul K. Conkin points out, "remain vivid reminders of a time, not so long past, when Americans still could dream of a better, more perfect world and could so believe in that dream that they dared set forth to realize it, unashamed of their zeal." [25] Almost all of the 100 communities were made up of subsistence homesteads.

With the backing of President Roosevelt and Congress, $25,000,000 was appropriated in 1933 to establish and put into working order the Division of Subsistence Homesteads, under Harold L. Ickes and his Department of the Interior. Ickes chose M. L. Wilson, who "always had a sentimental, as well as a rationalized, love for agriculture," to take charge of the program. Wilson did not have his head buried in the land, however: he earnestly hoped to restore "certain moral and spiritual values . . . coming from . . . contact with the soil" by making use of more and more technology and efficiency. The public response to the subsistence homestead appropriation was immediate and overwhelming. Wilson's division had $25 million to spend; by February 1934, requests for loans amounted to more than $4.5 *billion*. Wilson had a real problem in deciding how best to spend his appropriation, but he had made his basic decisions late in 1933. The typical community would contain "from 25 to 100 families living on individual homesteads of from one to five acres, which would accommodate an orchard, a vegetable garden, poultry, a pig, and, in some cases, a cow. Eventual ownership was promised for most colonists. . . ." Representative Ernest W. Marland, of Oklahoma, who was convinced that we must go back to the land "or we are lost," described the individual family's homestead somewhat more romantically:

> A small farm with a wood lot for fuel, a pasture for cows, an orchard with hives of bees, a dozen acres or so of plow land, and a garden for berries and annual vegetable crops.
> There is always plenty on a farm such as this.
> In winter a fat hog hangs in the smokehouse and from the cellar come jellies and jams and preserves, canned fruits, and dried vege-

[25] Conkin, pp. 6–7. In reviewing the community building programs of the New Deal, this essay relies heavily on Conkin's excellent book.

tables. In the summer there is a succession of fresh fruits from the orchard and fresh vegetables from the garden.

Heaven, indeed, was to be the destination of subsistence farmers. But dissension within Wilson's division kept the program from growing, and as the economy turned upward, the back-to-the-land movement, which "had been motivated largely by the hopelessness and despair of the depression," began to lose its appeal.[26]

The subsistence homesteads program faded into insignificance, but the community building program of the New Deal was far from dead. Rexford Tugwell spearheaded the second, final and most significant phase of the program. Tugwell, whose enormous ability was matched by his self-confidence, set about "rearranging the physical face of America." He spurned the emotional attractions of the family homestead, and thought instead in terms of the planning process. For example, he saw that farmers trying — and failing — to eke out a living on submarginal land would have to be resettled on better land. But there was not enough good land to go around, and the surplus farm population would find its way to the cities, where millions were already trapped in slums. The solution to both problems, both "the inevitable movement from farm to city" and the barren poverty of urban slum dwellers, Tugwell found in the suburban town or garden city, in a middle landscape planned in hard, cold, pragmatic terms by the hardest, coldest, most pragmatic of planners. Surplus farm families could resettle in these suburban garden cities, and so could slum families. The federal government, in the person of Rexford Tugwell, set about in 1934 to plan and build these modern "middle settlements."

As boss of the Resettlement Administration, Tugwell had originally sketched out a program for 25 suburban communities. But the courts and the reluctance of Congress to finance projects the Republican National Committee soon characterized as "communist farms" limited the number of such communities actually constructed to three — Greenbelt, Maryland, near Washington, D.C., the most famous; Greenhills, Ohio, near Cincinnati, and Greendale, Wisconsin, outside Milwaukee. Consciously working on behalf of collectivist goals, Tugwell's Resettlement Administration was chewed up in the meat-grinder of American politics. By June 1937, the agency was no more.

In the greenbelt towns, however, Tugwell had created the "three largest, most ambitious, and most significant communities of the New Deal." As Conkin comments, they "represented, and still do represent, the most daring, original, and ambitious experiments in public housing in the history of the United States." The three communities relocated low-income families, both from farm and from city, in a suburban environment which combined the advantages of country and city life. The suburbs, clearly, were the hope

[26] Conkin, pp. 87–130.

of the future for Tugwell, who believed there should be three thousand greenbelt cities, not three. In suburbia, still a relatively unexploited frontier in the mid-1930s, was to be found "the best chance ever offered for the governmental planning of a favorable working and living environment. Past opportunities for federal planning had been ignored, with urban slums and rural poverty the results. This new area offered a last chance." The city had turned out badly, and so had the farm. The suburb was the last place to plan for a viable environment, and Tugwell, his idealism showing beneath the pragmatic exterior, was determined not to let the chance go by.

The greenbelt city, as he conceived it, was to be a complete community, with its area and population strictly limited in size, surrounded by a greenbelt of farms. There was to be plenty of light, air and space, with safety assured for the children, plenty of gardens, and good schools and playgrounds. Jobs were either to be available within the community or close at hand, and the town and its utilities were to be owned collectively, not individually. Planning for the three greenbelt towns began in 1935, and construction was underway during the following three years. When completed the three projects contained 2,267 family units and complete community facilities. In many respects, the towns were successful: residents flocked to occupy the comfortable single-family and multiple dwellings in all three communities, and visitors from overseas were lavish in their praise. But the greenbelt towns never worked out, economically. At the low rents charged, it would have taken over three hundred years for Greenbelt, Maryland to pay for itself. In 1949, the Congress authorized the administration to sell the greenbelt cities at negotiated sale. By 1954, all three cities had been liquidated for $19.5 million, just over half the total cost to the federal government of $36 million, not taking interest or the devaluation of the dollar into account.[27]

However impractical they may have been in terms of dollars and cents, the greenbelt towns demonstrated what federal planning could accomplish in providing suburban housing for low-income families. Today, of course, the suburbs are full of people of all social classes, from the very wealthy to the nearly indigent. But the working-class suburb of the 1960s, conceived for profit and constructed in the same spirit, lacks many of the amenities of the greenbelt towns. Those who looked to the suburbs with stars in their eyes in the 1930s may be excused for disillusionment with the results of unplanned growth. Given enough money and time and the right political climate, Rexford Tugwell might have built a modern utopia in the suburbs of the United States. But there was not enough money or time, and the political climate, with its worship of individualism, was decidedly unfriendly. Tugwell's dream, like most, did not come true.

After the war, of course, came the deluge. The boys came marching home in 1945 and 1946, produced babies, and looked for homes to house their

[27] Conkin, pp. 153–325.

families. Instant suburbs, thrown up by developers with no professional planning or architectural assistance, supplied the homes, and the GI's moved out. To most of them, the new suburban homes, small and neat, seemed entirely adequate, but not to those intellectuals who, like Tugwell, saw in suburbia the last chance to create an ideal living environment. There were not enough playgrounds, not enough walkways, not enough trees — in short, not enough nature. In their disillusionment the intellectuals turned on the suburbs with a vengeance. Where once they had attacked the city for robbing America of it agrarian dream, now they zeroed in on the suburb, which had betrayed their fondest hopes for a twentieth-century restoration of the Jeffersonian ideal.

As the target of abuse shifted from downtown to the fringes of town, the city gained a respectability, a dignity, which it had never before enjoyed. Jane Jacobs, in her urban rhapsody, *The Death and Life of Great American Cities*, perceptively assesses the sentimentalization of nature as a major cause for "the bog of intellectual misconceptions about cities in which orthodox reformers and planners have mired themselves. . . ." Cities are just as natural as countryside, she maintains. Are not human beings part of nature? Are not cities the products of one form of nature, "as are the colonies of prairie dogs or the beds of oysters?" Of course they are, but Americans are not sentimental about cities. They are sentimental about the countryside, but they systematically destroy it in building an "insipid, standardized, suburbanized shadow of nature." Each day, the bulldozers flatten out the hills and tear up the trees; each day, acres of Grade I agricultural land are covered with pavement; each day, suburbanites kill "the thing they thought they came to find." Worst of all, it did not have to work out the way it has. There was no need for suburbs at all. Miss Jacobs would do away with the middle landscape, leaving only city and country:

> Big cities and countrysides can get along well together. Big cities need real countryside close by. And countryside — from man's point of view — needs big cities, with all their diverse opportunities and productivity, so human beings can be in a position to appreciate the rest of the natural world instead of to curse it.[28]

There is general critical agreement that suburbanization is systematically destroying America's priceless natural heritage. "These dormitory or bedroom communities displace the forests, the fruit orchards, and the fields of waving grain which up until a few years ago covered the countryside," a religious commentator writes, the echo of "My Country, 'Tis of Thee" sounding in his "fields of waving grain." [29] This accusation makes up only half of

[28] Jane Jacobs, *The Death and Life of Great American Cities* (New York, 1961), pp. 444–47.
[29] Frederick A. Shippey, *Protestantism in Suburban Life* (New York and Nashville, 1964), p. 117.

the indictment, though. For the suburbs are not only killing off the country; they are also doing away with the city. Nathan Glazer argues, for example, that suburbia is invading the city, not vice versa,[30] and political scientists complain that outlying communities are siphoning off the life blood of the city.

The suburbs, in short, have come to be regarded as combining the worst, not the best, of city and country. The dream of an ideal middle landscape has been transformed into the nightmare of a no man's land between two ideal extremes. In their suburbs, Americans have "succeeded in averaging down both the city and the [rural] village." [31] Nature only tantalizes the suburbanite:

> A fine spring or autumn morning in the city is nothing more than a "nice day," and in the country is something to drink to the deepest. But we suburbanites have to tear ourselves from such things and go climb a skyscraper. We'd like to stop and watch a brook run for a while and we don't feel too old to scuff autumn leaves. But no, the 8:19 is whistling around the bend and on we go.[32]

To some critics, the world of suburbia has become a dim, dull, basically *unreal world*. Children who live there, one commentator tells us, "need trips to both city and country to become acquainted with the world in which they live." [33] The implication is obvious. The suburbs, particularly the new postwar suburbs, are not meaningful places to live. They may exist, but they are not *real*. They represent a hazy half-world between the two real worlds of city and country.

But consigning the suburbs to a bland and opaque demimonde represents wishful thinking. The suburbs are highly visible and very much with us, as the census figures keep demonstrating; they are real places, and they have a meaning. The incredible speed with which the United States has become suburbanized testifies to this meaning. The flight from the city was entirely predictable in the light of the dominant mythology of American agrarianism. As two sociologists have remarked,

> what Suburbia means then, is a question that can be answered by viewing it more as a continuation of the older values that still exist rather than as a new phenomenon that has somehow taken the worst of all features of American life and encapsulated them within a split-level housing development. Perhaps the fact that Americans are moving in such numbers from the unplanned city to the poorly planned suburb

[30] Quoted in Anselm Strauss, "The Changing Imagery of American City and Suburb," *Sociological Quarterly*, 1 (Jan. 1960), 21.

[31] Burchard and Bush-Brown, p. 121.

[32] G. B. Palmer, *Slightly Cooler in the Suburbs* (Garden City, N.Y., 1950), pp. 214–15.

[33] Sidonie Matsner Gruenberg, "The Challenge of the New Suburbs," *Marriage and Family Living*, XVII (May 1955), 136.

is symbolic that really nothing much has changed except the time and the place.[34]

Nothing much, really, *has* changed. As much as ever, and despite the bitter lessons of history, America remains caught up in the Jeffersonian ideal, in the myth of the sturdy yeoman farmer plowing his own acres in self-sufficient independence, yet somehow part of a rural community. Conrad Knickerbocker has isolated the motivation which continues to produce the exodus to suburbia. The back-to-nature fixation, he writes, "has driven much . . . of the nation into street upon street of meaningless, tiny symbolic 'farms' stretching coast to coast." But these are farms with "60-foot frontages of crab grass," and no front porch on which to "set a spell" and fan yourself. "Rock-solid rural verities turn to sand in the treacherous climate of tract housing." Robert C. Wood, now Under Secretary of the Department of Housing and Urban Affairs, also blames "a rustic culture" for creating a decentralized governmental mess around our cities. "The need," he says, "is to develop a metropolitan conscience which demands something more than a rural shopkeeper's values." [35]

It would be reasonable to suppose, in the more heat than light of the tirade against the suburbs, that the concept of an ideal middle landscape might have disappeared from American thinking. But such a supposition underestimates the continuing pull of the country on the imagination of the urban intellectual. New Deal attempts to plan and construct the perfect community ended, if not in failure, at least in financial embarrassment. Now, the movers and shakers of the Great Society have determined to try once more, feeling again that there must be some way of happily marrying country and city. Following this goal, the administration has thrown its support behind the New Towns movement.

New Towns, of course, are really only another name for Garden Cities or greenbelt cities. But there are some differences. The New Towns of the Great Society are being constructed by private developers (often with government loans). And the New Towns will make a greater effort than was made in the cases of Greenbelt, Greendale and Greenhills to attract industry. As Wolf von Eckardt writes, the greenbelt program was abandoned "partly because . . . these towns could [not] attract sufficient employment so people could stay put." The success of the New Towns, he maintains, will depend largely on "whether they can actually attract employers." [36] For one goal of the New Towns, like that of Ebenezer Howard's Garden Cities, is to bring enough jobs out into the middle landscape between city

[34] Thomas Ktsanes and Leonard Reissman, "Suburbia — New Homes for Old Values," *Social Problems*, VII (May 1955), 136.

[35] *Life*, LIX (Dec. 24, 1965), 37, 139.

[36] Wolf von Eckardt, "New Towns in America," *New Republic*, CXLIX (Oct. 26, 1963), 17.

and country so that the tedious commutation from suburb to city can be eliminated. To the extent that they realize this goal, the communities will be able to keep "closely accessible the recreative values of Nature." (The capitalization is not Ralph Waldo Emerson's, but that of the *Architectural Record*, April 1964.) It is Henry Ford's idea all over again: men can and should be industrial workers eight hours a day and nature's noblemen the rest of the time. The New Towns are not to have any standard population, which can vary from 50,000 to several hundred thousand, but the limit will be predetermined by planning. Surrounding land will be purchased and kept essentially open, to serve as a natural greenbelt.[37]

Perhaps the best known of some 75 American New Towns is Reston, Virginia, a 10-square-mile site 17 miles from Washington, D.C. which is planned for a community of 75,000 persons. Robert E. Simon Jr., the developer, is frankly enamored of outdoor life, and instructed his planners to be certain that the growth of Reston did not "destroy the very rural amenities that its residents would seek." As a consequence, apartments and town houses have been built to cluster population and preserve more open land.[38]

New Town planners hope that their middle landscape, once created, will be hospitable to all:

> We hope to create a community that is economically and racially integrated — i.e., contains a substantial range of income and occupation, and a substantial number of nonwhite families.

But they lack confidence that such heterogeneous towns can be built, so long as private developers stay in charge. The developer must not only be willing to admit minority families; he must actively seek them, since they are not likely to apply in serious numbers. Besides, if housing is not subsidized, it is unlikely that many minority families could afford to move. The solution, as Albert Mayer and Clarence Stein see it, is to put "the government back in the real estate business," a business it was supposed to have given up with the sale of the greenbelt cities 15 years ago. So long as there is a possibility of speculative profit, they state, "large-scale logically related development is not going to take place. . . ." What is needed is a philosophy of long-range disinterested planning by a powerful New Town Committee or Commission.[39]

Stein, one of the developers of Radburn, New Jersey, is back where he and Rexford Tugwell and the other planners of the 1920s and 1930s always were — on the side of centralized government direction and control of new American utopias. Ada Louise Huxtable, the architectural critic for the

[37] Albert Mayer in consultation with Clarence Stein, "New Towns: and Fresh In-City Communities," *Architectural Record*, CXXXVI (Aug. 1964), 131–32.

[38] "Reston," *Architectural Record*, CXXXVI (July 1964), 120. The community needed re-financing in 1967.

[39] Mayer and Stein, pp. 134–36.

New York *Times*, is less insistent on federal control as well as less Panglossian. "Inevitably," she writes,

> New Towns may fall short of their objectives, and even share some of suburbia's sins. But only through professional community planning can the chaos of the country's growth be turned into order. Concern with the total community is a heartening sign of sanity, order, rationality and realism in the American approach to the problem of urban expansion. There may still be hope for the suburban dream.[40]

Serious, intelligent planning, serious, intelligent concern with the total community bodes well for the future. Planning is not going to cure all the ills of our cities and suburbs, Huxtable realizes, whether it is done privately or through government channels. The intellectual must be prepared to realize, with Huxtable, that New Towns and other ideal utopias will inevitably "fall short of their objectives." It is not going to be possible to restore rural America:

> The wilderness, the isolated farm, the plantation, the self-contained New England town, the detached neighborhood are things of the American past. All the world's a city now and there is no escaping urbanization, not even in outer space.[41]

To the very considerable extent that the modern ideal of the middle landscape looks backward to the Jeffersonian ideal for direction, it is doomed to failure, and its adherents to disillusionment. In any marriage between city and country today the city is going to be the dominant partner. Ebenezer Howard in 1898, like American intellectuals of any period, wanted it the other way around.

[40] Ada Louise Huxtable, " 'Clusters' Instead of 'Slurbs,' " *New York Times Magazine* (Feb. 9, 1964), p. 44.
[41] Whites, p. 238.

3

THE IMMIGRANT
IN AMERICAN LIFE AND THOUGHT

The word "immigrant" appears to have come into fairly common use only around 1820, when the census for the first time made note of the number of passengers arriving by ship from foreign shores. Between that date and 1930, the total number of immigrants entering the country is recorded as just under 37.8 million, of which an estimated 26.1 million settled. [W. F. Willcox, "Immigration into the U.S.," *International Migration*, 11, Willcox, ed. (1931), 89. Cf. E. W. Gilboy and E. M. Hoover, "Population and Immigration," in *American Economic History*, S. E. Harris, ed. (1961), pp. 265–266.] A plurality of immigrants have come from Germany (6.25 million as of 1950), with Italy (4.8 million), Ireland (4.6 million), Great Britain (4.4 million), and Austria-Hungary (4.2 million) following. (These figures are gross.)

"Immigration" is a word of American origin. Not coincidentally, so is "nativism." It has often been observed that the notion of "Americanism," with its quasi-religious qualities, has no real counterpart in other nations. It is something like a state or condition, which one can achieve, and (perhaps therefore) fall from, becoming "*un*-American." The great importance of immigration in American history has shaped these conceptions probably more than any other single force. [See S. M. Lipset, "Sources of the Radical Right," in *The Radical Right*, D. Bell, ed. (Anchor Edition, 1964), pp. 320–321.]

Much of the literature on American immigration has focused on the pathology of the "native-newcomer" relations, from general accounts of the problems caused by immigration, to broad studies of nativist movements [especially John Higham's *Strangers in the Land* (1955)] and somewhat defensive statistical efforts to calculate the contributions of immigrants to American life [notably, Brinley Thomas's "The Economic Aspect," in the UNESCO publication, *The Positive Contribution by Immigrants* Part II (1955), pp. 166–174]. Yet for a country populated so largely by immigrants of diverse backgrounds, the most noteworthy subject for attention might well be not the ethnopathology but the remarkable stability of American life. As Oscar Handlin has written, the diversity of sources of the American population "ruled out the possibility that some myth of common origin might supply a basis for creating communal order; it juxtaposed different and sometimes contradictory ideals of what that order should be like; and it left prominently embedded in society conflicting interests and values." ["Historical Perspectives on the American Ethnic Group," *Daedalus* (Spring 1962), p. 222.] Nevertheless, American society has managed to hold together with fewer serious schisms than almost any other society in the world (the violence of the 1960's notwithstanding). Part of the answer undoubtedly lies in the peculiar structure of American politics. But no less important is the manner of accommodation achieved by the hundreds of voluntary associations, churches, and subsocieties that exist within American society.

In the progressive era, immigration was a major preoccupation, and with good reason. New immigration (immigration minus emigration) during the period between 1881 and 1910 amounted to 12.5 million, or one-third of the total increase in United States population for the period. In that thirty-year span, too, the principal sources of immigration shifted from Germany, Great Britain, and Ireland to Italy, Austria-Hungary, and Russia. For almost half a century, until about 1925, foreign-born persons made up a constant 15 percent of the total population, while for the 15–55 age group, that percentage was much higher. The overwhelming number of the foreign-born resided in the cities of over 50,000. For the progressive reformers, the difficult problems created by urbanization were critically compounded by the influx of largely Latin- and Slavic-speaking Europeans whose religious affiliations as well as their languages contrasted with the American mode. There was no single response to massive immigration from among the progressives. Most assumed the virtue, indeed the necessity, of a homogeneous society, and many, such as Henry Demarest Lloyd, even began their analysis of social difficulties with the ostensible breakdown of homogeneity and the consequent paralysis of the "forces of good." To meet this problem, some progressives, like Wisconsin sociologist E. A. Ross, urged exclusion or severe restriction of immigrants. Many more advocated Americanization through the inculcation of Anglo-American values, though an important growing body of intellectuals argued that assimilation in America had been and should properly continue to be achieved by way of the melting pot. But there was also a small group led by John Dewey and Horace Kallen who argued that America's vitality had in fact derived from its *heterogeneity*, and that attempts to stifle cultural diversity would inevitably stifle America's creative power as well.

Milton M. Gordon's essay, "Assimilation in America," has many outstanding virtues. It surveys the sober and scholarly commentary on immigration throughout the course of American history. It has a freshness that only sociologists seem to be able to bring to the problem of group motivation. It presents in summary form, moreover, the major historical and historiographic views of immigration: Anglo-conformist, melting pot, and pluralist. And in the notes one may find a valuable bibliography of the most recent scholarship on the subject. Pluralism as a positive philosophical school has its origins in the progressive era, though as a fact of American life it goes far back into the colonial experience. Professor Gordon, of the Department of Sociology at the University of Massachusetts, Amherst, provides a framework that may help one to begin to understand the workability of American heterogeneity.

For a sharp, critical analysis of Gordon's book, *Assimilation in American Life* (1965), see Marshall Sklare's review in *Commentary* (May 1965), pp. 63–67. Maldwyn Jones, *American Immigration** (1966); Oscar Handlin, *The Uprooted** (1952); Barbara Solomon, *Ancestors and Immigrants* (1958); John Higham, *Strangers in the Land** (1955); and Marcus Hansen, *The Immigrant in American History* (1940), are the essential works. Earl Raab, ed., *Religious Conflict in America** (1964), and Lawrence H. Fuchs, ed., *American Ethnic Politics** (1968), are two superb collections of original essays.

Assimilation in America: Theory and Reality

Milton M. Gordon

Three ideologies or conceptual models have competed for attention on the American scene as explanations of the way in which a nation, in the beginning largely white, Anglo-Saxon, and Protestant, has absorbed over 41 million immigrants and their descendants from variegated sources and welded them into the contemporary American people. These ideologies are Anglo-conformity, the melting pot, and cultural pluralism. They have served at various times, and often simultaneously, as explanations of what has happened — descriptive models — and of what should happen — goal models. Not infrequently they have been used in such a fashion that it is difficult to tell which of these two usages the writer has had in mind. In fact, one of the more remarkable omissions in the history of American intellectual thought is the relative lack of close analytical attention given to the theory of immigrant adjustment in the United States by its social scientists.

The result has been that this field of discussion — an overridingly important one since it has significant implications for the more familiar problems of prejudice, discrimination, and majority-minority group relations generally — has been largely preempted by laymen, representatives of belles lettres, philosophers, and apologists of various persuasions. Even from these sources the amount of attention devoted to ideologies of assimilation is hardly extensive. Consequently, the work of improving intergroup relations in America is carried out by dedicated professional agencies and individuals who deal as best they can with day-to-day problems of discriminatory behavior,

Reprinted by permission from *Daedalus*, Journal of the American Academy of Arts and Sciences, Vol. 90, No. 2.

but who for the most part are unable to relate their efforts to an adequate conceptual apparatus. Such an apparatus would, at one and the same time, accurately describe the present structure of American society with respect to its ethnic groups (I shall use the term "ethnic group" to refer to any racial, religious, or national-origins collectivity), and allow for a considered formulation of its assimilation or integration goals for the foreseeable future. One is reminded of Alice's distraught question in her travels in Wonderland: "Would you tell me, please, which way I ought to go from here?" "That depends a good deal," replied the Cat with irrefutable logic, "on where you want to get to."

The story of America's immigration can be quickly told for our present purposes. The white American population at the time of the Revolution was largely English and Protestant in origin, but had already absorbed substantial groups of Germans and Scotch-Irish and smaller contingents of Frenchmen, Dutchmen, Swedes, Swiss, South Irish, Poles, and a handful of migrants from other European nations. Catholics were represented in modest numbers, particularly in the middle colonies, and a small number of Jews were residents of the incipient nation. With the exception of the Quakers and a few missionaries, the colonists had generally treated the Indians and their cultures with contempt and hostility, driving them from the coastal plains and making the western frontier a bloody battleground where eternal vigilance was the price of survival.

Although the Negro at that time made up nearly one-fifth of the total population, his predominantly slave status, together with racial and cultural prejudice, barred him from serious consideration as an assimilable element of the society. And while many groups of European origin started out as determined ethnic enclaves, eventually, most historians believe, considerable ethnic intermixture within the white population took place. "People of different blood" [sic] — write two American historians about the colonial period, "English, Irish, German, Huguenot, Dutch, Swedish — mingled and intermarried with little thought of any difference." [1] In such a society, its people predominantly English, its white immigrants of other ethnic origins either English-speaking or derived largely from countries of northern and western Europe whose cultural divergences from the English were not great, and its dominant white population excluding by fiat the claims and considerations of welfare of the non-Caucasian minorities, the problem of assimilation understandably did not loom unduly large or complex.

The unfolding events of the next century and a half with increasing momentum dispelled the complacency which rested upon the relative simplicity of colonial and immediate post-Revolutionary conditions. The large-scale immigration to America of the famine-fleeing Irish, the Germans, and later the Scandinavians (along with additional Englishmen and other peoples of northern and western Europe) in the middle of the nineteenth century (the

[1] Allan Nevins and Henry Steele Commager, *America: The Story of a Free People* (Boston, Little, Brown, 1942), p. 58.

so-called "old immigration"), the emancipation of the Negro slaves and the problems created by post–Civil War reconstruction, the placing of the conquered Indian with his broken culture on government reservations, the arrival of the Oriental, first attracted by the discovery of gold and other opportunities in the West, and finally, beginning in the last quarter of the nineteenth century and continuing to the early 1920's, the swelling to proportions hitherto unimagined of the tide of immigration from the peasantries and "pales" of southern and eastern Europe — the Italians, Jews, and Slavs of the so-called "new immigration," fleeing the persecutions and industrial dislocations of the day — all these events constitute the background against which we may consider the rise of the theories of assimilation mentioned above. After a necessarily foreshortened description of each of these theories and their historical emergence, we shall suggest analytical distinctions designed to aid in clarifying the nature of the assimilation process, and then conclude by focusing on the American scene.

ANGLO-CONFORMITY

"Anglo-conformity" [2] is a broad term used to cover a variety of viewpoints about assimilation and immigration; they all assume the desirability of maintaining English institutions (as modified by the American Revolution), the English language, and English-oriented cultural patterns as dominant and standard in American life. However, bound up with this assumption are related attitudes. These may range from discredited notions about race and "Nordic" and "Aryan" racial superiority, together with the nativist political programs and exclusionist immigration policies which such notions entail, through an intermediate position of favoring immigration from northern and western Europe on amorphous, unreflective grounds ("They are more like us"), to a lack of opposition to any source of immigration, as long as these immigrants and their descendants duly adopt the standard Anglo-Saxon cultural patterns. There is by no means any necessary equation between Anglo-conformity and racist attitudes.

It is quite likely that "Anglo-conformity" in its more moderate aspects, however explicit its formulation, has been the most prevalent ideology of assimilation goals in America throughout the nation's history. As far back as colonial times, Benjamin Franklin recorded concern about the clannishness of the Germans in Pennsylvania, their slowness in learning English, and the establishment of their own native-language press.[3] Others of the founding

[2] The phrase is the Coles'. See Stewart G. Cole and Mildred Wiese Cole, *Minorities and the American Promise* (New York, Harper & Brothers, 1954), ch. 6.
[3] Maurice R. Davie, *World Immigration* (New York, Macmillan, 1936), p. 36, and (cited therein) "Letter of Benjamin Franklin to Peter Collinson, 9th May, 1753, on the condition and character of the Germans in Pennsylvania," in *The Works of Benjamin Franklin, with notes and a life of the author,* by Jared Sparks (Boston, 1828), vol. 7, pp. 71–73.

fathers had similar reservations about large-scale immigration from Europe. In the context of their times they were unable to foresee the role such immigration was to play in creating the later greatness of the nation. They were not at all men of unthinking prejudices. The disestablishment of religion and the separation of church and state (so that no religious group — whether New England Congregationalists, Virginian Anglicans, or even all Protestants combined — could call upon the federal government for special favors or support, and so that man's religious conscience should be free) were cardinal points of the new national policy they fostered. "The Government of the United States," George Washington had written to the Jewish congregation of Newport during his first term as president, "gives to bigotry no sanction, to persecution no assistance."

Political differences with ancestral England had just been written in blood; but there is no reason to suppose that these men looked upon their fledgling country as an impartial melting pot for the merging of the various cultures of Europe, or as a new "nation of nations," or as anything but a society in which, with important political modifications, Anglo-Saxon speech and institutional forms would be standard. Indeed, their newly won victory for democracy and republicanism made them especially anxious that these still precarious fruits of revolution should not be threatened by a large influx of European peoples whose life experiences had accustomed them to the bonds of despotic monarchy. Thus, although they explicitly conceived of the new United States of America as a haven for those unfortunates of Europe who were persecuted and oppressed, they had characteristic reservations about the effects of too free a policy. "My opinion, with respect to immigration," Washington wrote to John Adams in 1794, "is that except of useful mechanics and some particular descriptions of men or professions, there is no need of encouragement, while the policy or advantage of its taking place in a body (I mean the settling of them in a body) may be much questioned; for, by so doing, they retain the language, habits and principles (good or bad) which they bring with them." [4] Thomas Jefferson, whose views on race and attitudes towards slavery were notably liberal and advanced for his time, had similar doubts concerning the effects of mass immigration on American institutions, while conceding that immigrants, "if they come of themselves . . . are entitled to all the rights of citizenship." [5]

The attitudes of Americans toward foreign immigration in the first three-quarters of the nineteenth century may correctly be described as ambiguous. On the one hand, immigrants were much desired, so as to swell the population and importance of states and territories, to man the farms of expanding

[4] *The Writings of George Washington*, collected and edited by W. C. Ford (New York, G. P. Putnam's Sons, 1889), vol. 12, p. 489.

[5] Thomas Jefferson, "Notes on Virginia, Query 8," in *The Writing of Thomas Jefferson*, ed. A. E. Bergh (Washington, The Thomas Jefferson Memorial Association, 1907), vol. 2, p. 121.

prairie settlement, to work the mines, build the railroads and canals, and take their place in expanding industry. This was a period in which no federal legislation of any consequence prevented the entry of aliens, and such state legislation as existed attempted to bar on an individual basis only those who were likely to become a burden on the community, such as convicts and paupers. On the other hand, the arrival in an overwhelmingly Protestant society of large numbers of poverty-stricken Irish Catholics, who settled in groups in the slums of Eastern cities, roused dormant fears of "Popery" and Rome. Another source of anxiety was the substantial influx of Germans, who made their way to the cities and farms of the mid-West and whose different language, separate communal life, and freer ideas on temperance and sabbath observance brought them into conflict with the Anglo-Saxon bearers of the Puritan and Evangelical traditions. Fear of foreign "radicals" and suspicion of the economic demands of the occasionally aroused workingmen added fuel to the nativist fires. In their extreme form these fears resulted in the Native-American movement of the 1830's and 1840's and the "American" or "Know-Nothing" party of the 1850's, with their anti-Catholic campaigns and their demands for restrictive laws on naturalization procedures and for keeping the foreign-born out of political office. While these movements scored local political successes and their turbulences so rent the national social fabric that the patches are not yet entirely invisible, they failed to influence national legislative policy on immigration and immigrants; and their fulminations inevitably provoked the expected reactions from thoughtful observers.

The flood of newcomers to the westward expanding nation grew larger, reaching over one and two-thirds million between 1841 and 1850 and over two and one-half million in the decade before the Civil War. Throughout the entire period, quite apart from the excesses of the Know-Nothings, the predominant (though not exclusive) conception of what the ideal immigrant adjustment should be was probably summed up in a letter written in 1818 by John Quincy Adams, then Secretary of State, in answer to the inquiries of the Baron von Fürstenwaerther. If not the earliest, it is certainly the most elegant version of the sentiment, "If they don't like it here, they can go back where they came from." Adams declared: [6]

> They [immigrants to America] come to a life of independence, but to a life of labor — and, if they cannot accommodate themselves to the character, moral, political and physical, of this country with all its compensating balances of good and evil, the Atlantic is always open to them to return to the land of their nativity and their fathers. To one thing they must make up their minds, or they will be disappointed in every expectation of happiness as Americans. They must cast off the European skin, never to resume it. They must look forward to their

[6] Niles' Weekly Register, vol. 18, 29 April 1820, pp. 157–158; also, Marcus L. Hansen, The Atlantic Migration, 1607–1860, pp. 96–97.

posterity rather than backward to their ancestors; they must be sure that whatever their own feelings may be, those of their children will cling to the prejudices of this country.

The events that followed the Civil War created their own ambiguities in attitude toward the immigrant. A nation undergoing wholesale industrial expansion and not yet finished with the march of westward settlement could make good use of the never faltering waves of newcomers. But sporadic bursts of labor unrest, attributed to foreign radicals, the growth of Catholic institutions and the rise of Catholics to municipal political power, and the continuing association of immigrant settlement with urban slums revived familiar fears. The first federal selective law restricting immigration was passed in 1882, and Chinese immigration was cut off in the same year. The most significant development of all, barely recognized at first, was the change in the source of European migrants. Beginning in the 1880's, the countries of southern and eastern Europe began to be represented in substantial numbers for the first time, and in the next decade immigrants from these sources became numerically dominant. Now the notes of a new, or at least hitherto unemphasized, chord from the nativist lyre began to sound — the ugly chord, or discord, of racism. Previously vague and romantic notions of Anglo-Saxon peoplehood, combined with general ethnocentrism, rudimentary wisps of genetics, selected tidbits of evolutionary theory, and naive assumptions from an early and crude imported anthropology produced the doctrine that the English, Germans, and others of the "old immigration" constituted a superior race of tall, blonde, blue-eyed "Nordics" or "Aryans," whereas the people of eastern and southern Europe made up the darker Alpines or Mediterraneans — both "inferior" breeds whose presence in America threatened, either by intermixture or supplementation, the traditional American stock and culture. The obvious corollary to this doctrine was to exclude the allegedly inferior breeds; but if the new type of immigrant could not be excluded, then everything must be done to instill Anglo-Saxon virtues in these benighted creatures. Thus, one educator writing in 1909 could state: [7]

> These southern and eastern Europeans are of a very different type from the north Europeans who preceded them. Illiterate, docile, lacking in self-reliance and initiative, and not possessing the Anglo-Teutonic conceptions of law, order, and government, their coming has served to dilute tremendously our national stock, and to corrupt our civic life. . . . Everywhere these people tend to settle in groups or settlements, and to set up here their national manners, customs, and observances. Our task is to break up these groups or settlements, to assimilate and amalgamate these people as a part of our American race, and to implant in their children, so far as can be done, the

[7] Ellwood P. Cubberly, *Changing Conceptions of Education* (Boston, Houghton Mifflin, 1909), pp. 15–16.

Anglo-Saxon conception of righteousness, law and order, and popular government, and to awaken in them a reverence for our democratic institutions and for those things in our national life which we as a people hold to be of abiding worth.

Anglo-conformity received its fullest expression in the so-called Americanization movement which gripped the nation during World War I. While "Americanization" in its various stages had more than one emphasis, it was essentially a consciously articulated movement to strip the immigrant of his native culture and attachments and make him over into an American along Anglo-Saxon lines — all this to be accomplished with great rapidity. To use an image of a later day, it was an attempt at "pressure-cooking assimilation." It had prewar antecedents, but it was during the height of the world conflict that federal agencies, state governments, municipalities, and a host of private organizations joined in the effort to persuade the immigrant to learn English, take out naturalization papers, buy war bonds, forget his former origins and culture, and give himself over to patriotic hysteria.

After the war and the "Red scare" which followed, the excesses of the Americanization movement subsided. In its place, however, came the restriction of immigration through federal law. Foiled at first by presidential vetoes, and later by the failure of the 1917 literacy test to halt the immigrant tide, the proponents of restriction finally put through in the early 1920's a series of acts culminating in the well-known national-origins formula for immigrant quotas which went into effect in 1929. Whatever the merits of a quantitative limit on the number of immigrants to be admitted to the United States, the provisions of the formula, which discriminated sharply against the countries of southern and eastern Europe, in effect institutionalized the assumptions of the rightful dominance of Anglo-Saxon patterns in the land. Reaffirmed with only slight modifications in the McCarran-Walter Act of 1952, these laws, then, stand as a legal monument to the creed of Anglo-conformity and a telling reminder that this ideological system still has numerous and powerful adherents on the American scene.

THE MELTING POT

While Anglo-conformity in various guises has probably been the most prevalent ideology of assimilation in the American historical experience, a competing viewpoint with more generous and idealistic overtones has had its adherents and exponents from the eighteenth century onward. Conditions in the virgin continent, it was clear, were modifying the institutions which the English colonists brought with them from the mother country. Arrivals from non-English homelands such as Germany, Sweden, and France were similarly exposed to this fresh environment. Was it not possible, then, to think of the evolving American society not as a slightly modified England but rather as a totally new blend, culturally and biologically, in which the stocks and folkways of Europe, figuratively speaking, were indiscriminately mixed in the political pot of the emerging nation and fused by the fires of American influence and interaction into a distinctly new type?

Such, at any rate, was the conception of the new society which motivated that eighteenth-century French-born writer and agriculturalist, J. Hector St. John de Crèvecoeur, who, after many years of American residence, published his reflections and observations in *Letters from an American Farmer*.[8] Who, he asks, is the American?

> He is either an European, or the descendant of an European, hence that strange mixture of blood, which you will find in no other country. I could point out to you a family whose grandfather was an Englishman, whose wife was Dutch, whose son married a French woman, and whose present four sons have now four wives of different nations. *He* is an American, who leaving behind him all his ancient prejudices and manners, receives new ones from the new mode of life he has embraced, the new government he obeys, and the new rank he holds. He becomes an American by being received in the broad lap of our great *Alma Mater*. Here individuals of all nations are melted into a new race of men, whose labours and posterity will one day cause great changes in the world.

Some observers have interpreted the open-door policy on immigration of the first three-quarters of the nineteenth century as reflecting an underlying faith in the effectiveness of the American melting pot, in the belief "that all could be absorbed and that all could contribute to an emerging national character." [9] No doubt many who observed with dismay the nativist agitation of the times felt as did Ralph Waldo Emerson that such conformity-demanding and immigrant-hating forces represented a perversion of the best American ideals. In 1845, Emerson wrote in his Journal: [10]

> I hate the narrowness of the Native American Party. It is the dog in the manger. It is precisely opposite to all the dictates of love and magnanimity; and therefore, of course, opposite to true wisdom. . . . Man is the most composite of all creatures. . . . Well, as in the old burning of the Temple at Corinth, by the melting and intermixture of silver and gold and other metals a new compound more precious than any, called Corinthian brass, was formed; so in this continent, — asylum of all nations, — the energy of Irish, Germans, Swedes, Poles, and Cossacks, and all the European tribes, — of the Africans, and of the Polynesians, — will construct a new race, a new religion, a new state,

---

[8] J. Hector St. John de Crèvecoeur, *Letters from an American Farmer* (New York, Albert and Charles Boni, 1925; reprinted from the 1st edn., London, 1782), pp. 54–55.

[9] Oscar Handlin, ed., *Immigration as a Factor in American History* (Englewood, Prentice-Hall, 1959), p. 146.

[10] Quoted by Stuart P. Sherman in his Introduction to *Essays and Poems of Emerson* (New York, Harcourt Brace, 1921), p. xxxiv.

a new literature, which will be as vigorous as the new Europe which came out of the smelting-pot of the Dark Ages, or that which earlier emerged from the Pelasgic and Etruscan barbarism. *La Nature aime les croisements.*

Eventually, the melting-pot hypothesis found its way into historical scholarship and interpretation. While many American historians of the late nineteenth century, some fresh from graduate study at German universities, tended to adopt the view that American institutions derived in essence from Anglo-Saxon (and ultimately Teutonic) sources, others were not so sure.[11] One of these was Frederick Jackson Turner, a young historian from Wisconsin, not long emerged from his graduate training at Johns Hopkins. Turner presented a paper to the American Historical Association, meeting in Chicago in 1893. Called "The Significance of the Frontier in American History," this paper proved to be one of the most influential essays in the history of American scholarship, and its point of view, supported by Turner's subsequent writings and his teaching, pervaded the field of American historical interpretation for at least a generation. Turner's thesis was that the dominant influence in the shaping of American institutions and American democracy was not this nation's European heritage in any of its forms, nor the forces emanating from the eastern seaboard cities, but rather the experiences created by a moving and variegated western frontier. Among the many effects attributed to the frontier environment and the challenges it presented was that it acted as a solvent for the national heritages and the separatist tendencies of the many nationality groups which had joined the trek westward, including the Germans and Scotch-Irish of the eighteenth century and the Scandinavians and Germans of the nineteenth. "The frontier," asserted Turner, "promoted the formation of a composite nationality for the American people. . . . In the crucible of the frontier the immigrants were Americanized, liberated, and fused into a mixed race, English in neither nationality nor characteristics. The process has gone on from the early days to our own." And later, in an essay on the role of the Mississippi Valley, he refers to "the tide of foreign immigration which has risen so steadily that it has made a composite American people whose amalgamation is destined to produce a new national stock." [12]

Thus far, the proponents of the melting pot idea had dealt largely with the diversity produced by the sizeable immigration from the countries of northern and western Europe alone — the "old immigration," consisting of peoples with cultures and physical appearance not greatly different from those of the Anglo-Saxon stock. Emerson, it is true, had impartially included Africans, Polynesians, and Cossacks in his conception of the mixture; but

[11] See Edward N. Saveth, *American Historians and European Immigrants, 1875–1925,* New York, Columbia University Press, 1948.

[12] Frederick Jackson Turner, *The Frontier in American History* (New York, Henry Holt, 1920), pp. 22–23, 190.

it was only in the last two decades of the nineteenth century that a large-scale influx of peoples from the countries of southern and eastern Europe imperatively posed the question of whether these uprooted newcomers who were crowding into the large cities of the nation and the industrial sector of the economy could also be successfully "melted." Would the "urban melting pot" work as well as the "frontier melting pot" of an essentially rural society was alleged to have done?

It remained for an English-Jewish writer with strong social convictions, moved by his observation of the role of the United States as a haven for the poor and oppressed of Europe, to give utterance to the broader view of the American melting pot in a way which attracted public attention. In 1908, Israel Zangwill's drama, *The Melting Pot*, was produced in this country and became a popular success. It is a play dominated by the dream of its protagonist, a young Russian-Jewish immigrant to America, a composer, whose goal is the completion of a vast "American" symphony which will express his deeply felt conception of his adopted country as a divinely appointed crucible in which all the ethnic divisions of mankind will divest themselves of their ancient animosities and differences and become fused into one group, signifying the brotherhood of man. In the process he falls in love with a beautiful and cultured Gentile girl. The play ends with the performance of the symphony and, after numerous vicissitudes and traditional family opposition from both sides, with the approaching marriage of David Quixano and his beloved. During the course of these developments, David, in the rhetoric of the time, delivers himself of such sentiments as these: [13]

> America is God's crucible, the great Melting Pot where all the races of Europe are melting and re-forming! Here you stand, good folk, think I, when I see them at Ellis Island, here you stand in your fifty groups, with your fifty languages and histories, and your fifty hatreds and rivalries. But you won't be long like that, brothers, for these are the fires of God you've come to — these are the fires of God. A fig for your feuds and vendettas! Germans and Frenchmen, Irishmen and Englishmen, Jews and Russians — into the Crucible with you all! God is making the American.

Here we have a conception of a melting pot which admits of no exceptions or qualifications with regard to the ethnic stocks which will fuse in the great crucible. Englishmen, Germans, Frenchmen, Slavs, Greeks, Syrians, Jews, Gentiles, even the black and yellow races, were specifically mentioned in Zangwill's rhapsodic enumeration. And this pot patently was to boil in the great cities of America.

Thus around the turn of the century the melting-pot idea became embedded in the ideals of the age as one response to the immigrant receiving experience of the nation. Soon to be challenged by a new philosophy of

[13] Israel Zangwill, *The Melting Pot* (New York, Macmillan, 1909), p. 37.

group adjustment (to be discussed below) and always competing with the more pervasive adherence to Anglo-conformity, the melting-pot image, however, continued to draw a portion of the attention consciously directed toward this aspect of the American scene in the first half of the twentieth century. In the mid-1940's a sociologist who had carried out an investigation of intermarriage trends in New Haven, Connecticut, described a revised conception of the melting process in that city and suggested a basic modification of the theory of that process. In New Haven, Ruby Jo Reeves Kennedy [14] reported from a study of intermarriages from 1870 to 1940 that there was a distinct tendency for the British-Americans, Germans, and Scandinavians to marry among themselves — that is, within a Protestant "pool"; for the Irish, Italians, and Poles to marry among themselves — a Catholic "pool"; and for the Jews to marry other Jews. In other words, intermarriage was taking place across lines of nationality background, but there was a strong tendency for it to stay confined within one or the other of the three major religious groups, Protestants, Catholics, and Jews. Thus, declared Mrs. Kennedy, the picture in New Haven resembled a "triple melting pot" based on religious divisions, rather than a single melting pot." Her study indicated, she stated, that "while strict endogamy is loosening, religious endogamy is persisting and the future cleavages will be along religious lines rather than along nationality lines as in the past. If this is the case, then the traditional 'single-melting-pot' idea must be abandoned, and a new conception, which we term the 'triple-melting-pot' theory of American assimilation, will take its place as the true expression of what is happening to the various nationality groups in the United States." [15] The triple melting-pot thesis was later taken up by the theologian, Will Herberg, and found an important sociological frame of reference for his analysis of religious trends in American society, *Protestant-Catholic-Jew*.[16] But the triple melting-pot hypothesis patently takes us into the realm of a society pluralistically conceived. We turn now to the rise of an ideology which attempts to justify such a conception.

CULTURAL PLURALISM

Probably all the non-English immigrants who came to American shores in any significant numbers from colonial times onward — settling either in the forbidding wilderness, the lonely prairie, or in some accessible urban slum — created ethnic enclaves and looked forward to the preservation of at least

[14] Ruby Jo Reeves Kennedy, "Single or Triple Melting-Pot? Intermarriage Trends in New Haven, 1870–1940," *American Journal of Sociology*, 1944, 49: 331–339. See also her "Single or Triple Melting Pot? Intermarriage in New Haven, 1870–1950," *ibid.*, 1952, 58: 56–59.

[15] Ruby Jo Reeves Kennedy, "Single or Triple Melting-Pot? . . . 1870–1940," p. 332 (author's italics omitted).

[16] Will Herberg, *Protestant-Catholic-Jew*, Garden City, Doubleday, 1955.

some of their native cultural patterns. Such a development, natural as breathing, was supported by the later accretion of friends, relatives, and countrymen seeking out oases of familiarity in a strange land, by the desire of the settlers to rebuild (necessarily in miniature) a society in which they could communicate in the familiar tongue and maintain familiar institutions, and finally, by the necessity to band together for mutual aid and mutual protection against the uncertainties of a strange and frequently hostile environment. This was as true of the "old" immigrants as of the "new." In fact, some of the liberal intellectuals who fled to America from an inhospitable political climate in Germany in the 1830's, 1840's, and 1850's looked forward to the creation of an all-German state within the union, or, even more hopefully, to the eventual formation of a separate German nation, as soon as the expected dissolution of the union under the impact of the slavery controversy should have taken place.[17] Oscar Handlin, writing of the sons of Erin in mid-nineteenth-century Boston, recent refugees from famine and economic degradation in their homeland, points out: "Unable to participate in the normal associational affairs of the community, the Irish felt obliged to erect a society within a society, to act together in their own way. In every contact therefore the group, acting apart from other sections of the community, became intensely aware of its peculiar and exclusive identity." [18] Thus cultural pluralism was a fact in American society before it became a theory — a theory with explicit relevance for the nation as a whole, and articulated and discussed in the English-speaking circles of American intellectual life.

Eventually, the cultural enclaves of the Germans (and the later arriving Scandinavians) were to decline in scope and significance as succeeding generations of their native-born attended public schools, left the farms and villages to strike out as individuals for the Americanizing city, and generally became subject to the influences of a standardizing industrial civilization. The German-American community, too, was struck a powerful blow by the accumulated passions generated by World War I — a blow from which it never fully recovered. The Irish were to be the dominant and pervasive element in the gradual emergence of a pan-Catholic group in America, but these developments would reveal themselves only in the twentieth century. In the meantime, in the last two decades of the nineteenth, the influx of immigrants from southern and eastern Europe had begun. These groups were all the more sociologically visible because the closing of the frontier,

[17] Nathan Glazer, "Ethnic Groups in America: From National Culture to Ideology," in Morroe Berger, Theodore Abel, and Charles H. Page, eds., *Freedom and Control in Modern Society* (New York, D. Van Nostrand, 1954), p. 161; Marcus Lee Hansen, *The Immigrant in American History* (Cambridge, Harvard University Press, 1940), pp. 129–140; John A. Hawgood, *The Tragedy of German-America* (New York, Putnam's, 1940), *passim*.

[18] Oscar Handlin, *Boston's Immigrants* (Cambridge, Harvard University Press, 1959, rev. edn.), p. 176.

the occupational demands of an expanding industrial economy, and their own poverty made it inevitable that they would remain in the urban areas of the nation. In the swirling fires of controversy and the steadier flame of experience created by these new events, the ideology of cultural pluralism as a philosophy for the nation was forged.

The first manifestations of an ideological counterattack against draconic Americanization came not from the beleaguered newcomers (who were, after all, more concerned with survival than with theories of adjustment), but from those idealistic members of the middle class who, in the decade or so before the turn of the century, had followed the example of their English predecessors and "settled" in the slums to "learn to sup sorrow with the poor." [19] Immediately, these workers in the "settlement houses" were forced to come to grips with the realities of immigrant life and adjustment. Not all reacted in the same way, but on the whole the settlements developed an approach to the immigrant which was sympathetic to his native cultural heritage and to his newly created ethnic institutions.[20] For one thing, their workers, necessarily in intimate contact with the lives of these often pathetic and bewildered newcomers and their daily problems, could see how unfortunate were the effects of those forces which impelled rapid Americanization in their impact on the immigrants' children, who not infrequently became alienated from their parents and the restraining influence of family authority. Were not their parents ignorant and uneducated "Hunkies," "Sheenies," or "Dagoes," as that limited portion of the American environment in which they moved defined the matter? Ethnic "self-hatred" with its debilitating psychological consequences, family disorganization, and juvenile delinquency, were not unusual results of this state of affairs. Furthermore, the immigrants themselves were adversely affected by the incessant attacks on their culture, their language, their institutions, their very conception of themselves. How were they to maintain their self-respect when all that they knew, felt, and dreamed, beyond their sheer capacity for manual labor — in other words, all that they *were* — was despised or scoffed at in America? And — unkindest cut of all — their own children had begun to adopt the contemptuous attitude of the "Americans." Jane Addams relates in a moving chapter of her *Twenty Years at Hull House* how, after coming to have some conception of the extent and depth of these problems, she created at the settlement a "Labor Museum," in which the immigrant women of the various nationalities crowded together in the slums of Chicago could illustrate their native methods of spinning and weaving, and in which the relation of these earlier techniques to contemporary factory meth-

[19] From a letter (1883) by Samuel A. Barnett; quoted in Arthur C. Holden, *The Settlement Idea* (New York, Macmillan, 1922), p. 12.
[20] Jane Addams, *Twenty Years at Hull House* (New York, Macmillan, 1914), pp. 231–258; Arthur C. Holden, *op. cit.*, pp. 109–131, 182–189; John Higham, *Strangers in the Land* (New Brunswick, Rutgers University Press, 1955), p. 236.

ods could be graphically shown. For the first time these peasant women were made to feel by some part of their American environment that they possessed valuable and interesting skills — that they too had something to offer — and for the first time, the daughters of these women who, after a long day's work at their dank "needletrade" sweatshops, came to Hull House to observe, began to appreciate the fact that their mothers, too, had a "culture," that this culture possessed its own merit, and that it was related to their own contemporary lives. How aptly Jane Addams concludes her chapter with the hope that "our American citizenship might be built without disturbing these foundations which were laid of old time." [21]

This appreciative view of the immigrant's cultural heritage and of its distinctive usefulness both to himself and his adopted country received additional sustenance from another source: those intellectual currents of the day which, however overborne by their currently more powerful opposites, emphasized liberalism, internationalism, and tolerance. From time to time, an occasional educator or publicist protested the demands of the "Americanizers," arguing that the immigrant, too, had an ancient and honorable culture, and that this culture had much to offer an America whose character and destiny were still in the process of formation, an America which must serve as an example of the harmonious cooperation of various heritages to a world inflamed by nationalism and war. In 1916 John Dewey, Norman Hapgood, and the young literary critic, Randolph Bourne, published articles or addresses elaborating various aspects of this theme.

The classic statement of the cultural pluralist position, however, had been made over a year before. Early in 1915 there appeared in the pages of *The Nation* two articles under the title "Democracy *versus* the Melting-Pot." Their author was Horace Kallen, a Harvard-educated philosopher with a concern for the application of philosophy to societal affairs, and, as an American Jew, himself derivative of an ethnic background which was subject to the contemporary pressures for dissolution implicit in the "Americanization," or Anglo-conformity, and the melting-pot theories. In these articles Kallen vigorously rejected the usefulness of these theories as models of what was actually transpiring in American life or as ideals for the future. Rather he was impressed by the way in which the various ethnic groups in America were coincident with particular areas and regions, and with the tendency for each group to preserve its own language, religion, communal institutions, and ancestral culture. All the while, he pointed out, the immigrant has been learning to speak English as the language of general communication, and has participated in the over-all economic and political life of the nation. These developments in which "the United States are in the process of becoming a federal state not merely as a union of geographical and administrative unities, but also as a cooperation of cultural diversities, as a federa-

[21] Jane Addams, *op. cit.*, p. 258.

tion or commonwealth of national cultures," [22] the author argued, far from constituting a violation of historic American political principles, as the "Americanizers" claimed, actually represented the inevitable consequences of democratic ideas, since individuals are implicated in groups, and since democracy for the individual must by extension also mean democracy for his group.

The processes just described, however, as Kallen develops his argument, are far from having been thoroughly realized. They are menaced by "Americanization" programs, assumptions of Anglo-Saxon superiority, and misguided attempts to promote "racial" amalgamation. Thus America stands at a kind of cultural crossroads. It can attempt to impose by force an artificial, Anglo-Saxon oriented uniformity on its peoples, or it can consciously allow and encourage its ethnic groups to develop democratically, each emphasizing its particular cultural heritage. If the latter course is followed, as Kallen puts it at the close of his essay, then,[23]

> The outlines of a possible great and truly democratic commonwealth become discernible. Its form would be that of the federal republic; its substance a democracy of nationalities, cooperating voluntarily and autonomously through common institutions in the enterprise of self-realization through the perfection of men according to their kind. The common language of the commonwealth, the language of its great tradition, would be English, but each nationality would have for its emotional and involuntary life its own peculiar dialect or speech, its own individual and inevitable esthetic and intellectual forms. The political and economic life of the commonwealth is a single unit and serves as the foundation and background for the realization of the distinctive individuality of each *natio* that composes it and of the pooling of these in a harmony above them all. Thus "American civilization" may come to mean the perfection of the cooperative harmonies of "European civilization" – the waste, the squalor and the distress of Europe being eliminated – a multiplicity in a unity, an orchestration of mankind.

Within the next decade Kallen published more essays dealing with the theme of American multiple-group life, later collected in a volume.[24] In the introductory note to this book he used for the first time the term "cultural pluralism" to refer to his position. These essays reflect both his increasingly sharp rejection of the onslaughts on the immigrant and his culture which the coming of World War I and its attendant fears, the "Red scare," the projection of themes of racial superiority, the continued exploitation of the

[22] Horace M. Kallen, "Democracy *versus* the Melting-Pot," *The Nation*, 18 and 25 February 1915; reprinted in his *Culture and Democracy in the United States*, New York, Boni and Liveright, 1924; the quotation is on p. 116.
[23] Kallen, *Culture and Democracy* . . . , p. 124.
[24] *Op. cit.*

newcomers, and the rise of the Ku Klux Klan all served to increase in intensity, and also his emphasis on cultural pluralism as the democratic antidote to these ills. He has since published other essays elaborating or annotating the theme of cultural pluralism. Thus, for at least forty-five years, most of them spent teaching at the New School for Social Research, Kallen has been acknowledged as the originator and leading philosophical exponent of the idea of cultural pluralism.

In the late 1930's and early 1940's the late Louis Adamic, the Yugoslav immigrant who had become an American writer, took up the theme of America's multicultural heritage and the role of these groups in forging the country's national character. Borrowing Walt Whitman's phrase, he described America as "a nation of nations," and while his ultimate goal was closer to the melting-pot idea than to cultural pluralism, he saw the immediate task as that of making America conscious of what it owed to all its ethnic groups, not just to the Anglo-Saxons. The children and grandchildren of immigrants of non-English origins, he was convinced, must be taught to be proud of the cultural heritage of their ancestral ethnic group and of its role in building the American nation; otherwise, they would not lose their sense of ethnic inferiority and the feeling of rootlessness he claimed to find in them.

Thus in the twentieth century, particularly since World War II, "cultural pluralism" has become a concept which has worked its way into the vocabulary and imagery of specialists in intergroup relations and leaders of ethnic communal groups. In view of this new pluralistic emphasis, some writers now prefer to speak of the "integration" of immigrants rather than of their "assimilation." [25] However, with a few exceptions,[26] no close analytical attention has been given either by social scientists or practitioners of intergroup relations to the meaning of cultural pluralism, its nature and relevance for a modern industrialized society, and its implications for problems of prejudice and discrimination — a point to which we referred at the outset of this discussion.

CONCLUSIONS

In the remaining pages I can make only a few analytical comments which I shall apply in context to the American scene, historical and current. My

[25] See W. D. Borrie *et al.*, *The Cultural Integration of Immigrants* (a survey based on the papers and proceedings of the UNESCO Conference in Havana, April 1956), Paris, UNESCO, 1959; and William S. Bernard, "The Integration of Immigrants in the United States" (mimeographed), one of the papers for this conference.

[26] See particularly Milton M. Gordon, "Social Structure and Goals in Group Relations"; and Nathan Glazer, "Ethnic Groups in America; From National Culture to Ideology," both articles in Berger, Abel, and Page, *op. cit.*; S. N. Eisenstadt, *The Absorption of Immigrants*, London, Routledge and Kegan Paul, 1954; and W. D. Borrie *et al.*, *op. cit.*

view of the American situation will not be documented here, but may be considered as a series of hypotheses in which I shall attempt to outline the American assimilation process.

First of all, it must be realized that "assimilation" is a blanket term which in reality covers a multitude of subprocesses. The most crucial distinction is one often ignored — the distinction between what I have elsewhere called "behavioral assimilation" and "structural assimilation." [27] The first refers to the absorption of the cultural behavior patterns of the "host" society. (At the same time, there is frequently some modification of the cultural patterns of the immigrant-receiving country, as well.) There is a special term for this process of cultural modification or "behavioral assimilation" — namely, "acculturation." "Structural assimilation," on the other hand, refers to the entrance of the immigrants and their descendants into the social cliques, organizations, institutional activities, and general civic life of the receiving society. If this process takes place on a large enough scale, then a high frequency of intermarriage must result. A further distinction must be made between, on the one hand, those activities of the general civic life which involve earning a living, carrying out political responsibilities, and engaging in the instrumental affairs of the larger community, and, on the other hand, activities which create personal friendship patterns, frequent home intervisiting, communal worship, and communal recreation. The first type usually develops so-called "secondary relationships," which tend to be relatively impersonal and segmental; the latter type leads to "primary relationships," which are warm, intimate, and personal.

With these various distinctions in mind, we may then proceed.

Built on the base of the original immigrant "colony" but frequently extending into the life of successive generations, the characteristic ethnic group experience is this: within the ethnic group there develops a network of organizations and informal social relationships which permits and encourages the members of the ethnic group to remain within the confines of the group for all of their primary relationships and some of their secondary relationships throughout all the stages of the life cycle. From the cradle in the sectarian hospital to the child's play group, the social clique in high school, the fraternity and religious center in college, the dating group within which he searches for a spouse, the marriage partner, the neighborhood of his residence, the church affiliation and the church clubs, the men's and the women's social and service organizations, the adult clique of "marrieds," the vacation resort, and then, as the age cycle nears completion, the rest home for the elderly and, finally, the sectarian cemetery — in all these activities and relationships which are close to the core of personality and selfhood — the member of the ethnic group may if he wishes follow a path which never takes him across the boundaries of his ethnic structural network.

The picture is made more complex by the existence of social class divi-

27 Milton M. Gordon, "Social Structure and Goals in Group Relations," p. 151.

sions which cut across ethnic group lines just as they do those of the white Protestant population in America. As each ethnic group which has been here for the requisite time has developed second, third, or in some cases, succeeding generations, it has produced a college-educated group which composes an upper middle class (and sometimes upper class, as well) segment of the larger groups. Such class divisions tend to restrict primary group relations even further, for although the ethnic-group member feels a general sense of identification with all the bearers of his ethnic heritage, he feels comfortable in intimate social relations only with those who also share his own class background or attainment.

In short, my point is that, while *behavioral assimilation* or acculturation has taken place in America to a considerable degree, *structural assimilation* with some important exceptions has not been extensive.[28] The exceptions are of two types. The first brings us back to the "triple melting pot" thesis of Ruby Jo Reeves Kennedy and Will Herberg. The "nationality" ethnic groups have tended to merge within each of the three major religious groups. This has been particularly true of the Protestant and Jewish communities. Those descendants of the "old" immigration of the nineteenth century, who were Protestant (many of the Germans and all the Scandinavians), have in considerable part gradually merged into the white Protestant "subsociety." Jews of Sephardic, German, and Eastern-European origins have similarly tended to come together in their communal life. The process of absorbing the various Catholic nationalities, such as the Italians, Poles, and French Canadians, into an American Catholic community hitherto dominated by the Irish has begun, although I do not believe that it is by any means close to completion. Racial and quasi-racial groups such as the Negroes, Indians, Mexican-Americans, and Puerto Ricans still retain their separate sociological structures. The outcome of all this in contemporary American life is thus pluralism — but it is more than "triple" and it is more accurately described as *structural pluralism* than as cultural pluralism, although some of the latter also remains.

My second exception refers to the social structures which implicate intellectuals. There is no space to develop the issue here, but I would argue that there is a social world or subsociety of the intellectuals in America in which true structural intermixture among persons of various ethnic backgrounds, including the religious, has markedly taken place.

My final point deals with the reasons for these developments. If structural assimilation has been retarded in America by religious and racial lines, we must ask why. The answer lies in the attitudes of both the majority and the minority groups and in the way these attitudes have interacted. A saying of the current day is, "It takes two to tango." To apply the analogy, there is no good reason to believe that white Protestant America has ever extended a firm and cordial invitation to its minorities to dance. Furthermore, the atti-

[28] See Erich Rosenthal, "Acculturation without Assimilation?" *American Journal of Sociology*, 1960, 66: 275–288.

tudes of the minority-group members themselves on the matter have been divided and ambiguous. Particularly for the minority religious groups, there is a certain logic in ethnic communality, since there is a commitment to the perpetuation of the religious ideology and since structural intermixture leads to intermarriage and the possible loss to the group of the intermarried family. Let us, then, examine the situation serially for various types of minorities.

With regard to the immigrant, in his characteristic numbers and socio-economic background, structural assimilation was out of the question. He did not want it, and he had a positive need for the comfort of his own communal institutions. The native American, moreover, whatever the implications of his public pronouncements, had no intention of opening up his primary group life to entrance by these hordes of alien newcomers. The situation was a functionally complementary standoff.

The second generation found a much more complex situation. Many believed they heard the siren call of welcome to the social cliques, clubs, and institutions of white Protestant America. After all, it was simply a matter of learning American ways, was it not? Had they not grown up as Americans, and were they not culturally different from their parents, the "greenhorns?" Or perhaps an especially eager one reasoned (like the Jewish protagonist of Myron Kaufmann's novel, *Remember Me To God*, aspiring to membership in the prestigious club system of Harvard undergraduate social life) "If only I can go the last few steps in Ivy League manners and behavior, they will surely recognize that I am one of them and take me in." But, alas, Brooks Brothers suit notwithstanding, the doors of the fraternity house, the city men's club, and the country club were slammed in the face of the immigrant's offspring. That invitation was not really there in the first place; or, to the extent it was, in Joshua Fishman's phrase, it was a " 'look me over but don't touch me' invitation to the American minority group child." [29] And so the rebuffed one returned to the homelier but dependable comfort of the communal institutions of his ancestral group. There he found his fellows of the same generation who had never stirred from the home fires. Some of these had been too timid to stray; others were ethnic ideologists committed to the group's survival; still others had never really believed in the authenticity of the siren call or were simply too passive to do more than go along the familiar way. All could now join in the task that was well within the realm of the sociologically possible — the build-up of social institutions and organizations within the ethnic enclave, manned increasingly by members of the second generation and suitably separated by social class.

Those who had for a time ventured out gingerly or confidently, as the case

---

[29] Joshua A. Fishman, "Childhood Indoctrination for Minority-Group Membership and the Quest for Minority-Group Biculturism in America," in Oscar Handlin, ed., *Group Life in America* (Cambridge, Harvard University Press, forthcoming).

might be, had been lured by the vision of an "American" social structure that was somehow larger than all subgroups and was ethnically neutral. Were they, too, not Americans? But they found to their dismay that at the primary group level a neutral American social structure was a mirage. What at a distance seemed to be a quasi-public edifice flying only the all-inclusive flag of American nationality turned out on closer inspection to be the club-house of a particular ethnic group — the white Anglo-Saxon Protestants, its operation shot through with the premises and expectations of its parental ethnicity. In these terms, the desirability of whatever invitation was grudgingly extended to those of other ethnic backgrounds could only become a considerably attenuated one.

With the racial minorities, there was not even the pretense of an invitation. Negroes, to take the most salient example, have for the most part been determinedly barred from the cliques, social clubs, and churches of white America. Consequently, with due allowance for internal class differences, they have constructed their own network of organizations and institutions, their own "social world." These are now many vested interests served by the preservation of this separate communal life, and doubtless many Negroes are psychologically comfortable in it, even though at the same time they keenly desire that discrimination in such areas as employment, education, housing, and public accommodations be eliminated. However, the ideological attachment of Negroes to their communal separation is not conspicuous. Their sense of identification with ancestral African national cultures is virtually nonexistent although Pan-Africanism engages the interest of some intellectuals and although "black nationalist" and "black racist" fringe groups have recently made an appearance at the other end of the communal spectrum. As for their religion, they are either Protestant or Catholic (overwhelmingly the former). Thus, there are no "logical" ideological reasons for their separate communality; dual social structures are created solely by the dynamics of prejudice and discrimination, rather than being reinforced by the ideological commitments of the minority itself.

Structural assimilation, then, has turned out to be the rock on which the ships of Anglo-conformity and the melting pot have foundered. To understand that behavioral assimilation (or acculturation) without massive structural intermingling in primary relationships has been the dominant motif in the American experience of creating and developing a nation out of diverse peoples is to comprehend the most essential sociological fact of that experience. It is against the background of "structural pluralism" that strategies of strengthening intergroup harmony, reducing ethnic discrimination and prejudice, and maintaining the rights of both those who stay within and those who venture beyond their ethnic boundaries must be thoughtfully devised.

4

CORPORATE AMERICA

In October 1901, shortly after J. P. Morgan announced the organization of the United States Steel Corporation with a capitalization of over a billion dollars, the *Boston Herald* commented: "If a limited financial group shall come to represent the capitalistic end of industry, the perils of socialism, even if brought about by some rude, because forcible, taking of the instruments of industry, may be looked upon by even intelligent people as possibly the lesser of two evils." It is a measure of the agitation evoked by the great business consolidations around the turn of the century that such a statement could come from so eminent a representative of conservative Eastern sentiment.

One reason for the agitation was the suddenness of the consolidation movement. Between 1879 and 1896 there had been only a dozen important combinations of mining or manufacturing companies: their aggregate capitalization did not amount to $1 billion. But in the six years between 1897 and 1902, there were 2,722 combinations of manufacturing and mining companies with an aggregate capitalization of almost $6.5 billion; in 1899 alone, there were 1,208 mergers totaling $2.3 billion. At no other time in American history has business enterprise gone in for consolidation on anything like that scale. In the fifteen-year period between 1906 and 1920, for example, the number of industrial mergers exceeded 100 only five times. A new record of 1,245 mergers was set in 1929, but the average of annual consolidations since 1905 has been only about 250. In short, it is not astonishing that in 1901 even conservatives had begun to fear that a small number of dubiously motivated businessmen might be assuming control of the economy.

A second reason for concern was the sudden and complete ascendancy of the corporate form of business organization, and especially the ominous possibilities for control that holding companies (such as U.S. Steel) possessed. Corporate organization provided the flexibility in finance and direction needed for large-scale business enterprise. But it also upset the traditional relationships of individuals to property. [For a short, sharp essay on this subject, see D. Bell, "The Breakup of Family Capitalism," in *The End of Ideology* (1960).] It placed a sturdy wall between ownership and control, and permitted motives other than profit to intrude into the conduct of business enterprise. Some hoped American business might thus be lifted from the meanness of small-time, competitive profit-grabbing. "The real news about business," wrote Walter Lippmann in 1914, "is that it is being administered by men who are not profiteers. The managers are on salary, divorced from ownership and from bargaining. . . . Their day's work is not measured in profit." [*Drift and Mastery* (1961 paperback reprint), p. 43.] But more often the separation seemed only to permit business leaders to indulge in reckless empire-building and stock manipulations for their own amusement and personal profit at the expense of the enterprises they controlled. [L. D. Brandeis's *Other People's Money and How the Bankers Use It* (1914) is the classic statement of this view.]

For a country that was still oriented to agriculture and small-town life, the development of "big business" and the ascendancy of the corporate form of business enterprise thus posed a dual threat. It is not hard to understand the references to the conspiratorial "they" which punctuate the speeches and editorials of the day. "They" invaded the natural markets of local retailers and processors. "They" rigged the price of kerosene and condiments, jute bags and implements, bathtubs and beefsteaks. "They" controlled property they did not own from offices thousands of miles away. "They" made money without working.

As we approach the last quarter of the twentieth century, most of the heat has gone out of the antimonopoly and anticorporation fight, despite the fact that the American economy is more highly concentrated than ever before and the power of the small oligarchy of corporate leaders who preside over most of industry has never been so well fused with the power of government. Perhaps the public has become inured to it. Perhaps the performance of corporate capitalism has successfully satisfied the public's principal needs. Or perhaps the apparent satisfaction is itself a function of corporate power and of the impact of sustained "public relations" efforts on the public's perspicacity as to its "true" self-interest. Whatever the case, if the growth of corporate power arose from some sort of collusion, either between government and business or among big business leaders, or from the exploitation of various economic victims, one will find little of that in the meticulous work of Johns Hopkins University Professor Alfred Chandler, probably the leading business historian in the country today.

In his renowned and much reprinted article, "The Beginnings of 'Big Business' in American Industry" [*Business History Review*, 33 (Spring 1959)], Chandler explained the growth of the giant corporations by emphasizing the demand for large-scale organization created by completion of a national transportation system and the growth of large urban markets. The natural growth of big business, he noted, quickly inspired defensive combinations and vertical integration to protect competitive positions and sources of supply as well as to reduce costs. Similarly, for optimal utilization of resources, skills, and market connections, as well as to hedge their investments, companies entered into ambitious diversification programs, adding another dimension to corporate growth. In his "The Structure of American Industry in the

20th Century: A Historical Perspective" [*ibid.*, 43 (Autumn 1969)], Chandler notes that at least through the 1930's, "government policies appear to have had even less effect on the development of the large firm or the overall structure of industry than have had individual entrepreneurs." Since then, however, government has significantly influenced at least the environment in which business decisions are made, by maintaining high effective demand for goods and services through policies designed to maximize employment, by providing the overwhelming portion of research and development resources, and by becoming a major consumer in its own right. Still, he concludes, in a passage that substantially confirms one important thesis of John Kenneth Galbraith's *The New Industrial State** (1968), "The modern diversified enterprise represents a calculated, rational response of technically trained professional managers to the needs and opportunities of changing technologies and markets. It is much less the product of ambitious and able individual entrepreneurs or of governmental policies."

Chandler is primarily interested in what has guided the decisions of the professional managers of modern industry. Although he rarely raises questions about the legitimacy of the enormous power that corporations wield or about the social efficiency of the industrial system he describes, wherein the technical needs of the "productive plans" seemingly have come to outweigh reasonable consumer needs, he is no apologist for the system. As he says at the end of the article reprinted below, "the first step in meeting these problems is the understanding of how the corporation developed the basic functions it has long enjoyed in the management of the American economy."

A bibliography on this subject would be endless, but the following are especially worth seeing: W. P. Adams, ed., *The Structure of American Industry** (1961); E. F. Cheit, ed., *The Business Establishment** (1964), esp. R. Hofstadter, "What Happened to the Antitrust Movement?" and R. Heilbroner, "The View from the Top: Reflections on a Changing Business Ideology"; E. S. Mason, ed., *The Corporation in Modern Society** (1959); and R. Eells, *The Government of Corporations* (1962).

The Large Industrial Corporation
and the Making of the Modern American Economy

ALFRED D. CHANDLER, JR.

. . . The corporation is . . . the most important single economic organization in the American economy.[1] Because of its functions and because of the types of decisions made by its managers, I believe that its influence is more pervasive than the labor union, the regulatory commission, or other public bodies concerned with the economy. My focus will be on the most influential and the most complex species of this institutional genus — the integrated and diversified industrial corporation.[2] The large industrial corporation is more varied in its activities and more difficult to manage than are the highly specialized financial, transportation, and public utilities corporations.

Let me begin by reminding you of the dominating position which the giant corporation has acquired in our economy. Consider the statistics on earnings. In 1960 six hundred American corporations had annual earnings of over $10 million. These six hundred represented only 0.5 per cent of the total corporations in the country; yet they accounted for 53 per cent of the total corporate income. Or, if we look only at industrial corporations, in 1960 the four hundred largest of these, all of which had assets of over $100 million, earned 46 per cent of all income earned before taxes in the manu-

Reprinted by permission from *Institutions in Modern America: Innovation in Structure and Process*, edited by Stephen E. Ambrose, published by The Johns Hopkins Press, 1967.

[1] The sources of information of this essay come from extended researches, whose findings appear in my "Beginnings of Big Business in American Industry," in *Business History Review*, XXX (Spring, 1959), 1–31; "Development, Diversification and Decentralization," *Postwar Economic Trends in the United States*, ed. Ralph Freeman (Cambridge, 1960), ch. VII; "Le Rôle de la Firme dans l'Économie Américaine," in *Économie Appliquée*, XVII (1964), Nos. 2–3; and *Strategy and Structure: Chapters in the History of the Industrial Enterprise* (Cambridge, Mass., 1962), especially the chapters on Du Pont and General Motors. I am indebted to the Alfred P. Sloan Foundation for support of these studies and of the present one. In the past two years I have been working with Professor Stephen Salsbury on a biography of Pierre S. du Pont, which provides detailed information on the story of that pioneer in modern industrial management.

[2] Included in this definition of the industrial corporation are large marketing enterprises like Sears, Roebuck, Montgomery Ward, General Mills, National Dairy, and others that do their own manufacturing or through their purchasing policies determine the design and price of manufactured articles and so control the flow of goods from the producer of the raw and semi-finished materials to the ultimate consumer.

facturing sector and controlled 30 per cent of all assets. Of these the one hundred largest alone accounted for 54 per cent of all profits (not income) in the manufacturing sector.

Consider employment. In 1956 approximately 220 industrials employed more than ten thousand workers. In the aircraft industry 10 such firms employed 94 per cent of the total force; in petroleum 15 such firms employed 86 per cent; in steel 13 firms hired 85 per cent; in motor vehicles 8 firms employed 77 per cent; in office machinery 4 firms employed 71 per cent; in farm machinery 3 put to work 64 per cent; and in electrical machinery 6 employed 50 per cent. Much the same range of figures indicates that in value added, as in employment and income, a few giants handle most of the work in many major American industries. Rather than list more numbers, let me cite just one statistic given in the New York Times this fall, for it suggests the size of these giants in relation to other twentieth-century institutions. Last October the Times listed the world's largest units according to their gross revenues in the following order: United States, Russia, United Kingdom, France, and then General Motors, followed by West Germany, Japan, and Canada. General Motors' total revenues of just over $20 billion were greater than the combined revenues of Japan and Canada and were very close to United Kingdom's $21 billion and France's $20.5 billion.[3]

These statistics reflect the critical importance of the decisions made in the general offices of these industrial giants. In a large number of American industries a very small number of men make the final decisions on how much to produce and what prices to charge. Their actions, in turn, intimately affect the economic decisions of hundreds of suppliers, dealers, and retailers, as well as those managers of smaller firms producing or providing comparable or complementary goods for local or specialized markets. This small group also has much to say about employment and wages, although here the decisions are constrained by the desires and opinions of labor union representatives.

The decisions as to output, prices, and wages represent only one type of those made by the managers of large corporations. These and other types are usually tied into two larger and more comprehensive sets of decisions. One of these sets involves the co-ordination of the flow of goods through the various activities of the enterprise, from the production and purchase of the raw and semi-finished materials to the sale to the ultimate consumer. The second and even more critical set involves the allocation of the corporation's resources — money, personnel, and technical and administrative skills. It must be decided how, where, and when the corporation should expand, contract, or stabilize its business and whether it should move in or out of dif-

[3] New York Times (October 31, 1965); and General Motors Corporation 57th Annual Report, Year Ending December 31, 1965.

ferent geographical areas, economic functions, or end products and services. The first set of decisions — those affecting the co-ordination of flow —is determined by short-term estimates of the market and influences the day-to-day pace of the economy. Those involving the allocation of resources are made on the basis of estimates of long-range demand and affect the over-all direction and growth of the national economy.

I plan here to describe the methods and procedures developed over the years by corporation managers in making these two critically important types of decisions. In addition, I plan to indicate how the managers, by using these procedures, help determine the direction of the growth of their corporations, of their industries, and of the economy as a whole. In other words, I will first deal with the developing structure of the modern corporation and then with its changing strategy. But before considering these topics, I must say a little about how and why the large corporations came into being in the first place. This historical background is particularly essential because the institution was *not* created to carry out the critical functions it acquired. Therefore, among the most important tasks which faced the managers of the new institutions were those of devising methods to co-ordinate flow and to allocate resources. Only after these structural devices were completed were the managers able to concentrate on developing new strategies of growth.

The large integrated industrial corporation appeared suddenly and dramatically on the American scene during the last two decades of the nineteenth century. Before that time decisions affecting the flow of goods through the economy and the allocations of its resources were extremely decentralized. They were made in hundreds of thousands of small family firms. These firms normally handled a single product or function. The business decisions of their owners were normally affected by an impersonal market over which they had relatively little control, except possibly in nearby local areas. Price determined the volume of output and also the pace of the flow of goods from the producer of raw materials to the factory and then to the ultimate consumer via an intricate network of wholesalers.

The great transformation from decentralized decision-making to centralized co-ordination and control of production and distribution came at the very end of the last century. Between 1897 and 1902 there occurred the first and still the most significant merger movement in American history. In industry after industry the giant enterprise appeared. The merger movement which marked the beginning of the modern structure of American business was itself the culmination of a creative period of industrial and corporate growth.

The modern corporation had its beginnings in the eighteen fifties with the swift spread of the railroad network and the factory system during that decade. The railroads, as the nation's first big business, came to provide the only available model for financing and administering the giant industrial enterprises. The railroads played this role because their promoters, financers, and managers were the first to build, finance, and operate business enterprises requiring massive capital investment and calling for complex administrative arrangements. The financing of the railroads required such large amounts of money that it brought into being modern Wall Street and its specialized investment bankers. The instruments and methods later used to capitalize large industrial enterprises were all employed earlier by the railroads, for financial requirements forced the use of the corporate form. An individual or partnership simply could not supply enough capital to build even a small railroad. The sale of corporate stocks and bonds was essential. The modern holding company, too, had its start in the railroads, for the management of interstate business encouraged one railroad corporation to control others in other states by purchasing and holding their stock.

The railroads were forced to pioneer in modern business administration as well as in modern corporate finance. Their managers fashioned large functional departments to handle transportation, traffic, and finance. They set up central offices to supervise and co-ordinate the work of the departments and the railroads as a whole. They originated line and staff distinctions in business organization. They were the first to develop a flow of operating statistics used to control movement of traffic and also to evaluate the performance of operating departments. They also had to meet brand-new problems of modern cost accounting, to make the distinctions between variable, constant, and joint costs, to differentiate between working and fixed capital, and to account for depreciation and even obsolescence.

But the railroad was only the model. The parent of the large corporation was the factory. The modern factory with its power-driven machinery and its permanent working force, whose tasks were subdivided and specialized, appeared in the United States as early as 1814. Yet until the swift spread of an all-weather transportation network, including the railroad, the ocean-going steamship, and the telegraph, relatively few factories existed in the United States outside of the textile and related industries. Then in the late eighteen forties and fifties factory production began for the first time to be significant in the making of sewing machines, clocks, watches, ploughs, reapers, shoes, suits and other ready-made clothing, and rifles and pistols for commercial use. The same years saw the spread of the large integrated iron works, using coal and coke instead of charcoal for fuel. The Civil War further stimulated the growth in these industries. After the war the factory spread to others. By 1880 the census reported that of the three million people employed in industries using machines, four fifths worked under the factory system of production. "Remarkable applications of this system," the census added, "are to be found in the manufacture of boots, shoes, watches, musical instruments, clothing, metal goods, general firearms, carriages and wagons, woolen goods, rubber goods, and even the slaughtering of hogs." [4]

In the quarter of a century following the completion of this census, the factory was transformed in many industries into a vertically integrated, multifunctional enterprise. Let me explain what I mean by these terms. In 1880 nearly all manufacturing firms only manufactured. The factory owners purchased their raw materials and sold their finished goods through wholesalers, who were sometimes commission agents and at other times jobbers who took title to the goods. By the first years of the twentieth century, however, many American industries were dominated by enterprises that had created their own distributing organizations, sometimes including even retailing outlets, and had formed their own purchasing systems, in some cases controlling their supplies of semi-finished and raw materials.

Many reasons have been suggested for this fundamental change. These include the impact of new technology, the influence of shifting overseas demand for American goods, the development of the market for industrial securities, the desire for tighter market control, the tariff, and even the sinister motives of those energetic and somewhat romantic fellows, the Robber Barons.[5] I would like to propose two other more specific and, I believe, more significant reasons for the growth of the large integrated enterprise. One was the inability of factory owners to enforce and so maintain cartels. If the American cartels had had some kind of legal support or had been sanctioned by the government as was often true in Europe, the giant corporation would have been slower in developing. The other reason was the inadequacy of the existing wholesaler network to handle high volume distribution of goods.

The manufacturers who pioneered in building the integrated firm were those who first found the wholesaler network inadequate for their needs. They were of two types. First, there were the volume producers of durable goods, who discovered that the wholesaler was unable to handle the initial demonstration to customers, unable to provide the necessary consumer credit, and unable to ensure continuing repair and service of goods sold. Second, there were the producers of perishable goods for the mass market, and they found the wholesaler still more inadequate. Among the first type were the makers of sewing machines, agricultural implements, typewriters, cash registers, carriages, bicycles, and, most important of all, electrical machinery and equipment. The McCormicks in reapers, the Remingtons in

---

[4] Carroll D. Wright, "The Factory System of the United States," in U.S. Census Office, *Report on the Manufactures of the United States at the 10th Census, June 1, 1880* (Washington, D.C., 1883), p. 548.

[5] These views are well summarized in Ralph Andreano's comments on studies by Ralph Nelson and others in his *New Views on American Economic Development* (Cambridge, 1966), pp. 15–19. A recent study that gives further evidence of the inability of the pools to maintain price and production schedules is Peter Temin, *Iron and Steel in Nineteenth Century America — An Economic Inquiry* (Cambridge, 1965), pp. 175–89. Of all the products in the iron and steel industry the only effective pool for any amount of time was in rails, and even here it was successful for only short periods.

typewriters, Edward Clark of Singer Sewing Machine, James Patterson in cash registers, Albert Pope in bicycles, William C. Durant in carriages, and George Westinghouse and Charles Coffin in electrical machinery all pioneered in the creation of national and even international marketing organizations. Their new distributing networks usually included franchised retail dealers supported by branch offices which supplied the retailers with a flow of products, funds, spare parts and accessories, and with specialized repair and maintenance men. In order to assure supplies for the large volume of production needed to meet the demands of the new distributing system, these innovators also built large purchasing organizations, often bought or erected factories to manufacture parts and semi-finished materials, and sometimes came to own their own large tracts of lumber or iron and steel works.

In these same years, the eighties and nineties, the volume producers of perishable goods for the mass market created their own distributing and purchasing organizations. Among these Gustavus Swift, a New England wholesale butcher, was probably the most significant innovator. In the late seventies Swift appreciated, as had others, that the urbanizing East was outrunning its meat supply. Swift also saw the possibilities, which only a few others appreciated, of using the refrigerated car to bring western meat to the East. The shipment of live cattle east, which since the eighteen fifties had been the most lucrative eastbound trade for the railroads, was inefficient and costly. Sixty per cent of the animal was inedible. Cattle lost weight or died on the trip. What was equally important, concentration of butchering in Chicago would assure high volume operations and a much lower unit cost than the current method of shipping in small lots to wholesale butchers throughout the East.

Gustavus Swift's basic innovation was the creation of a distribution network. He realized that the refrigerated car was not enough. Carloads of fresh meat could hardly be dumped in Baltimore or Boston on a hot summer's day. So in the eighties he began to build branch houses in every major town or city in the East and in many other parts of the nation. A branch house included a refrigerated warehouse, a sales office, and men and equipment to deliver meat to retail butchers and food stores. In carrying out this plan, Swift met the most determined opposition. The railroads were startled by the prospect of losing a major business, so the Eastern Truck Line Association refused to carry his refrigerated cars. In 1886 the wholesalers organized the Butchers National Protection Association to fight the "trust."

But good meat at low price won out. Once the market was assured, Swift then set up large packing houses in the cities along the cattle frontier and even bought into the stockyards. By the end of the eighties wholesalers with ample energy and resources realized that unless they quickly followed Swift's example they would have to remain small local enterprises. Armour, Cudahy, Hammond, Morris, and the firm of Schwartzchild and Sulzberger (it became Wilson and Company in World War I) quickly built their branch networks and bought into stockyards. These remained the "big six" in the meat-packing industry until changes in transportation and refrigeration in the nineteen thirties and forties opened new opportunities.

What Swift did for meat, Andrew Preston did in the same years for the mass distribution of bananas through the creation of the United Fruit Company. Also in the eighties large brewers like Schlitz, Blatz, and Pabst in Milwaukee and Anheuser-Busch in St. Louis set up comparable distribution networks based on refrigeration. In the same decade James B. Duke did the same thing for a new non-refrigerated product — the cigarette.

These pioneers in high volume manufacturing and distribution of both perishable and relatively complex durable goods demonstrated the clear economies of scale. They provided obvious models for manufacturers who had until then found the existing wholesaler network quite satisfactory. Nevertheless, the factory owners in these industries were slow to follow the example of Swift, McCormick, and the others. They had to be pushed rather than attracted into adopting a strategy of vertical integration and with it the economies of mass production and mass distribution. It was the continuing oppressive pressure of falling prices between the mid-eighties and the mid-nineties that provided this push and forced many manufacturers to organize for the mass national market. The price decline, in turn, may have resulted largely from the coming of the factory itself. Far more efficient than hand or shop production, the widespread adoption of the factory after 1850, and particularly after the Civil War, had led to a sharply increasing output of goods and an excess of supply over demand.

In many American industries these falling prices resulted in a similar organizational response. The pattern was the same in producers' goods industries like iron, steel, brass, copper, rubber products, and explosives, and in consumers' goods industries like salt, sugar, matches, biscuits, kerosene, and rubber boots and shoes. This pattern — the second route to great size — was one of combination, consolidation, and then vertical integration. To meet the threat of falling prices and profits, the factory owners formed trade associations whose primary function was to control price and production. But these associations were rarely able to maintain their cartels. If the prices became stabilized, some manufacturers would leave the association and obtain business by selling below the established price. If prices rose temporarily, the members often disbanded until the downward trend began again. The associations proved to be, in the words of the first president of the Petroleum Refiners' Association, John D. Rockefeller, "ropes of sand." They failed for the same reason as did the railroad cartels in the seventies and eighties. The agreements could not be enforced. They did not have the binding effect of a legal contract.

While the railroad men turned unsuccessfully to advocating pooling legalized by state and national legislatures, the manufacturers devised new ways of acquiring firmer legal control of the factories in their industries. Initially they began to purchase stock in competing companies. Then came a new device, the trust. The stocks of the various manufacturing companies were turned over to a board of trustees, with the owners of the stock receiving trust certificates in return. Less cumbersome was the holding company, whose stock could be exchanged directly for that of an operating firm and could then be bought or sold in the security markets. Once New Jersey had passed a general incorporation law for holding companies in 1889, this instrument became the standard one by which a group of manufacturers obtained legal control over a large number of factories.

Administrative control and industrial reorganization often, though not always, followed legal consolidation. The factories controlled by the trust or the holding company were placed under a single manager with a specialized staff. The manager closed down the smaller, more inefficient plants and enlarged the more efficient ones. By running a much smaller number of much larger plants day and night, he quickly lowered unit costs. As a high volume producer, the consolidated enterprise now found it could no longer rely on the fragmented distributing network of wholesalers. The enterprise therefore quickly moved into setting up its own wholesalers and occasionally even its own retailers and its own purchasing organization, often moving back to control of raw material.

The petroleum industry was one of the very first to combine, then to consolidate legally and administratively, and then to integrate, because it was one of the very first to overproduce for the national and international markets. In the early seventies both refiners and producers of petroleum formed trade associations to control price and production. They were completely unsuccessful in enforcing their rulings throughout the industry. So in the mid-seventies Rockefeller, by using railroad rates as a weapon, was able to bring a large portion of the refiners under the legal control of his Standard Oil Company.

However, legal control proved to be insufficient. Standard's primary market was abroad (for in the eighteen seventies close to 90 per cent of refined petroleum went to Europe). Rockefeller therefore had to develop an efficient operating organization at home if he was to compete successfully abroad. So his company tightened up its legal control through the formation of the first modern business trust. Then between 1883 and 1885 the refineries were consolidated. Where the Standard Oil Trusts had operated fifty-five plants in 1882, it had only twenty-two in 1886. Three fourths of all its production was concentrated in three giant refineries. As a result, unit costs dropped dramatically. By 1884 Standard's average cost of refining a barrel of oil was already 0.534 cents, as compared to 1.5 cents in the rest of the industry.[6] The trust then began to set up its own extensive distributing

[6] Harold F. Williamson and Arnold R. Daum, *The American Petroleum Industry, The Age of Illumination, 1859–1899* (Evanston, Ill., 1959), pp. 475, 483–84.

network, and in the late eighties it started to integrate backwards, going for the first time into the production of crude; that is, taking the crude oil out of the ground.

In the late eighteen eighties and early nineties manufacturers in other industries began to follow the example of Standard Oil, Swift, and Mc-Cormick. The severe depression of the mid-nineties slowed the processes. Funds to finance the new holding companies, to help them tempt other manufacturers into the consolidation, to pay for the necessary reorganization of production and distribution facilities, and to finance the purchase or construction of plants and mines producing raw or semi-finished materials were hard to find. Indeed, some of the newly formed consolidations failed to survive the depression. Then as prosperity returned in 1897 and capital became easier to obtain, industry after industry came to be dominated by a handful of large integrated corporations.[7] The promise of handsome returns from high volume production and high volume distribution and the harsh memory of twenty years of falling prices made the prospect of consolidation and integration difficult to resist. The result was the first great merger movement in American history.

In the years immediately following this merger movement, one of the greatest challenges facing the managers of the newly integrated corporation was to develop procedures to assure their efficient operation. This was no easy task, for many of the factory managers had long been competitors, often bitter rivals. The wholesalers now transformed into sales executives had had in the past different interests and attitudes from those of the manufacturers. So too had the purchasing agents. Moreover, these men, long used to operating independently, did not take kindly either to personal or to accounting or statistical controls.

To unite these men and offices into a smooth working organization involved two basic tasks, the building of new functional departments and the creation of a central office. The formation of the functional departments often called for massive reorganization of an industry's production, distribution, and purchasing facilities. The setting up of the central office required the development of procedures to assure a steady and regular flow of goods and materials through the several departments in the interest of the corporation as a whole.

Some managers of the new integrated enterprises, like those of General Electric, International Harvester, Bethlehem Steel, and Du Pont, began almost immediately to work out their administrative structures. Others, like

[7] Hans B. Thorelli, *Federal Anti-Trust Policy* (Baltimore, 1957), pp. 275, 294–303, provides tables and lists of those companies formed before and after the depression of the nineties. Significantly, in industries where the wholesale network was deeply entrenched and had its own trade associations, such as in hardware, lumber, coal, furniture, textiles, and ready-made clothing industries, there was some consolidation but much less than in other industries.

those of Allis-Chalmers, Westinghouse, and United States Steel, moved more slowly, often acting only when forced by declining profits and financial difficulties. Let me indicate the administrative challenges facing these corporations and the nature of their responses by reviewing briefly the experience of one of the more energetic and imaginative pioneers in organization building, the E. I. du Pont de Nemours Powder Company.

In 1902 three young cousins — Coleman, Alfred, and Pierre du Pont — took over control of their family firm, then just a century old. They immediately arranged to consolidate with their largest and normally friendly rival, Laflin & Rand. Next they brought smaller firms into the consolidation by forming a holding company, the E. I. du Pont de Nemours Powder Company, and then exchanging its stock for that of the smaller companies who were members of the old Gunpowder Trade Association. Next they disbanded this trade association, which had been attempting to set price and production schedules fairly regularly since 1873 (and had been able to do so only because its leading members, Du Pont and Laflin & Rand, purchased stock of other members).

Department building quickly followed legal consolidation. The holding company became an operating one. The many factories were placed under one of three operating departments — black powder, high explosives (that is, dynamite), and smokeless powder. Branch sales offices were created in all parts of the country and placed under a central sales department. An essential materials department was formed to handle the new high volume purchasing of nitrates, glycerine, sulphur, and pyrites, for with consolidation the company had become the largest single purchaser in the United States of these materials. In fact, after 1902 the Du Pont Company alone accounted for 5 per cent of the world consumption and 30 per cent of the United States consumption of nitrate, and one sixth of the world and one third of the United States consumption of glycerine.[8]

The Du Pont cousins fashioned staff as well as line departments. The new development department concentrated on investigating and planning possibilities for capital expenditures and, until the formation of the chemical department, administered the research laboratories set up to improve the product. The engineering department specialized in plant and office construction and maintenance. The traffic department helped assure an efficient flow of materials from the nitrate beds of Chile to the mining and construction companies who used the finished explosives. In addition, there was a legal department and one for personnel. Finally, there was the treasury department, which had both line and staff duties. Besides taking on the routine work of handling funds coming in and out of the company,

---

[8] These figures come from internal reports of the Du Pont Company. They and their implications will be given in more detail in the forthcoming biography of Pierre S. du Pont.

it paid close attention to improving cost and accounting figures needed by the central office to carry on the administration of the company as a whole.

The process of department building required many persons in the new company to adopt new roles, new values, and new modes of action. In the case of Du Pont, the salesmen resisted the new ways more vehemently than did the factory managers. One highly respected agent considered the home office's request for systematic accounting information a direct slap at his business honor and soon retired in a huff. Another found reporting regularly to Wilmington so inhibiting to his taste that he left the company, taking with him all the records of the Gunpowder Trade Association (the old cartel), which he later used to bring an antitrust suit against Du Pont. Most of the men involved did not react so strongly, but in personal terms the transition from combination to consolidation and integration was by no means easy.

At the same time a central office had to be fashioned to administer the work of the departments. At Du Pont, as in most of the new giants, the company's ruling body was the executive committee, composed of the president and heads of the major departments. The committee considered its task one of appraising the performance and co-ordination of the work of the several departments and planning for the future growth of the company as a whole. And it was in carrying out these tasks that the committee became quickly involved in devising ways to co-ordinate flows and allocate resources.

The methods involved in the allocation of resources were the easiest to devise. First came procedures to provide information about each of the many requests for capital expenditures sent by the departments to the executive committee. Besides detailed data on costs, the committee asked for anticipated rate of return from the expenditure and estimates on how much the new construction or equipment would reduce current operating costs. In addition, each appropriation request had to be checked and approved by staff specialists in the engineering, traffic, and purchasing departments to see that all possible savings were achieved and specialized problems worked out.

The committee was soon getting the information it wanted, but the difficulty was that its members did not have time to digest it. So they delegated to plant managers and department heads the authorization of smaller capital expenditures. They appointed one full-time senior executive and his office staff to review appropriation requests and check on their execution. Finally, before the end of 1905, the committee decided to devote alternate weekly meetings to deciding on appropriations. This new emphasis of the powder-making industry's top decision-making body provides a striking demonstration of the functional differences between the old combination or cartel and the new consolidated, integrated enterprise. In 1902 the central committee of the Gunpowder Trade Association still met weekly. It discussed only specific adjustments of price and never considered the allocation of resources. In 1905 the executive committee of the new Powder Company was already concentrating over half its time on the allocation of resources. It rarely discussed prices, and then only in terms of general policy.[9] The specifics of pricing were left wholly to the sales department.

The next step in systematizing appropriation procedures was to tie the many departmental requests into a broad plan for company growth. This led to having each department submit annual estimates for capital expenditures as well as for their operating needs. On the basis of these estimates from the departments, the treasurer's financial forecasts, and a flow of information from the staff departments, particularly the development department, the executive committee made its decisions among the many claims of the several operating departments. To guide its decisions, the members began, after 1905, to work out a flexible long-term plan of growth based on extended long-range estimates of market demand.

The development of methods and techniques to co-ordinate flow of materials through the enterprise raised more critical challenges to the managers of Du Pont and other new giants than did the formulation of appropriation procedures. Such co-ordination of mass production and mass distribution involved several quite different but closely related matters, including the handling and adjusting of the fluctuating demands of working capital, the control of inventory at all stages of the flow, the physical movements of goods and materials from the sources of raw materials to the ultimate consumer, and finally the improvement and alteration of the quality and design of the product to meet the customers' changing needs and demands. All but the last of these problems became less difficult when supply or output was closely related to demand.[10] If materials could flow smoothly through the enterprise from the purchase of raw materials to the final sale of the product, working capital requirements could be reduced, inventories of raw materials and semi-finished goods could be kept at a minimum, retailers and customers could be assured of a steady and more certain supply, and employment could become more stable. Moreover, because a steady flow would permit the efficient use of all the company's facilities, it would help lower unit costs. To assure such a flow, an effective traffic department, concerned only with the physical flow of goods, was important but hardly in itself enough.

---

[9] For example, the executive committee agreed in 1905 on a pricing policy for black powder which would net the company a profit of fifteen cents a barrel and which would permit the most efficient small competitors five cents a barrel and the less efficient still less.

[10] To assure a liaison between the sales, operating, and development departments so that the products would be altered to meet customer needs and competitive developments, the Du Pont executive committee followed the example of the large electric and steel companies in forming a consumers' service office.

The problem of co-ordinating a massive flow of materials through all phases of an industry's activities was of course a brand-new one. Until the coming of the integrated firm there was no such central co-ordinating agency in any American industry. This function was not, as I have stressed, ever developed by the cartels or trade associations. Before the formation of the integrated firm, goods moved slowly in small lots from mine or farm to factory and then to customer through the extended wholesaler network. Each step normally involved a separate financial transaction and a delay in the wholesaler's warehouse or store. Three or four months from mine to factory and again from factory to customer was quite normal. During that period of time, demand for the finished goods and availability of raw and semi-finished materials often changed.

The meat packers, who created some of the very first of the integrated enterprises, were quickly able to assure an almost instantaneous connection between supply and demand. The branch houses telegraphed their orders daily to the packing plants. All messages were cleared through Chicago, where a complete record of all plants and yards was maintained. When one plant could not fill an order completely, the Chicago office would have the remainder supplied by another plant which had reported a surplus. The packing plans in turn had direct contact with the stockyards. So even as the cattle moved onto the disassembling line, the final destination of the many parts and accessories was already known.

Such co-ordination of flow of perishable refrigerated products was relatively simple. Other new enterprises had to obtain a variety of raw materials and other supplies from a great distance, often from overseas. They produced a greater number of products in widely scattered plants and marketed their line through an even more widespread distribution network. For these companies instantaneous communication linking supply and demand was not enough. Purchasing and production had to be based not on present but on future demand. An accurate forecast of the market had become essential.

For the makers of producers' goods, like the Du Ponts, forecasting was not too difficult. The number of customers was less than in consumers' goods industries and their needs easier to anticipate. Before World War I the Du Pont departments concerned — sales, operating, and purchasing — made their own separate forecasts based on careful consultation with one another. Immediately after World War I, however, when the Du Pont Company began to diversify into other lines, particularly into consumers' goods like paints and varnishes, these relatively informal arrangements broke down. The sharp postwar recession caught the Du Pont Company, as it did so many other large industrials, with a huge surplus of supplies of finished and unfinished materials. This depression, in fact, created the first modern inventory crisis in American industry, because it was the first really severe depression to occur since the coming of the integrated enterprise at the turn of the century. The overstocking of inventory and the resulting large losses brought a major administrative reorganization at Du Pont and other corporations.

For the volume producers of consumer durables the forecast of demand was even more critical than it was to those making producers' goods. This was particularly true of those firms whose products were relatively high-priced durables which involved a great number of materials, parts, and accessories in their production, as did, for example, household appliances and automobiles. It is hardly surprising, therefore, that the young, expanding automobile industry suffered a more serious inventory and accompanying financial crisis in 1921 than any other American business. Henry Ford rode out the storm by forcing his cars on his dealers, thereby making the local agents and their banks provide the necessary capital to carry the inventory. General Motors, with less market power and less executive nerve, had to write off $82 million worth of inventories as a dead loss.

Because of the heavy investment the Du Pont Company had made in General Motors, the Du Ponts then took over its management. The new president, Pierre du Pont, considered his first task as one of administrative reorganization. After defining the boundaries of the operating divisions and the new general office, he and his associates put into effect the appropriation procedures they had already developed in Wilmington. They also began to apply the Du Pont experience in co-ordinating the flow of goods through the enterprises to the more complex situation in the automobile industry.

By 1925 the General Motors managers had tied all the factors involved in mass production and mass distribution to an annual forecast of demand. These forecasts were employed to allocate working capital and to control inventory, production, employment and car delivery schedules, and the executive committee also used them to determine costs and prices, to appraise divisional performance, and to assist in the allocation of basic resources. This is the way the new forecasting procedures worked. Each year, every division regularly compiled a "divisional index" for the approval of the executive committee. It was based on long-term estimates of national growth, seasonal variations in demand, business fluctuations, and anticipated share of the market. These indices were constantly adjusted as ten-day reports from dealers and monthly reports of new car registrations indicated the precise nature of consumer demand.[11] On the first day of each month the estimates of output, inventory, purchases, etc., were made definite for the next month and made more exact for the following three months. The approval of the monthly schedule thus provided authorization for the following month's purchases. "The usual practice," reported one General Motors

[11] The monthly reports of new car registration were supplied by the R. L. Polk Company, which, by showing the exact figures on all new cars registered, gave the executive committee constant information on each division's share of the market.

executive in 1926, "is to release immediately upon adoption of the schedule the materials required for the following month, and to make definite commitments beyond that time, that is, one month, only for those items which require a longer period for their manufacture and delivery to the plant." [12]

In addition, the annual division indices provided detailed estimates on cost, prices, and profits, which the executive committee used in allocating the company's resources. Because unit costs varied so directly with volume in this largest of all mass production industries, costs came to be based on standard volume of 80 per cent of capacity. But satisfactory cost data could only be acquired after Pierre du Pont had instituted a uniform and detailed system of cost accounting throughout the entire huge corporation. On the basis of uniform costs and of both standard and estimated volume, the executive committee approved prices recommended by the division. On the basis of the resulting profit margins and volume of sales, the committee evaluated the performance of the divisions. Finally, by using these evaluations, the divisional forecasts, and staff-prepared long-term estimates of the market and the economy, the committee allocated the resources it controlled by reviewing, reworking, and approving capital and operating budgets and by promoting and transferring top operating personnel.

During the nineteen twenties similar complex techniques were worked out and adopted by other giant enterprises for controlling flows and allocating resources. The recession of 1921 provided the initial impetus to a number of large corporations other than Du Pont and General Motors.[13] General Motors executives themselves encouraged the spread of these methods by describing their achievements at professional meetings and in professional journals. In the mid-twenties the large oil firms, which had not been so hard hit by the 1921 recession, started to work out details of such procedures as they began to be caught in a squeeze resulting from a leveling off of demand for gasoline at the very moment when the opening of the mid-continent fields greatly increased supply. Standard Oil was the first, when it set up its co-ordination and budgeting departments in 1925. Others soon followed its example. After 1929 the coming of the great depression hastened the adoption of these new cost-cutting procedures in this and other industries.

In the thirties and forties these and other corporate techniques even spread to the public sector of the economy. As national income contracted after the 1929 stock market crash, those corporations which had adopted the new co-ordinating procedures were able to roll with the punch. (For example, in 1931 General Motors still made a profit of $117 million, while

[12] Albert Bradley, "Setting Up a Forecasting Program," *Annual Convention Series,* American Management Association, No. 41 (March, 1926), reprinted in Alfred D. Chandler, Jr. (ed.), *Giant Enterprise* (New York, 1964), p. 136.

[13] *Strategy and Structure,* pp. 231–32, suggests the impact of the recession on the development of inventory and other controls at Sears, Roebuck.

Henry Ford, who never had any use for these bureaucratic methods, lost $32 million.) But even these enterprises could do little to retard the economy's headlong decline. Only the government was in a position to take strong positive action. As it began to play a larger role in the economy, government officials increasingly made use of the legal and administrative advantages of the corporation. Where in 1932 there had been less than a dozen government corporations, there were ninety by 1937 and just over one hundred at the end of World War II.[14] While a majority of these were financial corporations, a good number did handle the production and distribution of goods and quickly adopted the procedures developed earlier by the private corporations.

World War II encouraged in other ways the spread of these procedures in both the private and public sectors of the economy. One was through government contracts for war production. The system of payment under these contracts required a multitude of businesses, particularly relatively small ones, to adopt for the first time effective cost accounting methods, which are the essential basis of all statistical controls. Far more important was the fact that by late 1942 the war economy came to be managed by means of the business forecast. In 1942, when war needs replaced consumer markets as the determinant of end products, the War Production Board attempted to allocate scarce materials by the use of priorities. Priorities, however, did not work at all. The basic difficulty was that the Board issued priorities on materials and components that did not yet exist. Such priorities became only hunting licenses. In the complex production of durable goods, as industrialists had earlier discovered, supply simply could not respond that quickly to demand, even to demand created by government fiat. A lead time was necessary.

The solution to these difficulties was suggested in the summer of 1942 by Ferdinand Eberstadt, an investment banker who was in charge of naval procurement. He proposed what became known as the Controlled Materials Plan, which tied the allocation of critically scarce metals like iron, steel, copper, and aluminum, and, a little later, of components like motors, generators, and compressors, into the forecasting procedures developed by General Motors and other large corporations.[15] By this plan, the makers of the few most critical materials and components forwarded to the War Production Board forecasts of their output for the next three months. At the same time, the major claimant agencies — the Army, Navy, Shipping Board,

---

[14] The growth and uses of the corporation in the federal government is summarized in John C. James, "A Report on Public Corporations in the Federal Government," an unpublished study prepared in the summer of 1965 at the Center for the Study of Recent American History at The Johns Hopkins University.

[15] The story of the formation, adoption, and operation of the Controlled Material Plan and its counterpart, the Component Scheduling Plan, is well told in J. Elberton Smith, *The Army and Economic Mobilization* (Washington, D.C., 1959), ch. XXV, pp. 597-99.

Lend-Lease, synthetic rubber, and high-octane gasoline programs — sent the Board three-month estimates of their needs. The Requirements Committee of the War Production Board then worked out allocations of the output of the critical items, notifying the claimant agencies of their quotas two months in advance of actual production. The agencies then allocated their quotas among the prime contractors, who received them one month in advance of production. These prime contractors, usually the large corporations, then adjusted their production schedules and those of most of their subcontractors and suppliers in accordance with their allocation. Thus, when the basic materials were produced, they went directly to the prime and subcontractors for immediate use.

As Eberstadt explained when he proposed his plan to the W.P.B.: "The above system has the merit of confining decisions at the highest levels to broad questions and decentralizing the detail. . . . The basic distribution of materials between the military, basic economic, Lend-Lease, and other exports would be made by the War Production Board . . . but the actual scheduling and directing of materials, particularly in the military field, would be taken over by those responsible for procurement and production, which cannot be carried out without control of the flow of materials in accordance with their schedules." [16] In nearly all cases the large corporations continued to co-ordinate the flow from the initial supplier to the claimant agency. But where production had not yet come under the large corporation, as in the case of landing craft, the responsible agency, in this case the Navy, had to work out the co-ordination of flows at the cost of a great deal of time and energy.

In this way, then, the war helped to make the forecast, like modern cost accounting, a standard operating procedure for much of American industry. The success of the Controlled Materials Plan and the Component Scheduling Plan, particularly when compared to the earlier chaos in war production, emphasized the key role the large corporation had played in co-ordinating the flow of materials through the American economy. Their successes also suggest the value of the procedures which the corporation managers had developed for the management of a command as well as a market economy.

With the return of peace the War Production Board was disbanded, and market demand again became the basic criterion for decisions concerning the allocation of resources and the co-ordination of flows. And these critical economic decisions remained concentrated, as they had been since 1900, in the hands of corporation managers. As the procedures for co-ordinating flows became increasingly systematized and routinized, the senior executives of these large corporations were able to concentrate more and more on the most significant of their functions, the allocation of the resources under

[16] *Ibid.*, pp. 567–70.

their control. I want now to consider briefly how the managers used their long- and short-term forecasts and their appropriation procedures to allocate funds, personnel, and technical and managerial know-how. In particular, I want to examine the underlying business strategies which the managers used as criteria for allocating their resources. I want also to explain why the managers shifted from one basic strategy, that of vertical integration, to another, that of diversification.

During the first two decades of the twentieth century, the men in charge of the large corporations continued to follow the strategy of vertical integration, which had been so critical to the formation of their corporations. This strategy particularly continued to dominate the new industries, such as automobiles and chemicals, which only began to move into high volume production and distribution in these decades. The strategy was also significant to companies in industries like petroleum and rubber, which were transformed by the coming of the automobile. But even the corporations that had come into being during the great merger movement at the turn of the century at first continued to grow largely by integrating backwards.

The reasons for specific moves varied. Rate of return on investment was a critical criterion. Often, however, the move to purchase or build a factory making semi-finished materials or a mine producing raw materials was made for defensive reasons. The need to assure the steady flow of raw and semi-finished materials at a reasonable price led to the buying or building of facilities at below the normal expected rate of return. This was true when the Du Ponts moved into the manufacture of glycerine and fusel oil and when the United States Rubber Company purchased rubber plantations in Sumatra. Sometimes the mere threat of backward integration was enough to assure materials from suppliers on reasonable schedules and at reasonable prices. General Motors, for example, used this threat successfully in obtaining its tires, as did Du Pont in getting its supplies of sulphuric and nitric acid. Companies often found the production of raw or semi-finished materials quite profitable, as did Du Pont in its Chilean nitrate production, Jersey Standard and Socony in the production of crude oil, and General Motors in its parts and accessory business. If this were so, their managers would allocate further resources to these areas even before they would expand their more traditional manufacturing and distributing activities.

Very few corporations, however, advocated complete and total integration — that is, the ownership and control of all activities involved in the production and distribution of their products. The General Motors executives emphatically opposed Henry Ford's example of building one massive manufacturing plant to produce a single model and of owning the sources of nearly all the supplies that went into its production. They believed that the forecasting and other procedures they were developing were as efficient in assuring a steady volume of production, as well as being far more flexible in meeting changing market demands, than were Ford's technological achievements in physical co-ordination. In fact, the effective control of their integrated operation by statistical means helped make General Motors one of the most profitable in the nation after 1925, while Ford's attempt at physical rather than statistical co-ordination was one basic reason for his astonishingly poor profit performance in the same years.

When the nation's economy began to level off in the twenties and when it stumbled badly in the thirties, firms in the more technologically advanced industries began to shift from a strategy of integration to one of diversification; that is, they began to allocate resources for the development of new products for new kinds of markets. Those that took up the new strategy did so precisely because the leveling and then the decline in demand left their managers faced with the threat of a decreasing rate of return from their resources. Companies whose resources were most easily transferable to the production and distribution of new products were the first to diversify. A few firms with a large investment in research and development started on the new strategy in the twenties. Those with resources concentrated in distribution facilities began hesitantly to follow suit in the thirties, while those whose primary investment was in production facilities made few attempts to diversify, even after World War II.

In 1938 five industries employed three fourths of all persons working in organized American industrial research. They were the chemical, electrical, rubber, petroleum, and power machinery industries. (The last group included automobile and agricultural machinery companies.) In the twenties chemical and electrical companies began to develop new end products for markets quite different from those of their traditional lines. The Du Pont Company pioneered by turning its skills and organization developed in nitrocellulose technology into the mass production and distribution of paints, artificial leather, films, synthetic fibers, dyestuffs, and heavy chemicals. Later in the twenties Hercules developed several lines of products on a naval stores base. Dow soon began to diversify on the basis of salt chemistry, while Monsanto did the same on sugar. Union Carbide in its early diversification relied on calcium carbide, and Tennessee Eastman on cellulose acetate.

The story of the electrical industry is comparable. Until the twenties General Electric and Westinghouse had concentrated almost wholly on the development, manufacturing, and marketing of electric power and light. Then after World War I they began to develop household appliances such as stoves, washing machines, heaters, vacuum cleaners, and refrigerators. The explicit reason given for the move was that appliances would use excess capacity in the small motor and other divisions and at the same time increase the demand for power-generating equipment. In addition, the research laboratories turned out a number of new products such as radio tubes, X-rays, and alloys. Where, on the basis of rate of return on investment, the new product could make use of some existing facilities and personnel, the company took on its manufacture and distribution. If it could not, then it licensed the product to be manufactured elsewhere.

The continuing rapid growth of automobile production up to 1925 delayed diversification in the petroleum and rubber industries. However, the two large rubber firms, United States Rubber and Goodrich, which were formed before the development of the tire did begin to diversify after World War I. So too did the large power machinery makers who were not involved in producing passenger cars, such as International Harvester and Allis-Chalmers. With the beginning of the depression, however, the automobile and allied industries began to diversify. The tire companies started to develop products based on rubber chemistry. General Motors moved into airplanes, aircraft engines, and diesels. In the latter case, it revolutionized the American locomotive industry. The petroleum companies moved more slowly than the other two industries, but by the end of the thirties two or three companies were producing petrochemicals. In the thirties, too, General Foods, General Mills, and Borden's (milk) began to use their marketing organizations to sell a number of new products. So did International Paper, American Can, and Pittsburgh Plate Glass. These last three had a heavier investment in distribution than in production facilities.

The war had a far greater impact than the depression on bringing on diversification, and for very different reasons. The war permitted companies in a wide range of industries to amass resources used for the manufacture of products quite different from their traditional lines. For example, the huge synthetic rubber program fully committed rubber and petroleum corporations to the production of chemicals. After the war, nearly all the major oil and rubber companies began producing petrochemicals, rubber chemicals, plastics, and many sorts of synthetics; and the automobile companies began turning out tractors, farm equipment, marine engines, and other nonautomotive products. At the same time the war-stimulated electronics revolution had opened new fields for General Electric, Westinghouse, and the smaller electrical manufacturers in television, computers, and transistors.

Corporation managers soon discovered that the new strategy required a new administrative structure. The first to devise it were those rational executives in charge of the Du Pont Company, one of the very first companies to diversify. The basic reason for the reorganization was that the move from operating in one industry to operating in many industries sharply increased both the short-range and long-term decisions made at the central office, and particularly those concerned with the co-ordination of flows and the allocation of resources. The Du Pont executives therefore created a new structure consisting of autonomous, integrated product divisions and a general office consisting of general and staff executives concerned with the operations of the corporation as a whole. The primary task of the division managers was to assure effective co-ordination of flow. The integrated divisions were usually defined by the market they served, since the demands of the different markets so profoundly affected the decisions involved in the co-ordination of flow. The executives in the general office, relieved of day-to-day operating decisions, were to concentrate on appraising the performance of the different divisions and determining the present and future allocation of the company's resources.

The new decentralized structure had become fairly well known and understood by the end of the thirties. Chemical firms, including Hercules, Monsanto, and to some extent Union Carbide, had adopted it before World War II. Westinghouse began to move toward a decentralized structure in 1934 and General Electric in 1939. In both giant electric companies the move came initially because of the difficulty of controlling the flow of consumer durables. United States Rubber and Goodrich both applied the Du Pont principles in the late twenties, while General Motors had a similar organization after the Du Pont-supervised reorganization of 1921. International Harvester, explicitly following the General Motors model, made the changes during the war, while Ford and Chrysler did the same immediately afterwards.

In the postwar years the strategy of diversification spread quickly to other less technologically oriented industries. Swift, National Dairy, Procter and Gamble, and other corporations in feed and consumer perishables followed the earlier example of General Foods and General Mills. In time even the steel and aluminum companies started to develop new products. In nearly every case these firms also turned to the decentralized structure. By the nineteen fifties diversification and decentralization had become the compelling fashion in American industry.

In the years since World War II American corporations have widely accepted the organizational innovations and the operational procedures worked out before 1940 by the pioneers in modern corporate management. These same postwar years have been ones of impressive growth for the national economy and of rapid expansion for the industrial corporations. They have been years of economic stability as well as growth for the economy and for the corporations. The direct relationship between the spread of the new administrative forms and procedures and economic and corporate growth and stability would be difficult to define with any precision. Yet let me suggest some possible connections.

By complementing the policies and procedures developed in the federal government by the Council of Economic Advisers, by the Treasury, and by the Federal Reserve Board, the new controls over inventory and working capital may have helped to even out the business cycle and to make business fluctuations less severe and less dangerous than they have been in any other period of American history.

Certainly the institutionalizing of industrial innovation has been vitally significant to the continued growth of the economy and the corporation. And nothing has contributed more to the systematizing of such innovation than the increased use of the research laboratory in American industry and the adoption of the decentralized administrative structure. The research department of a corporation develops and tests the commercial value of a new product or process. The executives in the general office, free from routine activities, decide, on the basis of detailed information provided by their staff and by the divisions, whether to produce and market the product or process. If its production and distribution makes full use of the firm's existing resources, it will be manufactured and sold through an existing division. If it uses similar production facilities but requires quite different distributive ones, or vice versa — that is, if it can use existing distributing facilities but requires new production ones — then a new division can be formed. If its output employs very few of the company's existing resources, then the senior executives can decide to lease its manufacture and sale to another company. Moreover, the institutionalizing of product or process innovation has been concentrated more in producers' goods than in consumers' goods industries. The products of the chemical and electronics industries are purchased by customers not because of their style, comforts, or status-bringing qualities but because they cut the costs and improve the quality of their purchasers' own processes or products.

If competition encourages growth, the strategy of diversification and the decentralized structure have had an additional impact on postwar economic performance, for they have increased competition between large corporations. Compare the competitive situation in the old copper and the new plastics industries. In the copper industry, production and distribution are still dominated as they were forty years ago by the "big four." In the plastics business, most of the large firms in the technologically advanced industries are competing with one another. Not only do nearly all the large chemical electrical, rubber, and petroleum companies have plastics divisions but General Foods, General Mills, Borden, and Swift do as well. Within the past few months even United States Steel has moved into the competition. Where four giants produce by far the largest share of the nation's copper, ten times that many industrial giants are in the plastics business.

Although the direct connection between organizational and administrative innovation and economic growth cannot be precisely defined, it seems safe to say that the constant efforts which I have been describing to cut the costs of production and distribution, to assure a smooth flow of goods from the suppliers of raw materials to the final customer, to allocate economic resources rationally, and to develop and apply new processes and products systematically have been and continue to be essential to the health and growth of the American economy. By innovating in these areas, the corporation has surely played a major role in making the American economy the most productive in the world.

On the other hand, the overwhelming dominance of the large corporation in the modern American economy has raised problems and issues, some of which are still totally unresolved. The extreme concentration of power in a society committed to democratic values is one such issue. Another is the difficulty, if not the impossibility, of the corporation's allocating resources to meet socially desirable needs which bring only a low rate of return on investment. However, the first step in meeting these problems is the understanding of how the corporation developed the basic functions it has long enjoyed in the management of the American economy. Such an understanding is essential if the nation is to achieve the full promise of a consumer-oriented mass production, mass distribution economy operating within an open society.

5

THE ISSUE OF WOMEN'S EQUALITY

Many commentators have noted that the place of women in America probably most closely resembles that of Negroes. Both constitute groups with highly visible and irremovable distinguishing attributes that have served as the basis for myths concerning their distinctive propensities and capabilities. Discriminatory laws and customs may be seen as attempts to accommodate the putative qualities of each group, but at the same time, for women, as for Negroes, the discriminatory treatment accorded by law and custom has tended to evoke and to perpetuate behavioral traits that in turn serve to confirm the underlying myths. To break the circle, the myths themselves must undergo challenge, but since the empirical evidence can be used as much to support the myths as to refute them, the challenge must be ideological — that is, it must envisage a social order built upon contrasting premises regarding human differentiation. Thus, it is scarcely a coincidence that feminism has experienced renewed vitality at a time when nearly all the conventional myths of social order have been undergoing test throughout the world.

The analogy between women and Negroes cannot be pressed very far, since clearly the inequalities in treatment experienced by women because of the difference of their sex offer many positive, privileged, and even luxurious advantages that are scarcely shared by black people on account of the difference of their color. Yet it has been argued that even these advantages have been "enslaving," precisely as for most American black people the "reward" of being allowed to live with minimal daily humiliations has served to enforce subservient roles and behavior patterns for most of the last few centuries. In a way, the price of "happiness" for members of each group has been their acceptance of their subordination, and even of the belief that their difference impels deference. Although it cannot be assumed that Negroes have to any substantial degree accepted their subordination, except as the "better part of valor" in the face of an always potentially murderous repression, all the evidence suggests that most women have.

Part of the evidence is that women have not exploited as thoroughly as might have been expected the opportunities opened to them half a century ago by the first emancipation movement. Not all the laws have been fully implemented, to be sure, and prejudice continues to place discriminatory obstacles in the way, but most women have not taken advantage of their opportunities. Thus, although the proportion of women in the work force has increased (37 percent in

1967 as opposed to 25 percent in 1940), women's engagement in the prestigious professions, business leadership, and even politics has shown almost no significant increase since 1900; moreover, there are proportionately fewer women seeking advanced degrees today than there were thirty years ago.

Since feminism has been an extraordinarily ambiguous movement, it is difficult to attribute to any single factor the reasons for the low degree of activity of women in the political and economic scene. Some have suggested that female militants of the early twentieth century actually never sought more than the symbolic political equality that the Nineteenth Amendment gave them (so that they would have recognition as human beings at least on a par with lower-class and immigrant males for whom so many woman suffragists expressed their contempt). Even sexual equality — meaning the right to enjoy sex with or without the sanction of marriage — came eventually for those who wanted it, at least once Freud had bared the universality of the human sexual urge. (Curiously, one of the strikingly new features of the current feminist militancy is that the slogan "sexual *equality*" has been replaced by "sexual *freedom*," meaning the right *not* to enjoy sex.) Probably more important, though (as Carl Degler, Professor of History at Stanford University, observes in the article reprinted below), is that the movement in America for women's equality has lacked any ideological content. Implicitly this means that most of the traditional assumptions or myths about the distinctive qualities of women have remained intact. Consequently, although women have sought "equality," the goal has been modified by the assumption that there are irreducible qualities attached to womanhood that place certain irremediable handicaps upon women, at least with regard to their participation in economic and intellectual endeavors. Among these, a woman's role as a mother and as the focus of the family has probably played a more decisive part in prescribing secondary place for women in politics and in the economy than the obvious physical differences have.

For this reason, the new feminism has often come to focus specifically on the conventional family structure as the key to the oppression of women. For, in its conventional form at least, the family ties a woman's energy and time to child care and household duties. This fact alone denies her the equal opportunity to compete for place and status with males in the political and economic arenas. In addition, it invites job discrimination on account of the tentative commitment a woman appears to have to a career during the child-rearing period. Perhaps most "insidious" (from the modern feminist viewpoint at least) is the high status that the family enjoys in the society at large, a fact that, on the one hand, conditions the female child to plan her life with the expectation of being a wife and mother herself, and, on the other, invites job discrimination on the grounds that an unmarried but "eligible" young woman may be expected to marry and therefore would give secondary consideration to her job.

To break out of this binding circle, feminists of the post-1960's have pressed for changes in child-rearing and marital relationships. State-supported, full-time, child-care and even child-rearing facilities may join The Pill and easier divorce and abortion laws in liberating women from some specific burdens of their womanhood. Such changes have already touched on serious ideological and moral issues concerning the relationship of the individual to the state as well as one's relationships and obligations to other human beings. Beyond this, so far the scene is highly confused, with a lot of personal and political axe-grinding mixing in with more straightforward feminist demands. For example, the conventional family has come under attack not merely because it tends to condition females to suffer all too gladly the subordination to males that feminists deplore, but also, for many, because it is another institution that presumably may have to be toppled in the cause of some sort of revolution. Of course, from the viewpoint of some militants, devotion to feminism necessarily makes one a "revolutionary" in all respects. From an observer's viewpoint, however, it is not always clear when a feminist proposal is made for the purpose of the further liberation of women as human beings, and when for the purpose of merely recruiting women into a more general revolutionary movement in which "emancipation" may be subordinate to some other social or political objective. But whatever the case, it is becoming clear that a new attitude between the sexes is evolving that will likely afford women a more dignified place than they have generally enjoyed in the human family to date.

For more extended survey treatment of feminism in America than offered in the article reprinted below, see: W. L. O'Neill, *Everyone Was Brave: The Rise and Fall of Feminism in America* (1969); or Andrew Sinclair, *The Emancipation of the American Woman** (1965). Aileen S. Kraditor, *The Ideas of the Woman Suffrage Movement, 1890–1920* (1965); J. R. McGovern, "The American Woman's Pre-World War I Freedom in Manners and Morals," *Journal of American History*, 55 (Sept. 1968); and C. Degler's introduction to Charlotte Perkins Gilman, *Women and Economics** (reissued by Torchbooks, 1966), are useful works on the earlier feminist movement. The *Daedalus* issue from which the article reprinted below is taken is devoted entirely to "The Woman in America," with perceptive articles by Erik Erikson, David Riesman, and Alice Rossi, among others. Betty Friedan's *The Feminine Mystique** (1963), and Kate Millett's *Sexual Politics* (1970), are the key works of two leading feminist militants, but both owe much to Simone de Beauvoir's much earlier *The Second Sex** (1949). Irving Howe's "The Middle-Class Mind of Kate Millett," *Harper's*, December 1970, is an exceptionally incisive critique that offers more than just a review of Dr. Millett's book. See also, Midge Decter, "The Liberated Woman," *Commentary*, October 1970.

Revolution Without Ideology: The Changing Place of Women in America

CARL N. DEGLER

If feminism is defined as the belief that women are human beings and entitled to the same opportunities for self-expression as men, then America has harbored a feminist bias from the beginning. In both the eighteenth and nineteenth centuries foreign travelers remarked on the freedom for women in America. "A paradise for women," one eighteenth-century German called America, and toward the close of the nineteenth century Lord Bryce wrote that in the United States "it is easier for women to find a career, to obtain work of an intellectual as of a commercial kind, than in any part of Europe."

Certainly the long history of a frontier in America helps to account for this feminist bias. In a society being carved out of a wilderness, women were active and important contributors to the process of settlement and civilization. Moreover, because women have been scarce in America they have been highly valued. During almost the whole of the colonial period men outnumbered women, and even in the nineteenth century women remained scarce in the West. As late as 1865, for example, there were three men for each woman in California; in Colorado the ratio was as high as 20 to 1. Such disparities in the sex ratio undoubtedly account for the West's favorable attitude toward women as in an Oregon law of 1850 that granted land to single women and, even more significant for the time, to married women; or in the willingness of western territories like Wyoming (1869) and Utah (1870) to grant the suffrage to women long before other regions where the sex ratio was more nearly equal.

Another measure of women's high esteem in American society was the rapidity with which the doors of higher education opened to women. Even without counting forerunners like Oberlin College, which admitted women in 1837, the bars against women came down faster and earlier in America than anywhere. The breakthrough came during the Civil War era, when women's colleges like Elmira, Vassar and Smith were founded, and universities like Michigan and Cornell became coeducational. The process was later and slower in Europe. Girton College, Cambridge, for example, which opened in 1869, was the sole English institution of higher education available to women until London University accorded women full privileges in

Reprinted by permission from *Daedalus*, Journal of the American Academy of Arts and Sciences, Vol. 93, No. 2.

1879. Heidelberg, which was the first German university to accept women, did not do so until 1900. More striking was the fact that at its opening Girton provided six places for young women; Vassar alone, when it opened in 1865, counted some 350 students in residence. Another indication of the American feminist bias was that at the end of the century girls outnumbered boys among high school graduates.

But if the frontier experience of America helped to create a vague feminist bias that accorded women more privileges than in settled Europe, the really potent force changing women's place had little to do with the frontier or the newness of the country. It was the industrial revolution that provided the impetus to women's aspirations for equality of opportunity; it was the industrial revolution that carried through the first stage in the changing position of women — the removal of legal and customary barriers to women's full participation in the activities of the world.

Today it is axiomatic that men work outside the home. But before the industrial revolution of the nineteenth century, the great majority of men and women were co-workers on the land and in the home. Women worked in the fields when the chores of the home and child-rearing permitted, so that there was not only close association between work and home for both sexes, but even a certain amount of overlap in the sexual division of labor. The coming of machine production changed all that. For a time, it is true, many unmarried women and children — the surplus labor of the day — were the mainstay of the new factory system, but that was only temporary. By the middle of the nineteenth century the bulk of industrial labor was male. The coming of the factory and the city thus wholly changed the nature of men's work. For the first time in history, work for most men was something done outside the family, psychologically as well as physically separated from the home.

The same industrial process that separated work and home also provided the opportunities for women to follow men out of the home. For that reason the feminist movement, both socially and intellectually, was a direct consequence of the industrial changes of the nineteenth century. Furthermore, just as the new industrial system was reshaping the rural men who came under its influence, so it reshaped the nature of women.

The process began with the home, which, in the early years of industrialization, was still the site of most women's work. Because of high land values, the city home was smaller than the farm house, and with less work for children, the size of the urban family was smaller than the rural. Moreover, in the city work in the home changed. Machines in factories now performed many of the tasks that had long been women's. In truth, the feminist movement began not when women felt a desire for men's jobs, but when men in factories began to take away women's traditional work. Factory-produced clothing, commercial laundries, prepared foods (e.g. prepared cereals, canned vegetables, condensed milk, bakery bread) were already available in the years after the Civil War. Toward the end of the century an advanced feminist like Charlotte Perkins Gilman, impressed by the accelerating exodus of women's chores from the middle-class home, predicted that the whole kitchen would soon be gone. She was wrong there, but even today the flight continues with precooked and frozen foods, TV dinners, cake mixes, special packaging for easy disposal, diaper services and the like.

Middle-class women were the main beneficiaries of the lightening of the chores of the home; few working-class or immigrant women could as yet take advantage of the new services and products. These middle-class women became the bone and sinew of the feminist movement, which was almost entirely an urban affair. They joined the women's clubs, organized the temperance crusades and marched in the suffrage parades. With an increasing amount of time available to them in the city, and imbued with the historic American value of work, they sought to do good. And there was much to be done in the raw, sometimes savage, urban environment of the late nineteenth century. For example, public playgrounds in the United States began in Boston only in the 1880's, when two public-spirited middle-class women caused a cartload of sand to be piled on an empty lot and set the neighborhood children loose upon it. Many a city and small town at the turn of the century owed its public library or its park to the dedicated work of women's clubs. The venerable giant redwood trees of northern California survive today because clubwomen of San Francisco and nearby towns successfully campaigned in 1900 to save them from being cut down for lumber. The saloon and prostitution were two other prevalent urban blights that prompted study and action by women's organizations.

More important than women's opposition to social evils was the widening of women's knowledge and concerns that inevitably accompanied it. What began as a simple effort to rid the community of a threat to its purity often turned into a discovery of the economic exploitation that drove young working girls into brothels and harried working men into saloons. Frances Willard for example, while head of the Women's Christian Temperance Union, broadened the WCTU's reform interests far beyond the liquor question, causing it to advocate protective legislation for working women, kindergartens and training programs for young working girls. Jane Addams, at Hull-House in Chicago's slums, quickly learned what historians have only recently discovered, that it was the urban boss's undeniable services to the immigrants that were the true sources of his great political power and the real secret of his successful survival of municipal reform campaigns.

The most direct way in which industrialization altered the social function of women was by providing work for women outside the home. Production by machine, of course, widened enormously the uses to which women's labor could be put once physical strength was no longer a consideration. And toward the end of the century, as business enterprises grew and record-keeping, communications and public relations expanded, new opportunities for women opened up in business offices. The telephone operator, the typist, the clerical worker and the stenographer now took places beside the seam-stress, the cotton mill operator and the teacher.

As workers outside the home, women buried the Victorian stereotype of the lady under a mountain of reality. After all, it was difficult to argue that women as a sex were weak, timid, incompetent, fragile vessels of spirituality when thousands of them could be seen trudging to work in the early hours of the day in any city of the nation. Nor could a girl who worked in a fac-tory or office help but become more worldly. A young woman new to a shop might have been embarrassed to ask a male foreman for the ladies' room, as some working girls' autobiographies report, but such maidenly reticence could hardly survive very long. Even gentle, naïve farm girls soon found out how to handle the inevitable, improper advances of foremen. They also learned the discipline of the clock, the managing of their own money, the excitement of life outside the home, the exhilaration of financial indepen-dence along with the drudgery of machine labor. Having learned something of the ways of the world, women could not be treated then, nor later in mar-riage, as the hopeless dependents Victorian ideals prescribed.

In time work transformed the outer woman, too. First to go were the hobbling, trailing skirts, which in a factory were a hazard and a nuisance. Even before the Civil War, Amelia Bloomer and other feminists had pointed out that women, if they were to work in the world as human beings, needed looser and lighter garments than those then in fashion. Until work-ing women were numbered in the millions, no change took place. After 1890 women's skirts gradually crept up from the floor, and the neat and simple shirtwaist became the uniform of the working girl. A costume very like the original bloomer was widely worn by women factory workers during the First World War. Later the overall and the coverall continued the adaptation of women's clothes to the machine.

The most dramatic alteration in the image of woman came after the First World War, when there was a new upsurge in women's employment. The twenties witnessed the emergence of the white-collar class, and women were a large part of it. Over twice as many women entered the labor force that decade as in the previous one; the number of typists alone in 1930 was three-quarters of a million, a tenfold increase since 1900. And woman's ap-pearance reflected the requirements of work. Except for some of the extreme flapper fashions, which were transient, the contemporary woman still dresses much as the woman of the 1920's did. In the 1920's women threw out the corset and the numerous petticoats in favor of light undergarments, a single slip, silk or rayon stockings, short skirts and bobbed hair. So rapid and wide-spread was the change that an investigation in the 1920's revealed that even most working-class girls no longer wore corsets, and the new interest in bobbed hair resulted between 1920 and 1930 in an increase of 400 per cent in the number of women hair dressers.

The physical freedom of dress that women acquired during the 1920's was but the superficial mark of a new social equality. The social forces behind this new equality are several. Some of these forces, like the growing number of college-trained women and the increasing number of women in the working force, go back far into the past; others, like the impact of the war and the arduous campaign for women's suffrage, were more recent. But whatever the causes, the consequences were obvious. Indeed, what is generally spoken of as the revolution in morals of the 1920's is more accurately a revolution in the position of women. Within a few short years a spectrum of taboos was shed. For the first time women began to smoke and drink in public; cigarette manufacturers discovered and exploited in advertising a virtually untouched market. As recently as 1918 it was considered daring for a New York hotel to permit women to sit at a bar. In the twenties, despite prohibition, both sexes drank in public.

Perhaps most significant, as well as symbolic, of the new stage in the position of women was their new sexual freedom. The twenties have long been associated with the discovery of Freud and a fresh, publicly acknowledged interest in sex. But insofar as these attitudes were new they represented changes in women, particularly those of the middle and upper classes. Premarital and extramarital sexuality by men had never been severely criticized, and discussion of sexual matters was commonplace where men gathered. Now, though, middle-class women also enjoyed that freedom. For the first time, it has been said, middle-class men carried on their extramarital affairs with women of their own social class instead of with cooks, maids, and prostitutes.

An easier sexuality outside of marriage was only the most sensational side of the revolution in morals; more important, if only because more broadly based, was a new, informal, equal relationship between the sexes, culminating in a new conception of marriage. The day was long since past when Jennie June Croly could be barred, as she was in 1868, from a dinner in honor of Charles Dickens at a men's club even though her husband was a member and she was a professional writer. (Indeed, so thoroughly has such separation of the sexes been abandoned that the new Princeton Club in New York City has closed all but one of its public rooms to any man who is not accompanied by a woman!) And at least in the gatherings of the educated middle class, talk between the sexes was often free, frank and wide-ranging. The same mutual acceptance of the sexes was visible in the prevalent talk about the "new marriage," in which the woman was a partner and a companion, not simply a mother, a social convenience and a housekeeper.

The reality of the new conception of marriage was reflected in the sharp increase in the divorce rate. Because marriage, legally as well as socially, in the nineteenth century was more confining for women than for men, the early feminists had often advocated more liberal divorce laws. And even though divorce in the nineteenth century was more common in the United States than in any European country, the divorce rate in the 1920's shot up 50 per cent over what it had been only ten years before. One sign that women in the 1920's were seeking freedom from marriage if they could not secure equality in marriage was that two thirds of the divorces in that decade were instituted by women.

By the close of the twenties the ordinary woman in America was closer to a man in the social behavior expected of her, in the economic opportunities open to her and in the intellectual freedom enjoyed by her than at any time in history. To be sure there still was a double standard, but now its existence was neither taken for granted nor confidently asserted by men.

In truth, the years since the twenties have witnessed few alterations in the position of women that were not first evident in that crucial decade. The changes have penetrated more deeply and spread more widely through the social structure, but their central tendency was then already spelled out. Even the upsurge in women's employment, which was so striking in the twenties, continued in subsequent years. Each decade thereafter has counted a larger number of working women than the previous one. During the depression decade of the 1930's, even, half a million more women entered the labor force than in the prosperous twenties. By 1960 some 38 per cent of all women of working age — almost two out of five women — were employed outside the home.

The movement of women out of the home into remunerative work, however, has been neither steady nor unopposed. Undoubtedly one of the underlying conditions is an expanding economy's need for labor. But something more than that is needed to break society's traditional habits of mind about the proper work for women. Certainly here the feminist demands for equality for women played a part. But a social factor of equal importance was war. By their very disruption of the steady pulse of everyday living, wars break the cake of custom, shake up society and compel people to look afresh at old habits and attitudes. It is not accidental, for instance, that women's suffrage in England, Russia and Germany, as well as the United States, was achieved immediately after the First World War and in France and Italy after the Second.

At the very least, by making large and new demands upon the established work force, war draws hitherto unused labor into the economic process. During the Civil War, for example, young women assumed new roles in the economy as workers in metal and munitions factories, as clerks in the expanded bureaucracy in Washington and as nurses in war hospitals. Moreover, when the war was over women had permanently replaced men as the dominant sex in the teaching profession. Furthermore, since many women found a new usefulness in the Sanitary Fairs and other volunteer work, the end of hostilities left many women unwilling to slip back into the seclusion of the Victorian home. It is not simply coincidental that the women's club movement began very soon after the war.

When the First World War came to the United States, feminist leaders, perhaps recalling the gains of the Civil War, anticipated new and broad advances for their sex. And the demand for labor, especially after the United States entered the war, did open many jobs to women, just as it was doing in contemporary Great Britain and Germany. All over the United States during the war customary and legal restrictions on the employment of women fell away. Women could be seen doing everything from laying railroad ties to working in airplane factories. The war also brought to a successful climax the struggle for the suffrage. Pointedly women had argued that a war for democracy abroad should at least remedy the deficiencies of democracy at home.

If politically the war was a boon to women, economically it failed to live up to feminist anticipations. The First World War, unlike the Civil War, did not result in a large permanent increase in the number of working women. Indeed, by 1920 there were only 800,000 more women working than in 1910. But as a result of war-time demands, women did get permanent places in new job categories, like elevator operators and theater ushers. (But women street car conductors disappeared soon after the armistice.) Certain traditional professions for women, like music teaching, lost members between 1910 and 1920, while professions that required more training and provided steadier income, like library and social work and college teaching, doubled or tripled their numbers in the same period.

The Second World War, with its even more massive demands for labor and skills, brought almost four million new women workers into the nation's factories and offices. Once again jobs usually not filled by women were opened to them. For example, the number of women bank officers rose 40 per cent during the four years of the war and the number of women employees in finance has continued to rise ever since. Furthermore, unlike the situation after the First World War, the female work force after 1945 not only stayed up but then went higher.

Measured in the number of women working, the changes in the economic position of women add up to a feminist success. Twenty-four million working women cannot be ignored. But weighed in the scales of quality instead of quantity, the change in women's economic status is not so striking. It is true that women now work in virtually every job listed by the Bureau of the Census. Moreover, the popular press repeatedly tells of the inroads women are making into what used to be thought of as men's jobs. Three years ago, for example, a woman won a prize as the mutual fund salesman of the year. Women are widely represented in advertising and in real estate, and even women taxicab drivers are no longer rare. Yet the fact remains that the occupations in which the vast majority of women actually engage are remarkably similar to those historically held by women. In 1950 almost three quarters of all employed women fell into twenty occupational categories, of which the largest was stenographers, typists and secretaries — a category that first became prominent as a woman's occupation over a half century ago.

Other occupations which have traditionally been women's, like domestic service, teaching, clerical work, nursing and telephone service, are also conspicuous among the twenty categories. Further than that, the great majority of women are employed in occupations in which they predominate. This sexual division of labor is clearly evident in the professions, even though women are only a small proportion of total professional workers. Two thirds of all professional women are either nurses or teachers; and even in teaching there is a division between the sexes. Most women teach in the primary grades; most men teach in high school. Women are notoriously underrepresented in the top professions like law, medicine, engineering and scientific research. No more than 7 per cent of all professional women in 1950 were in the four of these categories together. Only 6 per cent of medical doctors and 4 per cent of lawyers and judges were women. In contrast, almost three quarters of medical doctors are women in the Soviet Union; in England the figure is 16 per cent. In both France and Sweden women make up a high proportion of pharmacists and dentists; neither of those professions attracts many women in the United States.

One consequence as well as manifestation of the sexual division of labor in the United States has been the differences in pay for men and women. That difference has been a historical complaint of feminist leaders. In 1900 one study found women's wages to be, on the average, only 53 per cent of men's. The reason was, of course, that women were concentrated in the poorer paying jobs and industries of the economy. The disparity in pay between the sexes has been somewhat reduced today, but not very much. In 1955 among full-time women workers of all types the median wage was about two thirds of that for men. In short, women are still supplying the low-paid in the economy just as they were in the last century. (In substance, women workers and Negroes of both sexes perform a similar function in the economy.) The willingness of women to supply cheap labor may well account for their getting the large number of jobs they do; men often will not work for the wages that women will accept.

Today, there does not seem to be very much disparity between men's and women's wages for the same work, though the sexual division of labor is so nearly complete that it is difficult to find comparable jobs of the two sexes to make a definitive study.

There has been no improvement in women's position in higher education; indeed, it can be argued that women have failed to maintain the place reached much earlier. As we have seen, the United States led the world in opening higher education to women. This country also led in broadening the social base of education for women. No other country educated such a large proportion of women in its universities and colleges as did the United States. At the close of the nineteenth century, one third of American college students were women; by 1937 women made up almost 40 per cent of the students in American institutions of higher learning. In Germany, just before Hitler took power, no more than one out of ten university students was a woman; in Swedish universities in 1937 only 17 per cent of the students were women; in British universities the ratio was 22 per cent.

But since the Second World War the gap between American and European proportions of women in higher education has narrowed considerably. In 1952–1953 women constituted only 35 per cent of the American college population, while France counted women as 36 per cent of its university students and Sweden 26 per cent. The *number* of women in American colleges, of course, is considerably greater than it was in the 1920's and 1930's, but in proportion to men, women have lost ground in America while gaining it in Europe.

A further sign of the regression in the educational position of women in the United States is that in the early 1950's women earned about 10 per cent of the doctoral degrees in this country as compared with almost 15 per cent in the 1920's.

How is one to explain this uneven, almost contradictory record of women in America? How does it happen that a country with a kind of built-in feminism from the frontier falls behind more traditional countries in its training of college women; that a country with one of the highest proportions of working women in the world ends up with such a small proportion of its women in medicine, in law and in the sciences? Perhaps the correct answer is that the question should not be asked — at least not by Americans. For like so much else in American society, such contradictions are a manifestation of the national avoidance of any ideological principle, whether it be in feminist reform or in anything else. To be sure there has been no lack of feminist argument or rationale for women's work outside the home, for women's education and for other activities by women. But American women, like American society in general, have been more concerned with individual practice than with a consistent feminist ideology. If women have entered the labor force or taken jobs during a war they have done so for reasons related to the immediate individual or social circumstances and not for reasons of feminist ideology. The women who have been concerned about showing that women's capabilities can match men's have been the exception. As the limited, and low-paying, kinds of jobs women occupy demonstrate, there is not now and never has been any strong feminist push behind the massive and continuing movement of women into jobs. Most American women have been interested in jobs, not careers. To say, as many feminists have, that men have opposed and resisted the opening of opportunities to women is to utter only a half truth. The whole truth is that American society in general, which includes women, shuns like a disease any feminist ideology.

Another way of showing that the historical changes in the status of women in America bear little relation to a feminist ideology is to examine one of those rare instances when women did effect a social improvement through an appeal to ideology, for instance, the struggle for the suffrage. By the early twentieth century the feminist demand for the vote overrode every other feminist goal. Once women achieved the vote, it was argued, the evils of society would be routed, for women, because of their peculiar attributes, would bring a fresh, needed and wholesome element into political life. In form, and in the minds of many women leaders, the arguments for the suffrage came close to being a full-blown ideology of feminism.

In point of fact, of course, the Nineteenth Amendment ushered in no millennium. But that fact is of less importance than the reason why it did not. When American women obtained the vote they simply did not use it ideologically; they voted not as women but as individuals. Evidence of this was the failure of many women to vote at all. At the end of the first decade of national suffrage women still did not exercise the franchise to the extent that men did. Nor did many women run for or hold political offices. The first woman to serve in Congress was elected in 1916; in 1920, the first year of national women's suffrage, four women were elected to Congress, but until 1940 no more than nine women served at one time in the House of Representatives and the Senate together. That we are here observing an American and not simply a sexual phenomenon is shown by a comparison with European countries. In nonfeminist Germany, where the ballot came to women at about the same time as in the United States, the first Reichstag after suffrage counted forty-one women as members. In 1951 seventeen women sat in the British House of Commons as compared with ten in the United States House of Representatives. Twice the number of women have served as cabinet ministers in Britain between 1928 and 1951 as have served in the United States down to the present.

Another instance in which social change was effected by feminist ideology was prohibition. The achievement of national prohibition ran second only to the suffrage movement as a prime goal of the organized women's movement; the Eighteenth Amendment was as much a product of feminist ideology as the Nineteenth. Yet like the suffrage movement, prohibition, despite its feminist backing, failed to receive the support of women. It was *after* prohibition was enacted, after all, that women drank in public.

In the cases of both suffrage and prohibition, women acted as individuals, not as members of a sex. And so they have continued to act. It is not without relevance that the women's political organization that is most respected — the League of Women Voters — is not only nonpartisan but studiously avoids questions pertaining only to women. To do otherwise would be feminist and therefore ideological.

One further conclusion might be drawn from this examination of the non-ideological character of American women. That the changes that have come to the position of women have been devoid of ideological intent may well explain why there has been so little opposition to them. The most successful of American reforms have always been those of an impromptu and practical nature. The great revolution of the New Deal is a classic example. The American people, like F. D. R. himself, simply tried one thing after another, looking for something — anything — that would get the nation out of the depression. If lasting reforms took place too, so much the better. On the other hand, reforms that have been justified by an elaborate rationale or ideology, like abolition, have aroused strong and long-drawn-out opposition. By the same token, when women became ideological in support of suffrage and prohibition, they faced their greatest opposition and scored their most disappointing triumphs.

The achievement of the suffrage in 1920 is a convenient date for marking the end of the first phase in the changing position of women, for by then women were accorded virtually the same rights as men even if they did not always exercise them. The second phase began at about the same time. It was the participation of married women in the work force. During the nineteenth century few married women worked; when they did it was because they were childless or because their husbands were inadequate providers. Even among the poor, married women normally did not work. A survey of the slum districts in five large cities in 1893 revealed that no more than 5 per cent of the wives were employed. Only Negro wives in the South and immigrant wives in big northern cities provided any significant exceptions to this generalization.

Before the First World War, the movement of wives into the working force was barely noticeable. During the 1920's there was an acceleration, but as late as 1940 less than 17 per cent of all married women were working. Among working women in 1940, 48 per cent were single and only 31 per cent were married. The Second World War dramatically reversed these proportions — another instance of the influence of war on the position of women. By 1950 the proportion of married women living with their husbands had risen to 48 per cent of all working women while that of single women had fallen to 32 per cent. In 1960 the Census reported that almost 32 per cent of all married women were employed outside the home and that they comprised 54 per cent of all working women. No industrial country of Europe, with the exception of the Soviet Union, counted such a high proportion. Today, married women are the greatest source of new labor in the American economy. Between 1949 and 1959, for example, over four million married women entered the labor force, some 60 per cent of *all* additions, male and female.

Such a massive movement of married women out of the home was a development few of the early feminists could have anticipated. That it has taken place is at once a sign and a yardstick of the enormous change in women's position in society and in the family. In the nineteenth century work outside the home was unthinkable for the married woman. Not only were there children to care for, but there were objections from husbands and society to consider. That is why the convinced feminist of the nineteenth century often spurned marriage. Indeed, it is often forgotten that the feminist movement was a form of revolt against marriage. For it was through marriage, with the legal and social dominance of the husband, that women were most obviously denied opportunities for self-expression. Even after the legal superiority of the husband had been largely eliminated from the law, middle-class social conventions could still scarcely accommodate the working wife. To the woman interested in realizing her human capabilities marriage in the nineteenth century was not an opportunity but a dead end. And it was indeed a minor scandal of the time that many of the "new women" did in fact reject marriage. The tendency was most pronounced, as was to be expected, among highly educated women, many of whom felt strongly their obligation to serve society through careers. Around 1900 more than one fourth of women who graduated from college never married; more than half of the women medical doctors in 1890 were single.

Like other changes in the position of women, the movement of married women into the work force — the reconciliation of marriage and work — must be related to the social changes of the last three decades. One of these social changes was the increase in contraceptive knowledge, for until married women could limit their families they could not become steady and reliable industrial workers. Information about contraceptive techniques which had been known for a generation or more to educated middle-class women did not seep down to the working class until the years of the Great Depression. In 1931, for instance, there were only 81 clinics disseminating birth control information in the United States; in 1943 there were 549, of which 166 were under public auspices. As the number of public clinics suggest, by the end of the 1930's birth control was both socially and religiously acceptable, at least among Protestants. And a method was also available then to Roman Catholics, since it was in the same decade that the rhythm method, the only one acceptable to the Roman Catholic Church, was first brought to popular attention with the approval of ecclesiastical authorities.

Another social force underlying the movement of wives and mothers in the work force was the growing affluence of an industrial society, especially after 1940. Higher health standards, enlarged incomes of husbands and a better standard of living in general permitted a marked alteration in the temporal cycle of women's lives. Women now lived longer, stayed in school later and married earlier. In 1890 half the girls left school at 14 or before — that is, when they finished grammar school; in 1957 the median age was 18 — after graduation from high school. The girl of 1890, typically, did not marry until she was 22; the age of her counterpart in 1957 was 20, leaving no more than two years for work between the end of school and marriage. Among other things this fact explains the fall in the proportion of single women in the work force in the United States as compared with other industrial societies. Few other countries have such an early median age of marriage for girls.

Early marriages for women produce another effect. With knowledge of contraceptive techniques providing a measure of control over child-bearing, women are now having their children early and rapidly. When this tendency is combined with a younger age of marriage, the result is an early end to child-bearing. In 1890 the median age of a mother when her last child was born was 32, in 1957 it was 26. A modern mother thus has her children off to school by the time she is in her middle thirties, leaving her as much as thirty-five years free for work outside the home. And the fact is that almost half of working women today are over forty years of age. Put another way, 34 per cent of married women between the ages of thirty-five and forty-four years are gainfully employed.

Unquestionably, as the practical character of the woman's movement would lead us to expect, an important force behind the influx of married women into the work force is economic need. But simple poverty is not the only force. Several studies, for example, have documented the conclusion that many women who work are married to men who earn salaries in the upper income brackets, suggesting that poverty is not the controlling factor in the wife's decision to work. A similar conclusion is to be drawn from the positive correlation between education and work for married women. The more education a wife has (and therefore the better salary her husband is likely to earn) the more likely she is to be working herself. Many of these women work undoubtedly in order to raise an adequate standard of living to a comfortable one. Many others work probably because they want to realize their potentialities in the world. But that women are so poorly represented in the professions and other careers suggests that most married women who work are realizing their full capabilities neither for themselves nor for society.

Over sixty years ago, in *Women and Economics*, the feminist Charlotte Perkins Gilman cogently traced the connection between work and the fulfillment of women as human beings. In subsequent writings she grappled with the problem of how this aim might be realized for married women. As a mother herself, raising a child under the trying circumstances of divorce, Gilman knew first hand that work outside the home and child-rearing constituted *two* full-time jobs. No man, she knew, was expected or required to shoulder such a double burden. Gilman's remedies of professional domestic service and kitchenless apartments never received much of a hearing, and considering the utopian if not bizarre character of her solutions, that is not surprising. Yet the problem she raised remained without any solution other than the eminently individualistic and inadequate one of permitting a woman to assume the double burden if she was so minded. Meanwhile, as the economy has grown, the problem has entered the lives of an ever increasing number of women. Unlike most of her feminist contemporaries, who were mainly concerned with the suffrage and the final elimination of legal and customary barriers to women's opportunities, Gilman recognized that the logic of feminism led unavoidably to the working mother as the typical woman. For if women were to be free to express themselves, then they should be able to marry as well as to work. Women should not have to make a choice any more than men. To make that possible, though, would require that some way be found to mitigate the double burden which biology and society had combined to place only on women.

As women moved into the second stage of their development — the reconciliation of work and marriage — the problem which Gilman saw so early was increasingly recognized as the central issue. Virginia Collier, for example, in a book *Marriage and Careers*, published in 1926, wrote that since so many married women were working, "The question therefore is no longer should women combine marriage with careers, but how do they manage it and how does it work." Interestingly enough, her study shows that what today Betty Friedan, in *The Feminine Mystique*, has called the "problem that has no name," was already apparent in the 1920's. One working wife explained her reasons for taking a job in these words, "I am burning up with energy and it is rather hard on the family to use it up in angry frustration." Another said, "I had done everything for Polly for six years. Suddenly she was in school all day and I had nothing to do. My engine was running just as hard as ever, but my car was standing still." A year after Collier's book appeared, President William A. Neilson of Smith College observed "that the outstanding problem confronting women is how to reconcile a normal life of marriage and motherhood with intellectual activity such as her college education has fitted her for." That the issue was taken seriously is attested by an action of the Board of Trustees of Barnard College in 1932. The board voted to grant six months' maternity leave with pay to members of the staff and faculty. In announcing the decision, Dean Virginia Gildersleeve clearly voiced its import. "Neither the men nor the women of our staff," she said, "should be forced into celibacy, and cut off from that great source of experience, of joy, sorrow and wisdom which marriage and parenthood offer."

With one out of three married women working today, the problem of reconciling marriage and work for women is of a social dimension considerably larger than in the days of Charlotte Gilman or even in the 1930's. But the fundamental issue is still the same: how to make it possible, as Dean Gildersleeve said, to pursue a career or hold a job while enjoying the "experience . . . joy, sorrow and wisdom" of marriage and parenthood. The practical solutions to this central problem of the second stage in the changing position of women seem mainly collective or governmental, not individual. Child-care centers, efficient and readily available house-keeping services, and emergency child-care service such as the Swedes have instituted are obviously a minimal requirement if women are to have the double burdens of homemaking and employment lightened. The individual working woman cannot be expected to compensate for the temporary disabilities consequent upon her role as mother any more than the individual farmer or industrial worker can be expected single-handedly to overcome the imbalance between himself and the market. Today both farmers and workers have government and their own organizations to assist them in righting the balance.

But as the history of farmers and industrial labor makes evident, to enact legislation or to change mores requires persuasion of those who do not appreciate the necessity for change. Those who would do so must organize the like-minded and mobilize power, which is to say they need a rationale, an ideology. And here is the rub; in pragmatic America, as we have seen, any ideology must leap high hurdles. And one in support of working wives is additionally handicapped because women themselves, despite the profound changes in their status in the last century, do not acknowledge such an ideology. Most American women simply do not want work outside the home to be justified as a normal activity for married women. Despite the counter-argument of overwhelming numbers of working wives, they like to think of it as special and exceptional. And so long as they do not advance such an ideology, American society surely will not do so, though other societies, like Israel's and the Soviet Union's, which are more ideological than ours, obviously have.

Perhaps . . . gradual, piecemeal advance toward a feminist ideology . . . may contain the seeds of change. But a reading of the past reminds us forcefully that in America the soil is thin and the climate uncongenial for the growth of any seedlings of ideology.

6

BLACK RESISTANCE

The focus of the following article by Lawrence Levine is upon Negro folk songs but its central point extends to every area of American history and culture. Most historians of the United States are faced with an embarrassing wealth of materials, both printed and manuscript. This has enabled them to reconstruct in great detail various segments of the economic, political, and social history of the nation. Unfortunately, it has also tempted them to ignore the history of those who were not represented by the prolific traditional sources – those who might most accurately be referred to as the "historically inarticulate," not because they were necessarily inarticulate in their own lifetimes, but because they have been rendered so by the neglect of historians. The result has been that we have many histories of labor unions and union leaders but few of workers; minute descriptions of the thought and actions of political spokesmen but few of their constituents; numerous studies of intellectuals, artists, and humorists, but a depressing dearth of studies of popular fiction, folklore, folk humor, folk song, and an almost complete absence of historical studies of the mass media – which Marshall McLuhan has called the folklore of industrial man. We know infinitely more about the clergy than about their parishoners; more about troop movements during America's various wars than about the actual migrations that transformed the face of the United States from generation to generation; more about the aspirations and life styles of large entrepreneurs than about those of small shopkeepers, merchants, or artisans; more about social workers than about the poor to whom they ministered; more about men of all kinds than about women.

This catalog – which of course could be extended – is not meant as an indictment of the kind of history that has been written most frequently. Obviously, there can be no meaningful historiography which does not take as one of its central tasks the re-creation of the background, thought, and action of those who direct the important institutions and movements of any society. No one who understands history would plead seriously that all groups should receive equal time. We know more about some groups than others not only because of the predilections of historians or the nature of their sources, but frequently because we *should* know more about some groups or individuals in terms of their importance and their effects upon others. The problem is that historians have tended to spend too much of their time in the company of the "movers and shakers" and too little time in the universe of the mass of mankind. It is time to restore a greater balance in historical writing, but the shift will not be an easy one. The re-creation of the life styles, thought, and actions of the historically inarticulate will call for the more conscious use of interdisciplinary techniques. The skills of the anthropologist, sociologist, psychologist, demographer, statistician, and folklorist will have to be learned and applied. And even then the nature of the sources will, more often than not, prove troublesome. With reference to the use of folk materials, for instance, Levine has written elsewhere:

> Having worked my way carefully through thousands of Negro songs, folktales, jokes, games, and the like, I am painfully aware of the problems inherent in the use of such materials. They are difficult, often impossible, to date with any precision. Their geographical distribution is usually unclear. They were collected belatedly, most frequently by men and women who had little understanding of the culture from which they sprang and little scruple about altering or suppressing them. Such major collectors as John Lomax, Howard Odum, and Newman White, all admitted openly and even cheerfully that many of the songs they collected were "unprintable" by the moral standards which guided them and presumably their readers. But historians have overcome imperfect records before. They have learned how to deal with altered documents, with consciously or unconsciously biased first-hand accounts, with manuscript collections that were deposited in archives only after being filtered through the over-protective hands of fearful relatives, with the comparative lack of contemporary sources and the need to use their materials retrospectively. The materials of folk and popular culture present a challenge, to be sure, but one that is neither totally unique nor insurmountable. ["Slave Songs and Slave Consciousness," in Tamara Hareven, ed., *Anonymous Americans: Explorations in Nineteenth Century History** (1971).]

There is of course no one approach to the problem of widening the historian's net to take in a larger number of people and social groups. Henry Nash Smith, in *Virgin Land** (1950), and John William Ward, in *Andrew Jackson: Symbol for an Age** (1955) and in his analysis of Charles Lindbergh (see below, pp. 343–354), have done so through the study of popular symbols and myths. Stephen Thernstrom, in his study of Newburyport, Massachusetts, workers, *Poverty and Progress* (1964),* has utilized the quantitative materials of the manuscript census reports. Philip Greven, in *Four Generations: Population, Land, and Family in Colonial Andover, Massachusetts* (1970), and John Demos, in *A Little Commonwealth: Family Life in Plymouth Colony* (1970), have used demographic techniques to reconstruct the history of families in the colonial period. Herbert Gutman, in a number of articles, has looked more closely than most historians have at the culture of workers in late nineteenth-century America (see, for example, "Protestantism and the American Labor Movement," *American Historical Review*, 72 [October 1966], 74–101; and "Class, Status, and Community Power in Nineteenth-Century American Industrial Cities — Paterson, New Jersey: A Case Study," in Fred Jaher, ed., *The Age of Industrialism in America* [1968]). That there are many other possible approaches is indicated by the articles in such journals as *American Quarterly* and the *Journal of Popular Culture*. At this stage, the approach is less important than the attempt itself.

The Concept of the New Negro
and the Realities of Black Culture

LAWRENCE W. LEVINE

I. THE UBIQUITOUS NEW NEGRO

Americans in general and American scholars in particular have not yet really come to terms with a challenge posed by Ralph Ellison a number of years ago: "Everybody wants to tell us what a Negro is. . . . But if you would tell me who I am, at least take the trouble to discover what I have been." [1] Most scholars have failed to penetrate with sufficient energy and imagination the rich and varied cultural sources of the black masses. I want to consider not the reasons for but the effects of this failure. It has left scholars as vulnerable as other Americans to the mood that prevailed in the decades following World War II, which might well be called the period of the rediscovery of the Negro in American life.

White Americans, to be sure, have always been preoccupied with Negroes, but rarely since the years immediately preceding and following the Civil War have black people occupied so important a place in the national consciousness as they have in the past several decades. The standard mechanisms by which whites were able to repress their recognition of the Negro's plight were rendered increasingly ineffective by the middle of the twentieth century. The belief that Negroes, being inferior, could not really object to an inferior status, that they were in fact quite content with the caste-ridden life they were thrust into after the Civil War, and that if there was any problem, it centered around a handful of white and black radicals, agitators, and neurotic malcontents, was undermined as black Americans became more and more able to articulate and act upon their dissatisfactions and their aspirations. The fantasy, indulged in by so many whites at the turn of the century, that what they liked to call the "Negro problem" was at best

Reprinted by permission of Harcourt Brace Jovanovich, Inc., from *Key Issues in the Afro-American Experience*, Vol. II, edited by Nathan I. Huggins, Martin Kilson, and Daniel M. Fox, © 1971 by Harcourt Brace Jovanovich, Inc.

[1] Ralph Ellison, *Shadow and Act* (New York: Random House, 1964), p. 115.

temporary, since Negroes, unable to stand the rigors of either the northern climate or of free competition, were in the process of extinction as a people, was belied by the increasing presence of blacks in all parts of the country. Not even the comfortable conviction that, since the United States was an open society, those Negroes on the bottom of the socioeconomic ladder had no one to blame but themselves (though it is a conviction that retains potency to this day) could be totally persuasive to a people who had just experienced the irrationality and injustice of the Great Depression.

That Negroes came to occupy an increasingly prominent place in the national consciousness has been one of the healthier aspects of the postwar era. Nevertheless, it is important to recognize that this rediscovery has taken place in a historical vacuum. Knowledge of the historical Negro is still obscured by the myths and stereotypes of the past. Whites have construed their dawning awareness of the feelings of blacks as a change in Negroes rather than as a change in themselves. This has given rise to the tendency to think in cataclysmic terms such as the "New Negro" when characterizing black people in contemporary America.

In one sense the concept of the New Negro is undeniably valid. The twentieth century has witnessed striking changes in the status and situation of black Americans. While at the beginning of the century 90 percent of the Negroes in the United States lived in the South and 75 percent were rural, by the middle of the century more than 50 percent lived in the North and 73 percent were urban. These demographic changes have had important social, economic, and political implications. As Negroes moved from rural to urban areas their economic position and occupational opportunities increased markedly. As they moved from the South to the North their political position improved greatly. And both shifts enhanced their opportunities for an improved education. Thus by mid-century Negroes were in a better position to make their demands felt than ever before in American history. But this has been a gradual and cumulative change; it has not been cataclysmic and its effects have been manifest throughout the twentieth century. If black people were more and more able to confront the white man directly and to articulate their feelings, this was not necessarily an indication that the feelings were new.

The problem with the concept of the New Negro is that it has not centered upon these crucial external developments but has taken more important internal changes for granted. It is predicated on the assumption that Negroes before World War II had internalized the white man's image of themselves so that they believed they were somehow inferior and deserving of their fate and consequently did not protest in any effective way. Blacks, to borrow Norbert Wiener's telling phrase, have been seen as reaching up to kiss the whip that lashed them. This image has been enhanced by much of the scholarship of the past few decades. One study, which has had enormous influence in spite of the fact that it totally ignored almost every aspect of slave culture from religion to music to folklore, concluded that Negroes were infantilized by the system of slavery, that they were virtually reduced to a state of perpetual childhood in which their sense of self was derived from the master class upon whom they depended and who constituted their only "significant others." [2] Other studies, paying equally little attention to black culture, have projected this picture into the era of freedom. Confusing group consciousness and a firm sense of self with political consciousness and organization, manhood with armed rebellion, and resistance with the building of a revolutionary tradition, these scholars have been able to find little more than dependence, servility, and apathy in the black masses until relatively recently.[3]

The tendency to see Negroes primarily as reactors to white society rather than as actors in their own right has been intensified by contemporary social scientists who have been unable to perceive a distinctive set of black folkways or institutions at least potentially capable of sustaining Negroes against the worst ravages of the system they live in. "The key to much in the Negro world," two sociologists maintained in their study of ethnic groups in New York City, is that "the Negro is only an American, and nothing else. He has no values and culture to guard and protect." [4] A 1965 government report on the Negro family found that "it was by destroying the Negro family under slavery that white America broke the will of the Negro people. *Although that will has reasserted itself in our time*, it is a resurgence doomed to frustration unless the viability of the Negro family is restored." [5] "Being a Negro in America," a psychologist asserted in 1964, "is less of a racial identity than a necessity to adopt a subordinate social role." [6] Nor has this line of argument been confined to white scholars. The sociologist E. Franklin Frazier summed up much of his research by concluding in 1957 that "unlike any other racial or cultural minority, the Negro is not distinguished by culture from the dominant group. Having completely lost his ancestral culture, he speaks the same language, practices the same religion, and accepts the same values and political ideals as the dominant group." [7]

[2] Stanley Elkins, *Slavery* (Chicago: University of Chicago Press, 1959), Chapter 3.
[3] See, for example, Eugene D. Genovese, "The Legacy of Slavery and the Roots of Black Nationalism," *Studies on the Left* 6 (November-December 1966): 3–26. Ironically, Genovese has been one of the most perceptive and effective critics of the Elkins thesis for the period of slavery. See his article "Rebelliousness and Docility in the Negro Slave: A Critique of the Elkins Thesis," *Civil War History* 13 (December 1967): 293–314, in which he criticizes "Elkins' inability to see the slaves as active forces capable of tempering the authority of the master."
[4] Nathan Glazer and Daniel Moynihan, *Beyond the Melting Pot* (Cambridge, Mass.: MIT Press, 1963), p. 53.
[5] [Daniel Moynihan], *The Negro Family: The Case for National Action* (Washington, D.C.: Office of Policy Planning and Research, Department of Labor, March 1965), p. 30. Italics added.
[6] Thomas F. Pettigrew, *A Profile of the Negro American* (Princeton, N.J.: D. Van Nostrand, 1964), p. 25.
[7] E. Franklin Frazier, *The Negro in the United States*, revised ed. (New York: Macmillan, 1957), pp. 680–81.

The thrust of these studies has been to see black history in the United States as an almost straight line from slavery to the recent past and to envision the distinctive features of that history not as cultural forms but as disorganization or pathology. Thus a scholarly foundation for the concept of the New Negro has been constructed. That it is a foundation without much substance is due not to the necessary invalidity of its central arguments but to the narrow and culture-bound research that has gone into the construction of these arguments. The easy assumption that black history has merely been a pathological version of white history and that the Negro has been little more than "an exaggerated American," as Gunnar Myrdal put it, has worked to inhibit the open and painstaking study of all areas of Negro life and history, without which a complete understanding of the validity of the concept of the New Negro is impossible.

In fact, of course, Negro protest is not new. Indeed, as August Meier has shown, the term New Negro itself has been a ubiquitous one. It was used at least as early as 1895 by the *Cleveland Gazette* to describe a group of Negroes who had just secured a New York civil rights law. Booker T. Washington spoke of a New Negro who was emerging as a result of his policies of self-help and economic betterment. The journalist Ray Stannard Baker wrote in 1908 that while "the old-fashioned Negro preferred to go to the white man for everything . . . the New Negro . . . urges his friends to patronize Negro doctors and dentists, and to trade with Negro storekeepers." In 1916 Dean William Pickens of Morgan College wrote a series of essays entitled *The New Negro*, in which he saw the Negro on the threshold of a renaissance of civilization and culture. For W. E. B. Du Bois, the New Negro was embodied in the group of businessmen who were developing a group economy.[8] The term was used most frequently in the decade after World War I to describe the young artists and poets who were engaged in what was hopefully called a Negro Renaissance. Alain Locke, in his 1925 anthology of Negro writing, *The New Negro*, was virtually alive with the possibilities of the golden day that was dawning:

> There is ample evidence of a New Negro in the latest phases of social change and progress, but still more in the internal world of the Negro mind and spirit. . . . We are witnessing the resurgence of a people. . . . Negro life is not only establishing new contacts and founding new centers, it is finding a new soul. . . . There is a renewed race-spirit that consciously and proudly sets itself apart. . . . The day of "aunties," "uncles" and "mammies" is equally gone. Uncle Tom and Sambo have passed on, . . . the Negro is becoming transformed. . . . The American mind must reckon with a fundamentally changed Negro.[9]

[8] August Meier, *Negro Thought in America, 1880–1915* (Ann Arbor, Mich.: University of Michigan Press, 1963), Chapter 14.

[9] See the foreword and "The New Negro," Alain Locke, *The New Negro* (New York: Albert & Charles Boni, 1925), pp. xv, xvii, 5, 6, 8.

Statements like these stemmed not only from the demographic changes already referred to, but also from the ferment that was taking place among Negroes throughout the nation. Although this ferment was not often marked by direct mass action, there was nonetheless more action than has been recognized. August Meier and Elliott Rudwick have demonstrated that the bus boycotts in Montgomery, Alabama, and other Southern cities during the mid-1950's were by no means a radical break with the past. Negroes had adopted similar tactics in the late nineteenth and early twentieth centuries to oppose segregation in Southern transportation and Northern education. As early as Reconstruction, Negroes in Richmond, New Orleans, Charleston, and Louisville conducted successful boycotts against the introduction of segregated horsecars. During the 1890's, Negroes in Atlanta, Augusta, and Savannah successfully boycotted attempts to segregate local transportation facilities. Between 1900 and 1906, similar protest movements occurred in more than twenty-five cities in every state of the former Confederacy. For periods ranging from several weeks to several years, Negroes in these cities refused to ride on newly segregated streetcars. Negro hackmen and draymen developed informal transit systems to accommodate the protesters, and in Portsmouth, Norfolk, Chattanooga, and Nashville all-black transportation lines were created. Similarly, in Alton, Illinois, in 1897 and in East Orange, New Jersey, in 1899, Negro residents refused to send their children to schools in which they were being segregated. Identical movements took place in Springfield and Dayton, Ohio, in the 1920's. All these movements were ultimately suppressed, as they had to be, with no aid or encouragement from the courts or the government. But, considering the power relationships existing at the time, the important thing about them, as Meier and Rudwick have concluded, is not that they failed "but that they happened in so many places and lasted as long as they often did." [10]

In all this protest there was so great a diversity of means and ends, so frequent a blurring of tactical differences, that it is hard to categorize it without oversimplifying. Bearing this in mind and recalling also that throughout the twentieth century there has always been an important strain of militant action — from the boycotts at the turn of the century, to the campaigns during the Great Depression to force stores in black neighborhoods to employ Negroes, to the 1941 March on Washington Movement to bring about the hiring of Negroes in defense industries, to the accelerating activities of the postwar years — it is possible to isolate several major streams of action that predominated at different times. The political abandonment of the freedmen by the Republican party in the 1870's and 1880's abruptly

[10] August Meier and Elliott Rudwick, "The Boycott Movement Against Jim Crow Streetcars in the South, 1900–1906," *Journal of American History* 55 (March 1969): 756–75; "Negro Boycotts of Jim Crow Streetcars in Tennessee," *American Quarterly* 21 (Winter 1969): 755–63; and "Negro Boycotts of Jim Crow Schools in the North, 1897–1925," *Integrated Education* 5 (August-September 1967): 1–12.

ended the dream that Negro rights could be secured through conventional political behavior and gave rise to the line of thought epitomized by Booker T. Washington's emphasis upon self-help and economic activity. Operating in an age imbued with the belief that man could progress according to the Horatio Alger model and confronted with the blocking of political channels by federal indifference and Southern disfranchisement, Negro leadership preached the possibilities of advancement through moral and economic development: Negroes must band together and further their own cause through mutual aid and self-help; Negroes must show themselves the equal of white men by developing their own capabilities. Although this philosophy of Negro progress persists with some interesting variations on the theme, World War I dealt it a blow from which it never fully recovered.

With few exceptions, Negroes flocked into the American army during the war and served with enthusiasm and hope. When 200 Negro college graduates were asked to volunteer for officer training, 1,500 responded almost immediately. Here was a situation made to order for the Alger philosophy, whose heroes had always proved their worth through inspired acts of heroism and devotion. "We believe that our second emancipation will be the outcome of this war," the Texas Grand Master of the Negro Masons announced in 1918.[11] This loyalty and hope was rewarded by a hardening of the lines of discrimination, by increased humiliation, and by the bloody Red Summer of 1919, which saw major race riots in city after city. Blacks had played the game by the rules and had discovered definitively that the rules simply did not apply to them. The anxiety that accompanied this discovery was marked by the dramatic rise of Marcus Garvey and his Back to Africa movement and by the Negro Renaissance, whose poets and writers flirted with the dream of Africa and a separate Negro people. In organizational terms it was marked by the emergence of the NAACP, with its emphasis upon legalism as the dominant form of protest. If black leaders in the Reconstruction era put their faith in the political process, and those of Booker T. Washington's time stressed the American dream of self-help and success, the new postwar spokesmen turned to the American system of justice. There were endless appeals to the courts to force the application of the rules of the game to Negroes as well as everyone else.

Ironically, it was the very success of this movement that brought about its demise. In the wake of its greatest legal victory, the *Brown v. Board of Education of Topeka* school desegregation decision of 1954, the NAACP found itself beleaguered by the challenges of new organizations and new tactics. It was not long before it began to appear as though the school victory had only symbolic importance. More than ten years after the court spoke, only 8 percent of the Negro youths in the South attended integrated schools. New

11 William Muraskin, "Black Masons: The Role of Fraternal Orders in the Creation of a Middle-Class Black Community" (Ph.D. diss., University of California, Berkeley, 1970), p. 186.

organizations — CORE, SNCC, SCLC — abandoned legalism for direct action, the courts for the streets. Their appeal was directly to the American conscience; their tactic was the graphic demonstration of the injustices and brutalities of the system, along with added economic pressure from boycotts and picket lines. Their results were in many ways impressive, and yet in the more than ten years in which they dominated the Civil Rights movement the relative economic position of the Negro masses declined and the stubborn problems of the urban ghettos became even more intense. As a result of these developments there is the crisis of our own day, in which we are witnessing the rise of new leadership and the use of new methods lumped under the rubric "Black Power."

The variegated and shifting spectrum of Negro protest thought and action has provided still another fertile seedbed for the concept of the New Negro. It has been in periods of transition from the dominance of one set of leaders and tactics to that of another that we have most frequently heard the assertion that a New Negro was arising in the land. The failure to see the Negro rights movements as a totality has made it easy to confuse the rise of new organizations and the adoption of new methods with the birth of a New Negro. But there has been an even greater error. In attempting to understand the reaction of Negroes to the society in which they lived, there has been far too great a concentration on organized movements and on the articulate middle-class and upper-class Negroes upon whom the title of "Negro leaders" has been bestowed. The larger masses of lower-class and lower-middle-class Negroes, who are anything but inarticulate in their own lives, have thus been rendered silent, and this silence in turn has been interpreted as acquiescence or apathy. Failure to understand the reaction of the Negro masses has stemmed directly from failure to look seriously at their lives and their culture. It is precisely at this point that the concept of the New Negro is weakest.

The long-standing notion that blacks have understood whites far better than whites have understood blacks can be overdone, but there is much to substantiate its essential validity. It has been true not simply because of white indifference to Negro feelings but because Negroes have taken pains — have had to take pains — not to let whites understand them too well. W. E. B. Du Bois spoke of a "veil" that prevented whites from seeing the inner world of blacks.[12] Paul Laurence Dunbar spoke of a mask:

> Why should the world be overwise,
> In counting all our tears and sighs?
> Nay, let them only see us, while
>   We wear the mask.[13]

[12] W. E. B. Du Bois, The Souls of Black Folk (1903; reprint ed., New York: Fawcett, 1961).
[13] Paul Laurence Dunbar, The Complete Poems of Paul Laurence Dunbar (New York: Dodd, Mead, 1922), p. 71.

This has been a constant message in Negro letters from the late nineteenth century to the present. Ralph Ellison wrote in 1964:

> I found the greatest difficulty for a Negro writer was the problem of revealing what he truly felt, rather than serving up what Negroes were supposed to feel, and were encouraged to feel. And linked to this was the difficulty, based upon our long habit of deception and evasion, of depicting what really happened within our areas of American life, and putting down with honesty and without bowing to ideological expediencies the attitudes and values which give Negro American life its sense of wholeness and which render it bearable and human and, when measured by our own terms, desirable.[14]

The pervasiveness of this phenomenon has been amply demonstrated by the radically different results that research pollsters and social scientists have gotten when using black rather than white investigators. During World War II, Memphis Negroes were asked, "Would Negroes be treated better or worse if the Japanese conquered the U.S.A.?" While 45 percent answered "worse" when the interviewer was white, only 25 percent did so when the interviewer was black. North Carolina Negroes in the early 1960's demonstrated higher educational aspirations, agreed more readily that there had to be changes "in the way our country is run," and were more prone to support student sit-ins when they were questioned by black interviewers. Of the Boston Negroes questioned during the same period, 87 percent were willing to agree that "the trouble with most white people is that they think they are better than other people" when questioned by other Negroes; only 66 percent admitted this to whites. Studies made of black youths from two year olds to college students have confirmed these results.[15] All this bears out the truth of a song sung by generations of blacks:

> Got one mind for white folks to see,
> 'Nother for what I know is me;
> He don't know, he don't know my mind.

Unfortunately, this truth has not yet sufficiently penetrated the methodologies and perceptions of scholars who have too facilely summed up the attitudes and reactions of blacks. In *The Peculiar Institution*, the most important and perceptive history of United States slavery yet written, Kenneth Stampp anticipated recent theories about the process of "infantilization" by which white masters attempted to produce a childlike race, but he did not commit the mistake of confusing the planters' ideal with reality. His study contains a wealth of suggestions about the private and *sub rosa* tactics used by slaves to resist the white man's design, maintain a sense of individual integrity and self-respect, and manifest a spirit of communal conscious-

---

[14] Ellison, *Shadow and Act*, p. xxi.
[15] The results of these tests and interviews are conveniently summarized in Pettigrew, *A Profile of the Negro American*, pp. 50–51.

ness and solidarity with their fellow blacks.[16] Surprisingly few scholars have attempted this kind of analysis for the postslavery era.

For millions of Negroes in the decades after Emancipation, the normal outlets for protest were closed. They were denied the right of political expression and active demonstration. To understand their reaction to the system under which they lived it is necessary to broaden our definition of protest and resistance, to make it less restrictive and more realistic. This is particularly important because so much of the recent discussion has been concerned with the effects of American racial patterns upon Negro psychic and emotional development. Scholars have written about the psychic effects of the role that many blacks have had to assume among whites without having a full understanding of the roles Negroes have been able to play in black society. The assumption has been that the crucial roles for blacks have been the ones they have played before whites, but this must remain an untested hypothesis until the racial veil has been penetrated and the functions of such institutions as Negro churches and fraternal organizations have been understood. In these institutional enclaves blacks were able to assume many of the social, economic, and political roles denied them in the outside society. What effects these surrogates have had upon black psychic development and concepts of self cannot be understood until scholars drop their assumption that the white stage has been the central one for the development of Negro personality and study in a more open and detailed way the alternatives blacks have been able to construct for themselves.

Similarly, scholars have spoken too easily of Negro apathy and acquiescence without looking in any systematic way at the role spatial mobility has played for blacks. Precisely what has been the meaning of the migrations that have sent millions of Negroes from the South to the North and from rural to urban centers? How have Negroes perceived these demographic shifts? What effects have they had upon black social and psychic life? There have been equally superficial and incomplete discussions of the available peer group models upon which Negro youth could pattern their lives and aspirations. On the whole, such discussions have ignored the evidence of black folklore, black music, and black humor, with their array of such heroes and models as tricksters, bad men, and signifiers, and the evidence of lower-class black culture in which entertainers, preachers, and underworld hustlers often occupy central positions.[17]

One can easily extend this list of omissions, but it should be evident that,

[16] Kenneth M. Stampp, *The Peculiar Institution* (New York: Alfred A. Knopf, 1955), Chapters 3, 8.

[17] There have been a number of recent studies which have focused upon the central elements of black culture. Among the most notable are Charles Keil, *Urban Blues* (Chicago: University of Chicago Press, 1966); LeRoi Jones, *Blues People* (New York: William Morrow, 1963); Roger D. Abrahams, *Positively Black* (Englewood Cliffs, N.J.: Prentice-Hall, 1970); and Bruce A. Rosenberg, *The Art of the American Folk Preacher* (New York: Oxford University Press, 1970).

for all their contributions, too many studies of black history and society have been written in a cultural vacuum, have ignored whole areas of black life and culture, and have emphasized one stratum of Negro society to the exclusion of the masses of blacks. Surely, this is too frail a framework upon which to base hypotheses about the internal life of Negroes in the United States. The remainder of this essay will use the example of early twentieth-century black music to indicate the kind of evidence scholars must consult before indulging in generalizations about Negroes — old or New.

II. Black Songs and Black Consciousness

In exasperation with a reporter who was questioning him about the nature of the music he played, Big Bill Broonzy once remarked: "All music's gotta be 'folk' music. I ain't never heard no horse sing a song." While his interpretation of folk music may have been too all-inclusive, Broonzy was reflecting the fact that for Negroes, probably more than for any other group in the United States, music has been historically (and for large numbers has remained) a *participant* activity rather than primarily a performer-audience phenomenon. It is precisely this folk quality of Negro music that makes it such a good medium for getting at the thought, spirit, and history of the very segment of the Negro community that historians have rendered inarticulate through their neglect. This is evident in Muddy Waters' recollections of his boyhood in Clarksdale, Mississippi during the 1920's:

> I was just a boy and they put me to workin' right along side the men. I handled the plough, chopped cotton, did all of them things. Every man would be hollerin' but you don't pay that no mind. Yeah, course I'd holler too. You might call them blues but they was just made-up things. Like a feller be workin' or most likely some gal be workin' near and you want to say somethin' to 'em. So you holler it. Sing it. Or maybe to your mule or something or it's gettin' late and you wanna go home. I can't remember much of what I was singin' now 'ceptin' I do remember I was always singin', "I cain't be satisfied, I be all troubled in mind." Seems to me like I was always singin' that, because I was always singin' jest the way I felt, and maybe I didn't exactly *know* it, but I jest didn't like the way things were down there — in Mississippi.

This participant role was true not only of those who "hollered" in the fields, sang in the churches, or picked a guitar at home, but also of those who went out to listen and respond to professional entertainers. Norman Mason, a trumpet player who backed up such classic blues singers as Ida Cox, Mamie Smith, and Ma Rainey, has testified that he liked the blues

> because it do express the feelings of people and when we used to play around through Mississippi in those cotton sections of the country we

had the people *with* us! They hadn't much outlet for their enjoyment and they get together in those honkytonks and you should hear them. That's where they let out their suppressed desires, and the more suppressed they are the better the blues they put out, seems to me.[18]

What emerges from these statements — and they could be multiplied many times — is the important role music played in the lives of lower-class Negroes, both urban and rural.

Black songs were rarely completely formalized — handed down from generation to generation with no changes — or wholly spontaneous. Most often they were products of that folk process which has been called "communal re-creation," through which old songs are constantly reworked into essentially new entities.[19] The white sociologist and song collector Howard Odum, hearing the singing of a Negro road gang working in front of his Georgia home, promptly sat on a rock wall nearby in an effort to record the lyrics of their songs. When he finally made out the words, they were:

> White man settin' on wall,
> White man settin' on wall,
> White man settin' on wall all day long,
> Wastin' his time, wastin' his time.[20]

Utilizing a familiar structure and probably also a familiar tune, these black workers left themselves ample scope to improvise new words that fit their surroundings and their mood. An even better example of this process has been provided by the blues and jazz pianist Sam Price in relating an incident from his Texas boyhood:

> I'll never forget the first song I ever heard to remember. A man had been lynched near my home in a town called Robinson, Texas. And at that time we were living in Waco, Texas — my mother, brother and myself. And they made a parody of this song and the words were something like this:
>
> > I never have, and I never will
> > Pick no more cotton in Robinsonville,
> >   Tell me how long will I have to wait,
> >   Can I get you now or must I hesitate?[21]

The importance of this communal spontaneity is evident: the songs sung at work and at play constitute a record of events, impressions, and reactions which is rarely available through other sources.

To comprehend the importance of this record does not ensure that it will

[18] Paul Oliver, *Conversation with the Blues* (New York: Horizon Press, 1965), pp. 29–30, 121–23.

[19] Bruno Nettl, *Folk and Traditional Music of the Western Continents* (Englewood Cliffs, N.J.: Prentice-Hall, 1965), pp. 4–5.

[20] Howard W. Odum and Guy B. Johnson, *The Negro and His Songs* (1925; reprint ed., Hatboro, Pa.: Folklore Associates, 1964), pp. 2–3.

[21] Oliver, *Conversation with the Blues*, pp. 34–35.

be read correctly. Despite their precocity in recognizing the centrality of music in black culture and their unremitting zeal in collecting that music, some of the most important students of early twentieth-century Negro folk music proved to be too deeply rooted in their own cultural milieu to comprehend the implications of much of what they had gathered. John Lomax, for instance, argued in a 1917 article that the prevailing mood of black songs "is one of introspection — self-pity is the theme that, perhaps above all others, dominates his singing," and printed lyrics like these:

> White folks go to college, niggers to de fiel';
> White folks learn to read an' write, niggers learn to steal.
> Well, it make no diff'ence how you make out yo' time,
> White man sho' to bring a nigger out behin'.

> Ain't it hard, ain't it hard,
> Ain't it hard to be a nigger, nigger, nigger?
> Ain't it hard, ain't it hard,
> Caze you can't git yo' money when it's due?

Or:

> Ought for ought an' figger for figger,
> All for white man an' nothin' for nigger.
> Nigger an' white man playin' seben-up, O my hon,
> Nigger win de money but 'fraid to pick it up, O my hon.

Yet, in spite of these songs and of his own perception of the introspective nature of Negro song, Lomax found the stereotypes of the past too much to overcome. Why blacks should sing songs of discontent, he concluded, "is difficult to say. There surely exists no merrier-hearted race than the negro, especially in his natural home, the warm climate of the South. The negro's loud laugh may sometimes speak the empty mind, but at the same time it reveals a nature upon which trouble and want sit but lightly." [22]

In their 1926 collection, *Negro Workaday Songs*, Howard Odum and Guy Johnson entitled one of their chapters "Just Songs to Help With Work" and characterized the songs presented as "songs for song's sake, expression for expression's sake, and 'hollerin' jes' to he'p me wid my work.' " Yet this chapter contains lyrics like these:

> I'm gonna buy me,
> Buy me a winchester rifle,
> Box o' balls,
> Lawd, Lawd, box o' balls.

> I'm gonna back my,
> Back myself in the mountains
> To play bad,
> Lawd, Lawd, to play bad.

[22] John A. Lomax, "Self-Pity in Negro Folk-Songs," *Nation* 105 (9 August 1917): 141–45.

Or this pick-and-shovel song for which the authors can find no "historical base" and in which they see little "sense":

> Well I can stan',
> Lookin' 'way over in Georgia,
> O-eh-he, Lawd, Lawd,
> She's burnin' down,
> Lawd, she's burnin' down.[23]

Perhaps the best example of this selective myopia can be found in one of the most valuable and scholarly collections of early twentieth-century black music, *American Negro Folk-Songs*. Its compiler, Newman I. White, concluded:

> In his songs I find him [the Negro] as I have found him elsewhere, a most naive and unanalytical-minded person, with a sensuous joy in his religion; thoughtless, careless, unidealistic, rather fond of boasting, predominantly cheerful, but able to derive considerable pleasure from a grouch; occasionally suspicious, charitably inclined toward the white man, and capable of a gorgeously humorous view of anything, particularly himself.

Professor White's view of Negroes was hardly original. What was new is that it was accompanied by a good number of songs like these:

> Some o' these mornings, and 'twon't be long,
> Capt'n gwine ter call me and I be gone. (1915–1916)

> The times are hard and money is sca'ce;
> Soon as I sell my cotton and corn
> I am bound to leave this place. (1915–1916)

> If a white man kills a negro, they hardly carry it to court,
> If a negro kills a white man, they hang him like a goat. (1915–1916)

> The old bee makes de honey-comb,
> The young bee makes de honey;
> Colored folks plant de cotton and corn,
> And de white folks gits de money. (1919)

> White man in the parlor reading latest news,
> Negro in the kitchen blacking Roosevelt's shoes. (1915–1916)

> But God loves yo', yo' little black baby,
> Jes' de same as if yo' wuz white,
> God made yo', yo' little black baby,
> So I jes' says yo's all right. (1915–1916)

White was scholarly enough to print these songs and others like them and thoughtful enough to feel the need to explain them, since they failed to fit his conclusions about black people. First, he discounted them quantita-

---

23 Howard W. Odum and Guy B. Johnson, *Negro Workaday Songs* (Chapel Hill: University of North Carolina Press, 1926), pp. 120–21.

tively, arguing that "the very small number of such songs in my whole collection of nearly a thousand . . . is a matter of really primary significance."
The impressive thing, of course, was not the small number of such songs
(which were more numerous than White ever admitted) but the fact that
in the repressive climate of the early twentieth century Negroes in the Deep
South were willing to sing any of these songs openly. White himself must
have realized this, for he constructed a more elaborate explanation in his
theory of the "transcending of verbal meaning" in black songs. "It is very
easy, in fact," he wrote, "to over-interpret all Negro folk-songs through forgetting that to the folk Negro the music, and not the words, is the important matter." [24] This is a particularly fascinating argument, coming as it
did from a man who spent some ten years collecting the lyrics — not the
music — of black songs and who, in the five hundred pages of his text, devoted only one seven-page appendix to "Specimens of Tunes." Newman
White understood fully the importance of Negro folk lyrics; he resorted to
the tortured logic and wishful thinking of arguments like verbal transcen-
dence only when those lyrics threatened an image he needed to preserve.

Indeed, it is extremely doubtful that someone as familiar with black songs
as Newman White could have failed to perceive that their most important
element was the words, not the music. As Harold Courlander has argued for
the blues — and his argument applies to the other basic forms of Negro
song as well — "it is easy to overlook the reality that genuine blues in its
natural setting is not primarily conceived as 'music' but as a verbalization of
deeply felt personal meanings. It is a convention that this verbalization is
sung." One finds this theme in the testimony of one Negro blues singer after
another. As one of them put it:

> When you make a new blues and it says exactly what you got on
> your mind, you feel like it's pay day. Some blues, now, they get
> *towards* it, but if they don't quite get to what you got on your mind,
> you just got to keep on trying. There have been times when I sang
> till my throat was hoarse without really putting my difficulties in the
> song the way I felt them. Other times, it comes out just right on the
> first try.[25]

The concentration on content underlines the functional nature of most
black music. This functionality stemmed from the fact that for black
Americans, as for their African forebears, music was not primarily an art

[24] Newman I. White, *American Negro Folk Songs* (1928; reprint ed., Hatboro, Pa.:
Folklore Associates, 1965), pp. 30, 258, 286, 382, 384, 377, 27.
[25] Harold Courlander, *Negro Folk Music, U.S.A.* (New York: Columbia University
Press, 1963), p. 145. For similar arguments, see James Weldon Johnson's preface to
The Second Book of Negro Spirituals (New York: Viking Press, 1926) and Jones, *Blues
People*, p. 28. Jones goes even further and argues: "Even the purely instrumental music
of the American Negro contains constant reference to vocal music. Blues-playing is the
closest imitation of the human voice of any music I've heard; the vocal effects that jazz
musicians have delighted in from Bunk Johnson to Ornette Coleman are evidence of
this."

form but an integral part of life. One of the most important functions of black songs was the verbalization of personal and group feelings which had few, if any, other outlets. This too has been documented by black singers. Lil Son Jackson recalled the massive burden of economic and social injustice his sharecropper father labored under:

> That was the onliest way he could get relief from it, by singin' them blues. Just like me or anybody. I can get vexed up or somethin' or I have a sad feelin'; seems like to me that if I can sing, I feel better. But my father, he only just played at home and around. More or less at home is all I did know him to play. . . . They all played music, my father and mother too. . . . I never did take music to be a thing that I could make a livin' of; . . . I never did take interest enough in it to go to school and try to learn somethin' from the book, I more or less played what I felt.

"I tell you," Henry Townsend agreed,

> in most cases the way I feel, the song will come to you when you are really depressed you know. I mean, words'll come to you and you feel them and you decide you'll do something about it, so the thing that you do about it is more or less to put it in rhymes and words and make them come out. It gives you relief — it kinda helps somehow. I don't know — it kinda helps.[26]

If our understanding of the meaning of Negro folk songs has been hampered frequently by the predispositions of the pioneer analysts and collectors, it has been impeded as well by the nature of the songs themselves, which are often indirect and ambiguous. From the time Negroes first arrived in America, conditions have made it imperative for them to disguise their feelings from the white man and perhaps at times from themselves as well. As I have argued elsewhere, music has always provided one of the primary means for transcending the restrictions imposed by external, and even internal, censors. Through the use of innuendo, metaphor, and circumlocution, Negroes, could utilize their songs as outlets for individual and communal release.[27]

The existence of double meaning in Negro folk songs has long been recognized. Howard Odum, for example, reflected upon the "paradoxes and contradictions" contained in the songs he collected, admitted that "the negro is very secretive," and spoke of "the resourcefulness and adaptability of the negro" and of "his hypocrisy and two-faced survival mechanisms." [28] The only instance in which this phenomenon was studied in any detail by the

---

[26] Oliver, *Conversation with the Blues*, pp. 24, 33–34.

[27] Lawrence W. Levine, "Slave Songs and Slave Consciousness," in Tamara Hareven, ed., *Anonymous Americans* (Englewood Cliffs, N.J.: Prentice-Hall, 1971).

[28] Howard W. Odum, "Religious Folk-Songs of the Southern Negroes," *American Journal of Religious Psychology and Education* 3 (July 1909): 269. Odum and Johnson, *The Negro and His Songs*, pp. xvii, 9.

early twentieth-century collectors, however, focused upon sexual relations. In 1927 Guy Johnson pointed out that when black songs depict men stealing, cheating, and dying for a piece of their woman's jelly roll, angel food cake, or shortening bread, it is difficult to believe that these terms are meant to refer to food:

> Dupree was a bandit,
> He was brave an' bol',
> He stole that diamon' ring
> For some of Betty's jelly roll.

> Two little niggers layin' in bed,
> One turned over to the other an' said,
> "My baby loves short'nin', short'nin' bread,
> My baby loves short'nin' bread."

Johnson found that words like "cabbage," "keyhole," "cookie," and "cake" were frequently used as symbols for the female sexual organs, and it would be possible to add many similar metaphors to his list. Johnson never claimed that all double meanings in Negro music were of a sexual nature, and in a footnote he indicated: "There are, for example, many hidden references to the white man in the Negro's songs. This is an interesting field of research in which little has been done." [29] But it was doubtless easier for him and many of his colleagues to admit the existence of double meaning in sexual relations, since it merely confirmed their image of the low moral state of the Negro. They were much less ready to analyze double meaning that reflected lack of contentment or anything less than total adjustment. Once the door is opened, however, it is difficult to close again. Once the existence of *double-entendre* and veiled meaning is admitted in one area, it is hard to rule it out in others.

What precisely have Negroes meant in their twentieth-century religious music when they complained continuously, "Why doan de debbil let-a me be?" or asked, "What makes ole Satan hate me so?" and answered, "Cause he got me once an' let me go," or boasted, "Ole Satan thought he had me fast, / Broke his chain an' I'm free at last," or observed:

> Just let me tell you how this world is fixed:
> Satan has got it so full of tricks,
> You can go from place to place,
> Everybody's runnin' down the colored race.

In freedom, as in slavery, the Devil — over whom Negroes generally triumphed in their songs — often looked suspiciously like a surrogate for the white man. Similarly, while Negroes had long sung of "letters from the Lord" and "trains to glory," and while there can be no doubt that these

---

[29] Guy B. Johnson, "Double Meaning in the Popular Negro Blues," *Journal of Abnormal Psychology* 22 (April–June 1927): 12–20.

phrases were frequently meant literally, during the early twentieth-century migration of blacks from the South to the North — which many Southern states desperately tried to stop — it is difficult to imagine that these metaphors did not assume contemporary connotations.

> Well, my mother got a letter, oh, yes;
> Well, she could not read it, oh, yes.
> What you reckon that letter said?
> That she didn't have long to stay here.

> Yes, I 'bleeged to leave this world,
> Yes, I 'bleeged to leave this world.
> Sister, I's 'bleeged to leave this world,
> For it's a hell to me.[30]

Nonreligious work songs and blues are a bit less of a dilemma, since they tend to be more direct and open, but this is by no means invariable. Even in as relatively formalized and popular a Negro work song as "John Henry," the meaning is by no means clear cut:

> This old hammer killed John Henry,
> But it can't kill me.
> Take this hammer, take it to the Captain,
> Tell him I'm gone, babe, tell him I'm gone.[31]

The possible meanings of the following lyrics are also intriguing:

> Niggers gettin' mo' like white fo'ks,
> Mo' like white fo'ks eve'y day.
> Niggers learnin' Greek an' Latin,
> Niggers wearin' silk an' satin,
> Niggers gettin' mo' like white fo'ks eve'y day.[32]

In 1917 John Lomax interpreted those lines as presenting "the cheerful side of improving social conditions." But they could as easily, and perhaps more meaningfully, be seen as an example of lower-class black satire and anger directed at those Negroes who were trying to become culturally "white." An even greater interpretive challenge is presented by these lyrics, sung by a black Georgia worker:

> Ever see bear cat
> Turn to lion,
> Lawd, Lawd,
> Down in Georgia?

---

[30] Odum and Johnson, *The Negro and His Songs*, pp. 41, 42, 124, 131, 120, 116. For many similar songs, see Chapters 2–4.

[31] For many examples of "John Henry" songs, see Guy B. Johnson, *John Henry: Tracking Down a Negro Legend* (Chapel Hill: University of North Carolina Press, 1929).

[32] Lomax, *Nation*, 105 (9 August 1917): 144.

My ol' bear cat,
My ol' bear cat
Turn to lion,
Lawd, Lawd, Lawd.

'Fo' long, Lawd,
Yes, 'fo' long, Lawd,
I'll be back here,
I'll be back here.[33]

The number of songs containing ambiguous metaphors and intriguing but obscure symbolism could be extended indefinitely. Still, as many of the lyrics quoted indicate, there are hollers, work songs, field songs, and blues whose meaning is really not subject to a great deal of interpretation. There are hundreds of songs from the first two decades of this century that make it unmistakably clear that Negro music has been a crucial, and perhaps central, vehicle for the expression of protest and discontent. There were constant complaints about the white "captain," about working conditions, about the unfairness of the sharecropping system. Sometimes these were expressed satirically:

Reason I love my captain so,
'Cause I ast him for a dollah,
Lawd, he give me fo'.

But often they were presented openly and baldly:

Niggers plant the cotton,
Niggers pick it out,
White man pockets money,
Niggers does without.[34]

During these years, blacks were still singing the words of a song first reported by Frederick Douglass during slavery:

She sift de meal, she gimme de dust,
She bake de bread, she gimme de crust,
She eat de meat, she gimme de skin,
An' dat's de way she tuck me in.[35]

There was often, one song admitted, "Plenty to eat, / Place to sleep," but "nothin' fer a feller, / Lawd, nothin' fer / A feller to keep." [36]

This sense of injustice, which certainly embodied no illusions about the

[33] Odum and Johnson, *Negro Workaday Songs*, pp. 121–22.
[34] Ibid., pp. 112, 115.
[35] Dorothy Scarborough, *On the Trail of Negro Folk-Songs* (1925; reprint ed., Hatboro, Pa.: Folklore Associates, 1963), p. 99. White, *American Negro Folk Songs*, p. 161.
[36] Odum and Johnson, *Negro Workaday Songs*, pp. 115–16.

American racial situation or the black man's place in it, was often accompanied by a great deal of anger, aggression, and self-pride:

> Well, if I had my weight in lime,
> I'd whip my captain till I went stone-blind.

> Well, you can't do me like you do po' Shine,
> You take Shine's money, but you can't take mine.[37]

Lines like "I wish my captain would go blind," "I didn't come here to be
nobody's dog," "Ain't let nobody treat me dis way," "Ain't gonna be bossed
aroun' no mo'," "Ain't gwine let you humbug me," "You call me dog, I
don' ker," "I ain't gonna let nobody, / Nobody make a fool out o' me," were
ubiquitous:

> If you don't like the way I work, jus' pay me off.
> I want to speak one luvin' word before I go:
> I know you think I'm pow'ful easy, but I ain't so sof';
> I can git another job an' be my boss.[38]

Often this anger took the form not of aggression so much as of refusing
to play the game by the white man's rules: "Cap'n says, hurry, I say take my
time," "Dere ain't no use in my workin' so hard," "When you think I'm
workin', I ain't doin' a thing." [39]

> If you work all the week,
>   An' work all the time,
> White man sho to bring
>   Nigger out behin'.[40]

These lyrics are important because they are an assertion of a break with the
idealized Puritan values and mores of white society. The "Bad Man" songs
like "Stagolee" and "Dupree" ("I'm de bad nigger, / If you wants to know;
. . . Shoot, nigger, / Shoot to kill") and the blues, especially in their depiction of sexual conduct, are similarly filled with assertions of independence
from the cold, mocking world of bourgeois values and dicta that seemed so
hypocritical.[41]

The same independence from the values of the larger society can be seen
with regard to color. Certainly, Negro songs were often marked by the color
preferences of white American society. What is more important, given the
stereotype that most blacks during this period longed to be white, is that at
least as often they were characterized by color pride. Negro troops in France

[37] Odum and Johnson, *The Negro and His Songs*, p. 253.
[38] Ibid., pp. 171, 257. Odum and Johnson, *Negro Workaday Songs*, pp. 76, 128.
White, *American Negro Folk Songs*, pp. 255, 258. Scarborough, *On the Trail of Negro
Folk-Songs*, p. 190.
[39] White, *American Negro Folk Songs*, pp. 255, 302. Scarborough, *On the Trail of
Negro Folk-Songs*, p. 235. Odum and Johnson, *The Negro and His Songs*, p. 163.
[40] Odum and Johnson, *The Negro and His Songs*, p. 255.
[41] For example, see Odum and Johnson, *Negro Workaday Songs*, Chapter 4, and
Paul Oliver, *Blues Fell This Morning* (New York: Horizon Press, 1960).

during World War I were often heard singing: "It takes a long, tall, slim, black man to make a German lay his rifle down." [42] Again and again, black-skinned and brown-skinned women and men were held up as objects of desire and admiration:

> Some says yellow
> While others say brown,
> But for me I'll take the blackest in town.[43]

> A yellow girl I do despise,
> But a jut-black girl I can't denies.[44]

> Ain't crazy 'bout no high yellows, worried about no brown,
> Come to picking my choice, gimme
> The blackest man in town.[45]

> Some say, give me a high yaller,
> I say give me a teasin' brown,
> For it takes a teasin' brown,
> To satisfy my soul.[46]

Black songs of the early twentieth century could be accompanied by a deadening sense of fatalism and despair: "I didn't bring nuthin' in dis bright worl'; / Nuthin' I'll carry away," or "Trouble, trouble, / Been had it all my day; / Believe to my soul / Trouble gonna kill me dead." [47] This mood, however, was often modified by the strong sense of change, freedom of movement, and mobility that pervaded these songs: "I jest come here to stay a little while," "Gwine whar' I never been befo'," "Oh, goin' down dat lonesome road, / An' I won't be treated this-a way," "I'm gonna row here few days longer, / Then, Lawd, I'm goin' on." [48] Frequently there seemed to be a new self-consciousness about movement and a need to distinguish it from mere running away. Thus in "John Henry" and similar work songs the request to "Take my hammer . . . to my captain, / Tell him I'm gone," was accompanied by this admonition:

> If he asks you was I running,
> Tell him no,
> Tell him no.
> Tell him I was going across the Blue Ridge Mountains
> Walking slow, yes, walking slow.[49]

---

[42] White, *American Negro Folk Songs*, p. 355.
[43] Ibid., p. 316.
[44] Odum and Johnson, *The Negro and His Songs*, p. 193.
[45] White, *American Negro Folk Songs*, p. 326.
[46] Odum and Johnson, *Negro Workaday Songs*, p. 146.
[47] Odum and Johnson, *The Negro and His Songs*, p. 162. Odum and Johnson, *Negro Workaday Songs*, p. 40.
[48] Odum and Johnson, *The Negro and His Songs*, pp. 171, 176. Odum and Johnson, *Negro Workaday Songs*, pp. 46, 112–113.
[49] White, *American Negro Folk Songs*, p. 259.

Occasionally there was even a sense of the possibility of turning the tables on the whites:

> Well, I'm goin' to buy me a little railroad of my own,
> Ain't goin' to let nobody ride but de chocolate to de bone.
> Well, I'm goin' to buy me a hotel of my own,
> Ain't goin' to let nobody eat but de chocolate to de bone.[50]

III. Conclusion

The purpose of this essay is not to argue that Negro music has functioned primarily as a medium of protest. To state this would distort black music and black culture. Negroes have not spent all their time reacting to whites, and their songs are filled with comments on all aspects of life. But it would be an even greater distortion to assume that a people occupying the position that Negroes have in this society could produce a music as rich and varied as they have with few allusions to their situation or only slight indications of their reactions to the treatment they were accorded. While black music is not dominated by such reactions, it is a rich repository of them and offers a new window onto the lives and into the minds of a large segment of the black community that has been ignored because its members have not left behind the kind of sources that historians are used to working with.

To argue that music constituted a form of black protest does not mean that it necessarily led to any tangible and specific actions, but rather that it served as a mechanism by which Negroes could be relatively candid in a society that rarely accorded them that privilege, could communicate with other Negroes whom they would in no other way be able to reach, and could assert their own individuality, aspirations, and sense of being. Certainly, if nothing else, black music makes it difficult to believe that early twentieth-century Negroes internalized their situation so completely, accepted the values of the larger society so totally, or manifested so pervasive an apathy as we have been led to believe.

As it has been applied both implicitly and explicitly, then, the concept of the New Negro requires serious modification. As a historical phenomenon, of course, it retains great importance. For almost every generation of blacks since Emancipation, the idea of the New Negro, in all its varying forms, has been a crucial rallying cry and a source of great optimism and ego gratification. But its very ubiquity should make scholars wary of taking it too literally. It has had unquestionable utility as a vehicle for action, but as a means of historical understanding it has tended to obscure as much as it has revealed. And it will continue to do so until it is made to encompass not merely select groups of historically articulate Negroes but the entire spectrum of black society and all the realities of black culture.

[50] Lomax, *Nation*, 105 (9 August 1917): 144.

PART II

THE OPENING DECADES

7

THE RELIGIOUS THEME
IN AMERICAN THOUGHT

"It is a commonplace," Sidney Mead says in an earlier article than the one that follows, "that in the period roughly from 1870 to 1900 evangelical Protestant Christianity largely dominated the American culture, setting the prevailing mores and the moral standards by which personal and public, individual and group, conduct was judged." ["American Protestantism Since the Civil War. I. From Denominationalism to Americanism," *Journal of Religion*, 36 (Jan. 1956).] Dr. Mead argues, however, that "domination" was possible only because of the amalgamation of "scholastic Protestant orthodoxy" with "the religion of the democratic society and nation . . . articulated in terms of the destiny of America, under God, to be fulfilled by perfecting the democratic way of life for the example and betterment of all mankind." In effect, by the latter part of the 19th century, Protestantism had become little more than a sanctimonious justification for the status quo with almost no independent intellectual content. Three developments had served to emasculate Protestant theology: (1) the triumph of pietistic revivalism in the denominations following the Revolution; (2) "the almost universal reaction in the free churches against the whole ethos of the Enlightenment"; and (3) "the lack of intellectual interests and structure of the pietistic Protestantism which came to dominance." Thus, Protestantism [Mead approvingly quotes John Herman Randall, Jr.] "tended to become largely an emotional force in support of the reigning secular social ideals."

It is difficult for us today to understand just how potent a force Protestantism was at the turn of the century. Within it lay the often inarticulate but fundamental assumptions about original sin, the demonstrable harmony of God's purpose, and the natural hierarchy of men based upon their relative morality. The assumptions set the contemporary definitions of truth and evil, justice and injustice. They were shared, moreover, by Catholic orthodoxy as well, though Catholic thought rejected evangelical Protestantism's identification of the course of American democracy with God's purpose.

The assumptions were manifested in the expressed attitudes toward women and children, to say nothing of *sotto voce* attitudes toward the lower classes. Children no less than adults were held responsible for the good works that indicated the reception of grace; they were, however, morally incomplete and thus vulnerable to the devil's temptations, and so they had to be disciplined, by punishment as well as by labor that was to divert their energies from doing the devil's work. Women were regarded in much the same manner — though as adults they might be humored rather than disciplined or worked — but they were to be kept in their place in any event. As for the poor, their very poverty proved their moral incapacity — especially in this, God's own country. "The truth," averred Henry Ward Beecher, is that "no man in this land suffers from poverty unless it be more than his fault — unless it be his *sin*." [See Mead below.] Not only did America provide a special opportunity for men to test their mettle, but, as Episcopal Bishop William Lawrence put it even more generally: "In the long run, it is only to the men of morality that wealth comes. We believe in the harmony of God's Universe. . . . We . . . occasionally see the wicked prosper, but only occasionally." ["The Relationship of Wealth to Morals," *World's Work*, I (Jan. 1901).]

Although, as Dr. Mead notes, Henry Adams lamented in 1900 that he felt like an alien in the America he had once called his own, at least the dominant elements of Adams's America in 1900 still used essentially the same thought constellations and the same criteria for "truth" and "evil" as his illustrious ancestors had done even a hundred years earlier. Religious, especially Protestant, principles remained the key. Adams was a perceptive man who had taken note of the moral revolution of his day brought on by the high level of social mobility, political change, and philosophical controversy. Adams himself had hailed Darwinism as a "substitute for religion," while the pronounced increase in social violence during the last decades of the nineteenth century had put conventional normative definitions to severe pragmatic tests. Yet, for most contemporaries the revolution was only a challenge still inchoate and repressible. As late as 1912, Henry May has observed, "words like truth, justice, patriotism, unselfishness, and decency were used constantly without any sense of embarrassment, and ordinarily without any suggestion that their meaning might be only of a time and place." Most Americans, moreover, "did not argue about the essential morality of the universe — they assumed it." [*The End of American Innocence** (1959), pp. 9, 14.]

Unless it is understood how much the norms of 1900 owed to the prevailing religious notions, the statements of some leading spokesmen for the America of the turn of the century often appear merely fatuous. Perhaps the most notorious example is that of George F. Baer, the mining tycoon, in his reply to criticism of his company's stand in the coal strike of 1902. "I do not know who you are," Baer wrote to the remonstrator. "I see that you are a religious man. . . . I beg you not to be discouraged. The rights and interests of the laboring man will be protected and cared for — not by the labor agitators, but by the Christian men to whom God in his infinite wisdom has given the control of the property interests of this country." Although George Baer may well have been a fatuous man, his self-arrogated stewardship was commonplace in his day. It was not the archaism of the sentiment so much as the timing and phrasing of his letter (which he certainly did not expect would be made public) that evoked the contemporary uproar and helped make him the butt of historians' derision. [Cf. E. C. Kirkland, "The Robber Barons Revisited," *American Historical Review*, 66 (Oct. 1960).]

That God rewarded his elect with earthly gifts of money or power and that the ascendant classes must serve as God's "stewards" were in fact old Calvinist notions that leading progressives (most obviously Theodore Roosevelt and Woodrow Wilson) shared fully with the apologists for the status quo. The beliefs help explain the moral dogmatism and the underlying elitism of so much of progressive thought. They help also to explain the bitter dismay among many of the progressives following the collapse of the movement after World War I: the people, it seemed, would not be led, would not be uplifted, would not be *right*; the people be damned.

The power of evangelical Protestantism remained great in the 1920's. Religious fundamentalism was its chief manifestation. Prohibitionism and nativism, two of the most striking phenomena of the 'twenties, owed much to it, as did the Ku Klux Klan. In many ways, these movements represented the terminal efforts of a progressive society to maintain fixed standards of value. Their inevitable failure forced American Protestantism to reexamine its tenets, and to become transformed, as Dr. Mead puts it, "from Americanism to Christianity."

H. R. Niebuhr's "Fundamentalism," in *The Encyclopedia of the Social Sciences*, is a brief but highly informative account that should not be overlooked. Among the many works cited in Dr. Mead's article, below, students should see especially P. Carter's *The Decline and Revival of the Social Gospel** (1954). Winthrop S. Hudson, *American Protestantism** (1961), a brief survey, has a valuable annotated bibliography. S. M. Lipset, "Religion and Politics in American History," and Earl Raab, "The Nature of the Conflict," in Raab, ed., *Religious Conflict in America** (1964), will introduce the student to some vital problems concerning the religious themes in American thought that Mead touches only tangentially.

Dr. Mead is Professor of Religion and History at the University of Iowa.

American Protestantism Since the Civil War
II. From Americanism to Christianity

SIDNEY E. MEAD

In the preceding article* we described a metamorphosis of Protestantism in the United States, exemplified in its ideological amalgamation with "Americanism." In America this was still a period of "fervent devotion," but the object of devotion has been subtly changed under the appearance of enlargement to include a particular system of social, political, and economic life. "In ages of fervent devotion," Tocqueville noted, "men sometimes abandon their religion, but they only shake it off to adopt another. Their faith changes the objects to which it is directed, but it suffers no decline." [1] This was the kind of change we have described. Hence there was no outward appearance of decline in religious activities or denominational prosperity. Indeed, contemporary statistical studies suggested a period of organizational vitality and exceptional growth, during which the denominations were rapidly bringing the unchurched into their folds. For this reason the rightness of the general outlook and practice seemed to pass the pragmatic test — the system worked, as serious and able students like Daniel Dorchester took pains to point out.[2]

Nevertheless, the ideological amalgamation of Protestant denominationalism and Americanism went on. The situation was not untouched with irony, since, while the Protestant denominations remained very conscious of the evils due to a formal connection between church and state as demonstrated in history, they were rendered by circumstances described in the preceding article less critically conscious of the equally grave evils contingent upon ideological amalgamation with a particular way of life. Hence, while abhorring Erastianism and being skeptical of theocracy — in their overt forms — the free churches eventually found themselves entangled in a more subtle form of identification of Christianity, nationalism, and economic system than Christendom had ever known before.

Reprinted by permission of The University of Chicago Press and the author from *The Journal of Religion*, 36 (April 1956).
* [See Sidney E. Mead, "American Protestantism Since the Civil War. I. From Denominationalism to Americanism," *Journal of Religion*, 36 (Jan. 1956). — Eds.]
[1] Alexis de Tocqueville, *Democracy in America*, trans. Henry Reeve (4th ed.; New York: J. & H. G. Langley, 1841), I, 341.
[2] Daniel Dorchester, *The Problem of Religious Progress* (New York: Phillips & Hunt, 1881), see particularly chap. iii and the Appendix containing "Ecclesiastical Statistics."

Not unnaturally, a crisis in the life of the denomination resulted when events occurred that were spectacular and explosive enough to raise the question in many minds of the adequacy of the current conceptual order and of the modes of practice. It is clear that the crisis, of which we speak in this article, was a matter of both the denominationalism and the Americanism, which ideologically had achieved such a high degree of amalgamation. We may take, as a text for the discussion of this development, the simple thesis of A. M. Schlesinger, Sr., that during the last quarter of the nineteenth century organized religion in America met two great challenges — "the one to its system of thought, the other to its social program." [3]

The challenge to the "system of thought" in the denominations was spearheaded by the persuasive sway of evolutionary thinking, appearing first in the work of Darwin and Spencer and soon pervading all areas of intellectual life. The challenge to the "social program" of the denominations came first in the form of unbearable conditions in the expanding industrial cities and then in a series of spectacular upheavals that shook the social and economic structure to its foundations.

It is important to note that these two challenges, which threatened completely to shatter both the ideological and the practical worlds of the denominations, were concurrent. In this perspective the wonder is not that there was a great deal of confusion, inanity, and hysteria but that as much sanity and order prevailed in them as actually did, so that one of the most thorough students of the era can conclude that "during this period of recurrent depression, doubt and struggle the Protestant churches still maintained, to a greater extent than is usually realized, their historic position of intellectual and moral leadership." [4]

I

The social program of the denominations was firmly rooted in the long Christian tradition of "charity" — the amelioration of distress, feeding the hungry, clothing the naked, visiting the sick and imprisoned, and giving the cup of cold water for Jesus' sake and not the titillation of human pride. The ideal in this respect was "the man of feeling . . . the feeling of the renewed heart, enlarged as is the range of human wretchedness, purified by the indwelling Spirit of God, and ennobled by the model on which it is

[3] A. M. Schlesinger, Sr., "A Critical Period in American Protestantism, 1875–1900," in *Massachusetts Historical Society Proceedings*, LXIV (June, 1932) (New York: Macmillan Co., 1922), p. 140. The questions, said Brown, are: "Can the old religion still maintain itself under the strain of the new conditions? Can it sustain the theoretical test of the intellectual movement which we call modern science? Can it meet the practical test of the social and economic movement which we call industrialism, with its political counterpart in the rivalry of races and of nations for prestige and for power?" These, he suggests, are aspects of the same scientific movement.

[4] Henry F. May, *Protestant Churches and Industrial America* (New York: Harper & Bros., 1949), p. ix.

formed," as two Scotch ministers wrote of the Rev. Ezra Stiles Ely in 1829.[5]

But the exercise of Christian charity came to be hemmed in and conditioned by current modes of thinking. In the first place, it was to be exercised wisely, which meant with a realistic understanding of what Horace Bushnell called "those higher laws" of trade — for example, "the laws of current price," which automatically set the price of "the productions of agriculture" as well as "the wages of hand labor." [6] These laws were thought to be immutable, and hence, as the Rev. John Bascom of Williams College explained in 1868 in arguing against eight-hour-day legislation, any attempt to interfere in the interests of abstract justice or the amelioration of distress was to attempt "a substitution of civil for natural law" and to demonstrate "the impossibility of affecting favorably or shifting the conditions of society except in connection with the forces that give rise to them." [7]

Recognizing this, Bushnell continued that "the merchant . . . should do his trade by the strict law principles of trade, and never let his operations be mixed up with charities." Hence his two ideal merchants

> were never known to veer by a hair from integrity in any transaction of business, but they would have veered a hundred times a day, falling into a muddle where all distinctions of principle are lost, if they had not done their trade as trade, under the laws of trade, and reserved their charities — all their sympathies, allowances, mitigations, merciful accommodations — for a separate chapter of life.[8]

Andrew Carnegie, in his famous article on "Wealth," intimated clearly enough that to pay higher wages than the market demanded in an effort to distribute wealth more equitably was just such a mistaken mixing of trade and charity and violated the rich man's responsibility to administer his wealth "for the community far better than it could or would have done for itself." [9]

In this view he was backed by the "natural theology" of Professor Bascom, who held that, while ultimately "selfishness" will be "steadily softened into a just and generous regard of the good of others," meanwhile the only "basis of simple justice, of pure economic right, and . . . the only one on which the claims of all parties can find firm, constant, and conclusive adjustment" is that of "sharp competition, of a stern and unscrupulous use of the ad-

[5] Ezra Stiles Ely, *Visits of Mercy; or the Journals of the Rev. Ezra Stiles Ely* (6th ed., revised by the author; Philadelphia: Samuel F. Bradford, 1829), I, iii.

[6] Horace Bushnell, "How To Be a Christian in Trade," in *Sermons on Living Subjects* (New York: Charles Scribner's Sons, 1903), p. 251.

[7] John Bascom, "The Natural Theology of Social Science. IV. Labor and Capital," *Bibliotheca sacra*, XXV (October, 1868), 680, 683.

[8] Bushnell, *op. cit.*, pp. 263, 248.

[9] The article appeared in the *North American Review*, CXLVIII (June, 1889), 653–64. For convenience I have used it as reprinted in Gail Kennedy (ed.), *Democracy and the Gospel of Wealth* (Boston: D. C. Heath & Co., 1949), a volume in the Amherst College "Problems in American Civilization Series." The quotation is from p. 8.

vantages which the market affords." Therefore, for example, "if a workman wishes higher wages than the employer is willing to pay, he has but one test of the validity of his claim . . . and that is his ability to secure elsewhere the sum demanded." This, he explained, "is commercial law, commercial justice, a practical and final decision of all questions, beyond which there is the opportunity for no claim, as there is for no coercion." [10]

Under these rubrics Carnegie castigated the "writer of philosophic books" who confessed that he had given a quarter "to a man who approached him as he was coming to visit the house of a friend." This, thought Carnegie, was a flagrant example of "indiscriminate charity" and was probably "one of the most selfish and very worst actions" of this man's generally "worthy" life.[11] The Rev. Charles Wood was even more dogmatic than Carnegie. He was convinced that "begging on the streets, and from door to door, is a *habit*, acquired after an experience of its success. . . . In nine cases out of ten there is no pressure of want at all." Rather, it is prompted by a low, indolent spirit, which seeks to gratify its selfish lusts, at the expense of the virtuous and good." Furthermore, he added, revealing a widespread prejudice, "four-fifths, if not nine-tenths, of all our street beggars and paupers are of one nationality and of one form of religion." Therefore, he argued, "street begging should be made an offence in the eyes of the law, and should be strictly visited by a suitable penalty." [12]

In the second place, the exercise of charity was limited and conditioned by the prevalent view that since "Godliness is in league with riches," most poverty is the direct result of vice and sin. Hence Carnegie was convinced that "in alms-giving more injury is probably done by rewarding vice than by relieving virtue," and his "true reformer" was "as careful and as anxious not to aid the unworthy as he [was] to aid the worthy." [13]

These views also had clerical approval in high places. Henry Ward Beecher thought that, while "there may be reasons of poverty which do not involve wrong," nevertheless, "looking comprehensively through city and town and village and country, the general truth will stand, that no man in this land suffers from poverty unless it be more than his fault — unless it be his *sin*." Happily, he added, "there is enough and to spare thrice over; and if men have not enough, it is owing to the want of provident care, and foresight, and industry, and frugality, and wise saving. This is the general truth." [14] In 1873 the reviewer of Charles Loring Brace's *The Dangerous Classes of New York* . . . in the *Presbyterian Quarterly and Princeton Re-*

[10] Bascom, op. cit., p. 675.

[11] Carnegie, *op. cit.*, p. 7.

[12] Charles Wood, "The Pauperism of Our Cities: Its Character, Condition, Causes, and Relief," *Presbyterian Quarterly and Princeton Review*, III (new ser.; April, 1874), 225.

[13] Carnegie, *op. cit.*, p. 7.

[14] Henry Ward Beecher, "Economy in Small Things," in *Plymouth Pulpit*, IV (March–September, 1875) (New York: Fords, Howard & Hulbert, 1892), 463–64.

view, commented that "in this city . . . as a general rule, poverty comes from vice, rather than vice from poverty," [15] while the Rev. Charles Wood, writing in the same *Quarterly* a year later, was positive that "pauperism and vagrancy are *crimes*, and should be *prevented* or *punished*." And, he added, "it is even doubtful whether the indirect *injury* done by our voluntary, benevolent associations, and 'missions for the relief of the poor' . . . does not overbalance the good which they accomplish." For, he continued, perhaps with a tinge of professional jealousy, "the only institutions, or organized societies" which can insure the punishment or prevention of vagrancy and pauperism are the "divine institutions" of "the family, the *church* and the state," and "all other institutions should be associated with and subordinated to these." Only "good homes, pure churches, and well administered laws, will either prevent or punish the crimes of our lowest classes." [16]

John Bascom was made of even sterner stuff. "The staple with which Providence has to deal with in the races of men," he pontificated, "is ignorance and indolence interstratified with sin — stupidity made heavy, solid, opaque, and gritty with a wicked will" until

> the unpliant and stubborn mass can only be broken and ground and reformed by the strongest and harshest of machinery. Unpitying poverty, absolute and severe want, must be allowed to force action, to sharpen instincts, to strengthen the will. War and pestilence must winnow the feeble races, lest they swarm in vile, unprofitable life.

Hence "God's method," with which Bascom seemed to be completely familiar, is the "melancholy work of scourging on the backs of the blind and perverse," and wisdom recognizes that "the loitering, unambitious poor still reserve for themselves the lash of necessity, are checked in increase . . . by hardship and disease, and left under the severe hand of physical law," which treats them "according to the dulness and sin that is in them." Hence

> outside philanthrophy finds itself in the dilemma of either robbing intelligence and industry of their reward . . . or of casting off the unworthy, hemming them in once more to the fruits of their folly, till the bitterness of sin shall aid in working its cure, and help to create an appetite for something better.

How foolish, he concluded, for "hasty philanthropy" to try to "undo by a trick of management and new relations the work of sin, and unbind its heavy burdens." [17]

Thus Christian charity came to be incased in a hard shell of sanctified realism that sought to protect it from foolishness. Nevertheless, the sheer existence of conditions in the growing industrial cities [18] increasingly consti-

---

[15] *Presbyterian Quarterly and Princeton Review*, II (January, 1873), 189.
[16] Wood, *op. cit.*, p. 226.
[17] Bascom, *op. cit.*; the quotations, in order, are from pp. 659, 662, 658.
[18] See, e.g., Wood, *op. cit.*, 218–19. For a contemporary account see May, *op. cit.*, chapter on "The Face of the City," pp. 112–24.

tuted a challenge to human decency as well as to Christian conscience, which made its impact. Walter Rauschenbusch, who apparently went to the Second German Baptist Church on West Forty-fifth Street in New York in 1886 to save individual souls, there found himself confronted with "the endless procession of men 'out of work, out of clothes, out of shoes, and out of hope,' that wore down the threshold and wore away the hearts of the sensitive young pastor and his wife." And no doubt this experience put him in a receptive mood to be awakened "to the world of social problems" by Henry George,[19] who was reminding the clergy that kindness, generosity, and other amiable virtues were no longer sufficient — that "what is needed is justice." [20]

In this situation and while at the same time the denominations were rapidly becoming "middle-class" in outlook and constituency, their social program was also challenged by the obvious loss of working people. This was a fact that could not be ignored, and many church leaders became concerned about it. "We make the statement without fear of contradiction, and therefore without apology," said Charles Wood in 1874, "that the poor are not provided for, nor are they wanted as a part of the congregations which worship in the majority of our city churches." And "this indifference," he thought, "taken in connection with that of the poor themselves to their own spiritual instruction, only shows the pitiable condition in which they are placed." [21] Even Henry Ward Beecher, although less obviously perturbed by it, recognized in 1874 that in "the average churches in New York and Brooklyn, from Murray Hill downward . . . it will be found that the aristocratic and prosperous elements have possession of them, and if the great under-class, the poor and needy, go to them at all, they go sparsely, and not as to a home." And, he added with surprising candor, "our churches are largely for the mutual insurance of prosperous families, and not for the upbuilding of the great under-class of humanity." [22]

Out of these factors created by the rise of great industrial cities came the many movements of charity and philanthropy and definite attempts to appeal to workers which are delineated so well by Aaron I. Abell in his study of *The Urban Impact on American Protestantism, 1865–1900.*[23] City rescue missions, homes of various kinds, the Salvation Army, the Volunteers of America, institutional churches, and a host of other instruments for meeting the situation were devised and grew apace. And these, in turn, had their effect. The efforts expended through them were somewhat successful in alleviating distress but were more important in holding significant numbers of

[19] Charles Howard Hopkins, *The Rise of the Social Gospel in American Protestantism, 1865–1915* (New Haven: Yale University Press, 1940), pp. 216, 217.

[20] May, *op. cit.*, p. 220.

[21] Wood, *op. cit.*, p. 224.

[22] Henry Ward Beecher, "Liberty in the Churches," *Plymouth Pulpit*, II (March–September, 1874) (New York: Fords, Howard & Hulbert, 1896), 209.

[23] Aaron I. Abell, *The Urban Impact on American Protestantism, 1865–1900* (Cambridge: Harvard University Press, 1943).

the workers. And the urban workers who were won and retained exerted an influence in the churches, since, as Abell says, "the wage-earning masses expected religion to establish ultimately a more equitable economic and industrial order." [24] And this, in turn, bolstered the emerging concern for social justice.

Nevertheless, as Henry May notes, "until they were shocked by a series of violent social conflicts, most Protestant spokesmen continued to insist that all was well." Until then, by those standing on the teleological escalator of progress," "greed at the top could be ignored or accepted as a tool of progress," while "misery at the bottom could be waved aside as inevitable or, at most, treated by a program of guarded and labeled philanthropy." [25]

The upheavals which challenged the magnificently complacent outlook of the period came out of the discontent smoldering in agriculture and labor. Speaking broadly, the woes of the farmer were attributable to the rapid industrialization of the country, with the attendant ascendance of a "business" mentality and the lure of "business-like" practices. This is the situation which a textbook writer discusses in the aptly titled chapter, "Capitalism Captures the Farmer," in which, after picturing the farmers' plight, he concludes that "in the placid language of economics this was marginal living; in the realistic language of life it meant futility and desperation." [26] Hamlin Garland, that exemplification of the sons of "the middle border" in revolt, used such realistic language in dedicating his *Main Travelled Roads*, published in 1891, to "my father and mother whose half century of pilgrimage on the main travelled road has brought them only pain and weariness." Out of the "pain and weariness," the "futility and desperation," came the somewhat mild and sporadic movements of "revolt" — the Grange movement (Patrons of Husbandry) of 1867 and following; Greenbackism in the middle of the seventies; the Farmers' Alliance movement following 1880; the merging of these movements in Populism (the Peoples' party) in 1891; and their final culmination in merger with the Bryan Democrats for the great "free-silver" campaign of 1896.

But Protestant spokesmen, as revealed in the religious press, actually gave these "manifestations of farmer unrest" relatively little attention. No doubt this was largely because their attention was centered upon the more spectacular uprisings of labor. The Bureau of Labor reported 23,798 strikes in the nineteen years from 1881 to 1900, involving 6,610,000 workers in 132,442 plants. Four of these strikes were particularly explosive and rocked the social structure to its foundations. First, the railroad strikes in 1877 — called by the author of *Raintree County* "another Sumpter" — which spread out over

[24] *Ibid.*, p. vii.
[25] May, *op. cit.*, p. 63.
[26] Loewenberg, in Ray A. Billington, Bert J. Loewenberg, and Samuel H. Brockunier, *The United States: American Democracy in World Perspective* (New York: Rinehart & Co., Inc., 1947), p. 358; hereafter cited as "B. L. & B."

the Pennsylvania, the Baltimore and Ohio, and the New York Central. Pitched battles involving workers, police, militia, and federal troops were fought in many cities; property damage was immense, and sober men had visions of mobocracy and revolution. Second was the "Haymarket affair" in Chicago. In a clash between pickets and police at the McCormick Harvester Plant early in May, 1886, six of the former were killed and several wounded. At a protest meeting held the following day in Haymarket Square a bomb was thrown which killed eight policemen and injured twenty-seven persons. The trial, which resulted in seven "anarchists" being condemned to death (four were hanged, one committed suicide, two were given life-imprisonment), revealed widespread alarm bordering on hysteria. Third was the great strike at the Carnegie Steel Plant in Homestead, Pennsylvania, in 1892, during which a battle between three hundred Pinkerton "detectives" and workers resulted in ten deaths and sixty wounded. This strike was finally ended only when eight thousand state militia were called out. Fourth was the great strike at the Pullman Palace Car Company in 1894, when President Cleveland — over the protests of Governor Altgeld of Illinois — sent two thousand federal troops to "guard the mails," and the injunction was effectively used against the unions. Henry May holds that "no strike had so alarmed the middle-class public" [27] — perhaps this was because the strikers cut their Pullman cars out of the trains.

Meanwhile, the depression of 1893 gripped the country — "in many ways . . . the most serious challenge of American political and economic institutions between the Civil War and the depression of 1929–37." [28] It was "a black year . . . with thousands upon thousands out of work, and want, and suffering and hopelessness to be seen everywhere." Revolution was scented when "bands of unemployed, of which 'General' Jacob S. Coxey's 'army' is the best known, descended upon Washington seeking redress and relief." [29]

Religious leaders were ideologically prepared, after a fashion, to meet even such unprecedented upheavals in the nation. Regarding strikes, John Bascom had argued that, while they represent "the simple assertion of a right" and therefore "cannot be condemned on moral and commercial grounds," yet they are "rarely necessary," because "the causes which justify a rise of wages will usually, by the inevitable laws of trade, quietly secure the result." Therefore, in those cases where "the clamor becomes loud and the measures violent," this fact alone is almost sufficient to mark "the absence . . . in the relation of the parties, of those grounds which render the claim just." [30] And in the midst of the troubles of 1893, Andrew Preston Peabody, who taught ethics and religion at Harvard, dismissed labor organizations with the remark: "That they are tolerated in what pretends to be a free country, or by

[27] May, *op. cit.*, p. 108.
[28] *Ibid.*, p. 107.
[29] B. L. & B., p. 450.
[30] Bascom, *op. cit.*, p. 678.

any government less barbarous than that of Dahomey or Ashantee, is to me an unsolvable mystery." [31]

We are not surprised to note that men of such preparation reacted first with amazement, hurt, and fear and cried out for the suppression of the "mobs." Not untypical were the comments of the *Christian Union* in 1877: "There are times when mercy is a mistake, and this is one of them," and the hysterical outburst of the *Independent:*

> If the club of the policeman, knocking out the brains of the rioter, will answer, then well and good; but if it does not promptly meet the exigency, then bullets and bayonets, canister and grape — with no sham or pretense, in order to frighten men, but with fearful and destructive reality — constitute the one remedy and the one duty of the hour. . . . Napoleon was right when he said that the way to deal with a mob was to exterminate it.

And as late as 1892 a writer in the *Christian Advocate* thought that the duty of "every patriot" was to "hope for the best, and say only those words which will tend to the maintenance of law," and meanwhile, "if he has any abstract theories for bettering the human race, this is no time to ventilate them." [32]

But by that time many religious leaders were already deeply troubled. "In the darkest hours of the Civil War," said a writer in the *New York Christian Advocate* in 1886, "we never felt more sober than today." [33] Even John Bascom had noted in 1868 that in the contest between capital and labor "employers, frequently few in number, can easily come to a tacit understanding without attracting public attention, and steadily resist the natural forces which are tending to press up the price of labor," while "the workmen, on the contrary . . . feel keenly the immediate necessity of continuing labor on the best terms they can make." [34] Hence, he had argued, "on any sudden inflation of prices laborers are sure to be relatively the losers," and, indeed, "in the years of [the Civil] war . . . profits in most branches

[31] Andrew Preston Peabody, "Wealth," *Andover Review*, XIX (May, 1893), 329. The September, 1877, issue of the *North American Review* carried an article by Thomas A. Scott, president of the Pennsylvania Railroad Company, entitled "The Recent Strikes" (CXXV, 351–62). Speaking of the railroad strikes in terms such as "a mob," "riot, arson, and bloodshed," and "insurrection" and arguing that "the conduct of the rioters is entirely inconsistent with the idea that this movement could have been directed by serious, right-minded men bent on improving the condition of the laboring classes," Mr. Scott suggested, first, the use of the injunction and, second, the systematic disposal of federal troops throughout the nation (pp. 359–61). The same issue (pp. 322–26) also carried an anonymous article signed "A 'Striker,'" and entitled "Fair Wages." Unlike the handling of the Scott article, the editor appended the following (p. 326): "Note. — In this case, as in all others, the Editor disclaims responsibility for the opinions of contributors, whether their articles are signed or anonymous."

[32] These quotations from the *Christian Union*, the *Independent*, and the *Christian Advocate* are taken from May, *op. cit.*, pp. 92–93, 105.

[33] *Ibid.*, p. 100.

[34] Bascom, *op. cit.*, p. 678.

of manufacture were very unusual; while the advance of wages, though considerable, by no means kept pace with the prices"; and hence "the condition of workmen became, and remains, more trying than before."

The first reaction of the editors of the *Congregationalist* to "The Strike at Homestead" was to compare the owners' hiring "the Pinkerton men . . . to shoot the strikers" to "lynchers . . . taking the law into their own hands" because "impatient of the slow processes of justice." Further, "some legal requirement and provision of arbitration" is "absolutely necessary," they argued, because "these great business enterprises, employing many thousands of men and affecting widely the interests of the people . . . are not merely private property." Therefore, the "skilled workmen" at Homestead "cannot rightly be dispossessed of their positions by mere arbitrary conditions imposed by their employers," any more than "a great corporation [can] be rightfully blocked in carrying on its business by the arbitrary demands of labor organizations." [35]

In the September, 1892, issue, the editors of the *Andover Review*, commenting on "the tragic events at Homestead," held that while "law and order" must be given "immediate and absolute precedence," nevertheless, "the maintenance of order in congested labor districts is not the settlement of the labor question." The question of the day, they continued, is that of the "personal rights in equity in the plant which the men had contributed so much to build up by their skill and character." For, contrary to Carnegie's "benevolent millionairism," the growth and "reputation of the Carnegie works . . . are due, not simply to the energy and business sagacity of the owners, not simply the enterprise in the managers, not simply to improved machinery, but equally to the cooperation of the skilled workmen employed." And while it may be legal, it just isn't equitable "whenever a question of work or wage arises, for the management to say, if you don't like the place you can quit."

Hence, the editors concluded, "there can be no further progress in the adjustment of labor and capital, and no permanent safety for the wage system, as the method of industrialism, until these rights in equity are in some way acknowledged." And unless they are, "the wage system will certainly and justly lose its place as the accredited method of industrial business, and something will be devised which will express in larger degree than wages the

[35] *Congregationalist*, LXXVII (July 14, 1892), 224, col. 4. In fairness it should be noted that on the first page of the same issue (p. 221, col. 6), the editors condemned the views allegedly expressed by Senator Palmer of Illinois as "nationalistic," and thought that, if enforced upon capital by law, they would "cause . . . temporary, if not permanent, disaster." Palmer was reputed to have said that "hereafter manufacturing establishments will have to be regarded as semipublic property, their owners to be regarded as holding the property subject to the correlative rights of those without whose services the property would be valueless. Laboring men are conscious of the right to continuous employment during good behavior. They will insist upon it. If employers have the right to hold over the heads of their employes the rod of dismissal American freedom will be gone."

interest of labor in the means and agencies of production." Finally, the editors muttered, in what sounds like a threat, if management continues to insist upon "legal rights" in the wage system "against rights in equity, the appeal will be taken to politics, and the appeal of industrialism to politics is the first and a long step toward State Socialism." [36] Here, then, were emerging cogent criticisms of the existing American way of life based on a rejection of some of the most sacred doctrines of the "gospel of wealth."

So far as the Protestant denominations were concerned, the significance of the great social upheavals was that they forced in many minds consideration of the question of the adequacy of "charity" as then understood and interpreted, either to guide the social program of the free churches or to suggest ways to meet the vast new problems of the industrialized civilization. "Do I mean to say that Christian philanthropy is a failure?" asked Charles Worcester Clark in an article published posthumously in 1893.[37] "Certainly not; only that the time has come earnestly to consider whether its field ought not to be extended so as to cover the cause of the evils it is already doing so much to alleviate." "Charity," he explained, "whether public or private, mainly deals with results, to mitigate effects; public action must be applied to the industrial system itself, in order to prevent a continuation of their causes." In brief, "our philanthropy must concern itself not only with private helpfulness, but with public reform and economic reorganization." This, he thought, will be objected to as "wholly unprecedented" by those who "do not even try to solve the social problem, save in the same old way," but "I merely contend that, in view of the industrial revolution wrought by science and invention during the past century, the burden of proof rests on those who maintain that the old ways are sufficient under the new conditions, no less than on those who demand a change."

In this general context we are better able to understand the great gulf between the views of John Bascom and Henry Ward Beecher and those of Francis Greenwood Peabody, professor of Christian morals at conservative Harvard, who in 1900 in a book called *Jesus Christ and the Social Question*, argued that "the social question of the present age is not a question of mitigating the evils of the existing order, but a question whether the existing order itself shall last. It is not so much a problem of social amelioration which occupies the modern mind, as a problem of social transformation

[36] "The Impending Question in the Industrial World," *Andover Review*, XVIII (September, 1892), 272–78.

[37] Charles W. Clark, "Applied Christianity: Who Shall Apply It First?" *Andover Review*, XIX (January, 1893), 20, 23, 24, 25. The editor, noting that the author "died in 1891, at the age of twenty-seven," held the article to be "typical of the aim of the better mind of his generation as the more earnest of our younger men are seeking to interpret Christianity to themselves and to their time." In the May issue, the *Review* carried an article by A. P. Peabody entitled "Wealth" (see n. 31) which has the appearance of being conceived by the author as a reply to Clark's article. Peabody is described in the recent history of the Harvard Divinity School as "a sage Unitarian . . . defender of a conservative version of the Liberal Faith."

and reconstruction." The demands, he continued, are "not patronage, but justice; not the general distribution of superfluous wealth, but the righteous restitution of wealth to those who have created it." [38] This indicates a mood or temper widely prevalent at the turn of the century, which is in sharp contrast to the prevailing ideology of the seventies and eighties wherein Protestant Christianity was largely amalgamated with the outlook of the burgeoning acquisitive society. It suggests the emergence of the so-called "social-gospel" movement in the denominations.

II

Meanwhile, referring to Schlesinger's thesis, the denominations' "system of thought" was also being challenged and shaken as never before in America, even during the heyday of "infidelity." For, concurrent with the social upheavals which attended the "economic revolution" and "industrial metamorphosis," [39] came the full impact of Darwinian evolutionary thinking, which appeared to strike at the very root of Christianity and all religion. Because it was posited upon the induction that "all life developed from pre-existing life," [40] evolutionism seemed to remove the creating Deity and his providence from the origin and direction of the world and to erase the created boundary between man and the other animals, placing all upon a continuum. This appeared to do away with the object of Christian devotion and to destroy the foundations of Christian ethics.[41]

It was this evolutionism which "germinated ideas wherever it penetrated, and it penetrated everywhere." [42] The so-called "new history," which appeared, was based upon the application of evolutionary theories to the understanding of the past, and the so-called "higher criticism" of the Bible was largely the application of the new history to the sacred volume.[43]

Evolutionary thinking was certainly nothing new in Western civilization, and its sudden sway in America is not accounted for simply by the convincing empirical documentation of Darwin and the persuasive universality of Spencer's systematization. It was a period of great changes in the structures of the culture, but it is "the rate rather than the fact of change [which] en-

[38] Francis G. Peabody, *Jesus Christ and the Social Question* (New York: Macmillan Co., reprinting, 1930; copyright, 1900), pp. 5, 6.

[39] Bert James Loewenberg, "Darwinism Comes to America, 1859–1900," *Mississippi Valley Historical Review*, XXVIII (December 1941), 342.

[40] *Ibid.*, p. 349.

[41] See W. H. Roberts, "The Reaction of the American Protestant Churches to the Darwinian Philosophy, 1860–1900" (Ph.D. dissertation, University of Chicago, March, 1936). Stow Persons discusses the way in which the theory of natural selection tended to undermine belief in design in *Evolutionary Thought in America*, of which he was the editor (New Haven: Yale University Press, 1950), pp. 425 ff.

[42] Loewenberg, *op. cit.*, p. 339.

[43] See, e.g., George H. Williams (ed.), *The Harvard Divinity School* (Boston: Beacon Press, 1954), pp. 169–72.

dows the forty years after 1860 with epochal attributes." [44] It was evolution-ary theories, sanctified by mingling with the traditional Christian doctrine of Providence, which spawned the general idea of "progress" and made the rapid change tolerable and even exhilarating. Hence its tremendous appeal and almost universal sway.

Evolutionary theories were an aspect of the world-view of modern science and at the time gave structure to its cosmology. Hence their tremendous appeal forced theology at last to try to come to terms intellectually with the world-view of modern science. Since the end of the eighteenth century the bulk of the Protestant denominations had cultivated scholastic orthodoxy, enlivened and more or less sentimentalized by pietistic revivalism *and* apart from the spirit and mind of modern civilization. The forcing of the issue by evolutionism was therefore, in effect, a forcing of the denominations to take up again the intellectual business laid on the table at the opening of the nineteenth century and largely ignored during the intervening busy years of institutional proliferation and growth. Now the issue between science and theology could no longer be ignored. And the pathetic nature of the de-nominations' position is revealed in the fact that when in 1926, in Dayton, Tennessee, "twelve unlettered hill-men were constituted a jury to decide the most momentous issue of modern thought," Tom Stewart, the public prosecutor, could ask in all seriousness — "Who says we can't bar science that deprives us of all hope of the future life to come?" [45] There indeed is the place for tears.

Struck by what appeared to be mutiny in the social and economic areas at the very time when ideological winds were sweeping them from their old theological anchorages, the denominations seemed in danger of floundering. Derisive gods might have found grounds for sardonic laughter in the situa-tion. The social outlook of the denominations was hard pressed during this period because it was too "modern" — too immediately immersed in the contemporary outlook, while their theology was hit because it was too "ancient," too out of touch with the modern currents of thought, too anachronistic.

The two challenges, to return to Schlesinger's terms, went hand in hand.[46] The bourgeoning industrial system created the great cities, which became the centers for the development and easy dissemination of new knowledge and havens for the new religious, social, and economic heretics. Meanwhile, some of the denominationally supported educational institutions, including church-related seminaries, were reaping a harvest from the acquisitive, ex-ploitive, middle-class social structure in the form of large gifts from Car-negie's peculiarly endowed individuals who, willy-nilly, accumulated wealth.

[44] Loewenberg, *op. cit.*, p. 341.
[45] Gaius Glenn Atkins, *Religion in Our Times* (New York: Round Table Press, Inc., 1932), pp. 249–51.
[46] Loewenberg in the article cited in n. 39 spells this out in some detail.

Such gifts, by making these schools financially independent of their denominations, had the effect of freeing their administrations and professors from direct denominational control. This, of course, was not entirely unappreciated. Thus one suspects a bit of existential involvement in the statement of Andrew Preston Peabody, Professor at Harvard, that his "intercourse with rich men has been such as to make me thank God for them, and deprecate with my whole soul the leveling doctrines" now abroad in the land, especially since on the next page he notes the number of schools and professorships such men had endowed.[47]

Thus at just the time when so many young men from America were imbibing "advanced" theological ideas in the German universities and returning to teaching positions in the theological schools of America, these schools had opened before them the possibility of freeing their professors from church discipline. Hence in several instances, when denominations attempted to censure or discipline "heretical" professors, their schools, in effect, declared their independence from such churchly control.

This permitted the cultivation in America of "modern" or "liberal" approaches to the several disciplines in the theological schools which were not necessarily responsibly related to the churches at all and were always in danger of becoming preciously exotic and even contemptuous of the denominations' level of enlightenment. This helps to explain why the controversy between sciences and theology in America was not settled when and because a handful of such professors in the seminaries accepted evolutionism, any more than it was settled when and because several outstanding, but practically independent, ministers, such as Henry Ward Beecher and his worthy successor, Lyman Abbott, decided in sweet reasonableness that it was "God's way of doing things."

When they were forced at last to consider the complex theoretical and practical issues between science and theology, the religious leaders reacted according to their individual lights, which in turn (to mix the metaphor) depended upon the theological stream or tradition in which they were immersed.

One can distinguish clearly enough for our purposes three outstanding strands in American Protestant thought during this period.[48] The first was traditional orthodoxy or biblical authoritarianism, which provided what Hopkins aptly calls the "frozen foundation of complacency" characteristic of "conventional, institutionalized, orthodox Protestantism." [49] It was frankly supernaturalistic in outlook, and it maintained a solid core of doctrine. But it had long been conditioned and modified by pietism and revival-

---

[47] Carnegie, *op. cit.*, pp. 327–28.
[48] Compare E. E. Aubrey, "Religious Bearings of the Modern Scientific Movement," in J. T. McNeill *et al.* (eds.), *Environmental Factors in Christian History* (Chicago: University of Chicago, 1939), pp. 361–79.
[49] Hopkins, *op. cit.*, p. 14.

ism, and the doctrinal outlines might be fuzzy, except in such uncorruptedly staunch men as Charles Hodge, professor of theology at Princeton from 1822 to 1878, who possessed an uncanny ability to reduce the profound complexities of the Christian walk in the modern world to a kind of rough-hewn, orthodox simplicity.

In general, the men in this tradition met the challenge to their way of thinking with pietistic indifference, with strong dogmatic denials, or with open contempt, as when Hodge declared that "we can even afford to acknowledge our incompetence to meet them in argument, or to answer their objections; and yet our faith remains unshaken and rational." [50] They tended to meet the challenges to the churches' social program first with surprise and anger and then with increased efforts through charity. By and large, they were slow and reluctant to criticize the social system and inclined to be critical of those who did.

The second strand was that of romantic liberalism — or "progressive religion" [51] — which was rooted in philosophic idealism and appealed in one way or another to intuition. The romantic movement in America during the early nineteenth century spawned transcendentalism among New England Unitarians, which, for this reason, was two steps removed from the main stream of American Protestantism. Hence the descendants of transcendentalism in America have, by and large, been outside the regular denominations. To be sure, Unitarianism later digested Emerson and even Parker — under pressures from the ill-fated Free Religious Association organized in 1867.[52] But the real religious descendants of the transcendentalist movement in America would seem to be the host of "cults" bred of the "new-thought" movement, whose thought has only recently been slipping into the Protestant churches through the back door [53] and may result in revolutionary changes.

Meanwhile, the comet's tail of romanticism swept across Horace Bushnell in the fold of "orthodoxy" as defined in Connecticut-centered Congregational Calvinism, and, as Perry Miller has suggested, with Bushnell this "Calvinism itself was, as it were, transcendentalized." [54] Granted this, perhaps the most significant thing Bushnell did, so far as the immediate future

[50] Charles Hodge, "Inspiration," *Princeton Review*, XXIX (1857), 662.

[51] See, for example, John Wright Buckham, *Progressive Religious Thought in America: A Survey of the Enlarging Pilgrim Faith* (New York: Houghton Mifflin Co., 1919).

[52] See Stow Persons, *Free Religion: An American Faith* (New Haven: Yale University Press, 1947).

[53] For a treatment of transcendentalism as a religious movement see Perry Miller's Introduction in his *The Transcendentalists: An Anthology* (Cambridge: Harvard University Press, 1950). In my review of this work I stressed the relationship of transcendentalism to the present "cults" (*Journal of Religion*, XXXI [January, 1951], 52–54). For a sympathetic treatment of these "cults" see Charles S. Braden, *These Also Believe* (New York: Macmillan Co., 1949). In my review of this book I pointed out how New Thought was beginning to invade the Protestant churches (*Journal of Religion*, XXX [April, 1950], 142–44).

[54] Perry Miller, "Jonathan Edwards to Emerson," *New England Quarterly*, XIII (December, 1940), 616.

of American Protestantism was concerned, was to maintain this position within "orthodox" Congregationalism, which gradually over the years managed to digest this form of romanticized orthodoxy. In the long view, Emerson and Bushnell represent aspects of the same religious movement in America, but, thanks to Bushnell, it took root in the denominations and flowered as "liberalism."

For Bushnell the central problem of his early life was that of the relationship between the dogmatic formulations of his inherited orthodoxy and the world of science. Thus torn, as he put it, between his head and his heart, he chose to follow his heart; and finally his solution "came to him at last, after all his thought and study, not as something reasoned out, but as an inspiration, — a revelation from the mind of God himself." He had experienced the direct, intuitive perception of "the Gospel" — of "God in Christ." [55] For him this was the Christian experience and, as such, was as real and unassailable as were all other direct perceptions.

This it was that provided succeeding generations of romantic liberals in American Protestantism a basis for Christian faith that could not be harmed by all the "acids of modernity." Men of this sentiment during the nineteenth century moved in one of two possible directions in meeting the challenge of science to theology: they might "abstract religion from the realm of scientific verification" — and hence of criticism — or they might "claim for the data of religious experience the same scientific status as the data of the physical sciences and build thereon an empirical science of theology." [56] Hence the doctrine of immanence became central — God was seen as revealing himself through all of history, and religion as "the gradually developed experiences of men who had some perception of the infinite in nature and in human life." [57]

Men in this tradition faced evolutionism with an equanimity of soul that bordered on the blasé, as witness Lyman Abbott's *Theology of an Evolutionist*, published in 1897. Beginning with a romantic teleology, they produced a facile harmonization of science with Christianity over which one's mind may glide unruffled by any angularities of meaning. But perhaps because their minds were unshackled from tradition (we are "to look for our experience of God in our own times and in our own souls," said Abbott) [58] and because they believed in developmental progress and because, rooted in

---

[55] [Mary Bushnell Cheney], *Life and Letters of Horace Bushnell* (New York: Harper & Bros., 1880), pp. 56, 192. *God in Christ: Three Discourses Delivered at New Haven, Cambridge, and Andover* was published at Hartford (Brown & Parsons) in 1849. It contains the famous "Dissertation on Language."

[56] Aubrey, *op. cit.*, p. 368. Compare Lyman Abbott, *Reminiscences* (New York: Houghton Mifflin Co., 1915), p. 451, where he says he could disregard "the scientific arguments for Christian truth" and appeal "directly to human experience and . . . find evidence for Christianity in the hearts and consciousnesses of my hearers," for "the foundation of spiritual faith is neither in the church nor in the Bible, but in the spiritual consciousness of man."

[57] Abbott, *op. cit.*, p. 461.

[58] *Ibid.*

Bushnell, they retained a sense of the importance of nurture in a community and hence were sensitive to the ill effects of adverse environments, when men in this tradition faced the challenge to the churches' social program they tended to become social critics and even prophets. Commonly it is these men, of whom Washington Gladden is an outstanding example, who come to mind when we think of the "social gospel."

The third strand to be noted is that of scientific modernism — the way of building "a religion out of the materials furnished by the several sciences." [59] Perhaps this position was most pithily put by Shailer Mathews in his *The Faith of Modernism*,[60] when he said that modernism "is the use of the methods of modern science to find, state and use the permanent and central values of inherited orthodoxy in meeting the needs of a modern world." Of course, at this time "science" included the burgeoning disciplines of "scientific" psychology, sociology, anthropology, and history.

While romantic liberalism seems to have been characteristic of ministers in the churches, scientific modernism was the forte of professors in the schools. Men in this stream adopted evolutionism as a scientific hypothesis, on the basis of which they became socio-historians, developed the psychology and sociology of religion, or expounded a "scientific" philosophy of religion that threatened sometimes to crowd Christian theology out of the seminaries. When they faced the social crisis, they tended to maintain a proper "scientific" objectivity — became "social scientists" or sociologists, and, under the compelling impulsion of the "endeavor to reach beliefs and their application in the same way that chemists or historians reach and apply their conclusions," [61] they tended to abandon normative pretensions and become increasingly descriptive. One of their characteristic "social" products was the kind of settlement houses which were founded as middle-class outposts in the urban slums, where students might become acquainted at first hand with the life of the lower classes and study conditions among the denizens of these modern jungles,[62] perhaps even salvaging some wrecked lives.

Each of these strands had origins far back in the history of America and, indeed, of Christendom, and, of course, on the generally amorphous topography of the American religious mind they did not run as discrete streams. They crossed and recrossed in complex ways in different individuals and groups. Elements of each were mingled in ever changing kaleidoscopic patterns by the host of highly individualistic thinkers. Nevertheless, the strands are definable — these traditions existed in the American Protestant churches,

---

[59] Aubrey, *op. cit.*, p. 368.

[60] Shailer Mathews, *The Faith of Modernism* (New York: Macmillan Co., 1924), p. 23.

[61] *Ibid.*

[62] Compare B. J. Loewenberg, in B. L. & B., p. 425; "The settlement houses were remedial agencies devoted to the salvage of wrecked lives, but they gave scarcely any attention to the economic whirlpools that produced social catastrophe." However, "conceived as laboratories for social workers . . . they came to be infinitely more."

and no doubt parties would have grown up around them in the denominations in any case. But the impact of evolutionism accentuated their differences by giving them a common center of interest — or of opposition — and led to controversies that, in general, augmented the prevailing ideological turmoil. However that may be, it is clear that when the denominations' way of thinking and social program were challenged, there was a great deal of confusion in Protestant theology in America, and Schlesinger's "organized religion" was by no means a massive unity either organizationally or ideologically.

In 1881 Daniel Dorchester, noting the several signs of "religious progress," enthused that "theology is less scholastic and repulsive, has less of pagan adulteration, has been lubricated and broadened, and is better for its siftings." [63] But from the standpoint of the mid-twentieth century the lubrication appears less salutary, and we are more inclined to agree with H. S. Commager that "during the nineteenth century and well into the twentieth, [organized] religion prospered while theology went slowly bankrupt." [64]

III

If we look into this extremely complex situation for one central thread upon which to string our interpretation, I think we find it in the change of attitude toward laissez faire individualism rooted in the doctrine of automatic harmony,[65] which was then taking place. In the September 8, 1892, issue, the *Congregationalist*, in quoting Professor H. C. Adams, of the University of Michigan, with tacit approval, struck the keynote of the changing time: "Modern economy has . . . made the mistake of assuming that free competition would guarantee just exchanges and hence realize industrial jus-

[63] Dorchester, *op. cit.*, p. 41.

[64] H. S. Commager, *The American Mind* (New Haven: Yale University Press, 1950), p. 165. The "bankruptcy" of theology among the Congregationalists is made explicit, for example, by Washington Gladden in his *Recollections*, published in 1909. "My theology," he noted (p. 163), "had to be hammered out on the anvil for daily use in the pulpit. The pragmatic test was the only one that could be applied to it: 'Will it work?' " He recalled with relish that Dr. John Todd, moderator of the council which installed him in the church in North Adams, in 1866 "skillfully conducted the examination over ground on which there was no chance of discussion, and after about twenty minutes, brought it to an abrupt conclusion. It was a palpable evasion, but I was not responsible for it. 'I thought,' said Dr. Todd to me after the examination, 'that you were a great heretic.' 'Perhaps I am,' I answered, 'but you didn't bore in the right place' " (p. 168).

Finally, he notes with obvious approval that, in the "creed" drawn up by the "committee of twenty-five" in 1883, "all the distinctively Calvinistic dogmas . . . were eliminated; there was no formal doctrine of the Trinity . . . election, in the Calvinistic sense, was not in it, nor was original sin, nor Biblical infallibility; and the sufferings of Christ on the cross were described as his 'sacrifice of himself' " (p. 288).

[65] See Paul Tillich, "The World Situation," in H. P. Van Dusen (ed.), *The Christian Answer* (New York: Charles Scribner's Sons, 1945). This change of attitude is exemplified in Washington Gladden, *Recollections* (Boston: Houghton Mifflin Co., 1909), pp. 295–97.

tice." But "the trust in free competition has failed to realize the Christian idea of fair exchange." [66] Even more pointed was the statement of Charles Worcester Clark in the article quoted earlier: "In the early part of this century . . . the conditions essential for the justification of the *laissez faire* theory of political economy were present: freedom to move from place to place, and from industry to industry, wherever the best chance offered." But "that fair field for individual merit to prove itself and win its due reward has been our pride so long that it is hard to believe it gone. But it is gone." [67] And some clergymen, at least, were canny enough to take the attitude expressed by Washington Gladden: "If the old order changeth giving place to new, we may as well have our eyes open to what is going on and make our peace with the new order on the best possible terms." [68]

If it be asked what was the "cause" of the extremely rapid change that was taking place, the reply must be that the important thing was modern science — science as an outlook or way of thinking — and the consequent technological development.[69] It was science in these senses that transformed the outward face of human living more in about two generations than had been the case in all the previous centuries. It was this that Woodrow Wilson had in mind when he told the members of the G.A.R. in 1915 that "the nation in which you now live is not the nation for whose union you fought." And Henry Adams had already muttered, "My country in 1900 is something totally different from my own country in 1860."

On the technological side, the symbol of the science which created this new world came to be the "machine," which may stand broadly for the instruments created by man for the control and use of physical nature. In this, man was tremendously successful — so successful, indeed, that modern man's fears are not primarily his fears of "nature," of epidemic disease, earthquake, wind, flood, and fire. Rather, modern man's fears are those of the "machine" he somehow created, which seemed to take on a life of its own, becoming the monster of Frankenstein. Henry Adams pictured the predicament of modern man as that of the creator of the "Dynamo" who has inadvertently grasped the two poles and can thereafter neither let go nor control his own actions.[70] Now the flower and hence the symbol of the "machine" was the modern city, the product of technological industrialism.

[66] *Congregationalist*, p. 289, col. 5.

[67] Clark, *op. cit.*, p. 20.

[68] Washington Gladden, "A Question That Ought To Be Settled," *Congregationalist*, LXXVII (July 28, 1892), 237, col. 3.

[69] Compare William Adams Brown, *The Church in America* (New York: Macmillan Co., 1922), p. 141: "There are two ways in which modern science has affected the task of the church. It has affected it as pure science by its challenge to the assumptions on which the older theology is based. It has affected it even more profoundly as applied science by the changes which it has brought about in the external environment in which the church must work."

[70] Compare Charles A. and Mary R. Beard, *The Rise of American Civilization*, Vol. IV: *The American Spirit* (New York: Macmillan Co., 1948), p. 18.

And the problems created by the machine were accentuated and seen in relief in the urban centers.

Hence during this period of increasing recognition of the Frankenstein possibilities of the "machine" — of the sense that increasing control of physical nature was paralleled by decreasing control of the "machine" — probably the most common way of stating the basic problem of the age was to say that it was the problem of control. Looking back from the vantage point of 1909, Washington Gladden recalled how, as early as 1860, "the amount of titanic energy which was even then finding vent in the life of . . . greater New York" impressed upon him "a vivid sense of the impersonality and brutality of the whole movement, of the lack of coordinating intelligence," and placed one in a position where one

> could not help wondering whether in liberating the force which gathers men into cities, and equipping it with steam and electricity, a power had not been created which was stronger than the intelligence which seeks to control it; whether such aggregations of humanity, with wills no better socialized than those of the average nineteenth-century American, are not by their own action self-destructive.[71]

In September, 1892, the editors of the *Congregationalist* approved Professor H. C. Adams' statement of the question: "The monopoly problem of today is really this — shall organized industry, with its positive benefits and great possibilities, be directed for personal or for public ends?" And "shall this tremendous industrial power be in the arbitrary control of individuals, or be exercised under conditions of responsibility?" [72]

This way of looking at things became widespread during the last quarter of the nineteenth century and, broadly speaking, gave shape and meaning to "the social question" and defined for many the nature of the crisis. An English writer, surveying in 1901 "a century's progress in religious life," summed it up very well: "The first half of the [19th] century was individualistic; the second half has tended to become collectivistic. Freedom was the earlier ideal, brotherhood is the latter." For "the policy of *laissez-faire* is thought to have broken down, and the State is repeatedly called upon to take over and control the interests of the Community." [73]

---

[71] Gladden, *op. cit.*, pp. 90–91. It is interesting to note that Gladden, who frankly advocated overhead control of the social and economic realms (see p. 314), as frankly indorsed the regnant anarchistic Congregational individualism in theological and ecclesiastical affairs. "It had come to be recognized as Congregational doctrine," he said with reference to the "creed" of 1883, "that no ecclesiastical body existed, or could be created, with power to frame such a creed and impose it upon the churches — each church, by the primary Congregational principle, having the right to make its own creed" (p. 287).

[72] "The Monopoly Problem," *Congregationalist*, LXXVII (September 8, 1892), 289, col. 5.

[73] Walter F. Adeney, *A Century's Progress in Religious Life and Thought* (London: James Clarke & Co., 1901), p. 183.

IV

Now then, the so-called "social-gospel" movement must be seen within the broad context of this widespread sentiment that the social problem was that of instrumenting planned social and economic controls in the interests of justice and that this would involve a revolution in thinking and attitudes as well as in practice. There would have to be such a change in thinking and attitudes because the mind that had so successfully created the "machine" and which was still predominant was individualistic and laissez faire and hence constitutionally opposed to planning and control in the social and economic spheres. Further, these attitudes had accumulated powerful pragmatic and religious sanctions.

Recognition that there was a "social question" was almost universal. A. I. Abell makes the point that so large did it loom over the denominations' life that, for the time at least, doctrinal, creedal, and polity questions both within and between denominations tended to be subordinated. Even the Episcopalians, he notes, toned down or dropped their differences to make the keynote of their General Convention in 1880 " 'not the restatement of dogma, but the urgency of Christian work.' " [74] All, of course, did not accept the view of the nature of the "social question" noted above. *The social-gospel movement was the response in the denominations on the part of those who did.* This seems to be the one common characteristic useful in defining what "movement" there was.

This is to suggest that the social-gospel movement cannot be defined theologically or institutionally. It was never incorporated in any independent new organizations; it did not result in any new denominations. The theologies associated with the movement were many and as diverse as the diverse and individualistic religious pattern in America could provide. Indeed, down at least to the 1930's, theology in relation to the movement was in a real sense fortuitous and instrumental. It was, in reality, a movement in the denominations looking for theological roots.

Walter Rauschenbusch recognized this clearly enough in opening his *Theology for the Social Gospel* published in 1917, with the statement that "we have a social gospel. We need a systematic theology large enough to match it and vital enough to back it." Therefore, as he says, he devoted the first three chapters to the attempt "to show that a readjustment and expansion of theology so that it will furnish an adequate intellectual basis for the social gospel, is necessary, feasible, desirable and legitimate."

To be sure, the general situation we have described tended to give the movement a kind of theological complexion. The leaders found that the prevailing individualistic outlook of pietistic revivalism and the "gospel of wealth" rooted in traditional orthodoxy was not a congenial atmosphere for

[74] Abell, *op. cit.*, pp. 16–17.

their views, and hence they were almost forced into the paths of the burgeoning reconstructive movement in theology. The "social gospel" became the church party platform of all "progressives," "liberals," or "modernists" — of all those movements that represented attempts to come to terms with the ideas and spirit of modern civilization while maintaining continuity with the Christian tradition. There was never the one-to-one relationship suggested by G. G. Atkins however: "The 'social gospel' and liberal theology were as interlocking as were the 'old gospel,' economic conservatism and a general despair of the future of the world." [75] This situation tended to place leadership of the movement in the hands of informed people, the educated, those in the churches who were most in touch with current intellectual life, and hence to give the movement itself an "eggheadish" aspect which was to prove a fertile seed bed for opposition in the denominations.

Once the concern for social reconstruction in the interests of equity and justice became widespread among individuals, two factors in the religious situation in America became very important in shaping the emerging movement. The first was the nature of the denominations as voluntary associations. This meant that any man who could gain a pulpit and the backing of a local congregation, a denominational post, or even a professorship had a secure platform from which to speak and propagandize. Hence all views were bound to be aired.

Further, every such concern or idea, in order to live and have power in a denomination, had to be incarnated in a movement, and eventually the drive of the movement had to be to capture the denominational machinery itself. Finally, since the evangelistic or missionary enterprise was central in each denomination, it was recognized that those who could define its nature would control the denomination's life. Hence the movement generated the drive to shift the conception of the evangelistic work of the churches from individualistic revivalism to social reconstruction — and its success in this respect should not be underestimated. "It is true the work of the Church has been markedly individualistic," a speaker patiently explained to Plymouth Church, Brooklyn, New York, in 1897, but now changed conditions have served "to make it alive to its social obligations and duties." This, he thought, was "the difference between *remedial* Christianity and *preventive* Christianity." "That is to say, the social work of the Church in the past . . . has been to remedy the effects of evils which have been left to work themselves out and multiply themselves in fresh evil effects." However, "to-day the Church has aroused itself to this: it is our business to strike deeper, to get at the roots of these evils and remove them, — and then we shall be under no necessity to remedy their effects." [76]

The second important factor was the theological confusion and turmoil

[75] Atkins, *op. cit.*, p. 230.
[76] Charles A. Berry, "Retrospect and Outlook," in Rossiter W. Raymond (ed.), *The New Puritanism* (New York, 1898), pp. 245–46.

that prevailed — or, perhaps better, "the absence of theology in the supreme sense of that word," as George A. Gordon suggested in 1897,[77] at the time when the "acids of modernity" were eating away the possibility of religious belief in the traditional sense. However, people thus set afloat, mentally and spiritually, could still cling to belief in "Christian" work which was relevant to immediate situations. For those religiously adrift, there was assurance and comfort to be found in the thought that perhaps the Christian could not go too far astray when feeding the hungry, clothing the naked, visiting the sick and imprisoned, giving the cup of cold water for Christ's sake. Perhaps it was never formulated in just this fashion, but one profound appeal of the social-gospel movement was that it made possible for many idealistic Americans continued belief in Christianity "for the work's sake." No doubt what many nominally Christian people really came to believe in was the work of social betterment and renovation.

In order to understand the sweep and scope of the movement in the denominations, it is helpful to see it through the eyes of one of its most active leaders in the years just before the first World War. Writing the Foreword for his book *Christianizing the Social Order* in October, 1912, Walter Rauschenbusch gave as one reason for such a work that "outsiders misjudge the part which the churches are taking in the impending social transformation because they are ignorant of the quiet revolution that is going on in the spirit and aims of the American churches." Indeed, "few, probably, even of those who are taking an active part in their social awakening, realize fully the far-reaching importance of this great historic movement." There was taking place, he thought, "a great change" in "the life of this nation," which he compared to an individual's experience of conversion and interpreted as "the stirring of God in the souls of men." Among "the people in the churches, who have long been consciously religious, the new thing is the social application of their religious life." For the old current of their religion is pouring into a broader channel of social purpose, and running with swift flow toward the achievement of public justice and love." Indeed, this is increasingly felt to be "the great business of religion."

Rauschenbusch was elated at the change that had taken place. He could, as he said, look back to the time before 1900, which "pioneers of Christian social thought in America" recalled "as a time of lonesomeness [when] we were few and we shouted in a wilderness." But since 1900, he thought, "the able ministers who were not already physically or mentally old by 1900, and who were not rendered impervious by doctrinal rubbercasting of some kind, have been permeated by the social interest almost in a body," until, today, "perhaps the most convincing proof of the spread of the social interest in the ministry is the fact that the old men and the timid men are falling in line." But what pleased him most of all perhaps was that "the social interest in

[77] *Ibid.*, p. 143.

the Church has now run beyond the stage of the solitary pioneer. It has been admitted within the organizations of the Church." Indeed, as C. Howard Hopkins puts it, social Christianity had become "official." [78] For between 1901, when the General Convention of the Protestant Episcopal Church and the National Council of Congregational Churches "took preliminary action leading toward official social-service programs," and 1912, when Rauschenbusch was writing, all the great denominations took official action through the creation of boards, committees, councils, and so on — of social action.[79] Outstanding was the Methodist Federation for Social Service, organized in Washington, D.C., in December, 1907, as "an effort to apply the sane and fervid spirit of Methodism to the social needs of our time." [80]

The "climax of the official recognition of social Christianity was attained in the organization of the Federal Council of the Churches of Christ in America in 1908." In 1912 it adopted its famous "social creed," patterned after the Methodist "creed" of 1908.[81] Hopkins concludes that perhaps social Christianity reached its popular peak with the Men and Religion Forward Movement of 1911–12 — the very time when Rauschenbusch was writing. This movement Hopkins describes as "the most comprehensive evangelistic effort ever undertaken in the United States," and, he adds, it was "virtually converted . . . into a social gospel campaign." [82] Rauschenbusch had concluded in 1912 that "the movement has probably done more than any other single agency to lodge the social gospel in the common mind of the church." [83]

It is indicated that the social-gospel movement was one of great proportions in the denominations on the eve of the first World War. A revolution in outlook was taking place in the churches, which is epitomized in the comment of an English writer: "A hundred years ago the dominant idea in religion was the salvation of the individual soul; to-day it is the redemption of society." "Formerly," he added, "it was said that attendance at the weekly prayer meeting was the test of the vitality of a church; now we look for the gauge in its social activities." However, "there is no need for these to supersede the prayer meeting," although "it is now the case that the Church best reveals the energy of its spiritual life by the self-sacrificing devotion of its social work." [84]

Keeping in mind that an important aspect of the background of this social-gospel movement in the denominations was a reaction against the

[78] Hopkins, *op. cit.*, chap. xvii, pp. 280–301.
[79] *Ibid.*, p. 284.
[80] *Ibid.*, p. 289.
[81] *Ibid.*, pp. 302, 316–17.
[82] *Ibid.*, p. 296.
[83] Walter Rauschenbusch, *Christianizing the Social Order* (New York: Macmillan Co., 1914), p. 20.
[84] Adeney, *op. cit.*, pp. 171, 186.

individualism of pietistic revivalism and the amalgamation of Protestant Christianity with the social outlook of industrial capitalism helps us to understand how and why the movement tended to swing to the opposite extremes of substituting social concern for individual Christian experience and commitment; of identifying the Christian gospel with current schemes for reconstructing society; of judging the work of the Christian church on the basis of its effectiveness in furthering social work and social renovation; of substituting sociology for theology. How far this tendency ran it would be very difficult to ascertain. That it existed is beyond question, and it suggests the emergence of a new syncretistic outlook in reaction against that of the "gospel of wealth" era. By around 1932 the "informed" and "liberal" Protestant clergyman in America was about as blindly a Democrat or Socialist as his predecessor around 1885 had been a Republican.

V

It is against this background that we are to understand the emergence and development of the so-called "fundamentalist movement" in the denominations. Most simply, it is to be seen as the movement generated in opposition to the tendencies of the social-gospel movement noted earlier; and, by the same token, it was as broad, complex, and amorphous as its opponent.

The rise of self-conscious "liberal" or "modernist" movements — meaning thereby all the various attempts to reconcile Christian thinking and practice with the spirit and mind of the modern world — indicates that many people were being torn loose from traditional formulations of belief. And there was generated in some of them, as they sensed that they were being set adrift on uncharted waters, a strong tendency to cling to what appeared to be steadfast and sure.

On the one hand, then, fundamentalism was a genuinely "conservative" movement in the denominations — that is, a movement whose intention was to conserve the truly valuable elements of Christian tradition — to conserve continuity with historic Christianity in a way that common folk in the churches could understand. The sound, positive sentiment of fundamentalism was that the basis for the Christian church ought to be recognizable Christian experience and belief, explained and defended systematically in a theology having direct continuity with the Christian past. But, on the other hand, the movement was, as the self-styled "liberals" liked to see it, a movement of recalcitrant resistance to the ideas and spirit of the modern world — a truly reactionary movement spearheaded by what Shailer Mathews is reputed to have called his "contemporary theological ancestors." The fundamentalist was one who, being swept willy-nilly into the currents of modern life, grasped desperately and usually uncritically at whatever seemed able to stand immovable in the general flood.

In a sense the fundamentalist was more theologically minded than his liberal opponent. But so desperate was he to defend and preserve his parochial view of Christian belief that he tended to suspect and to by-pass thinking completely and to assert on the basis of supported traditional authority what was conceived to be essential to the being of a Christian and a church. The so-called "fundamentals" [85] that were asserted were not theological at all, but pretheological assumptions — and, by the same token, they were to be posttheological. The "fundamentals" were the firmly planted posts that defined the limits of the corral in which Christianity was to be fenced, and whatever thinking was to be permitted was limited to placing the bars between these posts.

This attitude was, of course, contrary to the whole spirit and mind of the modern world. Therefore, it was natural for evolution to become the theological shibboleth (or perhaps I ought to say "sibboleth" — see Judges, chap. 12) of the movement. For evolutionism was the symbol of the modern mind. Hence, as E. E. Aubrey put it, the fundamentalist attacks on the Darwinian theory of evolution are not merely superstitious recalcitrance. "They are based on sound suspicions that to yield an inch is to expose the citadel of their system to destruction." For "it is not merely the origin of man which is involved but the scientific approach as such; and the evolutionary point of view spells destruction to dogmatic finality." [86]

It is suggested, then, that the fundamentalist movement is to be seen as the movement generated in opposition to real and/or supposed tendencies in the social-gospel movement which was sweeping through the denominations on the eve of World War I. It was, on the one hand, soundly based — its essential sentiment was right. But, rooted in that side of American Protestantism that had never come to terms with the currents of the modern world, its theology and modes of thinking were so obsolete and anachronistic that it soon lost (if it had ever had) the appearance of intellectual leadership and constituency. The tragedy is that, in intelligence and imagination, real religious conservatism was about as bankrupt at the time as political conservatism appears to be today. All its checks drawn on pietistic revivalism and literalistic orthodoxy bounced. For this reason the fundamentalist movement became (as all conservative movements lacking imagination and intelligent leadership become) merely a political power-group movement in the denominations. One prototype of all American fundamentalists is the Congregational minister in Connecticut, who more than a hundred years ago told Lyman Beecher and Nathaniel W. Taylor — the

[85] Although the statement of "fundamentals" varied somewhat, the following six would usually be included: the inerrancy of Scripture in every detail; the deity of Jesus; the virgin birth; the substitutionary theory of the atonement; the physical resurrection; the imminent, bodily return of Jesus to earth (see Steward G. Cole, *The History of Fundamentalism* [New York: Richard R. Smith, Inc., 1931], and Norman F. Furniss, *The Fundamentalist Controversy, 1918–1931* [New Haven: Yale University Press, 1954]).

[86] Aubrey, *op. cit.*, p. 375.

current "liberals" — "I may not be able to think and argue as well as you can, but I know what the people in the churches — the constituency — will stand." And he did. And he created a great deal of trouble.

Fundamentalism is, I suppose, as old as Christianity. But the historians of what we call the fundamentalist movement in America commonly trace its origins to Bible, prophecy, and premillennialism conferences in the 1870's. But the crystallization of such a definable power movement in the denominations, as we have noted, may conveniently be dated with the publication of the twelve small volumes of *The Fundamentals* between 1909 and 1912. It is significant that this is precisely the period of the height of the social-gospel movement. Publication of these volumes was financed by two laymen, and by the time that the twelfth volume had appeared it was claimed that some three million copies had been distributed to religious leaders all over the world — about one million outside the United States.

In 1919 the World Christian Fundamentals Association was formed, because "it was no longer deemed sufficient to carry on a general propaganda through conservative interdenominational agencies, but the denominational machinery must now be captured for the same end." [87]

It is unnecessary to rehearse the movement in each of the denominations. Essentially, the aims of the movement were the same in each; the strategies and techniques varied largely according to the general cultural level of the group and the form of church polity. In each denomination the fundamentalists attempted to gain control of theological education, the missionary enterprises of the group, and the denominational machinery and to affirm and impose doctrinal standards that would successfully exclude those who did not accept the "fundamentals."

Fundamentalism did not actually win in any denomination. But it was defeated primarily not by direct discussion and debate of controverted theological issues but by the clever maneuvering of astute denominational politicians, who, like the poor, are always with us. These, to be sure, were riding the crest of the wave that finally broke beneath them in the decade 1929–39. Some of them, of course, do not know it yet.

It was these ten years that shook the world of the social-gospel "liberals" and "modernists" and broke their confident march along the path toward the "brave new world" to be achieved by social reconstruction, in which they had tended to make God the omnipotent ally who guaranteed a successful culmination. For, as Shailer Mathews told the Stockholm conference in 1925, "to recognize the divine presence as furthering and assuring the permanent success of a sacrificial social-mindedness is the modern equivalent of the apostolic preaching of the Kingdom of God." [88]

---

[87] Winfred E. Garrison, *The March of Faith: The Story of Religion in America since 1865* (New York: Harper & Bros., 1933), p. 277.

[88] G. K. A. Bell (ed.), *The Stockholm Conference, 1925* (London: Oxford University Press, 1926), p. 140.

Since around 1930, capable intellectual leaders in the denominations have, in effect, been in a mood to appreciate what the best side of the fundamentalist movement really stood for as a genuinely "conservative" Christian movement. Beginning early in the 1930's and continuing into the present, there has been a general stirring in the denominations, characterized by attempts critically to evaluate the life and work, faith and order, of the free churches in America on the basis of a re-evaluation of their historical traditions and in the context of a theological renaissance.

Although appearing in different garbs in different denominations and groups, so that one cannot speak of a precisely definable general movement, the stirrings seem to share a common spirit, characterized by a heightened theological consciousness, a willingness to re-examine traditional formulations of the Christian faith of Protestants in the traditional terms, a critical attitude toward the "liberalism" and "modernism" of the immediate past, and attempts to revitalize the life of the denominations on the basis of theological formulations of the nature of the church and its relationship to the general culture. It is within this context and in this spirit that the historical examination of the free churches in America is now proceeding.

Finally, in keeping with a current mode, I should like to close with a paradox: the crisis is as yet not past, but the patient is not resting easily, and this, in a church, is a basis for hope.

8

BUSINESS AND POLITICS

Historians have debated just how much the progressives really wanted change. The usual picture of the "typical progressive" is that he was a rather conservative and even nostalgic fellow who would reform in order to preserve. Woodrow Wilson revealed much about progressivism when he compared the movement to Lewis Carroll's Red Queen, who was impelled to run twice as fast in order to remain in the same place; and Louis Post's quip that likened Theodore Roosevelt's program to a rocking horse — "much motion and no progress" — struck an apt note. By and large, it seems the progressives were very much devoted to the notion of keeping American society, at least as they imagined it, intact.

At the same time, many substantial changes, however "superficial," unquestionably were made, and historians have further debated just whom those changes were intended to benefit as well as who in fact benefited from them. Although there was a strong anticommercial bias in the progressive impulse, R. H. Wiebe [*Businessmen and Reform** (1962)] and others have shown that business groups themselves initiated many of the most important progressive reforms; without at least the support of merchants and small businessmen who suffered at the hands of the railroads and the giant corporations, measures such as the Federal Trade Commission and the several railroad reform bills could never have passed. On the other hand, some — notably J. Chamberlain [*Farewell to Reform** (1931)] and M. Josephson [*The President Makers* (1940)] — have contended that the creation of governmental regulatory agencies (for example) merely gave the dominant business groups new sources of power for dictating to the rest of the people so that the practical consequence of that class of progressive reform was to make conditions worse. Gabriel Kolko [*The Triumph of Conservatism** (1963)] has carried this contention still further, arguing that the dominant business groups themselves shaped the economic reforms of the era so as to ensure their own continued dominance. That representatives of the "Business Establishment," such as Richard Olney and Elbert H. Gary, spoke seriously of using the new government agencies for their own purposes — both to protect private price and market agreements and to buffer popular criticism — lends support to Kolko's thesis. So does the fact that agencies such as the ICC and FTC have, during certain eras, served precisely such purposes. [See, e.g., G. C. Davis, "The Transformation of the Federal Trade Commission, 1914–1929," *Mississippi Valley Historical*

Review, 49 (Dec. 1962).] But it remains to be demonstrated that the reforms themselves either had their origins in or usually became the instruments of such purposes.

For an intelligent presentation of the problem, see M. H. Bernstein, *Regulating Business by Independent Commission** (1955). K. A. Kerr, *American Railroad Politics, 1914–1920* (1968), is extremely suggestive in its treatment of the several group interests that jostled for position within and around the railroad industry: management, stockholders, labor, shippers, and the state and federal regulatory agencies. S. P. Hays, *Conservation and the Gospel of Efficiency** (1959), similarly presents the problem of governmental regulations in the context of the intra-industrial political struggles and the rivalry of government agencies. S. Caine, "Why Railroads Supported Regulation: The Case of Wisconsin, 1905–1910," *Business History Review*, 44 (Summer 1970), is an able case study that shows how railroad managers discovered the advantages of regulatory agencies once they were established, though they had fought their establishment. R. G. Tugwell and R. Banfield, "Grass Roots Democracy — Myth or Reality?" *Public Administration Review* (Winter 1950), a review of P. Selznick's brilliant *TVA and the Grass Roots* (1949), similarly focuses on the successful accommodation of powerful private interests to ambitious reform programs.

Businessmen have always had a keen interest in new political developments. The weight of the evidence tends to deny that in most cases, during the progressive era at least, businessmen actively sought government regulations, but it is clear they hastened to accommodate themselves to it, at least to protect themselves and at best in the hope of influencing it. On the whole the accommodations were successful. But this should come as no surprise, since (except for the socialists) in no event did reformers propose regulation in order to destroy either private business as an institution or private businesses in particular. Indeed, progressive reformers often explicitly derided the obtuseness of businessmen for clinging to the prerogatives of individual, private policy-making and for failing to see the advantages of a more efficient, "rationalized" economy.

In the following article, Robert H. Wiebe, Professor of History at Northwestern University, discusses the impact upon "Wall Street" of the movement for federal regulation. Because the Morgan interests held dominance over much of the American economy at the start of the century, they regarded federal ascendancy as a distinct threat. Mr. Wiebe shows how the Morgan group managed to protect itself during the Roosevelt Administration, only to run afoul of the highly traditionalistic William Howard Taft. The article is important not only for the insights it affords into the "antitrust" policies of the Roosevelt and Taft Administrations, but also for its suggestions about how business attitudes toward the federal government underwent change during the progressive era.

Students should also see Wiebe's "Business Disunity and the Progressive Movement, 1901–1914," *Mississippi Valley Historical Review*, 44 (March 1958).

The House of Morgan and the Executive, 1905–1913

Robert H. Wiebe

Early in 1902, when Theodore Roosevelt's administration began antitrust proceedings, against the Northern Securities Company, John Pierpont Morgan, its organizer, reputedly complained to Roosevelt, "If we have done anything wrong . . . send your man to my man and they can fix it up." [1] Several years later, in the midst of the Panic of 1907, Elbert H. Gary and Henry Clay Frick hurried to Washington to ask Roosevelt's advice. The two men, who represented Morgan interests in the United States Steel Corporation, told Roosevelt about a plan to purchase for United States Steel a controlling interest in the Tennessee Coal and Iron Company. Presenting the proposal as a bit of altruism designed to save a hard-pressed brokerage firm that owned the stock, they requested assurances that the purchase would not bring antitrust prosecution against the Steel Corporation. Roosevelt gave vague blessings, and the House of Morgan completed the transaction. [2]

Such familiar anecdotes are the material used to describe Wall Street–Washington relations during the progressive era. Contemporary reformers popularized these stories as illustrations of big business incorrigibility and unscrupulousness. Historians, denied access to most buinessmen's records and primarily concerned with the course of liberal reform, have accepted them as anecdotes.

Back of these stories lay a consistent pattern, unified by Wall Street's view of the federal government. According to an official biographer, Roosevelt, after listening to Morgan's ideas on corporation control, commented, "Mr. Morgan could not help regarding me as a big rival operator, who either intended to ruin all his interests, or else could be induced to come to an agreement to ruin none." [3] That insight held the essence of Wall

Reprinted by permission of the American Historical Association and the author from the *American Historical Review*, 65, No. 1 (October 1959), 49–60.

[1] Quoted in Mark Sullivan, *Our Times: The United States 1900–1925* (6 vols., New York, 1927), II (*America Finding Herself*), 414. See also Joseph Bucklin Bishop, *Theodore Roosevelt and His Times* (2 vols., New York, 1920), I, 184.

[2] Frederick Lewis Allen, *The Lords of Creation* (New York, 1935), 139–40; Henry F. Pringle, *Theodore Roosevelt: A Bibliography* (New York, 1931), 441–43. As Roosevelt phrased it, "I felt it no public duty of mine to interpose any objections." Bishop, *Roosevelt*, II, 55. Gary later called this "tacit acquiescence." House Committee on Investigation of United States Steel Corporation (May 27, 1911–Apr. 13, 1912, 62 Cong., 2 sess.), *United States Steel Corporation, Hearings* (53 pts., Washington, D.C., 1911–12), June 7, 1911, pt. 4, p. 167.

[3] Bishop, *Roosevelt*, I, 185.

Street's attitude. The New York magnates included the federal government among the autonomous blocs they found in American society. Generically, the government belonged with the Standard Oil Company and the American Federation of Labor. As a corollary, each bloc enjoyed primary power within its particular sphere, which meant that relations among these units roughly paralleled diplomacy among sovereign states.

Wall Street's leaders, reflecting their own involvement, usually spoke of the government in economic language. To the railroad magnate James J. Hill, the President served as chairman of the board for the "great economic corporation known as the United States of America." [4] Applying Wall Street logic, Hill argued that government regulation equaled federal ownership. The government, through the Interstate Commerce Commission, would have the seat of power on the boards of all railroads and could then determine policy.[5] Business journals, reasoning from similar premises, hoped for a "reconciliation" between the administration and the railroads and, more generally, "a proper 'balance of power' between the government and the corporations." [6]

In this theory the government was intrinsically neither good nor evil. Its worth varied with circumstances. In the wrong hands — Bryan's, for example — the government became, like the labor unions, an enemy. With the right men in office, it operated like a friendly corporation cooperating under a community of interest agreement.

The magnates did not sharpen their ideas with precise definitions. They had a flexible approach rather than a pat theory. Yet their orientation clearly obviated a government that arises from the whole society and in turn promotes the general welfare. Nor would their approach enable the government to act as a dispenser of justice above society's units. Early in the century, in fact, Wall Street's leaders ranked the government among the second-rate powers. When speculating about a battle between Washington and Standard Oil, Wall Street odds lay with John D. Rockefeller.[7]

At no time, however, did the magnates leave the government's disposition to chance. In various ways they cultivated the political influence they had inherited from the nineteenth century. Some, like the steel leaders Henry Clay Frick, worked intimately with local party leaders.[8] George W. Perkins, a Morgan partner, preferred the free play of Washington, where in 1908 he lobbied simultaneously for corporation, financial, and tariff legislation.[9] Political involvement sometimes bred contempt ("I suppose," sighed J. P.

---

[4] Quoted in George Mowry, *The Era of Theodore Roosevelt*, The New American Nation Series, ed. Henry Steele Commager and Richard B. Morris (New York, 1958), 216.

[5] "Address Delivered June 4, 1902," James J. Hill, *Addresses* (n.p., n.d.).

[6] *Railway Age*, XLIII (Mar. 22, 1907), 373; *Wall Street Journal*, Feb. 24, 1904.

[7] New York *Journal of Commerce and Commercial Bulletin*, June 25, 1906.

[8] Frick to Philander C. Knox, Nov. 11, 1901, Philander C. Knox Papers, Manuscript Division, Library of Congress.

[9] Perkins to Morgan, Mar. 16, 1908, George W. Perkins Papers, Michigan State University.

Morgan, Jr., "that when one deals with politicians one must expect to be lied to."),[10] and other Wall Street men joined Frank A. Vanderlip, vice-president of the National City Bank, who sat in his office and read reports from his two Washington agents.[11] Only the elder Morgan could call Senator Nelson W. Aldrich into his office and present him with a currency bill or have Aldrich telegraph political news while he vacationed on his yacht.[12] All of them toughened the fiber of their political connections by distributing the funds that made effective campaigning possible.

With the magnates' nineteenth-century inheritance came an emphasis upon Congressional connections. Congress made the government's economic policy in the days of Benjamin Harrison and William McKinley, and at the turn of the century the Republican Big Four — Nelson W. Aldrich, Orville H. Platt, John C. Spooner, and William B. Allison — still held sway with Mark Hanna in the Senate. Then Roosevelt tipped the balance. He sprang the Northern Securities prosecution, intervened in the anthracite coal strike, and forced the Department of Commerce and Labor bill through a reluctant Congress. Both his methods and his acts transformed the executive into a formidable power. Wall Street, in order to maintain its influence, either had to remove the rambunctious Roosevelt as soon as possible, or it had to establish strong bonds with the executive. By 1904, the first alternative — if many Wall Street men ever seriously entertained it — had vanished. Roosevelt, financed by Wall Street contributions, was triumphantly returned to office with the largest percentage of the popular vote since Monroe.[13]

On January 28, 1905, Secretary of Commerce and Labor Victor Metcalf ordered Commissioner of Corporations James R. Garfield to investigate United States Steel.[14] After some months' delay, Garfield sent a subordinate to the offices of Elbert Gary, chairman of the corporation's board, to discuss the matter. Gary used this opportunity to open negotiations for a general understanding with the executive. Through Garfield, always cordial to Morgan's men, Gary arranged a personal conference with Roosevelt.[15]

On the evening of November 2, 1905, Gary and an assistant met with Roosevelt, Metcalf, and Garfield at the White House. Gary stated "that

10 J. P. Morgan, Jr., to Perkins, Oct. 28, 1907, ibid.
11 Jerome J. Wilbur and Ailes Files, Frank A. Vanderlip Papers, Butler Library, Columbia University.
12 Vanderlip to George E. Roberts, Dec. 23, 1907, ibid.; Aldrich to Morgan (typed copy of telegram), Aug. 5, 1909, Albert J. Beveridge Papers, Manuscript Division, Library of Congress.
13 For a good discussion of this transition, see Mowry, Era of Theodore Roosevelt, 115–40.
14 Metcalf to Garfield, Jan. 28, 1905, File 42395, Records of the Department of Commerce, National Archives. A House resolution that day had called for the investigation.
15 Garfield to Z. Lewis Dalby, Sept. 20, 1905, File 3641, Records of the Federal Trade Commission, National Archives (hereafter cited as Records FTC); Garfield to Gary, Oct. 27, 1905, File 2604–1–1, ibid. See also Garfield to Perkins, Dec. 24, 1904, Perkins Papers.

[United States Steel] does not raise the question of the constitutionality of the law [empowering the Bureau of Corporations to investigate]; it desires to co-operate with the Government in every possible way that is consistent with the proper protection of . . . [the stockholders'] rights and property." [16] He promised to open all books and records of the corporation to the Bureau's investigators. In return for this cooperation, Gary asked that the information gleaned from the files be used "by the President alone for his guidance in making such suggestions to Congress concerning legislation as might be proper, expedient, and for the actual benefits of the general public"; and that "any questions relative to the use, publication, and disposition of material which Judge Gary might deem confidential would be considered by him and Commissioner Garfield, and that if there should be a disagreement between them the matter should be referred to Secretary Metcalf and, if necessary, ultimately to the President for determination." [17] Gary and Roosevelt read a memorandum of the conference and seemed satisfied. Gary's first gentlemen's agreement with the administration was consummated.

On December 18, 1906, Oscar S. Straus, then Secretary of Commerce and Labor, directed the Bureau to investigate the International Harvester Company.[18] The Morgan interests were almost as involved in this company as in United States Steel: Perkins had been instrumental in organizing it, and Gary owned a large bloc of its stock.[19] This time the Wall Street leaders had prepared in advance. On December 8 the board of directors of International Harvester had authorized government investigators full access to its files.[20] Then, as soon as news of the investigation broke, Perkins and Cyrus H. McCormick, Harvester's president, wrote to the Department suggesting "a personal conference on the subject." [21] With a precedent established, it was not necessary to see Roosevelt. On January 18, 1907, Garfield and Deputy Commissioner of Corporations Herbert Knox Smith came to Gary's Waldorf-Astoria suite in New York for a two-day conference with representatives from International Harvester.[22] Morgan's men were meeting Roosevelt's men in order to arrange matters.

---

[16] White House Conference, Nov. 2, 1905, File 2605, Records FTC.

[17] *Ibid*. When Roosevelt brought up the subject of overcapitalization, Gary replied that, if the Bureau believed United States Steel guilty after its study, it should say so and "the Steel Corporation could not be punished in any more severe way than by such publicity." *Ibid*.

[18] Straus to Garfield, Dec. 18, 1906, File 64606, Records Commerce Department. A Senate resolution of December 17 asked for the study.

[19] Memorandum, agreement among George W. Perkins, Elbert H. Gary, John P. Wilson, and Cyrus H. McCormick, Oct. 29, 1906, File 4921–23, Records FTC. For duplication between United States Steel and International Harvester officials, see House Committee on Investigation of United States Steel Corporation, *United States Steel Corporation, Hearings*, July 26, 1911, pt. 12, p. 802.

[20] Memorandum, Aug. 23, 1907, File 4902–1, Records FTC.

[21] Perkins to Straus, Dec. 18, 1906; McCormick to Garfield, Dec. 28, 1906, in File 4902–2, *ibid*.

[22] Memorandum of First International Harvester Conference, Jan. 18, 1907, File 4902–1, *ibid*.

Gary praised the administration in the language of the contented customer. United States Steel "had been absolutely satisfied with the treatment it had received from the Bureau," and he hoped "that the Harvester Company would receive the same treatment." [23] In the hands of Roosevelt and the Bureau's staff, Gary said, federal supervision became "a strong safeguard . . . to the prevention of violent attacks on private rights in general that might otherwise come." [24] On that pleasant note, the negotiators completed a second gentlemen's agreement, identical with the one concerning United States Steel.

During these years the Morgan men watched other corporations run afoul of the administration. A few months after the Steel agreement, the Justice Department charged Rockefeller's Standard Oil Company with violations of the antirebate law. Perkins reported to Morgan that as a result of Gary's "wise and vigilant" policies, "we have anticipated a great many questions and situations that might have been unpleasant and . . . [United States Steel] is looked upon in Washington with more favor than perhaps any other one concerned." [25] In 1907, when the government began antitrust prosecution of James B. Duke's American Tobacco Company, Perkins again assured Morgan that this was "about the limit to which the Government can go in the direction of trust smashing." [26] If some business interests remained vulnerable, the Morgan men felt secure behind their private arrangements with the administration.

Why was Perkins so confident? Ostensibly these agreements covered only procedural details for two government investigations, with special emphasis upon protecting the corporations' trade secrets. The answer lay in a Wall Street assumption that, in community of interest understandings, the actual words spoken carried certain automatic implications. Perkins and Gary later spelled these out. In August 1907 Roosevelt asked Perkins whether International Harvester would "be satisfied with whatever the findings [of the Bureau's investigation] were?" Perkins replied that the company expected "the Department frankly [to] come to us and point out any mistakes or technical violations of any law; then give us a chance to correct them, if we could or would, and that if we did, then we would expect the Attorney General not to bring proceedings. . . ." [27] Perkins cited a precedent. In 1904 International Harvester had asked Secretary of Commerce and Labor George B. Cortelyou to find out whether the company was breaking the law. The Interstate Commerce Commission decided that International Harvester had illegally accepted rebates. Representatives of the company then reached an understanding with Attorney General William H. Moody whereby the com-

---

[23] *Ibid.*
[24] Memorandum of Second International Harvester Interview, Jan. 19, 1907, *ibid.*
[25] Perkins to Morgan, June 25, 1906, Perkins Papers.
[26] Perkins to Morgan, July 12, 1907, *ibid.*
[27] Memorandum, Aug. 28, 1907, *ibid.*

pany stopped its improper practices and the government in turn forgot the matter.[28]

Gary's interpretation matched that of Perkins. In 1911 an agent of the Bureau of Corporations reported Gary's reconstruction of the Steel conference:

> Somewhere about 1905, Judge Gary said, he had a talk with President Roosevelt. This talk seems to have been pretty general in terms. In substance, he told the President that he wished to lay before him whatever the Corporation was doing; that if anything were wrong he wished to be advised of it, and the Corporation would change it; and the President replied that this seemed to him a fair proposition.[29]

Although nothing in the gentlemen's agreements said so, the magnates pictured them as a buffer between the corporations and the courts. The executive would issue private rulings on the corporations' legality and then allow them to avoid suits by cleaning house.

Roosevelt neither accepted nor denied this construction. When Perkins presented his gloss on the International Harvester agreement, Roosevelt evaded the issue. He assured Perkins that the Justice Department would not prosecute until the Attorney General had cleared it with him — a normal procedure — and later promised to postpone all legal action until the Bureau has completed its investigation.[30]

Despite the evasion, the Morgan men had confidence in the President's intentions. A number of Roosevelt's characteristics justified their faith. The idea of blocs within society came naturally to a politician, and Roosevelt added a personal enjoyment for the game of diplomacy. Respecting the magnates' power and their importance to the Republican party, he wanted peace between Wall Street and Washington. Because he believed so firmly in his own judgment, Roosevelt gladly committed his administration once he had determined that a course of action was right.

Roosevelt, like the Morgan men, was groping for a new definition of the government's relationship with big business. Early in his administration the President had indicated his dissatisfaction with the negativism of the Sher-

---

[28] *Ibid.*; memorandum, Aug. 23, 1907, Records FTC. In the latter memorandum, Perkins' assistant William C. Beer said that "the Government has but to point out in what respect it thinks the Company is not obeying the laws to have them obeyed immediately."

[29] Memorandum, interview with E. H. Gary, Oct. 6, 1911, File 1940–1, Records FTC. Needless to say, this résumé does not agree with the official memorandum of the conference. At the time of the agreement, Gary only alluded to his thoughts. He wrote to Garfield (Nov. 10, 1905, File 2605, *ibid.*) that "there has been no disposition on my part to endeavor to bind the Government to any promise or undertaking for the protection of our Corporation," but, he added, Roosevelt certainly did not want to harm the Steel Corporation, or business in general. He repeatedly emphasized the man-to-man character of the agreement. See also second letter to Garfield, Nov. 10, 1905, *ibid.*

[30] Memoranda, Aug. 28 and Nov. 7, 1907, in Perkins Papers.

man Act. While he welcomed the popularity of the trust buster, he also made clear his preference for a less destructive law. By 1908 he was cooperating with Wall Street in a drive behind the so-called Hepburn amendments to the Sherman Act, bills drawn up in New York that would give the executive the discretion to distinguish between good and bad trusts.[31] Four years later, Roosevelt canvassed the nation as a presidential candidate with this idea fundamental to his platform.

Behind these areas of agreement, however, lay a distinct difference between the President and the magnates. Wall Street initially regarded the government as a mediocre power and at no time recognized it as more than an equal. From the beginning Roosevelt had considered the government above the nation's private groups.[32] Under the gentlemen's agreements he expected the government — in this case, Roosevelt — to have a free hand in making all final decisions. This conviction showed first in the corrections Roosevelt made when he reviewed the original memorandum of the United States Steel agreement. Where the copy read, "That the general business conditions of the country would naturally be damaged if our Corporation were injured; that it was not intended to take any unnecessary action which would be calculated to be injurious . . . ," Roosevelt changed the latter part to read, "that it was not intended to take any action which would be calculated to be injurious unless it was shown to be the Government's clear duty to take it. . . ." [33] Roosevelt's equivocal answer to Perkins in August 1907 implied the same desire to judge as he saw fit.

In this light the most important development of the agreements under Roosevelt, the Tennessee Coal and Iron episode, represented a defeat for the President. The Morgan men regarded the understandings as the foundation for general cooperation with the executive, upon which they would build as new situations arose. When, during the Panic of 1907, the House of Morgan planned to purchase the Tennessee Coal and Iron Company, it naturally sent Gary and Frick to sound out Roosevelt first. The very heart of the agreements, as Gary and Perkins construed them, involved an advance executive ruling to safeguard against later court action. For the House of Morgan, Roosevelt's approval logically extended the existing agreements. But Roosevelt suffered a reverse. Caught in a politically and economically

[31] The magnates continued to campaign for a federal agency that would regularize the executive cooperation they tried to achieve through the gentlemen's agreements. See Robert H. Wiebe, "Business Disunity and the Progressive Movement, 1901–1914," *Mississippi Valley Historical Review*, XLIV (Mar. 1958), 681–84.

[32] The Progressive party platform in 1912 indicated that by this time Roosevelt's concept of the government as a dispenser of justice had matured. George Perkins, who worked so closely with Roosevelt in the campaign, had apparently accepted Roosevelt's view that the government was a power superior to the corporations.

[33] Copy in second letter Gary to Garfield, Nov. 10, 1905, Records FTC. For another example of Roosevelt's differences with the House of Morgan over the proper function of government, see Mowry, *Era of Theodore Roosevelt*, 217.

dangerous panic he did not understand, he allowed the Morgan men to assume the initiative and thereby lost control over the agreements.[34]

Otherwise relations between the magnates and Washington were cordial and uneventful during the last Roosevelt years, partly because the Bureau of Corporations did little investigating. The new Commissioner Herbert Knox Smith repeatedly showed his friendliness towards the magnates. Seconded by Secretary Straus, he offered to publicize International Harvester's cooperative attitude toward the Bureau's investigation.[35] When Attorney General Charles J. Bonaparte made threatening gestures toward International Harvester, it was Smith who extracted Roosevelt's promise to withhold any prosecution until the Bureau had finished investigating.[36] At the same time he confided in Harvester's chief counsel that all available evidence pointed toward the company's legality.[37] Roosevelt, seemingly convinced that United States Steel and International Harvester were good corporations, did not press the Bureau for action.

Left in peace, the Morgan men responded in kind. Perkins chatted often with Roosevelt and always found him congenial.[38] In March 1907, when other businessmen were blaming Roosevelt for an unsettled stock market, Gary wrote the President a letter flattering his reform record.[39] Only once did Gary experience a moment of doubt. In January 1909 Roosevelt turned

[34] For comments on the meeting by two participants, see Gary to Elihu Root, Nov. 7, 1907, and Root to Gary, Nov. 11, 1907, both in Elihu Root Papers, Manuscript Division, Library of Congress. Gary's letter includes veiled references to the United States Steel agreement. Gary later claimed that early in the panic he had also requested executive approval for his plan to stabilize prices throughout the iron and steel industry and that Roosevelt had raised no objections (Memorandum of interview with E. H. Gary, Oct. 6, 1911, File 1940–1, Records FTC). Thus Gary considered his famous "dinners" as well as the purchase of Tennessee Coal and Iron a part of the expanding Steel agreement. Perhaps encouraged by success, Frick wrote to Roosevelt (Nov. 30, 1907, Theodore Roosevelt Papers, Manuscript Division, Library of Congress) offering his and Gary's services as mediators in the court battles between the government and Standard Oil. The bloc approach to government had many applications.

Emphasizing the executive's retreat during the financial crisis, Secretary of the Treasury George B. Cortelyou turned over to the House of Morgan government funds which the bankers used at their discretion to fight the panic. See Cortelyou's later testimony in the House subcommittee of the Committee on Banking and Currency (62 Cong. 3 sess., May 16, 1912–Feb. 26, 1913), *Money Trust Investigation, Investigation of Financial and Monetary Conditions in the United States under House Resolutions Nos. 429 and 504* (3 vols., Washington, D.C., 1912–13), June 13, 1912, I, 430–54.

[35] Smith to McCormick, Aug. 8, 1907, Perkins Papers; Straus to Redfield Proctor, Jan. 25, 1908, File 64606, Records Commerce Department.

[36] Memorandum, Nov. 7, 1907, Perkins Papers. See also Henry F. Pringle, *The Life and Times of William Howard Taft: A Biography* (2 vols., New York, 1939), II, 790–91.

[37] Edgar A. Bancroft to Perkins, Feb. 4, 1908, Perkins Papers. See also Perkins to Smith, Apr. 18, 1908, File 5589, Records FTC; Smith to Perkins, Apr. 20, 1908, Perkins Papers.

[38] Perkins to Morgan, July 31, 1908, Perkins Papers. See also Perkins to Roosevelt, June 10, 1908, *ibid.*

[39] Gary to Roosevelt, Mar. 15, 1907, Roosevelt Papers.

over nonconfidential data from the Steel investigation to the Senate Judiciary Committee. Although the Bureau dutifully sent Gary a list of the documents divulged, Gary felt impelled "to call the attention . . . of Commissioner Smith to original correspondence between Secretary Garfield and myself. I hope our understanding will not be overlooked." Smith assured Gary that "we have in mind the matter of which you speak," and the incident passed.[40]

When Roosevelt selected William Howard Taft as his heir, Wall Street applauded;[41] he appeared far safer than Roosevelt. Asked during the 1908 campaign whether he anticipated any action against United States Steel, Taft replied that he saw no reason for an investigation, and added, "Indeed, Secretary Garfield tells me there is not [any reason for one]."[42] The candidate did not even know that the Steel Corporation, along with International Harvester, was already under investigation. Taft's victory, coinciding with court decisions favorable to big business, made the Morgan men certain that their agreements with the executive were secure.[43]

The House of Morgan, in company with much of the nation, misjudged the new President. The agreements, in order to function properly, required a strong President whose word bound his administration. Taft was a follower who diffused responsibility among his subordinates and relied upon them for much of his policy. The agreements, as the Morgan men understood them, also depended upon a pragmatic executive, willing to bend them to fit any new developments. Where Roosevelt enjoyed the leeway of private negotiations, Taft's administration lacked the necessary flexibility. Taft's mind worked in legal channels, and in revamping the cabinet he surrounded himself with lawyers who shared his outlook. Finally, the magnates needed a President who, like Roosevelt, could accept big business as a positive good for America. Neither Taft nor Attorney General George W. Wickersham qualified. Both men believed that the dissolution of overlarge corporations would bring back old-time competition. For Taft, who wanted to continue Roosevelt's progressivism by administering rather than innovat-

---

[40] William H. Baldwin to Gary, Jan. 30, 1909; Gary to Baldwin, Feb. 1, 1909; Baldwin to Gary, Feb. 2, 1909; Gary to Baldwin, Feb. 4, 1909; Baldwin to Gary, Feb. 5, 1909; all in File 6296, Records FTC. Later, when the Stanley Committee asked Gary if he knew whether the President had received any information from the Bureau of Corporation's investigation of United States Steel, Gary disingenuously replied, "I have no knowledge as to whether or not the Department of Commerce and Labor has furnished any of this information to the President. There is no way I could know that." House Committee on Investigation of United State Steel Corporation, *United States Steel Corporation, Hearings,* June 1, 1911, pt. 2, p. 71. See also *ibid.,* June 2, 1911, pt. 3, p. 139; July 20, 1911, pt. 9, pp. 495–98.

[41] Pringle, *Taft,* I, 347, 355.

[42] Quoted in Mowry, *Era of Theodore Roosevelt,* 288. The remark indicates that, if Taft reported him correctly, Garfield discounted the investigations as a formality.

[43] For comments on the courts, see Perkins to J. P. Morgan, Jr., Nov. 10, 1908, Perkins Papers.

ing, the trust issue proved a godsend. With Wickersham showing the way, the government mined the Sherman Act for all it was worth.[44]

In Roosevelt's last years a Department of Commerce and Labor sympathetic to Wall Street had counterbalanced the aggressive Attorney General Charles Bonaparte. Under Taft, Secretary Charles Nagel gave the Justice Department every possible assistance. When Nagel discovered that the Steel investigation had lagged under Roosevelt and that the International Harvester study had scarcely begun, he immediately concentrated the Department's energies on those two projects.[45] Bypassing Commissioner of Corporations Herbert Knox Smth, a confirmed friend of the Morgan men, Nagel relied upon a pair of Smith's subordinates, who distrusted Gary's motives, to manage the investigations.[46] Contrary to his predecessor's policy, Nagel never insisted that the Justice Department wait for a completed investigation before prosecuting. At the same time that he placed his Department at the service of the Attorney General, Nagel turned his back on Wall Street and, by silencing Smith, cut off the magnates' main source of unofficial information.[47]

Commissioner Smith was an anachronism in the new administration. As the only participant in the original agreements still in office, he did his best to keep them operative. He prodded Nagel to destroy copies of confidential data that the Bureau had used in its investigations and reminded his superiors of the corporations' cooperativeness. Citing Roosevelt, he tried to delay antitrust suits until the Bureau had completed its studies.[48] But he cried into the wind. Although he remained in office until 1912, he wielded no power. Taft and Nagel privately rejoiced when Smith resigned to join Roosevelt's Progressive party.[49]

Meanwhile, the Morgan men could only await developments. When the Supreme Court in May 1911 ruled that the Standard Oil and American Tobacco Companies violated the Sherman Act, the magnates read the decisions as an invitation to Wickersham and Taft to try their luck with United States Steel and International Harvester.[50] Hearing rumors of imminent

[44] Mowry, *Era of Theodore Roosevelt*, 231–38; and Pringle *Taft*, I, 248, 523; II, 604–606, 655–59, 669–73, 718 ff., contain suggestive information on Taft and the nature of his administration.

[45] Memorandum, Aug. 22, 1912, File 64606, Records Commerce Department.

[46] William H. Baldwin to Garfield, Nov. 28, Dec. 3, 1906, File 3641, Records FTC; Luther Conant, Jr., to Smith, Dec. 25, 1908, File 2604–1–1, *ibid.*

[47] Perkins to Smith, July 3, 1911, File 4902–2, *ibid.*; Smith to Perkins, July 8, 1911, Perkins Papers.

[48] Smith to Nagel, June 30, Oct. 27, 1910, and Conant to Nagel, Nov. 1, 1910, in File 69445, Records Commerce Department; Smith to Taft, Apr. 28, 1912, File 64606, *ibid.* See also E. A. Bancroft to Smith, Nov. 6, 1909, and Smith to Bancroft, Nov. 12, 1909, in File 6419, Records FTC.

[49] Taft to Nagel, July 17, 1912, File 64606, Records Commerce Department.

[50] Memorandum for Mr. Roosevelt, Mar. 11, 1912, Perkins Papers, shows Perkins' distaste, shared by other men from Wall Street, for the Supreme Court's so-called rule of reason, distinguishing between acceptable and unacceptable restraint of trade.

prosecutions, Perkins went to Wickersham in July 1911 to revitalize the agreements. He promised Wickersham that if the Justice Department uncovered any practices which "in his judgment, should be corrected, we would all meet him half way in an effort to [correct them] by agreement rather than through a suit." [51] The magnates had come full circle; Perkins' offer exactly matched the one made to Attorney General Moody seven years earlier. But what had made sense in 1904 no longer applied in 1911. Wickersham answered Perkins on October 26 when the Justice Department, without waiting for the Bureau to finish its study, began antitrust proceedings against United States Steel.

The next day Gary sadly but firmly told the Bureau's agents that United States Steel could no longer cooperate in their investigations.[52] The corporation's attorneys received no more satisfaction from the Taft administration. When they asked the government to respect the confidential information it had at its disposal, Nagel told them they would "have to trust him to use it discreetly and to publish only what [was] necessary," and Taft added, "That is right." [53] Shortly afterward, the Justice Department brought suit against the International Harvester Company. Again the Bureau had not yet issued its report, and Harvester's attorney worked to the last minute to breathe life into the second gentlemen's agreement. He reminded the Bureau of "the very fair offer" Smith had made to allow the company to correct the report for "any inadvertent errors or [to] present further information on any point upon which I may believe you to have been misinformed." [54] Despite rebuffs from the new Commissioner of Corporations Luther Conant, Jr., the attorney persisted until Nagel had told him twice that the report's publication could not wait for his proofreading.[55] The Taft administration left office amid bitter complaints from the prosecuted corporations.[56]

In 1911 Gary called the Steel suit "the irony of Fate." [57] Considering his misplaced faith in Taft three years before, the judgment sounded reasonable. More accurately, the Steel prosecution, marking the end of one gentle-

---

[51] Memorandum, July 13, 1911, Perkins Papers.

[52] Memorandum, conference between Gary and Bureau of Corporations officials, Oct. 27, 1911, 1940–1, Records FTC, includes Gary's emotions.

[53] Memorandum, Nov. 29, 1911, Presidential Ser. no. 2, William Howard Taft Papers, Manuscript Division, Library of Congress. Ironically, the administration's decision still followed the letter of agreement: the Secretary, then the President, arbitrated differences between the Bureau and the Steel Corporation.

[54] E. A. Bancroft to Luther Conant, Jr., Sept. 10, 1912, File 6419, Records FTC. Just before he resigned, Smith had allowed Gary's rejoinders to be included in the Bureau's report on United States Steel. Memorandum, conference at Gary's office, Oct. 13, 1911, File 1940–1, *ibid.*

[55] Conant to Bancroft, Sept. 18, 1912, File 6419, *ibid.*; Bancroft to Nagel, Feb. 21, 1913; Nagel to Bancroft, Feb. 22, 26, 1913, File 64606, Records Commerce Department.

[56] Statement of Cyrus H. McCormick, Mar. 2, 1913, File 6963–1, Records FTC.

[57] Gary to Perkins, Aug. 1, 1911, Perkins Papers. As the date shows, this comment was written just before the government suit began, when prosecution was certain.

men's agreement, was the casualty of a transition period. The Wall Street approach to the federal government, as embodied in the agreements, required more abnegation than the progressive era's administrations would accept. It fitted neither Roosevelt's view of a government above society nor Taft's legalistic, administrating executive.

Before they collapsed, the gentlemen's agreements gave Wall Street valuable experience. They taught the magnates the importance of adapting their approach to new circumstances. Even before entering the agreements, the Morgan men had made an important concession. By elevating the government from secondary power to a position of equality with the House of Morgan, they extended the executive's domain to include a study of their hitherto sacred records and, in the process, partially recognized the government's right to regulate corporations. This facilitated a later concession to Woodrow Wilson's administration by which the magnates temporarily accepted the government as a superior power with unquestioned rights to regulate business. On that basis, the American Telephone and Telegraph Company and the New York, New Haven and Hartford Railroad arranged private settlements with Attorney General James C. McReynolds that forestalled prosecution.[58] Moreover, the painful changes from Roosevelt to Taft to Wilson pointed up the value of continuity in the government's personnel and philosophy to any private understandings. The progressive era's irregular course made the magnates more appreciative of Republican consistency during the 1920's when the business of government always remained business. In defeat, Wall Street was learning.

[58] Arthur S. Link, *Woodrow Wilson and the Progressive Era, 1910–1917*, The New American Nation Series, ed. Henry Steele Commager and Richard B. Morris (New York, 1954), 76 and fn. 56; and a slightly different presentation in Link, *Wilson: The New Freedom* (Princeton, N.J., 1956), 418–23.

9

PROBLEMS OF PROGRESS

In the prosperous first year of the twentieth century, Episcopal Bishop William Lawrence of Massachusetts beamed the message that seemed Truth for its time and place: "Material prosperity," he said, "is helping to make the national character sweeter, more joyous, more unselfish, more Christlike." As in the past, America's phenomenal success tended to cloak potent discontents, such as had burst into small-scale civil warfare during the 1890's. Although it is clear that prosperity did "sweeten" the long-standing discontents of the nation's underprivileged, it was the sweetening effect upon the dominant classes that had the most lasting significance. Repression gave way to accommodation as the policy of the nation's chief policy-makers. A threatened strike by coal miners in 1900, for example, brought pressure from the White House, through Mark Hanna, not on the labor leaders but on the mine owners to settle the issue with concessions to labor. When the mine owners refused a second accommodation in 1902 and the strike ensued, the president invoked not the military, as Presidents Hayes, Harrison, and Cleveland had done in similar circumstances, but a mediation that again exacted concessions from the mine owners. [See R. H. Wiebe, "The Anthracite Strike of 1902: A Record of Confusion," *Mississippi Valley Historical Review*, 48 (Sept. 1961).] These events were indicative of a substantial change in policy by those who held power in the country. In the 1890's, men like Roosevelt and Taft had spoken readily of using Gatling guns to make short work of agitators, but in the prosperous year of the new century they spoke at least as readily of the "dull, purblind folly of the very rich men, their greed and their arrogance," which "tended to produce a very unhealthy condition of excitement and irritation in the popular mind" and which showed itself "in the great increase in socialistic propaganda." [Roosevelt to Taft (March 1906).] "The friends of property," Roosevelt declared in 1904, "must realize that the surest way to provoke an explosion of wrong and injustice is to be short-sighted, narrow-minded, greedy and arrogant." [To P. Knox (Nov. 10, 1904).]

The fear of socialism, violence, and possibly worse lay behind many of the major achievements of the progressive movement. There was some truth, for example, in Lincoln Steffens's accusation that Roosevelt wanted only *a* railroad law, one that would mollify the public without substantially altering the power of railroad management. TR candidly acknowledged precisely that tactic on the issue of tariff reform; when he negotiated a reciprocity treaty with Newfoundland in 1904 (his one important concession to the tariff reformers), he wrote to intimates that he had acted only because there was "a sentiment which demands a [tariff] revision" that no longer could be ignored, and not because there was any "material need."

Roosevelt sought to discriminate between "moral issues" (which he believed were the principal issues of his time) and matters of expediency. He placed tariff reform in the second category because he could not see that one could determine the measure of justice or injustice done when tariff favors were bestowed on or taken away from some particular economic interest; it was merely a question of reshuffling advantages among competing business groups, with the best favors going to those who wielded the greatest power. Similarly, he could understand the "immorality" of extortionate railroad rates, but he tended to dismiss the more complex issues of freight classification or less-than-carload and long- and short-haul rate differentials simply as matters of which interest had the power to make the best deal in a competitive situation. As J. M. Blum has noted (while making a different point), TR understood that the maximum rate provision of the Hepburn Act (1906) would afford little remedy for discrimination between commodities or between localities, "but such discrimination seemed to him relatively impersonal. He cared less about freight classification and long- and short-haul differentials because he could not readily associate those matters with a doer of evil and a victim." [*The Republican Roosevelt** (1954), p. 90.]

Roosevelt's aversion to such problems did not, of course, remove them. Tariff reform remained one of the two leading issues of the day, while the agitation for railroad reform focused precisely on the issue of discriminations that TR considered to have little "moral meaning." Actually, the most significant political developments of the era took place in just that sector of human conflict where such matters as "evil," "justice," and "morality" have no appropriate application — or at least where their definitions tend to be a direct function of self-interest. (Possibly this is true for any era. See Link, p. 267, below.) In some measure, Roosevelt noticed this contradiction himself. "Curiously enough," he wrote to Steffens in 1908, "events have forced me to make my chief fights in public life against privilege, [though] I know from actual experience . . . that what is needed is the *fundamental fight for morality*." [TR's emphasis.] Roosevelt was in many ways among the most sophisticated of the progressives. Yet he seems to have resisted stubbornly the necessity for grappling with a world of politics in which the principal stakes were not whether good men or bad men were to prevail, but who was to get how much of what the society had to offer.

The contending interests in America were indeed competing for *privilege*, in the legal sense of what forms of social or commercial behavior were to be privileged or legitimated even though they might cause injury to others. (In this respect, Roosevelt's statement to

Steffens said more than he knew; for Roosevelt used the word "privilege" essentially in the opprobrious sense that was common in his day.) A grocer who opens a store across the street from another grocer does injury to the latter's business and consequently to his standard of living. But the society *privileges* such injury in the interest of maintaining a competitive marketplace. More to the point: a labor union and its weapon, the strike, do injury to the profit margins of an employer, to the free flow of commerce, and even to the liberties of antiunion workers, but society may privilege it (it was a major issue in the progressive era) in the interest of balancing corporate power and of bringing a form of order to labor-management relations. Other issues of the same nature included these: Should the society privilege railroad rate differentials that impair the industrial potentialities of a region in the interest of unencumbered private enterprise and of the previously established claims of businessmen elsewhere? Should commercial pools and monopolies be excluded from the privileges society grants to other competing business forms? Or, as it was most often put in the progressive era: Should certain business consolidations be exempted from the proscriptions against combinations in restraint of trade in the interest of industrial efficiency and the enhancement of our international trade?

Other equally knotty problems of a somewhat different order also beset the policy-makers of the progressive era. In the interest of decentralized political power, should American society permit the states and their local interests to decide policy for the exploitation of natural resources; or should the federal government set such policy in the interest of efficiency and the total national need? Should society restrict the flow of immigration in the interest of greater social order; or would such restriction too seriously impair our industrial vitality? Should the society strive to maximize homogeneity through integrationist and assimilationist programs in the interest of reducing social conflict, or should it encourage ethnic diversity in the interest of maintaining a "free market in ideas" and life styles? (See Gordon, pp. 70–89, above.) Should our inefficient agricultural system be allowed to crumble from its own deficiencies; or should part of the social surplus be used to maintain the family farm as a major source of social stability?

These were crucial questions of social policy, yet few progressives were equipped intellectually to grapple with them because of a fundamental premise most of them seemed to share with Roosevelt: that the most important social problems could be solved by integrity, ability, and simple morality. [Cf. D. W. Noble, "The Paradox of Progressive Thought," *American Quarterly*, 5 (Fall 1953).] It was perhaps natural for progressives to place such emphasis upon the fight for morality, since the progressive movement in general was conceived in the interest of ending the brutality to human decencies and conventional values that industrialism seemed to have inflicted. The conventions of decency, right, and justice were simply assumed. It was, indeed, primarily through their constant appeal for common-place virtues in social affairs that the progressives achieved their most durable success: the blunting of the sharper edges of self-interest among the major forces in American life. But we cannot begin to understand the era if we assume that the appeal to common virtues was generally successful. Roosevelt's experience gives point to this fact. Insofar as the problems noted above were solved at all, it was through the interplay of political power, modified only slightly by the influence of the progressive ethos — that is, by the then conventional standards of "fair play," "justice," or legitimated privilege.

And therein lies the key to the ultimate failure of progressivism. The progressives' efforts to resolve major social and economic con-flicts were foredoomed by the fact that the very conventions to which the progressives appealed could offer little advantage to the chief insurgent interests of the day.

For a view of the failure of urban progressivism, see Roy Lubove, "The 20th Century City: The Progressive as Municipal Reformer," *Mid-America*, 41 (October 1959), 195–209, and his *The Urban Community: Housing and Planning in the Progressive Era** (1967). Herbert F. Margulies, "Recent Opinion on the Decline of the Pro-gressive Movement," *Mid-America* 45 (October 1963), is a simple survey of how some leading historians have treated the subject.

The Failure of Progressivism

RICHARD M. ABRAMS

Our first task is definitional, because clearly it would be possible to beg the whole question of "failure" by means of semantical niceties. I have no in-tention of being caught in that kind of critics' trap. I hope to establish that there was a distinctive major reform movement that took place during most of the first two decades of this century, that it had a mostly coherent set of characteristics and long-term objectives, and that, measured by its own cri-teria — not criteria I should wish, through hindsight and preference, to im-pose on it — it fell drastically short of its chief goals.[1]

One can, of course, define a reform movement so broadly that merely to acknowledge that we are where we are and that we enjoy some advantages

© 1971 by Richard M. Abrams.

This essay is a modified version of a paper delivered before the Organization of American Historians in Cincinnati in May 1966.

[1] For a more substantial treatment of this subject, see my *The Burdens of Progress* (Scott, Foresman, forthcoming), esp. chs. 2, 4, and 5.

over where we were would be to prove the "success" of the movement. In many respects, Arthur Link does this sort of thing, both in his and William B. Catton's popular textbook, *American Epoch*, and in his article, "What Happened to the Progressive Movement in the 1920's?" [2] In the latter, Link defines "progressivism" as a movement that "began convulsively in the 1890's and waxed and waned afterward to our own time, to insure the survival of democracy in the United States by the enlargement of governmental power to control and offset the power of private economic groups over the nation's institutions and life." Such a definition may be useful to classify data gathered to show the liberal sources of the enlargement of governmental power since the 1890's; but such data would not be finely classified enough to tell us much about the *non*liberal sources of governmental power (which were numerous and important), about the distinctive styles of different generations of reformers concerned with a liberal society, or even about vital distinctions among divergent reform groups in the era that contemporaries and the conventional historical wisdom have designated as progressive.

Curiously, in the work of Gabriel Kolko — an extreme critic of "liberal-orthodox historiography" — we find apparent agreement that progressivism was a success. While emphatically denying that the power of big business "over the nation's institutions and life" has ever been controlled or offset, Professor Kolko ascribes to progressivism so narrow and unique a purpose as to foretell its consummate "triumph." According to him, "progressivism" was "a movement for the political rationalization of business and industrial conditions, a movement that operated on the assumption that the general welfare of the community could be best served by satisfying the concrete needs of business." [3] To be sure, this definition is useful for focusing on a significant development of the era, namely, the increasing politicization of business and industrial decision-making — that is, the replacement of the market to a significant degree by decisions emanating from government regulatory agencies. Yet it leaves us without ready categories to describe the hundreds of leading reformers in the center of the era's activities for whom business and industrial conditions were secondary to humanitarian, social, and political concerns, and who tended moreover to oppose the "rationalization" of business and industrial conditions altogether. One could, conceivably, find other words than "progressives" to describe such reformers and reform impulses — such as "moral reformers" or "humanitarianists," "civicists," or "political reformers," and so on — but this would not only proliferate the categories of contemporary reform movements, it would

---

[2] Arthur Link and William B. Catton, *American Epoch*, 3 vols. (Knopf, 1967). Link's article appears in this volume, pp. 267–283; see also the introduction to it by the editors, pp. 265–267.

[3] *The Triumph of Conservatism* (Free Press, 1964), pp. 2–3.

also mean using words in a way that neither contemporaries nor historians would easily recognize.[4]

Now, without going any further into the problem of historians' definitions which are too broad or too narrow — there is no space here for such an effort — I shall attempt a definition of my own, beginning with the problem that contemporaries set themselves to solve and that gave the era its cognomen, "progressive." That problem was *progress* — or more specifically, how American society was to continue to enjoy the fruits of material progress without the accompanying assault upon human dignity and the erosion of the conventional values and moral assumptions on which the social order appeared to rest.

This, I think, is the key to the major reform efforts of the early twentieth century. It contains two principal concerns: (1) the maintenance of the values and moral assumptions that resided at the center of contemporary conventional thought, in the face of vast demographic, technological, and commercial changes;[5] and (2) the mitigation of the harsher cruelties of life for those who remained beyond the boundaries of society's privileges and the preponderance of its rewards. The second represented, moreover, a subsumption of the first — first, because a distinct humanitarianism inhered in those values, and second, because unless the unprivileged or underprivileged (who comprised a growing and increasingly restive segment of American society) were given special considerations, they would likely jeopardize by violence the entire structure of conventional values.

In the 1890's, for a great many of those who later became leaders of the progressive movement, the threat that social violence presented to the system they sought to preserve had seemed the most immediate problem. Fear of social and political instability had peaked during those disorderly years. ("The time has come," cried Lyman Abbott in 1894, "when forebearance has ceased to be a virtue. There must be some shooting, men must be killed, and then there will be an end of this defiance of the law and destruction of property. . . . The soldiers [at Pullman] must use their guns. They must shoot to kill."[6]) With the return of prosperity after 1897, the attention of

---

[4] Many other things are wrong with Kolko's definitions, but I am concerned here merely with the usefulness of his definition of "progressivism" as a way of classifying historical data.

[5] It is impossible here to spell out the nature of the conventional values I refer to. But others — notably George Mowry, Richard Hofstadter, and Henry F. May — have done the job generally to my satisfaction, and I can lean on them for present purposes (without necessarily accepting *every* part of these gentlemen's arguments or even suggesting that they agree in every respect with each other). May, *The End of American Innocence* (Knopf, 1959), especially chs. 1–3; Mowry, *The Era of Theodore Roosevelt* (Harper, 1958), esp. chs. 2, 5; Hofstadter, *The Age of Reform* (Knopf, 1955), esp. ch. 4. See also Sidney Mead, "American Protestantism Since the Civil War II. From Americanism to Christianity," reprinted in this volume, pp. 162–189, and the editors' introduction to the essay, pp. 159–161.

[6] Quoted in Ray Ginger, *Eugene Debs* (Collier Books edition), p. 161.

these same people turned toward removing or modifying the conditions that underlay the violence that so threatened the social order and its concomitant values. They sought a peaceful, legal substitute for Gatling guns and bayonets, and, moreover, a more morally perfect society. Toward those ends they would make common cause with any interests, even those they feared the most among the deprived, underprivileged elements, as long as the commitment they had to their special view of civilization was not seriously compromised.

To put it briefly and yet more specifically, a very large body of men and women entered into reform activities at the end of the nineteenth century to translate "the national credo" (as Henry May calls it) into a general program for social action. Their actions, according to Richard Hofstadter, were "founded upon the indigenous Yankee-Protestant political tradition [that] assumed and demanded the constant disinterested activity of the citizen in public affairs, argued that political life ought to be run, to a greater degree than it was, in accordance with general principles and abstract laws apart from and superior to personal needs, and expressed a common feeling that government should be in good part an effort to moralize the lives of individuals while economic life should be intimately related to the stimulation and development of individual character." [7]

The most consistently important reform impulse, among *many* reform impulses, during the progressive era grew directly from these considerations. It is this reform thrust that we should properly call "the progressive movement." We should distinguish it carefully from reform movements in the era committed primarily to other considerations.

The progressive movement drew its strength from the old mugwump reform impulse, civil service reform, female emancipationists, prohibitionists, the social gospel, the settlement-house movement, some national expansionists, some world peace advocates, conservation advocates, technical efficiency experts, and a wide variety of intellectuals who helped cut through the stifling, obstructionist smokescreen of systematized ignorance. It gained powerful allies from many disadvantaged business interests that appealed to politics to redress unfavorable trade positions; from some ascendant business interests seeking institutional protection; from publishers who discovered the promotional value of exposés; and from politicians-on-the-make who sought issues with which to dislodge longlived incumbents from their place. Objectively it focused on or expressed (1) a concern for responsive, honest, and efficient government, on the local and state levels especially; (2) recognition of the obligations of society — particularly of an affluent society — to its underprivileged; (3) a desire for more rational use of the nation's resources and economic energies; (4) a rejection, on at least intellectual grounds, of certain social principles that had long obstructed social remedies for what

[7] *The Age of Reform,* pp. 139–40.

had traditionally been regarded as irremediable evils, such as poverty; and, above all, (5) a concern for the maintenance or restoration of a consensus on what conventionally had been regarded as *fixed moral* principles. "The first and central faith in the national credo," writes Professor May, "was, as it always had been, the reality, certainty, and eternity of moral values. . . . A few thought and said that ultimate values and goals were unnecessary, but in most cases this meant that they believed so deeply in a consensus on these matters that they could not imagine a serious challenge." [8] Progressives shared this faith with most of the rest of the country, but they also conceived of themselves, with a grand sense of stewardship, as its heralds, and its agents.

The progressive movement was (and is) distinguishable from other contemporary reform movements not only by its devotion to social conditions regarded, by those within it as well as by much of the generality, as *normative*, but also by its definition of what forces threatened that order. More specifically, progressivism directed its shafts at five principal enemies, each in its own way representing reform:

1. *The socialist reform movement* — because, despite socialism's usually praiseworthy concern for human dignity, it represented the subordination of the rights of private property and of individualistic options to objectives that often explicitly threatened common religious beliefs and conventional standards of justice and excellence.

2. The corporate reorganization of American business, which I should call *the corporate reform movement* (its consequence has, after all, been called "the corporate revolution") — because it challenged the traditional relationship of ownership and control of private property, because it represented a shift from production to profits in the entrepreneurial definition of efficiency, because it threatened the proprietary small-business character of the American social structure, because it had already demonstrated a capacity for highly concentrated and socially irresponsible power, and because it sanctioned practices that strained the limits of conventionality and even legality.

3. *The labor union movement* — because despite the virtues of unionized labor as a source of countervailing force against the corporations and as a basis for a more orderly labor force, unionism (like corporate capitalism and socialism) suggested a reduction of individualistic options (at least for wage-earners and especially for small employers), and a demand for a partnership with business management in the decision-making process by a class that convention excluded from such a role.

4. *Agrarian radicalism*, and populism in particular — because it, too, represented (at least in appearance) the insurgency of a class convention-

---

[8] *The End of American Innocence*, p. 9.

ally believed to be properly excluded from a policy-making role in the society, a class graphically represented by the "Pitchfork" Bens and "Sockless" Jerrys, the "Cyclone" Davises and "Alfalfa" Bills, the wool hat brigade and the rednecks.

5. *The ethnic movement* — the demand for specific political and social recognition of ethnic or ex-national affiliations — because accession to the demand meant acknowledgment of the fragmentation of American society as well as a retreat from official standards of integrity, honesty, and efficiency in government in favor of standards based on personal loyalty, partisanship, and sectarian provincialism.

Probably no two progressives opposed all of these forces with equal animus, and most had a noteworthy sympathy for one or more of them. Theodore Roosevelt, for example, sympathized generally with the corporation revolution because it seemed likely to serve the cause of American power and affluence. It is worth noting, at the same time, that this sympathy produced the greatest "static" among his progressive supporters, and it seems clear that (for better or worse) the "New Nationalist" approach to the corporation problems was distinctly a minority view among the mass of progressives.[9] More to the point is that TR himself stressed subordinating this new source of private power to transcendant national (nationalist) purposes, and in the deluge of revisionist historiography on Roosevelt it is sometimes forgotten that his program was the first since the earliest years of the republic to place broad political *restraints* upon private entrepreneurial energies.[10] Roosevelt spoke in favor of the corporate reorganization of business, but he acted to *control*, not to augment it. The point is that Roosevelt, in common with the progressive impulse and his progressive-reformer colleagues, maintained a serious anxiety over corporate power and a will to constrict it in the interest of traditional values.

In their acceptance of the notion that monopolistic power in industry meant greater industrial efficiency and greater economic growth, some whom we should properly call progressives flirted with socialism, especially those most keenly indignant over the folly, the crudity, and the brutality of the country's economic and political "rulers." Some, such as Walter Weyl, refused to avoid the words "socialism" and "socialization" in describing their position.[11] But this made them socialists neither in party politics nor in philosophical outlook. Weyl was specifically critical of Marxian socialism for emphasizing class division and for underestimating "those common interests

[9] See George Mowry, *Theodore Roosevelt and the Progressive Movement* (Hill and Wang, 1949), p. 270; John Garraty, *Right Hand Man* (Harper, 1957), chs. 14, 15; my own "Woodrow Wilson and the Southern Congressmen, 1913–1916," *Journal of Southern History*, 22 (November 1956), 425, 427.

[10] Cf. James Willard Hurst, *Law and the Conditions of Freedom in the Nineteenth Century* (University of Wisconsin Press, 1956), esp. ch. 1.

[11] "The industrial goal of the democracy is the socialization of industry." *The New Democracy* (Harper Torchbook), p. 276.

of classes, those broad, unifying bonds in society which inspire certain national ideals and race purposes." [12] Indeed, Weyl and other progressives used the word "socialization" in a way that suggested the meaning "to make more socially responsible" — and though that might have meant public ownership of particular industries, it did not mean that public ownership was an integral requirement for reforming The System.

Jane Addams's work with immigrant groups evidenced a remarkably advanced understanding of divergent ethnic traits and aspirations — or at least of their utilitarian, clinical value — but on the whole, Addams's colleagues in the settlement-house and social-gospel movements emphasized "civilizing" the "weaker" and "barbaric" classes in order to assimilate (i.e., Anglo-Americanize) them.[13] Even so sympathetic a humanitarian and labor advocate as Louis Brandeis was asserting in 1905, "Habits of living or of thought which tend to keep alive differences of origin or to classify men according to their religious beliefs are inconsistent with the American ideal of brotherhood, and are disloyal." [14] And Walter Weyl was urging restricting immigration to 100,000 or 200,000 of the most readily "assimilable" Europeans each year, or almost exactly what the National Origins Act of 1924 would prescribe.[15]

Toward unionism, most progressives expressed a variety of views, ranging from open hostility (many of the California progressives, for example) to *acceptance* of unions and of collective bargaining as the best answer to a bad situation created by the ascendancy of the corporation in economic life. Most progressives probably shared a genuine sympathy for workers as underprivileged. But, as Professor Mowry has put it, it was one thing "to be benevolent to the underdog as an individual"; it was quite another to have to confront labor "as a competing social class." [16] On the whole, what Charles Howard Hopkins has said of the social gospellers' attitude toward unionism applies equally well to other progressives: "Social Christianity did not bestow upon [unions] an unqualified blessing. The same attitude that prompted comparison of corporate authority to the rule of Louis XIV also cautioned the unions against abuse of power and privilege." [17] Indeed, in

[12] *Ibid.*, pp. 169–70.
[13] See, e.g., Robert Woods, *Americans in Process* (Houghton Mifflin, 1902), pp. 147–50, 368–70; J. Higham, *Strangers in the Land* (Rutgers University Press, 1955), esp. pp. 239–49. Cf. William Petersen, "The 'Scientific' Basis of Our Immigration Policy," in *The Politics of Population* (Anchor Book, 1965), esp. p. 212.
[14] See my "Brandeis and the Ascendancy of Corporate Capitalism," in the Harper Torchbook reprint of Brandeis's *Other People's Money* (1967), esp. pp. xix–xxix.
[15] Weyl, *New Democracy*, p. 347.
[16] *The California Progressives* (Quadrangle Books, 1952), p. 143. Cf. Michael Rogin, "Progressivism and the California Electorate," *The Journal of American History*, 55 (September 1968). Rogin shows that workers, organized and unorganized, tended to support progressive reform candidates. But this does not really challenge my (or George Mowry's) point that progressive-reformers remained suspicious — to say the least — of the growth of union power.
[17] *The Rise of the Social Gospel in American Protestantism*, 1865–1915 (Yale University Press, 1940), p. 324.

his full-length study of the relationship of the New York progressive movement to labor and labor unionism, Irwin Yellowitz notes that the only "social Progressive group" — his term for the social worker–social gospel complex of progressive reformers — that consistently supported unionism was
CAIL (the Church Association for the Advancement of the Interests of
Labor). And even when a progressive reform group did give lip-service to
unionist initiative in obtaining labor gains, it was for reasons the unionists
themselves must have regarded as fatuous and irrelevant, having little to do
with the unionists' own contention that they must build organizational
power in order to force themselves into the policy-making councils of business and government. The New York Consumers League, for example,
asserted its support of labor union organization for the reason that the
League was "convinced that such associated activity develops both the
moral and the intellectual nature of those who take part in it, and also
the advantages gained by self-effort are better appreciated and more lasting
than those conferred in consequence of the exertion of others." [18]

There were, finally, many progressives who would easily qualify as "agrarians" (if the word is not too narrowly defined). But not all agrarians qualify
as progressives, and here the difference between, say, Robert La Follette and
even so moderate a "populistic" agrarian as William Jennings Bryan can be
instructive.[19] Whereas Bryan stressed evangelical imagery and fundamentalist morality, sought rural support with attacks upon the great cities of the
nation, and gained notoriety for his assault on modern scientific thought,
La Follette stressed liberal education, made systematic use of university-
trained and -centered experts, and generally sought a solution to the problems of modern society through modern intelligence. One can make
comparable observations in distinguishing progressive agrarians, such as
Charles B. Aycock and Clarence Poe of the south, from radical agrarians,
such as "Sockless Jerry" Simpson and "Pitchfork Ben" Tillman, whom Poe
(for one) described as "rough, primeval, untrained men" whom the south
would be well rid of.[20]

[18] Yellowitz, *Labor and the Progressive Movement in New York State, 1897–1916*
(Cornell University Press, 1965), p. 45; see also pp. 44–47, 55, 63. Yellowitz points out
that despite such paternalistic gestures of support, when it came to strikes — as in 1905
and 1909 — the League fought the unions, and its president finally attempted to deny
that the League had ever supported unionism even "sentimentally."
[19] One can argue, with confidence I think, that Bryan does not really belong in the
same category with the "Cyclone" Davises, that he belongs properly in the progressive
category, despite his distance from La Follette. See Lawrence W. Levine, *Defender of
the Faith* (Oxford University Press, 1965).
[20] Poe, "The South: Backward and Sectional or Progressive and National?" *Outlook*,
114 (October 11, 1916), pp. 328–31. It is striking that only a handful of those active
in progressive reform had even been noticeably sympathetic to Populism in the 1890's.
The outstanding progressives — Roosevelt, Woodrow Wilson, La Follette, Lincoln Steffens, Albert Cummins, George Norris, William Allen White, Addams, Brandeis — had
not only not been Populists, but most had fought the Populists with a special ve-
hemence.

So much for what progressivism was not. Let me sum it up by noting that what it rejected and sought to oppose necessarily says much about what it was — perhaps even more than can be ascertained by the more direct approach.

My thesis is that progressivism failed. It failed in what it — or what those who shaped it — conceived to be its principal objective. And that was, over and above everything else, to restore or maintain the conventional consensus on a particular view of the universe, a particular set of values, and a particular constellation of behavioral modes in the country's commerce, its industry, its social relations, and its politics. Such a view, such values, such modes were challenged by the influx of diverse religious and ethnic elements into the nation's social and intellectual stream, by the overwhelming economic success and power of the corporate form of business organization, by the subordination of the work-ethic bound up within the old proprietary and craft enterprise system, and by the increasing centrality of a growing proportion of low-income, unskilled, wage-earning classes in the nation's economy and social structure. Ironically, the *coup de grâce* would be struck by the emergence of a philosophical and scientific rationale for the existence of cultural diversity within a single social system, a rationale that largely grew out of the very intellectual ferment to which progressivism so substantially contributed.

Progressivism sought to save the old view, and the old values and modes, by educating the immigrants and the poor so as to facilitate their acceptance of and absorption into the Anglo-American mode of life, or by excluding the "unassimilable" altogether; by instituting antitrust legislation or, at the least, by imposing regulations upon corporate practices in order to preserve a minimal base for small proprietary business enterprise; by making legislative accommodations to the newly important wage-earning classes — accommodations that might provide some measure of wealth and income redistribution, on the job safety, occupational security, and the like — so as to forestall a forcible transfer of policy-making power away from the groups that had conventionally exercised that power; and by broadening the political selection process, through direct elections, direct nominations, and direct legislation, in order to reduce tensions caused unnecessarily by excessively narrow and provincial cliques of policy-makers. When the economic and political reforms failed to restore the consensus by giving the previously unprivileged an ostensible stake in it, progressive energies turned increasingly toward using the force of the state to proscribe or restrict specifically opprobrious modes of social behavior, such as gaming habits, drinking habits, sexual habits, and Sabbatarian habits. In the ultimate resort, with the proliferation of sedition and criminal syndicalist laws, it sought to constrict political discourse itself. And (except perhaps for the disintegration of the socialist movement) *that* failed, too.

One measure of progressivism's failure lies in the xenophobic racism that reappeared on a large scale even by 1910. In many parts of the country, for example, in the far west and the south, racism and nativism had been fully blended with reform movements even at the height of progressive activities there. The alleged threats of "coolie labor" to American living standards, and of "venal" immigrant and Negro voting to republican institutions generally, underlay the alliance of racism and reform in this period. By and large, however, for the early progressive era the alliance was conspicuous only in the south and on the west coast. By 1910, signs of heightening ethnic animosities, most notably anti-Catholicism, began appearing in other areas of the country as well. As John Higham has written, "It is hard to explain the rebirth of anti-Catholic ferment [at this time] except as an outlet for expectations which progressivism raised and then failed to fulfill." [21] The failure here was in part the inability of reform to deliver a meaningful share of the social surplus to the groups left out of the general national progress, and in part the inability of reform to achieve its objective of assimilation and consensus.

The growing ethnic animus, moreover, operated to compound the difficulty of achieving assimilation. By the second decade of the century, the objects of the antagonism were beginning to adopt a frankly assertive posture. The World War, and the ethnic cleavages it accentuated and aggravated, represented only the final blow to the assimilationist idea; "hyphenate" tendencies had already been growing during the years before 1914. It had only been in 1905 that the Louisville-born and secular-minded Louis Brandeis had branded as "disloyal" all who "keep alive" their differences of origin or religion. By 1912, by now a victim of anti-Semitism and aware of a rising hostility toward Jews in the country, Brandeis had become an active Zionist; before a Jewish audience in 1913, he remarked how "practical experience" had convinced him that "to be good Americans, we must be better Jews, and to be better Jews, we must become Zionists." [22]

Similarly, American Negroes also began to adopt a more aggressive public stance after having been subdued for more than a decade by antiblack violence and the accommodationist tactics suggested in 1895 by Booker T. Washington. As early as 1905, many black leaders had broken with Washington in founding the Niagara Movement for a more vigorous assertion of Negro demands for equality. But most historians seem to agree that it was probably the Springfield race riot of 1908 that ended illusions that black people could gain an equitable share in the rewards of American culture by accommodationist or assimilationist methods. The organization of the NAACP in 1909 gave substantive force for the first time to the three-year-old Niagara Movement. The year 1915 symbolically concluded the demise of accommodationism. That year, the Negro-baiting movie, "The Birth of

---

21 *Strangers in the Land*, p. 179.
22 See my "Brandeis," *op. cit.*, pp. xxiii–xxiv; cf. Horace Kallen, *Zionism and World Politics* (Doubleday, Page, 1921), p. 139.

a Nation," played to massive, enthusiastic audiences that included notably the president of the United States and the chief justice of the Supreme Court; the KKK was revived; and Booker T. Washington died. The next year, black nationalist Marcus Garvey arrived in New York from Jamaica.

Meanwhile, scientific knowledge about race and culture was undergoing a crucial revision. At least in small part stimulated by a keen self-consciousness of his own "outsider" status in American culture, the German-Jewish immigrant Franz Boas was pioneering in the new anthropological concept of "cultures," based on the idea that human behavioral traits are conditioned by historical traditions. The new view of culture was in time to undermine completely the prevailing evolutionary view that ethnic differences must mean racial inequality. The significance of Boas's work after 1910, and that of his students A. L. Kroeber and Clyde Kluckhohn in particular, rests on the fact that the racist thought of the progressive era had founded its intellectual rationale on the monistic, evolutionary view of culture; and indeed much of the progressives' anxiety over the threatened demise of "the American culture" had been founded on that view.[23]

Other intellectual developments as well had for a long time been whittling away at the notion that American society had to stand or fall on the unimpaired coherence of its cultural consensus. Yet the new work in anthropology, law, philosophy, physics, psychology, and literature only unwittingly undermined that assumption. Rather, it was only as the ethnic hostilities grew, and especially as the power of the state came increasingly to be invoked against dissenting groups whose ethnic "peculiarities" provided an excuse for repression, that the new intelligence came to be developed. "The world has thought that it must have its culture and its political unity coincide," wrote Randolph Bourne in 1916 while chauvinism, nativism, and anti-radicalism were mounting; now it was seeing that cultural diversity might yet be the salvation of the liberal society — that it might even serve to provide the necessary countervailing force to the power of the state that private property had once served (in the schema of Locke, Harrington, and Smith) before the interests of private property became so highly concentrated and so well blended with the state itself.[24]

The telltale sign of progressivism's failure was the violent crusade against

[23] I am indebted to my friend and former colleague, George W. Stocking, Jr., for sharing with me at an early date some of his findings on Boas and on the history of American anthropology. See his *Race, Culture, and Evolution* (Free Press, 1968), esp. ch. 9: "Franz Boas and the Culture Concept in Historical Perspective." "Boas," he writes, "began his career with a notion of culture that was . . . still a singular phenomenon, present to a higher or lower degree in all peoples. By 1911, this meaning . . . is given instead to 'civilization.' It would seem that by this time, Boas sensed that the word *culture* was better reserved for the 'cultures' of individual human groups. . . . The plural appears with regularity only in the first generation of Boas' students around 1910." (P. 203.)

[24] The quotation is from Bourne's, "The Jew and Trans-National America," reprinted in *War and the Intellectuals*, edited by Carl Resek (Harper Torchbook, 1964), p. 129.

dissent that took place in the closing years of the Wilson administration. It is too easy to ascribe the literal hysteria of the postwar years to the dislocations of the War alone. Incidents of violent repression of labor and radical activities had been growing remarkably, often in step with xenophobic outbreaks, for several years before America's intervention in the War. To quote Professor Higham once more: "The seemingly unpropitious circumstances under which antiradicalism and anti-Catholicism came to life [after 1910] make their renewal a subject of moment." [25] It seems clear that they both arose out of the sources of the reform ferment itself. When reform failed to enlarge the consensus, or to make it more relevant to the needs of the still disadvantaged and disaffected, and when in fact reform seemed to be encouraging more radical challenges to the social order, the old anxieties of the 1890's returned.

The postwar hysteria represented a reaction to a confluence of anxiety-laden developments, including the high cost of living, the physical and social dislocations of war mobilization and the recruitment of women and Negroes into war production jobs in the big northern cities, the Bolshevik Revolution, a series of labor strikes, and a flood of radical literature that exaggerated the capabilities of radical action. "One Hundred Per Cent Americanism" seemed the only effective way of meeting all these challenges at once. As Stanley Coben has written, making use of recent psychological studies and anthropological work on cultural "revitalization movements": "Citizens who joined the crusade for one hundred per cent Americanism sought, primarily, a unifying force which would halt the apparent disintegration of their culture. . . . The slight evidence of danger from radical organizations aroused such wild fear only because Americans had already encountered other threats to cultural stability." [26]

Now, certainly during the progressive era a lot of reform legislation was passed, much that contributed genuinely to a more liberal society, though more that contributed to the more absolutistic moral objectives of progressivism. Progressivism indeed had real, lasting effects for the blunting of the sharper edges of self-interest in American life, and for the reduction of the harsher cruelties suffered by the society's underprivileged. These achievements deserve emphasis, not least because they derived directly from the progressive habit of looking to standards of conventional morality and human decency for the solution of diverse social conflicts. But the deeper nature of the problem confronting American society required more than the invocation of conventional standards; the conventions themselves were at stake, especially as they bore upon the allocation of privileges and rewards.

[25] *Strangers in the Land,* p. 176.
[26] "A Study in Nativism: The American Red Scare of 1919–20," reprinted in this volume, pp. 289–306.

Because most of the progressives never confronted that problem, in a way their efforts were doomed to failure.

In sum, the overall effect of the period's legislation is not so impressive. For example, all the popular government measures put together have not conspicuously raised the quality of American political life. Direct nominations and elections have tended to make political campaigns so expensive as to reduce the number of eligible candidates for public office to (1) the independently wealthy; (2) the ideologues, especially on the right, who can raise the needed campaign money from independently wealthy ideologues like themselves, or from the organizations set up to promote a particular ideology; and (3) party hacks who pay off their debt to the party treasury by whistle-stopping and chicken dinner speeches. Direct legislation through the Initiative and Referendum device has made cities and states prey to the best-financed and -organized special-interest group pressures, as have so-called nonpartisan elections. Which is not to say that things are worse than before, but only that they are not conspicuously better. The popular government measures did have the effect of shaking up the established political organizations of the day, and that may well have been their only real purpose.[27]

But as Arthur Link has said, in his text, *The American Epoch*, the popular government measures "were merely instruments to facilitate the capture of political machinery. . . . They must be judged for what they accomplished or failed to accomplish on the higher level of substantive reform." [28] Without disparaging the long list of reform measures that passed during the progressive era, the question remains whether all the "substantive reforms" together accomplished what the progressives wanted them to accomplish.

Certain social and economic advantages were indeed shuffled about, but this must be regarded as a short-term achievement for special groups at best. Certain commercial interests, for example, achieved greater political leverage in railroad policy-making than they had had in 1900 through measures such as the Hepburn and Mann-Elkins Acts — though it was not until the 1940's that any real change occurred in the general rate structure, as some broad regional interests had been demanding at the beginning of the century.[29] Warehouse, farm credits, and land-bank acts gave the diminishing numbers of farm owners enhanced opportunities to mortgage their property, and some business groups had persuaded the federal government to use

[27] See, e.g., Grant McConnell, "California Conundrum," *The Nation,* 179 (December 4, 1954), 477–78; and Eugene C. Lee, *The Politics of Nonpartisanship* (University of California Press, 1960).

[28] *American Epoch,* vol. I, p. 90.

[29] See David M. Potter, "The Historical Development of Eastern-Southern Freight Rate Relationships," *Law and Contemporary Problems,* 12 (Summer 1947); and Robert A. Lively, "The South and Freight Rates: Political Settlement of an Economic Argument," *Journal of Southern History,* 14 (August 1948).

national revenues to educate farmers on how to increase their productivity (Smith-Lever Act, 1914); but most farmers remained as dependent as ever upon forces beyond their control — the bankers, the middlemen, the international market. The FTC, and the Tariff Commission established in 1916, extended the principle of using government agencies to adjudicate intra-industrial conflicts ostensibly in the national interest, but these agencies would develop a lamentable tendency of deferring to and even confirming rather than moderating the power of each industry's dominant interests.[30] The Federal Reserve Act made the currency more flexible, and that certainly made more sense than the old system, as even the bankers agreed. But depositers would be as prey to defaulting banks as they had been in the days of the Pharoah — bank deposit insurance somehow was "socialism" to even the best of men in this generation. And despite Woodrow Wilson's brave promise to end the bankers' stifling hold on innovative small business, one searches in vain for some provision in the FRA designed specifically to encourage small or new businesses. In fact, the only constraints on the bankers' power that emerged from the era came primarily from the ability of the larger corporations to finance their own expansion out of capital surpluses they had accumulated from extortionate profits during the War.

A major change almost occurred during the war years when organized labor and the principle of collective bargaining received official recognition and a handful of labor leaders was taken, temporarily, into policy-making councils (e.g., in the War Labor Board). But actually, as already indicated, such a development, if it had been made permanent, would have represented a defeat, not a triumph, for progressivism. The progressives may have fought for improved labor conditions, but they jealously fought against the enlargement of union power. It was no aberration that once the need for wartime productive efficiency evaporated, leading progressives such as A. Mitchell Palmer, Miles Poindexter, and Woodrow Wilson himself helped civic and employer organizations to bludgeon the labor movement into disunity and docility. (It is possible, I suppose, to argue that such progressives were simply inconsistent, but if we understand progressivism in the terms I have outlined above I think the consistency is more evident.) Nevertheless, a double irony is worth noting with respect to progressivism's objectives and the wartime labor developments. On the one hand, the progressives' hostility to labor unions defeated their own objectives of (1) counterbalancing the power of collectivized capital (i.e., corporations), and (2) enhancing workers' share of the nation's wealth. On the other hand, under wartime duress, the progressives did grant concessions to organized labor (e.g., the Adamson Eight-Hour Railway Labor Act, as well as the WLB) that would

---

[30] For a thoughtful study of this issue, see Marver H. Bernstein, *Regulating Business by Independent Commission* (Princeton University Press, 1955). G. Kolko, *The Triumph of Conservatism*, which makes a related point, has to be read with great care.

later serve as precedents for the very "collectivization" of the economic situation that they were dedicated to oppose.

Meanwhile, the distribution of advantages in the society did not change much at all. In some cases, from the progressive reformers' viewpoint at least, it may even have changed for the worse. According to the figures of the National Industrial Conference Board, even income was as badly distributed at the end of the era as before. In 1921, the highest 10 percent of income recipients received 38 percent of total personal income, and that figure was only 34 percent in 1910. (Since the share of the top 5 percent of income recipients probably declined in the 1910–20 period, the figures for the top 10 percent group suggest a certain improvement in income distribution at the top. But the fact that the share of the lowest 60 percent also declined in that period, from 35 percent to 30 percent, confirms the view that no meaningful improvement can be shown.) Maldistribution was to grow worse until after 1929.

American farmers on the whole and in particular seemed to suffer increasing disadvantages. Farm life was one of the institutional bulwarks of the mode of life the progressives ostensibly cherished. "The farmer who owns his land," averred Gifford Pinchot, "is still the backbone of the Nation; and one of the things we want most is more of him, . . . [for] he is the first of home-makers." [31] If only in the sense that there were relatively fewer farmers in the total population at the end of the progressive era, one would have to say farm life in the United States had suffered. But, moreover, fewer owned their own farms. The number of farm tenants increased by 21 percent from 1900 to 1920; 38.1 percent of all farm operators in 1921 were tenants; and the figures look even worse when one notices that tenancy *declined* in the most *impoverished* areas during this period, suggesting that the family farm was surviving mostly in the more marginal agricultural areas. Finally, although agriculture had enjoyed some of its most prosperous years in history in the 1910–20 period, the 21 percent of the nation's gainfully employed who were in agriculture in 1919 (a peak year) earned only 16 percent of the national income.

While progressivism failed to restore vitality to American farming, it failed also to stop the vigorous ascendancy of corporate capitalism, the most conspicuous challenge to conventional values and modes that the society faced at the beginning of the era. The corporation had drastically undermined the very basis of the traditional rationale that had supported the nation's freewheeling system of resource allocation and had underwritten the permissiveness of the laws governing economic activities in the nineteenth century. The new capitalism by-passed the privately-owned proprietary firm, it featured a separation of ownership and control, it subordinated the profit motive to varied and variable other objectives such as empire-

[31] Gifford Pinchot, *The Fight for Conservation* (Doubleday, Page, 1910), pp. 22–23.

building, and, in many of the techniques developed by financial brokers and investment bankers, it appeared to create a great gulf between the making of money and the producing of useful goods and services. Through a remarkable series of judicial sophistries, this nonconventional form of business enterprise had become, in law, a *person*, and had won privileges and liberties once entrusted only to men, who were presumed to be conditioned and restrained by the moral qualities that inhere in human nature.[32] Although gaining legal dispensations from an obliging Supreme Court, the corporation could claim no theoretical legitimacy beyond the fact of its power and its apparently inextricable entanglement in the business order that had produced America's seemingly unbounded material success.[33]

Although much has been written about the supposed continuing vitality of small proprietary business enterprise in the United States,[34] there is no gainsaying the continued ascendancy of the big corporation nor the fact that it still lacks legitimation. The fact that in the last sixty years the number of small proprietary businesses has grown at a rate that slightly exceeds the rate of population growth says little about the character of small business enterprise today as compared with that of the era of the American industrial revolution; it does nothing to disparage the apprehensions expressed in the antitrust campaigns of the progressives. To focus on the vast numbers of automobile dealers and gasoline service station owners, for example, is to miss completely their truly humble dependence upon the very few giant automobile and oil companies, a foretold dependence that was the very point of the progressives' anticorporation, antitrust sentiments. The progressive movement must indeed be credited with placing real restraints upon monopolistic tendencies in the United States, for most statistics indicate that at least until the 1950's business concentration showed no substantial increase from the turn of the century (though it may be pertinent to note that concentration ratios did increase significantly in the decade immediately following the progressive era).[35] But the statistics of concentration remain

[32] As John Tipple writes, "In establishing the legal fiction [of the corporation as a person], the court not only undermined the ideal of the morally responsible individual by extending the individualistic ethic to the amoral impersonality of the modern corporation, but in the long run subordinated the ideal to the right of property." "The Robber Barons in the Gilded Age: Entrepreneurs or Iconoclasts?" in H. W. Morgan, ed., *The Gilded Age: A Reappraisal* (Syracuse University Press, 1963), p. 31.

[33] See, e.g., A. A. Berle, Jr., "Economic Power and the Free Society," in Andrew Hacker, ed., *The Corporation Take-Over* (Anchor, 1965), pp. 86–102, esp. pp. 91, 95–98.

[34] See Hacker, p. 1; Thomas C. Cochran, *The American Business System* (Harper Torchbook, 1955), pp. 164–65; R. Hofstadter, "What Happened to the Antitrust Movement?" in Earl F. Cheit, ed., *The Business Establishment* (Wiley, 1964), esp. p. 137.

[35] See M. A. Adelman, "The Measurement of Industrial Concentration," *The Review of Economics and Statistics*, 33 (1951); and G. C. Means, "The Growth in the Relative Importance of the Large Corporation in American Life," *American Economic Review*, 21 (1931).

impressive — just as they were when John Moody wrote *The Truth About the Trusts* in 1904 and Louis Brandeis followed it with *Other People's Money* in 1914. That two hundred corporations (many of them inter-related) held almost one-quarter of all business assets, and more than 40 percent of all corporate assets in the country in 1948; that the fifty largest manufacturing corporations held 35 percent of all industrial assets in 1948, and 38 percent by 1962; and that a mere twenty-eight corporations or one one-thousandth of a percentage of all nonfinancial firms in 1956 employed 10 percent of all those employed in the nonfinancial industries, should be sufficient statistical support for the apprehensions of the progressive era — *just as it is testimony to the failure of the progressive movement to achieve anything substantial to alter the situation.*[36]

Perhaps the crowning failure of progressivism was the American role in World War I. It is true that many progressives opposed America's interven-tion, but it is also true that a great many more supported it. The failure in progressivism lies not in the decision to intervene but in the futility of inter-vention measured by progressive expectations. (It is worth noting, by the way, that the influence of ethnic and ex-nationalistic emotions on how each progressive viewed the decision to intervene is not merely an incidental part of the failure: it suggests the fact that such emotions, and the identifications they expressed, were after all stronger than the presumed consensus even among the progressives. It must have been a revelation to most.) For those who supported Wilson's decision to intervene — as well as for those who early urged a more militant posture — the European conflagration appeared to have created an opportunity to work for essentially the same ideals abroad as the progressives had been serving at home. The idea of *mission* had in fact always been a part of the cultural consensus to which the progressives had been devoting their energies. It is, moreover, becoming increasingly clear from the biographical masterwork on Wilson that Arthur Link is com-pleting that nothing was quite so important in shaping the Wilson policies toward Germany as Wilson's commitment to the Anglo-American system of values by which he defined "civilization." Wilson's decision to intervene ultimately rested, it seems clear now, not only on his unwillingness to see England defeated but on his desire to make certain that America would have a major decision-making role at the peace table — where it could help shape

---

[36] The figures are from Adelman, *op. cit.*; Carl Kaysen, "The Corporation: How Much Power? What Scope?" in E. S. Mason, ed., *The Corporation in Modern Society* (Harvard Press, 1959); and Richard A. Miller, "Conglomerate Mergers: A Monopoly Problem?" *St. John's Law Review*, 44 (Special Edition, Spring 1970), 211–34. But see, too, A. D. Chandler, "The Large Industrial Corporation and the Making of the Modern American Economy," reprinted in this volume, pp. 93–115; and Chandler, "The Structure of American Industry in the Twentieth Century: A Historical Overview," *Business History Review*, 43 (Autumn 1969).

the world according to the same principles of stewardship that guided the Wilsonian program at home.[37]

Of course there were many who protested that America's mission might better be served by staying out, and Wilson himself had, until almost the very end, believed that, too. "This country does not intend to become involved in this war," he wrote to House on January 4, 1917. "We are the only one of the great white nations that is free from war today, and it would be a crime against civilization for us to go in." [38] We do not know yet precisely what changed Wilson's mind — perhaps it was the contemptuousness with which both the British and the Germans rejected his mediation offers as long as the United States remained neutral. But once the decision was made, Wilson succeeded in persuading others (such as John Dewey) who had resisted intervention until then to commit themselves to the same cause. But this will take us too far afield, and space will not permit.

Let me conclude with a bit of an epilogue. The inability of progressive reform to solve the problems of a society riven by industrial alienation, by the community-dissolving experience of the industrial process, by the convention-defying influence of massive immigration, by the faith-shattering impact of modern science, and by the consensus-destroying effect of rival nationalisms at war, helps us to understand the estrangement from all causes and social purpose that seems to have characterized the generation of Americans that came out of the War era. Many had gone off to the War at the height of the enthusiasm to do something for civilization (such as Hemingway), or had enlisted at home in government work (such as Veblen). And when it was over, and it had all seemed futile, they were prepared to concede that Randolph Bourne had been right — that one could *not* have the War and the American promise, too; that now something in American life had been extinguished forever: "The dream of a new community, all the tokens of that brave and expectant fraternalism which had at one period marked the emergence of the modern spirit in America." [39]

For younger men, such as F. Scott Fitzgerald, who were just emerging from college, it seemed that they had come on the scene "with all gods dead, with all wars fought, with all faiths shaken." For progressives, the god that was dead was the one that had made them "stewards" of the people; the faith that was shaken was what had given them the criteria upon which they could confidently assert their definition of the "general interest"; and the war (to end all wars) that had been fought — to make the world safe for democracy — had been a mockery, an exercise in futility, a grand illusion, especially because even the object no longer had the hallowed shimmer they thought they had perceived.

[37] See esp. Link, *Wilson the Diplomatist* (Quadrangle edition, 1965), p. xv. For a summary of the evolution of Link's assessment of Wilson's motivations, see Daniel M. Smith, "National Interest and American Intervention, 1917: An Historiographical Appraisal," *Journal of American History*, 52 (June 1965).

[38] Link, *Wilson the Diplomatist*, p. 81.

[39] Quoting Alfred Kazin, *On Native Grounds* (Anchor edition, 1956), p. 149.

10

WHY WE WENT TO WAR

The outbreak of World War I came as a tremendous shock to the Western world. Not that war was unexpected; rather it was *unbelievable*. "What shall we say," asked the director of the World Peace Foundation a year before Sarajevo, "of the Great War of Europe, ever threatening, ever impending and which never comes? We shall say that it will never come. Humanly speaking, it is impossible." After a century of peace (not counting border wars, colonial wars, and wars for national unity), it seemed unthinkable that the world's most civilized people could ever again indulge in the barbarism of full-scale warfare among themselves. "If civilized Europe were holding back India, for example," said Norman Hapgood after the War broke, "it would be comprehensible. [But] for Germans and French, with a whole complex of delicate civilization in common, to be using huge death engines to mow down men and cities is so unthinkable that we go about in a daze, hoping to awake from the most horrid of nightmares." [*Harper's Weekly*, Sept. 12, 1914.]

But if the onset of the war was shocking, the war itself produced a still greater trauma. U-boats, poison gas, aerial bombings, and the direct involvement of civilians in war brutality tended to jolt a society that, at the outbreak, had still lingered on the notion that even barbarism must adhere to rules of decency. Then, of course, there were the actual casualties: counting the military dead only, Germany lost 1.8 million men, Russia 1.7 million, France, 1.4 million, Austria-Hungary, 1.2 million, Great Britain, 947,000, and on down to the United States' losses of 107,000 men dead in less than a year of actual military engagement. Back home, the "walking dead" with their missing limbs and mutilated faces advertised war's triumph over valor, while the words "shell shock" entered the language to describe the suffering of those who left their sanity somewhere in the trenches as hostage to the genius of military technology.

From the beginning, the American inclination was to keep out of it. President Woodrow Wilson implored the American people to remain "impartial in thought as well as in action" and to "put a curb upon our sentiments as well as upon every transaction that might be construed as a preference of one party to the struggle before another." But the nationalistic, ethnic, economic, and other pressures for intervention proved too great, and in less than three years we were in it. As Paul Birdsall notes in the article that follows, the German decision to wage unlimited submarine warfare in February 1917 unquestionably was the immediate cause of American intervention, but how the Germans came to back into that corner has remained a source of major controversy among historians and laymen.

Essentially, the controversy focuses on two points: (1) the role played by Wilson's pro-Allied predilections, and (2) the role played by American economic interests. That Wilson sympathized with the Allies — particularly with Britain — defies refutation; that these sympathies bore directly upon our involvement remains to be demonstrated. It may be true that Wilson's prejudices made it impossible for him to play the role of mediator (which he so zealously coveted) on terms reasonably acceptable to the Germans. Yet it is at least equally true that the British had little desire for a Wilsonian mediation on any terms. Wilson might have been able to avoid eventual American participation by refusing United States assistance to the Allies early in the war (either by an embargo or, the equivalent, by banning credit arrangements), forcing them to capitulate to German military power for want of supplies. But even if Wilson had been willing to accept a British defeat, it seems highly unlikely that the American electorate would have allowed him to do it. Here, even the most anti-Wilson partisans have to concede that German behavior had something to do with "taking us to war." The sinking in May 1915 of the *Lusitania*, that era's approximate equivalent to the *Queen Elizabeth* of our time, and the Germans' mishandling of the negotiations that followed, served to heighten an already hostile sentiment in this country. It was on the night after he learned of the *Lusitania*'s destruction and the loss of 124 American lives that Wilson made the speech in which he said, "There is such a thing as being too proud to fight." In effect, he was pleading with the country to keep its head. But so violent was the public reaction that Wilson was forced to retract the substance of his point the next day. For a long time thereafter, it was impossible for him to attempt any rapprochement with Germany.

But aside from the pressure of pro-Allied sentiments in the United States, Wilson was restrained from restricting American credit and shipments for two reasons. One was his possibly ill-advised (though far from unreasonable) interpretation of international law that made such a move appear to be a relinquishment of our neutral rights and specifically anti-British as well. The other was that such a move would almost certainly have resulted in the immediate collapse of American prosperity. It is to the role of the American economic commitment that the late Mr. Birdsall (at the time, Professor of History at Williams College) addresses himself in the article that follows.

The influence of economic interests has long been a subject for opprobrious comment by politicians and historians. That the United States could have become entangled in World War I because of its economic interests continues to smell bad to those who grew up in what intellectuals call "the progressive tradition." Paul Birdsall's article is especially remarkable because he tends to regard the economic motive as entirely legitimate, although he wrote in an era that was especially critical of pecuniary motivation. With the American economic stake in international commerce, and particularly in its commerce with the Allies, what other policy could the United States government have been expected to take?

For a long time, Wilson suffered severely from critics for ostensibly pandering to economic interests, and his defenders have spilled much ink saying it wasn't so. But in this age of *realpolitik* Wilson has required a new defense. Among the historians who have endorsed the Wilsonian course, Ernest May has confronted the economic issue most bluntly. Noting that Wilson himself had argued before a Kansas audience that in addition to the moral obligation to stay out of war there was also "a moral obligation . . . to keep free the courses of our commerce and of our finance," May concludes: "The government did have an overriding obligation to protect the business and the rights and the safety of its citizens. It would have been unfaithful to its trust, as well as to the national tradition, if it had failed to help Americans make money out of the war." [*The World War and American Isolationism, 1914–1917* (1959), p. 184.]

It is probably unnecessary to go quite so far to recognize that German maritime policy represented a distinct threat to America's sizable commerce with Europe, whereas Britain's blockade, for all practical purposes, did not; moreover, if at that point the United States failed to assert and protect its stake in international commerce, it would have seriously jeopardized its economic growth and would have become committed to secondary status among the world powers. But it is one thing to justify United States intervention on these grounds, and another to contend that Wilson had a clear understanding of such realities. Despite the efforts of Ernest May, A. S. Link [*Wilson: The Struggle for Neutrality** (1960), *Wilson: Campaigns for Progressivism and Peace, 1916–1917* (1965), and *Wilson the Diplomatist** (1957)] and E. H. Buehrig [*Woodrow Wilson and the Balance of Power* (1955)], Wilson's intermittent concern for economic self-interest or for national security does not seem to outweigh his far more usual preoccupation with universal principles and his ambition to sit at the peace table to help set the terms of the settlement. [See R. E. Osgood, *Ideals and Self-Interest in America's Foreign Relations** (1953); Osgood's "Woodrow Wilson, Collective Security, and the Lessons of History," *Confluence*, 5 (Winter 1957); and Link's 1963 preface to the Quadrangle paperback reissue of *The Diplomatist*.] That Wilson worked to hold American intervention to the principles of universal law and altruism with which he justified it surely stands as one of the noblest acts of civilization; that a major power could enter a major war seeking "no conquest, no dominion . . . no indemnities for ourselves, no material compensation for the sacrifices we shall freely make" is probably unique in all history. Unfortunately, this achievement left the American people unprepared for the *realpolitik* of Versailles and thereafter. As Henry F. May has remarked, the assumptions and purposes of the Wilson War Message "had little to do with the particular war Wilson was talking about, and, in their most literal aspects, little to do with history itself." [*The End of American Innocence* (1959), p. 386.]

D. M. Smith, "Robert Lansing and the Formulation of American Neutrality Policies, 1914–1915," *Mississippi Valley Historical Review*, 42 (June 1956); and R. W. Leopold, "The Problem of American Intervention, 1917: An Historical Retrospect," *World Politics*, 2 (April 1950), are first-rate articles still worth reading, though each has written more recent historiographical analyses. Smith's "National Interest and American Intervention, 1917," *Journal of American History*, 52 (June 1965) is equally useful for tracing the development of many scholars' views on the problems; and Leopold's, "The Emergence of America as a World Power: Some Second Thoughts," in J. Braeman et al., eds., *Change and Continuity in Twentieth-Century America* (1964), treats the issue in a broader perspective. N. Gordon Levin, Jr., *Woodrow Wilson and World Politics: America's Response to War and Revolution** (1968), is an especially bright interpretation.

Neutrality and Economic Pressures, 1914–1917

PAUL BIRDSALL

Twenty years of debate have not yet produced a satisfactory or even a coherent neutrality policy for the United States, nor have they yet offered any real understanding of the problem of neutrality in the modern world to serve as a basis for policy making. Until we have some adequate analysis of the forces which destroyed President Wilson's neutrality policy between 1914 and 1917 no government is likely to be more successful than his in future efforts to master such forces. Nor will the neutrality legislation of the past years help very much if it simply ignores these forces.

The trouble with much of the writing on the World War period is that it deals with separate aspects of the problem in watertight compartments with complete disregard of the complex interrelations between economic and political phenomena. Thus Charles Seymour deals almost exclusively with the diplomatic record of our relations with Imperial Germany and from that record draws the only possible conclusion, that "It was the German submarine warfare and nothing else that forced him [Wilson] to lead America

Reprinted by permission from *Science and Society*, 3 (Spring 1939), 217–28.

into war." [1] The late Newton D. Baker arrives by the same route at the same conclusion: "Certainly the occasion of the United States entering the World War was the resumption of submarine warfare." That Baker had a glimpse of more remote and subtile causation is indicated by his choice of the word "occasion" and by his admission that critics may with some justification charge him with oversimplification by confusing "occasion" with "cause." "This," he says, "I may to some extent have done." [2] Each of these authors is content with a surface record of diplomacy and politics without reference to the fundamental context of economic and social phenomena which alone can give it significance for analysis of the large problem of neutrality.

Nor does it advance the investigation to turn one's back completely on the diplomatic record and resort to a narrow economic determinism, as does Senator Nye. Ignoring the inescapable evidence that German submarine warfare was the immediate "occasion" for American entry into the war, he argues the simple thesis that American bankers first forced the American Government to authorize large loans to France and Great Britain, and when those countries were faced with defeat, then forced the American Government into the war to protect the bankers' investments. I have heard Senator Nye publicly express embarrassment at the lack of any direct evidence to support the second, and for his purposes the essential, part of his thesis, but what he lacks in evidence he makes up in faith.[3]

What is most needed is careful synthesis of the accurate and valid parts of the diplomatic and economic theses. Senator Nye's committee has given us invaluable data on the development of close economic ties with the Entente Powers in the face of a government policy of neutrality designed to prevent just that development, even if the committee failed to analyze the precise forces at work.[4] We have accurate and scholarly studies explaining the *immediate* cause of American intervention as due to the German decision to wage unrestricted submarine warfare. But no one has yet demonstrated the connection between American economic ties with Germany's enemies and Germany's submarine campaign which provoked American intervention. It is precisely this connection which reveals the true significance of the economic relationship, namely that it makes neutrality in modern war impossible — unless the economic relationships with bellig-

---

[1] *American Diplomacy during the World War* (Baltimore, The Johns Hopkins Press, 1934), p. 210. See also *American Neutrality, 1914–1917* (New Haven, Yale University Press, 1935).
[2] *Foreign Affairs*, xv (Oct., 1936), p. 85.
[3] C. C. Tansill, *America Goes to War* (Boston, 1938), p. 133.
[4] *Hearings before the Special Senate Committee on the Investigation of the Munitions Industry.* United States Senate. 74th Cong., 2nd sess. (Washington, 1937). Many of the same documents were published in the New York *Times* (Jan. 8–12, 1936). Many are to be found in R. S. Baker, *Woodrow Wilson* (Garden City, 1935), v.

erents can somehow be prevented. And that must be the first subject of investigation.

II

If Senator Nye is right in contending that it was primarily the intrigues of the banking interests which prevented a genuine neutrality policy, then the present legislation to curb such activity in the future should prove adequate. But careful study of the evidence he has himself unearthed does not bear him out.

The Wilson administration attempted to enforce a neutrality policy identical with that now prescribed by statute in respect to loans to belligerents. To be sure there was no effort to prevent the sale of munitions to belligerents, and Secretary of State Bryan explained why in a letter of January 20, 1915 to Senator Stone of the Senate Committee on Foreign Relations. He said that "the duty of a neutral to restrict trade in munitions of war has never been imposed by international law or municipal statute. . . . [It] has never been the policy of this government to prevent the shipment of arms or ammunition into belligerent territory, except in the case of the American Republics, and then only when civil strife prevailed." [5] Moreover the German government admitted the legality of the munitions traffic as late as December 15, 1914 even while they complained of its disadvantage to their cause.

Very different was the official attitude toward loans to belligerent governments. The State Department recognized no greater legal obligation to prevent them than the sale of munitions. Lansing, Bryan's subordinate and successor, said he knew of no legal objection but agreed with Bryan in urging that the United States government refuse to approve loans to belligerents. Bryan said that "money is the worst of all contrabands," and on August 15, 1914, wrote J. P. Morgan, who wished to finance a French loan, "There is no reason why loans should not be made to the governments of neutral nations, but in the judgment of this government, *loans by American bankers to any foreign nation which is at war are inconsistent with the spirit of true neutrality.*" [6] Our State Department has never received the credit it deserves for its realistic appraisal of the issues of neutrality and its refusal to take refuge in the technicalities of international law. It is scarcely the fault of the State Department that powerful economic forces almost at once began to undermine its policy and within the year forced its abandonment. Nor can it be denied that the German government itself helped destroy the policy by sinking the *Lusitania*.

The first efforts to modify the State Department's policy came from the bankers, specifically the house of J. P. Morgan. Lamont testifies that Mor-

[5] Baker, *Wilson*, v, p. 179–184 and 189.
[6] New York *Times*, Jan. 8, 1936; Baker, *Wilson*, v, p. 175 f.

gan's firm accepted the State Department ruling but asked permission at least to extend credits to foreign governments to facilitate purchases in the United States, on the theory that this was purely a bookkeeping arrangement very different from the sale of belligerent bonds on the open market. On October 23, 1914 Lansing recorded a conversation he had with President Wilson dealing with this request, in which Wilson accepted the distinction as valid. "There is a decided difference between an issue of government bonds, sold in the open market to investors, and an arrangement for easy exchange in meeting debts incurred between the government and American merchants." The latter was merely a means of facilitating trade. Accordingly Straight of the firm of Morgan was authorized to open credits of this character for belligerent governments, particularly the French. On March 31, 1915 the State Department issued a public statement of its policy in the following press release. "While loans to belligerents have been disapproved, this government has not felt that it was justified in interposing objections.to the credit arrangements which have been brought to its attention. It has neither approved these nor disapproved — it has simply taken no action and expressed no opinion." [7]

The destruction of the *Lusitania* by a German submarine undermined the State Department's neutrality policy in two ways, by causing the resignation of Bryan (who refused to take responsibility for Wilson's stiff notes of protest to Germany), and by establishing in the post of Secretary of State his former subordinate Lansing. Lansing says in his memoirs that after the *Lusitania* there was always in his mind the "conviction that we would ultimately become the ally of Britain." [8] He was therefore less disposed to maintain the rigid standards of neutrality set by Bryan. Yet in the event it was economic pressures that overwhelmed the policy.

In August of 1915 the British pound sterling began to sag in the exchange market under the pressure of war finance, and the first note of warning of threat to American export business appears in a letter of August 14 from Governor Strong of the New York Federal Reserve Bank to Col. House. Strong said that the drop of sterling to below $4.71 had already led to cancellation of many foreign contracts for the purchase of American grain. He predicted more to follow and feared for the drastic curtailment of all American exports. On August 21 Secretary of the Treasury McAdoo wrote to President Wilson, "Great Britain is and always has been our best customer. . . . The high prices for food products have brought great prosperity to the farmers, while the purchasers of war munitions have stimulated industry and have set factories going to full capacity. . . . Great prosperity is coming. It is, in large measure, already here. It will be tremendously increased if we can extend reasonable credits to our customers." It was therefore imperative, he said, that Great Britain be permitted to float a loan of $500,-

[7] New York *Times*, Jan. 8, 1936. Also Baker, *op. cit.*, p. 186 f.
[8] *War Memoirs of Robert Lansing* (Indianapolis, 1935), p. 128.

000,000 at once. "To maintain our prosperity we must finance it." Unfortunately, according to him, the way was barred by the State Department ban on foreign loans, and by the pro-German attitude of two members of the Federal Reserve Board, Miller and Warburg.[9]

Wilson's reply was an evasion. On August 26, he wrote Lansing, "My opinion is that we should say that 'parties would take no action either for or against such a transaction,' but that this should be orally conveyed, and not put in writing. Yrs. W. W." But Lansing wanted something more definite and wrote a long letter rehearsing all McAdoo's arguments. "Doubtless Sec'y McAdoo has discussed with you the necessity of floating government loans for the belligerent nations, which are purchasing such great quantities of goods in this country, in order to avoid a serious financial situation which will not only affect them but this country as well." He estimated excess of American exports over imports for the entire year at $2,500,000,000 and alleged that the figure from December 1, 1914 to June 30, 1915 was only slightly less than $1,000,000,000. "If the European countries cannot find the means to pay for the excess of goods sold them over those purchased from them, they will have to stop buying and our present export trade will shrink proportionately. The result would be restriction of output, industrial depression, idle capital, idle labor, numerous failures, financial demoralization, and general unrest and suffering among the laboring classes. . . . Can we afford to let a declaration as to our conception of the 'true spirit of neutrality,' made in the early days of the war, stand in the way of our national interests which seem to be seriously threatened?" McAdoo had stressed the opportunity for national prosperity; Lansing threatened the horrors of national depression. Wilson replied two days later, on September 8, "I have no doubt that our oral discussion of this letter suffices. If it does not, will you let me know that you would like a written reply? W. W." Shortly after this the house of Morgan floated a loan of $500,000,000 on behalf of the British and French governments.[10]

What of Senator Nye's contention that the bankers got us into the war by exerting direct pressure on Washington to protect their "investment"? It remains to be proved that the investment did get us into the war, and it is perfectly clear that direct pressure on Washington ceased when their desire to float loans for belligerent governments was granted. It is likewise clear that the government did not relinquish its ban on such loans out of any tender concern for the bankers as a group. What McAdoo, Lansing, and Wilson feared was a national economic depression. The bankers were in the happy position of being able to serve both God and Mammon. The situation is summarized in a single paragraph of Lansing's letter of September 6: "I believe that Secretary McAdoo is convinced, and I agree with him, that there is only one means of avoiding this situation which would so seriously

9 New York *Times*, Jan. 10, 1936. *Cf.* Baker, *op. cit.*, p. 380 f.
10 New York *Times*, Jan. 10 and 11, 1936. Baker, *op. cit.*, p. 381–383.

affect economic conditions in this country, and that is the flotation of large bond issues by the belligerent governments. Our financial institutions have the money to loan and wish to do so." [11]

At this point the conclusions of Seymour and Baker seem irresistible. They conclusively demonstrate from the diplomatic record that German resort to unrestricted submarine warfare was the immediate cause of American participation in the war. Yet they are strangely incurious about the reasons for the German decision, which have a very direct connection with the American departure from its own deliberately adopted policy of forbidding loans to belligerents. The fact that the German decision was made with full realization that it would force the United States into the war is certainly something that needs to be explained and the search for an explanation is revealing.

III

There were two forces struggling for control within Germany, the civilian government of Chancellor Bethmann-Hollweg, and the naval-military element. The latter favored extreme military policies without regard to diplomatic consequences, while Bethmann waged a losing fight on behalf of elementary political common-sense. In regard to the specific issue of submarine warfare the military group were uncompromising advocates of its unrestricted use as against Bethmann's warnings that such a policy was certain to bring the United States into the war in the ranks of Germany's enemies. After the sinking of the *Sussex* in March 1916 Bethmann was able to dominate the situation for the rest of the year. On May 4, 1916 the German Government gave to the United States a pledge to abide by the rules of cruiser warfare, abandoning the attacks on passenger ships, and promising to obey the rules of visit and search as they applied to merchant vessels. That the pledge was conditional on American enforcement of international law on Great Britain was a clear indication that Bethmann's victory was not decisive. The military element opposed the pledge from the beginning and fought for its abrogation from May throughout the rest of the year, with ultimate success. [12]

They did not in the least contest the civilian thesis that unrestricted submarine warfare would force the United States into the war. They blithely admitted it — and said it did not matter! Here is the reasoning. On May 4, the very day of the *Sussex* pledge, General Falkenhayn wrote Bethmann: "I consider unrestricted U-boat warfare not only one, but the *only* effective instrument of war at our disposal capable of bringing England to consider peace negotiations. . . . So far as this situation is concerned [the probable

[11] *Ibid.*
[12] Carnegie Endowment, *Official German Documents Relating to the World War* (New York, Oxford University Press, 1923), II, p. 1151, no. 155.

entry of the United States into the war] *America's step from secret war in which it has long been engaged against us, to an openly declared hostility can effect no real change.*" [13] Hindenburg and Ludendorff grew more and more impatient of the civilians' incurable timidity about war with the United States. They renewed their attack at the end of August, and Holtzendorff of the Admiralty Staff carried their complaints to Bethmann. "The objections to this mode of warfare are not considered mainly from the standpoint of the effect upon England, but from that of the reaction upon the United States. . . . *The United States can scarcely engage in more hostile activities than she has already done up to this time.*" [14] On August 31 at Pless, the civilian and military elements fought it out, with Jagow, Helferrich, and Bethmann standing firmly together against the generals. All three warned that war with the United States must inevitably follow resumption of submarine warfare, and that active American participation would be fatal to Germany. For the time being they again won their point, and it was agreed that final decision might await the outcome of the Rumanian campaign.[15] Even after that Bethmann was permitted to try his hand at peace negotiations in December, but their complete failure, coupled with Wilson's inability to mediate, inevitably brought renewed pressure from the military. Ludendorff on December 22 told the Foreign Office again that formal American participation in the war would alter nothing, and on the same day Holtzendorf brought in an Admiralty report to much the same effect. It dismissed the danger of American troops by showing how much time was needed for their training and transport; it calculated that the American supply of munitions — already at capacity — would be less rather than more available to Germany's enemies because they would be reserved for American use. Positive advantage would accrue to Germany from restored freedom of action in sinking even passenger ships which carried munitions. The only disadvantage conceded by the report was the possible increase in American loans to the belligerents, but the amount of these was already so tremendous a factor in the economic strength of the hostile coalition that little additional danger from that source was to be anticipated.[16] Bethmann had for some time been yielding to the arguments and the importunities of the military, and the conference at Pless on January 9, 1917 sealed his defeat by the decision to renew unrestricted submarine warfare. Hindenburg's final words were, "It simply must be. We are counting on the possibility of war with the United States, and have made all preparations to meet it. *Things cannot be worse than they now are.* The war must be brought to an end by the use of all means as soon as possible." [17] The United States declared war on April 6, 1917.

[13] *Ibid.*, p. 1151 f., no. 156.
[14] *Ibid.*, p. 1153, no. 157.
[15] *Ibid.*, p. 1154–1163, no. 158.
[16] *Ibid.*, p. 1200 f., no. 177, and p. 1218 f., no. 190.
[17] *Ibid.*, p. 1317–1319, no. 212.

The civilians were right and the military were wrong in their calculations as to the ultimate importance of a formal declaration of war by the United States. But the arguments of the military were plausible and they carried the day. Their promise to reduce England speedily to prostration was tempting, but it was essentially a gamble, and it is hard to see how they could have overborne civilian opposition if they had not had so plausible an answer to the one serious argument that the civilians presented. The answer was always that formal participation of the United States in the war would bring no change in the fundamental situation of American economic support to the Allies. The major influence in shaping the decision which brought the United States into the war is to be found in American policy in the economic sphere, specifically the decision of the Wilson administration in August, 1915 to abandon a policy deliberately adopted in the interest of neutrality early in the war. It was government permission to bankers to float loans for belligerent governments in order to finance American export trade that provided the Allies with resources which Germany could not obtain. That in turn weighted the scales in favor of the extremists and against the moderates in Germany, and provoked the decision which forced the United States into the war.

It is equally clear that the administration yielded to pressures which no administration is likely to withstand. The alternative policy of strict adherence to its earlier standards of neutrality meant economic depression on a national scale. It is scarcely drawing the long bow to say that the fundamental cause of the failure of American neutrality policy was economic, nor is it unreasonable to suppose that the same economic factors will again in the future make a genuine and strict policy of neutrality unworkable, no matter what laws may be written on the statute books to enforce it. The only sensible course is to renounce our illusions and to face the world of reality where there is no longer any such thing as neutrality. In the face of a possible collapse of the collective security system as an alternative to ostrich isolationism and "neutrality" the area of choice is tragically narrowed. It would seem to involve a choice between deciding whether we should now affirm our decision publicly that we will align ourselves with the democracies of the world in the event of war on the long chance of preventing the war, or follow that policy of drift which will sooner or later involve us in inevitable war without our having any very clear cut program of war aims to achieve.

IV

Is such realism conceivable in the present state of confusion of mind? Probably not, because of the tenacity of outworn but hallowed concepts and policies. Neutrality has a long history and its own particular folklore. Two of its high priests, Borchard and Lage, treat it as an all-sufficient decalogue when rightly interpreted and strictly adhered to. ". . . Neutral rights were as clear in 1914 as was any other branch of public law, and while the law was grossly violated during the war, it has not thereby been ended or modified." [18] The real difficulty they discover in Wilson's repudiation of "the very basis of American tradition in foreign policy." The submarine controversy with Germany is made to turn on Wilson's "insistence as a matter of National Honor that American citizens were privileged to travel unmolested on belligerent vessels." [19] It follows that there was no adequate excuse for the United States to break "with its fundamental principles by the unprecedented decision to participate in a European war. . . ." [20] Consequently there is no need to explore the economic background against which the drama of neutrality was played out, unless indeed there was no such drama at all, but only a skillful bit of play acting. Borchard and Lage devote exactly one page out of a total of three hundred and fifty to the administration's retreat from its original prohibition of loans to belligerent governments, with the remark that "No more than casual reference needs to be made to one of the more egregious lurches into unneutrality, whereby the United States and its people were led into financing the munitions supply of one set of the belligerents, the Allies." [21] In their account this appears as but a minor detail in a general policy of partisanship of the Allies' cause. And so at the end they reject the argument that the conditions of the modern world make American neutrality impossible as "humiliating to American independence." [22] Denying the efficacy of any improvised formula, they recommend "an honest intention to remain aloof from foreign conflict, a refusal to be stampeded by unneutral propaganda, *a knowledge of the law and capacity to stand upon it*, meeting emergencies and problems not romantically but wisely." [23] It can be argued plausibly that President Wilson fought against overwhelming odds to realize exactly that program.

At least historians should not become victims of the legal exegesis that obscures the unreality of the neutrality concept. But the latest and most comprehensive account of American intervention in the World War, Tansill's *America Goes to War*, is almost totally lacking in interpretative treatment and completely lacking in synthesis. His very full chapters on the events leading to abandonment of the administration's loan policy are written largely in terms of "War Profits Beckon to 'Big Business,' " [24] with very little reference to the administration's concern with the economic condition of the country as a whole. Moreover he fails completely to show the politi-

---

[18] *Neutrality for the United States* (New Haven, Yale University Press, 1937), p. 345.

[19] *Ibid.*, p. 346.

[20] *Ibid.*, p. 344.

[21] *Ibid.*, p. 40. The authors say, p. 41, that ". . . only public lending could meet the need, and that meant war." They do not explain why.

[22] *Ibid.*, p. 345.

[23] *Ibid.*, p. 350. (The italics are mine.)

[24] Title of chapter 3, p. 67–89.

cal and diplomatic implications of the economic ties in his concluding paragraph that deals with them. "The real reasons why America went to war cannot be found in any single set of circumstances. There was no clear-cut road to war that the President followed with certain steps that knew no hesitation. There were many dim trails of doubtful promise, and one along which he travelled with early misgivings and reluctant tread was that which led to American economic solidarity with the Allies." [25] Tansill leaves it at that without any attempt to pursue the profound effect of this economic solidarity on the equilibrium of political forces in Germany which I have been at pains to trace in the central portion of this essay. This is all the more remarkable because Tansill is the only writer on the subject who has conscientiously studied that unstable equilibrium extensively in the German official documents. He has used most if not all of the documents I have cited to prove the decisive effect of the economic argument on the submarine decision — and many more — without ever apparently noting the presence of that argument at all. In his quotations from the documents he simply does not quote the passages where the argument appears. Despite his failure to see relationships, and his avoidance of interpretation, his account is still the fullest treatment available of all the complex phenomena, economic, political, psychological, inherent in the neutrality problem. But it is a compendium devoid of significance for an intelligent understanding of the neutrality problem.

The definitive study at once analytical and interpretative as well as comprehensive has yet to appear, and until it does appear there is small hope of enlightenment.[26]

[25] C. C. Tansill, *America Goes to War*, p. 134.

[26] I have deliberately omitted from consideration in these pages one of the most colorful of the historical accounts, Walter Millis's *Road to War* (Cambridge, 1935). It is journalistic and dramatic with little pretense at analysis. There is recognition that economic relations with the Allies were dangerous to neutrality, but no attempt to show precisely how. For example, p. 336, ". . . the United States was enmeshed more deeply than ever in the cause of Allied victory." But there is no effort to explain the submarine decision in these terms (p. 372 f.).

11

A MODERN WAR ECONOMY:
FIRST EFFORTS

The image evoked by the phrase "Military-Industrial Complex" might seem the product of a paranoid radical's rhetoric if it were not that it comes from President Dwight David Eisenhower's farewell address to the nation on January 17, 1961. The address was written for him at his direction by Malcolm C. Moos, a conservative political scientist who later became president of the University of Minnesota. Eisenhower declared:

> A vital element in keeping the peace is our military establishment. . . . Our military organization today bears little relation to that known by any of my predecessors. . . . We can no longer risk emergency improvisation of national defense. . . . We annually spend on military security more than the net income of all U.S. corporations. . . . The total influence — economic, political, even spiritual — is felt in every city, every statehouse, every office of the Federal Government. . . . In the councils of government we must guard against the acquisition of unwarranted influence, whether sought or unsought, by the military-industrial complex. The potential for the disastrous rise of misplaced power exists and will persist. We must never let the weight of this combination endanger our liberties or democratic processes. We should take nothing for granted.

As the reference to the threat of "unwarranted influence" in the councils of government suggests, Eisenhower had in mind mostly the inevitable pressures that would continue to be exerted by the private armaments industry on the political agencies. It has become evident, however, that the menace posed by the MIC is tremendously greater. For one thing, when we notice that in 1969 the Pentagon spent more than $4 million on 339 congressional lobbyists, 6,140 public relations men, and other forms of assistance to promote what it regarded as its special interests, it should be clear that "unwarranted influence" can emanate from within the government as readily as from without. But the problem goes still further. As of 1969, almost $80 billion of the federal budget went to defense and defense-oriented work, with approximately 22,000 prime contractors, 200,000 subcontractors, and 5,300 different cities and towns sharing in the largesse. Meanwhile, congressmen actively vied for the chance to "favor" their own constituencies with such economic opportunities, and of course they faced serious political repercussions whenever defense work lagged or was withdrawn from their district. By 1970, about 9 percent of the GNP and 10 percent of the nation's work force had been engaged annually in defense-oriented programs for almost a decade. Two major universities — M.I.T. and John Hopkins — counted among the top hundred defense contractors with $95 million and $71 million in contracts respectively in 1967, and just about every important university in the country owed a major share of its research funds to the Department of Defense.

It comes as no surprise that the aircraft and shipbuilding industries are largely if not wholly dependent on defense contracts — from a high of 88 percent of Lockheed's sales during 1961–67 to a low of 45 percent of Boeing's. But it is alarming that among the older, giant corporations, a growing proportion of sales by the end of the 1960's seemed significantly dependent on defense expenditures. During 1961–67, in descending order of total defense business performed, the proportion of company sales accounted for by defense business was as follows: General Electric, 19 percent; General Tire, 37 percent; Westinghouse Electric, 13 percent; RCA, 16 percent; Bendix, 42 percent; I.T.&T., 19 percent; Kaiser Industries, 45 percent; Honeywell, 24 percent; and General Telephone, 25 percent. The danger here can best be appreciated when one observes that in the past, before World War II, the principal effective deterrent of United States military ascendancy in public life came from the leading sectors of the business community which, with typical conservatism, feared the disruptions and uncertainties for business that military "adventures" might cause, and above all, the tax costs that military expenditures require. With major sections of the country's most powerful corporations becoming increasingly dependent on defense appropriations, the United States may well be losing one of its chief institutional bulwarks against "adventurism."

There is a large literature blossoming on the MIC. [Among the best are: J. L. Clayton, ed., *The Economic Impact of the Cold War: Sources and Readings** (1970); S. Lens, *The Military-Industrial Complex** (1970); Senator William Proxmire, *Report from Wasteland: America's Military-Industrial Complex* (1970); and *The Congressional Quarterly Weekly Report*, No. 21, Part I, May 24, 1968, all of which emphasize the dangers, as does *Newsweek's* able report in its June 9, 1969, issue. J. S. Baumgartner, *The Lonely Warriors: The Case for the Military-Industrial Complex* (1970) is a noteworthy rebuttal.] But so far there is little on the historical background of the issue. One important exception is the work of Professor Paul Koistinen of San Fernando Valley State College. Koistinen's doctoral dissertation, "The Hammer and the Sword: Labor, the Military, and Industrial Mobilization" (University of California at Berkeley, 1964) covered the years 1920 to 1945. [See his "The 'Industrial-Military Complex' in Historical Perspective: The Interwar Years," *The Journal of American History*, 56 (March 1970), for a brief published version. R. Schaffer, "The War Department's Defense of ROTC, 1920–1940," *Wisconsin Maga-*

zine of History, 53 (Winter 1969–70), has valuable material on the military's effort to overcome public resistance to its ambitions for a more central place in American life in the same period.] In the article reprinted below, Koistinen pushes his study back to the mobilization for World War I.

At that time, the country had nothing that could be remotely called a "Military-Industrial Complex," and indeed virtually no experience in preparing for a major war. It is significant that as late as December 1915, President Woodrow Wilson argued that war preparations would be "a reversal of the whole history and character of our polity," even though his neutrality policies at the time seemed tenuous in the extreme. The story Professor Koistinen tells is largely one of conflict between the military and some preparedness-minded members of the business community. A combination of self-acclaimed patriotism and a traditional conservatism about the likelihood of chaotic business conditions seems to have stimulated certain individual business leaders to press for the coordination of business and military requirements. The effort met with the jealous opposition of the military and War Department bureaucracies, but some of their objectives were achieved in 1918 with the creation of the War Industries Board under Bernard Baruch. Although it is clear that the War Industries Board and the scores of quasi-governmental war service committees bore the earmarks of a nascent MIC, the apparatus was hastily dismantled once peace was achieved.

Much work has yet to be done on the response of the American business community to the rising importance of the military in American life. For a start, S. P. Huntington, *The Soldier and the State** (1957), is superb, though the author's idealization of military life and ideals may trouble some readers. For the World War I era, R. F. Himmelberg, "The War Industries Board and the Antitrust Question in November 1918," *Journal of American History*, 52 (June 1965), is an incisive piece of greater significance than the title may suggest, as is his "Business, Antitrust Policy, and the Industrial Board of the Department of Commerce, 1919," *Business History Review*, 42 (Spring 1968). See also D. R. Beaver, "Newton D. Baker and the Genesis of the War Industries Board," in the issue of the *Journal of American History* just cited; Beaver's biography of Baker, *Newton D. Baker and the American War Effort, 1917–1919* (1966); R. D. Cuff, "Bernard Baruch: Symbol and Myth in Industrial Mobilization," *Business History Review*, 43 (Summer 1969); and Cuff's "A 'Dollar-A-Year Man' in Government: George N. Peek and the War Industries Board," *ibid.*, 41 (Winter 1967). G. B. Clarkson, *Industrial America in the World War* (1923), is the "official" history. M. Janowitz, *The Professional Soldier: A Social and Political Portrait** (1960), is a nearly unique sociological study of the American military.

The "Industrial-Military Complex" in Historical Perspective: World War I

Paul A. C. Koistinen

The rubric "military-industrial complex" has gained widespread currency in the United States since being coined by President Dwight D. Eisenhower in 1961. Though imprecise, the term usually refers to the partial integration of economic and military institutions for the purpose of national security. The nature and consequences of the "complex" remain matters of dispute, but few contest that modern, industrialized warfare has had far-reaching effects upon American life at all levels. Scientific and technological advances have dictated a revolution in weaponry — a revolution which has broken down the distinction between both the civilian and military worlds and the private and public economic functions. Massive spending for war and defense has spread the influence of the "managers of violence" far and wide.

Numerous studies treating the "industrial-military complex" directly and indirectly already exist. Almost without exception, all have concentrated upon the World War II and Cold War years. To focus on those years is quite natural, for it is then that the most blatant manifestations of the "complex" are evident. Nevertheless, to neglect the years before 1940 greatly limits our understanding of the subject for several reasons. In the first place, the so-called "complex" is more difficult to penetrate after 1940 than before. So comprehensive are the effects of twentieth century warfare that it is often difficult to distinguish the central from the peripheral. Moreover, in many instances essential documents are still denied the scholar. In the second place, and more importantly, the years after 1940 mark not a start but rather a culmination in the process of partially integrating economic and military institutions.

World War I is the watershed. In 1917, the United States had to mobilize its economy totally for the first time. Since a large share of the nation's industrial productivity went to the armed services, their supply and procurement systems had to be integrated into civilian mobilization agencies. The means for doing so were determined by a very chaotic interaction of the federal government as a whole, the industrial community, and the military services. From the wartime experience, the foundations for the so-called "complex" were laid. But the armistice ended the experiment in industrial-

Reprinted by permission from *Business History Review*, 41 (Winter 1967), 378–403. Copyright 1967 by the President and Fellows of Harvard College.

ized warfare before it was complete. What began with the war, however, did not end with it. Directly and indirectly, the 1920's and 1930's were years of consolidation for the government, for industry, and for the armed services in terms of fighting a war under modern conditions. The present article deals with these processes during World War I; the inter-war years will be the subject of a future essay.

According to Professor Ellis W. Hawley, three schools have dominated American thinking about what should be the government's policy toward the concentration of economic power: maintaining competition through the antitrust laws; economic regulation and planning by the federal government; and industrial self-regulation through cooperation within business and between it and the government.[1] Of course, the three schools have never been mutually exclusive; numerous shadings within and among them exist. Industrial self-regulation as the middle way probably best characterizes the political economy of twentieth-century America. The antitrust impulse has had widespread appeal but inadequate political support. Economic planning and regulation has lacked both popularity and sustained backing. For a nation torn between its competitive, *laissez faire* ideology and the massive problems of consolidated economic power, the drift towards industrial self-regulation was quite natural. To varying degrees it found favor in the business community. For the nation at large, cooperation, or a "new competition" as it was often called, had the attraction of meeting the dictates of ideology while still solving some practical economic problems.

In theory and practice, industrial self-rule, policed by the federal government, made impressive gains during the Progressive Era.[2] But its hold was far from absolute. Antitrust sentiments were still strong; numerous divisions still existed within business and the government over matters of political economy. Despite various attempts, industry was not granted immunity from the antitrust laws by having the federal government determine in advance the legality of business practices.

What was not possible during peace became imperative during war. Even if it was politically possible, the federal government lacked the personnel, the information, or the experience necessary for the massive economic regulation World War I demanded. Under the auspices of the government, businessmen had to do it themselves. War created the ideal conditions for industrial self-regulation. The demand for maximum munitions production and the lavish prosperity federal spending brought about quieted temporarily antitrust and anti-business dissent. Wartime opportunities for

[1] *The New Deal and the Problem of Monopoly: A Study in Economic Ambivalence* (Princeton, 1966).

[2] Robert Wiebe, *Businessmen and Reform: A Study of the Progressive Movement* (Cambridge, 1962); Gabriel Kolko, *The Triumph of Conservatism: A Reinterpretation of American History, 1900–1916* (New York, 1963); Arthur M. Johnson, "Anti-trust Policy in Transition, 1908: Ideal and Reality," *Mississippi Valley Historical Review,* XLVIII (Dec., 1961), 415–34.

rationalizing the economy, however, were matched by grave risks. Converting the huge American economic machine to war production could end disastrously unless exactly the right means were employed.

Neither the Wilson administration, Congress, nor prominent American industrialists, financiers, and the firms they represented appeared excessively concerned about the economics of warfare between 1914 and 1917. Less prominent members of the business community led in the drive for economic preparedness. The Chamber of Commerce of the United States was in the vanguard. Since its organization in 1912, the Chamber was an outstanding advocate for government-policed industrial self-regulation. Backed by the nearly unanimous vote of its membership, the Chamber was consistently far ahead of the administration, the Congress, and the general public in policies it supported for industrial mobilization between 1915 and 1918.[3] Legitimately concerned about the economic effects of war, the Chamber also perceived that a state of hostility would further its peacetime goal. A mobilized economy "will make individual manufacturers and business men and the Government share equally in responsibility for the safety of the nation," declared *The Nation's Business* in mid-1916.[4] Chamber spokesmen never tired of reiterating that the national emergency was the perfect opportunity for businessmen to prove their new morality and patriotism to the country. Writing to the DuPonts in December 1916, the chairman of the Chamber's Executive Committee on National Defense stated: [5]

> The Chamber of Commerce of the United States has been keenly interested in the attempt to create an entirely new relationship between the Government of the United States and the industries of the United States. It is hoped that the atmosphere of confidence and cooperation which is beginning in this country, as shown by the Federal Trade Commission, the Federal Reserve Board and other points of contact which are now in existence, may be further developed, and this munitions question would seem to be the greatest opportunity to foster the new spirit.

Though the Chamber of Commerce was the prominent advocate of economic preparedness, other members of the commercial world initiated the specific action in behalf of industrial preparedness. Their first opportunity came in mid-1915 when Secretary of the Navy Josephus Daniels called upon members of leading engineering and industrial societies to serve as

---

[3] Galen R. Fisher, "The Chamber of Commerce of the United States and the Laissez-Faire Rationale, 1912–1919" (Ph.D. dissertation, University of California, Berkeley, 1960).

[4] *The Nation's Business*, June, 1916, 4.

[5] Reproduced in U.S. Congress, Senate, Special Committee Investigating the Munitions Industry, *Hearings, Munitions Industry*, 73rd Cong., 1935, Part 15, 3661 — hereafter cited as Nye Committee, *Hearings*.

unofficial industrial consultants for the expanding Navy. Called the Naval Consulting Board, this group ultimately organized down to the local level.

The most dynamic accomplishments of the Naval Consulting Board were performed by a subdivision called the Industrial Preparedness Committee. Discovering that neither the Army nor the Navy had adequate information about the nation's industrial potential, the committee during 1916 inventoried thousands of industrial facilities for the services. The detailed work was done by voluntary effort and private financing under the direction of the then virtually unknown Walter S. Gifford, chief statistician for the American Telephone and Telegraph Company. But the real moving spirit behind the project was Howard E. Coffin, vice-president of the Hudson Motor Car Company.[6]

For Coffin, efforts in behalf of preparedness were only an extension of his peacetime endeavors. In 1910, as president of the Society of Automotive Engineers, he had, with the help of others, transformed the society and the auto industry by bringing about the standardization of specifications and materials.[7] Rationalizing the productive process and promoting industrial organization were continuing interests of this restless individual. As few others, he foresaw the threats as well as the possibilities of industrial mobilization.

"Twentieth century warfare," Coffin insisted, "demands that the blood of the soldier must be mingled with from three to five parts of the sweat of the man in the factories, mills, mines, and fields of the nation in arms." [8] World War I was "the greatest business proposition since time began." [9] In the Progressive rhetoric, he and other industrialists were moved by "patriotism." Just as important, however, was the "cold-blooded" desire to protect their own interests.[10] Only industrialists and engineers were qualified to run a mobilized economy, Coffin averred. Under such leadership, war could be fought without untoward damage to the economy.

Coffin and his colleagues had plans for gradually expanding the activities of the Industrial Preparedness Committee as an agency for industrial mobilization. But a committee of unofficial industrial consultants was unsuited for such grandiose responsibilities. In August 1916, the Council of National

[6] Lloyd N. Scott, *Naval Consulting Board of the United States* (Washington, 1920), 7–37, 220–23.

[7] George V. Thompson, "Intercompany Technical Standardization in the Early American Automobile Industry," *Journal of Economic History*, XIV (Winter, 1954), 1–12.

[8] Quoted in, Franklin H. Martin, *Digest of the Proceedings of the Council of National Defense during the World War*, U.S. Congress, Senate, 73rd Cong., 2nd Sess., Document No. 193 (Washington, 1934), 512.

[9] U.S. Congress, Senate, Committee on Military Affairs, *Hearings, Investigation of the War Department*, 65th Cong., 2nd Sess., 1917–1918, 2281 — hereafter cited as Chamberlain Committee, *Hearings*.

[10] U.S. Congress, House, Committee on Naval Affairs, *Hearings, Estimates Submitted by the Secretary of the Navy — 1916*, 64th Cong., 1st Sess., 1916, 3360.

Defense was created; the council ultimately absorbed the Naval Consulting Board.

The Council of National Defense was the brain child of Dr. Hollis Godfrey, president of the Drexel Institute of Philadelphia — an industrial training and management education institution. As early as 1899, Godfrey was nearly obsessed with the idea of management education as the high road to industrial efficiency and progress. Even before 1914, Godfrey reasoned that his ideas concerning management could serve the nation in war as well as in peace.

Early in 1916, unable to sit by while the nation drifted unprepared into war, Godfrey outlined to General Leonard Wood a plan for applying the principles of management to the economy in order to achieve optimum performance. The two sketched out a proposal for a council of national defense. Over a period of weeks, Godfrey then consulted with numerous industrial colleagues, influential friends, and administrative officials.[11] The final legislation was drafted in the War Department under Secretary Newton D. Baker's instructions. It was shepherded through Congress by the respective chairmen and influential members of the two Military Affairs committees. No meaningful congressional debate took place.

Passed in August 1916, as part of the Army Appropriations Act, the legislation provided for a Council of National Defense consisting of six Cabinet officers. Council members would nominate and the President appoint seven experts in various fields to act as a National Defense Advisory Commission (NDAC) to the Council. Together with the NDAC, the Council would serve as the President's advisory body on all aspects of industrial mobilization.

The creation of the NDAC was actually a formalization of the procedures adopted by the Naval Consulting Board: industrial experts voluntarily donated their talents as public officials without surrendering their positions or incomes as private citizens. The precedent was an important one. It provided the wherewithal for industrialists to guide the process of mobilizing the economy. Moreover, the personnel selected for the National Defense Advisory Commission revealed that it was more an expansion of the Naval Consulting Board than a new agency. Walter S. Gifford was selected as director and Grosvenor B. Clarkson, a journalist, advertising executive, and former civil servant who had handled publicity for the Board, was ultimately to become secretary. Both Coffin and Godfrey were chosen as members along with Bernard M. Baruch and others.

The legislation for the Council of National Defense was predicated on the assumption that private industry would be the primary source of munitions supply in the event of war. Nevertheless, opponents of preparedness

[11] U.S. Congress, House, Subcommittee No. 2 (Camps), Select Committee on Expenditures in the War Department, *Hearings, War Expenditures*, Serial 3, 66th Cong., 1st Sess., 1920, 880–90 — hereafter cited as Graham Committee, *Hearings*.

zeroed in on the munitions makers in an effort to discredit the drive for an enlarged military force. War mongering, profiteering at the nation's expense, it was charged, would be reduced if the government alone produced munitions. Almost to a man, military personnel opposed the proposition as impractical. It would be prohibitively expensive and would not provide the armed forces the quantity of munitions needed once war was fought, they maintained.[12] Industry, of course, took a similar stand, especially since the armaments industry was threatened as Allied orders were cut back.

To settle the issue, the National Defense Act of 1916 authorized a board of three military officers and two civilians to study the matter and make recommendations. They met in November–December 1916, under the direction of Colonel Francis J. Kernan. Benedict Crowell, chairman of Crowell and Little Construction Company of Cleveland and later Assistant Secretary of War, and R. Goodwyn Rhett, former mayor of Charleston, S.C., president of the People's National Bank of Charleston, and president of the Chamber of Commerce of the United States, served as the civilian members. In its study, the Kernan Board relied heavily on the work of the Naval Consulting Board. Coffin, along with others involved in industrial preparedness, lent their advice.

After inspecting government arsenals and consulting with some leading industrialists, the board reported that it was "not desirable for the Government to undertake, unaided by private plants, to provide for its needs in arms, munitions, and equipment." In the event of war the government should depend "largely upon private plants for war material. . . ." But the board did not stop there. Reading like an editorial from *The Nation's Business*, its report praised businessmen for their patriotism in helping to prepare for an emergency and assured the nation that industry would continue to cooperate in the future. Concerning more immediate problems, the board recommended that plants producing munitions for the Allies not be permitted to remain idle when orders were terminated. It concluded by calling for a comprehensive plan for industrial mobilization.[13]

Though only beginning steps in the long trek toward a mobilized economy, the work of the Naval Consulting Board, the organization of the Council of National Defense and its National Defense Advisory Commission, and the conclusions of the Kernan Board were of the greatest significance. They signaled the beginning of a government-industry partnership for

[12] Arthur A. Ekirch, Jr., *The Civilian and the Military* (New York, 1956), 160; U.S. Congress, House, Committee on Military Affairs, *Hearings, To Increase the Efficiency of the Military Establishment of the United States*, 64th Cong., 1st Sess., 1916, 62–64, 342, 347, 498–513, 518–20, 532–35, 550–51, 738–39 — hereafter cited as HMAC, *Hearings*, 1916; U.S. Congress, Senate, Committee on Military Affairs, *Hearings, Preparedness for National Defense*, 64th Cong., 1st Sess., 1916, 84–85, 519–20, 524–30 — hereafter cited as SMAC, *Hearings*, 1916; Marvin A. Kreidberg and Merton G. Henry, *History of Military Mobilization in the United States Army, 1775–1945*, U.S. Dept. of Army Pamphlet No. 20–212 (Washington, 1955), 336–37.

[13] U.S. Congress, Senate, *Government Manufacture of Arms, Munitions, and Equipment*, 64th Cong., 2nd Sess., 1917, Document 664, 5–17.

the purpose of national security. The initiative came from industry, but, out of necessity, the federal government, and specifically the military services, appeared willing to go along. When announcing the appointment of the NDAC members in October 1916, President Wilson observed: "The organization of the Council [of National Defense] . . . opens up a new and direct channel of communication and cooperation between business and scientific men and all departments of the Government. . . ." [14] Howard E. Coffin had ambitious plans for the Council of National Defense. He wrote to the DuPonts in December 1916: [15]

> Private industry in all the varied lines of Governmental supply must be encouraged and not discouraged. It must be educated, organized, and trained for the national emergency service. A closer and more mutually satisfactory business relation [sic] must be established between the industrial lines and every Department of the Government, and the work of the newly created Council of National Defense must be directed to this end.
>
> . . .
>
> The first meeting of the Council of National Defense and its Advisory Commission will be held in the office of the Secretary of War, December 6th, and within six months thereafter it is our hope that we may lay the foundation for that closely knit structure, industrial, civil and military, which every thinking American has come to realize is vital to the future life of this country, in peace and in commerce, no less than in possible war.

Organized in December 1916, the Council of National Defense and its National Defense Advisory Commission did not actively function until March. When war was declared, the Council and the NDAC, authorized only to investigate, advise, and recommend policies to the President and his administration, also assumed responsibilities for mobilizing the economy.

Lack of experience explains in part the failure to create a better, more powerful agency. No one was fully able to anticipate what was required. The nation had to go through the pragmatic process of working out solutions as problems arose. More importantly, there was the widespread desire to avoid permanent political and economic change during the war. Hopefully, a makeshift organization like the Council of National Defense, without clearly defined authority and consisting mainly of existing department heads, would be sufficient to meet war needs. When hostilities ceased, it could easily be disbanded.[16] Moreover, vital issues of political economy were central to any scheme for industrial mobilization. With Progressive divisions

14 New York Times, Oct. 12, 1916, 10.
15 Reproduced in Nye Committee, Hearings, Part 16, 4056–57.
16 For the best expression of this sentiment see: U.S. Congress, Subcommittee of the House Committee on Appropriations, Hearings, Council of National Defense, 65th Cong., 1st Sess., 1917, 37–38, 42–43 — hereafter cited as Appropriations Subcommittee, Hearings. See also, Daniel R. Beaver, Newton D. Baker and the American War Effort, 1917–1919 (Lincoln, 1966), 51–52, 71–76.

still great over the government's role in the economy, any attempt to set up new, powerful mobilization machinery could end in paralyzing debate in Congress and in the nation. Consistently, the President and the Congress avoided facing issues of economic mobilization whenever possible. Not until the mobilization program was on the verge of collapse during the winter of 1917–1918 did President Wilson strengthen the nation's industrial mobilization apparatus. Even then, only the minimal changes essential to the continued operation of the economy were made.

Consistent with prewar precedents, business representatives of the NDAC, not the Cabinet members of the Council of National Defense, led in mobilizing the economy. Haltingly, the commissioners groped their way in search of the proper means. At the outset, they chose to create the most efficient organization possible with the least disturbance to the *status quo*. That meant the federal government would accept, use, and adjust itself to the configuration of power in and the basic pattern of the private sector of the economy.[17]

Several months after its creation, the NDAC divided itself into semiautonomous committees corresponding to the natural subdivisions of the economy: the most important were transportation, raw materials, munitions and manufacturing, and general supplies. In order to relate commission activities to those of the economy as a whole, the commissioners selected or had various industries choose members to represent their interests on committees within the commission. Over 100 such committees were ultimately organized. Almost inevitably, major firms were dominant. Where a trade association like the American Iron and Steel Institute was supreme in its field, it provided the representatives. The Cooperative Committee on Canned Goods, for example, consisted of individuals from the California Packing Corporation, Libby, McNeil & Libby, the H. J. Heinz Company, and others; the steel committee included Elbert H. Gray as chairman and other members from Bethlehem Steel Corporation, Jones and Laughlin Steel Company, Republic Iron and Steel Company, and Lackawanna Steel Company.

The "dollar-a-year" man system was devised to provide the government with the services of experts without undue sacrifice on their part. Because appropriations were limited, businessmen often paid for their own expenses, clerical help, and even office space. Though far from a perfect solution, the system worked for a while. It assured industry's cooperation at a time when

---

[17] Preserving the economic *status quo* during wartime was a central idea of Coffin and was a basic assumption of the Kernan Board. See the discussion of Baruch below and also: Nye Committee, *Minutes of the General Munitions Board From April 4 to August 9, 1917,* 74th Cong., 2nd Sess., 1936, Senate Committee Print No. 6, 1, 2, 4, 6, 39; Nye Committee, *Final Report of the Chairman of the United States War Industries Board to the President of the United States, February, 1919,* 74th Cong., 1st Sess., 1935, Senate Committee Print No. 3, 43–44; Fisher, "Chamber of Commerce," 435–36.

the nation's mobilization agency was without authority. Industrialists and merchandisers worked hand in hand with the commissioners. Information on the capacity of the essential industries was collected, the means for curtailing production for civilian uses and converting industry to meet governmental needs were considered, and rudimentary price, priority, and other controls were developed.[18]

Quite early in the war, therefore, the NDAC devised the means for organizing and controlling the private sector of the economy. The methods were often crude and piecemeal, but they could be perfected. Rapid progress was possible because the cooperative efforts of industry and the federal government on behalf of economic regulation during the Progressive Era prepared them to a degree for wartime conditions. Nevertheless, the economic mobilization program floundered for almost a year. Organizing supply — the civilian economy — was not enough. Demand — the multiple needs of claimant agencies like the Army and Navy — also had to be controlled. Throughout the war, demand exceeded supply. Consequently, unless war contracts were distributed with care and in order of precedence, the equilibrium of the economy could not be maintained. The NDAC, however, had no authority over the procurement agencies. They were free to do as they liked. A crisis was avoidable as long as claimant agencies procured in an orderly manner and cooperated with the NDAC. To a degree, most did. The Navy Department adjusted to hostilities without major difficulty. That was possible because it was always in a state of semi-preparedness and had an efficient supply system dating back to the late nineteenth century. Other private and public civilian agencies like the American Red Cross, the Emergency Fleet Corporation, and the Fuel and Food Administration also proved to be sufficiently flexible. But not the War Department. The flagrant inadequacies of its supply apparatus undermined the efforts of the NDAC.

When war broke out, five, and later eight, bureaus — the Quartermaster Corps, the Ordnance Department, and the like — independently procured for the Army. Each had its own purchasing staff, handled its own funds, stored its own goods, and transported its supplies. Determined to meet their own needs, the bureaus competed with one another and other claimant agencies. Contracts were let indiscriminately, facilities commandeered without plan, and equipment transported without regard to need. With such a system, it was virtually impossible for the War Department to come up with reliable statistics concerning requirements.

[18] For a complete list of NDAC committees see: U.S. Council of National Defense, *First Annual Report* (Washington, 1917), 97–127. See also, Nye Committee, *Minutes of the Council of National Defense*, 11–14, 18–19, 30, and *Minutes of the Advisory Commission of the Council of National Defense and Minutes of the Munitions Standard Board*, 3, 11, 28, 30–32, 74th Cong., 2nd Sess., 1936, Senate Committee Prints 7 and 8; Appropriations Subcommittee, *Hearings*, 3–157; Grosvenor B. Clarkson, *Industrial America in the World War: The Strategy Behind the Line*, 1917–1918 (New York, 1923), 26–29.

War Department difficulties did not start with the war. The politics of supply had been a constant source of aggravation within the department for decades.[19] The strife became especially intense around the turn of the century when the Chief of Staff-General Staff system was created by the reforms of Elihu Root (Secretary of War, 1899–1904). Supervising the bureaus and bringing them under some centralized control were part of the responsibility of the Chief of Staff. But the tenaciously independent bureaus successfully resisted control. The staff-bureau conflict continued into the war years. Secretary of War Baker would not move forcefully to resolve it. A Progressive dedicated to applying local solutions to modern problems, Baker opposed temporary changes in the federal government during the war out of fear they might become permanent. Moreover, the former mayor of Cleveland consistently avoided controversy. Attempting to compromise nearly irreconcilable differences between the General Staff and the bureaus, Baker allowed the War Department to drift hopelessly toward disaster.[20]

The General Staff-bureau controversy in part was responsible for the Army failing to anticipate the nature of twentieth-century warfare. Industrial production was as important, or more important, to military success as tactics or strategy. Relating its supply and procurement apparatus to a mobilized economy had to be part of the military mission in modern times.[21] Had the staff-bureau conflict ended with the war and an efficient supply system been fashioned, the Army could have adjusted to emergency conditions with relative ease. Since neither took place, the Army came close to losing its control of supply by threatening the entire civilian economy.

Out of war costs approximating $32,000,000,000, the Army spent

[19] Testimony of military and other witnesses before congressional committees is the best source for military supply operation immediately before and during World War I. See the relevant portions of: HMAC, *Hearings*, 1916; SMAC, *Hearings*, 1916; Graham Committee, *Hearings*, Serial 1 and 3; Chamberlain Committee, *Hearings*; U.S. Congress, Senate Subcommittee of the Committee on Military Affairs, *Hearings, Reorganization of the Army*, 66th Cong., 2nd Sess., 1919; U.S. Congress, House, Committee on Military Affairs, *Hearings, Army Reorganization*, 66th Cong., 1st Sess., 1919–1920 — hereafter cited as HMAC, *Hearings*, 1920.

Secondary sources on the Army are legion. None of them treat adequately with supply factors. The better ones include: John Dickinson, *The Building of an Army: A Detailed Account of Legislation, Administration and Opinion in the United States, 1915–1920* (New York, 1922); J. Franklin Crowell, *Government War Contracts* (New York, 1920); Paul Y. Hammond, *Organizing for Defense: The American Military Establishment in the Twentieth Century* (Princeton, 1961); Samuel P. Huntington, *The Soldier and the State: The Theory and Politics of Civil-Military Relations* (New York, 1964); Otto L. Nelson, Jr., *National Security and the General Staff* (Washington, 1946); Kreidberg and Henry, *Military Mobilization*; Erna Risch, *The Quartermaster Corps: Organization, Supply, and Services* (Washington, 1953); Constance McLaughlin Green, Harry C. Thomson, and Peter C. Roots, *The Ordnance Department: Planning Munitions for War* (Washington, 1955).

[20] Beaver, *Baker*, 5–7, 51–52, 71–72, 80–81, 108–109, 152, 178, 210–11, 215–17, 243–46; C. H. Cramer, *Newton D. Baker: A Biography* (New York, 1961), 136–37.

[21] Industrial Mobilization Plan, 1933 — contained in U.S. War Policies Commission, *Hearings*, 72nd Cong., 1st Sess., House Document No. 163, 401–402.

$14,500,000,000 between April 1916 and June 1919.[22] Pouring such vast amounts of money into the economy through the department's antiquated supply system unavoidably produced havoc.

To mitigate the effect, the National Defense Advisory Commission, while still organizing supply and attempting to perfect wartime economic controls, was forced to assume responsibility for coordinating supply and demand. No other agency existed for the purpose. Its task was almost impossible. The procurement agencies had the statutory authority; the NDAC had no more than advisory powers. They were not enough to hold the largest of the procurement agencies in line.

The NDAC's difficulties with the War Department stemmed from two sources. In the first place, according to military dictum, those who controlled strategy must also control supply. The Army looked upon civilian mobilization agencies as a threat to its supply prerogatives. The very weakness of the Army supply system served only to strengthen the suspicion. Secondly, the War Department's supply network did not correspond with that of the civilian economy. The bureaus were organized along functional lines — ordnance, quartermaster, and the like; the economy was informally structured according to commodities — raw materials, industrial products, and so forth.[23] With the NDAC patterned after the economy, effectively coordinating supply and demand was out of the question. Logically, the Army had not only to reform its supply system but also restructure it along commodity lines. It stubbornly resisted until early in 1918.

The Army was able to resist not only because of its statutory authority, but also because Baker was selected as chairman of the Council of National Defense and served as President Wilson's chief adviser on industrial mobilization. Unable to bring order out of confusion in the War Department, Baker failed to rise above departmental interests as chairman of the Council. He used his position to maintain the Army's prerogatives undiminished.[24] For almost a year after the outbreak of war, therefore, the War Department insisted that the civilian economy adjust to its decentralized, inefficient, functional supply system rather than *vice versa*. The tail was attempting to wag the dog.

At first the NDAC accepted the War Department terms. It attempted to make the War Department system work by serving more or less as a bridge between the industrial and military worlds. With the Army bureaus unable

[22] John M. Clark, *The Cost of the World War to the American People* (New Haven, 1931), 30; Crowell, *War Contracts*, 63. For comparative purposes, the War Department figures would be slightly lower if estimated normal expenses for the war years were subtracted.

[23] U.S. War Department, Purchase, Storage, and Traffic Division, General Staff, Supply Bulletin No. 29, Nov. 7, 1918 — reproduced in, Graham Committee, *Hearings*, Serial 1, 128–32.

[24] Cramer, *Baker*, 122–23; Frederick Palmer, *Newton D. Baker: America at War* (2 vols., New York, 1931), I, 372; Beaver, *Baker*, 71–76; Clarkson, *Industrial America*, 41–42.

to keep up, the recently organized Cooperative Committees of the NDAC performed procurement activities. Individuals and committees aided the Army in distributing contracts within the industries they represented. In the case of the Quartermaster Corps, the Committee on Supplies literally built a procurement system around the corps and assumed many of its functions. NDAC aid unquestionably kept the Army bureaus from being totally swamped. But as worked out, the system was not an unmixed blessing. Indeed, commission operations were often illegal. Actually, if not nominally, industrialists awarded contracts to themselves and their colleagues. Small groups of businessmen admittedly engaged in collusive activity — activity sanctioned by the government. Army regulations and the antitrust laws were being violated.

The expediency, not the legality, of the NDAC's operations was what bothered its members. Out of need, the NDAC was forced to assume the responsibilities of a general mobilization agency without that authority. The Army, and the Navy as well, used or ignored the NDAC to suit its own purposes. Frustrated, the commissioners began pressing the Council of National Defense to sanction a more effective organization. The latter yielded to NDAC entreaties only reluctantly. At first, a Munitions Standards Board, later a General Munitions Board, was created. Both were intended to facilitate military procurement; neither had much effect. As creatures of the Council of National Defense, they lacked authority. Technically independent of the NDAC, they were really only extensions of it. After months of turmoil, the hopelessly inadequate NDAC still remained the principal mobilization agency.[25] As spring gave way to summer in 1917, confusion was rife and the efforts to harness the economy were bogging down.

By July 1917, change was essential. The NDAC structure could not maintain economic balance. Backed by influential members of the administration like William G. McAdoo, the Secretary of the Treasury and President Wilson's son-in-law, the commissioners made a plea for the creation of a mobilization agency freed from military control and able to centralize and enforce its decisions.[26]

The impetus for change was strengthened by the first extended debate

[25] Testimony of various members of the NDAC before Congressional Committees is one of the best sources on Commission activities: Chamberlain Committee, *Hearings*, 1850–1884 — Gifford; Graham Committee, *Hearings*, Serial 3, 869–79, 987–1019 — Gifford and Frank A. Scott; Graham Committee, *Hearings*, Serial 1, 333–447, 1793–1857 — Clarkson, Charles Eiseman, and Baruch; Appropriations Subcommittee, *Hearings*, 3–157. The day to day evolution of the Council of National Defense and its Advisory Commission are traced out in: *Council of National Defense Minutes*; *NDAC Minutes*; *General Munitions Board Minutes*; Nye Committee, *Minutes of the War Industries Board from August 1, 1917, to December 19, 1918*, 74th Cong., 1st Sess., 1935, Senate Committee Print No. 4; Council of National Defense, *First Annual Report*, and *Second Annual Report* (Washington, 1918).

[26] *Council of National Defense Minutes*, 140; *NDAC Minutes*, 75–78, 80–81; Martin, *Digest*, 234; Beaver, *Baker*, 71.

in Congress involving economic mobilization. NDAC operations, where favored businessmen could serve simultaneously as government agents and contractors, took on the proportions of a national scandal when publicized. The agitation was triggered by those business interests who found themselves excluded from a decision-making process which affected their interests. After acrimonious debate, Congress included in the Lever Act a provision restricting individuals from serving or acting in a capacity to influence the awarding of contracts beneficial to themselves or their firms.[27]

The drive for a more effective mobilization agency combined with congressional criticism led to a general reorganization in July 1917. The Council of National Defense replaced the NDAC structure with the War Industries Board (WIB). As its name implied, the board was to regulate the entire industrial might of the nation, not simply to expedite munitions production. The WIB absorbed the various committees and boards that had proliferated over the months under the Council of National Defense. For the first time, the federal government had one centralized organization for controlling industry.

In order to meet Congressional and business criticism, the WIB between August and December 1918, disbanded the Cooperative Committees of Industries. It then turned to the Chamber of Commerce of the United States to supervise and certify the formation of new industrial committees. Industries with trade associations or similar societies "democratically" elected members to represent them before the WIB. Precautions were exercised to insure that nonmember firms had a voice. For unorganized industries, the Chamber facilitated organization. The elected bodies were called War Service Committees. Unlike the NDAC committees, their members were private, not public, representatives; industry financed their operations. Many of the committees were new, some — e.g. steel — were the old group with a new name and only minor changes. The Chamber of Commerce had been advocating such a system since before the war. In part it was based on the English mobilization experience.[28]

---

[27] Cong. Rec., 65th Cong., 1st Sess., Vol. 55, Part 4, 3335–41, Part 5, 4590–4610, 4651–79, 4814–15, 5001–5049 (intermittent), 5169–89 (intermittent), 5214–25; Cong. Rec., 66th Cong., 2nd Sess., Vol. 59, Part 4, 4089–4091; Council of National Defense Minutes, 129; NDAC Minutes, 80, 82, 85; General Munitions Board Minutes, 131, 142–43, 208–209. For an extended investigation of NDAC committees involving alleged conflict of interest in general and the Committee on Supplies in particular, see: Chamberlain Committee, Hearings, 593–1604 (intermittent), 1791–98. See also, Seward W. Livermore, Politics is Adjourned: Woodrow Wilson and the War Congress, 1916–1918 (Middletown, 1966), 52–57.

[28] For the creation of the WIB and its War Service Committees, see: Council of National Defense Minutes, 151–52, 170–71, 196–97, 215–16; WIB Minutes, 31, 38, 50, 69, 78, 93, 111–12, 208, 504–505; Chamberlain Committee, Hearings, 1850–84 — Gifford testimony; Fisher, "Chamber of Commerce," 335–40, 343–461; William F. Willoughby, Government Organization in War Time and After: A Survey of the Federal Civil Agencies Created for the Prosecution of the War (New York, 1919), 80–91; Bernard M. Baruch, American Industry in the War: A Report of the War Industries

The War Service Committees granted business far more immunity from the antitrust laws than even the most sanguine advocates of industrial co-operation espoused during the Progressive years. A private, commercial body, not the federal government, certified committees to represent the collective interests of business. As a result, the modern trade association movement began to come of age. Associations grew rapidly in number and importance during the war years.[29]

The change from the informal, legally tenuous NDAC Cooperative Committees, reminiscent of the ambiguous relations between the government and industry during the Progressive years, was essential. Without the full support of all industrial elements, economic mobilization was difficult, if not impossible. Out of need, the federal government dropped its reservations about trade associations. Indeed, industry could treat with the government only on an organized basis. Writing in *The Nation's Business* in August 1918, Chamber of Commerce President Harry A. Wheeler (vice-president, Union Trust Company of Chicago) declared: [30]

> Creation of the War Service Committees promises to furnish the basis for a truly national organization of industry whose proportions and opportunities are unlimited.
>
> .   .   .
>
> The integration of business, the expressed aim of the National Chamber, is in sight. War is the stern teacher that is driving home the lesson of cooperative effort.

Representing private interests, the War Service Committees were not officially a part of the WIB. Subdivisions of the board, called Commodity Committees, determined policy for and administered the various industries. The committees were usually staffed with industrialists on a "dollar-a-year" basis but allegedly free from conflicts of interest. Claimant agencies such as the Army and Navy also had representatives on the committees. To maintain a clear line of demarcation between the public and private domains, War Service Committees only "advised" the Commodity Committees. Some 57 Commodity Committees and over 300 War Service Committees were ultimately organized. The former were grouped according to the

---

Board (March, 1921), ed. by Richard H. Hippelheuser (New York, 1941), 20–23, 109–116; Clarkson, *Industrial America*, 240, 300–314; Benedict Crowell and Robert F. Wilson, *The Giant Hand: Our Mobilization and Control of Industry and Natural Resources, 1917–1918* (New Haven, 1921), 24–27, 99–103; *Final Report of the WIB*, 13–15, 40–41, 50–51.

[29] There is no one outstanding comprehensive work on trade associations. Several of the better volumes include: Joseph H. Foth, *Trade Associations: Their Service to Industry* (New York, 1930); National Industrial Conference Board, *Trade Associations: Their Economic Significance and Legal Status* (New York, 1925); U.S. Department of Commerce, *Trade Association Activities* (Washington, 1927).

[30] *The Nation's Business*, August, 1918, 9–10.

natural patterns of the economy: chemicals, textiles, finished products, and so forth. The latter operated with the Commodity Committee to which they corresponded.

The WIB never really got under way until early in 1918. By then it was clear that the distinction between public and private interests within the board was more apparent than real. The chief of the Agricultural Implements and Wood Products Section had been manager of the John Deere Wagon Company; at the head of Automotive Products was the former treasurer of the Studebaker Corporation; the former president of the Fisk Rubber Company was chief of the Rubber and Rubber Goods Section.[31] Serving in such capacities, industrialists were supposed to "dissociate" themselves from their firms. But in November, 1918, the acting chairman of the WIB observed that individuals could absent themselves from negotiations if their own firms were involved. Not until mid-1918 did the board begin to institute precautionary policies against compromising appointments.[32]

Even if no conflict of interest existed, the Commodity Committee–War Service Committee system was not the neat separation of private and public interests that its proponents maintained. At best, the decision-making process was organic. Grosvenor B. Clarkson described it at follows:

> Through the commodity sections on the side of Government and the war service committees on the side of business, all industry was merged in the War Industries Board. Subject to the veto of the chairman of the Board, as the supreme interpreter of the national good, industry imposed its own emergency laws and regulations and assumed nine tenths of the burden and responsibility of enforcing them.

Clarkson went on to say that the Commodity Committee–War Service Committee system was the very nerve center and major source of policy for the WIB.[33] The board was a form of industrial self-regulation writ large. Nonetheless, the organization of the WIB was a giant step forward. Effective industrial control was possible. Private industry was organized, an agency capable of coordinating mobilization existed, and trained personnel were available.

Regardless of the progress, the reorganization did not deal with the fundamental flaw. The WIB was without authority. Created by the Council of National Defense, it had only advisory powers. Actually the board's creation was a victory for Secretary Baker and the War Department. They had resisted the concerted drive for an agency independent of and superior to the

---

[31] Principal WIB officials, their affiliations, and sources of income, are given in Nye Committee, *Hearings*, Part 16, 4142–45. Complete lists of WIB personnel and members of the War Service Committees are conveniently available in Clarkson, *Industrial America*, 501–543.

[32] Michael D. Reagen, "Serving Two Masters: Problems in the Employment of Dollar-A-Year and Without Compensation Personnel" (Ph.D. dissertation, Princeton University, 1959), 7–8, 17.

[33] Clarkson, *Industrial America*, 98, 303–311.

military services. Wilson upheld them.[34] The Army still had the authority to force its methods on the economy. The WIB stood by helplessly. An impasse had been reached. Either the Army had to give way or the mobilization program would halt. The latter occurred before the former.

Chaired by Frank A. Scott, president of Warner and Swasey Company, a Cleveland precision equipment manufacturer, the WIB first faltered and then stumbled. Deterioration was rapid after October, 1917, when Scott resigned, his health broken through agonizing months spent in government service. Daniel Willard, president of the Baltimore and Ohio Railroad Company, was practically drafted to replace him. But on January 11, 1918, he also quit in disgust over the board's impotence. A crippled WIB simply could not fulfill its functions. Various sections remained active but without over-all direction. Like a convulsed person, the WIB's limbs twitched without central motor control. For a time, a so-called War Council, made up of representatives from leading war agencies and others, tried without much success to provide leadership. The crisis was at hand. A new chairman for the WIB was not appointed until March. No one who was considered qualified would take the job without sweeping changes.[35]

The paralysis that gripped the board was matched by that of the economy. Uncontrolled procurement overloaded the Northeast with contracts far beyond its capacity to produce. With the unusually severe winter of 1917–1918, fuel was critically short and the railroad and shipping industries virtually halted in some sections of the nation. The mobilization effort, indeed the entire economy, appeared on the brink of collapse. To remedy the crisis, the administration was forced to bring the railroads under national control in December 1917. But overall coordination of procurement and production was essential to resolve the critical economic conditions. On that crucial issue the administration was stalemated.[36]

In the absense of executive leadership, the Senate Military Affairs Committee, under the leadership of a Democratic maverick, Senator George E. Chamberlain, of Oregon, moved on its own. The committee conducted an investigation of the War Department from December 12, 1917, until the

[34] Beaver, *Baker*, 71–75.

[35] *Ibid.*, 75–78; WIB *Minutes*, 2, 6, 13–15, 94, 146; *Council of National Defense Minutes*, 200; Chamberlain Committee, *Hearings*, 2282–83 — Coffin testimony; War Policies Commission, *Hearings*, 169–70, 177–78 — Daniel Willard testimony; Palmer, *Baker*, I, 378–79; Clarkson, *Industrial America*, 36–49, 83–84, 202–203; Crowell and Wilson, *The Giant Hand*, 22–27.

[36] See the following secondary sources for the winter crisis and its resolution: Beaver, *Baker*, 79–109; Alexander D. Noyes, *The War Period of American Finance, 1908–1925* (New York, 1926), 244–78; L. C. Marshall, "A Nation of Economic Amateurs," *Readings in the Economics of War*, ed. by J. Maurice Clark, Walton H. Hamilton, and Harold G. Moulton (Chicago, 1918), 221–24; Clarkson, *Industrial America*, 42–45, 51–59, 138–39, 199–200, 234–35, 453; Benedict Crowell and Forrest Wilson, *The Armies of Industry*, I (New Haven, 1921), 4–6; Livermore, *Politics is Adjourned*, 62–104; Palmer, *Baker*, II, 66–84; Frederic L. Paxson, *America at War: 1917–1918* (Boston, 1939), 210–228, 250–53.

end of March. It established beyond question the chaos in Army supply and highlighted its effects on the economy.

The Chamberlain Committee was greatly influenced by Waddill Catchings, formerly of J. P. Morgan and Company, now chairman of the War Committee of the Chamber of Commerce of the United States, and president of ironworks in New York and Ohio. For months, argued Catchings, Chamber members had devoted full-time effort to perfecting the nation's mobilization machinery only to have conditions deteriorate rather than improve. Businessmen found their economic fortunes threatened not by government regulation but by government chaos. With a united Chamber behind him, Catchings recommended that the United States follow the British experience: separate procurement from the military and place it under a civilian-controlled ministry of munitions; and create a War Cabinet to direct the over-all national war effort.[37]

In January 1918, the Chamberlain Committee presented two bills to Congress incorporating the Chamber of Commerce recommendations.[38] The proposed legislation led to the most extended and knowledgeable debate on economic mobilization heard in the halls of Congress during World War I. Legislation for a ministry of munitions, but not the war cabinet, was seriously considered. In order to circumvent it, the Army began to reform its supply system and the administration came forth with the Overman Act: a sweeping grant of authority for the President to reshuffle his administration to meet the demands of warfare. With the full weight of the administration behind the compromise proposal, the Chamberlain Committee legislation never stood a chance. In May 1918, the Overman bill passed with only slight opposition.[39]

The compromise succeeded only because Wilson ended the War Department's domination of the mobilization program in March. Under his general powers as President and Commander in Chief, Wilson separated the WIB from the Council of National Defense and placed it directly under himself. After the passage of the Overman Act, the President confirmed his action with an Executive Order. To chair the strengthened board, Wilson selected Bernard M. Baruch. According to the latter's instructions, the WIB's specific and general powers were great indeed. They included general coordinating authority over procurement. Without *statutory* authority, much of the board's action remained legally tenuous. Moreover, the President's directive was vaguely qualified at many points. Nevertheless, with

---

[37] Chamberlain Committee, *Hearings*, 1885–1924.

[38] *Cong. Rec.*, 65th Cong., 2nd Sess., Vol. 56, Part 1, 557, 1004, Part 2, 1077–78; U.S. Congress, Senate, Committee on Military Affairs, *Director of Munitions*, 65th Cong., 2nd Sess., 1918, Senate Report No. 200 to accompany S. 3311, 1–2.

[39] *Cong. Rec.*, 65th Cong., 2nd Sess., Vol. 56, Part 1, 977–79, 980–83, Part 2, 1194–1211, 1242–44, 1607–21, 1686–95, 1747, 1819–32, 1842–52, 2095–2105, Part 3, 2136–49, Part 4, 3815, 4504–26, 4572–83, 4945–73, 5013–23, 5551–71, 5739–66, Part 9, 8616.

Wilson's full backing, the nearly complete support of business, and the critical conditions the nation faced, the WIB was able to enforce its decisions in most instances. The winter crisis, therefore, was resolved with the military services maintaining control of supply but not of the economy.

Probably without anyone being fully aware of its consequences, the Overman Act set a most important precedent for twentieth-century warfare. Unlike most belligerent nations, in the United States the military services continued to procure their own munitions and, therefore, remained in a position to affect the economy most directly and vitally during war as well as peace. To varying degrees Great Britain and France separated procurement from the services and placed it under civilian-controlled munitions ministries. Even in pre-revolutionary Russia the armed services did not maintain unqualified control of their own purchasing. In Germany, quite a different pattern emerged. The economy was largely mobilized under military authorities in league with large industrial elements.[40]

Maintaining procurement in the hands of the armed services was dictated more by political economy than military necessity. Businessmen had directed economic mobilization since April 1917, because they were the only ones qualified to do so. Yet, Wilson, members of his administration, and the public at large, doubted the ability of business to place the interests of the nation above its own.[41] Such attitudes, combined with the desire to avoid political and economic changes during the war, led to granting industry a great deal of latitude for perfecting the mobilization machinery, while ultimate authority was continued with the traditional procurement agencies. Only when that expedient failed, did the business-dominated WIB gain some authority under the Overman Act.

To many government officials, going further than the Overman legislation, by separating supply from the armed services, was both undesirable and politically hazardous. It would have meant turning over to industry directly billions of dollars of contracts. The ministry of munitions legislation supported by the Chamberlain Committee was no more than a general grant of authority for a Director of Munitions to perform procurement functions. Out of necessity, the director would have to use the WIB or a similar agency controlled by businessmen to fulfill his responsibilities. Of course, under WIB operations, contracts were virtually in industry's hand anyway. None-

[40] E. M. H. Lloyd, *Experiments in State Control at the War Office and the Ministry of Food* (London, 1924); John A. Fairle, *British War Administration* (New York, 1919); Pierre Renouvin, *The Forms of War Government in France* (New Haven, 1927); S. O. Zagorsky, *State Control of Industry in Russia during the War* (New Haven, 1928); Robert B. Armeson, *Total Warfare and Compulsory Labor: A Study of the Military-Industrial Complex in Germany during World War I* (The Hague, 1964).

[41] Beaver, *Baker*, 52, 96 (and footnote 64), 105–106. Revering, yet suspecting, the business community has been a long-run trend in American life. See: Thomas C. Cochran, *The American Business System: A Historical Perspective, 1900–1955* (New York, 1962), 2–10, 194–205.

theless, as long as the armed services maintained the legal right of contracting, ceremonial distinctions between government and business operations were preserved.

Since the Commodity Committee–War Service Committee system nominally separated private and public interests, Congress appeared satisfied with the WIB. Nevertheless, the "dollar-a-year" man and War Service Committee practices — the very life blood of the WIB — were vulnerable. During 1917 they came under repeated attack; in January 1918, legislation was introduced to prohibit the use of industrial advisory committees and government officials serving on a nominal salary. Instead, the wartime economy would be run by paid employees free of compromising affiliations.[42] For the most part, critics of the NDAC and WIB were conveniently ignored. Had Congress moved to place procurement in the hands of the WIB or attempted to write detailed legislation as to how civilians would perform procurement functions, WIB methods at least would have been in jeopardy.

The Overman Act allowed the administration and the Congress to dodge the vexacious problems of industrial mobilization. The WIB was strengthened without in any way disturbing its operations or clearly defining its authority. Moreover, the War Department — the major obstacle to successful mobilization — was forced into line. Issues almost too complex for direct resolution were, thereby, avoided.

Business representatives had every reason to support the Overman compromise and did so. Before the Chamberlain Committee, no one from among the business members on the Council of National Defense or on the WIB favored a ministry of munitions.[43] As members of the Wilson administration they could not have done otherwise. But as long as the President was willing to strengthen the WIB they had no reason to press for the ministry idea. Furthermore, businessmen within government were not unconscious of the threat of a ministry of munitions to the existing mobilization machinery. While still chairman of the crippled and helpless WIB during the winter crisis of 1917–1918, Daniel Willard pleaded with business not to support a supply ministry. It was a risky experiment requiring legislation, he argued. Such legislation, Willard implied, was undesirable.[44] Both Grosvenor B. Clarkson and General Hugh S. Johnson, intimately involved with the wartime economic experience, concluded that the flexibility granted the NDAC and the WIB by the lack of specific statues was a decided advantage, if not imperative.[45] The attitude of businessmen within the Administration

---

[42] *Cong. Rec.*, 65th Cong., 2nd Sess., Vol. 56, Part 1, 558; New York *Times*, January 5, 1918, 3. See also citations for the *Cong. Rec.* in footnotes 27 and 39.

[43] See the testimony of Willard, Baruch, Gifford, and Coffin, Chamberlain Committee, *Hearings*, 1799–1847, 1850–84, 2253–89.

[44] *The Nation's Business*, Feb., 1918, 7–9.

[45] Clarkson, *Industrial America*, 5–9, 20, 215–16; *Final Report of the WIB*, 3–4 — for authorship of the *Report* see Nye Committee, *Hearings*, Part 22, 6393–95, 6642.

apparently influenced the business community. In February 1918, the Chamber of Commerce of the United States, largely responsible for the Senate Military Affairs Committee's legislation, not only switched its support to the Overman Act, but also defended the bill against its critics. "Those in charge of the administrative machinery of the Government" were opposed to more extended legislation, announced a Chamber member. Through the Overman Act, the desired ends could be achieved without weathering the cumbersome legislative process.[46]

Baruch's selection as chairman was as important to the WIB as its new grant of authority. From the day the NDAC was organized, Baruch was a prominent figure. His intimate but detached knowledge and understanding of the American economy and the men who ran it was central to his success. Long before war was declared, Baruch reasoned that successful mobilization depended upon winning industry's voluntary cooperation and maintaining the existing power structure. That meant industry would virtually have to be incorporated into the government. While a member of the NDAC, Baruch was instrumental in devising what ultimately became the Commodity Committee–War Service Committee system.[47]

The nature of the WIB demanded that its chairman have the confidence of industry and yet be above charges of conflict of interests or of favoring private over public welfare. Ironically, Baruch, the "Wolf of Wall Street," was tailor-made for the job. Before joining the NDAC, he divested himself of any connections that could compromise his activities. His speculative career raised opposition to his appointment in some circles, but a congressional committee gave Baruch a clean bill of health. Henceforth, his public image improved. For a time industrialists and financiers approached him with reservation because of his unorthodox occupation. However, uncertainty gradually gave way to trust as Baruch proved his abilities. Because he was largely above suspicion in the eyes of the public and the business community, Baruch could guide the risky process of incorporating industry into government while mostly giving industry its way. A more suspect individual would have met impossible obstacles.

When appointed chairman of the WIB, Baruch instituted policies which he had successfully applied in private business. He selected knowledgeable, competent young men to direct the major subdivisions of the WIB and gave them maximum freedom for carrying out their responsibilities. Authority

---

[46] New York *Times*, Feb. 27, 1918, 4; Fisher, "Chamber of Commerce," 378–80.

[47] Concerning Baruch, the NDAC, and his qualifications for the WIB chairmanship, see: sources cited in footnote No. 18; Bernard M. Baruch, *My Own Story* (New York, 1957), 308–312; Bernard M. Baruch, *Baruch, The Public Years* (New York, 1960), 20–25, 28–33, 48–49; Clarkson, *Industrial America*, 66–73, 89, 301–302; Crowell and Wilson, *The Giant Hand*, 24–25, 27–31; Palmer, *Baker*, II, 201–202; Hugh S. Johnson, *The Blue Eagle From Egg to Earth* (New York, 1935), 113–14; Margaret L. Coit, *Mr. Baruch* (Boston, 1957), 147–52, 167–76; Beaver, *Baker*, 104–108.

was centralized, administration decentralized. The Commodity Committees were enlarged and strengthened. In effect they became small war industries boards for the various industries of the nation.[48]

By early 1918, then, a mobilization agency with authority had been perfected. Organized supply was integrated into its structure. But the system would not operate unless demand, and particularly the War Department, was fitted into it. The prospect for a successful merger was better in March 1918, than ever before.

Actually, Baker began patchwork reform of the Army supply network in late summer, 1917. When it became clear, during the winter crisis of 1917–1918, that fundamental change was essential to prevent complete severance of supply from the War Department, the General Staff was reorganized to establish more effective supervision of the bureaus and to better coordinate the Army's operations with those of the WIB.[49]

The more radical reforms Baker initiated did not produce the desired results until March 1918, when General Peyton C. March was appointed first Acting, and later Chief of Staff. In record time, the dynamic, aggressive March fashioned a powerful agency out of the withered General Staff he inherited.[50]

General George W. Goethals became March's chief lieutenant for supply and procurement. Basing his authority on the Overman Act, he directed a near-revolution by managing to break down the old bureau structure and replacing it with a centralized supply system. It was a herculean task that met with intense resistance from the bureaus. At the time of the armistice the job was incomplete.

Ultimately Goethals became an assistant chief of staff and directed supply through a subdivision of the General Staff called the Division of Purchase, Storage, and Traffic. All of the Quartermaster Corps and the supply functions of the other bureaus, including purchase, storage, transportation, and finance were incorporated into the division. In the process, Army supply operations were reorganized along commodity, instead of functional, lines. The War Department's system now paralleled that of the WIB. At last, the Army was adjusting to the civilian economy. Reforms also included methods for obtaining reliable requirements information, centralized procurement of

[48] The WIB Minutes are helpful in tracing the board's development, as are Crowell and Wilson's volumes, The Giant Hand and The Armies of Industry, I. The 52-page introductory essay to the Final Report of the WIB is the one best source on the board. Clarkson, Industrial America and Baruch, American Industry are indispensable despite their very numerous limitations.

[49] Graham Committee, Hearings, Serial 1, 518–20 — Goethals testimony; Nelson, National Security and the General Staff, 242–43; Beaver, Baker, 93–97.

[50] The quality of March's leadership is a main theme of Edward M. Coffman, The Hilt of the Sword: The Career of Peyton C. March (Madison, 1966) — see especially, 67–68, 76–77, 149, 151, 247–49. See also, Peyton C. Marsh, The Nation at War (New York, 1932), 56.

common items, and the standardization of contract forms and procedures.[51]

War Department reforms were originally intended to head off a strengthened civilian agency in order to safeguard Army supply independence.[52] Nevertheless, Army and Navy operations were slowly integrated into those of the WIB. For the Army, that was possible because of new vitality and new personnel. When selected to work with the WIB, officers like General Hugh S. Johnson at first approached the board with typical military suspicion. Soon they came to appreciate that the civilian agency helped secure rather than threaten military prerogatives by aiding the Army in fulfilling its responsibilities.[53] Antagonism gradually gave way to harmony. Flexibility within the WIB helped. At the outset, authority in the Commodity Committees rested exclusively with the civilian section chief. Army members on various committees felt that under the circumstances they were unable to protect War Department interests. Upon the plea of General Johnson, the entire committee was made the source of authority.[54] With similar organization, with a spirit of cooperation, the civilian mobilization agency and the War Department had finally reached a *modus operandi*. From March 1918, forward, the crisis of the economy was resolved.

That is not to say that the mobilization machinery ran without flaws or that the munitions picture was bright at war's end. Procurement agencies still set their own requirements; the WIB only determined how they were met. The board lacked the authority, and often the information, for working out a production program that was feasible for the economy. When hostilities ceased, the WIB faced the need to limit demand in order to avoid another crisis.[55]

All of the claimant agencies affected WIB operations, but none as greatly as the War Department. Chief of Staff March looked upon the board as no better than the War Department's equal, perhaps its inferior. As shifts in military requirements took place, March refused to inform the WIB. Only a major showdown between Baruch and March resolved the matter in favor of the board. Realizing that the services tenaciously guarded the right to determine their needs, the WIB never even attempted to institute review procedures. Had the war continued with demand multiplying faster than supply, the explosive military requirements riddle would have become a

---

[51] The one best secondary source for analyzing and describing the modernization of the Army's supply structure is, Dickinson, *Building of an Army*, 284–307. For primary sources and other secondary sources, see citations in footnote 19.

[52] Clarkson, *Industrial America*, 42, 54, 84–85, 128–31; Beaver, *Baker*, 95, 97.

[53] Johnson, *Blue Eagle*, 90–93; Clarkson, *Industrial America*, 128–32. Not only did Johnson become an enthusiastic supporter of the WIB, but he was also instrumental in drafting the proposals for restructuring the Army supply system to parallel that of the WIB. See Goethals testimony, Graham Committee, *Hearings*, Serial 1, 529.

[54] *WIB Minutes*, 427–28; *Final Report of the WIB*, 14–15; Baruch, *American Industry*, 111–12.

[55] David Novick, Melvin Anshen, and W. C. Truppner, *Wartime Production Controls* (New York, 1949), 28–30; Beaver, *Baker*, 172–73.

major divisive issue. The thirty-division American Expeditionary Force program for 1918 was to be increased to eighty for 1919; General John J. Pershing was holding out for even more. Throughout 1918, Pershing's forces were critically short of needed supplies, including ordnance, signal equipment, motor vehicles, and medical provisions; by fall conditions were becoming desperate. Only the armistice saved the day.[56]

Nonetheless, when hostilities ceased, there existed a mobilization scheme that worked. The armed services had preserved control of supply; the business community had experienced a return to stability despite the exigencies of war. The basic pattern was sound even if the mechanics needed perfecting and the lines of authority required clarification.

Scholars and other writers have generally interpreted the War Department's encounter with the WIB and predecessor agencies as a struggle between civilian and military elements over domination of economic mobilization.[57] That is a misconception. The conflict arose as civilian and military institutions were going through the throes of adjusting to modern warfare where economically the rigid lines of demarcation between them were no longer possible. Civilian administrations adapted with greater ease to the new conditions. The War Department, however, resisted the minimum changes essential for the successful mobilization of the economy.

Throughout a good part of World War I, the War Department was barely able to manage its own affairs, let alone extend its control over the economy. Its resistance to civilian mobilization agencies was more a result of isolation from, suspicion of, and ignorance about the civilian economy than a desire to dominate it. The Army supply bureaus, really more civilian than military with their close congressional ties and detachment from the line, and Baker's fear of bringing them under control, were a central cause of the friction. Even Chief of Staff March's arrogant attitude toward civilian institutions reflected a failure to grasp the fact that it was no longer possible to compartmentalize civilian and military functions with finality.

Civilians were not anxious to take over military roles. The business community and its representatives were largely responsible for industrial mobilization. Their first concern was finding the means for mobilizing the economy without endangering the status quo. Some saw the war as an opportunity for strengthening the Progressive ties between government and industry. From the beginning, however, circumstances made the military services central to any mobilization scheme. While perfecting their own institutions, therefore, members of the NDAC, WIB, and private businessmen worked hand in hand with Army personnel to modernize military sup-

---

[56] *Ibid.*, 156–61, 165–69, 171–79, 186–88; Baruch, *Public Years*, 56–58; Clarkson, *Industrial America*, 100–102, 128, 132–35; Johnson, *Blue Eagle*, 91; Coffman, *Hilt of the Sword*, 73–74, 76, 84–94, 104–110, 136–41.
[57] For the most recent example, see: Beaver, *Baker*, 76.

ply procedures.[58] Ultimately the War Industries Board proved to be the right means for harnessing the economy. Civilians in general, but business-men in particular, would not permit the War Department to ruin what they had carefully worked out to protect their own and the nation's inter-ests. Either the Army had to adjust to the WIB or lose its procurement prerogatives. Since separating procurement from the armed services was politically undesirable, the former rather than the latter solution was adopted with the Overman Act. Wartime industrial self-rule was possible because of the emergency, but only when left undefined. Severing supply from the Army and Navy could have threatened the entire enterprise. Out of those conditions, economic and military institutions were integrated for the duration of the war and the foundation for the "industrial-military com-plex" was laid.

[58] Businessmen, in and out of government service, before and after the winter crisis of 1917–1918, devoted many hours to War Department supply problems. Before war was declared, the Chamber of Commerce organized advisory boards to facilitate the opera-tions of local quartermasters. The following were among those who aided the Army in setting up the Purchase, Storage, and Traffic Division of the General Staff: Otto H. Kahn, of Kuhn, Loeb & Company, C. D. Norton, president of the First National Bank of New York; R. J. Thorne, president of Montgomery Ward & Company, Inc.; H. H. Lehman of Lehman Brothers; Girard Swope, president of Western Electric Company, Inc.; and F. C. Weems, of J. P. Morgan & Company. See: Fisher, "Chamber of Com-merce," 331–34; HMAC, Hearings, 1920, 447; Graham Committee, Hearings, Serial 1, 293; Dickinson, Building of an Army, 305–306.

12

FROM "GENERAL-INTEREST" TO "SPECIAL-INTEREST" POLITICS

An era that featured or produced cubism, Coué, Capone, the Klan, the Charleston, the chemise, speakeasies, tommy-guns, and Teapot Dome — as well as the only paternity case ever to have emerged from the White House — hardly deserves the designation "Normalcy" which the hapless Warren Harding bestowed upon it. If one looks beyond the "politics-as-usual," "business-as-usual" tone that seems to have dominated government, there is much about the 1920's that makes that period appear remarkably dynamic and germinal. Historians are now rescuing the decade from its "retrograde" reputation. George Mowry, for example, has described the period as "one of the major formulative epochs in American history"; he points to the ascendancy of the urban "cast of mind," to the reorientation of American industry to mass-marketing needs, to technological changes, and to the revolution in sexual mores. [*The Twenties: Fords, Flappers, and Fanatics* (1963).]

In the article that follows, Arthur Link (Professor of History, Princeton University) shows the way toward a possible rehabilitation of the political history of the era as well. Link produces evidence that the progressive movement was very much alive in the 1920's though, to be sure, its successes were few. The continued presence of large numbers of reformers in Congress and in state and city administrations represents one type of evidence of this nature. The vigorous promotion of agricultural relief measures and of public power projects constitutes another.

His inclusion of Prohibition and of immigration restriction among progressive successes reminds us that progressive objectives were not always liberal objectives. Unfortunately, Link makes no further distinctions among reform impulses, in the nature of noting, for example, that not all reform objectives were progressive objectives. He tends thereby to miss the distinctiveness of the progressive reform movement.

Link alludes to that distinctiveness when he mentions the altruistic motivation "even of the special interest groups" within the progressive coalition; it was the rhetoric and self-conviction of selflessness among the reform groups that served to relieve tensions within the movement and to elevate certain common objectives to the stature of principles. Whatever else it may have stood for, the progressive movement pre-eminently disavowed the legitimacy of special-interest or pressure-group politics. Although it is probably true, as Link says, that by 1913 "the work of special interest groups or classes seeking greater political status and economic security" had become the progressive movement's "most important characteristic," it was characteristic of the progressives themselves — whether they were businessmen, farmers, or professionals — that they refused to recognize this fact and fervently fought all measures that they could not fit within the "general interest" rubric. This characteristic above all distinguishes the progressive from the reformer of other eras and other causes.

One may well explain a great deal about the progressives' demoralization after 1918 by noting their discovery of the fragility of their "general-interest politics" hypothesis. The notion of a "general interest" tends to exclude new, inchoate, and innovative interests. It is a static idea which in any long view suggests the preclusion of new consensuses. In the long run, therefore, it is inappropriate for an open and mobile society such as ours. As an activating political "myth," it served the progressive cause well for nearly a generation. But, as Eric Goldman points out, once fictions come to be known as fictions they lose their power. "Once your own movement as well as the other fellow's is stripped of the Truth and the Good . . . the trouble comes." [*Rendezvous with Destiny* (1953), pp. 313, 200.] The progressive movement leaned heavily on such fictional absolutes. When they went, progressivism collapsed.

Though progressivism did survive in the 'twenties in many of the ways that Link says it did, most of the reform thrusts were of a different character. Deprived of its principal rationale, and deserted by the intellectuals, the progressive movement fragmented into its constituent elements, each self-consciously assertive of its own special interest. (The Farm Bloc, especially, followed this path; Link credits it — inappropriately — with much of what he calls "progressive" in the 'twenties. [See Grant McConnell, *The Decline of Agrarian Democracy** (1953), and C. B. Anderson, "The Metamorphosis of American Agrarian Idealism in the 1920s and 1930s," *Agricultural History*, 35 (Oct. 1961).] Perhaps even more important, the major energies for reform now came from sources that, at least until 1915, had played no significant part in the movement, namely, the ethnic minority groups, centered especially in the big cities. Al Smith symbolized this development, just as Bryan and William McAdoo, Smith's great Democratic antagonists, symbolized the expiring progressive impulse of the 'twenties.

W. E. Leuchtenburg's *Perils of Prosperity** (1958) is a balanced synthesis of the decade that emphasizes the antiprogressive tone of the era even as it notes certain of the remaining progressive impulses. H. F. May, "Shifting Perspectives on the 1920's," *Mississippi Valley Historical Review*, 43 (Dec. 1956) is a historiographical essay with valuable insights of its own. J. J. Huthmacher's "Urban Liberalism and the Age of Reform," *ibid.*, 49 (Sept. 1962), is an often cited but unconvincing effort to establish the "progressiveness" of urban minority groups in the progressive era. D. Burner's "The Breakup of the Wilson Coalition of 1916," *Mid-America*, 45 (Jan. 1963), and S. W. Livermore, "The Sectional Issue in the 1918 Congressional Election," *Mississippi Valley Historical Review*, 35 (June 1948), treat some of the political reasons for the old-guard Republican return to power after 1918. P. W. Glad, "Progressives and the Business Culture of the 1920's," *Journal of American History*, 53 (June 1966), indirectly suggests that business groups, in adopting progressive rhetoric, created the appearance but little substance of progressive survival. For more of the same, see G. B. Tindall, "Business Progressivism: Southern Politics in the Twenties," *South Atlantic Quarterly*, 62 (Winter 1963); and M. Heald, "Business Thought in the Twenties: Social Responsibility," *American Quarterly*, 13 (Summer 1963).

What Happened to the
Progressive Movement in the 1920's?

Arthur S. Link

If the day has not yet arrived when we can make a definite synthesis of political developments between the Armistice and the Great Depression, it is surely high time for historians to begin to clear away the accumulated heap of mistaken and half-mistaken hypotheses about this important transitional period. Writing often without fear or much research (to paraphrase Carl Becker's remark), we recent American historians have gone on indefatigably to perpetuate hypotheses that either reflected the disillusionment and despair of contemporaries, or once served their purpose in exposing the alleged hiatus in the great continuum of twentieth-century reform.

Stated briefly, the following are what might be called the governing hypotheses of the period under discussion: The 1920's were a period made almost unique by an extraordinary reaction against idealism and reform. They were a time when the political representatives of big business and Wall Street executed a relentless and successful campaign in state and nation to subvert the regulatory structure that had been built at the cost of so much toil and sweat since the 1870's, and to restore a Hanna-like reign of special privilege to benefit business, industry, and finance. The surging tides of nationalism and mass hatreds generated by World War I continued

Reprinted by permission of the author from the *American Historical Review*, 64, No. 4 (July 1959), 833–51.

to engulf the land and were manifested, among other things, in fear of communism, suppression of civil liberties, revival of nativism and anti-Semitism most crudely exemplified by the Ku Klux Klan, and in the triumph of racism and prejudice in immigration legislation. The 1920's were an era when great traditions and ideals were repudiated or forgotten, when the American people, propelled by a crass materialism in their scramble for wealth, uttered a curse on twenty-five years of reform endeavor. As a result, progressives were stunned and everywhere in retreat along the entire political front, their forces disorganized and leaderless, their movement shattered, their dreams of a new America turned into agonizing nightmares.

To be sure, the total picture that emerges from these generalizations is overdrawn. Yet it seems fair to say that leading historians have advanced each of these generalizations, that the total picture is the one that most of us younger historians saw during the years of our training, and that these hypotheses to a greater or lesser degree still control the way in which we write and teach about the 1920's, as a reading of textbooks and general works will quickly show.

This paper has not been written, however, to quarrel with anyone or to make an indictment. Its purposes are, first, to attempt to determine the degree to which the governing hypotheses, as stated, are adequate or inadequate to explain the political phenomena of the period, and, second, to discover whether any new and sounder hypotheses might be suggested. Such an effort, of course, must be tentative and above all imperfect in view of the absence of sufficient foundations for a synthesis.

Happily, however, we do not have to proceed entirely in the dark. Historians young and old, but mostly young, have already discovered that the period of the 1920's is the exciting new frontier of American historical research and that its opportunities are almost limitless in view of the mass of manuscript materials that are becoming available. Thus we have (the following examples are mentioned only at random) excellent recent studies of agrarian discontent and farm movements by Theodore Saloutos, John D. Hicks, Gilbert C. Fite, Robert L. Morlan, and James H. Shideler; of nativism and problems of immigration and assimilation by John Higham, Oscar Handlin, Robert A. Devine, and Edmund D. Cronon; of intellectual currents, the social gospel, and religious controversies by Henry F. May, Paul A. Carter, Robert M. Miller, and Norman F. Furniss; of left-wing politics and labor developments by Theodore Draper, David A. Shannon, Daniel Bell, Paul M. Angle, and Matthew Josephson; of the campaign of 1928 by Edmund A. Moore; and of political and judicial leaders by Alpheus T. Mason, Frank Freidel, Arthur M. Schlesinger, Jr., Merlo J. Pusey, and Joel F. Paschal.[1] Moreover, we can look forward to the early

[1] Theodore Saloutos and John D. Hicks, *Agrarian Discontent in the Middle West, 1900–1939* (Madison, Wis., 1951); Gilbert C. Fite, *Peter Norbeck: Prairie Statesman* (Columbia, Mo., 1948), and *George N. Peek and the Fight for Farm Parity* (Norman,

publication of studies that will be equally illuminating for the period, like the biographies of George W. Norris, Thomas J. Walsh, and Albert B. Fall now being prepared by Richard Lowitt, Leonard Bates, and David Stratton, respectively, and the recently completed study of the campaign and election of 1920 by Wesley M. Bagby.[2]

Obviously, we are not only at a point in the progress of our research into the political history of the 1920's when we can begin to generalize, but we have reached the time when we should attempt to find some consensus, however tentative it must now be, concerning the larger political dimensions and meanings of the period.

In answering the question of what happened to the progressive movement in the 1920's, we should begin by looking briefly at some fundamental facts about the movement before 1918, facts that in large measure predetermined its fate in the 1920's, given the political climate and circumstances that prevailed.

The first of these was the elementary fact that the progressive movement never really existed as a recognizable organization with common goals and a political machinery geared to achieve them. Generally speaking (and for the purposes of this paper), progressivism might be defined as the popular effort, which began convulsively in the 1890's and waxed and waned afterward

---

Okla., 1954); Robert L. Moran, *Political Prairie Fire: The Nonpartisan League, 1915–1922* (Minneapolis, Minn., 1955); James H. Shideler, *Farm Crisis, 1919–1923* (Berkeley, Calif., 1957); John Higham, *Strangers in the Land: Patterns of American Nativism, 1860–1925* (New Brunswick, N.J., 1955); Oscar Handlin, *The American People in the Twentieth Century* (Cambridge, Mass., 1954); Robert A. Devine, *American Immigration Policy, 1924–1952* (New Haven, Conn., 1957); Edmund D. Cronon, *Black Moses: The Story of Marcus Garvey and the Universal Negro Improvement Association* (Madison, Wis., 1955); Henry F. May, "Shifting Perspectives on the 1920's," *Mississippi Valley Historical Review*, XLIII (Dec., 1956), 405–27; Paul A. Carter, *The Decline and Revival of the Social Gospel* (Ithaca, N.Y., 1956); Robert M. Miller, "An Inquiry into the Social Attitudes of American Protestantism, 1919–1939," doctoral dissertation, Northwestern University, 1955; Norman F. Furniss, *The Fundamentalist Controversy, 1918–1931* (New Haven, Conn., 1954); Theodore Draper, *The Roots of American Communism* (New York, 1957); David A. Shannon, *The Socialist Party of America: A History* (New York, 1955); Daniel Bell, "The Background and Development of Marxian Socialism in the United States," *Socialism and American Life*, ed. Donald D. Egbert and Stow Persons (2 vols., Princeton, N.J., 1952), I, 215–405; Paul M. Angle, *Bloody Williamson* (New York, 1952); Matthew Josephson, *Sidney Hillman: Statesman of American Labor* (New York, 1952); Edmund A. Moore, *A Catholic Runs for President: The Campaign of 1928* (New York, 1956); Alpheus Thomas Mason, *Brandeis: A Free Man's Life* (New York, 1946), and *Harlan Fiske Stone: Pillar of the Law* (New York, 1956); Frank Freidel, *Franklin D. Roosevelt: The Ordeal* (Boston, 1954); Arthur M. Schlesinger, Jr., *The Age of Roosevelt: The Crisis of the Old Order* (Boston, 1957); Merlo J. Pusey, *Charles Evans Hughes* (2 vols., New York, 1951); Joel Francis Paschal, *Mr. Justice Sutherland: A Man against the State* (Princeton, N.J., 1951).

2 Wesley M. Bagby, "Woodrow Wilson and the Great Debate of 1920," MS in the possession of Professor Bagby; see also his "The 'Smoke-Filled Room' and the Nomination of Warren G. Harding," *Mississippi Valley Historical Review*, XLI (Mar., 1955), 657–74, and "Woodrow Wilson, a Third Term, and the Solemn Referendum," *American Historical Review*, LX (Apr., 1955), 567–75.

to our own time, to insure the survival of democracy in the United States by the enlargement of governmental power to control and offset the power of private economic groups over the nation's institutions and life. Actually, of course, from the 1890's on there were many "progressive" movements on many levels seeking sometimes contradictory objectives. Not all, but most of these campaigns were the work of special interest groups or classes seeking greater political status and economic security. This was true from the beginning of the progressive movement in the 1890's; by 1913 it was that movement's most important characteristic.

The second fundamental fact — that the progressive movements were often largely middle class in constituency and orientation — is of course well known, but an important corollary has often been ignored. It was that several of the most important reform movements were inspired, staffed, and led by businessmen with very specific or special-interest objectives in view. Because they hated waste, mismanagement, and high taxes, they, together with their friends in the legal profession, often furnished the leadership of good government campaigns. Because they feared industrial monopoly, abuse of power by railroads, and the growth of financial oligarchy, they were the backbone of the movements that culminated in the adoption of the Hepburn and later acts for railroad regulation, the Federal Reserve Act, and the Federal Trade Commission Act. Among the many consequences of their participation in the progressive movement, two should be mentioned because of their significance for developments in the 1920's: First, the strong identification of businessmen with good government and economic reforms for which the general public also had a lively concern helped preserve the good reputation of the middle-class business community (as opposed to its alleged natural enemies, monopolists, malefactors of great wealth, and railroad barons) and helped to direct the energies of the progressive movement toward the strengthening instead of the shackling of the business community. Second, their activities and influence served to intensify the tensions within the broad reform movement, because they often opposed the demands of farm groups, labor unions, and advocates of social justice.

The third remark to be made about the progressive movement before 1918 is that despite its actual diversity and inner tensions it did seem to have unity; that is, it seemed to share common ideals and objectives. This was true in part because much of the motivation even of the special-interest groups was altruistic (at least they succeeded in convincing themselves that they sought the welfare of society rather than their own interests primarily); in part because political leadership generally succeeded in subordinating inner tensions. It was true, above all, because there were in fact important idealistic elements in the progressive ranks — social gospel leaders, social justice elements, and intellectuals and philosophers — who worked hard at the task of defining and elevating common principles and goals.

Fourth and finally, the substantial progressive achievements before 1918 had been gained, at least on the federal level, only because of the temporary dislocations of the national political structure caused by successive popular uprisings, not because progressives had found or created a viable organization for perpetuating their control. Or, to put the matter another way, before 1918 the various progressive elements had failed to destroy the existing party structure by organizing a national party of their own that could survive. They, or at least many of them, tried in 1912; and it seemed for a time in 1916 that Woodrow Wilson had succeeded in drawing the important progressive groups permanently into the Democratic party. But Wilson's accomplishment did not survive even to the end of the war, and by 1920 traditional partisan loyalties were reasserting themselves with extraordinary vigor.

With this introduction, we can now ask what happened to the progressive movement or movements in the 1920's. Surely no one would contend that after 1916 the political scene did not change significantly, both on the state and national levels. There was the seemingly obvious fact that the Wilsonian coalition had been wrecked by the election of 1920, and that the progressive elements were divided and afterward unable to agree upon a program or to control the national government. There was the even more "obvious" fact that conservative Republican presidents and their cabinets controlled the executive branch throughout the period. There was Congress, as Eric F. Goldman has said, allegedly whooping through procorporation legislation, and the Supreme Court interpreting the New Freedom laws in a way that harassed unions and encouraged trusts.[3] There were, to outraged idealists and intellectuals, the more disgusting spectacles of Red hunts, mass arrests and deportations, the survival deep into the 1920's of arrogant nationalism, crusades against the teaching of evolution, the attempted suppression of the right to drink, and myriad other manifestations of what would now be called a repressive reaction.[4]

Like the hypotheses suggested at the beginning, this picture is overdrawn in some particulars. But it is accurate in part, for progressivism was certainly on the downgrade if not in decay after 1918. This is an obvious fact that needs explanation and understanding rather than elaborate proof. We can go a long way toward answering our question if we can explain, at least partially, the extraordinarily complex developments that converge to produce the "obvious" result.

For this explanation we must begin by looking at the several progressive elements and their relation to each other and to the two major parties after 1916. Since national progressivism was never an organized or independent movement (except imperfectly and then only temporarily in 1912), it could succeed only when its constituent elements formed a coalition strong enough to control one of the major parties. This had happened in 1916,

---

[3] Eric F. Goldman, *Rendezvous with Destiny* (New York, 1953), 284. The "allegedly" in this sentence is mine, not Professor Goldman's.

[4] H. C. Peterson and Gilbert C. Fite, *Opponents of War, 1917–1918* (Norman, Okla., 1957); Robert K. Murray, *Red Scare: A Study in National Hysteria, 1919–1920* (Minneapolis, Minn., 1955).

when southern and western farmers, organized labor, the social justice elements, and a large part of the independent radicals who had heretofore voted the Socialist ticket coalesced to continue the control of Wilson and the Democratic party.

The important fact about the progressive coalition of 1916, however, was not its strength but its weakness. It was not a new party but a temporary alliance, welded in the heat of the most extraordinary domestic and external events. To be sure, it functioned for the most part successfully during the war, in providing the necessary support for a program of heavy taxation, relatively stringent controls over business and industry, and extensive new benefits to labor. Surviving in a crippled way even in the months following the Armistice, it put across a program that constituted a sizable triumph for the progressive movement — continued heavy taxation, the Transportation Act of 1920, the culmination of the long fight for railroad regulation, a new child labor act, amendments for prohibition and woman suffrage, immigration restriction, and water power and conservation legislation.

Even so, the progressive coalition of 1916 was inherently unstable. Indeed, it was so wracked by inner tensions that it could not survive, and destruction came inexorably, it seemed systematically, from 1917 to 1920. Why was this true?

First, the independent radicals and antiwar agrarians were alienated by the war declaration and the government's suppression of dissent and civil liberties during the war and the Red scare. Organized labor was disaffected by the administration's coercion of the coal miners in 1919, its lukewarm if not hostile attitude during the great strikes of 1919 and 1920, and its failure to support the Plumb Plan for nationalization of the railroads. Isolationists and idealists were outraged by what they thought was the President's betrayal of American traditions or the liberal peace program at Paris. These tensions were strong enough to disrupt the coalition, but a final one would have been fatal even if the others had never existed. This was the alienation of farmers in the Plains and western states produced by the administration's refusal to impose price controls on cotton while it maintained ceilings on the prices of other agricultural commodities,[5] and especially by the administration's failure to do anything decisive to stem the downward plunge of farm prices that began in the summer of 1920.[6] Under the impact of all these stresses, the Wilsonian coalition gradually disintegrated from 1917 to 1920 and disappeared entirely during the campaign of 1920.

The progressive coalition was thus destroyed, but the components of a potential movement remained. As we will see, these elements were neither inactive nor entirely unsuccessful in the 1920's. But they obviously failed to

[5] On this point, see Seward W. Livermore, "The Sectional Issue in the 1918 Congressional Elections," *Mississippi Valley Historical Review*, XXXV (June, 1948), 29–60.

[6] Arthur S. Link, "The Federal Reserve Policy and the Agricultural Depression of 1920–1921," *Agricultural History*, XX (July, 1946), 166–75; and Herbert F. Margulies, "The Election of 1920 in Wisconsin: The Return to 'Normalcy' Reappraised," *Wisconsin Magazine of History*, XXXVIII (Autumn, 1954), 15–22.

find common principles and a program, much less to unite effectively for political action on a national scale. I suggest that this was true, in part at least, for the following reasons:

First, the progressive elements could never create or gain control of a political organization capable of carrying them into national office. The Republican party was patently an impossible instrument because control of the GOP was too much in the hands of the eastern and midwestern industrial, oil, and financial interests, as it had been since about 1910. There was always the hope of a third party. Several progressive groups — insurgent midwestern Republicans, the railroad brotherhoods, a segment of the AF of L, and the moderate Socialists under Robert M. La Follette — tried to realize this goal in 1924, only to discover that third party movements in the United States are doomed to failure except in periods of enormous national turmoil, and that the 1920's were not such a time. Thus the Democratic party remained the only vehicle that conceivably could have been used by a new progressive coalition. But that party was simply not capable of such service in the 1920's. It was so torn by conflicts between its eastern, big city wing and its southern and western rural majority that it literally ceased to be a national party. It remained strong in its sectional and metropolitan components, but it was so divided that it barely succeeded in nominating a presidential candidate at all in 1924 and nominated one in 1928 only at the cost of temporary disruption.[7]

Progressivism declined in the 1920's, in the second place, because, as has been suggested, the tensions that had wrecked the coalition of 1916 not only persisted but actually grew in number and intensity. The two most numerous progressive elements, the southern and western farmers, strongly supported the Eighteenth Amendment, were heavily tinged with nativism and therefore supported immigration restriction, were either members of, friendly to, or politically afraid of the Ku Klux Klan, and demanded as the principal plank in their platform legislation to guarantee them a larger share of the national income. On all these points and issues the lower and lower middle classes in the large cities stood in direct and often violent opposition to their potential allies in the rural areas. Moreover, the liaison between the farm groups and organized labor, which had been productive of much significant legislation during the Wilson period, virtually ceased to exist in the 1920's. There were many reasons for this development, and I mention only one — the fact that the preeminent spokesmen of farmers in the 1920's, the new Farm Bureau Federation, represented the larger commercial farmers who (in contrast to the members of the leading farm organization in Wilson's day, the National Farmers' Union) were often employers themselves and felt no identification with the rank and file of labor.

It was little wonder, therefore (and this is a third reason for the weakness

[7] For a highly partisan account of the events see Karl Schriftgiesser, *This Was Normalcy* (Boston, 1948). More balanced are the already cited Freidel, *Franklin D. Roosevelt: The Ordeal,* and Schlesinger, *The Age of Roosevelt: The Crisis of the Old Order.*

of progressivism in the 1920's), that the tension-ridden progressive groups were never able to agree upon a program that, like the Democratic platform of 1916, could provide the basis for a revived coalition. So long as progressive groups fought one another more fiercely than they fought their natural opponents, such agreement was impossible; and so long as common goals were impossible to achieve, a national progressive movement could not take effective form. Nothing illustrates this better than the failure of the Democratic conventions of 1924 and 1928 to adopt platforms that could rally and unite the discontented elements. One result, among others, was that southern farmers voted as Democrats and western farmers as Republicans. And, as Professor Frank Freidel once commented to the author, much of the failure of progressivism in the 1920's can be explained by this elementary fact.

A deeper reason for the failure of progressives to unite ideologically in the 1920's was what might be called a substantial paralysis of the progressive mind. This was partly the result of the repudiation of progressive ideals by many intellectuals and the defection from the progressive movement of the urban middle classes and professional groups, as will be demonstrated. It was the result, even more importantly, of the fact that progressivism as an organized body of political thought found itself at a crossroads in the 1920's, like progressivism today, and did not know which way to turn. The major objectives of the progressive movement of the prewar years had in fact been largely achieved by 1920. In what direction should progressivism now move? Should it remain in the channels already deeply cut by its own traditions, and, while giving sincere allegiance to the ideal of democratic capitalism, work for more comprehensive programs of business regulation and assistance to disadvantaged classes like farmers and submerged industrial workers? Should it abandon these traditions and, like most similar European movements, take the road toward a moderate socialism with a predominantly labor orientation? Should it attempt merely to revive the goals of more democracy through changes in the political machinery? Or should it become mainly an agrarian movement with purely agrarian goals?

These were real dilemmas, not academic ones, and one can see numerous examples of how they confused and almost paralyzed progressives in the 1920's. The platform of La Follette's Progressive party of 1924 offers one revealing illustration. It embodied much that was old and meaningless by this time (the direct election of the president and a national referendum before the adoption of a war resolution, for example) and little that had any real significance for the future.[8] And yet it was the best that a vigorous and idealistic movement could offer. A second example was the plight of the agrarians and insurgents in Congress who fought so hard all through the 1920's

---

[8] For a different picture see Belle C. La Follette and Fola La Follette, *Robert M. La Follette* (2 vols., New York, 1953); and Russel B. Nye, *Midwestern Progressive Politics*, 1870–1950 (East Lansing, Mich., 1951). Both works contribute to an understanding of progressive politics in the 1920's.

against Andrew Mellon's proposals to abolish the inheritance tax and to make drastic reductions in the taxes on large incomes. In view of the rapid reduction of the federal debt, the progressives were hard pressed to justify the continuation of nearly confiscatory tax levels, simply because few of them realized the wide social and economic uses to which the income tax could be put. Lacking any programs for the redistribution of the national income (except to farmers), they were plagued and overwhelmed by the surpluses in the federal Treasury until, for want of any good arguments, they finally gave Secretary Andrew Mellon the legislation he had been demanding.[9] A third and final example of this virtual paralysis of the progressive mind was perhaps the most revealing of all. It was the attempt that Woodrow Wilson, Louis D. Brandeis, and other Democratic leaders made from 1921 to 1924 to draft a new charter for progressivism. Except for its inevitable proposals for an idealistic world leadership, the document that emerged from this interchange included little or nothing that would have sounded new to a western progressive in 1912.

A fourth reason for the disintegration and decline of the progressive movement in the 1920's was the lack of any effective leadership. Given the political temper and circumstances of the 1920's, it is possible that such leadership could not have operated successfully in any event. Perhaps the various progressive elements were so mutually hostile and so self-centered in interests and objectives that even a Theodore Roosevelt or a Woodrow Wilson, had they been at the zenith of their powers in the 1920's, could not have drawn them together in a common front. We will never know what a strong national leader might have done because by a trick of fate no such leader emerged before Franklin D. Roosevelt.

Four factors, then, contributed to the failure of the progressive components to unite successfully after 1918 and, as things turned out, before 1932: the lack of a suitable political vehicle, the severity of the tensions that kept progressives apart, the failure of progressives to agree upon a common program, and the absence of a national leadership, without which a united movement could never be created and sustained. These were all weaknesses that stemmed to a large degree from the instability and failures of the progressive movement itself.

There were, besides, a number of what might be called external causes for the movement's decline. In considering them one must begin with what was seemingly the most important — the alleged fact that the 1920's were a very unpropitious time for any new progressive revolt because of the ever-increasing level of economic prosperity, the materialism, and the general contentment of the decade 1919 to 1929. Part of this generalization is valid when applied to specific elements in the population. For example, the rapid rise in the real wages of industrial workers, coupled with generally full employ-

[9] Here indebtedness is acknowledged to Sidney Ratner, *American Taxation: Its History as a Social Force in Democracy* (New York, 1942).

ment and the spread of so-called welfare practices among management, certainly did much to weaken and avert the further spread of organized labor, and thus to debilitate one of the important progressive components. But to say that it was prosperity per se that created a climate unfriendly to progressive ideals would be inaccurate. There was little prosperity and much depression during the 1920's for the single largest economic group, the farmers, as well as for numerous other groups. Progressivism, moreover, can flourish as much during periods of prosperity as during periods of discontent, as the history of the development of the progressive movement from 1901 to 1917 and of its triumph from 1945 to 1956 prove.

Vastly more important among the external factors in the decline of progressivism was the widespread, almost wholesale, defection from its ranks of the middle classes — the middling businessmen, bankers, and manufacturers, and the professional people closely associated with them in ideals and habits — in American cities large and small. For an understanding of this phenomenon no simple explanations like "prosperity" or the "temper of the times" will suffice, although they give some insight. The important fact was that these groups found a new economic and social status as a consequence of the flowering of American enterprise under the impact of the technological, financial, and other revolutions of the 1920's. If, as Professor Richard Hofstadter has claimed,[10] the urban middle classes were progressive (that is, they demanded governmental relief from various anxieties) in the early 1900's because they resented their loss of social prestige to the *nouveaux riches* and feared being ground under by monopolists in industry, banking, and labor — if this is true, then the urban middle classes were not progressive in the 1920's for inverse reasons. Their temper was dynamic, expansive, and supremely confident. They knew that they were building a new America, a business civilization based not upon monopoly and restriction but upon a whole new set of business values — mass production and consumption, short hours and high wages, full employment, welfare capitalism. And what was more important, virtually the entire country (at least the journalists, writers in popular magazines, and many preachers and professors) acknowledged that the nation's destiny was in good hands. It was little wonder, therefore, that the whole complex of groups constituting the urban middle classes, whether in New York, Zenith, or Middletown, had little interest in rebellion or even in mild reform proposals that seemed to imperil their leadership and control.

Other important factors, of course, contributed to the contentment of the urban middle classes. The professionalization of business and the full-blown emergence of a large managerial class had a profound impact upon social and political ideals. The acceleration of mass advertising played its role, as did also the beginning disintegration of the great cities with the spread of

[10] Richard Hofstadter, *The Age of Reform: From Bryan to F.D.R.* (New York, 1955), 131 ff.

middle- and upper-middle-class suburbs, a factor that diffused the remaining reform energies among the urban leaders.

A second external factor in the decline of the progressive movement after 1918 was the desertion from its ranks of a good part of the intellectual leadership of the country. Indeed, more than simple desertion was involved here; it was often a matter of a cynical repudiation of the ideals from which progressivism derived its strength. I do not mean to imply too much by this generalization. I know that what has been called intellectual progressivism not only survived in the 1920's but actually flourished in many fields.[11] I know that the intellectual foundations of our present quasi-welfare state were either being laid or reinforced during the decade. Even so, one cannot evade the conclusion that the intellectual-political climate of the 1920's was vastly different from the one that had prevailed in the preceding two decades.

During the years of the great progressive revolt, intellectuals — novelists, journalists, political thinkers, social scientists, historians, and the like — had made a deeply personal commitment to the cause of democracy, first in domestic and then in foreign affairs. Their leadership in and impact on many phases of the progressive movement had been profound. By contrast, in the 1920's a large body of this intellectual phalanx turned against the very ideals they had once deified. One could cite, for example, the reaction of the idealists against the Versailles settlement; the disenchantment of the intellectuals with the extension of government authority when it could be used to justify the Eighteenth Amendment or the suppression of free speech; or the inevitable loss of faith in the "people" when en masse they hounded so-called radicals, joined Bryan's crusade against evolution, or regaled themselves as Knights of the Ku Klux Klan. Whatever the cause, many alienated intellectuals simply withdrew or repudiated any identification with the groups they had once helped to lead. The result was not fatal to progressivism, but it was serious. The spark plugs had been removed from the engine of reform.

The progressive movement, then, unquestionably declined, but was it defunct in the 1920's? Much, of course, depends upon the definition of terms. If we accept the usual definition for "defunct" as "dead" or "ceasing to have any life or strength," we must recognize that the progressive movement was certainly not defunct in the 1920's; that on the contrary at least important parts of it were very much alive; and that it is just as important to know how and why progressivism survived as it is to know how and why it declined.

To state the matter briefly, progressivism survived in the 1920's because several important elements of the movement remained either in full vigor

11 *Ibid.*, 5, 131, 135 ff. For a recent excellent survey, previously cited, see Henry F. May, "Shifting Perspectives on the 1920's." Schlesinger's previously cited *Age of Roosevelt* sheds much new light on the economic thought of the 1920's.

or in only slightly diminished strength. These were the farmers, after 1918 better organized and more powerful than during the high tide of the progressive revolt; the politically conscious elements among organized labor, particularly the railroad brotherhoods, who wielded a power all out of proportion to their numbers; the Democratic organizations in the large cities, usually vitally concerned with the welfare of the so-called lower classes; a remnant of independent radicals, social workers, and social gospel writers and preachers; and finally, an emerging new vocal element, the champions of public power and regional developments.

Although they never united effectively enough to capture a major party and the national government before 1932, these progressive elements controlled Congress from 1921 to about 1927 and continued to exercise a near control during the period of their greatest weakness in the legislative branch, from 1927 to about 1930.

Indeed, the single most powerful and consistently successful group in Congress during the entire decade from 1919 to 1929 were the spokesmen of the farmers. Spurred by an unrest in the country areas more intense than at any time since the 1890's,[12] in 1920 and 1921 southern Democrats and midwestern and western insurgents, nominally Republican, joined forces in an alliance called the Farm Bloc. By maintaining a common front from 1921 to 1924 they succeeded in enacting the most advanced agricultural legislation to that date, legislation that completed the program begun under Wilsonian auspices. It included measures for high tariffs on agricultural products, thoroughgoing federal regulation of stockyards, packing houses, and grain exchanges, the exemption of agricultural cooperatives from the application of the antitrust laws, stimulation of the export of agricultural commodities, and the establishment of an entirely new federal system of intermediate rural credit.

When prosperity failed to return to the countryside, rural leaders in Congress espoused a new and bolder plan for relief — the proposal made by George N. Peck and Hugh S. Johnson in 1922 to use the federal power to obtain "fair exchange" or "parity" prices for farm products. Embodied in the McNary-Haugen bill in 1924, this measure was approved by Congress in 1927 and 1928, only to encounter vetoes by President Calvin Coolidge.

In spite of its momentary failure, the McNary-Haugen bill had a momentous significance for the American progressive movement. Its wholesale espousal by the great mass of farm leaders and spokesmen meant that the politically most powerful class in the country had come full scale to the conviction that the taxing power should be used directly and specifically for the purpose of underwriting (some persons called it subsidizing) agriculture. It was a milestone in the development of a comprehensive political

---

[12] It derived from the fact that farm prices plummeted in 1920 and 1921, and remained so low that farmers, generally speaking, operated at a net capital loss throughout the balance of the decade.

doctrine that it was government's duty to protect the economic security of all classes and particularly depressed ones. McNary-Haugenism can be seen in its proper perspective if it is remembered that it would have been considered almost absurd in the Wilson period, that it was regarded as radical by non-farm elements in the 1920's, and that it, or at any rate its fundamental objective, was incorporated almost as a matter of course into basic federal policy in the 1930's.

A second significant manifestation of the survival of progressivism in the 1920's came during the long controversy over public ownership or regulation of the burgeoning electric power industry. In this, as in most of the conflicts that eventually culminated on Capitol Hill, the agrarian element constituted the core of progressive strength. At the same time a sizable and well-organized independent movement developed that emanated from urban centers and was vigorous on the municipal and state levels. Throughout the decade this relatively new progressive group fought with mounting success to expose the propaganda of the private utilities, to strengthen state and federal regulatory agencies, and to win municipal ownership for distributive facilities. Like the advocates of railroad regulation in an earlier period, these proponents of regulation or ownership of a great new natural monopoly failed almost as much as they had succeeded in the 1920's. But their activities and exposures (the Federal Trade Commission's devastating investigation of the electric power industry in the late 1920's and early 1930's was the prime example) laid secure foundations for movements that in the 1930's would reach various culminations.

Even more significant for the future of American progressivism was the emergence in the 1920's of a new objective, that of committing the federal government to plans for large hydroelectric projects in the Tennessee Valley, the Columbia River watershed, the Southwest, and the St. Lawrence Valley for the purpose, some progressives said, of establishing "yardsticks" for rates, or for the further purpose, as other progressives declared, of beginning a movement for the eventual nationalization of the entire electric power industry. The development of this movement in its emerging stages affords a good case study in the natural history of American progressivism. It began when Harding and Coolidge administrations attempted to dispose of the government's hydroelectric and nitrate facilities at Muscle Shoals, Alabama, to private interests. In the first stage of the controversy, the progressive objective was merely federal operation of these facilities for the production of cheap fertilizer — a reflection of its exclusive special-interest orientation. Then, as new groups joined the fight to save Muscle Shoals, the objective of public production of cheap electric power came to the fore. Finally, by the end of the 1920's, the objective of a multipurpose regional development in the Tennessee Valley and in other areas as well had taken firm shape.

In addition, by 1928 the agrarians in Congress led by Senator George W.

Norris had found enough allies in the two houses and enough support in the country at large to adopt a bill for limited federal development of the Tennessee Valley. Thwarted by President Coolidge's pocket veto, the progressives tried again in 1931, only to meet a second rebuff at the hands of President Herbert Hoover.

All this might be regarded as another milestone in the maturing of American progressivism. It signified a deviation from the older traditions of mere regulation, as President Hoover had said in his veto of the second Muscle Shoals bill, and the triumph of new concepts of direct federal leadership in large-scale development of resources. If progressives had not won their goal by the end of the 1920's, they had at least succeeded in writing what would become perhaps the most important plank in their program for the future.

The maturing of an advanced farm program and the formulation of plans for public power and regional developments may be termed the two most significant progressive achievements on the national level in the 1920's. Others merit only brief consideration. One was the final winning of the old progressive goal of immigration restriction through limited and selective admission. The fact that this movement was motivated in part by racism, nativism, and anti-Semitism (with which, incidentally, a great many if not a majority of progressives were imbued in the 1920's) should not blind us to the fact that it was also progressive. It sought to substitute a so-called scientific and a planned policy of laissez faire. Its purpose was admittedly to disturb the free operation of the international labor market. Organized labor and social workers had long supported it against the opposition of large employers. And there was prohibition, the most ambitious and revealing progressive experiment of the twentieth century. Even the contemned anti-evolution crusade of Bryan and the fundamentalists and the surging drives for conformity of thought and action in other fields should be mentioned. All these movements stemmed from the conviction that organized public power could and should be used purposefully to achieve fundamental social and so-called moral change. The fact that they were potentially or actively repressive does not mean that they were not progressive. On the contrary, they superbly illustrated the repressive tendencies that inhered in progressivism precisely because it was grounded so much upon majoritarian principles.

Three other developments on the national level that have often been cited as evidences of the failure of progressivism in the 1920's appear in a somewhat different light at second glance. The first was the reversal of the tariff-for-revenue-only tendencies of the Underwood Act with the enactment of the Emergency Tariff Act of 1921 and the Fordney-McCumber Act of 1922. Actually, the adoption of these measures signified, on the whole, not a repudiation but a revival of progressive principles in the realm of federal fiscal policy. A revenue tariff had never been an authentic progressive objective. Indeed, at least by 1913, many progressives, except for some southern agrarians, had concluded that it was retrogressive and had agreed that the tariff laws should be used deliberately to achieve certain national objectives — for example, the crippling of noncompetitive big business by the free admission of articles manufactured by so-called trusts, or benefits to farmers by the free entry of farm implements. Wilson himself had been at least partially converted to these principles by 1916, as his insistence upon the creation of the Federal Tariff Commission and his promise of protection to the domestic chemical industry revealed. As for the tariff legislation of the early 1920's, its only important changes were increased protection for aluminum, chemical products, and agricultural commodities. It left the Underwood rates on the great mass of raw materials and manufactured goods largely undisturbed. It may have been economically shortsighted and a bad example for the rest of the world, but for the most part it was progressive in principle and was the handiwork of the progressive coalition in Congress.

Another development that has often been misunderstood in its relation to the progressive movement was the policies of consistent support that the Harding and Coolidge administrations adopted for business enterprise, particularly the policy of the Federal Trade Commission in encouraging the formation of trade associations and the diminution of certain traditional competitive practices. The significance of all this can easily be overrated. Such policies as these two administrations executed had substantial justification in progressive theory and in precedents clearly established by the Wilson administration.

A third challenge to usual interpretations concerns implications to be drawn from the election of Harding and Coolidge in 1920 and 1924. These elections seem to indicate the triumph of reaction among the mass of American voters. Yet one could argue that both Harding and Coolidge were political accidents, the beneficiaries of grave defects in the American political and constitutional systems. The rank and file of Republican voters demonstrated during the preconvention campaign that they wanted vigorous leadership and a moderately progressive candidate in 1920. They got Harding instead, not because they wanted him, but because unusual circumstances permitted a small clique to thwart the will of the majority.[13] They took Coolidge as their candidate in 1924 simply because Harding died in the middle of his term and there seemed to be no alternative to nominating the man who had succeeded him in the White House. Further, an analysis of the election returns in 1920 and 1924 will show that the really decisive factor in the victories of Harding and Coolidge was the fragmentation of the progressive movement and the fact that an opposition strong enough to rally and unite the progressive majority simply did not exist.

There remains, finally, a vast area of progressive activity about which we

[13] Much that is new on the Republican preconvention campaign and convention of 1920 may be found in William T. Hutchinson, *Lowden of Illinois: The Life of Frank O. Lowden* (2 vols., Chicago, 1957).

yet know very little. One could mention the continuation of old reform movements and the development of new ones in the cities and states during the years following the Armistice: For example, the steady spread of the city manager form of government, the beginning of zoning and planning movements, and the efforts of the great cities to keep abreast of the transportation revolution then in full swing. Throughout the country the educational and welfare activities of the cities and states steadily increased. Factory legislation matured, while social insurance had its experimental beginnings. Whether such reform impulses were generally weak or strong, one cannot say; but what we do know about developments in cities like Cincinnati and states like New York, Wisconsin, and Louisiana [14] justifies a challenge to the assumption that municipal and state reform energies were dead after 1918 and, incidentally, a plea to young scholars to plow this unworked field of recent American history.

Let us, then, suggest a tentative synthesis as an explanation of what happened to the progressive movement after 1918:

First, the national progressive movement, which had found its most effective embodiment in the coalition of forces that reelected Woodrow Wilson in 1916, was shattered by certain policies that the administration pursued from 1917 to 1920, and by some developments over which the administration had no or only slight control. The collapse that occurred in 1920 was not inevitable and cannot be explained by merely saying that "the war killed the progressive movement."

Second, large and aggressive components of a potential new progressive coalition remained after 1920. These elements never succeeded in uniting effectively before the end of the decade, not because they did not exist, but because they were divided by conflicts among themselves. National leadership, which in any event did not emerge in the 1920's, perhaps could not have succeeded in subduing these tensions and in creating a new common front.

Third, as a result of the foregoing, progressivism as an organized national force suffered a serious decline in the 1920's. This decline was heightened by the defection of large elements among the urban middle classes and the intellectuals, a desertion induced by technological, economic, and demographic changes, and by the outcropping of certain repressive tendencies in progressivism after 1917.

Fourth, in spite of reversals and failures, important components of the national progressive movement survived in considerable vigor and succeeded to a varying degree, not merely in keeping the movement alive, but even in broadening its horizons. This was true particularly of the farm groups and of the coalition concerned with public regulation or ownership of electric

[14] See, e.g., Allen P. Sindler, *Huey Long's Louisiana: State Politics, 1920–1952* (Baltimore, Md., 1956).

power resources. These two groups laid the groundwork in the 1920's for significant new programs in the 1930's and beyond.

Fifth, various progressive coalitions controlled Congress for the greater part of the 1920's and were always a serious threat to the conservative administrations that controlled the executive branch. Because this was true, most of the legislation adopted by Congress during this period, including many measures that historians have inaccurately called reactionary, was progressive in character.

Sixth, the progressive movement in the cities and states was far from dead in the 1920's, although we do not have sufficient evidence to justify any generalizations about the degree of its vigor.

If this tentative and imperfect synthesis has any value, perhaps it is high time that we discard the sweeping generalizations, false hypotheses, and clichés that we have so often used in explaining and characterizing political developments from 1918 to 1929. Perhaps we should try to see these developments for what they were — the normal and ordinary political behavior of groups and classes caught up in a swirl of social and economic change. When we do this we will no longer ask whether the progressive movement was defunct in the 1920's. We will ask only what happened to it and why.

PART III

FROM THE NEW ERA
TO THE NEW DEAL

13

THE FAILED PROPHECY:
REVITALIZATION IN POSTWAR AMERICA

Our understanding of the 1920's cannot be complete until we give full recognition to the fact that the decade began with a failed prophecy. Specifically, Woodrow Wilson's prophetic assurance to his countrymen that he was leading "this great peaceful people into war" in order to foster the universal adoption of American democratic ideals: "for democracy, for the right of those who submit to authority to have a voice in their own Governments, for the rights and liberties of small nations, for a universal dominion of right." It was not enough, then, to portray Germany as a nation whose activities conflicted with the vital interests of the United States. Germany had to be converted into the very antithesis of everything America stood for. "This war," a member of George Creel's Committee of Public Information wrote, "is being fought in the minds of great masses of people as truly as it is being fought on the battle fields of Europe."

How profound this messianic fervor was can be seen in the American reaction to the February Revolution in Russia. The United States was the first nation to extend diplomatic recognition to Kerensky's provisional government for, as Wilson put it, the overthrow of autocracy in Russia now gave the United States "a fit partner for a League of Honor." From the beginning Americans viewed the Russian Revolution through the prism of American ideology. "It was the American flag that has brought about the peaceable revolution in Russia," the *Des Moines Register* observed on March 23, 1917, "And it is the American flag that will bring about the revolution in Germany, peaceable or violent, for that revolution is bound to come. It is American ideals that dominate the world."

The October Revolution, which overthrew Kerensky and established Lenin and Trotsky in power, and the Versailles Treaty, which indicated that the war aims of the Allies were not in concord with those of Wilson, left the messianic prophecies of the United States everywhere in ruins. The resulting disappointment supposedly impelled a disillusioned American people to turn inward, to abandon their former dreams, to forsake idealism for hedonism. Lloyd Morris has stated this traditional interpretation concisely: "Feeling cheated, the war generation was cynical rather than revolutionary. It was tired of Great Causes. . . . It wanted slices of the national cake. There resulted the general decision to be amused."

In actuality, the immediate aftermath of World War I exhibited

287

the opposite tendencies. Americans did not abandon their old verities and values but reasserted them with renewed vigor. In their study, *When Prophecy Fails** (1964), the psychologist Leon Festinger and his associates have demonstrated that the clash between a belief system and facts that tend to disconfirm it produces anxiety which leaves the believers three general options: to discard the disconfirmed belief; to blind themselves to the fact that the prophecy in which they had placed their faith has not been fulfilled; to reconfirm their belief and increase proselytizing in the hope that "if more and more people can be persuaded that the system of belief is correct, then clearly it must be correct."

Although Americans exercised all three options during the 1920's, the latter two, and especially the third, constituted by far the most prevalent responses. There was, for instance, no disposition to recognize that Americans had misinterpreted the direction and meaning of the Russian Revolution of 1917. America's ultimate response was in effect to deny the existence of the Bolsheviks by withholding recognition. Perhaps the purest example of this postwar urge to reassert the old verities was the Red Scare of 1919–20. In the following article, Professor Stanley Coben (who teaches in the Department of History at the University of California, Los Angeles) utilizes the anthropological theories of Anthony F. C. Wallace to liken the Red Scare to a "revitalization movement" and demonstrates that its full significance cannot be grasped unless it is perceived as an attempt to purify the nation and to call it back to its historic mission by ridding it of intruding ideologies and groups.

This emphasis upon revivification was manifest not only in the crusade against almost every possible form of radicalism but also in the reaction against strikes and unionization; in the race riots of 1919 that struck out against the changed image and status of black Americans; in the repudiation of America's open door to immigration and the adoption of a national origins formula that reversed the tide of immigration from southern and eastern Europe and Asia in favor of the more familiar northern European countries; in Warren Harding's assurance to his countrymen that theirs was a time for "not heroics but healing; not nostrums but normalcy; not revolution but restoration."

For more discussion on a number of these themes see the essays by Joseph Gusfield (pp. 309–341) and John William Ward (pp. 343–354). See also: Lawrence W. Levine, "Progress and Nostalgia: The Self Image of the 1920's," in Malcolm Bradbury, ed., *The American Novel: The Writers of the 1920's** (1971); Paul Murphy, "The Sources and Nature of Intolerance in the 1920's," *Journal of American History*, 51 (June, 1964), 60–76; Stanley Coben, *A. Mitchell Palmer: Politician* (1963); Robert K. Murray, *Red Scare** (1955); John Higham, *Strangers in the Land: Patterns of American Nativism, 1860–1925** (1954); and William Preston, *Aliens and Dissenters: Federal Suppression of Radicals, 1903–1933** (1963).

A *Study in Nativism:*
The American Red Scare of 1919–20

STANLEY COBEN

At a victory loan pageant in the District of Columbia on May 6, 1919, a man refused to rise for the playing of "The Star-Spangled Banner." As soon as the national anthem was completed an enraged sailor fired three shots into the unpatriotic spectator's back. When the man fell, the *Washington Post* reported, "the crowd burst into cheering and handclapping." In February of the same year, a jury in Hammond, Indiana, took two minutes to acquit the assassin of an alien who yelled, "To Hell with the United States." Early in 1920, a clothing store salesman in Waterbury, Connecticut, was sentenced to six months in jail for having remarked to a customer that Lenin was "the brainiest," or "one of the brainiest" of the world's political leaders.[1] Dramatic episodes like these, or the better known Centralia Massacre, Palmer Raids, or May Day riots, were not everyday occurrences, even at the height of the Red Scare. But the fanatical one hundred per cent Americanism reflected by the Washington crowd, the Hammond jury, and the Waterbury judge pervaded a large part of our society between early 1919 and mid-1920.

Recently, social scientists have produced illuminating evidence about the causes of eruptions like that of 1919–20. They have attempted to identify experimentally the individuals most responsive to nativistic appeals, to explain their susceptibility, and to propose general theories of nativistic and related movements. These studies suggest a fuller, more coherent picture of nativistic upheavals and their causes than we now possess, and they provide the framework for this attempt to reinterpret the Red Scare.

Reprinted by permission of The Academy of Political Science and the author from *Political Science Quarterly*, 79 (March 1964), 52–75.

I am grateful to Robert D. Cross and Clyde C. Griffen for their critical reading of this article, and to Anthony F. C. Wallace and Abram Kardiner for their helpful comments on my use of anthropological and psychological material.

[1] *Washington Post*, May 7, 1919; Mark Sullivan, *Our Times, The United States 1900–1925* (New York, 1935), VI, 169; *The Nation*, CX (April 17, 1920), 510–11. The most complete account of the Red Scare is Robert K. Murray, *Red Scare, A Study in National Hysteria* (Minneapolis, 1955). But see the critical review of Murray's book by John M. Blum in *Mississippi Valley Historical Review*, XLII (1955), 145. Blum comments that Murray failed to explain "the susceptibility of the American people and of their elite to the 'national hysteria.' . . . About hysteria, after all, psychology and social psychology in particular have had considerable to say." John Higham places the postwar movement in historical perspective in his superb *Strangers in the Land, Patterns of American Nativism, 1860–1925* (New Brunswick, 1955), especially Chaps. 8 and 9.

Psychological experiments indicate that a great many Americans — at least several million — are always ready to participate in a "red scare." These people permanently hold attitudes which characterized the nativists of 1919–20: hostility toward certain minority groups, especially radicals and recent immigrants, fanatical patriotism, and a belief that internal enemies seriously threaten national security.[2]

In one of the most comprehensive of these experiments, psychologists Nancy C. Morse and Floyd H. Allport tested seven hypotheses about the causes of prejudice and found that one, national involvement or patriotism, proved to be "by far the most important factor" associated with prejudice. Other widely held theories about prejudice — status rivalry, frustration-aggression, and scapegoat hypotheses, for example — were found to be of only secondary importance.[3] Summarizing the results of this and a number of other psychological experiments, Gordon W. Allport, a pioneer in the scientific study of prejudice, concluded that in a large proportion of cases the prejudiced person is attempting to defend himself against severe inner turmoil by enforcing order in his external life. Any disturbance in the social *status quo* threatens the precarious psychic equilibrium of this type of individual, who, according to Allport, seeks "an island of institutional safety and security. The nation is the island he selects. . . . It has the definiteness he needs."

Allport pointed out that many apprehensive and frustrated people are not especially prejudiced. What is important, he found,

> is the way fear and frustration are handled. The institutionalistic way — especially the nationalistic — seems to be the nub of the matter. What happens is that the prejudiced person defines "nation" to fit his needs. The nation is first of all a protection (the chief protection) of him as an individual. It is his in-group. He sees no contradiction in ruling out of its beneficent orbit those whom he regards as threatening intruders and enemies (namely, American minorities). What is more, the nation stands for the status quo. It is a conservative agent;

---

[2] On the incidence of prejudice against minorities in the United States, see Gordon W. Allport and Bernard M. Kramer, "Some Roots of Prejudice," *Journal of Psychology*, XXII (1946), 9–39; Morris Janowitz and Dwaine Marvick, "Authoritarianism and Political Behavior," *Public Opinion Quarterly*, XVII (1953), 185–201; Bruno Bettelheim and Morris Janowitz, *Dynamics of Prejudice, A Psychological and Sociological Study of Veterans* (New York, 1950), 16, 26, and *passim*.

[3] Nancy M. Morse and F. H. Allport, "The Causation of Anti-Semitism: An Investigation of Seven Hypotheses," *Journal of Psychology*, XXXIV (1952), 197–233. For further experimental evidence indicating that prejudiced individuals are no more anxious, neurotic, or intolerant of ambiguity than those with more "liberal" attitudes, Anthony Davids, "Some Personality and Intellectual Correlates to Intolerance of Ambiguity," *Journal of Abnormal and Social Psychology*, LI (1955), 415–20; Ross Stagner and Clyde S. Congdon, "Another Failure to Demonstrate Displacement of Aggression," *Journal of Abnormal and Social Psychology*, LI (1955), 695–96; Dean Peabody, "Attitude Content and Agreement Set in Scales of Authoritarianism, Dogmatism, Anti-Semitism and Economic Conservatism," *Journal of Abnormal and Social Psychology*, LXIII (1961), 1–11.

within it are all the devices for safe living that he approves. His nationalism is a form of conservatism.[4]

Substantial evidence, then, suggests that millions of Americans are both extraordinarily fearful of social change and prejudiced against those minority groups which they perceive as "threatening intruders." Societal disruption, especially if it can easily be connected with the "intruders," not only will intensify the hostility of highly prejudiced individuals, but also will provoke many others, whose antagonism in more stable times had been mild or incipient, into the extreme group.

A number of anthropologists have come to conclusions about the roots of nativism which complement these psychological studies. Since the late nineteenth century, anthropologists have been studying the religious and nativistic cults of American Indian tribes and of Melanesian and Papuan groups in the South Pacific. Recently, several anthropologists have attempted to synthesize their findings and have shown striking parallels in the cultural conditions out of which these movements arose.[5] In every case, severe societal disruption preceded the outbreak of widespread nativistic cult behavior. According to Anthony F. C. Wallace, who has gone farthest toward constructing a general theory of cult formation, when the disruption has proceeded so far that many members of a society find it difficult or impossible to fulfill their physical and psychological needs, or to relieve severe anxiety through the ordinary culturally approved methods, the society will be susceptible to what Wallace has termed a "revitalization movement." This is a convulsive attempt to change or revivify important cultural beliefs and values, and frequently to eliminate alien influences. Such movements promise and often provide participants with better means of dealing with

---

[4] Gordon W. Allport, *The Nature of Prejudice* (Cambridge, 1955), 406; see Boyd C. Shafer, *Nationalism, Myth and Reality* (New York, 1955), 181.

[5] See, especially, the works of Anthony F. C. Wallace: "Revitalization Movements," *American Anthropologist*, LVIII (1956), 264–81; "Handsome Lake and the Great Revival in the West," *American Quarterly*, IV (1952), 149–65; "Stress and Rapid Personality Change," *International Record of Medicine and General Practice Clinics*, CLXIX (1956), 761–73; "New Religions Among the Delaware Indians, 1600–1900," *Southwest Journal of Anthropology*, XII (1956), 1–21. Also, Michael M. Ames, "Reaction to Stress: A Comparative Study of Nativism," *Davidson Journal of Anthropology*, III (1957), 16–30; C. S. Belshaw, "The Significance of Modern Cults in Melanesian Development," *Australian Outlook*, IV (1950), 116–25; Raymond Firth, "The Theory of 'Cargo' Cults: A Note on Tikopia," *Man*, LV (1955), 130–32; Lawrence Krader, "A Nativistic Movement in Western Siberia," *American Anthropologist*, LVIII (1956), 282–92; Ralph Linton, "Nativistic Movements," *American Anthropologist*, XLV (1943), 220–43; Margaret Mead, *New Lives for Old* (New York, 1956); Peter Worsley, *The Trumpet Shall Sound* (London, 1957). Several sociologists and psychologists have come to conclusions about the causes of these movements that are similar in important respects to Wallace's, although less comprehensive. See Leon Festinger, *A Theory of Cognitive Dissonance* (New York, 1957); Hadley Cantril, *The Psychology of Social Movements* (New York, 1941), especially pp. 3–4, Chaps. 5, 8, and 9; Hans H. Toch, "Crisis Situations and Ideological Revaluation," *Public Opinion Quarterly*, XVIX (1955), 53–67.

their changed circumstances, thus reducing their very high level of internal stress.[6]

American Indian tribes, for example, experienced a series of such convulsions as the tide of white settlers rolled west. The Indians were pushed onto reservations and provided with Indian agents, missionaries, and physicians, who took over many of the functions hitherto assumed by chiefs and medicine men. Indian craftsmen (and craftswomen) were replaced by dealers in the white man's implements. Most hunters and warriors also lost their vocations and consequently their self-respect. What an anthropologist wrote of one tribe was true of many others: "From cultural maturity as Pawnees they were reduced to cultural infancy as civilized men." [7]

One of the last major religious upheavals among the Indians was the Ghost Dance cult which spread from Nevada through Oregon and northern California in the eighteen-seventies, and a similar movement among the Rocky Mountain and western plains Indians about 1890. Although cult beliefs varied somewhat from tribe to tribe, converts generally were persuaded that if they followed certain prescribed rituals, including the dance, they would soon return to their old ways of living. Even their dead relatives would be restored to life. Most Indians were too conscious of their military weakness to challenge their white masters directly. Ghost Dancers among the Dakota Sioux, however, influenced by the militant proselyter Sitting Bull, became convinced that true believers could not be harmed by the white man's bullets and that Sioux warriors would drive the intruders from Indian lands. Their dreams were rudely smashed at the massacre of Wounded Knee Creek in December 1890.[8]

[6] Wallace, "Revitalization Movements." For a recent verification of Wallace's theories see Thomas Rhys Williams, "The Form of a North Borneo Nativistic Behavior," *American Anthropologist*, LXV (1963), 543–51. On the psychological results of socially caused stress, Wallace, "Stress and Rapid Personality Change"; William Caudill, *Effects of Social and Cultural Systems in Reactions to Stress*, Social Science Research Council Pamphlet No. 14 (New York, 1958); Caudill, "Cultural Perspectives on Stress," Army Medical Service Graduate School, *Symposium on Stress* (Washington, D.C., 1953); Hans Selye, *The Stress of Life* (New York, 1956); Roland Fischer and Neil Agnew, "A Hierarchy of Stressors," *Journal of Mental Science*, CI (1955), 383–86; Daniel H. Funkenstein, Stanley H. King, and Margaret E. Drolette, *Mastery of Stress* (Cambridge, 1957); M. Basowitz et al., *Anxiety and Stress: An Interdisciplinary Study of a Life Situation* (New York, 1955).

[7] Alexander Lesser, *The Pawnee Ghost Dance Hand Game. A Study of Cultural Change* (New York, 1933), 44.

[8] Cora DuBois, *The 1870 Ghost Dance*, Anthropological Records, III (Berkeley, 1946); Leslie Spier, *The Ghost Dance of 1870 Among the Klamath of Oregon*, University of Washington Publications in Anthropology, II (Seattle, 1927); Lesser, *Ghost Dance*; A. L. Kroeber, *Handbook of the Indians of California*, Bureau of American Ethnology Bulletin 78 (Washington, D.C., 1925). Anthropologists recently have argued about the origins of the Ghost Dance cults. Both sides agree, however, that whatever their origins, the cults took the form they did because of intolerable cultural conditions caused largely by white encroachments. David F. Aberle, "The Prophet Dance and Reactions to White Contact," *Southwest Journal of Anthropology*, XV (1959), 74–83; Leslie Spier, Wayne Suttles, and Melvin Herskovits, "Comment on Aberle's Thesis of Deprivation," *Southwest Journal of Anthropology*, XV (1959), 84–88.

The Boxer movement in China, 1898 to 1900, resembled in many aspects the Indian Ghost Dance cults; however, the Boxers, more numerous and perhaps less demoralized than the Indians, aimed more directly at removing foreign influences from their land. The movement erupted first in Shantung province where foreigners, especially Japanese, British, and Germans, were most aggressive. A flood of the Yellow River had recently deprived about a million people in the province of food and shelter. Banditry was rampant, organized government ineffective. The Boxer movement, based on the belief that these tragic conditions were due almost entirely to the "foreign devils" and their agents, determined to drive the enemy out of China. Boxers went into action carrying charms and chanting incantations supposed to make them invulnerable to the foreigners' bullets. The first object of the Boxers' nativistic fury were Chinese who had converted to Christianity, the intruders' religion. The patriots then attacked railroad and telegraph lines, leading symbols of foreign influence. Finally, the Boxers turned against the foreigners themselves, slaughtering many. Not until after the Boxers carried on a two-month siege of the foreign community in Peking did American, European, and Japanese armies crush the movement.[9]

Other revitalization attempts proved more successful than the Boxers or Ghost Dancers. The Gaiwiio movement, for example, helped the Iroquois Indians of western New York State to retain their identity as a culture while adjusting successfully to an encroaching white civilization during the first decade of the nineteenth century. The movement implanted a new moral code among the Indians, enjoining sobriety and family stability and encouraging acceptance of Western technology, while revivifying cohesive Indian traditions.[10]

Dominant as well as conquered peoples, Ralph Linton has pointed out, undergo nativistic movements. Dominant groups, he observed, are sometimes threatened "not only by foreign invasion or domestic revolt but also by the invidious process of assimilation which might, in the long run, destroy their distinctive powers and privileges." Under such circumstances, Linton concluded, "the frustrations which motivate nativistic movements in inferior or dominated groups" are "replaced by anxieties which produce very much the same [nativistic] result" in dominant groups.[11]

Communist "brainwashers" have consciously attempted to achieve results

[9] The best account of the Boxer movement is Chester C. Tan, *The Boxer Catastrophe* (New York, 1955). Also, George N. Steiger, *China and the Occident, the Origin and Development of the Boxer Movement* (New Haven, 1927); Peter Fleming, *The Siege at Peking* (New York, 1959).

[10] Wallace, "Handsome Lake." Wallace compared the Gaiwiio with a Chinese attempt to accommodate their society to Western civilization in "Stress and Rapid Personality Change." For a successful movement in the South Pacific see Mead, *New Lives for Old*.

[11] Linton, 237. Also, Carroll L. Riley and John Hobgood, "A Recent Nativistic Movement Among the Southern Tepehuan Indians," *Southwest Journal of Anthropology*, XV (1959), 355–60.

comparable to those obtained by prophets of movements like the Ghost Dance cult and the Boxers. They create intolerable stress within individuals, not through rapid societal change, but by intentional physical debilitation and continual accusations, cross-examinations, and use of other anxiety-provoking techniques. Then they offer their prisoners an escape from the induced psychological torment: conversion to the new gospel.[12]

The similarity in the mental processes involved in "brainwashing" and in the formation of nativistic movements becomes even clearer upon examination of the Chinese Communist attempt to establish their doctrines in mainland China. Again, the Communists intentionally have created conditions like those out of which nativistic cults have arisen more spontaneously in other societies. In addition to the stress which ordinarily would accompany rapid industrialization of an economically backward society, the Chinese leaders have provoked additional anxiety through the systematic use of group confessions and denunciations and have intentionally disrupted family life. Hostility toward the American enemy has been purposely aroused and used to unify the masses, as well as to justify the repression of millions of alleged internal enemies. The whole population has been continually urged to repent their sins and to adopt wholeheartedly the Communist gospel, which has a strong nativistic component. As a psychologist has remarked, to a large extent the Chinese Communists provide both the disease and the cure.[13]

The ferocious outbreak of nativism in the United States after World War I was not consciously planned or provoked by any individual or group, although some Americans took advantage of the movement once it started. Rather, the Red Scare, like the Gaiwiio and Boxer movements described above, was brought on largely by a number of severe social and economic dislocations which threatened the national equilibrium. The full extent and the shocking effects of these disturbances of 1919 have not yet been adequately described. Runaway prices, a brief but sharp stock market crash and business depression, revolutions throughout Europe, widespread fear of domestic revolt, bomb explosions, and an outpouring of radical literature were distressing enough. These sudden difficulties, moreover, served to exaggerate the disruptive effects already produced by the social and intellectual ravages of the World War and the preceding reform era, and by the arrival, before the war, of millions of new immigrants. This added stress intensified the hostility of Americans strongly antagonistic to minority

---

[12] Robert J. Lifton, "Thought Reform in Western Civilians in Chinese Communist Prisons," *Psychiatry*, XIX (1956), 173–95; Edgar H. Schein, "The Chinese Indoctrination Program for Prisoners of War, A Study of Attempted Brainwashing," *Psychiatry*, XIX (1956), 149–72.

[13] Edgar H. Schein, with Inge Schneier and Curtis H. Bark, *Coercive Persuasion* (New York, 1961); William Sargent, *Battle for the Mind* (New York, 1957), 150–65; Robert J. Lifton, *Thought Reform and the Psychology of Totalism* (New York, 1961); R. L. Walker, *China Under Communism* (London, 1946).

groups, and brought new converts to blatant nativism from among those who ordinarily were not overtly hostile toward radicals or recent immigrants.

Citizens who joined the crusade for one hundred per cent Americanism sought, primarily, a unifying force which would halt the apparent disintegration of their culture. The movement, they felt, would eliminate those foreign influences which the one hundred per centers believed were the major cause of their anxiety.

Many of the postwar sources of stress were also present during World War I, and the Red Scare, as John Higham has observed, was partly an exaggeration of wartime passions.[14] In 1917–18 German-Americans served as the object of almost all our nativistic fervor; they were the threatening intruders who refused to become good citizens. "They used America," a patriotic author declared in 1918 of two million German-Americans, "they never loved her. They clung to their old language, their old customs, and cared nothing for ours. . . . As a class they were clannish beyond all other races coming here." [15] Fear of subversion by German agents was almost as extravagant in 1917–18 as anxiety about "reds" in the postwar period. Attorney General Thomas Watt Gregory reported to a friend in May 1918 that "we not infrequently receive as many as fifteen hundred letters in a single day suggesting disloyalty and the making of investigations." [16]

Opposition to the war by radical groups helped smooth the transition among American nativists from hatred of everything German to fear of radical revolution. The two groups of enemies were associated also for other reasons. High government officials declared after the war that German leaders planned and subsidized the Bolshevik Revolution.[17] When bombs blasted homes and public buildings in nine cities in June 1919, the director of the Justice Department's Bureau of Investigation asserted that the bombers were "connected with Russian bolshevism, aided by Hun money." [18] In November 1919, a year after the armistice, a popular magazine warned of "the Russo-German movement that is now trying to dominate America. . . ." [19]

Even the wartime hostility toward German-Americans, however, is more

[14] Higham, 222.

[15] Emerson Hough, *The Web* (Chicago, 1919), 23. Hough was a rabid one hundred per center during the Red Scare also.

[16] T. W. Gregory to R. E. Vinson, May 13, 1918, Papers of Thomas Watt Gregory (Library of Congress, Washington, D.C.).

[17] Subcommittee of Senate Committee on the Judiciary, *Hearings, Brewing and Liquor Interests and German and Bolshevik Propaganda*, 66th Congress, 1st Session, 1919, 2669 ff.; *The New York Times*, July 7, August 11 and 29, September 15–21, 1918.

[18] *Washington Post*, July 3, 1919. Bureau Director William J. Flynn produced no evidence to back this assertion. Later he claimed to have conclusive proof that the bombers were Italian anarchists. Flynn to Attorney General Harry Daugherty, April 4, 1922, Department of Justice Records, File 202600, Sect. 5 (National Archives, Washington, D.C.).

[19] *Saturday Evening Post*, CXCII (November 1, 1919), 28. For similar assertions in other publications, Meno Lovenstein, *American Opinion of Soviet Russia* (Washington, D.C., 1941), Chap. 1, *passim*.

understandable when seen in the light of recent anthropological and psychological studies. World War I disturbed Americans not only because of the real threat posed by enemy armies and a foreign ideology. For many citizens it had the further effect of shattering an already weakened intellectual tradition. When the European governments decided to fight, they provided shocking evidence that man was not, as most educated members of Western society had believed, a rational creature progressing steadily, if slowly, toward control of his environment. When the great powers declared war in 1914, many Americans as well as many Europeans were stunned. The *New York Times* proclaimed a common theme — European civilization had collapsed: The supposedly advanced nations, declared the *Times*, "have reverted to the condition of savage tribes roaming the forests and falling upon each other in a fury of blood and carnage to achieve the ambitious designs of chieftains clad in skins and drunk with mead." [20] Franz Alexander, director for twenty-five years of the Chicago Institute of Psychoanalysis, recently recalled his response to the outbreak of the World War:

> The first impact of this news is [*sic*] unforgettable. It was the sudden intuitive realization that a chapter of history had ended. . . . Since then, I have discussed this matter with some of my contemporaries and heard about it a great deal in my early postwar psychoanalytic treatments of patients. To my amazement, the others who went through the same events had quite a similar reaction. . . . It was an immediate vivid and prophetic realization that something irrevocable of immense importance had happened in history.[21]

Americans were jolted by new blows to their equilibrium after entering the war. Four million men were drafted away from familiar surroundings and some of them experienced the terrible carnage of trench warfare. Great numbers of women left home to work in war industries or to replace men in other jobs. Negroes flocked to Northern industrial areas by the hundreds of thousands, and their first mass migration from the South created violent racial antagonism in Northern cities.

During the war, also, Americans sanctioned a degree of government control over the economy which deviated sharply from traditional economic individualism. Again, fears aroused before the war were aggravated, for the reform legislation of the Progressive era had tended to increase government intervention, and many citizens were further perturbed by demands that

---

[20] Quoted in William E. Leuchtenburg, *The Perils of Prosperity, 1914–32* (Chicago, 1958), 13. There is no comprehensive study of the effects of the war on the American mind. For brief treatments, Henry F. May, *The End of American Innocence* (New York, 1959), 361–67; Merle Curti, *The Growth of American Thought* (New York, 1951), 687–705; Ralph Henry Gabriel, *The Course of American Democratic Thought* (New York, 1956), 387, 404; André Siegfried, *America Comes of Age* (New York, 1927), 3; Walter Lord, *The Good Years, From 1900 to the First War* (New York, 1960), 339–41.

[21] Franz Alexander, *The Western Mind in Transition* (New York, 1960), 73–74. Also see William Barrett, *Irrational Man* (Garden City, N.Y., 1961), 32–33.

the federal government enforce even higher standards of economic and social morality. By 1919, therefore, some prewar progressives as well as conservatives feared the gradual disappearance of highly valued individual opportunity and responsibility. Their fears were fed by strong postwar calls for continued large-scale government controls — extension of federal operation of railroads and of the Food Administration, for example.

The prime threat to these long-held individualistic values, however, and the most powerful immediate stimulus to the revitalistic response, came from Russia. There the Bolshevik conquerors proclaimed their intention of exporting Marxist ideology. If millions of Americans were disturbed in 1919 by the specter of communism, the underlying reason was not fear of foreign invasion — Russia, after all, was still a backward nation recently badly defeated by German armies. The real threat was the potential spread of communist ideas. These, the one hundred per centers realized with horror, possessed a genuine appeal for reformers and for the economically underprivileged, and if accepted they would complete the transformation of America.

A clear picture of the Bolshevik tyranny was not yet available; therefore, as after the French Revolution, those who feared the newly successful ideology turned to fight the revolutionary ideals. So the *Saturday Evening Post* declared editorially in November 1919 that "History will see our present state of mind as one with that preceding the burning of witches, the children's crusade, the great tulip craze and other examples of softening of the world brain." The *Post* referred not to the Red Scare or the impending Palmer Raids, but to the spread of communist ideology. Its editorial concluded: "The need of the country is not more idealism, but more pragmatism; not communism, but common sense." [22] One of the most powerful patriotic groups, the National Security League, called upon members early in 1919 to "teach 'Americanism.' This means the fighting of Bolshevism . . . by the creation of well defined National Ideals." Members "must preach Americanism and instil the idealism of America's Wars, and that American spirit of service which believes in giving as well as getting." [23] New York attorney, author, and educator Henry Waters Taft warned a Carnegie Hall audience late in 1919 that Americans must battle "a propaganda which is tending to undermine our most cherished social and political institutions and is having the effect of producing widespread unrest among the poor and the ignorant, especially those of foreign birth." [24]

When the war ended Americans also confronted the disturbing possibility, pointed up in 1919 by the struggle over the League of Nations, that Europe's struggles would continue to be their own. These factors combined

[22] *Saturday Evening Post*, CXCII (November 1, 1919), 28.
[23] National Security League, *Future Work* (New York, 1919), 6.
[24] Henry Waters Taft, *Aspects of Bolshevism and Americanism, Address before the League for Political Education at Carnegie Hall, New York, December 6, 1919* (New York, 1919), 21.

to make the First World War a traumatic experience for millions of citizens. As Senator James Reed of Missouri observed in August 1919, "This country is still suffering from shell shock. Hardly anyone is in a normal state ravages and disturbances still exist." [25]
of mind. . . . A great storm has swept over the intellectual world and its
The wartime "shell shock" left many Americans extraordinarily susceptible to psychological stress caused by postwar social and economic turbulence. Most important for the course of the Red Scare, many of these disturbances had their greatest effect on individuals already antagonistic toward minorities. First of all, there was some real evidence of danger to the nation in 1919, and the nation provided the chief emotional support for many Americans who responded easily to charges of an alien radical menace. Violence flared throughout Europe after the war and revolt lifted radicals to power in several Eastern and Central European nations. Combined with the earlier Bolshevik triumph in Russia these revolutions made Americans look more anxiously at radicals here. Domestic radicals encouraged these fears; they became unduly optimistic about their own chances of success and boasted openly of their coming triumph. Scores of new foreign language anarchist and communist journals, most of them written by and for Southern and Eastern European immigrants, commenced publication, and the established radical press became more exuberant. These periodicals never tired of assuring readers in 1919 that "the United States seems to be on the verge of a revolutionary crisis." [26] American newspapers and magazines reprinted selections from radical speeches, pamphlets, and periodicals so their readers could see what dangerous ideas were abroad in the land.[27] Several mysterious bomb explosions and bombing attempts, reported in bold front page headlines in newspapers across the country, frightened the public in 1919. To many citizens these seemed part of an organized campaign of terror carried on by alien radicals intending to bring down the federal government. The great strikes of 1919 and early 1920 aroused similar fears.[28]

[25] U.S., *Congressional Record*, 66th Congress, 1st Session, August 15, 1919, 3892.
[26] Robert E. Park, *The Immigrant Press and Its Control* (New York, 1922), 214, 230–38, 241–45; R. E. Park and Herbert A. Miller, *Old World Traits Transplanted* (New York, 1921), 99–101; Daniel Bell, "The Background and Development of Marxian Socialism in the United States," in Donald Drew Egbert and Stow Persons, *Socialism in American Life* (Princeton, 1952), I, 334; Lovenstein, 7–50; Leuchtenburg, 67–68; Murray, 33–36.
[27] The Justice Department distributed pamphlets containing such material to all American newspapers and magazines; *Red Radicalism, as Described by Its Own Leaders* (Washington, D.C., 1920); National Popular Government League, *To the American People, Report Upon the Illegal Practices of the Department of Justice* (Washington, D.C., 1920), 64–66. The staunchly anti-radical *New York Times* published translations from a large sample of foreign language radical newspapers on June 8, 1919.
[28] Murray, Chaps. 5, 7–10. Asked by a congressional committee a few weeks after the spate of bombings in June 1919 whether there was real evidence of an organized effort to destroy the federal government, Assistant Attorney General Francis P. Garvan replied, "Certainly." Garvan was in charge of federal prosecution of radicals. *Washington Post*, June 27, 1919.

Actually American radical organizations in 1919 were disorganized and poverty-stricken. The Communists were inept, almost without contact with American workers and not yet dominated or subsidized by Moscow. The IWW was shorn of its effective leaders, distrusted by labor, and generally declining in influence and power. Violent anarchists were isolated in a handful of tiny, unconnected local organizations.[29] One or two of these anarchist groups probably carried out the "bomb conspiracy" of 1919; but the extent of the "conspiracy" can be judged from the fact that the bombs killed a total of two men during the year, a night watchman and one of the bomb throwers, and seriously wounded one person, a maid in the home of a Georgia senator.[30]

Nevertheless, prophecies of national disaster abounded in 1919, even among high government officials. Secretary of State Robert Lansing confided to his diary that we were in real peril of social revolution. Attorney General A. Mitchell Palmer advised the House Appropriations Committee that "on a certain day, which we have been advised of," radicals would attempt "to rise up and destroy the Government at one fell swoop." Senator Charles Thomas of Colorado warned that "the country is on the verge of a volcanic upheaval." And Senator Miles Poindexter of Washington declared, "There is real danger that the government will fall." [31] A West Virginia wholesaler, with offices throughout the state, informed the Justice Department in October 1919 that "there is hardly a respectable citizen of my acquaintance who does not believe that we are on the verge of armed conflict in this country." William G. McAdoo was told by a trusted friend that "Chicago, which has always been a very liberal minded place, seems to me to have gone mad on the question of the 'Reds.' " Delegates to the Farmers National Congress in November 1919 pledged that farmers would assist the government in meeting the threat of revolution.[32]

---

[29] Theodore Draper, *The Roots of American Communism* (New York, 1957), 198–200, 302, 312–14; David J. Saposs, *Left Wing Unionism, A Study in Policies and Tactics* (New York, 1926), 49–50, 152–57; Selig Perlman and Philip Taft (eds.), *Labor Movements* in John R. Commons (ed.), *History of Labour in the United States 1896–1932*, IV (New York, 1935), 621, 431–32; Jerome Davis, *The Russian Immigrant* (New York, 1922), 114–18; Kate Holladay Claghorn, *The Immigrant's Day in Court* (New York, 1923), 363–73; John S. Gambs, *The Decline of the I.W.W.* (New York, 1932), 133; Murray, 107–10.

[30] *The New York Times*, May 1, June 3, 4, 1919.

[31] "The Spread of Bolshevism in the United States," private memorandum, dated July 26, 1919, Papers of Robert Lansing (Library of Congress, Washington, D.C.); "One Point of View of the Murders at Centralia, Washington," private memorandum, dated November 13, 1919, Lansing Papers; U.S., *Congressional Record*, 66th Congress, 1st Session, October 14, 1919, 6869; *Washington Post*, February 16, 1919; New York *World*, June 19, 1919.

[32] Henry Barham to Palmer, October 27, 1919, Justice Department Records, File 202600; unidentified correspondent to McAdoo, February 10, 1920, McAdoo Papers (Library of Congress, Washington, D.C.); A. P. Sanders to Palmer, November 12, 1919, Justice Department Records, File 202600; *The New York Times*, October 31, 1919.

The slight evidence of danger from radical organizations aroused such wild fear only because Americans had already encountered other threats to cultural stability. However, the dislocations caused by the war and the menace of communism alone would not have produced such a vehement nativistic response. Other postwar challenges to the social and economic order made the crucial difference.

Of considerable importance was the skyrocketing cost of living. Retail prices more than doubled between 1915 and 1920, and the price rise began gathering momentum in the spring of 1919.[33] During the summer of 1919 the dominant political issue in America was not the League of Nations; not even the "red menace" or the threat of a series of major strikes disturbed the public as much as did the climbing cost of living. The *Washington Post* early in August 1919 called rising prices "the burning domestic issue. . . ." Democratic National Chairman Homer Cummings, after a trip around the country, told President Woodrow Wilson that more Americans were worried about prices than about any other public issue and that they demanded government action. When Wilson decided to address Congress on the question the Philadelphia *Public Ledger* observed that the administration had "come rather tardily to a realization of what is uppermost in the minds of the American people." [34]

Then the wave of postwar strikes — there were 3,600 of them in 1919 involving over 4,000,000 workers [35] — reached a climax in the fall of 1919. A national steel strike began in September and nationwide coal and rail walkouts were scheduled for November 1. Unions gained in membership and power during the war, and in 1919 labor leaders were under strong pressure to help workers catch up to or go ahead of mounting living costs. Nevertheless, influential government officials attributed the walkouts to radical activities. Early in 1919, Secretary of Labor William B. Wilson declared in a public speech that recent major strikes in Seattle, Butte, Montana, and Lawrence, Massachusetts, had been instituted by the Bolsheviks and the IWW for the sole purpose of bringing about a nationwide revolution in the United States.[36] During the steel strike of early fall, 1919, a Senate investigating committee reported that "behind this strike there is massed a consid-

---

[33] U.S. Bureau of the Census, *Historical Statistics of the United States, Colonial Times to 1952, A Statistical Abstract Supplement* (Washington, D.C., 1960), 91, 92, 126; U.S. Department of Labor, Bureau of Labor Statistics, Bulletin Number 300, *Retail Prices 1913 to December, 1920* (Washington, D.C., 1922), 4; Daniel J. Ahearn, Jr., *The Wages of Farm and Factory Laborers 1914–1944* (New York, 1945), 227.

[34] *Washington Post*, August 1, 4, 1919; *The New York Times*, July 30, August 1, 1919; Philadelphia *Public Ledger*, August 5, 1919.

[35] Florence Peterson, *Strikes in the United States, 1880–1936*, U.S. Department of Labor Bulletin Number 651 (Washington, D.C., 1938), 21. More employees engaged in strikes in 1919 than the total over the ten-year period 1923–32.

[36] *Washington Post*, February 21, 1919. As late as April 1920, Secretary Wilson agreed with Palmer during a Cabinet meeting that the nationwide rail walkout had been caused by Communists and the IWW. Entry in Josephus Daniels' Diary for April 14, 1920, Papers of Josephus Daniels (Library of Congress, Washington, D.C.).

erable element of I.W.W.'s, anarchists, revolutionists, and Russian soviets. . . ."[37] In April 1920 the head of the Justice Department's General Intelligence Division, J. Edgar Hoover, declared in a public hearing that at least fifty per cent of the influence behind the recent series of strikes was traceable directly to communist agents.[38]

Furthermore, the nation suffered a sharp economic depression in late 1918 and early 1919, caused largely by sudden cancellations of war orders. Returning servicemen found it difficult to obtain jobs during this period, which coincided with the beginning of the Red Scare. The former soldiers had been uprooted from their homes and told that they were engaged in a patriotic crusade. Now they came back to find "reds" criticizing their country and threatening the government with violence, Negroes holding good jobs in the big cities, prices terribly high, and workers who had not served in the armed forces striking for higher wages.[39] A delegate won prolonged applause from the 1919 American Legion Convention when he denounced radical aliens, exclaiming, "Now that the war is over and they are in lucrative positions while our boys haven't a job, we've got to send those scamps to hell." The major part of the mobs which invaded meeting halls of immigrant organizations and broke up radical parades, especially during the first half of 1919, was comprised of men in uniform.[40]

A variety of other circumstances combined to add even more force to the postwar nativistic movement. Long before the new immigrants were seen as potential revolutionists they became the objects of widespread hostility. The peak of immigration from Southern and Eastern Europe occurred in the fifteen years before the war; during that period almost ten million immigrants from those areas entered the country. Before the anxious eyes of members of all classes of Americans, the newcomers crowded the cities and began to disturb the economic and social order.[41] Even without other postwar disturbances a nativistic movement of some strength could have been predicted when the wartime solidarity against the German enemy began to wear off in 1919.

In addition, not only were the European revolutions most successful in Eastern and to a lesser extent in Southern Europe, but aliens from these

[37] U.S. Senate, Committee on Education and Labor, *Report, Investigation on Strike in Steel Industry*, 66th Congress, 1st Session, 1919, 14.

[38] *The New York Times*, April 25, 1920, 23.

[39] George Soule, *Prosperity Decade, From War to Depression: 1917–1929* (New York, 1947), 81–84; Murray, 125, 182–83.

[40] *Proceedings and Committees, Caucus of the American Legion* (St. Louis, 1919), 117; *The New York Times*, May 2, 1919; *Washington Post*, May 2, 1919. Ex-servicemen also played major roles in the great Negro-white race riots of mid-1919. *Washington Post*, July 20–23, 28–31.

[41] *Historical Statistics of the United States*, 56. On the causes of American hostility to recent immigrants see John Higham's probing and provocative essay "Another Look at Nativism," *Catholic Historical Review*, XLIV (1958), 147–58. Higham stresses status conflicts, but does not explain why some competitors on the crowded social ladder were much more antagonistic to the new immigrants than were others.

areas predominated in American radical organizations. At least ninety per cent of the members of the two American Communist parties formed in 1919 were born in Eastern Europe. The anarchist groups whose literature and bombs captured the imagination of the American public in 1919 were composed almost entirely of Italian, Spanish, and Slavic aliens. Justice Department announcements and statements by politicians and the press stressed the predominance of recent immigrants in radical organizations.[42] Smoldering prejudice against new immigrants and identification of these immigrants with European as well as American radical movements, combined with other sources of postwar stress to create one of the most frenzied and one of the most widespread nativistic movements in the nation's history.

The result, akin to the movements incited by the Chinese Boxers or the Indian Ghost Dancers, was called Americanism or one hundred per cent Americanism.[43] Its objective was to end the apparent erosion of American values and the disintegration of American culture. By reaffirming those beliefs, customs, symbols, and traditions felt to be the foundation of our way of life, by enforcing conformity among the population, and by purging the nation of dangerous foreigners, the one hundred per centers expected to heal societal divisions and to tighten defenses against cultural change.

Panegyrics celebrating our history and institutions were delivered regularly in almost every American school, church, and public hall in 1919 and 1920. Many of these fervent addresses went far beyond the usual patriotic declarations. Audiences were usually urged to join a crusade to protect our hallowed institutions. Typical of the more moderate statements was Columbia University President Nicholas Murray Butler's insistence in April 1919 that "America will be saved, not by those who have only contempt and despite for her founders and her history, but by those who look with respect and reverence upon the great series of happenings extending from the voyage of the Mayflower. . . ." [44]

What one historian has called "a riot of biographies of American heroes — statesmen, cowboys, and pioneers" [45] appeared in this brief period. Immigrants as well as citizens produced many autobiographical testimonials to the superiority of American institutions. These patriotic tendencies in our

[42] Draper, 189–90; *Annual Report of the Attorney General for 1920* (Washington, D.C., 1920), 177; Higham, *Strangers in the Land*, 226–27.

[43] The word "Americanism" was used by the nativists of the eighteen-forties and eighteen-fifties. During World War I, the stronger phrase "100 per cent Americanism" was invented to suit the belligerent drive for universal conformity.

[44] Horace M. Kallen, *Culture and Democracy in the United States* (New York, 1924), Chap. 3, 154–55; Edward G. Hartman, *The Movement to Americanize the Immigrant* (New York, 1948), Chap. 9; Nicholas Murray Butler, *Is America Worth Saving? An Address Delivered Before the Commercial Club of Cincinnati, Ohio, April 19, 1919* (New York, 1919), 20.

[45] Emerson Hunsberger Loucks, *The Ku Klux Klan in Pennsylvania* (New York, 1936), 163.

literature were as short-lived as the Red Scare, and have been concealed by "debunking" biographies of folk heroes and skeptical autobiographies so common later in the nineteen-twenties. An unusual number of motion pictures about our early history were turned out immediately after the war and the reconstruction of colonial Williamsburg and of Longfellow's Wayside Inn was begun. With great fanfare, Secretary of State Lansing placed the original documents of the Constitution and the Declaration of Independence on display in January 1920, and the State Department distributed movies of this ceremony to almost every town and city in the United States.[46] Organizations like the National Security League, the Association for Constitutional Government, the Sons and the Daughters of the American Revolution, the Colonial Dames of America, with the cooperation of the American Bar Association and many state Bar Associations, organized Constitution Day celebrations and distributed huge numbers of pamphlets on the subject throughout the country.

The American flag became a sacred symbol. Legionnaires demanded that citizens "Run the Reds out from the land whose flag they sully." [47] Men suspected of radical leanings were forced to kiss the stars and stripes. A Brooklyn truck driver decided in June 1919 that it was unpatriotic to obey a New York City law obliging him to fly a red cloth on lumber which projected from his vehicle. Instead he used as a danger signal a small American flag. A policeman, infuriated at the sight of the stars and stripes flying from a lumber pile, arrested the driver on a charge of disorderly conduct. Despite the Brooklyn patriot's insistence that he meant no offense to the flag, he was reprimanded and fined by the court.[48]

Recent immigrants, especially, were called upon to show evidence of real conversion. Great pressure was brought to bear upon the foreign-born to learn English and to forget their native tongues. As Senator William S. Kenyon of Iowa declared in October 1919, "The time has come to make this a one-language nation." [49] An editorial in the American Legion Weekly took a further step and insisted that the one language must be called "American. Why even in Mexico they do not stand for calling the language the Spanish language." [50]

Immigrants were also expected to adopt our customs and to snuff out remnants of Old World cultures. Genteel prewar and wartime movements to speed up assimilation took on a "frightened and feverish aspect." [51] Welcoming members of an Americanization conference called by his depart-

[46] Kallen, Chap. 3, 154-55; Division of Foreign Intelligence, "Memorandum about Constitution Ceremonies," January 19, 1920, Lansing Papers; The New York Times, January 18, 1920.

[47] American Legion Weekly, I (November 14, 1919), 12.

[48] Sullivan, VI, 118; New York World, June 22, 1919.

[49] The New York Times, October 14, 1919.

[50] American Legion Weekly, I (November 14, 1919) 12.

[51] Higham, Strangers in the Land, 225.

ment, Secretary of the Interior Franklin K. Lane exclaimed in May 1919, "You have been gathered together as crusaders in a great cause. . . . There is no other question of such importance before the American people as the solidifying and strengthening of true American sentiment." A Harvard University official told the conference that "The Americanization movement . . . gives men a new and holy religion. . . . It challenges each one of us to a renewed consecration and devotion to the welfare of the nation." [52] The National Security League boasted, in 1919, of establishing one thousand study groups to teach teachers how to inculcate "Americanism" in their foreign-born students.[53] A critic of the prevailing mood protested against "one of our best advertised American mottoes, 'One country, one language, one flag,'" which, he complained, had become the basis for a fervent nationwide program.[54]

As the postwar movement for one hundred per cent Americanism gathered momentum, the deportation of alien nonconformists became increasingly its most compelling objective. Asked to suggest a remedy for the nationwide upsurge in radical activity, the Mayor of Gary, Indiana, replied, "Deportation is the answer, deportation of these leaders who talk treason in America and deportation of those who agree with them and work with them." "We must remake America," a popular author averred, "We must purify the source of America's population and keep it pure. . . . We must insist that there shall be an American loyalty, brooking no amendment or qualification." [55] As Higham noted, "In 1919, the clamor of 100 per centers for applying deportation as a purgative arose to an hysterical howl. . . . Through repression and deportation on the one hand and speedy total assimilation on the other, 100 per centers hoped to eradicate discontent and purify the nation." [56]

Politicians quickly sensed the possibilities of the popular frenzy for Americanism. Mayor Ole Hanson of Seattle, Governor Calvin Coolidge of Massachusetts, and General Leonard Wood became the early heroes of the

---

[52] United States Department of the Interior, Bureau of Education, *Organization Conference, Proceedings* (Washington, D.C., 1919), 293, 345–50.

[53] National Security League, 4.

[54] *Addresses and Proceedings of the Knights of Columbus Educational Convention* (New Haven, 1919), 71. Again note the family resemblance between the attempt to protect America through absolute conformity in 1919–20 and the more drastic, centrally-planned Chinese Communist efforts at national indoctrination. A student of Chinese "coercive persuasion" described the "elaborate unanimity rituals like parades, . . . 'spontaneous' mass demonstrations and society-wide campaigns, the extensive proselytizing among the 'heretics' or the 'infidels,' the purges, programs of re-education, and other repressive measures aimed at deviants." In China, also, past national glory is invoked as evidence of present and future greatness. Schein *et al.*, 62; Lifton, *Thought Reform and the Psychology of Totalism;* Walker, *China Under Communism.*

[55] Emerson Hough, "Round Our Town," *Saturday Evening Post,* CXCII (February 21, 1920), 102; Hough, *The Web,* 456.

[56] Higham, *Strangers in the Land,* 227, 255.

movement.[57] The man in the best political position to take advantage of the popular feeling, however, was Attorney General A. Mitchell Palmer.[58] In 1919, especially after the President's physical collapse, only Palmer had the authority, staff, and money necessary to arrest and deport huge numbers of radical aliens. The most virulent phase of the movement for one hundred per cent Americanism came early in 1920, when Palmer's agents rounded up for deportation over six thousand aliens and prepared to arrest thousands more suspected of membership in radical organizations. Most of these aliens were taken without warrants, many were detained for unjustifiably long periods of time, and some suffered incredible hardships. Almost all, however, were eventually released.[59]

After Palmer decided that he could ride the postwar fears into the presidency, he set out calculatingly to become the symbol of one hundred per cent Americanism. The Palmer raids, his anti-labor activities, and his frequent pious professions of patriotism during the campaign were all part of this effort. Palmer was introduced by a political associate to the Democratic party's annual Jackson Day dinner in January 1920 as "an American whose Americanism cannot be misunderstood." In a speech delivered in Georgia shortly before the primary election (in which Palmer won control of the state's delegation to the Democratic National Convention), the Attorney General asserted: "I am myself an American and I love to preach my doctrine before undiluted one hundred per cent Americans, because my platform is, in a word, undiluted Americanism and undying loyalty to the republic." The same theme dominated the address made by Palmer's old friend, John H. Bigelow of Hazleton, Pennsylvania, when he placed Palmer's name in nomination at the 1920 National Convention. Proclaimed Bigelow: "No party could survive today that did not write into its platform the magic word 'Americanism.' . . . The Attorney-General of the United States has not merely professed, but he has proved his true Americanism. . . . Behind him I see a solid phalanx of true Americanism that knows no divided allegiance." [60]

Unfortunately for political candidates like Palmer and Wood, most of the social and economic disturbances which had activated the movement they sought to lead gradually disappeared during the first half of 1920. The

---

[57] Murray, 62–65, 147–48, 159–60.

[58] For a full discussion of Palmer's role, Stanley Coben, A. *Mitchell Palmer: Politician* (New York, 1963).

[59] Coben, *Palmer*, Chaps. 11, 12; Claghorn, Chap. 10; Constantine Panunzio, *The Deportation Cases of 1919–1920* (New York, 1920); Zechariah Chafee, Jr., *Free Speech in the United States* (Cambridge, 1941), 204–17; Murray, Chap. 13.

[60] Coben, *Palmer*, Chap. 13; *The New York Times*, January 9, 1920; Atlanta *Constitution*, April 7, 1920; *Official Report of the Proceedings of the Democratic National Convention, 1920* (Indianapolis, 1920), 113–14. Palmer also launched a highly publicized campaign to hold down soaring prices in 1919–20, by fixing retail prices and bringing suits against profiteers and hoarders.

European revolutions were put down; by 1920 communism seemed to have been isolated in Russia. Bombings ceased abruptly after June 1919, and fear of new outrages gradually abated. Prices of food and clothing began to recede during the spring. Labor strife almost vanished from our major industries after a brief railroad walkout in April. Prosperity returned after mid-1919 and by early 1920 business activity and employment levels exceeded their wartime peaks.[61] At the same time, it became clear that the Senate would not pass Wilson's peace treaty and that America was free to turn its back on the responsibilities of world leadership. The problems associated with the new immigrants remained; so did the disillusionment with Europe and with many old intellectual ideals. Nativism did not disappear from the American scene; but the frenzied attempt to revitalize the culture did peter out in 1920. The handful of unintimidated men, especially Assistant Secretary of Labor Louis F. Post, who had used the safeguards provided by American law to protect many victims of the Red Scare, found increasing public support. On the other hand, politicians like Palmer, Wood, and Hanson were left high and dry, proclaiming the need for one hundred per cent Americanism to an audience which no longer urgently cared.

It is ironic that in 1920 the Russian leaders of the Comintern finally took charge of the American Communist movement, provided funds and leadership, and ordered the Communist factions to unite and participate actively in labor organizations and strikes. These facts were reported in the American press.[62] Thus a potentially serious foreign threat to national security appeared just as the Red Scare evaporated, providing a final illustration of the fact that the frenzied one hundred per centers of 1919–20 were affected less by the "red menace" than by a series of social and economic dislocations.

Although the Red Scare died out in 1920, its effects lingered. Hostility toward immigrants, mobilized in 1919–20, remained strong enough to force congressional passage of restrictive immigration laws. Some of the die-hard one hundred per centers found a temporary home in the Ku Klux Klan until that organization withered away during the mid-twenties. As its most lasting accomplishments, the movement for one hundred per cent Americanism fostered a spirit of conformity in the country, a satisfaction with the status quo, and the equation of reform ideologies with foreign enemies. Revitalization movements have helped many societies adapt successfully to new conditions. The movement associated with the American Red Scare, however, had no such effect. True, it unified the culture against the threats faced in 1919–20; but the basic problems — a damaged value system, an unrestrained business cycle, a hostile Russia, and communism — were left for future generations of Americans to deal with in their own fashion.

---

[61] Bell, 334; Soule, 83–88; *Seventh Annual Report of the Federal Reserve Board for the Year 1920* (Washington, D.C., 1920), 7.

[62] Draper, 244, 267–68; New York *World*, March 29, 1920.

14

CULTURAL SYMBOLS AND REFORM

The reexamination of the 1920's that has taken place during the past several years has gone a long way toward undermining the traditional view of the decade. In branding the 'twenties a period of indifference, materialism, and apathy, previous historians too easily ignored and misjudged much of the intense activity that marked the decade. For millions of Americans, both in and out of the Democratic Party, Al Smith came to symbolize the aspirations and ideals of urban, immigrant America and they rallied to his banner in 1924 and 1928. Millions of others joined or at least sympathized with the Ku Klux Klan, supported the efforts of militant fundamentalism to oust modernism from the church and evolution from the schoolroom, and were indignant over the widespread disregard of the Eighteenth Amendment and the increasing violations of traditional morality and conventions. If the term "idealism" is used to define not merely those movements of which historians approve but any movement that puts forward a set of principles about which people feel strongly enough to band together and fight for, then idealism and crusading zeal were still very much alive throughout the decade.

The gulf that separated the primarily rural followers of William G. McAdoo and the urban followers of Al Smith at the disastrous Democratic National Convention of 1924 was not economic, for there were few serious economic differences between the two factions that could not be reconciled. Rather, it was cultural, as symbolized by the heated battle over whether or not the Ku Klux Klan should be named specifically in a religious liberty plank. The Klan came to symbolize this widening cultural and sectional split because it stood for more than simply racial and religious exclusiveness. For a rural, small-town America that felt its very foundations being eroded by what Walter Lippmann referred to as the "acids of modernity," the Klan's emphasis upon the traditional moral and ethical code, its insistence that America had strayed from the paths and conventions that had made it great, its dire warnings of the continuing shredding of the traditional American fabric, its antipathy to urban mores and values, its opposition to the modernist movement within the churches, and its hearkening back to a golden age, seemed to offer relief from the apparently inexorable process of change that held the United States in its grip. This explains why the Klan of the 'twenties was at least as influential in the midwest and far west as it was in the south.

Robert Moats Miller maintains that the Klan of the 1920's was a genuine counterrevolutionary movement. Certainly, under the leadership of Hiram Wesley Evans, the Klan did promise to bring about "a return of power into the hands of the everyday, not highly cultured, not overly intellectualized, but entirely unspoiled and not de-Americanized average citizens of the old stock." In the long run, however, the movements for which Evans spoke were more ambivalent and defensive than Evans's rhetoric indicated. They were movements on the run that were struggling vainly to stave off the erosion of their cultures and life style — but not at the price of giving up all of the advantages of modernity. This is why they were so often content with the symbols rather than the substance of power.

The fundamentalist movement is a good example. By the middle of the decade, through the process of local pressure and intimidation, fundamentalists had made serious inroads upon the modernist advance within the churches and the teaching of evolution in the schools in large parts of the country. But this was not enough. Fundamentalists demanded statewide laws against the teaching of evolution because they craved the comfort of statutory symbols which would settle for all time the question of whose version of the good society was legitimate. Governor Austin Peay of Tennessee recognized this when, after signing the Tennessee Anti-Evolution Act of 1925, he told the legislature that he did not expect to see the law applied; its main purpose was to register "a distinct protest against an irreligious tendency to exalt so-called science, and deny the Bible in some schools and quarters."

The extent to which symbols had become paramount was manifest in the presidential election of 1928. It was not Al Smith's political or economic program, which met the needs of rural, small-town America better than that of the Republican Party, that induced such fear throughout the south and west, but his urban background, his appeal to the polyglot populations of the big cities, his very speech, dress, and manner. Thus although the nationalizing and standardizing forces of large-scale industry and the mass media were more deeply entrenched in the Republican Party of Herbert Hoover, Smith's defeat was greeted with widespread rejoicing. America, the *St. Paul Pioneer Press* announced jubilantly, "is not yet dominated by its great cities. . . . Control of its destinies still remains in the smaller communities and rural regions. . . . Main Street is still the principal thoroughfare of the nation."

No one has captured the symbolic nature of these movements better than Joseph Gusfield (Professor of Sociology at the University of Illinois, Urbana) in his studies of Prohibition. For an elaboration of the thesis he presents in the following article, see his book, *Symbolic Crusade: Status Politics and the American Temperance Movement** (1963). Andrew Sinclair, *Prohibition: An Era of Excess** (1962), is the most comprehensive account of the movement but is badly marred by its strong note of hostility to the Prohibitionists. James H. Timberlake, *Prohibition and the Progressive Movement, 1900–1920* (1962), is a good statement of Prohibition's reformist background. Gilman M. Ostrander, *The Prohibition Movement in California, 1848–1933* (1957), is an interesting state study. The best general account of the Klan in the 1920's is David Chalmers, *Hooded Americanism** (1965). E. H. Loucks, *The Ku Klux Klan in Pennsylvania* (1936), and C. C. Alexander, *The Ku Klux Klan in the Southwest** (1966), are valuable local and regional studies. Kenneth Jackson, *The Ku Klux Klan in the City, 1915–1930* (1968), has a wealth of detail on the Klan's urban activities but overstates the importance of its urban ethos. Hiram Wesley Evans, "The Klan's Fight for Americanism," *The North American Review*, 223 (March 1926), 33–61, remains a crucially important statement of what the Klan was all about. The most detailed and scholarly study of the fundamentalist movement is Norman F. Furniss, *The Fundamentalist Controversy, 1918–1931* (1954). Paul Carter, *The Decline and Revival of the Social Gospel* (1954), is an important study of the basic religious issues of the 1920's. Walter Lippmann's splendid evocation of some of the main cultural dilemmas of the 1920's can be found in his *A Preface to Morals** (1929). For an attempt to see all of these movements through the career of an important rural politician and spokesman, see Lawrence W. Levine, *Defender of the Faith: William Jennings Bryan, The Last Decade, 1915–1925** (1965).

Prohibition: The Impact of Political Utopianism

JOSEPH R. GUSFIELD

When Herbert Hoover labeled Prohibition "the experiment noble in purpose," he was only continuing to use a language of scientific procedure that made "success or failure" the dominant scholarly question to be asked about the attempt to create a dry America. Experiments are acts that resolve scientific issues, and the experience of the nation with Prohibition is trotted out and brought into the light of controversy whenever issues of law and public opinion are under the scrutiny of popular discussion. Often the 1920's and dry legislation are pointed to as evidence for William Graham Sumner's casual but powerful aphorism that "stateways cannot make folkways." In the heat of current debates about Negro civil rights we recognize that the matter is much more complex than such aphorisms would allow. As Gunnar

Reprinted by permission of the publisher from *Change and Continuity in Twentieth-Century America: The 1920's,* edited by John Braeman, Robert H. Bremer, and David Brody. Copyright © 1968 by the Ohio State University Press. All rights reserved.

Myrdal suggested in 1944, law may not regulate sentiment but it has much bearing on behavior and on the framework within which education and re-education go on.[1]

There is a greater significance to the experience of Prohibition than the issue of success or failure. Human experiments are by no means analogous to those performed in laboratories, nor was "the noble experiment" carried out in a hermetically sealed nation. Hopes and aspirations were aroused, fulfilled, and quashed; loyalties were developed and repelled; organizations were affected with particular and unique character. The United States was not the same after repeal as it had been before the Eighteenth Amendment was passed. Prohibition had some impact in producing that change. The analogy of the experiment that succeds or fails is at best a limited one for gauging the implications of dry legislation and dry activity on American life. We must be attuned to what *happened* as well as to what *lasted*. In any analysis of the Prohibition period in American history the acceptance or rejection of the Eighteenth Amendment is an essential part of the story. But it is not the whole story nor necessarily the most vital one. A concern for contemporary American life should make us sensitive to what the quest for the dry utopia has meant for later events and issues in American society.

The issue of national prohibition was a major focus of American politics for twenty years, from the beginnings of the Anti-Saloon League campaign for federal laws in 1913 to the repeal of the Eighteenth Amendment in 1933. Most candidates for national, state, or local office could not ignore being dry or wet, or using their political art to walk delicately between. By 1928, in Al Smith's campaign for the presidency, it was a dominating issue. Even in 1932, when repeal was in the air, it was still so vital a question that both presidential candidates thought it necessary to give it their attention. The impact of Prohibition upon behavior during the 1920's is evident. What we want to do in this paper is also to assess the influence of Prohibition upon the drinking habits of Americans after repeal. Was it only an experiment that lasted for fourteen years without any effects upon the climate of morality in the United States? What did it mean for the politics that came during and after Prohibition? Were the enemies of temperance and the advocates of repeal assuming a political identification that lasted even after beer and whiskey were again sold in the open? What did the demise of Prohibition mean to those for whom it had represented a triumph of reason and morality over the nefarious forces of sensuality and corruption? An assessment of the Prohibition Era and its place in American history cannot confine itself narrowly to the question of whether or not it succeeded in developing, for a short time, a world of sobriety and abstinence.

The debate over the Eighteenth Amendment was not, as some have sug-

---

[1] Gunnar Myrdal, *An American Dilemma* (New York, 1944), Appendix I.

gested, a sudden intrusion into American politics. It did not spring full-blown on the American scene as a conspiracy by which a small group of determined men foisted sobriety on a wet nation.

American experience with various efforts to curtail drinking and intoxication in the United States has a long and mercurial history. Licensing acts during colonial times regulated taverns and their use. From the 1820's on, a persistent temperance movement sought many and diverse ways to limit, if not abolish, the use of spirits, beer, and wine.[2] Under the leadership of New England Federalists the early temperance movement of the 1820's was less a movement for abstinence than a movement for moderate and temperate usage. Hence the name "temperance" for a movement that later came to be associated almost exclusively with abstention. During the 1830's, however, as the movement became infused with the spirit of evangelical religion and the problems of Midwestern and frontier people, it aimed more often at abstinence than at moderation.[3] The goal of abolishing the liquor traffic, rather than, and in addition to, the reform of the individual drinker, emerged during the 1840's and, in the famous Maine law of 1851, resulted in the first statewide legislation prohibiting the sale of "Demon Rum."[4]

The use of law as a means to achieve reform in drinking was by no means unknown before the twentieth century. Not only had statewide prohibition been tried in many places, but a great many parts of the United States had achieved prohibition through local option at the county, city, and township levels. American local and state politics was thus well filled with the issues of the legal regulation of liquor, beer, and wine. There were many vibrant controversies over the relative merits of legislation and exhortation; over moderation versus total abstinence; over political pressure-group actions versus the development of party legislation.[5]

Though the temperance movement had advocated statewide prohibition

[2] Though there is no single major history of temperance and prohibition in the United States, there are several works from which one gains an unbiased and scholarly account. John Krout, *The Origins of Prohibition* (New York, 1925) carries the history from colonial beginning to the Civil War. There is no adequate history of the movement during the last half of the nineteenth century. The period 1900–1933 has been well treated in James Timberlake, *Prohibition and the Progressive Movement* (Cambridge, 1963) and Andrew Sinclair, *Prohibition: The Era of Excess* (Boston, 1962). For an interpretation of the movement over the entire course of its history see Joseph Gusfield, *Symbolic Crusade: Status Politics and the American Temperance Movement* (Urbana, Ill., 1963). For a history of temperance in one state see Norman Clark, *The Dry Years: Prohibition and Social Change in Washington* (Seattle, 1965).

[3] The term "teetotalers" arose from the practice of placing a "T" beside one's name on temperance lists to designate a commitment to total abstinence.

[4] Colonial legislation existed in many areas licensing and regulating taverns. Krout, *The Origins of Prohibition*, chap. i.

[5] The argument over tactics was continuous in temperance history, and the rationale of various positions can be seen in the argument for a third party, the Prohibition party, and for a pressure group, the Anti-Saloon League. See D. Leigh Colvin, *Prohibition in the United States* (New York, 1926) and Peter Odegaard, *Pressure Politics* (New York, 1928), chap. iii.

at various times and had given such legislation a prominent part in its activities from time to time, agitation for national legislation prohibiting sales did not occur until well into the twentieth century. That it came about at all is therefore a matter of some question for analysis. A full discussion of how Prohibition came about is beyond the scope of this paper, but it is necessary to point to some of the ways in which it became possible at the federal level if we are to understand the Prohibition Era that came later.

Success in obtaining national prohibition owes much to the work and action of the Anti-Saloon League. The formation of the Anti-Saloon League, in 1896 in Ohio, brought with it two important elements to the temperance movement. First, it centered the attention of the movement on the eradication of the saloon. Second, it initiated an era of pressure politics that was divorced from the third-party tactics of the Prohibition party. The League utilized effective means for the mobilization of public opinion and political power in the American party structure.[6] Between 1906 and 1912 seven states passed prohibition laws. By 1919, before the passage of the Eighteenth Amendment, an additional nineteen states had passed restrictive legislation, and more than 50 per cent of the American population lived in dry areas. In 1913 the Anti-Saloon League reached its greatest success until then by managing the successful passage of the Webb-Kenyon Act, forbidding the transportation of intoxicating beverages into dry states. This was the first major national legislative victory of the temperance movement. When the Eighteenth Amendment was passed (January, 1919), a good deal of American society had already found such legislation appealing.

What brought about this new wave of dry sentiment and assured its political victories? In this paper I shall maintain that a common vision of a dry America underlay the two major strands of American reform in the late nineteenth and early twentieth centuries — the progressive impulse and the Populist movement. That vision expressed the world of nineteenth-century Protestant, nativist, and agrarian-commercial American society. The roots of national prohibition, we shall argue, lay in the urban middle-class reaction to a changing and industrialized city and in the rural antipathy to the growing dominance of the city. The issue between the drys and the wets was primarily one of cultural divergence in which the power and legitimacy of ways of life were symbolized by the acceptance or rejection of abstinence and sobriety as public ideals. A major thesis of this paper is that these two strands to American reform, and to drinking reform, separated and became opposed to each other during the 1920's in part over the issue of Prohibition itself.

It is important to recognize the coexistence of both strands, and their differences, in the surge of public sentiment producing the prohibitionist victories of the early twentieth century. Recently, several scholars have suggested a revision to the thesis that Prohibition ranged rural America against

6 Odegaard, *Pressure Politics, passim.*

the cities. Timberlake and others [7] have rightfully corrected an overstatement in pointing to the progressive and urban roots of dry belief. It is crucial, however, to recognize that the political power of rural populations was essential in securing dry supremacy at state and national levels. That power was the major source of dry political strength before, during, and after the Eighteenth Amendment wrote "Dry America" across the Statue of Liberty.

By the time the campaign for Prohibition began to gain force, the issues of drinking reform had developed their own sets of opposing supporters. Although Catholic sentiment for temperance existed in the late nineteenth and twentieth centuries, the support given to prohibition as a technique for reform was minimal, both from organized Catholic groups and from the large segments of Catholic populations in American cities.[8] The symbol of the saloon as a force of evil in American society made sense in an urban population that saw political corruption and vice at home in the saloons of urban America. Those aspects of the progressive movement that reacted to the threats of a big-business civilization and an immigrant population, saw the saloon as one source of evil, and the reform of drinking habits as a necessity for an America of Protestant virtues.[9] For the social worker, the drinking habits of the poor and the immigrant were both a slap at Protestant morality and a source of the deep-seated poverty of industrial America. The professional and small-business urban middle class had grown up and had found its dominant ideologies in a sober and disciplined framework of churchgoing people. The drinking habits of the new immigrant population were both a threat to their values and an object for deep moral concern.[10]

These considerations appear in the myriad arguments one can find in the vast mass of prohibitionist literature. In politics the argument for the sober electorate was a telling one. In the eye of the muckraker the dependence of the political machine on the saloon seemed self-evident. Just as Beecher had argued in 1820 that a whiskey-swilling electorate was a threat to the old aristocracy,[11] so too the progressives could argue that the demise of the saloon would help the cause of free and clean government.[12]

Prohibition appeared as a panacea for the economic ills of the society. Though liquor and beer brought in considerable revenue, it could be maintained that the worker would find his material salvation more rapidly through a change in consuming habits than in unionism or governmental welfare. Science and medicine also contributed to the growing debate over

[7] Timberlake, *Prohibition and the Progressive Movement*; Norton Mezvinsky, "The Temperance Movement: 1870–1920" (Paper presented to annual meeting of the Mississippi Valley Historical Society, Kansas City, Missouri, April, 1964).

[8] Sister Joan Bland, *Hibernian Crusade* (Washington, D.C., 1951).

[9] Timberlake, *Prohibition and the Progressive Movement*, chap. v; Odegaard, *Pressure Politics*, pp. 17–35.

[10] John Higham, *Strangers in the Land* (New Brunswick, N.J., 1955).

[11] Lyman Beecher, *Six Sermons on Intemperance* (New York, 1843), pp. 57–58.

[12] Bartlett C. Jones, "The Debate Over Prohibition: 1920–1933" (Ph.D. dissertation, Emory University, 1961); Timberlake, chap. iv.

the medical values of alcohol. The belief of the early nineteenth century that alcohol was essential to health received severe blows from "scientific temperance education" and the text material that the Women's Christian Temperance Union introduced into the American educational system during the early twentieth century. For employers in an industrial society, the need for safety and the prevention of accidents had in turn added to the force of temperance arguments. A number of companies, such as United Steel and the railroads, strongly supported efforts at temperance.[13]

We should be wary, however, of deriving the support of the movement from its arguments. The same arguments had been used many times in the past and had not always proved so effective. To be sure, the growth in drinking during the early twentieth century had been considerable, and in the period 1911–14 reached the peak since Americans began keeping records on these matters following the Civil War. The saloon itself had become not only the working man's club but certainly in many cases the hiring hall for crime, prostitution, and political corruption. The brewers and distillers had been late in recognizing the strength of the temperance movement and in taking any measures that might bring about a reform of the saloon. Nevertheless, we must be careful not to overestimate the degree to which Prohibition was an urban phenomenon or the degree to which the economic logic of an industrial society pushed for temperance legislation.

The United States is one of only three countries that have experimented with prohibition on a wide scale. Finland and India are the other two. We would be hard put to relate prohibition in these three countries to economic or geographical similarities. Though some American industrialists did support Prohibition, others did not. It is worthy of note that the American man of wealth who gave the greatest degree of effort to the support of the Prohibition movement both before and after the passage of the Eighteenth Amendment was S. S. Kresge, whose wealth was made not in manufacturing but in merchandising. There is little to indicate that manufacturing establishments, most clearly allied to an industrial society, saw in Prohibition so important a measure that they necessarily gave to it their united support.

Any analysis of the actual distribution of votes through which prohibition measures gained ascent must recognize the importance of both the rural states and the rural legislators in bringing about the passage of the Eighteenth Amendment. The South represented the greatest single source of legislative support for prohibitory measures.[14] Almost everywhere, the strength of the Anti-Saloon League represented the mobilization of church support more heavily in the rural than in the urban sectors.[15] The states that went prohibitionist earliest were not those with the highest but with the

[13] Jones, "The Debate over Prohibition," chap. vi.

[14] See my discussion of the political base of prohibitionist sentiment in *Symbolic Crusade*, pp. 117–126.

[15] Odegaard, *Pressure Politics*, pp. 29–35, 121–24.

smallest percentages of urban population.[16] The areas of national prohibition sentiment were strongest where the populations were Protestant, rural, and nativist. They were more likely to be found in the South and in the Midwest than in the East. Although states with high percentages of foreign-born were likely to oppose prohibition, this was less likely where the foreign population was Protestant and rural, as in Minnesota. In Mississippi, for example, it was in the rural areas with small Negro populations that one found the highest support for prohibition legislation both before and after the Eighteenth Amendment was passed and repeal had been initiated. In many of the states the ratification of the Eighteenth Amendment was brought about by votes in the state legislatures, controlled largely by rural legislators. Though the progressive movement played a role and responded well to the demands of the Anti-Saloon League, it was by no means able to wield the political power through which prohibition itself was implemented.

Both the urban middle class and agrarian America were substantially Protestant and nativist in their outlook. While they saw the cities engulfed by new groups of power, they responded both to demands of sentiment and concern for an urban and industrial poor and to the hostile threats of the cultural waves that distinguished eastern and Mediterranean Europe from Anglo-Saxon cultures. Although it was never dominant, the drys found room in their arguments for the sophisticated racism in the doctrines of eugenics and ethnic differentiation that resulted in the theories of Madison Grant and Lothrop Stoddard.[17]

In 1917 the Hobson resolution for submission of the prohibition amendment received the necessary two-thirds vote in Congress. The amendment was ratified on January 16, 1919, and went into effect one year later to date. The text of the amendment was as follows:

Section 1.

After one year from the ratification of this article the manufacture, sale, or transportation of intoxicating liquors within, the importation thereof into, or the exportation thereof from the United States and all territory subject to the jurisdiction thereof for beverage purposes is hereby prohibited.

Section 2.

The Congress and the several states shall have concurrent power to enforce this article by appropriate legislation.

A third section made the article inoperative until it had been ratified as an amendment to the Constitution by the legislatures of the several states.

The Eighteenth Amendment was aimed at the eradication of the saloon

[16] Gusfield, *Symbolic Crusade*, p. 109.
[17] Bartlett Jones, "Prohibition and Eugenics, 1920–33," *Journal of the History of Medicine*, XVIII (1963), 158–72.

and the distributor of liquor, wine, and beer. It was not an effort to govern the buyer but to get at intoxication by obstructing the seller. It was aimed at the saloon and at the liquor business.

Despite use of the Prohibition experience as a basis for offhand judgments about law and morality, the entire experience has seldom been analyzed to determine whether accounts of its impact are myth or reality. Dry adherents have persisted in the views that the friends of "Demon Rum" killed Prohibition by telling untruths about its impact. Those for whom it was unwelcome inhibition have, perhaps, had a greater influence in convincing most American historians that the enforcement of the Volstead Act ran aground on the sharp rocks of intense public resistance.

Even with difficulties in data, we are still able to give an accurate and qualified picture of what did happen to American drinking habits during the 1920's. That picture is a complicated one, suggesting different kinds of effects to different parts of the population. It does not support either the myth of increased drinking or the death of alcoholic indulgence.

Any effort to gauge the effectiveness of prohibition legislation must meet another problem in the analysis of the relation between law and human behavior. How much enforcement is *effective* enforcement? Laws may seek long-range and long-run changes in a society rather than short-range and short-run compliance. Laws may exist and function less as direct shapers of human behavior and more as means for symbolizing what is publicly legitimate and moral. Certainly prostitution, abortion, gambling, and drug addiction exist in the United States and have existed for many decades. The laws that forbid such behavior serve many functions. Perhaps they limit the degree to which such behavior would be discoverable without them. I have suggested, in *Symbolic Crusade*, that laws frequently serve highly symbolic functions, pointing to those groups in the society that achieve public recognition of their norms and values as the legitimate ones. This is certainly the case in relation to temperance legislation. If it was flouted by those who drank, it was clear whose law and whose culture was given dominant recognition as the legitimate and sanctioned modes of behavior. No politician could openly admit use of, or be seen using, alcohol. If public leaders gave only lip service to Prohibition, that itself was an indication of what was the public and official law of the land.

In short, the evasion of laws is by no means a telling argument against their effectiveness. As Robin Williams pointed out,[18] a patterned evasion of norms exists in many cases in American society and frequently preserves both law and illegality, side by side. Though the laws of abortion exist in American life, there is a structure that makes abortion possible for those who seek it. This patterned evasion is found in more or less frequency for a great many acts of government.

[18] Robin Williams, *American Society* (New York, 1960), chap. x.

What we need to know is the answer to a comparative question. Was there more or less excessive drinking than had existed before Prohibition? Were the effects such as to suggest a lessened degree of disapproval than had existed before Prohibition? In this way, the issue of the consequences of prohibitory legislation is rendered a little more capable of answer. On the other hand, it requires a greater degree of specific data often conspicuous by its absence.

The casual impressions of social workers, journalists, industrial executives, and temperance advocates is no substitute for the kind of careful measurement on which comparative analysis is based. We turn then to what we can say with a high degree of validity concerning the enforcement of Prohibition.

Having used considerable political power to effect the Eighteenth Amendment and its ratification, the dry forces had now to provide for its enforcement. Despite the considerable degree of support from public opinion and the rural-dominated state legislatures, the dry forces walked lightly. In this policy the federal and state legislatures were most co-operative. Having acceded to the intense pressure of the Anti-Saloon League and its supporters, Congress was in no mood to tweak the tail of the wets any more than it had to. The attitude toward enforcement was thus one that Charles Merz has effectively characterized as "nullification by non-enforcement." [19] The organization of the Prohibition Bureau, the appropriations granted to it and to various state agencies, and the limited disposition of courts to support Prohibition were all involved in a system of enforcement that appeared to seek compliance through patience rather than through authoritative action.[20]

The chief measure guiding enforcement was the National Prohibition Act, popularly known as the Volstead Act, after Congressman Volstead who had introduced it. Under this act the Commissioner of Internal Revenue of the Treasury Department, rather than the Department of Justice, was given the power to detect and suppress violations of Prohibition. The Prohibition Bureau itself was not brought under Civil Service — a fact that gave the dry forces effective power over the recruitment and maintenance of personnel. Under this situation the Prohibition Bureau and the salaries of Prohibition agents compared most unfavorably with other personnel. They were greatly dependent upon federal and state appropriations that were seldom large enough to make possible an effective legal and police organization. "It was not the business of the Prohibition Bureau to quarrel with its peers." [21]

[19] Charles Merz, *The Dry Decade* (Garden City, N.Y., 1937), p. 129.
[20] Similar accounts, using different data, are found in Merz, *The Dry Decade*; Sinclair, *Prohibition*, chap. x, pp. 13–14; Clark, *The Dry Years*, chaps. x–xii.
[21] Merz, *The Dry Decade*, p. 129.

The result, of course, was an ineffective organization whose morale was even further weakened by a succession of appointed heads. The first Prohibition commissioner, John F. Kramer, served for a year and a half until he was replaced by Roy A. Haines. Under Coolidge a new head, General Lincoln C. Andrews, was appointed. He resigned in March of 1927 and was replaced by several different people, including the assistant secretary of the treasury and the chief chemist of the Prohibition Bureau. Not until Herbert Hoover became President was the Bureau set upon a more regular basis, recruits required to pass the Civil Service examination, and the entire activity brought under the Department of Justice.

American impressions of drinking during the 1920's owe much to the description of a "lost generation" that novelists and journalists have done much to maintain. It is a picture of flaming youth in short skirts and bobbed hair dancing wickedly in speak-easies run by tough-looking gangsters. It is a picture of orgiastic drunkenness complete with wood alcohol, bathtub gin, and illicit sex. Like many myths, it mixes truth with falsity. The general shift in American morals during the 1920's is beyond our topic. Nevertheless, the generally accepted view suggests an increase in extensive drinking, especially among the young. A more sober analysis will recognize this as behavior that was decidedly not typical. Nevertheless, whether typical or not, its dramatic impact had a great deal to do with the setting of styles both during the Prohibition Era and afterward. It had a great deal to do with the ways in which people thought about drinking and Prohibition.

Any analysis of drinking during Prohibition should begin with what we know about American drinking habits before 1920. Table No. 1 presents data on the total amount of absolute alcohol consumed in the United States and the percentage of that alcohol contributed by various diverse components.[22] It should be noted that this data is based on United States tax returns and gives the gallons-per-capita population of drinking age, fourteen and over. For this reason it conflicts with the data presented in Warburton and other analyses of drinking during Prohibition.

Two things are significant in this analysis of American drinking before Prohibition. First, the first decade and a half of the twentieth century saw a considerably increased consumption of alcohol. The high point of alcohol consumption in the United States came in the years 1911–15. It is important, however, to recognize the second fact: there had been a great shift in the direction of beer-drinking and a great decrease in the use of distilled spirits. This indicates that there had been a movement away from a population consisting of a large stream of heavy drinkers (characterized by high rates of spirits-drinking) and many abstainers toward a population that indicated many less abstainers but relatively fewer heavy drinkers.[23]

[22] Reprinted from Raymond McCarthy, ed. *Drinking and Intoxication* (Glencoe, Ill., 1959), p. 180.
[23] E. M. Jellinek, "Recent Trends in Alcoholism and Alcohol Consumption," *Quarterly Journal of Studies on Alcohol*, VIII (July, 1947), 1–43.

TABLE 1

APPARENT CONSUMPTION OF ALCOHOLIC BEVERAGES,
PER CAPITA OF DRINKING AGE POPULATION (PERSONS AGED OVER
FOURTEEN YEARS), U.S.A., 1850–1957, IN U.S. GALLONS[a]

| YEAR | SPIRITS | | WINE | | BEER | | TOTAL |
	Beverage	Absolute alcohol	Beverage	Absolute alcohol	Beverage	Absolute alcohol	Absolute alcohol
1850	4.17	1.89	0.46	0.08	2.70	0.14	2.11
1860	4.79	2.16	0.57	0.10	5.39	0.27	2.53
1870	3.40	1.53	0.53	0.10	8.73	0.44	2.07
1871–80	2.27	1.02	0.77	0.14	11.26	0.56	1.72
1881–90	2.12	0.95	0.76	0.14	17.94	0.90	1.99
1891–95	2.12	0.95	0.60	0.11	23.42	1.17	2.23
1896–1900	1.72	0.77	0.55	0.10	23.72	1.19	2.06
1901–05	2.11	0.95	0.71	0.13	26.20	1.31	2.39
1906–10	2.14	0.96	0.92	0.17	29.27	1.47	2.60
1911–15	2.09	0.94	0.79	0.14	29.53	1.48	2.56
1916–19	1.68	0.76	0.69	0.12	21.63	1.08	1.96
. . . . . .	. . .		. . .		. . .		
1934	0.64	0.29	0.36	0.07	13.58	0.61	0.97
1935	0.96	0.43	0.50	0.09	15.13	0.68	1.20
1936	1.30	0.59	0.64	0.12	17.53	0.79	1.50
1937	1.43	0.64	0.71	0.13	18.21	0.82	1.59
1938	1.32	0.59	0.70	0.13	16.58	0.75	1.47
1939	1.38	0.62	0.79	0.14	16.77	0.75	1.51
1940	1.48	0.67	0.91	0.16	16.29	0.73	1.56
1941	1.58	0.71	1.02	0.18	17.97	0.81	1.70
1942	1.89	0.85	1.11	0.20	20.00	0.90	1.95
1943	1.46	0.66	0.94	0.17	22.26	1.00	1.83
1944	1.69	0.76	0.92	0.17	25.22	1.13	2.06
1945	1.95	0.88	1.13	0.20	25.97	1.17	2.25
1946	2.20	0.99	1.34	0.24	23.75	1.07	2.30
1947	1.69	0.76	0.90	0.16	24.56	1.11	2.03
1948	1.56	0.70	1.11	0.20	23.77	1.07	1.97
1949	1.55	0.70	1.21	0.22	23.48	1.06	1.98
1950	1.72	0.77	1.27	0.23	23.21	1.04	2.04
1951	1.73	0.78	1.13	0.20	22.92	1.03	2.01
1952	1.61	0.72	1.21	0.21	22.97	1.03	1.96
1953	1.68	0.76	1.18	0.20	22.81	1.03	1.99
1954	1.61	0.72	1.18	0.20	21.73	0.98	1.90
1955	1.66	0.75	1.18	0.20	21.74	0.98	1.94
1956	1.76	0.79	1.23	0.21	21.53	0.97	1.97
1957	1.70	0.77	1.21	0.21	20.62	0.93	1.91

[a] From Mark Keller and Vera Efron, *Selected Statistics on Alcoholic Beverages (1850–1957) and on Alcoholism (1910–1956)*, New Haven, Journal of Studies on Alcohol, 1958.

In analyzing the extent of drinking, we need to ask what kind of alcoholic beverages became prevalent during the dry era.[24] The most careful and impartial analysis of drinking during Prohibition is that contained in Clark

[24] It should also be noted that beer-drinking is associated less with drunkenness than is liquor, both because of its lower alcohol content and because it is more likely to be consumed in conjunction with eating.

TABLE 2

ESTIMATES OF THE CONSUMPTION OF PURE ALCOHOL
IN THE UNITED STATES, 1920–30 (GALLONS PER CAPITA)

YEAR	ESTIMATE FROM SOURCES OF PRODUCTION	ESTIMATE FROM DEATH RATES	ESTIMATE FROM ARRESTS FOR DRUNKENNESS	FINAL ESTIMATE	INDEX OF CONSUMPTION OF ALCOHOL 1911–14 = 100
1920	...	.64	.16	...	...
1921	.26	.82	.43	.54	32.0
1922	.90	.92	.81	.91	53.8
1923	1.17	.97	1.05	1.07	63.3
1924	1.08	1.02	1.05	1.05	62.1
1925	1.13	1.07	1.06	1.10	65.1
1926	1.24	1.11	1.11	1.18	69.8
1927	1.08	1.15	1.15	1.12	66.3
1928	1.23	1.13	1.25	1.18	69.8
1929	1.31	1.09	1.18	1.20	71.0
1930	1.03	1.09	...	1.06	62.7

Sources of data: Estimate from sources of production: Table 30, Warburton, *The Economic Results of Prohibition*, p. 72. Estimate from death rates: Table 37, *ibid.*, p. 89. Estimate from arrests for drunkenness: Table 44, *ibid.*, p. 102. Final estimate: Average of the estimate from sources of production and the estimate from death rates.

Warburton's *The Economic Results of Prohibition*. Even though it was conducted at the request of the Association Against the Prohibition Amendment, Warburton found a sharp decline in the total amount of alcohol consumed.[25] His analysis, furthermore, squares very well with that by Herman Feldman [26] and the later analysis by Jellinek in 1948.[27] Warburton estimated the amount of alcohol consumed by three methods — the analysis of components used for production, deaths from cirrhosis of the liver, and police arrests for drunkenness. All of these show the same general tendencies toward a sharp decline in the amount of alcohol consumed between 1920 and 1923 with an increase over the next seven years. Nevertheless, as Table 2 (above) indicates, the per capita usage at all times was considerably below that of the pre-Prohibition period of 1911–14. It remains evident, then, that Prohibition did succeed in curtailing, even if not stopping, the heavy drinking that had characterized the early twentieth century in the United States.

[25] Clark Warburton, *The Economic Results of Prohibition* (New York, 1932). Warburton utilized reports of the production of the components of alcoholic beverages, arrests from drunkenness, and estimates from death rates and from cirrhosis of the liver. All of these require major assumptions concerning other usages of the same components, the uniform validity of crime rates, and the relationship between cirrhosis of the liver and alcoholism and can best be considered as systematic estimates.

For another analysis of the effectiveness of Prohibition, see John Burnham, "The Prohibition Experiment of the 1920's" (Paper presented at the meeting of the Mississippi Valley Historical Society, Kansas City, Mo., April, 1964).

[26] Herman Feldman, *Prohibition: Its Economic and Industrial Aspects* (New York, 1930).

[27] Jellinek, "Recent Trends in Alcoholism and Alcohol Consumption."

Warburton's figures, based as they are on the general population rather than the population of age fourteen and over, probably overestimate the amount of alcohol usage during the 1920's as compared to the earlier period. Jellinek's later analysis of alcohol consumption in the United States (those in age groups of fourteen and over) suggests that the rate of alcohol consumption per capita during Prohibition for those of drinking age was about one-half of that for the average of the four years preceding Prohibition.[28] Jellinek has used later alcoholism rates to shed light on 1920's drinking. These rates for alcoholism from 1920 to 1945 show a decided drop as compared with 1910 and 1915 rates. Since chronic alcoholism is a reflection of past drinking habits (beginning approximately ten to fifteen years earlier), it is indicated by deaths of cirrhosis of the liver and is good evidence for changes brought about during state and national prohibition in the early twentieth century.

We can conclude then that Prohibition was effective in sharply reducing the rate of alcohol consumption in the United States. We may set the outer limit of this at about 50 per cent and the inner limit at about one-third less alcohol .consumed by the total population than had been the case before Prohibition and at the point of peak usage in the United States.

When we come to survey the different forms of alcohol usage, however, the picture becomes a little more complicated and a little closer to the lurid and impressionistic one of the novelist and the popular historian. It is highly significant, however, that the abolition of the liquor traffic had different effects at middle-class than at lower-class levels of the urban population.

We have already pointed out that the increase in total alcohol consumption during the first decade of the twentieth century was accompanied by a continuing drop in the percentage resulting from the consumption of distilled spirits. Prohibition succeeded in reversing that relationship. To a very large extent, according to Warburton, the decrease in total alcoholic consumption was the result of a great drop in the use of beer. As Table 3 shows, the diminished use of beer was as great as a total drop of 85 per cent during 1921–22 and a drop of more than two-thirds during 1927–30. According to Warburton's calculations, there was actually an increase in the gallons-per-capita usage of spirits. This seems reasonable given two facts about illicit sale of alcoholic beverages during the dry era. The first is that the price of alcohol increased enormously. The second is that, per unit, there was more money to be made in the sale of hard liquor than in the sale of beer. Both were difficult to manufacture at home, but liquor was just as easy as beer if not easier. As now, so too then, hard liquor was more often the choice of those in the higher-income levels than among lower-income groups.

Warburton concludes "that under Prohibition the working classes con-

[28] The American population of the 1920's contained a higher percentage of older people than it did in the previous decade. Consumption rates based on total population, as Warburton's are, actually ignore the fact that the population of the 1920's had a higher percentage of potential drinkers than did the earlier decade. Using only the population above fourteen would result in lowered rates for the 1920's.

TABLE 3

CONSUMPTION OF ALCOHOL BEVERAGES IN THE UNITED STATES
BEFORE AND AFTER THE ADOPTION OF PROHIBITION
(GALLONS PER CAPITA)

PERIOD	SPIRITS	BEER	WINE	PURE ALCOHOL
1911–14	1.47	20.53	.59	1.69
1921–22	.92	1.49	.51	.73
1927–30	1.62	6.27	.98	1.14

Sources of data: 1911–14, Table 2, Warburton, *The Economic Results of Prohibition*, p. 26; 1921–22 and 1927–30, Tables 45 and 46, *ibid.*, pp. 104, 106. Figures for spirits, wine, and beer taken from the estimates from sources of production.

sumed not more than half as much alcohol per capita as formerly; and that the expenditure of this class upon alcoholic beverages is probably a billion dollars less than it would be without national Prohibition.

"That the per capita consumption of alcohol by the business, professional and salaried classes has been affected but little by Prohibition; and that due to higher prices this class is spending at least a billion dollars a year more for alcoholic beverages than it would be spending without national Prohibition." [29] The differential between the classes has been noted as well in the impressions of social workers [30] and a testimony of executives observing workers.[31]

It would be fair to say then that Prohibition did affect drinking behavior. The impressionistic notion that rural areas were more clearly affected than urban is substantiated by the pattern of bootlegging. The total consumption of alcohol did drop. Even after the upsurge following the initial effects of the act, it still remained well below the rates of consumption in the pre-Prohibition years. It is also the case, however, that hard drinking was apparently substituted to some degree for beer, especially in those urban groups that represented high-income levels. Its greatest impact in eradicating drink was thus on the working classes, and, paradoxically, coinciding as it did with the shift of morals in the general prosperity of the 1920's, it may well have increased the hard and excessive drinking among precisely those groups that had in the past been pace-setters and style-setters. As may often happen, Prohibition was least effective in curtailing the drinking among precisely those groups that were most clearly visible to the mass media of communication.

If one attempts to adduce the economic results of Prohibition, he is in an even more difficult morass, one in which it is extraordinarily difficult to separate the general effects of historical conditions from those which are

[29] Warburton, *The Economic Results of Prohibition*, p. 262.
[30] Martha Bruère, *Does Prohibition Work?* (New York and London, 1927).
[31] Whiting Williams, testimony before the Wickersham Commission. Quoted in Burnham, "The Prohibition Experiment of the 1920's," p. 11.

specifically the results of legislation. The general increase in automobile usage in the United States was so great in 1920 as to mask any efforts to determine Prohibition's impact upon automobile accidents. What is true, however, and this became of considerable importance later, is that the national and state governments lost visible revenue as alcoholic beverages disappeared from the lists of taxable items. It was also coupled with the fact that the existence of Prohibition did lead to curtailment of certain specific jobs in the brewery and the distilling industries. To suggest that these were balanced by the ultimate economic gains is to pose an intangible and indirect effect against an immediate and visible one. For brewery and distillery workers such long-run considerations were cold comfort in the face of present unemployment.

During the 1920's the existence of the bootlegger and of syndicated crime made many headlines. The gangs and gang warfare of Chicago and the dramatic quality of Al Capone impressed themselves upon American mentality. American crime had begun to change considerably with the growth of large cities and the development of big business in crime — gambling, prostitution, and other economic services performed for clients rather than victims. That bootlegging was an industry of considerable magnitude is certainly unquestionable. Without Prohibition, of course, a bootlegging industry would have been nonexistent. It should be pointed out, however, that large gangs of a business nature had already been in existence before the advent of bootlegging. Capone himself came to Chicago from New York to function in the organization run at that time by Big Jim Colosimo, whose basic source of revenue came from the houses of prostitution in Chicago, well before Prohibition presented new opportunities.

The history of the underworld matches the history of American big business in many respects. It is one of increasing consolidation and centralization as small enterprises give way to large organizations.[32] In the complex and often ruthless competition by which the underworld became organized, there was increasing evidence that a high degree of central control would lead to a disappearance of the rougher tactics made necessary by an unregulated market economy. The last echoes of this can be found in the famous St. Valentine's Day Massacre, when the Capone gang reputedly brought the severest of all sanctions to bear against "unfair competition." The firm of "Bugs" Moran and Company was found operating outside the zone that had been agreed upon as their sales and merchandising territory, and seven executives died in defense of free enterprise.

To summarize this mass of evidence is not easy. Perhaps we may do best to quote Herman Feldman, who wrote in 1927:

> People who discuss the economic effects of Prohibition or, for that matter, any of the other effects of Prohibition, too often go to one of

[32] Daniel Bell, "Crime as an American Way of Life," in D. Bell, *The End of Ideology* (New York, 1960), chap. vii.

two extremes. The largest group attributes everything that had happened since about 1919 to 1920 to Prohibition, some finding the conditions insufferable while others are full of praise. The second group consists of skeptics who are so much impressed by the fact that other things could explain present day circumstances that they seem unwilling to admit that Prohibition has had any effects at all. . . . Its effects may well be exaggerated, but they should certainly not be waved aside as negligible.[33]

The full story of any law, moreover, is not to be found solely in what happened while it was on the books. If drinking behavior changed during the 1920's as this paper argues, we should expect that it did not readily return to what had existed before the 1920's. In short, we need to search for some more permanent and lasting effects of the Prohibition Era in the later experience of Americans with alcohol in the periods after repeal. Here again we should find that the United States by no means has gone to a drunkard's dubious reward with the advent of repeal, nor did the Prohibition Era succeed in drying up the wellsprings of drinking habits. Nevertheless, it does appear evident that the experience of a dry society, even though less than perfect, did not contribute to a wave of excessive alcoholism. What we find, instead, is that those cultural sources that had produced abstinence continued to play their role and those that had enforced moderate drinking continued to grow. In this respect the experience with Prohibition appears to have had little permanent effect on American drinking behavior per se.

In order to understand American drinking behavior, we must recognize the sharp differences in the various ways in which the different ethnic and religious groups of the United States utilize alcohol. Extensive use of beer was introduced into the United States largely by the Germans and Swedes. The use of beer, as we have pointed out above, reflects a strong relationship between eating and drinking as does the use of wine among the French and the Italians. A highly Protestantized country, such as the United States, has been given to more extreme patterns of use and non-use of alcohol, ranging from total abstinence to drunkenness. Studies of Italians and of Jews in the United States have shown that it is quite possible for cultures to sanction the use of alcohol and yet be surrounded with controls that limit the impact of alcoholism.[34] The Irish have represented still another motif of high rates of non-abstinence and high rates of chronic alcoholism.[35] These studies indicate that as immigration increased in the United States, it brought into American society patterns in the uses of alcohol different from those encompassed by Protestant virtues. As our society became increasingly an urban one, the styles of life of the middle class in turn reflected newer

[33] Feldman, *Prohibition*, p. 1.

[34] Charles Snyder, *Alcohol and The Jews* (Glencoe, Ill., 1958); Giorgio Lolli, *et al.*, *Alcohol in Italian Culture* (Glencoe, Ill., 1958).

[35] Robert F. Bales, "Attitudes Toward Drinking in the Irish Culture," in D. Pittman and C. Snyder (eds.), *Society, Culture and Drinking Patterns* (New York, 1962), pp. 157–87.

modes of entertainment and leisure in which liquor and beer came to play distinctly different roles.

Harold Pfautz has shown some of this in his study of the depictions of alcohol in popular fiction at the turn of the twentieth century and later at mid-century. Pfautz found that the earlier fiction was less likely to impute useful properties to drinking than were later works. Both periods in his mode-of-content analysis were equal in the frequency with which they perceived alcohol as harmful to the individual and as a focus for social interaction. What was true, however, was that the later fiction tended to place far more value on the social functions of alcohol than did the earlier literature.[36] Pfautz's work provides additional support to our general understanding of the use or place that alcohol has come to play in American entertainment and in the moderate drinking habits of the urban middle class. In a culture that has come to prize fellowship and ease of human relations, the relaxing effects of alcohol permit quicker dissolution of reserve among people and facilitate group formation.

It is this general tendency toward a more moderate drinking pattern that characterizes the drinking behavior of America today. The general alcohol consumption in the United States by no means has risen greatly in the post-Prohibition period, and the long-run trend toward moderation appears to have continued. Studies in 1945 and 1946 both demonstrated that about one-third of the American population considered themselves abstainers from all alcoholic beverages.[37] The Gallup Poll has remained, with one debatable exception, remarkably constant in its findings of abstinence. A recent national survey finds 29 per cent of its respondents indicating their commitment to total abstinence.[38] Even a 1962 study of San Francisco adults found 24 per cent were abstainers.[39] As Table 4 below shows, the total absolute alcohol consumed in the United States, although increased somewhat in recent years, has not fallen back to the 1911–15 levels. So, too, if one examines the components in American drinking, the substitution of beer for whiskey that occurred in the early twentieth century has continued. It is remarkable that a large amount of the increase in alcohol consumption since 1940 has been a function of the increased use of wines in American life. All this supports the general tendency toward a more moderate set of drinking habits in which both abstinence and indulgence are less normal.

Of course, it is impossible to know to what degree this is a function of the

[36] Harold Pfautz, "The Image of Alcohol in Popular Fiction: 1900–1904 & 1946–1950," *Quarterly Journal of Studies in Alcohol*, VIII (September, 1947), pp. 265–73.
[37] Raymond McCarthy, ed., *op. cit.*, p. 179.
[38] Harold Mulford, "Drinking and Deviant Drinking," *Quarterly Journal of Studies of Alcohol*, XXV (December, 1964), 634–50. Mulford's 1963 study shows 71 per cent of population drank. Riley and Marden (1946) found 65 per cent. Compared with Riley and Marden, Mulford found greatest increase among the small-town residents and among those over thirty-five.
[39] Genevieve Knupfer and Robin Room, "Drinking in a Metropolitan Community," *Social Problems*, XII (Fall, 1964), 224–40.

TABLE 4

PERCENTAGE CONTRIBUTION OF DISTILLED SPIRITS, WINE, AND BEER
TO THE APPARENT CONSUMPTION OF TOTAL ABSOLUTE ALCOHOL
IN THE UNITED STATES, 1850–1957,
BASED ON TABLE 1 ABOVE

YEAR	TOTAL ABSOLUTE ALCOHOL[a]	PERCENTAGE OF TOTAL		
		Distilled spirits	Wine	Beer
1850	2.07	89.6	3.7	6.7
1911–15[b]	2.56	36.7	5.9	57.4
1940	1.56	42.9	10.3	46.8
1957	1.91	40.3	11.0	48.7

[a] Gallons per capita population of drinking age, fourteen and over.
[b] Average figures.

Prohibition Era. What is important to recognize, however, is that neither the passage of the Eighteenth Amendment nor the repeal of it appeared to have had decisive effects upon American drinking habits or upon sentiment. If it did, we could only surmise that it tended to accentuate the moderate use of liquor and to some degree to diminish the high point in American alcohol use of the early nineteenth century, thus supporting the long-run trend toward moderate use of alcohol. Certainly the analysis of local-option elections since repeal, like the public opinion polls, does not indicate any remarkable shifts in basic sentiment. In 1939, 18.3 per cent of the American population lived in locally dry areas. In 1959 this percentage had only declined to 14.7 per cent.[40] During the period 1947–59 there were 12,114 local elections held in the United States on issues of liquor control, and most of these left the existing situation intact.[41] The conception of alcoholism as a moral imperfection rather than a disease still continues to persist in many areas. Thus Mulford and Miller found in an Iowa survey that 45 per cent of their respondents viewed the alcoholic as morally weak, although surveys in Connecticut have shown a much higher percentage who viewed alcoholism as a disease.[42] As compared with European countries, liquor in America is still limited in availability. The bars found in the theaters and museums of Europe are rarely encountered in America.

The Prohibition period, with the experience of hard drinking in the middle class, and the absence of beer and liquor among the working classes may, however, have contributed to a different kind of shift in American drinking habits. It is certainly the case that two things appear to have occurred: the middle-class components are more likely to be non-abstainers

[40] Based on annual reports of the Distilled Spirits Institute, 1939, 1959, p. 51.
[41] Gusfield, Symbolic Crusade, p. 161.
[42] Harold Mulford and Donald Miller, "Public Definitions of the Alcoholic," Quarterly Journal of Studies of Alcohol, XXII (June, 1961), 312–20.

today than might have been true at an earlier period before Prohibition, and lower classes appear to be more abstaining. Certainly all the surveys have indicated that middle and upper classes represent higher levels of drinking than working and lower classes.[43] Abstinence has declined among the college-educated groups, and with it the less evangelical and highly prestigious denominations such as the Presbyterians, the Congregationalists, and the Methodists, who had been so firm in their support of Prohibition, have wavered and became much less enamored of abstinence.

Although drinkers are perhaps no more frequent than was true in the pre-Prohibition Era, their character and status has considerably changed. As one informant put it: "There has been a breakdown in the middle classes. The upper classes have always used liquor; the lower classes have always used liquor. Now the middle class has taken it over. The thing is slopping over from both sides."

The Prohibition period did not serve to set in motion a vast antipathy to abstinence. It did not check the continued long-run trend away from the excessive use of distilled spirits in the United States. The 1920's experience of upper-middle-class urban drinking was consonant with the later shifts in the class usages of alcohol in the United States, resulting in moderate use by a formerly abstinent middle class. It was effective in diminishing the total of alcoholic consumption in the United States while it was in operation. Its lasting effects, then, in terms of American drinking and behavior appear to have been relatively few, although it may have to some degree acted to support other cultural shifts that were changing class patterns in the use of alcohol in the United States. In order to appreciate the impact of the Prohibition Era on American life we need also to look at its role as a political issue, a role that suggests other kinds of cultural meanings than those we have already examined in terms of direct effect upon drinking.

In many ways the movement for national prohibition was an inexpedient one. By 1913 an equitable arrangement seems to have developed in which temperance sentiment was recognized by both law and behavior in those areas where it was strongest. Where dry sentiments were weak, the populace continued to act in accord with what they thought to be culturally legitimate. Enforcement in urban areas, where cultural support was small, had been tried and had been shown to be a doubtful possibility. It should have seemed impossible to the reformer to enforce legislation against so deep a resistance. Instead of seeking a possible compromise on a national level, however, the Anti-Saloon League and its supporters pushed their power as

---

[43] John W. Riley, Jr., and Charles F. Marden, "The Social Pattern of Alcoholic Drinking," *Quarterly Journal of Studies on Alcohol*, VIII (September, 1947), 265–73; Knupfer and Room, "Drinking in a Metropolitan Community"; Mulford, "Drinking and Deviant Drinking." Mulford's story shows a slight *decrease* in percentage of drinkers among lower-educated persons when compared with Marden's 1946 study.

far as it could go into a law that made no distinctions between beer and liquor and gave no solace to those for whom drinking was part of the way of living.

The issue of enforcement, however, hides some crucial functions of Prohibition as a symbolic issue in American life. If the norm against alcohol was often evaded, there was no question after 1919 about whose law it was. The Eighteenth Amendment made very plain the legal and public commitment of the American society to the utopia of the dry. Perhaps Billy Sunday was carried away by his own moral fervor when he described a world in which "the reign of tears is over. The slums will soon be only a memory. We will turn our prisons into factories and our jails into storehouses and corn cribs. Men will walk upright now. Women will smile, and the children will laugh. Hell will be forever for rent." [44] The flamboyant orator's rhetoric expresses the fundamental moral conception of Prohibition that lies so deeply within the American and Protestant ethos. It is impossible to understand the politics of the 1920's adequately, and its consequences, without understanding the interrelationship between moral stands, cultural commitments, and political conflict.

In describing the myriad of forces that supported Prohibition, the one common denominator that united the sometimes disparate body of reformers was Protestant theology and its antipathy to the kinds of leisure that alcohol represented. If some overzealous supporters described the battle for Prohibition as a veritable Armaggedon, they were not without truth. They saw the drinkers and the opponents of Prohibition as people who stood for cultural values that were anathema to the dry. As one observer put it, "Criminals, bandits, ex-convicts and thugs; street-walkers, harlots, prostitutes and degenerates are against Prohibition. But the good church people, the humanitarians, those who try to uplift and help others are for Prohibition." [45]

In this disjuncture between the drinkers and the abstainers, we find the same kind of cultural dichotomy that Horace Greeley had recognized at the base of political loyalties and animosities in the 1844 elections in New York State when he wrote, "Upon those working men who stick to their business, hope to improve their circumstances by honest industry and go on Sundays to church rather than the grog shop, the appeals of Loco-Focoism fell comparatively harmless; while the opposite class were rallied with unprecedented unanimity against us." [46] As we have seen, this distinction had a certain validity. It was in the cities that one found the saloon at its height and the problem of alcohol consumption at its greatest. It was the immigrants and the Catholics who provided the greatest contrast in values to the sober

[44] Quoted in Harry Elmer Barnes, *Prohibition Versus Civilization* (New York, 1932), p. 68.

[45] *Ibid.*, p. 31.

[46] Quoted in Lee Benson, *The Concept of Jacksonian Democracy* (Princeton, N.J., 1961).

middle-class Protestant. These conflicts were focused around the issue of Prohibition. They were given sustenance by the nativism and racial theories that were then so current.[47]

In this context consumption and abstinence take on meanings as signs and symbols of group loyalty and differentiation. The styles of life to which people are committed in their status groups are signs to us of who they are. As important elements in the make-up of one's standards of living, they become symbols of membership and loyalty. Thorstein Veblen has shown this very clearly in his discussion of the theory of the leisure class. The furnishings we use, the clothes we wear, and the foods we eat are those that are part of our specific culture. They are also enjoined upon us as ways of demonstrating that we are what we claim to be. In American society, drinking, like sex, is also an aspect tinged with a high degree of moral judgment. Whether one is a "drunken bum" or a "dried-up blue nose" is a matter of considerable moral moment. Hence, drinking in American society is affected with an intensive set of cultural designations.

Politically, this implies that the designation of the public morality is also a determination of cultural dominance.[48] The quest for a given piece of legislation has meaning that is symbolic of, or in substitution for, instrumental goals. For cultural dominance to be symbolized by a piece of legislation, its mere existence is sufficient; enforcement is not essential. To have gained the legislative victory itself is to have gained the mark of cultural dominance; to be able to say, "Give deference to my way of living and degradation to yours."

As a code of living, temperance performed two functions vis-à-vis its opponents. First, it existed as a style of life that was set forth in opposition to less stern orientations to family, to neighbors, and to a hierarchial authority in which leisure involved a separation between work and play and not a preparation for it. In this sense the effort to make others temperate (abstinent) was an act of coercion, dominated by a defense against a threatened overwhelming new cultural impulse. Second, temperance was an invitation to those, especially the newly arrived in the United States, to adopt the habits that spelled success and prestige in American life. It was in this respect an invitation toward assimilation in which urban social problems were to be solved by the lower classes adopting the values by which middle-class citizens would permit them to enter their gates. The passage of Prohibition made clear that the cultural dominance of the old middle-class was proclaimed; Anna Gordon, president of the WCTU, put it in an address in 1915: "Total abstinence is no longer a ridiculed fanaticism. It sits in regal

[47] Jones, "Prohibition and Eugenics."
[48] Clark, *The Dry Years*, pp. 113–22, shows the split between middle class and lower class as deeply related to dry and wet antagonisms in the twentieth century in the state of Washington. The symbolic nature of the issue is discussed throughout my *Symbolic Crusade*.

state on the throne of empires and of kingdoms and sways, in ever increasing measure, the voting citizenship." [49]

If this cultural confrontation existed before Prohibition, it did so in a somewhat muted fashion. It was a major consequence of Prohibition and of the Prohibition Era that it served to make both sides more homogeneous and consequently to polarize the cultural diversities within American society. In understanding the ways in which Prohibition functioned as a symbol of cultural conflict, we must now turn to the sources of growing commitment and antipathy during the 1920's.

The polarizing effects of the campaign for national prohibition were made manifest in an editorial of the Anti-Saloon League's journal, the *American Issue*.[50] "The liquor issue is no longer one of Wet and Dry arguments. Henceforth, it is to be a question of Wet men and Dry men." The campaign for Prohibition had the effect of widening the gulf between the cultures involved in the defense of drinking and of abstinence. Because it sought political decisions, rather than moral suasion, the Anti-Saloon League and the dry forces tended to organize both sides around concrete issues. Because they sought a total victory, they made it extremely difficult for more moderate dry allies to stay in the same camp.

One aspect of this was the almost total demise of Catholic organizational support for prohibitionist legislation. Although the Catholic Abstinence Union and many of the Paulist fathers had been a source of aid in efforts to curtail drinking, they could not go along with the extreme position represented by Prohibition. When the Catholic Clergy Prohibition League of America was founded in 1919, it had relatively small backing in contrast to the earlier more moderate efforts. "Most Roman Catholics, however, opposed Prohibition and became especially hostile after the reform began to reach the larger cities where Catholic strength was concentrated." [51] Two major non-evangelical Protestant churches, the Episcopalian and both Lutheran synods, did not climb on board the dry wagon. The Jews, who also represented an immigrant population, were similarly hostile to prohibitory legislation. The effect, then, of the campaign for Prohibition was to stamp it even more clearly as a middle-class, Protestant, and nativist activity.

Despite the fact that the progressive movement was a major source for urban middle-class support for Prohibition, as Timberlake has shown, it yet remains the case that the drive for Prohibition tended to increase the gap along class lines between components within the progressive movement. Thus the labor movement, especially with the development of the American Federation of Labor, was by no means any longer a major ally of temperance. Although Terence Powderly, the founder and head of the Knights of Labor, had been actively allied with the temperance organizations of the

---

[49] *Annual Report*, National Woman's Christian Temperance Union, 1915, p. 93.
[50] *American Issue*, XX (January, 1912), 4.
[51] Timberlake, *Prohibition and the Progressive Movement*, p. 32.

late nineteenth century, his concern was by no means mirrored in the labor movement of the twentieth century. Gompers was concerned with moderating the use of liquor, but both he and most of the labor movement were by then, in culture and temperament, opposed to both abstinence and the tactics of legislative prohibition.[52]

The progressive movement, though it was dominated very much by the urban middle class, nevertheless gained very important strength from its general concern with the welfare of labor and the industrial worker. In this sympathy progressivism was anti-industrial and an opponent of the new business classes. Prohibition, so thoroughly identified in the urban areas with the Protestant middle class, split the progressive movement on the issue of drinking. To the worker it smacked of paternalism and class exploitation. Samuel Gompers, with considerable foresight, remarked to a Congressional committee that Prohibition would be discriminatory against the worker. "The cry is against this discrimination, which is almost inevitable, except so far as a business man or a man of means may be himself a total abstainer. Where a wage earner can not get a glass of beer, still a very large proportion of the men of means can have and do have a stock of intoxicating drinks to last men their lives." [53] The visible exemption of the urban rich from the restrictions of Prohibition made the gap evident to the urban poor.

Despite the activity of urban progressives, a major consequence of the Prohibition campaign was to intensify the conflict between the city and the country. As we have shown above, it was in the rural areas that the Prohibition forces found their greatest support. When the Webb-Kenyon Act was passed in Congress in 1913, the sources of support came far more from areas where old-stock middle classes were strong than from those of the industrial and immigrant population.[54] An analysis of percentage of state populations under prohibition by state or local laws in 1913 shows that dry laws were far less likely to occur in urbanized than in rural states.[55]

The same thing is true if one compares the Populist vote in the late nineteenth century to the prohibitionist status of states in 1919. In countries where the Populist vote had been high, there the prohibitionist support was strongest. The earliest of the states to be drawn into the wave of prohibitory legislation after 1906 were in the South, and it was in the South that one found the strongest support for national prohibition and prohibitory legislation. Those who were likely to see this as largely a reaction to the Negro are mistaken. County-by-county analysis in Mississippi and Alabama revealed that the strongest sources of support were in the rural counties that

---

[52] Despite Timberlake's assertion that Prohibition was a phase of progressive reform, he admits that "other Progressives, especially those identified with urban-labor-immigrant elements, disliked the reform and fought it" (*ibid.*, p. 2). Also see his discussion of labor and Prohibition, pp. 88–95.

[53] *Ibid.*, p. 94.

[54] *Ibid.*, p. 163; Sinclair, *Prohibition*, p. 154.

[55] Gusfield, *Symbolic Crusade*, pp. 102–3.

had been Populist in the late nineteenth century and that had a low percentage of Negroes. In the urban counties the support was much less, and in rural counties with high percentages of Negroes, largely disenfranchised, Prohibition found considerable opposition. What differentiated the Prohibitionist from the pro-wet forces in these southern areas was largely the existence of evangelical Protestant religion.

We are not implying here that Prohibition can be explained as a Populist reform. What we do suggest is that great opposition to Prohibition came from the eastern, urban states where large percentages of Catholics and immigrants were to be found. Major urban and industrial areas like Illinois, New York, and Pennsylvania were the last to ratify the Eighteenth Amendment. The strongest areas of national prohibition sentiment were not the industrialized states nor the industrialized sectors of rural states. They were largely areas that were Protestant, rural, and nativist; in the South and in the Midwest rather than in the East. This is not to deny that the progressives did play an important role in Prohibition campaigns. This they certainly did, as Timberlake has shown. In California they played perhaps the greatest role, but in Los Angeles County, where the Populist candidate for President in 1892 had pulled 14 per cent of the votes and the Prohibitionist 4 per cent, one found intense support for the Anti-Saloon League and the Progressive campaigns of 1909–13.[56]

The saloon and the drinker increasingly appeared to the Protestant middle class, both urban and rural, as a symbol of a culture alien to the ascetic character of American values. What was important was not so much that people drank but that they upheld the validity and the rightness of liquor and beer within an accepted way of life. There were many strands in the Prohibitionist campaign, derived from many ideological sources of a nineteenth century commercial and agrarian society. The reform movements that swept the United States in the late nineteenth and early twentieth centuries, especially in the form of progressivism and Populism, were important roots for the Prohibition movement. But in the process of pursuing Prohibition, both the gaps between the older social system and the newer one and the elements involved in these movements themselves came into conflict. At the root of these conflicts were cultural differences that were symbolized by the very effort to make the American Protestant version of the good life embedded in law.

The result was that what for one group was a part of its daily existence and a legitimate and welcome source of leisure was, to the dry forces, a vice whose eradication was essential. Consider the cultural overtones of superiority in the argument of a Prohibition advocate: "The hope of perpetuating our liberties is to help the foreigners correct any demoralizing custom, and

---

[56] *Ibid.*, p. 104; Gilman Ostrander, *The Prohibition Movement in California, 1848–1933* (Berkeley, Calif., 1957), p. 105.

through self-restraint assimilate American ideals." [57] The result of the Prohibition campaign was to increase the cultural conflict that had long been involved in temperance activity. "The Anglo-Saxon stock," declared the journal of the Anti-Saloon League, "is hardiest and fittest. . . . If we are to preserve this nation in the Anglo-Saxon type, we must abolish [saloons]." [58] For those who were the objects of such abolition, the attempt seemed only one of hostile aggressiveness.

As the nation entered the Prohibition Era on the night of January 16, 1920, the issues had already been drawn and the conflicts and symbols already stated. The only new argument to emerge for the drys was that abstinence was now the law of the land, and the devotees of law and order must obey. The wet rejoinder, after the first few years, was that Prohibition had been tried and was found to be unenforceable. Though the arguments from science, religion, economics, and other areas of knowledge were continuously stated and restated by friend and foe, the basic for and against positions of rural-urban, of middle-working class, and Protestant-Catholic were apparent and more evident day by day. What was new and what made the Prohibition Era so consequential for later American politics was the tendency toward an increasing and vigilant moralism among the drys and a fusion of these qualities with particular political parties and leaders. In the course of this, the moderates and the progressives were increasingly pushed to one or another side. When repeal came, it came to a country that was tired of the moralisms of the drys and the wets and preoccupied with a totally different kind of problem.

The progressive impulse had played a significant part in the Prohibition campaign. But even before Prohibition was achieved, there was a widening split. Although the urban, middle-class, and progressive supporters of Prohibition were highly visible, their role in the major Prohibitionist organizations was by no means this apparent. The WCTU, which had in the late 1890's been deeply committed to Frances Willard's Do-Everything policy, had been active in such diverse movements as female suffrage, the rights of labor, penal reform, and even cremation, as well as influenced by the general tenets of Christian socialism. After the Anti-Saloon League began its Prohibition campaigns in 1906, however, this ladies' wing of the temperance movement began to retreat from its wider concerns into a far more specific and concerted attack on the liquor traffic.[59] The Anti-Saloon League itself was based upon a very explicit policy of isolation from all other issues. The title of its major periodical, the *American Issue*, was its basic point of difference from the Prohibition party and from many earlier temperance organizations. Even the famed Methodist Board of Temperance, Morals,

[57] Barker, *The Saloon Problem*, pp. 49–50. Quoted in Timberlake, *Prohibition and the Progressive Movement*, p. 118.

[58] *American Issue*, XX (April, 1912), 1.

[59] Gusfield, *Symbolic Crusade*, chap. iv.

and Social Legislation was far less concerned with the latter two items than with the first. When Prohibition arrived, those organizations that had been so successful in mobilizing political strength had become isolated from other major progressive movements of the early twentieth century.

The urban middle classes, so much wedded to the progressive ideology of clean government and paternalism toward industrial workers, were far less hostile to the urban society than was the case among the rural components of Prohibition. As groups, they were less likely to be drawn into some of the highly bombastic and hostile attitudes that came to govern Prohibition rhetoric and action during the 1920's. As residents in urban America, they were quick to feel the consequences of Prohibition for middle-class drinking and for organized crime. The easier enforcement of Prohibition in the towns and country areas made rural people far less susceptible to the belief that Prohibition was unenforceable and productive of excessive crime. As the era continued, the defection of the moderate progressive left the field still further open to the neo-Populists. When the Federal Council of Churches of Christ, the leading organ of expression of the social gospel and high-status churches in the United States, announced its opposition to continued Prohibition, it sounded the beginnings of a shift that proved highly destructive to the drys.[60]

By the 1920's the progressive movement had run its course. Teddy Roosevelt and Woodrow Wilson had both departed, and the effort of La Follette was a last weak shot at revival. The alliance between temperance and nativism began to produce excessive and unsophisticated ideologies that pushed the urbanites further from identification with rural colleagues. It should be noted that in point of fact the northeastern urban progressives in the Progressive party of 1916, when the prohibition issue was raised, did not support it. The party convention opposed prohibition in its meetings in 1912.[61]

In this respect I am in agreement with Sinclair and in disagreement with Timberlake. Timberlake sees Prohibition as largely an extension of the progressive reform, whereas Sinclair and I are likely to see it as one element but much overshadowed by the rural political base and sentiments of anti-urbanism and nativism. During the Prohibition Era the forces of nativism, antiurbanism, and religious fundamentalism gained strength. Both defensiveness over the enforceability of Prohibition and the very success in achieving it added to an expansiveness that took the form of a strong effort to expand the rural virtues embodied in Prohibition into other areas. Perhaps, too, as Virginius Dabney has suggested, the dry leaders felt themselves threatened by the obviously increasing strength and numbers of the Catholic, immigrant, and working-class people of the big cities.

[60] Sinclair, *Prohibition*, pp. 290–91. It might also be suggested that this polarization among Protestants accentuated the shifts in drinking standards, distaste for the dry's single-minded political zeal undermining the standard he so zealously pursued.
[61] *Ibid.*, pp. 95–96.

In his rhetoric and in his career William Jennings Bryan embodied much of what Prohibitionists stood for. His action in the 1920's reflected a good deal of what was happening. Although he had carefully refrained from taking a stand on liquor questions during his presidential campaigns, despite his obvious personal pro-dry feelings, during the 1920's he came to feel that the Prohibition issue was now a dominant one. He spoke out most strongly in the effort to make the Democratic party a stauncher vehicle for Prohibition sentiment and to prevent its domination by urban and eastern forces. The 1924 convention was a bitter one. It linked Bryan and the drys to the support of the Ku Klux Klan. In this respect, as in so much of the rhetoric of the drys, the nativism and anti-Catholicism of the Prohibitionists were made to seem the central tenets of a wider movement. Those urban supporters who had found in Prohibition a significance given by concern for social welfare and for industrial efficiency were more likely to be rebuffed by legislation that had now been given a decidedly different kind of symbolic significance. In 1924 the Prohibition party even passed planks to support the placement of Bibles in the schools and for legislation to enforce the Americanization of aliens.[62]

The dry victory, and the later fight against repeal, made the conflicts between cultures more intense and polarized even more the forces of the urban and the rural, the Catholic and the Protestant, the immigrant and the native. Prohibition was thus not an isolated issue but one that pitted cultures against each other. Given the constitutionality of Prohibition and the experience with the denunciation of the German brewers during World War I, the loyal drys added patriotism to the other arrows in their quiver. It was a patriotism directed less against external enemies than toward the urban and immigrant cultures in American cities. Ella Boole, then the president of the WCTU, said in 1928 to its national convention that "this is the United States of America, my country and I love it. . . . As my forefathers worked and struggled to build it, so will I work and struggle to maintain it unsoiled by foreign influences, uncontaminated by vicious mind poison." [63]

Bryan's own qualities, so effective on the prairies, were not calculated to gain loyal followers on the cement sidewalks. He embodied the prejudices and the virtues of rural America. At the Scopes trial, he was not simply a pathetic old man; his effort to shore up fundamentalist religion against the attacks of sophisticated science in turn continued that resistance to the modern that is in part at the root of the antiurbanism in Prohibition. In a mania for purity in literature, attack on the cigarette, and the demand for the eradication of jazz, the drys moved increasingly to an alliance with a general movement of fundamentalist conservatism in American manners, morals, and politics. It is in this sense that we speak of the radicalization of

---

[62] *Ibid.*, p. 87.
[63] *Union Signal* (Dec. 15, 1928), p. 12.

Prohibition reform. Both sides moved toward a more rigid statement of diverse orientations toward life.

To some degree the increasing polarization was a function of the fact that the issues were posed as political choices. The split that Bryan had dramatized in the Democratic party began the set of events that tended increasingly to turn the Prohibition issue into one of party identifications. What the Anti-Saloon League had sought to avoid came into being — the identification of the Republicans with Prohibition and of the Democrats with Repeal. In large measure the national legislative victories had been a function of a coalition between southern Democrats and middlewestern and western Republicans. The Hobson resolution submitting the Eighteenth Amendment to the states was originally defeated in 1914. In 1917 its passage was secured by the increased votes that came from Republican gains in the House from midwestern states.[64] Nevertheless, neither the presidential campaigns of 1916, 1920, or 1924 had pivoted around the dry issue. Although Wilson and Harding had vetoed various pro-dry measures, such as Wilson's veto of the Volstead Act, they had all steered clear of any identification on either side of the issue.

The campaign of Alfred E. Smith for the presidency was a vital link in the processes by which repeal was achieved and by which the American political parties gained a great deal of their present stylistic differences. The conflict of cultures that Smith's candidacy mirrored had already been more than foreshadowed in the 1924 convention. The very fact that an urban Catholic, an avowed wet, was the candidate of a major political party was in itself an affront to the sober, Protestant middle classes that had put through Prohibition and that had for so long dominated American political life.

Theda Tray has written that while Hoover and Smith were talking about issues, "the rest of the population was talking about Al — where he went to church, what kind of a lid he wore, what liquids he took with his meals, how he was born and brought up in Tammany Hall and the way he pronounced 'foist.' "[65] In Smith the wets had found a perfect symbol of a way of life — a man who had championed social welfare, whose sentiments and speech showed clearly the sidewalks of New York on which he had been reared. He was the best of the machine politicians and a deep defender of the urban underdog who "worked in factories, spoke broken English, and wanted a good time on Sundays."[66] Herbert Hoover was, of course, the very opposite in manner and in speech. In so many ways he was the rural epitome of the American success story: the efficient engineer who had worked his way up from humble farm beginnings and who had made his

---

[64] Sinclair, *Prohibition*, p. 163.

[65] Quoted in *ibid.*, p. 304. For a general description of the 1928 campaign see Moore, *A Catholic Runs for President* (New York, 1956).

[66] Gusfield, *Symbolic Crusade*, p. 125. For an account of Smith's voting power in urban areas see Samuel Lubell, *The Future of American Politics* (New York, 1952).

mark in the effective organization of charity. At last the struggle was out in the open, and it led the Prohibitionist forces into a zealous fight against the devil. In a typical statement the Anti-Saloon League yearbook said in 1931, "When the great cities of America actually come to dominate the states and dictate the policies of the nation, the process of decay in our boasted American civilization will have begun." [67] Bishop Cannon, the Anti-Saloon League, the Methodist and other evangelical Protestant churches, the WCTU — all threw themselves behind Herbert Hoover, departing from their long policy of avoiding specific recommendations in presidential elections. Even the Prohibition party, for the first time since its beginning, in 1872, supported another party's presidential candidate and failed to nominate one of their own. Such a split made it extraordinarily difficult for the Progressive and social welfare–oriented urban Prohibitionists. The bigotry of the open anti-Catholicism in which Cannon and other Prohibition leaders engaged further turned the knife in the wounds that a vindictive policy of nativism had developed during the 1920's.

Hoover's victory, in a clear endorsement of Prohibition, should of course not hide what is evident today in Smith's defeat — the rise of Democratic majorities in the American big cities. These cities had already been the bastion of wet votes.[68] Samuel Lubell has recounted the importance of the Smith campaign in presaging the development of the Democratic party as the champion of the urban underdog ethnic minorities. Not only was it the case that the Catholic and Jewish populations were increasing more rapidly than were middle-class Protestants, but the cultural conflicts represented in part by prohibitionist issues tended to drive some of the immigrant groups that had been Republican closer to the Democratic party.[69]

What Smith had accomplished, in relation to the Prohibition issue, was to swing the wet centers of the population behind the Democrats. Sinclair's analysis of the vote in 1930 in the House of Representatives on the Jones Law shows this clearly. The drys, though winning a great victory in numbers (284–90), captured very little of the northern vote. Although the North had provided over half of the wet vote in 1917, now it provided just under two-thirds. The Republican party had become even more dry, whereas the Democrats were more split than ever.[70] In short, Prohibition had become identified with the Republican party. The basis for a compromise had increasingly diminished. When repeal came, it was as a vindication of all that urban and industrial America had come to stand for in the dialogue of American politics.

If Smith's defeat and the shifting nature of political polarization in the

---

[67] *Anti-Saloon League Yearbook.* 1931 (Westerville, Ohio, 1931), p. 9.

[68] With the exception of Los Angeles and several southern cities, no major American city was pro-dry.

[69] Lubell, *The Future of American Politics.*

[70] Sinclair, *Prohibition*, p. 353.

United States foreshadowed the possibility of repeal, the events of the 1920's had already begun to sharpen the opposition. The growth and development of the Association Against the Prohibition Amendment and the development of a Women's Auxiliary in the late 1920's had produced something that had not clearly existed before 1920 — an independent organization of wets. As long as the liquor and beer industries were behind all efforts to publicize a wet position, their hearing in public was limited. However, growing dissatisfaction with the law had brought into being groups of people of high social position who could not easily be dismissed. The early defection of the DuPonts from the ranks of temperance supporters and their enthusiastic backing of the Association Against the Prohibition Amendment represented a serious blow to dry forces. The championing of Repeal by Mrs. Charles Sabin, a woman of social prominence, was another blow to the dry cause.

The shifts in public opinion might have been borne and the amendment saved, at least in relationship to distilled spirits, had it not been for the major event of the depression. It was the Great Depression that killed the Eighteenth Amendment more than any other single act or process. In 1929 Prohibition was still part of the Constitution. It had survived the attack of the 1928 election. The Prohibition Bureau, under Hoover, for the first time was placed on a sound footing under Civil Service in the Department of Justice. A strong effort to enforce the law seemed in existence. The Wickersham Report, though critical of enforcement, laid the groundwork for an adequate discussion under which some compromise between wet and dry might have been achievable. That the dry forces were still quite strong has already been indicated in our analysis of the vote on the Jones Law. The depression, however, made the issue of Prohibition a minor one, less calculated to instil enthusiastic loyalties in either direction.

The argument of economic consideration now took precedence. In 1926 only a few unions had actively opposed the law in Congressional hearings. In 1930 and 1932 union representatives constituted a great source of the advocacy of Repeal, on the grounds that it would put men back to work in such jobs as lithography (making bottle labels), glass blowing, and among hotel and steward groups.[71] Further, the argument that new sources of tax revenues were necessary and needed appeared to play an extremely important role among businessmen who had championed Prohibition as the route to a sober and reliable work force. Even those great stalwarts of the dry reform John D. Rockefeller and S. S. Kresge had left the movement in 1932. For the first time in many, many years the Anti-Saloon League was suffering from a deficiency of funds.[72] More importantly, tangible economic issues became paramount, and the cultural differences between the lower-class

---

[71] See my discussion of these Congressional hearings in Gusfield, *Symbolic Crusade*, pp. 127–28.

[72] Clark, *The Dry Years*, pp. 227–29.

urban workers and the rural farmers became minimal when they were both so desperately in financial difficulty.

The depression, however, had another important effect upon the consequences of Prohibition for American life. Having so thoroughly identified the Republicans with dry sentiment and with Herbert Hoover, they quite clearly underlined the antipathy of the urban and immigrant masses for the party that appeared to be the spokesman of the white Anglo-Saxon Protestant. Not only did the Republican party come to be viewed as the party of big business, but it was also deeply associated with the party that had turned its back on the urban poor, the Catholic and the Jew and the working man whose leisure had little room for the dry utopia.

It is in its implications for the setting of styles in American politics that Prohibition has had a considerable importance in American life.

In becoming associated with the cause of the dry, the Republican party hardened its cultural overtones as the party whose heyday was the period of the 1920's — the high point of old middle-class political supremacy and a prosperity that celebrated the effectiveness and virtue of a business civilization. The Great Depression dissolved the magic power of the old symbols and set in its place a conception of government closer to the welfare orientations of the urban, immigrant, and industrial poor. In Al Smith and in the New Deal, the Democrats moved more clearly out of the 1920's and the world of William Jennings Bryan. These images of political parties have continued to play significant functions in voter perceptions of Republicans and Democrats — the Republicans as the party of "big business" and the Democrats as the party of the "underdog." Public opinion polls have been consistent in reporting such designations among American voters.[73]

We have already suggested that the era of Prohibition tended to polarize the cultural diversities in American life. In splitting off the welfare-oriented and progressive strands in Prohibition from the nativist and Populist strands, the 1920's more completely effected the bond between political party choices and cultural loyalties. The differential availability of beer and liquor for working and for middle classes underlined the symbolism of the Republicans as the party of the old middle class, the Protestant establishment, and the agrarian past.[74] The Democrats emerged more clearly as the party of the urban frontier, the champion of a good life of leisure and comradeship. Against the utopia of an efficient and moral civilization, soberly dedicated

[73] Bernard Berelson *et al.*, Voting (Chicago, 1954), p. 79; Angus Campbell *et al.*, *The American Voter* (New York, 1960), pp. 149–67; Lubell, *The Future of American Politics*.

[74] We should be careful not to confuse the farmer and the small town. Farmers show much less fealty to the Republican party than often supposed. Much of the solid Republican strength lies in the rural non-farm communities and does not display the erratic quality of the farm vote, which is more closely related to immediate farm prices. See Lubell, *The Future of American Politics*, chap. viii; Seymour Lipset, *Agrarian Socialism* (Berkeley and Los Angeles, 1950), chap. i.

to production and perfectability, there was clearly posed the utopia of the happy consumers, sharing in the fruits of the economy and practicing a "live and let live" attitude to the differences of a pluralistic society.

The linkages between party and cultural styles involve as well distinctly diverse views of government and its obligations and limits. Richard Hofstadter has described this in remarking on the contrast between the progressive's conception of government and that of the big city machine and its followers.[75] For the urban middle class that supported progressivism, government was a vehicle for achieving moral purposes and the public good. Clean government and the rational electorate were his virtues, and the corruption and organization of the machine were deeply vicious. The saloon, in its alliance with the political boss, was anathema. The good citizen, in the progressive utopia, saw government as a vehicle in which he was the driver, not the passenger. The urban immigrant, on the other hand, saw society as a hierarchical structure in which authority did favors for those on the bottom in return for favors toward those at the top. The impersonal, moralistic vision of politics that the drys upheld was the common property of the old middle class, both urban and rural. A more personal practice that mixed human concern with ethnic loyalty was the stuff on which the urban politician based his power. Lincoln Steffens quoted the Boston "boss" Martin Lomasny as saying that what people wanted was mercy, not law and justice.[76]

In their efforts to enshrine a Protestant Sunday as the ideal of American consumership, the drys set their face against the tolerant and indulgent cultures that had come to make up much of the new industrial populations. Their own logic and their intense need for the establishment of moral supremacy in public forms made compromises with the wets increasingly difficult. A politics of compromise was itself difficult for such moralists to accept. As the issues became sharper, became more clearly cultural in content, and became linked to political parties, political loyalties and ethnic identities were more clearly linked to stylistic differences.

Perhaps here we touch upon deeper shifts in American life that were beginning to emerge in the 1920's and in turn appear to have been in process of changing American orientations toward consumption, toward leisure, and toward the use of alcohol. We have already pointed out that America, over the past eighty years, has shifted from a nation of excessive drinkers and abstainers to one of far more moderate consumption of alcohol. The intensive use of alcohol as a means of escape (and consequently the defensive reaction against it) appears to have given way to the use of alcohol in facilitating social camaraderie. In this respect Americans, in their quest to extend and maintain good fellowship, are more inclined to accept playfulness and leisure and less inclined to show continuous concern with production and work. The general shifts in American character that David Ries-

---

[75] Richard Hofstadter, *The Age of Reform* (New York, 1956), pp. 180–84.
[76] Lincoln Steffens, *Autobiography* (New York, 1931), p. 618.

man has made so vivid are presaged in the 1920's. Kinsey, in his famous study of the sexual behavior of the human female, dates a sharp shift in American sexual morality from the appearance of the generation born after 1910.[77] Certainly the 1920's saw a tremendous increase in what may be called the cultural mobility of the American population, especially in urban centers. It was the era in which communication and transportation were greatly increased by the appearance of the automobile, the movies, and the radio. It was an era of affluence, in the main, and one in which the moralities of a sterner Protestantism were under attack both by the winds of change and by the appearance of whole new populations that were less committed to the utopia of the sober Sunday. After the 1920's the conflicts between the alien and the native, between urban and rural, Protestant and Catholic, became less vivid than those between adherents to styles of fundamentalism and modernism, conflicts that cut across the different religious and residence groups.[78]

The sentiments that American Prohibition expressed are by no means dead, although they have lost a great deal of their prestige and political dominance. Abstinence is still the commitment of a large segment of the American population. What is true, however, is that the domination in cultural and political terms that it represented, the domination of the nineteenth-century Anglo-Saxon Protestant, has ended in American life. It is this that was the meaning of the struggle over Prohibition and that has made its loss so bitter for those who have identified with it. "For when all the old Prohibs are dead — as soon they will be — one may look in vain for the old America." [79]

[77] Alfred Kinsey *et al.*, *Sexual Behavior in the Human Female* (Philadelphia, 1953).

[78] This has also been discussed recently in sociological literature as conflict between "cosmopolitans" and "locals." See the discussion of these cultural styles in Gusfield, *Symbolic Crusade*, Chapter VI.

[79] Clark, *The Dry Years*, p. 127.

15

NOSTALGIA AND PROGRESS
IN POPULAR THOUGHT

In his analysis of the reaction to Charles Lindbergh's transatlantic flight, John W. Ward, Professor of History at Amherst College, shows that in the 'twenties burning nostalgia for the past and fear of the increasing complexity of modern industrial society were by no means confined to rural America. In discussing the ambivalence that accompanied that nostalgia, Ward is treating a modern manifestation of a long-standing national paradox. From their colonial origins Americans have looked to the future even while they clung to the past, have sung of progress though they dreaded change, have assured themselves and the world of America's glorious destiny while they spoke ruefully of America's present decline. The dilemmas posed by Jefferson's earnest desire to foster the greatness of his country, coupled with his fear of the kind of urban, industrialized society without which no nation could hope to be a great power, have appeared again and again in American history. The will toward progress, so important to the American ethos, has forced the acceptance of societal and economic changes that seemed to underline the cherished values of individualism, agrarianism, and traditional Protestantism.

The desire to have things both ways — to accept the fruits of progress without relinquishing the fundamentals of the old order — goes a long way toward explaining many of the tensions in American life. But this dualism, though important, has not been totally static. If it had been, then, as Professor Ward puts it, we would truly be faced by a mass cultural neurosis. Instead, in spite of the lag between actuality and perception, there has been a gradual acceptance of changes and a reordering of desires, expectations, and action. Jefferson did, however belatedly and reluctantly, come to see the necessity for the promotion of domestic industry, which as he knew meant the proliferation of urban centers throughout the nation. The continued obsession of late nineteenth-century America with the symbols of superior agrarian virtue and self-determination appeared in the continued popularity of the McGuffey readers, which virtually ignored all aspects of urban, industrial society, and in the phenomenal success of the Horatio Alger stories, which overlooked most of the problems of the new society. Both persisted in the belief that success and failure were simply matters of the will; man, they insisted, made himself. Yet in spite of the obeisance paid to these symbols, the Americans of that era took a number of important steps to deal with the complexities of the age. However much the Populists may have yearned for the simpler problems of the past, they made no attempt to actually bring back the past. In the final analysis they sought to control, not to destroy, big business, the railroads, and finance capitalism. So too with the progressives after them, who defended competition and railed against big business but did relatively little to impede the growth of the large business organizations that a modern industrial technology fostered. Americans have dealt with the problems and complexities of their recent past not by seeking to abolish them but by enlarging the vast powers of the federal government, even though this recourse in turn seemed to violate many of their traditional beliefs in the virtues of individualism and local government.

Americans, then, have turned to the past in their sentiment and rhetoric more than in their actions. But the persistence of this gap is in itself important and enlightening. If the continuing dualism between a past and a future orientation in American ideology has not prevented action it has at least impeded and shaped action, and helps to make clearer the American approach to a host of modern problems. Using Lindbergh as a symbol to get at the heart of this dualism, Ward illuminates an important and much-neglected aspect of the American ethos.

Other articles that deal with aspects of this problem are C. B. Anderson, "The Metamorphosis of American Agrarian Idealism in the 1920's and 1930's," *Agricultural History*, 35 (Oct. 1961), 182–88; R. Hofstadter, "Antitrust in America," *Commentary*, 38 (Aug. 1964), 47–53; A. P. Dudden, "Nostalgia and the American," *The Journal of the History of Ideas*, 22 (Oct.–Dec. 1961), 515–30; and Paul Johnstone, "Old Ideals Versus New Ideas in Farm Life," reprinted in this volume, pp. 5–47. Important books that treat related problems include: Henry Nash Smith, *Virgin Land** (1950); Leo Marx, *The Machine in the Garden** (1964); John Cawelti, *Apostles of the Self-Made Man** (1965); and Richard Weiss, *The American Myth of Success* (1969).

The Meaning of Lindbergh's Flight

JOHN W. WARD

On Friday, May 20, 1927, at 7:52 A.M., Charles A. Lindbergh took off in a silver-winged monoplane and flew from the United States to France. With

Reprinted by permission of the University of Pennsylvania and the author from *American Quarterly*, 10, No. 1 (1958), 3–16. Copyright, 1958, Trustees of the University of Pennsylvania.

this flight Lindbergh became the first man to fly alone across the Atlantic Ocean. The log of flight 33 of "The Spirit of St. Louis" reads: "Roosevelt Field, Long Island, New York, to Le Bourget Aerodrome, Paris, France. 33 hrs. 30 min." Thus was the fact of Lindbergh's achievement easily put down. But the meaning of Lindbergh's flight lay hidden in the next sentence of the log: "(Fuselage fabric badly torn by souvenir hunters.)"

When Lindbergh landed at Le Bourget he is supposed to have said, "Well, we've done it." A contemporary writer asked "Did what?" Lindbergh "had no idea of what he had done. He thought he had simply flown from New York to Paris. What he had really done was something far greater. He had fired the imagination of mankind." From the moment of Lindbergh's flight people recognized that something more was involved than the mere fact of the physical leap from New York to Paris. "Lindbergh," wrote John Erskine, "served as a metaphor." But what the metaphor stood for was not easy to say. The *New York Times* remarked then that "there has been no complete and satisfactory explanation of the enthusiasm and acclaim for Captain Lindbergh." Looking back on the celebration of Lindbergh, one can see now that the American people were trying to understand Lindbergh's flight, to grasp its meaning, and through it, perhaps, to grasp the meaning of their own experience. Was the flight the achievement of a heroic, solitary, unaided individual? Or did the flight represent the triumph of the machine, the success of an industrially organized society? These questions were central to the meaning of Lindbergh's flight. They were also central to the lives of the people who made Lindbergh their hero.

The flight demanded attention in its own right, of course, quite apart from whatever significance it might have. Lindbergh's story had all the makings of great drama. Since 1919 there had been a standing prize of $25,000 to be awarded to the first aviator who could cross the Atlantic in either direction between the United States and France in a heavier-than-air craft. In the spring of 1927 there promised to be what the *New York Times* called "the most spectacular race ever held — 3,600 miles over the open sea to Paris." The scene was dominated by veteran pilots. On the European side were the French aces, Nungesser and Coli; on the American side, Commander Richard E. Byrd, in a big tri-motored Fokker monoplane, led a group of contestants. Besides Byrd, who had already flown over the North Pole, there were Commander Davis, flying a ship named in honor of the American Legion which had put up $100,000 to finance his attempt, Clarence Chamberlin, who had already set a world's endurance record of more than fifty-one hours in the air in a Bellanca tri-motored plane, and Captain René Fonck, the French war ace, who had come to America to fly a Sikorsky aircraft. The hero was unheard of and unknown. He was on the West Coast supervising the construction of a single-engined plane to cost only ten thousand dollars.

Then fate played its part. It seemed impossible that Lindbergh could get his plane built and east to New York in time to challenge his better equipped and more famous rivals. But in quick succession a series of disasters cleared his path. On April 16, Commander Byrd's "America" crashed on its test flight, crushing the leg of Floyd Bennett who was one of the crew and injuring Byrd's hand and wrist. On April 24, Clarence Chamberlin cracked up in his Bellanca, not seriously, but enough to delay his plans. Then on April 26, Commander Davis and his co-pilot lost their lives as the "American Legion" crashed on its final test flight. In ten days, accidents had stopped all of Lindbergh's American rivals. Nungesser and Coli, however, took off in their romantically named ship, "The White Bird," from Le Bourget on May 8. The world waited and Lindbergh, still on the West Coast, decided to try to fly the Pacific. But Nungesser and Coli were never seen again. As rumors filled the newspapers, as reports came in that the "White Bird" was seen over Newfoundland, over Boston, over the Atlantic, it soon became apparent that Nungesser and Coli had failed, dropping to their death in some unknown grave. Disaster had touched every ship entered in the trans-Atlantic race.

Now, with the stage cleared, Lindbergh entered. He swooped across the continent in two great strides, landing only at St. Louis. The first leg of his flight established a new distance record but all eyes were on the Atlantic and the feat received little notice. Curiously, the first time Lindbergh appeared in the headlines of the New York papers was Friday, the thirteenth. By this time Byrd and Chamberlin were ready once again but the weather had closed in and kept all planes on the ground. Then, after a week of fretful waiting, on the night of May 19, on the way into New York to see "Rio Rita," Lindbergh received a report that the weather was breaking over the ocean. He hurried back to Roosevelt Field to haul his plane out onto a wet, dripping runway. After mechanics painfully loaded the plane's gas by hand, the wind shifted, as fate played its last trick. A muddy runway and an adverse wind. Whatever the elements, whatever the fates, the decisive act is the hero's, and Lindbergh made his choice. Providing a chorus to the action, the *Herald Tribune* reported that Lindbergh lifted the overloaded plane into the sky "by his indomitable will alone."

The parabola of the action was as clean as the arc of Lindbergh's flight. The drama should have ended with the landing of "The Spirit of St. Louis" at Le Bourget. That is where Lindbergh wanted it to end. In "WE," written immediately after the flight, and in *The Spirit of St. Louis*, written twenty-six years later, Lindbergh chose to end his accounts there. But the flight turned out to be only the first act in the part Lindbergh was to play.

Lindbergh was so innocent of his future that on his flight he carried letters of introduction. The hysterical response, first of the French and then of his own countrymen, had been no part of his careful plans. In "WE," after Lindbergh's narrative of the flight, the publisher wrote: "When Lindbergh came to tell the story of his welcome at Paris, London, Brussels, Washington, New York, and St. Louis he found himself up against a tougher problem than flying the Atlantic." So another writer completed the account in the third person. He suggested that "the reason Lindbergh's story is different is that when his plane came to a halt on Le Bourget field that black night in Paris, Lindbergh the man kept on going. The phenomenon of Lindbergh took its start with his flight across the ocean; but in its entirety it was almost as distinct from that flight as though he had never flown at all."

Lindbergh's private life ended with his flight to Paris. The drama was no longer his, it was the public's. "The outburst of unanimous acclaim was at once personal and symbolic," said the *American Review of Reviews*. From the moment of success there were two Lindberghs, the private Lindbergh and the public Lindbergh. The latter was the construction of the imagination of Lindbergh's time, fastened on to an unwilling person. The tragedy of Lindbergh's career is that he could never accept the role assigned him. He always believed he might keep his two lives separate. But from the moment he landed at Le Bourget, Lindbergh became, as the *New Republic* noted, "*ours*. . . . He is no longer permitted to be himself. He is US personified. He is the United States." Ambassador Herrick introduced Lindbergh to the French, saying, "This young man from out of the West brings you better than anything else the spirit of America," and wired to President Coolidge, "Had we searched all America we could not have found a better type than young Lindbergh to represent the spirit and high purpose of our people." This was Lindbergh's fate, to be a type. A writer in the *North American Review* felt that Lindbergh represented "the dominant American character," he "images the best" about the United States. And an ecstatic female in the *American Magazine*, who began by saying that Lindbergh "is a sort of symbol. . . . He is the dream that is in our hearts," concluded that the American public responded so wildly to Lindbergh because of "the thrill of possessing, in him, our dream of what *we* really and truly want to be." The act of possession was so complete that articles since have attempted to discover the "real" Lindbergh, that enigmatic and taciturn figure behind the public mask. But it is no less difficult to discern the features of the public Lindbergh, that symbolic figure who presented to the imagination of his time all the yearnings and buried desires of its dream for itself.

Lindbergh's flight came at the end of a decade marked by social and political corruption and by a sense of moral loss. The heady idealism of the First World War had been succeeded by a deep cynicism as to the war's real purpose. The naïve belief that virtue could be legislated was violated by the vast discrepancy between the law and the social habits of prohibition. A philosophy of relativism had become the uneasy rationale of a nation which had formerly believed in moral absolutes. The newspapers agreed that Lindbergh's chief worth was his spiritual and moral value. His story was held to be "in striking contrast with the sordid unhallowed themes that have for months steeped the imaginations and thinking of the people." Or, as another had it, "there is good reason why people should hail Lindbergh and give him honor. He stands out in a grubby world as an inspiration."

Lindbergh gave the American people a glimpse of what they liked to think themselves to be at a time when they feared they had deserted their own vision of themselves. The grubbiness of the twenties had a good deal to do with the shining quality of Lindbergh's success, especially when one remembers that Lindbergh's flight was not as unexampled as our national memory would have it. The Atlantic was not unconquered when Lindbergh flew. A British dirigible had twice crossed the Atlantic before 1919 and on May 8 of that year three naval seaplanes left Rockaway, New York, and one, the NC–4 manned by a crew of five, got through to Plymouth, England. A month later, Captain John Alcock, an Englishman, with Arthur W. Browne, an American, flew the first heavier-than-air land plane across the Atlantic nonstop, from Newfoundland to Ireland, to win twice the money Lindbergh did, a prize of $50,000 offered by the London *Daily Mail*. Alcock's and Browne's misfortune was to land in a soft and somnolent Irish peat bog instead of before the cheering thousands of London or Paris. Or perhaps they should have flown in 1927.

The wild medley of public acclaim and the homeric strivings of editors make one realize that the response to Lindbergh involved a mass ritual in which America celebrated itself more than it celebrated Lindbergh. Lindbergh's flight was the occasion of a public act of regeneration in which the nation momentarily rededicated itself to something, the loss of which was keenly felt. It was said again and again that "Lindy" taught America "to lift its eyes up to Heaven." Heywood Broun, in his column in the *New York World*, wrote that this "tall young man raised up and let us see the potentialities of the human spirit." Broun felt that the flight proved that, though "we are small and fragile," it "isn't true that there is no health in us." Lindbergh's flight provided the moment, but the meaning of the flight is to be found in the deep and pervasive need for renewal which the flight brought to the surface of public feeling. When Lindbergh appeared at the nation's capital, the *Washington Post* observed, "He was given that frenzied acclaim which comes from the depths of the people." In New York, where 4,000,000 people saw him, a reporter wrote that the dense and vociferous crowds were swept, as Lindbergh passed, "with an emotion tense and inflammable." The *Literary Digest* suggested that the answer to the hero-worship of Lindbergh would "throw an interesting light on the psychology of our times and of the American people."

The *Nation* noted about Lindbergh that "there was something lyric as well as heroic about the apparition of this young Lochinvar who suddenly came out of the West and who flew all unarmed and all alone. It is the kind of stuff which the ancient Greeks would have worked into a myth and the medieval Scots into a border ballad. . . . But what we have in the case of

Lindbergh is an actual, an heroic and an exhaustively exposed experience which exists by suggestion in the form of poetry." The *Nation* quickly qualified its statement by observing that reporters were as far as possible from being poets and concluded that the discrepancy between the fact and the celebration of it was not poetry, perhaps, but "magic on a vast scale." Yet the *Nation* might have clung to its insight that the public meaning of Lindbergh's flight was somehow poetic. The vast publicity about Lindbergh corresponds in one vital particular with the poetic vision. Poetry, said William Butler Yeats, contains opposites; so did Lindbergh. Lindbergh did not mean one thing, he meant many things. The image of itself which America contemplated in the public person of Lindbergh was full of conflict; it was, in a word, dramatic.

To heighten the drama, Lindbergh did it alone. He was the "lone eagle" and a full exploration of that fact takes one deep into the emotional meaning of his success. Not only the *Nation* found Sir Walter Scott's lines on Lochinvar appropriate: "he rode all unarmed and he rode all alone." Newspapers and magazines were deluged with amateur poems that vindicated one rhymester's wry comment, "Go conquer the perils / That lurk in the skies — / And you'll get bum poems / Right up to your eyes." The *New York Times*, that alone received more than two hundred poems, observed in trying to summarize the poetic deluge that "the fact that he flew alone made the strongest impression." Another favorite tribute was Kipling's "The Winners," with its refrain, "He travels the fastest who travels alone." The others who had conquered the Atlantic and those like Byrd and Chamberlin who were trying at the same time were not traveling alone and they hardly rode unarmed. Other than Lindbergh, all the contestants in the trans-Atlantic race had unlimited backing, access to the best planes, and all were working in teams, carrying at least one co-pilot to share the long burden of flying the plane. So a writer in the New York *Sun*, in a poem called "The Flying Fool," a nickname that Lindbergh despised, celebrated Lindbergh's flight: ". . . no kingly plane for him; / No endless data, comrades, moneyed chums; / No boards, no councils, no directors grim — / He plans ALONE . . . and takes luck as it comes."

Upon second thought, it must seem strange that the long distance flight of an airplane, the achievement of a highly advanced and organized technology, should be the occasion for hymns of praise to the solitary unaided man. Yet the National Geographic Society, when it presented a medal to Lindbergh, wrote on the presentation scroll, "Courage, when it goes alone, has ever caught men's imagination," and compared Lindbergh to Robinson Crusoe and the trailmakers in our own West. But Lindbergh and Robinson Crusoe, the one in his helmet and fur-lined flying coat and the other in his wild goatskin, do not easily co-exist. Even if Robinson Crusoe did have a tidy capital investment in the form of a well-stocked shipwreck, he still did not have a ten thousand dollar machine under him.

Lindbergh, in nearly every remark about his flight and in his own writings about it, resisted the tendency to exploit the flight as the achievement of an individual. He never said "I," he always said "We." The plane was not to go unrecognized. Nevertheless, there persisted a tendency to seize upon the flight as a way of celebrating the self-sufficient individual, so that among many others an Ohio newspaper could describe Lindbergh as this "self-contained, self-reliant, courageous young man [who] ranks among the great pioneers of history." The strategy here was a common one, to make Lindbergh a "pioneer" and thus to link him with a long and vital tradition of individualism in the American experience. Colonel Theodore Roosevelt, himself the son of a famous exponent of self-reliance, said to reporters at his home in Oyster Bay that "Captain Lindbergh personifies the daring of youth. Daniel Boone, David Crocket [sic], and men of that type played a lone hand and made America. Lindbergh is their lineal descendant." In *Outlook* magazine, immediately below an enthusiastic endorsement of Lindbergh's own remarks on the importance of his machine and his scientific instruments, there was the statement, "Charles Lindbergh is the heir of all that we like to think is best in America. He is of the stuff out of which have been made the pioneers that opened up the wilderness, first on the Atlantic coast, and then in our great West. His are the qualities which we, as a people, must nourish." It is in this mood that one suspects it was important that Lindbergh came out of the West and rode all alone.

Another common metaphor in the attempt to place Lindbergh's exploit was to say that he had opened a new "frontier." To speak of the air as a "frontier" was to invoke an interpretation of the meaning of American history which had sources deep in American experience, but the frontier of the airplane is hardly the frontier of the trailmakers of the old West. Rather than an escape into the self-sufficient simplicity of the American past, the machine which made Lindbergh's flight possible represented an advance into a complex industrial present. The difficulty lay in using an instance of modern life to celebrate the virtues of the past, to use an extreme development of an urban industrial society to insist upon the significance of the frontier in American life.

A little more than a month after Lindbergh's flight, Joseph K. Hart in *Survey* magazine reached back to Walt Whitman's poem for the title of an article on Lindbergh: "O Pioneer." A school had made Lindbergh an honorary alumnus but Hart protested there was little available evidence "that he was educated in *schools*." "We must look elsewhere for our explanation," Hart wrote and he looked to the experience of Lindbergh's youth when "everything that he ever did . . . he did by himself. He lived more to himself than most boys." And, of course, Lindbergh lived to himself in the only place conceivably possible, in the world of nature, on a Minnesota farm. "There he developed in the companionship of woods and fields, animals and machines, his audaciously natural and simple personality." The word, "machines," jars as it intrudes into Hart's idyllic pastoral landscape and betrays Hart's difficulty in relating the setting of nature upon which he wishes to insist with the fact that its product spent his whole life tinkering with machines, from motorcycles to airplanes. But except for that one word, Hart proceeds in uncritical nostalgia to show that "a lone trip across the Atlantic was not impossible for a boy who had grown up in the solitude of the woods and waters." If Lindbergh was "clear-headed, naif, untrained in the ways of cities," it was because he had "that 'natural simplicity' which Fenimore Cooper used to attribute to the pioneer hero of his Leatherstocking Tales." Hart rejected the notion that any student "bent to all the conformities" of formal training could have done what Lindbergh did. "Must we not admit," he asked, "that this pioneering urge remained to this audacious youth because he had never submitted completely to the repressions of the world and its jealous institutions?"

Only those who insist on reason will find it strange that Hart should use the industrial achievement of the airplane to reject the urban, institutionalized world of industrialism. Hart was dealing with something other than reason; he was dealing with the emotion evoked by Lindbergh's solitude. He recognized that people wished to call Lindbergh a "genius" because that "would release him from the ordinary rules of existence." That way, "we could rejoice with him in his triumph, and then go back to the contracted routines of our institutional ways [because] ninety-nine percent of us must be content to be shaped and moulded by the routine ways and forms of the world to the routine tasks of life." It is in the word, "must," that the pathos of this interpretation of the phenomenon of Lindbergh lies. The world had changed from the open society of the pioneer to the close-knit, interdependent world of a modern machine-oriented civilization. The institutions of a highly corporate industrial society existed as a constant reproach to a people who liked to believe that the meaning of its experience was embodied in the formless, independent life of the frontier. Like Thomas Jefferson who identified American virtue with nature and saw the city as a "great sore" on the public body, Hart concluded that "certainly, in the response that the world — especially the world of great cities — has made to the performance of this mid-western boy, we can read of the homesickness of the human soul, immured in city canyons and routine tasks, for the freer world of youth, for the open spaces of the pioneer, for the joy of battling with nature and clean storms once more on the frontiers of the earth."

The social actuality which made the adulation of Lindbergh possible had its own irony for the notion that America's strength lay in its simple uncomplicated beginnings. For the public response to Lindbergh to have reached the proportions it did, the world had by necessity to be the intricately developed world of modern mass communications. But more than irony was involved. Ultimately, the emotion attached to Lindbergh's flight involved no less than a whole theory about American history. By singling out the fact that Lindbergh rode alone, and by naming him a pioneer of the frontier, the public projected its sense that the source of America's strength lay somewhere in the past and that Lindbergh somehow meant that America must look backward in time to rediscover some lost virtue. The mood was nostalgic and American history was read as a decline, a decline measured in terms of America's advance into an urban, institutionalized way of life which made solitary achievement increasingly beyond the reach of ninety-nine per cent of the people. Because Lindbergh's ancestors were Norse, it was easy to call him a "Viking" and extend the emotion far into the past when all frontiers were open. He became the "Columbus" of another new world to conquer as well as the "Lochinvar" who rode all alone. But there was always the brute, irreducible fact that Lindbergh's exploit was a victory of the machine over the barriers of nature. If the only response to Lindbergh had been a retreat to the past, we would be involved with a mass cultural neurosis, the inability of America to accept reality, the reality of the world in which it lived. But there was another aspect, one in which the public celebrated the machine and the highly organized society of which it was a product. The response to Lindbergh reveals that the American people were deeply torn between conflicting interpretations of their own experience. By calling Lindbergh a pioneer, the people could read into American history the necessity of turning back to the frontier past. Yet the people could also read American history in terms of progress into the industrial future. They could do this by emphasizing the machine which was involved in Lindbergh's flight.

Lindbergh came back from Europe in an American man-of-war, the cruiser *Memphis*. It seems he had contemplated flying on, around the whole world perhaps, but less adventurous heads prevailed and dictated a surer mode of travel for so valuable a piece of public property. The *New Republic* protested against bringing America's hero of romance home in a warship. If he had returned on a great liner, that would have been one thing. "One's first trip on an ocean-liner is a great adventure — the novelty of it, the many people of all kinds and conditions, floating for a week in a tiny compact world of their own." But to return on the *Memphis*, "to be put on a gray battleship with a collection of people all of the same stripe, in a kind of ship that has as much relation to the life of the sea as a Ford factory has! We might as well have put him in a pneumatic tube and shot him across the Atlantic." The interesting thing about the *New Republic*'s protest against the unromantic, regimented life of a battleship is that the image it found appropriate was the Ford assembly line. It was this reaction against the discipline of a mechanized society that probably led to the nostalgic image of Lindbergh as a remnant of a past when romance was possible for the individual, when life held novelty and society was variegated rather than uniform. But what the Ford Assembly Line represents, a society committed to the path of full mechanization, was what lay behind Lindbergh's romantic success. A long piece in the Sunday *New York Times,* "Lindbergh Symbolizes the Genius of America," reminded its readers of the too obvious fact that "without an airplane he could not have flown at all." Lindbergh "is, indeed, the Icarus of the twentieth century; not himself an inventor of his own wings, but a son of that omnipotent Daedalus whose ingenuity has created the modern world." The point was that modern America was the creation of modern industry. Lindbergh "reveres his 'ship' as a noble expression of mechanical wisdom. . . . Yet in this reverence . . . Lindbergh is not an exception. What he means by the Spirit of St. Louis is really the spirit of America. The mechanical genius, which is discerned in Henry Ford as well as in Charles A. Lindbergh, is in the very atmosphere of [the] country." In contrast to a sentiment that feared the enforced discipline of the machine there existed an attitude of reverence for its power.

Lindbergh led the way in the celebration of the machine, not only implicitly by including his plane when he said "we," but by direct statement. In Paris he told newspapermen, "You fellows have not said enough about that wonderful motor." Rarely have two more taciturn figures confronted one another than when Lindbergh returned to Washington and Calvin Coolidge pinned the Distinguished Flying Cross on him, but in his brief remarks Coolidge found room to express his particular delight that Lindbergh should have given equal credit to the airplane. "For we are proud," said the President, "that in every particular this silent partner represented American genius and industry. I am told that more than 100 separate companies furnished materials, parts or service in its construction."

The flight was not the heroic lone success of a single daring individual, but the climax of the co-operative effort of an elaborately interlocked technology. The day after Coolidge's speech, Lindbergh said at another ceremony in Washington that the honor should "not go to the pilot alone but to American science and genius which had given years of study to the advancement of aeronautics." "Some things," he said, "should be taken into due consideration in connection with our flight that have not heretofore been given due weight. That is just what made this flight possible. It was not the act of a single pilot. It was the culmination of twenty years of aeronautical research and the assembling together of all that was practicable and best in American aviation." "The flight," concluded Lindbergh, "represented American industry."

The worship of the machine which was embodied in the public's response to Lindbergh exalted those very aspects which were denigrated in the celebration of the flight as the work of a heroic individual. Organization and careful method were what lay behind the flight, not individual self-sufficiency and daring romance. One magazine hailed the flight as a "triumph of mechanical engineering." "It is not to be forgotten that this era is the work not so much of brave aviators as of engineers, who have through patient and protracted effort been steadily improving the construction of airplanes."

The lesson to be learned from Lindbergh's flight, thought a writer in the *Independent*, "is that the splendid human and material aspects of America need to be organized for the ordinary, matter of fact service of society." The machine meant organization, the careful rationalization of activity of a Ford assembly line, it meant planning, and, if it meant the loss of spontaneous individual action, it meant the material betterment of society. Lindbergh meant not a retreat to the free life of the frontier past but an emergence into the time when "the machine began to take first place in the public mind — the machine and the organization that made its operation possible on a large scale." A poet on this side of the matter wrote, "All day I felt the pull / Of the steel miracle." The machine was not a devilish engine which would enthrall mankind, it was the instrument which would lead to a new paradise. But the direction of history implicit in the machine was toward the future, not the past; the meaning of history was progress, not decline, and America should not lose faith in the future betterment of society. An address by a Harvard professor, picked up by the *Magazine of Business*, made all this explicit. "We commonly take Social Progress for granted," said Edwin F. Gay, "but the doctrine of Social Progress is one of the great revolutionary ideas which have powerfully affected our modern world." There was a danger, however, that the idea "may be in danger of becoming a commonplace or a butt of criticism." The speaker recognized why this might be. America was "worn and disillusioned after the Great War." Logically, contentment should have gone with so optimistic a creed, yet the American people were losing faith. So Lindbergh filled an emotional need even where a need should have been lacking. "He has come like a shining vision to revive the hope of mankind." The high ideals of faith in progress "had almost come to seem like hollow words to us — but now here he is, emblematic of heroes yet to inhabit this world. Our belief in Social Progress is justified symbolically in him."

It is a long flight from New York to Paris; it is a still longer flight from the fact of Lindbergh's achievement to the burden imposed upon it by the imagination of his time. But it is in that further flight that lies the full meaning of Lindbergh. His role was finally a double one. His flight provided an opportunity for the people to project their own emotions into his act and their emotions involved finally two attitudes toward the meaning of their own experience. One view had it that America represented a brief escape from the course of history, an emergence into a new and open world with the self-sufficient individual at its center. The other said that America represented a stage in historical evolution and that its fulfillment lay in the development of society. For one, the meaning of America lay in the past; for the other in the future. For one, the American ideal was an escape from institutions, from the forms of society, and from limitations put upon the free individual; for the other, the American ideal was the elaboration of the complex institutions which made modern society possible, an acceptance of the discipline of the machine, and the achievement of the individual within a context of which he was only a part. The two views were contradictory but both were possible and both were present in the public's reaction to Lindbergh's flight.

The Sunday newspapers announced that Lindbergh had reached Paris and in the very issue whose front pages were covered with Lindbergh's story the magazine section of the *New York Times* featured an article by the British philosopher, Bertrand Russell. The magazine had, of course, been made up too far in advance to take advantage of the news about Lindbergh. Yet, in a prophetic way, Russell's article was about Lindbergh. Russell hailed the rise to power of the United States because he felt that in the "new life that is America's" in the twentieth century "the new outlook appropriate to machinery [would] become more completely dominant than in the old world." Russell sensed that some might be unwilling to accept the machine, but "whether we like this new outlook or not," he wrote, "is of little importance." Why one might not was obvious. A society built on the machine, said Russell, meant "the diminution in the value and independence of the individual. Great enterprises tend more and more to be collective, and in an industrialized world the interference of the community with the individual must be more intense." Russell realized that while the cooperative effort involved in machine technology makes man collectively more lordly, it makes the individual more submissive. "I do not see how it is to be avoided," he concluded.

People are not philosophers. They did not see how conflict between a machine society and the free individual was to be avoided either. But neither were they ready to accept the philosopher's statement of the problem. In Lindbergh, the people celebrated both the self-sufficient individual and the machine. Americans still celebrate both. We cherish the individualism of the American creed at the same time that we worship the machine which increasingly enforces collectivized behavior. Whether we can have both, the freedom of the individual and the power of an organized society, is a question that still haunts our minds. To resolve the conflict that is present in America's celebration of Lindbergh in 1927 is still the task of America.

16

HERBERT HOOVER
AND THE GREAT DEPRESSION

Herbert Hoover's presidency has not been an easy one either for his contemporaries or for historians to evaluate. The difficulty, perhaps, has stemmed most directly from the dualism that pervaded both the actions and the rhetoric of the president. Hoover himself summed up the dualism concisely during the campaign of 1932:

> We have not feared boldly to adopt unprecedented measures to meet the unprecedented violence of the storm. But because we have kept ever before us these eternal principles of our nation, the American Government in its ideals is the same as it was when the people gave the Presidency into my trust.

Hoover was trying to convince his country, and himself, that he had successfully managed to break with tradition and maintain the eternal principles at the same time, and certainly many of his actions were shaped by his attempt to achieve both of these aims. Insofar as Hoover was given credit for anything, however, it was only for maintaining tradition, not for departing from it. "The crash came in October, 1929," Franklin Roosevelt charged during the 1932 campaign. "The President had at his disposal all the instrumentalities of government. . . . He did absolutely nothing." This interpretation of the Hoover presidency prevailed throughout the Great Depression and for many years thereafter.

In 1935, Walter Lippmann registered an important dissent from the popular image of Hoover in his article, "The Permanent New Deal" [*The Yale Review*, 24 (June 1935), 649–67]. If there had been anything in the nature of a sharp break with the past, Lippmann argued, that break came not with the inauguration of Roosevelt but during the autumn of 1929 when under Hoover "the national government undertook to make the whole economic order operate prosperously." Hoover, not his successor, first

> abandoned the principles of *laissez faire* in relation to the business cycle, established the conviction that prosperity and depression can be publicly controlled by political action, and drove out of the public consciousness the old idea that depressions must be overcome by private adjustment.

The importance of Lippmann's analysis lay in the evidence he marshalled to show that Hoover was never the totally incapable, do-nothing president of popular legend. Certainly, Lippmann was correct in arguing that Hoover was never an apostle of a simple-minded *laissez faire* policy. Unfortunately, in emphasizing one side of Hoover's dualism – the willingness to break with precedent – Lippmann failed to deal with the other – the need to maintain tradition. If Hoover was willing to countenance vigorous government initiative, he was equally insistent upon establishing clear and rigid demarcations between the proper spheres for federal, state, local, and individual (including corporate) action. Though the crisis of 1929 and after was to force him to violate his own precepts more than once, he was remarkably successful in adhering to them. In portraying Hoover as the New Deal's precursor, Lippmann ignored Hoover's reluctance to embark upon a federal relief program, his insistence upon self-liquidating public works, his refusal to have the government dispense direct aid to individuals, his unwillingness to depart from the voluntaristic principle in his agricultural, industrial, and labor programs, and the difficulty he had in admitting the seriousness of the situation.

Almost thirty years after Lippmann's article appeared, *The Yale Review* published the following essay by Carl Degler, Professor of History at Stanford University. The article, in arguing that Hoover was "a transitional figure in the development of the government as an active force in the economy in times of depression," comes remarkably close to Lippmann's. Degler, however, confronts Hoover's failures more directly. Rexford Guy Tugwell, one of the original members of Roosevelt's Brain Trust, has written that during the 1932 presidential contest, "it dawned on many of us, to whom it had simply not occurred before, that Hoover was not an engineer at all in any factual sense, but a man of principle." This proves to be Degler's point of departure as well. By comparing Hoover's actions with his well-enunciated principles, Degler attempts to explain both his achievements and his failures. Whether or not Degler is correct in arguing that "probably no government program then thought permissible could have been any more successful" than Hoover's, or in implying that without Hoover's transitional policies Roosevelt could not have moved as quickly or decisively as he did in the opening months of his administration, his essay is an important corrective to the traditional conception of Hoover and deserves careful consideration.

In *The American Political Tradition** (1948), Richard Hofstadter also analyzes Hoover's actions in the context of his beliefs but emerges with a much more negative picture of Hoover as an ideologue – a "Utopian Capitalist" who was paralyzed by his own philosophy. The best accounts of Hoover's presidency are Jordan A. Schwarz, *The Interregnum of Despair: Hoover, Congress, and the Depression* (1970); Albert Romasco, *The Poverty of Abundance: Hoover, the Nation, the Depression** (1965); and Harris G. Warren, *Herbert Hoover and the Great Depression** (1959). Two of Hoover's most important depression agencies are discussed in Gerald D. Nash, "Herbert Hoover and the Origins of the Reconstruction Finance

Corporation," *Mississippi Valley Historical Review*, 46 (December 1959), 455–68, and James H. Shideler, "Herbert Hoover and the Federal Farm Board Project," *ibid.*, 42 (March 1956), 710–29. For an interesting comparison of Hoover and Roosevelt, see R. G. Tugwell, "The Protagonists: Roosevelt and Hoover," *The Antioch Review*, 13 (December 1953), 419–39. The best statement of Hoover's philosophy is in his *American Individualism* (1922). For Hoover's own defense of his actions as president, see his *Memoirs* (3 volumes, 1951–52).

The Ordeal of Herbert Hoover

CARL N. DEGLER

In 1958 Herbert Hoover published a book about his old chief entitled *The Ordeal of Woodrow Wilson*. Wilson's struggle for the League was short and his part in it has gained lustre with passing years. Not so with the ordeal of Herbert Hoover. The Great Depression was considerably longer and his reputation has never been free from the memory of that ordeal. Today, in fact, there are two Hoovers. The first is the living man, the former President who has unstintingly and very capably served Democratic and Republican Administrations alike. He is the Hoover of nation-wide birthday celebrations, of rhapsodic editorials, of admiring Republican national conventions. That conception bears almost no relation to the second, the historical Hoover. In the history books his Administration is usually depicted as cold-hearted, when not pictured as totally devoid of heart, inept, or actionless in the face of the Great Depression. Simply because of the wide gulf between the two Hoovers it is time to try to answer the question William Allen White posed over thirty years ago. Writing an evaluation of Hoover's Administration in the *Saturday Evening Post* of March 4, 1933, White closed his piece with the following words: "So history stands hesitant waiting for time to tell whether Herbert Hoover . . . by pointing the way to social recovery . . . is the first of the new Presidents . . . or whether . . . he is the last of the old."

The notion of two Hoovers should never have grown up; his life and views were too consistent for that. During Hoover's tenure of office, Theodore Joslin, his press secretary, undertook to examine closely all the President's utterances and writings of the preceding ten or eleven years. "In all of those

Reprinted by permission of *The Yale Review* from *The Yale Review*, 52, No. 4 (Summer 1963). Copyright, 1963, by Yale University.

million-odd words, dealing with every important subject," Joslin reported in 1934, "the number of times he reversed himself or modified an important position could be counted on the fingers of one hand." And so it has remained even after March 4, 1933.

Nor were those principles, to which Hoover held so consistently, simply conservative ones, as has so often been assumed. In 1920, for example, when Hoover's political career began, he was the darling of the progressives who still clustered about the figure of the fallen Wilson. College and university faculties were calling upon Hoover to run for president that year — on either ticket. Indeed, his silence as to which party he belonged to, for a time caused his name to figure as prominently in Democratic primaries as in Republican. For example, he received the most votes by far in the Michigan Democratic primary that year. That year, too, Franklin Roosevelt, who was also a member of Woodrow Wilson's Administration, wrote Josephus Daniels that Herbert Hoover "is certainly a wonder, and I wish we could make him President of the United States. There could not be a better one." (Nor did Roosevelt's enthusiasm cool until much later. In 1928 he refused to write an article against Hoover's candidacy because Hoover was "an old personal friend.")

Hoover's principles were distinctly and publicly progressive. In 1920, for example, he defended the principle of collective bargaining and the right to strike — two very unpopular principles at that date — before a frosty Chamber of Commerce in Boston. As Secretary of Commerce in the Harding Administration he opposed the sweeping federal injunction against the railroad strikers and worked with Harding to have the steel industry abandon the twelve-hour day. In his book of guiding principles, *American Individualism*, which he published in 1922, he was careful to distinguish his views from laissez-faire capitalism. The American way, he insisted, "is not capitalism, or socialism, or syndicalism, nor a cross breed of them." It did include, though, government regulation in order to preserve equality of opportunity and individual rights. "This regulation is itself," he pointed out, "proof that we have gone a long way toward the abandonment of the 'capitalism' of Adam Smith. . . ." While Secretary of Commerce in the 1920's he instituted much needed regulations for the burgeoning radio and airplane industries. It was Herbert Hoover who said in 1922 at the first conference on radio that "the ether is a public medium and its use must be for the public benefit. The use of radio channels is justified only if there is public benefit. The dominant element of consideration in the radio field is, and always will be, the great body of the listening public, millions in number, country-wide in distribution." In the same address, he said, "It is inconceivable that we should allow so great a possibility for service to be drowned in advertising chatter." In 1928 he was recommending that a three billion dollar reserve of public works be built up to serve as an economic stabilizer in times of recession.

In short, though he served both Harding and Coolidge, Herbert Hoover was not of their stripe. As he himself said later in his memoirs, "Mr. Coolidge was a real conservative, probably the equal of Benjamin Harrison. . . . He was a fundamentalist in religion, in the economic and social order, and in fishing." (The last because Coolidge, the fishing tyro, used worms for bait.) Moreover, unlike Coolidge, Hoover did not publicly ignore the scandals that rocked the Harding Administration. In June 1931, while dedicating the Harding Memorial at Marion, Ohio, Hoover went out of his way to speak of the tragedy of Warren Harding and of the enormity of the betrayal of a public trust by Harding's friends.

Hoover's record as president contains a number of truly progressive achievements. Although he cannot take credit for initiating the Norris-La Guardia Act of 1932, the fact remains that one of the most important pro-labor acts in the whole history of American labor was signed by Herbert Hoover. Like other progressives, he sponsored legislation for conservation like the giant Boulder Dam project and the St. Lawrence Seaway.

But perhaps the most striking example of Hoover's willingness to recognize the new role of government in dealing with the complexities of an industrial economy was his breaking precedent to grapple directly with the Depression. From the outset Hoover rejected the advice of his Secretary of the Treasury, Andrew Mellon, who, as Hoover himself said, was a country-banker of narrow social vision. Mellon believed the crash should be permitted to run its course unmolested. His simple formula in a depression, as he told Hoover, was "Liquidate labor, liquidate stocks, liquidate farms, liquidate real estate." A panic, he told the President, was not so bad. "It will purge the rottenness out of the system. High costs of living and high living will come down. People will work harder, live more moral lives. Values will be adjusted, and enterprising people will pick up the wrecks from less competent people."

In contrast, Hoover's anti-depression action was swift in coming. Within a matter of weeks after the great crash of the stock market at the end of October, Hoover called a meeting of prominent business, labor, and farm leaders to work out plans for preventing the market crash from adversely affecting the rest of the economy. A week later he met for the same purpose with railway presidents. The economic leaders agreed to his plan of holding the line on wages and encouraging industrial expansion. In his annual message to Congress in December 1929, Hoover proudly told of these and other efforts his Administration had made to stem the economic decline. These efforts, he said, "must be vigorously pursued until normal conditions are restored." In January he continued to expand public works on Boulder Dam and on highway construction. By the end of July 1930, the Administration had got underway $800 million in public works, and the President called upon the states and local units of government to follow the national government's example in order to provide as much employment as possible.

The President was well aware of the unprecedented character of his swift anti-depression action. He said as much in his message to Congress in December 1929; he made the same point more explicitly at the Gridiron dinner in April 1930. The country, he said, had avoided the dole and other unsatisfactory devices to meet unemployment by "voluntary cooperation of industry with the Government in maintaining wages against reductions, and the intensification of construction work. Thereby we have inaugurated one of the greatest economic experiments in history on a basis of nation-wide cooperation not charity."

At first Hoover was optimistic about the effects of his program. Several times during the first year he compared the economic decline with that of 1921–22, usually with the observation that the earlier one was the more difficult. As he told the Chamber of Commerce in May 1930, the amount of public works contracted for was already three times the amount in the corresponding period of the previous "great depression."

Yet his optimism did not keep him from action. One thing he emphasized was the necessity of learning from this Depression about the prevention of future ones. He advocated better statistical measures and reform of the banking structure to prevent the drain of credit from productive to speculative enterprise, such as had led to the stock market boom and crash. Moreover, although he emphasized from the beginning that the Depression was "worldwide" and that its "causes and its effects lie only partly in the United States," he did not use this as an excuse for inactivity. There was no need simply to wait for the rest of the world to recover, he said. "We can make a very large degree of recovery independently of what may happen elsewhere." In October 1930 he told the American Bankers Association that depressions were not simply to be borne uncomplainingly. "The economic fatalist believes that these crises are inevitable and bound to be recurrent. I would remind these pessimists that exactly the same thing was once said of typhoid, cholera, and smallpox." But instead of being pessimistic, medical science went to work and conquered those diseases. "That should be our attitude toward these economic pestilences. They are not dispensations of Providence. I am confident in the faith that their control, so far as the cause lies within our own boundaries, is within the genius of modern business."

Hoover also told the bankers that he could not condone the argument which had been reported from some of them that the people would have to accept a lower standard of living in order to get through the Depression. Such a suggestion, he said, could not be countenanced either on idealistic or on practical grounds. To accept it would mean a "retreat into perpetual unemployment and the acceptance of a cesspool of poverty for some large part of our people." Several times during the Depression Hoover made it clear that the government had a responsibility to employ as many as possible as its contribution to the mitigation of the unemployment which was growing alarmingly.

The failure of the economy to respond to treatment and the loss of many Republican seats in the elections of 1930 caused Hoover for a while to place new emphasis upon the foreign sources of the Depression. At the end of 1930 he told the Congress that the "major forces of the depression now lie outside of the United States." In fact, though, the real collapse of the European economy was still almost six months away. Hoover was most fearful that the growing Congressional demands for new expenditures would throw the budget out of balance. His concern about the budget and his hostility toward the Congress were both measured in his tactless remark at a press conference in May 1931 that "I know of nothing that would so disturb the healing process now undoubtedly going on in the economic situation" as a special session of Congress. "We cannot legislate ourselves out of a world economic depression; we can and will work ourselves out."

The last sentence, because it was obviously too sweeping to be accurate, was to plague him for years. More important, he quite clearly did not believe it himself, since he later advocated legislation for just the purpose he said it could not serve. In the very next month, for example, he explained at some length to a group of Republican editors just how much the Administration had been doing to extricate the country from the Depression. "For the first time in history the Federal Government has taken an extensive and positive part in mitigating the effects of depression and expediting recovery. I have conceived that if we would preserve our democracy this leadership must take the part not of attempted dictatorship but of organizing cooperation in the constructive forces of the community and of stimulating every element of initiative and self-reliance in the country. There is no sudden stroke of either governmental or private action which can dissolve these world difficulties; patient, constructive action in a multitude of directions is the strategy of success. This battle is upon a thousand fronts." Unlike previous administrations, he continued, his had expanded, instead of curtailing, public works during a depression. Public works expenditures, both by the federal and state governments, he said, continued to increase. Some two billion dollars were being spent, and a million men were employed on these projects. Aid was also being given to farmers in the drought areas of the South and the Middle West.

That Hoover truly favored action over patient waiting for the storm to lift was further shown in his elaborate twelve-point program for recovery presented in his annual message in December 1931. Among his recommendations was the Reconstruction Finance Corporation, which would become one of the major agencies of his Administration and of the New Deal for stabilizing banks and aiding recovery. At a press conference the same month he emphasized anew the desirability of domestic action. "The major steps we must take are domestic. The action needed is in the home field and it is urgent. While reestablishment of stability abroad is helpful to us and to the world, and I am convinced that it is in progress, yet we must depend upon ourselves. If we devote ourselves to these urgent domestic questions we can make a very large measure of recovery irrespective of foreign influences." By early February 1932 the Reconstruction Finance Corporation was in operation. That same month he persuaded the Congress to enact the Glass-Steagall banking bill, which increased the bases for Federal Reserve bank reserves and thus expanded credit and conserved gold. The purpose of the RFC was to shore up failing banks and other financial institutions caught in runs upon their deposits. With the permission of the Interstate Commerce Commission, the RFC could also extend financial aid to railroads.

Beyond these operations, though, the President would not let the lending agency go. Especially did he resist federal aid to the unemployed, although the demands for it were growing monthly. He even opposed Congressional appropriations to the Red Cross on the ground that they would dry up private sources of relief funds. A dole, he said in 1931, must be avoided at all costs because "the net results of governmental doles are to lower wages toward the bare subsistence level and to endow the slacker." He did urge the citizenry generously to support, as he did himself, private charities, like the Red Cross, which were carrying so much of the burden of unemployment relief. At no time, of course, did Hoover object to helping the unemployed; he was no Social Darwinist arguing for the survival of only the fittest. Again and again, using the most idealistic language, he called upon Americans to extend a hand to those fellow citizens in need. But as much as he publicly and privately deplored the suffering which the economic crisis brought, he feared and deplored even more the effects which would be sure to follow if the federal government provided relief to the unemployed. Nowhere was the rigidity of Hoover's highly trained, agile, and well-stocked intellect more apparent than in this matter. Throughout his years as president, despite the cruelest of sarcastic barbs in the press and from the public platform, he held to his position.

Yet surprising as it may seem today, for a long time the country was with him. This was true even during 1931 and early 1932 when it was becoming increasingly evident that private charities, municipal relief funds, and even the resources of the states were inadequate to meet the costs of providing for ten or eleven million unemployed. Already in August 1931 Governor Franklin Roosevelt had told the New York legislature that unemployment relief "must be extended by government — not as a matter of charity but as a matter of social duty." Yet, as late as February 1932 the country was still following Hoover's view of relief and not Roosevelt's. This was shown by the fate of a bill sponsored by liberal Senators Robert M. La Follette, Jr. of Wisconsin and Edward F. Costigan of Colorado to provide federal money to the states for relief. The bill was defeated by a vote of 48 to 35. Democratic Senators made up some forty percent of the votes which killed the measure.

By May 1932, though, the pressure for some federal assistance in relief matters was building up fast. The National Conference of Social Workers, which in the previous year had refused to endorse the principle of federal relief, now switched to supporting it. More important from Hoover's standpoint was the announcement by Senator Joseph Robinson, the conservative Democratic leader in the Senate, that he was joining the liberals in favoring federal relief. Within two days the President announced, after consultation with Robinson, that the RFC would hereafter lend money to the states if their resources for relief were exhausted. The next day the President defended the extraordinary powers of the RFC as necessitated by the economic emergency. In words which sound in retrospect like those of his successor, he said, "We used such emergency powers to win the war; we can use them to fight the depression, the misery and suffering from which are equally great."

Soon thereafter, though, the President demonstrated that he would not take another step toward putting the federal government into the relief field. Two bills by Democrats which went beyond his limits were successfully vetoed. After Congress had adjourned in July 1932, he issued a nine-point program for economic recovery, but most of the items on it were old and the rest were only recommendations for exploratory conferences. By the summer of 1932, then, the Hoover program for recovery had been completed; his principles would permit him to go no further.

As one reviews the actions which Hoover took it is impossible to describe him as a do-nothing president. He was unquestionably one of the truly activist presidents of our history. But he was an activist within a very rigid framework of ideology. Of all American presidents, Herbert Hoover was probably the most singlemindedly committed to a system of beliefs. His pragmatism was well hidden and what there was of it emerged only after great prodding from events. To a remarkable degree, one can observe in his acts as president those principles of individualism which he set forth so simply in his book ten years before. The very same principle, for example, which prevented his sanctioning federal relief to the unemployed, dictated the tone and content of his veto of the bill to create a government corporation to operate Muscle Shoals. The government, he said, should not compete with private enterprise. Moreover, such a project, by being run by the federal government, abrogated the basic principle that all such enterprises should be "administered by the people upon the ground, responsible to their own communities, directing them solely for the benefit of their communities and not for the purposes of social theories or national politics. Any other course deprives them of liberty." It was this same belief in individual freedom and cooperation which kept him from accepting a governmental system of old age and unemployment insurance. He advocated such measures only when undertaken voluntarily and through private insurance companies.

Even the Reconstruction Finance Corporation, perhaps his most endur-ing anti-depression agency, was created to assist private business, not to sup-plant it. True, it was a credit agency in competition with private enterprise, but it was designed to perform tasks which no private institution dared risk; the competition was therefore minimal if not nonexistent. Moreover, al-though it has been frequently alleged that the RFC lent money to corpora-tions while the Administration denied relief to the unemployed, in Hoover's mind the distinction was crucial and real. The RFC was making loans which would be repaid — and most were — when the banks got back on their feet; it was not making grants. Even when Hoover did permit the RFC to lend money to the states for relief purposes he still insisted that no grants of federal funds be made.

But there was an even more important social justification for agencies like the RFC and the Federal Home Loan Board, which Congress created in July 1932 at the President's request. Hoover recognized as no president had before that the welfare of society was dependent upon business and that government, therefore, must step in. He did this, not because, as some critics said, he favored business over the common people, but because he recog-nized that if the banks failed the economy would collapse, savings would be lost, and jobs destroyed. The RFC and the Federal Home Loan Board, in effect, socialized the losses of financial institutions by using government to spread their obligations through society. Hoover was not prepared, though, to socialize the losses of the unemployed. That step in ameliorat-ing the impact of the Depression was undertaken by the New Deal through the WPA and other relief agencies. In this respect Hoover was a transitional figure in the development of the government as an active force in the econ-omy in times of depression. He was the first to smash the old shibboleth of govenment unconcern and impotence.

Perhaps his long-term role was even greater. In the face of great opposi-tion and much outright hostility, he made a determined and even coura-geous effort to give the business community and voluntary private agencies a chance to show whether they could bring the nation out of a depression. Their failure to do so gave a moral as well as a political impetus to the New Deal. Just as after Munich no one could say the West had not done its ut-most to meet Hitler halfway, so after Hoover's Administration no one could say that government had rushed in before other social or economic agencies had been given a try. That this was so goes a long way toward explaining the remarkable consensus among Americans ever since the 1930's that govern-ment has the prime responsibility for averting or cushioning the effects of a depression.

A second principle which stopped Hoover from permitting the federal government to provide relief was his conviction that the budget must not be unbalanced. As early as February 1930 he warned the Congress against extravagance and told of his own efforts to economize. Economy was essential, he emphasized, in order to avoid increasing taxes. But as decreasing revenues began to fall behind expenditures, Hoover's concern to keep the budget in balance overcame his reluctance to increase taxes. On July 1, 1931 the deficit was almost $500 million — an astronomical figure in those days when the total federal budget was less than $4 billion. In December of that same year Hoover recommended an increase in taxes. When Congress proved dilatory he told a press conference in March 1932 that a balanced budget "is the very keystone of recovery. It must be done." Anything less would undo all the recovery measures. "The Government," he warned, "no more than individual families can continue to expend more than it receives without inviting serious consequences."

Hoover recommended a manufacturers' sales tax as the chief new revenue device, in which suggestion he was joined by the new Democratic Speaker of the House, John Nance Garner of Texas. Garner enjoyed a reputation for being hostile to business and something of a radical in the old Populist tradition, but in the matter of bringing the budget into balance he stood four-square with the President. Congress did not pass the sales tax, but it did pass one of the largest peacetime tax increases in American history.

Today it seems incredible that in a time of economic slump when consumer purchasing power was the principal requirement for recovery, the nation should elect to take money out of the hands of consumers. Yet this was precisely what the bill, recommended and signed by the Republican President and passed by the Democratic House, entailed. In fact, when in the course of the debate the House seemed hesitant about increasing taxes, the Democratic Speaker, John Garner, could not contain his anxiety. Conspicuously forsaking the Speaker's chair, Garner advanced to the well of the House to make an earnest plea for more taxes. At the conclusion of his speech, he asked "every man and every woman in this House who . . . is willing to try to balance the budget to rise in their seats." Almost the whole House, with its majority of Democrats, rose to its feet, to a growing round of applause. When he asked those who did not want to balance the budget to rise, no one did. The overwhelming majority of the newspapers of the country strongly commended the Congress in June 1932 for its efforts to balance the budget through increased taxes.

During the campaign of 1932 the Democrats continued to equal or even outdo Hoover in their slavish adherence to the ideal of a balanced budget. Franklin Roosevelt, for example, unmercifully attacked the Administration for its extravagance and its unbalanced budget, calling the fifty percent increase in expenditures since 1927 "the most reckless and extravagant past that I have been able to discover in the statistical record of any peacetime government anywhere, any time." He promised a cut of 25 percent in the budget if he were elected. Nor was this simply campaign oratory. As Frank

Freidel has observed in his biography, Roosevelt was perfectly sincere in his dismay at the Hoover deficit and he would continue to be regretful about deficits until well after 1933.

From the record, then, it is evident that Democrats were in no better theoretical position to deal with the Depression than Hoover. Leaders of both parties thought of the government as a large household whose accounts must be balanced if national bankruptcy were to be avoided. Neither party could conceive of the central role which government must play in the economy in an industrial society in time of depression. It would take the whole decade of the New Deal and the continuance of the Depression before that fact would be learned by leaders and people alike.

Despite his fixation on the question of the budget, Hoover's conception of the Depression was sophisticated, rational, and coherent; the remedies he suggested were equally so, given his assumptions. In trying to find a way out, Hoover placed most reliance on what modern economists would call the "expectations" of businessmen. If businessmen feel that times are good or at least that they are getting better, they will invest in new plant and equipment, which in turn will employ men and create purchasing power. In substance, the remedies Hoover offered were designed to raise the expectations of businessmen and to maintain purchasing power until the economy picked up again. His first step was securing agreement among businessmen to hold the line on wages in order to keep purchasing power from falling. (And, by and large, as a result of his efforts, wage rates did not fall until the middle of 1931, but employment did, with, unfortunately, the same effect.) A second step in his program was to use government to help out with public work projects and, when private agencies proved inadequate, to provide credit through agencies like the RFC and the Home Loan Board. Finally, as a third arrow in his anti-depression quiver, Hoover sought, through the prestige of his office, to create that sense of confidence and approaching good times which would encourage businessmen to invest. As it turned out, though, he gambled and lost. For with each successive ineffectual statement, the value of his words dropped, until, like the worthless coins of a profligate monarch who debases his own coinage, they were hurled back at his head by a disenchanted press and people.

The Hoover recovery program failed, but probably no government program then thought permissible could have been any more successful. Certainly the New Deal with its more massive injection of government money into the economy succeeded little better. It ended the decade with 9.5 million still unemployed, and industrial production remained below the 1929 level throughout the 1930's except for a brief period in late 1936 and early 1937. On the other hand, most of the countries of Western and Central Europe regained the 1929 level of production by early 1935.

Part of Hoover's ordeal during the Great Depression undoubtedly derived from his personality, which, for a president, was unusual. Indeed, until he became President he had rarely been connected with government other than in an office which was nonpartisan or which he soon made so. Outwardly, at least, he was far removed from the stereotype of the politician; he could not slap a back or utter a guffaw. He appeared shy in public, though stolid was a more accurate description. A bulky man of over 200 pounds, standing almost six feet when he entered the White House, he gave a paradoxical impression of conservative solidity and beaming youth at the same time. His public speech, like his writing, was formal, often stiff, and sometimes bordered on the pedantic. Early in Hoover's Administration, soon after the stock market crash, William Allen White, a Hoover supporter, spotted the new President's weakness. "The President has great capacity to convince intellectuals," he wrote. "He has small capacity to stir people emotionally and through the emotions one gets to the will, not through the intellect." Even Hoover's press secretary recognized that he "experienced the greatest difficulty in interpreting himself and his acts to the public." Indeed, it was characteristic of Hoover that though he found speech writing one of the most laborious of his tasks, he insisted upon writing all his own speeches. The compulsion could be at least enervating, and at worst dangerous to his health. Often he traded sleep for time to work on his speeches and at least once, at St. Paul in the campaign of 1932, he was on the verge of collapse from fatigue. His method of writing was tedious and incredibly time-consuming, involving innumerable drafts, meticulously gone over by himself, only to have still further proofs run off for more rewriting. Yet, after all this effort, his final draft usually was dry, too long, and ponderous.

In view of his poor public image, it is not surprising that for most of his presidency, Hoover's relations with the press were strained when not downright painful. Although he continued the press conferences which Wilson had begun, they were formal affairs with written questions; many reporters were convinced that the President concealed more than he revealed in the meetings. But it was probably Hoover's sensitivity to criticism that worked the real damage. His annual addresses to newspapermen at the Gridiron Club, which, as was customary, mercilessly lampooned his administration, often carried an edge, betraying his sensitivity to the press corps' jibes. Only occasionally did his private wit break through in public. At the Gridiron Club dinner in December 1932, after his defeat for reelection, he puckishly said, "You will expect me to discuss the late election. Well, as nearly as I can learn, we did not have enough votes on our side. During the campaign I remarked that this Administration had been fighting on a thousand fronts; I learned since the campaign that we were fighting on 21 million fronts." (The size of the Democratic vote.) This was one of the rare times that Hoover poked fun at himself in public.

Yet, despite his difficulties as a public figure, in private Hoover was neither phlegmatic nor shy. In fact he was extremely convivial, seeking constant company, whether at the White House or at his retreat on the Rapidan in the Blue Ridge Mountains. His wife told Joslin that the President could not be happy without numbers of people around him. His friends cherished his constant flow of stories and he delighted in his cigars and pipe. He was an outdoor type of man, reveling in fishing and hiking. Although he liked a joke, he rarely laughed out loud, though his friends knew well his soft chuckle. His own brand of humor could be heavy-handed. Thus in January 1931, when addressing the National Automobile Chamber of Commerce, he observed, with a smile, that 3.5 million cars had been sold in the first year of the depression and that consumption of gasoline was up five percent. "This certainly means," he twitted, "that we have been cheerful in the use of automobiles; I do not assume they are being used for transportation to the poorhouse. While I am aware that many people are using the old automobile a little longer it is obvious that they are still using it and it is being worn out. Altogether the future for the industry does not warrant any despondency." Will Rogers was not so sure. Some months later in a radio broadcast, he drawled, "We are the first nation in the history of the world to go to the poorhouse in an automobile."

Part of the reason Hoover resented the barbed comments of the press was that he worked so hard. It was as characteristic of Herbert Hoover that he was the first president to have a telephone on his desk as it was characteristic of Calvin Coolidge that he refused to have one. Hoover rose at 6 A.M. each morning, joined a group of his friends for a brisk half-hour session with a five pound medicine ball on an improvised court on the White House grounds, then went in to breakfast. He was at his desk by 8:30. He worked steadily all day, smoking incessantly, and usually well into the night. Often he would wake up in the middle of the night and pore over papers or write for an hour or two before going back to sleep. Nevertheless, he rose at the same early hour. Subordinates were not always able to keep up with his pace; some had to be dispatched to rest, but Hoover, miraculously, never succumbed to his self-imposed regimen. His secretary reports that he was not sick a single day of the four years he spent in the White House. A few days at the camp on the Rapidan or a short trip usually sufficed to restore his energies and his will to work. But toward the end of his tenure, even the optimism and strength of a Hoover faltered, at least once. He told his secretary, "All the money in the world could not induce me to live over the last nine months. The conditions we have experienced make this office a compound hell."

Aside from the circumstances in which he found himself as President, one of the reasons the office was "hell" was that Hoover was a poor politician. Often it is said that he did not like politics, or even that he was above politics. Both statements describe the image he held of himself, but many of Hoover's actions while in office are clearly partisan and political. If, for example, he could objectively recognize the weaknesses of the Harding Administration once he was elected president, he could also say during the campaign of 1928 that "the record of the seven and one years" of Coolidge and Harding "constitutes a period of rare courage in leadership and constructive action. Never has a political party been able to look back upon a similar period with more satisfaction." In December 1931, when some voices were calling for a coalition government to deal with the worsening depression, Hoover made it clear that he would have nothing to do with Democrats. "The day that we begin coalition government you may know that our democracy has broken down," he told newspapermen at a Gridiron Club dinner. On the other hand, he could appoint Democrats to office, as he did former Senator Atlee Pomerene to head the RFC when he wanted that office to win support from Democrats. Nor was he devoid of political dramatics. In September 1931 he made a quick descent upon the American Legion Convention in Detroit in a successful effort to stop the Legion from going on record in favor of a bonus for veterans. By going all the way to Detroit, speaking for eleven minutes, and then immediately leaving for Washington again, he demonstrated the importance of his message and the weight of the schedule of work he pursued in Washington. Moreover, as the account written by his Press Secretary Joslin makes clear, he was no more above benefiting from parliamentary trickery in Congress than the next politically-minded president. As Joslin wrote, "It was characteristic of the President to hit back when attacked." Hoover suffered deeply when attacked, and he did not turn the other cheek. As William Allen White, who supported and admired the President, wrote in 1933, "he was no plaster saint politically. He had, during his three years, rather consistently and with a nice instinct chosen to honor in public office men of a conservative type of mind." Moreover, the behind-the-scenes circumstances of his nomination in 1928 and his renomination in 1932, both of which were steam-roller operations, should remove any doubts about his willingness and ability to use devices and tactics quite customary in politics.

No, it was not that he was above politics or that he really despised the operations of politicians. His difficulty was that he was temperamentally incapable of doing what a politician has to do — namely, to admit he could be wrong and to compromise. In the whole volume of his memoirs devoted to the Depression there is not a single mention of a major error on his part, though his opponents are taxed with errors in every chapter. Over a hundred pages of the volume are devoted to the answering of every charge of Franklin Roosevelt in 1932. Nowhere, though, does he notice that in 1932, he himself in his speech at Detroit incorrectly quoted Roosevelt and then proceeded to criticize at length his opponent for something he never said. This inability to admit error, to compromise, William Allen White recognized in 1931 as Hoover's undoing. After all, White wrote, "Politics . . . is one of the minor branches of harlotry, and Hoover's frigid desire to live a virtuous life and not follow the Pauline maxim and be all things to all men, is one of the things that has reduced the oil in his machinery and shot a bearing. . . ." Hoover's inability to admit error and the seriousness with which he viewed himself are both illustrated in another incident during the campaign of 1932. One of the Democrats' favorite sports that year was recalling, with appropriate sounds of derision, Hoover's remarks in 1928 to the effect that the United States was well on the way to abolishing poverty. Hoover, instead of admitting he had been somewhat optimistic, once again donned his hair shirt and stolidly endorsed the earlier statement because, as he said, it expressed the ideals for which Americans stood. Yet this was in the middle of the Depression and he was running for reelection.

In good times, Herbert Hoover's humble birth might have been an asset, but in the Great Depression it was not. Left an almost penniless orphan at nine, Hoover became a world figure and a millionaire before he was forty-five. With such spectacular success behind him it was understandable that he should think, albeit mistakenly, that anyone could achieve at least half as much as he. Undoubtedly his own experience fostered his insistence, throughout his life, that individual initiative was the prime motive force in a good society. What to other men appear as obstacles or handicaps, to the self-made man appear, at least in retrospect, as goads or incentives. Like most such men, Hoover attributed his success to will. When Theodore Joslin once asked him what had been his boyhood ambition, he replied without hesitation, "to be able to earn my own living without the help of anybody, anywhere." To such a man individual effort seems capable of moving mountains unaided; he is loath to see it shunted aside by collective action even in times of economic dislocation. The self-made man can indeed be the wrong man at such times.

Nor was it an accident that the other prominent self-made politician of the time, Alfred E. Smith, was also doubtful about the virtues of government aid to the unemployed, that he should attack Franklin Roosevelt for accusing the Hoover Administration of aiding the corporations and ignoring the poor. "I will take off my coat and vest," Smith vowed in the spring of 1932, "and fight to the end against any candidate who persists in any demagogic appeal to the masses of the working people of this country to destroy themselves by setting class against class and rich against poor." In a short time, Smith's views, like Hoover's, would bring him to outright opposition to the New Deal. It is not without significance in this respect that Roosevelt, who came to represent government benevolence toward the unemployed, was no self-made man, but lived securely and unadventurously on inherited wealth.

The differences in social origins of Roosevelt and Hoover, of course, are only one facet of the divergence between the Hoover Administration and the New Deal. Indeed, since the 1930's it has become commonplace to see Hoover and Roosevelt as opposites. Certainly there are differences — and important ones — between the administrations of the two Presidents, but we are now far enough removed from both to recognize also the real continuity between them that William Allen White was prescient enough to foresee dimly. When the two administrations are seen against the backdrop of previous administrations and earlier social attitudes, the gulf between them shrinks appreciably. Both men, it is worth recalling, were protégés of Woodrow Wilson; both of them, therefore, accepted a role for government in the economy which added up to a sharp departure from laissez-faire. Both, in the course of their respective administrations, drew upon their experiences in the First World War, where they had seen government intervening in the economy. Hoover's RFC, for example, was frankly modeled, as he said, after the War Finance Corporation. Both saw big business standing in need of controls, and, for a while, both believed that cooperation between business and government was the best way to achieve that control. Hoover, for instance, cited the Federal Reserve System as the ideal kind of business and government cooperation for purposes of regulating the economy; Roosevelt in the NRA also placed his trust in controls worked out through business and government cooperation. Moreover, both Roosevelt and Hoover took the view that it was government's responsibility to do something about a depression; neither man was willing to subscribe to the view which prevailed before 1929 — namely, that economic declines were simply natural phenomena through which the nation struggled as best it could and that government could not be expected to do much about them.

Finally, it is also worth noticing that the temperament of the two men, their conceptions of America and of its future are much closer than the conventional picture paints them. (It was Roosevelt, during the campaign of 1932, who created the erroneous image of Hoover as the man without faith or hope in the future.) All through the Depression, Hoover's unvarying theme was that all this would pass and the essential vigor of the American economy would reassert itself. Undoubtedly he counted too heavily on the influence of his words to overcome the lack of business confidence, but there is no question of his optimistic outlook. One measure of it was the shock he received when he read Roosevelt's address to the Commonwealth Club in San Francisco. That was the speech in which Roosevelt talked about the frontier being ended and opportunities for economic growth being limited. Hoover took up the challenge, denying "the whole idea that we have ended the advance of America, that this country has reached the zenith of its power, the height of its development. That is the counsel of despair for the future of America. That is not the spirit by which we shall emerge from this depression." The important point is that such pessimism was really not expressive of Roosevelt's thought, either. Although historians have frequently referred to the Commonwealth Club address as the one clear indication during the campaign of 1932 of the philosophy behind the New Deal, we now know that the speech was neither written by Roosevelt, nor read by him before he appeared before his audience. As Rexford Tugwell has pointed out, the Commonwealth Club address, which Berle and he wrote, did not reflect Roosevelt's true attitude toward the American economic future. Indeed, its very singularity among Roosevelt's campaign speeches demonstrates how foreign it was to Roosevelt's feelings and convictions. The speech belied his abundant enthusiasm for the future, and his deep faith in the country and its capacities. Moreover, he soon contradicted its import in his Inaugural Address, when he electrified the country with the cry, "All we have to fear is fear itself."

How ironical that these words of Roosevelt should be so well known, when it was Herbert Hoover who all along had been saying the same thing — in less graphic and less credible language, to be sure — but saying it nonetheless. That fact, too, contributed to the ordeal of Herbert Hoover.

17

THE CONTINUING EFFORT
TO CONTROL BIG BUSINESS

To focus upon the similarities between Herbert Hoover and Franklin
Roosevelt — who are commonly viewed as polar opposites — is not to
deny that there were important differences or to fall in with the consensus school of historiography that John Higham criticizes in another
article in this collection (see below, pp. 699–709). The differences in
the background, beliefs, milieu, and political connections of the two
presidents may help to explain why Roosevelt was able to go beyond
his predecessor's approaches in dealing with the Depression, but they
are of little help in explaining why he went only so far and no further.
Why, for instance, did he not take advantage of the early bleak days
of his administration to nationalize the banks and other segments of
industry, notably the coal mines whose operators were more than ame-
nable to government ownership or direction at that time? Why
was his initial approach to industry the National Recovery Administration, which institutionalized the trade-association pattern that industry had itself adopted in the freewheeling days of the previous
decade and which favored larger, more powerful business interests?
Why did he never embark upon a truly Keynesian program? Why did
he adopt the kind of cautious, economically regressive social security
program his administration belatedly came out for in 1935? Why was
he always so fearful of direct relief? Why did he have to be forced into
enacting labor legislation? Why was his first instinct frequently to turn
to programs of cooperative, voluntary action rather than to planned,
centralized, federal direction?

Certainly, the answers to such questions should be searched for in
the objective political situation that Roosevelt faced, but further elucidation may be found in a study of the points at which the beliefs,
aspirations, and environments of Roosevelt and Hoover conjoined.
For Roosevelt no less than his predecessor believed in such things as
the maintenance of capitalistic enterprise, the importance of individualism, the morality of fiscal orthodoxy, and the dangers of a hyper-
centralized state. If Herbert Hoover has too often been pictured as a
totally rigid, do-nothing president, our image of Franklin Roosevelt
suffers from the opposite extreme; he has been too easily labeled a
pragmatist — a free-and-easy exponent of anything that would work. It
is common to think of Roosevelt as a master politician who learned
early that "politics is the art of the possible," but one wonders not

only how accurate this label is but just what it really means. What a man *thinks* is possible reflects his general orientation more than it does reality. In the fluid, confused period of Roosevelt's first administration, many things were possible, but for the president they were not all desirable.

Roosevelt has been characterized as a man who could say with Ralph Waldo Emerson, whom Roosevelt so loved to quote, "No facts are to me sacred, none are profane, I simply experiment, an endless seeker with no past at my back." Roosevelt, of course, did have a past at his back and its roots were deeply embedded in the late nineteenth and early twentieth centuries. With the reformers of that era, Roosevelt shared a deep sense of morality and responsibility, believed in progress, the goodness of mankind, the virtues of the rural way of life, the existence of a harmony of interests, the benefits of capitalistic enterprise, and feared too much government intervention and too vigorous a break with the past. That Roosevelt was able to rise above many of his earlier beliefs to a much greater extent than many of his colleagues of the progressive era — including Herbert Hoover — is of the greatest importance and helps to explain many of the successes of the New Deal. But it should not obscure the fact that these beliefs continued to affect him and shape many of his actions and perceptions.

Much of the confusion and inconsistency so characteristic of the New Deal was created by the dichotomy between the things Roosevelt believed in and the steps he found himself having to take to bring about recovery. This dichotomy produced much of Roosevelt's so-called pragmatism. His pragmatic approach stemmed not from an absence of a prior faith but from the fact that the prior faith he held was inadequate to deal with the situation in which he found himself, and he was constantly searching for solutions that would alleviate the situation and do the least violence to the things in which he believed. No adherent of classical economics, Roosevelt did use certain Keynesian procedures, but he was never convinced that deficit spending and unbalanced budgets were not evils. Like Hoover before him, he was pushed by circumstances into spending larger sums of money than he wanted to, into constantly unbalancing the budget, but as Rexford Guy Tugwell has pointed out, it would be a mistake to minimize the agony these departures from economic orthodoxy caused Roosevelt or the sincerity of his perennial promise that he would balance the budget and reduce federal expenditures. The same tensions were manifest in his fears about the growth of the federal bureaucracy which circumstance forced him to expand constantly.

Only when we have a series of detailed studies of all aspects of the New Deal will the precise effects of these anxieties and the exact relationship between the beliefs and the actions of the New Dealers be fully understood. An important step toward this end is Ellis Hawley's superb book, *The New Deal and the Problem of Monopoly** (1966), which focuses upon the ambivalence of the New Deal and the American people toward industry and technology. The final chapter of the book is reprinted below. (Hawley is Professor of History at the University of Iowa.)

Thurman Arnold's *The Folklore of Capitalism** (1937) is an early attempt to trace the relationship between deeply ingrained traditional beliefs and perceptions of industry. Other studies which deal with the New Deal and business include: Broadus Mitchell, *Depression Decade** (1947); Sidney Fine, *The Automobile Under the Blue Eagle* (1963); James P. Johnson, "Drafting the NRA Code of Fair Competition for the Bituminous Coal Industry," *Journal of American History*, 53 (Dec. 1966), 521–41; Ralph DeBedts, *The New Deal's SEC: The Formative Years* (1964); Gene Gressley, "Thurman Arnold, Antitrust and the New Deal," *Business History Review*, 38 (Summer 1964), 214–31. James M. Burns, in his excellent biography, *Roosevelt: The Lion and the Fox** (1956), makes a good argument for Roosevelt as pragmatist, whereas William E. Leuchtenburg, in *Franklin D. Roosevelt and the New Deal** (1963), the best one-volume synthesis of the era, is more skeptical of the validity of the pragmatist label. See also Clark A. Chambers, "FDR, Pragmatist-Idealist: An Essay in Historiography," *Pacific Northwest Quarterly*, 52 (April 1961), 50–55.

The New Deal and the Problem of Monopoly

Ellis W. Hawley

"Two souls dwell in the bosom of this Administration," wrote Dorothy Thompson in 1938, "as indeed, they do in the bosom of the American people. The one loves the Abundant Life, as expressed in the cheap and plentiful products of large-scale mass production and distribution. . . . The other soul yearns for former simplicities, for decentralization, for the interests of the 'little man,' revolts against high-pressure salesmanship, denounces 'monopoly' and 'economic empires,' and seeks means of breaking them up." "Our Administration," she continued, "manages a remarkable . . . stunt of being . . . in favor of organizing and regulating the Economic Empires to greater and greater efficiency, and of breaking them up as a tribute to perennial American populist feeling." [1]

Dorothy Thompson was a persistent critic of the Roosevelt Administration; yet her remarks did show considerable insight into the dilemma that

Reprinted by permission of Princeton University Press from *The New Deal and the Problem of Monopoly: A Study in Economic Ambivalence* (copyright © 1969 by Princeton University Press; Princeton Paperback, 1969), pp. 472–94.
[1] Dorothy Thompson, in *New York Herald Tribune*, Jan. 24, 1938.

confronted New Dealers, and indeed, the dilemma that confronted industrial America. The problem of reconciling liberty and order, individualism and collective organization, was admittedly an ancient one, but the creation of a highly integrated industrial system in a land that had long cherished its liberal, democratic, and individualistic traditions presented the problem in a peculiarly acute form. Both the American people and their political leaders tended to view modern industrialism with mingled feelings of pride and regret. On one hand, they tended to associate large business units and economic organization with abundance, progress, and a rising standard of living. On the other, they associated them with a wide variety of economic abuses, which, because of past ideals and past standards, they felt to be injurious to society. Also, deep in their hearts, they retained a soft spot for the "little fellow." In moments of introspection, they looked upon the immense concentrations of economic power that they had created and accused them of destroying the good life, of destroying the independent businessman and the satisfactions that came from owning one's own business and working for oneself, of reducing Americans to a race of clerks and machine tenders, of creating an impersonal, mechanized world that destroyed man as an individual.[2]

The search in twentieth-century America, then, was for some solution that would reconcile the practical necessity with the individualistic ideal, some arrangement that would preserve the industrial order, necessarily based upon a high degree of collective organization, and yet would preserve America's democratic heritage at the same time. Americans wanted a stable, efficient industrial system, one that turned out a large quantity of material goods, insured full employment, and provided a relatively high degree of economic security. Yet at the same time they wanted a system as free as possible from centralized direction, one in which economic power was dispersed and economic opportunity was really open, one that preserved the dignity of the individual and adjusted itself automatically to market forces. And they were unwilling to renounce the hope of achieving both. In spite of periodic hurricanes of anti-big-business sentiment, they refused to follow the prophets that would destroy their industrial system and return to former simplicities. Nor did they pay much attention to those that would sacrifice democratic ideals and liberal traditions in order to create a more orderly and more rational system, one that promised greater security, greater stability, and possibly even greater material benefits.

There were times, of course, when this dilemma was virtually forgotten. During periods of economic prosperity, when Americans were imbued with a psychological sense of well-being and satiated with a steady outflow of ma-

---

[2] See Arthur R. Burns, in *American Economic Review*, June 1949, pp. 691–95; Burton R. Fisher and Stephen B. Withey, *Big Business as the People See It* (Ann Arbor: U. of Mich. Press, 1951), 21–22, 34–38; Rexford G. Tugwell, in *Western Political Quarterly*, Sept. 1950, pp. 392–400.

terial benefits, it was hard to convince them that their industrial organization was seriously out of step with their ideals. During such periods, the majority rallied to the support of the business system; so long as it continued to operate at a high level, they saw no need for any major reforms. So long as the competitive ideal was embodied in statutes and industrial and political leaders paid lip service to it, there was a general willingness to leave it at that. If there were troubled consciences left, these could be soothed by clothing collective organizations in the attributes of rugged individuals and by the assurances of economic experts that anything short of pure monopoly was "competition" and therefore assured the benefits that were supposed to flow from competition.

In a time of economic adversity, however, Americans became painfully aware of the gap between ideal and reality. Paradoxically, this awareness produced two conflicting and contradictory reactions. Some pointed to the gap, to the failure of business organizations to live by the competitive creed, and concluded that it was the cause of the economic debacle, that the breakdown of the industrial machine was the inevitable consequence of its failure to conform to competitive standards. Others pointed to the same gap and concluded that the ideal itself was at fault, that it had prevented the organization and conscious direction of a rational system that would provide stability and security. On one hand, the presence of depression conditions seemed to intensify anti-big-business sentiment and generate new demands for antitrust crusades. On the other, it inspired demands for planning, rationalization, and the creation of economic organizations that could weather deflationary forces. The first general effect grew directly out of the loss of confidence in business leadership, the conviction that industrial leaders had sinned against the economic creed, and the determination that they should be allowed to sin no more. The second grew out of the black fear of economic death, the urgent desire to stem the deflationary tide, and the mounting conviction that a policy of laissez-faire or real implementation of the competitive ideal would result in economic disaster.

During such a period, moreover, it would seem practically inevitable that the policy-making apparatus of a democracy should register both streams of sentiment. Regardless of their logical inconsistency, the two streams were so intermixed in the ideology of the average man that any administration, if it wished to retain political power, had to make concessions to both. It must move to check the deflationary spiral, to provide some sort of central direction, and to salvage economic groups through the erection of cartels and economic controls. Yet while it was doing this, it must make a proper show of maintaining competitive ideals. Its actions must be justified by an appeal to competitive traditions, by showing that they were designed to save the underdog, or if this was impossible, by an appeal to other arguments and other traditions that for the moment justified making an exception. Nor could antitrust action ever be much more than a matter of performing the proper rituals and manipulating the proper symbols. It might attack unusually privileged and widely hated groups, break up a few loose combinations, and set forth a general program that was presumably designed to make the competitive ideal a reality. But the limit of the program would, of necessity, be that point at which changes in business practice or business structures would cause serious economic dislocation. It could not risk the disruption of going concerns or a further shrinkage in employment and production, and it would not subject men to the logical working out of deflationary trends. To do so would amount to political suicide.

To condemn these policies for their inconsistency was to miss the point. From an economic standpoint, condemnation might very well be to the point. They *were* inconsistent. One line of action tended to cancel the other, with the result that little was accomplished. Yet from the political standpoint, this very inconsistency, so long as the dilemma persisted, was the safest method of retaining political power. President Roosevelt, it seems, never suffered politically from his reluctance to choose between planning and antitrust action. His mixed emotions so closely reflected the popular mind that they were a political asset rather than a liability.[3]

II

That New Deal policy was inconsistent, then, should occasion little surprise. Such inconsistency, in fact, was readily apparent in the National Industrial Recovery Act, the first major effort to deal with the problems of industrial organization. When Roosevelt took office in 1933, the depression had reached its most acute stage. Almost every economic group was crying for salvation through political means, for some sort of rationalization and planning, although they might differ as to just who was to do the planning and the type and amount of it that would be required. Pro-business planners, drawing upon the trade association ideology of the nineteen twenties and the precedent of the War Industries Board, envisioned a semi-cartelized business commonwealth in which industrial leaders would plan and the state would enforce the decisions. Other men, convinced that there was already too much planning by businessmen, hoped to create an order in which other economic groups would participate in the policy-making process. Even under these circumstances, however, the resulting legislation had to be clothed in competitive symbols. Proponents of the NRA advanced the theory that it would help small businessmen and industrial laborers by protecting them from predatory practices and monopolistic abuses. The devices used to erect

[3] See Adolf A. Berle, Jr., in *Virginia Quarterly Review*, Summer 1938, pp. 324–33; K. E. Boulding, in *Quarterly Journal of Economics*, Aug. 1945, pp. 524, 529–42; Arthur M. Schlesinger, Jr., *The Politics of Upheaval* (Boston: Houghton Mifflin, 1960), 650–54.

monopolistic controls became "codes of fair competition." And each such device contained the proper incantation against monopoly.

Consequently, the NRA was not a single program with a single objective, but rather a series of programs with a series of objectives, some of which were in direct conflict with each other. In effect, the National Industrial Recovery Act provided a phraseology that could be used to urge almost any approach to the problem of economic organization and an administrative machine that each of the conflicting economic and ideological groups might possibly use for their own ends. Under the circumstances, a bitter clash over basic policies was probably inevitable.

For a short period these inconsistencies were glossed over by the summer boomlet of 1933 and by a massive propaganda campaign appealing to wartime precedents and attempting to create a new set of cooperative symbols. As the propaganda wore off, however, and the economic indices turned downward again, the inconsistencies inherent in the program moved to the forefront of the picture. In the code-writing process, organized business had emerged as the dominant economic group, and once this became apparent, criticism of the NRA began to mount. Agrarians, convinced that rising industrial prices were canceling out any gains from the farm program, demanded that businessmen live up to the competitive faith. Labor spokesmen, bitterly disillusioned when the program failed to guarantee union recognition and collective bargaining, charged that the Administration had sold out to management. Small businessmen, certain that the new code authorities were only devices to increase the power of their larger rivals, raised the ancient cry of monopolistic exploitation. Antitrusters, convinced that the talk about strengthening competition was sheer hypocrisy, demanded that this disastrous trust-building program come to a halt. Economic planners, alienated by a process in which the businessmen did the planning, charged that the government was only sanctioning private monopolistic arrangements. And the American public, disillusioned with rising prices and the failure of the program to bring economic recovery, listened to the criticisms and demanded that its competitive ideals be made good.

The rising tide of public resentment greatly strengthened the hand of those that viewed the NRA primarily as a device for raising the plane of competition and securing social justice for labor. Picking up support from discontented groups, from other governmental agencies, and from such investigations as that conducted by Clarence Darrow's National Recovery Review Board, this group within the NRA had soon launched a campaign to bring about a reorientation in policy. By June 1934 it had obtained a formal written policy embodying its views, one that committed the NRA to the competitive ideal, renounced the use of price and production controls, and promised to subject the code authorities to strict public supervision. By this time, however, most of the major codes had been written, and the market restorers were never able to apply their policy to codes already approved. The chief effect of their efforts to do so was to antagonize businessmen and to complicate the difficulties of enforcing code provisions that were out of line with announced policy.

The result was a deadlock that persisted for the remainder of the agency's life. Putting the announced policy into effect would have meant, in all probability, the complete alienation of business support and the collapse of the whole structure. Yet accepting and enforcing the codes for what they were would have resulted, again in all probability, in an outraged public and congressional opinion that would have swept away the whole edifice. Thus the NRA tended to reflect the whole dilemma confronting the New Deal. Admittedly, declared policy was inconsistent with practice. Admittedly, the NRA was accomplishing little. Yet from a political standpoint, if the agency were to continue at all, a deadlock of this sort seemed to be the only solution. If the Supreme Court had not taken a hand in the matter, the probable outcome would have been either the abolition of the agency or a continuation of the deadlock.

The practical effect of the NRA, then, was to allow the erection, extension, and fortification of private monopolistic arrangements, particularly for groups that already possessed a fairly high degree of integration and monopoly power. Once these arrangements had been approved and vested interests had developed, the Administration found it difficult to deal with them. It could not move against them without alienating powerful interest groups, producing new economic dislocations, and running the risk of setting off the whole process of deflation again. Yet, because of the competitive ideal, it could not lend much support to the arrangements or provide much in the way of public supervision. Only in areas where other arguments, other ideals, and political pressure justified making an exception, in such areas as agriculture, natural resources, transportation, and to a certain extent labor, could the government lend its open support and direction.

Moreover, the policy dilemma, coupled with the sheer complexity of the undertaking, made it impossible to provide much central direction. There was little planning of a broad, general nature, either by businessmen or by the state; there was merely the half-hearted acceptance of a series of legalized, but generally uncoordinated, monopolistic combinations. The result was not over-all direction, but a type of partial, piecemeal, pressure-group planning, a type of planning designed by specific economic groups to balance production with consumption regardless of the dislocations produced elsewhere in the economy.

III

There were, certainly, proposals for other types of planning. But under the circumstances, they were and remained politically unfeasible, both during the NRA period and after. The idea of a government-supported business commonwealth still persisted, and a few men still felt that if the NRA had really applied it, the depression would have been over. Yet in the political context of the time, the idea was thoroughly unrealistic. For one thing, there was the growing gap between businessmen and New Dealers, the conviction of one side that cooperation would lead to bureaucratic socialism, of the other that it would lead to fascism or economic oppression. Even if this quarrel had not existed, the Administration could not have secured a program that ran directly counter to the anti-big-business sentiment of the time. The monopolistic implications in such a program were too obvious, and there was little that could be done to disguise them. Most industrial leaders recognized the situation, and the majority of them came to the conclusion that a political program of this sort was no longer necessary. With the crisis past and the deflationary process checked, private controls and such governmental aids as tariffs, subsidies, and loans would be sufficient.

The idea of national economic planning also persisted. A number of New Dealers continued to advocate the transfer of monopoly power from businessmen to the state or to other organized economic groups. Each major economic group, they argued, should be organized and allowed to participate in the formulation of a central plan, one that would result in expanded production, increased employment, a more equitable distribution, and a better balance of prices. Yet this idea, too, was thoroughly impractical when judged in terms of existing political realities. It ran counter to competitive and individualistic traditions. It threatened important vested interests. It largely ignored the complexities of the planning process or the tendency of regulated interests to dominate their regulators. And it was regarded by the majority of Americans as being overly radical, socialistic, and un-American.

Consequently, the planning of the New Deal was essentially single-industry planning, partial, piecemeal, and opportunistic, planning that could circumvent the competitive ideal or could be based on other ideals that justified making an exception. After the NRA experience, organized business groups found it increasingly difficult to devise these justifications. Some business leaders, to be sure, continued to talk about a public agency with power to waive the antitrust laws and sanction private controls. Yet few of them were willing to accept government participation in the planning process, and few were willing to come before the public with proposals that were immediately vulnerable to charges of monopoly. It was preferable, they felt, to let the whole issue lie quiet, to rely upon unauthorized private controls, and to hope that these would be little disturbed by antitrust action. Only a few peculiarly depressed groups, like the cotton textile industry, continued to agitate for government-supported cartels, and most of these groups lacked the cohesion, power, and alternative symbols that would have been necessary to put their programs through.

In some areas, however, especially in areas where alternative symbols were present and where private controls had broken down or proven impractical, it was possible to secure a type of partial planning. Agriculture was able to avoid most of the agitation against monopoly, and while retaining to a large extent its individualistic operations, to finds ways of using the state to fix prices, plan production, and regularize markets. Its ability to do so was attributable in part to the political power of the farmers, but it was also due to manipulation of certain symbols that effectively masked the monopolistic implications in the program. The ideal of the yeoman farmer — honest, independent, and morally upright — still had a strong appeal in America, and to many Americans it justified the salvation of farming as a "way of life," even at the cost of subsidies and the violation of competitive standards. Agriculture, moreover, was supposed to be the basic industry, the activity that supported all others. The country, so it was said, could not be prosperous unless its farmers were prosperous. Finally, there was the conservation argument, the great concern over conservation of the soil, which served to justify some degree of public planning and some type of production control.

Similar justifications were sometimes possible for other areas of the economy. Monopolistic arrangements in certain food-processing industries could be camouflaged as an essential part of the farm program. Departures from competitive standards in such natural resource industries as bituminous coal and crude oil production could be justified on the grounds of conservation. Public controls and economic cartelization in the fields of transportation and communication could be justified on the ground that these were "natural monopolies" in which the public had a vital interest. And in the distributive trades, it was possible to turn anti-big-business sentiment against the mass distributors, to brand them as "monopolies," and to obtain a series of essentially anti-competitive measures on the theory that they were designed to preserve competition by preserving small competitors. The small merchant, however, was never able to dodge the agitation against monopoly to the same extent that the farmer did. The supports granted him were weak to begin with, and to obtain them he had to make concessions to the competitive ideal, concessions that robbed his measures of much of their intended effectiveness.

In some ways, too, the Roosevelt Administration helped to create monopoly power for labor. Under the New Deal program, the government proceeded to absorb surplus labor and prescribe minimum labor standards; more important, it encouraged labor organization to the extent that it maintained a friendly attitude, required employer recognition of unions, and restrained certain practices that had been used to break unions in the past. For a time, the appeals to social justice, humanitarianism, and anti-big-business sentiment overrode the appeal of business spokesmen and classical economists to the competitive ideal and individualistic traditions. The doctrine that labor was not a commodity, that men who had worked and produced and kept their obligations to society were entitled to be taken care of, was widely accepted. Along with it went a growing belief that labor unions were necessary to maintain purchasing power and counterbalance big business. Consequently, even the New Dealers of an antitrust persuasion generally made a place in their program for social legislation and labor organization.

The general effect of this whole line of New Deal policy might be summed up in the word counterorganization, that is, the creation of monopoly power in areas previously unorganized. One can only conclude, however, that this did not happen according to any preconceived plan. Nor did it necessarily promote economic expansion or raise consumer purchasing power. Public support of monopolistic arrangements occurred in a piecemeal, haphazard fashion, in response to pressure from specific economic groups and as opportunities presented themselves. Since consumer organizations were weak and efforts to aid consumers made little progress, the benefits went primarily to producer groups interested in restricting production and raising prices. In the distributive trades, the efforts to help small merchants tended, insofar as they were successful, to impede technological changes, hamper mass distributors, and reduce consumer purchasing power. In the natural resource and transportation industries, most of the new legislation was designed to restrict production, reduce competition, and protect invested capital. And in the labor and agricultural fields, the strengthening of market controls was often at the expense of consumers and in conjunction with business groups. The whole tendency of interest-group planning, in fact, was toward the promotion of economic scarcity. Each group, it seemed, was trying to secure a larger piece from a pie that was steadily dwindling in size.

From an economic standpoint, then, the partial planning of the post-NRA type made little sense, and most economists, be they antitrusters, planners, or devotees of laissez-faire, felt that such an approach was doing more harm than good. It was understandable only in a political context, and as a political solution, it did possess obvious elements of strength. It retained the antitrust laws and avoided any direct attack upon the competitive ideal or competitive mythology. Yet by appealing to other goals and alternative ideals and by using these to justify special and presumably exceptional departures from competitive standards, it could make the necessary concessions to pressure groups interested in reducing competition and erecting government-sponsored cartels.[4] Such a program might be logically inconsistent and economically harmful. Perhaps, as one critic suggested at

[4] See Paul T. Homan, in American Economic Association, *Readings in the Social Control of Industry* (Philadelphia: Blakiston, 1942), 242–46, 252–54; and in *Political Science Quarterly*, June 1936, pp. 169–72, 178–84; Berle, in *Virginia Quarterly Review*, Summer 1938, pp. 330–31; Ernest Griffith, *Impasse of Democracy* (N.Y.: Harrison-Hilton, 1939), 231.

the time, it combined the worst features of both worlds, "an impairment of the efficiency of the competitive system without the compensating benefits of rationalized collective action." [5] But politically it was a going concern, and efforts to achieve theoretical consistency met with little success.

Perhaps the greatest defect in these limited planning measures was their tendency toward restriction, their failure to provide any incentive for expansion when an expanding economy was the crying need of the time. The easiest way to counteract this tendency, it seemed, was through government expenditures and deficit financing; in practice, this was essentially the path that the New Deal took. By 1938 Roosevelt seemed willing to accept the Keynesian arguments for a permanent spending program, and eventually, when war demands necessitated pump-priming on a gigantic scale, the spending solution worked. It overcame the restrictive tendencies in the economy, restored full employment, and brought rapid economic expansion. Drastic institutional reform, it seemed, was unnecessary. Limited, piecemeal, pressure-group planning could continue, and the spending weapon could be relied upon to stimulate expansion and maintain economic balance.

IV

One major stream of New Deal policy, then, ran toward partial planning. Yet this stream was shaped and altered, at least in a negative sense, by its encounters with the antitrust tradition and the competitive ideal. In a time when Americans distrusted business leadership and blamed big business for the prevailing economic misery, it was only natural that an antitrust approach should have wide political appeal. Concessions had to be made to it, and these concessions meant that planning had to be limited, piecemeal, and disguised. There could be no over-all program of centralized controls. There could be no government-sponsored business commonwealth. And there could be only a minimum of government participation in the planning process.

In and of itself, however, the antitrust approach did not offer a politically workable alternative. The antitrusters might set forth their own vision of the good society. They might blame the depression upon the departure from competitive standards and suggest measures to make industrial organization correspond more closely to the competitive model. But they could never ignore or explain away the deflationary and disruptive implications of their program. Nor could they enlist much support from the important political and economic pressure groups. Consequently, the antitrust approach, like that of planning, had to be applied on a limited basis. Action could be taken only in special or exceptional areas, against unusually privileged groups that were actively hated and particularly vulnerable, in fields where

[5] Homan, in *Political Science Quarterly*, June 1936, p. 181.

one business group was fighting another, in cases where no one would get hurt, or against practices that violated common standards of decency and fairness.

This was particularly true during the period prior to 1938. The power trust, for example, was a special demon in the progressive faith, one that was actively hated by large numbers of people and one that had not only violated competitive standards but had also outraged accepted canons of honesty and tampered with democratic political ideals. For such an institution, nothing was too bad, not even a little competition; and the resulting battle, limited though its gains might be, did provide a suitable outlet for popular antitrust feeling. Much the same was also true of the other anti-trust activities. Financial reform provided another outlet for antitrust sentiment, although its practical results were little more than regulation for the promotion of honesty and facilitation of the governmental spending program. The attacks upon such practices as collusive bidding, basing-point pricing, and block-booking benefited from a long history of past agitation. And the suits in the petroleum and auto-finance industries had the support of discontented business groups. The result of such activities, however, could hardly be more than marginal. When the antitrusters reached for real weapons, when they tried, for example, to use the taxing power or make drastic changes in corporate law, they found that any thorough-going pro-gram was simply not within the realm of political possibilities.

Under the circumstances, it appeared, neither planning nor antitrust ac-tion could be applied in a thorough-going fashion. Neither approach could completely eclipse the other. Yet the political climate and situation did change; and, as a result of these changes, policy vacillated between the two extremes. One period might see more emphasis on planning, the next on antitrust action, and considerable changes might also take place in the na-ture, content, and scope of each program.

Superficially, the crisis of 1937 was much like that of 1933. Again there were new demands for antitrust action, and again these demands were blended with new proposals for planning, rationalization, and monopolistic controls. In some respects, too, the results were similar. There was more partial planning in unorganized areas, and eventually, this was accom-panied by a resumption of large-scale federal spending. The big difference was in the greater emphasis on an antitrust approach, which could be attrib-uted primarily to the difference in political circumstances. The alienation of the business community, memories of NRA experiences, and the grow-ing influence of antimonopolists in the Roosevelt Administration made it difficult to work out any new scheme of business-government cooperation. These same factors, coupled with the direct appeal of New Dealers to the competitive ideal, made it difficult for business groups to secure public sanc-tion for monopolistic arrangements. The political repercussions of the re-cession, the fact that the new setback had occurred while the New Deal

was in power, made it necessary to appeal directly to anti-big-business sentiment and to use the administered price thesis to explain why the recession
had occurred and why the New Deal had failed to achieve sustained recovery. Under the circumstances, the initiative passed to the antitrusters,
and larger concessions had to be made to their point of view.

One such concession was the creation of the Temporary National Economic Committee. Yet this was not so much a victory for the antitrusters
as it was a way of avoiding the issue, a means of minimizing the policy conflict within the Administration and postponing any final decision. Essentially, the TNEC was a harmless device that could be used by each group
to urge a specific line of action or no action at all. Antimonopolists hoped
that it would generate the political sentiment necessary for a major breakthrough against concentrated economic power, but these hopes were never
realized. In practice, the investigation became largely an ineffective dupli-
cate of the frustrating debate that produced it, and by the time its report
was filed, the circumstances had changed. Most of the steam had gone out
of the monopoly issue, and antitrust sentiment was being replaced by war-
induced patriotism.

The second major concession to antimonopoly sentiment was Thurman
Arnold's revival of antitrust prosecutions, a program that presumably was
designed to restore a competitive system, one in which prices were flexible
and competition would provide the incentive for expansion. Actually, the
underlying assumptions behind such a program were of doubtful validity.
Price flexibility, even if attainable, might do more harm than good. The
Arnold approach had definite limitations, even assuming that the underlying theories were sound. It could and did break up a number of loose combinations; it could and did disrupt monopolistic arrangements that were no
necessary part of modern industrialism. It could and, in some cases, did succeed in convincing businessmen that they should adopt practices that corresponded a bit more closely to the competitive model. But it made no real
effort to rearrange the underlying industrial structure itself, no real attempt
to dislodge vested interests, disrupt controls that were actual checks against
deflation, or break up going concerns. And since the practices and policies
complained of would appear in many cases to be the outgrowth of this
underlying structure, the Arnold program had little success in achieving its
avowed goals.

Even within these limits, moreover, Arnold's antitrust campaign ran into
all sorts of difficulties. Often the combinations that he sought to break up
were the very ones that the earlier New Deal had fostered. Often, even
though the arrangements involved bore little relation to actual production,
their sponsors claimed that they did, that their disruption would set the
process of deflation in motion again and impair industrial efficiency. Arnold
claimed that his activities enjoyed great popular support, and as a symbol
and generality they probably did. But when they moved against specific
arrangements, it was a different story. There they succeeded in alienating

one political pressure group after another. Then, with the coming of the war, opposition became stronger than ever. As antitrust sentiment was replaced by wartime patriotism, it seemed indeed that the disruption of private controls would reduce efficiency and impair the war effort. Consequently, the Arnold program gradually faded from the scene.

It is doubtful, then, that the innovations of 1938 should be regarded as a basic reversal in economic policy. What actually happened was not the substitution of one set of policies for another, but rather a shift in emphasis between two sets of policies that had existed side by side throughout the entire period. Policies that attacked monopoly and those that fostered it, policies that reflected the underlying dilemma of industrial America, had long been inextricably intertwined in American history, and this basic inconsistency persisted in an acute form during the nineteen thirties. Policy might and did vacillate between the two extremes; but because of the limitations of the American political structure and of American economic ideology, it was virtually impossible for one set of policies to displace the other. The New Deal reform movement was forced to adjust to this basic fact. The practical outcome was an economy characterized by private controls, partial planning, compensatory government spending, and occasional gestures toward the competitive ideal.

V

In conclusion one might ask whether the experiences of the New Dealers have any relevance for the problems of today, and for various reasons he might doubt that they do. After all, the setting has changed. The concern with business power, mass unemployment, and rigid prices has given way to concern over inflation, labor power, and the price-wage spiral. In the increasingly affluent society of the organization man, there is less criticism of big business, less agitation for government-supported cartels, and less awareness of the gap between economic reality and the competitive ideal. Some economists, in fact, argue that the gap has largely disappeared. They claim that the process of economic concentration has been reversed, that technological innovation has stimulated a "revival of competition," and that any realistic definition of workable competition should include a variety of behavior patterns that economists in the nineteen thirties would have regarded as monopolistic.[6] Others disagree about the prevalence of competition, but maintain that the concentrations of economic power involved in big busi-

[6] See M. A. Adelman, in *Review of Economic Statistics*, Nov. 1951, pp. 293–96; Clair Wilcox and Shorey Peterson, in *AER*, May 1950, pp. 67–73; March 1957, pp. 60–78; Joseph A. Schumpeter, *Capitalism, Socialism, and Democracy* (N.Y.: Harper, 1942), 81–86; A. D. H. Kaplan, *Big Enterprise in a Competitive System* (Washington: Brookings, 1954), 231–48; Sumner H. Slichter, *The American Economy* (N.Y.: Knopf, 1950), 13–19; John M. Clark, *Competition as a Dynamic Process* (Washington: Brookings, 1961), 2–18, 465–90; *Fortune*, June 1952, pp. 98–99, 186, 188, 190, 192, 194, 197.

ness, big labor, big agriculture, and big government are not so bad after all. For example, they argue that the power is being used wisely, that one power concentrate tends to offset the other, or that excessive power can be checked by public opinion. Democracy, they seem to think, is still possible in an organizational system, and concentrated power can be used to liberate as well as oppress.[7]

The concern with monopoly as a major cause of economic depression has also faded from the scene. The majority of economists seem to doubt that there is much connection between concentration and rigid prices or that price flexibility, even if it could be attained, would insure full employment and sustained prosperity. In any event, they seem convinced that tampering with the price-wage structure is one of the most difficult and least desirable ways of controlling the business cycle. Consequently, most current discussions of countercyclical programs tend to revolve about the use of fiscal and monetary policies rather than central planning or antitrust action. The return of prosperity, however, has had less effect on the older indictment of monopoly. The fear of centralized economic power has not completely vanished. The older charges that monopoly is unfair, wasteful, uneconomic, and injurious to consumer welfare are still repeated. A number of economists, politicians, and scholars are still concerned about the gap between ideal and reality, about the continued growth of collectivization, planning, and administrative controls in a land that professes to believe in free markets and economic individualism.[8]

Those concerned with the problem, moreover, are still puzzled by the ambivalence of the attitudes involved and the inconsistency and irrationality of policies relating to competition and monopoly. The deep respect for efficiency, they point out, is counterbalanced by sympathy for the "little fellow" and concern about the political and economic power that giant suc-

---

[7] See John K. Galbraith, *American Capitalism* (Boston: Houghton Mifflin, 1952), 118–39; David E. Lilienthal, *Big Business* (N.Y.: Harper, 1952), 26–28, 47–57, 137–61, 198–201; Dexter M. Keezer, et al., *New Forces in American Business* (N.Y.: McGraw-Hill, 1959), 152–55; Oswald Knauth, *Managerial Enterprise* (N.Y.: Norton, 1948), 206–13; Adolf A. Berle, Jr., *The 20th Century Capitalist Revolution* (N.Y.: Harcourt, Brace, 1954), 43–60, 180–88; and in Thurman Arnold et al., *Future of Democratic Capitalism* (Philadelphia, 1950), 57–62; Bruce R. Morris, *Problems of American Economic Growth* (N.Y.: Oxford U. Press, 1961), 91–96, 154–55, 159–61, 223, 229–32, 246–49.

[8] See National Bureau of Economic Research, *Business Concentration and Price Policy* (Princeton: Princeton U. Press, 1955), 450–89; and *Policies to Combat Depression* (1956), 3–22, 60–74; Walter Adams and Horace Gray, *Monopoly in America* (N.Y.: Macmillan, 1955), 1–24, 173–78; T. K. Quinn, *Giant Business* (N.Y.: Exposition, 1953), 9–12, 300–1, 310–13; Henry A. Wells, *Monopoly and Social Control* (Washington: Public Affairs Press, 1952), VII, 2–7, 101–14; Knauth, *Managerial Enterprise*, 23–24, 203–13; A. D. Neale, *The Antitrust Laws of the U.S.A.* (Cambridge: Cambridge U. Press, 1960), 419–24; Donald Dewey, *Monopoly in Economics and Law* (Chicago: Rand McNally, 1959), 70–81; George W. Stocking, *Workable Competition and Antitrust Policy* (Nashville: Vanderbilt U. Press, 1961), 2–17, 408–28; Ben W. Lewis, in AER, June 1949, pp. 703–9.

cessful enterprises can wield. The belief in free competition is offset by substantial support for tariff barriers, private controls, and limitations on the entry of new entrepreneurs in a number of industries and trades. The desire for competitive incentives is tempered by a strong drive for economic security, for protection against such hazards as unemployment, declining incomes, shrinking markets, and price wars. And the general tradition in favor of a free market economy is combined with an amazing array of exceptions, with a wide range of activities designed to insulate economic groups from the rigors of market rivalry. Current policy, it seems, like that of the New Deal era, is still a maze of conflicting cross-currents, and so long as the intellectual heritage remains and conflicting goals persist, it seems doubtful that any set of simple, consistent policies can be drawn up and implemented.[9]

In some respects, then, the problems with which current policy-makers must deal are comparable to those facing the New Dealers. If the experiences of the nineteen thirties have any relevance at all, it is in illustrating the limitations of logical analysis, the pitfalls inherent in broad theoretical approaches, the difficulty of agreeing upon policy goals, and the necessity of making due allowances for the intellectual heritage, current trends of opinion, and the realities of pressure-group politics. The margin within which innovation could be made was considerably broader during the nineteen thirties than at present; yet the New Dealers were never able to agree upon a clear-cut program or to impose any rational and consistent pattern. The planners discovered that centralized, over-all planning was not really feasible, that because of political, practical, legal, and ideological considerations, any attempt to apply such an approach quickly degenerated into a type of single-industry, pressure-group planning that brought few of the benefits presumably associated with rationalized collective action. The antitrusters, too, discovered that their approach had to be economized, that it could be applied only on a limited basis or in special areas and special cases. The attempts to combine the two approaches, to work out pragmatic tests and choose between regulation and antitrust action on a case-by-case, industry-by-industry basis, ended typically in the same clash of values that lay behind the original battle of principles.

It seems doubtful, moreover, that research, investigation, and logical analysis can ever resolve this clash of values. In any event, decades of debate, coupled with massive investigations like that conducted by the TNEC, have failed to produce any general consensus about the causes of business concentration and combination, their results and effects, and the proper methods of dealing with them. Barring a revolution or drastic changes in techniques, attitudes, values, and institutions, it seems likely that policy in this area will remain confused and contradictory, that programs designed to

[9] See Mark S. Massel, *Competition and Monopoly* (Washington: Brookings, 1962), 16–20, 317–19.

combat monopoly will still be intermingled with those designed to promote it.

This is not to say, of course, that research and analysis are useless. Within limits they can be of great aid to the policy-maker. They can help to define the issues, identify points of pressure, and clarify national objectives. They can evaluate existing programs in terms of these goals and provide evidence as to the nature, feasibility, and relative effectiveness of the various methods whereby they might be attained. And they can acquaint the policy-maker with the range of alternatives at his disposal and the probable consequences of choosing any one of them.[10] This study, it is hoped, will contribute something in all of these areas, and further inquiries into particular periods, problems, or developments can contribute a good deal more. Yet such studies are unlikely to resolve the underlying policy dilemma. They are unlikely to come up with any line of policy that will be acceptable to all and that will really reconcile the conflicting goals, attitudes, and values that Americans have inherited from the past.

Consequently, the conflict in American ideology and American economic policy seems likely to continue. The gap between ideal and reality, particularly if the economy should falter, will continue to generate demands for economic reorganization and reform. Yet the possibilities for planning and rationalization will still be limited by the popular belief in free markets, and those for antitrust action by the realities of large-scale economies, vested interests, and pressure-group politics. The relative strength of the conflicting forces and ideologies may change, and new debates concerning the location, use, and control of power may develop; but so long as the competitive ideal and democratic heritage continue to mean anything, the dilemma itself seems likely to persist. And the problem of monopoly, in its broadest aspects, will remain unsolved.

[10] *Ibid.*, 40–41, 83–84, 108–22, 325–27, 337–39.

18

AGRICULTURAL POLITICS IN FDR'S "BROKER STATE"

It has frequently been argued that the New Deal set itself up as a "broker state," as a mediator between the often conflicting demands of the leading groups in American society. J. K. Galbraith, in his study *American Capitalism** (1952), has maintained that from the 1930's on, the United States has become a nation of "countervailing powers" working on and against one another, often through the auspices of the federal government, to achieve a rough kind of justice. It is certainly true that Franklin Roosevelt and most of his New Deal colleagues never really abandoned the progressive era's notion of a harmony of interests, a notion that eschewed all ideas of class conflict, stoutly denied that the "legitimate" interests of one group might necessarily conflict with those of another, and deemed it entirely appropriate that the federal government listen to the demands of all groups and help them to help themselves. Occasionally, minor surgery might have to be performed to eliminate or curb the small, selfish group of "male-factors of great wealth" — the "economic royalists" of Franklin Roosevelt's terminology — but overall justice could be achieved by simply balancing the needs of one group against those of another.

Many of the problems of the New Deal period and after arose from the difficulty of harmonizing a number of quite legitimate needs and demands of such antithetical groups as landed and landless farmers, skilled and unskilled workers, and large and small business-men. Equally important was the problem posed by those who, lacking organization and a national voice, found themselves without either influence or power in the new "broker state." Toward the close of the domestic New Deal, Louis Hacker, in his study *American Problems of Today* (1939), charged that the New Deal was primarily the agent of the organized and relatively powerful. Up to the present, historians have paid relatively scant attention to groups that fell outside the area of New Deal reforms and benefited little, if at all, from the major labor and social-welfare legislation of the 'thirties. One of the largest of these groups was the mass of depressed farmers, the migrant farm workers of John Steinbeck's *Grapes of Wrath** (1939), and the sharecroppers and tenant farmers of whom M. S. Venkataramani, who teaches American history at the Indian School of International Studies in New Delhi, writes in the following article.

The opposite side of the story, vis-à-vis the farmers, is told in G.

McConnell, *The Decline of Agrarian Democracy* (1959), which examines the most powerful and influential of the farm organizations, the American Farm Bureau Federation. During the New Deal, most Farm Bureau members were owner-operators who possessed twice as much land as did the average farm owner. This organization of large farmers, whose influence was most frequently felt in Washington, helped to shape many of the features of the two Agricultural Adjustment Acts and was largely responsible for destroying the Farm Security Administration, which despite its inadequacies was the final legislative hope for tenants and sharecroppers. The persisting plight of the latter groups is an indication that if there is a system of "countervailing powers" in the United States, the unorganized and marginal social and economic groups remain on its periphery today as they did four decades before.

In recent years, historians have devoted an increasing amount of study to the agricultural problems of the 'thirties. For more detail on the questions dealt with by Venkataramani, see David Conrad, *The Forgotten Farmer: The Story of Share Croppers and the New Deal* (1965), and Jerold Auerbach, "Southern Tenant Farmers: Socialist Critics of the New Deal," *Labor History*, 7 (Winter 1966), 3–18. Other aspects of the farmer's condition and the New Deal response are dealt with in the following: John Shover, *Cornbelt Rebellion: The Farmers' Holiday Association* (1965); Christiana M. Campbell, *The Farm Bureau and the New Deal* (1962); Richard S. Kirkendall, *Social Scientists and Farm Politics in the Age of Roosevelt* (1966); Bernard Sternsher, *Rexford Tugwell and the New Deal* (1964); and R. G. Tugwell, "The Resettlement Idea," *Agricultural History*, 33 (1959).

Norman Thomas, Arkansas Sharecroppers, and the Roosevelt Agricultural Policies, 1933–1937

M. S. VENKATARAMANI

The overwhelming victory of Franklin D. Roosevelt in 1932 led many Americans engaged in agriculture to hope that a "New Deal" would soon be forthcoming for them. Three years of depression had greatly injured the farmer, as prices of agricultural products dropped to levels that had not been known for several decades. Nowhere was this agrarian distress more

Reprinted by permission of the Organization of American Historians from *Mississippi Valley Historical Review*, 47 (September 1960), 225–46.

evident than among southern cotton producers. In July, 1932, cotton was selling at 5.1 cents a pound — the lowest price on record since 1897.[1] Landowners in the cotton states found their incomes sharply reduced, and the specter of bankruptcy stared many in the face. Leaders of farm organizations and members of Congress, speaking principally on behalf of the landowning interests, clamored for a program that would check the downward spiral of cotton prices. Asserting that the legitimate demands of those engaged in farming had long been neglected, they called for legislation that would insure "parity" for agriculture.

But landowners constituted only about one fourth of the population engaged in cotton farming in the South. Seventy-three per cent of the cotton farms in the United States, as classified in the census of 1930, were cultivated by tenants, and in the ten chief cotton-producing states there were 936,896 white and 670,665 Negro tenant families.[2] The most numerous and the least secure group among these tenants were the sharecroppers. The sharecropping system was a modification of the slave system of pre-Civil War days, and the Negro sharecropper was only a step removed from his previous status as a slave. Poor white farmers, too, had gradually been drawn into the system until, in time, they had become almost as numerous as Negroes. With little financial resources of their own, the sharecroppers were often heavily in debt to the landlord and were called upon to pay high rates of interest. The strict supervision exercised by the landlords over practically every phase of sharecropper life stultified initiative and enterprise. So meager were the financial returns from their labors that most of the sharecroppers had a standard of living that was "below any level of decency."[3]

The sharecroppers in the cotton states were thus among the most disadvantaged groups in American society and as such were least able to bear the added difficulties brought on by the depression. But because they had

---

[1] U.S. Department of Agriculture, *Agricultural Situation* (Washington), XVIII (August 1, 1933), 18.

[2] *Farm Tenancy: Report of the President's Committee* (Washington, 1937), Technical Supplement, p. 43, and Table I, p. 89. See also H. A. Turner, *A Graphic Summary of Farm Tenure*, U.S. Department of Agriculture, Miscellaneous Publication No. 261 (Washington, 1936), 2. According to the Census Bureau classification, the holding of each tenant or cropper in a plantation is a farm.

[3] *Farm Tenancy: Report of the President's Committee*, 7. For a description of the evolution of the sharecropping system, see Rupert B. Vance, *Human Geography of the South* (2nd ed., Chapel Hill, 1935), 186–90, 193–99, and Vance, *Farmers without Land* (New York, 1937), 12. Especially useful on the social and economic aspects of the life of sharecroppers are Charles S. Johnson, *Shadow of the Plantation* (Chicago, 1934); Charles S. Johnson, Edwin R. Embree, and Will W. Alexander, *The Collapse of Cotton Tenancy* (Chapel Hill, 1935); Thomas J. Woofter and others, *Landlord and Tenant on the Cotton Plantation* (Washington, 1936); and Arthur F. Raper and Ira DeA. Reid, *Sharecroppers All* (Chapel Hill, 1941). The most comprehensive bibliography on the subject of farm tenancy is U.S. Department of Agriculture, Bureau of Agricultural Economics, *Farm Tenancy in the United States, 1918–1936: A Selected List of References*, Agricultural Economic Bibliography No. 70 (Washington, 1937).

no organization to espouse their cause their political influence was negligible, and the early agricultural reform plans of the Roosevelt administration gave less attention to the needs of the tenants than to the interests of the landowners. Although Roosevelt, in his first major campaign address in 1932, had proclaimed himself the champion of the "forgotten man at the bottom of the economic pyramid," [4] it was not especially to the sharecropper that his administration directed its attention. The main features of the program subsequently embodied in the Agricultural Adjustment Act of 1933 were agreed upon in a conference between Roosevelt's advisers and "farm leaders" representing principally landowning interests. Henry A. Wallace, who played an important role in the conference and who was later named secretary of agriculture, earnestly sought to insure that the farm legislation of the new administration would be in conformity with "the wishes of the farm leaders' conference." [5]

The main objective of the Agricultural Adjustment Act was to raise farm prices by curtailing production. The secretary of agriculture was authorized to enter into contracts with individual landlords under which the latter were to receive "benefit payments" for reducing their acreage of cultivation. The funds for financing the program were to be raised by means of "processing taxes." Senator Joseph T. Robinson of Arkansas, who piloted the legislation through the Senate with great energy, reminded his colleagues that "as agriculture goes, so goes the nation"; [6] but neither he nor other spokesmen for the administration ventured to discuss publicly the manner in which the new program might affect the landless farmers of the South. Could any extensive program of acreage reduction be implemented without displacing tenants? Was it not essential to provide adequate safeguards to protect the tenants from eviction and to enable them to receive a fair share of the benefit payments? If the agricultural policy makers were concerned about those issues they gave little evidence of it in the "cotton contract" that they offered to the "farmers."

The contract proved to contain inadequate safeguards for the protection of the interests of non-landowning tenants. The tenant was not a party to the contract at all. It was left to the landlord to work out his own arrangements with his tenants. The contract merely contained an exhortation to the landlord to endeavor "in good faith to bring about the reduction of acreage . . . in such manner as to cause the least possible amount of labor,

[4] Radio speech from Albany, New York, April 7, 1932, Samuel I. Rosenman (ed.), *The Public Papers and Addresses of Franklin D. Roosevelt* (13 vols., New York, 1938–1950), I, 627.

[5] Henry A. Wallace, *New Frontiers* (New York, 1934), 164–65. Wallace regarded the AAA as "a new piece of social machinery." But George N. Peek who was named by President Roosevelt to head the agency was a conservative businessman who was opposed to "social experiments." For a description of the antecedents of the AAA and of Peek's views on agricultural policy see Gilbert C. Fite, *George N. Peek and the Fight for Farm Parity* (Norman, 1954), 253–55.

[6] *New York Times*, April 12, 1932, pp. 1, 2.

economic and social disturbance." The landlord was further called upon to effect the acreage reduction "as nearly ratably as practicable" among tenants and "in so far as possible" to maintain on his farm "the normal number of tenants and other employees." Obviously, security of tenure was not guaranteed in clear and unambiguous terms to the tenants. An unscrupulous landlord stood to gain financially if he could succeed in getting rid of some of his tenants or in reducing them to the status of wage hands.[7]

While the contract itself was thus weighted in favor of the landlords, the position of the tenants was not helped by the manner in which the machinery of enforcement was organized. The responsibility for insuring compliance with the contract was intrusted to county production control committees. These agencies were hailed by Secretary Wallace and his lieutenants as an innovation of profound significance for democratic progress in the United States.[8] In practice, however, the county committees in the South were dominated by the big landlords. Sharecroppers and tenants were seldom "elected" to serve on them, and small landowners fared no better.[9] This meant that the provisions of the contract were often interpreted in terms favorable to the landlords. Since the committees were also charged with the responsibility of investigating complaints, the landless farmer found it difficult to obtain redress of his grievances. The county agricultural agent, who was the official representative of the Secretary of Agriculture, was generally regarded by landless farmers as the ally and mouthpiece of the big landlords.[10]

The inadequacies of the legislation and the hardships it entailed for sharecroppers were brought to public attention mainly through the efforts of the Socialist party leader, Norman Thomas. Initially, Thomas was not intimately acquainted with the day-to-day problems of southern farmers and the party he headed had no significant following in the rural areas of the South. He had frequently spoken on agrarian topics, however, and as the Socialist presidential candidate in 1928 and 1932 he had campaigned against absentee landlordism and had advocated co-operative farming.[11] When the bill embodying the Agricultural Adjustment Administration program was being debated in Congress, Thomas criticized it on traditional Socialist lines

[7] Henry I. Richards, *Cotton and the AAA* (Washington, 1936), 146. For the text of the contract see U.S. Department of Agriculture, *Agricultural Adjustment: A Report of Administration of the Agricultual Adjustment Act, May, 1933, to February, 1934* (Washington, 1934), Appendix I, 331–32.

[8] Wallace, *New Frontiers*, 30, 159, 195, 200–201. Rexford G. Tugwell, Under Secretary of Agriculture, stated that the committees furnished "the life-blood" of the AAA. *New York Times*, April 22, 1934, p. 30.

[9] Richards, *Cotton and the AAA*, 78. See also Harold Hoffsommer, "The AAA and the Cropper," *Social Forces* (Chapel Hill), XIII (May, 1935), 494–502.

[10] Gladys Baker, *The County Agent* (Chicago, 1939), 74–76, 212.

[11] For a detailed account of the Socialist presidential campaign in 1932, see M. S. Venkataramani, "Some Aspects of Life and Politics in the United States of America in 1932," *International Review of Social History* (Amsterdam), III (December, 1958), 361–84.

and charged that "it will not cure any fundamental evil in capitalistic agriculture." [12] The Socialist leader's indignation was aroused when the Secretary of Agriculture ordered the "plowing under" of ten million acres of growing cotton and the slaughter of six million pigs as the first move to reduce "surpluses." Drawing attention to the tragic American phenomenon of "bread lines" in the midst of surpluses, Thomas declared that the government should have bought up the surpluses to relieve want and hunger at home and in famine-stricken countries abroad.[13]

Thomas soon discovered new and more disturbing ramifications of the New Deal's agricultural program. In November, 1933, he received a letter from Martha Johnson, a Socialist party organizer in Arkansas, asking him to visit the Arkansas town of Tyronza and see for himself the plight of sharecroppers. "Here you will find the true proletariat; here you will find inarticulate men moving irresistibly towards revolution and no less." [14] Thomas was impressed by the earnestness of the appeal and the urgency of its tone. In February, 1934, he arrived in Tyronza and was shocked by what he saw and heard about the distress of the sharecroppers. In a well-attended public meeting he denounced the inequities of the system of land tenure and exhorted the sharecroppers to organize and fight for their legitimate rights. From that day onward Thomas carried on an unceasing campaign to arouse the conscience of his countrymen about the plight of their brothers in the cotton fields. In numerous speeches and articles he pleaded for action to save the sharecroppers — "the Forgotten Men of the New Deal." [15]

After his first-hand study of the situation in Arkansas, Thomas came to the conclusion that the operation of the Agricultural Adjustment Act had intensified the difficulties of the sharecroppers. He asserted that while the cash payments for crop reduction had gone to the landlords, the program had driven a large number of sharecropper families off the land or had reduced them to the position of casual day laborers. In a letter to Secretary of Agriculture Henry A. Wallace, Thomas urged that action be taken to remedy the situation. "Has the Administration any plans for these sharecroppers other than pious hopes written into the contracts with landlords?" he asked. "What about the share-croppers driven from the land under any system of limitation?" "It is a social tragedy of the first magnitude," he insisted, "a tragedy that must be repaired, that we should be reducing a cotton crop

12 *New Leader* (New York), XV (March 25, 1933), 16.
13 Norman Thomas, *The Choice before Us: Mankind at the Crossroads* (New York, 1934), 7. See also report of a speech by Thomas at Princeton University, *New York Times*, January 22, 1934, p. 5.
14 Martha Johnson to Norman Thomas, November 7, 1933, Norman Thomas Papers (Manuscripts Division, New York Public Library). Mrs. Johnson and her husband, Edward, were sent by the national office of the Socialist party to Arkansas in September, 1933, to help the struggling Socialist locals in the state.
15 See, for example, his draft of a speech delivered over the C.B.S. network, February 21, 1935, *ibid.*

when the men who raise it lack a decent supply of cotton for their families. The whole country ought to be aroused to the social significance of the situation." [16]

In his reply Wallace did not challenge Thomas' description of the plight of the sharecroppers. He asserted, however, that their "extremely low standard of living" had existed for a long time and was not due to the new crop reduction program. The program, the Secretary declared, called for a contract that contained terms designed to prevent the landowner from evicting his tenants. "We are determined to avoid injustice," he added, "and to correct it to the full extent of our power where it may arise." [17]

While Wallace did not choose to take any vigorous action to safeguard the rights of the landless tenants and sharecroppers, he was quite active in claiming credit for the benefits that his program had conferred on "farmers." In numerous speeches he voiced an assurance that if Jefferson were alive he would wholeheartedly support the AAA; and Edward A. O'Neal, president of the American Farm Bureau Federation, expressed the sentiments of many landowners when he praised the program as "the Magna Charta of American Agriculture — its charter of freedom from the domination of predatory business interests, its guarantee of economic equality with other groups, its promise of a new day in American agriculture." [18] Wallace's lieutenants were equally enthusiastic in their public appraisals of the performance of the agency. It was reported, however, that a group of "liberals" within the AAA, under the leadership of Jerome Frank, were pressing for some positive action to relieve the distress of the sharecroppers. Their "rebellion" was speedily and decisively quelled, and on the demand of Chester Davis, the AAA administrator, the dissidents themselves were dismissed from the agency in February, 1935. Although President Roosevelt made no move to save the liberals, he stated that he was very sorry over the episode and that he had "the highest respect for all parties concerned." [19]

Thomas regarded Wallace and his associates as "high-minded and competent" men and conceded that partly as a result of their policies the prices

[16] Thomas to Henry A. Wallace, *February 22*, 1934, *ibid.*
[17] Wallace to Thomas, March 8, 1934, *ibid.*
[18] Quoted in Orville M. Kile, *The Farm Bureau through Three Decades* (Baltimore, 1948), 211. Some urban liberals were also impressed by the claim made on behalf of the program. See, for example, the comment that it was "the most brilliant success yet achieved by the Roosevelt administration," made in December, 1934, by Allan Nevins in the course of a lecture at University College, London. *New York Times*, December 30, 1934, Sec. IV, p. 2.
[19] Quoted in Arthur M. Schlesinger, Jr., *The Age of Roosevelt: The Coming of the New Deal* (Boston, 1958), 80. Schlesinger's account of the episode is based on his examination of the Department of Agriculture Papers as well as on other private papers and interviews. The present writer did not consult the Department of Agriculture Papers but examined carefully the extensive collection in the Widener Memorial Library, Harvard University, of press releases, statements, and other material put out by the Department. This material, while remarkable for its tone of self-praise, contains very little analysis of the problems of tenants.

of agricultural commodities, including cotton, had begun to rise. He felt, however, that they had failed to comprehend the gravity of human suffering in the cotton country.[20] He was reinforced in his conviction when he studied a report prepared by a group headed by Dr. William R. Amberson, professor of physiology at the University of Tennessee. The report stated that between 15 and 20 per cent of the sharecroppers had lost their employment as a result of the crop reduction program, adding that the contract prescribed by the government did not protect them from dismissal or exploitation as day laborers.[21] Thomas wrote to Wallace again in May, 1934, urging him to eliminate the loopholes in the contract forms, provide representation to sharecroppers on county production control committees, and insure for them the right of organization.[22] In his reply the Secretary reiterated his "serious concern" about the problem, but offered no assurance that the eviction of the sharecroppers would be stopped. He promised to strengthen the corps of investigators and to improve the system of enforcement, but added that it would be difficult to draw up a contract that would adequately protect the sharecropper's interests.[23]

Wallace did not lack information from his own sources regarding the position of the sharecroppers.[24] In January, 1935, Mrs. Mary Conner Myers, an attorney for the AAA, visited Arkansas and investigated complaints relating to the eviction of sharecroppers, but the Department of Agriculture did not release her report for publication. Dr. Calvin B. Hoover of Duke University, who conducted another investigation at the instance of Secretary Wallace, reported that the sharecropper had not shared equally with the landlord in the benefits of the AAA. The support of the landlords for the cotton contract, he said, had been secured "by an inducement obtained at the expense of the share-tenant and share cropper." Hoover asserted that the operation of the acreage reduction program "created a motive for reducing the number of tenants on farms" and added that the system of enforcement of the provisions of the contract did not adequately safeguard the rights of sharecroppers. "It is plainly the duty of the Agricultural Adjustment Administration . . . to spare no effort in preventing the unequal distribution of the advantages of the acreage reduction program, and particularly to prevent the operation of that program from making the situation of

---

[20] Thomas, The Choice before Us, 100.

[21] The Social and Economic Consequences of the Cotton Acreage Program (Memphis, 1934). See also William R. Amberson, "The New Deal for Share-Croppers," Nation (New York), CXL (February 13, 1935), 185–87; Norman Thomas, "Victims of Change," Current History (New York), XLII (April, 1935), 36–41.

[22] Thomas to Wallace, May 9, 1934, Thomas Papers.

[23] Wallace to Thomas, May 14, 1934, ibid.

[24] Wallace claimed credit for having set up suitable machinery for sounding farm opinion. Wallace, New Frontiers, 266–67. But since the machinery was based on the county production control associations, dominated by the big landlords, the point of view of the non-landowning farmer was perhaps not adequately conveyed to Washington.

any class of producers worse," Hoover declared.[25] No concrete action was taken by the Department of Agriculture, however, to safeguard the interests of sharecroppers.

Convinced that the disadvantaged farmers could hope to win their legitimate rights only by banding together in a strong organization, Thomas lent vigorous support to a new union started with his encouragement by a small group of Arkansas Socialists. The leader of the group was H. L. Mitchell, state secretary of the Socialist party, and associated with him were J. R. Butler, Howard Kester, and E. B. McKinney. The Southern Tenant Farmers' Union, as it was called, came into existence in Poinsett County in eastern Arkansas, which Thomas had visited earlier. The most important "farmers" in the area were corporations which controlled huge plantations. The largest landowner was the Chapman and Dewey Lumber Company with a plantation of 17,000 acres. The Poinsett Lumber Company, a subsidiary of the Singer Sewing Machine Company, and E. Ritter and Company owned farms of about 5,000 acres each. There were also some big farms owned by local landlords, such as the Hiram Norcross Plantation which covered about 5,000 acres. The resident managers of the corporation-owned plantations and the big local landlords, who were leaders of the community, were greatly angered by the temerity of the Socialists in attempting to organize the sharecroppers; and small farmers and merchants among the whites resented the efforts of the union leaders to hold non-segregated meetings. Sharecroppers who joined the union were subjected to intimidation and threats of eviction.[26]

While the local law enforcement authorities usually remained passive in the face of such activities, they sometimes swung into action on behalf of the landlords. Early in 1935, for example, Ward Rodgers, a young organizer for the union, was arrested at Marked Tree, in Poinsett County, on a charge of "anarchy" and was promptly sentenced to a fine of $500 and imprisonment for six months.[27] Released on bail, he was soon arrested again in another community and thrown into jail on a charge of "barratry," which was defined as exciting or maintaining "suits or quarrels in the courts or elsewhere in the country" and disturbing the peace by spreading "false rumors and calumnies whereby discord and disquiet may grow among neighbors." The fact that this restriction — originally directed against shysters in the legal profession — was now being used to thwart the efforts to organize

[25] *New York Times*, April 22, 1935, Sec. II, p. 7.

[26] H. L. Mitchell, "Organizing Southern Share-Croppers," *New Republic* (New York), LXXX (October 3, 1934), 217–18. For an account of the early history of the Union, see Howard Kester, *Revolt among the Sharecroppers* (New York, 1935), 55–56.

[27] For a quotation from a speech that Rodgers made to a meeting of sharecroppers, see Richards, *Cotton and the AAA*, 149 n., and for his statement to a reporter, Little Rock, *Arkansas Gazette*, January 31, 1935 (clipping in Thomas Papers).

the tenant farmers brought a protest from the American Civil Liberties Union, along with assistance in the conduct of Rodgers' defense.[28]

Meanwhile, landlords and local authorities sought to spread the impression that a serious "Red" menace had risen in Arkansas, and a Memphis newspaper echoed their agitation by proclaiming in a big headline: "Red Flag Spreading, Prosecutor Charges." [29] In Marked Tree, where the tenants' union began to gain substantial support, the city fathers promulgated an ordinance making it unlawful for any person "to make or deliver a public speech on any street, alley, park or other place" without securing permission from the local authorities. The ordinance was invoked to prevent organizers, and even such visitors as Roger Baldwin of the American Civil Liberties Union and Jennie Lee, the prominent British Socialist, from addressing meetings of sharecroppers.[30] "Of course the law don't mean that church people can't hold speakin', just the radicals, that's all," the mayor of Marked Tree told a visiting *New York Times* correspondent. "I'd give permission to most anybody to hold a street meeting so long as they haven't been mixed up with the union and ain't listed in the 'red network' book." [31]

Thomas, who had been striving to focus national attention on the developments in Arkansas, decided to make a tour of the area early in March, 1935. In many places he was told of evictions, intimidation, and violence; and in the little town of Birdsong armed intruders forcibly prevented him from addressing a meeting of sharecroppers.[32] Elsewhere vigilante squads harassed members and supporters of the Southern Tenant Farmers' Union, and Mitchell and other leaders of the union were forced to go "underground" to escape vigilante punishment. On March 25 a band of about forty masked "night riders" fired upon the house of C. T. Carpenter, a respected citizen who had incurred the wrath of the extremists by serving as an attorney for the union. Five days later another group of armed men "mobbed a group of Negro men and women returning home from church, beating several of them with pistol butts and flashlights." A Negro church

[28] See American Civil Liberties Union, *Annual Reports* (New York), 1935–1936, 1936–1937, and 1937–1938, for accounts of the Union's work on behalf of the sharecroppers. Norman Thomas was a member of its board of directors.

[29] Memphis *Commercial Appeal*, January 31, 1935 (clipping in Thomas Papers). In a letter of protest to the editor of the newspaper, Thomas charged that hysteria was being deliberately aroused over the efforts of sharecroppers to organize themselves into a union. Thomas to Editor of the Memphis *Commercial Appeal*, February 1, 1935, Thomas Papers.

[30] H. L. Mitchell to Thomas, February 25, 1935, Archives of the Socialist Party (Manuscripts Division, Duke University Library, Durham).

[31] *New York Times*, April 16, 1935, p. 18. See also Lucien Koch, "The War in Arkansas," *New Republic*, LXXXII (March 27, 1935), 182–84.

[32] "Norman Thomas Visits the Cotton Fields," mimeographed release by the Southern Tenant Farmers' Union, March, 1935, copy in Thomas Papers; "Norman Thomas Attacked in Arkansas," *Socialist Call* (New York), I (March 23, 1935), 1, 10; John Herling, "Field Notes from Arkansas," *Nation*, CXL (April 10, 1935), 419–20.

was fired upon in a neighboring community on the same night.[33] In order to prevent bloodshed Carpenter advised sharecroppers and organizers to obey the laws invoked by the landlords even though it meant a temporary cessation of the union's organizing drive. Thomas earnestly exhorted union leaders to strive to the best of their ability to avoid situations that might result in bloodshed.[34]

The hard-pressed leaders of the Southern Tenant Farmers' Union had other difficulties to contend with. A ruling by the Secretary of Agriculture and a decision of the Arkansas Supreme Court gravely affected the union's fight against arbitrary evictions. The union had contended that Section 7 of the cotton contract made it obligatory on the part of the landlords to maintain not only the same number of tenants but also the same tenants as at the time of the signing of the contract. The Secretary of Agriculture, however, supported the interpretation of landlords when he ruled in February, 1935, that the section "does not bind owners to keep the *same* tenants." [35] The union suffered another reverse when its petition for an injunction to restrain a landlord from evicting some tenants was rejected by the state supreme court on the ground that the tenants were not a party to the cotton contract.[36] The exhortations to the landlord contained in the cotton contract were thus shown to offer no real protection to the sharecroppers, and the situation in Arkansas at the time led a special correspondent of the *New York Times* to write:

> For many of them [the sharecroppers] the "Three A's" have spelled unemployment, shrunken incomes and a lowered standard of living, if the hand-to-mouth existence they have led since the war between the States may be called living at all. . . . Attempts to better their lot through organization in the Southern Tenant Farmers Union have taught them that they have few rights under the laws of Arkansas and no more security under the New Deal than they have had in the past. Scores have been evicted or "run off the place" for union activity, and

[33] The union issued a statement drawing attention to acts of violence against its members and supporters. "Acts of Tyranny and Terror Committed against Innocent Men, Women and Children of the Southern Tenant Farmers' Union in Northeast Arkansas," mimeographed, April, 1935, Thomas Papers. See also *New York Times*, April 16, 1935, p. 18; H. L. Mitchell and J. R. Butler, "The Cropper Learns His Fate," *Nation*, CXLI (September 18, 1935), 328–29; C. T. Carpenter, "King Cotton's Slaves: The Fate of the Share-Cropper Becomes a National Issue," *Scribner's Magazine* (New York), XCVIII (October, 1935), 193–99.

[34] Thomas to H. L. Mitchell and Howard Kester, April 5, 1935, Archives of the Socialist Party. Thomas suggested, however, that the union might acquire an armored car for protection against surprise attack on the road.

[35] Richards, *Cotton and the AAA*, 149. Richards states that there were differences of opinion over the issue within the AAA prior to its reorganization in 1935.

[36] *West et al. v. Norcross*, 190 Ark. 667 (1935); 80 Southwestern 2nd 67 (1935). For a discussion of regulations governing landlord-tenant relationships, see Albert H. Cotton, "Regulations of Farm Landlord-Tenant Relationships," *Law and Contemporary Problems* (Durham), IV (October, 1937), 508–38; A. B. Book, "A Note on the Legal Status of Share-Tenants and Share-Croppers in the South," *ibid.*, 539–45.

masked night riders have spread fear among union members, both white and Negro. In some communities the most fundamental rights of free speech and assemblage have been abridged.[37]

At the instance of Thomas the national executive committee of the Socialist party, meeting in Buffalo in March, 1935, sent a telegram to President Roosevelt calling for an investigation of the "reign of terror" directed against the Southern Tenant Farmers' Union in Arkansas; and when Secretary Wallace replied on behalf of the President that the situation was a difficult one for the federal government to step into, Thomas retorted: "A government that has interfered as extensively as yours has in the cotton economy of the South has a moral responsibility to act in view of the wholesale evictions I've seen with my own eyes." [38] Thomas also appealed to Under Secretary of Agriculture Rexford G. Tugwell, and to Chester Davis, AAA administrator, to use their good offices to bring about an open investigation. "I write earnestly," he wrote, "because I think it will only be a miracle that will prevent bloodshed . . . arising from the domineering arrogance of the planter class, unless public opinion and the federal government can take some sort of action." [39] Thomas went to Washington to present his case personally to representatives of the administration, but he soon became convinced that the officials of the Department of Agriculture, whatever their personal convictions in the matter, were restrained from taking vigorous action because of their fear of powerful southern senators.[40] As a consequence he wrote to Felix Frankfurter of Harvard University, urging him to bring the matter to the attention of the President; but Frankfurter replied that he did not know anything about agriculture and that it would not be proper for him to raise the matter with Roosevelt.[41]

In a final effort to reach the President, Thomas wrote a personal letter to him, describing the happenings in the cotton belt and voicing his opinion that high officials of the Department of Agriculture were "frankly in fear of the powers of Southern Senators." Roosevelt replied promptly and courteously, but neither acknowledged the existence of conditions as Thomas had described them nor offered any promise of early action. The President said that an appraisal of the conditions that Thomas had outlined would have to be based on careful investigations and that such investigations were under

[37] *New York Times*, April 15, 1935, p. 6. This quotation is from one of a series of news articles by F. Raymond Daniell, a reporter who made a special investigation of the situation in Arkansas in the spring of 1935. The *Times*, which had previously carried only brief reports of Thomas' charges about distress and injustice in the cotton fields, now commented editorially that the Daniell articles "constitute an interesting chapter in contemporary social history." *Ibid.*, April 16, 1935, p. 21.

[38] *Ibid.*, March 24, 1935, p. 12.

[39] Thomas to Chester Davis, March 22, 1935; Thomas to Rexford G. Tugwell, March 28, 1935, Thomas Papers.

[40] Thomas to H. L. Mitchell and Howard Kester, April 5, 1935, Archives of the Socialist Party.

[41] Felix Frankfurter to Thomas, March 27, 1935, Thomas Papers.

way. Thomas then wrote again to the President, appealing for some action to safeguard at least the elementary civil liberties of the sharecroppers and to protect "above everything else" the right of tenants and sharecroppers to organize. "That," he said, "is the dynamic force on which we must depend for real progress." [42]

Thomas also wrote to several United States senators, both Republicans and Democrats, urging them to give attention to the plight of the sharecroppers and to take steps to safeguard their civil liberties. He appealed especially to Senator Robert F. Wagner to extend the scope of his labor relations bill to include protection for agricultural workers. The condition of agricultural workers, Thomas wrote to Wagner, was worse than that of industrial workers. "A continuance of these conditions is preparing the way for a desperate revolt of virtual serfs," he added. "Unless the right to organize peacefully can be guaranteed we shall have a continuance of virtual slavery until the day of the revolt." [43] Wagner replied that agricultural workers had been excluded from the scope of his bill "only because I thought it would be better to pass the bill for the benefit of industrial workers than not to pass it at all." He was still convinced, he said, that the inclusion of agricultural workers was not desirable as it would lessen the likelihood of the bill's passage.[44] Not satisfied by Wagner's response, Thomas immediately sought the aid of organized labor. In a letter to William Green, president of the American Federation of Labor, he warned that industrial labor could not afford to remain a passive spectator of the events in the cotton belt. "As long as there is a reservoir of white and colored workers as badly exploited as these plantation workers," he declared, "the employers always have an advantage in the struggle with organized labor." [45] The AFL responded by adopting unanimously a resolution drawing attention to "the inhuman levels to which the workers employed in the cotton plantations had been reduced" and calling for a federal investigation of the condition of the workers.[46]

Democratic leaders acted swiftly to counteract Thomas' campaign to publicize the disabilities of the sharecroppers. In a special article in the *New York Times*, Secretary Wallace voiced his disapproval of the bitterness aroused by "Communist and Socialist agitators" in the South.[47] Senator Robinson, apparently irked by the spotlight focused on Arkansas by the So-

[42] Thomas to Roosevelt, April 9, 1935; Roosevelt to Thomas, April 22, 1935; Thomas to Roosevelt, April 23, 1935, *ibid.*

[43] Thomas to Leon Keyserling (Secretary to Senator Wagner), April 1, 1935; Thomas to Robert F. Wagner, April 3, 1935, *ibid.*

[44] Wagner to Thomas, April 2, 1935, *ibid.*

[45] Thomas to William Green, April 3, 1935, *ibid.*

[46] *Report of the Proceedings of the Fifty-fifth Annual Convention of the American Federation of Labor* (Washington, 1935), 588.

[47] *New York Times*, March 31, 1935, Sec. VII, pp. 4, 21. The Secretary admitted that displacement of tenants had increased and that the operation of the cotton contracts had probably added to their difficulties.

cialist leader, tried to discredit Republicans by alleging that they were giving encouragement and financial assistance to radical propagandists. President Roosevelt, in an "unscheduled address" before what was described as a spontaneous demonstration of farmers, held in Washington in May, 1935, charged that men with "special axes to grind" were trying to mislead the people by "lying" about the farm program.[48]

Administration tacticians apparently concluded, however, that the time had come for some action as proof of their solicitude for non-landowning farmers. "Respectable" groups as distinguished from Socialist "agitators" had begun to express misgivings concerning the plight of the sharecroppers. The Committee on Minority Groups in Economic Recovery, for instance, after more than a year's study of the problem, reported in March, 1935, that the southern tenant farmer was condemned to an economic and social life that was of a lower order than that of European peasants.[49] A number of articles about the hardships of the sharecroppers appeared in national magazines and northern newspapers.

The administration's response to such unfavorable publicity was twofold. On July 1, 1935, a new agency known as the Resettlement Administration was established to provide emergency relief to a selective group of farmers and to implement a long-range program for their rehabilitation.[50] The administration also announced its support of a farm tenancy bill sponsored in Congress by Senator John H. Bankhead of Alabama and Representative Marvin Jones of Texas. The bill called for the establishment of a federal agency to help selected tenants by providing long-term, low-interest loans for the purchase of farms. The agency, according to the bill, was to be capitalized at fifty million dollars and was to have potential authority to issue one billion dollars in bonds under government guarantee. Secretary Wallace hailed it as a "statesmanlike proposal" and pledged the full co-operation of the Department of Agriculture for the attainment of its objectives. The general philosophy of the Bankhead-Jones bill, said Wallace, was

[48] The object of the demonstration, according to its organizers, was "to counteract unfavorable impressions of the AAA which have been spread through the press by anti-administration propagandists." *Ibid.*, May 12, 1935, p. 9; May 15, pp. 1, 3. Edward F. Kennedy, secretary of the Farmers' Union, a national organization of small farmers, charged that county agents and minor officials had contributed funds to meet the expenses of persons who participated in the "trek" to Washington. Secretary Wallace denied the charge that the demonstration was inspired by the Department of Agriculture.

[49] *New York Times*, March 21, 1935, p. 25. The study was directed by Edwin R. Embree, president of the Julius Rosenwald Fund, Will W. Alexander, director of the Commission on Interracial Cooperation, and Charles S. Johnson, Negro educator and head of the Department of Social Research at Fisk University. Their report was published as *The Collapse of Cotton Tenancy* (Chapel Hill, 1935).

[50] The new agency functioned from July 1, 1935, to December 31, 1936. For an account of its work, see Clarence A. Wiley, "Settlement and Unsettlement in the Resettlement Administration Program," *Law and Contemporary Problems*, IV (October, 1937), 456–72.

"going back to the old principles, intended but not realized in our early land policy, of trying to get the good farm land of America into the hands of owner operators who live on family-size farms." [51]

"Farms for the Tenants" was an attractive slogan that evoked images of sturdy and independent yeomen diligently tilling their own homesteads. Newspapers described the tenancy bill — without any contradiction from its sponsors and supporters — as designed "to rehabilitate approximately 10,000,000 share-croppers and tenant farmers, Negro and white." [52] Roman Catholic, Protestant, and Jewish social welfare groups promptly endorsed the bill and William Green, head of the American Federation of Labor, expressed his support.

Thomas, on the other hand, regarded the Bankhead-Jones bill as a totally inappropriate method for meeting the problems of the sharecroppers. "It is simply a gesture," he said, "by which the leading advocates of the Bill in the Administration would like to divert attention from some results of the AAA and in particular the enormous hypocrisy of Section 7 of the cotton contracts." In a memorandum to the Senate Committee on Agriculture he stated that the bill as it stood would principally benefit land speculators while imposing a burden on the general public, and that the subsidization of an American peasantry on subsistence farms would be a step of questionable value. The bill "should at least be amended to allow the government to encourage cotton cooperatives under expert management," he contended. "That is to say, whole plantations should be organized as units, socially owned, with good working conditions and security of status for the present tenants who should be trained in cooperation." [53]

Nearly a year later the Southern Tenant Farmers' Union returned to the subject with a complaint that the bill's vague promise of homesteads for a few would not provide a solution of the problem of underprivileged groups in agriculture; [54] and within a few weeks a growing sentiment of protest against existing conditions flared into action. During May and June, 1936, approximately five thousand sharecroppers in Arkansas went on strike. Several cases of violence against strikers were reported, and many strikers were arrested on such charges as vagrancy, assault, and "interference with labor." [55] But when President Roosevelt visited Little Rock on June 10 to participate in the celebration of the centennial of Arkansas' admission to statehood, he made no reference to the strike, despite the fact that Thomas had wired him that all Americans "who care for liberty and justice to work-

[51] *New York Times,* March 31, 1935, Sec. VII, pp. 4, 21; April 22, 1935, p. 7.

[52] *Ibid.,* April 15, 1935, p. 6.

[53] Thomas to Senate Committee on Agriculture, May 1, 1935, Thomas Papers.

[54] *New York Times,* March 29, 1936, p. 25.

[55] For an account of the strike see "The Cotton Croppers Strike in Arkansas," Federal Council of Churches of Christ, *Information Service* (New York), XV (June, 1936).

ers" would anxiously wait to learn what the President would say concerning the disabilities of agricultural workers in Arkansas.[56]

The story of the strike received widespread notice when two Socialists, Miss Willie Sue Blagden and the Reverend Claude Williams, were subjected to a whipping by unknown assailants near the town of Earle.[57] The incident aroused considerable indignation in other sections of the country, and Thomas called upon the President to take effective action to deal with the situation. When Roosevelt replied that he had asked the governor of Arkansas to appoint a committee of citizens to investigate the matter, Thomas and the leaders of the tenant farmers' union asserted that no satisfactory investigation could be expected under the sponsorship of the governor, who had "shown himself fully the representative and tool of the planter class."[58] Their prediction was only partially confirmed when the report of the governor's committee, released in November, 1936, indorsed the objectives of the Bankhead-Jones bill and called for improvéd housing and long-term leases for sharecroppers.[59] But in the meantime a federal grand jury which had been investigating charges brought by the Southern Tenant Farmers' Union concerning the existence of peonage in Arkansas indicted the city marshal of Earle on eight counts of violating federal antislavery laws, one of which was that he had broken up a procession of strikers, arrested thirteen, and forced them to work on his own farm.

With such indications that public interest in the problem of tenancy was becoming aroused, and with the presidential campaign of 1936 in progress, Roosevelt apparently deemed it appropriate to demonstrate his solicitude for the tenants. In identical letters he called upon Senator Bankhead and Representative Jones to be ready by December with "plans for meeting the tenancy problem that might be undertaken by the Federal Government." The Republican presidential candidate, Alfred M. Landon, also proclaimed his resolve to promote a program to encourage the acquisition of lands by tenants. Thomas, again the standard-bearer of the Socialist party, mocked this "sudden concern for the tenant farmers" manifested on election eve by the Republican and Democratic candidates.[60] Roosevelt, he said, had not shown a real interest in redressing the grievances of the laboring men

[56] Roosevelt's speech is in Rosenman (ed.), *Public Papers and Addresses of Franklin D. Roosevelt*, V, 195–202; and for Thomas' comments see *Socialist Call*, II (June 20, 1936), 1.

[57] For a brief contemporary account of the incident see "Farmers: 'True Arkansas Hospitality'," *Time* (New York), XXVII (June 29, 1936), 12. Some additional detail appears in Oren Stephens, "Revolt in the Delta: What Happened to the Sharecroppers' Union," *Harper's Magazine* (New York), CLXXXIII (November, 1941), 658.

[58] Thomas wrote caustically that entrusting the governor of Arkansas with any responsibility for investigating the grievances of sharecroppers was like "asking Al Capone in his prime to investigate conditions in the underworld in Chicago." Norman Thomas, *After the New Deal, What?* (New York, 1936), 50.

[59] *New York Times*, November 20, 1936, p. 17.

[60] Speech at Waterloo, Iowa, *ibid.*, October 14, 1936, p. 11.

of the South. "He seems more interested in the labor problems of Pennsylvania where he needs their votes, than in the South, where he does not need the votes of the laboring man," Thomas charged.[61]

Shortly after his re-election, Roosevelt appointed a special committee, with Wallace as chairman, to report on "a long-term program of action to alleviate the shortcomings of our farm tenancy system," and a representative of the Southern Tenant Farmers' Union, W. L. Blackstone, was named as one of the members of the committee. Wallace undertook a trip through sharecropper territory and later spoke about workers "at the bottom of the pile" who constituted a majority of the population engaged in agriculture. Although he had ruled in 1935 that Section 7 of the cotton contract did not obligate the landlord to keep the same tenants, he now declared that security of tenure for tenant farmers was as important as security for other workers. He adhered, however, to his earlier stand that the regulation of the landlord-tenant relationship was outside the scope of federal action and was a matter to be handled at the state level.[62]

The Wallace committee submitted its report to President Roosevelt in February, 1937. It did not make a single criticism of federal agricultural policies or of the actions (or lack of them) of state governments. Nevertheless, its moderately worded findings constituted an admission of many of the charges that Thomas and leaders of the Southern Tenant Farmers' Union had leveled for over three years. One farm family out of every four "occupies a position in the Nation's social and economic structure that is precarious and should not be tolerated," the report said. Tenants, croppers, and farm laborers were the principal disadvantaged groups among farm families. The report added that the committee had "noted instances where disadvantaged groups in their attempts to organize and increase their bargaining power have been unlawfully prevented from exercising their civil liberties." It did not, however, seek to investigate them or to make any criticism of persons in a position of authority who had remained silent in the face of unlawful attacks on those engaged in lawful activities. The report also conceded, without attempting to apportion blame or responsibility, that the administration's agricultural policies had not provided security to the disadvantaged groups. "Croppers, who generally supply only their labor," it said, "are usually the most insecure group of tenants. Even the slender protection of the cropper contract has recently become less effective, as conditions have impelled landlords to convert many croppers into laborers, dependent on casual employment for wages." [63]

[61] *Ibid.*, September 23, 1936, p. 16.
[62] *Ibid.*, January 24, 1936, p. 2; November 23, 1936, p. 3; January 13, 1937, p. 13.
[63] *Farm Tenancy: Report of the President's Committee*, 4, 7. While the report confirmed the contention of Thomas and the leaders of the Southern Tenant Farmers' Union, concerning the conversion of sharecroppers into laborers, it did not estimate the extent to which this has been done. Considerable disagreement exists in the conclusions reached by writers who have published studies on this subject. See D. W. Watkins,

But the committee did not follow up its analysis with a demand for the elimination of the abuses in the landlord-tenant relationship. It held that while the federal government could do much to improve the conditions of tenant farmers "some of the most fruitful fields of endeavor are under the jurisdiction of State agencies." The report recommended that the federal government set up a Farm Security Administration in the Department of Agriculture to implement a program of "land for tenants." The Secretary of Agriculture should be authorized, through the new agency, to acquire suitable farm land to be made available to selected tenants, the report said.[64]

Blackstone, representative of the Southern Tenant Farmers' Union on the committee, filed a minority report expressing disagreement with the philosophy of "small homesteads" for tenants and offering a number of counter-suggestions.[65] In forwarding the committee's report to Congress, Roosevelt did not refer to or support any of these suggestions. Evoking the "American dream of the family-size farm, owned by the family which operates it," the President warned that the tenancy problem had reached such magnitude that action could no longer be postponed.[66] The program that the President commended to Congress was, however, a cautious and conservative one. Secretary Wallace himself had admitted on one occasion that with an annual outlay of $50,000,000 it would take 230 years to find farms for the existing number of tenants at a cost of $4,000 per farm.[67] According to Presi-

---

"Agricultural Adjustment and Farm Tenure," *Journal of Farm Economics* (Menasha, Wis.), XVIII (August, 1936), 469–76; Wilson Gee, "Acreage Reduction and the Displacement of Farm Labor," *ibid.*, XVII (August, 1935), 522–28; Gordon W. Blackwell, "The Displaced Tenant Farm Family in North Carolina," *Social Forces*, XIII (October, 1934), 69; Carl C. Taylor, Helen W. Wheeler, and Ellis L. Kirkpatrick, *Disadvantaged Classes in American Agriculture*, Farm Security Administration, Social Research Report No. VIII (Washington, 1938), 43; and Richards, *Cotton and the AAA*, 155–61. Figures compiled from Census Bureau publications show that between 1930 and 1935 the number of colored tenants declined in all the ten states in which cotton was an important crop. The number of white croppers declined in eight states and that of colored croppers in seven. In Arkansas the number of white croppers declined by 16.7 per cent and that of colored croppers by 9.9 per cent from 1930 to 1935. *Farm Tenancy: Report of the President's Committee*, Table VI, pp. 98–99. The extent to which the decline in the number of sharecroppers is attributable directly to the acreage reduction program cannot be determined from the census figures, but, as one study has suggested, there would be "few people gullible enough to believe that the acreage devoted to cotton can be reduced one-third without an accompanying decrease in the laborers engaged in its production." Fred C. Frey and T. Lynn Smith, "The Influence of the AAA Cotton Program upon the Tenant, Cropper, and Laborer," *Rural Sociology* (Baton Rouge), I (December, 1936), 489.

[64] *Farm Tenancy: Report of the President's Committee*, 12, 17–18.

[65] "Minority Report of W. L. Blackstone, Representing the Southern Tenant Farmers' Union on the President's Farm Tenancy Committee," *ibid.*, 20–22.

[66] *Ibid.*, 25–26.

[67] *New York Times*, December 17, 1936, p. 9. See also James G. Maddox, "The Bankhead-Jones Farm Tenant Act," *Law and Contemporary Problems*, IV (October, 1937), 451.

dent Roosevelt the number of tenants in the United States was increasing at the rate of 40,000 per year. But neither he nor many members of Congress gave firm support to even this modest program aiming at a partial solution of the tenancy problem. When the House Committee on Agriculture struck from the bill the section providing for an annual appropriation of $50,000,-000, Roosevelt contented himself with an attempt to obtain a smaller amount or even a mere recognition of the principle of assistance to tenants.[68]

The proposed deletion was not accepted, but the original allotment was scaled down to a more modest beginning. As finally adopted in July, 1937, the Bankhead-Jones Farm Tenancy Act provided for an appropriation of $10,000,000 in 1938; $25,000,000 in 1939; and $50,000,000 annually thereafter, out of which the Secretary of Agriculture was authorized to give low-interest loans to selected tenants for the purchase of farms. The loans were to be repaid over a period of forty years; and the newly organized Farm Security Administration became the agency through which the work was to be handled.

In theory this program meant a promise of opportunity for America's sharecroppers to improve their economic and social status; but in reality it could provide assistance to only a very small proportion of those who might wish to become the owners of the farms they cultivated. According to Census Bureau publications there were 2,865,155 tenants in the United States in 1935, representing 42.1 per cent of the total number of farmers.[69] By the end of 1941, the Farm Security Administration had given loans to only 20,748 tenants for the purchase of farms, and the agency reported that it had received about twenty applications for every loan that it was able to make out of the available funds. In Arkansas, which had a total of 151,759 tenant farmers in 1935, only 1,399 had been successful in obtaining loans during the period covered by this report.[70] With less than one per cent of its tenant-sharecropper population receiving any direct benefit from the government's program, it was obvious that little progress had been made toward a satisfactory solution of the state's problem.

The meagerness of these results, however, should not be permitted to obscure the more important fact that the problems of the sharecropper-tenant element in Arkansas served as a basis for the discussion and testing of two sharply divergent views of governmental power and responsibility in matters relating to social and economic affairs. That Norman Thomas drew upon his knowledge of the events in Arkansas to launch a general attack

[68] *New York Times*, April 1, 1937, p. 1. Arthur Krock, the well-informed Washington correspondent of the *Times*, interpreted Roosevelt's budget message for the year as "serving notice on tenancy enthusiasts to make a modest start." *Ibid.*, April 22, 1937, p. 22.

[69] *Farm Tenancy: Report of the President's Committee*, Table I, p. 89.

[70] *Report of the Administrator of the Farm Security Administration*, 1941 (Washington, 1942), 17, 31–32.

on New Deal agricultural policies seems clear. That the Roosevelt administration, despite its professed concern for "the forgotten man at the bottom of the economic pyramid," did not give adequate consideration to the needs of the tenants in framing and applying the Agricultural Adjustment Act is also apparent. But Thomas' unceasing efforts to focus public attention on the plight of the sharecroppers in Arkansas failed to bring about a correction of the features of the cotton program that adversely affected their interests.

When Secretary Wallace and the officials of the Agricultural Adjustment Administration took the position that the law did not permit them to do more than they were doing to protect the rights of the sharecroppers, they were technically correct. And in following up such a line of explanation it has been argued that any further governmental action would have amounted to an extension of control over the private property of landlords for the benefit of another group — a development that in 1933 was not a part of American practice or tradition. On the other hand, the critic might still legitimately ask whether it was really beyond the ingenuity and authority of Roosevelt and Wallace to have drawn up a program that would have assured a more equitable return to sharecroppers retained in employment and some protection to them against arbitrary eviction. But as the New Deal made way for the war effort after December, 1941, the farm tenancy picture improved in Arkansas, as in the nation as a whole. The military draft and employment opportunities in war plants in the South and elsewhere, together with the continuing progress of mechanization, were to have a far greater effect than either the proposals of Norman Thomas or the agricultural policies of the Roosevelt administration in reversing the growth of tenancy in the United States.

19

LABOR'S BID FOR POWER

On the eve of the New Deal, the labor movement was plainly on the decline. Fewer than 3 million members, less than 10 percent of the nonagricultural workforce, remained in the unions, and these figures were nearly 2.1 million members and 10 percentage points fewer than in 1920. To be sure, the 1920 figures should not be taken too seriously, because they represent the temporary impact of federal requirements during World War I that companies holding government contracts should engage in collective bargaining with their workers. When that requirement lapsed and when the Wilson administration used its power to crush major organizing efforts in the steel and other industries, union membership declined precipitously to about 3.6 million by 1923. From there, however, it continued to decline in an almost straight line. Among the reasons were: (1) a distinctly unfavorable government attitude, reflected in and reflecting the public's coolness to reformers and all sorts of "other troublemakers"; (2) high capital investment in technology that displaced large numbers of workers in the organized trades; (3) a significant increase in the percentage of women in the nonagricultural workforce; (4) the success of "welfare capitalism" – a combination of individual company pension and compensation plans, company unions, and public relations efforts that made independent unions seem unnecessary at best and more than a little sinister otherwise.

Underlying it all, moreover, was the conservative attitude of union leaders. Radical unionism had been all but destroyed by the repression of 1917–21 and by internecine warfare among the socialists. Virtually all that remained was the AFL leadership which, in its earlier contests with socialist union insurgents, had become committed against government intervention in the labor scene. Thus, the AFL was on record against, for example, legislation for job safeguards, unemployment insurance, minimum wages, and even the promotion of unionization itself. "In the demand for collective bargaining," the Federation declared in 1919, "labor has never asked that it be gained by law."

From an organizational standpoint, the AFL's emphasis on the voluntaristic character of labor unions made much sense. It served certain legal advantages during a period in which the courts refused to grant special status to unions *qua* unions on a par with corporations or religious institutions; and it also served to protect the authority of union leadership against the undermining influence of meliorative labor legislation. On the other hand, it left labor with no leverage for organizing the unorganized or indeed for anything beyond securing the leadership's control of already existing organizations. [Cf. M. Rogin, "Voluntarism: The Political Functions of an Antipolitical Doctrine," *Industrial and Labor Relations Review*, 15 (July 1962).]

With the advent of the New Deal, the political environment offered substantial opportunities for labor gains. Section 7(a) of the National Industrial Recovery Act lent federal authority to the principle of collective bargaining. But the unions, for the most part, were unprepared to exploit the opportunity. Where unions were already strong, as in the coal industry, the industrial codes established under the authority of the NRA tended to serve collective bargaining reasonably well; but where unions were weak, as in the automobile industry, the codes offered little. The codes, in other words, tended to reflect, rather than to improve, the existing balance of power within each industry. The effort of a few, such as John L. Lewis, Sidney Hillman, and Charles Howard, to accommodate union organization to the lines of force seemingly made available by the government immediately collided with the vested interests of the old line union leadership. As so often in the past, the crucial question was whether the latter would be able to maintain control of their constituents after unionization on an industrial basis, and the answer, as always, seemed to be no. As David Brody has commented, the craft unionists "always held realism in higher regard than compassion." They flatly refused Lewis's pleas to use their resources to organize the great mass of unskilled industrial workers. [Brody, "The Expansion of the American Labor Movement," in S. E. Ambrose, ed., *Institutions in Modern America* (1967).] The refusal precipitated the breakaway of the Congress of Industrial Organizations (CIO), and a long series of bitter conflicts not only between union organizers and employers, but between competing unions. In the course of those fights, the AFL joined with employer groups in attacking the CIO as a communist-dominated organization, and before long American patriots were rallying to anathematize CIO organizers, speakers, pamphleteers, and defenders.

Of course, what the unionists wanted broke fundamentally with the received conventions of the country with respect to a worker's right to influence the conditions of *his* job as against an employer's right to control *his* labor force. (Indeed, what the CIO was doing also broke with what had become "legitimate" within the main body of organized labor itself. Thus Dan Tobin of the Teamsters warned Lewis in May 1935, "We are not going to desert the fundamental principles on which [unions] have lived and are living to help you organize men who have never been organized.") And in contests that bear upon fundamental and contrasting concepts of "right," the balance of right can be determined only by superior power. When such contests engage the entire society, there is civil war; political agencies are incapable of resolving nonviolently, or within the boundaries of existing law, conflicts that divide the mass of the body politic. In more limited conflicts, as in this case, superior power develops on the side that can persuade the preponderance of *non*contestants that its cause has positive implications of vital significance for them. But in the course of the battle, the law and other conventional values and institutions are of use primarily as instruments of warfare.

Thus, in their struggle to maintain their control of the industrial labor force, employers strove to mobilize allies among elements in the society for whom modern industrialism and particularly the Depression had presented comparable threats to their sense of control over their lives and livelihoods. They appealed to "tradition" and "stability" and for "law and order," meanwhile blackmailing and bludgeoning their antagonists by means of labor spies, agents provocateurs, veritable armies of hired thugs, and even assassins. The unionists fought back perforce with many of the same techniques. Their most appealing device, however, became the sit-down strike. Certainly it was the most intriguing "instrument of war" to come out of the industrial strife of the 1930's. In graphic, symbolic fashion, it laid in the open the workers' claim that they had a rightful stake in *their* jobs — a principle not yet conceded by the property-oriented American legal system. But most particularly its appeal lay in its use of the principle of nonviolence while evoking violence from the forces of "law and order" — precisely in the style of the sit-ins of the 1950's and 1960's.

Ultimately, indeed, the employers' brute truculence handed the unionists their chief weapon: With the help of liberals concerned less with the specific objectives of unionized labor than with principles concerning the maintenance of an open society, the unionists were able to identify their struggle with the cause of civil liberties. [Cf. J. S. Auerbach, "The La Follette Committee: Labor and Civil Liberties in the New Deal," *The Journal of American History*, 51 (Dec. 1964); and his *Labor and Liberty* (1965).] There is, to be sure, something anomalous about this alliance. Blue-collar workers have rarely been conspicuous supporters of civil liberties (or civil rights, for that matter), except spuriously when the shoe pinched. Even the link between union organization and political democracy has always been tenuous, because union methods and internal procedures often bear little relationship to the principles of democratic consent. In fact, Sidney Fine's study of the General Motors sit-down strike (reprinted below) may have serious shortcomings in that it does not really face up to the small numbers of sit-downers involved, the issue of "rule by minority violence," and the case against Governor Murphy for having permitted the precedent of a successful sit-down strike.

Still, there is no doubt that the sit-down strike has earned a hallowed place in the history of the progress of American liberal democracy. And this is primarily because in the larger social context the unionists' success constituted a major gain for liberalism and for civil liberties, at least on two scores. First, it had become clear that in the absence of organized power of their own, wage-earners remained prey to the corporations not merely in economic matters but in political, social, and intellectual matters as well; the unions established a power base to offset the dominating power of the corporate sector of society. Second, because the struggle linked civil liberties firmly to the bread-and-butter pragmatism of the unionists, it provided a lasting and substantial popular base of support for the liberal political process.

Sidney Fine is Professor of History at the University of Michigan. His *The Automobile Under the Blue Eagle* (1963) is a major work valuable for economic and labor history as well as for political history. See also I. Bernstein, *The Lean Years** (1960), and *The New Deal Collective Bargaining Policy* (1950). For insights into the social and institutional constrictions on the growth of the American labor movement, see H. Pelling, *American Labor** (1960); M. Karson, *American Labor Unions and Politics, 1900–1918** (1958); and D. Brody, "The Emergence of Mass-Production Unionism," in J. Braeman et al., *Change and Continuity in Twentieth-Century America** (1964), as well as Brody's work already cited. M. Dubofsky, *We Shall Be All* (1969) is a comprehensive study of the Industrial Workers of the World. J. Laslett, *Labor and the Left* (1970) details the failure of socialist union techniques except when they adopted the short-term bread-and-butter objectives characteristic of American "business unionism." J. Weinstein, *The Decline of Socialism in America, 1912–1925* (1967), offers a competing view, to be compared also with D. Bell, *The End of Ideology** (1960), esp. chs. 10, 11, and 13. Paul Jacobs, *The State of the Unions* (1966), argues the "failure of collective bargaining" and challenges the view that American unions can be successful only when they concentrate on economic issues and eschew politics. J. O. Morris, *Conflict Within the AFL: A Study of Craft versus Industrial Unionism, 1901–1938* (1958), and W. Galenson, *The CIO Challenge to the AFL* (1960), cover that issue comprehensively, while L. Ulman's "The Development of Trades and Labor Unions" and "Unionism and Collective Bargaining in the Modern Period," in S. E. Harris, ed., *American Economic History* (1961), provide an elaborate though succinct original synthesis.

The General Motors Sit-Down Strike:
A Re-examination

SIDNEY FINE

Although the General Motors sit-down strike of 1937 has been correctly described as "the most critical labor conflict of the nineteen thirties" and as of crucial significance to the subsequent growth of automobile unionism

Reprinted by permission of the author from the *American Historical Review*, 70 (April 1965), 651–713.

in particular and industrial unionism in general,[1] a great many questions regarding the strike and the role of its principal participants remain unanswered. It is still not possible to resolve all the doubts concerning this greatest of all automotive strikes, but the relevant manuscript collections now available, and especially the recently opened Frank Murphy Papers, do permit one to speak about at least some aspects of the strike with a greater degree of certainty than was heretofore possible.[2]

The general outlines of the GM sit-down strike are familiar enough. Following the outbreak of sit-down strikes at the Atlanta Fisher Body plant on November 18, 1936, and the Kansas City Fisher Body plant on December 16, 1936, Homer Martin, president of the United Automobile Workers, sought an "immediate general conference" with the top management of GM. The corporation, however, insisted that the union should discuss its grievances at the local plant level, in accordance with GM's established procedure for collective bargaining. The union responded that the principal issues that it wished to discuss with the company — recognition for collective bargaining, seniority rights, minimum wages, and the speed of the production line — were national in scope and must consequently be dealt with by union and management representatives for GM as a whole. Affairs were thus deadlocked when on December 28 the Cleveland Fisher Body plant was tied up by a sit-down strike, and two days later the same strike tactic closed down the two Fisher Body plants in Flint. The strike eventually spread throughout the GM empire, affecting approximately 140,000 of the corporation's automotive employees and more than 50 of its plants, but the center of the conflict from the end of December was Flint, whose Fisher Body plants, along with Cleveland Fisher Body, produced bodies and parts on which perhaps three-fourths of GM's automotive production depended.[3]

The most significant of the union's official demands, which were submitted to GM on January 4, 1937, was the request that the UAW be recognized as the exclusive bargaining agency for all GM employees.[4] The issue

---

[1] Walter Galenson, *The CIO Challenge to the AFL: A History of the American Labor Movement, 1935–1941* (Cambridge, Mass., 1960), 134, 141; Edward Levinson, *Labor on the March* (New York, 1938, 1956), 168; Saul Alinsky, *John L. Lewis, an Unauthorized Biography* (New York, 1949), 96.

[2] The principal manuscript collections on which this article is based are the Frank Murphy Papers, Michigan Historical Collections; Records of the Michigan Military Establishment Relating to the Flint Sit-Down Strike, 1937 [hereafter cited as National Guard Records], microfilm copy in Michigan Historical Collections; the relevant files in the Franklin D. Roosevelt Library; General Motors, Labor Relations Diary and Appendix Documents, GM Building, Detroit, Michigan; the John Brophy Papers, Catholic University; and the Joe Brown Collection, Wayne State University Archives.

[3] GM, Labor Relations Diary, Sec. 1, 68–72; Martin to William S. Knudsen, Dec. 21, 1936, to Alfred P. Sloan, Jr., and to Knudsen, Dec. 24, 1936, Knudsen to Martin, Dec. 31, 1936, *ibid.*, Appendix Documents to Accompany Sec. 1; Henry Kraus, *The Many and the Few: A Chronicle of the Dynamic Auto Workers* (Los Angeles, 1947), 78–79; New York *Times*, Feb. 12, 1937.

[4] Martin to Sloan and Knudsen, Jan. 4, 1937, Murphy Papers.

of exclusive representation had been in contention between automobile labor and automobile management ever since Section 7(a) of the National Industrial Recovery Act had stimulated the growth of unionism in the industry. The National Labor Relations Act of 1935 had endorsed the union position on this question, but since the constitutionality of the statute had not yet been determined at the time the strike began, GM, like many other large employers, continued to adhere to the policy with regard to representation that it had evolved while the NIRA was in effect: union representatives would be permitted to bargain with the corporation only for union members.[5]

General Motors made its position clear with regard to the sit-down tactic on the last day of 1936. William S. Knudsen, the executive vice-president of the corporation, stated for GM that the sit-downers were "clearly trespassers and violators of the law of the land" and that there would be no bargaining with the UAW while the strikers remained in "illegal possession" of GM's plants.[6] On January 2, 1937, GM received from Judge Edward Black of the Genesee County Circuit Court in Flint an injunction ordering the strikers to evacuate the two Flint plants, to cease picketing, and not to interfere with those who wanted to enter the plants to work. The strikers ignored the injunction, but both Black and his writ were discredited a few days later when it was revealed that the Flint judge held $219,900 of GM stock. General Motors, caught unawares, transferred its injunction to Judge Paul Gadola's court, but it did not, for the moment, press the issue.[7]

On January 11, GM attempted to dislodge the strikers from the Fisher Body No. 2 plant, the smaller and the more weakly held of the two Flint Fisher Body factories. The heat in the plant was shut off, and company police tried to prevent food from being taken in to the strikers, but the sit-downers, who had held only the second floor of the factory, captured the plant gates from the company police to assure their supply of food. When Flint police sought to recapture the gates, the strikers drove them off with such improvised weapons as automobile door hinges and thus emerged the victors in what came to be known as "The Battle of the Running Bulls."[8]

The violence of January 11 prompted Michigan's newly elected governor, Frank Murphy, to send units of National Guard[9] into Flint to maintain order, and at the same time the governor invited union and management representatives to Lansing to bring an end to the strike. A truce was ar-

[5] The issue of representation in the automobile industry before the sit-down strikes is treated in Sidney Fine, *The Automobile under the Blue Eagle: Labor, Management, and the Automobile Manufacturing Code* (Ann Arbor, Mich., 1963), *passim*.

[6] Knudsen to Martin, Dec. 31, 1936, GM Appendix Documents, Sec. 1.

[7] Galenson, *CIO Challenge to AFL*, 136–37; Kraus, *Many and the Few*, 107–13; Detroit *News*, Jan. 3, 7, 25, 29, 1937.

[8] Kraus, *Many and the Few*, 125–41; Levinson, *Labor on the March*, 155–57; Detroit *News*, Jan. 12, 1937.

[9] The number of Guardsmen in Flint eventually reached 3,454. (G-1 Periodic Reports, Feb. 7, 1937, National Guard Records.)

ranged on January 15. The union, rejecting the advice of John Brophy, director of the CIO, that it was conceding too much, agreed to evacuate all GM plants held by the sit-down strikers, and GM consented to meet with UAW representatives on January 18 to bargain collectively on the proposals submitted to it by the union on January 4. Negotiations were to continue for at least fifteen days, unless a settlement had been effected earlier, and the corporation stated that it would not try to resume operations in any of the struck plants during this period nor would it remove from them any dies, tools, material (except for export), machinery, or equipment.[10]

Before the scheduled departure of the Flint workers from the two Fisher Body plants, the UAW learned that GM had agreed to meet with the Flint Alliance, a recently formed organization that had been sponsoring a back-to-back movement and that was viewed by the UAW as a company union. Charging the violation of the truce agreement, the UAW refused to evacuate the Flint plants, and a deadlock once again ensued. The scene of negotiations thereupon shifted to Washington, where Secretary of Labor Frances Perkins sought in vain to arrange a conference between GM's president, Alfred P. Sloan, Jr., and John L. Lewis, the CIO chieftain who was representing the UAW.[11]

In an effort to strengthen its position and gain the initiative in the strike, the UAW on February 1, after first drawing off the company police to the Chevrolet No. 9 plant by staging a decoy sit-down strike there, seized and occupied the Chevrolet No. 4 plant, which produced the engines for Chevrolet cars and was "the most important single unit" in the GM complex. The National Guard, on instructions from Governor Murphy, responded to this action by cordoning off the Chevrolet No. 4 plant and the nearby Fisher Body No. 2 plant.[12]

The day after the union captured the strategic Chevrolet No. 4 plant, Judge Gadola issued an injunction that ordered the union to evacuate the two Fisher Body plants and to cease picketing outside them. The injunction was again defied, but Murphy did not choose to use state troops to enforce the court order. In the meantime, GM agreed to confer with John L. Lewis, and a long series of talks began in Detroit on February 3. As Murphy later saw it, the crucial factor in breaking the strike deadlock was a letter that he read to Lewis on February 9 in which the Michigan governor stated that it was his duty to see to it that the laws were enforced.[13]

[10] Detroit *News*, Jan. 12–15, 1937; Knudsen *et al.* to Murphy, Jan. 15, 1937, Murphy Papers; John Brophy, A *Miner's Life: An Autobiography*, ed. and suppl. John O. P. Hall (Madison, Wis., 1964), 269.
[11] Detroit *News*, Jan. 18–31, 1937; Kraus, *Many and the Few*, 157–65.
[12] *Ibid.*, 189–219; Louis G. Seaton to H. W. Anderson, Feb. 2, 1937, GM Appendix Documents, Sec. 1; Executive Order, Feb. 1, 1937, Murphy Papers; Detroit *News*, Feb. 2, 3, 1937; *United Automobile Worker*, Feb. 25, 1937.
[13] Galenson, *CIO Challenge to AFL*, 139–40; Levinson, *Labor on the March*, 163–67; Kraus, *Many and the Few*, 229–34, 263–78; Detroit *News*, Feb. 3–11, 1937.

Agreement between union and management was reached on February 11, the corporation consenting to recognize the UAW as the bargaining agency for those of its employees who were union members and to commence negotiations with the UAW on the issues specified in its letter of January 4. The agreement was supplemented by a letter from Knudsen to Murphy in which GM agreed for a period of six months after work was resumed not to bargain or enter into agreements with any other employee organization with regard to such matters as were referred to in the union's January 4 letter unless this procedure was first sanctioned by Governor Murphy.[14] In effect, the UAW was given exclusive bargaining rights for a period of six months.

It seems clear from published accounts and from the transcripts of interviews with participants that have recently become available that the Flint sit-down occurred prematurely, and it would appear that the decision to conduct a sit-down rather than a conventional outside strike was made locally rather than by the UAW or CIO leadership. The UAW and the CIO regarded GM as "job number one" in the automobile industry, and there was at least talk among the leadership in the latter part of 1936 about striking the corporation as a whole by tying up the Cleveland and the Fisher Body No. 1 plants, but this was not to occur until after January 1, 1937. The holiday period between Christmas and New Year's, when the sit-down actually occurred, was regarded as "a very poor time psychologically to pull a strike" if only because the workers would be especially short of funds then and would be reluctant to lose any pay that they might otherwise earn. Also, Murphy was not scheduled to succeed Frank Fitzgerald as governor of Michigan until January 1, 1937, and the UAW expected Murphy to be more friendly to its position than Fitzgerald was likely to be.[15]

The conventional story as to why the strike began in Flint on December 30 is that Robert Travis, the director of organization for the UAW in Flint, learned that evening that GM, concerned about what might be impending because of the strikes in some of its plants, was planning to move some giant dies out of the Fisher Body No. 1 plant to Grand Rapids and Pontiac. Travis, according to the usual story, thereupon called the shop stewards together, and the decision was made to strike. Bud Simons, however, chairman of the Fisher Body No. 1 shop stewards, has recently challenged this version of the origins of the strike. As he recalls it, a strike at the time of

---

[14] There are copies in the Murphy Papers of the February 11 agreement and of Knudsen's letter to Murphy of February 11.

[15] Oral History Interview of Wyndham Mortimer, June 20, 1960, 27, 34–35, Michigan Historical Collections (there are copies of all the UAW oral history interviews in both the Michigan Historical Collections and the Wayne State University Archives); Oral History Interview of George F. Addes, June 25, 1960, 15–16; Statement of Mr. Martin . . . , Sept. 11, 1936, Brown Collection; *Time*, XXIX (Jan. 11, 1937), 16; John Brophy, "The Struggle for an Auto Union," 1–3, MS for chapter of book, Brophy Papers; Levinson, *Labor on the March*, 149; Kraus, *Many and the Few*, 78–81.

the flat-glass workers was causing a glass shortage that might in itself have forced the closing of the Flint plants in a few days without a strike. Travis, anxious for the union to seize the initiative rather than be the passive victim of a plant shutdown, came to Simons and declared: "We have got to find something to start a strike about around here." The story about the shipment of the dies was then fabricated and spread throughout the plant, and Travis and the shop stewards called for the sit-down.[16]

It was alleged before the Dies Committee in the fall of 1938 that the Communists inspired and organized the sit-down strikes, and Larry S. Davidow, who served as one of the attorneys for the UAW during the Flint sit-down, also voiced this opinion in a recent interview. "The major fact to keep in mind," he has charged, "is that the whole strategy of the sit-down strike was communist inspired, communist directed and communist controlled." [17]

That the Flint sit-down strike was part of a Communist plot would be difficult, if not impossible, to demonstrate, but that Communists and fellow travelers played crucial roles in the strike story is beyond dispute. It was Wyndham Mortimer, described by Benjamin Stolberg as "a Stalinist from the very beginning," who had begun the serious organization of automobile workers in Flint in July 1936 at a time when UAW strength in the city was at low ebb. When Mortimer was recalled from Flint in the fall of 1936, he was replaced by Travis, whom Max M. Kampelman has characterized as "a man with a long pedigree of Communist activity." Travis continued the work of organization begun by Mortimer, played the decisive part in calling the sit-down strike in the Fisher Body No. 1 plant, and has been accurately described as "The leading personality . . . in the strike." Inside the Fisher Body No. 1 plant, leadership was exercised by Simons, who had joined the Communist controlled Auto Workers Union in the late 1920's while working in Grand Rapids and had participated in at least one of the meetings arranged by Communists and "progressives" in 1934 to promote the establishment of an international, industrial union in the automobile industry.[18]

[16] Levinson, *Labor on the March*, 152; Kraus, *Many and the Few*, 86–88; Flint *Auto Worker*, Jan. 5, 1937; Mortimer Interview, 35–36; Oral History Interview of Bud Simons, Sept. 6, 1960, 28–30. The union claimed that it sat down in the Fisher Body No. 2 plant because GM had transferred three inspectors when they had refused to quit the union (Detroit *News*, Jan. 3, 1937); see William Weinstone, *The Great Sit-Down Strike* (New York, 1937), 21, for a Communist account of the strike that seems to support the Simons version of its origin.

[17] House Special Committee on Un-American Activities, *Investigation of the Un-American Propaganda Activities in the United States*, 75 Cong., 3 sess. (Washington, D.C., 1938), II, 1454, 1494–96, 1551, 1554, 1649, 1689; August Raymond Ogden, *The Dies Committee: A Study of the Special House Committee for the Investigation of Un-American Activities, 1938–1943* (Washington, D.C., 1943), 82, 106; Oral History Interview of Larry S. Davidow, July 14, 1960, 12–14, 22–23.

[18] Benjamin Stolberg, *The Story of the CIO* (New York, 1938), 164; Mortimer Interview, 28–33; UAW, Second Annual Convention, *Report of Wyndham Mortimer* (Aug. 23, 1937), 4–6, Joseph A. Labadie Collection, University of Michigan; Max M.

Communists or near Communists were also present at the UAW and CIO leadership levels during the strike. Maurice Sugar, characterized by Benjamin Gitlow as "top man for the Communist party in Detroit," served as a UAW counsel during the strike, and Lee Pressman, who later admitted his Communist connections, was one of John L. Lewis' closest advisers throughout the dispute, and his name, as well as Mortimer's, appears on the agreement that ended the strike.[19] It does not follow, though, that these men or any of the Communists and fellow travelers who played prominent roles in the GM strike pursued policies that conflicted with the organizational interests of the UAW or that they succeeded to any extent in reaping advantages from the strike for the Communist as distinct from the union cause. It is perfectly clear, moreover, that Murphy knew nothing about the Communist role in the strike and that the workers were striking because of their grievances against management rather than from any desire to promote Communist objectives.

As was suspected at the time and as recently made available evidence, including undercover reports, has substantiated, the Flint auto plants that were struck were held by a minority of the workers in these plants, on some days by a very small minority. The Fisher Body No. 1 plant, which employed as many as 6,500–7,500 workers, had as few as 90 men in the plant at one point during the strike, according to Simons, and the much smaller Fisher Body No. 2 plant, which had a normal complement of about 1,100 workers, was held by 17 strikers on January 26, according to the National Guard. Nor were all the workers inside the plants employees of these plants. Flint GM workers who were not on strike and automobile unionists from Detroit, Toledo, Cleveland, and elsewhere found their way into and out of the plants. Thus the morning after the UAW had seized the Chevrolet No. 4 plant, Colonel Joseph H. Lewis, the commanding officer of the National Guard in Flint, reported to Governor Murphy that of 850 workers in the plant, only 150 were employees of that plant.[20] Of course, if only because of the food problem, it was in the interests of the union to hold the plants with as few persons as possible, but the small numbers within the plants also reflect the very limited membership and strength of the UAW in Flint when the strike began.

Kampelman, *The Communist Party vs. the CIO: A Study in Power Politics* (New York, 1957), 64; Oral History Interview of Carl Haessler, Nov. 27, 1959–Oct. 24, 1960, 14; Simons Interview, 3–4, 11–13.

[19] Benjamin Gitlow, *The Whole of Their Lives: Communism in America — A Personal History and Intimate Portrayal of Its Leaders* (New York, 1948), 278–79; Oral History Interview of Len DeCaux, Mar. 11, 18, 1961, 29–30; Brophy, "Struggle for an Auto Union," 21, Brophy Papers.

[20] Simons Interview, 47; G-2 Journal, Jan. 26, 1937, National Guard Records; Strike Chronology [Feb. 1–8, 1937], Feb. 2, 1937, Murphy Papers; see also Norman Hill Memoranda to Murphy, Jan. 12, 15, 1937, *ibid.*; and Oral History Interviews of Arthur Case, Aug. 4, 1960, 6, Norman Bully, Oct. 12, 1961, 4–5, Joseph Ditzel, Sept. 25, 1960, 12, and Clayton Johnson, June 1, 1961, 9.

The major criticism leveled against Murphy with regard to his policy during the course of the sit-down strike in Flint was that he violated his oath of office by failing to eject the sit-downers who were illegally in possession of GM property and by refusing to enforce a court order requiring the evacuation of two of the corporation's plants. It must be recalled, however, that although the sit-down strikes were held by most, but not all, authorities to constitute an illegal trespass upon private property, the United States Supreme Court had not yet spoken on the matter, and the status of the tactic under the criminal laws was not altogether self-evident. As Murphy later wrote to a columnist, "Apart from private civil action, and owing to the novelty of the practice, it was not very certain what legal action was available or appropriate to deal with a body of men peacefully occupying their place of employment." [21]

Murphy informed the union negotiators more than once that the strikers were in illegal possession of the GM plants, and he referred publicly to "the unlawful seizure of private property." [22] He was not, however, prepared to push this point to its logical conclusion and thus impair the chances for a peaceful settlement. He saw the union as using the means at its disposal to safeguard its rights and as fighting back against employer violation of the Wagner Act and is thus understood to have told the GM negotiators that the occupation of their factories went "deeper into social and economic questions" than did the ordinary violation of property rights. Under the circumstances, he was content to follow the counsel of his legal advisers that the matter of legality was a problem at least initially for the local authorities to resolve; his own responsibility would not have to be considered until local officials called for his assistance in enforcing the law.[23]

As a matter of fact, Murphy has been less criticized for his failure to initiate action to dislodge the strikers than for his alleged refusal to act when the strikers were found in contempt of court. What is often ignored by Murphy's critics, however, is that only a few days actually elapsed between the time Murphy was requested by the sheriff to aid him in enforcing the court order and the settlement of the strike. From the start also, as is now evident, Murphy was painfully aware of his obligations with regard to the enforcement of the law.

Following the revelation of Judge Black's stockholdings, GM did not

[21] Edward G. Kemp, "Frank Murphy as Government Administrator," 1951, Edward G. Kemp Papers, Michigan Historical Collections; Murphy to Mark Sullivan, Jan. 4, 1939, Murphy Papers; for the argument that the sit-down strike was not illegal, see Leon Green, "The Case for the Sit-Down Strike," *New Republic*, XC (Mar. 24, 1937), 199–201.

[22] Murphy statement, Jan. 14, 1937, Murphy to Lewis and Martin, Feb. 9, 1937, to Albert H. Dale, Feb. 25, 1937, to Paul Block, Dec. 9, 1938, Murphy Papers; Kraus, *Many and the Few*, 268; Detroit *News*, Jan. 12, 1937; cf. Murphy to Octave P. Beauvais, July 7, 1937, Murphy Papers.

[23] Murphy to Dale, Feb. 25, 1937, Murphy speech, Oct. 21, 1938, Kemp Memorandum to Murphy, Jan. 27, 1937, *ibid.*; New York *Times*, Jan. 14, 1937.

file an amended bill of complaint and a motion for injunction until January 28, and it was not until February 2 that Judge Gadola issued his injunction, which was to take effect in twenty-four hours. Speaking to Perkins by phone on the evening of February 2, Murphy observed that consideration had to be given to the fact that "tomorrow afternoon I have got to say that I will be obedient to the law or not." [24] When the workers in the two Fisher Body plants defied the injunction and informed Murphy that the use of force would mean "a blood bath of unarmed workers" for which he would be responsible, Murphy had drawn up but did not issue a statement declaring that he had no "honorable alternative but to see that the laws of the state are faithfully executed and the lawful orders of its courts promptly and effectively enforced." [25]

Informed by affidavit that the injunction was being violated, Judge Gadola on February 5 issued a writ of attachment commanding the sheriff "to attach the bodies" of all occupants of the two Fisher Body plants, their "confederates" who were picketing the No. 1 plant, and local officers of the UAW for refusal to comply with the February 3 injunction. Thomas Wolcott, the Genesee County sheriff, thereupon sent Murphy a telegram asking for the assistance of the National Guard in the execution of the writ and inquiring whether, as an alternative, it would be necessary for the sheriff to swear in deputies to enforce the court order. It was only at this point, six days before the final settlement, that Murphy incurred any clear-cut obligation to ensure that a court order be obeyed. Murphy, who had authorized Maurice Sugar to inform Judge Gadola that a settlement was near, was perturbed that the judge had not delayed the issuance of the writ. He told Perkins, as notes made of their conversation indicate, that GM had made "a rather serious mistake" and was trying to "embarrass" him and put him in a "bad position. I am not a representative for the G.M. or for the labor group but for the people," he said, ". . . and the public interest requires peace." [26]

Intent upon preserving the peace and at the same time aware that the enforcement of the court order could not long be delayed, Murphy, we now know, took a series of steps to avoid disruption of the negotiations but, at the same time, to clarify to the union negotiators his position regarding law and order. He decided on Friday, February 5, the day the writ of attachment was issued, that the time had come to draft a letter to Lewis explain-

---

[24] Strike Chronology, Feb. 2, 1937, Murphy Papers. This document, covering the period February 1–8, contains a detailed, although incomplete, record of events relating to the strike as seen through Murphy's eyes. It was almost certainly prepared at the time of the strike.

[25] Fisher No. 1 Sit-In Employes to Murphy, Feb. 3, 1937, Stay In Strikes of the Fisher Body Plant No. 2 to Murphy, Feb. 3, 1937, Murphy statement, Feb. 3, 1937, *ibid.*

[26] Affidavit by E. J. Parker, Feb. 4, 1937, Writ of Attachment, Feb. 5, 1937, National Guard Records; Sugar to Murphy, Oct. 25, 1938, Murphy to Sugar, Nov. 2, 1938, Strike Chronology, Feb. 5, 1937, Murphy Papers.

ing that the order of a court was "the law of the land" and would have to be obeyed, but he also instructed the National Guard, if it deemed the action necessary, to cordon off the Fisher Body No. 1 plant as it had already surrounded the Fisher Body No. 2 and Chevrolet No. 4 plants and thus to make it impossible for the sheriff or "a mob of deputies" to get into the plants. Most important of all, he requested the sheriff to delay over the weekend any effort to enforce the writ since a settlement seemed imminent.[27] Actually, Sheriff Wolcott, a Democrat who "thoroughly hated his assignment," had no intention of taking any aggressive action without the approval of the governor.[28]

Murphy's decision to delay the enforcement of the writ of attachment was fully in accord with the wishes of the National Guard. As evidence recently made available indicates, Judge Advocate General Samuel D. Pepper, who disliked the idea of using the Guard at any time to make arrests under contempt orders, and Colonel Lewis and his staff were impressed with the difficulty under existing circumstances of apprehending and taking to court the several thousand persons against whom the writ of attachment was directed, and they advised the governor to delay an order to the Guard to aid the sheriff in executing the writ.[29]

On February 7, with a settlement not yet achieved, Murphy told President Roosevelt on the phone that he (Murphy) would have to make clear to Lewis the governor's responsibility as chief executive of the state to uphold the law, and on February 8 the famous letter to Lewis was drafted. The letter was read by Murphy to the CIO head at 9:15 P.M. the next day, with Conciliator James F. Dewey the only other person present. In the document, the original of which is preserved in the Murphy Papers,[30] Murphy informed Lewis that he wished to indicate in writing, as he had "already done verbally on several occasions," his position as chief executive of Michigan. It had been and still was his hope that the strike could be settled by negotiation, but since the parties had thus far been unable to

---

[27] Strike Chronology, Feb. 5, 1937, Murphy to the Rev. George H. Smith, July 22, 1937, *ibid.*; Detroit *News*, Feb. 6, 1937; Subcommittee of the Senate Committee on the Judiciary, *Nomination of Frank Murphy*, 76 Cong., 1 sess. (Washington, D.C., 1939), 3–4.

[28] Kraus, *Many and the Few*, 108; Wolcott to Murphy, Aug. 17, 1938, Statement by Wolcott, Oct. 21, 1938, Murphy Papers.

[29] Pepper to Raymond W. Starr, Mar. 22, 1937, Pepper to Kemp, Jan. 12, 1939, *ibid.*

[30] The original of the letter and the several carbon copies of it in the Murphy Papers bear the date February 9 rather than February 8. When the letter was typed, probably on February 8, the space for the day of the month was left blank, and the "9" was later added, presumably to make the date of the letter conform to the date of its presentation to Lewis. When a copy of the letter was first publicly revealed on January 13, 1939 (it was submitted by Murphy to a subcommittee of the Senate Committee on the Judiciary that was considering his nomination to be Attorney General), it bore the date February 8 and the notation that it had been read and delivered at 9:15 P.M. on February 9.

come to an agreement, "the time has come for all concerned to comply fully with the decision and order of the Court and take necessary steps to restore possession of the occupied plants to their rightful owners." It was his duty "to demand and require" obedience to the laws and court orders, and he would be faithful to that obligation.[31] After further prolonged negotiating sessions, the governor was able to announce the settlement of the strike early in the morning of February 11. The writ had not been enforced, but neither had a single life been lost in one of the most volatile strikes in all of American history.

As a matter of fact, Murphy's delay in enforcing the writ of attachment was not without precedent, and even Judge Gadola conceded at the time that the sheriff "had the authority to wait indefinitely before serving it." Commenting in 1938 on the delay, Wolcott agreed that there was "no hurry about it especially when such great issues were at stake." Sheriffs in Michigan and elsewhere, after all, regularly delayed the execution of writs of attachment issued after property had been foreclosed and writs of attachment requiring them to take action to satisfy judgments against merchants. "If the Governor is to be accused of obstructing justice," a member of the Michigan Parole Board wrote Murphy's brother George, "then every sheriff and public officer might be accused of the same thing." [32]

Among the factors that persuaded Frank Murphy to delay enforcement of a court order, none was more compelling than his great reluctance to take any step that might lead to violence and the loss of life. A man with a "deep reverence for human life," Murphy told his friend Mrs. Fielding H. Yost during the course of the strike, "I am not going to do it. I'm not going down in history as 'Bloody Murphy!' If I sent those soldiers right in on the men there'd be no telling how many would be killed. It would be inconsistent with everything I have ever stood for in my whole political life." In his first statement on the strike, the newly inaugurated governor declared on January 4 that he would see to it that "no force is used," and a few days later he wrote in a private letter to a Flint clergyman, "I abhor violence and you may be sure that the State of Michigan will do everything honorably within its power to prevent it." Throughout the strike, as the record indicates, Murphy did everything that could reasonably have been expected of him to remain faithful to the assurances with regard to violence that he had given.[33]

[31] Strike Chronology, Feb. 7, 1937, Murphy to Lewis and Martin, Feb. 9, 1937, Murphy Papers.

[32] Detroit News, Feb. 8, 1937; Statement by Wolcott, Oct. 21, 1938, John H. Eliasohn to George Murphy, Oct. 24, 1938, Murphy Papers.

[33] Kemp, "Murphy as Government Administrator"; transcript of interview with Mrs. Fielding H. Yost, Oct. 28, 1963, 6, in my possession; Strike Chronology, Feb. 8, 1937, Murphy Papers; Detroit News, Jan. 4, 1937; Murphy to the Rev. R. M. Atkins, Jan. 9, 1937, Murphy Papers.

When he was compelled by the Battle of the Running Bulls and the likelihood of further violence to send the National Guard into Flint, Murphy gave the command of the troops to Colonel Joseph H. Lewis, commander of the 119th Field Artillery and a seasoned soldier, rather than to the ranking officer of the Michigan Guard, General Heinrich Pickert, the police commissioner of Detroit. Pickert was passed over by the governor not only because the Detroit official had other duties but because his "militaristic policies" as police commissioner had antagonized labor and civil rights groups, and Murphy was afraid to rely on Pickert's discretion in an emergency.[34] Murphy also let it be known that "The state authorities will not take sides. They are here only to protect public peace . . . and for no other reason at all." John S. Bersey, Michigan's adjutant general, advised the area commander at the outset, as the records of the National Guard reveal, that Murphy was particularly concerned that "everything be done by the troops to avoid bringing on a conflict. He does not desire that anyone be shot or seriously injured." By maintaining "a calm and peaceful attitude," the troops, the governor hoped, would provide the opportunity for the disputants to reach an amicable settlement.[35]

Murphy's reluctance to use force was put to a severe test on February 1, when the union staged its attack on Chevrolet No. 9 to cover its seizure of Chevrolet No. 4. In his headquarters in a Detroit hotel, the governor received an almost blow-by-blow account of the unfolding developments in Flint. When Colonel Lewis suggested that the National Guard might be used to "scatter the crowd in a quiet manner," Murphy refused permission and declared, "I don't like the militia in it unless it is necessary but if it . . . [is] we have to go in strong." A short time later Sheriff Wolcott recommended that martial law be declared, but Murphy resisted taking such drastic action. In the evening Murphy made his decision and directed the National Guard "to take immediate and effective steps to bring the situation under the control of the public authorities, suppress and prevent any breach of the peace, and ensure that the laws of the state are faithfully executed." The "immediate and effective steps" taken by the Guard, at the instruction of the governor, were to establish a cordon guard around Chevrolet No. 4 and Fisher Body No. 2 — "Importance #1" in the parlance of the Guard, to prevent anyone from entering this area, and to deny supplies of any kind, including food, to the occupants of the two plants. Murphy made the decision to cut off the entry of food into the plants on the basis of early

[34] Frank Martel to Murphy, Apr. 28, 1936, *ibid.*; Detroit *News*, Jan. 28, 1937; Conference for Protection of Civil Rights, *Civil Rights Guardian* (1937), Brown Collection; Winston Wessels, "Importance #1: The Michigan National Guard and the 1937 Flint Sit-Down Strike," seminar paper, 1963, 10, MS in my possession.

[35] (Lansing) *State Journal*, Jan. 12, 1937; Bersey to Commanding Officer, Jan. 12, 1937, National Guard Records.

reports that the majority of the occupants of Chevrolet No. 4, which had been seized with the aid of outsiders, were not employees of the plant.[36]

When John Brophy learned that food was being denied the occupants of the two plants, he phoned Murphy and, according to Brophy's manuscript account of the event, "berated" the governor for his action and asked him whether he wanted to " 'starve to death poor workers who are only asking for their lawful rights.' " When Murphy explained the reason for his decision, Brophy asked for and received permission to enter the plant. By the time he visited the factory most of the outsiders had departed; Brophy found only four persons in the plant, including Walter and Roy Reuther, who were not employees, and all of them left the plant with him.

The National Guard conducted its own investigation of the personnel in Chevrolet No. 4, and when Colonel Lewis reported to Murphy on the evening of February 2 that he was "confident" that "practically all" the men in the plant were "regular employees," Murphy instructed the area commander to allow food to pass through the National Guard lines. Murphy spoke to Brophy on the phone that night and gave him a categorical and perhaps an unwise promise that "The military will never be used against you. I'd leave my office first." [37]

Writing to a clergyman a few months after peace terms had been arranged, Murphy observed that the Flint strike had been "loaded with dynamite that might have been touched off by a single injudicious act." [38] Whatever else might be said about Murphy's strike policy, he did avoid the "injudicious act" that could have led to the loss of life.

Some writers on the strike have pictured the National Guard as spoiling for a fight and as having been thwarted in its desire for action by a governor who was unwilling to use force.[39] Actually, the leadership of the Guard and the judge advocate general of the state were as anxious as Murphy to avoid provocative acts in Flint and were as reluctant as he to use the Guardsmen in a frontal assault on the plants to evict the strikers. At least some of the credit for the peaceful outcome of the Flint strike must go to the Michigan National Guard.

From the start, the troops in Flint were closely restricted to their billets and were "kept well in hand." Colonel Lewis left no doubt in the minds of the Guardsmen regarding the nature of their task in Flint.

[36] Strike Chronology, Feb. 1, 2, 1937, Executive Order, Feb. 1, 1937, Murphy Papers; G-2 Journal, Feb. 1, 1937, G-3 Periodic Reports, Feb. 1, 1937, 63rd Brigade S-3 Periodic Reports, Feb. 2, 1937, Pepper to Lewis, Feb. 20, 1937, National Guard Records; Kraus, *Many and the Few*, 219–22; Detroit *News*, Feb. 2, 1937.

[37] Brophy, "Struggle for an Auto Union," 18–19, and Brophy Diary, Feb. 2, 1937, Brophy Papers; G-3 Periodic Reports, Feb. 2, 1937, National Guard Records; Strike Chronology, Feb. 2, 1937, Murphy Papers; Official Strike Bulletin No. 10, Strike Bulletin, Feb. 2, 1937, Brown Collection; Kraus, *Many and the Few*, 222–26.

[38] Murphy to Smith, July 22, 1937, Murphy Papers.

[39] Levinson, *Labor on the March*, 163; Irving Howe and B. J. Widick, *The UAW and Walter Reuther* (New York, 1949), 61.

Our mission here in Flint [he informed them in the first bulletin issued to the men] is to protect life and property should the situation develop to a point where civil law enforcement agencies cannot do so. Unless and until such a situation develops, our task is that of mere watchful waiting. During this period of waiting, let me again emphasize the fact that officers and men must not, under any circumstances, enter into discussions or arguments with civilians regarding the strike. We must not take sides. We must lean backwards so as to avoid the semblance of seeming to take sides. Our troops include men of all walks of life and many of us are naturally sympathetic to one side or other. However, as long as we are in uniform, our personal leanings must be made secondary.

Guard leaders, as a matter of fact, tried not only to restrain their own men, but, in the words of Lieutenant Colonel John H. Steck, assistant chief of staff, to make all parties in Flint realize that "personal and group differences of opinion should be subordinated in an attempt to prevent any untoward act that might jeopardize the success of the conference being conducted by the Governor." [40]

On February 1, Colonel Lewis, Judge Advocate General Pepper, and Adjutant General Bersey conferred with Governor Murphy, and "certain studies were directed to be immediately made and decisions arrived at." [41] The records available do not tell any more than this about the February 1 conference, but almost certainly it was decided at that time that the National Guard should devise some plan for the possible eviction of the sit-in strikers. Responsibility for formulating the plan was assigned to Steck, and he was ready with his recommendations on February 5.

Steck considered three possible lines of action for the Guard to follow: the first involved the actual eviction of the strikers from both "Importance #1," (Chevrolet No. 4 and Fisher Body No. 2) and "Importance #2" (Fisher Body No. 1); the second called for containing "Importance #1" and the ejection of the occupants of "Importance #2"; and the third provided for containing "Importance #1" and isolating "Importance #2" by a cordon guard and then securing the ouster of the strikers, if desired, by denying them the necessities of life. Steck recommended the third option rather than a direct assault on either or both of the plants because he believed that it was likely to result in considerably fewer casualties. Steck must also have realized that if the strikers attacked to break the cordon around "Importance #2," the responsibility for violence would rest on them rather than on the Guard. Apparently agreeing with Steck's reasoning, Colonel Lewis endorsed his subordinate's recommendation.[42]

[40] Steck to Lewis, Feb. 20, 1937, Michigan National Guard Bulletin No. 1, Jan. 19, 1937, National Guard Records.
[41] Pepper to Lewis, Feb. 20, 1937, *ibid.*
[42] Steck to Lewis, Feb. 5, 1937, *ibid.* There is an "O.K.L." written on the plan recommended by Steck.

According to Pepper, the military staff also believed that the execution of its mission required a formal declaration of martial law, and the governor was so advised on February 8. Murphy, however, vetoed this proposal. On the afternoon of the next day Bersey called the governor and advised him that the "Investment [of "Importance #2"] can be made without weakening our position" and that it might strengthen the position of the Guard "in the event of orders to be enforced." [43]

When Murphy read his letter to John L. Lewis that evening, he spoke only of his obligation to enforce the law, but he carefully avoided any mention of the means he might employ to secure that end. It has been assumed that Murphy was delivering a veiled threat to use troops to eject the strikers forcibly from the plants,[44] and Lewis himself has given this interpretation currency by an account of his confrontation with Murphy which he delivered to the 1940 convention of the UAW. " 'I do not doubt your ability to call out your soldiers and shoot the members of our union out of those plants,' " Lewis told the delegates he had said to Murphy, " 'but let me say that when you issue that order I shall leave this conference and I shall enter one of those plants with my own people (Applause.) . . . And the militia will have the pleasure of shooting me out of the plants with you [them?].' " [45] Whether Lewis actually spoke these words to Murphy or was simply indulging in retrospective fiction we do not know, but at all events Murphy was not planning at that time to use the Guard to shoot anyone. The probability is that, following the advice of his military staff, he intended merely to place a cordon guard around "Importance #2" and then, if the negotiations broke down and if the isolation of the strikers from very much contact with the outside world failed to discourage them,[46] to deny the necessities of life to them and thus to compel their surrender.

As he surveyed the record of the National Guard in Flint some weeks after the troops had been demobilized, Colonel Lewis concluded that the experience had "demonstrated that effective use can be made of troops at such times without loss of life or distruction [sic] to property. . . ." [47] That

[43] Pepper to Kemp, Jan. 12, 1939, Strike Chronology, Feb. 5, 8, 1937, Murphy Papers; Record of Phone Conversation with Murphy, Feb. 9, 1937, National Guard Records.

[44] Kraus, Many and the Few, 275–76; Alinsky, Lewis, 144; Detroit News, Jan. 14, 1939; Richard D. Lunt, "The High Ministry of Government: The Political Career of Frank Murphy," doctoral dissertation, University of New Mexico, 1962, 229. Russell B. Porter reported in the New York Times of February 8, 1937, that if the strike talks failed, Murphy was likely to order the investment of the Fisher Body No. 1 plant rather than the forcible eviction of the strikers, but on February 10 Porter was reporting that the talk was that Murphy would declare a "state of insurrection" and that Colonel Lewis would then order the Guard to aid in evicting the strikers.

[45] UAW, Proceedings of the Fifth Annual Convention, 1940 (n.p:, n.d.), 105; there is a more embellished version of the Lewis story in Alinsky, Lewis, 144–46.

[46] Contact between the sit-in strikers in the plants that had been cordoned off and the outside world was being curtailed in the final days of the strike. (Regulations Nos. 1 and 2, Feb. 10, 1937, National Guard Records.)

[47] Lewis to Murphy, June 18, 1937, ibid.

violence had been avoided was pleasing not only to the colonel and the governor but also to the executives of GM, for it would be a mistake to assume that Knudsen and other officials were anxious to see the injunction they had sought enforced if it meant bloodshed. The loss of life was deplorable not only in itself, but it might have damaged the corporation's reputation and weakened its position in the race for sales with its two major competitors. Lawrence P. Fisher, of GM, a close friend of Murphy's, told the governor during the strike, as Norman H. Hill, Murphy's executive secretary, later remembered the governor's account of the conversation: "Frank, for God's sake if the Fisher . . . brothers never make another nickel, don't have any bloodshed in that plant. We don't want to have blood on our hands. . . . just keep things going and . . . it'll work out." There is every reason to believe that Knudsen fully shared these views.

When violence broke out in Flint on February 1, it was Fisher, we now know, who at first advised delay when Murphy asked if the GM executive thought it necessary "to put militia in there." On February 10, Arnold Lenz, the Flint Chevrolet plant manager, called Detroit for permission to use company police to eject the strikers in the No. 4 plant, but Lenz's superiors, the National Guard records reveal, vetoed the plan because they did not want to take responsibility for breaking up the negotiations.[48]

It is possible as the result of the manuscript resources now available to trace with greater accuracy than was previously possible the course of the negotiations that led to the settlement of the strike. The documents reveal that Murphy leaned toward the union, but, contrary to the popular image of him, was not an invariable supporter of the union point of view, that President Roosevelt involved himself in the negotiations to a greater extent than we have previously been led to believe, and that the importance of the Murphy-Lewis confrontation has been greatly exaggerated. The evidence also indicates that Murphy at the outbreak of the strike in all probability held 1,650 shares of GM stock, with a market value of more than $100,000 as of December 31, 1936.[49] One wonders if the UAW would have

[48] Speech by John Lovett, Apr. 1937, 6, Joseph H. Creighton Memorandum to Murphy, May 11, 1938, Speech by Murphy, Oct. 21, 1938, 12, Strike Chronology, Feb. 1, 1937, Murphy Papers; transcript of interview with Hill, Aug. 21, 1963, 22–23, in my possession; Lunt, "Career of Murphy," 247; New York *Times*, Jan. 29, 30, Feb. 3, 9, 1937; Norman Beasley, *Knudsen: A Biography* (New York, 1947), 168–69; G-2 Journal, Feb. 10, 1937, G-2 Periodic Reports, Feb. 10, 11, 1937, National Guard Records. There are several extant versions of Fisher's statement to Murphy regarding bloodshed.

[49] Murphy transferred 1,650 shares of GM stock from his Manila to his New York broker on October 3, 1936. He received the GM dividend of $1.50 per share on this same number of shares on December 12, 1936. The market value of GM stock as of December 31, 1936, was $63.50 per share. The stock subsequently seems to have been transferred to Murphy's sister, Mrs. William Teahan, and was sold by her on January 18, 1937, at an estimated profit of over $50,000. (Hayden, Stone and Co. to Murphy, Oct. 3, 5, 1936, Eleanor Bumgardner to Kemp [Dec. 31, 1936?], copy of Murphy's 1936 income tax return, J. E. Swan to Mrs. Margaret [Marguerite] Teahan, Dec. 29, 1937, Murphy Papers; GM, *Twenty-Eighth Annual Report, Year Ended Dec. 31, 1936* (n. p., 1937), 56; New York *Times*, Jan. 1, 1937.

sought to discredit Murphy, as it had succeeded in discrediting Judge Black, had it known that the Michigan governor was at the time of the strike, or at least very recently had been, the holder of a sizable block of GM stock.

Murphy, aided throughout by Conciliator James F. Dewey, involved himself in the strike as a mediator even before the Battle of the Running Bulls, but his efforts as a peacemaker came to naught since GM refused to negotiate while the strikers held its plants and the union was unwilling to withdraw from the plants unless GM first recognized it, agreed to keep the struck plants closed and not to remove any equipment from them until a national agreement was concluded, and promised not to coerce its employees.[50]

At the insistence of the governor, negotiations were resumed after the violence of January 11 had resulted in the dispatch of Guardsmen to Flint. When Murphy brought the negotiators face-to-face on January 14, he informed them that the strike would have to be settled in accordance with the principles of law and order. "No one," he declared, "should wish or attempt to place the Governor of this state in the position of suspending the law of the land. This is not right and he is not going to do it."

If Murphy followed the notes that he seems to have taken with him to this conference, he suggested that GM meet the union demand for exclusive bargaining rights by accepting the UAW as the representative of "a *large* if not the largest organized group of employees." The union, he apparently said, should withdraw from the plants since there could be "no serious dispute" that it was in "unlawful possession" of GM property. Similarly, the union could not insist that the corporation make a definite commitment regarding the removal of its equipment during the period of the truce lest this qualify GM's lawful control over its own property, but GM might nevertheless state its intentions in this regard. The next day, largely as the result of Murphy's efforts, a truce was concluded, with GM declaring its intention not to reopen its plans or remove equipment from them during the scheduled period of negotiations.[51]

Following the collapse of the January 15 truce agreement, Perkins took charge of the negotiations in Washington, but she was unable to bring Sloan and Lewis together. During the Washington talks, Murphy offered to surround the struck plants with the National Guard while negotiations were in progress if the strikers were evacuated. Lewis accepted a similar

[50] Draft of agreement, Jan. 7, 1937, Knudsen to Murphy, Jan. 8, 1937, Knudsen statements, Jan. 9, 1937, Martin to Murphy, Jan. 9, 1937, Murphy Papers; Detroit News, Jan. 10, 1937; Kraus, *Many and the Few*, 122.

[51] Murphy statement, Jan. 14, 1937, "Notes," Jan. 14, 1937, Knudsen *et al.* to Murphy, Jan. 15, 1937, Murphy Papers; Brophy, "Struggle for an Auto Union," 11–12, Brophy Papers. The "Notes" of January 14 and the law-and-order statement of February 3, noted above, were almost certainly prepared by Murphy's close friend and legal adviser, Edward G. Kemp, who had a more conventional view of law and order than Murphy did.

proposal during the Chrysler sit-down strike in March 1937, but he rejected Murphy's proposition in January. Although the proposal would appear to have been agreeable to many of the strikers, Lewis was unwilling to accept any plan for the evacuation of the plants that did not grant the union exclusive bargaining rights.[52]

When the UAW's seizure of the Chevrolet No. 4 plant markedly heightened strike tensions, Perkins asked Murphy to resume control of the negotiations in Michigan. She informed him on February 2 that Lewis would arrive in Detroit the next day, and she requested Murphy to summon Knudsen into conference with the CIO chief. Knudsen and Lawrence Fisher, however, advised Murphy that GM would not retreat from its position of refusing to negotiate with the union until the corporation's plants were evacuated unless ordered to do so by the President himself. Murphy very much opposed presidential intervention in this form since he believed that the intent was to embarrass Roosevelt, but the Secretary of Labor advised him that Roosevelt wanted him to tell the GM negotiators that it was the President's wish that they confer with the union representatives. Murphy transmitted this information to the management representatives, but still obviously unhappy with the idea, the governor tried to persuade Knudsen to omit any reference to the President from his letter agreeing to confer. General Motors, however, believing it necessary to explain to the public why it was now consenting to negotiate while the sit-down remained in effect, stated in its letter to Murphy of February 2 that it was agreeing to a conference because the governor had indicated that this was "In accordance with the wish of the President," and "The wish of the President of the United States leaves no alternative except compliance." [53]

Perkins makes it appear in her memoirs that President Roosevelt, after helping to arrange for the resumption of strike talks, played no significant part in the ensuing negotiations.[54] As we shall see, however, Roosevelt involved himself directly and indirectly in the strike talks that began on February 3 and almost certainly used his influence to help secure acceptance of the agreement that finally brought the strike to a close.

Mainly, Roosevelt worked behind the scenes, urging Murphy on and expressing a willingness to speak to the union and management representatives in support of one or another peace plan. At no time, however, did he evidence any desire to take charge of the negotiations personally. Possibly

[52] Perkins Memorandum to the President, Jan. 19, 1937, President's Secretary's File [hereafter cited as PSF], Roosevelt Library; G-2 Periodic Reports, Jan. 23, 1937, National Guard Records.

[53] Strike Chronology, Feb. 2, 1937, Murphy to Knudsen, Feb. 2, 1937, Knudsen to Murphy, Feb. 2, 1937, Murphy Papers; Donaldson Brown to Sidney Fine, Aug. 18, 1964.

[54] Frances Perkins, *The Roosevelt I Knew* (New York, 1946), 322, 323–24; Perkins to Fine, Apr. 30, 1964. It is possible that the former Secretary of Labor confuses two different events in her account of Roosevelt's intervention in the strike.

his caution was accounted for by his recollection of the prolonged criticism that organized labor had directed at the settlement that he had arranged for the automobile industry on March 25, 1934; [55] possibly he simply wanted to avoid becoming involved in the conflict between the AFL and the CIO that was being exacerbated by the UAW's quest for exclusive representation.[56] Had Murphy been a poor negotiator, the President might have been compelled to involve himself more openly in the efforts to settle the strike. As it was, he was delighted with the manner in which the Michigan governor was handling the negotiations, and he was as reluctant as Murphy to have the National Guard used to evict the strikers.[57]

The President called Murphy on February 4 and asked him to tell the negotiators that the public welfare demanded that they settle the strike. Roosevelt offered to convey this message personally to Knudsen or Lewis if Murphy thought this necessary. On that same day the union retreated a bit from its original position by proposing that GM recognize it as the bargaining agency only for the employees of the twenty plants then on strike rather than for all the corporation's employees. General Motors also took a step toward a settlement on the same day by declaring that it would not "sponsor, aid or abet" any organization in opposition to or paralleling the UAW. It stated that it recognized and would not interfere with the right of its employees to join the union and that it would not discriminate against or coerce any employees because of their union membership. It was also willing by this time to declare that it would not conclude an agreement with any other organization that contained more favorable terms than it granted the UAW.[58] But GM would not yield on the crucial issue of exclusive representation: it would recognize the union as the collective bargaining agency only for those employees in the struck plants who were members of the union. It would be necessary to resolve the difference between the company and the union on this point if the strike were to be terminated.

The next day, February 5, GM supplemented its statement on recognition of the previous day by agreeing to the conduct of a poll among the employees of the struck plants to determine the extent to which the UAW represented these workers. The election was to be conducted under the auspices of Murphy not less than sixty days after the resumption of work.

[55] The President's settlement provided for proportional representation in the choice of employee representatives rather than majority rule and exclusive representation.

[56] The AFL, from the start of the strike, opposed the grant of exclusive bargaining rights to the UAW. (See Galenson, CIO Challenge to AFL, 142–43; William Green et al. to Murphy, Feb. 6, 1937, Murphy Papers; and Kraus, Many and the Few, 269.)

[57] Detroit News, Jan. 31, 1937; Strike Chronology, Feb. 4, 5, 1937, Creighton Memorandum to Murphy, May 11, 1938, Murphy Papers; Roosevelt to Samuel I. Rosenman, Nov. 13, 1940, President's Personal File 64, Roosevelt Library.

[58] Strike Chronology, Feb. 4, 1937, Proposals of UAW, Feb. 4, 1937, "Recognition," Feb. 4, 1937, Murphy Papers; Proposal for General Motors-Lewis Agreement [Feb. 5, 1937?], PSF.

General Motors did not say that it would accept the UAW as the representative of all the workers in these plants should it win a majority in this poll, and its plan could readily have served as a basis for some form of proportional representation. The UAW was not, however, interested in any kind of poll of membership at this point since it was far from confident that it could make an impressive showing. Neither it nor GM, thus, for different reasons, was anxious to invoke the election procedure for which the National Labor Relations Act provided.[59]

It appears from the evidence in the Murphy Papers that the governor concluded on February 5 that the hope for a settlement lay in a formula that would afford the union the degree of recognition and the status in the struck plants that GM had already indicated it was willing to concede but that deferred any decision on the troublesome question of exclusive representation for several months, at which time it would be resolved by collective bargaining, the examination of union membership cards, a poll, or the appointment of a board by the President. Since Roosevelt had advised Murphy once again earlier in the day that he would be willing to talk to Knudsen and Lewis and to help reconcile what he thought was the small difference between them, the governor asked Perkins that afternoon to request the President to express to the two men his approval of the peace formula. Roosevelt might tell Lewis, Murphy advised, that the proposed plan would gain him exclusive representation and that he would therefore be yielding nothing in accepting it. Murphy did not indicate how he had arrived at this conclusion.[60]

On the basis of her conversation with Murphy, the Secretary of Labor prepared a memorandum for the President to use in speaking to Knudsen and Lewis, and, as Murphy had suggested, she advised the President to tell Lewis that the plan would, in effect, grant him the exclusive representation that he was seeking for the UAW.[61] The next day, February 6, Roosevelt spoke to Lewis and Knudsen on the phone, presumably following the memorandum that the Secretary of Labor had prepared for him.[62]

On the same day, but we do not know whether it was before or after the President spoke to Knudsen, GM handed Murphy a confidential letter setting forth its own alternative to the union's demand for exclusive representation. The UAW, GM declared, insisted that it must have exclusive

[59] GM to Murphy, Feb. 5, 1937, Murphy Papers; Alinsky, *Lewis*, 138; Detroit *News*, Jan. 13, Feb. 9, 1937; New York *Times*, Jan. 26, 1937.

[60] Strike Chronology, Feb. 5, 1937, Murphy Papers.

[61] Memorandum for the President, Feb. 5, 1937, Proposal for GM-Lewis Agreement [Feb. 5, 1937?], Memorandum for the President's conversation with John Lewis and with Knudsen and Brown [Feb. 5, 1937?], PSF. Whereas Murphy talked of a truce period of six to nine months, the memorandum Perkins prepared for the President limited the period to four months. The Perkins memorandum said nothing about how the issue of representation was to be resolved at the end of the truce period.

[62] Strike Chronology, Feb. 6, 1937, Murphy Papers.

representation because GM would otherwise proceed to bargain with other groups in order to undermine the UAW's position. The company had said that it had no intention of doing this, and, as evidence of its good faith, it would now agree with the governor for a period of ninety days after the basic agreement went into effect not to bargain with any other organization in the struck plants regarding matters of general corporation policy without first submitting the facts to Murphy and gaining his sanction for this procedure. This arrangement would leave the UAW, for all practical purposes, as the sole bargaining agency for a period of three months, but would permit GM to avoid any statement to that effect in the proposed agreement and did not commit it to accept any particular plan of representation once the truce period had expired.[63]

Lewis was willing to accept a ninety-day truce only if the true agreement specifically granted exclusive bargaining rights and thus at least recognized the principle for whose recognition the UAW was striving. Murphy supported Lewis on this issue, but, as the governor informed the Secretary of Labor, GM would "not under any circumstances agree to it." Murphy, sometime during the day on February 8, therefore suggested to Perkins that the President might ask Lewis to accept the GM proposal of February 6,[64] but the governor abandoned this approach that evening after he had had "a grand talk" with Lewis in which Lewis had agreed that if GM would extend the truce period from three months to six months, he would accept the February 6 proposal even though it did not, in so many words, concede the principle of exclusive representation.[65]

All that now remained to achieve a settlement was to secure GM's approval for the extension of the truce period. Since Knudsen and Fisher in Detroit were apparently unwilling to make this concession on their own, Murphy asked Perkins to speak to Sloan or, better still, to have the President do so.[66] It is possible that Murphy said at this time that if Roosevelt did not want to involve himself, Marvin McIntyre, the President's secretary, should "insist on it at the request of the president" since Knudsen had said, "if the president told them they would do it." [67] McIntyre called Knudsen that day, but the GM official was either unwilling or unable to agree to a longer truce period; for when McIntyre called Murphy a few minutes after he had

[63] GM to Murphy, Feb. 6, 1937, Strike Chronology, Feb. 6, 1937, *ibid.*

[64] Strike Chronology, Feb. 7, 1937, *ibid.*; Memorandum for the President, Feb. 8, 1937, Official File [hereafter cited as OF] 407-B, Roosevelt Library; GM Statement, Feb. 8, 1937, Brown Collection. Alinsky claims that Roosevelt tried to persuade Lewis to accept a truce period of three months or less. (Alinsky, *Lewis*, 133–34.)

[65] Strike Chronology, Feb. 8, 1937, Murphy Papers. Unlike the confrontation of the next day, the Murphy-Lewis meeting of February 8 seems to have been devoted to a discussion of the terms for settling the strike rather than to the issue of law and order.

[66] *Ibid.*

[67] Pencil notes attached to copy of Strike Chronology [Feb. 8, 1937?], *ibid.*

spoken to Knudsen, the governor said: "The Boss has to get in touch with Sloane [*sic*] or the Duponts [*sic*] — tell them this is okay." [68]

The next night, as GM continued to hold out for a ninety-day truce, Murphy confronted Lewis with his law-and-order letter and warned him that if a settlement were not immediately negotiated, the governor would read the statement to the other conferees the next morning and would also make it public. Carl Muller, a Detroit newspaperman and a close friend of Murphy, claims that Murphy on this occasion "grabbed Lewis by the coat collar, and in no uncertain terms told him the men would get out of the plants 'or else.'" George Murphy, the governor's brother, declared in an interview that Lewis told Murphy after the letter had been read, "Governor you win," and Murphy himself has described the event as "the turning point" in the strike.[69] The fact of the matter is, though, that Lewis did not alter his position in the slightest as the result of the February 9 confrontation with Murphy. The union leader had insisted on a six-month truce before the letter was read to him, and he continued to insist on a six-month truce after the letter had been read. It was GM that now had to be persuaded to yield.

Murphy had asked for the assistance of Washington in securing GM's consent to a truce period of six months, and that assistance was forthcoming. Not only had McIntyre spoken to Knudsen on February 8, but the next day Secretary of Commerce Daniel Roper talked to Donaldson Brown, a GM vice-president who represented Sloan in the negotiations with the union, and that same day or the next day S. Clay Williams, at Roper's request and in response to Perkins' desire that the aid of an "outstanding" business leader should also be enlisted, talked with Sloan and Brown. Brown explained to Roper that GM was less interested in the length of the "experiment" than in "the phraseology relating to a definition of the words 'exclusive bargaining agents' in such an experiment." [70] Brown was seemingly unaware that Lewis by this time had decided that the substance of the GM concession was more important that its form and no longer was insisting on an outright grant of exclusive bargaining rights.

It was probably more than the inclusion of satisfactory "phraseology" in the final agreement, however, that caused GM to retreat on the question of

---

[68] Strike Chronology, Feb. 8, 1937, *ibid.*; Beasley, *Knudsen*, 169.

[69] Subcommittee of Senate Committee on Judiciary, *Nomination of Frank Murphy*, 10; Carl Muller, "Frank Murphy, Ornament of the Bar," *Detroit Lawyer*, XVII (Sept. 1949), 183; Interview of George Murphy, Mar. 28, 1957, 4, Michigan Historical Collections; pencil notes by Murphy (Aug. 1938, undated folder), Murphy Papers. For Lewis' account of how he "frightened" Murphy into not executing the order, see Alinsky, *Lewis*, 144–46.

[70] Roper Memorandum for McIntyre, Feb. 10, 1937, OF 407-B; Donaldson Brown, *Some Reminiscences of an Industrialist* (n.p. [1957]), 96. Williams was given substantially the same information as was conveyed to Roper.

the length of the period during which the UAW would enjoy a favored position in its plants. The corporation's automotive production had dwindled to the vanishing point, and it must have appeared to GM negotiators, who were unaware of Murphy's law-and-order letter to Lewis,[71] that the sit-downers were simply not going to be dislodged from its plants in the near future and that the company's automotive production would not be resumed until an agreement with the UAW was reached. General Motors was also undoubtedly responding to the informal pressure being exerted from the White House through McIntyre and Roper. When Knudsen later reported that "the Government practically ordered" the settlement of the strike, it may well have been the President to whom he was referring. The corporation, after all, had been warned by one of its officials at the very outset of the strike that the temper of the times required it to adopt a reasonable posture toward unionism in its plants and not to forget that "there has been an election." [72]

The negotiations continued until 2:35 A.M. on February 11, when a weary Murphy was finally able to announce that peace terms had been arranged. The news that the strike had been ended made Murphy the hero of the hour, and praise was lavished upon him by government officials from the President on down, business and labor leaders, the press, and the general public. Murphy had "succeeded," as Josephus Daniels put it, "in what most people thought was an impossible achievement." *Time* reported that it was "apparent that the first vehicle to roll off General Motors' revived assembly lines will be a bandwagon label 'Frank Murphy for President in 1940.' " [73] Murphy's "star" seemed "in the ascendant" [74] on February 11, and had not the GM strike been followed by a rash of sit-downs across the land and especially in Michigan, it is unlikely that Murphy would have been subjected to the severe criticism that was soon to be directed at him and that was to plague him for the remainder of his days.

[71] Kemp, "Murphy as Government Administrator."

[72] Detroit *News*, Oct. 29, 1937; SMD [DuBrul], "The Problem of Union Agreements," Dec. 31, 1936, GM Appendix Documents, Sec. 1.

[73] Daniels to Murphy, Feb. 12, 1937, Murphy Papers; *Time*, XXIX (Feb. 22, 1937), 14; for praise of Murphy as a peacemaker, see the Murphy Papers for Feb. 12, 1937 ff., Murphy Scrapbook #12, and New York *Times*, Feb. 12, 1937.

[74] "Governor Murphy's Star Is in the Ascendant" is the title of an article by Russell B. Porter in the New York *Times Magazine*, Feb. 21, 1937.

20

THE AMERICAN INTELLIGENTSIA
AND THE COMMUNIST PARTY

One of the more interesting and neglected phenomena of the post–
World War II years was the almost total decline of a viable political
left in the United States. From the late 1940's to the mid-1960's, observers of the American scene found it increasingly appropriate to
apply the term "radical" to the extreme right rather than to its
seemingly moribund opposite numbers. The essays by a number of
eminent scholars in the 1963 collection, *The Radical Right**, edited
by Daniel Bell, are a good example of this tendency. The Communist party and a variety of socialist parties continued to exist, but
they became increasingly bereft of members, finances, and hope. (See,
for example, David Shannon, *The Decline of American Communism*
[1959]). To understand this decline it is necessary to examine not
only the angry and at times hysterical reaction that followed the disruption of the Soviet-American wartime alliance and the inception of
the Cold War, but the decade that preceded World War II as well,
a decade that, for the left at least, began in hope and ended in
disaster. Never again were the organizations and ideologies that had
dominated the American left throughout the twentieth century to
have as much force, appeal, or prospect.

The left not only failed to benefit in any meaningful way from the
mass privation, inequalities, and unemployment of the 'thirties, it
actually emerged from the depression decade far weaker than it had
entered it. The Socialist party had fewer members in 1937 than it had
at the party's birth in 1901. Though the Communist party's membership grew during the 'thirties, this increase was due more to the
party's support of the New Deal during the Popular Front honeymoon
than to any policy of militant, revolutionary action. In any case, its
membership never exceeded 100,000, hardly a formidable number.
Much of the left's thunder was stolen by various right-wing groups,
which during the 'thirties had a larger following and wider appeal
than any leftist organization – a fact that still needs explanation. The
material and psychological successes of the New Deal, which, as
Norman Thomas quipped, carried the Socialist party's platform out on
a stretcher, also greatly weakened the left.

These external factors, however, were no more important than the
internal weaknesses from which the major leftist organizations suffered.
The intense factionalism, always characteristic of the Socialist party,

437

reached a peak in the 'thirties. A group of labor leaders and intellectuals broke with the Socialists to form the American Labor party; additional factions split off, either to join other leftist organizations or to lapse into political quietude; a large group of Trotskyites entered the party in the late 'thirties and before departing helped to accelerate the process of internal disruption. All this, of course, left the party weak, demoralized, and frequently incapable of action. The Communist party was troubled less by factionalism than by a number of important and embarrassing policy gyrations that were determined more by the needs of the Soviet Union than by the realities of the situation in the United States. The most important of these sudden shifts is discussed by Norman Holmes Pearson, Professor of English at Yale University, in the article that follows.

But Pearson does more than merely point out one of the elements that helped to blunt the Communist appeal in the depression years. In an era in which it has become common to denounce as pseudo-intellectuals, frustrated elitists, or simple-minded dupes those writers, artists, and intellectuals who found the extreme left attractive, Pearson describes their actions with sensitivity and insight, speaking not only of the objective conditions that surrounded them but also of the literary and intellectual traditions in which they matured and worked. That so many literary, artistic, and intellectual figures of note found Communism the only, or at least the best, alternative during the depression, calls for understanding rather than epithets; and this Pearson attempts to supply. Other penetrating analyses of the literary and intellectual left in the 'thirties may be found in Daniel Aaron's essay, "A Decade of Convictions: The Appeal of Communism in the 1930's," *Massachusetts Review*, 2 (Summer 1961), 736–47; in his larger work, *Writers on the Left** (1961); and in James Gilbert, *Writers and Partisans* (1968). For a much different and less sympathetic picture, see L. Filler, "Political Literature: A Post-Mortem," *Southwest Review*, 39 (Summer 1954), 185–93.

The Nazi-Soviet Pact and the End of a Dream

Norman Holmes Pearson

To look back upon history is inevitably to distort it. As Ambrose Bierce morosely snarled: "God alone knows the future, but only an historian can alter the past." Bierce may have regarded historians as bumblers of facts.

Reprinted by permission of the publisher from *America in Crisis*, edited by Daniel Aaron. Copyright 1952 by Alfred A. Knopf, Inc.

We may view them simply as contrivers of necessary fictions that are the only approximate means we have for understanding yesterdays. The data historians choose from the web of events are usually those which lead directly to outcomes they already know. The tone they give is the tone they wish. The nearer we are to the present, the more difficult is the choice of material, since the less we can be sure that there are any true or discernible conclusions to form structures against. There are only steps (and many false ones) along the way to the uncertainties of an indeterminate future. The present is at least as difficult to assess as either the past or the future. It is as difficult to understand and to plan. That is why there are crises in the present, have been crises in the past, and unquestionably will continue to be crises in the future. They are the results of general failures of assessment. Yet in the necessity for making assessments, each of us is always a practicing fictionalist, whether or not we indite. We share in the process, and if we learn nothing else from the history of crises we may perhaps learn a decent humility in regarding them.

Such a crisis was the Nazi-Soviet Non-Aggression Pact of August 1939, which brought an end to the decade that had begun with the depression, and joined enemy to apparent friend in a confusion of loyalties that shattered the confidence of many writers. Today, the strong friendship with Russia in the 1930's seems somehow inexplicable to a generation whose mature life is a matter of years since World War II. Other factors have intervened to create a new situation, altered allegiances, and even new crises. What occurred then took place in a different scene. Regarded solely from the present, the affinities of the thirties appear in a sometimes dismal light; when they are looked at in terms of what had preceded them, a different tone prevails. For the writers of the thirties had a special conditioning and worked by values that first led them into such sympathies and then away. The values remained. What is now needed is an understanding of the impulsions.

Behind most writers lies their tradition, and there is much about the American tradition which is ambiguous, even paradoxical. It is a remarkable characteristic of the American psyche that, no matter how externally confident we may appear, we are always examining ourselves before mirrors, and our self-chosen classics of American writing are chiefly self-critical. Just as we are constantly discontented with our mechanical technologies and seek to improve upon them even at the cost of retooling, so we seek the same opportunity and find the same necessity with our nation and with our egos. Just as we seek for the truth of progress so we seek for the truth of self.

Something of this self-consciousness may be charged to a persistent psychology of national and personal adolescence. We are told, and tell ourselves, that we are a young nation. We live in a constant puberty, with our voices changing. We grope our way, like adolescents, without any easy confidence of acceptance as equals in a mature world. Such behavior may appear gauche, but it is also a source of strength, since our awareness of our youth encourages change and the possibility of change, and keeps us from an easy acceptance of things as they are simply because they are as they are. Progress for us is a continued disruption of the status quo, and our sense of innate youth gives us the energy, the daring, and the freedom for progress.

Yet the malaise goes deeper than mere awkwardness, and does not altogether find its compensation in the fact of achievement. The achievement always seems partial. There is an exhilaration in the process of "becoming," but there is a definable tension that comes from never arriving at the ideal stage that we envision. Americans are a race of sad young men because they dream of ideals without being able to achieve them in any absolute sense. Any momentary achievement is always overclouded by the further possibilities. Satisfaction is blended with unrest. The history of the American race shows how much has been altered for good; but when so much remains still to be done, the failure to accomplish it nourishes anguish. Such frustration accompanying such hope is a paradox of youth and Americans.

We have only to look briefly at American literary classics to see how dominant self-criticism has been. A substantial shelf of Cooper's books exist that scold Americans and American ways as severely as Sinclair Lewis was ever to do. Even Cooper's Natty Bumppo turned his primitive back to the increasingly dominant culture-patterns. Cooper felt such criticism to be his responsibility and a proper function of fiction. He was, as his literary ancestor Cotton Mather had put it, his brother's keeper as well as his own; and Cooper's books like Mather's were meant to do good. A cliché of consolation for us in many circumstances comes from a conviction that bitter medicine is administered for our own good. The criticisms of our materialistic way of life which Thoreau made in *Walden* are obvious, and still, we feel, pertinent. Mark Twain's Huckleberry Finn took to the river rather than the shores of the Mississippi, as Thoreau had taken to the pond. Huck hit out even farther at the end. "I reckon I got to light out for the Territory ahead of the rest, because Aunt Sally she's going to adopt me and civilize me, and I can't stand it. I been there before." The conclusion was more than comic; the book involved more than the ways of juveniles. Hawthorne's novel, *The House of the Seven Gables,* was an attack on the greed for property; and *The Marble Faun* a discussion of aspects of American immaturity. One does not have to read far in Melville to find characterizations of distrust. The preoccupation of Henry James with American cultural deficiencies was constant. Even Whitman pleaded for what was still latent rather than altogether realized. Yet none of these writers could be said not to have loved America; they were goading her toward the achievement of an ideal.

The writers of the 1930's were essentially the group who had been writing in the decade after World War I. One understands them as well by what they read as by what they wrote. An aspect of the 1920's was its awareness of such a literary tradition of self-criticism, and a certain dignity accompanied the writer who was willing to stand up against public criticism and complacency in order to point out the truths. Into the family of American classics, the intellectuals of the twenties adopted two books; and the adoption showed characteristics of the decade. One was *The Education of Henry Adams*; the other was Melville's *Moby Dick*.

The Education of Henry Adams was a depiction of shared plight, of isolation, of man's uneasiness and uncertainty, and of his agonized effort to understand himself, his heritage, and his age. The figure of Adams himself emerged as a Hamlet *de nos jours*: the prince who had been deprived of succession to kingship, who is in danger of being overcome by too much intellectualization and unable to adjust himself to a decayed court, yet persists in his education as though, even were the conclusions intolerable, the very achievement of them were an act of moral rectitude. One can hardly understand the tone of Adam's autobiography unless one reads it in the light of the implicit belief of Americans in the value of education. From the beginnings of the country there has been this reliance. From education comes the possibility of an enlightened electorate, the enlightened technologist, and the enlightened son of God. Henry Adams equates education with its goal, which is understanding. If there is no final understanding there has been, on these terms, no education. But this is really little more than to say that one has not been graduated; and for Americans the final examinations come only, if ever, at death. Yet Adams, in actual fact, was like most Americans and did believe in education as a process as well as an end. He uses the word in the sense both of attaining and of attainment. He relinquished neither meaning. He was always educating himself, and the goal was knowledge, not simply as a trophy but as an applicable science of history, which would serve as a technology of truth. "Any science of history must be absolute," he said, "and must fix with mathematical certainty the path which human society has got to follow." When Adam says "the path which human society has got to follow," he means it as an imperative only because it is the path of truth, which to the educated will be irresistible because it can be recognized through reasonable demonstration. Truth as a goal, and reason as a method, have been American tenets. If for Adams truth was in the world's decline, he was dignifying his countrymen by deeming them capable of being trained to a maturity that could bear the burden of pessimism.

In the literary myth, the figure of Adams was blended by T. S. Eliot into the Gerontion of "a dry month, being read to by a boy, waiting for rain." "After such knowledge, what forgiveness?" Eliot said of the situation. A Gerontion was incapable of action. "What will the spider do, suspend its operations, will the weevil delay?"

If [Adams had said in 1894 in speaking of his construction of history] an hypothesis is advanced

> that obviously brings into a direct sequence of cause and effect all the phenomena of human history, we must accept it, and if we accept it we must teach it. The mere fact that it overthrows social organization cannot affect our attitude. The rest of society can reject or ignore, but we must follow the new light no matter where it leads.

Such a light might seem to lead underground.

But Gerontion was only a facet of the psyche rather than the whole of it. Too much has been made of the "lostness" of the twenties, and too little of the spiritual daring, which was equally characteristic. The decade supplied a complementary answer to despondency by its admiration of Melville's Captain Ahab, whom it saw as a man of indomitable will, going gallantly even to death in his attempt to harpoon evil in the destructive body of the whale itself.

One way of expressing the indomitable will was through a reliance on youth, and the romantic powers of natural man. There was a freshening of the value of the romantic ego. The "mimic hootings" of Wordsworth's nature boy of Winander were being given new and blatant tones in the blare of the saxophone. The more "natural" one could become by casting aside encrusted hides of convention (tonal or otherwise) the closer one came to a modern adaptation of the state of Rousseau's primitive hero. Harlem became a convenient jungle in which inhibitions could be cast aside. To violate Prohibition was to assert one's natural freedom from legislation, and the recovered cocktail took on a sacramental glow. Sexual liberty became an asset, if for no other reason than that whatever was instinctive was right. Conventions were clichés of behavior, whose truth investigation denied. One of the characters in Dos Passos's *Manhattan Transfer* put the social case for the truth of reality:

> Everything would be so much better if suddenly a bell rang and everybody told everybody else honestly what they did about it, how they lived, how they loved. It's hiding things makes them putrefy.

Suddenly the bell had rung, and writers became bell-ringers. But it was not simply for the hullabaloo of clanging, though different ears heard it differently. It was a moral summons for the individuals to take out papers of naturalization.

Such a spiritual daring might lead to initial martyrdom at the hands of Philistines, who like whales took vengeance; but in the attempt lay the only hope for the destruction of sham, which by its deceitful nature was an evil. All this was in the sense of a dedication to the discovery of truth, based on the knowledge that even "whiteness" could not be accepted at surface appearance. Surface appearances had been profoundly altered since the previous century, though the public was not always quick to see what had happened. The scientific method, applied in various fields of knowledge, had toppled hitherto accepted definitions in physics, economics, politics, law, society, and religion. Secrets of the consciousness and subconsciousness of man had been laid bare. Writers, following this impulse and sharing in the dignity of scientists, were equally concerned with redefinitions in their attempts to deal with the description and analysis of life. Craftsmanship as a goal in writing was another aspect of the necessity for scientists to describe accurately the material they were dealing with. Truly accurate description in writing might, as Gertrude Stein had discovered in her portrayals of consciousness, lead to a rejection of established syntax. As science brought all data into the open as worthy of analysis, so writers broke down the barriers of censorship that inhibited subject-matter. The public's objections had nothing to do with the writer's necessity for presenting truth. Eventually, as writers knew, the public would come to accept it; because the public too, though more slowly than scientists or writers, believed as essentially in truth. Like Mather and Cooper, these moderns also were writing essays to do good. When a Hemingway character "was embarrassed by the words sacred, glorious, and sacrifice and the expression in vain," as he famously put it, and was out after the "concrete names of villages, the numbers of roads, the names of rivers, the numbers of regiments and the dates," he was acting in the scientific spirit that pursued truth. What Hemingway was not doing — though many asserted that he was — was carelessly tossing aside the concept of values. He was simply examining, as though the world were his laboratory, the silken or iron curtains of slick words that halted the vision of reality. He was also following a principle of free inquiry that gave him a right to express his conclusions. By his actions he was himself exemplifying a value.

On every side the privilege of free inquiry was maintained, with those unabashed questionings after what is really true which are characteristic of more than Congressional committees. Congressmen, after all, act for their constituents. An at least quasi-scientific method had gone into a general examination of such an overwhelming phenomenon as World War I. By one investigator after another, unrecognized economic factors were shown to exist alongside the urgencies of such idealistic slogans as H. G. Wells's phrase "the war to end war." Events during and after the war made such slogans seem little more than sham. But behind the irony that in histories, novels, and poems attacked the factual validity of the slogans lay a yearning belief in their ambitions. Irony, as Ezra Pound remarked, is never negative, because it always posits an ideal which has been corrupted. Pragmatic concepts notwithstanding, idealism has played a dramatic role, either as protagonist or antagonist, in the American drama of contradictions. Relief could have been found for the tensions. All that was required of American writers was that they relinquish their values. This would have brought a

lethargic and blinded contentment. But the values were too deeply ingrained, and the greatest enemy was inertia.

Something of the temper of the postwar years is to be found in an excerpt
from an unpublished letter from William Rose Benét to his younger
brother, written in November of 1919. Benét was working for a Washington
journal known as *The Nation's Business.* "Dear Steve," he wrote:

> This industrial situation makes me alternately feel Bolshevik and then
> just oh-what-the-hell's-the-use. This job is a good money-making job,
> but every once in so often I want to take the boat to Russia. I hate the
> way most things are going in this country and I am so damned tired
> of all this Americanization stuff I can hardly see straight. I have no
> illusions about the white purity of the working man, but the way these
> conferences have gone, and the attitude of the coal barons, and the
> [Versailles] Treaty all bitched to hell, and the League [of Nations] not
> even a ghost of itself — well, it seems to me as if all the world were
> ruled by mere stupid standpatness that just sits and sits and merely
> grunts when an idea comes along.

Here were the uneasinesses that the 1930's were to heighten for so many
writers.

The bell that *Manhattan Transfer* had called for as a summons to truth
began to toll like a tocsin in late October of 1929, when the stock market
crashed. Before the month was over fifteen billion dollars in market value
had been lost. By the end of the year, the total was "an estimated forty
billion." It was not too long afterwards, as history goes in time, when on
the 6th of March, 1933, the "bank holiday" was declared, and with it the
inviolability of economic clichés was shattered. Whatever else happened,
it was now obvious that the old reliances no longer obtained, and that more
and more people were beginning to realize this. What had seemed chiefly
an ideological dilemma now became a dilemma in fact.

The succession of shocks was overwhelming. It was not simply an American situation that was witnessed. In England had come the "dole"; in Germany, such a dislocation of economy that youth having finished college had
chiefly the choice between learning to play in the band of a cheap café or
drinking vermouth and plotting to migrate. In Germany there was at least
action. The Nazi Party began to emerge, following the Italian precedent;
and the same emotionally and physically hungry ones went to its rallies as
attended the meetings of the Communists. Over the speakers' stands at
both, the same appealing banner hung: *Arbeit und Brot* (Work and
Bread). But Hitler's stentorian nationalism was louder, and the roll of ket-
tledrums boomed a more intoxicating rhythm when the Führer strode, arms
folded across his brown-shirted breast, through public halls filled with men
whose palms were outstretched to touch a swastika'd savior.

Something was needed. As the troubled memory of writers played back
over the episodes from the first World War to the Great Depression and

afterwards, they could not help but be impressed by the absence of order and the lack of any binding ethics. There was only confusion. By 1932 at the Conference of Lausanne a despairing end was made to the frenzied financing by which American capital, depending upon a complacent view of its own powers, had lent money to Germany. By means of it, and while American capital winked, Germany had partly built up a new war potential and partly repaid reparations to countries that continued, by its means, to float their own American loans. By the summer of 1933 the flags flew at half-mast over the University of Berlin in mourning for the Versailles Treaty. Circles of young Nazis replaced the clustered *Studentenkorps* before the doors of learning. By now Germany was receiving apologies, and reviving young Germans were saying sometimes that the war had been lost by bad generalship, and anyhow that it was nothing for which their generation was responsible. Yet there was still little but sitting and grunting on the part of those others to whom the dangers of such a situation should have been obvious. No one seemed to listen to warnings. Japan, taking advantage of European confusion, had already in 1931 commenced her series of aggressions in Manchuria, but economic sanctions under the League Covenant were withheld because of the danger to British investments in Shanghai. No lessons had been learned from the first war. When it came time in 1935–6 for Mussolini to strike his fasces into Ethiopia, the same lack of principles prevented opposition. By the time of the Spanish War in 1936–9, the League of Nations was dead, not only because America had never joined in its initial idealism but also because Europe and Great Britain apparently did not want it either. From the moment in 1934 when Mussolini had marched his troops to the Brenner Pass to prevent Hitler from annexing Austria, and thousands waited at European radios for the news that war had been declared, it was only a question of time before, somewhere in the confusion, absolute calamity would break out. It did break out in Spain, when Germany and Italy ostentatiously used the peninsula as a practice ground. But even their bombings of civilians at Guernica and Barcelona could not overcome economic timidity. The word "time" had never seemed so important to those who desired to take measures against disorder.

Had there been anything like mutual good-will among nations in trying to work out on a truly rational basis any technologies for remedying situations, some progress towards order might have been made. A new force, however, had emerged, for which most American writers were ill prepared, but which they recognized for what it truly was long before its full significance was generally felt. This was Hitlerism as a positive force of deceit and evil. It had its testament in *Mein Kampf* and its affidavits in the slaughter of the Jews. To writers who believed not in the essential depravity of man but in his innate goodness, Nazi brutalities on street corners and in concentration camps acted not so much to change their belief as to rally them together against what was for the first time a common antagonist. Alongside such a foe, the earlier skirmishes of American writers in the twenties against Philistinism became trivial. But unless the values that had prompted them before were to be now relinquished, then they served as a basis for resistance against this more formidable opponent. The importance of demonstrating truths about a narrow range of local society became even greater in terms of the ubiquitous nature of Fascism. Echoes of Fascist-mindedness in America itself made Europe's problem one to be shared by us if we were not to be touched by the same cancer. That there was an indifference to the reception of truth was only an aspect of history repeating itself. Writers followed a moral imperative.

More and more the temper of writers had been altered. A dominantly personal ethic, as James Farrell was to point out, had shifted to a dominantly social ethic. Today when we wish to praise a book or insinuate unsuspected virtues in it, we say that it is basically religious. In the 1920's critical praise was reserved chiefly for originality and vitality and craftsmanship, with a premium for telling the truth. This was an expression of the morality of individualism. It was the individual who must be saved, and through his regeneration might come the regeneration of society. But in the 1930's the praise increasingly came for a book's social awareness or relevance, as though society could be directly manipulated and controlled. This was an expression of a developing sense of group involvement, and of the state as something separate from man. Under these circumstances the state was still man's servant. It was only later in America that the state began to be thought of as man's master or at least superior, and one could refer to such concepts as that of the state's duty to man. More and more as the 1930's developed, the role that a book can play in terms of social influence was recognized. Through his books, the writer could become a kind of social engineer, molding and reforming. This possibility of playing an active part in society gave writers and their books a new dignity, for they were now more than critical observers.

Against such forces of evil as the Spanish War, presented both actually and representationally, there was a sense of a literary crusade with a tangible objective. The Spanish War seemed to represent a moment in history which drew together the disturbing strands of tendencies that writers opposed. To join forces, whether by actual enlistment in such a group as the Abraham Lincoln Brigade, or by writing as social engineers, was to oppose moral inertia. Expressed in Hemingway's highest rhetoric in *For Whom the Bell Tolls*, the Spanish War offered

> a part in something which you could believe in wholly and completely and in which you felt an absolute brotherhood with the others who were engaged in it. . . . Your own death seemed of complete unimportance; only a thing to be avoided because it would interfere with the performance of your duty. But the best thing was that here was some-

thing you could do about this feeling and this necessity too. You could fight.

There were various ways of fighting and feeling, and most writers used words, which were their special weapons. They were working for peace, or at least for the achievement of an equilibrium on which organized peace could be maintained not by any balance of power but by the eventual coming together of rational minds, working in terms of common values and dedicated to truth and freedom. What they had learned was that nothing could be accomplished by doing nothing. They had come to know that active forces of evil must be actively opposed. "The point is clear enough," Archibald MacLeish said in an address:

> Those who fight against fascism are not fomenting war for the simple reason that the war is already fomented. The war is already made. Not a preliminary war. Not a local conflict. *The* war: the actual war: the war between the fascist powers and the things they could not destroy. Spain is no political allegory. Spain is not, as some would have us think, a dramatic spectacle in which the conflict of our time is acted out. These actors are not actors. They truly die. These cities are not stage sets. They burn with fire. These battles are not symbols of other battles to be fought elsewhere at some other time. They are the actual war itself. And in that war, that Spanish war on Spanish earth, we, writers who contend for freedom, are ourselves, and whether we so wish or not, engaged.

What was important was the objective, which was the crushing of the evil of Fascism. Mr. MacLeish's speech was made at the second Congress of American Writers in the summer of 1937. The first Congress had been held in 1935. As a chapter in American literary history, such gatherings, sponsored by names like those of Hemingway, Erskine Caldwell, Kenneth Burke, Malcolm Cowley, Theodore Dreiser, James T. Farrell, Horace Gregory, Lewis Mumford, and John Dos Passos, to name only an important few, were the first times when a substantial body of serious, though diversified, writers had come together with a sense of unity. Such gatherings were startling substitutions for those of the 1920's at the tables of the Dôme Café in Paris, but the functions of the two locales were not entirely unlike in serving the satisfaction for writers of being together with something in common. An un-Philistine idealism played a part at both meeting-houses. The sense of the importance of freedom of inquiry and a desire to reach toward truth were part of both. Only now the enemy was not intangible bigotry but tangible evil.

The political collapse of Europe, as Professor Hajo Holborn has called his newly published history of events, continued with increasing momentum. No matter what ennobling idealism the League of Nations may originally have represented, the League itself came tumbling down. The Spanish

Civil War kept Europe busy from 1936 to 1939, while Hitler grew strong. In 1936 the Rhineland was remilitarized. In the same year the Rome-Berlin Axis was established. By 1938 the annexation of Austria was achieved. Mussolini hurried this time only to be photographed at Hitler's side. In September of the same year came the pivotal Treaty of Munich, which, through Chamberlain's efforts at appeasement, gave Hitler the Sudetenland of Czechoslovakia, and eventually Czechoslovakia itself. Not even the United States, which through Wilson had helped to establish Czechoslovakia, made any tangible protest, though there were shudderings of nausea. Poland, which had once been freed like Czechoslovakia, put in a stained thumb for plums of territory, as though unaware of what greed would do against herself as the power of evil grew. The Spanish War ended as a failure for democratic values; the evils of Hitlerism had continued to flourish. The fiber of Europe was disintegrating.

But if during these years of the 1930's there was to be no effective formal association of nations to oppose what was increasingly evil, then at least there could be an informal association of right-minded peoples within nations, who could act together as a coercive force. They could form a protesting, if unauthorized, united front against a common enemy. As writers, when such was their skill, the people could continue to push aside the shams and false words and expose truth for truth. This was a goal; for American writers, joining such a movement, still retained their belief that truth, once revealed, would eventually triumph. That was perhaps their chief morality. So great was the force of the enemy that to join in opposition seemed in itself to be an affidavit of integrity.

The United Front as a name as well as an idea had been established in the summer of 1935, when the Third International decided that the U.S.S.R. would support democracies against the common Nazi enemy, and that Communists in countries other than Russia should support even bourgeois local governments. The role of the Community Party in the United States, which had been established in 1919, took on aspects of third-party protests that had long been a part of American politics, and whose strength came not so much through their own electoral victories as through their pressure on more established parties.

It was in the name of a united effort that the first American Writers' Congress was called together in 1935. Few who attended had any illusions about whether or not the American Communist Party, acting in the spirit of the Third International, was sponsoring the Congress. Many realized that the Congress had been developed at least partly to replace the John Reed clubs, which had been taken over by the Trotskyites. But the prevalent attitude of writers, not actually themselves involved in frictions within the Party, was that which MacLeish was to express for the laymen at the second Congress in 1937 in relation to the Spanish War. He was talking about those who felt "that the fascist issue is in actual fact nothing but a private squabble between fascism and communism, of no concern to anyone but the partisans, and of ulterior and purely factional concern to them." "The answer is, of course," Mr. MacLeish went on:

> that the man who refuses to defend his convictions for fear he may defend them in the wrong company, has no convictions. The further answer is that this fear of being used, this phobia of being maneuvered is itself a very curious thing. There is, to my mind, something about it unpleasantly squeamish and virginal — something indecently coy. Even if the danger of rape exists the tender spirit need not necessarily submit. Why *should* a man be "used" unless he pleases? Why should he not himself become the "user"? If a liberal really believes in the freedom of the mind and person which he protests, he will defend them against all comers and in any company and he will himself make the greatest possible *use* of those whom he finds at his side. All the great forays of the human spirit, whether by Marx or Rousseau, were originally one-man expeditions which gathered company from the bystanders as they moved. No writer worthy the name ever refused to make his position clear for fear that position might advantage others than himself — even others whom he had no wish to help.

Earl Browder, the head of the American Communist Party, welcomed the nondenominational writers to the first Congress of 1935, speaking of the struggle which writers had been engaged in from the beginning of the century, long before the name of Russia entered as a symbol either of admiration or suspicion. This, as Browder put it, was

> the struggle for a literature capable of satisfying the cultural needs of humanity in the period of break-up of the old social economic system, the period of chaos and readjustment, the period of searching for the values of the new society. This new society is not yet in existence in America, although we are powerfully affected by its glorious rise in the Soviet Union. The new literature must help to create a new society in America — that is its main function — giving it firm roots in our own traditional cultural life, holding fast to all that is of value in the old, saving it from the destruction threatened by the modern vandals brought forth by a rotting capitalism, the fascists, combining the new with the best of the old world heritage.

To such words of idealism few writers could be cold. A traditional role of American writers, when they wished to be more than entertainers, stood behind them as precept. Their own earlier efforts in the 1920's gave the validity of personal experience. It would be impossible to say precisely how many writers were actually to take out membership cards in the Party, but of those who lent their support to the United Front there were few who felt that they should turn their backs on a country like the Union of Soviet Socialist Republics, which the United States of America had officially recognized in 1933, and which more than any other nation seemed to be taking action in a time that needed it, an action apparently firm in its opposition to that form of action which Fascism had developed.

From the time when the Russian Czars had been overthrown, the revolutionary movement in that country seemed, in its youthful disdain of an intolerable status quo, congenial to the American youthful impatience with situations that could be bettered. Such a quality gave the appeal that men like Benét felt. The political opposition to the Russian revolutionists, on the part of other countries, appeared to be little more than a customary reluctance against progress, which in time would be overcome. Recognition of Russia did, to an extent, overcome the reluctance. What came to be said in opposition to Soviet idealism was often simply technological in tone: that the experiment would not work out. But whereas other nations seemed to be more or less content with themselves in the postwar period, Russia had already in 1928 made the beginnings of its much publicized first Five-Year Plan. This was societal and industrial planning in which technologically minded Americans could not help but be interested. America's own course in the crisis of economic depression or in catastrophes was not completely dissimilar. Whereas the Soviet Union had been held up before the general public as a bogy, increasingly in the 1930's her international actions seemed to be toward peace and working agreements between nations. In July of 1932 the U.S.S.R. signed non-aggression pacts with Poland, Estonia, Latvia, and Finland; and in November of the same year a similar pact was made with France. In 1934, as though bowing to the justice of international reason, she recognized the loss of Bessarabia and joined the League of Nations. In 1935 a Franco-Russian agreement of defensive alliance was concluded. Both internally and externally the pattern of Soviet movements was towards order. Western-Christian-Democratic values were ostensibly dominant, and the policy of the Third International for a United Front appeared to signify an ideological readiness for democratic action in a world that seemed otherwise morally inert.

The Soviet Union was excluded by the other powers from the negotiations at Munich, and so did not share in that symbol of culpability; she even seemed to gain in moral prestige by the fact of her absence. As "the war of nerves" between Germany and western Europe drew inevitably nearer to a war of weapons, Soviet spokesmen began to urge a hands-off. "Do you really believe that this is an ideological war?" a poet like Kenneth Rexroth, following the line, was to protest even after later events. "The only way this war can be stopped is by starving it to death." There had been many who, during these moments, were ready to follow such a path of rigid non-intervention, despite their criticism of similar policies at the time of the Spanish War. Too many broken treaties, too much appeasement now stood in the way. "A plague o' both your houses!" was reborn from the grave of Shakespeare to the stage of the modern world.

Then suddenly, for many, the top blew off! On August 23, 1939, non-

aggression and trade pacts were concluded between Germany and the Soviet Union. Variously the former was to be known as the Nazi-Soviet Pact,
the Russo-German Pact, or the Molotov-Ribbentrop Pact. The last two
titles only added diplomatic dignity to the description of a startling alliance
for which there was no preparation in the minds or sensibilities of American
writers. By it, Russia, although not actively entering the war on the side of
the Nazis, gave them the green light for their entry into Poland. The food
to be shipped proffered sustenance, not starvation. German Fascism, which
had been painted as Hell, with Hitler as Satan, now was said by the facts of
the Pact to be less culpable than the stand of those who were to be known
as the Allies. For American writers remembered what had been said ideologically at the time of the Spanish War, when only active participation
against evil counted, and when non-intervention of this kind was said to be
in reality sponsorship of Germany and Italy. Whatever weaknesses of policy
or even of motives could be laid at the door of the Allies, the truth about
Fascism far more than counterbalanced them. Without actively opposing
Hitlerism it was obvious that there would be no opportunity to accomplish
good. Russia was no longer in active opposition.

What the Nazi-Soviet Pact represented, diplomatically speaking, was
Realpolitik; but what it represented ideologically was the denial of the
primacy of morality in politics, which as a goal represented a significant aspect of American aspiration. To the sophisticated historian educated in the
diplomatic history of Russia and western Europe, such an agreement as had
now been completed was simply a continuation of the traditional manipulation of balance of power. The Czars had negotiated variously on such a
basis; the French and Germans and British had all done it. Most recently
in 1926, Germany and the U.S.S.R. had concluded a Treaty of Berlin, which
had established neutrality in the event of an unprovoked attack on either.
The Franco-Russian defensive agreement of 1935 had not been dissimilar.
The exclusion of Russia from the conversations at Munich had left her outside the group of western European powers, and, from the standpoint of
traditional European diplomacy, pushed her toward the alternatives of
either the throat or the arms of Germany. But such *Realpolitik*, though explainable on practical grounds of national expediency, has nothing to do
with the defense of idealism or the supremacy of ethics. It had been on
precisely these issues that American writers had listened to Russia. The
absence of morality in politics was what they had tried to oppose. The value
they placed on morality was a value they still clung to.

There were other values whose violation on the part of the Soviet Union
they now saw more clearly. Past policies by Russia seemed more than possibly to have been framed in terms of expediency rather than courageous belief. Not unity so much as a shattering disunity had been sponsored, not
order but disorder. The Nazi-Soviet Pact was to a very real degree a climax
of smaller but cumulative crises. In meeting them, even before the Pact,

more and more writers had slipped away from a belief in the "Bolshevik" alternative, which had once seemed so rosy. The Spanish War itself had demonstrated to many who participated in it, or knew it through less than a mist, that Russia had been as interested in fomenting dissension in Barcelona as in working for a speedy victory and peace. She herself had used Spain as a testing ground. Most significant of all these earlier repudiations of an ostensible idealism had been the long series of trials within Russia against internal dissidents. From 1927 on, when Trotsky and others were expelled from the Party and banished to the provinces, there was an increasing certainty that Russia herself would not permit the same encouragement of criticism she advocated abroad. Freedom of opinion, and the right of every man to search for and expose truth, could not be said to obtain under such circumstances. Education, in the American sense, was impossible unless man actually had the liberty for investigation which was promised him. In 1935, Zinoviev, Kamenev, and others were convicted and sentenced to prison; in 1936 some sixteen "self-reliants" were executed. In 1937 there were more trials, and in 1938 still others. The material achievements of which Russia boasted meant, if they existed, little more than Philistine achievements if idealism did not accompany them. Artists and writers began disconsolately watching the penned-in lot of their Soviet colleagues, with the feeling that Russia did not really respect intellectuals but found them only temporarily useful as pawns. Soviet Russia represented an orthodoxy more terrifying and oppressive than anything which American writers had termed as "Puritanism" or "Philistinism." What all these uneasinesses had begun, the Nazi-Soviet Pact brought to a climax. It was not a single crisis that had to be met, but a peak that was more than a monadnock.

The crisis that the Nazi-Soviet Pact represented for the American writer was spiritual, intellectual, and moral. He had been led by his training in the importance of truth; he was now met with a technique of deception. He believed in the primacy of the spirit, and was faced with the tactics of expediency. He had been instilled with a hatred of immorality, and was now asked to tolerate it. The very values that he had relied on, and been pledged to, were being betrayed. He had been tricked, led astray, and manipulated; and by these attitudes of distrust even his dignity as an individual had been shattered. Much more, however, than his self-respect and pride were involved, though these matters obviously came into play. The American writer had been trained too long in an American way. He had been educated in terms of a traditional role and responsibility of the writer. One of the responsibilities was the necessity of admitting errors of assessment when the truths of education pointed them out as false. It was not the least of the triumphs of the values impelling them that so many writers had the humility to admit the error of their assessment.

Not every writer did so immediately. Some were still learning and, even after the Pact, still clung to that which the United Front had promised. A public letter, in which the achievements and claims of Russia were still held forth, was published in *The Nation* in 1939, with some four hundred signatures of writers and intellectuals. The ten points of its argument were:

1. The Soviet Union continues as always to be a bulwark against war and aggression, and works unceasingly for a peaceful international order.

2. It has eliminated racial and national prejudices within its borders, freed the minority peoples enslaved under the czars, stimulated the culture and economic welfare of these peoples, and made the expression of anti-Semitism or any racial animosity a criminal offense.

3. It has socialized the means of production and distribution through the public ownership of industry and the collectivization of agriculture.

4. It has established nation-wide socialistic planning, resulting in increasingly higher living standards and the abolishment of unemployment.

5. It has built the trade unions, in which almost 24,000,000 workers are organized, into the very fabric of its society.

6. The Soviet Union has emancipated woman and the family, and has developed an advanced system of child care.

7. From the viewpoint of cultural freedom, the difference between the Soviet Union and the fascist countries is most striking. The Soviet Union has effected one of the most far-reaching cultural and educational advances in all history and among a population which at the start was almost three-fourths illiterate. Those writers and thinkers whose books have been burned by the Nazis are published in the Soviet Union. The best literature from Homer to Thomas Mann, the best thought from Aristotle to Lenin, are available to the masses of the Soviet people. . . .

8. It has replaced the myths and superstitions of old Russia with the truths and techniques of experimental science, extending scientific procedures to every field, from economics to public health.

9. The Soviet Union considers political dictatorship a transitional form and has shown a steadily expanding democracy in every sphere. Its epoch-making new constitution guarantees Soviet citizens universal suffrage, civil liberties, the right to employment, to leisure, to free education, to free medical care, to material security in sickness and old age, to equality of the sexes in all fields of activity, and to equality of all races and nationalities.

10. In relation to Russia's past, the country has been advancing rapidly along the road of material and cultural progress in a way that the American people can understand and appreciate.

This was a picture of the Soviet Union filled with appeals to the traditional American values, and by the nature of its appeal showed how strongly the values persisted as a judicial force. The assertions of the ten points did not coincide with whatever points would have clarified Fascism. Only the facts of the Soviet Union and its actions no longer seemed to fit the assertions either. Certainly they did not when Russia marched into Poland and the Baltic States, and invaded Finland. It was necessary to repeat once more the value-process of Hemingway's hero, who found abstract terms to be obscene when they did not jibe with what was actual and concrete. The error of American writers in the 1930's had not been so much that their method or values were fallacious as that putting them into effect had been only partial. Examining the abstract terms that had clouded the realities on one side, they had not pursued their method sufficiently to examine them on the other. They had for the moment drifted into a position where they were themselves properly suspect in thoroughness. But the vitality that had originally prompted them was maintained. They had demonstrated the possibility of error, but in their shift of position they showed the value of values. It was a better preservation of values to have used them than simply to have stood pat.

Nothing has restored Soviet Russia to the dream she once represented. Of his book, *I Like America*, published in 1938 when he was still a Party member, Granville Hicks could say after he had left the Party because of the Pact: "[It] contains only two or three pages, those dealing with the Soviet Union and the Party itself, that I could wish expunged." In 1950, William Rose Benét looked back on history, in a letter written little more than a week before his death. He himself had gone through many of the experiences which have been described in general terms. Now he could only say sadly:

> The situation abroad from what I can make out is pretty grim, though not to (apparently) the Daily Worker. What appalls me is that so many evil things are being done in the name of all we used to hold high-minded, for all of us at some time along the way have been taken by the dream of socialism. As poets when we were young we often inveighed against capitalism as a prison camp, and I was at first indignant at Hilaire Belloc's title for his book "The Slave State." Unfortunately he was right as rain.

What was importantly true for literary figures like Benét, and like Hicks, was not that any of their values had been proved wrong, but only the disheartening correlation of facts to them. To the values, they and others like them had stuck. It was not that being educated to truth, as Adams had put it, was incorrect, but only that their education had been incomplete. What was to be learned was — is — the true capacity to bear the burden of truth. If those writers were now old, there were others who were young and could learn from them and from history. But the endurance for both is inseparable from the iron help of the values themselves as a reliance. There is still the need for the values, and the values were not lost.

PART IV

THE AGE OF PERPETUAL CRISIS: WORLD WAR II AND ITS AFTERMATH

21

RACE AND POLITICS IN WARTIME

The events described by Eugene V. Rostow in the following article can be understood at least partly in the context of the concept of "Anglo-conformity" discussed by Milton Gordon (see above, pp. 70–89). Certainly, it is no coincidence that the groups who historically have been the most marginal in American society have been those racial and religious minorities (Negroes, Orientals, Jews, Catholics) who would not or could not fit completely the image of what an American was, an image that derived from the past and was perpetuated by the schools, mass media, popular literature, and the like. In 1910 the *San Francisco Chronicle* made it clear that so far as it was concerned the American dream was not for Asians:

> Had the Japanese laborer throttled his ambition to progress along the lines of American citizenship and industrial development, he probably would have attracted small attention of the public mind. Japanese ambition is to progress beyond mere servility to the plane of the better class of American workingmen and to own a home with him. The moment that this position is exercised, the Japanese ceases to be an ideal laborer.

By 1941 the *Chronicle* had come a long way and was one of the very few west coast newspapers that opposed Japanese evacuation. But its former point of view still characterized the bulk of California's citizens, or, at least, of their public officials. Being born in the United States did not make Americans out of Japanese, Mayor Bowron of Los Angeles maintained, for "there is a vast difference between the background of the European alien and the background of the Jap; the one is a Christian, the other a heathen." "When we are dealing with the Caucasian race," California Attorney General Earl Warren argued, "we have methods that will test the loyalty of them . . . but not of the Japanese."

This spirit was instrumental in bringing about the forced relocation of the *Issei* (those first-generation Japanese immigrants who were excluded from citizenship by the terms of the Naturalization Act of 1790, which has since been amended so that it no longer excludes any ethnic or racial group from naturalization), their American-born children, the *Nisei* (who were American citizens by virtue of their birth), and the *Kibei* (who, like the *Nisei*, were born in this country and were citizens but who had received a substantial part of their education in Japan). In spite of the emphasis upon military necessity, the racial basis of evacuation was understood from the very beginning by many Americans, especially those who themselves felt vulnerable. The NAACP's journal, *The Crisis*, warned in September, 1942, that what was happening to Japanese Americans "is of direct concern to the American Negro. . . . Americans of German or Italian descent are not being discriminated against. Wendell Willkie and Fiorello La-Guardia are not being stuck into filthy and noisome shacks in vile concentration camps because they are of German and Italian ancestry; they are white."

Though the proponents of Japanese American evacuation and internment got their way, their expectation that this would eliminate the Japanese Americans as a factor in the nation's society and economy remained unfulfilled. Ironically, as Harry Kitano has demonstrated in his *Japanese Americans** (1969), evacuation and internment actually accelerated the process of Japanese American acculturation. Evacuation ruined many Japanese families economically and helped reduce much of the power and authority of the father. The fact that in the relocation camps wives and children could work and earn as much as the father further reduced his power. The camps' policy of using only American citizens in positions of camp authority helped to shift the locus of power from the Issei to the Nisei. The regimen of the camps made it difficult and often impossible to perpetuate the old traditions and rituals that had characterized the Japanese family. Since most of the jobs in the camps were performed by the Japanese Americans themselves, a new range of occupations — policemen, firemen, foremen, supervisors, teachers — was opened and new ambitions were created. This was reflected in the postwar situation. Whereas in 1940 some 25 percent of Americans of Japanese ancestry were laborers and only 3.8 percent were professionals, by 1960 only 5 percent were laborers and 15 percent were professionals. Finally, evacuation led to greater diffusion throughout the nation which of course was still another acculturating factor. Some 35,000 of those interned in the camps refused to return to the west coast and resettled in the midwest and the east.

Wartime evacuation, then, had unexpected results. But if Japanese Americans have made striking progress since the war, their experience during it left a heritage of frustration and bitterness which has only recently begun to come out into the open, and, as Rostow's article emphasizes, the evacuation established a precedent that endangers the rights of every American.

Since Rostow's article appeared a number of valuable accounts of the Japanese-American experience have been published: Morton Grodzins, *Americans Betrayed* (1949); Dorothy S. Thomas and Richard S. Nishimoto, *The Spoilage** (1946); Dorothy S. Thomas et al., *The Salvage* (1952); Jacobus tenBroek et al., *Prejudice, War and the Constitution** (1954); Harry Kitano, *Japanese Americans** (1969); Bill Hosokawa, *Nisei* (1969); and Audrie Girdner and Anne Loftis, *The Great Betrayal* (1969).

The Japanese American Cases — A Disaster

EUGENE V. ROSTOW

> He [the King of Great Britain] has affected to render the Military independent of and superior to the Civil Power.
>> THE DECLARATION OF INDEPENDENCE

>> War is too serious a business to be left to generals.
>> CLEMENCEAU

I

Our war-time treatment of Japanese aliens and citizens of Japanese descent on the West Coast has been hasty, unnecessary and mistaken. The course of action which we undertook was in no way required or justified by the circumstances of the war. It was calculated to produce both individual injustice and deep-seated social maladjustments of a cumulative and sinister kind.

All in all, the internment of the West Coast Japanese is the worst blow our liberties have sustained in many years. Over one hundred thousand men, women and children have been imprisoned, some seventy thousand of them citizens of the United States, without indictment or the proffer of charges, pending inquiry into their "loyalty." They were taken into custody as a military measure on the ground that espionage and sabotage were especially to be feared from persons of Japanese blood. They were removed from the West Coast area because the military thought it would take too long to conduct individual loyalty investigations on the ground. They were arrested in an area where the courts were open, and freely functioning. They were held under prison conditions in uncomfortable camps, far from their homes, and for lengthy periods — several years in many cases. If found "disloyal" in administrative proceedings they were confined indefinitely, although no statute makes "disloyalty" a crime; it would be difficult indeed for a statute to do so under a Constitution which has been interpreted to minimize imprisonment for political opinions, both by defining the crime of treason in extremely rigid and explicit terms, and by limiting convictions for sedition and like offenses. In the course of relocation citizens have suffered severe property losses, despite some custodial assistance by the Government. Perhaps 70,000 persons are still in camps, "loyal" and "disloyal" citizens and

Reprinted, with footnotes omitted, by permission of the Yale Law Journal Company, Fred B. Rothman & Company, and the author from *The Yale Law Journal*, 54, pp. 489–533.

aliens alike, more than three years after the programs were instituted. Although the process of relocation has been recently accelerated, many will remain in the camps at least until January 2, 1946.

By the time the question reached the Supreme Court, the crisis which was supposed to justify the action had passed. The Court faced two issues: should it automatically accept the judgment of the military as to the need for the relocation program, or should it require a judicial investigation of the question? Was there factual support for the military judgment that the course of the war required the exclusion and confinement of the Japanese American population of the West Coast? Clearly, if such steps were not necessary to the prosecution of the war, they invaded rights protected by the Third Article of the Constitution, and the Fifth and Sixth Amendments.

If the Court had stepped forward in bold heart to vindicate the law and declare the entire program illegal, the episode would have been passed over as a national scandal, but a temporary one altogether capable of reparation. But the Court, after timid and evasive delays, has now upheld the main features of the program. That step converts a piece of war-time folly into political doctrine, and a permanent part of the law. Moreover, it affects a peculiarly important and sensitive part of the law. The relationship of civil to military authority is not often litigated. It is nonetheless one of the two or three most essential elements in the legal structure of a democratic society. The Court's few declarations on the subject govern the handling of vast affairs. They determine the essential organization of the military establishment, state and federal, in time of emergency or of war, as well as of peace. What the Supreme Court has done in these cases, and especially in *Korematsu v. United States*, is to increase the strength of the military in relation to civil government. It has upheld an act of military power without a factual record in which the justification for the act was analyzed. Thus it has created doubt as to the standards of responsibility to which the military power will be held. For the first time in American legal history, the Court has seriously weakened the protection of our basic civil right, the writ of habeas corpus. It has established a precedent which may well be used to encourage attacks on the civil rights of citizens and aliens, and may make it possible for some of those attacks to succeed. It will give aid to reactionary political programs which use social division and racial prejudice as tools for conquering power. As Mr. Justice Jackson points out, the principle of these cases "lies about like a loaded weapon ready for the hand of any authority that can bring forward a plausible claim of an urgent need."

The opinions of the Supreme Court in the Japanese American cases do not belong in the same political or intellectual universe with Ex parte *Milligan, DeJonge v. Oregon, Hague v. CIO,* or Mr. Justice Brandeis' opinion in the *Whitney* case. They threaten even more than the trial tradition of the common law and the status of individuals in relation to the state. By their acceptance of ethnic differences as a criterion for discrimination, these cases will make it more difficult to resolve one of the central problems in American life — the problem of minorities. They are a breach, potentially a major breach, in the principle of equality. Unless repudiated, they may encourage devastating and unforeseen social and political conflicts.

II

What General DeWitt did in the name of military precaution within his Western Defense Command was quite different from the security measures taken in Hawaii or on the East Coast — although both places were more active theatres of war in 1942 than the states of Washington, Oregon, California, and Arizona, which comprised the Western Defense Command.

On the East Coast, and in the United States generally, enemy aliens were controlled without mass arrests or evacuations, despite a considerable public agitation in favor of violent action. A registration of aliens had been accomplished under the Alien Registration Act of 1940, and the police authorities had compiled information about fascist sympathizers among the alien population, as well as about those who were citizens. "On the night of December 7, 1941," the Attorney General has reported, "the most dangerous of the persons in this group were taken into custody; in the following weeks a number of others were apprehended. Each arrest was made on the basis of information concerning the specific alien taken into custody. We have used no dragnet techniques and have conducted no indiscriminate, large-scale raids." Immediately after Pearl Harbor restrictions were imposed upon the conduct of all enemy aliens over 14 years of age. They were forbidden the Canal Zone and certain restricted military areas thereafter to be specified. They were not to leave the country, travel in a plane, change their place of abode, or travel about outside their own communities, without special permission. They were forbidden to own or use firearms, cameras, short-wave radio sets, codes, ciphers or invisible ink. The District Attorneys were given broad discretion to allow aliens of enemy nationality to carry on their usual occupations, under scrutiny, but without other restriction. A new registration of aliens of enemy nationality was conducted. The basic object of the control plan was to keep security officers informed, but otherwise to allow the aliens almost their normal share in the work and life of the community.

Aliens under suspicion, and those who violated the regulations, were subject to summary arrest on Presidential warrant. "The law," the Attorney General said, "does not require any hearing before the internment of an enemy alien. I believed that nevertheless, we should give each enemy alien who had been taken into custody an opportunity for a hearing on the question whether he should be interned." Those arrested were therefore promptly examined by voluntary Alien Enemy Hearing Boards, consisting of citizens appointed for the task by the Attorney General. These Boards could recommend that individuals be interned, paroled, or released unconditionally. This operation was smoothly conducted, with a minimal interference with the standards of justice in the community. Of the 1,100,000 enemy aliens in the United States, 9,080 had been examined by the end of the fiscal year 1943; 4,119 were then interned, 3,705 paroled, 1,256 released, and 9,341 were still in custody. On June 30, 1944, the number in custody had been reduced to 6,238. The number of those interned was then 2,525, those paroled, 4,840, and those released, 1,926.

In Hawaii a somewhat different procedure was followed, but one less drastic than the evacuation program pursued on the West Coast. Immediately after Pearl Harbor martial law was declared in Hawaii, and the commanding general assumed the role of military governor. Courts were reopened for some purposes shortly after the bombing raid, but the return of civil law to Hawaii has been a slow, controversial process, not yet complete. During the period of three and a half years after Pearl Harbor, military power was installed in Hawaii, constitutionally or not, and the normal controls against arrest on suspicion were not available. The population of Hawaii is 500,000, of whom some 160,000, or 32%, were of Japanese descent. Despite the confusions of the moment in Hawaii, only 700 to 800 Japanese aliens were arrested and sent to the mainland for internment. In addition, fewer than 1,100 persons of Japanese ancestry were transferred to the mainland to relocation centers. These Japanese were arrested on the basis of individual suspicion, resting on previous examination or observed behavior, or they were families of interned aliens, transferred voluntarily. Of those transferred from Hawaii to the mainland, 912 were citizens, the rest aliens. Even under a regime of martial law, men were arrested as individuals, and safety was assured without mass arrests.

These procedures compare favorably in their essential character with the precautions taken in Britain and France. The British procedure was the model for our general practice in dealing with enemy aliens. The British Government began in 1939 by interning only those enemy aliens who were on a "security list." Others were subjected to minor police restrictions, pending their individual examination by especially established tribunals. One hundred and twelve such tribunals were set up, under citizens with legal experience, to examine all enemy aliens in Britain. There was an appeals advisory committee to advise the Home Secretary in disputed cases. Aliens were divided into three classes: those judged dangerous were interned; if judged doubtful in their loyalty, they were subjected to certain continuing restrictions, especially as to travel, and the ownership of guns, cameras and radios; those deemed entirely loyal to the Allied cause were freed without further restraint. At first 2,000 enemy aliens on a black list were interned. But the entire group was then examined individually, and by March 1940 only 569 of approximately 75,000 aliens were ordered interned. During the panic period of 1940, a new screening was undertaken, to intern all those of doubtful loyalty, and other measures of mass internment were undertaken. Beginning as early as July 1940, however, the policy of wholesale internment was modified, and releases were granted, either generally, or on certain conditions — the proved politics of the internee, his joining the Auxiliary Pioneer Corps, his emigration, and so on. The maximum number interned, during July 1940, was about 27,000 of a total enemy alien population (German, Austrian and Italian) of about 93,000. By September 1941, the number of internees dropped to about 8,500. At the same time, the British undertook to arrest certain British subjects on suspicion alone, under the Emergency Powers Act of 1939. A constitutional storm was aroused by this procedure, which was finally resolved in favor of the government. The general pattern of British security practice was thus to treat enemy aliens on an individual basis, and to arrest British subjects of fascist tendencies in a limited number, and then only on strong personal suspicion.

In France all men enemy aliens between the ages of 17 and 65 were interned in 1939. After a good deal of confusion and complaint, and a vigorous parliamentary protest, many were screened out, either upon joining the Foreign Legion, or, for older men, upon examination, and sponsorship by French citizens. Further parliamentary criticism in December 1939 led to relief for the internees, but the crisis of May and June, 1940, produced mass internment. In France, though less effectively than in Britain, the principle of internment on an individual basis was the objective of policy, if not always its norm.

But on the West Coast the security program was something else again. A policy emerged piecemeal, apparently without sponsors or forethought. By May 1, 1942, it had become a policy of evacuating all persons of Japanese ancestry from the West Coast, and confining them indefinitely in camps located away from the coastal area. After some hesitation, General DeWitt proposed evacuation. Quite clearly, a conflict took place between the military authorities on the West Coast and some of the representatives of the Department of Justice over the justification for such action. But no one in the Government would take the responsibility for overruling General DeWitt and the War Department which backed him up.

The dominant factor in the development of this policy was not a military estimate of a military problem, but familiar West Coast attitudes of race prejudice. The program of excluding all persons of Japanese ancestry from the coastal area was conceived and put through by the organized minority whose business it has been for forty-five years to increase and exploit racial tensions on the West Coast. The Native Sons and Daughters of the Golden West, and their sympathizers, were lucky in their general, for General DeWitt amply proved himself to be one of them in opinion and values. As events happened, he became the chief policy maker in the situation, and he has caused more damage even than General Burnside in 1863, whose blunderings with Vallandigham, the Ohio Copperhead, were the previous high in American military officiousness.

In the period immediately after Pearl Harbor there was no special security program on the West Coast for persons of Japanese extraction, and no general conviction that a special program was needed. Known enemy sympathizers among the Japanese, like white traitors and enemy agents, were arrested. There was no sabotage on the part of persons of Japanese ancestry, either in Hawaii or on the West Coast. There was no reason to suppose that the 112,000 persons of Japanese descent on the West Coast, 1.2% of the population, constituted a greater menace to safety than such persons in Hawaii, 32% of the Territory's population. Their access to military installations was not substantially different in the two areas; their status in society was quite similar; their proved record of loyalty in the war has been the same. Although many white persons were arrested, and convicted, as Japanese agents, no resident Japanese American has so far been convicted of sabotage or espionage as an agent of Japan.

After a month's silence, the professional anti-Oriental agitators of the West Coast began a comprehensive campaign. There had been no sabotage in the area, although there was evidence of radio signaling from unknown persons within the area to enemy ships at sea. The West Coast Congressional delegation, led by Senator Hiram Johnson, memorialized the Administration in favor of excluding all persons of Japanese lineage from the coastal area. Anti-Oriental spokesmen appeared as witnesses before the Tolan Committee, and later the Dies Committee, and they explained the situation as they conceived of it to General DeWitt. Some of the coast newspapers, and particularly those owned by William Randolph Hearst, took up the cry. Politicians, fearful of an unknown public opinion, spoke out for white supremacy. Tension was intensified, and doubters, worried about the risks of another Pearl Harbor, remained silent, preferring too much caution to too little. An opinion crystallized in favor of evacuating the Japanese. Such action was at least action, promising greater relief from tension than the slow, patient work of military preparation for the defense and counter-attack. German and Italian aliens were too numerous to be arrested or severely confined, and they were closely connected with powerful blocs of voters. There were too many Japanese Americans in Hawaii to be moved. The 100,000 persons of Japanese descent on the West Coast thus became the chief available target for the release of frustration and aggression.

Despite the nature of the emergency, the military refused to act without fuller legal authority. Executive Order No. 9066 was issued on February 19, 1942, authorizing the Secretary of War, and military commanders he might designate, to prescribe "military areas" in their discretion, and either to exclude any or all persons from such areas, or to establish the conditions on which any or all such persons might enter, remain in or leave such areas. Lieutenant General J. L. DeWitt, head of the Western Defense Command, was ordered on February 20, 1942, to carry out the policy of the Executive Order. During the first two weeks of March; more than three months after Pearl Harbor, General DeWitt issued orders in which he announced that he would subsequently exclude "such persons or classes of persons as the situation may require" from the area.

But the Army's lawyers wanted more authority than the Executive Order. With inevitable further delays, a statute was therefore obtained prescribing that

> . . . whoever shall enter, remain in, leave, or commit any act in any military area or military zone prescribed, under the authority of an Executive order of the President, by the Secretary of War, or by any military commander designated by the Secretary of War, contrary to the restrictions applicable to any such area or zone or contrary to the order of the Secretary of War or any such military commander, shall, if it appears that he knew or should have known of the existence and extent of the restrictions or order and that his act was in violation thereof, be guilty of a misdemeanor and upon conviction shall be liable to a fine of not to exceed $5,000 or to imprisonment for not more than one year, or both, for each offense.

The statute thus authorized the exclusion of people from the military areas. It said nothing about their subsequent confinement in camps. This omission was seized upon in Ex parte *Endo* as a crucial fact limiting the power of the Government to hold persons shifted under military orders to relocation centers.

Starting on March 27, 1942, almost four months after Pearl Harbor, the first actual restrictions were imposed. A policy of encouraging the Japanese to move away on a voluntary and individual basis had shown signs of producing confusion and irritation. It was decided to have a uniform and comprehensive program of governmentally controlled migration. At first Japanese aliens and citizens of Japanese ancestry were subjected to the same controls applied to German and Italian aliens. Citizens of German and Italian descent were left free. Early in April, the first of a series of civilian exclusion orders were issued. They applied only to Japanese aliens and citizens of Japanese descent, who were to be excluded altogether from West Coast areas, ordered to report to control stations, and then confined in camps conducted by the newly organized War Relocation Authority, which became an agency of the Department of Interior on February 16, 1944.

The rules and policies of these camps were perhaps the most striking part of the entire program. Despite the humanitarian character of the WRA, which was from the beginning intrusted to high-minded and well-meaning men, a policy for discharging Japanese was developed which encouraged lawlessness and refused support to the simplest constitutional rights of citizens and aliens. It was originally thought that the camps would give temporary haven to some Japanese refugees from the West Coast who could not easily arrange new homes, jobs and lives for themselves. Then it was decided to make a stay in the camps compulsory, so as to facilitate the loyalty examinations which were supposed to have been too difficult and prolonged to conduct on the West Coast. Further, it was wisely decided that a loyalty "screening" would facilitate relocation and combat anti-Japanese agitation. The fact that all released evacuees had been approved, so far as loyalty was concerned, gave practical support to their position in new communities. Japanese aliens and citizens of Japanese origin found by this administrative process to be disloyal were confined indefinitely in a special camp. Persons of Japanese descent found to be loyal were to be released from the camps upon the satisfaction of certain conditions. As applied to citizens especially, those conditions upon the right to live and travel in the United States are so extraordinary as to require full statement:

> In the case of each application for indefinite leave, the Director, upon receipt of such file from the Project Director, will secure from the Federal Bureau of Investigation such information as may be obtainable, and will take such steps as may be necessary to satisfy himself concerning the applicant's means of support, his willingness to make the reports required of him under the provisions of this part, the conditions and factors affecting the applicant's opportunity for employment and residence at the proposed destination, the probable effect of the issuance of the leave upon the war program and upon the public peace and security, and such other conditions and factors as may be relevant. The Director will thereupon send instructions to the Project Director to issue or deny such leave in each case, and will inform the Regional Director of the instructions so issued. The Project Director shall issue indefinite leaves pursuant to such instructions.
>
> (f) A leave shall issue to an applicant in accordance with his application in each case, subject to the provisions of this Part and under the procedures herein provided, as a matter of right, where the applicant has made arrangements for employment or other means of support, where he agrees to make the reports required of him under the provisions of this Part and to comply with all other applicable provisions hereof, and where there is no reasonable cause to believe that applicant cannot successfully maintain employment and residence at the proposed destination, and no reasonable ground to believe that the issuance of a leave in the particular case will interfere with the war program or otherwise endanger the public peace and security.
>
> (g) The Director, the Regional Director, and the Project Director may at each such special conditions to the leave to be issued in a particular case as may be necessary in the public interest.

In other words, loyal citizens were required to have official approval of their homes, jobs and friends before they were allowed to move. They had to report subsequent changes of address, and remain under scrutiny almost amounting to parole. Officials were required to ascertain that community sentiment was not unfavorable to the presence of such citizens before they were permitted to enter the community. The briefs in behalf of the United States before the Supreme Court in the *Korematsu* and *Endo* cases explain the kind of evidence regarded as sufficient to uphold a finding of unfavorable community sentiment, and a suspension of the relocation process: the introduction of anti-Japanese bills in the local legislature, the occurrence of riots or other lawless episodes, and similar expressions of minority opinion.

This policy played a part in encouraging the growth and violent expression of race antagonisms in American society. The forces of the national government were not devoted to protecting and vindicating what *Edwards v. California* had recently upheld as the privilege of a United States citizen, or indeed of any resident, to move freely from state to state, without interference. Local lynch spirit was not controlled and punished by the agencies of law enforcement. On the contrary, it was encouraged to manifest itself in words and unpunished deeds. The threat of lawlessness was allowed to frustrate the legal rights of colored minorities unpopular with small and articulate minorities of white citizens. In March 1943, a small number of Japanese returned to their homes in Arizona, which had been removed from the military zone, without substantial incident. In the spring of 1945, however, the Ku Klux Klan spirit in California had been manifested in at least twenty major episodes of arson or intimidation. The War Relocation Authority has been consistently and effectively on the side of facilitating resettlement and combatting race prejudice. Yet the terms of its leave regulations constituted an extraordinary invasion of citizens' rights, as the Supreme Court later held. They were a practical compromise, under the circumstances, but a compromise nonetheless, with social forces which might better have been opposed head-on.

Studies are beginning to appear about conditions within the camps. They make it plain that the camps were in fact concentration camps, where the humiliation of evacuation was compounded by a regime which ignored citizens' rights, and the amenities which might have made the relocation process more palatable.

Thus there developed a system for the indefinite confinement and detention of Japanese aliens and citizens of Japanese descent, without charges or trial, without term, and without visible promise of relief. By May 1942, it was compulsory and self-contained. On pain of punishment under the Act of March 21, 1942, all had to leave the West Coast through Assembly Centers and the Relocation Centers. Counsel in the *Hirabayashi* case called it slavery; Mr. Justice Jackson said it was attainder of blood. The Japanese radio discussed it at length, finding in the system ample propaganda material for its thesis that American society was incapable of dealing justly with colored peoples.

III

Attempts were made at once to test the legality of the program. The district courts and the circuit courts of appeals had a good deal of difficulty with the issues. Although troubled, they generally upheld both the exclusion of Japanese aliens and citizens from the West Coast, and at least their temporary confinement in WRA camps.

The question of how and on what grounds the Supreme Court should dispose of the cases was one of broad political policy. Would a repudiation of the Congress, the President and the military in one aspect of their conduct of the war affect the people's will to fight? Would it create a campaign issue for 1944? Would it affect the power, status and prestige of the Supreme Court as a political institution? How would a decision upholding the Government influence civil liberties and the condition of minorities? A bench of sedentary civilians was reluctant to overrule the military decision of those charged with carrying on the war. Conflicting loyalties, ambitions and conceptions of the Court's duty undoubtedly had their part in the positions the justices took.

The issue first came before the Supreme Court in May 1943, and the first cases, *Hirabayashi v. United States* and *Yasui v. United States*, were decided on June 21, 1943. No Japanese submarines had been detected off the West Coast for many months. Midway was won; Libya, Tripolitania and Tunisia had been conquered. Guadalcanal and a good deal of New Guinea were in Allied hands. The posture of the war had changed profoundly in a year. We had suffered no defeats since the fall of Tobruk in July 1942, and we had won a long series of preliminary victories. Our forces were poised for the offensive. The phase of aggressive deployment was over.

The problem presented to the Supreme Court was thus completely different from that which confronted worried legislators and officials in the bleak winter and spring of 1942. Invalidation of the exclusion and confinement programs would do no possible harm to the prosecution of the war. The Court could afford to view the issues in full perspective. The war powers of the legislative and executive must of course be amply protected. But the special concerns of the Supreme Court for the development of constitutional law as a whole could be given proper weight, free of the pressure of the Pearl Harbor emergency.

It was only half the truth to say that the cases had to be decided as if the date of decision were February 1942. It was not in fact the date of decision, and could not be made so. The issue was not only whether the military should have excluded the Japanese in the spring of 1942, but whether the Court should now validate what had been done. As many episodes in the history of the United States eloquently attest, these are different issues. The problem of the Court in the *Hirabayashi* case was not that of General De-Witt in 1942, but an infinitely more complex one. Whether it faced the issues or tried to ignore them, whether it decided the cases frankly or obliquely, by decision or evasion, the Court could not escape the fact that it was the Supreme Court, arbiter of a vast system of rules, habits, customs and relationships. No matter how inarticulate, its decision could not be confined in its effect to the United States Reports. It would necessarily alter the balance of forces determining the condition of every social interest within range of the problems of the cases — the power of the military and the police; our developing law of emergencies, which is beginning to resemble the French and German law of the state of siege; the status of minorities and of groups which live by attacking minorities; the future decision of cases in police stations and lower courts, involving the writ of habeas corpus, the equal rights of citizens, the protection of aliens, the segregation of racial groups, and like questions.

In a bewildering and unimpressive series of opinions, relieved only by the dissents of Mr. Justice Roberts and of Mr. Justice Murphy in *Korematsu v. United States*, the Court chose to assume that the main issue of the cases — the scope and method of judicial review of military decisions — did not exist. In the political process of American life, these decisions were a negative and reactionary act. The Court avoided the risks of overruling the Government on an issue of war policy. But it weakened society's control over military authority — one of the polarizing forces on which the organization of our society depends. And it solemnly accepted and gave the prestige of its support to dangerous racial myths about a minority group, in arguments which can be applied easily to any other minority in our society.

The cases are worth separate statement, for they are by no means alike. In *Hirabayashi v. United States* the Court considered a conviction based on the Act of March 21, 1942, for violating two orders issued by General DeWitt under authority of the Executive Order of February 19, 1942. Gordon Hirabayashi, a citizen of the United States and a senior in the University of Washington, was sentenced to three months in prison on each of two counts, the sentences running concurrently. The first count was that Hirabayashi failed to report to a control station on May 11 or May 12, 1942, for exclusion from the duly designated military area including Seattle, his home. The first count thus raised the legality of the compulsory transportation of an American citizen from one of the military areas to a WRA camp, and of his indefinite incarceration there. The second count was that on May 9, 1942, he had violated a curfew order, by failing to remain at home after 8 P.M., within a designated military area, in contravention of a regulation promulgated by the military authority. The Court considered the violation of the second count first, upheld the curfew order and the sentence imposed for violating it. Since the two sentences were concurrent, it said, there was no need to consider the conviction on the first count.

In fact, of course, the Court was entirely free to consider the first count if it wanted to. It would have been normal practice to do so. Its refusal to pass on the more serious controversy cannot be put down to wise and for-bearing judicial statesmanship. This was not the occasion for prudent withdrawal on the part of the Supreme Court, but for affirmative leadership in causes peculiarly within its sphere of primary responsibility. The social problems created by the exclusion and confinement of the Japanese Ameri-cans of the West Coast states increased in seriousness with every day of their continued exclusion. The rabble-rousers of California now were de-manding the permanent exclusion of all persons of Japanese ancestry from the West Coast area. They were living at peace, altogether free of the threat of Japanese invasion. Yet they were still successful in their efforts to keep the Japanese out. The business and professional capital of the Japanese was being profitably used by others. Intelligent and resourceful competitors had been removed from many markets. At the expense of the Japanese, vested interests were being created, entrenched, and endowed with political power. All these interests would resist the return of the Japanese by law if possible, if not, by terror. The refusal of the Supreme Court to face the problem was itself a positive decision on the merits. It gave strength to the anti-Oriental forces on the West Coast, and made a difficult social situation more and more tense. A full assertion of the ordinary rights of citizenship would have shamed and weakened the lynch spirit. It would have fortified the party of law and order. Instead, that party was confused and weakened by the vacillation of the Court.

The reasoning of the Court itself contributed to the intensification of so-cial pressure.

In the *Hirabayashi* case the Court held that its problem was the scope of the war power of the national government. The extent of Presidential dis-cretion was not presented as a separate issue, because the statute of March 21, 1942, and appropriation acts under it, were passed with full knowledge of the action taken and proposed by General DeWitt, and thus fully au-thorized the curfew. Both Congress and the Executive were held to have approved the curfew as a war measure, required in their judgment because espionage and sabotage were especially to be feared from persons of Japa-nese origin or descent on the West Coast during the spring of 1942.

The premise from which the Court's argument proceeded was the incon-testable proposition that the war power is the power to wage war successfully. The States must have every facility and the widest latitude in defending itself against destruction. The issue for the Court, the Chief Justice said, was whether at the time "there was any substantial basis for the conclusion" that the curfew as applied to a citizen of Japanese ancestry was "a protective mea-sure necessary to meet the threat of sabotage and espionage which would sub-stantially affect the war effort and which might reasonably be expected to aid a threatened enemy invasion." The formulation of the test followed the lines of the Court's familiar doctrine in passing on the action of administrative bodies: was there "reasonable ground" for those charged with the responsibility of national defense to believe that the threat was real, and the remedy useful? The orders of the commander, the Court held, were based on findings of fact which supported action within the contemplation of the statute. The findings were based on an informed appraisal of the relevant facts in the light of the statutory standard, and published as proclamations. The circumstances, the Court said, afforded a sufficiently rational basis for the decision made.

The "facts" which were thus held to "afford a rational basis for decision" were that in time of war "residents having ethnic affiliations with an invading enemy may be a greater source of danger than those of different ancestry," and that in time of war such persons could not readily be isolated and dealt with individually. This is the basic factual hypothesis on which all three cases rest.

The first part of this double-headed proposition of fact is contrary to the experience of American society, in war and peace. Imagine applying an ethnic presumption of disloyalty in the circumstances of the Revolution or the Civil War! In the World War and in the present war, soldiers who had ethnic affiliations with the enemy — German, Austrian, Hungarian, Finnish, Roumanian, Bulgarian, Japanese and Italian — fought uniformly as Americans in our armed forces, without any suggestion of group disloyalty. As a generalization about the consequences of inheritance, as compared with experience, in determining political opinions, the Supreme Court's doctrine of ethnic disloyalty belongs with folk proverbs — "blood is thicker than water" — and the pseudo-genetics of the Nazis. It is flatly contradicted by the evidence of the biological sciences, of cultural anthropology, sociology, and every other branch of systematic social study, both in general, and with specific reference to the position of Japanese groups on the West Coast. The most important driving urge of such minority groups is to conform, not to rebel. This is true even for the American minorities which are partially isolated from the rest of society by the bar of color. The desire to conform is stronger than resentments and counter-reactions to prejudice and discrimination. Insecure and conscious of the environment as a threat, such minorities seek to establish their status by proving themselves to be good Americans. The younger generation rejects the language, customs and attitudes of the older. The exemplary combat records of the Japanese American regiments in Italy and in France is a normal symbol of their quest for security within the environment. It is an expected part of the process of social adjustment, repeated again and again in our experience with minorities within American society. By and large, men and women who grow up in the American cultural community are Americans in outlook, values and basic social attitudes. This is the conclusion of the scientific literature on the subject. It has been the first tenet of American law, the ideal if not always the practice of American life.

To support its contrary opinion, the Supreme Court undertook a review of its own intuitions, without a judicial record before it, and without serious recourse to available scientific studies of the problem. Kiplingesque folklore about East and West is close to the heart of the opinions. The Japanese, the Court said, had been imperfectly assimilated; they constituted an isolated group in the community; their Japanese language schools might be sources of Japanese propaganda. Moreover, the discriminatory way in which the Japanese on the West Coast were treated may have been regarded as contributing to Japanese solidarity, preventing their assimilation, and increasing in many instances their attachments to Japan and its institutions.

There was no testimony or other evidence in the record as to the facts which governed the judgment of the military in entering the orders in question. They were not required to support the action they had taken by producing evidence as to the need for it. Nor were they exposed to cross-examination. By way of judicial research and notice the Court wrote four short paragraphs to explain "some of the many considerations" which in its view might have been considered by the military in making their decision to institute a discriminatory curfew.

The second part of the Court's basic premise of fact was that it was impossible to investigate the question of loyalty individually. As to the validity of this proposition there was neither evidence in the record nor even discussion by the Court to indicate a basis for the conclusion which might appeal to a reasonable man, or even to a choleric and harassed general, faced with the danger of invasion and the specter of his own court martial. The issue was dismissed in a sentence. "We cannot say that the war-making branches of the Government did not have ground for believing that in a critical hour such persons could not readily be isolated and separately dealt with, and constituted a menace to the national defense and safety, which demanded that prompt and adequate measures be taken to guard against it." In view of the history of security measures during the war, it would not have been easy to establish strong grounds for such a belief. There were about 110,000 persons subject to the exclusion orders, 43% of them being over 50 or under 15. At the time of the exclusion orders, they had lived in California without committing sabotage for five months after Pearl Harbor. The number of persons to be examined was not beyond the capacities of individual examination processes, in the light of experience with such security measures, both in the United States and abroad. The fact was that the loyalty examinations finally undertaken in the Relocation Authority camps consisted in large part of filling out a questionnaire, and little more, except in cases of serious doubt as to loyalty. Most of those released from the camps were given their freedom on the basis of little information which was not available on the West Coast in 1942.

Actually, the exclusion program was undertaken not because the Japanese were too numerous to be examined individually, but because they were a small enough group to be punished by confinement. It would have been physically impossible to confine the Japanese and Japanese Americans in Hawaii, and it would have been both physically and politically impossible to undertake comparable measures against the 690,000 Italians or the 314,000 Germans living in the United States. The Japanese were being attacked because for some they provided the only possible outlet and expression for sentiments of group hostility. Others were unable or unwilling to accept the burden of urging the repudiation of a general's judgment which he placed on grounds of military need.

The *Hirabayashi* case states a rule which permits some judicial control over action purporting to be taken under military authority. It proposes that such action be treated in the courts like that of administrative agencies generally, and upheld if supported by "facts" which afford "a rational basis" for the decision. For all practical purposes, it is true, the *Hirabayashi* case ignores the rule; but the Court did go to great lengths to assert the principle of protecting society against unwarranted and dictatorial military action. *Korematsu v. United States* seems sharply to relax even the formal requirement of judicial review over military conduct. Korematsu, an American citizen of Japanese descent, was convicted under the Act of March 21, 1942 for violating an order requiring his exclusion from the coastal area. The Court held the problem of exclusion to be identical with the issue of discriminatory curfew presented in the *Hirabayashi* case. There, it said, the Court had decided that it was not unreasonable for the military to impose a curfew in order to guard against the special dangers of sabotage and espionage anticipated from the Japanese group. The military had found, and the Court refused to reject the finding, that it was impossible to bring about an immediate segregation of the disloyal from the loyal. According to Mr. Justice Black, the exclusion orders merely apply these two findings — that the Japanese are a dangerous lot, and that there was no time to screen them individually. Actually, there was a new "finding" of fact in this case, going far beyond the situation considered in the *Hirabayashi* case. The military had "found" that the curfew provided inadequate protection against the danger of sabotage and espionage. Therefore the exclusion of all Japanese, citizens and aliens alike, was thought to be a reasonable way to protect the Coast against sabotage and espionage. Mr. Justice Black does not pretend to review even the possible foundations of such a judgment. There is no attempt in the *Korematsu* case to show a reasonable connection between the factual situation and the program adopted to deal with it.

The Court refused to regard the validity of the detention features of the relocation policy as raised by the case. Korematsu had not yet been taken to a camp, and the Court would not pass on the issues presented by such imprisonment. Those issues, the Court said, are "momentous questions not contained within the framework of the pleadings or the evidence in this case. It will be time enough to decide the serious constitutional issues which petitioner seeks to raise when an assembly or relocation order is applied or is certain to be applied to him, and we have its terms before us." This is a good deal like saying in an ordinary criminal case that the appeal raises the validity of the trial and verdict, but not the sentence, since the defendant may be out on probation or bail. It is difficult to understand in any event why this consideration did not apply equally to the evidence before the Court on the issue which the Court conceded was raised by the pleadings, i.e., the decision of the General to exclude all Japanese from the Defense Area. On this problem there was literally no trial record or other form of evidence in the case.

There were four other opinions in *Korematsu v. United States*. Mr. Justice Roberts and Mr. Justice Murphy dissented on the merits, in separate opinions. Mr. Justice Roberts said that while he might agree that a temporary or emergency exclusion of the Japanese was a legitimate exercise of military power, this case presented a plan for imprisoning the Japanese in concentration camps, solely because of their ancestry, and "without evidence or inquiry" as to their "loyalty and good disposition towards the United States." Such action, he said, was clearly unconstitutional.

Mr. Justice Murphy's substantial opinion does not join issue with the opinion of the Court on the central problem of how to review military decisions, but it does contend that the military decisions involved in this case were unjustified in fact. The military power, he agreed, must have wide and appropriate discretion in carrying out military duties. But, "like other claims conflicting with the asserted constitutional rights of the individual, the military claim must subject itself to the judicial process of having its reasonableness determined and its conflicts with other interests reconciled. . . ."

> The judicial test of whether the Government, on a plea of military necessity, can validly deprive an individual of any of his constitutional rights is whether the deprivation is reasonably related to a public danger that is so "immediate, imminent, and impending" as not to admit of delay and not to permit the intervention of ordinary constitutional processes to alleviate the danger. . . . Civilian Exclusion Order No. 34, banishing from a prescribed area of the Pacific Coast "all persons of Japanese ancestry, both alien and nonalien," clearly does not meet that test. Being an obvious racial discrimination, the order deprives all those within its scope of the equal protection of the laws as guaranteed by the Fifth Amendment. It further deprives these individuals of their constitutional rights to live and work where they will, to establish a home where they choose and to move about freely. In excommunicating them without benefit of hearings, this order also deprives them of all their constitutional rights to procedural due process. Yet no reasonable relation to an "immediate, imminent, and

impending" public danger is evident to support this racial restriction which is one of the most sweeping and complete deprivations of constitutional rights in the history of this nation in the absence of martial law.

The action taken does not meet such a test, Justice Murphy argues, because there was no reasonable ground for supposing that all persons of Japanese blood have a tendency to commit sabotage or espionage, nor was there any ground for supposing that their loyalty could not have been tested individually where they lived. A review of statements made by General DeWitt before Congressional committees and in his Final Report to the Secretary of War clearly reveals that the basis of his action was "an accumulation of much of the misinformation, half-truths and insinuations that for years have been directed against Japanese Americans by people with racial and economic prejudices." These are compared with the independent studies of experts, and shown to be nonsensical. The supposed basis for the exercise of military discretion disappears, and the case for the order falls.

Mr. Justice Jackson wrote a fascinating and fantastic essay in nihilism. Nothing in the record of the case, he said very properly, permits the Court to judge the military reasonableness of the order. But even if the orders were permissible and reasonable as military measures, he said, "I deny that it follows that they are constitutional."

> I should hold that a civil court cannot be made to enforce an order which violates constitutional limitations even if it is a reasonable exercise of military authority. The courts can exercise only the judicial power, can apply only law, and must abide by the Constitution, or they cease to be civil courts and become instruments of military policy.
>
> Of course the existence of a military power resting on force, so vagrant, so centralized, so necessarily heedless of the individual, is an inherent threat to liberty. But I would not lead people to rely on this Court for a review that seems to me wholly delusive. The military reasonableness of these orders can only be determined by military superiors. If the people ever let command of the war power fall into irresponsible and unscrupulous hands, the courts wield no power equal to its restraint. The chief restraint upon those who command the physical forces of the country, in the future as in the past, must be their responsibility to the political judgments of their contemporaries and to the moral judgments of history.
>
> My duties as a justice as I see them do not require me to make a military judgment as to whether General DeWitt's evacuation and detention program was a reasonable military necessity. I do not suggest that the courts should have attempted to interfere with the Army in carrying out its task. But I do not think that they may be asked to execute a military expedient that has no place in law under the Constitution. I would reverse the judgment and discharge the prisoner.

Thus the Justice proposes to refuse enforcement of the statute of March 21, 1942. Apparently, in this regard at least, the statute would be treated as unconstitutional. The prisoner would then be taken to the camp and kept there by the military, and all judicial relief would be denied him.

It is hard to imagine what courts are for if not to protect people against unconstitutional arrest. If the Supreme Court washed its hands of such problems, for what purposes would it sit? The idea that military officers whose only authority rests on that of the President and the Congress, both creatures of the Constitution, can be considered to be acting "unconstitutionally" when they carry out concededly legitimate military policies is Pickwickian, to say the least. For judges to pass by on the other side, when men are imprisoned without charge or trial, suggests a less appealing analogy. The action of Chief Justice Taney in Ex parte *Merryman* is in a more heroic tradition of the judge's responsibility.

What Justice Jackson is saying seems to be this: Courts should refuse to decide hard cases, for in the hands of foolish judges they make bad law. The ark of the law must be protected against contamination. Therefore law should not be allowed to grow through its application to the serious and intensely difficult problems of modern life, such as the punishment of war criminals or the imprisonment of Japanese Americans. It should be kept in orderly seclusion, and confined to problems like the logical adumbration of the full faith and credit clause, and other lawyers' issues. The problems which deeply concern us should be decided outside the courts, even when they arise as the principal and inescapable issues of law suits. Judges are thus to be relieved of the political responsibilities of their citizenship and their office. They will be allowed to pretend that the judicial function is to "interpret" the law, and that law itself is a technical and antiquarian hobby, not the central institution of a changing society.

Mr. Justice Frankfurter concurred specially, answering Mr. Justice Jackson's dissent. "To talk about a military order that expresses an allowable judgment of war needs by those entrusted with the duty of conducting war as 'an unconstitutional order' is to suffuse a part of the Constitution with an atmosphere of unconstitutionality," he said. But one of the first issues of the case was whether or not the military order in question did express an "allowable judgment of war needs." That was the question which the Court was compelled to decide, and did decide, without benefit of the testimony of witnesses, or a factual record, and without substantial independent study on its own motion.

Ex parte *Endo* was the next stage in the judicial elucidation of the problem. In Ex parte *Endo*, decided on December 18, 1944, an adjudication was finally obtained on about one half the question of the validity of confining Japanese aliens and citizens in camps. The case was a habeas corpus proceeding in which an American citizen of Japanese ancestry sought freedom from a War Relocation Center where she was detained, after having been found loyal, until the Authority could place her in an area of the country where local disorder would not be anticipated as a result of her arrival. The Court held that the statute, as rather strenuously construed, did not authorize the detention of persons in the petitioner's situation, although temporary detention for the purpose of investigating loyalty was assumed to be valid as an incident to the program of "orderly" evacuation approved in the *Korematsu* case.

The purpose of the statute under which exclusion and detention were accomplished, the Court said, was to help prevent sabotage and espionage. The act talks only of excluding persons from defense areas. It does not mention the possibility of their detention. While the Court assumes that an implied power of temporary detention may be accepted, as an incident in the program of exclusion, for the purpose of facilitating loyalty examinations, such an implied power should be narrowly confined to the precise purpose of the statute, in order to minimize the impact of the statute on the liberties of the individual citizen. The authority to detain a citizen as a measure of protection against sabotage and espionage is exhausted when his loyalty is established. The persistence of community hostility to citizens of Japanese descent is not a ground for holding them in camp under the present statute. The disclosure of the full scope of the detention program to various committees of the Congress, including appropriation committees, was held not to support a ratification by the Congress of what was done. The basis of this conclusion was the extraordinarily technical proposition that the appropriation acts which might have been considered to ratify the entire program were lump-sum appropiations, and were not broken down by items to earmark a specific sum for the specific cost of detaining citizens found to be loyal pending their relocation in friendly communities. In this respect the reasoning of the Court is contrary to that in the *Hirabayashi* case, where Congressional ratification of the plans of the executive branch was established in a broad and common-sense way. Justices Roberts and Murphy concurred specially, urging that the decision be based on the constitutional grounds stated in their opinions in the *Korematsu* case, rather than on the statutory interpretation underlying Justice Douglas' opinion.

IV

The many opinions of the three Japanese cases do not consider the primary constitutional issues which are raised by the West Coast anti-Japanese program as a whole. This was a program which included (a) a discriminatory curfew against Japanese persons; (b) their exclusion from the West Coast; (c) their confinement pending investigations of loyalty; and (d) the indefinite confinement of those persons found to be disloyal. These measures were proposed and accepted as military necessities. Their validity as military measures was an issue in litigation. By what standards are courts to pass on the justification for such military action? Were those standards satisfied here?

The conception of the war power under the American Constitution rests on the experience of the Revolution and the Civil War. It rests on basic political principles which men who had endured those times of trouble had fully discussed and carefully articulated. The chief architects of the conception were men of affairs who had participated in war, and had definite and sophisticated ideas about the role of the professional military mind in the conduct of war.

The first and dominating proposition about the war power under the Constitution is that the Commander-in-Chief of the armed forces is a civilian and must be a civilian, elected and not promoted to his office. The subordination of the military to the civil power is thus primarily assured. In every democracy the relationship between civil and military power is the crucial social and political issue on which its capacity to survive a crisis ultimately depends. Inadequate analysis of this problem, and inadequate measures to deal with it, led to the downfall of the Spanish Republic, and gravely weakened the Third French Republic. British experience, especially during the first World War, puts the problem in dramatic perspective. In its own proper sphere of tactics, the professional military judgment is decisive. In waging war the larger decisions — the choice of generals, the organization of command, the allocation of forces, the political, economic and often strategic aspects of war — these have to be made by responsible civilian ministers. Clemenceau's famous remark, quoted at the head of this article, is not a witticism, but the first principle of organizing democracy for war. It reflects a balanced view of the proper relation in policy-making between the expert and the practical man. It expresses a keen sense of the supremacy of civil power in a republic. The image of Napoleon is never far from the surface of French political consciousness. France's experience with Pétain has once more underscored the danger. In our own national life recurring waste and incompetence in the handling of war problems — in the Mexican War, the Civil War, and the Spanish-American War — led to important reforms in the organization of the War Department under Elihu Root, and further developments under later Secretaries of War. The process of achieving adequate organization and control is by no means complete.

The second political principle governing the exercise of the war power in a democracy is that of responsibility. Like every other officer of government, soldiers must answer for their decisions to the system of law, and not to the Chief of Staff alone. Where, as in the Japanese exclusion program, military decisions lead to conflicts between individuals and authority, the courts must adjudicate them. Even if Mr. Justice Jackson's doctrine of the judicial function is accepted, the courts will adjudicate nonetheless, by refusing relief, and thus decide cases in favor of the military power. The problem is the scope of the military power, and means for assuring its responsible exercise. It is not a problem which can be avoided by any verbal formula.

Most occasions for the exercise of authority in the name of military need will not present justiciable controversy. When a general attacks or retreats in the field, sends his troops to the right or to the left, he may have to justify his decision to a court martial, but not often to a court. On the other hand some steps deemed to be required in war do raise the kind of conflict over property or personal rights which can be presented to the courts. A factory or business may be taken into custody, prices and wages may be established, whole classes of activity, like horse-racing, temporarily forbidden. Without stopping for an over-nice definition of the terms, these are justiciable occasions — situations in which courts have customarily decided controversies, and determined the legality of official action when such problems were implicit in the conflicts presented to them. It is essential to every democratic value in society that official action taken in the name of the war power be held to standards of responsibility under such circumstances. The courts have not in the past, and should not now, declare the whole category of problems to be political questions beyond the reach of judicial review. The present Supreme Court is dominated by the conviction that in the past judicial review has unduly limited the freedom of administrative action. But surely the permissible response to bad law is good law, not no law at all. The Court must review the exercise of military power in a way which permits ample freedom to the Executive, yet assures society as a whole that appropriate standards of responsibility have been met.

The issue for judicial decision in these cases is not lessened or changed by saying that the war power includes any steps required to win the war. The problem is still one of judgment as to what helps win a war. Who is to decide whether there was a sensible reason for doing what was done? Is it enough for the General to say that at the time he acted, he honestly thought it was a good idea to do what he did? Is this an example of "expertise," to which the courts must give blind deference? Or must there be "objective" evidence, beyond the General's state of mind, to show "the reasonable ground for belief" which the *Hirabayashi* case says is necessary? Should such evidence be available before the action is taken? Should the rule be a procedural one that the general has to consider evidence, and then come to a decision, or should it be only that at the subsequent trial suitable evidence is available to justify the result? As the Chief Justice remarked, the Constitution "does not demand the impossible or the impractical." The inquiry should be addressed to the rationality of the general's exercise of his judgment as a general, not as a master in chancery. It should give full and sympathetic weight to the confusion and danger which are inevitable elements in any problem presented for military decision.

Unless the courts require a showing, in cases like these, of an intelligible relationship between means and ends, society has lost its basic protection against the abuse of military power. The general's good intentions must be irrelevant. There should be evidence in court that his military judgment had a suitable basis in fact. As Colonel Fairman, a strong proponent of widened military discretion, points out: "When the executive fails or is unable to satisfy the court of the evident necessity for the extraordinary measures it has taken, it can hardly expect the court to assume it on faith."

The *Hirabayashi* case proposes one test for the validity of an exercise of military power. Even though that test is not applied in the *Hirabayashi* case, and is roughly handled in the *Korematsu* case, it is not hopelessly lost. As the Court said in *Sterling v. Constantin*, the necessity under all the circumstances for a use of martial power "is necessarily one for judicial inquiry in an appropriate proceeding directed against the individuals charged with the transgression."

Perhaps the closest judicial precedent and analogy for the Japanese American cases is *Mitchell v. Harmony*, which arose out of the Doniphan raid during the Mexican war. The plaintiff was a trader, whose wagons, mules, and goods were seized by the defendant, a lieutenant colonel of the United States Army, during the course of the expedition. The plaintiff, who wanted to leave the Army column and trade with the Mexicans, was forced to accompany the troops. All his property was lost on the march and in battle. The action was of trespass, for the value of the property taken, and for damages. The defenses were that the control of the trader and the destruction of his property were a military necessity, justified by the circumstances of the situation. After a full trial, featured by depositions of the commanding officers, the jury found for the plaintiff.

> The defence has been placed . . . on rumors which reached the commanding officer and suspicions which he appears to have entertained of a secret design in the plaintiff to leave the American forces and carry on an illicit trade with the enemy, injurious to the interests of the United States. And if such a design had been shown, and that he was preparing to leave the American troops for that purpose, the seizure and detention of his property, to prevent its execution, would have been fully justified. But there is no evidence in the record tending to show that these rumors and suspicions had any foundation. And certainly mere suspicions of an illegal intention will not authorize a military officer to seize and detain the property of an American citizen. The fact that such an intention existed must be shown; and of that there is no evidence.
>
> The 2d and 3d objections will be considered together, as they depend on the same principles. Upon these two grounds of defence the Circuit Court instructed the jury, that the defendant might lawfully take possession of the goods of the plaintiff, to prevent them from falling into the hands of the public enemy; but in order to justify the seizure the danger must be immediate and impending, and not remote or contingent. And that he might also take them for public use and

impress them into the public service, in case of an immediate and pressing danger or urgent necessity existing at the time, but not otherwise.

In the argument of these two points, the circumstances under which the goods of the plaintiff were taken have been much discussed, and the evidence examined for the purpose of showing the nature and character of the danger which actually existed at the time or was apprehended by the commander of the American forces. But this question is not before us. It is a question of fact upon which the jury have passed, and their verdict has decided that a danger or necessity, such as the court described, did not exist when the property of the plaintiff was taken by the defendant. And the only subject for inquiry in this court is whether the law was correctly stated in the instruction of the court; and whether any thing short of an immediate and impending danger from the public enemy, or an urgent necessity for the public service, can justify the taking of private property by a military commander to prevent it from falling into the hands of the enemy or for the purpose of converting it to the use of the public.

The instruction is objected to on the ground, that it restricts the power of the officer within narrower limits than the law will justify. And that when the troops are employed in an expedition into the enemy's country, where the dangers that meet them cannot always be foreseen, and where they are cut off from aid from their own government, the commanding officer must necessarily be intrusted with some discretionary power as to the measures he should adopt; and if he acts honestly, and to the best of his judgment, the law will protect him. But it must be remembered that the question here, is not as to the discretion he may exercise in his military operations or in relation to those who are under his command. His distance from home, and the duties in which he is engaged, cannot enlarge his power over the property of a citizen, nor give to him, in that respect, any authority which he would not, under similar circumstances, possess at home. And where the owner has done nothing to forfeit his rights, every officer is bound to respect them, whether he finds the property in a foreign or hostile country, or in his own.

There are, without doubt, occasions in which private property may lawfully be taken possession of or destroyed to prevent it from falling into the hands of the public enemy; and also where a military officer, charged with a particular duty, may impress private property into the public service or take it for public use. Unquestionably, in such cases, the government is bound to make full compensation to the owner; but the officer is not a trespasser.

But we are clearly of opinion, that in all of these cases the danger must be immediate and impending; or the necessity urgent for the public service, such as will not admit of delay, and where the action of the civil authority would be too late in providing the means which the occasion calls for. It is impossible to define the particular circumstances of danger or necessity in which this power may be lawfully exercised. Every case must depend on its own circumstances. It is the emergency that gives the right, and the emergency must be shown to exist before the taking can be justified.

In deciding upon this necessity, however, the state of the facts, as they appeared to the officer at the time he acted, must govern the decision; for he must necessarily act upon the information of others as well as his own observation. And if, with such information as he had a right to rely upon, there is reasonable ground for believing that the peril is immediate and menacing, or the necessity urgent, he is justified in acting upon it; and the discovery afterwards that it was false or erroneous, will not make him a trespasser. But it is not sufficient to show that he exercised an honest judgment, and took the property to promote the public service; he must show by proof the nature and character of the emergency, such as he had reasonable grounds to believe it to be, and it is then for a jury to say, whether it was so pressing as not to admit of delay; and the occasion such, according to the information upon which he acted, that private rights must for the time give way to the common and public good.

But it is not alleged that Colonel Doniphan was deceived by false intelligence as to the movements or strength of the enemy at the time the property was taken. His camp at San Elisario was not threatened. He was well informed upon the state of affairs in his rear, as well as of the dangers before him. And the property was seized, not to defend his position, nor to place his troops in a safer one, nor to anticipate the attack of an approaching enemy, but to insure the success of a distant and hazardous expedition, upon which he was about to march.

The movement upon Chihuahua was undoubtedly undertaken from high and patriotic motives. It was boldly planned and gallantly executed, and contributed to the successful issue of the war. But it is not for the court to say what protection or indemnity is due from the public to an officer who, in his zeal for the honor and interest of his country, and in the excitement of military operations, has trespassed on private rights. That question belongs to the political department of the government. Our duty is to determine under what circumstances private property may be taken from the owner by a military officer in a time of war. And the question here is, whether the law permits it to be taken to insure the success of any enterprise against a public enemy which the commanding officer may deem it advisable to undertake. And we think it very clear that the law does not permit it.

Applied to the circumstances of the Japanese exclusion cases, these precedents require that there be a showing to the trial court of the evidence upon which General DeWitt acted, or evidence which justifies his action under the statute and the constitution. Nor will it do to say that there need be only enough evidence to prove his good faith, or to provide a possible basis for the decision. This was the contention expressly overruled in *Mitchell v.*

Harmony. The varying formulae about presumptions, and the quantum of proof required in different classes of cases, merely conceal the court's problem. There must be evidence enough to satisfy the court as to the need for the grave and disagreeable action taken — arrest on vague suspicion, denial of trial, and permanent incarceration for opinions alone. The standard of reasonableness, here as elsewhere, is one requiring a full evaluation of all circumstances. But the law is not neutral. It has a positive preference for protecting civil rights where possible, and a long-standing suspicion of the military mind when acting outside its own sphere. In protecting important social values against frivolous or unnecessary interference by generals, the courts' obligations cannot be satisfied by a scintilla of evidence, or any other mechanical rule supposed to explain the process of proof. There must be a convincing and substantial factual case, in Colonel Fairman's phrase, to satisfy the court of "the evident necessity" for the measures taken.

No matter how narrowly the rule of proof is formulated, it could not have been satisfied in either the *Hirabayashi* or the *Korematsu* cases. Not only was there insufficient evidence in those cases to satisfy a reasonably prudent judge or a reasonably prudent general: there was no evidence whatever by which a court might test the responsibility of General DeWitt's action, either under the statute of March 21, 1942, or on more general considerations. True, in the *Hirabayashi* case the Court carefully identified certain of General DeWitt's proclamations as "findings," which established the conformity of his actions to the standard of the statute — the protection of military resources against the risk of sabotage and espionage. But the military proclamations record conclusions, not evidence. And in both cases the record is bare of testimony on either side about the policy of the curfew or the exclusion orders. There was every reason to have regarded this omission as a fatal defect, and to have remanded in each case for a trial on the justification of the discriminatory curfew, and of the exclusion orders.

Such an inquiry would have been illuminating. General DeWitt's Final Report and his testimony before committees of the Congress clearly indicate that his motivation was ignorant race prejudice, not facts to support the hypothesis that there was a greater risk of sabotage among the Japanese than among residents of German, Italian, or any other ethnic affiliation. The most significant comment on the quality of the General's report is contained in the Government's brief in *Korematsu v. United States*. There the Solicitor General said that the report was relied upon "for statistics and other details concerning the actual evacuation and the events that took place subsequent thereto. We have specifically recited in this brief the facts relating to the justification for the evacuation, of which we ask the Court to take judicial notice, and we rely upon the Final Report only to the extent that it relates such facts." Yet the Final Report embodies the basic decision under review, and states the reasons why it was actually undertaken. General De-Witt's Final Recommendation to the Secretary of War, dated February 14,

1942, included in the Final Report, is the closest approximation we have in these cases to an authoritative determination of fact. In that Recommendation, General DeWitt says:

> In the war in which we are now engaged racial affinities are not severed by migration. The Japanese race is an enemy race and while many second and third generation Japanese born on United States soil, possessed of United States citizenship, have become "Americanized," the racial strains are undiluted. To conclude otherwise is to expect that children born of white parents on Japanese soil sever all racial affinity and become loyal Japanese subjects, ready to fight and, if necessary, to die for Japan in a war against the nation of their parents. That Japan is allied with Germany and Italy in this struggle is no ground for assuming that any Japanese, barred from assimilation by convention as he is, though born and raised in the United States, will not turn against this nation when the final test of loyalty comes. It, therefore, follows that along the vital Pacific Coast over 112,000 potential enemies, of Japanese extraction, are at large today. There are indications that these are organized and ready for concerted action at a favorable opportunity. The very fact that no sabotage has taken place to date is a disturbing and confirming indication that such action will be taken.

In his Final Report to the Secretary of War General DeWitt adduces somewhat more evidence than the absence of sabotage to prove its special danger. His report, and the briefs for the United States in *Hirabayashi v. United States* and *Korematsu v. United States* emphasize these points as well: The Japanese lived together, often concentrated around harbors and other strategic areas. They had been discriminated against, and it was suggested that their resentment at such treatment might give rise to disloyalty. Japanese clubs and religious institutions played an important part in their social life. Japanese language schools were maintained to preserve for the American-born children something of the cultural heritage of Japan. The Japanese Government, like that of Italy, France, and many other countries, asserted a doctrine of nationality which was thought to result in claims of dual citizenship, and thus to cast doubt on the loyalty of American citizens of Japanese descent. There were some 10,000 Kibei among the population of the West Coast, Japanese Americans who had returned to Japan for an important part of their education, and who were thought to be more strongly affiliated with Japan in their political outlook than the others.

Much of the suspicion inferentially based on these statements disappears when they are more closely examined. In many instances the concentration of Japanese homes around strategic areas had come about years before, and for entirely innocent reasons. Japanese fishing and cannery workers, for example, were compelled by the canneries to live on the waterfront, in order to be near the plants in which they worked. Japanese truck gardeners rented land in the industrial outskirts of large cities in order to be as close as possible to their markets. They rented land for agricultural purposes under high tension lines — regarded as a very suspicious circumstance — because the company could not use the land for other purposes. The initiative in starting the practice came from the utility companies, not from the Japanese. Despite discrimination against the Japanese, many had done well in America. They were substantial property owners. Their children participated normally and actively in the schools and universities of the West Coast. Their unions and social organizations had passed resolutions of loyalty in great number, before and after the Pearl Harbor disaster. It is difficult to find real evidence that either religious or social institutions among the Japanese had successfully fostered Japanese militarism, or other dangerous sentiments, among the Japanese American population. The Japanese language schools, which the Japanese Americans themselves had long sought to put under state control, seem to represent little more than the familiar desire of many immigrant groups to keep alive the language and tradition of the "old country"; in the case of Japanese Americans, knowledge of the Japanese language was of particular economic importance, since so much of their working life was spent with other Japanese on the West Coast.

There were of course suspicious elements among the Japanese. They were known to the authorities, which had for several years been checking the security of the Japanese American population. Many had been individually arrested immediately after Pearl Harbor, and the others were under constant surveillance. We had many intelligence officers who knew both the language and the people well. So far as the police were concerned, there was no substance to the man-in-the-street's belief that all Orientals "look alike." On the contrary, the Japanese were a small and conspicuous minority on the West Coast, both individually and as a group. They would have been an unlikely source of sabotage agents for an intelligent enemy in any case.

Apart from the members of the group known to be under suspicion, there was no evidence beyond the vaguest fear to connect the Japanese on the West Coast with the unfavorable military events of 1941 and 1942. Both at Pearl Harbor and in sporadic attacks on the West Coast the enemy had shown that he had knowledge of our dispositions. There was some signaling to enemy ships at sea, both by radio and by lights, along the West Coast. It was said to be difficult to trace such signals because of limitations on the power of search without warrant. There had been several episodes of shelling the coast by submarine, although two of the three such episodes mentioned by General DeWitt as tending to create suspicion of the Japanese Americans had taken place after their removal from the Coast. These were the only such items in the Final Report which were not identified by data. And it was positively known that no suspicions attached to the Japanese residents for sabotage at Pearl Harbor before, during or after the raid. Those subsequently arrested as Japanese agents were all white men. "To focus attention on local residents of Japanese descent, actually diverted attention from those who were busily engaged in espionage activity."

It is possible that the absence of a trial on the facts may permit the Court in the future to distinguish or to extinguish the Japanese American cases; for in these cases the defendants did not bring forth evidence, nor require the Government to produce evidence, on the factual justification of the military action. Whoever had the burden of going forward, or of proof, Government or defendant, the burden was not met. Not even the *Korematsu* case would justify the exclusion of such evidence, nor the denial of a defendant's request to call the General as a witness. A future case may therefore create a better record for establishing appropriate criteria of judicial control over military conduct, and for applying such criteria to better purpose.

A trial on the factual justification of the curfew and exclusion orders would require the Court to confront Ex parte *Milligan*, which it sought to avoid in all three of the Japanese cases. Ex parte *Milligan* represents an application to a large and common class of semi-military situations of what Chief Justice Stone articulated in the *Hirabayashi* case as a "rule of reason" governing the scope of military power. The military power, the Chief Justice said, included any steps needed to wage war successfully. The justices in the majority in Ex parte *Milligan* declared in effect that it would be difficult, if not impossible, to convince them that there was or could be a military necessity for allowing the military to hold, try, or punish civilians while the civil courts were open and functioning. And it held further that it is for the judges, not the generals, to say when it is proper under the Constitution to shut the courts, or to deny access to them.

Ex parte *Milligan* is a monument in the democratic tradition, and should be the animating force of this branch of our law. At a time when national emergency, mobilization and war are more frequent occurrences than at any previous period of our history, it would be difficult to name a single decision of more fundamental importance to society. Yet there is a tendency to treat Ex parte *Milligan* as outmoded, as if new methods of "total" warfare made the case an anachronism. Those who take this view have forgotten the circumstances of the Civil War. Fifth columns, propaganda, sabotage and espionage were more generally used than in any war since the siege of Troy, and certainly more widely used than in the second World War.

Ex parte *Milligan* illustrates the point. Milligan was convincingly charged with active participation in a fifth column plot worthy of Hitler or Alfred Hitchcock. A group of armed and determined men were to seize federal arsenals at Columbus, Indianapolis and at three points in Illinois, and then to release Confederate prisoners of war held in those states. Thus they would create a Confederate army behind the Union lines in Tennessee. Milligan and his alleged co-conspirators acted in Indiana, Missouri, Illinois, and in other border states. Their strategy had a political arm. The Union was to be split politically, and a Northwest Confederation was to be declared, friendly to the South, and embracing Illinois, Wisconsin, Iowa, Kansas, Indiana and Minnesota. This plan was not an idle dream. It was sponsored by a well-financed society, the Sons of Liberty, thought to have 300,000 members, many of them rich and respectable; the planned uprising would coincide with the Chicago convention of the Democratic Party, which was sympathetic to abandoning the war, and recognizing the Confederacy.

The unanimous Court which freed Milligan for civil trial was a court of fire-eating Unionists. Mr. Justice Davis, who wrote for the majority, was one of President Lincoln's closest friends, supporters and admirers. The Chief Justice, who wrote the opinion for the concurring minority, was a valiant and resolute supporter of the war, whatever his shortcomings in other respects. The Court had no difficulty in freeing Milligan, and facing down the outcry of radical Republicans which was provoked by the decision. The issue dividing the Court in the *Milligan* case was parallel in some ways to the problem presented by the Japanese exclusion program under the statute of March 21, 1942. Congress had passed a statute in 1863 permitting the President to suspend the privilege of habeas corpus in a limited way whenever, in his judgment, the public safety required it, holding prisoners without trial for a short period. If the next sitting of the grand jury did not indict those held in its district, they were entitled to release under the statute.

The statute was in fact a dead letter, although the Court did not consider that aspect of the situation in deciding Milligan's case. Milligan had been arrested by the military. The grand jury had not returned an indictment against him at its next sitting. He had nonetheless been tried by a military commission, and sentenced to death. The minority of the Court urged his release according to the terms of the statute, because no indictment had been presented against him. The Court, however, freed him for normal criminal trial on broader grounds. The controlling question of the case, the Court said, was whether the military commission had jurisdiction to try Milligan. This question was considered without express reference to the statute of 1863, as such, but on the evidence which might justify the exercise of martial law powers either under the statute or otherwise. The only constitutional reason, the Court said, for denying Milligan the trial provided for in the Third Article of the Constitution, and in the Fifth and Sixth Amendments, is that such a trial could not physically be conducted. So long as the courts are open, persons accused of crime, and not subject to the laws of war as members of the armed forces or enemy belligerents, must be brought before the courts, or discharged. Ex parte *Milligan* therefore holds Milligan's trial before a military commission to be unconstitutional, despite the President's action under the first section of the Act of 1863. The factual situation was not such as to justify the exercise of martial law powers, even for temporary detention, and certainly not for trial. Ordinary civilians could be held for military trial only when the civil power was incapable of acting — during an invasion, for example, or during a period of severe riot or insurrection.

> It is difficult to see how the *safety* of the country required martial law in Indiana. If any of her citizens were plotting treason, the power of arrest could secure them, until the government was prepared for their trial, when the courts were open and ready to try them. It was as easy to protect witnesses before a civil as a military tribunal; and as there could be no wish to convict, except on sufficient legal evidence, surely an ordained and established court was better able to judge of this than a military tribunal composed of gentlemen not trained to the profession of the law.
>
> It is claimed that martial law covers with its broad mantle the proceedings of this military commission. The proposition is this: that in a time of war the commander of an armed force (if in his opinion the exigencies of the country demand it, and of which he is to judge) has the power, within the lines of his military district, to suspend all civil rights and their remedies, and subject citizens as well as soldiers to the rule of *his will*; and in the exercise of his lawful authority cannot be restrained, except by his superior officer or the President of the United States.
>
> If this position is sound to the extent claimed, then when war exists, foreign or domestic, and the country is subdivided into military departments for mere convenience, the commander of one of them can, if he chooses, within his limits, on the plea of necessity, with the approval of the Executive, substitute military force for and to the exclusion of the laws, and punish all persons, as he thinks right and proper, without fixed or certain rules.
>
> The statement of this proposition shows its importance; for, if true, republican government is a failure, and there is an end of liberty regulated by law. Martial law, established on such a basis, destroys every guarantee of the Constitution, and effectually renders the "military independent of and superior to the civil power" — the attempt to do which by the King of Great Britain was deemed by our fathers such an offence, that they assigned it to the world as one of the causes which impelled them to declare their independence. Civil liberty and this kind of martial law cannot endure together; the antagonism is irreconcilable; and, in the conflict, one or the other must perish.

The Court's dismissal of Ex parte *Milligan* in Ex parte *Endo* requires some analysis. The Court said, "It should be noted at the outset that we do not have here a question such as was presented in Ex parte *Milligan*, 4 Wall. 2, or in Ex parte *Quirin*, 317 U.S. 1, where the jurisdiction of military tribunals to try persons according to the law of war was challenged in *habeas corpus* proceedings. Mitsuye Endo is detained by a civilian agency, the War Relocation Authority, not by the military. Moreover, the evaluation program was not left exclusively to the military; the Authority was given a large measure of responsibility for its execution and Congress made its enforcement subject to civil penalties by the Act of March 21, 1942. Accordingly, no questions of military law are involved."

The proposition is extraordinary. Under penalty of imprisonment, the orders before the Court in Ex parte *Endo* required that enemy aliens and citizens of Japanese blood be removed from their home and confined in camps. If found to be "disloyal," they were kept in the camps indefinitely. If found to be "loyal," they were kept in the camps as long as was necessary for the Authority to place them in friendly communities.

The problems of Ex parte *Milligan* are avoided by the simplest of expedients. In Ex parte *Milligan* the Court said that the military could not constitutionally arrest, nor could a military tribunal constitutionally try, civilians charged with treason and conspiracy to destroy the state by force, at a time when the civil courts were open and functioning. Under the plan considered in the Japanese American cases, people not charged with crime are imprisoned for several years without even a military trial, on the ground that they have the taint of Japanese blood. Why doesn't the *Milligan* case apply *a fortiori?* If it is illegal to arrest and confine people after an unwarranted military trial, it is surely even more illegal to arrest and confine them without any trial at all. The Supreme Court says that the issues of the *Milligan* case are not involved because the evacuees were committed to camps by military orders, not by military tribunals, and because their jailers did not wear uniforms. It is hard to see any sequence in the sentences. The Japanese Americans were ordered detained by a general, purporting to act on military grounds. The military order was enforceable, on pain of imprisonment. While a United States marshal, rather than a military policeman, assured obedience to the order, the ultimate sanction behind the marshal's writ is the same as that of the military police: the bayonets of United States troops. It is hardly a ground for distinction that the general's command was backed by the penalty of civil imprisonment, or that he obtained civilian aid in running the relocation camps. The starting point for the program was a military order, which had to be obeyed. It required enemy aliens and citizens of Japanese blood to be removed from their homes and confined in camps. As events developed, the general's command imposed confinement for three years on most of the people who were evacuated under it.

There are then two basic constitutional problems concealed in the Court's easy dismissal of Ex parte *Milligan:* the arrest, removal and confinement of persons without trial, pending examination of their loyalty; and the indefinite confinement of persons found to be disloyal. On both counts, at least as to citizens, the moral of Ex parte *Milligan* is plain. The *Milligan* case says little about the propriety of a curfew, or perhaps even of the exclusion orders as such. The military necessity of such steps are to be tested independently in the light of all the relevant circumstances. The *Milligan* case does say, however, that arrest and confinement are forms of action which cannot be taken as military necessities while courts are open. For such punitive measures it proposes a clear and forceful rule of thumb: the protection of the individual by normal trial does not under such circumstances interfere with the conduct of war.

Much was made in the Japanese American cases of the analogy of temporary preventive arrest or other restriction, approved for material witnesses, the protection of the public at fires, the detention of typhoid carriers, mentally ill persons, and so on. The analogy has little or no application to the problems presented in these cases, except perhaps for the curfew or conceivably the abstract issue of exclusion, as distinguished from detention. The restrictions involved here were not temporary emergency measures, justified by the breakdown of more orderly facilities for protecting society against espionage and sabotage. As interferences with the liberty of the individual, they go well beyond the minimal forms of precautionary arrest without warrant which were permitted by the statute of 1863, discussed in the *Milligan* case; they are closely comparable to the forms of arbitrary action which were actually presented by the facts of the *Milligan* case, and strongly disapproved by the Court.

As for Japanese aliens, it is orthodox, though not very accurate, to say that as persons of enemy nationality they are subject only to the Government's will in time of war. But the protection of the Fifth and Sixth Amendments extends generally to aliens. Should arbitrary distinctions be permitted in our policy for enemy aliens, distinctions without reasonable basis? Is it permissible to intern all the Japanese who live on the West Coast, but to allow German and Italian aliens, and Japanese who live elsewhere, general freedom? Lower courts have said they would refuse to review executive action directed at the control of enemy aliens. Such a view is far from necessary. The courts go to great lengths to assure reasonable protection to the property rights of enemy aliens, their privilege of pursuing litigation, and the like. It requires no extension of doctrine to propose that their control and custody in time of war be reasonably equal, and even-handed. So far as accepted notions of international law are concerned, the "single aim" of specialized enemy alien controls is to prevent enemy aliens from aiding the enemy. The present pattern of discriminatory controls bears no relation to the end of safety.

V

These cases represent deep-seated and largely inarticulate responses to the problems they raise. In part they express the justices' reluctance to interfere in any way with the prosecution of the war. In part they stem from widely shared fears and uncertainties about the technical possibilities of new means of warfare. Such fears were strongly felt everywhere on the Allied side after the German victories of 1940 and 1941. It was common then, and still is common, to believe in a vague but positive way that the restoration of mobility in warfare, and the appearance of new weapons, have somehow made all older thought on the subject of war obsolete. We expected fifth-columns and paratroops to drop near San Francisco at any moment. In the panic of the time, it seemed almost rational to lock up Japanese Americans as potential enemy agents.

But the airplane, the tank, and the rocket have not made it necessary to abandon the principles of Ex parte *Milligan*. Whatever the effect of such developments may be on Infantry Field Regulations and the Manual of Arms, they do not compel us to deny suspects the right of trial, to hold people for years in preventive custody, or to substitute military commissions for the civil courts. The need for democratic control of the management of war has not been reduced by advances in the technique of fighting. The accelerated rate of technical advance emphasizes anew the importance of civil control to guard against resistance to novelty, and the other occupational diseases of the higher staffs of all armies. And as warfare becomes more dangerous, and as it embraces more and more of the life of the community, the problem of assuring a sensible choice of war policies, and of preserving democratic social values under conditions of general mobilization, becomes steadily more urgent.

What lies behind Ex parte *Milligan*, *Mitchell v. Harmony*, and *Sterling v. Constantin* is the principle of responsibility. The war power is the power to wage war successfully, as Chief Justice Hughes once remarked. But it is the power to wage war, not a license to do unnecessary and dictatorial things in the name of the war power. The decision as to where the boundaries of military discretion lie in particular cases has to be made differently in different circumstances. Sometimes the issue will arise in law suits, more often in courts martial, Congressional investigations, reports of the Inspector General, or other law-enforcement procedures. When a court confronts the problem of determining the permissible limit of military discretion, it must test the question by the same methods of judicial inquiry it uses in other cases. There is no special reason why witnesses, depositions, cross-examination and other familiar techniques of investigation are less available in these cases than in others. As *Mitchell v. Harmony* and many other cases indicate, Mr. Justice Jackson is plainly wrong in asserting that judicial control of military discretion is impossible. Mr. Justice Jackson said:

> The limitation under which courts always will labor in examining the necessity for a military order are illustrated by this case. How does the Court know that these orders have a reasonable basis in necessity? No evidence whatever on that subject has been taken by this or any other court. There is sharp controversy as to the credibility of the DeWitt report. So the Court, having no real evidence before it, has

no choice but to accept General DeWitt's own unsworn, self-serving statement, untested by any cross-examination, that what he did was reasonable. And thus it will always be when courts try to look into the reasonableness of a military order.

The Supreme Court had a real alternative in the *Korematsu* case: it could have remanded for trial on the necessity of the orders. The courts have found no special difficulty in investigating such questions, and there is no reason why they should.

The first and greatest anomaly of the *Hirabayashi, Korematsu* and *Endo* cases is that they seem to abandon the requirement of a judicial inquiry into the factual justification for General DeWitt's decisions. Despite the careful language of the Chief Justice, these cases treat the decisions of military officials, unlike those of other government officers, as almost immune from ordinary rules of public responsibility. The judges were convinced by the *ipse dixit* of a general, not the factual record of a court proceeding. On this ground alone, the Japanese American cases should be most strenuously reconsidered.

An appropriate procedure for reviewing decisions taken in the name of the war power is an indispensable step towards assuring a sensible result. But the ultimate problem left by these cases is not one of procedure. In these cases the Supreme Court of the United States has upheld a decision to incarcerate 100,000 people for a term of several years. The reason for this action was the extraordinary proposition that all persons of Japanese ancestry are enemies, that the war is not directed at the Japanese state, but at the Japanese "race." General DeWitt's views on this subject are formally presented in his Final Recommendations and his Final Report to the War Department. They are reiterated in his later testimony to a subcommittee of the Naval Affairs Committee. After testifying about soldier delinquency and other problems involving the welfare of his troops, General DeWitt was asked whether he had any suggestions he wanted to leave with the Congressmen. He responded:

> I haven't any except one – that is the development of a false sentiment on the part of certain individuals and some organizations to get the Japanese back on the west coast. I don't want any of them here. They are a dangerous element. There is no way to determine their loyalty. The west coast contains too many vital installations essential to the defense of the country to allow any Japanese on this coast. There is a feeling developing, I think, in certain sections of the country that the Japanese should be allowed to return. I am opposing it with every proper means at my disposal.
>
> MR. BATES: I was going to ask — would you base your determined stand on experience as a result of sabotage or racial history or what is it?
>
> GENERAL DeWITT: I first of all base it on my responsibility. I

have the mission of defending this coast and securing vital installations. The danger of the Japanese was, and is now — if they are permitted to come back — espionage and sabotage. It makes no difference whether he is an American citizen, he is still a Japanese. American citizenship does not necessarily determine loyalty.

MR. BATES: You draw a distinction then between Japanese and Italians and Germans? We have a great number of Italians and Germans and we think they are fine citizens. There may be exceptions.

GENERAL DeWITT: You needn't worry about the Italians at all except in certain cases. Also, the same for the Germans except in individual cases. But we must worry about the Japanese all the time until he is wiped off the map. Sabotage and espionage will make problems as long as he is allowed in this area — problems which I don't want to have to worry about.

The Japanese exclusion program thus rests on five propositions of the utmost potential menace: (1) protective custody, extending over three or four years, is a permitted form of imprisonment in the United States; (2) political opinions, not criminal acts, may contain enough clear and present danger to justify such imprisonment; (3) men, women and children of a given ethnic group, both Americans and resident aliens, can be presumed to possess the kind of dangerous ideas which require their imprisonment; (4) in time of war or emergency the military, perhaps without even the concurrence of the legislature, can decide what political opinions require imprisonment, and which ethnic groups are infected with them; and (5) the decision of the military can be carried out without indictment, trial examination, jury, the confrontation of witnesses, counsel for the defense, the privilege against self-incrimination, or any of the other safeguards of the Bill of Rights.

The idea of punishment only for individual behavior is basic to all systems of civilized law. A great principle was never lost so casually. Mr. Justice Black's comment was weak to the point of impotence: "Hardships are a part of war, and war is an aggregation of hardships." It was an answer in the spirit of cliché: "Don't you know there's a war going on?" It is hard to reconcile with the purposes of his dissent in *Williams v. North Carolina*, where he said that a conviction for bigamy in North Carolina of two people who had been validly divorced and remarried in Nevada "makes of human liberty a very cheap thing — too cheap to be consistent with the principles of free government."

That the Supreme Court has upheld imprisonment on such a basis constitutes an expansion of military discretion beyond the limit of tolerance in democratic society. It ignores the rights of citizenship, and the safeguards of trial practice which have been the historical attributes of liberty. Beyond that, it is an injustice, and therefore, like the trials of Sacco, Vanzetti, and Dreyfus, a threat to society, and to all men. We believe that the German people bear a common political responsibility for outrages secretly committed by the Gestapo and the SS. What are we to think of our own part in a program which violates every democratic social value, yet has been approved by the Congress, the President and the Supreme Court?

Three forms of reparation are available, and should be pursued. The first is the inescapable obligation of the Federal Government to protect the civil rights of Japanese Americans against organized and unorganized hooliganism. If local law enforcement fails, prosecutions under the Civil Rights Act should be undertaken. Secondly, generous financial indemnity should be sought, for the Japanese Americans have suffered and will suffer heavy property losses as a consequence of their evacuation. Finally, the basic issues should be presented to the Supreme Court again, in an effort to obtain a reversal of these war-time cases. In the history of the Supreme Court there have been important occasions when the Court itself corrected a decision occasioned by the excitement of a tense and patriotic moment. After the end of the Civil War, Ex parte *Vallandigham* was followed by Ex parte *Milligan*. The *Gobitis* case has recently been overruled by *West Virginia v. Barnette*. Similar public expiation in the case of the internment of Japanese Americans from the West Coast would be good for the Court, and for the country.

22

THE ECONOMIC IMPACT

The American experience during World War II has inspired a large number of books dealing with military strategy and policy and foreign affairs. Historical controversies have raged about the nature of American involvement in the war and America's conduct of the war — especially in terms of its relations to its allies, the motivation behind the dropping of atomic bombs on Japan, and the role of World War II in bringing on the Cold War. Unfortunately, the domestic side of the war years has yet to be related in sufficient detail. We have had very few studies of economic, political, or social developments in the United States from 1940 to 1945. The same has also been true of other major war periods. The inundation of volumes dealing with the military history of the Civil War, for instance, has not been equalled by the relative trickle of studies of the domestic side of the war. The same has been true of World War I. American historians obviously have found the military and foreign affairs aspects of war infinitely more glamorous than the home front, but they are not necessarily more important in terms of understanding the American past or gaining a better perspective from which to view postwar developments. The following essay by Robert Lekachman, taken from his study of the English economist John Maynard Keynes, makes clear how closely related wartime attitudes and actions were to the postwar economic developments and demonstrates how important it would be to have an array of similar studies for every aspect of American society during the war.

The story of Keynes's impact upon the United States in peace and war is particularly interesting and revealing. As we pointed out in our introduction to Ellis Hawley's article (see above, pp. 373–375), Franklin Roosevelt never became a convert to Keynes's theories; he was always uncomfortable with deficit spending and unbalanced budgets, and he was eager to reduce expenditures at the least sign of an economic upturn. Only with the advent of the war did Roosevelt more completely pursue some of the policies that Keynes had long urged upon him: a massive injection of funds into the economy, the creation of jobs on a huge scale, and a much greater degree of central planning and economic rationalization. When Roosevelt's conservative critics charged that the New Deal failed to end the depression and only the coming of war saved the nation, they were correct, but for the wrong reasons. The New Deal failed to bring about full-scale economic recovery not because its economic policies were necessarily wrong, as conservatives charged, but because the policies that did help to bring about a large measure of recovery were pursued only half-heartedly and on a limited scale. Nor was there anything mystical or even inevitable about wartime recovery. It came about because under the impetus of war Roosevelt was both willing and able to broaden and enlarge those very economic devices that he had used very reluctantly in peacetime. As Lekachman shows, the end of the war brought about a renewal of this reluctance and hesitance among Roosevelt's successors.

The contrast between the economic policies pursued during the Depression and the war raises a number of interesting and important questions. Why were Americans and their leaders willing to utilize techniques to meet a wartime crisis that they were not willing to use to solve an equally urgent and critical domestic crisis? Can Americans solve their economic problems without the existence of a wartime economy and the creation of economic waste in the form of a quickly outmoded weaponry that fulfills none of the pressing economic and social needs of a large segment of the population? The answers to questions like these may lie only in the future, but we can perceive the problems much more clearly once we have gathered more information and understanding of our experiences during and after World War II.

For an interesting inquiry into the impact of World War I upon New Deal governmental agencies and experiments, see William E. Leuchtenburg, "The New Deal and the Analogue of War," in J. Braeman et al., eds., *Change and Continuity in Twentieth-Century America** (1964). The following studies all throw light upon the home front during World War II: W. F. Ogburn, ed., *American Society in Wartime* (1943); Jack Goodman, ed., *While You Were Gone: A Report on Wartime Life in the United States* (1946); Bruce Catton, *War Lords of Washington* (1948); Eliot Janeway, *The Struggle for Survival* (1951); Jonathan Daniels, *Frontier on the Potomac* (1946); Roland Young, *Congressional Politics in the Second World War* (1956); Walter W. Wilcox, *The Farmer in the Second World War* (1947); Joel Seidman, *American Labor from Defense to Reconversion* (1953); E. S. Corwin, *Total War and the Constitution* (1947); L. S. Wittner, *Rebels Against War: The American Peace Movement, 1941–1960* (1969); and Reuben Hill, *Families Under Stress* (1949). Two useful collections of documents are: Richard Polenberg, *America at War** (1968), and Chester Eisinger, *The 1940's** (1969).

Robert Lekachman is Professor of Economics at the State University of New York, Stony Brook.

The Trial of War

ROBERT LEKACHMAN

How Keynesian was the American conduct of the war? How willing were Americans to accept doctrines in war that they had resisted in peace? How much of American planning for the post-war era bore the marks of Keynes's ideas? A good place to begin consideration of such questions is with the spectacular transformation of the American economy from depression and under-employment to overfull employment and massive output of every kind of good and service.

Between 1939 and 1944, the peak of the war effort, the real value of the nation's output rose over seventy per cent. Still more remarkable, private product expanded by over half at the same time that the value of the government's output more than trebled and its share of total output rose from slightly more than ten per cent in 1939 to between a fifth and a quarter in 1944.

Accompanying these shifts in the national product was a nationwide redeployment of the labour force. In 1939 the total membership of the armed forces was a meagre 370,000. At the cessation of hostilities in 1945, some 11,410,000 men and women were in uniform. Nevertheless, the total civilian labour force numbering 55,230,000 individuals in 1939 dropped only to 53,860,000 in 1945. The numbers contain no mystery. The elderly, the maimed and the drunken, housewives, pensioners and students turned out in the missions at the call of patriotism and high wages. And suddenly there was no unemployment problem. By 1942 the rate was 4.7 per cent, but in 1943 it was 1.9 per cent and in the succeeding year a wartime low of 1.2 per cent. The miracles of war production were a tribute to the energies and the organizational talents of millions of Americans. But they were made possible by the tremendous slack which existed in the 1939 economy.

As that slack was taken up, the same problems of resource allocation and price restraint concerned American administrators as had earlier challenged their British colleagues. In a liberal democracy, the minimum objectives of wartime finance are the efficient allocation of resources to the military, the avoidance of economic scandal, and the uncoerced movement of workers into the right jobs and capital into the appropriate industries. In the management of economic resources, patriotism must be supplemented

Reprinted by permission of Random House, Inc., from *The Age of Keynes*, Ch. 6, by Robert Lekachman. Copyright © 1966 by Robert Lekachman.

with more tangible rewards. At least the appearance if not the reality of equality of sacrifice is essential.

No more than England was the United States able to finance wartime expenditure out of wartime taxation. This inability can be traced in the upward movement of the national debt from $40.4 billion in 1939 to $258.7 billion by the end of 1949, a more than six-fold increase. Taxes were nevertheless an indispensable supplement to borrowing. Taxes diminished the purchasing power which the expansion of the economy generated. And taxes were deployed as a technique of social equity. The record of taxes, expenditures, deficits and federal debt during the years 1939–45 makes plain the decision of American leaders to tax equitably and heavily. An almost tenfold increase in tax receipts between 1939 and 1945 measures the impact of this decision (see Table 1).

TABLE 1

FEDERAL TAXES, EXPENDITURES, DEFICITS, AND NATIONAL DEBT: 1939–45 (IN MILLIONS OF DOLLARS)

YEAR	TAXES	EXPENDITURES	DEFICIT	NATIONAL DEBT
1939	$ 4,979	$ 8,841	$ 3,862	$ 40,440
1940	5,137	9,055	3,918	42,968
1941	7,096	13,255	6,159	48,961
1942	12,547	34,037	21,490	72,422
1943	21,948	79,368	57,420	136,696
1944	43,563	94,986	51,423	201,003
1945	44,362	98,303	53,941	258,682

SOURCE: Adapted from *The Economic Report of the President* (Washington, D.C.: U.S. Government Printing Office, January, 1964).

Taxes rose because the economy expanded, but they rose also because in 1942 an excess profits tax was enacted and because each year the rates applied to personal income were elevated. In 1939 the income tax was paid by only four million prosperous Americans, but in 1942 no fewer than forty-two million Americans filed returns.[1] The bulk of the increases in personal and corporate income-tax rates occurred in the later years of the Second World War, after idle men and resources had been absorbed. Nevertheless, with the single exception of 1944, the tax increases failed to keep pace with mounting government spending on the war. In consequence both deficits and the national debt made spectacular leaps.

Quite possibly tax rates could have been increased more sharply, although no one can be certain that adverse effects upon incentives to labour and investment might not have followed. It is conceivable that some version of

---

[1] Norman F. Keiser, *Macroeconomics, Fiscal Policy, and Economic Growth* (New York: Wiley, 1964).

forced saving might have been installed. This is conjecture. The fact is the failure of taxes to remove enough of the extra spending power generated by wartime production to obviate the need for rationing and price controls. It quickly became essential to supplement these with wage and salary restraints.

In these events and decisions, what was the Keynesian influence? Keynes himself was pleased with the extent to which his ideas had spread among the younger officials of the administration. On his 1941 visit to the United States, Keynes addressed a National Press Club dinner which had been arranged so that he could meet Leon Henderson and Henderson's principal associates in the Office of Price Administration. In his talk Keynes urged higher taxes as an anti-inflation device. One of the dinner's sequels was a correspondence with Walter S. Salant in which Salant explained that American economists were taking into account both the multiplier and the acceleration impact upon the economy of defence spending. "It was satisfactory to Keynes to find that his own tools of analysis were being used by those responsible for framing policy with characteristic American statistical thoroughness." [2] As Keynes's comment in a letter to Salant noted, it was the young who were the most receptive:

> There is too wide a gap between the intellectual outlook of the older people and that of the younger. I have been greatly struck during my visit by the quality of the younger economists and civil servants in the Administration. I am sure that the best hope for good government of America is to be found there. The war will be a great sifter and will bring the right people to the top. We have a few good people in London, but nothing like the *numbers* you can produce here.[3]

Although Morgenthau remained as untouched by the New Economics as ever, young Keynesians were fairly numerous in the Treasury, especially in Harry Dexter White's division. And they were scattered through other agencies, including the special agencies of wartime control — the Office of Price Administration and the War Production Board. These economists routinely applied income analysis to wartime problems. According to an observer of later eminence, the quality of wartime economics in Washington was high, significantly superior to the German level of economic analysis.[4] Like their confrères in England, the American economists conducted their investigations in terms of the real raw materials, labour and capital available to the community. The aggregative technique was a truer guide for resource allocation than purely financial measures.

The war pointed a sharp Keynesian moral. As a public works project, all

[2] Sir Roy Harrod, *The Life of John Maynard Keynes* (London: Macmillan, 1951).
[3] Quoted in ibid.
[4] See Paul A. Samuelson, "The Modern Scene," in Ralph E. Freeman (ed.) *Postwar Economic Trends in the United States* (New York: Harper & Row, 1960).

wars (before the nuclear era) are ideal. Since all war production is sheer economic waste, there is never a danger of producing too much. Even an enlightened nation might build enough schools, roads, houses, parks and hospitals to meet its own standards. What happens when the demand for perfectly useless objects is multiplied almost without limit? What happens when this demand is financed in reality if not in appearance by the printing of new money? In the world of 1941–5, what occurred was full employment, bustling factories and an increase in the production of useful as well as useless things. In real life these were the consequences of waste. They were also the consequences predicted by Keynes. In the Second World War the equivalent of the Egyptian pyramids, the medieval cathedrals, and the buried bottles full of money were the tanks, the bombers and the aircraft carriers.

Both by their numbers and by their influence, American Keynesians did much in Washington to enhance the reputation of American economics. Samuelson conjectures (plausibly for other economists at least) that the nature of their graduate training prepares economists to cope effectively with the issues of choice and allocation which are at the centre of wartime economic decision. In the early war years, these indeed were practically the only problems on which economists worked. There was a war to be won. However, by 1944 when victory was over the horizon, their focus of interest shifted increasingly to the planning of the post-war world.

It was probably inevitable that the renewed concern for a peacetime economy took its point of departure from the immediate prewar discussions on the apparently intractable "normal" dilemmas of deficient private investment, inadequate rates of economic expansion and persistent unemployment. Alvin Hansen's doctrine of secular stagnation had been accorded its boldest and most radical amplification in a polemic by a group of Harvard and Tufts economists writing in the gloom of the 1937–8 recession.[5] These seven young Keynesians took it for granted that "The economic development of America may be divided into two periods. The first, beginning when the earliest colonists set foot on our shores, was the period of economic expansion. It came to a dramatic close with the collapse of 1929. The second period has so far been one of economic stagnation."[6]

Obviously, the New Deal had not defeated stagnation, but as far as it had gone, it had found the right track in expanded deficit spending: "One of the lessons of the past five years has been the striking demonstration of the efficacy of public spending in promoting national well being."[7] If the New Deal had spent more, the results undoubtedly would have been more

---

[5] Richard Gilbert, *et al.*, *An Economic Program for American Democracy* (New York: Vanguard, 1938).
[6] Ibid.
[7] Ibid.

satisfactory. However, the 1937–8 recession implied the need for a more substantial change in the American economy than deficit spending by itself. Resumption of public spending as a temporary measure was not enough. Since "Today the country is faced with a long-run change in trend," [8] what was required was a coordinated government attempt to repair the institutional arrangements which had caused the deficiencies of aggregate demand that in turn generated high unemployment.

Such a programme divided itself into two major sections. The first featured a drastic redistribution of national income. The seven authors argued less from attachment to social justice and more from Keynesian principle. Since the wealthy saved relatively large proportions of their incomes and spent relatively small proportions, funds taken away from them and transferred to the bulk of the population, whose marginal propensity to consume was much higher and whose marginal propensity to save was accordingly much lower, would have the desirable effect of raising consumer expenditure on goods and services and diminishing aggregate saving. If saving was smaller, then full employment was consistent with a lower level of private investment than was necessary before the income redistribution. Since the crux of the problem of stagnation was deficient private investment, income redistribution was a large portion of the effective treatment. And if only the few suffered while the many benefited, surely this was no argument against the proposal.

The poor would gain still more from the complementary proposal of public investment which the Harvard-Tufts group advanced. The principal argument for public investment was the failure of private markets to satisfy urgent public demands. In the words of the manifesto,

> Since private enterprise has been unsuccessful in the provision of new housing for the lower-income families, public agencies must themselves undertake extensive housing construction if the dwelling standards of these families are to be raised. Large public investment in building schools and hospitals will be similarly necessary if the country is to provide itself with more adequate education and health services.[9]

Possibly as a prudential afterthought, the seven economists finally got around to reassuring their readers that their programme was not red socialism, but indeed was designed to "protect private enterprise in the traditional private sector of the economy." [10] Nevertheless, businessmen and other naturally conservative types were unlikely to rejoice at the list of necessities for the preservation of private enterprise. These included a vigorous expansion of the public sector of the economy, sharp increases in the progression of the tax system, indefinite increases in the public debt, enlarge-

[8] Ibid.
[9] Ibid.
[10] Ibid.

ment of old-age benefits, assistance programmes for health and education, and massive commitments to housing and urban development.

All the same the Harvard-Tufts group had done no more than emphasize clearly and firmly the implications of the stagnation doctrine, and economists of their general habit of thought were scattered through the wartime agencies as well as the old-line departments. It was natural for them to become increasingly apprehensive about the future as the war neared its end, since the dangers of stagnation had been postponed and not diminished by the war.

For a time it seemed that every articulate soul in the United States had something to say about the shape of the post-war era and the policies required to make it attractive. When the Pabst Brewing Company organized an essay contest on the topic of post-war employment, it was inundated by 36,000 entries, including contributions from leading economists and social thinkers. The Legislative Reference Service's annotated bibliography of *important* books and articles on employment written between 1943 and 1945 covers fifty-six closely printed pages. Within the government post-war planning was the rage. Projects were undertaken by the Department of Commerce, the Department of Agriculture, the War Production Board, the Public Works Administration, the Maritime Commission, the Defense Plant Corporation, the Bureau of the Budget, the Rural Electrification Administration, the National Housing Agency, the Treasury Department and the State Department — among others. This was a sample, not the complete list.[11]

The agency which had made the most persistent attempt to prepare for the peace was the National Resources Planning Board, which even possessed the temerity to include the word *planning* blatantly in its name. Completely an idea agency, the N.R.P.B. had neither administrative responsibility nor control over the direction of public funds. Possibly for these reasons, it was somewhat freer in its speculations than the more conventional government departments. The price of its freedom was to be high, for in 1943 Congress effectively silenced it by denying it further appropriations.

But not before it produced in March of that year its *magnum opus*, a 400,000-word report on *Security, Work and Relief Policies*. This report was Keynesian in its reasoning, not very distant in its initial assumptions from the Harvard-Tufts group. Like the seven economists, the N.R.P.B. favoured redistributive tax policies, continuing programmes of public works, broadened social security and assault upon monopolies. Their argument bore the marks of Keynesian preferences for the manipulation of aggregate demand, Wisconsin's experiment in the preceding decade with welfare legislation, a Brandeisian suspicion of giant corporations and Harvard fears of stagnation.

[11] On this topic see Stephen Kemp Bailey, *Congress Makes a Law* (New York: Columbia University Press, 1964).

The most striking bit of rhetoric in the long document was a New Bill of Rights, whose nine points made inspiring reading:

> 1. The right to work, usefully and creatively through the productive years.
> 2. The right to fair play, adequate to command the necessities and amenities of life in exchange for work, ideas, thrift and other socially valuable service.
> 3. The right to adequate food, clothing, shelter and medical care.
> 4. The right to security, with freedom from fear of old age, want, dependency, sickness, unemployment and accident.
> 5. The right to live in a system of free enterprise, free from compulsory labour, irresponsible private power, arbitrary public authority and unregulated monopolies.
> 6. The right to come and go, to speak and to be silent, free from the spying of secret police.
> 7. The right to equality before the law, with equal access to justice in fact.
> 8. The right to education for work, for citizenship and for personal growth and happiness.
> 9. The right to rest, recreation and adventure, the opportunity to enjoy and take part in an advancing civilization.[12]

The brew contained echoes of the Rooseveltian Four Freedoms, but the economic ingredients were sufficiently prominent and far-reaching to imply a considerable departure from prior government attitudes.

Liberal reaction was joyous. *The New Republic*'s editors, Bruce Bliven, Max Lerner and George Soule, celebrated the New Bill of Rights in a special eighteen-page section entitled "Charter for America." Emphasizing and reiterating the major propositions of *Security, Work and Relief Policies*, *The New Republic* started from the premise that "No action likely to be taken in the United States in the visible future will do away with long-range unemployment, which will be particularly acute after the war." [13] It adopted a Keynesian analysis of the triumphs and the failures of economic policy during the 1930s:

> During the last depression, the incurring of a public deficit to pay relief was accompanied by a steady increase in the national income from 1933 to 1937. Then social security taxes began, while deficit-financed relief payments fell, so that in 1938 the federal budget was practically in balance. Result − a halt in the growth of the national income; indeed a drop for 1938 and 1939.[14]

In *The New Republic*'s judgement, what was now required included "a permanent policy of large-scale public works," "comparatively heavy taxa-

12 Quoted in ibid.
13 "Charter for America," supplement, *The New Republic*, 19 April 1943.
14 Ibid.

tion emphasizing individual incomes and inheritance," and "effective measures against monopoly." [15] The major belief which permeated *The New Republic*'s reasoning was in a continuity between pre-war and post-war experience. The same trends, especially declining population growth and stronger institutional obstacles to innovation, must be expected to intensify the same problems: inadequate investment, deficient aggregate demand and unbearable rates of unemployment. Therefore, it was none too soon to sketch an American programme far more ambitious than the Beveridge proposals for "cradle to grave" social security which had just emerged in England. Although the editors of *The New Republic*, like the N.R.P.B. in its report, conceded a substantial role to private business, they firmly declared that "It had better be recognized at the very start that the old ideal of laissez-faire is no longer possible. . . . Some sort of planning and control there will have to be, *to an increasing degree*." [16] According to the editors, American choices lay among a corporate economy run by business, full-scale government planning as in the Soviet Union, and cooperation between business and government. On the public's terms the third was infinitely the preferable outcome.

As the prospect of victory brightened, *The New Republic*'s editors and the Keynesians who were its contributors, among them Seymour Harris, Alvin Hansen, Paul Samuelson and Oscar Gass, became increasingly worried about post-war unemployment, the equities of demobilization, the quality of post-war planning and the danger that business could appropriate a disproportionate share of the good things of the peacetime world. Business intentions were much on *The New Republic*'s mind in 1944 and 1945.

Initially, the journal had welcomed a new, liberal business group, the Committee for Economic Development, which had been chartered within ten days of the congressional extermination of the National Resources Planning Board. The magazine applauded the C.E.D.'s promise "to promote and aid planning for high level employment and production by commerce and industry in the post-war period." [17] *The New Republic* also found itself impressed by the C.E.D.'s able research group, which included Theodore Yntema, then of the University of Chicago; Gardiner C. Means, the foe of monopoly; and Howard Myers, formerly of the W.P.A. staff. Suspicion soon replaced approval. Oscar Gass said of the C.E.D.'s 1944 tax programme that "they have written a 'Postwar federal tax program for high employment' that is, in fact, an Intelligent Rich Man's Guide to Profits and Prosperity." [18] Gass found more to approve in the C.E.D.'s willingness to contemplate peacetime federal spending of between $16 and $18 billion annually. Although this was "refreshing," he himself estimated that $25 to $30 billion was a true measure of national need.

[15] Ibid.
[16] Ibid. The italic is added.
[17] *The New Republic*, 26 July 1943.
[18] Oscar Gass, *The New Republic*, 16 October 1944.

The New Republic did not entirely lose hope in the enlightenment of business opinion. It gave space to Macy's ingenious Beardsley Ruml, who went a good distance for a businessman in declaring that "We require for success in the attack by business and government on the danger of mass un-employment a commitment on the part of government that, through an explicit fiscal and monetary policy, it will act when business, as business, can-not act to sustain employment and effective demand." [19] *The New Republic* was happy that a leading businessman had accepted the government's neces-sary role as an agent of full employment. It was much less pleased with Ruml's more conventional business pleas for lower taxes and his wish to limit public works to the stabilization not of the entire economy but of the construction industry only.

Liberal opinion grew increasingly alarmed that the pace of reconversion might cause unemployment to soar once more. Paul Samuelson, in 1944 a Washington official on leave from M.I.T., wrote gloomily about the produc-tion slashes which were planned for the final three months of the year. As Samuelson described the prospect, with V-E Day and the reduction of the war to a single front, this country should "anticipate unemployment or underemployment of around five million men." [20] His Washington col-leagues were amazingly complacent: "The experts have not perceived the magnitude of the storm ahead. The executive branch of the government does not have even a normal year's amount of public works in a processed form ready to go into quick operation." This was all the more a pity be-cause up to this time the economists' role in the national effort had been so valuable: "It has been said that the last war was the chemist's war and that this one is the physicist's. It might equally be said that this is an economist's war." [21] But unless the peace also was directed by sound economic princi-ples, the nation was in for troubled times. Samuelson's concluding summary contained a stern warning:

> Every month, every day, every hour the federal government is pump-ing millions and billions of dollars into the bloodstream of the Ameri-can economy. . . . We have reached the present high levels of output and employment only by means of $100 billion of government ex-penditures, of which $50 billion represents deficits. . . . Any simple statistical calculation will show that the automobile, aircraft, ship-building and electronics industries combined, comprising the fields with the rosiest postwar prospects, cannot possibly maintain their present level of employment or one-half, or one-third of it.[22]

Samuelson properly ranked as only a moderate pessimist. James G. Patton of the liberal National Farmers Union predicted nineteen million unem-ployed unless a bill that he had drawn up was enacted by Congress. Patton's

[19] Beardsley Ruml, *The New Republic*, 28 February 1944.
[20] Paul Samuelson, *The New Republic*, 11 September 1944.
[21] Ibid.
[22] Paul Samuelson, *The New Republic*, 18 September 1944.

plan directed the government to increase its own spending by amounts equal to any decreases in private investment: "The bill I have proposed would call for quarterly adjustment, up or down, of the rate of government invest-ment so that, as private investment decreased, that of the national govern-ment would move in the opposite direction." [23] *The New Republic*'s own programme took serious note of such cries of alarm. Its five points were unusually concrete in presentation:

> 1. Avoid postwar inflation essentially by retaining price controls and rationing, and, if necessary, by extending rationing to additional com-modities;
> 2. Minimize and compensate postwar unemployment by offering more generous unemployment insurance and social security, making retraining programs available, and filling any remaining gaps with construction expenditures;
> 3. Adopt a compensatory fiscal policy for the long term as an anti-stagnationist measure;
> 4. See that big business does not throttle production;
> 5. Back an expanding economy on a worldwide scale.[24]

To *The New Republic*'s Keynesians, the 1945 outlook had in no way improved. At the beginning of the year Seymour Harris wondered, "Are we likely to find profitable investments at the rate of $30 billion (say) a year?" Were consumers dependable? Possibly not: "Consumption expenditures of $115–135 billion which are required at a full-employment income may not be attained." The moral was easy to draw: "Many in Washington will concur that the prospects for a high level of employment are not too bright unless the government is prepared to step in. To many it appears that an investment program of $10–15 billion annually is inevitable." [25] So spoke most liberal economists, social reformers and New Deal Democrats.

As always liberal sentiment was a mixture of attitude, social valuation, political affiliation and legislative proposal. In 1945 liberal opinions of American business were shaped by the disasters of 1929–33, whose causes, in the liberal judgement, were the financial immorality and social irresponsi-bility of stockbrokers, industrialists and plain millionaires. These opinions were solidified by the scurrility of the conservative assault on Franklin Roosevelt, after New Deal policies had checked economic disaster and initiated recovery in sales and profits. Liberal hostility to business was rein-forced by the resistance of some industrialists to wartime arrangements and the desire of some business leaders to reap rapid profits from reconversion. Liberals invariably favoured the "victims" of business selfishness — factory workers and their unions, the indigent elderly, small farmers, and racial

[23] *The New Republic*, 6 November 1944.
[24] "A Program in Brief," *The New Republic*, 27 November 1944.
[25] Seymour Harris, *The New Republic*, 15 January 1945.

minorities denied equal access to jobs by their employers. Within this context of opinion, the Keynesian mechanisms were perceived as the means to income redistribution, larger public investment and public control of private enterprise. In the 1940s Keynesianism and liberalism were very nearly symbiotic. The 1960s were to give a surprising twist to this relationship.

What liberals wanted and needed in 1944 and 1945 was a cause, a legislative embodiment of the apprehensions and the hopes which spurred their discussions. In particular they needed reassurance that the aftermath of the Second World War would be less disruptive than the sharp recession which followed the First World War. As the forecasts came flooding in, predicting anywhere from five million to eleven million unemployed in the spring that followed peace, preventive government action appeared more and more urgent.

An honourable exception to the general pessimism was the late W. S. Woytinsky, who in July, 1944, concluded that the aftermath of the Second World War would differ substantially from its predecessor. The central differences, as Woytinsky accurately foresaw them, were the existence of $250 billion in savings and liquid consumer reserve and a very large volume of long-deferred demand for consumer goods of every variety.[26]

But in general the same economists who had done a competent job of forecasting under controlled wartime conditions did much less well in their sketches of the immediate post-war picture. Indeed, if economic policy had been based literally upon some of the more pessimistic forecasts, the consequence would have been a major post-war inflation.

Why the prognosticators went so badly wrong is a long story, not without a touch of *hubris* in its ramifications. There were, to begin with, far too many uncertainties in the period between V-E Day in May, 1945, and V-J Day in August, 1945 (when many of the forecasts were made), to permit as much dogmatism as the rasher forecasters expressed. No one knew how rapidly military expenditures would be cut back, how many soldiers and sailors would be brought home in what length of time, how tax policy would be revised and how effectively industry could reconvert its machines and factories from wartime production to peacetime output of automobiles, appliances and civilian amenities. And there was only the dimmest awareness of the scale of immediate assistance that our allies and our defeated enemies would require.

Many of the forecasts suffered from significant errors of analysis. These centered upon the consumption function. Before and during the war, Keynesians had been accustomed to relating the consumer spending of a particular period to the disposable income paid out to consumers in that same period. If this rule was extended to the post-war era, it was very natural to

26 W. S. Woytinsky, *The New Republic*, 31 July 1944.

argue that incomes would drop because of sharp curtailments of war production, and that when incomes did drop, consumer expenditure would decline
in the percentage determined by the pre-war value of the marginal propensity to consume. If the M.P.C. was two thirds — a common pre-war estimate
— then a $30 billion drop in income would produce a $20 billion drop in
consumption.

Woytinsky was almost alone in perceiving that there were at least two
other major influences working on consumer behavior. The first was the
tremendous expansion of liquid wealth in the hands of a very large proportion of the community. This was wealth accumulated by workers labouring
long hours at overtime rates, soldiers unable to spend their pay on the barren
islands of the Pacific, wives and mothers who had saved the allotments
which their husbands and sons had directed to them, and citizens of every
category who had responded to patriotic appeals by purchasing over $65
billion of readily negotiable war bonds.

Here was approximately $250 billion readily available, if ordinary Ameri-
cans wanted to spend it. Why should they not have wanted to spend it? The
1930s had been a decade of uncertainty and despair. Many families had run
their cars to the last wheeze, worn their clothes to the last thread, and lived
among increasingly rickety bits and pieces of household furnishings. During
the war they had acquired the means to buy what they had so long deferred,
but the means had been useless. Steel had gone into cannons, not automobiles and electrical appliances. Cloth had gone into uniforms, not civilian
clothing. When the war at last ended, most Americans were eager to gratify
the thwarted tastes of fifteen years.

All that was needed was the goods. And American manufactures poured
out of the factories more rapidly than the wildest optimism had ever contemplated. Reconversion was a matter of months, not of years. The
economists could console themselves later that after a wild buying spree,
consumers did return to a normal relation between income and consumption. Under the circumstances the consolation was slender compensation
for massive error.

The error had at least one additional root. This was the stagnationist
orientation of too many of the analysts. Stagnation had been on their minds,
and no present evidence served to remove it. If disaster is an axiom, it can
scarcely help becoming part of a forecast.[27] It was an axiom reinforced by
historical analogy: if a recession had followed the smaller conflict of the
First World War, a still larger recession ought to succeed the Second World
War — larger in every dimension.

In due time the mistakes of the forecasters became public property and
the occasion for that special glee which accompanies the public discomfiture

---

[27] Sir Roy Harrod has observed that economists are born little inflationists or little
deflationists, and go through their lives fearing the onset of inflation or deflation respectively. For the most part, the Washington forecasters belonged in the second
category.

of any variety of expert. In 1945 these forecasts were taken seriously, for they expressed in deceptively exact terms the post-war economic fears of a good many Americans. Liberals naturally used the forecasts to bolster programmes of public works and social amelioration which they supported on ethical and humanitarian grounds. As for businessmen, many perceived in the cheerless predictions an excellent argument for greater official understanding of the special problems of industry, more favourable tax treatment, generous terms of sale to private buyers of government plants, and elimination of price and rationing controls.

The quest for a legislative cause on the part of liberals and the divided opinions of the business community came to focus on the Full Employment Bill of 1945 as it began its legislative history, and on the Employment Act of 1946 as it terminated that history. The stormy congressional course of this measure accurately measured the powerful economic and ideological interests which clashed over the government's future role in the economy.[28] The record begins on 22 January, 1945, when Senator James E. Murray introduced the full employment measure in the names of Senators Robert Wagner of New York, Elbert Thomas of Utah and Joseph O'Mahoney of Wyoming, as well as his own. The four were possibly the Senate's most effective liberal voices and the sponsors of some of the most significant of the New Deal's legislative projects. From the outset the sponsors endeavoured to broaden support for their project beyond the liberal periodicals and organizations which had long busied themselves with post-war employment. Stephen K. Bailey analyses the bill's friends in these words:

> The proponents of S. 380 were from the beginning conscious of the fact that they had an uphill fight on their hands. The war was still on and public attention was riveted to military news. Labor and liberal organizations, although interested in full employment as a goal, were split on methods and divided among themselves institutionally and power-politically. Opposition to S. 380 was to be expected from a large part of business, conservative farm organizations, to a lesser extent from the old-line veterans' organizations, and strangely enough from an influential left-wing group in the C.I.O. Strategically, therefore, the proponents of the Full Employment Bill had three major jobs on their hands outside of Congress: (1) to arouse public interest, (2) to mobilize and unify the friends of the Full Employment Bill and (3) to split the opposition.[29]

The contrast between the original and the final measure will be made later in some detail. Here it is enough to state the conclusion of the comparison: S. 380 became law only at the price of much of its substance.

[28] Stephen Kemp Bailey's *Congress Makes a Law* is an extremely useful history of the antecedents and history of the Employment Act of 1946. In the pages that follow I have drawn upon it substantially.
[29] Ibid.

How this occurred is a case study in political warfare. Realizing just how hard the fight was, advocates of the bill began to arouse public interest with a barrage of speeches, articles and letter campaigns. They enlisted the Press and radio, and encouraged state legislators to formulate miniature full employment measures of their own. There was also the touchy job of holding liberals in line. Liberal groups tend to be quarrelsome. Their strength is in their capacity to generate fruitful ideas as the basis of public action, but their corresponding weakness is excessive attachment to these same ideas and extreme reluctance to compromise or surrender them in a common effort. Liberals, like the college faculties of which they are often members, too readily translate matters of tactics or detail into issues of principle. A Continuations Group was organized by Senators Murray and Wagner in an attempt to coordinate liberal pressure. The Continuations Group met regularly from June to December, 1945.

Its activities were reasonably successful. The liberals infrequently strayed from the reservation. Even the two quarrelsome organizations of labour unions were persuaded to support the bill instead of automatically choosing opposite sides after their usual fashion. The attempt to split the enemies of the legislation was less effective. The liberal National Farmers Union did indeed militantly favour full employment, a cause that its president had been preaching for years. But the old-line farm organizations were disappointing. The National Grange issued a statement and offered testimony so ambiguous that Congressmen were uncertain whether the organization favoured or opposed the legislation. However, there was no doubt about the powerful American Farm Bureau Federation's stand. From first to last, its representatives opposed the bill.

Business was still more hostile. Although two small groups of businessmen, several individuals and the Committee for Economic Development favoured some sort of legislation, the most powerful business groups, led by the National Association of Manufacturers and the Chamber of Commerce, mounted a militant campaign soon after the Senate passed a version of the bill and the House of Representatives in the autumn of 1945 began its debates. The quality of the business arguments appears in the section headings of a major piece of N.A.M. literature called A *Compilation in Excerpt Form of Statements and Expressions of Views Exposing Inherent Fallacies and Contradictions of the So-called "Full Employment Bill," S. 380,* a descriptive title but surely not one that will live in the annals of literature. The eight section headings were:

> Section 1: The Full Employment Bill (S. 380) Means Government Controls.
> Section 2: The Full Employment Bill (S. 380) Destroys Private Enterprise.
> Section 3: The Full Employment Bill (S. 380) Will Increase the Powers of the Executive.

Section 4: "Full" Employment Guaranteed – Criticisms – Terms.

Section 5: The Full Employment Bill (S. 380) Legalizes a Compensatory Fiscal Policy – Federal Spending and Pump Priming.

Section 6: The Full Employment Bill (S. 380) Leads to Socialism.

Section 7: The Full Employment Bill (S. 380) Is Unworkable, Impractical, and Promises Too Much.

Section 8: The Full Employment Bill (S. 380) – Items for Ridicule.

The faithful reader of this piece of literature would end at least by knowing the bill's legislative number. A sample of "ridicule" can complete the illustration of the business contribution to the public discussion:

> RIDICULE AND LAUGH AT THEM
>
> The Majority Report Observes:
>
> "Witnesses before the subcommittees and correspondents whose letters are in the Record emphasized that the present postwar outlook is *as unstable as our past experience*" (Senate Report on S. 380, p. 2).
>
> What! In the face of the abundant life brought in by the New Deal?
>
> What! After fifteen years of super-efforts of the New Deal for "recovery and reform"?
>
> What! After spending $23 billions of government money in peacetime and over $250 billion in war? [30]

While less ludicrous and virulent in its opposition, the Chamber of Commerce may have been more effective. Its 1,700 local organizations represented a larger number and wider variety of businessmen than the relatively small number of very big industrialists banded together in the N.A.M.'s crusade against the twentieth century.

Although business maintained a very nearly united front, there is question whether business opposition alone could have emasculated the bill. Fighting on business's side was the continuing lack of public interest. The excitement at the termination of the Pacific war took precedence over anything that Congress was doing, certainly including this measure. American support for some legislative action was at best wide but not deep. In 1944, for example, a *Fortune* poll reported that 67.7 per cent of the respondents believed that the federal government should take up the job slack when necessary. Moreover, both political parties, Thomas Dewey's Republicans and Franklin Roosevelt's Democrats, had pledged themselves during the 1944 campaign to all the government action that might be needed to stimulate full employment. Evidently, however, the supporters of S. 380 had not succeeded in making the link between such sentiments and the actual legislation which sought to give them meaning. Public apathy was great. An Illinois poll taken in July of 1945 found that sixty-nine per cent of the voters had never heard of the bill; of those who had heard of it, nineteen per cent

[30] Quoted in *ibid.*

hadn't the slightest idea what it contained, and four per cent had a seriously erroneous opinion of its contents; and only eight per cent both had heard of the measure and held accurate information on its contents.[31] Ignorance and misinformation offered a clear field to business propaganda and the obstructionist talents of conservative members of the House of Representatives.

Even so, this ignorance might have been dispelled as the emotions of V-J Day waned had it not been for the embarrassing buoyancy of the economy. The dire projections of massive unemployment were fulfilled neither after V-E Day nor after V-J Day. Civilian industry proved unexpectedly capable of absorbing hordes of returning veterans and legions of discharged war workers. Given these circumstances, the public, rejoicing at the unexpectedly abrupt conclusion to a long war, might have been forgiven a certain indifference to the fate of a technical piece of legislation on a difficult and complex subject. Possibly the sponsors and the supporters of S. 380 were fortunate to push any bill at all through an increasingly reluctant Congress.

What finally emerged was a very different animal from the depression-eater of 1945. The initial bill boldly used the fearsome words "full employment" in its statement of purpose:

> A BILL to establish a national policy and program for assuring continuing full employment in a free competitive economy, through the concerted efforts of industry, agriculture, labor, State and local governments, and the Federal Government.[32]

In title and underlying thrust, the Murray measure, despite pleasant verbal assurances of devotion to free enterprise, accorded well with the international discussions of full employment, exemplified in England by the Conservative government's White Paper of 1944 and Lord Beveridge's *Full Employment in a Free Society*.

By contrast, consider the Employment Act of 1946's "Declaration of Policy":

> The Congress hereby declares that it is the continuing policy and responsibility of the Federal Government to use all practicable means consistent with its needs and obligations and other essential considerations of national policy with the assistance and cooperation of industry, agriculture, labor, and State and local governments, to coordinate and utilize all its plans, functions, and resources for the purpose of creating and maintaining, in a manner calculated to foster and promote free competitive enterprise and the general welfare, conditions under which there will be afforded useful employment, for those able, will-

---

[31] Ibid.
[32] Ibid.

ing, and seeking work, and to promote maximum employment, production, and purchasing power.[33]

The non-stop sentence pursued a tortuous path to an ambiguous conclusion, that other things equal, the federal government really ought to assist the industrious poor to find jobs, if other national objectives did not interfere. "Full Employment," that phrase of semantic charm, vanished entirely from the title and the declaration of purpose. Also sunk without trace was the notion of right to employment, which in the original draft maintained that "all Americans able to work and seeking work have the right to useful, remunerative, regular and full-time employment, and it is the policy of the United States to assure the existence at all times of sufficient employment opportunities to enable all Americans who have finished schooling and who do not have full-time housekeeping responsibilities freely to exercise this right." [34]

These were only the preliminaries. The original and final drafts differed still more dramatically in their substantive clauses. The framers of S. 380 intended to make the federal government responsible for the preservation of full employment, and if federal spending was needed to fulfil that responsibility, the bill directed federal funds to be spent. Section 2(d) declared it "the responsibility of the Federal Government to pursue such consistent and openly arrived at economic policies and programs as will stimulate and encourage the highest feasible levels of employment opportunities through private and other non-Federal investment and expenditure"; and Section 2(e), hard upon its heels, made it plain that "to the extent that continuing full employment cannot otherwise be achieved, it is the further responsibility of the Federal Government to provide such volume of Federal investment and expenditure as may be needed to assure continuing full employment." [35]

The bill's authors stopped just short of openly accepting deficit spending and deliberately unbalanced budgets, but they deceived no one. Still, such statements might have been discounted as nine parts rhetoric and one part action had it not been for the next major section, entitled "The National Production and Employment Budget." This was the heart of S. 380. This section prescribed a procedure and imposed a new responsibility upon both the President and the Congress.

As usual the section pursued the soothing strategy of starting with the stimulation of increased private investment and employment. But the pieties disposed of, the drafters' attachment to public spending was unmistakable. The section first directed the President to submit a national production and employment budget at the beginning of each congressional

[33] Ibid.
[34] Ibid.
[35] Ibid.

session. For the ensuing fiscal year at least, this budget was to be a forecast of the size of the labour force, private investment, government spending and consumer expenditure. From these forecasts the President was supposed to infer a policy on which he was to base appropriate legislative proposals. In guarded but explicit language, the framers of the bill ordered that

> To the extent, if any, that such increased non-Federal investment and expenditures as may be expected to result from actions taken under the program set forth . . . are deemed insufficient to provide a full employment volume of production, the President shall transmit a general program for such Federal investment and expenditure as will be sufficient to bring the aggregate volume of investment and expenditure by private business, consumers, State and local governments, and the Federal Government, up to the level required to assure a full employment volume of production.[36]

The words were unlikely to cause riots in the streets, but the bill meant business nevertheless. A timetable was set for congressional action whenever the President's national production and employment budget contained a deficit. A new high-level Joint Committee on the National Production and Employment Budget was instructed to report not only its observations on the President's budget but also a general policy which was to guide other congressional committees in their preparation of legislation to ensure full employment.

Whether this mechanism could ever have worked is an open question. Political responsibility was shared between a President responsible for the forecasts and programme and a Congress charged with making its own analyses and legislative proposals. Nor did any possible sanction ensure congressional adherence to the timetable written into the measure. However, at the very least, S.380's friends were offering the voters the right to hold their President and their Congress responsible for unemployment, lagging economic growth and the general malfunction of the economy.

Nothing was plainer than the commitment to Keynesian national income accounting, a Keynesian emphasis upon aggregate demand and Keynesian fiscal policy. Indeed, the commitment was probably excessive. As soon became evident, forecasting in the 1945 state of the art failed to project the movement of the economy with enough precision to define appropriate compensatory action. As far as the legislative prospects of the measure were concerned, it was a misfortune that the doleful predictions of early and mid-1945 were already being disproved by the strength of the economy in the autumn and early winter of the same year. It is even conceivable that Congress did an unwitting service to the reputation of economists by its refusal to retain this key section of the bill.

Whatever Congress's intentions, its surgery was radical. The new law

[36] Ibid.

dropped overboard the entire national production and employment budget. The responsibilities of the President and Congress alike were made much less burdensome. The President was directed to favour Congress within sixty days of its convening with an economic report designed to carry out the extraordinarily vague "Declaration of Policy" (see pp. 512–513) and to provide a general review of economic conditions. Congress graciously extended permission to the President, at his own discretion, to convey to Congress any supplementary reports which he cared to make. All that the law retained of the stellar Joint Committee on the National Production and Employment Budget was the pale shadow of a Joint Committee on the Economic Report. And all that this Committee was enjoined to do was study and assess, not prepare new legislation.

The act also established a new executive instrument, the Council of Economic Advisers, whose "duty" and "function" included advising the President on the preparation of an economic report, collecting current business and economic information, appraising the employment and income activities of other federal agencies, and preparing "national economic policies to foster and promote free competitive enterprise, to avoid economic fluctuations, or to diminish the effects thereof, and to maintain employment, production and purchasing power." [37] Congress had carefully removed the political sting from S. 380's tail. A President was asked only to prepare one more report. Congress was directed to do no more than study it. Neither was compelled to do more than implement a policy so vague that it could be construed to mean almost anything at all.

Who had won? The valiant liberals, who had fought long and hard for full employment legislation and ended with an Employment Act which nowhere used the words "full employment"? Or the National Association of Manufacturers, which had opposed legislation of any kind on this topic? Senator Taft, among other intelligent conservatives, was able to vote for the final measure because the teeth and claws of S. 380 had been removed; Congress's practice of considering economic legislation in its own way and its own time was unimpaired. The national budget and the awesome Joint Committee which was to evaluate it were guillotined. Nobody really had to do much more than he was currently doing. Any rational opponent of S. 380 would have been fully entitled to conclude that he had helped defeat the compensatory spending devices of Keynesians in and out of the administration.

The other side of the case depends upon the importance one gives to symbols and beginnings. However reluctantly and even ambiguously, Congress for the first time had accepted some responsibility for maintaining, if not full employment, at least "high levels of employment." Moreover, the

[37] Ibid.

Council of Economic Advisers and *The Economic Report of the President* were instruments which in the hands of a determined chief executive could be turned into powerful agents of public action. Although S. 380's explicit commitment to public spending and expansionary deficits was sheared away, at the least the President and his Council were not debarred from recommending a compensatory tax or expenditure policy in the name of "high levels of employment." The influence of Arthur F. Burns in the councils of the Eisenhower administration and the role played by Walter W. Heller in the education of President Kennedy both attest to the opportunities that the act opened to astute Chairmen of the Council of Economic Advisers. And at a minimum the existence of the Council hastened the introduction of the Tax Reduction Act of 1964 and facilitated the open declarations of both Presidents Kennedy and Johnson to the principle of deficit financing.

There is a more subtle point. Each national administration since the end of the Second World War has tacitly accepted a vital political proposition: the public will not maintain in office a President and a Congress who permit unemployment to rise very high and last very long. This recognition is far more significant than any possible piece of legislation, for it converts into activists even conservative Presidents and old-fashioned Congressmen. The debate over S. 380 and the Employment Act of 1946 which resulted from it in their way helped to create this political fact of life. In the end it is the electorate and their expectations of action, more than the theories of economists or the personal prejudices of politicians, which determine the shape of national economic policy.

23

BLACK AMERICANS
IN WORLD WAR II

The following article by Richard Dalfiume (Associate Professor of History, SUNY, Binghamton), like the article by Lawrence Levine (see above, pp. 136–156), stresses the all too frequent failure to see the Negro protest movements of the 1950's and 1960's in historical perspective. Although Dalfiume himself focuses upon the "forgotten years" of World War II, which he seems to agree was a watershed in recent Negro history, he is fully aware of earlier developments. As he points out, much of what happened among blacks during World War II had its origins in the experiences of World War I. The high hopes of millions of Negroes who had come to believe in the message of Booker T. Washington that if Negroes showed themselves worthy of freedom they would achieve it, were cruelly disappointed. These crushed expectations led to an inward-turning and a lessened faith in the American dream which, upon further investigation, may well prove that World War I was an even more important turning point than World War II.

It is, of course, fruitless to argue about which "watershed" or "turning point" was more important. It is sufficient to say that no comprehension of black ferment and protest during the past two decades can be complete without an understanding of the impact of both wars upon the Negro population of the United States. In addition to the attitudes and actions discussed by Dalfiume, the wars had crucial demographic effects. They accelerated the mass movement of blacks from country to city and from south to north and in so doing they greatly increased the political power of Negroes. This was already apparent during the New Deal. Negroes tended to benefit from the New Deal not primarily as a race but rather as a class — as part of the one-third of the nation that Roosevelt wanted to rehabilitate. Although Roosevelt denounced lynching and ended segregation in the federal civil service, at no time did he make civil rights part of the New Deal program. Nevertheless, the increased political power of Negroes throughout the 'thirties and the growing amount of grass-roots militance, such as the boycotts of white-owned stores in Chicago, St. Louis, Pittsburgh, Cleveland, and New York which forced the hiring of black employees, led Roosevelt to consult with more Negro leaders, appoint more Negroes to federal office, and pay more attention to Negro political demands than any previous president in Ameri-

..

can history. These were important steps in the process that was to make racial equality part of the reformist movement in the United States for the first time.

Both wars had crucial economic effects upon Negroes as well. At the outset of World War II, for instance, Negroes constituted only 4.4 percent of all skilled workers: by 1945 they constituted 7.3 percent. In semiskilled occupations the number of Negroes increased from 12 percent to 22 percent. The number of Negro women in industry increased from less than 5 percent to over 8 percent. By the end of World War II, then, the stage had been more than amply set for the emergence of the movements and tactics that characterize our own period.

For the depression years, see Leslie H. Fishel, Jr., "The Negro in the New Deal Era," *Wisconsin Magazine of History*, 48 (Winter 1964–65), 111–21; Allan Morrison, "The Secret Papers of FDR," *Negro Digest*, 9 (January 1951), 3–13; Robert Zangrando, "The NAACP and a Federal Anti-Lynching Bill, 1934–1940," *Journal of Negro History*, 50 (April 1946), 106–117; and Wilson Record's two studies: *The Negro and the Communist Party* (1951) and *Race and Radicalism: The NAACP and the Communist Party* (1964). For the World War II years, see Herbert Garfinkel, *When Negroes March: The March on Washington Movement in the Organizational Politics for FEPC* (1959); Ulysses Lee, *United States Army in World War II: The Employment of Negro Troops* (1966); S. Stouffer et al., *The American Soldier: Adjustment During Army Life* (1949), ch. 10; Kenneth B. Clark, "Morale of the Negro on the Home Front: World Wars I and II," *Journal of Negro Education*, 12 (Summer 1943), 417–28; Roi Ottley, 'New World A-Coming' (1943); St. Clair Drake and Horace Cayton, *Black Metropolis* (1945).

The "Forgotten Years"
of the Negro Revolution

RICHARD M. DALFIUME

A recent president of the American Sociological Society addressed himself to a puzzling question about what we know as the Civil Rights Revolution: "Why did social scientists — and sociologists in particular — not foresee the explosion of collective action of Negro Americans toward full integration

Reprinted by permission of the Organization of American Historians from *Journal of American History*, 55 (June 1968), 90–106.

into American society?" He pointed out that "it is the vigor and urgency of the Negro demand that is new, not its direction or supporting ideas." [1] Without arguing the point further, the lack of knowledge can be attributed to two groups — the ahistorical social scientists, and the historians who, until recently, have neglected modern Negro history.

The search for a "watershed" in recent Negro history ends at the years that comprised World War II, 1939–1945. James Baldwin has written of this period: "The treatment accorded the Negro during the Second World War marks, for me, a turning point in the Negro's relation to America. To put it briefly, and somewhat too simply, a certain hope died, a certain respect for white Americans faded." [2] Writing during World War II, Gunnar Myrdal predicted that the war would act as a "stimulant" to Negro protest, and he felt that "There is bound to be a redefinition of the Negro's status in America as a result of this War." [3] The Negro sociologist E. Franklin Frazier states that World War II marked the point where "The Negro was no longer willing to accept discrimination in employment and in housing without protest." [4] Charles E. Silberman writes that the war was a "turning point" in American race relations, in which "the seeds of the protest movements of the 1950s and 1960s were sown." [5] While a few writers have indicated the importance of these years in the recent Negro protest movement, the majority have failed to do so. Overlooking what went before, most recent books on the subject claim that a Negro "revolution" or "revolt" occurred in 1954, 1955, 1960, or 1963. [6] Because of the neglect of the war period, these years of transition in American race relations comprise the "forgotten years" of the Negro revolution.

To understand how the American Negro reacted to World War II, it is necessary to have some idea of the discrimination he faced. The defense build-up begun by the United States in 1940 was welcomed by Negroes who were disproportionately represented among the unemployed. Employment discrimination in the revived industries, however, was rampant. When Negroes sought jobs at aircraft factories where employers begged for workers, they were informed that "the Negro will be considered only as janitors and

---

[1] Everett C. Hughes, "Race Relations and the Sociological Imagination," *American Sociological Review*, XXVIII (Dec. 1963), 879.

[2] Quoted in J. Milton Yinger, *A Minority Group in American Society* (New York, 1965), 52. Many Negroes agreed with James Baldwin in recalling the bitterness they experienced. William Brink and Louis Harris, *The Negro Revolution in America* (New York, 1964), 50.

[3] Gunnar Myrdal, *An American Dilemma: The Negro Problem and Modern Democracy* (New York, 1944), 756, 997.

[4] E. Franklin Frazier, *The Negro in the United States* (rev. ed., New York, 1957), 682.

[5] Charles E. Silberman, *Crisis in Black and White* (New York, 1964), 60, 65.

[6] See, for example, Lewis M. Killian and Charles Grigg, *Racial Crisis in America* (Englewood Cliffs, 1964); Louis E. Lomax, *The Negro Revolt* (New York, 1962); Leonard Broom and Norval D. Glenn, *Transformation of the Negro American* (New York, 1965); Brink and Harris, *Negro Revolution in America*.

in other similar capacities. . . ." [7] Government financed training programs to overcome the shortages of skilled workers discriminated against Negro trainees. When government agencies issued orders against such discrimination, they were ignored.[8]

Increasing defense preparations also meant an expansion of the armed forces. Here, as in industry, however, Negroes faced restrictions. Black Americans were assigned a minimal role and rigidly segregated. In the navy, Negroes could enlist only in the all-Negro messman's branch. The marine and the air corps excluded Negroes entirely. In the army, black Americans were prevented from enlisting, except for a few vacancies in the four regular army Negro units that had been created shortly after the Civil War; and the strength of these had been reduced drastically in the 1920s and 1930s.[9]

Although the most important bread-and-butter issue for Negroes in this period was employment discrimination, their position in the armed forces was an important symbol. If one could not participate fully in the defense of his country, he could not lay claim to the rights of a full-fledged citizen. The NAACP organ, the *Crisis*, expressed this idea in its demand for unrestricted participation in the armed forces: "this is no fight merely to wear a uniform. This is a struggle for status, a struggle to take democracy off of parchment and give it life." [10] Herbert Garfinkel, a student of Negro protest during this period, points out that "in many respects, the discriminatory practices against Negroes which characterized the military programs . . . cut deeper into Negro feelings than did employment discrimination." [11]

Added to the rebuffs from industry and the armed services were a hundred others. Negroes, anxious to contribute to the Red Cross blood program, were turned away. Despite the fact that white and Negro blood is the same biologically, it was deemed inadvisable "to collect and mix caucasian and Negro blood indiscriminately." [12] When Negro citizens called upon the governor of Tennessee to appoint some black members to the state's draft boards, he told them: "This is a white man's country. . . . The

[7] Quoted in Louis Coleridge Kesselman, *The Social Politics of FEPC: A Study in Reform Pressure Movements* (Chapel Hill, 1948), 7.

[8] Charles H. Thompson, "The American Negro and the National Defense," *Journal of Negro Education*, IX (Oct. 1940), 547–52; Frazier, *Negro in the United States*, 599–606; Robert C. Weaver, "Racial Employment Trends in National Defense," *Phylon*, II (4th Quarter, 1941), 337–58.

[9] See Richard M. Dalfiume, "Desegregation of the United States Armed Forces, 1939–1953" (doctoral dissertation, University of Missouri, 1966), 30–57; Ulysses Lee, *United States Army in World War II: Special Studies: The Employment of Negro Troops* (Washington, 1966), 32–87.

[10] "For Manhood in National Defense," *Crisis*, 47 (Dec. 1940), 375.

[11] Herbert Garfinkel, *When Negroes March: The March on Washington Movement in the Organizational Politics for FEPC* (Glencoe, Ill., 1959), 20.

[12] General James C. Magee, Surgeon General, to Assistant Secretary of War John J. McCloy, Sept. 3, 1941, ASW 291.2, Record Group 335 (National Archives); Pittsburgh *Courier*, Jan. 3, 1942.

Negro had nothing to do with the settling of America." [13] At a time when the United States claimed to be the last bulwark of democracy in a war-torn world, the legislature of Mississippi passed a law requiring different text-books for Negro schools: all references to voting, elections, and democracy were to be excluded from the black student's books.[14]

The Negro's morale at the beginning of World War II is also partly explained by his experience in World War I. Black America had gone into that war with high morale, generated by the belief that the democratic slogans literally meant what they said. Most Negroes succumbed to the "close ranks" strategy announced by the crusading NAACP editor, W. E. B. Du Bois, who advocated subduing racial grievances in order to give full support to winning the war. But the image of a new democratic order was smashed by the race riots, lynchings, and continued rigid discrimination. The result was a mass trauma and a series of movements among Negroes in the 1920s which were characterized by a desire to withdraw from a white society which wanted little to do with them. When the war crisis of the 1940s came along, the bitter memories of World War I were recalled with the result that there was a built-in cynicism among Negroes toward the democratic slogans of the new war.[15]

Nevertheless, Negroes were part of the general population being stimulated to come to the defense of democracy in the world. When they responded and attempted to do their share, they were turned away. The result was a widespread feeling of frustration and a general decline of the Negro's morale toward the war effort, as compared with the rest of American society. But paradoxically, the Negro's general morale was both low and high.

While the morale of the Negro, as an American, was low in regard to the war effort, the Negro, as a member of a minority group, had high morale in his heightened race consciousness and determination to fight for a better position in American society. The same slogans which caused the Negro to react cynically also served to emphasize the disparity between the creed and the practice of democracy as far as the Negro in America was concerned. Because of his position in society, the Negro reacted to the war both as an American and as a Negro. Discrimination against him had given rise to "a sickly, negative attitude toward national goals, but at the same time a vibrantly positive attitude toward racial aims and aspirations." [16]

---

[13] Pittsburgh *Courier*, Nov. 2, 1940.

[14] "Text Books in Mississippi," *Opportunity*, XVIII (April 1940), 99.

[15] Kenneth B. Clark, "Morale of the Negro on the Home Front: World Wars I and II," *Journal of Negro Education*, XII (Summer 1943), 417–28; Walter White, " 'It's Our Country, Too': The Negro Demands the Right to be Allowed to Fight for It," *Saturday Evening Post*, 213 (Dec. 14, 1940), 27, 61, 63, 66, 68; Metz T. P. Lochard, "Negroes and Defense," *Nation*, 152 (Jan. 4, 1941), 14–16.

[16] Cornelius L. Golightly, "Negro Higher Education and Democratic Negro Morale," *Journal of Negro Education*, XI (July 1942), 324. See also Horace R. Cayton, "Negro Morale," *Opportunity*, XIX (Dec. 1941), 371–75; Louis Wirth, "Morale and Minority Groups," *American Journal of Sociology*, XLVII (Nov. 1941), 415–33; Kenneth B.

When war broke out in Europe in 1939, many black Americans tended to adopt an isolationist attitude. Those taking this position viewed the war as a "white man's war." George Schuyler, the iconoclastic columnist, was a typical spokesman for this view: "So far as the colored peoples of the earth are concerned," Schuyler wrote, "it is a toss-up between the 'democracies' and the dictatorships. . . . [W]hat is there to choose between the rule of the British in Africa and the rule of the Germans in Austria?" [17] Another Negro columnist claimed that it was a blessing to have war so that whites could "mow one another down" rather than "have them quietly murder hundreds of thousands of Africans, East Indians and Chinese. . . ." [18] This kind of isolation took the form of anti-colonialism, particularly against the British. There was some sympathy for France, however, because of its more liberal treatment of black citizens. [19]

Another spur to isolationist sentiment was the obvious hypocrisy of calling for the defense of democracy abroad while it was not a reality at home. The NAACP bitterly expressed this point:

> THE CRISIS is sorry for brutality, blood, and death among the peoples of Europe, just as we were sorry for China and Ethiopia. But the hysterical cries of the preachers of democracy for Europe leave us cold. We want democracy in Alabama and Arkansas, in Mississippi and Michigan, in the District of Columbia — *in the Senate of the United States.* [20]

The editor of the Pittsburgh *Courier* proclaimed that Negroes had their "own war" at home "against oppression and exploitation from without and against disorganization and lack of confidence within"; and the Chicago *Defender* thought that "peace at home" should be the main concern of black Americans. [21]

Many Negroes agreed with columnist Schuyler that "Our war is not against Hitler in Europe, but against the Hitlers in America." [22] The isolationist view of the war in Europe and the antagonism toward Great Britain led to an attitude that was rather neutral toward the Nazis and the Japanese, or, in some extreme cases, pro-Axis. Appealing to this latent feeling, isolationist periodicals tried to gain Negro support in their struggle against American entrance into the war. [23] By 1940 there were also Negro cults

---

Clark, "Morale Among Negroes," Goodwin Watson, ed., *Civilian Morale* (Boston, 1942), 228–48; Arnold M. Rose, *The Negro's Morale: Group Identification and Protest* (Minneapolis, 1949), 5–7, 54–55, 122–24, 141–44.

[17] Pittsburgh *Courier*, Sept. 9, 1939.

[18] P. L. Prattis in *ibid.*, Sept. 2, 1939. Similar sentiments were expressed by Chicago *Defender* editorials, May 25, June 15, 1940.

[19] Pittsburgh *Courier*, Sept. 9, 16, 1939.

[20] "Lynching and Liberty," *Crisis*, 47 (July 1940), 209.

[21] Pittsburgh *Courier*, Sept. 9, 1939; Chicago *Defender*, May 25, 1940.

[22] Pittsburgh *Courier*, Dec. 21, 1940.

[23] Lee, *The Employment of Negro Troops*, 65–67; Horace Mann Bond, "Should the Negro Care Who Wins the War?" *Annals*, CCXXIII (Sept. 1942), 81–84; Adam

such as the Ethiopian Pacific Movement, the World Wide Friends of Africa, the Brotherhood of Liberty for the Black People of America, and many others, which preached unity among the world's darker people, including Japanese. Many of these groups exploited the latent anti-semitism common among Negroes in the urban ghettos by claiming that the racial policies of Germany were correct.[24]

Reports reached the public that some black Americans were expressing a vicarious pleasure over successes by the "yellow" Japanese and by Germany. In a quarrel with her employer in North Carolina, a Negro woman retorted: "I hope Hitler does come, because if he does he will get you first!" A Negro truck driver in Philadelphia was held on charges of treason after he was accused of telling a Negro soldier that he should not be in uniform and that "This is a white man's government and war and it's no damned good." After Pearl Harbor, a Negro share cropper told his landlord: "By the way, Captain, I hear the Japs done declared war on you white folks." Another Negro declared that he was going to get his eyes slanted so that the next time a white man shoved him around he could fight back.[25]

It is impossible to determine the extent of this kind of pro-Axis sentiment among Negroes, but it was widespread enough for the Negro press to make rather frequent mention of it.[26] In 1942 and 1943 the federal government did arrest the members of several pro-Japanese Negro cults in Chicago, New York, Newark, New Jersey, and East St. Louis, Illinois. Although the numbers involved were small, the evidence indicated that Japanese agents had been at work among these groups and had capitalized on Negro grievances.[27]

By the time of the Pearl Harbor attack, certain fundamental changes were taking place among American Negroes. Nowhere is this more evident than in a comparison of Negroes' reactions to World Wars I and II. The dominant opinion among them toward World War I was expressed by Du Bois. In World War II, most Negroes looked upon the earlier stand as a great mistake. The dominant attitude during World War II was that the Negro must fight for democracy on two fronts — at home as well as

---

Clayton Powell, Jr., "Is This a 'White Man's War'?" *Common Sense*, XI (April 1942), 111–13.

[24] Roi Ottley, "A White Folk's War?" *Common Ground*, II (Spring 1942), 28–31, and '*New World A-Coming*' (Boston, 1943), 322–42; Lunnabelle Wedlock, *The Reaction of Negro Publications and Organizations to German Anti-Semitism* (Washington, 1942), 116–93; Alfred M. Lee, "Subversive Individuals of Minority Status," *Annals*, CCXXIII (Sept. 1942), 167–68.

[25] St. Clair Drake and Horace R. Cayton, *Black Metropolis* (New York, 1945), 744–45; Ottley, '*New World A-Coming*,' 306–10; Horace R. Cayton, "Fighting for White Folks?" *Nation*, 155 (Sept. 26, 1942), 267–70.

[26] "The Negro and Nazism," *Opportunity*, XVIII (July 1940), 194–95; Horace R. Cayton in Pittsburgh *Courier*, Dec. 20, 1941; J. A. Rodgers in *ibid.*, Dec. 27, 1941; Chandler Owen in Norfolk *Journal and Guide*, Dec. 13, 1941; report in Baltimore *Afro-American*, Nov. 21, 1942.

[27] New York *Times*, Sept. 15, 22, 1942, Jan. 14, 28, 1943.

abroad. This opinion had first appeared in reaction to the discriminatory treatment of Negro soldiers; [28] but with the attack on Pearl Harbor, this idea, stated in many different ways, became the slogan of black America.[29]

American Negroes took advantage of the war to tie their racial demands to the ideology for which the war was being fought. Before Pearl Harbor, the Negro press frequently pointed out the similarity of American treatment of Negroes and Nazi Germany's treatment of minorities. In 1940, the Chicago *Defender* featured a mock invasion of the United States by Germany in which the Nazis were victorious because a fifth column of southern senators and other racists aided them.[30] Later the *Crisis* printed an editorial which compared the white supremacy doctrine in America to the Nazi plan for Negroes, a comparison which indicated a marked similarity.[31] Even the periodical of the conservative Urban League made such comparisons.[32]

Many Negroes adopted a paradoxical stand on the meaning of the war. At the same time that it was labeled a "white man's war," Negroes often stated that they were bound to benefit from it. For example, Schuyler could argue that the war was not for democracy, but "Peace means . . . a continuation of the status quo . . . which must be ended if the Negro is to get free." And accordingly, the longer the war the better: "Perhaps in the shuffle we who have been on the bottom of the deck for so long will find ourselves at the top." [33]

Cynicism and hope existed side by side in the Negro mind. Cynicism was often the attitude expressed after some outrageous example of discrimination. After Pearl Harbor, however, a mixture of hope and certainty — great

[28] "Conference Resolutions," *Crisis*, 47 (Sept. 1940), 296; "Where the Negro Stands," *Opportunity*, XIX (April 1941), 98; Lester M. Jones, "The Editorial Policy of Negro Newspapers of 1917–18 as Compared with That of 1941–42," *Journal of Negro History*, XXIX (Jan. 1944), 24–31.

[29] Baltimore *Afro-American*, Dec. 20, 1941, Feb. 7, 1942; Norfolk *Journal and Guide*, March 21, 1942; "Now Is the Time Not to Be Silent," *Crisis*, 49 (Jan. 1942), 7; "The Fate of Democracy," *Opportunity*, XX (Jan. 1942), 2. Two Negro newspapers adopted this theme for their war slogans. The Pittsburgh *Courier*, Feb. 14, 1942, initiated a "Double V" campaign — "victory over our enemies at home and victory over our enemies on the battlefields abroad." When a Negro was brutally lynched in Sikeston, Missouri, a few weeks after Pearl Harbor, the Chicago *Defender*, March 14, 1942, adopted as its war slogan: "Remember Pearl Harbor and Sikeston too." See also Ralph N. Davis, "The Negro Newspapers and the War," *Sociology and Social Research*, XXVII (May–June 1943), 373–80.

[30] Chicago *Defender*, Sept. 25, 1940.

[31] "Nazi Plan for Negroes Copies Southern U.S.A.," *Crisis*, 48 (March 1941), 71.

[32] "American Nazism," *Opportunity*, XIX (Feb. 1941), 35. See also editorials in Pittsburgh *Courier*, March 15, April 19, 26, 1941, May 30, 1942; Chicago *Defender*, Sept. 7, 1940; Norfolk *Journal and Guide*, April 19, 1941; Baltimore *Afro-American*, Feb. 17, 1940, Sept. 6, 1941.

[33] Pittsburgh *Courier*, Oct. 5, 1940; George S. Schuyler, "A Long War Will Aid the Negro," *Crisis*, 50 (Nov. 1943), 328–29, 344. See also J. A. Rodgers in Pittsburgh *Courier*, June 28, 1941; Horace R. Cayton in *ibid.*, March 22, 1941; Baltimore *Afro-American*, Sept. 12, 16, 1939; Guion Griffis Johnson, "The Impact of War Upon the Negro," *Journal of Negro Education*, X (July 1941), 596–611.

changes favorable to the Negro would result from the war and things would never be the same again — became the dominant attitude. Hope was evident in the growing realization that the war provided the Negro with an excellent opportunity to prick the conscience of white America. "What an opportunity the crisis has been . . . for one to persuade, embarrass, compel and shame our government and our nation . . . into a more enlightened attitude toward a tenth of its people!" the Pittsburgh *Courier* proclaimed.[34] Certainty that a better life would result from the war was based on the belief that revolutionary forces had been released throughout the world. It was no longer a "white man's world," and the "myth of white invincibility" had been shattered for good.[35]

There was a growing protest against the racial status quo by black Americans; this was evidenced by the reevaluation of segregation in all sections of the country. In the North there was self-criticism of past acceptance of certain forms of segregation.[36] Southern Negroes became bolder in openly questioning the sacredness of segregation. In October 1942, a group of southern Negro leaders met in Durham, North Carolina, and issued a statement on race relations. In addition to endorsing the idea that the Negro should fight for democracy at home as well as abroad, these leaders called for complete equality for the Negro in American life. While recognizing the "strength and age" of the South's racial customs, the Durham meeting was "fundamentally opposed to the principle and practice of compulsory segregation in our American society." In addition, there were reports of deep discontent among southern Negro college students and evidence that political activity among the blacks of the South, particularly on the local level, was increasing.[37]

The American Negro, stimulated by the democratic ideology of the war,

[34] Pittsburgh *Courier*, Jan. 10, Aug. 8, 1942. Charles S. Johnson, "The Negro and the Present Crisis," *Journal of Negro Education*, X (July 1941), 585–95. Opinion surveys indicated that most Negro soldiers expressed support for this kind of opportunism. Samuel A. Stouffer and others, *The American Soldier* (2 vols., Princeton, 1949), I, 516–17.

[35] Baltimore *Afro-American*, June 12, Oct. 31, 1942; Walter White in Pittsburgh *Courier*, May 23, 1942. The impact of world affairs on the American Negro is detailed in Harold R. Isaacs, *The New World of Negro Americans* (New York, 1963).

[36] See editorials in Pittsburgh *Courier*, Dec. 28, 1940; Feb. 1, June 28, 1941; May 30, 1942; Baltimore *Afro-American*, May 23, 1942.

[37] Charles S. Johnson, *To Stem This Tide* (Boston, 1943), 131–39; Malcolm S. MacLean, president of Hampton Institute, to Marvin H. McIntyre, Nov. 20, 1942, OF 93, Roosevelt Papers (Franklin D. Roosevelt Library, Hyde Park); George B. Tindall, "The Significance of Howard W. Odum to Southern History: A Preliminary Estimate," *Journal of Southern History*, XXIV (Aug. 1958), 302. Anthropologist Hortense Powdermaker, *After Freedom: A Cultural Study of the Deep South* (New York, 1939), 331–33, 353, supports the observations of a tendency to rebel among the younger Negroes of the South. See also Ralph J. Bunche, "The Negro in the Political Life of the United States," *Journal of Negro Education*, X (July 1941), 567–84; Myrdal, *American Dilemma*, 499; Henry Lee Moon, *Balance of Power: The Negro Vote* (Garden City, 1948), 178–79.

was reexamining his position in American society. "It cannot be doubted that the spirit of American Negroes in all classes is different today from what it was a generation ago," Myrdal observed.[38] Part of this new spirit was an increased militancy, a readiness to protest loud and strong against grievances. The crisis gave Negroes more reason and opportunity to protest. Representative of all of the trends of black thought and action — the cynicism, the hope, the heightened race consciousness, the militancy — was the March on Washington Movement (MOWM).

The general idea of exerting mass pressure upon the government to end defense discrimination did not originate with A. Philip Randolph's call for a march on Washington, D.C., in early 1941.[39] Agitation for mass pressure had grown since the failure of a group of Negro leaders to gain any major concessions from President Franklin D. Roosevelt in September 1940.[40] Various organizations, such as the NAACP, the Committee for Participation of Negroes in the National Defense, and the Allied Committees on National Defense, held mass protest meetings around the country in late 1940 and early 1941.[41] The weeks passed and these efforts did not seem to have any appreciable impact on the government; Walter White, Randolph, and other Negro leaders could not even secure an appointment to see the President. "Bitterness grew at an alarming pace throughout the country," White recalled.[42]

It remained, however, for Randolph to consolidate this protest. In January 1941, he wrote an article for the Negro press which pointed out the failure of committees and individuals to achieve action against defense discrimination. "Only power can effect the enforcement and adoption of a given policy," Randolph noted; and "Power is the active principle of only the organized masses, the masses united for a definite purpose." To focus the weight of the black masses, he suggested that 10,000 Negroes march on Washington, D.C., with the slogan: "We loyal Negro-American citizens demand the right to work and fight for our country." [43]

This march appeal led to the formation of one of the most significant — though today almost forgotten — Negro protest movements. The MOWM pioneered what has become the common denominator of today's Negro revolt — "the spontaneous involvement of large masses of Negroes in a political protest." [44] Furthermore, as August Meier and Elliott Rudwick have recently pointed out, the MOWM clearly foreshadowed "the goals, tactics,

[38] Myrdal, *American Dilemma*, 744.

[39] Garfinkel, *When Negroes March*, fails to emphasize this point.

[40] Walter White, *A Man Called White* (New York, 1948), 186–87; "White House Blesses Jim Crow," *Crisis*, 47 (Nov. 1940), 350–51, 357; Dalfiume, "Desegregation of the United States Armed Forces, 1939–1953," 46–51.

[41] Pittsburgh *Courier*, Dec. 7, 14, 21, 1940; Jan. 4, 25, Feb. 8, 1941.

[42] White, *A Man Called White*, 189–90.

[43] Pittsburgh *Courier*, Jan. 25, 1941.

[44] Garfinkel, *When Negroes March*, 8.

and strategy of the mid-twentieth-century civil rights movement." Whites were excluded purposely to make it an all-Negro movement; its main weapon was direct action on the part of the black masses. Furthermore, the MOWM took as its major concern the economic problems of urban slum-dwellers.[45]

Randolph's tactic of mass pressure through a demonstration of black power struck a response among the Negro masses. The number to march on Washington on July 1, 1941, was increased to 50,000, and only Roosevelt's agreement to issue an executive order establishing a President's Committee on Fair Employment Practices led to a cancellation of the march. Negroes then, and scholars later, generally interpreted this as a great victory. But the magnitude of the victory is diminished when one examines the original MOWM demands: an executive order forbidding government contracts to be awarded to a firm which practiced discrimination in hiring, an executive order abolishing discrimination in government defense training courses, an executive order requiring the United States Employment Service to supply workers without regard to race, an executive order abolishing segregation in the armed forces, an executive order abolishing discrimination and segregation on account of race in all departments of the federal government, and a request from the President to Congress to pass a law forbidding benefits of the National Labor Relations Act to unions denying Negroes membership. Regardless of the extent of the success of the MOWM, however, it represented something different in black protest. Unlike the older Negro movements, the MOWM had captured the imagination of the masses.[46]

Although overlooked by most recent writers on civil rights, a mass militancy became characteristic of the American Negro in World War II. This was symbolized by the MOWM and was the reason for its wide appeal. Furthermore, older Negro organizations found themselves pushed into militant stands. For example, the NAACP underwent a tremendous growth in its membership and became representative of the Negro masses for the first time in its history. From 355 branches and a membership of 50,556 in

[45] August Meier and Elliott M. Rudwick, *From Plantation to Ghetto: An Interpretative History of American Negroes* (New York, 1966), 222.

[46] "Proposals of the Negro March-On-Washington Committee to President Roosevelt for Urgent Consideration," June 21, 1941, OF 391, Roosevelt Papers. The standard versions of a Negro "victory" are Garfinkel, *When Negroes March*; Kesselman, *The Social Politics of FEPC*; and Louis Ruchames, *Race, Jobs, & Politics: The Story of FEPC* (New York, 1953). For a different interpretation, see Dalfiume, "Desegregation of the United States Armed Forces, 1939–1953," 172–77. The Negro press generally recognized that the MOWM represented something new. The Pittsburgh *Courier*, July 5, 1941, claimed: "We begin to feel at last that the day when we shall gain full rights . . . of American citizenship is now not far distant." The Chicago *Defender*, June 28, July 12, 1941, felt that the white man will be convinced that "the American black man has decided henceforth and forever to abandon the timid role of Uncle-Tomism in his struggle. . . ." The tactics of the MOWM had "demonstrated to the doubting Thomases among us that only mass action can pry open the iron doors that have been erected against America's black minority."

1940, the NAACP grew to 1,073 branches with a membership of slightly less than 450,000 in 1946.[47] The editors of the Pittsburgh *Courier* recognized that a new spirit was present in black America. In the past, Negroes

> made the mistake of relying entirely upon the gratitude and sense of fair play of the American people. Now we are disillusioned. We have neither faith in promises, nor a high opinion of the integrity of the American people, where race is involved. Experience has taught us that we must rely primarily upon our own efforts. . . . That is why we protest, agitate, and demand that all forms of color prejudice be blotted out. . . .[48]

By the time of the Japanese attack on Pearl Harbor, many in America, both inside and outside of the government, were worried over the state of Negro morale. There was fear that the Negro would be disloyal.[49] The depth of white ignorance about the causes for the Negro's cynicism and low morale is obvious from the fact that the black press was blamed for the widespread discontent. The double victory attitude constantly displayed in Negro newspapers throughout the war, and supported by most black Americans, was considered as verging on disloyalty by most whites. White America, ignorant of the American Negroes' reaction to World War I, thought that black citizens should subdue their grievances for the duration.

During World War II, there was pressure upon the White House and the justice department from within the federal government to indict some Negro editors for sedition and interference with the war effort. President

[47] Frazier, *The Negro in the United States*, 537; Charles Radford Lawrence, "Negro Organizations in Crisis: Depression, New Deal, World War II (doctoral dissertation, Columbia University, 1953), 103; Myrdal, *American Dilemma*, 851–52. Such close observers of American race relations as Will Alexander, Edwin Embree, and Charles S. Johnson recognized the changing character of Negro protest. They believed that "the characteristic movements among Negroes are now for the first time becoming proletarian, as contrasted to upper class or intellectual influence that was typical of previous movements. The present proletarian direction grows out of the increasing general feelings of protest against discrimination, especially in the armed forces and in our war activities generally. The present movements are led in part by such established leaders as A. Philip Randolph, Walter White, etc. There is likelihood (and danger) that the movement may be seized upon by some much more picturesque figure who may be less responsible and less interested in actual improvement of conditions. One of the most likely of the potential leaders is A. Clayton Powell, Jr." Memorandum of Conferences of Alexander, Johnson, and Embree on the Rosenwald Fund's Program in Race Relations, June 27, 1942, Race Relations folder, Rosenwald Fund Papers (Fisk University).

[48] Pittsburgh *Courier*, Sept. 12, 1942. See also Roscoe E. Lewis, "The Role of Pressure Groups in Maintaining Morale Among Negroes," *Journal of Negro Education*, XII (Summer 1943), 464–73; Earl Brown, "American Negroes and the War," *Harper's Magazine*, 184 (April 1942), 545–52; Roi Ottley, "Negro Morale," *New Republic*, 105 (Nov. 10, 1941), 613–15; Thomas Sancton, "Something's Happened to the Negro," *New Republic*, 108 (Feb. 8, 1943), 175–79; Stanley High, "How the Negro Fights for Freedom," *Reader's Digest*, 41 (July 1942), 113–18; H. C. Brearley, "The Negro's New Belligerency," *Phylon*, V (4th Quarter 1944), 339–45.

[49] Memorandum to Assistant Secretary of War McCloy from G-2, June 27, 1942, ASW 291.2, Record Group 335.

Roosevelt refused to sanction this, however. There was also an attempt to deny newsprint to the more militant Negro newspapers, but the President put an end to this when the matter was brought to his attention.[50] The restriction of Negro newspapers from military installations became so widespread that the war department had to call a halt to this practice in 1943.[51] These critics failed to realize that, although serving to unify black opinion, the Negro press simply reflected the Negro mind.

One of the most widely publicized attacks on the Negro press was made by the southern white liberal, Virginius Dabney, editor of the Richmond *Times Dispatch*. He charged that "extremist" Negro newspapers and Negro leaders were "demanding an overnight revolution in race relations," and as a consequence they were "stirring up interracial hate." Dabney concluded Norfolk *Journal and Guide* claimed they were created by the "nothing-attempt is made forcibly to abolish segregation throughout the South, violence and bloodshed will result." [52] The Negro press reacted vigorously to such charges. Admitting that there were "all-or-nothing" Negro leaders, the Norfolk *Journal and Guide* claimed they were created by the "northing-at-all" attitude of whites.[53] The Chicago *Defender* and Baltimore *Afro-American* took the position that they were only pointing out the shortcomings of American democracy, and this was certainly not disloyal.[54] The NAACP and the Urban League claimed that it was patriotic for Negroes to protest against undemocratic practices, and those who sought to stifle this protest were the unpatriotic ones.[55]

[50] White, *A Man Called White*, 207–08; R. Keith Kane to Ulric Bell, May 14, 1942, OFF 992.11, Record Group 208; Memorandum to Robert A. Lovett from McCloy, March 6, 1942, ASW 291.2, Record Group 335.

[51] Baltimore *Afro-American*, Sept. 30, 1941; Pittsburgh *Courier*, March 8, 1941, Nov. 13, 1943. Assistant Secretary of War McCloy, who was also head of the war department's Advisory Committee on Negro Troop Policies, held a critical view of the Negro press that was common in the army. McCloy to Herbert Elliston, editor of the Washington *Post*, Aug. 5, 1943, ASW 292.2, Record Group 335.

[52] Virginius Dabney, "Nearer and Nearer the Precipice," *Atlantic Monthly*, 171 (Jan. 1943), 94–100; Virginius Dabney, "Press and Morale," *Saturday Review of Literature*, XXV (July 4, 1942), 5–6, 24–25.

[53] Norfolk *Journal and Guide*, Aug. 15, 1942. See also *Journal and Guide* editorials of Oct. 17, April 25, 1942; and March 6, 1943, for a defense of Negro militancy.

[54] Chicago *Defender*, Dec. 20, 1941; Baltimore *Afro-American*, Jan. 9, 1943.

[55] Pittsburgh *Courier*, May 8, June 19, 1943. A few conservative Negroes joined whites in criticizing the growing militancy. James E. Shepard, Negro president of North Carolina College for Negroes, asked the administration to do something to undercut the growing support of the militants among young Negroes: "Those who seek to stir them up about rights and not duties are their enemies." Shepard to Secretary of the Navy Frank Knox, Sept. 28, 1940, OF 93, Roosevelt Papers. Frederick D. Patterson, president of Tuskegee Institute, made it clear in his newspaper column and in talks with administration officials that he believed in all-out support for the war effort by Negroes regardless of segregation and discrimination. "Stimson Diary," Jan. 29, 1943 (Yale University Library), and columns by Patterson in the Pittsburgh *Courier*, Jan. 16, July 3, 1943. Such conservatives were bitterly attacked in the Negro press. The black leader who urged his people to relax their determination to win full participation in American life was a "misleader and a false prophet," the Norfolk *Journal and Guide*, May 2,

The Negro masses simply did not support a strategy of moderating their grievances for the duration of the war. After attending an Office of Facts and Figures conference for Negro leaders in March 1942, Roy Wilkins of the NAACP wrote:

> . . . it is a plain fact that no Negro leader with a constituency can face his members today and ask full support for the war in the light of the atmosphere the government has created. Some Negro educators who are responsible only to their boards or trustees might do so, but the heads of no organized groups would dare do so.[56]

By 1942, the federal government began investigating Negro morale in order to find out what could be done to improve it. This project was undertaken by the Office of Facts and Figures and its successor, the Office of War Information.[57] Surveys by these agencies indicated that the great amount of national publicity given the defense program only served to increase the Negro's awareness that he was not participating fully in that program. Black Americans found it increasingly difficult to reconcile their treatment with the announced war aims. Urban Negroes were the most resentful over defense discrimination, particularly against the treatment accorded black members of the armed forces. Never before had Negroes been so united behind a cause: the war had served to focus their attention on their unequal status in American society. Black Americans were almost unanimous in wanting a show of good intention from the federal government that changes would be made in the racial status quo.[58]

The government's inclination to take steps to improve Negro morale, and the Negro's desire for change, were frustrated by the general attitude of white Americans. In 1942, after two years of militant agitation by Ne-

---

1942, proclaimed. Such people "endangered" the interests of Negroes by "compromising with the forces that promote and uphold segregation and discrimination," wrote the editor of the Chicago *Defender*, April 5, 1941. The *Crisis* charged that those Negroes who succumbed to segregation as "realism" provided a rationale for those whites who sought to perpetuate segregation. "Government Blesses Separatism," *Crisis*, 50 (April 1943), 105.

[56] Memorandum to White from Roy Wilkins, March 24, 1942, Stephen J. Spingarn Papers (Harry S Truman Library, Independence).

[57] Memorandum to Archibald MacLeish from Kane, Feb. 14, 1942; Bell to Embree, Feb. 23, 1942, OFF 002.11, Record Group 208. Some government agencies displayed timidity when it came to a subject as controversial as the race question. Jonathan Daniels, Assistant Director in Charge of Civilian Mobilization, Office of Civilian Defense, urged the creation of a Division of American Unity within the OCD, but his superiors decided Negro morale was "too hot a potato." Memoranda to James Landis, April 1, 7, 1942; Daniels to Howard W. Odum, Aug. 24, 1942, Jonathan Daniels Papers (University of North Carolina).

[58] "Reports from the Special Services Division Submitted April 23, 1942: Negro Organizations and the War Effort"; Cornelius Golightly, "Negro Morale in Boston," Special Services Division Report No. 7, May 19, 1942; Special Services Division Report No. 5, May 15, 1942: "Negro Conference at Lincoln University"; Special Services Division Memorandum, "Report on Recent Factors Increasing Negro-White Tension," Nov. 2, 1942. All are in OFF and OWI files in Record Group 44.

groes, six out of ten white Americans felt that black Americans were satisfied with things the way they were and that Negroes were receiving all of the opportunities they deserved. More than half of all whites interviewed in the Northwest and West believed that there should be separate schools, separate restaurants, and separate neighborhoods for the races. A majority of whites in all parts of the country believed that the Negro would not be treated any better after the war than in 1942 and that the Negro's lesser role in society was due to his own shortcomings rather than anything the whites had done.[59] The white opposition to racial change may have provided the rationale for governmental inactivity. Furthermore, the white obstinance must have added to the bitterness of black Americans.

Although few people recognized it, the war was working a revolution in American race relations. Sociologist Robert E. Park felt that the racial structure of society was "cracking," and the equilibrium reached after the Civil War seemed "to be under attack at a time and under conditions when it is particularly difficult to defend it." [60] Sociologist Howard W. Odum wrote from the South that there was "an unmeasurable and unbridgeable distance between the white South and the reasonable expectation of the Negro." [61] White southerners opposed to change in the racial mores sensed changes occurring among "their" Negroes. "Outsiders" from the North, Mrs. Franklin Roosevelt, and the Roosevelt Administration were all accused of attempting to undermine segregation under the pretense of wartime necessity.[62]

Racial tensions were common in all sections of the country during the war.[63] There were riots in 1943. Tensions were high because Negro Americans were challenging the status quo. When fourteen prominent Negroes, conservatives and liberals, southerners and northerners, were asked in 1944 what they thought the black American wanted, their responses were almost unanimous. Twelve of the fourteen said they thought that Negroes wanted full political equality, economic equality, equality of opportunity, and full social equality with the abolition of legal segregation.[64] The war had stimulated the race consciousness and the desire for change among Negroes.

Most American Negroes and their leaders wanted the government to in-

[59] "Intelligence Report: White Attitudes Toward Negroes," OWI, Bureau of Intelligence, Aug. 5, 1942; same title dated July 28, 1942, Record Group 44. Hazel Gaudet Erskine, "The Polls: Race Relations," *Public Opinion Quarterly*, XXVI (Spring 1962), 137–48.

[60] Robert E. Park, "Racial Ideologies," William Fielding Ogburn, ed., *American Society In Wartime* (Chicago, 1943), 174.

[61] Howard W. Odum, *Race and Rumors of Race: Challenge to American Crisis* (Chapel Hill, 1943), 7; for a similar view, see Johnson, *To Stem This Tide*, 67–68, 73, 89–107, 113, 117.

[62] John Temple Graves, "The Southern Negro and the War Crisis," *Virginia Quarterly Review*, 18 (Autumn 1942), 500–17; Clark Foreman, "Race Tension in the South," *New Republic*, 107 (Sept. 21, 1942), 340–42.

[63] Alfred McClung Lee and Norman Daymond Humphrey, *Race Riot* (New York, 1943); Carey McWilliams, "Race Tensions: Second Phase," *Common Ground*, IV (Autumn 1943), 7–12.

[64] Rayford W. Logan, ed., *What the Negro Wants* (Chapel Hill, 1944).

stitute a revolutionary change in its race policy. Whereas the policy had been acquiescence in segregation since the end of Reconstruction, the government was now asked to set the example for the rest of the nation by supporting integration. This was the demand voiced by the great majority of the Negro leaders called together in March 1942 by the Office of Facts and Figures.[65] *Crisis* magazine summarized the feelings of many black Americans: Negroes have "waited thus far in vain for some sharp and dramatic notice that this war is not to maintain the status quo here." [66]

The White House, and it was not alone, failed to respond to the revolutionary changes occurring among the nation's largest minority. When the Fraternal Council of Negro Churches called upon President Roosevelt to end discrimination in the defense industries and armed forces, the position taken was that "it would be very bad to give encouragement beyond the point where actual results can be accomplished." [67] Roosevelt did bestir himself over particularly outrageous incidents. When Roland Hayes, a noted Negro singer, was beaten and jailed in a Georgia town, the President dashed off a note to his attorney general: "Will you have someone go down and check up . . . and see if any law was violated. I suggest you send a northerner." [68]

Roosevelt was not enthusiastic about major steps in the race relations field proposed by interested individuals within and without the government.[69] In February 1942 Edwin R. Embree of the Julius Rosenwald Fund, acutely aware of the growing crisis in American race relations, urged Roosevelt to create a commission of experts on race relations to advise him on what steps the government should take to improve matters. FDR's answer to this proposal indicates that he felt race relations was one of the reform areas that had to be sacrificed for the present in order to prosecute the war. He thought

[65] Memorandum to White from Wilkins, March 23, 1942, Spingarn Papers; Pittsburgh *Courier*, March 28, 1942; Norfolk *Journal and Guide*, March 28, 1942.

[66] "U. S. A. Needs Sharp Break With the Past," *Crisis*, 49 (May 1942), 151.

[67] "A Statement to the President of the United States Concerning the Present World Crisis by Negro Church Leaders Called by the Executive Committee of the Fraternal Council of Negro Churches of America," Feb. 17, 1942; McIntyre to MacLean, Chairman of the President's Committee on Fair Employment Practice, Feb. 19, 1942, OF 93, Roosevelt Papers.

[68] Memorandum to the Attorney General from the President, Aug. 26, 1942, OF 93, *ibid.*

[69] Franklin Roosevelt's conservative and "leave well enough alone" attitude toward Negro rights is discussed in Arthur M. Schlesinger, Jr., *The Age of Roosevelt: The Politics of Upheaval* (Boston, 1960), 431; Frank Freidel, *F. D. R. and the South* (Baton Rouge, 1965), 73, 81, 97; Mary McLeod Bethune, "My Secret Talks with F. D. R.," *Ebony*, IV (April 1949), 42–51. Perhaps Roosevelt's conservative attitude is responsible for his privately expressed dislike of the NAACP. In 1943 Arthur B. Spingarn, president of the NAACP, asked him to write a letter praising the twenty-five years of service by White to that organization. On one version of the proposed letter there is an attached note which reads: "Miss Tully brought this in. Says the President doesn't think too much of this organization — not to be to[o] fullsome — tone it down a bit." Roosevelt to Spingarn, Oct. 1, 1943, PPF 1226, Roosevelt Papers.

such a commission was "premature" and that "we must start winning the war . . . before we do much general planning for the future." The President believed that "there is a danger of such long-range planning becoming projects of wide influence in escape from the realities of war. I am not convinced that we can be realists about the war and planners for the future at this critical time." [70]

After the race riots of 1943, numerous proposals for a national committee on race relations were put forward; but FDR refused to change his position. Instead, the President simply appointed Jonathan Daniels to gather information from all government departments on current race tensions and what they were doing to combat them.[71] This suggestion for what would eventually become a President's Committee on Civil Rights would have to wait until a President recognized that a revolution in race relations was occurring and that action by the government could no longer be put off. In the in-

[70] Roosevelt to Embree, March 16, 1942, in answer to Embree to Roosevelt, Feb. 3, 1942, OF 93, Roosevelt Papers. In his covering letter to the President's secretary, Embree emphasized that his proposed commission should address itself to the problem of race around the world as well as at home: "A serious weakness both in America and among the united nations is the low morale of the 'colored peoples' to whom this war is being pictured as simply another struggle of the white man for domination of the world. This condition is becoming acute among the Negro group at home and among important allies abroad, especially the Chinese and the residents of Malaya, the East Indies, and the Philippines." Embree to McIntyre, Feb. 3, 1942, Commission on Race and Color folder, Rosenwald Fund Papers.

[71] In June 1943, Embree and John Collier, Commissioner of Indian Affairs, developed an idea for a committee established by the President "to assume special responsibility in implementing the Bill of Rights of the Constitution, particularly in defending racial minorities at a time of crisis." Memorandum to Johnson and Alexander from Embree, June 16, 1943, Race Relations folder, Rosenwald Fund Papers. See also John Collier and Saul K. Padover, "An Institute for Ethnic Democracy," *Common Ground*, IV (Autumn 1943), 3–7, for a more elaborate proposal.

Embree probably passed along his idea to Odum of the University of North Carolina so that he could discuss it with a fellow North Carolinian in the White House, Daniels, administrative assistant to the President. Odum and Daniels had a conference in August 1943 from which emerged a recommendation for a "President's Committee on Race and Minority Groups." Odum to Daniels, Aug. 23, 1943; Memorandum to Daniels from Odum, Aug. 30, 1943, Howard W. Odum Papers (University of North Carolina).

Although Daniels apparently gave Odum the impression that he was interested in a national committee, this was not the case. "It has been suggested that a committee of prominent men be named to study this situation," he wrote the President. "I am sure the naming of such a committee would not now halt the procession of angry outbreaks which are occurring. I doubt that any report could be made which would be so effective as a statement now from you would be. I am very much afraid, indeed, that any committee report would only serve as a new ground for controversy." Memorandum to the President from Daniels, Aug. 2, 1943, Daniels Papers. Roosevelt apparently agreed with Daniels, and Odum was informed that "My boss does not think well of the idea that we discussed." Daniels to Odum, Sept. 1, 1943, Odum Papers.

Daniels' appointment as White House coordinator of information on race relations was actually suggested by him to the President in June 1943. Memorandum to the President from Daniels, June 29, 1943, Daniels Papers. By July 1943, Roosevelt had approved of the new role for his administrative assistant, and Daniels was hard at work gathering information. Daniels to Secretary of War Stimson, July 28, 1943, ASW 291.2, Record Group 335.

terim, many would share the shallow reasoning of Secretary of War Stimson that the cause of racial tension was "the deliberate effort . . . on the part of certain radical leaders of the colored race to use the war for obtaining . . . race equality and interracial marriages. . . ." [72]

The hypocrisy and paradox involved in fighting a world war for the four freedoms and against aggression by an enemy preaching a master race ideology, while at the same time upholding racial segregation and white supremacy, were too obvious. The war crisis provided American Negroes with a unique opportunity to point out, for all to see, the difference between the American creed and practice. The democratic ideology and rhetoric with which the war was fought stimulated a sense of hope and certainty in black Americans that the old race structure was destroyed forever. In part, this confidence was also the result of the mass militancy and race consciousness that developed in these years. When the expected white acquiescence in a new racial order did not occur, the ground was prepared for the civil rights revolution of the 1950s and 1960s; the seeds were indeed sown in the World War II years.

[72] "Stimson Diary," June 24, 1943.

24

THE RISE OF CIVIL RIGHTS

For most Americans who were of political age during the Truman Era, the fight for civil rights launched by the national leaders of the Democratic party stood — and perhaps still stands — as one of the outstanding events of Truman's second administration. In the perspective of twenty years, however, with all that has happened since the Supreme Court's (post-Truman) school desegregation decision, it has come to seem, to many, a very poor beginning indeed. In the following article, Professor Barton Bernstein of Stanford University, one of the country's leading Truman scholars, details the severe limits of Truman's civil rights commitment. For those who would complain that the country has been moving "too fast" in the direction of meeting its own avowed standards on equality, Bernstein reveals just how slow, just how reluctant, and even how disingenuous much of this "movement" has been. The uncertain beginning may help us to understand why twenty years and four presidential administrations later, full equality remains an elusive goal.

In another respect, though, American society *has* moved fast. Even for many Americans over forty it must now appear astounding that the nation's leaders could have been so obtuse, and the leaders of the black community so acquiescent, about the hideous political, economic, and social penalties officially sanctioned and even inflicted by law upon nonwhite American citizens scarcely a quarter-century ago. To notice this is to begin to appreciate the distance between the tenets of thought of the 1940's and those of the 1960's. In a way, Bernstein misses a marvelous historiographical opportunity to highlight the distinctiveness of different eras. For, one of the key points about historical change is the way in which it presents the same phenomena to a given society on a radically different scale of importance. For example, it may well be another measure of Truman's insensitivity that inflation, foreign policy, and labor unions placed higher among his administration's priorities than the oppression of black Americans, but only when we note that fact can we readily understand why the small gains made for civil rights seemed so impressive at the time. To neglect the context within which the civil rights issue began its slow progress *toward* the center of the political stage is to contribute to a misreading of contemporary motivations. It is one thing to point out the limits of the contemporary imagination on what was socially and politically possible; but it is redundant to find contemporaries culpable because their proposals failed to go beyond those limits.

536   *The Rise of Civil Rights*

At times, Bernstein seems aware of this problem, as when he says, belatedly, "The point is not to judge the liberalism of those years by current standards"; but even then he negates his own purpose when he concludes that he only wants "to emphasize how little the liberals asked" — the word "little" betraying his 1970 judgment. To the extent that students in the 1970's may erroneously believe that the civil rights plank of the 1948 Democratic platform did "explicitly promise social equality," Bernstein does an important service in nailing the error; but at the same time it should be made clear that for most contemporaries the "promise" of "social equality" was not so much rejected as it was *unimaginable*.

This is important because (among other things) it bears on the tendency of New Left historians to read "the failure of liberalism" into every historical instance where the democratic consensus on an issue precluded action compatible with an avant-garde elite's notions of humanitarian justice. Partisan political considerations did indeed dictate Truman's less than heroic postures on civil rights, but this scarcely "reveals" the "shortcomings . . . of liberal democracy in America" (to quote Bernstein). It seems, rather, that given the limits of the contemporary imagination on the issue, the American *democracy* worked only too well — too well, that is, because the democracy was altogether less than generous in its commitment to liberalism.

For perspective on the place of the civil rights issue in the politics of the 1940's, Gunnar Myrdal's *An American Dilemma*, 2 vols. (1944), Arnold Rose's condensed version of the same, *The Negro in America** (1948; paper ed. 1964), and A. M. Schlesinger, Jr.'s, *The Vital Center* (1949; paper ed. 1962), are still worth reading, even if as "historical documents." See E. F. Goldman, *The Crucial Decade** (1956; revised ed. 1960), and S. Lubell, *The Future of American Politics** (1951; 3rd revised ed. 1965), for further detail on the American scene in the late 1940's. Cabell Phillips, *The Truman Presidency** (1966), is a readable and mostly sympathetic account. But Barton Bernstein's own numerous articles on the Truman administration should serve as the student's best guide to the subject. William C. Berman, *The Politics of Civil Rights in the Truman Administration* (1970), cited by Bernstein as a doctoral dissertation, was published too late for the editors to read, but students should know at least that it is now in print.

The Ambiguous Legacy:
The Truman Administration and Civil Rights

Barton J. Bernstein

Harry S. Truman, unexpectedly thrust into the presidency, was the heir of an ambiguous legacy in civil rights. As the successor of Franklin D. Roosevelt, he inherited some of the Negro's loyalty and the torn Democratic coalition as well. The party, rent by factionalism between liberals and conservatives, was a product of history and not logic. Its strong Southern wing opposed Negro rights while the national party relied upon the Negro vote for biennial electoral success. Despite the power of Southern Democrats within Congress, Negroes had slowly abandoned the Republican party to become Roosevelt's staunch supporters. His New Deal had rescued them from starvation and desperation. Though never receiving their fair share, they were grateful to their benefactor in the White House. His government had bestowed benefits upon them as poor, not as Negroes, but its reasons and motives were not important to the majority of black men, who had never before received much assistance from any government. And the Roosevelt administration had done more: it had recognized them. Courted by Northern Democrats, flattered by the much-heralded invitation of their leaders to the White House and the appointment of some of their race to prominent federal offices, Negroes had achieved belatedly some gains which the society and earlier governments had denied them. Yet, despite the changes, their advance during the depression had been marked more by promise than by substance.[1]

Negroes were still unprotected from lynching and were often victims of

Reprinted by permission of Quadrangle Books, Inc., from *Politics and Policies of the Truman Administration*, edited by Barton J. Bernstein. Copyright © 1970 by Quadrangle Books, Inc.

The author wishes to express his gratitude to Oscar Handlin, David M. Potter, Hugh D. Graham, Richard S. Kirkendall, Allen J. Matusow, Alonzo Hamby, Athan Theoharis, and Tamara Hareven for their criticisms. Research on this subject was initiated under a grant from the Harry S. Truman Library Institute, and continued with assistance from the Samuel S. Fels Fund, the American Philosophical Society, the Rabinowitz Foundation, the American Council of Learned Societies, and the Institute of American History (Stanford). A more heavily documented copy of an earlier version of this paper (presented at the American Historical Association meeting in 1966) is available at the Truman Library.

[1] On the Negro and the New Deal, see Allen Kifer, "The Negro Under the New Deal, 1933–1941" (unpublished Ph.D. dissertation, University of Wisconsin, 1961); and Arthur M. Schlesinger, Jr., *The Politics of Upheaval* (Boston, 1960), pp. 409–446.

violence, and they received only faltering aid from the federal government in their lonely quest for equal protection of the laws. Roosevelt, generally assured of their support, was not prepared to risk his popularity or power by aiding the struggle for equality. Nor did he move far even to protect their economic interests. Not until they threatened a march on Washington were they able even to wring from the government a federal Fair Employment Practice Committee (FEPC) and a significant share of the jobs and prosperity generated by a war economy. Nor would Roosevelt yield further and desegregate the armed forces. Yet Negroes achieved new dignity as some fought for the nation and others worked in defense production. They flocked into Northern cities and discovered new opportunities, new possibilities, new freedoms — and new and more subtle forms of discrimination. Freed of Southern oppression, many were still thwarted, still denied equality in neighborhoods, schools, unions, factories, and offices. Negroes, as the Urban League emphasized, did "not enjoy equal opportunities and services in the fields of employment, education, health, housing, and civil liberties." They encountered lingering and deep-rooted prejudices, but also they found reason for hope, and their expectations rose. Struggling for advantages, gaining new political power, they became a more important force in urban politics and hence in American political life. They constituted a political and moral challenge which neither the government nor the nation could ultimately deny. ("The Negro problem," wrote Gunnar Myrdal in 1944, "is not only America's greatest failure but also America's incomparably great opportunity for the future. . . . America can demonstrate that justice, equality and cooperation are possible between white and colored people.") [2]

I

Harry S. Truman, a border-state senator and a moderate on racial and economic issues, had been the compromise candidate in 1944 for the vice-presidency. Selected partly because he had offended no one, he seemed ill equipped to face this new challenge. He was a man of great decency and of limited education. His uncle had served in the Confederate Army, his mother still condemned Republicans as abolitionists. Only slowly and falteringly did he move beyond the racial prejudices of his section. Before the war he had (reluctantly) endorsed an anti-lynching bill, probably because he was dependent on the Negro vote of Kansas City and St. Louis. In his later

[2] On FEPC, see Barton J. Bernstein, "America in War and Peace," in Bernstein, ed., *Towards a New Past* (New York, 1968), pp. 296–299; and Gunnar Myrdal, *An American Dilemma: The Negro Problem in Modern Democracy* (New York, 1944), also at p. 1021 for the quotation. Urban League, "Racial Aspects of Reconversion," August 27, 1945, PPF 2685, Truman Library (source of all of the President's Personal Files). On new aspirations, see Richard M. Dalfiume, "The 'Forgotten Years' of the Negro Revolution," *Journal of American History*, LV (June 1968), 90–106.

years as senator, when his nation struggled against Nazi racism, political necessity may have begun to fuse into a new moral conviction for Harry S. Truman. During the war he voted for FEPC, signed an unsuccessful petition to end a filibuster on an anti–poll tax measure, and agreed to investigations of racial discrimination on war contracts and in the armed services. But he was never severely tested and surely not sympathetic to demands for bold social reform; he was not deeply troubled by the plight of American Negroes, and he did not oppose racial segregation. Like many Americans, he believed that Negroes did not want to end segregation, only inequality. He failed to acknowledge that in many ways America denigrated her black citizens and condemned them to define their quest for dignity as a denial of their color and a plea for color-blindness. He shared the views of many decent men of his generation and thought that equality before the law could be achieved within the framework of "separate but equal" ("I am not appealing for social equality of the Negro," he had said. "The Negro himself knows better than that. . . . Negroes want justice, not social relations.") His vision was parochial and his bias clear. Like many Americans, he found racial matters peripheral to his interests and considered the problem only when it was thrust upon him.[3]

The issue which Truman and his generation had largely avoided forced its way into the national forum during his presidency, and disrupted American politics. Shortly after entering the White House, when asked about his plans to advance the rights of Negroes and his attitude toward FEPC and the poll tax, he side-stepped the question. "All you need to do is read the Senate record of one Harry S. Truman," he replied. Soon he would struggle briefly before acquiescing while Congress killed FEPC. Roosevelt, just before his death, had sought a large appropriation for the temporary FEPC, but a subcommittee cut the request in half and then the House Appropriations Committee eliminated all funds. Truman, though apparently unwilling to expend much effort or risk much prestige, tried to reverse the committee's action. Defeated in the House, he let the proponents of FEPC battle without his support in the Senate. Indeed, when they seemed near victory, a compromise by Senator Alben Barkley, the Majority Leader, allowed their enemies to settle on a small appropriation, and the House ultimately agreed. The committee, left without sufficient funds, cut its staff, closed offices, and quickly declined, as FEPC officials had predicted.[4]

[3] On Truman's vote in 1938, see Samuel Lubell, *The Future of American Politics* (New York, 1951), p. 9; the quote is from his speech of July 14, 1940, to the Convention of the National Colored Democratic Association, in David Horton, ed., *Freedom and Equality: Addresses by Harry S. Truman* (Columbia, Mo., 1960), pp. xi–xxx; for a similar view in 1944, see *Common Sense* (October 1944), quoted in John O'Donnell, *Boston Daily Record*, September 15, 1948. See also interview in *Pittsburgh Courier*, August 5, 1944. For public attitudes toward the Negro, see Hadley Cantril, with Mildred Strunk, eds., *Public Opinion, 1935–1946* (Princeton, 1951), pp. 508–510.

[4] President's News Conference, April 17, 1945, Files of the White House Reporter, Truman Library (all future news conferences cited are from the same source); Will

Truman, while unable to stop Congress from strangling the *temporary* wartime agency, did publicly endorse a *permanent* FEPC. His support was cautious, and again he was careful not to invest much political capital. He pleased both wings of the party and avoided fragmenting the crumbling Democratic coalition. Probably fearing the antagonism of Southern Democrats, he refused even to meet with A. Philip Randolph, determined Negro leader of the Brotherhood of Sleeping Car Porters and organizer of the threatened march on Washington in 1941 which had led to FEPC, and others who urged the President to prod the Congress. He was unwilling to take a politically unnecessary risk in a cause which did not enlist great sympathy, although he mildly endorsed FEPC in his twenty-one-point speech of September 6, 1945, which ended his honeymoon with Congress.[5]

His "declaration of independence" from congressional conservatives, as he privately described this liberal speech, promised to continue and extend the New Deal; his requests for such welfare measures as a full employment act, increased unemployment compensation, and a higher minimum wage were valued by civil rights leaders who believed this legislation would be particularly useful to Negroes during the anticipated postwar depression. Indeed, the NAACP was so fearful of a depression that it placed the full employment bill first on its list of priorities, and FEPC second. But Truman's commitment to the employment bill and other welfare measures seemed halfhearted, and his efforts specifically on behalf of the Negro were occasional and usually ambiguous. Like Roosevelt, he did not emphasize the nation's obligation to the Negro.[6]

(Nor did Truman's wife, unlike Eleanor Roosevelt, ever champion the

---

Maslow, "FEPC — A Case History in Parliamentary Maneuver," *University of Chicago Law Review*, XIII (April 1946), 422–433; *Congressional Record*, 79th Cong., 1st sess., pp. 5734–5735, 5751, 5794–5798, 5812, 6820–6822, 7062–7065; FEPC, *Final Report* (Washington, 1947), pp. ix–x. Also, Walter White to Truman, June 1, Official File (OF) 413, Truman Papers, Truman Library (the source of all future citations of OF); Representative Mary Norton to Truman, June 1, OF40; Truman to Fred Vinson, June 2, OF122; Truman to Rep. Adolph Sabath, June 5 (and an identical letter to Senator Denis Chavez), OF40; Malcolm Ross (FEPC chairman) to Truman, June 7, OF40. Cf. Louis Ruchames, *Race, Jobs and Politics: The Story of FEPC* (New York, 1953), pp. 122–135.

[5] Of about four thousand letters between June 1 and June 23, only nineteen opposed FEPC. "Analysis of Presidential Mail on FEPC," OF40. On Truman's avoidance of antagonism and meetings with partisans, see Frank Boykin to Truman, and reply, June 29, 1945; Randolph to Truman, August 31, September 30; Matthew Connelly to Randolph, September 4, 6, 10, October 16, 1945; Randolph to Matthew Connelly, October 10 and 19, all in OF40. For Truman's speech of September 6, see *Public Papers of the Presidents: Harry S. Truman* (hereafter *Truman Papers*), 1945 (Washington, D.C., 1961), pp. 263–309. For Truman's later interpretation, see his *Memoirs* (Garden City, 1955), I, 481–485.

[6] On Negro fears of depression, see *Negro Digest*, III (November 1944), 36. On the NAACP, see *NAACP Bulletin*, January 1946, and Walter White's testimony, in Senate Banking and Currency Committee Hearings, *Full Employment Act of 1946*, 79th Cong., 2nd sess., pp. 615–621.

Negro. Indeed, when the Daughters of the American Revolution refused to rent Constitution Hall to Hazel Scott, the Negro pianist, Bess Truman, departing from her predecessor's response to a similar provocation, refused even to stay away from a DAR tea given in her honor. Miss Scott's husband, a Negro congressman, Adam Clayton Powell, scorned the First Lady as "the last lady.") [7]

Late in the fall of 1945, Truman dealt the already weakened FEPC another blow. When the government seized the strikebound Capital Transit Company and the FEPC decided to order the company to end discriminatory hiring, the President halted the directive and then ignored the committee's request for a conference. One member resigned in protest, charging that the government "is not only empowered to, but must enforce the national policy of non-discrimination in employment." He emphasized that Truman was condoning racial discrimination and repudiating the committee. Truman, defending his action, explained that the law empowering seizure required him to maintain the term of employment during government operation.[8]

Meanwhile, the President continued to appeal publicly for a *permanent* FEPC. On January 3, 1946, he complained to the nation that congressmen were blocking his reform program, and he lashed out at "a small handful of Congressmen in the Rules Committee" who had prevented a number of measures, including the FEPC bill, from reaching the House floor. Truman continued to give FEPC some support, but his efforts did not seem designed to spur Congress. He ultimately acquiesced in the refusal of the Rules Committee to release the measure, and he never openly criticized a Senate filibuster against FEPC in January and February, nor rallied support for cloture. After some sparring, when cloture failed, the advocates of FEPC abandoned their attempt. To many observers, the struggle of the civil rights advocates appeared halfhearted, their efforts "a sham if not a fraud." They did not press for extra sessions or harass those filibustering, as parliamentary rules permitted. Instead, meeting largely during banking hours, the Senate appeared to follow an expected routine. Civil rights measures, including fed-

[7] On the Hazel Scott affair, see Powell to Truman, October 1; Truman to Powell, and reply, October 12; Powell to Mrs. Truman, October 11, and reply, October 12, 1945, all in OF93; *Newsweek*, XXVI (October 22, 1945), 31; *Crisis*, LII (November 1945), 313.

[8] On the dispute, see Charles Houston to Truman, December 3, and reply, December 7; White House press release (Truman to Houston), December 17, 1945, all in OF40. For an affirmation of the committee, see Executive Order 9664 of December 20, 10 Federal Register 15301; Thomas Emerson to John Snyder, August 30, 1945, Office of War Mobilization and Reconversion (OWMR) Records, Box 116, Record Group (RG) 240, National Archives (NA); Tom Clark to Truman, November 29; Ross to Harold Smith, November 9; Samuel Rosenman to Truman, December 3; and Rosenman, undated memo, all in OF40; cf. White to Truman, December 19, 1945, OF40; *Crisis*, LIII (January 1946), 9; Ruchames, *Race, Jobs*, p. 134; William Berman, "The Politics of Civil Rights in the Truman Administration" (unpublished Ph.D. dissertation, Ohio State University, 1963), pp. 23–25.

eral anti-lynching and anti–poll tax laws, did not receive support from either the Democratic or Republican leadership in Congress, although both parties had pledged support for FEPC. And with the President on the sidelines, hopes for reform crumbled.[9]

By the middle of 1946 it was clear that Truman's government, despite his words, was not as active in the struggle for civil rights as Roosevelt's had been during the war. When FEPC expired at the end of June, for example, a presidential assistant drafted a directive "to insure compliance with . . . [the] policy of nondiscrimination in Federal service and by government contractors," but apparently the President rejected the measure and discrimination as well as segregation continued. While Truman had expressed "friendship for the Negro people" (according to the largest Negro paper), he had not acted significantly to advance their welfare. Yet, when violence against Negroes erupted, Truman's words were important. When advances made by minorities during the New Deal and the war seemed in doubt, his public commitment was important. By appointing a few Negroes to office, he reaffirmed racial equality in symbolic form and recognized the Negro's political power. His efforts also generated mild sympathy among Northern liberals, although he sidestepped conflict and avoided a direct clash with Southern interests.[10]

Truman's occasional support of FEPC and abolition of the poll tax kept these issues alive. By his words he even encouraged the hopes of civil rights advocates. "The right to use [the ballot] must be protected," he wrote to the

[9] Speech of January 3 is reprinted in *Truman Papers 1946*, pp. 1–8, and see particularly pp. 3–4. For pressure on Truman to support FEPC vigorously and condemn the filibuster, see Mary McLeod Bethune to Truman, February 3, 1946; National Council for FEPC to Truman, February 6, 1946, both in OF40. On Truman's responses, see Truman to Randolph, February 6, 1946, and Truman to Mrs. J. Borden Harriman, January 29, 1946, OF40. On Truman and the filibuster, see also I. F. Stone, "Where There Is No Vision," *Nation*, CLXII (February 9, 1946), 111–119; Maslow, "FEPC," p. 440, which is the source of the quotation about the filibuster. On the defection of liberals, see NAACP Minutes, February 11, 1946, NAACP Papers, Library of Congress. At the FEPC rally of February 28 in Madison Square Garden, Secretary of Labor Lewis Schwellenbach represented the administration. Department of Labor press release, February 28, 1946, Philleo Nash Files, No. 21, Truman Library (all Nash Files are in the Truman Library).

[10] Truman to Niles, July 22, 1946, and drafts (undated); and Nash to Niles, July 19, 1946, Nash Files, No. 20; and see Executive Order 9346, May 27, 1943. On segregation in federal employment, see President's Committee on Civil Rights, *To Secure These Rights* (Washington, D.C., 1947), pp. 57–61; on segregation in USES, see "Memorandum on the Washington Office, USES," August 26, 1946, Office of the Secretary (Schwellenbach) Files, Records of the Department of Labor, RG174, NA, and on Labor's promise to correct the situation, NAACP press release, September 19, 1946, NAACP Files, Schomburg Library (source of all NAACP Files). Quotation from *Pittsburgh Courier*, April 27, 1946, called to my attention in Berman, "Civil Rights," p. 33. On violence against Negroes, see *To Secure These Rights*, p. 22; and *Pittsburgh Courier*, October 6, 1945; February 2, March 9, 1946. On Truman and the poll tax, see News Conferences, April 6 and 11, 1946; and Truman to Irving Brant, March 29, 1946, OF465B.

NAACP national convention in June 1946. He condemned the upsurge of violence, the outbreak of racial lynchings and assaults upon Negroes. Every citizen, he declared, "must be protected from all forms of organized terrorism." Yet, earlier in the year, when law enforcement officers in Columbia, Tennessee, had attacked Negroes, he had been silent; when a returning Negro veteran was removed from a bus in South Carolina, and beaten and blinded, he had been silent. Even shortly after his message to the NAACP, he waited a few days, until angry protests reached his office, before condemning an unmasked white mob in Georgia which had seized two Negro couples in broad daylight and murdered them. ("Three volleys of shots," later reported an investigating committee, "were fired as if by a squad of professional executioners." "Speak! Speak! Mr. President, where is Democracy?" asked angry pickets at the White House.) Spurred on by national shame, troubled that racial violence was providing ammunition for Russian propaganda, Truman directed the Justice Department to investigate whether a federal crime had been committed. But he did not use the opportunity to launch protective legislation. He was already scrapping with Congress and unwilling to antagonize the South or move ahead of national sentiment. Though the liberalism of the postwar years was slowly finding a central place in its "ideology" for a crusade against racial injustice and inequality, and even the national conscience was growing more sensitive to racial violence, only a few white reformers and a handful of Negro leaders were pushing Truman to move beyond the occasional rhetoric of condemnation. They were too few and too weak, without great prestige or substantial power, to be effective.[11]

But events were conspiring to move Truman. In mid-September 1946 the National Emergency Committee Against Mob Violence sent a delegation, including, among others, Walter White, Negro executive secretary of the NAACP, Channing Tobias, Negro executive of the Phelps-Stokes Fund, James Carey, secretary-treasurer of the CIO, and Boris Shiskin, AFL economist, to confer with the President. They told him grimly of lynchings of Negroes in Georgia and Louisiana, and asked him to use the authority of his office to halt the terror. What they hoped for was not action but, as Walter White confided, "so strong a statement in denunciation of lynchings and the Ku Klux Klan that it will make real news." (Actually, Truman had already prepared a formal message for the annual meeting of the Urban League in which he declared that America "must not . . . and shall not remain indifferent in the face of acts of intimidation and violence in our . . . communities.") While Truman replied that he "had no idea it was as

11 For NAACP message, Truman to White, June 11, 1946, President's Personal File (PPF) 393, Truman Library (source for all PPF citations). The white press virtually disregarded the incident in Tennessee, *New York Times*, February 27, 1946, p. 44. *To Secure These Rights*, p. 22, is the source of the first quotation. See OF93 for more than two hundred telegrams protesting violence in Georgia, and NAACP press release, August 8, 1946. Other quotation from *New York Times*, July 31, 1946.

terrible as all that," it is clear that he had known of the terror and had already formulated a plan. Like Roosevelt, he was distressed when the nation fell so far short of its pledge of law and order. He lacked his predecessor's political capital among white liberals and black men, and there were political and moral reasons for doing more about civil rights. It was not just to appease his visitors and the groups they represented (to which he attributed more power than they really had) that he promised to create a civil rights committee. White and his colleagues had no guarantee that Truman's proposed committee was not simply a tactic of delay, but they could do little other than accept the gesture and regard it publicly as a minor triumph. Committed to working through the political process and the Democratic party, they had nowhere else to go for help. They had to rely upon the man in the White House.[12]

It is true that Truman could have used the promise to gain time and avoid a decision before the autumn election and perhaps even afterward. The appointment of a committee entailed some risks, but they could be minimized: the President had the power to select members, shape the investigations, influence conclusions, and perhaps even prevent publication of the ensuing report. Rather than creating unwanted pressures and nurturing uncontrollable aspirations, he might, through a committee, stall and restrain disruptive demands for reform. In government, where studies are designed more frequently to divert energies and impede action than to promote reform, appointment of another panel can be a clever maneuver, not evidence of concern or promise of remedy. But by promising to act, by creating a committee, Truman could temporarily affirm his commitment to legal equality without antagonizing the South. If he appointed prominent men of liberal faith, however, the committee could be a political danger and commit him to a course of action, and cost him more than he cared to spend. These, then, were some of the influences shaping his decision.

On October 11 Attorney General Tom Clark privately urged Truman to establish the committee, for it "would be of the utmost value in the task of preserving civil rights." Within ten days Truman's assistant for civil rights, David K. Niles, began selecting members for the special investigation, and he secured commitments from Franklin D. Roosevelt, Jr., who

[12] For the quotation, see White to Donald Harrington, September 12, 1946, White Papers, Yale University. For the message to the Urban League, see Truman to Lester Granger, September 12, 1946, PPF2868. On the meeting, see *Pittsburgh Courier*, September 28, 1946; NAACP press release, September 20, 1946; Walter White, *A Man Called White* (New York, 1948), pp. 330–332, also the source of the quotation attributed to Truman. Nash, in an interview of September 19, 1966, revealed that the plan was formulated in advance. Negro leaders were viewed by the administration as men of considerable power, as leaders of a bloc vote. For evidence of this belief, see Clark Clifford, "Memorandum for the President," November 19, 1947, Clifford Papers (used while in his possession but now at the Truman Library). For Negro grievances with the Democratic party, see *New York Times*, October 18, 1946.

served as vice-chairman; Reverend Francis J. Haas, Bishop of Grand Rapids and former chairman of the FEPC; Francis Matthews, former executive of the Chamber of Commerce and head of the Knights of Columbus; and apparently Charles E. Wilson, the president of General Electric who served as chairman. In the short time before the election in early November, the administration probably was not able to find willing, suitable candidates for many of the other positions, and perhaps the quest continued well after the voters' overwhelming repudiation of the Democrats. Whatever the reasons for delay, not until December 5 did the President announce the appointment of his Committee on Civil Rights, and by the standards of the forties it was a group of liberal, prominent citizens. Within the administration it was described as "Noah's Ark" because it included two Negroes, two women, two Catholics, two Jews, two businessmen, two Southerners, two labor leaders, and two college presidents. Chaired by Wilson, the committee also included: Sadie T. Alexander, Philadelphia city solicitor and a Negro; James B. Carey, secretary-treasurer of the CIO and a member of the National Emergency Committee Against Mob Violence; John S. Dickey, president of Dartmouth College; Charles Luckman, president of Lever Brothers; Morris Ernst, prominent New York attorney and an active member of the ACLU; Rabbi Roland B. Gittelson of Rockville Center, New York; Frank Graham, liberal president of the University of North Carolina; Henry Knox Sherrill, Presiding Bishop of the Episcopal Church; Boris Shishkin, AFL economist and a member of the National Emergency Committee Against Mob Violence; Mrs. M. E. Tilly, a prominent Methodist and Southern friend of the Negro; and Channing Tobias, Negro executive of the Phelps-Stokes Fund and a member of the National Emergency Committee Against Mob Violence. Robert K. Carr, a political scientist at Dartmouth and a liberal student of civil rights, became the executive secretary and guiding spirit of the committee.[13]

In publicly establishing the committee, Truman's executive order declared that democratic institutions could not survive "where law and order have broken down and individuals . . . have been killed, maimed or intimidated." He concluded that inadequate civil rights statutes hampered the federal government in discharging its constitutional obligations, and called upon the committee to recommend whatever legislation and administrative actions were necessary for protecting civil rights. Significantly, his action provoked little interest among Southerners. There were no dramatic outbursts, no threats or warnings, no expressed fears of betrayal; nor did his

[13] Clark to Truman, October 11, 1946, OF596A; on the dating of the first three appointments, see Francis Matthews, "Memorandum" (n.d.), Matthews Papers No. 15, Truman Library. "Noah's Ark" was Nash's characterization. On Wilson, see White House Appointment Book, October 18, 1946. On Carr's appointment, see Nash to Charles Mazley, Nash Files, No. 24. Luckman because of the pressure of other commitments, later withdrew from the committee.

State of the Union message, which included a section on civil rights, alarm the South.[14]

Despite Truman's expressed concern about restrictions of the franchise and racial bars to employment, his own government continued to discriminate against Negroes. In part, the government was too large, the system too intractable, to reverse direction abruptly; in part, the President was not *committed* to ending discrimination in federal employment. But by the summer of 1947, as he despaired of compromise with Congress and struggled to mend the tattered Democratic coalition, he spoke more vigorously on civil rights and courted more energetically the Negro vote. Agreeing to address an NAACP rally in June, he rejected an assistant's cautious advice that he limit civil rights to the last paragraph, "not to exceed a minute"; instead he asked two staff members of the civil rights committee to draft his speech. In his address, at the Lincoln Memorial, he openly acknowledged some of the shortcomings of American society and affirmed the need for federal remedies ("vigilant defender of the rights and equalities of all Americans") — but he omitted specific proposals.[15]

Without seriously antagonizing the South, Truman had won the praise of much of the Negro press, the NAACP, and other white liberals. But some Negro leaders were eager to push him from rhetoric to action. Encouraged to seek a better life for their people, they were guided by vocal support for racial equality from prominent social scientists. These Negro leaders were aware of Truman's political weakness at home and were able to exploit his fear that mistreatment of Negroes could mean Russian propaganda victories abroad. Moreover, they knew that Truman was not as insulated from their pressures as was his predecessor, whose popularity with the mass of Negroes sometimes inhibited Negro leaders in pressing their demands. Perhaps to spur Truman to action, the NAACP in October petitioned the United Nations, outlining the plight of the American Negro and pleading with "the nations of the world to persuade . . . [America] to be just to its people." [16]

[14] Executive Order 9809, 11 F.R. 14153. Also see Truman, *Memoirs*, II, 180–182. *Atlanta Constitution, Atlanta Journal, Mobile Register, Gulfport* (Miss.) *Daily Herald, Nashville Banner*, and *Charlotte Observer*, December 5–8, 1946, neither reported the President's act nor commented upon it. *Birmingham News*, December 7, was favorable, and the *Raleigh News and Observer*, December 6, 1946, mentioned it. The White House received about forty letters, and all but three were favorable. OF596. Address of January 6, 1947, is in *Truman Papers 1947*, p. 9. For Southern responses, see *New York Times, Washington Post, Baltimore Sun*, January 7–9, 1947.

[15] On discrimination in the federal government, see n. 8 and complaints of the United Public Workers, in *New York Times*, January 11, 1947; also *Pittsburgh Courier*, May 18, 1946; October 18, 1947. On his statement of January 15, 1947 (to the committee), see *Truman Papers 1947*, pp. 98–99; there was no Southern response. *Charleston* (S.C.) *News and Courier, New Orleans Times-Picayune, Birmingham News, Mobile Register*, and *Atlanta Journal*, January 15–20, 1947. Advice on Truman's speech is in Niles to Connelly, June 4, 1947, OF419B, and June 16, 1947, Clifford Files, Truman Library. Truman's address of June 29 is in *Truman Papers 1947*, 311–313.

[16] On responses to the speech, see *Pittsburgh Courier*, July 5, 1947; "Truman to the NAACP," *Crisis*, LIV (August 1947), 233. In 1946 the National Negro Congress had

Six days after this petition, by releasing the long-awaited study of the Committee on Civil Rights, Truman publicized charges that America treated its Negroes as second-class citizens. In nearly every sector of American life, concluded the report, practice violated traditional ideals. Negroes were subject to lynchings and police brutality. They were frequently denied equal protection of the law. In the armed services they were segregated and restricted mostly to menial tasks. They were also effectively barred from many professions and denied equality in education, housing, medical care, and in the allocation of government assistance and services. They were, the committee concluded, victims of the "separate-but-equal" doctrine, virtually abandoned by the society. By attacking Jim Crow, the committee moved beyond the issue of federal protection of civil rights (for example, the right to life which lynching threatened) to a redefinition of the conditions for equality.[17]

The federal government must act to *secure* civil rights, asserted the committee. Left unprotected and sometimes persecuted by local and state officials, Negroes needed federal safeguards. "By mobilizing the idealism and prestige of our whole people," the committee reasoned, the government could "check the wayward tendencies of part of them," for the nation could not afford to delay "until the most backward country has learned to prize civil liberty." Nor could America neglect the "growing international implications" of civil rights violations. While admitting that legislation might not eliminate prejudice and intolerance, the committee avoided the trap of conservative thought — that change must *await* education and conversion — and concluded that the government should move to abolish discriminatory practices.[18]

To protect civil rights, the committee unanimously recommended federal machinery: expansion of the Civil Rights Section of the Department of Justice to a division; creation of a permanent commission on civil rights in the Executive and a joint committee on civil rights in Congress. The committee also proposed national legislation: increasing penalties and revising the requirements of evidence in cases of violation of federal civil rights statutes by private individuals or public officials; outlawing police brutality; barring segregation in interstate transportation; making lynching a federal crime; abolishing the poll tax; protecting participants in federal elections and primaries; ending (also by administrative action) discrimination and

---

filed a complaint with the U.N. Economic and Social Council. The NAACP petition, "A Statement on the Denial of Human Rights to Minorities in the Case of Citizens of Negro Descent in the United States of America and an Appeal to the United Nations for Redress," was first submitted in preliminary form on January 27, 1947, and, after revisions, formally presented on October 23. The council, rejecting a Soviet motion, refused to investigate. Carey McWilliams, *Brothers Under the Skin* (New York, 1951), p. 38. On NAACP pressure, see White to Niles, November 5, 1947, Nash Files.

[17] *To Secure These Rights*, pp. 1–95.

[18] *Ibid.*, pp. 100–103.

segregation in the military; eliminating public discrimination against members of the armed forces; establishing FEPC; and terminating federal discrimination and segregation in public schools and other publicly supported institutions in the District of Columbia. The committee looked forward to the end of racial segregation in American life, and a majority advised Congress to bar financial aid to any government agency (even in the states and communities) guilty of racial discrimination. Tilly and Graham, both Southerners, would not endorse compulsory FEPC or the cutting off of federal aid to government agencies which discriminated. At first the committee had split almost evenly on the latter issue, but by limiting the recommendation to discrimination and excluding segregation, the other members of the committee were able to reach agreement.[19]

Truman, in appointing liberals, had established a committee likely to recommend *some* federal legislation to protect the rights of black citizens. By selecting prominent men the President had forfeited the option of shaping their recommendations or quashing their report. It was not a committee he could control or silence. During its ten months of meetings, neither Truman nor his assistants, surprisingly, sought to influence the report. Cynics may attribute the choice of a liberal commission to sloppy staff work in the White House or to the excessive influence of liberal assistants, and cynics may attribute the failure to keep the commission within safe channels to assistants pushing the President beyond his desires, but it seems more likely that Truman wanted a report urging *some* action. Such a report from respected Americans could serve as a partial mandate and make his political course easier. Be that as it may, the extent of the committee's recommendations surprised many citizens, including Truman's assistant on civil rights and presumably the President himself. Yet he should have known what was coming. Already, in May, the Compton Commission on Universal Military Training had condemned segregation in the military, and in December the President's Commission on Higher Education would assail the "separate-but-equal doctrine" and would recommend abolishing segregation in higher education.[20]

---

[19] *Ibid.*, pp. 139–173. On the compromise, Stephen Spingarn, "Recommendations of the President's Committee on Civil Rights," [n.d.], Spingarn Papers, No. 37, Truman Library. On FEPC, see "Telephone Conversation Between Mr. Matthews and Mr. Lowenstein," April 26, 1950, Matthews Papers, No. 43.

[20] Curiously, there is no record — in the files of the Bureau of the Budget or in the papers at the Truman Library — of the recommendations which led to the selection of the committee's personnel. Perhaps there is information in the papers of David K. Niles at Brandeis University, but the collection is closed. On the committee's independence and the expectation throughout its history that the report would be published, see Robert Carr to Bernstein, August 11, 1966; Henry Knox Sherrill to Bernstein, July 2, 1966; "Minutes, the President's Committee on Civil Rights," March 6, 1947, p. 15, and April 17, 1947, pp. 179–180, Nash Files, No. 28; Carr to Maurice Latta, September 15, 1947, Nash Files, No. 24; Carr to Latta, October 21, 1947, files of the President's Commission on Civil Rights, No. 4, Truman Library; Nash to Niles, September 29, 1947, Nash Files No. 4. On surprise at the course of the committee, see interview with

Truman, while offering the report of his Committee on Civil Rights as "an American charter of human freedom . . . [and] a guide for action," claimed publicly that he had not read the brief study. (One member of the committee, Channing Tobias, reported to the NAACP that the President, upon being presented with the report, privately told the committee, "I have already read the report and I want you to know that . . . you have done what I wanted you to do.") He was still cautious. He seemed sympathetic but promised nothing. Soon, though, he would have to choose. Compelled by the report to take a position, he might have to request vigorous legislation or risk losing pivotal Negro votes. He found his alternatives narrowed, his room for maneuvering limited. No longer could he easily remain an ally of Southern Democrats and maintain the wary allegiance of Negro leaders and urban liberals. Forced to yield to demands for the advancement of the Negro — pressures which he did not wish fully to resist — Truman had encouraged these forces which were now moving beyond his control. His political future might rest precariously on his decision.[21]

For a few months he seemed to hesitate. The issue was not whether he would do nothing — the hour was far too late for inaction — but how much of the report he would endorse. In large measure Truman's decision was influenced by the prospect of a new third party led by Henry Wallace, Roosevelt's vice-president whom Truman had dismissed as Secretary of Commerce. Estimates of Wallace's likely support in 1948 were mixtures of conjecture and anxiety, but early polls suggested that he might capture about 10 per cent of the vote. Wallace's candidacy compelled the President to take a stronger position on civil rights. Only by moving to the left could Truman prevent a bolt of important numbers of urban Negroes and some white liberals from the uneasy Democratic coalition; without their substantial support, he and many urban Democrats were doomed to defeat.

Though Wallace's candidacy would spur the administration to greater liberalism, the new threat did not alter the basic form of that liberalism. Ever since the Democrats suffered defeat in the 1946 elections, advisers had been pressing Truman to reshape the coalition by courting labor and minority groups. Analyzing the situation after the committee's report, Clark Clifford, probably the President's closest and wisest political counselor, recommended that the administration move to the left to pick up disgruntled New Dealers, and build the party on Western farmers, urban workers, and Negroes. Truman, by picking his issues carefully, could avoid clashes between these groups. The administration might antagonize Southern voters,

Nash. For the committee reports, *A Program for National Security: Report of the President's Advisory Commission on Universal Training* (Washington, D.C., 1947), p. 42; *A Report of the President's Commission on Higher Education, Higher Education for American Democracy* (Washington, D.C., 1947), II, 29–35.

[21] Truman's statement of October 29, 1947 is in *Truman Papers 1947*, pp. 479–480; cf. report by Tobias, NAACP Minutes, November 17, 1947, NAACP Papers.

Clifford reasoned, but he foresaw no risk of losing Southern Democrats, no possibility of a bolt by dissidents. The mild Southern response to the civil rights report seemed to confirm his judgment. There was no torrent of protest, and many Southerners who objected to the report restricted their objections to the committee's attack upon segregation.[22]

Clifford sketched the strategy which Truman would follow in his uphill battle for re-election:

> Insofar as it has control of the situation, the Administration should select the issues upon which there will be conflict with the majority in Congress. It can assume that it will get no major part of its own program approved. Its tactics must, therefore, be entirely different than if there were any real point to bargaining and compromise. Its recommendations — in the State of the Union message and elsewhere — must be tailored for the voter, not the Congressman; they must display a label which reads "no compromise." [That strategy worked with Taft-Hartley and] should be expanded in the next session to include all the *domestic* issues.[23]

II

Truman launched his campaign in 1948 with his message on the State of the Union. He reaffirmed the reform program Congress had thwarted, added a few more items, and promised a special message on civil rights. Though liberals greeted his speech with cynicism and conservatives with hostility, prominent Southern politicians paid little attention to the statement about civil rights. On both sides, in the Executive and among Dixie's responsible leaders, there was some misreading of intention and perhaps of sentiment.[24]

Within a few weeks the President surprised the South. On February 2, shortly after two hundred Negro ministers had prayed publicly at the Capitol for the end of Jim Crow, Truman asked Congress to enact most of the

[22] On Wallace's strength, see American Institute of Public Opinion poll of June 1947, in *Public Opinion Quarterly*, XII (Fall 1947), 490. On the efforts of advisers, see author's interviews with Clifford and Nash; Ewing to Bernstein, December 1, 1966; and interviews by Berman, "Civil Rights," pp. 64–70. For strategy, see Clifford, "Memorandum for the President," November 17, 1947. On Southern reactions, see *New York Times, Baltimore Sun, Washington Post, New Orleans Times-Picayune, Atlanta Journal, Atlanta Constitution, Greensboro* (N.C.) *News, Richmond Times-Dispatch, Birmingham News, Louisville Courier-Journal, Alexandria* (Va.) *Gazette*, October 29–November 10, 1947; *Nashville Banner*, October 30; *Gulfport* (Miss.) *Daily Herald*, October 31; *Mobile Register*, October 30; *Charlotte Observer*, October 30; and F. H. Vass to Harry Vaughn, October 30, 1947, OF596A. The mail on the report was about 5 to 1 in favor. OF596A. Also see Jack Redding, *Inside the Democratic Party* (New York, 1958), p. 76.

[23] Clifford, "Memorandum for the President," November 19, 1947.

[24] Speech of January 7, in *Truman Papers 1948*, pp. 1–10. On responses, see *New York Times, Washington Post, Birmingham News*, January 7–10, 1948. For misreading of sentiment, see interviews with Clifford and Nash.

recommendations offered by his Civil Rights Committee (except most of those attacking segregation). His boldness won praise from friends of the Negro and provoked attacks by Southerners, although most did not notice that, with the exception of opposing segregation in interstate transportation, he had barely challenged Jim Crow. Despite his executive power and the recommendation of the Civil Rights Committee, he did not even act to wipe out segregation in federal employment or within the military. Instead, he announced that he had instructed the Secretary of Defense to end discrimination (but not specifically Jim Crow) in the armed services "as rapidly as possible," and he *promised* to issue an order restating and enforcing Roosevelt's policy of nondiscrimination (but not nonsegregation) in federal employment. (Truman had also requested expansion of the Civil Rights Section into a division in the Justice Department, but an Assistant Attorney General, T. Vincent Quinn, was opposing the reorganization, and the Bureau of the Budget even reduced the appropriations for civil rights attorneys.) The strategy seemed to be one of reasonably bold requests in the legislative arena, where they could not succeed, and more cautious proposals in the executive arena, where the President had greater power.[25]

Undeterred by threats of a Southern rebellion, Truman and his advisers undoubtedly anticipated the brief flurry of loud Southern protests that occurred well before the Democratic national convention. Of course, some intransigent Southerners such as Senator James Eastland of Mississippi and Representative Eugene Cox of Georgia would continue to denounce the report and Truman's endorsement of it. But they were simply racists, full of hatred, and with constituencies admiring their pyrotechnics; he could discount their wrath and their threats. Others, however, were more moderate: to strengthen their bargaining position with the administration and the liberal wing of the party, they would threaten; to persuade their constituents of their devotion to the Southern heritage, they would protest. But they, as well as the administration, knew that Truman's legislative program did not endanger the Southern way of life, for they could block civil rights legislation by filibustering in the Senate. As long as passions did not blind men, as long as substance remained more important than symbols, Truman could count upon Southern leaders to support the party.[26]

Briefly, the counsel of moderation seemed to prevail. Senator Barkley,

---

[25] On the ministers, see *Pittsburgh Courier*, January 19, 1948. Truman's address of February 2 is in *Truman Papers 1948*, pp. 121–126. The mail received at the White House was about 4 to 1 in favor of the President's speech (OF596A). On Truman's move left, see William Helm, ed., *Mr. President* (New York, 1952), p. 134, and Jules Abels, *Out of the Jaws of Victory* (New York, 1959), pp. 4–6. On the Civil Rights Section, see *New York Times*, November 28, December 8, 1947; May 9, 1948. On the contents of the legislative program, see Stephen Spingarn, "Suggested Outline of the Omnibus and Rights Bill of 1948," January 22, 1948, Spingarn Papers, No. 36. For support of FEPC by prominent businessmen, see *New York Times*, February 16, 1948.

[26] See Arthur Krock, *New York Times*, February 4, 1948. On the South, see *New Orleans Times-Picayune, Mobile Register, Atlanta Constitution*, February 2–10, 1948.

who had not been consulted about the proposed legislation, decided not to risk a party rift and estrange the South: he refused to sponsor the measure. In turn, Southern governors, at a long-scheduled conference, overrode a few extremists and endorsed the mechanics of compromise. They appointed a committee to confer with the Democratic national chairman, Senator J. Howard McGrath. Though Truman's press secretary announced that the President would not retreat on any point, McGrath at first seemed conciliatory; but a few days later he appeared less willing to compromise. In the interim, a Wallace candidate had won a surprising victory in a special congressional election in New York City, and the Progressive party loomed as an increasingly powerful threat, likely to gain as much as 7 per cent of the vote. McGrath, fearful of Wallace, rebuffed Southern demands that Truman withdraw his civil rights measures. Nevertheless, the national chairman did emphasize the moderation of the President's program, which would leave segregation largely intact, and he suggested a concession — the mild Democratic plank of 1944 as the model for the 1948 platform. The governors, refusing publicly to be mollified, warned that "the South is no longer 'in the bag.'" Sharpening the threat, Governor Ben Laney of Arkansas warned, "The Democratic Party doesn't want to run the race with a politically dead Missouri mule." [27]

Southern politicians began girding for battle. Most were still maneuvering to improve their leverage within the party; only a few were planning rebellion. In seven Southern states, governors recommended that presidential electors not vote for a candidate favoring civil rights and that delegates to the national convention be instructed to oppose Truman's position. In two states, Mississippi and Alabama, the party's executive committees threatened to bolt if the convention endorsed a civil rights plank. Though no one in the administration expected a rebellion, many advised moderation.[28]

Truman, now an avowed candidate for re-election, was reluctant to press his program. He was unwilling to risk schism or even bad feelings and tried to rest on his laurels and let passions cool. ("The strategy," an assistant later explained, "was to start with a bold measure and then temporize to pick up the rightwing forces. Simply stated, backtrack after the bang.") Explaining that Congress would reject legislation recommended by his office, the President admitted that he did not plan to submit a civil rights bill. But A. Philip Randolph, with the Reverend Grant Reynolds, director of the five-month-old Committee Against Jim Crow in Military Service and Training, tried to upset the presidential strategy of conciliation. They were persuaded that Truman was primarily a politician eager to avoid conflict and to escape

[27] On Barkley, see New York Times, March 10, 1948. On the maneuvering, see V. O. Key, Southern Politics (New York, 1949), pp. 329–334; New York Times, February 7–11, 24, 1948, and February 24 for the first quote. Laney, quoted in Hugh Gloster, "The Southern Revolt," Crisis, LV (May 1948), 137. On the Progressive victory, see Lubell, Future of American Politics, pp. 85–87.

[28] Key, Southern Politics, pp. 332–336; New York Times, February 24, 1948.

moral and political challenges, and so they continued to threaten him, and with him, white America. On March 22 at the White House they informed Truman that unless he ended Jim Crow in the military they would lead a massive campaign of civil disobedience; Negroes would not shoulder "a gun to fight for democracy abroad" while they were denied democracy here, Randolph declared. A week later, Reynolds and Randolph delivered the same message to the Senate Armed Services Committee, and Randolph pledged "to openly counsel, aid, and abet youth . . . to quarantine any Jim Crow conscription system." Negroes, they warned, were prepared for sacrifices, suffering, terrorism, even concentration camps, in order to achieve their rights. A poll of Negro college students (mostly veterans) concluded that 71 per cent supported the campaign. Leaders of the Urban League and the NAACP, while abhorring the tactics of disobedience and preferring to work within the political system, gave the movement mild and indirect support.[29]

The administration arranged for moderate Negro leaders to confer with the military and serve as consultants to the services, but the session ended in disaster for the President. While the Navy promised to improve its program and the Air Force agreed to reexamine its policies of discrimination and segregation, the Secretary of the Army, Kenneth Royall, from North Carolina, refused to revise the Army's policy of segregation. Enraged by Royall, these prominent Negroes refused the offer of consultantships, and they publicly renewed the challenge: they wanted both segregation and discrimination eliminated in the military, for "segregation is a form of discrimination." Without naming Royall, the Negro leaders of twenty organizations, including the Urban League and the NAACP, demanded the removal of public officials who would not end segregation and discrimination in the federal government. "Our nation, to its shame," they declared, "is condemned throughout the world for speaking of freedom while continuing to permit the perpetuation of gross discrimination against its own minorities." [30]

Despite these demands, Truman remained cautious and still did nothing about civil rights. Obviously delaying and perhaps intending to abandon the promised directive ending discrimination in federal agencies, he was

[29] On Truman, see *New York Times*, March 8, 1948; and news conference, March 11, 1948. The assistant is Nash, in an interview. The quotations are from Randolph, *New York Times*, March 23, 1948, and Senate Committee on Armed Services, *Hearings on Universal Military Training*, 80th Cong., 2nd sess., p. 688; and see p. 677 for Reynolds' agreement. For the (possibly unreliable) poll, see *Negro Digest*, VI (August 1948), 7. On the NAACP's response, see "Fighting the Jim Crow Army," *Crisis*, LV (May 1948), 136; and *Congressional Record*, 80th Cong., 2nd sess., pp. 4317–4318; and see pp. 4314–4318 for other Negro responses.

[30] On the meeting, see transcript of National Defense Conference on Negro Affairs, April 26, 1948, Records of the President's Committee on Equality of Treatment and Opportunity in the Armed Services, Truman Library. For the quotes, see *New York Times*, April 27, 1948; March 28, 1948.

moving toward a compromise with the South. In May, apparently with Royall's approval, the keynote speaker told the Democratic convention in North Carolina, "The Republican Party has gone much, much further in its advocacy of Federal interference in racial adjustments than has the Democratic Party," and he implied that the administration would not alter racial policies in the military. Truman apparently found this speech useful, for he did not dissent privately or publicly. The President retreated further from the boldness of February and sought to ease Southern doubts by inserting in the 1948 platform the party's moderate 1944 plank on civil rights. It was a mild statement, declaring simply that Congress should "exert its full constitutional powers to protect . . . the right [of minorities] to live, develop and vote equally with all citizens and share the rights that are guaranteed by our Constitution." [31]

This plank was not strong enough to keep some Negroes from moving into the camps of Henry Wallace or Thomas Dewey, the Republican standard bearer. Dewey, as governor of New York, had won acclaim for securing a state FEPC and appointing a few Negroes to prominent office. By pledging in the Republican platform support of an anti-lynching bill, equality of opportunity in employment, abolition of the poll tax, and elimination of segregation in the military, the GOP threatened to cut into Democratic strength in Negro ghettos. In addition, Dewey, according to the pundits, would receive indirect aid from Wallace. Charges of communist domination were weakening the Progressive party, but Truman faced a foe whose strength in traditional Democratic urban areas could throw the election to the Republicans. Wallace's earlier concern with civil rights had been questionable, but in 1948 he wore the mantle of a crusader for Negro rights. By condemning segregation and discrimination "in all forms and in all places," and thereby drawing curses and taunts, and some rotten fruit, Wallace courted the Negro vote and castigated Truman for his hypocrisy. So great was the feared defection of Negro voters from the Democratic party that two of the best ward leaders in Brooklyn and Harlem expected that about 75 per cent of the voters in their wards might support Wallace.[32]

In the NAACP, also, local support for Wallace was developing. In In-

[31] For the statement of William Joyner, see Royall to Truman, June 21, 1948, Clifford Papers. On the delayed orders, see news conference, May 13, 1948. For protests, see White to Truman, April 7, 1948, OF413; NAACP press release, July 22, 1948, and William Batt, Jr., to Gael Sullivan, April 20, 1948, Clifford Papers. For the plank, see Kirk Porter and Donald Johnson, eds., *National Party Platforms* (Urbana, Ill., 1956), p. 404. On thoughts about the order, see Oscar Ewing to Charles Murphy, January 2, 1948, Murphy Papers; Nash to Clifford, April 9, 1948, Nash Files No. 10; Niles to Clifford, May 12, 1948, Nash Files No. 11.

[32] See Porter and Johnson, *National Party Platforms*, pp. 452–453. On Dewey's record, see Lubell, *Future of American Politics*, pp. 94–95. On Wallace quotation, see *New York Times*, June 22, 1948; on defections, see Batt to Sullivan, April 20. On the parties and FEPC, see Lee McDonald, "Congress and F.E.P.C.: A Case Study in the Legislative Process" (unpublished PH.D. dissertation, Harvard University). For fears of the GOP and not the Progressives in Philadelphia, see Raymond P. Alexander to Sen. Frank Myers, May 11, 1948, McGrath Papers.

diana the state president was supporting Wallace, and in many of the large cities, including San Francisco and Philadelphia, local officials were backing the third-party ticket. Unlike these local leaders and the black people trapped in the ghettos, most prominent Negro civil rights leaders feared the taint of Wallace. And they were willing to return to the Republican party. They knew that the GOP, through its congressional party's involvement in the conservative coalition, was closely tied to the Southern Democrats and could not be depended upon to support the quest for equality. So Negro leaders stayed with the Democrats and Truman. They might press him to act with more boldness, they might demand that he fire subordinates who supported segregation, but most would not abandon him at the convention, for his advocacy of rights for the Negroes was unmatched by any twentieth-century President. To turn their backs on him in his time of need, most Negro leaders feared, would be injuring their own cause: no President might ever again risk supporting civil rights.[33]

While the national officials of the NAACP and most prominent Negro leaders were prepared to support the President, others in the party were ready for revolt. Urban bosses, persuaded that Truman would lose, hoped to save their local tickets, and prominent white Northern liberals sought power and principle. Their desperate boom for Dwight D. Eisenhower had collapsed when the general refused to run, but they battled at the convention to pledge the wavering President and the party to the civil rights recommendations he had submitted to Congress in February. They were unwilling to let Truman placate the Southern Democrats with the 1944 plank. Even though the platform committee had approved his compromise, the liberals and the bosses, supported by Negro leaders, pressed their case on the convention floor. Theirs was a struggle not for legislation but at best for technical commitment; for them the plank was an expression of considerable political value as well as a symbol of great moral importance. Spurred on by the Americans for Democratic Action, galvanized by one of that liberal organization's leaders, Hubert Humphrey, then mayor of Minneapolis, the convention endorsed a firm civil rights plank. It praised Truman for his courageous vision and called for federal laws guaranteeing political participation, equal opportunity in employment, security of person, and equal treatment in the services. Despite the drama and the passion, the convention did not directly attack Jim Crow: it did not promise social equality. By offering equality when it was still regarded as compatible with segregation, the convention was offering far less than the "walk forthrightly into the bright sunshine of human rights" which Humphrey had pledged.[34]

Nonetheless, the civil rights plank split the convention. The Mississippi

[33] On the NAACP's splits, see *New York Times*, March 20, June 27, 1948; "Annual Meeting," *Crisis*, LV (August 1948), 246–247.

[34] On the battle, see Clifton Brock, *Americans for Democratic Action: Its Role in National Politics* (Washington, D.C., 1962), pp. 94–99; cf. Truman, *Memoirs*, II, 181–182; William Batt, Jr., to Clifford, July 9 (?), 1948, Clifford Papers. For the platform, see Porter and Johnson, *National Party Platforms*, p. 435.

delegation and about half of the Alabama delegates walked out. Convening at Birmingham a few days later, the states righters, according to V. O. Key, were composed of "the big brass" of the Mississippi and Alabama parties, Governor J. Strom Thurmond of South Carolina and his entourage, and "a miscellaneous assortment of persons of no particular importance." These disgruntled Democrats briefly challenged the existing party framework and struck fear in the ranks of many organization regulars by forming the States Rights party.[35]

The addition of the popular Alben Barkley of Kentucky to the national Democratic ticket helped to salve some wounds. A loyal New Dealer, a moderate on racial matters, and a skilled tactician of compromise, he was an ideal candidate as a native of a border state. But even Barkley failed to lift the convention out of the clutches of despair; the party was convinced it could not win in November. Truman, facing challenges from the left and right, acted to puncture the gloom and in his acceptance speech hammered at the Republican-dominated Congress. The "Do-Nothing Congress," as he castigated it, would be called into special session to accomplish unfinished business, to test the promises of the Republican platform. By necessity, Truman had taken the bold approach.[36]

In 1948 there was no white backlash to fear in urban America outside the South, and a Democratic politician could court the Negro vote without risking the estrangement of Northern white voters. To most of the nation, America's racial problem was a Southern problem, and that conception shaped Truman's tactics. No longer in bondage to the South, he could follow but one political path. He had to capture the urban vote outside the South, for his chances of success rested heavily upon the cities. Without further stalling, Truman acted: on July 26 he barred discrimination in federal employment and created a board to consider complaints, and he declared a policy of equality of opportunity in the armed forces and established a committee (with members to be designated) to advise on the implementation of this vaguely formulated policy. In his executive orders the President still avoided an open legal assault on Jim Crow, promising only to end federal discrimination, not segregation. In the armed services the process would prove to be slow. But when General Omar Bradley, Army Chief of Staff, declared that the Army "is not out to make any social reform" and would continue segregation until the nation revised its racial policies, Truman publicly rebuked him and acknowledged that he wanted segregation ended. Within the week, McGrath conferred with Negro leaders, promising that the President was committed to the elimination of segregation in the armed forces and that he would soon appoint the committee to advise the military in its revision of race policies. On September 18, without fanfare,

[35] Key, *Southern Politics*, pp. 321–335.
[36] Truman's speech is in *Truman Papers 1948*, pp. 406–409.

Truman appointed the seven-man committee, which was liberal and included two Negroes.[37]

Truman, though eager to win Negro votes, was careful not to emphasize the differences on civil rights between the party's sectional wings or to antagonize loyal Southerners. When he addressed the special session of Congress in late July, he carefully tucked civil rights into a single paragraph. So close to the election, he was eager to prevent further disputes within the party over civil rights and unwilling to risk a Southern filibuster. To dramatize the failure of the Republican Congress, particularly its responsibility for inflation, he had asked for price controls which he did not want, and shifted attention from civil rights. His strategy almost miscarried in the Senate when a Southern filibuster against an anti–poll tax bill dragged on for nearly a week and blocked other legislation. Truman predictably was rebuffed by the Congress, which rejected price controls. He was also denied other requests — a housing program, aid to education, a higher minimum wage, relaxed immigration policies, and the civil rights program of February — on which he planned to conduct his campaign.

During the campaign, Truman played politics carefully and generally stayed away from civil rights. Following Clifford's strategy, the President concentrated on the Western farm states, where he talked primarily about public power and farm problems, and the Eastern and Midwestern industrial centers, where he spoke mostly of inflation, public housing, and the Taft-Hartley law. A campaign adviser urged the President to mention his accomplishments in civil rights "to prove that he acts as well as talks civil rights. The Negro votes in the crucial states will more than cancel out any votes he may lose in the South." Toward the end of his campaign Truman openly courted the Negro. He became the first President to speak in Negro Harlem.

An aggressive campaigner, a master of invective, Truman lusted for combat and gleefully condemned the GOP-dominated "Do-Nothing Congress." In a story generally familiar to Americans, he refuted the pollsters and won a close election. Battling the silent, evasive, seemingly smug Dewey, who avoided the issues, he "gave 'em hell." At least briefly, he had reshaped the

---

[37] For a weaker order on federal employment, see Donald Dawson to Clifford, March 8, 1948, OF596. Executive Orders 9980, 9981, in 13 F.R., 4311, 4314; for the Bradley episode, see news conference, July 29, 1948; Bradley to Truman, July 30, 1948, and Truman to Bradley, August 4, 1948, CS291.2, Army General Staff Papers, RG319, NA; last two items called to my attention in Richard M. Dalfiume, "Desegregation of the United States Armed Forces, 1939–1945" (unpublished Ph.D. dissertation, University of Missouri, 1966). For Randolph's renewed threat, see Pittsburgh Courier, July 3, 1948; for other pressures, see Leon Henderson to Truman, July 22, 1948, OF93B. On the meeting, see Grant Reynolds, "A Triumph of Civil Disobedience," Nation, CLXXVII (August 28, 1948), 365–366, and Black Worker, November 1948. On the announcement of the committee, see New York Times, September 19, 1948, p. 61; Pittsburgh Courier, September 25. For an earlier judgment, see Dawson to Truman, September 9, 1948, Nash Files No. 1.

Democratic coalition. It is easy in such tight races to demonstrate that the votes of any one group were critical: without the upsurge of farm support, Truman would have lost; without strong labor support, he would have lost. The NAACP concluded that 69 per cent of the Negro vote in twenty-seven major cities supported the President. The election revealed that the urban Negro vote, in a close election, could be more important than Southern solidarity and even suggested that Southern loyalty to the party could survive the struggle over civil rights.[38]

III

Truman, the confident recipient of a mandate, had great expectations as he awaited the new Congress. He did not disappoint Negro leaders, who were encouraged by the election and anticipated that the government would move closer toward advancing equality for their race. The President, promising the nation a "fair deal" (largely the policies he had urged during his first term), asked the Eighty-First Congress for the civil rights legislation its predecessor had refused. To secure these statutes, Democrats had to cut a path through the legislative bramble bush. In the House they weakened the Rules Committee, long an impediment to civil rights. But in the Senate liberal Democrats struggled without success.[39]

Their aim was liberalization of Senate rules to halt filibusters on motions (procedural issues) and measures; but poor strategy and party defections contributed to a serious defeat. To cut off unlimited debate, a bipartisan group proposed that two-thirds of the senators *present* could invoke cloture on motions. By choosing two-thirds, rather than a simple majority, they were offering the Southern Democrats a compromise, which was rejected. Democratic leaders, fearing a party split which could block Truman's other domestic legislation, moved cautiously. When the Senate bogged down in a filibuster preventing consideration of a rules change, Truman suggested a simple majority for cloture, thereby upsetting all hopes for the two-thirds compromise. Ultimately a coalition of Northern Republicans and Southern Democrats, joined by many Northern Democrats, triumphed and wrote an even tougher cloture rule, which required two-thirds of the *entire* membership.[40]

[38] For Truman's speeches, *Truman Papers 1948*, pp. 462–939, particularly 923–925. Advice from Batt to Clifford, August 11, 1948, Clifford Papers. On the campaign and election, also see Cecelia Van Auken, "The Negro Press in the 1948 Presidential Election," *Journalism Quarterly*, XXVI (December 1949), 431–435. For NAACP's estimates, see Henry Moon, "What Chance for Civil Rights," *Crisis*, LVI (February 1949), 42–45.

[39] On Negro leaders, see *Pittsburgh Courier*, January 8, 1949. Truman's message of January 5, 1949, is in *Truman Papers 1949*, pp. 1–7. On the House, see *Congressional Record*, 81st Cong., 1st sess., pp. 10–12.

[40] On the Senate, see *Congressional Record*, 81st Cong., 1st sess., pp. 863–866, 2724; McDonald, "Congress and F.E.P.C.," pp. 361–371; Berman, "Civil Rights," pp. 130–

Defeated on procedures, the administration soon failed in its quest for civil rights legislation outlawing the poll tax, making lynching a federal crime, establishing FEPC, and prohibiting segregation and discrimination in interstate transportation. Truman, though blocked by the Southern Democrat–Republican coalition, rejected a compromise — a voluntary FEPC, a constitutional amendment eliminating the poll tax, and an anti-lynching bill resting on state action — offered by Senator Richard Russell, the coalition's leader.[41]

Perhaps the President still believed he could marshal enough votes for a victory on civil rights; certainly some of his assistants still hoped for success. But Truman's action was also influenced, and perhaps even shaped, by the demands and expectations of white liberals and Negro leaders. To them the compromise would have seemed a "sell-out," for the states might never pass the amendment outlawing the poll tax, and the anti-lynching bill might suffer a similar fate. The President could not risk estranging the advocates of civil rights, for, without their support, this settlement would be of no political value. They, in turn, were apparently still optimistic that Congress would grant much of the civil rights legislation, and they certainly would not settle for a voluntary FEPC, much less *only* a voluntary FEPC. On that they were probably wrong, for the Congress would not grant more, and experience with the wartime FEPC suggested that negotiations and education by FEPC were more important than a sanction because they were more likely to be tried.[42]

The advocates of civil rights would not compromise and accept Russell's proposal, and they could not win on their own terms. Yet at times many of them would compromise, as for example in the spring of 1949, when they confronted the choice of an expanded, but segregated, public-housing program or no new program at all. (Presumably they also did not realize that slum clearance meant "Negro clearance.") Though the NAACP voted to "withhold active support from any federal legislation in . . . housing, health or education which does not expressly forbid segregation," the organization was unwilling to oppose such laws, and its liberal friends in Congress generally voted for such legislation. By the standards of these years, they were frequently practical liberals willing to sacrifice the goal of integra-

---

143. On Truman, see news conference, March 3, 1949; *New York Times*, March 16, 1949; and Jay Franklin [John Franklin Carter], "What Truman Really Thinks of Negroes," *Negro Digest*, VII (June 1949), 10–12.

41 On the Russell offer, see Malcolm Ross to Truman, February 5, 1949, OF596A; Jack Allen in *Washington Post*, July 13, 1949; Brooks Hays, *A Southern Moderate Speaks* (Chapel Hill, 1959), pp. 45–50; and Henry Silver to Truman, September 28, 1949, Clifford Files, Truman Library.

42 On Truman's hopes, see Truman to Representative Mary Norton, April 5, 1949, OF596. On FEPC, see Herbert Northrup, "Progress Without Federal Compulsion," *Commentary*, XIV (September 1952), 206–211; cf. Ruchames, *Race, Jobs*, pp. 142–143, 183–184. On FEPC and competing priorities, see NAACP Minutes, July 14 and September 12, 1949.

tion to meet what seemed to be some of the more immediate needs of the poor and disadvantaged. With liberal support, Congress also passed some of Truman's other Fair Deal proposals — public power, expanded social security, and higher minimum wages.[43]

Most liberals did not realize that these welfare measures did not effectively help the neglected millions suffering in poverty. Ironically, while the liberals chafed at Truman's limitations and believed that another President might lead Congress effectively and rally the nation to a crusade, they frequently failed to recognize the shallowness of the Fair Deal proposals. White liberals and black leaders were effectively isolated from the poor and the slums, and in the absence of militancy among lower-class blacks, there was little recognition of their needs — almost no communication from the bottom to the top. Like the President and his advisers, most liberals were unaware of the extent of poverty in America, or of the economic plight of many Negroes; they did not urge special programs to assist Negroes left unemployed (at roughly double the white rate) in the mild recession of 1949–1950. Concentrating on limited measures to restore a modicum of human dignity, the liberals and their allies emphasized legislation, primarily FEPC, which could not solve the deeper problems they failed to understand. To some, of course, FEPC itself had become a rallying ground for civil rights, an issue to dramatize the quest. Yet, not only was it an unsatisfactory issue, but civil rights leaders, because of their loose alliance with some labor leaders, were unwilling to acknowledge the discriminatory practices of many unions and the deep hatred of Negroes upon which these practices often rested. At least eighteen unions — eleven in the AFL and seven others, including four major railway brotherhoods — barred Negroes. Nor were white liberals generally concerned to seek social equality for the Negro. Perhaps it is an added irony that such liberals as Henry Wallace, Max Ascoli, Isador Lubin, and Oswald Garrison Villard could comfortably be members of the Cosmos Club, which excluded Negroes.[44]

---

[43] On public housing, see (unsigned) "The Housing Bill of 1949 and the Struggle over Segregation," July 7, 1949, Clifford Files; on "Negro clearance," see NAACP press release, July 2, 1952. Negro leaders did not generally protest segregation in public housing, but for an exception see NAACP press release, February 2, 1950. On January 3, 1949, the NAACP withheld active support for federal legislation in housing, health, or education which required segregation. NAACP Minutes, May 9, 1949. For occasional concern in the administration about "Negro clearance," see Richard Neustadt to Nash, June 5, 1950, Spingarn Papers, No. 38.

[44] For a more complete discussion, see Barton J. Bernstein, "Economic Policies," in Richard S. Kirkendall, ed., The Truman Period as a Research Field (Columbia, Mo., 1967), pp. 86–147. On labor unions, see John A. Davis, "Negro Employment: A Progress Report," Fortune, LXVI (July 1952), 102 ff; CIO News, April 17, May 1 and 22, 1950. On Negro income, see Marion Hayes, "A Century of Change: Negroes in the U.S. Economy, 1860–1960," Monthly Labor Review, LXXXV (December 1962), 1364; Arthur Ross, "The Negro in the American Economy," in Ross and R. A. Gordon, eds., Employment, Race and Poverty (New York, 1967), p. 18. On the Cosmos Club, see its List of Members (Washington, D.C., 1945).

If faulty or limited vision was one of the obvious defects of American liberalism in these years, perhaps its greatest flaw was a heavy emphasis on change through legislation and judicial decisions affirming equality or outlawing segregation. In a sense, the proponents of civil rights allowed their means to be shaped partly by their conservative opponents, who favored old laws and older social patterns and denied the capacity of new laws to alter social behavior. The liberal way was the legal way, and it was seldom measured against radical demands, never against bold new tactics. Only occa- sionally — in some ride-ins in 1947 and in the campaign of civil disobedience against the draft in 1948 — had there been bolder means. Nor was the organized left — the Communists, the Socialists, and the Progressives — more profound in its analysis, more visionary in the choice of tactics; it was only more demanding in the egalitarian legislation it sought. The point is not to judge the liberalism of those years anachronistically by current standards, nor to expect techniques which would probably have failed, but rather to emphasize from the perspective of our own time how little the liberals asked and how little their success would have accomplished in structural terms.[45]

They continued to struggle for the shallow reforms that Truman had requested. Despite some achievements in the new Congress, by late summer the President's hopes faded for even a piece of his civil rights program. He acknowledged defeat in October and agreed to postpone civil rights until the next session. Soon Negro leaders began to organize a mass lobby for civil rights legislation, and particularly for FEPC. At a publicized White House meeting with the leaders in January 1950, Truman promised that FEPC would reach a vote "if it takes all summer." Despite his pledge, Truman "was reluctant to invest much executive capital in a legislative enterprise that could bankrupt the rest of his program." When Speaker Sam Rayburn blocked FEPC in the House, the President did not prod him, but friends of the legislation managed to pry the bill loose. A few weeks later its foes cut out the provision for enforcement, and the House passed the measure.[46]

It expired in a filibuster in the Senate. The proceedings were a "parliamentary sham," concluded Arthur Krock. "Leaders of the Democratic party, boasting a majority in the Senate, were bold and vigorous in their public affirmations of support for FEPC, but singularly weak, hesitant, and inactive on the Senate floor." Rather than waging a determined battle against

[45] On the ride-in, see George M. Houser and Bayard Rustin, "Journey of Reconciliation" (mimeo, n.d., probably 1947), CORE files, Schomburg Library. Also see address by Walter White, June 29, 1947, Clifford Files. In 1951 the NAACP asked U.S. Steel to use its influence, through its subsidiary, Tennessee Coal and Iron, to stop "the reign of terror [in Birmingham] against Negro citizens." U.S. Steel "misunderstood" the request and shunted the NAACP to its subsidiary, which did nothing. (NAACP press release, July 12, 1951. Also see *ibid.*, March 26, 1950.)

[46] On sincerity of Democratic legislators, see *New York Times*, July 13, October 4, 1949. Truman's statement is in NAACP press release, January 19, 1950. On the course of the measure, see Ruchames, *Race, Jobs*, pp. 206–213. The quote is from Berman, "Civil Rights," p. 152.

the filibuster, as the new Majority Leader, Senator Scott Lucas, had promised, FEPC's friends participated in what the *Times* derided as "rocking-chair affair . . . no all night sessions . . . no laryngitis or body strain." (A. Philip Randolph criticized Lucas for "transparent, hypocritical tactics.") After this mild setback, Truman in July endorsed a second attempt to secure FEPC, but again his efforts were inadequate to rally his own party.[47]

By the summer of 1950 the administration's response to the challenge of civil rights was becoming clear. Truman would go on record in support of civil rights, but he could not press his program on a recalcitrant Congress and a torn party which he sought to patch. As a legislative leader on domestic issues he was a failure, unable to get Congress to do his bidding. He gave priority to foreign policy and had to temper his domestic program and offer concessions to Southern Democrats who endorsed his conduct of foreign affairs. As a moral leader he was limited. His sense of indignation was restricted, his voice muted. In his demands and actions he did seek to end Jim Crow in interstate transportation and in the military, but he avoided opportunities to condemn segregation or to lead a crusade. When, for example, Negroes were attacked at an integrated swimming pool in the nation's capital, the White House did not protest or even publicly express sympathy. Political wisdom dictated caution and frequently silence, but the recognition of these political necessities revealed the shortcomings of Truman's administration and of liberal democracy in America.[48]

Despite these equivocations and neglected opportunities, the administration was not without its achievements on behalf of civil rights. During these years of legislative stalemate, Truman's Department of Justice, despite his apparent indifference, was an active warrior in the battle against Jim Crow. It entered cases as an *amicus curiae* and submitted briefs arguing the unconstitutionality of enforcing restrictive covenants and of requiring separate-but-equal facilities in interstate transportation and in higher education. Prodded by Justice, and particularly the Solicitor General's office, the Supreme Court continued to chip away at racial discrimination. It struck down state laws requiring segregation in interstate travel and declared en-

---

[47] Krock in the *New York Times*, May 8, 1950, and see NAACP press releases, March 16, April 13, 1950. The second quotation is from *New York Times*, May 8, 1950; A Philip Randolph's comment is in *Chicago Defender*, May 6, 1950. On Truman's reluctance to battle for FEPC, see Spingarn to Charles Murphy, March 11, 1950; *Washington Post*, April 14, 1950; Spingarn to Truman, May 16 and 19, 1950, all manuscripts in Spingarn Papers, Truman Library. On the July efforts, see Spingarn, "Memorandum for the FEPC File," July 5, 1950, Nash Files, No. 4; *Pittsburgh Courier*, July 22, 1950. For public attitudes to FEPC, see Scott Fowler, "Congress Blocks the Civil Rights Program," *Commentary*, IX (May 1950), 397–406. On continued complaints about segregation in federal employment, see Thomas Richardson to David Niles, January 29, 1949, Nash Files, No. 8; Therese Robinson to Truman, April 19, 1949, OF93; NAACP press release, March 22, 1951; Dan Kimball to Lester Granger, Admiral Dennison Papers, Truman Library.

[48] On the swimming pool, see *Washington Post*, July 13, 1949.

forcement of restrictive covenants unconstitutional. (Two years after the court's decision, and after pressure from members of the administration and civil rights groups, the Federal Housing Administration finally declared it would not issue mortgages on property with restrictive covenants. But it continued, by its policies, to protect residential segregation.)[49]

Perhaps most important, Truman had moved to integrate the armed services. On September 18, 1948, he had initiated this program by appointing a committee of Charles Fahy, former Solicitor General; Lester Granger, Negro executive secretary of the Urban League; John Sengstacke, Negro editor of the *Chicago Defender*; Dwight Palmer, president of General Cable Corporation and member of the Urban League; and William Stevenson, president of Oberlin College. At their first meeting, Truman declared he wanted desegregation accomplished "in such a way that it is not a publicity stunt." For nearly two years the committee investigated the military and quietly sought cooperation for racial integration. From the beginning the members emphasized that racial segregation denied equal opportunity, and they found ample evidence that segregation used personnel inefficiently and injured morale. Backed by the President, the committee slowly made headway toward equal opportunity and integration. The Navy, which had few Negroes and did not officially segregate, agreed to seek more Negroes. The Marine Corps abolished segregated basic training but still retained some all-Negro units. The Air Force, while retaining a racial quota for some units and keeping some all-Negro forces, agreed to end most segregation and to open opportunities to both races. The Army lagged behind the other services, partly because it relied upon the draft and had more Negroes. After first seeking to deceive the committee, it moved slowly toward integration.

[49] Justice Department in brief for *Shelley* vs. *Kraemer* (signed by Tom Clark, Attorney General, and Philip Perlman, Solicitor General), 334 U.S. 1 (1948), which is a minor landmark because of the federal government's decision to intervene in a private case involving construction of the Fourteenth Amendment; brief for *Henderson* vs. *United States* (signed by Perlman and McGrath, Attorney General), 339 U.S. 816 (1950), the first federal attack on the *Plessy* doctrine; brief for *McLaurin* vs. *Board of Regents* (signed by Perlman and Philip Elman), 339 U.S. 629 (1950); brief for *Sweatt* vs. *Painter* (signed by Perlman and Elman), 339 U.S., 629 (1950). On the President's apparent lack of interest, see interview with Philip Elman, December 21, 1966. Charles Murphy, a close presidential advisor, as well as Nash and Spingarn, two White House assistants on civil rights, disclaimed any contact with the Solicitor General's office, but Spingarn, at a public meeting on December 28, 1966, belatedly claimed almost daily contact with Perlman. On Charles Murphy, see letter to Bernstein, October 25, 1967; cf. Arnold Raum to Bernstein, October 23, 1967. According to the White House appointment book, Perlman never had a business appointment with the President until August 17, 1949, and then he had only eighteen in the next three years. On FHA, see NAACP press release, February 4, 1949, and Nash to Dawson, June 16, 1952, Nash Files, No. 8. The revision of FHA policy applied only to new houses, and FHA was not scrupulous in enforcing it. (Hortense Gabel to Raymond Foley, February 26, 1953, Foley Papers, Truman Library.) Also see White to Truman, December 28, 1951, Nash Files, No. 6; Housing and Home Finance Agency, *Fifth Annual Report* (Washington, D.C., 1952), p. 413; U.S. Commission on Civil Rights, *Civil Rights '63* (Washington, D.C., 1963), pp. 95–98.

Even then, however, Truman had to promise the Secretary secretly that the Army could restore its restrictive Negro quota if it received a disproportionately high number of Negroes. Well into the Korean War the Army retained many segregated units, and integration in Europe did not even begin until April 1952, more than four years after Truman had promised to issue his executive order.[50]

Negro leaders recognized the government's efforts in their behalf, but they and their white allies realized sadly that Truman's efforts were not enlisted fully in the struggle for equality. When the Korean War erupted in June 1950, Negro leaders and white liberals urged Truman to emulate Roosevelt and create an FEPC "as an integral factor in mobilization of manpower . . . against . . . aggression." But Truman was blocked from establishing an FEPC by a legislative rider (which barred funds for an FEPC without explicit congressional approval), and he never explained the statutory impediment, never acted to inform the nation, and failed to create an FEPC-type agency which would be legal. Perhaps the civil rights groups knew of the statutory restriction to an executive-created FEPC, but probably they did not. That the President did not explain his position to them indicates the widening gap between him and the liberals. And it is symptomatic of Truman's conception of his office that he did not regard educating the people as part of the responsibility of presidential leadership.[51]

While urging Congress to approve FEPC legislation, Truman still did not act for months in this area where he had some effective power. On February 2, 1951, the third anniversary of his original civil rights message and after nearly seven months of war, the President moved only part way. Reaffirming Roosevelt's executive order, Truman authorized the Secretaries of Defense and Commerce to require and enforce non-discriminatory clauses in their government contracts. Proponents of FEPC were still dissatisfied. They suspected that federal agencies would continue to countenance discrimination by contractors, and they organized a vigorous campaign to spur the President to greater activity. On June 25, the tenth anniversary of Roosevelt's creation of FEPC, seven governors and eight mayors pro-

[50] Two other members were later unavailable for service. On the first meeting, see "Meeting of the President and the Four Service Secretaries with the President's Committee on Equality of Treatment and Opportunity in the Armed Services," January 12, 1949, OF1285(o). Report by the President's Committee on Equality of Treatment and Opportunity in the Armed Forces, *Freedom to Serve* (Washington, D.C., 1950), pp. 11–13, 24–29, 52–55, 67. On the promise, see Gordon Gray to Truman, March 1, 1950, OF1285B. In his news conferences of February 9 and April 13, 1950, Truman avoided attacking segregation, and he continued this policy in his address of May 15, 1950, reprinted in *Truman Papers 1950*, p. 413.

[51] The telegram is excerpted in *CIO News*, June 25, 1951. For continued demands, Senator Hubert Humphrey to Truman, January 12, 1951; National Council of Negro Women, November 18, 1950; Albert Fitzgerald to Truman, October 25, 1950, all in Nash Files, No. 17; also many letters in OF40; *Chicago Defender*, November 25, 1950; and *Pittsburgh Courier*, January 6 and 13, 1951. The legislative impediment, the so-called Russell amendment, was Public Law 358, sec. 213, 78th Cong., 2nd sess. On Truman, see also news conference of January 18, 1951.

claimed "Fair Employment Practice Day," and Mrs. Roosevelt supported the effort by commemorating FEPC in a ceremony at the grave of her husband. Only after vigorous liberal demands continued for another six months did Truman create a Committee on Government Contracts Compliance (from funds of participating federal agencies) to review adherence to the non-discriminatory provisions required in government contracts. The committee found that the clause was "almost forgotten," that most contractors "made little, if any attempt to adhere to its standards," and that officials of many federal agencies lacked "even the will" to enforce the requirement. With a small budget and few personnel, without power of enforcement or the right to hold public hearings, in effect without presidential support, the committee was not very effective in halting discrimination.[52]

In this area of executive action, as in others, Truman was never as bold as Negro leaders or staunch proponents of civil rights desired. A decade had passed in the assault upon discrimination, but the Democratic administration remained a cautious friend of civil rights. The President would not use his great powers fully even in his last years in the White House; yet he continued to ask Congress to pass the legislation he had recommended in 1948. The Democratic Congress, dominated on domestic issues by the bipartisan conservative alliance, was unwilling to cooperate with the President and blocked most of the Fair Deal. After the Korean War began, Congress balked at all social reform. The Democratic defeats in the congressional races of 1950 made Truman and the legislature bitter antagonists. Long-standing differences on domestic issues paled before the cleavage on foreign policy. In 1951 committees in each house even refused to report a civil rights measure, and the prospects dimmed for legislation on lynching, the poll tax, and FEPC.[53]

The nation was succumbing to vicious illiberalism, and McCarthy seemed

[52] Executive Order 10210, in 16 F.R. 1049. For demands, see "Statement [by Negro Americans] to President Truman at the White House Conference on February 28, 1951," Nash Files, No. 17; Senator William Benton to Truman, October 21, 1951, OF526B; James Carey to Truman, April 12, 1951; *CIO News*, June 25, 1951; and Patrick M. Malin, Francis Biddle, Walter White, *et al.* (leaders of twelve other liberal organizations) to Truman, June 24, 1951, OF40, which includes many more letters of complaint; *Chicago Defender*, April 28, May 19, June 2 and 30, December 8, 1951; *Pittsburgh Courier*, June 8, 1951; "Where Is FEPC?" *Crisis*, LVIII (April 1, 1951), 258. Executive Order 10308, in 16 F.R. 12303. For criticisms that Truman had not created an FEPC, see *Pittsburgh Courier*, December 15, 1951; NAACP press releases, December 6, 1951, January 3, 1952; Randolph to Truman, December 4, 1951, OF526. Cf. Channing Tobias to Truman, December 6, 1951, and other correspondence in OF526 and 526B. On the committee's experiences, see "Résumé of the Committee's letter of January 30, 1952 . . . ," March 17, 1952; for resistance by officials of the Department of Defense, see "Suggestions from Contracting Agencies" (n.d., about July 1952); Palmer to Nash, September 2, 1952, all in Records of Committee on Government Compliance, No. 3, RG325, NA. See its *Equal Economic Opportunity* (Washington, D.C., 1953), pp. 3–5, for quotations, and also pp. 42–46 and 63–76.

[53] State of the Union message of January 8, 1951, calling for "equal rights and equal opportunities," is in *Truman Papers 1951*, and the quotation is on p. 12; the budget message, which asked for FEPC, is in *ibid.*, and see particularly p. 80.

to be running rampant. With Americans fearful of communism, suspicious of reform, and identifying most opponents of segregation as reds, Truman remained cautious. His prestige was damaged, his influence waning; he had almost no political capital. But despite his plight, his administration did not retreat before these new tides. When the citizens and officials of Cicero, a Chicago suburb, attacked a Negro war veteran who moved into the previously all-white area, Truman's Attorney General, prodded by public outrage, sought action after a local grand jury had exonerated the hoodlums and officials and had indicted the Negro's attorney for defending his client's right to rent a home.[54]

There was much to admire in Truman's willingness to allow the Department of Justice to place the government on the side of Negro rights, but some Americans wanted even more vigorous action. A handful demanded that the President act as energetically to advance the Negro's cause as had the government in opposing communism at home and abroad. (Walter White pointed to one of the disturbing paradoxes of Truman's government — "an increasing tendency on the part of government agencies to associate activity on interracial matters with disloyalty." Even Negroes working for the federal government and opposing segregation were frequently investigated as security risks.) Though Truman's interest in civil rights never approached his commitment to anti-communism, he did refuse to let the forces of reaction and segregation triumph. He pocket-vetoed a bill requiring some integrated federal schools in the South (such as those in Oak Ridge) to accept segregation. Continuing the struggle, in his 1952 State of the Union message he told Congress, "As we build our strength to defend the freedom in the world, we ourselves must extend the benefits of freedom more widely among all our own people." He was careful not to antagonize the South and generally silent about racial violence, but he did not abandon his occasional pleading for equality. Nevertheless, the Democratic record, when judged by legislative accomplishment, was bleak indeed. In 1952 civil rights bills were again bottled up in hostile committees and did not reach the floor of either house.[55]

IV

For Truman the promise of equality and protection against discrimination (though he construed these rights narrowly) remained the "essence of the

[54] Events at Cicero are discussed by Charles Abrams in *Forbidden Neighbors: A Study of Prejudice in Housing* (New York, 1955), pp. 103–106; also see pp. 150–164 for the code of the National Association of Real Estate Boards, which asserted as a principle that realtors should not act to establish interracial neighborhoods.

[55] White to Truman, November 26, 1948, OF258K; and Carl Murphy to Truman, April 10, 1950, OF93 misc.; NAACP Minutes, November 8, 1947. The bill was HR 5411, and advice from officials is in bill file 107 and Nash Files, No. 31. Veto is in the White House press release, November 2, 1951. Address of January 9 is in *Truman Papers 1952–1953*, p. 16.

American ideal and the American Constitution." In the spring and early summer of 1952 he campaigned sporadically for a strong civil rights plank. He was unwilling to see his party split again, and he seemed conscious of his record and perhaps anxious about how historians would judge him. But he yielded to exigency, and he succumbed ultimately, but uncomfortably, to the politics of accommodation. He gave up trying to place pledges for compulsory FEPC and a simple majority for cloture in the party's 1952 platform, and let other party leaders work out a compromise with the Southern wing. Whatever fears, however mild, had lingered of a Southern bolt in civil rights, the actions of the Democratic chiefs soon quashed them.[56]

The party retreated from the platform of 1948. By promising "equal opportunities for education, for economic advancement, and for decent living conditions," and leaving unspecified its efforts to eradicate racial discrimination, the Democrats yielded to caution. Their standard bearer, Adlai Stevenson, opposed compulsory federal FEPC, and John Sparkman of Alabama was placed on the national ticket. The party recognized its obligation to the South and restored temporarily the uneasy sectional alliance. At the convention, liberals won a weak loyalty pledge to the party, but when delegates from three Southern states balked, they did not bolt, nor did they lose their voting rights. In 1952 the bolters on civil rights were few, and they were not disgruntled Southerners but Negroes. Unable to halt the politics of capitulation, lacking adequate support from liberal allies who were anxious to heal the party, Adam Clayton Powell, Negro congressman from Harlem, and some other Negro delegates left in dismay. "Juggling with the favor of one group as against another, and maneuvering toward the tolerable compromise, the [white] politicians equivocated and lost sight of principle," concluded Oscar Handlin.[57]

In the campaign both parties competed for the important Negro vote which could swing the election. Stevenson moved beyond the platform and agreed, if elected, to try to influence the Senate to reform its rule on filibusters. Though the party had not endorsed the civil rights plank that Truman had urged, the President continued to condemn the Republicans for shying away from civil rights and for refusing to join the struggle for equality. He criticized the General and the GOP, but actually there was little to choose (at least as judged by promises) between the positions of Eisenhower and

[56] The quotation is from his address to the Jefferson-Jackson Day dinner on March 29 and repeated to the ADA on May 17, 1952, *Truman Papers 1952–1953*, pp. 224, 346; and Truman reaffirmed his position in a speech at Howard University on June 13, 1952, White House press release, and in his news conference of June 19, 1952. For Negro praise, see *Chicago Defender*, May 24, June 21, 1952. On the efforts in May by the chairman, see *Nation*, CLXXIV (May 24, 1952), 489.

[57] The Democratic platform is in Porter and Johnson, *National Party Platforms*, pp. 473–489, and the Republican is on pp. 496–505. For *Chicago Defender*, July 12, 1952 [*sic*]. On the convention, see *New York Times* and *Washington Post*, July 16–28, 1952; *Chicago Defender* and *Pittsburgh Courier*, July 19–August 9, 1952; Oscar Handlin, "Party Maneuvers and Civil Rights Restrictions," *Commentary*, XIV (September 1952), 197–206.

Stevenson on civil rights. Nevertheless, Truman went to Harlem and to the Negro section of Chicago to assail the Republicans on civil rights, to emphasize the achievements of his administration, and to plead for Democratic votes. He had become a conscience for the Democrats. He was bolder on civil rights than his party and its presidential candidate. Pushed years before to take a stand on civil rights and eager to defend his own record (which included many defeats on civil rights by the Congress), the President was now unwilling to abandon the issue. "You can't cure a moral problem, or a social problem, by ignoring it," he warned the nation.[58]

But the issue in 1952 was not civil rights. That challenge could not rekindle the passions of 1948. Instead, as the nation moved from the domestic-oriented politics of the thirties and the postwar forties to a new politics, the issues were communism, corruption, and Korea. No Democratic candidate, certainly not the scholarly and reflective Stevenson, aided by the slashing and discredited Truman, could have prevented the triumph of Dwight D. Eisenhower and the Republican party. The new President and his victorious party would face many challenges in the next eight years. On the domestic front, aside from McCarthyism, the major test would be in civil rights, and later generations might well judge the Republicans more by their failure and lack of vision in this realm than even by their ability to vanquish McCarthy, to cleanse politics, and to protect dissent. Truman, in some measure, had dimly foreseen the future. Appraising his own contributions, he had concluded:

> The civil rights report and the civil rights program give voice and expression to this great change of sentiment. They are the necessary instrument of progress. They are the trumpet blast outside the Walls of Jericho — the crumbling walls of prejudice.[59]

V

"No occupant of the White House since the nation was born has taken so frontal or constant a stand against racial discrimination as has Harry S. Truman," Walter White said in 1952. Truman's rhetoric and his efforts fell far short of the promise of American democracy, and his actions were not even as bold as his words. But his contributions were still significant. He was the first President in the twentieth century to assail discrimination against Negroes, to condemn violence and intimidation directed at them, to pro-

---

[58] On Stevenson, see *New York Times*, August 5, September 3, 1952; Stuart Brown, *Conscience in Politics: Adlai E. Stevenson in the 1950's* (Syracuse, 1961), pp. 76–112; NAACP press release, September 11, 1952. Powell returned to the Stevenson camp. (*New York Times*, August 30, 1952.) For Truman's statement, see speech of June 13.

[59] Quotation from speech of June 13. Also see his farewell address, White House press release, January 15, 1953. On the Negro vote, see Henry Moon, "Election Post-Mortem," *Crisis*, LXIV (December 1952), 616–617; Louis Harris, *Is There a Republican Majority?* (New York, 1954), pp. 152–153.

claim their legal equality. Though his vision was limited and his motives frequently political; though his concern about the American image abroad influenced his actions; though he was reluctant to lead the nation on a crusade for equality and never vigorously attacked Jim Crow, he did advance the quest for civil rights. As President he started to desegregate the armed services and moved to end federal discrimination in federal employment. It was his Department of Justice, despite Truman's apparent lack of interest, that placed the weight of the national government against segregated schools and argued that separate-but-equal was self-contradictory and unconstitutional. The government had moved to a redefinition, a broader view of equality which presaged the end of the *Plessy* doctrine.[60]

In all, the Truman program was moderate, and its defects left the nation with a great burden of unresolved problems. Viewed from the perspective of today, Truman's views seem unduly restrained and his government excessively cautious; viewed even by the standards of his own time, he was a reluctant liberal, troubled by terror and eager to establish limited equality. He was ahead of public opinion in his legislative requests, but not usually in his actions. In that imbalance there is some evidence to support cynical charges but not enough to minimize his contributions. While lagging behind the new liberalism which found an important place for racial equality, Truman struggled with the racial problems of America.

The recipient of an ambiguous heritage, Truman bestowed a similar legacy upon the generation which followed. In emphasizing the ambiguity of that legacy, he focused American attention on the moral dimension of its dilemma. By his occasional advocacy, he educated the nation and held high the promise of equality. By kindling hope, he also may have prevented rebellion and restrained or delayed impulses to work outside the political system. In a limited sense he encouraged the reform forces which relied upon legalism; by yielding partly to their pleas and by granting them frequent audiences, he dignified them and their methods. He also helped — often in spite of himself — to educate a nation to its obligations and its failures. In another sense, he unleashed expectations he could not foresee, desires he could not understand, and forces which future governments would not be able to restrain. The injustices he revealed, the evils he tried occasionally to correct would soon demand new efforts and a new vision which would leave an aging Truman an embarrassing anachronism and many Negro leaders and

[60] White's statement began, "Although he has appeared to soft-pedal the civil rights issue in recent months . . ." It is from NAACP press release, April 3, 1952. For other praise, see Wilkins to Truman, January 12, 1953, OF596. When the first of the primary school cases arose, Perlman, the Solicitor General, had boggled at filing a brief urging desegregation at the primary level, though he had previously endorsed briefs for integrated higher education. When he resigned, the new Attorney General, James P. McGranery, endorsed this brief. The Department waited until after the election before filing it in order to keep the issue removed from any appearance of partisan politics. Interview with Elman.

their white allies as painfully outdated as their techniques. To remedy the injustices which the federal government did not correct and would not protest, some Americans would take to the streets to dramatize the evils a nation had too long endured. Ultimately these failures would compel blacks to reconsider their assumptions about the promise of American life and their quest for a color-blind society. Many would conclude that dignity and racial pride could be achieved only in separation from, and in antagonism to, white America. For too long, Americans had reneged on their commitment to equality; for too long they had denied human aspirations. The bold efforts and the troubling events of the late fifties and the sixties may have been at least as much the result of the failure of Harry S. Truman's administration as of its successes.[61]

[61] On Truman's responses to new tactics and demands, see *New York Times*, June 3, 1961; March 3, 1965.

25

THE COLD WAR, THE ATOMIC BOMB, AND THE "REVISIONISTS"

A perilous tension between the United States and the Soviet Union has dominated international policy-making since the end of World War II and, especially during the 'fifties, has had nearly as much importance for American domestic politics as well. For a quarter of a century now the world's two mightiest powers, once partners in the destruction of the Nazi war machine, have been virtually implacable foes. How did the great wartime allies develop such mutual hostility so soon after a triumphant partnership? This is the question to which a small army of American scholars, many young and much alienated, have been devoting their energies.

A simple answer, generally popular with the American press and with some older scholars as well, is that the Cold War originated with the Soviet Union's avowed dedication to the eventual conversion of the world to the communist system. This is a comforting answer in the sense that it thoroughly exonerates United States diplomacy; but such an answer offers no hope of an end to the tension — to "the balance of terror," as it has become — short of the triumph, by persuasion or by war, of one or the other of the great conflicting systems. Other answers are at least more interesting because they permit a broader scope for self-questioning and because they offer the possibility of a workable solution short of the unlikely or the catastrophic. One is that an aggressive United States policy unnecessarily drove the Russians into an understandably suspicious and defensive posture even before the war was over. Among other things, this view argues that the Russians are not so dedicated to international communism that they would willingly risk war to promote it forcibly, that they are and have usually been first of all concerned with their own national security and particularly with the security of their western frontier, and that tensions could be subsantially reduced if the West would consent to a more or less formal division of Europe, and perhaps the globe, into "spheres of influence."

In this interpretation, American ideology shares with Soviet ideology responsibility for the tensions and frequent "brinkmanship" of recent diplomacy. America's deeply-rooted commitment to a foreign policy governed by the liberal ideology, in which diplomacy must be handmaiden to principle, not politics, rejected outright, as immoral, suggestions that the destinies of small nations be set within spheres of

major-power influence. The United States insisted on self-determination for all the central European nations liberated from Nazism, including eventually Germany itself. Yet because of still-fresh memories
of national and ethnic enmities, to say nothing for the moment of the
issue of communism, "self-determination" for Russia's western neighbors suggested to the Soviet Union the reestablishment of hostile
nations on its frontier, and essentially the recreation of the status quo
ante at least so far as considerations of national security governed
Soviet foreign policy. From this viewpoint, American insistence on
self-determination tended to be seen only as evidence of calculated
ill will; whereas American rejection of spheres of influence in Europe
while we were busy establishing our influence in Japan, Korea, Greece,
and elsewhere could be considered evidence of duplicity.

All our insistence upon principle, of course, could not roll back the
Russian army in central Europe. We retrenched with a policy of
"containment," which was ostensibly designed to meet Soviet expansionist thrusts where they might appear. Thus we accepted of necessity what we had rejected in principle. The alternative was to make
war on the Soviet Union.

United States domestic politics meanwhile precluded the surrender
of self-determination in principle even while Soviet military power
precluded self-determination in fact. The political opposition especially, growing bitter and perhaps even irresponsible because of its
long deprivation of power, compelled the incumbent administration
in Washington to put on its boldest face. Congressional demands
that President Truman take a "tough line" against Soviet efforts to
create sympathetic ("satellite") governments in the countries occupied by her troops were matched only by the demands for rapid demobilization of our military immediately following the surrender of
the Axis. The weaker the West became militarily, the more belligerent became the diplomatic exchanges. The communist coup in Czechoslovakia (February 1948), the Berlin blockade (July 1948–May 1949),
the communist victory in China (Fall 1949), and the outbreak of
the Korean War (June 1950) tended to give substantial force to
the interpretation that laid the blame for international tensions on
Soviet intransigence. When, on American initiative, the "tough line"
took substantive form in the North Atlantic Treaty Organization
(NATO) and German rearmament, Western foreign policy had come
in effect to confirm the very division of Europe that the United States
had in principle refused to countenance.

Communist belligerency in Europe and Asia and partisan politics
in the United States continued to preclude a settlement with Russia
on the principal divisive issues. The Republican party victory in 1952
somewhat reduced the factor of domestic partisanship in this tense
standoff. This change was indicated when President Eisenhower was
able to negotiate a settlement of the Korean conflict on terms that
partisan attacks had made impossible for the Truman administration.
The verbal "tough line" meanwhile had gravitated to its logical cul-

mination in John Foster Dulles's formulation of the policy of "Liberation" (first set forth in "A Policy of Boldness," *Life*, May 19, 1952), which was frankly shaped to encourage rebellion within the Soviet orbit. But whatever force a policy of moral exhortation might ever have had was expunged in 1956 when Dulles, then secretary of state, refused to commit American power to assist the Hungarian revolution. (Dulles had shown similar restraint during the Polish uprising earlier in 1956 and in the East Berlin riots of 1953.)

By declining to assist the rebelling Germans, Poles, and Hungarians (and, in 1968, the Czechs), the United States effectively conceded the spheres-of-influence principle outright. The noticeable "thaw" in Russo-American relations since 1956 may owe as much to that de facto concession as to Russia's grave difficulties with Red China. That none of the factors underlying the "thaw" can be said to derive from a "tough line" policy lends weight to the proposals for "disengagement" urged by foreign-policy experts such as George Kennan. If the relaxation of repressive conditions in the "satellite" countries is ever to take place (without a major war, that is), it can only come about if the change is not regarded by the Russians as a defeat or humiliation.

On the other hand, experts such as Dean Acheson, former secretary of state, and Henry Kissinger, top foreign policy advisor to President Nixon, insist that Soviet national purposes extend far beyond the mere confirmation of the status quo in Europe and elsewhere. From this viewpoint, the "thaw" can only be temporary, and the West must maintain a position of strength from which it may not only negotiate confidently with the Russians but also contain the intrinsic expansionist tendencies of the Soviet system.

This description of the evolution of the Cold War sketches only the surface of the problem. Beneath lies the more fundamental problem of premises and motives that governed the crucial decisions of Cold War diplomacy. In the first of the following articles, Charles Maier, Assistant Professor of History at Harvard University, closely scrutinizes the vigorous and sometimes vitriolic clash between those historians who generally have attributed the Cold War to an aggressive, uncompromising Soviet foreign policy that has been continuously distrustful of "capitalist" diplomacy, and those called "revisionists" who have placed the onus on United States aggression and, more particularly, on the expansionist "needs" of liberal capitalism. The roots of revisionism lie in the work of historian William Appleman Williams, particularly his *American-Russian Relations, 1871–1947* (1952) and *The Tragedy of American Diplomacy** (1959), though, as Maier suggests, the remarkable enthusiasm for revisionism in recent years may owe more to the alienation evoked by United States policy in Indochina than to the cogency of Williams's presentation. Indeed, American engagement in Vietnam, Laos, and Cambodia has aroused such vehement controversy that it is probably unreasonable to expect any recent account to avoid reading current partisan arguments into history. Maier's article is noteworthy not only for its comprehensiveness and its use of European source materials, but also for its incisive isolation of the premises – in part, mutually exclusive – on which the revisionist and "orthodox" treatments rest. His point that the revisionist argument depends unusually heavily on preestablished values, and is thus unusually independent of evidential test, contains a very serious indictment. Yet it is one that will scarcely disturb those who are prepared to argue that the Cold War is itself largely a conflict over value systems that permit no "neutral" vantage point.

The second article reprinted below, by Martin J. Sherwin of the University of California History Department at Berkeley, is a brief but sharp review essay of three major books concerning "the most important consequence of the Second World War": the advent of atomic energy and the revolution in modern diplomacy that it evoked. Sherwin adds another dimension to Gar Alperovitz's treatment of *Atomic Diplomacy*, and moreover calls attention to the awesome dilemma of the scientific community facing the conflict between the modern demands of national security and the age-old requirement of science for free access to knowledge.

The best bibliography on the Cold War can be found in Maier's and Sherwin's footnotes. Beyond that, Diane Shaver Clemens, *Yalta* (1970), is outstanding among the few important works to appear since the articles below were written. N. A. Graebner, "Dean G. Acheson (1949–1953)," and H. J. Morgenthau, "John Foster Dulles (1953–1959)," both in Graebner, ed., *An Uncertain Tradition: American Secretaries of State in the Twentieth Century** (1961), and H. J. Morgenthau's review of G. Kolko's *The Politics of War* (1969), "The Cold War as History," in *The New York Review of Books*, July 10, 1969, are of especial interest. Thomas G. Paterson, ed., *The Origins of the Cold War* (1970), contains an interesting selection of viewpoints and an extensive bibliography.

Revisionism and the Interpretation
of Cold War Origins

CHARLES S. MAIER

Few historical reappraisals have achieved such sudden popularity as the current revisionist critique of American foreign policy and the origins of the Cold War. Much of this impact is clearly due to Vietnam. Although

Reprinted by permission of the author and the President and Fellows of Harvard College from *Perspectives in American History*, 4 (1970), 313–47, published by the Charles Warren Center for Studies in American History, Harvard University.

the work of revision began before the United States became deeply involved in that country, the war has eroded so many national self-conceptions that many assumptions behind traditional Cold War history have been cast into doubt. For twenty years the Soviet-American conflict was attributed to Stalin's effort to expand Soviet control through revolutionary subversion,[1] or, as in a more recent formulation, to "the logic of his position as the ruler of a totalitarian society and as the supreme head of a movement that seeks security through constant expansion." [2] Revisionist assailants of this view have now found readers receptive to the contrary idea that the United States must bear the blame for the Cold War. The preoccupation with America's historical guilt distinguishes the new authors not only from anti-communist historians but from earlier writers who felt the question of blame was inappropriate. William McNeill, for example, in an outstanding account written at the height of the Cold War, stressed a nearly inevitable falling-out among allies who had never been united save to fight a common enemy.[3] This viewpoint has been preserved in some recent accounts; but since Denna Fleming's massive Cold War history of 1961, the revisionists have gone on to indict the United States for long-term antipathy to communism, insensitivity to legitimate Soviet security needs, and generally belligerent behavior after World War II.[4]

The revisionist version of Cold War history includes three major elements: an interpretation of Eastern European developments; an allegation of anti-Soviet motives in the Americans' use of the atomic bomb; and a general Marxian critique of the alleged American search for a world capitalist hegemony. Since these three elements comprise a detailed reassessment of the role of the United States in world politics they deserve to be discussed and evaluated in turn; but in the end one must consider the more fundamental question of the conceptual bases of revisionist history.

The revisionists are divided among themselves about the turning points and the causes of American aggressiveness, but all agree that the traditional

---

[1] Herbert Feis, *Roosevelt-Churchill-Stalin. The War They Waged and the Peace They Sought* (Princeton, 1957), p. 655.

[2] Adam Ulam, *Expansion and Coexistence: The History of Soviet Foreign Policy, 1917–1967* (New York, 1968), p. 377.

[3] William H. McNeill, *America, Britain, and Russia, Their Cooperation and Conflict, 1941–1946* (London, 1953). For recent explorations in the same spirit: Walter LaFeber, *America, Russia, and the Cold War, 1945–1966* (New York, 1967), which stresses growing ideological militancy; Louis J. Halle, *The Cold War as History* (London, 1967), a treatment that verges on fatalism; Martin F. Herz, *Beginnings of the Cold War* (Bloomington, Ind., 1966); William L. Neumann, *After Victory: Churchill, Roosevelt, Stalin, and the Making of the Peace* (New York, 1967); André Fontaine, *History of the Cold War*, trans. D. D. Paige (2 vols.: New York, 1968); cf. also Arthur Schlesinger, Jr., "Origins of the Cold War," *Foreign Affairs*, 46 (1967), 22–52.

[4] Denna F. Fleming, *The Cold War and Its Origins, 1917–1960* (2 vols.: Garden City, N.Y., 1961). Unfortunately the book relies almost exclusively on newspaper accounts and commentary. Relying heavily on Fleming for its historical analysis is David Horowitz, *The Free World Colossus* (New York, 1965).

description of the crucial events in Eastern Europe must be radically altered. The old version of the roots of the Cold War charged Soviet Russia with progressively tightening totalitarian control from mid-1944. In effect the earlier historians only confirmed the diagnosis of Ambassador Averell Harriman in Moscow, whose cables between late 1943 and early 1945 changed from emphasizing the needs of a functioning wartime alliance to stressing the difficulties of prolonging cooperation in the face of Soviet ambitions.[5] In this evolution of views, the Russian refusal to facilitate Anglo-American supply flights to the Warsaw uprising of August 1944 and Moscow's backing for its own Polish government later in that year provoked major Western disillusionment. It was agreed after 1945 that the germs of the Cold War lay in Stalin's intransigence on the Polish issue.

In contrast to this interpretation, the revisionists charge that the United States forced Stalin into his stubborn Polish policy by backing the excessive aspirations of the exile Polish government in London. Revisionist accounts emphasize how antagonistic the State Department's refusal to sanction any territorial changes during the war must have appeared in Moscow. They point out that the territory that the Soviets had annexed in 1939, and which the Poles were contesting, had restored the 1919 Curzon line of mediation and merely reversed Poland's own acquisitions by war in 1920– 1921. At the Teheran Conference in December 1943, Churchill and Roosevelt had loosely consented to Poland's borders being shifted westward. Even Harriman backed the British in counseling the London Poles to accept the terms the Soviets were offering in October 1944.[6] Only when the Russians produced their own so-called Lublin Committee and thereafter Polish government — allegedly out of frustration and bitterness at the unyielding stance of the London Poles — did the focus switch from the question of territory to that of regimes.[7] At the Yalta conference, Stalin agreed to add some Western Poles to the communist-based government and to move toward free elections; and if the United States had continued to accept the

---

[5] Harriman's assessments in Department of State, *Foreign Relations of the United States* (henceforth: *FRUS*), especially November 5, 1943 foreseeing disagreements on reparations and Poland but generally pleased with Russian cooperation (*FRUS*, 1943, III, 589–593), August 15, and August 21, 1944 (*FRUS*, 1944, III, 1376, 1382 n.1), March 17, 1945 (*FRUS*, 1945, III, 732), and April 4, 1945 — "the Soviet program is the establishment of totalitarianism," — (*FRUS*, 1945, V, 819).

[6] For the Teheran discussions of the Polish frontier, Feis, *Churchill-Roosevelt-Stalin*, pp. 284–285. Harriman advice in *FRUS*, 1944, III, 1322 ff.

[7] For the revisionist view of the Polish dispute, Gabriel Kolko, *The Politics of War, The World and United States Foreign Policy*, 1943–1945 (New York, 1968), pp. 99– 122, 147–152; Gar Alperovitz, *Atomic Diplomacy: Hiroshima and Potsdam* (New York, 1965), esp. pp. 243–256; Fleming, *The Cold War and Its Origins*, I, 222–248. Cf. Feis, *Churchill-Roosevelt-Stalin*, pp. 283–301, 453–460, 518–529; official summary in *FRUS*, *The Conferences at Malta and Yalta* (1945), p. 202 ff.; and for strong anticommunist presentations, Arthur Bliss Lane, *I Saw Poland Betrayed* (Indianapolis, 1948), and Edward J. Rozek, *Allied Wartime Diplomacy: A Pattern in Poland* (London, 1958).

Yalta provisions in a generous spirit, the revisionists maintain, the earlier disputes might have been overcome. Gar Alperovitz argues in detail that after Yalta Roosevelt sought to persuade Churchill to move toward the Soviet position on the key question of who would determine which Western Polish leaders might be invited to join the expanded Warsaw government. But Roosevelt's successors, notably President Truman and Secretary of State James Byrnes, put up a harsh fight to reverse this supposed acquiescence in the creation of a basically communist-dominated government.[8]

This American attitude toward Polish issues, the revisionists claim, was typical of a wide range of Eastern European questions where the United States appeared to be set upon frustrating Russia's international security. From the summer of 1945 Truman and Byrnes, it is charged, sought to reverse the pro-Soviet governments in Rumania and Bulgaria by blustering with atomic weapons.[9] The American opposition to Soviet demands for territorial security and friendly neighboring states allegedly forced the Russians away from their minimal aims of 1943–1945, which envisaged United Front coalition regimes, to the ruthless communization they imposed by 1947–1948. Had the United States not demanded total openness to Western influence, the revisionists imply, Poland, Bulgaria, and Rumania might have survived as Hungary and Czechoslovakia did until 1947–1948 and Finland thereafter. But in fact, they argue, the parties and social groups that Washington desired to entrench could only intensify Stalin's mistrust. In revisionist eyes these groups were either unworthy or unviable: unworthy because they regrouped pre-war reactionary elements who had often been pro-German, unviable because even when democratic they were doomed to fall between the more intransigent right and the Russian-backed left.[10]

---

[8] Alperovitz, *Atomic Diplomacy*, pp. 250–253, 261–267, on Roosevelt after Yalta, and 188–225 on post-Hiroshima aggressiveness. In judging Roosevelt's correspondence it is important to remember that by March 1945 the Polish issue was just part of a larger concern about keeping the alliance together in view of the upcoming United Nations conference and preventing broad public disillusion about the Crimean agreements. Roosevelt was acting more as a mediator than as a defender of a particular Polish position. For the President's misgivings about the agreement even at Yalta see William D. Leahy, *I Was There* (New York, 1950), pp. 315–316; the mingled exultation and disillusion in the post-Yalta atmosphere is conveyed in Robert Sherwood, *Roosevelt and Hopkins* (New York, 1948), pp. 869–876. For the quarrel about the composition of the Polish government, Winston S. Churchill, *The Second World War*, vol. VI, *Triumph and Tragedy* (Boston, 1953), pp. 418–439; cf. also the reports from the Commission of Poland sitting in Moscow: *FRUS*, 1945, V, 134 ff.

[9] But see the American point of view in James F. Byrnes, *Speaking Frankly* (New York, 1947), pp. 72 ff., 89–101, 115 ff.; also the critical reports of Byrnes's observer in Rumania, Mark Ethridge, who urged firm resistance to growing aggression: *FRUS*, 1945, V, 627–630, 633–641.

[10] See Kolko, *The Politics of War*, pp. 168–171 (an analysis marred by the remarkable judgment that absence of civil war in Eastern Europe showed the "flexibility and subtlety of the various Communist parties and the Russians"); also Alperovitz, *Atomic Diplomacy*, pp. 217 ff.; Fleming, *The Cold War and Its Origins*, I, 203, 208–210, 242–243, 250–258.

Even more fundamental from the revisionist point of view, there was no legitimacy for any American concern with affairs in that distant region. However ugly the results in Eastern Europe, they should not really have worried Washington. Russia should have been willingly accorded unchallenged primacy because of her massive wartime sacrifices, her need for territorial security, and the long history of the area's reactionary politics and bitter anti-bolshevism. Only when Moscow's deserved primacy was contested did Stalin embark upon a search for exclusive control.[11]

These revisionist assessments of the United States's political choices in Eastern Europe are valid in some respects, simplistic in others. It is true that American policy makers sought to establish agrarian democracies and based their hopes upon peasant proprietors and populist-like parties whose adherents had oscillated between left and right before the war. As revisionist accounts suggest, these occupied a precarious middle ground in Polish politics and an even narrower one in the former Axis satellites, Rumania and Bulgaria, where the Russians may have felt entitled to complete hegemony. Churchill for one felt that his "percentages" agreement of October 1944 had sanctioned Soviet control over these countries as a *quid pro quo* for the Russians' acceptance of British dominance in Greece. And whatever the effective status of that arrangement, Stalin might well have considered his domination of Rumania no more than the counterpart of Allied exclusion of the Soviets from any effective voice in Italy.[12]

But despite revisionist implications to the contrary, the major offense of the middle- and pro-Western groups in Soviet eyes was not really their collusion with rightists. The Russians themselves, after all, supported the far more fascist-tainted Marshall Badoglio as Italian premier. The major crime of the pro-Western elements seems really to have been the desire to stay independent of Soviet influence in a situation of Soviet-American polarization that made independence seem enmity. Perhaps the pro-Westerners acted imprudently by looking to Washington: Benes won three years of Czech democracy by collaboration with Moscow — but one might argue from his example that either the collaboration prolonged the Czech respite or that it helped contribute to the final undermining of Prague's indepen-

[11] For a spectrum of opinions on Stalinist objectives see Ulam, *Expansion and Coexistence*, pp. 377, 381, 388–408, an anti-revisionist but rich and subtle account; J. M. Mackintosh, *Strategy and Tactics of Soviet Foreign Policy* (London, 1962), pp. 1–17, for a traditional view; also Philip E. Mosely, "Soviet Policy in a Two-World System," *The Kremlin and World Politics* (New York, 1960), who sees the Russians reverting to revolutionary goals from November 1944; Kolko, *The Politics of War*, pp. 164–165, stressing Soviet conservatism; McNeill, *America, Britain, and Russia*, pp. 564–565, 609–610; LaFeber, *America, Russia, and the Cold War*, pp. 14–18, 23, 28–32, which couples Stalin's electoral address and Churchill's speech at Fulton, Missouri; Isaac Deutscher, *Stalin, A Political Biography* (New York, 1960), pp. 518–521, 529 ff.

[12] Cf. Kolko, *The Politics of War*, pp. 37–39, 128–131 for the Italian-Rumanian parallel; Churchill, *Triumph and Tragedy*, pp. 227–235, for the percentages agreement; cf. Alperovitz, *Atomic Diplomacy*, pp. 133–134.

dence. In any case the outcome throughout the area was communist dictatorship. Between 1945 and 1947 the peasant party and social democratic leaders were harassed in their assemblies and organizations, tried for treason by communist interior ministries, driven abroad or into silence, and finally, as with the case of Nikola Petkov, the Bulgarian agrarian party leader, executed.[13]

This bleak result naturally undercut those who advocated voluntarily relinquishing United States influence in the area. Opposing the official American rejection of spheres of influence, Henry Wallace on one side, and Henry Stimson and George Kennan on the other, counseled restraint and acceptance of the new status quo; [14] but few contemporary advocates could wholeheartedly celebrate a policy of spheres of influence. It was justified from expedience and as a second-best alternative. As a former advocate recalls, it had always to be advanced as a melancholy necessity, especially as the men for whom Western liberals felt most sympathy were liquidated.[15] To follow a policy of abnegation might indeed have allowed more openness in Eastern Europe; on the other hand, the Stalinist tendencies toward repression might well have followed their own Moscow-determined momentum.

If as a group the revisionists condemn the American role in Eastern Europe, they diverge beyond that point of criticism. One major area of debate among them concerns the use of the atomic bomb, which while it must be weighed as an important issue in its own right also signals a basic methodological division. Although the revisionist writing that often seems most hostile to received opinion is that of Gar Alperovitz he is not the most radical of the dissenting historians. His writings involve a less thoroughgoing critique of United States institutions than the contributions of either William Appleman Williams or Gabriel Kolko. What has elevated Alperovitz to the role of the revisionist *enfant terrible* is his thesis that the United States used nuclear weapons against the Japanese largely to overawe the Soviets. Still, his version of events hinges less on structural elements in American life than on the contingent roles of personality and technological opportunity.

There are two aspects of Alperovitz's thesis: first, that before Hiroshima,

[13] For a pro-Western account of Balkan party politics: Hugh Seton-Watson, *The East European Revolution* (New York, 3rd ed., 1956), pp. 31–36, 174–175, 184, 197–198, 202–219.

[14] For official American disavowal of spheres of influence, Cordell Hull, *The Memoirs of Cordell Hull* (London, 1948), II, 1168, 1298; FRUS, *The Conference of Berlin (The Potsdam Conference)* 1945, I, 262–264. For Stimson's dissent, Alperovitz, *Atomic Diplomacy*, p. 54; for Kennan's, George F. Kennan, *Memoirs, 1925–1950* (Boston, 1967), pp. 211–213, 222, 250; for Henry Wallace's coupling of political spheres of influence with economic universalism, LaFeber, *America, Russia, and the Cold War*, pp. 37–39.

[15] H. Stuart Hughes, "The Second Year of the Cold War: A Memoir & an Anticipation," *Commentary*, 48 (1969), 27–32, esp. 31.

expectation of the bomb's availability caused decisive tactical changes in American diplomacy; second, that the weapon was used wantonly when it became available, in part to limit Soviet penetration into the Far East, and more generally because only a combat demonstration would create a sufficient impression to prevent absolute Soviet control over Eastern Europe. Only the desire to have the atomic bomb in hand, Alperovitz argues, led Truman to reverse his harsh diplomatic approach of late April 1945, to dispatch Harry Hopkins to Moscow, and to delay the Potsdam conference despite Churchill's misgivings.[16]

More disturbing than this charge is Alperovitz's subsequent argument that Americans did not merely wish to possess the bomb but actually used it to enhance the country's position vis-à-vis the Soviets. Alperovitz repeats the charge that by the spring of 1945 most Washington officials believed neither the bomb nor an invasion was necessary to end the war. Either continued blockade or a Russian declaration of war could achieve victory. The bomb, however, would obviate the need for Soviet participation in the Pacific war, and, allegedly, the United States wanted desperately to keep Russia out. Along with hastening the technical preparations for Hiroshima, the United States supposedly had the Chinese Nationalists prolong their negotiations with Moscow so that the Sino-Soviet treaty would remain a stumbling block to Stalin's entry.[17]

Interestingly enough, the historiographical factions in this debate have crossed the usual lines. Kolko offers the most cogent response to Alperovitz and the most plausible reconstruction of Potsdam. On the other hand, Herbert Feis — the major traditionalist historian of wartime diplomacy — has so tempered his conclusions that despite himself he grudgingly gives the Alperovitz view considerable credence.[18] Alperovitz has indeed documented a reversal in May 1945 of some initial efforts at confrontation and then a renewed American toughness after Potsdam. But whether calculations about

---

[16] Alperovitz, *Atomic Diplomacy*, pp. 19–33, 55–90, 270–275.

[17] *Ibid.*, pp. 117–120 on military estimates, 176–187 and 226–242 on nuclear calculations, 120–126 and 183–186 on the Sino-Soviet treaty. The delays in the final arrangements of the treaty, however, did not all stem from the American or Chinese side; the Russians themselves were raising the price of a treaty with Chiang's government. Cf. Kolko, *The Politics of War*, pp. 556–560.

[18] Kolko, *The Politics of War*, pp. 560–565: "Mechanism prevailed"; Herbert Feis, *The Atomic Bomb and the End of World War II* (Princeton, N.J., 1966), p. 194, who now feels that "to monitor" Russian behavior may have been a motive for using the weapon. Cf. Alperovitz's critique of Feis's vacillation now included as "The Use of the Atomic Bomb," in his collection of *New York Review of Books* pieces: Gar Alperovitz, *Cold War Essays* (Garden City, N.Y., 1970), pp. 51–74. A variant of the Alperovitz thesis was first advanced by P.M.S. Blackett, *Fear, War, and the Bomb* (New York, 1949). Important in the earlier debate was Henry L. Stimson's justification, "The Decision to Use the Atomic Bomb," *Harper's Magazine*, February 1947, reprinted in H. L. Stimson and McGeorge Bundy, *On Active Service in Peace and War* (New York, 1948); also Louis Morton, "The Decision to Use the Atomic Bomb," *Foreign Affairs*, 35 (1957), 334–353.

the bomb were decisive remains unproven. The evidence adduced must remain circumstantial: the increased hostility to Russia that was thrust upon the new President; Stimson's and Byrnes' awareness that possession of nuclear weapons might bestow significant diplomatic leverage; and the pushing back of a Big Three parley. In light of this conjunction of events a calculated strategy of delay, such as Alperovitz develops, does remain a possible component of Truman's motivation. But the initial months of the new administration formed a period of contradictory needs and approaches. For a while Truman may have been thinking in terms of disengaging from the disquieting Soviet repression in Bulgaria and Rumania by withdrawing from the Allied Control Commission rather than attempting to reverse the course of events by exerting pressure within it.[19] The Hopkins mission was well suited to many purposes: perhaps an effort to appease Stalin until nuclear weapons were at hand, but more immediately an attempt to secure agreements in their own right and to halt further deterioration of relations as a worthy goal in itself. For Truman, as even Alperovitz realizes, the Hopkins trip was probably viewed not as a reversal of his earlier harsh language to Molotov on April 23, but as a complementary démarche, another approach to a dramatic unjamming of issues.[20]

What also makes the Alperovitz view so difficult to evaluate is the fact, as the author himself admits, that the debate has been largely a retrospective one. Actors at the time hardly saw the significance of the alternatives as later historians have. The place that the idea of using the bomb might have been thrashed out was in the so-called Interim Committee dominated by Stimson and Byrnes, both of whom were committed to dropping the weapon. In this forum it was easy to dismiss any alternative to the incineration of a real city as beset with one fatal obstacle or another. And beyond the Interim Committee except for a group of scientific dissenters at Chicago who felt they had been turned into sorcerers' apprentices, there was no fundamental challenge to using the weapon. Moreover, if the bomb repre-

[19] See Memorandum of Conversation, May 2, 1945 with President Truman, Generals Schuyler and Crane, in Joseph Grew MSS., Conversations, vol. 7, Houghton Library, Harvard University.

[20] Alperovitz, *Atomic Diplomacy*, p. 80. As ground for pushing back a summit conference, Truman himself claimed newness to office and the need to complete the preparation of a budget before the end of the fiscal year (Grew-Eden-Truman conversation, March 14, 1945, Joseph Grew MSS, Conversations, vol. 7). Alperovitz dismisses the budget considerations as implausible (p. 67). Much of Alperovitz's case hinges upon the timing and intent of the Hopkins mission. Truman's decision to dispatch Hopkins was made earlier than Sherwood said, although the suggestion was still Harriman's; hence Alperovitz argues it should be read as a response to Stimson's atomic briefings and not the disputes usually cited. Cf. Harry Truman, *Year of Decisions* (Garden City, N.Y., 1955), pp. 108–110 for April 30 date; Sherwood, *Roosevelt and Hopkins*, p. 885, for mid-May, and cf. Alperovitz, *Atomic Diplomacy*, p. 71n, and pp. 270–275. In fact by the end of April there were many indications of urgent troubles warranting an envoy's talk with Stalin: see Churchill's major letter of April 29 to Stalin, which foresaw a divided Europe and a quarrel "that would tear the world to pieces." *Triumph and Tragedy*, pp. 494–497.

sented a threshold in terms of weapons technology, it no longer represented one in terms of casualties: the Tokyo incendiary raids in March of 1945 produced about 84,000 deaths; Dresden, between 60,000 and 130,000; Hiroshima, about 70,000. The significant ethical question was that of area versus precision bombing, and the allies had long since steeled their conscience on that issue. If the Navy and Air Force, moreover, were confident that they could starve the Japanese into submission, the Joint Chiefs never gave their collective imprimatur to such a view because the Army would not endorse it. Many thought the collapse of Japan was likely; official plans were drawn up to deal with a sudden surrender; but no one in authority felt he could assume official responsibility for advocating restraint so long as some prolonged Japanese resistance was remotely possible. If Byrnes, Harriman, and Admiral Leahy would have preferred to complete the Pacific war without obligations to Moscow, Truman still felt it his duty to cling to the contingency plans of the Joint Chiefs of Staff and seek Soviet help at Potsdam. Even at Potsdam when Japanese capitulation seemed near, a host of factors militated against reappraisal: the ambivalence of the Tokyo response to the Potsdam ultimatum (itself only the vaguest of warnings); concern that diehard Japanese militarists would seek to "protect" their monarch against those who counseled surrender; the debate in Washington over retention of the Emperor, which delayed a surrender formula both sides might accept; the belief that the nation responsible for the Pearl Harbor attack could be requited from the air hundreds of times over without any injustice; and no doubt the vested interests in making the bomb contribute to the war effort.[21] If in addition to these pressures Byrnes also entertained an ulterior anti-Soviet motive, it probably represented a marginal, additional payoff of a policy long established on other grounds.

Alperovitz seems to feel it wrong that the atomic bomb became a major factor in American policy calculations. Certainly, however, it was natural to give deep consideration to the new weapon's diplomatic implications. And despite Alperovitz's linkage, there is insufficient evidence that possession of nuclear weapons was decisive in motivating a hard line on Bulgaria and Rumania in the latter half of 1945. This approach followed naturally from the administration's view of Eastern European developments since

[21] For the recommendations of the Joint Chiefs of Staff see FRUS, The Conference of Berlin (Potsdam), I, 903–910, which records the White House meeting of June 18, 1945, where Marshall outlined a November 1 landing on Kyushu, and the President said he would seek Russian help at Potsdam and wanted to prevent an "Okinawa from one end of Japan to another." See also the text of the JCS report, pp. 910–911, and the Combined Chiefs of Staff report as approved by Truman and the Prime Minister on July 24, in Vol. II, 1462–1463. Cf. Alperovitz, Atomic Diplomacy, pp. 117–120, for discussion of this point. For divisions on the surrender debates within the respective combatants: Waldo H. Heinrichs, Jr., American Ambassador: Joseph C. Grew and the Development of the United States Diplomatic Tradition (Boston, 1966), pp. 372–380; Robert J. C. Butow, Japan's Decision to Surrender (Stanford, 1954), pp. 158 ff. for the post-Hiroshima situation.

Yalta and would have been pursued without an atomic monopoly. It is questionable, too, whether the United States could have utilized a veiled atomic threat except in regard to the distant future, for Washington was not prepared to threaten the use of nuclear weapons over Russian targets in 1945.[22] Despite the revisionist view that the United States enjoyed a preponderance of power and therefore must be charged with the greater responsibility in the generation of the Cold War, the Soviet Union still exerted effective control over the area that was central to the dispute. This is not to deny that outside its borders the United States seemed to be flaunting its nuclear capacity. Harriman reported from Moscow in November that the Soviets felt America was trying to intimidate them with the atomic bomb, while to observers in Washington Truman and Byrnes often seemed bolstered by an inner assurance of American invincibility.[23]

Indeed it may have appeared by late 1945 and early 1946 as if the United States were wrapping iron fist in iron glove; but even had there been a far more sophisticated and reserved approach, the simple fact of one-sided possession of the bomb was bound to evoke mistrust. There was no way for its influence to be exorcized from international relations.

Alperovitz's charges are, of course, profoundly disquieting. But at least he suggests that things might have been different. Had Roosevelt lived he might have smoothed out differences with Moscow. Had Stimson been heeded, the United States might have bargained by offering to share atomic secrets and not by seeking, as it is alleged to have done, to intimidate with the weapon itself. Gabriel Kolko, in contrast, can dismiss Alperovitz's arguments about atomic diplomacy because they are unnecessary for what he considers the more important indictment, namely, that the United States, in order to serve its economic needs and ambitions, opposed any threat to its world-wide military and political power.

This view produces a more radical interpretation of both American foreign relations and the country's internal history. William Appleman Williams, for instance, argues that the long-term American quest for universal market and investment arenas, even into Eastern Europe, naturally collided with quite moderate Soviet wartime aspirations and thereby helped the Kremlin's own hard-liners and ideologues to prevail.[24] For both Williams and Kolko, moreover, a critique of United States foreign policy forms only part of a wider reassessment of American liberal institutions. The

---

[22] Cf. Kolko, *The Politics of War*, p. 560; Halle, *The Cold War as History*, p. 173.

[23] Harriman's assessment is in *FRUS*, 1945, V, 922–924. On Truman and the bomb, see Alperovitz, *Atomic Diplomacy*, p. 227; cf. Nuel Pharr Davis, *Lawrence and Oppenheimer* (Greenwich, Conn., Fawcett ed., 1969), pp. 257–260.

[24] William Appleman Williams, *The Tragedy of American Diplomacy* (New York, rev. ed., 1962); for similar analysis as applied to the whole Roosevelt period cf. the work of Williams' student, Lloyd C. Gardner, *Economic Aspects of New Deal Diplomacy* (Madison, 1964).

anti-communist effort is depicted as the natural product of an industrial society in which even major reform efforts have been intended only to rationalize corporate capitalism.[25]

The more the revisionists stress the continuity of American capitalist goals and de-emphasize the importance of the Roosevelt-Truman transition, the more they tend to condemn all of America's earlier policies as contributing to the Cold War. The revisionists in general have stressed the direct pre-1945 clashes with the Soviets. They emphasize the significance of the Allies' delay in opening a Second Front in Europe;[26] and while anti-Soviet historians duly cite Russia's non-aggression pact with Germany, the revisionists usually argue that the Soviets were forced into this arrangement by the Western powers' appeasement policies and their exclusion of Moscow from any common defense plans.[27] Finally, revisionists like Fleming recall the United States' original hostility to bolshevism and the interventions of 1918–1920.[28] In short, all revisionists are mindful of the Western treatment of the Soviets as a pariah regime.

The more radical revisionists, however, go on to depict all of twentieth-century foreign policy as woven into a large counter-revolutionary fabric of which the Cold War itself is only one portion. Their logic links a hesitant and ineffective anti-Nazi foreign policy with a zealous anti-communism and thus finds that the issues of the 1930's adumbrate Cold War attitudes. Similarly, revisionists who discuss pre-war diplomacy have attacked the usual image of American isolationism by stressing the country's persistent economic stakes abroad. All this vaguely serves to hint that the lateness of United States enlistment against Nazism is no longer explainable in terms of deep internal divisions about involvement in European quarrels: the

[25] For this theme, Gabriel Kolko, *The Triumph of Conservatism* (Chicago, 1963); William A. Williams, *The Contours of American History* (Chicago, 1966), pp. 390 ff.; James Weinstein, *The Corporate Ideal in the Liberal State, 1900–1918* (Boston, 1968); Barton J. Bernstein, "The New Deal: The Conservative Achievements of Liberal Reform," in Barton J. Bernstein, ed., *Towards a New Past: Dissenting Essays in American History* (New York, 1969), pp. 262–288.

[26] See John Bagulley, "The World War and the Cold War," David Horowitz, ed., *Containment and Revolution* (Boston, 1968), pp. 77–97; Kolko, *The Politics of War*, pp. 12–30. For non-revisionist discussions of this thorny issue cf. Feis, *Churchill-Roosevelt-Stalin*, pp. 47–80, 93–102, 114–119, 134–136; Maurice Matloff and Edwin M. Snell, *Strategic Planning for Coalition Warfare, 1941–1942* (Washington, 1953), pp. 229–244, 328–349; also Maurice Matloff, *Strategic Planning for Coalition Warfare, 1943–1944* (Washington, 1959). Valuable insight into the "technical" restraints on Allied policy is provided by Robert W. Coakley and Richard M. Leighton, *Global Logistics and Strategy, 1943–1945* (Washington, 1968), pp. 3–6, 173–245.

[27] See Fleming, *The Cold War and Its Origins*, I, 106–134; also A. J. P. Taylor, *The Origins of the Second World War* (New York, 1962), pp. 240–241, for defenses of Stalinist diplomacy, and George F. Kennan, *Russia and the West under Lenin and Stalin* (Boston, 1960), pp. 312–336, 347–348, for a harsh critique. The recent accounts on both sides — Kolko, *The Politics of War*, pp. 13–14, and Ulam, *Expansion and Coexistence*, pp. 250–279 — stress the prevailing Machiavellism and cynicism of the late 1930's and sensibly tend to divorce the period from an integral role in Cold War origins.

[28] Fleming, *The Cold War and Its Origins*, I, 20–35.

United States responded only as it perceived threats to foreign economic interests.[29] Receding even further, the revisionists view Woodrow Wilson as a major architect of liberal but counter-revolutionary interventionism.[30] And even before Wilson the roots of the Cold War can be discerned, they feel, in the economic lobbying that backed the Open Door policy and the capitalist expansion of the late nineteenth century.[31] Finally, under the stresses of a market economy, even the otherwise virtuous farmers felt it necessary to seek world markets and back imperialist expansionism. The private economy, for Williams and others, taints with acquisitiveness the Jeffersonian Eden that America might have been.[32]

There is a further aspect of this radical revisionism. Since it concentrates on American expansionism in general, its focus shifts from the Soviet-American conflict to the alleged American imperialist drive against all forces of radicalism, or what Kolko loosely calls the New Order. Not an insouciant blundering, and not the arrogance of power, but only capitalist megalomania suffices to explain American efforts to prop up an international Old Order of discredited and outworn parties and elites. Within this perspective, Kolko's explanation of the events of 1943–1945 becomes most clear. He offers three major areas of evidence: United States policy in respect to its future enemy, that is, the effort to reduce Russia to dependency; United States policy against its own ally, that is, the insistence on an economic multilateralism designed to reduce Great Britain to dependency; and United States policy in respect to the "Third World" and the Resistance, the effort to smash all truly independent challenges to American hegemony.

Under Kolko's scrutiny the policies once adjudged to be among the most enlightened emerge as the most imperialistic. Where, for example, previous

[29] One can usefully separate those accounts that stress the ineffectiveness and hesitations of Roosevelt's foreign policy — Arnold Offner, *American Appeasement: United States Foreign Policy and Germany, 1933–1938* (Cambridge, Mass., 1969); Robert A. Divine, *The Illusion of Neutrality* (Chicago, 1962) — from those questioning the old view of isolationism from economic or ideological criteria: Gardner, *Economic Aspects of New Deal Diplomacy*, pp. 86–98; Williams, "The Legend of Isolationism," in *The Tragedy of American Diplomacy*, pp. 104–159; Robert Freeman Smith, "American Foreign Relations, 1920–1942," in Bernstein, *Towards a New Past*, pp. 232–256.

[30] For a presentation of Wilsonian aspirations parallel in some respects to Kolko, Arno J. Mayer, *Politics and Diplomacy of Peacemaking: Containment and Counterrevolution at Versailles, 1918–1919* (New York, 1967). Cf. also N. Gordon Levin, Jr., *Woodrow Wilson and World Politics* (New York, 1968). Common to both Mayer and Kolko, is the subordination of the German problem to the Russian one; on the other hand, Wilson exerted a more genuinely reformist impulse in Europe according to Mayer than Roosevelt did according to Kolko.

[31] See Marilyn B. Young, "American Expansion, 1870–1900: The Far East," in Bernstein, *Towards a New Past*, esp. pp. 186–198, for a tempered interpretation; also Williams, *The Tragedy of American Diplomacy*, pp. 37–50; Walter LaFeber, *The New Empire: An Interpretation of American Expansion, 1860–1898* (Ithaca, N.Y., 1963).

[32] See William A. Williams, *The Roots of the Modern American Empire* (New York, 1969), based upon an extensive reading of agrarian opinion, and a learned and moving, if problematic, book.

critics attacked the abandonment of Morgenthau's intended ten-billion-dollar loan to Russia, Kolko sees the proposal itself as devious. Coupled with the destruction of German industry, the contemplated loan was allegedly designed to prevent Russia from refurbishing her industrial base from German factories and thus to force her into a dependency on United States capital for which she could return raw materials. Ironically enough, the plans of Harry Dexter White — abused as a communist in the 1950's — represented a massive effort to place the USSR in a state of semi-colonial subservience.[33]

American aid to England emanates from analogous motives, according to Kolko and Lloyd Gardner who have concentrated most closely on this issue. Kolko asserts that American policy aimed at keeping Britain in a viable second-rank position: rescuing her from utter collapse for reasons of world economic stability yet profiting from her distress. State Department officials, congressmen, and businessmen supporting assistance to Britain intended to penetrate the sterling bloc and the Commonwealth markets protected by tariffs since the 1930's. The celebrated Article Seven of the Mutual Aid Agreement of February 1942, the revisionists emphasize, demanded that Britain consider reduction of Commonwealth trade barriers in return for Lend-Lease, a stipulation repeated with each renewal of Lend-Lease. Finally, all the projects for post-war financial credits and arrangements, as they took form at Bretton Woods and in the 3.75-billion dollar loan negotiated in December 1945, envisaged a sterling-dollar convertibility that would also open the Commonwealth to American goods and severely test the pound.[34]

As the revisionists see it, the interest in convertibility and multilateralism represented the answer of post-Depression America to the chronic domestic under-consumption of a capitalist economy. In the final analysis American efforts amounted to a subtle neo-colonialism. While classical economic theorists helped to justify the international division of labor by comparative-advantage doctrine no matter how unequal the partners, the revisionists evidently feel that the costs to the less powerful or industrial nation outweigh the benefits. They emphasize that specialization can act to perpetuate relations of dependency, and they view American policy as dedicated throughout the twentieth century to fostering the bonds of economic subordination.[35] In this interpretative framework the Cold War, in its Euro-

---

[33] Kolko, *The Politics of War*, pp. 323–340.

[34] For detailed treatment of these issues, see Richard N. Gardner, *Sterling-Dollar Diplomacy* (Oxford, 1956), which covers the entire wartime period; cf. also E. F. Penrose, *Economic Planning for Peace* (Princeton, 1953). Revisionist critiques are in Lloyd Gardner, *Economic Aspects of New Deal Diplomacy*, pp. 275–291, and Kolko, *The Politics of War*, pp. 280–294, 488–492, 623–624.

[35] For critiques of "exploitative" international economic relations from a Marxist viewpoint, see Harry Magdoff, *The Age of Imperialism: The Economics of United States Foreign Policy* (New York, 1969); and Paul A. Baran, *The Political Economy of Growth* (New York and London, 1957), pp. 177 ff.

pean aspects, arose because Soviet Russia refused to allow herself or Eastern Europe to be integrated into the American neo-colonial network.

This analysis is often illuminating but sometimes exaggerated and tendentious. One can certainly differentiate between the values of the arguments about the Soviet Union and Britain. To see debolshevizing Russia as Morgenthau's underlying concern in 1944–1945 is simply to ignore the central quest of his public life, which was to deny Germany any future as a world industrial power. In the policy alternatives shaping up in Washington, a bitterly anti-German policy could, moreover, only mean a desire to collaborate with the Soviet Union and not to dominate it. And by late 1944 Morgenthau viewed those opposing his projects as themselves motivated primarily by anti-communism. The major purpose of the loan to Russia was, in fact, to make it easier for the Soviets to accede to the dismantling of German industry. The economic destruction of the Reich was not designed to make the Russians dependent upon America: if the Soviets would receive no reparation from future German exports they would get many factories that would have produced the exports.[36]

Revisionist analysis of American economic relations with Great Britain is more convincing. Kolko's discussion of Anglo-American financial relations in the framework of overall United States goals probably forms the most innovative and substantive contribution of his study. Americans did push against British trade barriers and mentally relegated the country to a secondary role in a Western economic system. The pressure upon the beleaguered Ally could be harsh: "What do you want me to do," Churchill asked about Lend-Lease renewal at Quebec in the fall of 1944, "stand up and beg like Fala?"[37] Nevertheless, revisionist judgments tend to neglect the powerful ties of sentiment that motivated Roosevelt's policy, and they minimize the critical fact that British financial commitments were overextended in terms of her own resources. Moreover, the focus by the revisionists on the free-trade rapacity of an Eastern banking establishment is inappropriate. Insofar as banking representatives formed a coherent interest it was often the friendliest to London's needs. Pressures came as much from a conservative Congress as from Wall Street.[38]

Still, as the revisionists stress, economic self-interest was woven into American policy even when it was most generous. The hard fact is that until

---

[36] John Morton Blum, *From the Morgenthau Diaries: Years of War, 1941–1945* (Cambridge, Mass., 1967), pp. 323–347; Paul Y. Hammond, "Directives for the Occupation of Germany: The Washington Controversy," in Harold Stein, ed., *American Civil-Military Decisions* (Birmingham, Ala., 1963), pp. 348–388.

[37] Cited in Blum, *From the Morgenthau Diaries*, III, 273.

[38] For impulses to cooperation, Richard Gardner, *Sterling-Dollar Diplomacy*, pp. 54–58; for the spectrum of domestic opinion on aid to Britain, *ibid.*, pp. 192–199, 226–253, 208–210; cf. also Thomas Lamont's call for restoration of British prosperity, cited in Lloyd Gardner, *Economic Aspects of New Deal Diplomacy*, pp. 275–276; also Blum, *From the Morgenthau Diaries*, III, 324–326 for opposed views (Morgenthau's and Baruch's) on what to demand of Britain.

they both felt mortally threatened by Soviet power London and Washington had conflicting economic interests. There was a desire for currency convertibility on the part of the United States Treasury which Britain naturally felt was potentially disastrous. For Britain to meet the American wishes for sterling convertibility at a moment when she had liquidated four billion pounds of overseas assets in order to fight the war meant subjecting her economy to great deflationary pressure. During the war Keynes had already asked priority for full employment and strong domestic demands over considerations of exports and stable exchanges. After the war the Labour government even more fervently stressed easy money to banish the specter of unemployment. They did not want planning, investment, and new social-service transfers to be impeded by worries about sterling outflow. The American enthusiasm for currency convertibility threatened havoc to all the delicate equilibriums in London; and it was only dire necessity that led the English to pledge an effort at convertibility as a condition for the massive credits the United States extended in late 1945. When finally the dissenting historians reach the story of 1947–1950, they will no doubt be able to depict in their terms a further effort at world economic supremacy. For similar Treasury pressures for convertibility were to continue into the America-sponsored negotiations for intra-European payments agreements in 1949 and the European Payments Union of 1950. Once again, Britain feared a flanking attack on the sterling area, and once again many of her Labour leaders worried about a deflationary thrust against schemes of economic planning.[39]

One can agree that American objectives clashed with British economic policy without accepting the larger revisionist accusation of a pervasive neo-colonialism. As of 1945, American thinking on foreign trade and investment (as well as more general questions of colonialism) was often marked by reformist ideas. American spokesmen such as Eric Johnston of the Chamber of Commerce or Donald Nelson of the War Production Board certainly emphasized the need for sustained American exports as a safeguard against renewed depression,[40] but a sense of the need for exports assumed that countries rich and industrialized enough to offer extensive markets were more helpful to the United States than economies kept in perpetual under-development or one-sided dependency.[41]

[39] Richard Gardner, *Sterling-Dollar Diplomacy*, pp. 306–347; J. Keith Horsefield, *History of the International Monetary Fund* (Washington, D.C., 1970), I, 3–118. For the difficulties that convertibility presented to English policies: Sidney Pollard, *The Development of the British Economy, 1914–1950* (London, 1962), pp. 365–407; Hugh Dalton, *High Tide and After: Memoirs, 1945–1960* (London, 1962), pp. 68–89, 178–184, 254 ff. For American policies of 1949–1950, William Diebold, Jr., *Trade and Payments in Western Europe: A Study in Economic Cooperation, 1947–1951* (New York, 1952), pp. 34–110.

[40] See Thomas G. Paterson, "The Abortive American Loan to Russia and the Origins of the Cold War, 1943–1946," *The Journal of American History*, 56 (1969), pp. 71–72, 75–77.

[41] Cf. Sumner Welles, *The Time for Decision* (New York, 1944), p. 409.

Underlying much revisionist criticism of United States foreign economic relations is a desire for socialist self-sufficiency: a virtuous autarchy inflicts the least damage on the rest of the world. Indeed, in theory, there might have been one alternative for the American economy that did not require either unemployment or international trade: a great program of domestic investment to remedy urban blight, improve transportation, build new TVA's — in short an expansion of the New Deal into a semi-socialized economy. But after the domestic emphasis upon small business and competition in the "Second New Deal," and after the massive infusion of business leaders into the government to run the war economy, such a public-sector commitment was not likely.[42] In the absence of such a program the stress on international trade was probably the most reasonable United States response. Finally, one must note that a United States public-sector solution for full employment would not necessarily have benefited foreign countries. Their problems were not entirely owing to outsiders' exploitation; they needed investments, and socialist governments, whether British or Soviet, were no less likely to draw profits from abroad where they could.

The revisionists' reasoning on this point fits in analytically with one of their major current preoccupations: the role of the United States in the third world of peasant movements. The same revisionist argument that sees foreign trade as a means to subordination and control also suggests that the United States had to be hostile to movements seeking genuine self-determination and local independence. Thus American hostility to popular resistance movements, including those of World War II, forms one more logical extension of the country's counter-revolutionary and imperialist drive in the wake of World War II. Kolko makes much of the British suppression of the Greek resistance movement in December 1944, of the American preference for continued dealings with Vichy, of the dislike of Tito's partisans, and of the joint Anglo-American efforts to restrain the left-wing forces in the Italian resistance. When it is remembered that the United States is still fighting the heirs of the Vietnamese resistance to the Japanese and later the French, or that the Haiphong incidents between French and Vietminh occurred within two years after the British put down the Greek resistance cadres in Athens, the emotional thrust of the revisionist argument becomes more understandable.[43]

This concern with the continuities of counter-revolution arises in part from the natural fact that revisionists want to explain the origins of cold

[42] See Under-Secretary of State Dean Acheson's condemnation of any such tendency as bordering on Soviet autarchy cited in Williams, *The Tragedy of American Diplomacy*, p. 236; for a spectrum of economists' thinking about post-war possibilities, see Seymour Harris, ed., *Postwar Economic Problems* (New York, 1943).

[43] Cf. Kolko, *The Politics of War*, pp. 55–71, 154–155, 172–193. For a pointed Greek EAM-NLF comparison, see Todd Gitlin, "Counter-Insurgency: Myth and Reality in Greece," in Horowitz, *Containment and Revolution*, pp. 140–181. The major pro-EAM Greek account is now André Kédros, *La résistance grècque* (1940–1944) (Paris, 1966).

war against the background of Vietnam. Ironically enough, the result is to downgrade the importance of the Soviet-American antagonism that originally preoccupied revisionist authors. What in fact increasingly distinguishes the more radical historians is their emphasis upon a Soviet "conservatism" that sought to discourage revolutionary action for the sake of acquiring territorial buffers. Stalin's treaty with Chiang at the expense of Mao, his distrust of Tito, and his abandonment of the Greek Communists, complement American objectives. In view of this supposed convergence of Moscow and Washington, the Cold War becomes little more than a mistaken enmity deriving from the United States' panicky identification of Soviet policies with indigenous Marxist or merely democratic movements. This finding confirms a "third world" viewpoint which can indict both major world powers and supply a "usable past" for those morally overwhelmed by an updated Holy Alliance between Moscow and Washington.[44] Through the mid 1960's, in short, the revisionists could still be fixed upon explaining the origins of conflict with Moscow; by the end of the decade they were concerned with the antagonism with Havana, Hanoi, and Peking.

Attractive though it may be in light of current events, this third-world perspective has serious analytical deficiencies. First of all, its Marxian basis imposes an overly schematic view of motivation; it precludes any possibility that American policy-makers might have acted from genuine emancipatory impulses or even in uncertainty. The war had united the country around democratic ideas that were genuinely held, even if too abstract for implementation in the areas they were aimed at. It can be argued that the economic aspirations that State Department draftsmen grated onto the policy statements the revisionists cite were just as ritualistic as the political formulas,[45] and that there was still cause for a genuine dismay at the developments

---

[44] Cf. Isaac Deutscher, "Myths of the Cold War," in Horowitz, *Containment and Revolution*, pp. 17–19; Gabriel Kolko, *The Roots of American Foreign Policy* (Boston, 1969), esp. pp. xi–xii and 85–87 on the United States relation to the third world; also Kolko, *The Politics of War*, pp. 449–451, 594–595 ff. For an extensive critical discussion of the American attitudes toward the third world and Greece since the 1940's see Richard J. Barnet, *Intervention and Revolution: The United States in the Third World* (New York and Cleveland, 1968).

[45] For a view of economically determined aims for Eastern Europe, see Kolko, *The Politics of War*, pp. 167–171. But is it really so true, as Kolko claims, that trade and investment were "so central to objectives in that area"? The aims stated by Stetinnius (*FRUS*, 1944, IV, 1025–1026) that Kolko cities were more inconsistent than imperialist: their cardinal point was self-determination of political and social systems. Briefing papers prepared for Yalta also said that the United States should insist on access for trade and investment, but still recognized that the Soviets would exert predominant political influence in the area. They expressed a willingness to accept the fact so long as American influence was not completely nullified, and ventured, furthermore, to say that precisely the safe assurance of a pro-Russian political orientation would let the Soviets admit United States loans. (See *FRUS, The Conferences at Malta and Yalta*, pp. 234–235.) For definition of aspirations in a concrete situation see Harriman's report on the Polish agreement, June 28, 1945, in *FRUS, The Conference of Berlin (Potsdam)*, I, 728, where the matter of concern cited is administration of the Ministry

in Eastern Europe. The revisionist presentation conveys no sense of America's anti-totalitarian commitment and thus little understanding of the seeds of the post-1945 disillusionment.

Furthermore, the new revisionist writings composed under the impact of Vietnam attribute too consistently ideological an opposition to the resistance movements in Western Europe. For anyone with sympathy for the "vision" of the Resistance, vague as it was, American policy often does appear as misguided or willful. At times tactical considerations were influential; at times the wartime authority that devolved upon conservative proconsuls such as Robert Murphy was critical; at times United States policy acquiesced in a joint allied position more rightist than Washington alone would have preferred, as when the exigencies of coalition warfare led Roosevelt to accede to Churchill's reactionary policies in Italy and Greece.[46] Yet most basically what militated against the Resistance was a big-power paternalism and the wartime habit of viewing military success as an end in itself. United States spokesmen accused Resistance leaders of seeking their own political advantage above the destruction of the Germans, though what Americans saw as narrow partisanship was to Resistance leaders a battle against collaborators and a fascist or semi-fascist right — a struggle for regeneration within to match the fight against the occupying power. The British and Americans preferred to think of the Resistance as a vanguard of saboteurs who might soften up the Germans and pin down their troops but not as an army or regime in embryo. Centralization and control, the distrust of independent authority and pretensions, characterized all three great powers. But unless decentralization itself is made synonymous with radicalism while centralization is defined as reactionary *per se*, it is misleading to condemn American behavior toward the Resistance movements as consistently conservative.[47]

---

of Internal Security: "the crux of whether Poland will have her independence, whether reasonable personal freedoms will be permitted and whether reasonably free elections can be held."

[46] On Vichy policy: William L. Langer, *Our Vichy Gamble* (New York, 1947); Robert Murphy, *Diplomat Among Warriors* (Garden City, N.Y., 1964), pp. 49–64, 124–185; Cordell Hull, *The Memoirs of Cordell Hull*, II, 1127–1138, 1222–1226, 1241–1246. For allied differences in Italy: Norman Kogan, *Italy and the Allies* (Cambridge, Mass., 1956); for British policy in Greece, Kédros, *La résistance grècque* (1940–1944), pp. 479–513; William H. McNeill, *The Greek Dilemma* (London, 1947); and Churchill's defense in *Triumph and Tragedy*, pp. 283–325.

[47] Cf. Norman Kogan, "American Policies toward European Resistance Movements," *European Resistance Movements, 1939–1945. Proceedings of the Second International Conference on the History of the Resistance Movements Held at Milan, 26–29 March 1961* (London, 1964), pp. 74–93; cf. F. W. Deakin, "Great Britain and European Resistance," and the veiled criticisms of Allied policy by Feruccio Parri and Franco Venturi, "The Italian Resistance and the Allies," in the same collection, xxvii–xxxvii.

For a critique from the Left of Allied pressure against the Northern Resistance movement in Italy (the CLNAI) see Franco Catalano, *Storia del C.L.N.A.I.* (Bari, 1956), pp. 283–315, 326–350; Kogan, *Italy and the Allies*, pp. 90–110; Kolko, *The Politics of War*, pp. 53–63.

Finally, what is perhaps most misleading about the neo-Marxian point of view is its suggestion that Europe in 1945 was as socially malleable as underdeveloped societies today. By projecting a third-world image upon the West the revisionists overestimate the power of the radical forces and the structural possibilities for change. The United States did help to brake fundamental change especially after V-E Day, but the major limits on reconstruction were set by the internal divisions within the Resistance and the conservative attitude of the Communist parties and the other two allies.[48]

No more in institutional than in political terms did America alone abort a New Order. Kolko's New Order represents a normative image of revolution borrowed from predominantly peasant countries or Yugoslavia and applied to industrial Europe. But not even 1945 Europe was so shaky: the Germans, not the Russians, had occupied the area and left most elites intact. Even where nominally socialist remedies such as nationalization were to be tried, they rarely incorporated any revolutionary tendencies.[49] Pre-war economies had already evolved toward pluralist balances among labor, heavy industry, and small producers and merchandisers. The communists were concerned primarily with retaining their share of the trade-union component in this equilibrium of forces. They sought a social and economic buffer as Stalin sought territorial buffers. A renovation of society

---

[48] It is often overlooked that the political decisions of late 1944, which led to the British suppression of the Greek resistance and the Allied pressure for a compromise between the reformist Northern Italian resistance groups (the CLNAI) and the more conservative Rome government, grew out of Anglo-American differences as much as out of any quarrel with the Soviets. At the second Quebec Conference in September 1944 Roosevelt had pressed the Morgenthau plan upon the reluctant British and had threatened Lend-Lease curtailment. At the same time the President, in view of the upcoming elections, was advocating an Italian policy more favorable to the Rome government or the Resistance parties than Churchill desired and was more obdurate on the Polish issue. It was immediately after Quebec that Churchill flew to Moscow to make his "percentages" agreement with Stalin on the demarcation of Balkan spheres of influence. In the months to come Stalin increased his own domination over the Eastern European countries, but in contrast reaffirmed his policy of having Western communist leaders support the established forces in Rome and Paris. Churchill and Eden could act with a freer hand in the Mediterranean and also explore a West European bloc. In short, both Allies adopted policies that envisaged a possible falling-out with America, although the Soviet push into Central Europe was to bring Churchill quickly back into an anti-Russian posture. In the interim it was the independent forces of the local Resistance movements that bore the cost. But for the divisions within the Resistance forces themselves, which was also an important factor, see Kolko, *The Politics of War*, pp. 428–456, esp. 450–456; Franco Catalano, "Presentazione," and "Italia," in *Aspetti sociali ed economici della Resistenza in Europa: Atti del convegno . . . (Milano 26–27 marzo 1966)*, pp. xviii, 114 ff., 121 ff.; Georgio Bocca, *Storia dell'Italia partigiana* (Bari, 1966), pp. 466–484; cf. also Leo Valiani, "Sulla storia sociale della resistanza," *Il movimento di Liberazione in Italia*, 88 (1967), 87–92 on the limits of the Resistance Left. For France, Henri Michel sees American and inherent limits on the resistance: "France," *Aspetti sociali ed economici*, pp. 17, 32–33; cf. also his *Les courants de pensée de la résistance* (Paris, 1962), pp. 387–410, 518–529, 685–706, 711–721.

[49] A brief exception may have been the Communist efforts at syndical control in France, but even these appear to have been only a means to entrench the Party in a new labor fief. See Maurice Bye, Ernest Rossi, Mario Einaudi, *Nationalization in France and Italy* (Ithaca, N.Y., 1955), pp. 96–109.

on new principles would have required smashing the corporate pluralism in which left-wing as well as conservative leaders found comfort. America did not really have to rescue Europe from radical change because no significant mass-based elements advocated a radical transformation. The so-called New Order — an amalgam in the revisionist mind of Yugoslavian factory councils and Algerian, Vietnamese, or Greek national resistance movements — had no solid peacetime constituency in the West.

What in fact was new in the West was precisely the conglomeration of business, labor, and government that the revisionists lament. In America the New Deal and the wartime economic effort worked to dissolve many of the old lines between public and private spheres.[50] In Fascist Italy, Vichy France, and Nazi Germany a similar interweaving occurred, as it did in a democratic Britain that submitted to extensive planning and welfare measures.[51] Revisionists such as Kolko would accept this description of trends — in fact, Kolko examined the precursor of this private-public interpenetration in his critique of Progressivism — but the revisionists regard these developments as clearly elitist and conservative. Ultimately their general interpretation conceives of the issues behind the Cold War in terms of inequality and class: the Cold War represents to them a continuation of an international civil war in which Russian and later peasant revolutionary forces have successively championed the cause of the oppressed in all countries, while the United States has become the leader of the world's elites.

But no matter what importance this conceptualization may have for today's world, it obscures the historical development. If there has been a growth in international class conflict over the past generation, so too in Western societies there has been an increase of bureaucratic and administrative solutions for social conflict — solutions to which labor contributed, solutions that were conservative in leaving intact private control and ownership, yet still social compromises that commanded wide assent. The forces for compromise sprang from the bureaucratic trends of modern industrial

[50] Ellis Hawley, *The New Deal and the Problems of Monopoly* (Princeton, 1966), pp. 449 ff., 489; Sherwood, *Roosevelt and Hopkins*, pp. 157–164; Barton J. Bernstein, "America in War and Peace: The Test of Liberalism," in Bernstein, *Towards a New Past*, pp. 292–295; also his "Industrial Reconversion: The Protection of Oligopoly and Military Control of the War Machine," *American Journal of Economics and Sociology*, 26 (1967), 159–172. For a good case study of military-industrial collaboration, Robert H. Connery, *The Navy and the Industrial Mobilization in World War II* (Princeton, N.J., 1951).

[51] Derek H. Aldcroft, "The Development of the Managed Economy before 1939," *Journal of Contemporary History*, 4 (October 1969), 117–137; W. K. Hancock and M. M. Growing, *British War Economy* (London, 1949). For French initiatives, Stanley Hoffmann, "Paradoxes of the French Political Community," in Stanley H. Hoffmann, et al., *In Search of France* (New York, Harper Torchbooks, 1965), pp. 38–39. For descriptions of the German situation, Arthur Schweitzer, *Big Business in the Third Reich* (Bloomington, Ind., 1954); Franz Neumann, *Behemoth, The Structure and Practice of National Socialism* (New York, Harper Torchbook ed., 1966), pp. 221–361; David S. Landes, *The Unbound Prometheus* (Cambridge, Eng., 1969), pp. 402–417. For the origins of the IRI, Rossi, Bye, Einaudi, *Nationalization in France and Italy*, pp. 191–200.

society as they existed in Europe as well as in the United States. The revisionist view splits the world into an industrial half that America supposedly stabilized on behalf of a bureaucratic capitalism and a peasant world where the United States has since met its match. But if peasant society has proved hard to manipulate, Western industrial society has also proved refractory; the neo-Marxians overestimate the fragility of its capitalist order, and overvalue the American contribution to counter-revolution as well as the will to impose it. There is still no well-modulated portrayal of what the United States sought in the world, even less of the real possibilities of institutional change.

No full evaluation of revisionist history, however, can be content with weighing particular interpretations against available evidence. For beneath the details of specific revisionist arguments are more fundamental historiographical problems — implicit conceptual models and underlying assumptions about the decisive factors in American foreign relations.

The revisionists' approach to international conflict and foreign policy formation is a narrow one. They are interested in certain specific modes of explanation and no others. Rejecting any model of international society that sees crucial impulses to conflict as inherent in the international system itself, they seek explanations in American domestic conditions. But for them all domestic conditions are not equally valid. They are unwilling to accept any description that tends to stress the decentralized nature of decision-making or that envisages the possibility of expansionist policy taking shape by imperceptible commitments and bureaucratic momentum. Above all, they approach history with a value system and a vocabulary that appear to make meaningful historical dialogue with those who do not share their framework impossible.

The revisionists presuppose international harmony as a normal state and have a deep sense of grievance against whatever factors disturb it. This common assumption shapes their work from the outset in terms of both analysis and tone. But is international harmony a normal state? The division of sovereignty among nation-states makes it difficult to eliminate friction and tension, as theorists from the time of Machiavelli and Hobbes have pointed out.[52] The disputes of 1944–1945 especially were not easy to avoid.

[52] For an introduction to the large body of theory that stresses the inherent logic of the international system in shaping bipolar or balance-of-power competition, see Morton Kaplan, *System and Process in International Politics* (New York, 1957), also his "Variants on Six Models of the International System," in James N. Rosenau, ed., *International Politics and Foreign Policy* (New York, 1969 ed.), pp. 291–303; cf. Karl W. Deutsch, *The Analysis of International Relations* (Englewood Cliffs, N.J., 1969), pp. 112–140. In its most abstract form in terms of an international system, the Cold War to 1948 can be reconstructed as a transition in which each side raised its criteria of tolerable political conditions in third countries from acceptance of regimes so long as they allowed some influence for their own respective supporters to an insistence on regimes that excluded their opponents' clients from any voice in policy. For elaboration

With a power vacuum in Central Europe created by the defeat of Germany and with the expansion of American and Soviet influence into new, overlapping regions, some underlying level of dispute was likely. Angered by the scope that the Cold War finally assumed, the revisionists do not really ask whether conflict might have been totally avoided or what level of residual disagreement was likely to emerge even with the best intentions on both sides.

Once mutual mistrust was unchained — and much already existed — all disputes were burdened by it. The initiatives that would have been required to assuage incipient conflict appeared too risky to venture in terms either of domestic public opinion or international security. By late 1945 the United States and Russia each felt itself to be at a competitive disadvantage in key disputes. Each felt that the other, being ahead, could best afford to make initial concessions, while gestures on its part would entail disproportionate or unilateral sacrifice. Perhaps more far-sighted leaders could have sought different outcomes, but there were pressures on all policy makers to take decisions that would harden conflict rather than alleviate it. Some details on this point are particularly worth considering.

In retrospect there appear to have been several areas of negotiation where compromise might at least have been possible, where accommodation demanded relatively little cost, and where the continued absence of greater concession probably deepened suspicion. Some additional flexibility on the issues of both atomic control and financial assistance might have helped to alleviate the growing estrangement. Innovative and generous as our plans for atomic energy control appeared to Americans at the time, the provisions for holding all United States weapons until controls were complete, as well as the demand that the Russians renounce their United Nations veto on all atomic-energy matters, probably doomed the proposal. With such an imbalance of obligations the Soviet advocates of their own country's atomic arsenal were likely to prevail over those willing to acquiesce in nuclear inferiority for a decade or so. As so often after 1946, the reluctance to give up an advantage that at best could only be transitory led to a further spiral in the arms race.[53]

---

of a similar logic in mathematical terms as applied to arms races, see Anatol Rapoport, "Lewis M. Richardson's Mathematical Theory of War," now included as "The Mathematics of Arms Races," in James N. Rosenau, ed., *International Politics and Foreign Policy* (New York, 1961 ed.). For a useful discrimination between causal models of war according to their focus on international, domestic, or psychological factors see Kenneth Waltz, *Man, the State, and War* (New York, 1959).

[53] Richard G. Hewlett and Oscar E. Anderson, *The New World, 1939–1946* (University Park, Pa., 1962), pp. 455–481, 531–619; David Lilienthal, *The Journals of David E. Lilienthal: The Atomic Energy Years, 1945–1950* (New York, 1964), pp. 27 ff.; Dean Acheson, *Present at the Creation: My Years in the State Department* (New York, 1969), pp. 151–156; critical views in Fleming, *The Cold War and Its Origins*, I, 363–379; cf. also Robert Gilpin, *American Scientists and Nuclear Weapons Policy* (Princeton, 1962), pp. 52–63.

With far less objective risk than was presented by the nuclear issue, liberality with aid might also have offered United States policy makers a chance to dissipate quarrels. Unfortunately Lend-Lease was brusquely cut off in a way that could not help but offend the Russians, although it was slated to end with the close of the war in any case.[54] Had transitional aid or a significant post-war loan been available, the termination of Lend-Lease might not have proved so abrasive. But the loan proposal was always keyed to the extraction of political concessions, and the Russians had no need to become a suppliant.[55] As it turned out a post-war credit was less crucial to the Soviets than to the British who faced a mammoth balance of payments crisis that Russia did not have to cope with. Washington could not really use the loan to wrest concessions, instead her failure to provide funds precluded any chance for post-war credits to help improve the general international atmosphere and re-establish some minimal trust.

Disagreement at the start over Eastern Europe had undermined the chances of those peripheral initiatives that might in turn have helped to alleviate overall tension. By becoming trapped in a position where apparently unilateral démarches were needed to break a growing deadlock, policy was far more likely to be vetoed by State Department, Congress, or the President's immediate advisers. It was far harder to justify financial assistance or atomic renunciation when Russia was already felt to be uncooperative. Domestic constraints and the suspicions fed by international rivalry interacted to intensify a serious deadlock.

Although the revisionists do not readily soften their judgments about American policy makers in light of these pressures, they do use them to make Soviet responses appear more acceptable. They explain that the Russians had to reckon with the death of an exceptionally friendly President and the replacement of his key policy makers by tougher spokesmen; with a tooth-and-nail resistance to the German reparations that Russia felt she clearly deserved; and with the curt United States dismissal of a Soviet voice in the occupation of Japan, an influence over the Dardanelles, and a base in the Mediterranean. Neither side was likely to see in the opposing moves anything but a calculated effort to expand power, or, with a little more subtlety, the upshot of a contest between the other power's doves and hawks with the doves increasingly impotent. Such interpretations tended to pro-

[54] The best recent summary is in George C. Herring, Jr., "Lend-Lease to Russia and the Origins of the Cold War, 1944–1945," *The Journal of American History*, 56 (1969), 93–114. Herring emphasizes that Lend-Lease to Russia always depended upon Roosevelt's constant intervention to smooth requirements that might have disqualified the Soviets. The 3(c) clause of the Lend-Lease agreement provided for transitional aid after the war, but the negotiations were dropped in March 1945 on the recommendation of Joseph Grew and Leo Crowley — who also engineered the cut-off in May. Grew and Crowley pleaded Congressional difficulty, but this seems exaggerated. Cf. Morgenthau's objections to 3(c) delays in *FRUS, The Conferences at Malta and Yalta*, p. 320.

[55] See Paterson, "The Abortive American Loan to Russia and the Origins of the Cold War, 1943–1946," pp. 70–92.

duce a response in kind. In the absence of any overriding commitment to conciliation, the Cold War thus contained its own momentum toward polarization and deadlock.

It would, however, also be inappropriate to fix too much blame for the origins of the Cold War upon the Hobbesian nature of the international system, though it is a major element the revisionists ignore. As revisionists insist, domestic factors are clearly required to explain the timing and trajectory of the Soviet-American antagonism. But significantly absent from revisionist writing is any sense of the bureaucratic determinants of policy — an element of increasing interest to historians and social scientists seeking to respond to the revisionist indictment. In the view of these writers, decisions are seen as the outcome of organizational disputes within an overall government structure. Policy emerges not so much as a way of maximizing a well-defined national "interest" as the outcome of struggles among bureaucratic forces each seeking to perpetuate its own *raison d'être* and to expand its corporate influence. Recent studies have shown for instance that much of the impulse toward a cold-war defense posture after 1945 came from the fact that both the Air Force and the Navy sought out new strategic conceptions and justifications to preserve their wartime size and status.[56]

Study of the German and reparations issues also reveals how American foreign policy emerged from inter-departmental contention, in this case between Henry Morgenthau and the Treasury on the one hand, and on the other a more conservative State Department desirous of recreating economic stability in Central Europe. After V-E day the Army military government agencies also demanded that their American occupation zone be as economically self-sufficient as possible. The result of these pressures, and of Morgenthau's loss of influence under Truman, was that the United States quarreled bitterly with the Soviets to limit reparations. The American insistence at Potsdam that each power largely confine its reparations to its own zone helped lead to the division of Germany that the United States officially deplored. The intent was not to build Germany up at the expense of Russia: Byrnes after all offered the Soviets a 25- or 40-year treaty against German aggression in late 1945 and the spring of 1946. But each agency's struggle for the priorities it set in terms of its own organizational interest helped shape a narrow policy that was not subordinated to a clear sense of our more general relations with the Soviet Union.[57]

[56] Vincent Davis, *Postwar Defense Policy and the U.S. Navy, 1943–1946* (Chapel Hill, 1966), pp. 164 ff., 186 ff., 219 ff.; Perry M. Smith, *The Air Force Plans for Peace, 1943–1945* (Baltimore, Md., 1970). The Army, on the other hand, was interested in maintaining Soviet participation in the war because they were unwilling to concede that air and naval power would defeat Japan; moreover Eisenhower needed Russian cooperation in administering Germany, and was personally impressed by Marshall Zhukov. See Dwight D. Eisenhower, *Crusade in Europe* (New York, 1948), pp. 458–475; Feis, *Between War and Peace*, pp. 74–76, 141–144.

[57] For inter-agency contention on Germany see Hammond, "Directives for the Occupation of Germany," pp. 408–443. State Department conservatism and backwardness are

This approach to policy analysis, which opens up a new range of motivation and offers an alternative to an undue emphasis on personal factors, contrasts with the explanatory model suggested by the neo-Marxist revisionists.[58] For the latter group what ultimately explain policy is a "system" arising out of the property and power relations within a society, a system causative in its own right and within which institutions and organizations do not lead independent lives but relate to each other dialectically. For these revisionists the explanation of events in terms of intra-governmental structure and struggles is simply formalistic, oriented to the procedural aspects of policy formation and begging the substantive questions. For them, the processes of government might as well be a black box: if one understands the distribution of wealth and influence then policy follows by an almost deductive logic. To attribute decisive influence to bureaucratic pressures seems additionally frivolous to the revisionists since allegedly only certain elites ever rise to the top of those bureaucracies.[59] For those, on the other hand, who stress the political infighting among bureaucracies what is important about history tends to be the successive modifications of action — in short, political process not social structure.

Both of these approaches are deceptive and limiting if taken to extremes. For those who stress history as bureaucratic process, all questions of historical responsibility can appear ambiguous and even irrelevant. Foreign policy emerges as the result of a competition for fiefs within governmental empires. Bureaucratic emphases can produce a neo-Rankean acquiescence in the use of power that is no less deterministic than the revisionist tendency to make all policies exploitative in a liberal capitalist order. But what is perhaps most significant about these alternative causal models is that they are addressed to different questions. The non-revisionists are asking how poli-

---

well evoked in Acheson, *Present at the Creation*, pp. 17, 22–36, 38–47, 64 ff.; Kolko, *The Politics of War*, pp. 511–521, 569–575, and for criticism of reparations policy, 578; John M. Gimbel, *The American Occupation of Germany: Politics and the Military, 1945–1949* (Stanford, 1968), pp. xii, 9–30, 52–61, 85–87, stresses the economic needs of the American zonal administrators and the resistance of the French. For the hard-fought reparations negotiations, see also Feis, *Between War and Peace*, pp. 234, 246–258, and FRUS, *Conference of Berlin* (*Potsdam*), I, 510–511, 519–554; II, 274–275, 277–287, 295–298 and passim to 512–518, 830–949. Cf. Alperovitz, "How Did the Cold War Begin?" *Cold War Essays*, p. 48, for recognition of the complexities of the German questions.

58 For some examples of this approach see Hammond's and other studies in Stein, *American Civil-Military Decisions;* also the studies in Werner Schilling, P. Y. Hammond, and G. H. Snyder, eds., *Strategy, Politics and Defense Budgets* (New York, 1962); Werner Schilling, "The H Bomb Decision: How to Decide Without Actually Choosing," *Political Science Quarterly*, 76 (1961), 24–46. For a methodological statement, see Graham T. Allison, "Conceptual Models and the Cuban Missile Crisis," *The American Political Science Review*, 63 (1969), 689–718.

59 See most recently Gabriel Kolko's emphasis on the permeation of business influence in the United States foreign-policy elite and his attack on bureaucratic formalism in *The Roots of American Foreign Policy*, esp. pp. xii–xiii, 3–26.

cies are formed and assume that this also covers the question why. The revisionists see the two questions as different and are interested in the why. And by "why?" revisionists are asking what the meaning of policies is in terms of values imposed from outside the historical narrative. The revisionists charge that the historian must pose this question of meaning consciously or he will pose it unconsciously and accept the values that help to uphold a given social system. History, they suggest, must serve the oppressors or the oppressed, if not by intent then by default. The historian who wishes to avoid this iron polarity can reply that social systems rarely divide their members into clear-cut oppressors and oppressed. He can also insist that even when one despairs of absolute objectivity there are criteria for minimizing subjectivity. On the other hand, he must also take care that the history of policy making not become so focused on organizational processes that the idea of social choice and responsibility is precluded.

In the end it is this attempt by the revisionists to analyze specific historical issues on the basis of *a priori* values about the political system that most strongly affects the controversies their writings have touched off. For their values cannot be derived from the mere amassment of historical data nor do they follow from strictly historical judgments, but rather underlie such judgments. This is true in some sense, no doubt, of history in general, but the whole of Cold War historiography seems particularly dependent upon defined value systems.

For the revisionists, on the one hand, the key issues hinge not upon facts or evidence but upon assessments as to how repressive or non-repressive contemporary liberal institutions are. These judgments in turn must be made within ground rules that allow only polar alternatives for evaluating political action. What is non-revolutionary must be condemned as counter-revolutionary, and reformist political aspirations are dismissed in advance. Similarly, the foreign policies of Western powers cannot escape the stigma of imperialism, for imperialism and exploitation are defined by the revisionists as virtually inherent in any economic intercourse between industrialized and less developed states, or just between unequals. But how can one decide whether the economic reconstruction that America financed was beneficial or "exploitative" for countries brought into a cooperative if not subordinate relationship to the United States? How does one judge the value of multilateral or bilateral trading relations that benefit each side differentially? Judgments must rest upon definitions of exploitation or fairness that logically precede the historical narrative and cannot be derived from it.

The non-revisionist, on the other hand, can refuse to accept the ground rules that presuppose exploitation, dependency, or automatic neo-colonialism; he can refuse to accept the definitions that allow no choice between revolution and reaction. But traditional Cold War historians no less than the revisionists have been involved in tautologies. Historical explanations are normally tested by efforts to find and weigh contradictory evidence, but Cold War analyses on both sides have relied upon propositions that cannot be disproven. Sometimes disproof is precluded by prior assumptions, and while revisionists may believe America's capitalist economy necessitates a voracious expansionism, Cold War theorists have similarly argued that any commitment to communism is *ipso facto* destructive of a "moderate" or "legitimate" international order.[60] Often disproof is impossible because the explanations are totalistic enough to accommodate all contradictory phenomena into one all-embracing explanatory structure. So writers who condemned the Soviets cited Marxist ideology as evidence of real intention when it preached revolution and as evidence of deviousness when it envisaged United-Front coalitions. Conversely, according to the revisionists, when the United States withdrew foreign assistance it was seeking to bring nations to heel; when it was generous, it sought to suborn. When the United States bowed to British desires to delay the Second Front it justified Soviet suspicions; when it opposed Churchill's imperial designs it did so in order to erect a new economic hegemony over what England (and likewise France or the Netherlands) controlled by direct dominion. Spokesmen for each side present the reader with a total explanatory system that accounts for all phenomena, eliminates the possibility of disproof, and thus transcends the usual processes of historical reasoning. More than in most historical controversies, the questions about what happened are transformed into concealed debate about the nature of freedom and duress, exploitation and hegemony. As a result much Cold War historiography has become a confrontation *manqué* — debatable philosophy taught by dismaying example.

The Atomic Bomb as History: An Essay Review

MARTIN J. SHERWIN

The atomic bombings of Hiroshima and Nagasaki dramatized the most important consequence of the Second World War: through a revolution in weapons technology, Man's very survival had become linked to international relations. "Suddenly the day of judgment was the next day and has been ever since," a veteran of the Manhattan Project observed. The impact of

[60] See Henry Kissinger's influence distinction between legitimate and revolutionary orders in *Nuclear Weapons and Foreign Policy* (Garden City, N.Y., 1958), pp. 43–49; also Henry Kissinger, "Conditions of World Order," *Daedalus*, 45 (1966), pp. 503–529.

Reprinted by permission of the publisher from *Wisconsin Magazine of History* (Winter 1969–1970), 128–34.

this awesome development has hardly begun to be investigated by historians interested in the postwar years. A great deal of their recent effort has been devoted instead to the economic and ideological motivations that direct the policies of the government of the United States. But the roots of many of the most significant changes that have occurred during the Cold War are embedded in the weapons revolution that preceded it. The books under review suggest some of the significant changes that atomic weapons brought to the politics and diplomacy of the atomic age.

Atomic Diplomacy: Hiroshima and Potsdam, by Gar Alperovitz [Random House, New York, 1965], is an account of the influence of the atomic bomb on the policies of the Truman Administration toward the Soviet Union through September, 1945. It is a scholarly challenge to the generally accepted view of Soviet responsibility for the Cold War. *The Atomic Age: Scientists in National and World Affairs,* edited by Morton Grodzins and Eugene Rabinowitch [Basic Books, New York, 1963], is a collection of sixty-five articles from the *Bulletin of the Atomic Scientists* (1945–1962) dealing with the major issues involving nuclear weapons that have commanded the attention of scientists. *Lawrence and Oppenheimer,* by Nuel Pharr Davis [Simon and Schuster, New York, 1968], adds several hundred more pages to a growing genre of literature — the scientific gossip column. In spite of their diversity of purpose and subject matter, their contrasting styles and their different publication dates, these three books have a historical unity — all owe their existence to the development of the atomic bomb. Taken together, they raise two fundamental questions: What effect did the revolution in weapons technology have on American politics and diplomacy, and how did it affect American science? The two issues are intimately related.

The confluence of weapons that could destroy the world with a foreign policy of global proportions removed the physical and psychological barriers that had protected the United States from the full force of international affairs before World War II. In the context of the Cold War, politics no longer stopped at the water's edge; on the contrary, it is not too much to suggest that it began there. No group of Americans was more keenly aware of this change than the scientists of the Manhattan Project who did so much to help bring it about. To J. Robert Oppenheimer, wartime director of the Nuclear Weapons Laboratory at Los Alamos, New Mexico, it was an occurrence that threatened "the life of science [and] the life of the world." It involved scientists more, he said, "than any other group in the world." The existence of the atomic bomb linked science to national security and scientists to military control; the intellectual freedom and institutional independence of American science were thus put in jeopardy. The twin "evils of secrecy and control strike at the very roots of what science is and what it is for," Oppenheimer warned his former colleagues at Los Alamos.[1]

---

[1] "A Speech Given by J. R. Oppenheimer at a Meeting of the Association of Los Alamos Scientists" (November 2, 1945), in the Papers of J. H. Rush, University of Chicago Library. Hereinafter referred to as JRO, November 2, 1945.

The question of the meaning and uses of science raised by Oppenheimer took on a new sense of immediacy for all scientists after the war. With the advent of the atomic age, the answer to that question inevitably became tied to the political and national defense issues generated by the Cold War. As a result, the boundary between science and politics blurred, and the public's attitude toward science was defined by political rather than scientific criteria. Thus, Bernard Baruch could suggest that "science should be free but only when the world has been freed from the menaces which hang over us." [2] Science emerged from the war the first political victim of its own success, an outcome Percy W. Bridgman had anticipated in 1943. As president of the American Physical Society, he responded to the threat of external control of science with the declaration that "society is the servant of science. . . . Any control which society exerts over science and invention must be subject to this condition." [3] With this professional scientific view at one pole and the converse political view expressed by Baruch at the other, it is not too much to suggest that there arose a split between "two cultures." But it was not, as C. P. Snow argued, a division having to do with a non-scientist's knowledge of the Second Law of Thermodynamics or a scientist's ability to quote Shakespeare. It touched upon a deeper issue — the nature of freedom in a democratic society.

Oppenheimer spoke of this issue from a scientific perspective in answering the question he had raised. "If you are a scientist," he said, "you believe that it is good to find out how the world works . . . that it is good to turn over to mankind at large the greatest possible power to control the world and to deal with it according to its lights and its values." It was not for the scientist to judge, he implied, whether those lights and values were adequate to control new understandings. Nor was it for society to judge, he added explicitly, what the scientist should and should not seek to discover. Any such external control "is based on a philosophy incompatible with that by which we live, and have learned to live in the past." [4] If society was not the servant of science it certainly was a collaborator; to politicize Man's most exciting intellectual pursuit would destroy it. A free state could only be well served by science if scientists were free to publish and discuss their research. A state could only remain free, he implied, if its intellectual life was free.

To keep politics out of science scientists responded politically to the challenges they recognized. Some counseled the administration privately against policies that would lead to military control, while others led a successful public campaign against an Atomic Energy Commission dominated by the War Department.[5] However, in the ensuing events of the Cold War

2 Baruch to David Lilienthal, January 10, 1949, in the Papers of Bernard M. Baruch, Princeton University Library, Princeton, New Jersey.

3 Percy W. Bridgman, *Reflections of a Physicist* (New York, 1950), 270.

4 JRO, November 2, 1945.

5 Alice K. Smith, *A Peril and a Hope: The Scientists' Movement, 1945–1947* (Chicago, 1965) is the best study of the public response. The behind the scenes activities of

civilian control of atomic energy development proved to be illusory. Military requirements held sway, loyalty and security programs were vigorously prosecuted, and government support led to far more control than anticipated. Though scientists gained greater opportunities to participate in policy formulation, their advice was expected to do little more than modify basic policies decided by others. This is the lesson revealed by the public careers of J. Robert Oppenheimer and Lawrence.

Ernest O. Lawrence, the founder of big-machine physics in America, and Oppenheimer were two of the most prominent scientists catapulted by the wartime weapons revolution into policy-making circles. Their careers ought to disclose a great deal about the relationship between science and government in America but, unfortunately, Davis has ignored the issue. *Lawrence and Oppenheimer* begins with the collaboration of the two young scientists at Berkeley in the 1930's, traces their growing antagonism through the war, and reaches its absorbing climax with Oppenheimer's security hearing in 1954, when only ill health prevented Lawrence from testifying against him. Though Davis has added to our understanding of the mundane and petty motives of scientists, he has only increased our misunderstanding of the history that shaped their lives. He exhibits no interest in probing beneath the surface of the events he describes. The book is constructed in large part out of slick quotations selected from many interviews with scientists, though no attempt has been made to isolate fact from fiction, anecdote from malicious gossip.[6] Davis' sole criterion appears to have been good copy, and if this was indeed his primary goal, he has succeeded. But a historian cannot consider this readable and entertaining book as serious scholarship. It is marred by a lack of perspective, numerous misleading thumbnail sketches of important scientists like Edward U. Condon, an unconvincing nonanalysis of Oppenheimer as a "simple" man, and a total disregard for Lawrence's role as the founder and guiding spirit of modern physics in America. In sum, Davis has ignored the basic tenets of historical scholarship. He has approached Oppenheimer and Lawrence as political symbols of the 1950's, telling us more about his own well-taken indignation for the injustices of those years than about his subjects.

Though the feud between Oppenheimer and Lawrence animates Davis' book, he fails to trace it beyond personality differences and Oppenheimer's opposition after the war to Lawrence's cherished Materials Testing Accelerator. With this giant machine, Lawrence promised to turn uranium 238 into

---

scientists are documented in what is probably the best official history published in the United States: Richard G. Hewlett and Oscar E. Anderson, Jr., *The New World, 1939–1946: A History of the United States Atomic Energy Commission* (University Park, Pennsylvania, 1962), Vol. I. See chapters 12–17.

[6] See the following reviews of *Lawrence and Oppenheimer* for specific examples: Frank Oppenheimer, in *Physics Today* (February, 1969), 77–80; Jeremy Berstein, in *The New Yorker* (May 10, 1969), 141 and continued; Jane Wilson, in *The Bulletin of the Atomic Scientists* (January, 1969), 31–32.

plutonium. It was an expensive, humiliating failure, as Oppenheimer and others predicted, and Lawrence never forgave him his prescience. "It shaped his attitude toward Oppenheimer and everything he judged Oppenheimer stood for," Davis observes. (p. 272) But he has overlooked a larger point of their dispute. Though both men shared a common faith in science, they came to disagree over how its interests were best protected. Lawrence fought a rearguard action to keep politics, as he narrowly defined the term, out of the laboratory by joining with the government on every major scientific issue. Oppenheimer, on the other hand, understood that modern warfare had already blurred the distinction between science and politics. To protect the future of science, he first developed a plan for the international control of atomic energy; when that failed he chose to oppose those policies he considered dangerous. As Davis concludes after describing the decision of the AEC to deny Oppenheimer security clearance: "Thus ended Oppenheimer's strong, often successful seven-year endeavor to turn the country to sane nuclear courses." (p. 351) Though he has exaggerated Oppenheimer's leadership, Davis has recognized that politics was not absent from his scientific considerations. But in a world engaged in an insane nuclear arms race, one is left to ponder what made a scientist believe that his country might be made to act sanely.

Perhaps some insight into the politics of science and the postwar political actions of scientists will be found in the private papers of scientists that have been opened recently to scholars. The availability of the Oppenheimer and Vannevar Bush papers at the Library of Congress and the Lawrence papers soon to be opened at Berkeley may reveal answers to questions Davis overlooked. A deeper understanding of the political actions of scientists may even emerge from a study of the pre-atomic age values of science and the "cultural" division those values helped to create.

After the war the scientific community itself appeared to divide "culturally." Scientists like Oppenheimer, Lawrence, Bush, and James B. Conant worked closely with the government, in contrast to others like Eugene Rabinowitch and Leo Szilard who became vocal critics of the Truman Administration's policies. In 1945 Rabinowitch and other troubled veterans of the Manhattan Project's Metallurgical Laboratory at the University of Chicago founded the *Bulletin of the Atomic Scientists*. The publication grew rapidly from a newsletter into a national journal with a circulation currently exceeding 30,000. Its editors sought to educate scientists about national and international politics and to educate the public about nuclear energy and the significance of its application to war. But, as the excellent selection of articles for *The Atomic Age* reveals, this stated commitment took the form of arguing for an alternative to established Cold War policies. Yet the "cultural" division among scientists was merely political. The scientists who criticized government policies and those who co-operated with the administration in their development shared an abiding faith in science. The scientific community was united by an unstated, perhaps even unconscious, assumption that the best interests of science defined the best interests of world peace. All scientists seem to have agreed that the salvation of man could only come through science, and that the salvation of science depended upon mankind's acceptance of that proposition. The real split in the scientific community was over how salvation should be attained.

The salvation of science after the war, like the salvation of the world, appeared to depend upon avoiding an atomic arms race with the Soviet Union. Scientists argued that the international control of atomic energy was the most important issue of recent world history. The revolution in weapons technology, they maintained, could lead either to a peaceful diplomatic revolution or a nuclear armed world. If international control was not adopted and an arms race ensued, American science would be the servant of American foreign policy. Thus, the life of science in the atomic age seemed to depend upon the foreign policy decisions made shortly after the war by the Soviet Union and the United States. But in 1948, the British scientist P. M. S. Blackett looked back beyond the debates in the United Nations over the international control of atomic energy to the atomic bombings of Hiroshima and Nagasaki. These bombings, he charged, were the "first major operation in the cold diplomatic war." [7] This observation suggests that the postwar political efforts of scientists were in vain, and, furthermore, that the origins of the Cold War cannot be understood without careful attention to the influence of the atomic bomb on American diplomacy.

Following Blackett and the later suggestive work of William Appleman Williams, Gar Alperovitz in *Atomic Diplomacy* has reinforced this point of view.[8] He has relied heavily on a close (and at times strained) analysis of the diaries of Secretary of War Henry Stimson, the Cabinet officer responsible for atomic energy matters. But in spite of its carefully constructed and cautiously phrased argument, supported by some 1,300 citations, *Atomic Diplomacy* is important more for the questions it raises than for the answers it gives. The chronological scope of the work is too narrow and Alperovitz's formulation of the problem too inadequate to unravel the most basic aspects of the relationship between the atomic bomb, the war against Japan, and the origins of the Cold War. Nevertheless, the care he has taken to develop his challenge to an established series of views — that American wartime diplomacy was naive, that the Cold War began in 1947, and that the overriding diplomatic issue was the threat of the communization of western Europe — has altered some of the simpler notions that have dominated our views of the origins of the Cold War.

---

[7] P. M. S. Blackett, *Fear, War, and the Bomb: Military and Political Consequences of Atomic Energy* (New York, 1948), 139.

[8] William Appleman Williams, *The Tragedy of American Diplomacy* (New York, 1962). See chapters 5 and 6.

Alperovitz argues that a basic no-compromise strategy of opposition to the Soviet Union underlay all the diplomatic maneuvers of the Truman Administration, almost from the moment of Roosevelt's death. Apparently friendly gestures like the visit of Harry Hopkins to Moscow in May, 1945, were merely covers for a "strategy of delayed showdown," a subtle diplomatic policy designed by Stimson and allegedly accepted by Truman. The plan was to avoid an open confrontation with the Soviet Union over the control of eastern Europe until American power could be backed up by the testing and use of the atomic bomb. Thus, the Big Three Conference was delayed by Truman until the middle of July, and at Potsdam, when the President received the results of the first atomic test, he felt no compulsion to compromise with Stalin. Therefore, the interesting question about the final Allied wartime conference "is not what happened at the meeting, but why very little happened at all." (p. 231) The answer Alperovitz implies for Potsdam he explicitly states for the London Foreign Ministers' Conference in September: "The atomic bomb not only influenced the attitude American policy makers took in their approach to the confrontation . . . [it] completely overshadowed the discussions." (pp. 226–227)

Alperovitz's judgments about Potsdam are persuasive, but in attempting to establish a "strategy of delayed showdown" to that conference, he has strained his evidence. Rather than explaining the President's profound uncertainty, he has projected Truman's false confidence of July back to April. Still, this probing book has forced a reconsideration of the proposition that the Cold War began sometime before the hot one ended, and that the point at issue was not the imminent threat of Soviet expansion to the Pyrenees, but competition for the control of eastern Europe.

To explain the use of the atomic bomb against Japan in terms of Truman's "atomic diplomacy," Alperovitz constructs a chain of events that ignores the influence of the first and most vital link — the assumption that the bomb would be used. Curiously enough, however, he states in his preface that he set out to understand just that: "The issue is not why it was decided to use the bomb, but rather, how policy makers came to assume the bomb would be used, and why they never questioned this assumption . . . ." (p. 14) The answer is well worth a historian's labors. His research, however, must take into account the origins and influence of this assumption inherited by Truman — that the Allies would "make effective use of the weapon as soon as it had been manufactured," as Oppenheimer was informed by the general in charge of the Manhattan Project.[9] Because *Atomic Diplomacy* begins with Roosevelt's death, the author has necessarily ignored the development of this assumption and he appears insensitive to its profound influence. Furthermore, he has relied too heavily on the views of

[9] Leslie Groves to Oppenheimer, January 6, 1944, in the Papers of J. Robert Oppenheimer, Library of Congress.

Stimson. To understand what the Secretary of War thought and what he suggested to Truman is not necessarily to understand American foreign policy. Though he was a highly regarded elder statesman, Stimson's own diaries indicate that his advice was offered more than sought; his influence appears to have been less than Alperovitz suggests.

The limited scope of *Atomic Diplomacy* has also led Alperovitz to misunderstand the significance of Stimson's views about the atomic bomb. Those views reveal less about American diplomacy than Alperovitz believes, and far more about the concerns of Stimson's science advisors. The Secretary of War's background and responsibilities led him to regard the atomic bomb merely as a weapon, but Vannevar Bush, director of the Office of Scientific Research and Development, and James B. Conant, chairman of the National Defense Research Committee, added another dimension to Stimson's understanding. Though they shared with the Secretary the view that the atomic bomb was a legitimate weapon, they understood more of its profound postwar implications. As early as 1942 Bush first discussed the need for the international control of atomic energy with Roosevelt. In the fall of 1944 Bush and Conant began to educate Stimson to the dangers of a postwar atomic arms race. Under their guidance Stimson came to look upon his atomic responsibility as "a revolutionary change in the relations of man to the universe." On May 31, 1945, he told the Interim Committee on atomic energy matters "that [the atomic bomb] might even mean the doom of civilization or it might mean the perfection of civilization." He expressed his hope that policy makers would approach the problem of the atomic bomb like "statesmen and not like merely soldiers anxious to win the war at any cost." [10] Yet, in spite of this misunderstanding, Stimson isolated the use of the bomb in war from the related political problems it was likely to create in the postwar relations with the Soviet Union. The implications of the weapon for Soviet-American relations were discussed by scientists and policy makers alike, *quite apart from whether or in what manner it was used in war.*

To discover why a decision was never taken to prevent the use of the atomic bomb, a historian must view the problem in its broadest perspective. He must investigate the political, personal, social, and institutional forces, not just the diplomatic considerations, that influenced policy makers. The dynamics of the transfer of power from Roosevelt to Truman cannot be ignored, nor can the views of scientists like Bush and Conant, Oppenheimer and Lawrence, among others, be overlooked if the problem of the atomic bomb, and its use, is to be understood today, as it was understood by these men before Hiroshima. By formulating the problem narrowly, Alperovitz

---

[10] Stimson Diaries, May 31, 1945, in the Yale University Library, New Haven, Connecticut.

has unraveled only a single important (though not necessarily the most important) thread among the many that tied the use of the bomb to the *non-military* issues of the war. Though he disclaims any attempt to describe the influence of diplomacy on the use of the atomic bomb, his disclaimer is unconvincing.[11] What is implied throughout the study is clearly stated in his last paragraph: the assumption that the bomb would be used was not questioned because "our possessing and demonstrating the bomb would make Russia more manageable in Europe," as Secretary of State-designate James F. Byrnes told Leo Szilard. (p. 242)

But the most important point of *Atomic Diplomacy*, as the author himself understands it, is the most general: "It is abundantly clear that the atomic bomb profoundly influenced the way American policy makers viewed political problems." (p. 227) As McGeorge Bundy has noted in a different context, international relations came to turn to a remarkable degree on how men saw and valued nuclear weapons. As a result the historic relationship between weaponry and diplomacy was reversed: the tail began to wag the dog.

The books by Davis and Alperovitz, and the essays selected by Grodzins and Rabinowitch, suggest a series of important themes American historians will have to investigate. But studies of the impact of the development of the atomic bomb should not be limited to biography or political and diplomatic history. The psychic and social life of the nation has been affected so profoundly by the scientific and technological weapons revolution that traditional historical divisions have lost their value. Beyond politics and diplomacy the threat of nuclear warfare has contributed to a new way of life and thought for a new generation of Americans. Some of its most articulate members have sought a new politics, a new science and a new history to help shape their future; others a new astrology merely to read it. Raised in an unconventional nuclear world, this postwar generation has been frustrated by the persistence of conventional ideas and has rebelled against being the medium for a message it dislikes. It is not necessary to accept completely either their analysis of the present or their prescriptions for the future to recognize the historical validity of at least one of their anxieties. Henry Adams articulated it over a hundred years ago: "Man has mounted science, and is now run away with."

---

[11] "This essay has attempted to describe the influence of the atomic bomb on certain questions of diplomacy. I do not believe that the reverse question — the influence of diplomacy upon the decision to use the atomic bomb — can be answered on the basis of the presently available evidence." Alperovitz, *Atomic Diplomacy*, 236.

PART V

CONTEMPORARY AMERICAN HISTORY

26

THE REDISCOVERY OF POVERTY

It may be that the 'fifties will become known in history books as the Era of Great Complacency. Certainly reformers, intellectuals, and innovators generally, were on the defensive during most of the decade. Much of the outstanding commentary and scholarship during the period was concerned with the pressures of conformity in American society and with the popular resistance to liberal objectives (sometimes to liberalism itself). Vance Packard's *Hidden Persuaders* (1957), William Whyte's *Organization Man* (1956), David Reisman's *Lonely Crowd* (1950) and *Individualism Reconsidered* (1954), Richard Hofstadter's *Age of Reform* (1956), Daniel Boorstin's *The Genius of American Politics* (1953), Daniel Bell's *The New American Right* (1955), and Samuel Lubell's *Revolt of the Moderates* (1956) are some examples.

What may have underlain the attitude was another feature of the era: America's apparent opulence. The 'fifties, it seems, was a time for self-congratulation about the great material success of American civilization. American abundance was the general theme upon which scholars began their searches into the quality of American life as well as into the problem of how the new nations of the world might come to enjoy similar success. In his effort to define the American national character, for example, historian D. M. Potter found abundance the key:

> The compilation of statistics might be extended endlessly, but it would only prove repetitively that in every aspect of material plenty America possesses unprecedented riches and that these are very widely distributed among one hundred and fifty million people. If few can cite the figures, everyone knows that we have, per capita, more automobiles, more telephones, more radios, more vacuum cleaners, more electric lights, more supermarkets and movie palaces and hospitals, than any other nation. Even at mid-century prices we can afford college educations and T-bone steaks for a far higher proportion of our people than receive them anywhere else on the globe.
>
> It approaches the commonplace, then, to observe that the factor of relative abundance is, by general consent, a basic condition of American life.

The theme of Potter's book, *People of Plenty* (1954), is that "economic abundance . . . has exercised a pervasive influence in the shaping of the American character."

611

The theme of contemporary abundance was given its fullest treatment in J. K. Galbraith's *The Affluent Society* (1958). Interestingly,
Galbraith considered it necessary to forewarn his contemporary readers that his book might be upsetting: "these are . . . days in which
even the mildly critical individual is likely to seem a lion in contrast
with the general mood." For, though the Harvard economist remarked
that American civilization had essentially solved the age-old problems
of scarcity and poverty, he argued that recognition of this accomplishment required a drastic revision of the "conventional wisdom" on
political economy. Galbraith's point about poverty in America was
not that it was too minimal to concern us but, on the contrary, that
its survival in such an affluent society as ours is "remarkable" and "a
disgrace." Nevertheless, because Galbraith stressed affluence and designated poverty as uniquely a "minority problem" in our society, *The
Affluent Society* has not escaped a place on the shelf with the literature of complacency of the 'fifties. (Galbraith's *American Capitalism*
[1952], A. A. Berle's *The 20th Century Capitalist Revolution* [1954],
and David Lilienthal's *Big Business; A New Era* [1952] belong more
certainly on that shelf.)

During the 'sixties people experienced a different mood. To some
degree, the Kennedy administration deserves credit for this change.
Although in its domestic efforts that administration may have been
the least successful since that of Andrew Johnson, it did convey a
sense of vitality and urgency in its approach to some long-ignored problems. The presence of extensive poverty in the midst of our "affluent society" was one case in point. But there are other reasons for the
change. One is that the poverty of a great proportion of the poor derives from social and legal discrimination against the colored people
of our country, a fact that it was no longer possible to ignore when
the civil rights movement at last achieved a militant stage by the end
of the complacent 'fifties. America, as Michael Harrington says (in
one of the books reviewed in the article that follows), had long *expected* Negroes to be poor; they were considered a "given" when one
contemplated the problem of poverty in America. This attitude is no
longer permissible.

The release of the 1960 census figures, of course, provided economists and statisticians with the raw materials for a rediscovery of poverty in America. One set of statistics in particular cast a pall on the
exuberant optimism of the 'fifties; that is, the figures showing trends
of income distribution. The statistics revealed: (1) that the share of
income received by the lower 40 percent of income recipients had not
changed for twenty years; (2) that occupational differentials in earnings (between skilled and unskilled laborers) were no longer narrowing; (3) that white-nonwhite income differentials were beginning to
widen after decades of gradual narrowing – in 1962, the median wage
or salary income for nonwhite workers was 55 percent of that received
by whites, or about what it was in 1947 and 3 percent lower than in
1958. The major reason for all three phenomena was the displace-

ment, by technological innovation, of a great part of the unskilled labor force. Although nonwhite workers suffered disproportionately in this development, masses of previously "well-off" whites suffered as well, which gave the problem the appearance of especial urgency in the eyes of the rest of the country. (It was the white mining communities of West Virginia and Kentucky, not chronically impoverished Harlem, which received the earliest attention of the "antipoverty" proposals.)

In the following article essayist Dwight Macdonald reviews several studies of poverty in America and, in his inimitable fashion, uses the findings for a broad commentary on the American scene.

For an exceptionally readable and reliable presentation of the problem of poverty in America, see *Rich Man, Poor Man** (1964) by Herman P. Miller, who for almost two decades was a researcher for the Bureau of the Census. Since poverty has become a crucial political issue in recent years, the literature on the subject has swelled embarrassingly. It is perhaps best to start with some of the excellent anthologies, notably, M. S. Gordon, ed., *Poverty in America** (1965); and L. A. Ferman, J. L. Kornbluh, and A. Haber, eds., *Poverty in America** (1968).

Our Invisible Poor

Dwight Macdonald

In his significantly titled *The Affluent Society* (1958) Professor J. K. Galbraith states that poverty in this country is no longer "a massive affliction [but] more nearly an afterthought." Dr. Galbraith is a humane critic of the American capitalist system, and he is generously indignant about the continued existence of even this nonmassive and afterthoughtish poverty. But the interesting thing about his pronouncement, aside from the fact that it is inaccurate, is that it was generally accepted as obvious. For a long time now, almost everybody has assumed that, because of the New Deal's social legislation and — more important — the prosperity we have enjoyed since 1940, mass poverty no longer exists in this country.

Dr. Galbraith states that our poor have dwindled to two hard-core categories. One is the "insular poverty" of those who live in the rural South or in depressed areas like West Virginia. The other category is "case poverty," which he says is "commonly and properly related to [such] characteristics of the individuals so afflicted [as] mental deficiency, bad health, inability to adapt to the discipline of modern economic life, excessive procreation, alcohol, insufficient education." He reasons that such poverty must be due to individual defects, since "nearly everyone else has mastered his environment; this proves that it is not intractable." Without pressing the similarity of this concept to the "Social Darwinism" whose fallacies Dr. Galbraith easily disposes of elsewhere in his book, one may observe that most of these characteristics are as much the result of poverty as its cause.

Dr. Galbraith's error is understandable, and common. Last April the newspapers reported some exhilarating statistics in a Department of Commerce study: the average family income increased from $2,340 in 1929 to $7,020 in 1961. (These figures are calculated in current dollars, as are all the others I shall cite.) But the papers did not report the fine type, so to speak, which showed that almost all the recent gain was made by families with incomes of over $7,500, and that the rate at which poverty is being eliminated has slowed down alarmingly since 1953. Only the specialists and the statisticians read the fine type, which is why illusions continue to exist about American poverty.

Now Michael Harrington, an alumnus of the *Catholic Worker* and the Fund for the Republic who is at present a contributing editor of *Dissent* and the chief editor of the Socialist Party biweekly, *New America*, has written *The Other America: Poverty in the United States* (Macmillan). In the admirably short space of under two hundred pages, he outlines the problem, describes in imaginative detail what it means to be poor in this country today, summarizes the findings of recent studies by economists and sociologists, and analyzes the reasons for the persistence of mass poverty in the midst of general prosperity. It is an excellent book — and a most important one.

My only serious criticism is that Mr. Harrington has popularized the treatment a bit too much. Not in the writing, which is on a decent level, but in a certain vagueness. There are no index, no bibliography, no reference footnotes. In our overspecialized culture, books like this tend to fall into two categories: Popular (no scholarly "apparatus") and Academic (too much). I favor something intermediate — why should the academics have *all* the footnotes? The lack of references means that the book is of limited use to future researchers and writers. A pity, since the author has brought together a great range of material.

I must also object that Mr. Harrington's treatment of statistics is more than a little impressionistic. His appendix, which he calls a coming to grips with the professional material, doesn't live up to its billing. "If my interpretation is bleak and grim," he writes, "and even if it overstates the case slightly, that is intentional. My moral point of departure is a sense of outrage. . . . In such a discussion it is inevitable that one gets mixed up with dry, graceless, technical matters. That should not conceal the crucial fact that these numbers represent people and that any tendency toward under-statement is an intellectual way of acquiescing in suffering." But a fact is a fact, and Mr. Harrington confuses the issue when he writes that "these num-bers represent people." They do — and one virtue of his book is that he never forgets it — but in dealing with statistics, this truism must be firmly repressed lest one begin to think from the heart rather than from the head, as he seems to do when he charges those statisticians who "understate" the numbers of the poor with having found "an intellectual way of acquiescing in suffering." This is moral bullying, and it reminds me, *toutes proportions gardées*, of the habitual confusion in Communist thinking between facts and political inferences from them. "A sense of outrage" is proper for a "moral point of departure," but statistics are the appropriate *factual* point of departure, as in the writings of Marx and Engels on the agony of the nineteenth-century English working class — writings that are by no means lacking in a sense of moral outrage, either.

These objections, however, do not affect Mr. Harrington's two main con-tentions: that mass poverty still exists in the United States, and that it is disappearing more slowly than is commonly thought. Two recent dry, grace-less, and technical reports bear him out. One is that Commerce Department study, already mentioned. More important is *Poverty and Deprivation in the U.S.*, a bulky pamphlet issued by the Conference on Economic Prog-ress, in Washington, whose national committee includes Thurman Arnold, Leon H. Keyserling (said to be the principal author of the pamphlet), and Walter P. Reuther.

In the last year we seem to have suddenly awakened, rubbing our eyes like Rip van Winkle, to the fact that mass poverty persists, and that it is one of our two gravest social problems. (The other is related: While only eleven per cent of our population is non-white, twenty-five per cent of our poor are.) Two other current books confirm Mr. Harrington's thesis: *Wealth and Power in America* (Praeger), by Dr. Gabriel Kolko, a social historian who has recently been at Harvard and the University of Mel-bourne, Australia, and *Income and Welfare in the United States* (Mc-Graw-Hill), compiled by an imposing battery of four socio-economists headed by Dr. James N. Morgan, who rejoices in the title of Program Di-rector of the Survey Research Center of the Institute for Social Research at the University of Michigan.

Dr. Kolko's book resembles Mr. Harrington's in several ways: It is short, it is based on earlier studies, and it is liberally inclined. It is less readable, because it is written in an academic jargon that is merely a vehicle for the clinching Statistic. Although it is impossible to write seriously about pov-erty without a copious use of statistics — as this review will demonstrate — it *is* possible to bring thought and feeling to bear on such raw material. Mr. Harrington does this more successfully than Dr. Kolko, whose prose is af-flicted not only with academic blight but also with creeping ideology. Dr.

Kolko leans so far to the socialist side that he sometimes falls on his nose, as when he clinches the inequality of wealth in the United States with a statistic: "In 1959, 23% of those earning less than $1,000 [a year] owned a car, compared to 95% of those earning more than $10,000." The real point is just the opposite, as any citizen of Iran, Ghana, Yemen, or the U.S.S.R. would appreciate — not that the rich have cars but that almost a quarter of the extremely poor do. Similarly, although Dr. Kolko has two chapters on poverty that confirm Mr. Harrington's argument, his main point is a different and more vulnerable one: "The basic distribution of income and wealth in the United States is essentially the same now as it was in 1939, or even 1910." This is a half fact. The rich are almost as rich as ever and the poor are even poorer, in the percentage of the national income they receive. Yet, as will become apparent later, there have been major changes in the distribution of wealth, and there has been a general improvement in living standards, so that the poor are much fewer today than they were in 1939. "Most low-income groups live substantially better today," Dr. Kolko admits. "But even though their real wages have mounted, their percentage of the national income has not changed." That in the last half century the rich have kept their riches and the poor their poverty is indeed a scandal. But it is theoretically possible, assuming enough general increase in wealth, that the relatively poor might by now have achieved a decent standard of living, no matter how inferior to that of the rich. As the books under consideration show, however, this theoretical possibility has not been realized.

Inequality of wealth is not necessarily a major social problem per se. Poverty is. The late French philosopher Charles Péguy remarks, in his classic essay on poverty, "The duty of tearing the destitute from their destitution and the duty of distributing goods equitably are not of the same order. The first is an urgent duty, the second is a duty of convenience. . . . When all men are provided with the necessities . . . what do we care about the distribution of luxury?" What indeed? Envy and emulation are the motives — and not very good ones — for the equalization of wealth. The problem of poverty goes much deeper.

Income and Welfare in the United States differs from the other works reviewed here in length (531 big pages) and in being the result of original research; 2,800 families were interviewed "in depth." I must confess that, aside from a few interesting bits of data, I got almost nothing out of it. I assume the authors think poverty is still an important social problem, else why would they have gone to all this labor, but I'm not at all sure what their general conclusions are; maybe there aren't supposed to be any, in the best tradition of American scholarship. Their book is one of those behemoths of collective research financed by a foundation (in this case, largely by Ford) that daunt the stoutest-hearted lay reader (in this case, me). Based on "a multi-stage area probability sample that gives equal chance of selection to all non-institutional dwelling units in the conterminous United States [and that] was clustered geographically at each stage and stratified with inter-laced controls," it is a specimen of what Charles Lamb called *biblia abiblia* — things that have the outward appearance of books but are not books, since they cannot be read. Methodologically, it employs something called the "multivariate analysis," which is explained in Appendix E. Typograph-ically, Appendix E looks like language, but it turns out to be strewn with booby traps, all doubtless well known in the trade, like "dummy variables," "F ratios," "regression coefficients," "beta coefficients" (and "partial beta coefficients"), and two kinds of "standard deviations" — "of explanatory variable A" and "of the dependent variable."

My experience with such works may be summarized as follows: (alpha) the coefficient of comprehensibility decreases in direct ratio to the increase in length, or the longer the incomprehensibler, a notion that is illustrated here by the fact that Dr. Kolko's short work is more understandable than Dr. Morgan et al.'s long one; (beta) the standard deviation from truism is inversely related to the magnitude of the generalization, or the bigger the statement the more obvious. (Beta) is illustrated by the authors' five general proposals for action ("Implications for Public Policy"). The second of these is: "Fuller employment and the elimination of discrimination based on prejudice would contribute greatly to the independence of non-white per-sons, women, teen-agers, and some of the aged." That is, if Negroes and the rest had jobs and were not discriminated against, they would be better off — a point that doesn't need to be argued or, for that matter, stated. The au-thors have achieved such a mastery of truism that they sometimes achieve the same monumental effect even in non-magnitudinous statements, as: "Table 28–1 shows that the proportion of parents who indicated that their children will attend private colleges is approximately twice as large for those with incomes over $10,000 as for those with incomes under $3,000." Could be.

What is "poverty"? It is a historically relative concept, first of all. "There are new definitions [in America] of what man can achieve, of what a human standard of life should be," Mr. Harrington writes. "Those who suffer levels of life well below those that are possible, even though they live better than medieval knights or Asian peasants, are poor. . . . Poverty should be de-fined in terms of those who are denied the minimal levels of health, hous-ing, food, and education that our present stage of scientific knowledge specifies as necessary for life as it is now lived in the United States." His dividing line follows that proposed in recent studies by the United States Bureau of Labor Statistics: $4,000 a year for a family of four and $2,000 for an individual living alone. (All kinds of income are included, such as food grown and consumed on farms.) This is the cutoff line generally drawn today.

Mr. Harrington estimates that between forty and fifty million Americans, or about a fourth of the population, are now living in poverty. Not just below the level of comfortable living, but real poverty, in the old-fashioned sense of the word — that they are hard put to it to get the mere necessities, beginning with enough to eat. This is difficult to believe in the United States of 1963, but one has to make the effort, and it is now being made. The extent of our poverty has suddenly become visible. The same thing has happened in England, where working-class gains as a result of the Labour Party's post-1945 welfare state blinded almost everybody to the continued existence of mass poverty. It was not until Professor Richard M. Titmuss, of the London School of Economics, published a series of articles in the *New Statesman* last fall, based on his new book, *Income Distribution and Social Change* (Allen & Unwin), that even the liberal public in England became aware that the problem still persists on a scale that is "statistically significant," as the economists put it.

Statistics on poverty are even trickier than most. For example, age and geography make a difference. There is a distinction, which cannot be rendered arithmetically, between poverty and low income. A childless young couple with $3,000 a year is not poor in the way an elderly couple might be with the same income. The young couple's statistical poverty may be a temporary inconvenience; if the husband is a graduate student or a skilled worker, there are prospects of latter affluence or at least comfort. But the old couple can look forward only to diminishing earnings and increasing medical expenses. So also geographically: A family of four in a small town with $4,000 a year may be better off than a like family in a city — lower rent, no bus fares to get to work, fewer occasions (or temptations) to spend money. Even more so with a rural family. Although allowance is made for the value of the vegetables they may raise to feed themselves, it is impossible to calculate how much money they *don't* spend on clothes, say, or furniture, because they don't have to keep up with the Joneses. Lurking in the crevices of a city, like piranha fish in a Brazilian stream, are numerous tempting opportunities for expenditure, small but voracious, which can strip a budget to its bones in a surprisingly short time. The subtlety and complexity of poverty statistics may be discovered by a look at Dr. Kolko's statement that in 1959 "23% of those earning less than $1,000 owned a car." Does this include college students, or are they included in their families' statistics? If the first is true, then Dr. Kolko's figure loses much of its meaning. If the second is, then it is almost *too* meaningful, since it says that one-fourth of those earning less than twenty dollars a week are able to afford a car. Which it is, deponent sayeth not.

It is not, therefore, surprising to find that there is some disagreement about just how many millions of Americans are poor. The point is that all these recent studies agree that American poverty is still a mass phenomenon. One of the lowest estimates appears in the University of Michigan's *Income and Welfare*, which states, "Poor families comprise one-fifth of the nation's families." The authors do not develop this large and crucial statement, or even give sources for it, despite their meticulous pedantry in all unimportant matters. So one can only murmur that the other experts put the number of poor much higher. (Though even a fifth is still over 35,000,-000 people.) The lowness of the Michigan estimate is especially puzzling since its cutoff figure for poverty is $4,330, which is slightly higher than the commonly accepted one. The tendentious Dr. Kolko is also unconvincing, in the opposite direction. "Since 1947," he writes, "one-half of the nation's families and unattached individuals have had an income too small to provide them with a maintenance standard of living," which he sets at $4,500 a year for a family. He does gives a table, with a long supporting footnote that failed to make clear to me how he could have possibly decided that 90,000,000 Americans are now living on less than $4,500 a year; I suspect some confusion between a "maintenance" and a "minimum-comfort" budget.

More persuasive estimates appear in the Conference on Economic Progress pamphlet, *Poverty and Deprivation*. Using the $4,000 cutoff, the authors conclude that 38,000,000 persons are now living in poverty, which is slightly less than Mr. Harrington's lowest estimate. One reason may be that the pamphlet discriminates, as most studies don't, between "multiple-person families" and "unattached individuals," rating the latter as poor only if they have less than $2,000 a year. But there is more to it than that, including a few things I don't feel competent to judge. Income statistics are never compiled on exactly the same bases and there are all kinds of refinements, which vary from one study to another. Thus the Commerce Department's April report estimates there are 17,500,000 families *and* "unattached individuals" with incomes of less than $4,000. How many of the latter are there? *Poverty and Deprivation* puts the number of single persons with under $2,000 at 4,000,000. Let us say that in the 17,500,000 under $4,000 there are 6,500,-000 single persons — the proportion of unattached individuals tends to go down as income rises. This homemade estimate gives us 11,000,000 families with incomes of under $4,000. Figuring the average American family at three and a half persons — which it is — this makes 38,500,000 individuals in families, or a grand total, if we add in the 4,000,000 "unattached individuals" with under $2,000 a year, of 42,500,000 Americans now living in poverty, which is close to a fourth of the total population.

The reason Dr. Galbraith was able to see poverty as no longer "a massive affliction" is that he used a cutoff of $1,000, which even in 1949, when it was adopted in a Congressional study, was probably too low (the C.I.O. argued for $2,000) and in 1958, when *The Affluent Society* appeared, was simply fantastic.

The model postwar budgets drawn up in 1951 by the Bureau of Labor Statistics to "maintain a level of adequate living" give a concrete idea of what poverty means in this country — or would mean if poor families lived within their income and spent it wisely, which they don't. Dr. Kolko summarizes the kind of living these budgets provide:

> Three members of the family see a movie once every three weeks, and one member sees a movie once every two weeks. There is no telephone in the house, but the family makes three pay calls a week. They buy one book a year and write one letter a week.
>
> The father buys one heavy wool suit every two years and a light wool suit every three years; the wife, one suit every ten years or one skirt every five years. Every three or four years, depending on the distance and time involved, the family takes a vacation outside their own city. In 1950, the family spent a total of $80 to $90 on all types of home furnishings, electrical appliances, and laundry equipment. . . . The family eats cheaper cuts of meat several times a week, but has more expensive cuts on holidays. The entire family consumes a total of two five-cent ice cream cones, one five-cent candy bar, two bottles of soda, and one bottle of beer a week. The family owes no money, but has no savings except for a small insurance policy.

One other item is included in the B.L.S. "maintenance" budget: a new car every twelve to eighteen years.

This is an ideal picture, drawn up by social workers, of how a poor family *should* spend its money. But the poor are much less provident — installment debts take up a lot of their cash, and only a statistician could expect an actual live woman, however poor, to buy new clothes at intervals of five or ten years. Also, one suspects that a lot more movies are seen and ice-cream cones and bottles of beer are consumed than in the Spartan ideal. But these necessary luxuries are had only at the cost of displacing other items — necessary necessities, so to speak — in the B.L.S. budget.

The Conference on Economic Progress's *Poverty and Deprivation* deals not only with the poor but also with another large section of the "underprivileged," which is an American euphemism almost as good as "senior citizen"; namely, the 37,000,000 persons whose family income is between $4,000 and $5,999 and the 2,000,000 singles who have from $2,000 to $2,999. The authors define "deprivation" as "above poverty but short of minimum requirements for a modestly comfortable level of living." They claim that 77,000,000 Americans, or *almost half the population*, live in poverty or deprivation. One recalls the furor Roosevelt aroused with his "one-third of a nation — ill-housed, ill-clad, ill-nourished." But the political climate was different then.

The distinction between a family income of $3,500 ("poverty") and $4,500 ("deprivation") is not vivid to those who run things — the 31 per cent whose incomes are between $7,500 and $14,999 and the 7 per cent of the topmost top dogs, who get $15,000 or more. These two minorities, sizable enough to feel they *are* the nation, have been as unaware of the continued existence of mass poverty as this reviewer was until he read Mr. Harrington's book. They are businessmen, congressmen, judges, government officials, politicians, lawyers, doctors, engineers, scientists, editors, journalists, and administrators in colleges, churches, and foundations. Since their education, income, and social status are superior, they, if anybody, might be expected to accept responsibility for what the Constitution calls "the general welfare." They have not done so in the case of the poor. And they have a good excuse. It is becoming harder and harder simply to *see* the one-fourth of our fellow-citizens who live below the poverty line.

> The poor are increasingly slipping out of the very experience and consciousness of the nation. [Mr. Harrington writes]. If the middle class never did like ugliness and poverty, it was at least aware of them. "Across the tracks" was not a very long way to go. . . . Now the American city has been transformed. The poor still inhabit the miserable housing in the central area, but they are increasingly isolated from contact with, or sight of, anybody else. . . . Living out in the suburbs, it is easy to assume that ours is, indeed, an affluent society. . . .
>
> Clothes make the poor invisible too: America has the best-dressed poverty the world has ever known. . . . It is much easier in the United States to be decently dressed than it is to be decently housed, fed, or doctored. . . .
>
> Many of the poor are the wrong age to be seen. A good number of them are sixty-five years of age or better; an even larger number are under eighteen. . . .
>
> And finally, the poor are politically invisible. . . . They are without lobbies of their own; they put forward no legislative program. As a group, they are atomized. They have no face; they have no voice. . . . Only the social agencies have a really direct involvement with the other America, and they are without any great political power. . . .
>
> Forty to fifty million people are becoming increasingly invisible.

These invisible people fall mostly into the following categories, some of them overlapping: poor farmers, who operate 40 per cent of the farms and get 7 per cent of the farm cash income; migratory farm workers; unskilled, unorganized workers in offices, hotels, restaurants, hospitals, laundries, and other service jobs; inhabitants of areas where poverty is either endemic ("peculiar to a people or district"), as in the rural South, or epidemic ("prevalent among a community at a special time and produced by some special causes"), as in West Virginia, where the special cause was the closing of coal mines and steel plants; Negroes and Puerto Ricans, who are a fourth of the total poor; the alcoholic derelicts in the big-city skid rows; the hillbillies from Kentucky, Tennessee, and Oklahoma who have migrated to Midwestern cities in search of better jobs. And, finally, almost half our "senior citizens."

The only pages in *Poverty and Deprivation* that can be read are the statistical tables. The rest is a jungle of inchoate data that seems deliberately to eschew, like other collective research projects, such human qualities as reason (the reader has to do most of the work of ordering the material) and feeling (if Mr. Harrington sometimes has too much, it is a venial sin compared to the bleakness of this prose). My hypothesis is that *Poverty and Deprivation* was composed on that TX-o "electronic brain" at M.I.T. This would account both for the vitality of the tables and for the deadness of the text.

And what shall one say about the University of Michigan's *Income and Welfare in the United States?* Even its *tables* are not readable. And its text makes *Poverty and Deprivation* look like the Federalist Papers. On the first page, the authors unloose a generalization of stupefying generality: "The United States has arrived at the point where poverty could be abolished easily and simply by a stroke of the pen. [Where have we heard *that* before?] To raise every individual and family in the nation now below a subsistence income to the subsistence level would cost about $10 billion a year. This is less than 2 per cent of the gross national product. It is less than 10 per cent of tax revenues. [They mean, but forgot to say so, *federal* taxes, since if state and local taxes were added, the total would be much higher than $100 billion.] It is about one-fifth of the cost of national defense." (They might have added that it is slightly more than three times the $3 billion Americans spend on their dogs and cats and canaries every year.) This got big headlines in the press, as must have been expected: " 'STROKE OF PEN' COULD ELIMINATE POVERTY IN U.S., 4 SCIENTISTS SAY." But the authors, having dropped the $10 billion figure on the first page, never explain its meaning — is it a seedbed operation or a permanent dole? They are not clear even on how they arrived at it. At their own estimate of 35,000,000 poor, $10 billion would work out to slightly less than $300 per person. This seems too little to abolish poverty "easily and simply by a stroke of the pen."

There are other vaguenesses: "A careful analysis of the characteristics of families whose incomes are inadequate reveals that they should earn considerably more than they do on the basis of their education and other characteristics. The multivariate analysis . . . indicates that heads of poor families should average $2,204 in earnings. In fact heads of poor families earned an average of only $932 in 1959." I have already confessed my inability to understand the multivariate analysis, but the compilers seem to be saying that according to the variables in their study (race, age, sex, education, physical disabilities, and locale), heads of poor families should now be making twice as much as they are. And why don't they? "The discrepancy may arise from psychological dependency, lack of motivation, lack of intelligence, and a variety of other factors that were not studied." One wonders why they were not studied — and what those "other factors" were, exactly. Also, whether such a discrepancy — the earnings the researchers expected to find were actually less than half those they *did* find — may not indicate some ghastly flaw in that "multivariate analysis." There is, of course, no suggestion in the book that Dr. Morgan and his team are in any way worried.

The most obvious citizens of the Other America are those whose skins are the wrong color. The folk slogans are realistic: "Last to be hired, first to be fired" and "If you're black, stay back." There has been some progress. In 1939, the non-white worker's wage averaged 41.4 per cent of the white worker's; by 1958 it had climbed to 58 per cent. A famous victory, but the non-whites still average only slightly more than half as much as the whites. Even this modest gain was due not to any Rooseveltian or Trumanian social reform but merely to the fact that for some years there was a war on and workers were in demand, whether black, white, or violet. By 1947, the non-whites had achieved most of their advance — to 54 per cent of white earnings, which means they have gained, in the last fifteen years, just 4 per cent.

The least obvious poverty affects our "senior citizens" — those over sixty-five. Mr. Harrington estimates that half of them — 8,000,000 — live in poverty, and he thinks they are even more atomized and politically helpless than the rest of the Other America. He estimates that one-fourth of the "unrelated" individuals" among them, or a million persons, have less than $580 a year, which is about what is allotted *for food alone* in the Department of Agriculture's minimum-subsistence budget. (The average American family now spends only 20 per cent of its income for food — an indication of the remarkable prosperity we are all enjoying, except for one-quarter of us.) One can imagine, or perhaps one can't, what it would be like to live on $580 a year, or $11 a week. It is only fair to note that most of our senior citizens do better: The average per-capita income of those over sixty-five is now estimated to be slightly over $20 a week. That is, about $1,000 a year.

The aged poor have two sources of income besides their earnings or savings. One is contributions by relatives. A 1961 White House Conference Report put this at 10 per cent of income, which works out to $8 a week for an income of $4,000 — and the 8,000,000 aged poor all have less than that. The other is Social Security, whose benefits in 1959 averaged $18 a week. Even this modest sum is more than any of the under-$4,000 got, since payments are proportionate to earnings and the poor, of course, earned less than the rest. A quarter of them, and those in general the neediest, are not covered by Social Security. The last report is relief, and Mr. Harrington describes most vividly the humiliations the poor often have to put up with to get that.

The problem of the aged poor is aggravated by the fact that, unlike the Italians or the English, we seem to have little respect for or interest in our "senior citizens," beyond giving them that honorific title, and we don't include them in family life. If we can afford it, we are likely to send them to nursing homes — "a storage-bin philosophy," a Senate report calls it — and if we can't, which is the case with the poor, they must make do with the resources noted above. The Michigan study has a depressing chapter on "The Economics of Living with Relatives." Nearly two-thirds of the heads of families queried were opposed to having their aged parents live with their children. "The old do not understand the young, and the young do not understand the old or the young," observed one respondent, who must have had a sense of humor. Other replies were "Old people are pretty hard to get along with" and "The parents and the children try to boss each other and when they live with you there's always fighting." The minority in favor gave practical reasons, like "It's a good thing to have them with you so you can see after them" and "The old folks might get a pension or something, so they could help you out." Hardly anyone expressed any particular respect for the old, or a feeling that their experience might enrich family life. The most depressing finding was "People most able to provide support for relatives are most opposed to it. Older people with some college education are eleven to one against it." The most favorable toward including older people in the home were Negroes, and even they were mostly against it.

The whole problem of poverty and the aged is especially serious today because Americans are living longer. In the first half of this century, life expectancy increased 17.6 years for men and 20.3 years for women. And between 1950 and 1960 the over-sixty-five group increased twice as fast as the population as a whole.

The worst part of being old and poor in this country is the loneliness. Mr. Harrington notes that we have not only racial ghettos but geriatric ones, in the cheap rooming-house districts of large cities. He gives one peculiarly disturbing statistic: "One-third of the aged in the United States, some 5,000,000 or more human beings, have no phone in their place of residence. They are literally cut off from the rest of America."

Ernest Hemingway's celebrated deflation of Scott Fitzgerald's romantic notion that the rich are "different" somehow — "Yes, they have money" — doesn't apply to the poor. They are different in more important ways than their lack of money, as Mr. Harrington demonstrates:

> Emotional upset is one of the main forms of the vicious circle of impoverishment. The structure of the society is hostile to these people. The poor tend to become pessimistic and depressed; they seek immediate gratification instead of saving; they act out.
>
> Once this mood, this unarticulated philosophy becomes a fact, society can change, the recession can end, and yet there is no motive for movement. The depression has become internalized. The middle class looks upon this process and sees "lazy" people who "just don't want to get ahead." People who are much too sensitive to demand of cripples that they run races ask of the poor that they get up and act just like everyone else in the society.

> The poor are not like everyone else. . . . They think and feel differently; they look upon a different America than the middle class looks upon.

The poor are also different in a physical sense: they are much less healthy. According to *Poverty and Deprivation*, the proportion of those "disabled or limited in their major activity by chronic ill health" rises sharply as income sinks. In reasonably well-off families ($7,000 and up), 4.3 per cent are so disabled; in reasonably poor families ($2,000 to $3,999), the proportion doubles, to 8 per cent; and in unreasonably poor families (under $2,000), it doubles again, to 16.5 per cent. An obvious cause, among others, for the very poor being four times as much disabled by "chronic ill health" as the well-to-do is that they have much less money to spend for medical care — in fact, almost nothing. This weighs with special heaviness on the aged poor. During the fifties, Mr. Harrington notes, "all costs on the Consumer Price Index went up by 12 per cent. But medical costs, that terrible staple of the aged, went up by 36 per cent, hospitalization rose by 65 per cent, and group hospitalization costs (Blue Cross premiums) were up by 83 per cent."

This last figure is particularly interesting, since Blue Cross and such plans are the A.M.A.'s alternative to socialized medicine, or, rather, to the timid fumblings toward it that even our most liberal politicians have dared to propose. Such figures throw an unpleasant light on the Senate's rejection of Medicare. The defeat was all the more bitter because, in the usual effort to appease the conservatives (with the usual lack of success — only five Republicans and only four Southern Democrats voted pro), the bill was watered down in advance. Not until he had spent $90 of his own money — which is 10 per cent of the annual income of some 3,000,000 aged poor — would a patient have been eligible. And the original program included only people already covered by Social Security or Railroad Retirement pensions and excluded the neediest of all — the 2,500,000 aged poor who are left out of both these systems. These untouchables were finally included in order to placate five liberal Republican senators, led by Javits of New York. They did vote for Medicare, but they were the only Republicans who did.

Mental as well as physical illness is much greater among the poor, even though our complacent cliché is that nervous breakdowns are a prerogative of the rich because the poor "can't afford" them. (They can't, but they have them anyway.) This bit of middle-class folklore should be laid to rest by a study made in New Haven: *Social Class and Mental Illness*, by August B. Hollingshead and Fredrick C. Redlich (Wiley). They found that the rate of "treated psychiatric illness" is about the same from the rich down through decently paid workers — an average of 573 per 100,000. But in the bottom fifth it shoots up to 1,659 per 100,000. There is an even more striking difference in the *kind* of mental illness. Of those in the four top income groups who had undergone psychiatric treatment, 65 per cent had been treated for neurotic problems and 35 per cent for psychotic disturbances. In the bottom fifth, the treated illnesses were almost all psychotic (90 per cent). This shows there is something to the notion that the poor "can't afford" nervous breakdowns — the milder kind, that is — since the reason the proportion of *treated* neuroses among the poor is only 10 per cent is that a neurotic can keep going, after a fashion. But the argument cuts deeper the other way. The poor go to a psychiatrist (or, more commonly, are committed to a mental institution) only when they are completely unable to function because of psychotic symptoms. Therefore, even that nearly threefold increase in mental disorders among the poor is probably an underestimate.

The poor are different, then, both physically and psychologically. During the fifties, a team of psychiatrists from Cornell studied "Midtown," a residential area in this city that contained 170,000 people, of all social classes. The area was 99 per cent white, so the findings may be presumed to understate the problem of poverty. The description of the poor — the "low social economic status individual" — is blunt: "[They are] rigid, suspicious, and have a fatalistic outlook on life. They do not plan ahead. . . . They are prone to depression, have feelings of futility, lack of belongingness, friendliness, and a lack of trust in others." Only a Dr. Pangloss would expect anything else. As Mr. Harrington points out, such characteristics are "a realistic adaptation to a socially perverse situation."

As for the isolation that is the lot of the American poor, that is a point on which Mr. Harrington is very good:

> America has a self-image of itself as a nation of joiners and doers. There are social clubs, charities, community drives, and the like. [One might add organizations like the Elks and Masons, Rotary and Kiwanis, cultural groups like our women's clubs, also alumni associations and professional organizations.] And yet this entire structure is a phenomenon of the middle class. Some time ago, a study in Franklin, Indiana [this vagueness of reference is all too typical of *The Other America*], reported that the percentage of people in the bottom class who were without affiliations of any kind was eight times as great as the percentage in the high-income class.
>
> Paradoxically, one of the factors that intensifies the social isolation of the poor is that America thinks of itself as a nation without social classes. As a result, there are few social or civic organizations that are separated on the basis of income and class. The "working-class culture" that sociologists have described in a country like England does not exist here. . . . The poor person who might want to join an organization is afraid. Because he or she will have less education, less money, less competence to articulate ideas than anyone else in the group, they stay away.

One reason our society is a comparatively violent one is that the French and Italian and British poor have a communal life and culture that the American poor lack. As one reads *The Other America*, one wonders why there is not even more violence than there is.

The richest city of all, New York, has been steadily growing poorer, if one looks beyond Park Avenue and Wall Street. Of its 2,080,000 families, just under half (49 per cent) had incomes in 1959 of less than $6,000; for the city's non-white families, the percentage was 71. And a fourth of all New York families in 1959 were below the poverty line of $4,000. These percentages are at present slightly higher than the national average — an ominous reversal of the city's earlier position. In 1932, the average national weekly wage was only 67 per cent of the New York City average. In 1960, it was 108 per cent. The city's manufacturing workers in 1946 earned $11 more a week than the national average; in 1960 they earned $6.55 a week less. The two chief reasons are probably the postwar influx of Puerto Ricans and the exodus to the suburbs of the well-to-do. But whatever the reasons, the city seems to be turning into an economically backward area, like Arkansas or New Hampshire. Even the bankers — the "non-supervisory" ones, that is — are modestly paid: 54 per cent of the males and 78 per cent of the females make less than $80 a week. All these statistics come from John O'Rourke, president of Joint Council 16, International Brotherhood of Teamsters, which has 168,000 members in the area. Mr. O'Rourke has been campaigning to persuade Mayor Wagner to raise the city's minimum hourly wage to $1.50. (The Mayor has gone as far as $1.25.) The New York teamsters are motivated by enlightened self-interest: the more other wages stagnate, the harder it will be to maintain their own comparatively high level of pay. They complain especially about the low wages in the highly organized garment trade, to which Mr. Dubinsky's International Ladies' Garment Workers' Union replies that if it presses for higher wages the manufacturers will simply move to low-wage, non-union areas, mostly in the South, as the New England textile manufacturers did many years ago — a riposte that is as realistic as it is uncheering. However, Mr. O'Rourke has an enterprising research staff, plenty of persistence, and a sharp tongue. "New Yorkers," he says, "are accustomed to thinking of themselves as pacesetters in an allegedly affluent society [but] at the rate we are going, we will soon qualify for the title 'Sweatshop Capital of the Nation.' "

The main reason the American poor have become invisible is that since 1936 their numbers have been reduced by two-thirds. Astounding as it may seem, the fact is that President Roosevelt's "one-third of a nation" was a considerable understatement; over two-thirds of us then lived below the poverty line, as is shown by the tables that follow. But today the poor are a minority, and minorities can be ignored if they are so heterogeneous that they cannot be organized. When the poor were a majority, they simply could not be overlooked. Poverty is also hard to see today because the middle class ($6,000 to $14,999) has vastly increased — from 13 per cent of all families in 1936 to a near-majority (47 per cent) today. That mass poverty can persist despite this rise to affluence is hard to believe, or see, especially if one is among those who have risen.

Two tables in *Poverty and Deprivation* summarize what has been happening in the last thirty years. They cover only multiple-person families; all figures are converted to 1960 dollars; and the income is before taxes. I have omitted, for clarity, all fractions.

The first table is the percentage of families with a given income:

	1935–6	1947	1953	1960
Under $ 4,000	68%	37%	28%	23%
$4,000 to $ 5,999	17	29	28	23
$6,000 to $ 7,499	6	12	17	16
$7,500 to $14,999	7	17	23	31
Over $15,000	2	4	5	7

The second table is the share each group had in the family income of the nation:

	1935–6	1947	1953	1960
Under $ 4,000	35%	16%	11%	7%
$4,000 to $ 5,999	21	24	21	15
$6,000 to $ 7,499	10	14	17	14
$7,500 to $14,999	16	28	33	40
Over $15,000	18	18	19	24

Several interesting conclusions can be drawn from these tables:

1. The New Deal didn't do anything about poverty: The under-$4,000 families in 1936 were 68 per cent of the total population, which was slightly *more* than the 1929 figure of 65 per cent.

2. The war economy (hot and cold) did do something about poverty: Between 1936 and 1960 the proportion of all families who were poor was reduced from 68 per cent to 23 per cent.

3. If the percentage of under-$4,000 families decreased by two-thirds between 1936 and 1960, their share of the national income dropped a great deal more — from 35 per cent to 7 per cent.

4. The well-to-do ($7,500 to $14,999) have enormously increased, from 7 per cent of all families in 1936 to 31 per cent today. The rich ($15,00 and over) have also multiplied — from 2 to 7 per cent. But it should be noted that the very rich, according to another new study, *The Share of Top Wealth-Holders in National Wealth*, 1922–1956, by Robert J. Lampman (Princeton), have experienced a decline. He finds that the top 1 per cent of wealth-holders owned 38 per cent of the national wealth in 1929 and own only 28 per cent today. (Though let's not get sentimental over that "only.") Thus, *pace* Dr. Kolko, there has in fact been a redistribution of wealth — in favor of the well-to-do and the rich at the expense of the poor and the very rich.

5. The reduction of poverty has slowed down. In the six years 1947–53, the number of poor families declined 9 per cent, but in the following seven years only 5 per cent. The economic stasis that set in with Eisenhower and that still persists under Kennedy was responsible. (This stagnation, however, did not affect the over-$7,500 families, who increased from 28 per cent to 38 per cent between 1953 and 1960.) In the New York *Times Magazine* for last November 11th, Herman P. Miller, of the Bureau of the Census, wrote, "During the forties, the lower-paid occupations made the greatest relative gains in average income. Laborers and service workers . . . had increases of about 180% . . . and professional and managerial workers, the highest paid workers of all, had the lowest relative gain — 96%." But in the last decade the trend has been reversed; laborers and service workers have gained 39% while professional-managerial workers have gained 68%. This is because in the wartime forties the unskilled were in great demand, while now they are being replaced by machines. Automation is today the same kind of menace to the unskilled — that is, the poor — that the enclosure movement was to the British agricultural population centuries ago. "The facts show that our 'social revolution' ended nearly twenty years ago," Mr. Miller concludes, "yet important segments of the American public, many of them highly placed Government officials and prominent educators, think and act as though it were a continuing process."

"A reduction of about 19% [in the under-$6,000 families] in more than thirty years, or at a rate of about 0.7% per year, is no ground for complacency," the authors of *Poverty and Deprivation* justly observe. There is even less ground for complacency in the recent figures on *extreme* poverty. The authors estimate the number of families in 1929 with incomes of under $2,000 (in current dollars) at 7,500,000. By 1947 there were less than 4,000,000, not because of any philanthropic effort by their more prosperous fellow-citizens but entirely because of those first glorious years of a war economy. Six years later, in 1953, when the economy had begun to slow down, there were still 3,300,000 of these families with incomes of less than $2,000, and seven years later, in 1960, "there had been no further reduction." Thus in the last fifteen years the bottom dogs have remained on the bottom, sharing hardly at all in the advances that the income groups above them have made in an ascending scale that is exquisitely adjusted, by the automatic workings of capitalism, so that it is inversely proportionate to need.

There are, finally, the bottomest bottom dogs; i.e., *families* with incomes of *under $1,000*. I apologize for the italics, but some facts insist on them. According to *Poverty and Deprivation*, the numbers of these families "appear to have risen slightly" of late (1953–60), from 800,000 to about 1,000,-000. It is only fair, and patriotic, to add that according to the Commerce Department study, about 10,000,000 of our families and unattached individuals now enjoy incomes of $10,000 a year and up. So while some 3,500,-

ooo Americans are in under-$1,000 families, ten times as many are in over-$10,000 families. Not bad at all — in a way.

The post-1940 decrease in poverty was not due to the policies or actions of those who are not poor, those in positions of power and responsibility. The war economy needed workers, wages went up, and the poor became less poor. When economic stasis set in, the rate of decrease in poverty slowed down proportionately, and it is still slow. Kennedy's efforts to "get the country moving again" have been unsuccessful, possibly because he has, despite the suggestions of many of his economic advisers, not yet advocated the one big step that might push the economy off dead center: a massive increase in government spending. This would be politically courageous, perhaps even dangerous, because of the superstitious fear of "deficit spending" and an "unbalanced" federal budget. American folklore insists that a government's budget must be arranged like a private family's. Walter Lippmann wrote, after the collapse of the stock market last spring:

> There is mounting evidence that those economists were right who told the Administration last winter that it was making the mistake of trying to balance the budget too soon. It will be said that the budget is not balanced: it shows a deficit in fiscal 1962 of $7 billion. . . . But . . . the budget that matters is the Department of Commerce's income and product accounts budget. Nobody looks at it except the economists [but] while the Administrative budget is necessary for administration and is like a man's checkbook, the income budget tells the real story. . . .
> [It] shows that at the end of 1962 the outgo and ingo accounts will be virtually in balance, with a deficit of only about half a billion dollars. Thus, in reality, the Kennedy administration is no longer stimulating the economy, and the economy is stagnating for lack of stimulation. We have one of the lowest rates of growth among the advanced industrial nations of the world.

One shouldn't be hard on the President. Franklin Roosevelt, a more daring and experimental politician, at least in his domestic policy, listened to the American disciples of J. M. Keynes in the early New Deal years and unbalanced his budgets, with splendid results. But by 1936 he had lost his nerve. He cut back government spending and there ensued the 1937 recession, from which the economy recovered only when war orders began to make up for the deficiency in domestic buying power. *Poverty and Deprivation* estimates that between 1953 and 1961 the annual growth rate of our economy was "only 2.5 per cent per annum contrasted with an estimated 4.2 per cent required to maintain utilization of manpower and other productive resources." The poor, who always experience the worst the first, understand quite personally the meaning of that dry statistic, as they understand Kipling's "The toad beneath the harrow knows / Exactly where each toothpoint goes." They are also most intimately acquainted with another set of statistics: the steady postwar rise in the unemployment rate, from 3.1 per cent in 1949 to 4.3 per cent in 1954 to 5.1 per cent in 1958 to over 7 per cent in 1961. (The Tory Government is worried because British unemployment is now at its highest point for the last three years. This point is 2.1 per cent, which is less than our lowest rate in the last fifteen years.)

Some of the post-1940 gains of the poor have been their own doing. "Moonlighting" — or holding two or more jobs at once — was practiced by about 3 per cent of the employed in 1950; today this percentage has almost doubled. Far more important is what might be called "wife-flitting": Between 1940 and 1957, the percentage of wives with jobs outside the home doubled, from 15 per cent to 30 per cent. The head of the United States Children's Bureau, Mrs. Katherine B. Oettinger, announced last summer, not at all triumphantly, that there are now two-thirds more working mothers than there were ten years ago and that these mothers have about 15,000,000 children under eighteen — of whom 4,000,000 are under six. This kind of economic enterprise ought to impress Senator Goldwater and the ideologues of the *National Review*, whose reaction to the poor, when they think about such an uninspiring subject, is "Why don't they *do* something about it?" The poor have done something about it and the family pay check is bigger and the statistics on poverty look better. But the effects on family life and on those 4,000,000 pre-school children is something else. Mrs. Oettinger quoted a roadside sign, "IRONING, DAY CARE AND WORMS FOR FISHING BAIT," and mentioned a baby-sitter who pacified her charge with sleeping pills and another who met the problem of a cold apartment by putting the baby in the oven. "The situation has become a 'national disgrace,' with many unfortunate conditions that do not come to public attention until a crisis arises," the *Times* summed up her conclusion. This crisis has finally penetrated to public attention. The President recently signed a law that might be called Day-care. It provides $5,000,000 for such facilities this fiscal year, which works out to $1.25 for each of the 4,000,000 under-six children with working mothers. Next year, the program will provide all of $2.50 per child. This is a free, democratic society's notion of an adequate response. Almost a century ago, Bismarck instituted in Germany state-financed social benefits far beyond anything we have yet ventured. Granted that he did it merely to take the play away from the Social Democratic Party founded by Marx and Engels. Still, one imagines that Count Bismarck must be amused — in the circle of Hell reserved for reactionaries — by that $2.50 a child.

It's not that Public Opinion doesn't become aroused every now and then. But the arousement never leads to much. It was aroused twenty-four years ago when John Steinbeck published *The Grapes of Wrath*, but Mr. Harrington reports that things in the Imperial Valley are still much the same: low wages, bad housing, no effective union. Public Opinion is too public — that is, too general; of its very nature, it can have no sustained interest in California agriculture. The only groups with such a continuing interest are the workers and the farmers who hire them. Once Public Opinion ceased to be Aroused, the battle was again between the two antagonists with a real, personal stake in the outcome, and there was no question about which was stronger. So with the rural poor in general. In the late fifties, the average annual wage for white male American farm workers was slightly over $1,000; women, children, Negroes, and Mexicans got less. One recalls Edward R. Murrow's celebrated television program about these people, "Harvest of Shame." Once more everybody was shocked, but the harvest is still shameful. One also recalls that Mr. Murrow, after President Kennedy had appointed him head of the United States Information Agency, tried to persuade the B.B.C. not to show "Harvest of Shame." His argument was that it would give an undesirable "image" of America to foreign audiences.

There is a monotony about the injustices suffered by the poor that perhaps accounts for the lack of interest the rest of society shows in them. Everything seems to go wrong with them. They never win. It's just boring.

Public housing turns out not to be for them. The 1949 Housing Act authorized 810,000 new units of low-cost housing in the following four years. Twelve years later, in 1961, the A.F.L.-C.I.O. proposed 400,000 units to complete the lagging 1949 program. The Kennedy administration ventured to recommend 100,000 to Congress. Thus, instead of 810,000 low-cost units by 1953, the poor will get, if they are lucky, 500,000 by 1963. And they are more likely to be injured than helped by slum clearance, since the new projects usually have higher rents than the displaced slum-dwellers can afford. (There has been no dearth of government-financed *middle*-income housing since 1949.) These refugees from the bulldozers for the most part simply emigrate to other slums. They also become invisible; Mr. Harrington notes that half of them are recorded as "address unknown." Several years ago, Charles Abrams, who was New York State Rent Administrator under Harriman and who is now president of the National Committee Against Discrimination in Housing, summed up what he had learned in two decades in public housing: "Once social reforms have won tonal appeal in the public mind, their slogans and goal-symbols may degenerate into tools of the dominant class for beleaguering the minority and often for defeating the very aims which the original sponsors had intended for their reforms." Mr. Abrams was probably thinking, in part, of the Title I adventures of Robert Moses in dealing with New York housing. There is a Moses or two in every American city, determined to lead us away from the promised land.

And this is not the end of tribulation. The poor, who can least afford to lose pay because of ill health, lose the most. A National Health Survey, made a few years ago, found that workers earning under $2,000 a year had twice as many "restricted-activity days" as those earning over $4,000.

The poor are even fatter than the rich. (The cartoonists will have to revise their clichés.) "Obesity is seven times more frequent among women of the lowest socio-economic level than it is among those of the highest level," state Drs. Moore, Stunkard, and Srole in a recent issue of the *Journal of the*

American Medical Association. (The proportion is almost the same for men.) They also found that overweight associated with poverty is related to mental disease. Fatness used to be a sign of wealth, as it still is in some parts of Africa, but in more advanced societies it is now a stigma of poverty, since it means too many cheap carbohydrates and too little exercise — which has changed from a necessity for the poor into a luxury for the rich, as may be confirmed by a glance at the models in any fashion magazine.

Although they are the most in need of hospital insurance, the poor have the least, since they can't afford the premiums; only 40 per cent of poor families have it, as against 63 per cent of all families. (It should be noted, however, that the poor who are war veterans can get free treatment, at government expense, in Veterans Administration Hospitals.)

The poor actually pay more taxes, in proportion to their income, than the rich. A recent study by the Tax Foundation estimates that 28 per cent of incomes under $2,000 goes for taxes, as against 24 per cent of the incomes of families earning five to seven times as much. Sales and other excise taxes are largely responsible for this curious statistic. It is true that such taxes fall impartially on all, like the blessed rain from heaven, but it is a form of egalitarianism that perhaps only Senator Goldwater can fully appreciate.

The final irony is that the Welfare State, which Roosevelt erected and which Eisenhower, no matter how strongly he felt about it, didn't attempt to pull down, is not for the poor, either. Agricultural workers are not covered by Social Security, nor are many of the desperately poor among the aged, such as "unrelated individuals" with incomes of less than $1,000, of whom only 37 per cent are covered, which is just half the percentage of coverage among the aged in general. Of the Welfare State, Mr. Harrington says, "Its creation had been stimulated by mass impoverishment and misery, yet it helped the poor least of all. Laws like unemployment compensation, the Wagner Act, the various farm programs, all these were designed for the middle third in the cities, for the organized workers, and for the . . . big market farmers. . . . [It] benefits those least who need help most." The industrial workers, led by John L. Lewis, mobilized enough political force to put through Section 7(a) of the National Industrial Recovery Act, which, with the Wagner Act, made the C.I.O. possible. The big farmers put enough pressure on Henry Wallace, Roosevelt's first Secretary of Agriculture — who talked a good fight for liberal principles but was a Hamlet when it came to action — to establish the two basic propositions of Welfare State agriculture: subsidies that now cost $3 billion a year and that chiefly benefit the big farmers; and the exclusion of sharecroppers, tenant farmers, and migratory workers from the protection of minimum-wage and Social Security laws.

No doubt the Kennedy administration would like to do more for the poor that it has, but it is hampered by the cabal of Republicans and Southern Democrats in Congress. The 1961 revision of the Fair Labor Standards Act, which raised the national minimum wage to the not exorbitant figure of

$1.15 an hour, was a slight improvement over the previous act. For instance, it increased coverage of retail-trade workers from 3 per cent to 33 per cent. (But one-fourth of the retail workers still excluded earn less than $1 an hour.) There was also a considerable amount of shadowboxing involved: Of the 3,600,000 workers newly covered, only 663,000 were making less than $1 an hour. And there was the exclusion of a particularly ill-paid group of workers. Nobody had anything against the laundry workers *personally*. It was just that they were weak, unorganized, and politically expendable. To appease the conservatives in Congress, whose votes were needed to get the revision through, they were therefore expended. The result is that of the 500,000 workers in the laundry, dry-cleaning, and dyeing industries, just 17,000 are now protected by the Fair Labor Standards Act.

In short, one reaches the unstartling conclusion that rewards in class societies, including Communist ones, are according to power rather than need. A recent illustration is the campaign of an obscure organization called Veterans of World War I of the U.S.A. to get a bill through Congress for pensions of about $25 a week. It was formed by older men who think other veterans' organizations (such as the American Legion, which claims 2,500,-000 members to their 200,000) are dominated by the relatively young. It asks for pensions for veterans of the First World War with incomes of under $2,400 (if single) or $3,600 (if married) — that is, only for *poor* veterans. The editorials have been violent: "STOP THIS VETERANS' GRAB," implored the *Herald Tribune*; "WORLD WAR I PENSION GRAB," echoed the *Saturday Evening Post*. Their objection was, in part, that many of the beneficiaries would not be bonafide poor, since pensions, annuities, and Social Security benefits were excluded from the maximum income needed to qualify. Considering that the average Social Security payment is about $1,000 a year, this would not put any potential beneficiary into the rich or even the comfortably-off class, even if one assumes another $1,000, which is surely too high, from annuities and pensions. It's all very confusing. The one clear aspect is that the minuscule Veterans of World War I of the U.S.A. came very near to bringing it off. Although their bill was opposed by both the White House and by the chairman of the House Committee on Veterans' Affairs, two hundred and one members of the House signed a petition to bring the measure to a vote, only eighteen less than needed "to accomplish this unusual parliamentary strategy," as the *Times* put it. These congressmen were motivated by politics rather than charity, one may assume. Many were up for reëlection last November, and the two hundred thousand Veterans of World War I had two advantages over the fifty million poor: They were organized, and they had a patriotic appeal only a wink away from the demagogic. Their "unusual parliamentary strategy" failed by eighteen votes in the Congress. But there will be another Congress.

It seems likely that mass poverty will continue in this country for a long time. The more it is reduced, the harder it is to keep on reducing it. The poor, having dwindled from two-thirds of the population in 1936 to one-quarter today, no longer are a significant political force, as is shown by the Senate's rejection of Medicare and by the Democrats' dropping it as an issue in the elections last year. Also, as poverty decreases, those left behind tend more and more to be the ones who have for so long accepted poverty as their destiny that they need outside help to climb out of it. This new minority mass poverty, so much more isolated and hopeless than the old majority poverty, shows signs of becoming chronic. "The permanence of low incomes is inferred from a variety of findings," write the authors of the Michigan survey. "In many poor families the head has never earned enough to cover the family's present needs." They give a vignette of what the statistics mean in human terms:

> For most families, however, the problem of chronic poverty is serious. One such family is headed by a thirty-two-year-old man who is employed as a dishwasher. Though he works steadily and more than full time, he earned slightly over $2,000 in 1959. His wife earned $300 more, but their combined incomes are not enough to support themselves and their three children. Although the head of the family is only thirty-two, he feels that he has no chance of advancement partly because he finished only seven grades of school. . . . The possibility of such families leaving the ranks of the poor is not high.

Children born into poor families today have less chance of "improving themselves" than the children of the pre-1940 poor. Rags to riches is now more likely to be rags to rags. "Indeed," the Michigan surveyors conclude, "it appears that a number of the heads of poor families have moved into less skilled jobs than their fathers had." Over a third of the children of the poor, according to the survey, don't go beyond the eighth grade and "will probably perpetuate the poverty of their parents." There are a great many of these children. In an important study of poverty, made for a Congressional committee in 1959, Dr. Robert J. Lampman estimated that eleven million of the poor were under eighteen. "A considerable number of younger persons are starting life in a condition of 'inherited poverty,' " he observed. To which Mr. Harrington adds, "The character of poverty has changed, and it has become more deadly for the young. It is no longer associated with immigrant groups with high aspirations; it is now identified with those whose social existence makes it more and more difficult to break out into the larger society." Even when children from poor families show intellectual promise, there is nothing in the values of their friends or families to encourage them to make use of it. Dr. Kolko, citing impressive sources, states that of the top 16 per cent of high-school students — those scoring 120 and over in I.Q. tests — only half go on to college. The explanation for this amazing — and alarming — situation is as much cultural as economic. The children of the poor now tend to lack what the sociologists call "motivation." At least one foundation is working on the problem of why so many bright children from poor families don't ever try to go beyond high school.

Mr. Raymond M. Hilliard, at present director of the Cook County (i.e., Chicago) Department of Public Aid and formerly Commissioner of Welfare for New York City, recently directed a "representative-sample" investigation, which showed that more than half of the 225,000 able-bodied Cook County residents who were on relief were "functionally illiterate." One reason Cook County has to spend $16,500,000 a month on relief is "the lack of basic educational skills of relief recipients which are essential to compete in our modern society." An interesting footnote, apropos of recent happenings at "Ole Miss," is that the illiteracy rate of the relief recipients who were educated in Chicago is 33 per cent, while among those who were educated in Mississippi and later moved to Chicago it is 77 per cent.

The problem of educating the poor has changed since 1900. Then it was the language and cultural difficulties of immigrants from foreign countries; now it is the subtler but more intractable problems of internal migration from backward regions, mostly in the South. The old immigrants wanted to Better Themselves and to Get Ahead. The new migrants are less ambitious, and they come into a less ambitious atmosphere. "When they arrive in the city," wrote Christopher Jencks in an excellent two-part survey, "Slums and Schools," in the *New Republic* last fall, "they join others equally unprepared for urban life in the slums — a milieu which is in many ways utterly dissociated from the rest of America. Often this milieu is self-perpetuating. I have been unable to find any statistics on how many of these migrants' children and grandchildren have become middle-class, but it is probably not too inaccurate to estimate that about 30,000,000 people live in urban slums, and that about half are second-generation residents." The immigrants of 1890–1910 also arrived in a milieu that was "in many ways utterly dissociated from the rest of America," yet they had a vision — a rather materialistic one, but still a vision — of what life in America could be if they worked hard enough; and they did work, and they did aspire to something more than they had; and they did get out of the slums. The disturbing thing about the poor today is that so many of them seem to lack any such vision. Mr. Jencks remarks:

> While the economy is changing in a way which makes the eventual liquidation of the slums at least conceivable, young people are not seizing the opportunities this change presents. Too many are dropping out of school before graduation (more than half in many slums); too few are going to college. . . . As a result there are serious shortages of teachers, nurses, doctors, technicians, and scientifically trained executives, but 4,500,000 unemployables.

"Poverty is the parent of revolution and crime," Aristotle wrote. This is now a half truth — the last half. Our poor are alienated; they don't consider themselves part of society. But precisely because they don't they are not politically dangerous. It is people with "a stake in the country" who make revolutions. The best — though by no means the only — reason for worrying about the Other America is that its existence should make us feel uncomfortable.

The federal government is the only purposeful force — I assume wars are not purposeful — that can reduce the numbers of the poor and make their lives more bearable. The authors of *Poverty and Deprivation* take a dim view of the Kennedy administration's efforts to date:

> The Federal Budget is the most important single instrument available to us as a free people to induce satisfactory economic performance, and to reduce poverty and deprivation. . . .
> Projected Federal outlays in the fiscal 1963 Budget are too small. The items in this Budget covering programs directly related to human improvement and the reduction of mass poverty and deprivation allocate far too small a portion of our total national production to these great purposes.

The effect of government policy on poverty has two quite distinct aspects. One is the indirect effect of the stimulation of the economy by federal spending. Such stimulation — though by war-time demands rather than government policy — has in the past produced a prosperity that did cut down American poverty by almost two-thirds. But I am inclined to agree with Dr. Galbraith that it would not have a comparable effect on present-day poverty:

> It is assumed that with increasing output poverty must disappear [he writes]. Increased output eliminated the general poverty of all who worked. Accordingly it must, sooner or later, eliminate the special poverty that still remains. . . . Yet just as the arithmetic of modern politics makes it tempting to overlook the very poor, so the supposition that increasing output will remedy their case has made it easy to do so too.

He underestimates the massiveness of American poverty, but he is right when he says there is now a hard core of the specially disadvantaged — because of age, race, environment, physical or mental defects, etc. — that would not be significantly reduced by general prosperity. (Although I think the majority of our present poor *would* benefit, if only by a reduction in the present high rate of unemployment.)

To do something about this hard core, a second line of government policy would be required; namely, direct intervention to help the poor. We have had this since the New Deal, but it has always been grudging and miserly, and we have never accepted the principle that every citizen should be provided, at state expense, with a reasonable minimum standard of living regardless of any other considerations. It should not depend on earnings, as does Social Security, which continues the inequalities and inequities and so tends to keep the poor forever poor. Nor should it exclude millions of our poorest citizens because they lack the political pressure to force their way into the Welfare State. The governmental obligation to provide, out of taxes, such a minimum living standard for all who need it should be taken as much for granted as free public schools have always been in our history.

It may be objected that the economy cannot bear the cost, and certainly costs must be calculated. But the point is not the calculation but the principle. Statistics — and especially statistical forecasts — can be pushed one way or the other. Who can determine in advance to what extent the extra expense of giving our 40,000,000 poor enough income to rise above the poverty line would be offset by the lift to the economy from their increased purchasing power? We really don't know. Nor did we know what the budgetary effects would be when we established the principle of free public education. The rationale then was that all citizens should have an equal chance of competing for a better status. The rationale now is different: that every citizen has a right to become or remain part of our society because if this right is denied, as it is in the case of at least one-fourth of our citizens, it impoverishes us all. Since 1932, "the government" — local, state, and federal — has recognized a responsibility to provide its citizens with a subsistence living. Apples will never again be sold on the street by jobless accountants, it seems safe to predict, nor will any serious political leader ever again suggest that share-the-work and local charity can solve the problem of unemployment. "Nobody starves" in this country any more, but, like every social statistic, this is a tricky business. Nobody starves, but who can measure the starvation, not to be calculated by daily intake of proteins and calories, that reduces life for many of our poor to a long vestibule to death? Nobody starves, but every fourth citizen rubs along on a standard of living that is below what Mr. Harrington defines as "the minimal levels of health, housing, food, and education that our present stage of scientific knowledge specifies as necessary for life as it is now lived in the United States." Nobody starves, but a fourth of us are excluded from the common social existence. Not to be able to afford a movie or a glass of beer is a kind of starvation — if everybody else can.

The problem is obvious: the persistence of mass poverty in a prosperous country. The solution is also obvious: to provide, out of taxes, the kind of subsidies that have always been given to the public schools (not to mention the police and fire departments and the post office) — subsidies that would raise incomes above the poverty level, so that every citizen could feel he is indeed such. "*Civis Romanus sum!*" cried St. Paul when he was threatened with flogging — and he was not flogged. Until our poor can be proud to say "*Civis Americanus sum!*," until the act of justice that would make this possible has been performed by the three-quarters of Americans who are not poor — until then the shame of the Other America will continue.

27

RACIAL VIOLENCE IN THE CITIES

The importance of Joseph Boskin's essay lies in his attempt to relate the urban riots of the 1960's not only to American racial attitudes but also to American attitudes toward the city. As a number of articles in this collection make clear, Americans have used the city but they never have been completely comfortable with it. The city has provided generations of Americans with a safety valve which offered release from the diminishing rewards and limited opportunities of the farm and village. But though Americans have flocked to the city in the millions, large numbers of them always have remained imperfectly acculturated to the urban ethos; their ideals remained, in the words of F. Scott Fitzgerald, "somewhere back in that vast obscurity beyond the city, where the dark fields of the republic rolled on under the night." The city, then, was gradually transformed from a place to which one escaped into a place from which one escaped. Since in an industrial nation opportunity remained in cities, escape took the form of attempting to create within or, more frequently, near the city some form of quasi-rural enclave. Americans, as Scott Donaldson has demonstrated, have attempted to marry the city and the country (see above, pp. 49–67). Suburban America has been the most common offspring of this rather improbable union.

How central this movement away from the cities has been in the past few decades is demonstrated by the preliminary reports of the 1970 census which indicate that the majority of Americans may now live in the suburbs that have proliferated around and between all of America's urban centers. The census of 1970 may prove to have been as premature in declaring America a suburban nation as was the census of 1890 in announcing that the frontier was closed or the census of 1920 in declaring America an urban nation (counting every community with more than 2,500 people in it as "urban"). But like these earlier censuses, the census of 1970 is important not so much as an accurate statement of what exists but as a portent of what soon must come if some major reversal does not take place.

The national unwillingness or incapacity to accept the city on its own terms and, starting with its limitations and opportunities, to build within it places in which men and women can live with dignity and pleasure, is increasing. The white middle classes, who until now have been the only groups with sufficient political power to demand the expenditures of money and energy necessary to reclaim and rebuild the city, have fled to suburban enclaves from which they frequently act as a counter-pressure against these very expenditures. As a result, cities are rapidly becoming transformed into unwieldy conglomerations of the very wealthy who have no need to escape and the very poor who have no means of escape.

The urban riots of the 1960's were partly a direct product of these developments. They were also, of course, race riots, and as such they were an indication of an important new means of black protest. In the nineteenth and early twentieth centuries, when Negroes still constituted only small minorities within urban centers, race riots resembled pogroms in which angry white mobs would charge into a black section of the city burning, looting, and killing. By the time the riots of 1919 occurred, the pattern had changed markedly. Riots were still precipitated for the most part by whites but the larger Negro urban settlements now had increased means of resistance, and in Chicago, Washington, D.C., and other cities, the riots often turned into pitched racial battles with whites as well as blacks among the fatalities. As the historian Joseph Boskin points out in the article below, the Harlem riots of 1935 and 1943 were the first major race riots precipitated by Negroes themselves, and they set the pattern that predominated throughout the last decade.

Nor have Negroes been the only central actors in these riots. Major riots have taken place in Puerto Rican and Mexican-American neighborhoods in New York and Los Angeles, and there have been angry rumblings from young inhabitants of San Francisco's large Chinese-American enclave. Without some major change in the pattern of American attitudes and action, there is every reason to expect that these riots will continue and even proliferate in the future. The point of this introduction and of Boskin's article is that this change must take place not only in America's racial patterns but also in its historic approach to the city.

There is as yet no comprehensive study of race riots in the United States. The Chicago Commission on Race Relation's report on the Chicago riot of 1919, *The Negro in Chicago* (1922), is the most profound study of a race riot yet published. Elliott Rudwick, *Race Riot at East St. Louis** (1964), provides an excellent picture of the 1917 riot in that city. Arthur Waskow, *From Race Riot to Sit-In** (1966), contains a great deal of information on the riots of 1919. There have been a number of contemporary accounts of individual race riots during the 1960's. See, for example, Jerry Cohen and William Murphy, *Burn, Baby, Burn!** (1966), and Robert Conot, *Rivers of Blood, Years of Darkness** (1967), on the Los Angeles riot of 1965; John Hersey, *The Algiers Motel Incident** (1968), on the Detroit riot of 1967; and Fred C. Shapiro and James W. Sullivan, *Race Riots New York, 1964* (1964). Even more important are the numerous reports of government commissions and study groups, which contain invaluable information. The most comprehensive is the *Report of the National Advisory Commission on Civil Disorders** (1968). Important also are the following two reports to the National

Commission on the Causes and Prevention of Violence: J. H. Skolnick, *The Politics of Protest** (1969); and H. D. Graham and T. R. Gurr, eds., *The History of Violence in America** (1969). R. H. Connery, ed., *Urban Riots** (1969), is a useful collection of essays.

The Revolt of the Urban Ghettos, 1964–1967

JOSEPH BOSKIN

Alternating extremes of elation and despair have characterized black protest in the 1960's. Vacillating between the studied nonviolent and the spontaneous violent approaches to the entrapments of ghetto life, Negro behavior has mirrored the dilemma of the exploited, dark-skinned person: whether to withstand the rejection of the majority in the hope that ameliorative actions would bring rewards within the system or to lash out and destroy the hated environment, thus bringing abrupt awareness to the majority and release for oneself. Over one hundred major revolts in as many cities in the incredibly short space of three years have demonstrated that for those blacks outside of the civil rights and other allied protest movements of the mid-1950's and early 1960's, the course of protest was to be disruptive and violent. Clearly, the behavior of blacks in the large and small ghettos connoted a consensus of attitude toward their own communities, one another, and the larger society. Their actions signified the most important underclass revolt [1] in recent American history.

THE CONTINUING CONFLICT OF RACE

The urban protest riots proved to be the pivotal black response. The riots affected the course of the civil rights movement; they coalesced the young, lower- and middle-class Negroes in the cities; they marked the growing conflict between the generations and the classes in Negro communities throughout the nation. Further, they symbolized the inability of American democracy to cope effectively with the historical-psychological problem of racism. The riots, in fact, split the nation in the 1960's and prompted the period of polarization. The clashes of the summer of 1967, however, marked

Reprinted by permission of the author from *The Annals of the American Academy of Political and Social Science*, 382 (March 1969).

[1] The term "riot" and "revolt" are used interchangeably in this study. They describe acts of assault on the status quo and its tangible legitimate authorities, in this instance, the police and business establishments.

an end to the spontaneous outbursts of the previous period of urban violence. A new stance was effected, as militant groups fashioned a framework of sociopolitical objectives essentially absent in the earlier period of protest.

As the incidence of riots marked the departure from the civil rights period, this new expression of protest in the 1960's can be differentiated from the more characteristic form of urban racial violence which prevailed in the past. With the exception of the Harlem riots of 1935 and 1943, which seemed more clearly to be the consequence of economic and wartime conditions, the riots of the past two centuries were initiated by Caucasians and were motivated by racist attitudes.

In these racial episodes, Negroes suffered the bulk of personal and property damage, with little restitution offered from civil authorities. Between 1900 and 1949, there were thirty-three major interracial clashes. Of these, eighteen occurred during the period of World War I and its aftermath, whereas five occurred during World War II. Obviously, the majority of these occurrences reflected situations of a critical nature.

From the end of World War II until 1964, there were several large-scale urban disturbances which reflected the underlying potential for social violence. None of these conflicts expanded into major urban conflagrations. Rather, most of the clashes were manifestations of what Allen Grimshaw has called "assaults upon the accommodative structure," that is, Negro challenges to the socioeconomic structure of a community. The most intense violence occurred when minority groups attempted to change residential patterns or when a number of Caucasians defined the situation as one in which such an attempt was being made.

The volatility of these situations was constantly reflected in the years following the termination of the war. Resentment against Negroes who moved into all-white neighborhoods resulted in more than a hundred incidents: the Airport Homes violence in Chicago in November 1945; the Fernwood Project violence, also in Chicago, August 1947; the Georgia house-bombings in May 1947; and the highly publicized violence of 1951 in Cicero, Illinois. Some of the weapons employed by white assaulters — bricks, guns, sniping, Molotov cocktails — were those which were utilized by blacks in the 1960's. Racial violence also occurred when Negroes attempted to use public recreational facilities traditionally reserved for Caucasians in northern and midwestern cities. In sum, the race riots which raged in American society from the turn of the century until the mid-1960's reflected extensions of white racism. The rebellions which began in 1964 represented a major response to that racism.

The explosion of the blacks in the urban ghettos from 1964 to 1967 was presaged three decades ago in the lines of poet Langston Hughes:

Negroes,
Sweet and docile,
Meek, humble, and kind:

Beware the day
They change their minds! [2]

As late as the year of the first riots came the powerful words of Kenneth
Clark, the eminent psychologist, in his work *Dark Ghetto:*

> The poor are always alienated from normal society, and when the
> poor are Negro, as they increasingly are in the American cities, a
> double trauma exists — rejection on the basis of class and race is a
> danger to the stability of the society as a whole.[3]

And, in 1965, a shocked but largely lethargic suburban society was admon-
ished by Mayor Robert Wagner of New York:

> There are lions in the streets, angry lions, aggrieved lions, lions who
> have been caged until the cages crumbled. We had better do some-
> thing about those lions, and when I speak of lions I do not mean in-
> dividuals. I mean the spirit of the people. Those who have been
> neglected and oppressed and discriminated against and misunderstood
> and forgotten.[4]

Yet, despite a year of violent urban disruptions and countless admonitions
from leaders in the Caucasian and black communities, the disturbances
were ascribed to a minority of disgruntled blacks. Few were prepared — even
after studies had demonstrated that a sizable proportion of Negroes were
actively involved in the rebellions — to accept the fact that Negroes were
indeed alienated from American society and angry enough to destroy the
environments immediately surrounding them which represented the outside repressive world.

That blacks vented their antagonism on the buildings, streets, and businesses within their immediate reach and avoided these same places in exclusively white areas is crucial to an understanding of their motivations.
Central to the development of the *zeitgeist* of the revolts were the attitudes
of the Caucasian not only regarding the Negro — which, to understate the
situation, is well understood as being antagonistic — but regarding the Negro's environment, that is, the city itself. The experience of the blacks in
their mass migration into the core cities was inextricably related to the attitudes of whites toward the cities. For it is not merely the fact of high-density
populations living in slum conditions which brought blacks to convulsive
actions but, more importantly, the approach which predominates in relation
to those enclaves which we call the city. The riot was a response to the interaction of both majority and minority in their respective attitudes toward
the ghetto and the city. An essential component of its origin was the majority's rejection of the city as a viable and creative environment within

[2] Langston Hughes, "Roland Hayes Beaten," *One-Way Ticket* (New York: Alfred
A. Knopf, 1949), p. 86.

[3] Kenneth Clark, *Dark Ghetto* (New York: Harper and Row, 1964), p. 21.

[4] Quoted in Gurston D. Goldin, "Violence: The Integration of Psychiatric and
Sociological Concepts," *Notre Dame Lawyer*, Vol. XL, No. 5, 1965, p. 513.

which to live. Thus, an ecological malaise was one of the primary causes of the violent protest.

The City: Never the Promised Land

One of the most poignant and enduring conflicts in our national life, frequently subtle, yet constantly gnawing, has been the antagonism between rural and urban America. This has been far more than a conflict between the political and power interests of divergent human locales; it has been a conflict in the American consciousness, and is implicit in the American value system. Since the early nineteenth century, millions of Americans have yielded to a seemingly fatal attraction to make the great migration from farm and village to the city. Whatever may have been the harsh imperatives which guided them, there was a persistent tendency to look back, with a degree of nostalgia and with a sense of irreparable loss, to an idyllic rural setting. In a nation in which the forces of urbanization were unrelenting, where urban living was clearly the shape of the future, there was a deep conviction, as Walter Lippmann wrote, that the city should not be acknowledged as the American ideal. This mood was not limited merely to those who had strayed from the intended ways, but was shared by those who were born in the city environs. The city has never been conceived as being the preferred place to inhabit permanently, nor has it been romanticized in the arts and mass media. It has rarely been regarded as a focus for creative living.

The burgeoning of industry, and the expansion of the middle class, with its increased financial and physical mobility, enabled the nostalgic rural life to be transplanted into suburbia and exurbia. Thus, for this group of urban dwellers, alternatives of living were possible. The actuality of choice, however, gave rise to an ambivalence in which the best and worst of feelings conjoined: the desire for the idealized rural life-style and a strong desire to partake in the activities of the city.

The movement into the cities in the past two centuries, then, was not accomplished without the creation of a basic paradox. The economic means to achieve a fuller life, though associated with the city, was not fulfilled within the city. The compromise of the suburban community seemed to provide a solution to the uncomfortable dilemma of rural versus urban life. Seemingly, one could have the best of both styles. Several difficulties, however, prevented the suburb from becoming the American middle-class nirvana. The magnitude of the march to the suburbs necessitated mass transportation to and from the central cities. The city administrators' choice, the freeway, soon became a strangulated contact with the city, bringing it not close enough, yet too far away. Yet, many who lived in suburbia were economically dependent upon the city, so that contact with the core city was never physically far removed. Ironically, too, transportation arteries made possible the invisibility of the ghettos.

The development of a sophisticated mass communications system, in the form of television, in the early 1950's reinforced the ambivalent antagonisms towards the city. Throughout the 1950's and 1960's, television portrayed the city as a violent, unhealthy, dirty, corrupt, lonely, unseemly place for people to live, develop, and grow. Survival appeared to be the main component dramatized in series after series. With the exceptions of such productions as were borrowed from earlier successful radio shows, the bulk of television performances were antiurban in substance. In such medical series as "Ben Casey," "The Young Interns," and "The Nurses," psychological maladies or life and death were constant themes. The decade of the 1920's, depicted in such series as "The Roaring Twenties" and "The Untouchables," consistently associated the city with gang violence. In such outstanding series as "Naked City," which dealt with some realistic problems of life in New York, and "East Side, West Side," a series based on the experiences of a social worker, the promise and potential of the city were lacking. Television largely reinforced the image of the city earlier perpetuated by literature and the movies. As Herbert Kosower has correctly noted: "Almost all of Hollywood's films deal with contemporary urban life on a superficial fantasy plane." [5] Even *Street Scene, On the Waterfront, The Naked City, The Pawnbroker*, and *A Thousand Clowns* tended to reflect the harsh aspects of urban life.

Resistance to city living grew from several sources. The organization of the city was felt to be antagonistic to basic American values. It bred impersonality, detachment, and unhealthy conditions. Criticism stemmed from the conception of the city as being anti-individualistic. Groups of people were herded together in living and working conditions which placed a premium on co-operative and collectivistic solutions to social problems.

The city was further indicted for altering the landscape of America, for denying its past and playing havoc with its future. As Anselm Strauss has accurately written, the United States managed to develop an industrial economy without developing a thoroughly urbanized citizenry. Americans, he noted, entered upon the great urbanization of the nineteenth century "protestingly, metaphorically walking backward." [6]

The image of the city was capped in the catch phrase originally ascribed to New York City: "It's a nice place to visit but I wouldn't want to live there." Living was to be done in the suburbs, away from the source of corruptions. The "Promised Land," then, was to be sought outside the city.

Aided by affluence, millions fled from the city into the landscaped suburbs — leaving the core cities to the newer migrant and immigrant groups. Negro-, Puerto Rican-, Mexican-, and Japanese-Americans, and other smaller

[5] Herbert Kosower, King Vidor, and Joseph Boshur, "The Arts," *Psychology Today*, Vol. II, No. 3 (August 1968), p. 16.

[6] Anselm Strauss, *Images of the American City* (New York: Free Press, 1961), p. 123.

American minority groups with dark or nonwhite skins, filled the central cities. By the 1960's, all major and most smaller cities had sizable numbers of various ethnic groups in the downtown areas, living in slum ghettos, breathing the increasingly foul urban air, and becoming increasingly alienated. They gradually developed an urban consciousness — a consciousness of the entrapped underclass.

The sense of entrapment stemmed from the inability of the ethnic groups to break out of the urban ghetto and become part of the burgeoning middle classes. Alienation grew out of the anger of betrayal, a betrayal that began when the inner-city dwellers were made the inheritors of decaying cities. That they were being deserted, that the promised land in the North and West was drying up, as Langston Hughes caustically expressed it, "like a raisin in the sun," became increasingly clear in the decades of the 1950's and 1960's. Claude Brown, in his *Manchild in the Promised Land*, an affectionate portrayal of Harlem, began his sketch with this denial of the promise:

> I want to talk about the first Northern urban generation of Negroes. I want to talk about the experiences of a misplaced generation, of a misplaced people in an extremely complex, confused society. This is a story of their searching, their dreams, their sorrows, their small and futile rebellions, and their endless battle to establish their own place in America's greatest metropolis — and in America itself.
>
> The characters are sons and daughters of former Southern sharecroppers. These were the poorest people of the South, who poured into New York City during the decade following the Great Depression. These migrants were told that unlimited opportunities for prosperity existed in New York and that there was no "color problem" there. They were told that Negroes lived in houses with bathrooms, electricity, running water, and indoor toilets. To them, this was the "promised land" that Mammy had been singing about in the cotton fields for many years. . . . It seems that Cousin Willie, in his lying haste, had neglected to tell the folks down home about one of the most important aspects of the promised land: it was a slum ghetto. There was a tremendous difference in the way life was lived up North. There were too many people full of hate and bitterness crowded into a dirty, stinky, uncared-for closet-size section of a great city.
>
> Before the soreness of the cotton fields had left Mama's back, her knees were getting sore from scrubbing "Goldberg's" floor. Nevertheless, she was better off; she had gone from the fire into the frying pan.
>
> The children of these disillusioned colored pioneers inherited the total lot of their parents — the disappointments, the anger. To add to their misery, they had little hope of deliverance. For where does one run to when he's already in the promised land? [7]

One runs to one's soul brother.

[7] Claude Brown, *Manchild in the Promised Land* (New York: New American Library, 1965), pp. vii–viii.

The significant consequences of the great migration along the hallelujah trail was the development of an urban consciousness in the ghettos of the industrial cities. Alain Locke, in his important book in the 1920's, *The New Negro*, took cognizance of the ecological forces at work in Harlem. Proscription and prejudice, he noted, had thrown dissimilar black elements into a common area of contact and interaction. Prior to the movement into Harlem, the Negro was "a race more in name than in fact, or to be exact, more in sentiment than in experience." The central experience between these groups, he continued, was that of "a common condition rather than a life in common. In Harlem, Negro life is seizing upon its first chances for group expression and self-determination." [8] The fusing of sentiment and experience in Harlem was repeated over and again in ghettos across the country. Indeed, ghetto experience became a common denominator, its life-style and language and conditions a similarity of experiences.

Had the ghetto become a viable environment within a dynamic city existence, the level of grievance-consciousness shared by Negroes would have been muted. But the opposite occurred. Instead, the ghetto became a dead-end to those who lived in it. It became an object of loathing, a mirror of a squalid existence. Feelings of hopelessness and isolation were recurrent themes in the testimony of the slum residents, wrote the United States Commission on Civil Rights in 1967. When asked what she would do if she had sufficient income, one resident declared, "The first thing I would do myself is move out of the neighborhood. I feel the entire neighborhood is more or less a trap." [9]

Compounding these antagonisms were, of course, the intensifying anti-urban attitudes of whites. "The people in Harlem," wrote James Baldwin in *Nobody Knows My Name*, two years before the first protest riot, "know they are living there because white people do not think they are good enough to live elsewhere. No amount of 'improvement' can sweeten this fact. . . . A ghetto can be improved in one way only: out of existence." [10] These resentments were further exacerbated by the obvious disparity between the Caucasian and black neighborhoods. Said a young man to Budd Schulberg in the Watts Happening Coffee House immediately after the riots:

> The contrast: the spectacular growth of central and west L.A. vs. the stagnation of Watts. . . . You've conquered it, baby. You've got it made. Some nights on the roof of our rotten falling down buildings we can actually see your lights shining in the distance. So near and

[8] Alain Locke, *The New Negro* (New York: Albert and Charles Boni, 1925), pp. 6–7.
[9] U.S., Commission on Civil Rights, *A Time to Listen . . . A Time to Act* (Washington, D.C.: U.S. Government Printing Office, 1967), p. 6.
[10] James Baldwin, *Nobody Knows My Name* (New York: Delta Books, 1962), p. 65.

yet so far. We want to reach out and grab it and punch it on the nose.[11]

The mythical urban melting pot began to simmer and finally boiled over.

The protest riots which occurred in massive profusion were thus the consequence of a myriad of historical and ecological factors which fused in the 1960's. Their outstanding feature was a collective mode of attitude, behavior, and sense of power.

THE CRY: BURN, BABY, BURN

The sudden burst of rage which rent Harlem in July 1964 was the third mass outburst in that community in the twentieth century. On two previous occasions, the first time during the Great Depression and the second during World War II, blacks in one of the most highly concentrated, racially, ethnic ghettos in the nation signified their protest in spontaneous rioting. Unlike the earlier uprisings which were confined to Harlem, however, the actions in 1964 proved to be the beginning of an urban black protest throughout the country. In city after city, summer after summer, blacks took vengeance by wrecking the hated symbols within their own ghetto areas.

The violent protest in Harlem was rapidly repeated in seven other urban Negro ghettos in the next two months: Bedford-Stuyvesant (Brooklyn), Rochester, Paterson, Jersey City, Elizabeth, Philadelphia, and Dixmoor (Chicago). In 1965, eruptions occurred in five cities, the major conflagrations taking place in Chicago and especially in Los Angeles. Large-scale rioting increased in intensity in the following year, when blacks took to the streets in twenty cities, including Cleveland, Chicago, Omaha, East Oakland, and San Francisco. The year 1967 began on a volatile note as disturbances occurred in the spring in the Southern cities of Nashville, Jackson, and Houston. As the heat of the summer increased, so did the temper for violence. There were mass assaults in Roxbury (Boston), Tampa, Dayton, Atlanta, Buffalo, and Cincinnati in the month of June. Within the next two months, Negroes swarmed through the ghettos of twenty-two cities in the North, Midwest, and South, with the largest riots taking place in Toledo, Grand Rapids, Plainfield (New Jersey), Milwaukee, and especially in Newark and Detroit. By 1968 the rioting had subsided, suggesting that the anger had been channeled into aggressive community programs.

The toll of the rioting over the four-year period was devastating. Between 1964 and 1967, approximately 130 civilians, mainly Negroes, and 12 civil personnel, mainly Caucasian, were killed. Approximately 4,700 Negroes and civil personnel were injured. Over 20,000 persons were arrested during the

---

[11] "Watts — End or Beginning," *Los Angeles Times*, Calendar, May 15, 1966, p. 3, col. 2.

melees; property damages mounted into the hundreds of millions of dollars; many cities resembled the hollowed remnants of war-torn cities.[12]

Despite the disparity of distance, there was a consensus of attitudes and a similarity of actions among those urban blacks who revolted and those who supported the violent protest.[13] Significantly, the riots were largely unplanned, unorganized, and unscheduled. Ray Lewis, a Cleveland youth worker, explained the origins of the outbreak in that city:

> It wasn't that people planned our riot so consciously. But take a Negro ghetto where men sit around for years saying, "we gonna get whitey," and you build up a group knowledge of what to do.[14]

Taken together, the riots were the actions of a people, poor and dispossessed and crushed in huge numbers into large slum ghettos, who rose up in wrath against a society committed to democratic ideals. Their outburst was an expression of class antagonism, resentment against racial prejudice, anger at the unreachable affluence around them, and frustration at their sociopolitical powerlessness. "What are these people riotin' about in other cities?" exclaimed Efelka Brown, of the "Sons of Watts," an organization set up to train young males in trade skills. "They want *recognition* and the only way they goin' get it is to riot. We don't want to overthrow the country — we just want what we ain't got." [15]

The sense of betrayal of expectations brought about a focus on the grievances of the past and present. The visibility of an affluent, comfortable, middle-class life, made possible by a powerful mass communications system, was in itself enough to induce dual feelings of resentment and emulation. Pronouncements by the political establishment, however, served only to increase these emotions. Thus, enticed by advertising of the leisure life, excited by legislative programs such as the Civil Rights Acts and the War on Poverty, lured by television programs depicting middle-class life, and hopeful of change in their environment, the poor anticipated an imminent improvement in their socioeconomic position. The failure of society effectively to raise the status of those trapped in the cities contributed immensely to the smoldering resentments.

The urge to retaliate, to return the hurts and the injustices, played an integral part of the protest. By itself, the riot was not "a major thing," stated

[12] The rioting which occurred following the assassination of Dr. Martin Luther King in April 1968 is not covered in this paper. These actions were not specifically related to the origins and spread of the urban revolt.

[13] For a further analysis of the 'consensus of attitudes and behavior,' see Joseph Boskin, "Violence in the Ghettos: A Consensus of Attitudes," in *Violence in Contemporary Society*, ed. Joseph Frank, *New Mexico Quarterly*, Vol. XXXVII, No. 4 (Winter 1968), pp. 317–334.

[14] John Allan Long, "After the Midwest Riots," *Christian Science Monitor*, November 10, 1966, p. 11.

[15] "The Hard-Core Ghetto Mood," *Newsweek*, Vol. LXX, No. 8, August 21, 1967, p. 21.

James Richards to the United States Commission on Civil Rights after the
Hunter's Point riot in San Francisco in 1966:

> It was just an idea to strike out at something and someone. Even if
> you don't do anything but break a window or a chair or something
> like this, you feel that you are hurting a white man or something like
> this because the white man is the one that is doing everything to you
> that causes you to have all these problems on you now.[16]

Similar expressions of deep-welled anger were heard from Puerto Ricans in
Spanish Harlem. Piri Thomas, author of *Down These Mean Streets*, in
testimony before the National Advisory Commission on Civil Disorders, described the origins of the explosion in that area:

> Did you ever stand on street corners and look the other way, at the
> world of muchos ricos and think, I ain't got a damn? Did you ever
> count the garbage that flowed down dirty streets, or dig in the back
> yards who in their glory were a garbage dumps dream? Did you ever
> stand on rooftops and watch night time cover the bad below? Did
> you ever put your hand around your throat and feel your pulse beat
> say, "I do belong and there's not gonna be nobody can tell me, I'm
> wrong?" [17]

Intense grievances vis-à-vis their inability to achieve even the basic promises of American life of work, status, and housing combined with other
minor factors to make the cities highly combustible. The National Advisory
Commission found in almost all the cities surveyed "the same major grievance topic among Negro communities." [18] The Commission ranked three
levels of grievances among Negroes:

First Level of Intensity:
1. Police practices
2. Unemployment and underemployment
3. Inadequate housing

Second Level of Intensity:
1. Inadequate education
2. Poor recreational facilities and programs
3. Ineffectiveness of the political structure and grievance mechanisms

Third Level of Intensity:
1. Disrespectful white attitudes
2. Discriminatory administration of justice
3. Inadequacy of federal programs
4. Inadequacy of municipal services

[16] *A Time to Listen . . . A Time to Act*, p. 5.
[17] Piri Thomas, in testimony before the National Advisory Commission on Civil Disorders, September 21, 1967.
[18] U.S., Riot Commission, *Report of the National Advisory Commission on Civil
Disorders* (New York: Bantam Books, 1968), p. 143.

5. Discriminatory consumer and credit practices
6. Inadequate welfare programs [19]

To strike out against the visible symbols of white society became a sign of brotherhood. In more than one instance, rock-throwing blacks placed missiles into the hands of residents of the community, saying, "You're either with us or against us, man." In the Watts riot, Mervin Dymally, a Negro assemblyman, was asked by one of the rioters to prove his loyalty by heaving an object at a police car. Dymally refused, saying, "No, man, I'm for peace." The boy quickly replied, "No, you're with the man." [20] Many residents of ghetto areas who did not participate in the actions shouted their approval to those on the streets.

That a general approval, a collective behavior, pervaded the ghettos can be borne out by analysis of the actions of blacks. The two groups singled out for attack were the police and Caucasian-owned businesses. Relations between the police and the minorities, particularly members of the dark-skinned ethnic groups, have always been volatile. As an institution, the police have reflected the attitudes of the majority. To have expected the police to act as a social agency oriented towards reform or conflict-amelioration is to misconstrue their primary function as they view it; namely, the maintenance of law and order. Thus, the police have practiced physical attacks and verbal harassment on minority-group members without interference. Though the public was generally unaware of the treatment accorded minority-ethnic-group members, a prejudicial attitude on its part sanctioned police actions. The language of the police vis-à-vis Negroes — "nigger," "monkey," "them," "boy" — were terms in general usage in American culture. For many years, blacks have attempted to bring to light the ample evidence of discriminatory beatings and humiliations. One such attempt in 1965, by furious blacks in the South-Central area of Los Angeles, compiled a listing of the discriminatory remarks of the then Los Angeles Chief of Police William H. Parker — which resulted in a fifteen-page report entitled "Police Chief William H. Parker speaks" — and distributed it in the community.[21]

Yet, the police became a main local point for attack not only because of their attitude toward and behavior with minority groups, but primarily because they came to symbolize the despised invisible white power structure. Of the institutional contacts with which ghetto-dwellers have intimate contact — schools, social welfare and employment agencies, medical facilities, business owners — the police embody the most crushing authority. For many blacks, the police had come to represent more than enforcement of law; they were viewed as members of an occupying army and as an oppres-

[19] *Ibid.*, pp. 143–144.
[20] *Report of the Governor's Commission on the Los Angeles Riot*, Vol. II (Sacramento, 1966), pp. 88–89.
[21] William H. Parker, "Police Chief William H. Parker Speaks" (Los Angeles: Community Relations Conference of Southern California, 1965).

sive force acting on behalf of those who rule their environment but who fled it for the greener pastures. "A policeman is an object of contempt," Ernie W. Chambers of Omaha bitterly stated in testimony given before the National Advisory Committee on Civil Disorders.[22] The system represented by the police has been oppressivee, the method of rule has been heavy with force, and the phrase "maintain law and order" has been directed basically towards the control of Negroes. "Like why, man, should I get home?" angrily inquired a young black during the Watts riot. "These cops have been pushin' me 'round all my life. Kickin' my ——— and things like that. Whitey ain't no damn good, he talks 'bout law and order, it's his law and order, it ain't mine [word deleted by the Commission]." [23]

That a collective wrath directed against the police goaded ghetto residents is evident from an analysis of the early stages of the riots. It is significant that most revolts began as a consequence of an incident in which the police were, in some manner, involved. In several instances, the initiating episode was in the line of routine activity. In the Watts situation, for instance, police stopped two men who were driving in an intoxicated condition. Nevertheless, the significance of the specific event bore no relation to the more serious undercurrent of animosity which had been previously created. In other cases, verbal and physical actions by the police were instrumental in increasing a tense situation by inflaming the ghetto people, as happened in the Newark riot of 1967, which really began when the police charged out of the station house towards a large group of demonstrating and jeering Negroes.

Equally instructive is the fact that snipers, despite their numbers, hit extremely few policemen and firemen during the three years of rioting. The low number of deaths of law officials could hardly be ascribed to poor marksmanship. By 1967, especially in Detroit, the incidence of sniper fire had increased considerably; yet, only four law officers were killed, as compared to thirty-nine civilians. Indeed, of the eighty-three persons who died in seventy-five disorders analyzed by the Permanent Sub-committee on Investigations of the Senate Committee on Government Operations in 1967, approximately ten persons were public officials, primarily law officers and firemen, whereas the remainder were civilians, primarily Negroes.[24]

White businessmen were the second most exposed group singled out for attack. Resentment against the practices of exploitation, in the form of hidden and higher interest rates, shoddy goods and lower quality, higher prices and questionable service, had likewise been building for many years.

---

[22] Ernie W. Chambers, in testimony before the National Advisory Commission on Civil Disorders, September 23, 1967. The Commission described Chambers as a "grass-roots leader."

[23] *Report of the Governor's Commission on the Los Angeles Riot*, Vol. I (Sacramento, 1966), p. 43.

[24] *Report of the National Advisory Commission on Civil Disorders*, pp. 115–116.

The communications system in the community had long isolated such business establishments. Consequently, the majority of stores damaged and looted were those against which ill-feelings had developed. Negro stores frequently were protected by identifying signs: "Blood Brother," "Soul Brother," "Negro-owned." Not only were black businesses generally left untouched, but so, too, were libraries, schools, hospitals, clinics, and, surprisingly, governmental agencies. There were instances of bricks and sniper fire hitting these various buildings; however, no concerted attack was conducted. Many places burned down because of the refusal of the rioters to permit fire engines into the area.

Nevertheless, retail businesses suffered a much greater proportion of the damage during the violence than public institutions, industrial properties, or private residences. In Newark in 1967, 1,029 establishments listed damage to buildings or loss of inventory or both.[25] Those businesses which were hardest hit by rioters were those which were felt to be the most exploitative in their business practices: liquor, clothing, food, and furniture stores. Indeed, in at least nine of the riots studied by the President's National Advisory Commission on Civil Disorders, the damage was, in part, the result of "deliberate attacks on white-owned businesses characterized in the Negro community as unfair or disrespectful toward Negroes." [26]

The riot brought a sense of exultation in the community. It served as a release of frustration, anger, and helplessness. Even those participants who afterwards regretted their actions admitted to the joy that they had personally experienced. In testimony before the McCone Commission, conducted after the riot in central Los Angeles, Winston Slaughter, age twenty, a junior college student, responded to the question: "Do you think the riot helped or hurt the Negro cause?"

> Well, you can say regret and then you can say there are some who are glad it happened. Now, me personally, I feel that I regret it, yes. But, deep down inside I know I was feeling some joy while it was going on, simply because I am a Negro.[27]

Others felt no regret, but a sense of pride. As the riots spread to other ghetto areas, those communities which experienced no turmoil felt the need to emulate their brothers. An exchange between three young blacks after the Detroit riot indicated the fulfilling exuberance of the historical moment:

> "Those buildings goin' up was a pretty sight," a long-legged kid said. "I sat right here and watched them go. And there wasn't nothin' them honkies could do but sweat and strain to put it out."

[25] *Ibid.*
[26] *Ibid.*
[27] *Report of Governor's Commission on the Los Angeles Riot,* Vol. XIII (Sacramento, 1966), pp. 28–29.

"Yeah, man," a pal chimed in, "it's about time those honkies started earnin' their money in this neighborhood."

"You know," said Long Legs, "we made big news. They called this the country's worst race riot in history."

"Yeah," said another gangly kid, straddling the railing. "My kids goin' to study about that in school, and they'll know their old man was part of it."

"We got the record man," exulted another youth. . . . "They can forget all about Watts and Newark and Harlem. This is where the riot to end all riots was held." [28]

Further, the protest riot assumed certain features of conventional warfare. The weapons and tactics employed were those standardized in the past thirty years: Molotov cocktails, selected targets, visible enemies, harassing tactics, sniping, mobility, and a capitulation to a more powerful military force in the form of national guardsmen or federal troops. Parallels between war as a means of confronting an enemy and the protest riot could also be observed in the attitudes of ghetto residents. Although the term "riot" was used by blacks, it became clear that they meant to describe their actions in a larger sense. "We in a war," a black youth told a reporter. "Or hasn't anybody told you that?" [29]

The attitude of immediacy was heard from many persons. "Many Negroes would rather die than live under conditions as they are now," exclaimed a male at a youth symposium. "For these people, riots present the only chance of ever achieving equality." [30] An absence of fear was notable among those who actively participated in the streets. "The cops think we are scared of them because they got guns," stated a male in testimony before the McCone Commission, "but you can only die once: if I get a few of them I don't mind dying." [31] Thus, the riots were emotionally liberating. The joy in retaliating and the fun in looting reinforced the feelings of communal action. The individual acts fused with the collective act. The term "we" was used with frequency among the protesting rioters: "We put ourselves on the map." "We were whole again." During the civil violences, there was a partial suspension of conscience. "This liberation from conscience and from conscientiousness made possible for the rioters an involvement and an extreme commitment usually denied them." [32] Moreover, the pride in action played an integral role in the historical consciousness of the community.

[28] "The Hard-Core Ghetto Mood," p. 20.

[29] *Ibid.*

[30] California, Alameda County, Human Relations Commission, "Youth Discuss Racial Problems," *Human Relations News*, Vol. I, No. 2 (September 1967), p. 1.

[31] *Report of Governor's Commission on the Los Angeles Riot*, Vol. I, p. 16.

[32] Frederick J. Hacker and Aljean Harmetz, "What the McCone Commission Didn't See," *Frontier*, Vol. XVII, No. 5 (March 1966), p. 13.

Two years after the Watts riot, black and brown high school students, selected to participate in an upward-bound educational project, were asked to complete a form which contained the question: "What kinds of civil rights activities have you participated in?" One student answered: "Watts Riot." Such statements and actions indicate a high degree of participation in the protest disturbances.

Several significant studies have pointedly noted a high degree of community participation in the violence of the small and large riots in the 1960's. The Los Angeles Riot Study (LARS), initiated immediately after the 1965 riot, collated the interviews of 2,070 persons living within the curfew area.[33] The group of Negroes interviewed was a random sample, stratified by age, sex, and income. Interviews were approximately two hours in length; the interview covered questions of attitude toward the riot, activity in the riot, general social and political attitudes, and background information. The LARS survey noted that the majority of Negroes had spent their childhood in the South but that over 60 per cent of the sample had matured in urban areas. Significantly, about the same percentage had lived in Los Angeles ten years or longer at the time of the riot. Contrary to reports about the low educational level of the rioters, the study indicated that over half of the sample had completed high school. Contrary to popular assumptions as well, the study indicated that 72 per cent of the males and 35 per cent of the females were employed in August 1965.

With regard to participation in the riot, the LARS survey demonstrated that up to 15 per cent of the Negro adult population, or about 22,000 persons, were active at some point during the rioting; that an additional 35 or 40 per cent, or 51,000 persons, were active spectators. Support for the violence was greater among the younger persons, was greater among men than women, and was as great among relatively long-time residents of South-Central Los Angeles as it was among the more recent migrants from the South. The latter point is of particular importance, inasmuch as it undercut the notion that the riot was largely the work of the unacculturated and of the recent influx of migrants from the South.

A high percentage of the community supported the violence, in attitude if not in action. Approximately 34 per cent of the sample were favorably disposed toward the actions, and 38 per cent of the population in the curfew area felt that the revolt would help in their quest to improve their positions. Only 20 per cent indicated that the riot hurt the community. In sum, a high proportion of persons in the riot area participated in, or gave support to, the action of fellow residents.

Studies undertaken after the LARS report substantially corroborated its conclusions. The National Advisory Commission on Civil Disorders con-

---

[33] Institute of Government and Public Affairs, University of California, Los Angeles, 1967.

ducted 1,200 interviews in approximately twenty cities, studied arrest records in twenty-two cities, and elicited additional reports from participants. According to the Report of the Commission, the typical rioter was an unmarried male, between the ages of fifteen and twenty-four, born in the state, and a lifelong resident of the city in which the riot occurred. His education was substantially good, have attended high school, and, economically, his position was approximately the same as his counterpart who did not actively participate in the riot. Nonetheless, he was more likely to be working in a menial or low-status job as an unskilled laborer. In special surveys taken after the Newark and Detroit revolts, interviewers noted strong feelings of racial pride, "if not racial superiority." [34] The riot experience was a definite factor in increased self- and communal pride:

> INTERVIEWER: You said you were feeling good when you followed the crowd?
> RESPONDENT: I was feeling proud, man, at the fact that I was a Negro. I felt like I was a first-class citizen. I didn't feel ashamed of my race because of what they did [Detroit, 1967].[35]

The nature of the rioting which marked the mid-1960's appeared to undergo serious change by the end of the decade. Two indications of this change were, firstly, the Detroit riot of 1967 in which a sizable proportion of Caucasians joined with the Negroes in burning and looting, thus indicating a meshing of an economic underclass; and, secondly, the development and intensity of the Black Power movement. The activists have been concerned with developing cultural, economic, and political programs within the community. These activist organizations have, on more than one occasion, prevented violent outbreaks by ghetto residents who were angered by representatives of the power structure, particularly the police. Within the broad Black Power movement, moreover, militant groups have counseled for the termination of nonviolence as a technique of bringing about necessary change. "We know that we cannot change violent people by nonviolence," read a mimeographed sheet handed out by the Black Student Union at the University of California, San Diego, immediately after the assassination of Dr. Martin Luther King in April 1968. "We must build mass armed self-defense groups. We must unite to get rid of the government and people that oppress and murder Black People." Thus, by the end of the decade, the energies of the younger blacks were oriented towards more specific, militant goals.

In sum, the revolts in the mid-1960's — more than the nonviolent movement of Dr. Martin Luther King and the extraordinarily powerful civil rights movement of the early 1960's — directed attention to the anguished plights of millions of Negroes, Puerto Ricans, and Mexican-Americans liv-

---

[34] *Report of the National Advisory Commission on Civil Disorders*, p. 133.
[35] *Ibid.*

ing in the urban centers of the country. The spontaneous outbursts, the collective actions, and the consensual attitudes of blacks and browns highlighted the failure of American society to recognize the problems of the racial minority groups in the cities. The events stemmed not only from the tradition of racist mentality but also from the ambiguous attitudes towards the city itself. The enormity of the failure led to one of the most intense social crises in American society in the twentieth century.

28

YOUNG REBELS

By 1970, the costs of United States intervention in Indochina had mounted so high — measured by the loss of life and limbs, by the disruption of the economy, by the substantial damage done domestically to confidence in the political system, by the apprehensions raised among our allies abroad, and perhaps also by the delay at a crucial moment in history of a multilateral nuclear arms treaty — that it is difficult to explain the American procrastination in, or indeed the positive resistance to, a conclusive pullout. To be sure, many foreign policy experts, such as Henry Kissinger and Dean Rusk, still clung to the logic that had impelled the initial military commitment; and indeed the logic of "negotiating from strength," of "fidelity to commitment" and of falling Asian dominoes continued to serve official policy. Yet the force of that logic had evidently vanished, not only for those who had long regarded "anticommunism" as a poor excuse for a foreign policy, but also for such noteworthy, "hard-headed," anticommunist policy experts as Defense Secretaries Robert McNamara and Clark Clifford, National Security Council head McGeorge Bundy, and Paris Peace conferees Averill Harriman and Cyrus Vance. Though many of these men had helped shape the policies of intervention, they had come to change their minds even before they had left their respective offices. By the time the Nixon administration was two years old, notables from the business world, such as the head of the Bank of America, had added their own public denunciations of the war. And in certain large eastern states, such as New York, Pennsylvania, and Massachusetts — usually identified with the capitalist ogres of Wall Street — the Republicans seemed to be trying to outdo the Democrats in their antiwar fervor, while Republican Senators Percy (Illinois), Hatfield (Oregon), Mathias (Maryland), and Cooper (Kentucky) showed that the sentiment was not merely regional. In sum, whatever logic the initial intervention had had, its costs (at least) had dictated to a remarkable array of decidedly conservative leaders a prompt reversal. And still we persisted.

It would seem that to explain the resistance to withdrawal, one must turn away from foreign policy objectives to the domestic predicament. At the lowest level, two sources of resistance are obvious: (1) How could old-line political leaders, trained in Cold War demonology themselves, explain to a public they had helped condition to the holiness of anticommunist sacrifice, that it was necessary to withdraw in Indochina without having substantially defeated "the communists" there? (2) More trenchantly, how could political leaders responsible for, or at least on record in support of, intervention explain to the voting-age friends and relatives of the 45,000 American dead and the 300,000 American wounded that they had made a mistake? But it is important not to focus exclusively on the politicians. To press the second point just a step further: How could those who had made such enormous sacrifices admit *to themselves* that it was all in vain? — especially, one must add, in the face of the strikingly numerous and articulate people in the country who had decried the folly and vanity of it all in advance, and had — often with great courage — refused to endure such sacrifices themselves? If it was all in vain, the "cop outs" were right and they were *dupes*; but if the war could be sustained and justified, the "cop outs" were bums and they were *heroes*.

Indeed, in a vital sense, the popular reaction to, or rather *against*, the antiwar campaign may be the key to it all. In this respect, it is essential to understand that the Vietnam issue developed against the background of a complex set of anxieties that arose out of an extraordinary confluence of social upheavals during the 1960's. These included the so-called black revolution; the emergence of a "particularistic" militancy among blacks, Chicanos, American Indians, Puerto Ricans, students, and women; and the flowering of an aggressive (and often irritatingly self-righteous) youth culture. Altogether these developments contributed to a longer-standing and manifold challenge to conventional behavioral standards with regard to authority, sex, race relations, and the work ethic. (For example, in 1965 probably most people over thirty-five — black, brown, and white, male and female — had grown up with certain expectations about how Negroes, *latinos*, minors, and females "are supposed" to behave, but these expectations were meeting with broad, deliberate confrontations that would multiply in the next few years. Again, most people over thirty-five had implicitly focused their relationships to their families, to their livelihood, and to the society in general on their orientation to "the job"; but large numbers of younger people, most of them untouched by economic anxieties such as had tormented their parents in the 'thirties and earlier, would indict the work ethic as responsible for the mean competitiveness that eventuates in brutality and war and for the egregious wastes of a production-mad culture that point to potential ecological disaster.)

Although American universities did not "originate" any of these developments, they did for the most part lead the way in calling attention to them. For example, although the youth rebellion traces back at least to the 1940's (when it was often identified with "juvenile delinquency"), it did not become a part of the national scene or attain political significance until college students adopted it at the end of the 'fifties. More to the point, by 1965 the antiwar movement had taken hold most dramatically on the college campuses, which significantly served as both legitimate sanctuaries from the draft and staging areas for the youth culture. With the universities as focal points, the antiwar posture became easily identified with all the challenges that conventional society had been forced to contend with over the previous painful decade and more. As of 1970, United States intervention in Indochina appeared to be sustained less by the principled "commitments" frequently avowed by its advocates than by an *anti-antiwar* animus fed by acute anxieties over the social upheavals of the 1960's.

Of all the upheavals, that of the young is probably the most important because it is the most fundamental and transcendant. It sustains the contemporary racial rebellion and sexual radicalism, and has motivated the rejection of conventional law, politics, wisdom, and life styles. It is the subject of the analysis that is reprinted below.

"Change, Affluence, and Violence" by Kenneth Keniston, Professor of Psychology at the Yale University Medical School and author of *The Uncommitted* (1965), is taken from his book, *Young Radicals: Notes on Committed Youth** (1968). The book mostly reports his observations based on interviews at the Cambridge, Massachusetts, National Headquarters of Vietnam Summer — the name given to a massive antiwar project of the summer of 1967 during which several thousand individuals, mostly students, engaged in "field work" to develop antiwar "constituencies" in middle-class and wage-earner communities. However, Chapter 7, reprinted below, reflects a broader scene with keen historical perspective.

Keniston uses no footnotes, but he acknowledges his debt especially to the works of Erik Erikson, Robert Jay Lifton, Frederick Wyatt, and Christopher Jencks. See especially Erikson, *Youth: Change and Challenge* (1963), and *Insight and Responsibility* (1964); Jencks, "Limits of the New Left," *The New Republic* (Oct. 21, 1967); and Wyatt, "The Reconstruction of the Individual and of the Collective Past," in R. W. White, ed., *The Study of Lives* (1963), and "In Quest of Change," *Comparative Studies in Society and History,* 7 (1965), 384–92. See also Robert Coles, *Children of Crisis* (1967). S. M. Lipset, "Student Opposition in the United States," *Government and Opposition,* 1 (1966), compares student dissent in the 1930's and 1960's. H. D. Graham and T. R. Gurr, eds., *The History of Violence in America: A Report to the National Commission on the Causes and Prevention of Violence** (1969); L. Veysey, ed., *Law and Resistance: American Attitudes toward Authority** (1960); R. S. Cavan, ed., *Readings in Juvenile Delinquency** (1969); and T. Rose, ed., *Violence in America: A Historical and Contemporary Reader** (1969), are all extremely valuable collections of scholarly articles and some documents.

Change, Affluence, and Violence

Kenneth Keniston

The young radicals I interviewed were born near the end of the Second World War, and their earliest memories date from the years just after it. Their parents were born around the time of the First World War; their grandparents are, without exception, the children of the nineteenth century. Their parents are thus members of the first modern generation to emerge from the Victorian era. And these young radicals are the first products of the post-war world, the first post-modern generation. In tracing the story of their lives, I have discussed the personal meaning of three central themes: change, affluence, and violence; in each, the psychological, the social, the political, and the historical are fused. And each of these issues was so much a part of the young radicals' lives that it is only by stepping aside to consider the historical ground on which they grew that we can perceive the impact on these lives of the history of the post-war era.

In the last chapter, I argued that the issue of change is pervasive in the development of these young men and women. Despite their underlying ties to their personal and familial pasts, their development has involved major alterations, reversals, and reassimilations of that past. As young adults, they remain acutely aware of how far they have come, of the differences between their generation and their parents'. More than that, they have in their own lives witnessed and experienced social and historical changes on an unprecedented scale, lived through the Cold War, the McCarthy era, the Eisenhower period, the short administration of Kennedy and the long one of Johnson. By becoming involved with the New Left, they have linked themselves to a moving, changing movement of dissenting youth. And as individuals, even in their early adulthood, they remain open to the future, eager to change, "in motion."

Similarly, the fact of affluence is crucial to their lives. Not one of these young men and women comes from a background of deprivation, poverty, discrimination, or want. From their earliest years they have simply taken for granted that there would be enough — not only enough to survive, but enough for a vacation every year, a television set, a family car, and a good education. They grew up in a world where they and virtually everyone they knew took prosperity and the luxuries it provides most Americans totally

Reprinted by permission of Harcourt Brace Jovanovich, Inc., from *Young Radicals*, ch. 7, by Kenneth Keniston. Copyright © 1968 by Kenneth Keniston.

for granted. Until they reached adolescence and social consciousness, few of them were immediately aware of the facts of poverty, discrimination, and hunger. Their affluence provided them not only with economic security, but with the preconditions for the independence they exhibit in later life: families generally free from acute anxiety over status, thoughtful and well-educated parents, schools and colleges that — whatever their limitations — exposed them to many of the riches of world tradition, and the extraordinary privilege of a lengthy adolescence and youth in which to grow, to become more complex, to arrive at a more separate selfhood.

The issue of violence, and of the fear and anger it inspired, starts with the earliest memories of many of these young radicals. Recall the young man whose first memory involves his backyard parade at the end of World War II, and whose second memory is of his hysterical terror at the encyclopedia pictures of an atomic-bomb explosion and an army tank. Remember the angry and menacing mob in one early memory, the jealous rage at a younger brother in another, the "gruesome" fights in the playground in still another. Such early memories, of course, mean many things. They point to themes of lifelong importance; they can serve as a "screen" for other less conscious issues — as symbolic alternatives to what is not remembered — and they indicate something about the fears of the dreamer both when he was small and as an adult. Taken with the rest of what we now know about these young radicals, these memories indicate a special sensitivity to the issue of violence — inner and outer — that continues as a central theme in their lives.

These young radicals, then, are members of the first post-modern generation, and their lives are permeated with the history of the past two decades. They, and I as their interviewer, took such changes completely for granted, and rarely felt compelled to note their occurrence and significance. Indeed, in the last third of the twentieth century, we all take for granted the revolutionarily changing world in which we have lived from birth. Yet to understand better what these radicals have done and are attempting to do, to comprehend the style they are creating, requires that we also examine the historical ground of their development.

Change and the Credibility Gap

The twentieth century, as a whole, has been a period of unprecedentedly rapid social, industrial, ideological, and political change. But during the post-war era, the pace of change has increased still further, transforming the world in a way that no one, twenty-five years ago, could have anticipated. These post-war years have brought to the more advanced nations of the world a kind of affluence rarely even dreamed of before. They have seen the often violent liberation of the majority of the world's population from colonial rule. They have been a time of extraordinary scientific and techno-logical innovation that has profoundly transformed our physical, human, social, and cultural environment. And no one can foresee the end of change.

In the last two decades, it has become increasingly obvious that extremely rapid social change is endemic to the modern world. It is unnecessary to chronicle in detail the specific changes that have occurred. Suffice it to note that the material and technological changes that are easiest to pinpoint and discuss constitute but a small part of the over-all process of social change. Even more important have been the less tangible, more gradual, often unnoticed yet radical transformations in social institutions, in the ways men relate to each other and their society, in interpretations of the world and of history, and in the definitions of the goals of life itself. Increasingly, we take such changes for granted, welcoming them, accommodating ourselves to them as best we can, growing used to a world where nothing is permanent. Partly for this reason, we have barely begun to understand the human effects of rapid, continual social change. Especially for the post-war generation, who have always known a world of flux and transformation, change is so much a part of life that they seldom reflect on its meaning. It is like the grammar of our language, or the quality of the air, or the face of a family member: we seldom stand back to notice.

Yet the forces that affect us most profoundly are often those we never stop to notice. In *The Uncommitted* I have discussed at greater length some of the human effect of chronic social change. All of these effects are evident in the lives of the young radicals who led Vietnam Summer. Even in these young men and women, for example, we see a gap between the generations, such that each generation must reconsider and re-examine the values of its heritage for itself. The parents of these particular young radicals have been able to establish a continuity in what I have called core values between themselves and their children. In this respect, there is probably *less* of a generational gap in the families of these young radicals than in the families of most of their contemporaries. But this continuity is at the level of basic personal values like honesty and responsibility, rather than at the level of specific political programs and social creeds. Even the children of old radicals simply take it for granted that their political values and goals will be different from those of their parents. As far as formal values are concerned, then, the prime symptom of the generation gap is apparent: both generations take more or less for granted that the public philosophies of parents are largely irrelevant to their children. In a time of rapid value change, it may be that the only possible value continuities between the generations must involve core values so broad, general, and basic that they can remain relevant despite a radically transformed human and social world.

Another corollary of rapid social change is a focus on the present as contrasted with the past and future. As the pace in social change accelerates, the relevance of the past (and of those like parents who are a part of it) decreases; similarly, the predictability and stability of the future as an object of planning lessens. No traditional verity can be accepted without testing its continuing validity: the skills, styles, rules, and truths of the past become quickly old-fashioned. Since the rate of social change is continually accelerating, and since, in the past, most efforts to predict the future have been dismal failures, the possibility of making concrete plans for the future decreases steadily. Whatever its many other meanings, the focus on the short range and the tactical in the New Left reflects the consciousness of many of today's youths that long-range planning is virtually impossible, given the many imponderables that make the best laid plans go astray. And the absence of utopian visions of the future among young radicals may not reflect a failure of imagination as much as an awareness that the future is simply impossible to anticipate.

Another consequence of a rapidly changing world is the emphasis placed on such psychological qualities as flexibility, openness, adaptability, and personal change. Men always identify themselves with what they take to be the nature of the historical process in which they are immersed: in a time of rapid social and historical change, psychological changeability is therefore stressed. But flexibility is also a way of coping with the demands of the modern historical process. In a stable society, changing individuals must at each stage of their psychological development accommodate themselves to the same static society. But in a rapidly changing society, individuals must adapt themselves at each stage of their personal development to a constantly different physical, human, and social environment. Fixed positions — be they fixed character traits, rigid defenses, absolutely held dogmas, or tenaciously acquired skills — are a commitment to obsolescence. To "keep up with the times," men and women must be ready to change — often radically — throughout their lives. This readiness is, of course, a salient quality in young radicals.

Even the ambivalences of these young radicals toward their parents of the same sex, and the extreme selectivity of their identifications with these parents, are connected to the fact of social change. In an era when the life-situations of children differ so drastically from the environments of their parents as children, simple and "total" identification between generations is rarely possible. Children recognize intuitively that their parents are the products of a different social and historical matrix, and become more selective about following in their footsteps. Parents, in turn, also tend to acknowledge these generational differences, and no longer dare demand the same filial loyalty, obedience, or imitation. Children must learn to winnow the historical chaff from the grain in identifying with their parents, just as these young radicals chose a few core values as their inheritance, rejecting the rest. The particular content of parental identifications among young radicals has many special features, but the need to be selective in identifying is inherent in an era of rapid change.

The major transformations of the past decades also contribute to a widespread sensitivity of today's youth to the *discrepancy between principle and practice*, and may help explain why the charges of insincerity, manipulation, and dishonesty are today so often leveled by the young against the old. During a time when values change with each generation, the values most deeply embedded in parents and expressed in their behavior in times of crisis are often very different from the more "modern" principles, ideals, and values that parents profess and attempt to practice in bringing up their children. Filial perception of this discrepancy between parental practice and principle may help explain the very widespread sensitivity amongst contemporary youth to the "hypocrisy" of the previous generation. Among the young radicals interviewed, the schism in the parental image seems related not only to the idiosyncratic behavior of specific parents, but to this broader problem of transmission of values in a time of rapid change.

The grandparents of today's twenty-year-olds were generally brought up during the pre–World War I years, heirs of a Victorian tradition as yet unaffected by the value revolutions of the twentieth century. They reared their own children, the parents of today's youth, in families that emphasized respect, the control of impulse, obedience to authority, and the traditional "inner-directed" values of hard work, deferred gratification and self-restraint. Their children, born around the time of the First World War, were thus raised in families that remained largely Victorian in outlook.

During their lifetimes, however, these parents (and in particular the most intelligent, well educated, and privileged of them) were exposed to a great variety of new values that often changed their formal convictions. During their youths in the 1920's and 1930's, major changes in American behavior and American values took place. For example, the "emancipation of women" in the 1920's, marked by the achievement of suffrage for women, coincided with the last major change in actual sexual behavior in America: during this period, women started to become the equal partners of men, who no longer sought premarital sexual gratification solely with women of a lower class. More important, the 1920's and 1930's were an era when older Victorian values were challenged, attacked, and all but discredited, especially in educated middle-class families. Young men and women who went to college during this period were influenced by "progressive," "liberal," and even psychoanalytic ideas that contrasted sharply with the values of their childhood families. Moreover, during the 1930's, many of the parents of today's upper-middle-class youth were exposed to, or involved with, the ideals of the New Deal, and sometimes to more radical interpretations of man, society, and history. And in the 1940's and 1950's, when it came time to raise their own children, the parents to today's youth were strongly influenced by "permissive" views of child-rearing that again clashed with the techniques by which they themselves had been raised. Thus, many middle-class parents moved during their lifetimes from the Victorian ethos in which they had been brought up to the less moralistic, more humanitarian, and more "expressive" values of their own adulthoods.

But major changes in values, when they occur in adult life, are likely to be less than complete. To have grown up in a family where unquestioning obedience to parents was expected, but to rear one's own children in an atmosphere of "democratic" permissiveness and self-actualization — and never to revert to the practices of one's own childhood — requires a change of values more comprehensive than most adults can achieve. Furthermore, behavior that springs from values acquired in adulthood often appears somewhat forced, artificial, or insincere to the sensitive observer. Children, always the most perceptive observers of their own parents, are likely to sense a discrepancy between their parents' avowed and consciously held values and their "basic instincts," especially with regard to child-rearing. In addition, the parental tendency to "revert to form" is greatest in times of family crisis, which, of course, have the weightiest effect upon children. No matter how "genuinely" parents hold their "new" values, many of them, when the chips are down, fall back on the lessons of their own childhoods.

In a time of rapid social change, then, a *credibility gap* is likely to open between the generations. Children are likely to perceive a discrepancy between what the parents avow as their values and the actual assumptions from which parental behavior springs in times of crisis. In the young radicals interviewed, the focal issue of adolescent rebellion against parents seems to have been just this discrepancy: the children argued that their parents' endorsement of independence and self-determination for their children was "hypocritical" because it did not correspond with the parents' actual behavior when their children seized the independence offered them. Similar perceptions of "hypocrisy" occurred for others around racial matters: there were a few parents who supported racial and religious equality in principle, but became upset when their children dated someone of another race or religion. Around political activity similar issues arose, especially during the 1950's. For example, many of the parents of today's youth espoused in principle the cause of political freedom; but most were not involved in politics themselves and some opposed their children's involvement lest they "jeopardize their records."

Of course, in no society do parents (or anyone else) ever fully live up to their own professed ideals. In every society, there is a gap between creedal values and actual practices; and everywhere the recognition of this gap constitutes a powerful motor for social change. But in most societies, especially when social change is slow and social institutions are powerful and unchanged, there occurs what can be called the *institutionalization of hypocrisy*. Children and adolescents routinely learn when it is "reasonable" to expect that the values parents profess will be implemented in their behavior, and when it is not reasonable. There develops an elaborate system of exegesis and commentary upon the society's creedal values, excluding certain people or situations from the full weight of these values or "demonstrating" that apparent inconsistencies are not really inconsistencies at all.

Thus, in almost all societies, a "sincere" man who "honestly" believes one set of values is frequently allowed to ignore them completely, for example, in the practice of his business, in his interpersonal relationships, in dealings with foreigners, in relationships of his children, and so on — all because these situations have been defined by social consensus as exempt from the application of his creedal values.

In a time of rapid social change and value change, however, the institutionalization of hypocrisy tends to break down. "New" values have been in existence for so brief a period that the exemptions to them have not yet been defined, the situations to be excluded have not yet been determined. The universal gap between principle and practice appears without disguise. Thus, the mere fact of a discrepancy between creedal values and practice is not at all unusual. But what is special about the present situation of rapid value change is, first, that parents themselves tend to have two conflicting sets of values, one related to the experience of their early childhood, the other to the ideologies and principles acquired in adulthood; and, second, that no stable institutions or rules for defining hypocrisy out of existence have yet been fully evolved. In such a situation, the young see the Emperor in all his nakedness, recognizing the value conflict within their parents and perceiving clearly the "hypocritical" gap between ideal and behavior.

This argument suggests that the post-modern youth may not be confronted with a gap between parental preaching and practice that is "objectively" any greater than that facing most generations. But they do confront an unusual internal ambivalence within the parental generation over the very values that parents successfully inculcated in their children, and they are "deprived" of a system of social interpretation that rationalizes the discrepancy between creed and deed. It seems likely, then, that today's youth may simply be able to perceive the universal gulf between principle and practice more clearly than previous generations have done.

This points to one of the central characteristics of today's youth in general and young radicals in particular: they insist on taking seriously a great variety of political, personal, and social principles that "no one in his right mind" ever before thought of attempting to extend to such situations as dealings with strangers, relations between the races, or international politics. For example, peaceable openness has long been a creedal virtue in our society, but it has rarely been extended to foreigners, particularly those with dark skins. Similarly, equality has long been preached, but the "American dilemma" has been resolved by a series of institutionalized hypocrisies that exempted Negroes from the application of this principle. Love has always been a formal value in Christian societies, but really to love one's enemies — to be generous to policemen, customers, criminals, servants, or foreigners — has been considered folly.

The fact of social change, then, is not only distantly perceived by those who are growing up, but immediately interwoven with the texture of their daily lives as they develop. Many of the seemingly "special" characteristics of this small group of young radicals are connected not only to the vicissitudes of their individual histories, but to the history of their generation and of the modern world. The tenacity with which these young men and women adhere to a small number of the core values from their early family lives, their short-range plans, their absence of political program and visions of the future, and their enormous emphasis on openness, change, and process is both a reflection of, and a response to, a world changing at a dizzy rate in a direction that no one can foresee.

And these speculations on the credibility gap and the "deinstitutionalization of hypocrisy" in a time of rapid change may help explain two further facts about young radicals: first, they frequently come from highly principled families with whose core principles they continue to agree, but they often see their parents as somehow ineffectual in the practice of these principles; second, they have the outrageous temerity to insist that individuals and societies live by the values they preach. And these speculations may also explain the frequent feeling of many who have worked intensively with today's dissenting youth that, apart from the "impracticality" of some of their views, these sometimes seem to be the only clear-eyed and sane people in a society and a world where most of us are systematically blind to the traditional gap between personal principle and practice, national creed and policy.

The Advent of Automatic Affluence

To any American who has grown up since the Second World War, one of the most important facts of life has been the continually increasing affluence around him. For all middle- and upper-class young Americans, as for increasing numbers of working-class youth, the fact of affluence is simply taken for granted — prosperity has become automatic. For example, although one or two of the young radicals who led Vietnam Summer came from lower-middle-class families and considered themselves "poor" during childhood, questions of income, security, social status, upward mobility, and finding a job were largely irrelevant when the time came for them to consider adult commitments. And when they realized during their adolescences that the affluence they so took for granted did not extend to all Americans — much less to the impoverished two-thirds of the world — they reacted with surprise, shock, and dismay. Material prosperity alone has made a difference in the development of this generation. The "luxuries" of an affluent age — electronic communications, rapid transport, good housing, physical comfort, readily available music, art, and literature, good health care and longevity — have helped give this generation its distinctive style. Without material affluence, the restlessness, mobility, and "wastefulness" of today's youth could hardly be understood.

But the impact of affluence extends considerably beyond its material benefits. "Affluence" can stand as shorthand for a variety of other changes in American institutions, the economy, family life, education, and the definition of the stages of life, all of which have affected the outlook of this generation. Material affluence is made possible by a system of production, innovation, and organization that defines the options open to today's young men and women, just as it has been the framework for their development to date. Affluence, in a broad sense, has both opened new doors and closed old ones.

Social criticism in the past decades has emphasized the destructive aspects of technology, bureaucracy, specialization, centralization, and bigness. Yet we have also begun to realize that these ambivalently viewed features of our society may be necessary conditions for the advantages of affluence. Our prosperity is built upon high technology, as upon complex and bureaucratic social organization. And both technology and differentiated social roles involve specialization and technical competence far beyond the basic requisites of literacy and fluency with numbers. Furthermore, in any highly specialized society, complex systems of co-ordination, social control, and communication must be developed to harmonize the work of specialized role-holders. Even sheer size sometimes increases affluence: centralization not only can permit industrial efficiencies, but sometimes facilitates administrative co-ordination. The advent of electronic communications and rapid transportation had made it increasingly possible for a small number of men to co-ordinate and control the activities of vast numbers of their fellows. For better and for worse, then, our affluent society is technological, specialized, bureaucratized, and complexly controlled. In such a society, most educated adults not only do highly specialized work, but are involved in complex networks of social co-ordination that they must accept if the System is to function smoothly.

All of these characteristics of modern society contribute to the malaise and reluctance of many of today's youth when they confront the System. Yet these same young men and women, like all of us, consider the many benefits of affluence as "givens" of modern life. They take for granted that just as the machine and factory production made possible the industrial revolution by multiplying each man's physical efforts a dozenfold, so now, in the technological era, the computer is increasingly freeing men from routine and repetitive mental work. Men and women need no longer work in the fields or factories from dawn to dusk to produce the requisites for survival. For affluent Americans (who are the majority), survival, subsistence, and starvation are no longer at issue. A small part of the population can produce the essentials of life, while the rest produce goods and services that, to previous generations, would have appeared unprecedented luxuries.

These "luxuries" include not only the material commodities that fill American life, but less tangible opportunities for education, the cultivation of the mind, and the fulfillment of psychological needs beyond the need for subsistence, security, and status. By vastly extending the power and reach of each individual, the affluent society both permits and requires men to be "unproductive" for many years of their lives. The labor of children, adolescents, and, increasingly, post-adolescents is no longer needed by the economy. On the contrary, keeping young men and women off the labor market is a net social gain because it allows fuller employment of their elders. In addition, an affluent society increasingly requires the young to stay off the labor market in order to learn the high technological skills required to maintain affluence. The result, of course, is the historically unprecedented situation of prolonged higher education, extending well into the twenties, for a larger and larger proportion of the American population.

The postponement of entry into the labor force has contributed to a redefinition of the life cycle, underlining the connection between social opportunity and developmental stage. Giving large numbers of young men and women the opportunity to have an adolescence is an achievement of industrial societies. In many preindustrial societies, even childhood was forcibly aborted by the requirement that children begin to work before puberty. When this happens, the full psychological experience of childhood as we define it in modern society is inevitably cut short: childen are small adults — by our modern standards, old before their time. But even in those societies where psychological childhood continues until biological puberty, adolescence as a psychological experience is rarely permitted.

To be sure, the physiological changes that announce the possibility of an adolescent experience occur in every society, regardless of what the society chooses to make of these changes. But in most previous societies, only the extraordinarily wealthy, talented, or fortunate were allowed anything like an adolescence. Even the wellborn Romeo and Juliet were thirteen years old; in the Middle Ages, kings assumed their thrones in their teens; and most children of the common people began working in the fields (in later times, in factories) well before they reached puberty. Allowing the possibility of adolescent development is only one possible reaction to the approach of biological adulthood: historically it is a relatively rare reaction. Even today, in primitive societies, puberty rites more often serve to hasten the child toward adulthood than to permit him anything like the possibility of adolescent turmoil, emotional growth, and independence. Although from the beginnings of history, the old have deplored the irreverence of the young, adolescence as a distinctive stage of life that *should* be made available to all young men and women has only begun to be recognized during the past two centuries in advanced societies.

By creating a vast surplus of wealth, modern societies have freed first children and then teen-agers from the requirements of farm and factory labor. Even before the industrial revolution, of course, a small number of young men and women were allowed a deferment of full involvement in adult work. And a few of them — a few from among the pages and princes, novices and apprentices — were sometimes able to create for themselves what we now recognize as an adolescence. But most, lacking opportunity and social sanction, moved directly from childhood to adulthood. The industrial revolution, however, created a new bourgeoisie with a commitment to education as a pathway to success for their children. This new middle class also had the means to allow children freedom from labor after puberty. There began to develop — for the middle classes at least — a vague concept, at first, of a post-childhood, preadult stage of life, a stage of continuing education that was initially modeled after the apprenticeship. Little by little, however, it became clear that this stage of life had qualities of its own. The adolescent gradually emerged as something more than a cross between a child and an adult.

First for the upper middle class, then for the lower middle class, and then, increasingly, for the working-class youth, adolescence became routinely available. And although the precise definition of the expected qualities of the adolescent is sensitive to the particular values of each society, in most affluent societies today, adolescence is recognized as *sui generis,* as important for the fullest possible unfolding of human potentials, and as a right to be guaranteed through compulsory education and anti-child-labor laws.

We should not forget how recently all of this has taken place, nor how incomplete it still is. Some of Marx's most vehement strictures in the middle of the nineteenth century were directed against the use of children in factories. And in America, the child-labor laws were passed only in the twentieth century. For many young Americans, and for an even greater proportion of the young in other nations, the psychological experience of adolescence is still aborted by the failure of education or the assumption of major economic responsibilities in the mid-teens — years that by our modern reckoning are only the beginning of adolescence. For large numbers of the poor, the deprived, the undermotivated, the psychologically or intellectually handicapped, adolescence still does not take place.

Even if it has not yet been extended to all, making the experience of adolescence available to most young men and women in modern society must be counted among the achievements of affluence. The possibility of adolescence as a psychological experience is dependent on economic conditions that free adolescents from the need to work, as upon the development of new values that make child or adolescent labor seem "outrageous" to right-thinking men and women. Only when a society produces enough to liberate young men and women between the ages of twelve and eighteen from labor can it demand that they continue their educations and allow them to continue their psychological development; only then can abhorrence of the "exploitation" of adolescents develop.

Affluence has also permitted changes in the quality of family life, especially among better-educated Americans. During the twentieth century, growing numbers of men and women, responding to the opportunities and demands of industrial society, have at least begun college, with many completing it and continuing on for their Ph.D. Higher education changes the outlooks and styles of at least some of those who pass through it. Its impact is difficult to describe precisely, but at best it allows greater freedom to express underlying feelings and impulses, greater independence of outlook and thought, and increased sympathy for the underdog. Also, since the best educated are generally those who attain greatest affluence in their own lives, higher education indirectly gives its graduates an adult life that is more secure, freer from the struggle for subsistence and status, and more open to the pursuit of non-material, self-expressive goals. Educated parents who have attained professional and economic security are in turn able to develop a distinctive family style that has important effects upon children.

Although they themselves may have had to struggle out of poverty, today's well-educated and affluent parents have generally "arrived" by the time they raise their own children. Compared to their own parents, they are more likely to instill in their children the special values of self-actualization — independence, sensitivity to feelings, concern for others, free expression of emotion, openness, and spontaneity. And since such parents tend to have relatively few children, they are able to lavish on each child an enormous amount of individual attention. Upper-middle-class educated women need not work to support the family: most devote themselves entirely to bringing up their small children. Even those who do work are likely to feel restored by their work rather than depleted. All of this means that affluent mothers are increasingly free to devote themselves to their small brood of children. Such devotion can have the bad consequences we see in the familiar stereotype of "Momism." But its good consequences are equally important: in many affluent families, children grow up unusually well cared for emotionally and psychologically, the objects of thoughtful attention and informed devotion. Increasingly, affluent middle-class parents *educate* their children, rather than merely training them. And in some affluent families, one finds a parental devotion to the autonomy, self-determination, and dignity of children that is without precedent, even in American history.

Obviously, not all affluent middle-class families fit this rosy description: such families are clearly in a minority. A full account of the impact of affluence and education of the American family would have to discuss other parental responses, among them family styles that lead to filial apathy, alienation, neurosis, or conformity. But affluence means that families like those I am describing — devoted, principled, expressive, thoughtful, humanitarian, and permissive — are increasing in number. Whatever the other satisfactions they derive from their children, parents in these families genuinely desire them to be independent, thoughtful, honorable, and resourceful men and women. To be sure, in these as all families, parents are full of foibles, contradictions, inconsistencies, and faults. And as I suggested, in a time of rapid value change, the values that parents attempt to apply in bringing up their children may contrast with the more "instinctive" values that have their roots in the parents' own upbringing.

Yet for all their characteristic faults, the families of the educated and affluent have freed a growing number of today's youth to concern themselves with the welfare of others and the wider society. Their security makes possible an identification with others who are insecure; their affluence permits them to worry about those who are poor; their freedom allows them to care about those who are enslaved. Families like the families of the radicals who led Vietnam Summer are impressively *good*. They have given their children great strength, integrity, and warmth. The devotion to family core values that we see in many young radicals derives from parents who have principles and care lovingly for their children. Even the ability of young radicals to be different from their parents may stem partly from their parents' genuine willingness to let them be different. These are children, then, who have been taught from an early age to value independence, to think for themselves, to seek rational solutions, and to believe that principles should be practiced. As Richard Flacks, one of the most astute observers of the contemporary New Left, has put it, these young men and women are members of a "liberated generation."

This argument suggests that in an affluent society, the psychological and social underpinnings of radicalism have begun to change. In non-affluent societies, radicals and revolutionaries — who almost invariably come from relatively privileged backgrounds — tend to react with guilt to the "discovery" of poverty, tyranny, and misery. Furthermore, many radical and revolutionary groups have in the past sought social and political changes that would improve their own position, giving them freedom, power, or benefits they did not possess. In a society like our own — where affluence, economic opportunity, and considerable political freedom are the rule — radicalism is less likely to be built upon personal feelings of deprivation or a desire to improve one's own position. Nor is the guilt of the wealthy when confronted with the poor as likely a motivation for the radical's commitments. While radical leaders of all eras have typically been men of high principle, the role of principle increases further in an affluent era. The radical's basic goal is not to achieve new freedoms, opportunities, or benefits for himself, but rather to extend to all the freedoms, opportunities, and benefits he himself has always experienced. In an affluent world, the radical feels indignation rather than guilt; outrage rather than oppression.

VIOLENCE: SADISM AND CATACLYSM

The focal issue in Vietnam Summer was ending American involvement in violence in Southeast Asia. And the issue of violence is central not only for young radicals, but for the modern world. Hanging over the lives of all men and women during the past decade has been the Bomb, and the terrifying possibilities of *technological death* it summarizes and symbolizes. These include not only holocaustal destruction by thermonuclear blast and radiation, but the equally gruesome possibilities of the deliberate spread of virulent man-perfected disease or the use of lethal chemicals to destroy the functioning of the human body.

Premature death has, of course, always been a fearful possibility in human life. But technological death is new in a variety of ways. It is now realistic to imagine not only one's own unannounced death and perhaps the death of one's intimates through natural catastrophe, but to envision the "deliberate" destruction of all civilization, all human life, or, indeed, all living things on earth. Furthermore, technological death has a peculiar quality of impersonality, automaticity, and absurdity to it. Until the relatively recent past, most man-inflicted deaths have at least been personal acts: the jealous husband murders his wife's lover, the soldier shoots the enemy on the battlefield, the cannibal kills the member of a neighboring tribe, the sadist butchers his victim. Technological death, in contrast, requires no contact between man and man. One well-intentioned bureaucrat (who means no harm, is only following orders and is doing his duty for his country) can press a button and set in motion a chain of events that could mean the burning, maiming, and death of most of those now alive. Paradoxically, malice, anger, and hostility are no longer necessary to create a cataclysm beyond the imaginings of the darkest sadist. It only takes an understandable inability to visualize the human meanings of a "megadeath."

The technology of death has hung like a sword over the lives of this post-modern generation. Recall, once again, how in the early memories of these young radicals, the violence of the outside world found echo and counterpart in the violence of inner feelings: on the one hand, the atomic bomb, the menacing mob, the gruesome playground fights; on the other hand, rage, fear, and anger. The word "violence" itself suggests both of these possibilities: the *psychological* violence of sadism, exploitation, and aggression, and the *historical* violence of war, cataclysm, and holocaust. In the lives of these young radicals, as in much of their generation, the threats of inner and outer violence are fused, each exciting the other. To summarize a complex thesis in a few words: *the issue of violence is to this generation what the issue of sex was to the Victorian world.*

The context of development for the post-war generation must again be recalled. These young men and women were born near the end of the most savage, wanton, and destructive war in the history of the world. Perhaps 100,000,000 men, women, and children, most of them "non-combatants," were killed, maimed, or wounded. All of Europe and large parts of Asia and North Africa were laid waste. The lessons of that war for this generation are summarized in the names of three cities: Auschwitz, Hiroshima, Nuremberg. At Auschwitz and the other Nazi concentration camps, more than six million Jews were systematically exterminated. Although their executioners were sometimes brutal sadists, acts of personal cruelty were the least momentous part of the extermination of European Jewry. Even more impressive are the numbers of "decent," well-educated Germans (who loved their wives, children, and dogs) who learned to take part in, or blind themselves to, this genocide. Murder became depersonalized and dissociated, performed by a System of cold, efficient precision whose members were only following orders in doing a distasteful job well. Bureaucracy, technology, and science were linked in the service of death. Evil became "banal," in Hannah Arendt's words; it was impersonal, dissociated from its human perpetrators, and institutionalized in an efficient and "scientific" organization. It became clear that science and civilization, far from deterring technological death, were its preconditions.

The Second World War ended not with the discovery of the Nazi concentration camps, but with the American use of atomic bombs on the cities of Hiroshima and Nagasaki. This act, which in retrospect hardly seems to have been necessary, helped define the nightmare of the past two decades. Just as the experience of the concentration camp showed that the apparently civilized and "advanced" nations of the world could perform barbarities more cruel than any heretofore imagined, so the atomic bomb and its even more frightening thermonuclear successors provided the concrete imagery for the collective terror of the world. Germany had shown that civilized nations could do the unthinkable; Hiroshima demonstrated how simple, clean, and easy (from the point of view of the perpetrator) doing the unthinkable could be.

In Nuremberg after the war, the German leaders were tried and convicted for their crimes. Here the principle was enunciated and affirmed that there is a law above national interest, an ethic above national purpose, and an accountability above obedience to national leaders. Policies that have the full support of national law may be, nonetheless, criminal and illegal. Confronted with such policies, it is the duty of an ethical man to resist. The principle of collective responsibility was also proposed, and many maintained that the German people, by silence, acquiescence, or deliberate ignorance, had assented to and facilitated the crimes of Nazism.

Auschwitz, Hiroshima, and Nuremberg are the birth pangs of the post-war generation, and their lessons — the bureaucratization of genocide, the clean ease of the unthinkable, and the ethic above nationality — have marked post-modern youth. But despite the nightmare of retaliation that has so far deterred men from the use of their most destructive weapons, the post-war years have not been calm or peaceful. On the contrary, these have been decades of constant international unrest, of continual wars of containment, civil violence, and revolutionary liberation. Since the war, the oppressed two-thirds of the world have largely achieved independence, often through strife, violence, and cruelty. Millions were killed in the civil war that followed the partition of India; more millions in the victory of the Communist revolution in China; and the struggles for independence in nations like Algeria, Kenya, and Vietnam were cruel and violent. American involvement first in Korea and then in Vietnam, the American "military presence" in dozens of nations across the world, our national policies of "massive retaliation" premised upon city-annihilating thermonuclear weapons, the continually unsuccessful attempt to prevent, limit or control the manufacture of atomic, biological, and chemical weapons — these have been the context for this generation's growth. The marvels of electronic communication have brought these violent realities of the post-war world into the living rooms of almost every young American, concretizing and making emotionally immediate — at least to those who are capable of identification — the absurd violence of the modern world, and the even more frightening possibilities of world-wide cataclysm.

In the lives of young radicals and of their generation, the threat of outer violence has been not only a backdrop, but a constant fact of life. It is reflected not only in childhood terrors of the Bomb, but in the routine experience of air-raid drills in school, in constant exposure to discussions of fallout shelters, preventive warfare, ballistic missiles, and anti-missile defenses, and sometimes in a compulsive fascination with the technology of destruction. The Bomb and what it symbolizes has set the tone for this generation, even for the majority who make a semideliberate point of trying not to think about it. There are relatively few young Americans who, upon hearing a distant explosion, seeing a bright flash of light, or hearing a faraway sound of jets overhead at night, have not wondered for a brief instant whether this might not be "It." And there are a surprising number who have thought, often with horror and dismay, that they wished "It" were over so they would no longer live in fear. Most thoughtful members of the post-war generation have had elaborate fantasies — usually wishful fantasies of survival and rebirth — about what would become of them if "It" happened. All of this points to a great investment of energy, attention, and thought around the issue of violence, although most find the issue too painful to discuss or even to think about.

Continual confrontation with the fact and possibility of violence in the world has activated and become joined with the universal human potential for aggression, anger, and rage: the psychological and historical possibilities of violence have come to strengthen each other. Witnessing the acting out of violence on a scale more gigantic than ever before, or imaginatively participating in holocaust — both activate the fear of inner violence; while heightened awareness of the inner potential for rage, anger, and destructiveness in turn increases sensitivity to violence in the world. It therefore does not require an assumption of increased biological aggression to account for the importance of violence to post-war youth. Starting with the Second World War, we have witnessed violence and imagined violence on a scale more frightening than ever before. Like the angry children in a violent home who fear that their rage will destroy the warring adults around them, we have become vastly more fearful of our inner angers. In fact, we live in a world where even the mildest irritation, multiplied a billionfold by modern technology, might destroy all civilization.

The fear of violence has led to a fascination with it that further surrounds us with its symptoms. Our society is preoccupied with the violence of organized crime, the violence of urban rioting, the violence of an assassinated President and the televised murder of his alleged murderer, the violence of madmen, the oppressed and the rage-filled. And to have been an American child in the past two decades is, as many have noted, to have watched the violence of television, both as it reports the bloodshed of the American and non-American world, and as it skillfully elaborates in repetitive dramas the potential for brutality and aggression in each of us. We have been repeatedly reminded in the past decade that our society, despite its claims to peaceableness and justice, is in fact one of the most violent societies in the history of the world.

In the Victorian era, what was most deeply repressed, rejected, feared, controlled, projected onto others, or compulsively acted out was related to the issue of sex. The personal and social symptomatology of that era — the hysterical ladies who consulted Freud, the repressive moralism of middle-class life, and the sordid underlife of the "other Victorians" — can only be understood in the context of the preoccupation of the Victorian era with human sexuality. The post-war generation, in contrast, is freer, more open, less guilt- and anxiety-ridden about sex. Sex obviously remains important, as befits one of the primary human drives. But increasing numbers of post-modern youth, like these young radicals, have been able to overcome even the asceticism and puritanism of their own adolescences and to move toward a sexuality that is less obsessional, less dissociated, less driven, more integrated with other human experiences and relationships. Inner and outer violence is replacing sex as a prime object of fear, terror, projection, displacement, repression, suppression, acting out, and efforts at control.

At the same time, the symptomatology of violence and repressed violence is becoming more visible. In the complex and highly organized modern world, open displays of rage, anger, and fury are increasingly tabooed: they are considered "irrational"; they threaten to disrupt the finely tuned system in which we live out our working lives; we consider them "childish" or "dangerous." Driven underground, our inevitable angers sometimes seek less direct forms of expression: they heighten autonomic activity to the point of psychosomatic illness; they are turned against the self, producing angry depression; and they are expressed interpersonally in subtle undercutting, backbiting, viciousness, and pettiness. The repression of inner violence makes us eager consumers of the packaged violence of television and the trashy novel. Equally important, our suppressed aggression is projected onto others. We grossly exaggerate the violence of the oppressed, of our enemies, and even of those to whom our society has given good grounds for anger. Consider, for example, the white fear of black violence. Until the summers of 1966 and 1967, it was the Negroes and their friends whose churches were bombed, who were shot, beaten, and injured by whites, and rarely, if ever, vice versa. And even in the urban rioting of 1966 and 1967, the number of black men killed by white men far outweighed the toll of whites. Yet it is the fear of *black* violence that preoccupies the white public.

To connect the fear of black violence, or the war in Vietnam, or the assassination of a President, or the violence of television solely to the threat of technological death would be a gross oversimplification. My argument here is simply that we live in an unusually violent society, in an unprecedentedly violent world. In our society — as in others — the fears and facts of violence are self-stimulating. The greater the outer reality of violence, the more the inner fear of it, and for many, the greater the need to create or find external situations in which violence can be experienced vicariously outside themselves. The way men react to constant confrontation with violence in the world of course differs: some tolerate it; others develop symptoms related to their inability to confront directly their own inner anger; others project their inner aggression onto others; still others develop a "neurotic" preoccupation with the possibilities of world holocaust. And, most dangerous of all, some need to act violently in order to discharge their own excited rage. If we are to choose one issue as central to our own time, one danger as most frightening, one possibility as most to be avoided and yet most fascinating, one psychological issue that both rationally and irrationally preoccupies us, it is the issue of violence.

In tracing the development of the young radicals who led Vietnam Summer, I have underlined the related themes that center on the concept of violence. Many of their earliest memories involve conflict, outer anger, and inner fear. They were, throughout their childhoods, especially sensitive to the issue of struggle within their families and communities. Although in behavior most of these young radicals were rather *less* violent than their contemporaries, this was not because they were indifferent to the issue, but because their early experience and family values had taught them how to control, modulate, oppose, and avoid violence. Verbal aggression took the place of physical attack. They learned to argue, to compromise, and to make peace when confronted with conflict. So, too, although their adolescent experience was full of inner conflict, they acted on their often violent feelings only during a brief period of indignant rebellion against the inconsistencies of their parents. These young radicals are unusual in their sensitivity to violence, as in their need and ability to oppose it.

I have mentioned the many tensions — psychological, interpersonal, and organizational — that are related to this issue in their work. The avoidance and control of violence, whether in international warfare, political organizations, small groups, or face-to-face personal relations, is a central goal and a key psychological orientation in the New Left. Many of the problems of the Movement are related to the zealous effort to avoid actions and relations in which inner aggression or outer conflict may be evoked. Recall, for example, the extraordinary efforts made to avoid domination within the Movement, the distrust of "totalitarian intimidation," the suppression of leadership lest it lead to manipulation, the avoidance of "flashiness" that might exploit the organized. Remember, too, the deliberate efforts of many of these young men and women to overcome their own angers, their capacity to stay "cool" when provoked, their initial preference for "non-violent" forms of protest, and their largely successful struggle to overcome in themselves any vestige of sadism, cruelty, domination, or power-seeking in human relationships.

I do not mean to suggest that young radicals in particular, or their generation in general, are rage-filled deniers of their own inner angers. On the contrary, amongst these young radicals, exuberance and zest are the rule rather than the exception. Nor are these young radicals incapable of anger and resentment — although they find these emotions easiest to tolerate when, as in their adolescent rebellions, they can be buttressed by a sense of outraged principle. But young radicals, even more than most young men and women of their generation, learned early in their lives the fruitlessness of conflict; and this lesson, in later years, was among the many forces that went into their decision to work for Vietnam Summer.

The position of the psychologically non-violent revolutionary in opposition to a violent world is paradoxical. On the one hand, he seeks to minimize violence, but, on the other, his efforts often elicit violence from others. He works toward a vague vision of a peaceful world, but he must confront more directly than most of his peers the warfare of the world. The frustrations of his work repetitively reawaken his rage, which must continually be redirected into peaceful paths. Combating destructiveness and exploitation in others, his own destructiveness and desire to exploit are inevitably aroused. Furthermore, he is a citizen of a nation whose international policies seem to him only slightly less barbarous than the policies of the Nazis toward the Jews. He has been recently reminded that, with the support of world opinion, the State of Israel executed Adolf Eichmann because of his complicity in the extermination of the Jews (despite his plea that he was only following orders). Rather than be an accomplice in a comparable enterprise, should the radical not move toward the violent resistance that the world would have preferred from Eichmann? For all his efforts to control violence, cataclysm, and sadism, the young radical continually runs the danger of identifying himself with what he seeks to control, and through a militant struggle against violence, creating more violence than he overcomes. The issue of violence is not resolved for these young men and women. Nor can it be.

29

THE VIETNAM WAR

At least since the Civil War, nothing has rocked the American nation so cataclysmically as its own military intervention in the seemingly incessant warfare within and among the countries of the former "French Indochina." Between 1967 and 1970 alone, the intervention cost the United States about $25 billion per year in direct military expenditures in Vietnam, and about $100 billion in all for the decade of the 'sixties. In addition, up to 1970 we had suffered about 350,000 casualties, of which more than 45,000 were fatalities, making Vietnam the fourth bloodiest war in United States history, following the two World Wars and the Civil War. Still, this is only to touch on the more obvious of the real costs of the intervention. The American political system is still reeling from the strains of the most enduring war in United States history. No society committed to the nonviolent resolution of social conflicts can long survive noncompromising, mutually exclusive claims upon its decision-making agencies. But the war evoked precisely this kind of polarization among the interest groups making claims for social priorities, and as the country entered the decade of the 'seventies social violence increased to frightening dimensions. In addition, the war accelerated the development of an unprecedentedly powerful military establishment within the political and economic structures of the country. By 1970, with more than 9 percent of our gross national product, more than 85 percent of the federal budget, and about 10 percent of the total work force annually devoted to or engaged in defense industries, the commitment had become threatening as well as almost certainly irreversible in any "short run." Finally the brutalizing impact of continuing warfare cost the American spirit at home, and its image abroad, in ways that have not yet been fully reckoned.

Defenders of the intervention usually attribute it to America's ob-ligation to defend the "free world" against "communist aggression." Opponents (such as the "revisionists" discussed by Charles S. Maier in his article on the Cold War, pp. 574–600) typically have had little difficulty attributing United States policy to the inexorable demands of "liberal-capitalist-imperialism." Whereas the defenders usually point to the individual decisions governed by a rational commitment to principle and national security, the revisionists have tended to argue from certain institutional and ideological imperatives. They have usually rejected heatedly any suggestion that interventionism followed from some "mistake," but have insisted that the historical logic of a

The Vietnam War 681

capitalist society impels the kind of "expansionism" that eventuates in a Vietnam situation; if one can infer individual will at all, it operates through crucial decisions made with a conscious, even cynical, eye on the self-interest of America's "ruling classes."

After 1965 and particularly after 1967, increasing numbers of "non-revisionists" joined the opposition to continued intervention in the Indochinese wars. The opposition now included many who initially supported intervention, at least before the major troop commitments, but who came to view the matter in the light of different facts and a different appreciation of the facts. James C. Thomson, Jr., who served on White House and State Department staffs during the 1961–66 period, is one of these (although he evidently entertained doubts about American policy in Indochina at an early date). His article, reprinted below, tends to bear out the revisionists' argument that a thoughtless "anticommunist" (though not particularly "pro-capitalist" or "imperialist") commitment precluded judicious treatment of the facts by the chief policy-makers. Yet the thoughtlessness seems to have arisen from personal, human traits having more to do with the general resistance of the mind to new premises, and with the thought-stifling pressures of large organizations, than with the imperatives of ideology or class.

That the inexorable incursions of bureaucracy upon the decision-making process must be added to the more ancient human frailties can only diminish hopes for a rational foreign policy. Even before the major escalations in Vietnam, John Mecklin, public affairs officer for the United States embassy in Saigon, warned of the State Department's bureaucratic habit of dismissing information that "complicated" its policy deliberations. "The root of the problem," he wrote in his book, *Mission in Torment* (1965), "was the fact that much of what the newsmen took to be lies was exactly what the [U.S.] Mission genuinely believed, and was reporting to Washington. Events were to prove that the Mission itself was unaware of how badly the war was going, operating in a world of illusion. Our feud with the newsmen was an angry symptom of bureaucratic sickness." [Quoted in Bernard Fall, *Viet-Nam Witness 1953–66* (1966), p. 11.] If "liberal-capitalist" interests were served by the Vietnam policies that the "liberal-capitalist rulers" of American foreign policy set in the 1960's, it can only have been by the sheerest coincidence. For it would seem that those policies were founded mostly on tragically inappropriate assumptions and even worse information.

We are still so close to the events that analyses that are in large part memoirs serve as among the most valuable historical works. Townsend Hoopes, *The Limits of Intervention* (1969), is in many ways the most astute. It focuses in detail on the process by which the policy of escalation in Vietnam was reversed early in 1968. The first chapter, which puts the problem in historical perspective, closely complements the account Thomson gives us.

For other "inside accounts" of foreign policy making in the 1960's, see George Ball, *The Discipline of Power* (1968), and Roger Hilsman, *To Move a Nation* (1967). George F. Kennan, "America's Administrative Response to Its World Problems," in E. E. Morison, ed., *The American Style* (1958), is an earlier commentary on "bureaucratic imperatives." R. J. Barnet's *Intervention and Revolution: America's Confrontation with Insurgent Movements Around the World** (1968) is an intelligent though sometimes glib survey of United States policy assumptions and of four interventions — Greece, Lebanon, the Dominican Republic, and Vietnam. In the same genre, Theodore Draper's *Abuse of Power** (1969) is more closely argued. Barnet's *The Economy of Death** (1969), a hostile commentary on "the Defense Budget and the Military-Industrial Complex," is similarly incisive though a bit burdened by the author's commitment. J. L. Clayton, ed., *The Economic Impact of the War: Sources and Readings** (1970), is an excellent collection of government documents and scholarly articles, with valuable statistical tables. Bernard Fall, *The Two Viet-Nams: A Political and Military Analysis* (rev. ed. 1964), is sometimes referred to as the "standard work." Fall, a French scholar and journalist who occasionally taught in American universities, knew both Vietnams probably better than anyone in the Western world, and his judgments are balanced and judicious. He was killed in 1967 when he stepped on a land mine in South Vietnam. See also his *Street Without Joy* (1967), a military history from 1946 to 1954, and *The Vietnam Reader* (1965), edited with Marcus Raskin. Jean Lacouture, *Vietnam: Between Two Truces* (1966), and David Halberstam, *The Making of a Quagmire* (1965), are two similarly sharp and judicious studies by men who know Vietnam intimately. F. Schurmann, P. D. Scott, and R. Zelnik, *The Politics of Escalation** (1966), is a useful chronicle that makes considerable use of Asian and European sources. For more "orthodox" views of American foreign policy, see Dean Acheson, *Present at the Creation* (1969); H. A. Kissinger, ed., *Problems of National Strategy: A Book of Readings** (1965); and Kissinger's original contribution to the debate, *Nuclear Weapons and Foreign Policy** (1957), which is still well worth reading. I. L. Horowitz, *The New Civilian Militarists** (1963), is a biased but provocative study of the group of civilian intellectuals (Kissinger included) who advise the government on the strategy of war diplomacy. Finally, W. Bunge et al., "Johnson's Information Strategy for Vietnam: An Evaluation," *Journalism Quarterly*, 45 (Autumn 1968), is a suggestive though not altogether successful article.

How Could Vietnam Happen?
An Autopsy

James C. Thomson, Jr.

As a case study in the making of foreign policy, the Vietnam War will fascinate historians and social scientists for many decades to come. One question that will certainly be asked: How did men of superior ability, sound training, and high ideals — American policy-makers of the 1960s — create such costly and divisive policy?

As one who watched the decision-making process in Washington from 1961 to 1966 under Presidents Kennedy and Johnson, I can suggest a preliminary answer. I can do so by briefly listing some of the factors that seemed to me to shape our Vietnam policy during my years as an East Asia specialist at the State Department and the White House. I shall deal largely with Washington as I saw or sensed it, and not with Saigon, where I have spent but a scant three days, in the entourage of the Vice President, or with other decision centers, the capitals of interested parties. Nor will I deal with other important parts of the record: Vietnam's history prior to 1961, for instance, or the overall course of America's relations with Vietnam.

Yet a first and central ingredient in these years of Vietnam decisions does involve history. The ingredient was *the legacy of the 1950s* — by which I mean the so-called "loss of China," the Korean War, and the Far East policy of Secretary of State Dulles.

This legacy had an institutional by-product for the Kennedy Administration: in 1961 the U.S. government's East Asian establishment was undoubtedly the most rigid and doctrinaire of Washington's regional divisions in foreign affairs. This was especially true at the Department of State, where the incoming Administration found the Bureau of Far Eastern Affairs the hardest nut to crack. It was a bureau that had been purged of its best China expertise, and of farsighted, dispassionate men, as a result of McCarthyism. Its members were generally committed to one policy line: the close containment and isolation of mainland China, the harassment of "neutralist" nations which sought to avoid alignment with either Washington or Peking, and the maintenance of a network of alliances with anti-Communist client states on China's periphery.

Another aspect of the legacy was the special vulnerability and sensitivity of the new Democratic Administration on Far East policy issues. The memory of the McCarthy era was still very sharp, and Kennedy's margin of victory was too thin. The 1960 Offshore Islands TV debate between Kennedy and Nixon had shown the President-elect the perils of "fresh thinking." The Administration was inherently leery of moving too fast on Asia. As a result, the Far East Bureau (now the Bureau of East Asian and Pacific Affairs) was the last one to be overhauled. Not until Averell Harriman was brought in as Assistant Secretary in December, 1961, were significant personnel changes attempted, and it took Harriman several months to make a deep imprint on the bureau because of his necessary preoccupation with the Laos settlement. Once he did so, there was virtually no effort to bring back the purged or exiled East Asia experts.

There were other important by-products of this "legacy of the fifties":

The new Administration inherited and somewhat shared *a general perception of China-on-the-march* — a sense of China's vastness, its numbers, its belligerence; a revived sense, perhaps, of the Golden Horde. This was a perception fed by Chinese intervention in the Korean War (an intervention actually based on appallingly bad communications and mutual miscalculation on the part of Washington and Peking; but the careful unraveling of that tragedy, which scholars have accomplished, had not yet become part of the conventional wisdom).

The new Administration inherited and briefly accepted *a monolithic conception of the Communist bloc*. Despite much earlier predictions and reports by outside analysts, policy-makers did not begin to accept the reality and possible finality of the Sino-Soviet split until the first weeks of 1962. The inevitably corrosive impact of competing nationalisms on Communism was largely ignored.

The new Administration inherited and to some extent shared *the "domino theory" about Asia*. This theory resulted from profound ignorance of Asian history and hence ignorance of the radical differences among Asian nations and societies. It resulted from a blindness to the power and resilience of Asian nationalisms. (It may also have resulted from a subconscious sense that, since "all Asians look alike," all Asian nations will act alike.) As a theory, the domino fallacy was not merely inaccurate but also insulting to Asian nations; yet it has continued to this day to beguile men who should know better.

Finally, the legacy of the fifties was apparently compounded by an uneasy sense of a worldwide Communist challenge to the new Administration after the Bay of Pigs fiasco. A first manifestation was the President's traumatic Vienna meeting with Khrushchev in June, 1961; then came the Berlin crisis of the summer. All this created an atmosphere in which President Kennedy undoubtedly felt under special pressure to show his nation's mettle in Vietnam — if the Vietnamese, unlike the people of Laos, were willing to fight.

In general, the legacy of the fifties shaped such early moves of the new Administration as the decisions to maintain a high-visibility SEATO (by sending the Secretary of State himself instead of some underling to its first meeting in 1961), to back away from diplomatic recognition of Mongolia in the summer of 1961, and most important, to expand U.S. military assistance to South Vietnam that winter on the basis of the much more tentative Eisenhower commitment. It should be added that the increased commitment to Vietnam was also fueled by a new breed of military strategists and academic social scientists (some of whom had entered the new Administration) who had developed theories of counterguerrilla warfare and were eager to see them put to the test. To some, "counterinsurgency" seemed a new panacea for coping with the world's instability.

So much for the legacy and the history. Any new Administration inherits both complicated problems and simplistic views of the world. But surely among the policy-makers of the Kennedy and Johnson Administrations there were men who would warn of the dangers of an open-ended commitment to the Vietnam quagmire?

This raises a central question, at the heart of the policy process: Where were the experts, the doubters, and the dissenters? Were they there at all, and if so, what happened to them?

The answer is complex but instructive.

In the first place, the American government was sorely *lacking in real Vietnam or Indochina expertise.* Originally treated as an adjunct of Embassy Paris, our Saigon embassy and the Vietnam Desk at State were largely staffed from 1954 onward by French-speaking Foreign Service personnel of narrowly European experience. Such diplomats were even more closely restricted than the normal embassy officer — by cast of mind as well as language — to contacts with Vietnam's French-speaking urban elites. For instance, Foreign Service linguists in Portugal are able to speak with the peasantry if they get out of Lisbon and choose to do so; not so the French speakers of Embassy Saigon.

In addition, the *shadow of the "loss of China"* distorted Vietnam reporting. Career officers in the Department, and especially those in the field, had not forgotten the fate of their World War II colleagues who wrote in frankness from China and were later pilloried by Senate committees for critical comments on the Chinese Nationalists. Candid reporting on the strengths of the Viet Cong and the weaknesses of the Diem government was inhibited by the memory. It was also inhibited by some higher officials, notably Ambassador Nolting in Saigon, who refused to sign off on such cables.

In due course, to be sure, some Vietnam talent was discovered or developed. But a recurrent and increasingly important factor in the decision-making process was *the banishment of real expertise.* Here the underlying cause was the "closed politics" of policy-making as issues become hot: the more sensitive the issue, and the higher it rises in the bureaucracy, the more completely the experts are excluded while the harassed senior generalists take over (that is, the Secretaries, Undersecretaries, and Presidential Assistants). The frantic skimming of briefing papers in the back seats of limousines is no substitute for the presence of specialists; furthermore, in times of crisis such papers are deemed "too sensitive" even for review by the specialists. Another underlying cause of this banishment, as Vietnam became more critical, was the replacement of the experts, who were generally and increasingly pessimistic, by men described as "can-do guys," loyal and energetic fixers unsoured by expertise. In early 1965, when I confided my growing policy doubts to an older colleague on the NSC staff, he assured me that the smartest thing both of us could do was to "steer clear of the whole Vietnam mess"; the gentleman in question had the misfortune to be a "can-do guy," however, and is now highly placed in Vietnam, under orders to solve the mess.

Despite the banishment of the experts, internal doubters and dissenters did indeed appear and persist. Yet as I watched the process, such men were effectively neutralized by a subtle dynamic: *the domestication of dissenters.* Such "domestication" arose out of a twofold clubbish need: on the one hand, the dissenter's desire to stay aboard; and on the other hand, the nondissenter's conscience. Simply stated, dissent, when recognized, was made to feel at home. On the lowest possible scale of importance, I must confess my own considerable sense of dignity and acceptance (both vital) when my senior White House employer would refer to me as his "favorite dove." Far more significant was the case of the former Undersecretary of State, George Ball. Once Mr. Ball began to express doubts, he was warmly institutionalized: he was encouraged to become the inhouse devil's advocate on Vietnam. The upshot was inevitable: the process of escalation allowed for periodic requests to Mr. Ball to speak his piece; Ball felt good, I assume (he had fought for righteousness); the others felt good (they had given a full hearing to the dovish option); and there was minimal unpleasantness. The club remained intact; and it is of course possible that matters would have gotten worse faster if Mr. Ball had kept silent, or left before his final departure in the fall of 1966. There was also, of course, the case of the last institutionalized doubter, Bill Moyers. The President is said to have greeted his arrival at meetings with an affectionate, "Well, here comes Mr. Stop-the-Bombing . . ." Here again the dynamics of domesticated dissent sustained the relationship for a while.

A related point — and crucial, I suppose, to government at all times — was *the "effectiveness" trap,* the trap that keeps men from speaking out, as clearly or often as they might, within the government. And it is the trap that keeps men from resigning in protest and airing their dissent outside the government. The most important asset that a man brings to bureaucratic life is his "effectiveness," a mysterious combination of training, style, and connections. The most ominous complaint that can be whispered of a bureaucrat is: "I'm afraid Charlie's beginning to lose his effectiveness." To preserve your effectiveness, you must decide where and when to fight the mainstream of policy; the opportunities range from pillow talk with your wife, to private drinks with your friends, to meetings with the Secretary of State or the President. The inclination to remain silent or to acquiesce in the presence of the great men — to live to fight another day, to give on this issue so that you can be "effective" on later issues — is overwhelming. Nor is it the tendency of youth alone; some of our most senior officials, men of wealth and fame, whose place in history is secure, have remained silent lest their connection with power be terminated. As for the disinclination to resign in protest: while not necessarily a Washington or even American specialty, it seems more true of a government in which ministers have no parliamentary backbench to which to retreat. In the absence of such a refuge, it is easy to rationalize the decision to stay aboard. By doing so, one may be able to prevent a few bad things from happening and perhaps even make a few good things happen. To exit is to lose even those marginal chances for "effectiveness."

Another factor must be noted: as the Vietnam controversy escalated at home, there developed *a preoccupation with Vietnam public relations as opposed to Vietnam policy-making.* And here, ironically, internal doubters and dissenters were heavily employed. For such men, by virtue of their own doubts, were often deemed best able to "massage" the doubting intelligentsia. My senior East Asia colleague at the White House, a brilliant and humane doubter who had dealt with Indochina since 1954, spent three quarters of his working days on Vietnam public relations: drafting presidential responses to letters from important critics, writing conciliatory language for presidential speeches, and meeting quite interminably with delegations of outraged Quakers, clergymen, academics, and housewives. His regular callers were the late A. J. Muste and Norman Thomas; mine were members of the Women's Strike for Peace. Our orders from above: keep them off the backs of busy policy-makers (who usually happened to be nondoubters). Incidentally, my most discouraging assignment in the realm of public relations was the preparation of a White House pamphlet entitled *Why Vietnam,* in September, 1965; in a gesture toward my conscience, I fought — and lost — a battle to have the title followed by a question mark.

Through a variety of procedures, both institutional and personal, doubt, dissent, and expertise were effectively neutralized in the making of policy. But what can be said of the men "in charge"? It is patently absurd to suggest that they produced such tragedy by intention and calculation. But it is neither absurd nor difficult to discern certain forces at work that caused decent and honorable men to do great harm.

Here I would stress the paramount role of *executive fatigue.* No factor seems to me more crucial and underrated in the making of foreign policy. The physical and emotional toll of executive responsibility in State, the Pentagon, the White House, and other executive agencies is enormous; that toll is of course compounded by extended service. Many of today's Vietnam policy-makers have been on the job for from four to seven years. Complaints may be few, and physical health may remain unimpaired, though emotional health is far harder to gauge. But what is most seriously eroded in the deadening process of fatigue is freshness of thought, imagination, a sense of possibility, a sense of priorities and perspective — those rare assets of a new Administration in its first year or two of office. The tired policy-maker becomes a prisoner of his own narrowed view of the world and his own clichéd rhetoric. He becomes irritable and defensive — short on sleep, short on family ties, short on patience. Such men make bad policy and then compound it. They have neither the time nor the temperament for new ideas or preventive diplomacy.

Below the level of the fatigued executives in the making of Vietnam policy was a widespread phenomenon: *the curator mentality* in the Department of State. By this I mean the collective inertia produced by the bureaucrat's view of his job. At State, the average "desk officer" inherits from his predecessor our policy toward Country X; he regards it as his function to keep that policy intact — under glass, untampered with, and dusted — so that he may pass it on in two to four years to his successor. And such curatorial service generally merits promotion within the system. (Maintain the status quo, and you will stay out of trouble.) In some circumstances, the inertia bred by such an outlook can act as a brake against rash innovation. But on many issues, this inertia sustains the momentum of bad policy and unwise commitments — momentum that might otherwise have been resisted within the ranks. Clearly, Vietnam is such an issue.

To fatigue and inertia must be added the factor of internal confusion. Even among the "architects" of our Vietnam commitment, there has been persistent *confusion as to what type of war we were fighting* and, as a direct consequence, *confusion as to how to end that war*. (The "credibility gap" is, in part, a reflection of such internal confusion.) Was it, for instance, a civil war, in which case counterinsurgency might suffice? Or was it a war of international aggression? (This might invoke SEATO or UN commitment.) Who was the aggressor — and the "real enemy"? The Viet Cong? Hanoi? Peking? Moscow? International Communism? Or maybe "Asian Communism"? Differing enemies dictated differing strategies and tactics. And confused throughout, in like fashion, was the question of American objectives; your objectives depended on whom you were fighting and why. I shall not forget my assignment from an Assistant Secretary of State in March, 1964: to draft a speech for Secretary McNamara which would, *inter alia*, once and for all dispose of the canard that the Vietnam conflict was a civil war. "But in some ways, of course," I mused, "it *is* a civil war." "Don't play word games with me!" snapped the Assistant Secretary.

Similar confusion beset the concept of "negotiations" — anathema to much of official Washington from 1961 to 1965. Not until April, 1965, did "unconditional discussions" become respectable, via a presidential speech; even then the Secretary of State stressed privately to newsmen that nothing had changed, since "discussions" were by no means the same as "negotiations." Months later that issue was resolved. But it took even longer to obtain a fragile internal agreement that negotiations might include the Viet Cong as something other than an appendage to Hanoi's delegation. Given such confusion as to the whos and whys of our Vietnam commitment, it is not surprising, as Theodore Draper has written, that policy-makers find it so difficult to agree on how to end the war.

Of course, one force — a constant in the vortex of commitment — was that of *wishful thinking.* I partook of it myself at many times. I did so especially during Washington's struggle with Diem in the autumn of 1963 when some of us at State believed that for once, in dealing with a difficult client state, the U.S. government could use the leverage of our economic and military assistance to make good things happen, instead of being led around by the nose by men like Chiang Kai-shek and Syngman Rhee (and, in that particular instance, by Diem). If we could prove that point, I thought, and move into a new day, with or without Diem, then Vietnam was well worth the effort. Later came the wishful thinking of the air-strike planners in the late autumn of 1964; there were those who actually thought that after six weeks of air strikes, the North Vietnamese would come crawling to us to ask for peace talks. And what, someone asked in one of the meetings of the time, if they don't? The answer was that we would bomb for another four weeks, and that would do the trick. And a few weeks later came one instance of wishful thinking that was symptomatic of good men misled: in January, 1965, I encountered one of the very highest figures in the Administration at a dinner, drew him aside, and told him of my worries about the air-strike option. He told me that I really shouldn't worry; it was his conviction that before any such plans could be put into effect, a neutralist government would come to power in Saigon that would politely invite us out. And finally, there was the recurrent wishful thinking that sustained many of us through the trying months of 1965–1966 after the air strikes had begun: that surely, somehow, one way or another, we would "be in a conference in six months," and the escalatory spiral would be suspended. The basis of our hope: "It simply can't go on."

As a further influence on policy-makers I would cite the factor of *bureaucratic detachment.* By this I mean what at best might be termed the professional callousness of the surgeon (and indeed, medical lingo — the "surgical strike" for instance — seemed to crop up in the euphemisms of the times). In Washington the semantics of the military muted the reality of war for the civilian policy-makers. In quiet, air-conditioned, thick-carpeted rooms, such terms as "systematic pressure," "armed reconnaissance," "targets of opportunity," and even "body count" seemed to breed a sort of games-theory detachment. Most memorable to me was a moment in the late 1964 target planning when the question under discussion was how heavy our bombing should be, and how extensive our strafing, at some midpoint in the projected pattern of systematic pressure. An Assistant Secretary of State resolved the point in the following words: "It seems to me that our orchestration should be mainly violins, but with periodic touches of brass." Perhaps the biggest shock of my return to Cambridge, Massachusetts, was the realization that the young men, the flesh and blood I taught and saw on these university streets, were potentially some of the numbers on the charts of those faraway planners. In a curious sense, Cambridge is closer to this war than Washington.

There is an unprovable factor that relates to bureaucratic detachment: the ingredient of *crypto-racism*. I do not mean to imply any conscious contempt for Asian loss of life on the part of Washington officials. But I do mean to imply that bureaucratic detachment may well be compounded by a traditional Western sense that there are so many Asians, after all; that Asians have a fatalism about life and a disregard for its loss; that they are cruel and barbaric to their own people; and that they are very different from us (and all look alike?). And I *do* mean to imply that the upshot of such subliminal views is a subliminal question whether Asians, and particularly Asian peasants, and most particularly Asian Communists, are really people — like you and me. To put the matter another way: would we have pursued quite such policies — and quite such military tactics — if the Vietnamese were white?

It is impossible to write of Vietnam decision-making without writing about language. Throughout the conflict, words have been of paramount importance. I refer here to the impact of *rhetorical escalation* and to the *problem of oversell*. In an important sense, Vietnam has become of crucial significance to us *because we have said that it is of crucial significance*. (The issue obviously relates to the public relations preoccupation described earlier.)

The key here is domestic politics: the need to sell the American people, press, and Congress on support for an unpopular and costly war in which the objectives themselves have been in flux. To sell means to persuade, and to persuade means rhetoric. As the difficulties and costs have mounted, so has the definition of the stakes. This is not to say that rhetorical escalation is an orderly process; executive prose is the product of many writers, and some concepts — North Vietnamese infiltration, America's "national honor," Red China as the chief enemy — have entered the rhetoric only gradually and even sporadically. But there is an upward spiral nonetheless. And once you have *said* that the American Experiment itself stands or falls on the Vietnam outcome, you have thereby created a national stake far beyond any earlier stakes.

Crucial throughout the process of Vietnam decision-making was a conviction among many policy-makers: that Vietnam posed a *fundamental test of America's national will*. Time and again I was told by men reared in the tradition of Henry L. Stimson that all we needed was the will, and we would then prevail. Implicit in such a view, it seemed to me, was a curious assumption that Asians lacked will, or at least that in a contest between Asian and Anglo-Saxon wills, the non-Asians must prevail. A corollary to the persistent belief in will was a *fascination with power* and an awe in the face of the power America possessed as no nation or civilization ever before. Those who doubted our role in Vietnam were said to shrink from the burdens of power, the obligations of power, the uses of power, the responsibility of power. By implication, such men were soft-headed and effete.

Finally, no discussion of the factors and forces at work on Vietnam policy-makers can ignore the central fact of *human ego investment*. Men who have participated in a decision develop a stake in that decision. As they participate in further, related decisions, their stake increases. It might have been possible to dissuade a man of strong self-confidence at an early stage of the ladder of decision; but it is infinitely harder at later stages since a change of mind there usually involves implicit or explicit repudiation of a chain of previous decisions.

To put it bluntly: at the heart of the Vietnam calamity is a group of able, dedicated men who have been regularly and repeatedly wrong — and whose standing with their contemporaries, and more important, with history, depends, as they see it, on being proven right. These are not men who can be asked to extricate themselves from error.

The various ingredients I have cited in the making of Vietnam policy have created a variety of results, most of them fairly obvious. Here are some that seem to me most central:

Throughout the conflict, there has been *persistent and repeated miscalculation* by virtually all the actors, in high echelons and low, whether dove, hawk, or something else. To cite one simple example among many: in late 1964 and early 1965, some peace-seeking planners at State who strongly opposed the projected bombing of the North urged that, instead, American ground forces be sent to South Vietnam; this would, they said, increase our bargaining leverage against the North — our "chips" — and would give us something to negotiate about (the withdrawal of our forces) at an early peace conference. Simultaneously, the air-strike option was urged by many in the military who were dead set against American participation in "another land war in Asia"; they were joined by other civilian peace-seekers who wanted to bomb Hanoi into early negotiations. By late 1965, we had ended up with the worst of all worlds: ineffective and costly air strikes against the North, spiraling ground forces in the South, and no negotiations in sight.

Throughout the conflict as well, there has been *a steady give-in to pressures for a military solution* and only minimal and sporadic efforts at a diplomatic and political solution. In part this resulted from the confusion (earlier cited) among the civilians — confusion regarding objectives and strategy. And in part this resulted from the self-enlarging nature of military investment. Once air strikes and particularly ground forces were introduced, our investment itself had transformed the original stakes. More air power was needed to protect the ground forces; and then more ground forces to protect the ground forces. And needless to say, the military mind develops its own momentum in the absence of clear guidelines from the civilians. Once asked to save South Vietnam, rather than to "advise" it, the American military could not but press for escalation. In addition, sad to report, assorted military constituencies, once involved in Vietnam, have had a series of cases to prove: for instance, the utility not only of air power (the Air Force) but of supercarrier-based air power (the Navy). Also, Vietnam policy has suffered from one ironic by-product of Secretary McNamara's establishment of civilian control at the Pentagon: in the face of such control, interservice rivalry has given way to a united front among the military — reflected in the new but recurrent phenomenon of JCS unanimity. In conjunction with traditional congressional allies (mostly Southern senators and representatives) such a united front would pose a formidable problem for any President.

Throughout the conflict, there have been *missed opportunities, large and small, to disengage ourselves from Vietnam on increasingly unpleasant but still acceptable terms.* Of the many moments from 1961 onward, I shall cite only one, the last and most important opportunity that was lost: in the summer of 1964 the President instructed his chief advisers to prepare for him as wide a range of Vietnam options as possible for postelection consideration and decision. He explicitly asked that all options be laid out. What happened next was, in effect, Lyndon Johnson's slow-motion Bay of Pigs. For the advisers so effectively converged on one single option — juxtaposed against two other, phony options (in effect, blowing up the world, or scuttle-and-run) — that the President was confronted with unanimity for bombing the North from all his trusted counselors. Had he been more confident in foreign affairs, had he been deeply informed on Vietnam and Southeast Asia, and had he raised some hard questions that unanimity had submerged, this President could have used the largest electoral mandate in history to de-escalate in Vietnam, in the clear expectation that at the worst a neutralist government would come to power in Saigon and politely invite us out. Today, many lives and dollars later, such an alternative has become an elusive and infinitely more expensive possibility.

In the course of these years, another result of Vietnam decision-making has been *the abuse and distortion of history*. Vietnamese, Southeast Asian, and Far Eastern history has been rewritten by our policy-makers, and their spokesmen, to conform with the alleged necessity of our presence in Vietnam. Highly dubious analogies from our experience elsewhere — the "Munich" sellout and "containment" from Europe, the Malayan insurgency and the Korean War from Asia — have been imported in order to justify our actions. And more recent events have been fitted to the Procrustean bed of Vietnam. Most notably, the change of power in Indonesia in 1965–1966 has been ascribed to our Vietnam presence; and virtually all progress in the Pacific region — the rise of regionalism, new forms of cooperation, and mounting growth rates — has been similarly explained. The Indonesian allegation is undoubtedly false (I tried to prove it, during six months of careful investigation at the White House, and had to confess failure); the regional allegation is patently unprovable in either direction (except, of course, for the clear fact that the economies of both Japan and Korea have profited enormously from our Vietnam-related procurement in these countries; but that is a costly and highly dubious form of foreign aid).

There is a final result of Vietnam policy I would cite that holds potential danger for the future of American foreign policy: *the rise of a new breed of American ideologues who see Vietnam as the ultimate test of their doctrine.* I have in mind those men in Washington who have given a new life to the missionary impulse in American foreign relations: who believe that this nation, in this era, has received a threefold endowment that can transform the world. As they see it, that endowment is composed of, first, our unsurpassed military might; second, our clear technological supremacy; and third, our allegedly invincible benevolence (our "altruism," our affluence, our lack of territorial aspirations). Together, it is argued, this threefold endowment provides us with the opportunity and the obligation to ease the nations of the earth toward modernization and stability: toward a full-fledged *Pax Americana Technocratica*. In reaching toward this goal, Vietnam is viewed as the last and crucial test. Once we have succeeded there, the road ahead is clear. In a sense, these men are our counterpart to the visionaries of Communism's radical left: they are technocracy's own Maoists. They do not govern Washington today. But their doctrine rides high.

Long before I went into government, I was told a story about Henry L. Stimson that seemed to me pertinent during the years that I watched the Vietnam tragedy unfold — and participated in that tragedy. It seems to me more pertinent than ever as we move toward the election of 1968.

In his waning years Stimson was asked by an anxious questioner, "Mr. Secretary, how on earth can we ever bring peace to the world?" Stimson is said to have answered: "You begin by bringing to Washington a small handful of able men who believe that the achievement of peace is possible.

"You work them to the bone until they no longer believe that it is possible.

"And then you throw them out — and bring in a new bunch who believe that it is possible."

PART VI

THE HISTORIAN
AND THE TWENTIETH CENTURY

30

THE HISTORIOGRAPHY
OF THE 1950'S: AN ANALYSIS

In the following essay, written in 1959, Professor John Higham of the University of Michigan saw and appreciated much of what was healthy and vital about the historical writing of the 1950's. He remained, however, more troubled than appreciative. For all their accomplishments, he argued, the historians of the post–World War II years went too far in revising the work of their predecessors and in the process allowed themselves to be affected too profoundly by the conservative tenor of the period in which they wrote.

Higham's article in itself is evidence that all American historians in the 1950's did not succumb to the hypnotic attraction of conservatism. His central point — that American history has not been one long, happy voyage in a homogeneous vessel with few differences and with a joyful consensus — was a point worth making. But in hammering this message home, Higham himself was frequently guilty of a bit of "homogenizing." He too easily lumped the majority of modern historians together with Daniel Boorstin whose work he subjected to close analysis. It may well be that Boorstin's ideas were motivated by philosophical conservatism, but whether this was true of the other "homogenizers" is not quite so clear. It is clear that they were deeply influenced by the sociological and psychological ideas and theories that permeate our age. This influence led them to ask questions concerning status, ideology, and motivation, which historians in the past have too frequently ignored. It led them also to overlook too easily the validity contained in the analyses of their predecessors. At times, as Higham maintained, they stood Beard, Turner, and Parrington on their heads and distorted the past a bit by seemingly reducing it all to one continuous plateau.

This kind of distortion, of course, is by no means unique. "Any written history," Charles Beard once argued, "inevitably reflects the thought of the author in his time and cultural setting." Beard himself is a good example. Nurtured in an age of reform, an age convinced of the potency of economic motivation, Beard saw the past partially through the spectacles of the present. But though his method was often faulty, his evidence often inadequate, his thesis often imperfect, though, in short, he often distorted the past, his contribution to our knowledge of ourselves and our history was immense and enduring. This is not to say that the historian is the prisoner of the present but rather that he can and should learn from the present and apply that learning to his understanding of the past. To be true to his calling, the historian must attempt to rise above the present, but he can ignore it only at his peril. The historian, of course, is affected not merely by the ideological currents of his age but also, and perhaps to an even greater extent, by its scholarly methodologies and techniques. Historians, as J. H. Hexter has pointed out, "use all the tracking devices available to them at the time. . . . And of course the adequacy of the historical search at any time is in some degree limited by the adequacy of the tracking devices." Viewed in this perspective, rather than in the ideological framework that Higham employed, the strengths and weaknesses of the historical works of the 1950's might become clearer.

It may well be that the social science "tracking devices" of the 1950's led historians to ask questions and examine phenomena that more naturally tended to focus upon problems of consensus and continuity than upon problems of change, but the bias did not necessarily result in a conservative interpretation of the American past. It is possible to maintain that Democrats and Republicans, agrarians and urbanites, westerners and easterners, have shared a certain set of values without denying the real differences between them. But if these shared values have not eliminated meaningful conflict in America, they have been extremely influential in shaping the course and resolution of that conflict. One need not join Boorstin in celebrating the existence of this consensus. Insofar as it has served to prevent the rise of a meaningful two-party system, to limit the resolution of the real conflicts that have taken place, to blind Americans to the needs of their society, and to inhibit them from solving their persistent problems, one may well deplore it, but to deplore it is not to deny its existence.

We can, in short, echo Higham's pleas for "an appreciation of the crusading spirit, a responsiveness to indignation, a sense of injustice," without forgetting that these values can go hand in hand with, and can even be enhanced by, a deeper understanding of the existence of a certain degree of continuity and consensus in American history.

John Higham would undoubtedly agree with a number of the criticisms we have directed at his 1959 analysis of the state of American historiography. During the decade following the publication of this essay, Higham continued and intensified his studies of American historiography. In his major study, *History* (1965), written in collaboration with Leonard Krieger and Felix Gilbert, Higham placed the historical writing of the 1950's in a richer intellectual context and showed a heightened sense of the variations within that historiography and a greater appreciation for its accomplishments. In his most recent book, *Writing American History: Essays on Modern Scholarship* (1970), a collection of his historiographical essays, changes in his point of view are even more evident. He now writes:

Distinctions between today's consensus historians and their progressive predecessors were not nearly as sharp as I had believed. In fact, I discovered that the trend I had perceived so suddenly in the 1950's as a major movement had really originated in the 1930's. It stemmed from a crisis within progressive thought, not from an assault from outside the pale. Moreover, the significant changes since World War II seemed less and less the possession of an identifiable group. They were in the air. They affected everyone but it different degrees and ways. There was indeed too much stress on consensus among some leading writers, but American historical thought had not congealed into distinct schools. Instead, it was swirling around a few central problems. Evidently I had underestimated both the degree of continuity and the range of diversity in our historiography (pp. 159–60).

The problem for the contemporary historian, Higham feels, is "somehow to bring together a renewed appreciation of conflict in our history with the understanding of consensus which was so heavily stressed in the scholarship of the 1950's" (p. 73).

We are particularly indebted to Professor Higham for allowing us to reprint an article which he himself chose not to include in his recent collection because, as he puts it in his preface, he finds it "embarrassing to reread in the light of subsequent scholarship and my own present understanding of the issues . . ." (p. ix). We have made a different decision since, for all the differences we have with the point of view he then expressed, we still think there is much to be learned from this essay in terms of both its delineation of some of the salient points of departure between the historians of the postwar years and their predecessors and its expression of a disquiet with the historical writing of those years that was common to a significant number of historians and graduate students and that was to become intensified during the 1960's, as the last essay in this volume illustrates.

The Cult of the "American Consensus": Homogenizing Our History

JOHN HIGHAM

In retrospect, it is becoming apparent that the decade of the 1940's marked a fundamental change of direction in the exploration of the American past. At the time nothing very unusual seemed to be happening in the minds of American historians, in spite of the clamor in the world around them. The usual outpouring of conventional monographs continued. Our endless fas-

Reprinted by permission of the author and the publisher from *Commentary* (February 1959), copyright © 1959 by the American Jewish Committee.

cination with the pageant of the Civil War produced a new but not a very different crop of narratives. There was, to be sure, a rising volume of criticism of the giants who had dominated American historical scholarship in the period between the wars: Frederick Jackson Turner, Charles A. Beard, and Vernon L. Parrington. But the image they had fixed on the screen of the American past had only begun to dissolve. As late as 1950, when Henry Steele Commager's *The American Mind* carried our intellectual history down to date in the spirit of Parrington, the result sounded only a trifle old-fashioned.

In the last few years, however, the critical attacks of the 40's have matured into a full-scale reappraisal of the main themes in American history. The great trio of yesteryear has gone into eclipse. Their vision of an America in which democracy, vaguely associated with the West, battled against entrenched economic privilege no longer seems basic enough to define the shape of our national development. On the whole, the distinctive interpretations of Turner, Beard, and Parrington no longer appear persuasive enough to evoke really lively controversy. They linger on, flattened and desiccated, in the pages of many a textbook, where they may occasionally inflame the Daughters of the American Revolution, the *Daily News*, and others who specialize in discovering the menace of dead issues. Meanwhile, our living historical awareness has moved so far from the interests of Turner, Beard, and Parrington that interpretive historians now feel less need to criticize or defend them than to supersede them.

Giants being notoriously oversized, no one has yet stepped into their shoes. The new books that are giving us an altered sense of who we are lack either the scale or the density or the architectural strength that history of the first order of importance must have. Still, some lively work is being done. Some important books that try to fit fragmentary research into a new pattern, plausible to contemporary sensibilities, are being written. The dominant image they project bears few resemblances to the turbulent picture that prevailed before the 1940's.

An earlier generation of historians, inspired by Turner, Beard, and Parrington and nurtured in a restless atmosphere of reform, had painted America in the bold hues of conflict. Sometimes their interpretations pitted class against class, sometimes section against section; and increasingly they aligned both sections and classes behind the banners of clashing ideologies. It was East vs. West, with the South gravitating from one to the other; farmers vs. businessmen, with urban workers in the pivotal position; city vs. country; property rights vs. human rights; Hamiltonianism vs. Jeffersonianism. These lines of cleavage were charted continuously from the Colonial period to the present. They gave a sense of depth to the social struggles which historians in the early 20th century observed all around them.

The divisions between periods loomed as large as those between groups. Among scholars attuned to conflict, American history appeared jagged and discontinuous. Historians like Beard had an eye for the convulsive moments in history, and they dramatized vividly the turning points when one side or the other seemed to seize control. To them, America had had several revolutions, usually triumphant over formidable resistance, and always big with unfulfilled promise. They saw the revolution of 1776 not simply as a war for independence but as a drastic redistribution of power within the Colonies. They called the Civil War the "Second American Revolution," and in between they acclaimed the "Revolution of 1800," when Jefferson came to power, and the militant rise of the common man behind Andrew Jackson. There was, of course, the Industrial Revolution, followed by the heroic Populist Revolt; and similar social conflicts throughout the Colonial period caught their attention.

With some lapse of consistency these connoisseurs of change often played down the newness of the New Deal. The closer they looked to the present, the more clearly they observed the traditional elements in a movement of protest. The issues of their own day, they knew, were anchored in a long heritage, the changes no more than might be expected; the transitions of the past looked much more radical. Over all, however, the crises of American history stood out as the milestones of progress, when men shed outworn beliefs and remade their institutions in response to the demands of a changed environment.

In contrast, the new look of American history is strikingly conservative. More than at any time before, historians are discovering a placid, unexciting past. To an impressive degree, the dominant interpretations have recaptured the spirit of Alexis de Tocqueville, whose *Democracy in America* has emerged in recent years from a characteristic neglect during the early 20th century. As Tocqueville did more than a century ago, today's historians are exhibiting a happy land, adventurous in manner but conservative in substance, and — above all — remarkably homogeneous.

For one thing, current scholarship is carrying out a massive grading operation to smooth over America's social convulsions. The American Revolution has lost its revolutionary character, becoming again what genteel historians had always said it was: a reluctant resistance of sober Englishmen to infringements on English liberties. We have learned that the Jacksonians yearned nostalgically to restore the stable simplicity of a bygone age, and that the Populists were rural businessmen deluded by a similar pastoral mythology. Paradoxically, we have even grown conservative enough to recognize fairly radical changes in the recent past and so to probe, with Richard Hofstadter, for elements of social revolution in the New Deal. Hofstadter's very influential book, *The Age of Reform: From Bryan to F.D.R.* (1955) neatly reverses the older views. It presents Populism in the 1890's and Progressivism in the early 20th century not as mighty upheavals but as archaic efforts to recapture the past. On the other hand, it shows the New Deal as an abrupt break with the past.

Among earlier crises, the Civil War alone has resisted somewhat the flattening process. Yet a significant decline has occurred in the number of important contributions to Civil War history from professional scholars. One is tempted to conclude that disturbances which cannot be minimized must be neglected. On the other hand, the growing attraction of the Civil War to journalists suggests that it provides a large public with a kind of surrogate for all of the other dramatic moments that historians are deflating.

By reducing the importance of these turning points, the newer interpretations have enabled us to rediscover the continuity of American history, the stability of basic institutions, the toughness of the social fabric. The same result is also being attained by dissolving the persistent dualisms, which Parrington and Beard emphasized, and substituting a monistic pattern. Instead of two traditions or sections or classes deployed against one another all along the line of national development, we are told that America in the largest sense has had one unified culture. Classes have turned into myths, sections have lost their solidarity, ideologies have vaporized into climates of opinion. The phrase *"the* American experience" has become an incantation.

To fill in its meaning, historians have joined social scientists in a new fascination with the concept of national character. Since definitions of national character necessarily concern the pervasive, persistent features of a whole culture, progressive scholars distrusted them. Today, however, the study of national character brings out the unifying effects of forces that formerly impressed us as disruptive. Thus David Potter's *People of Plenty: Economic Abundance and the American Character* (1954) advances an economic interpretation of our similarities instead of our differences. Whereas the generation of Parrington and Beard had explained basic cleavages on economic grounds, Potter shows our wealth shaping our common ways of life.

Of course, the new interpreters have to face a considerable amount of real strife at various times in the history of the nation. They must also recognize that many Americans at such times have *thought* their country cleft between "haves" and "have-nots." But an emphasis on the belief can help to minimize the reality. A psychological approach to conflict enables historians to substitute a schism in the soul for a schism in society. Certainly present-day scholars tend to subjectivize the stresses in American life. Divisions, which the previous generation understood as basic opposition between distinct groups, turn into generalized psychological tensions running through the society as a whole. John Dos Passos's bitter outburst in the 1930's — "all right we are two nations" — becomes the record of a state of mind. An able synthesis of recent research on the age of the great tycoons explains the popular outcries against them as a projection upon one group of responsibility for the rapid industrial changes into which all were thrown.[1]

[1] Samuel Hays, *The Response to Industrialism, 1885–1914* (1957).

Accordingly, when historians today write critically, they scrupulously avoid singling out any one segment of the population for blame. They either criticize the myths and stereotypes that have exaggerated the differences between competing groups; or they attack our uniformities and hanker for more variety. Louis Hartz, in what was perhaps the most outstanding of the new interpretive books, *The Liberal Tradition in America: An Interpretation of American Political Thought Since the Revolution* (1955), worried because we have no other tradition. A regime of freedom has had so unchallenged a sway in America, Hartz contended, that most American political debate has been shadow-boxing. "America must look to its contact with other nations to provide that spark of philosophy, that grain of relative insight that its own history has denied it."

Hartz's own sympathies lay with dissent and diversity. He was clearly disturbed by the soporific intellectual implications of the liberal consensus he described. To take full advantage of the new monolithic approach to American history would require a point of view much more complacent, much less internationally oriented, and much less respectful of the value of ideas. About the time when Hartz was first publishing the early chapters of his book in scholarly journals, Daniel J. Boorstin was making a similar but more drastic revision of American history in a conservative direction. Boorstin wrote in a mood thoroughly in tune with the unphilosophic harmony which he and Hartz were independently appraising.

A slim volume of lectures published in 1953, *The Genius of American Politics*, stated the essence of Boorstin's thesis. Ostensibly, the book concerned a relatively limited problem: why has America produced almost no systematic, fundamental political theory? Boorstin was not the first, of course, to brood over this question. Most American intellectual historians try pretty hard to deny the charge. Boorstin, however, had no apologies to make. He presented this supposed shortcoming as a triumphant demonstration of our success as a nation. With sour, sidelong glances at Europe, he argued that Americans did not need basic theories. Having no deep antagonisms, they could dispense with metaphysical defenses. Never having repudiated their past, they could discuss their problems as lawyers rather than political philosophers. American values had emerged from happy experience; here the "ought" derived from the "is." In the 20th century, he admitted, Americans could no longer take themselves for granted; but let them not therefore try to acquire an ideology and become crusaders. American political thought need only consult the wisdom imbedded in our historic institutions. In spite of the author's contempt for European theory, a bit of Edmund Burke proved useful in the end.

This celebration of the mindlessness of American life came from no provincial lowbrow. Boorstin is one of the very few native students of American history who possesses European culture, and participates in it with easy familiarity. A Rhodes Scholar, a student at various times of the humanities and the biological sciences, a barrister of the Inner Temple, author of a study in English intellectual history, he knows of what he scorns. Yet the view he advanced in *The Genius of American Politics* cannot be dismissed simply as an intellectual's self-hatred — the perversity of a man somehow driven to revulsion from what he had cherished. The book was more than this. It crisply summarized and foreshadowed the new trend of American historiography: the appeal to homogeneity, continuity, and national character. Above all, it swept aside the characteristically progressive approach to American intellectual history as a dialectic of warring ideologies.

Louis Hartz was already doing the same thing in the articles later reprinted in his *Liberal Tradition in America*, though Hartz's appraisal showed the intellectual deficiencies produced by the homogeneity and continuity of American society. Having no such qualms about our supposedly one-track culture, Boorstin went a step beyond Hartz. The latter at least conceded to America one system of ideas; Boorstin admitted none at all.

In their different but overlapping ways, the two books sketched the general outlines of an anti-progressive interpretation of American history. While other scholars were rewriting specific episodes in the story, Boorstin and Hartz revised the plot. Boorstin did not leave the matter there, however. He has now come forth with the first volume of a projected trilogy, ambitiously entitled *The Americans*,[2] which brilliantly elaborates the thesis stated in his previous book. The new volume ranges lightly but learnedly across the Colonial period. Far from being confined to political forms, about which it says relatively little, it has sections on religion, science, the professions, styles of speech, the press, and the art of war. On each of these subjects Boorstin presses the central theme that America flourished by scrapping European blueprints, dissolving the social and intellectual distinctions of European life, and moving toward a homogeneous society of undifferentiated men. The whole work amounts to a running demonstration that a naive practicality enabled Americans from a very early date to unite in a stable way of life, undisturbed by divisive principles.

Let it be said at once that this first volume seems to me a collection of sparkling fragments rather than an enduring monument, a fascinating miscellany rather than a grand achievement. Though clearly the most provocative book of the year in American history, it selects waywardly — even willfully — an assortment of topics for the illustration of a thesis which is both too simple and too elusive to embrace the complex experience of a nation. Since Boorstin's book assumes the continuity of American history, it has none itself. Since it revels in the unsystematic character of American culture, it has little plan or system. It is a series of incisive, original improvisations, which never become a symphony. (From the author's point of view the metaphor may be unfair: symphonies are European, he likes jazz.)

---

[2] *The Americans: The Colonial Experience*, Random House, 434 pp., $6.00. An excerpt from this volume appeared in *Commentary*, October 1958.

Boorstin's ingenuity in turning intellectual limitations into social virtues never flags. Beginning with the Puritans, he promptly deflates the exaggerated claims recently made for their philosophic stature. Having done their creative thinking in Europe, they could concentrate in America on organizing a community. Having a wilderness at their doorstep, they could expel dissenters and so did not need to think out fine-spun theories on toleration. Having the Bible and the English common law to guide them, they could act on precedents instead of losing themselves in utopian abstractions. Whereas other writers have liked the Puritans for their piety or disliked them for their fanaticism, Boorstin loves their sober practicality.

The one American group that is roughly handled in this generally indulgent book is the Quakers. They represent resistance to the American way of life: they refused to bend religious principle to social expediency. Focusing as always on men's attitudes rather than their ideas, Boorstin presents the Quakers as self-righteous dogmatists in their mental habits in spite of the absence of dogma in their formal creed. As missionaries, they panted after martyrdom instead of seeking converts. As rulers of Pennsylvania, they sacrificed some humane legislation and otherwise abdicated responsibility in order to preserve their personal purity. Through these unworldly and un-American proclivities, the Quakers grew insular toward their neighbors and so failed to become "undifferentiated" Americans. To make matters worse, they remained cosmopolitan in spirit and so failed to achieve a "good" kind of insularity, i.e., from Europe. Nothing is said of Quaker leadership in the anti-slavery movement, and almost nothing of their religious toleration, doubtless because these activities were too deep-dyed in principle. Boorstin acclaims toleration in Virginia because it arose there from a practical compromising spirit, not from any theory; he tells us that intolerance in Massachusetts was "useful" in maintaining the unity of the community; but for either tolerance or intolerance as a principle his book has no place.

This is too thoughtful a book to ignore consistently the dangers of the opportunistic and parochial qualities it celebrates. Particularly in the final section, dealing with military institutions, the debits of a short-sighted amateurism are plainly entered. This is also too widely informed a book to rest entirely on the soundness of its general argument. Some of the topics treated here, such as the practice of medicine and of law in the Colonies, have hitherto received the attention of only a few specialists. Although the experts will undoubtedly pick at many of Boorstin's statements, any reader who can control his exasperation at the anti-intellectual bias of the book will find arresting insights into phases of early American life that diverged significantly from English patterns. On the whole, I know of no other book that combines so effectively a grasp of large features of American culture with the intimate, functional detail that makes a social order come to life.

Yet the deeper one goes in this book, the more perplexed one becomes about the criteria it applies in measuring American achievements. The notion that a "pragmatic temper" distinguishes American culture, setting it apart from the bookish and contemplative culture of Europe, is one of our commonest national stereotypes. In 1893 Frederick Jackson Turner lyricized "that practical, inventive turn of mind, quick to find expedients; that masterful grasp of material things, lacking in the artistic but powerful to effect great ends." The same image of America was held by most of the progressive historians whose views Boorstin has clearly undertaken to revise. Is his perspective really much different from that of an old-fashioned liberal pragmatist, devoted to a tough-minded respect for experience?

Often the outlook seems very similar indeed. Like Parrington and Beard, Boorstin associates belles-lettres with an aristocratic society, an oppressive class system, and a stagnant regime of privilege. Like John Dewey' philosophy, Boorstin's history celebrates the empirical thinker-doer who is uninhibited by the formal learning of the past — the early American physician, for example, who was fortunately unschooled in the learned ignorance of European medicine. Like any good pragmatist, Boorstin identifies America with innovation, experiment, and a fluid response to the novelties of experience. His democratic rhetoric sometimes exceeds that of the pragmatists themselves: his image of the American as an "undifferentiated man" harks back to Whitman's glorification of the "divine average."

But the substance of this book bears no consistent relation to these rhetorical overtones. If we look at what Boorstin is really writing about, we find very little evidence of experimentation, no innovations except those which circumstances forced the colonists to make, and almost no interest on the author's part in democracy in any positive sense. One of the best sections of the book discusses the extraordinary standardization that the English language underwent in America under the influence of English literary models. To describe this linguistic uniformity as "the vernacular for equality" helps along one part of the argument of the book, but hardly testifies to innovation or experiment. As for the theme of equality, another section of the book lovingly describes the Virginia aristocracy, whose special virtue according to Boorstin lay in maintaining an English aristocratic pattern in a businesslike and unreflective way. Or, to take another example, consider the section entitled "A Conservative Press." It begins by saying that Colonial printers could serve the general public since they did not need to print good books; it ends by showing that the printers actually served the ruling groups who subsidized and controlled them.

Clearly, the pragmatism that informs this bland approval of American institutions resembles only superficially the fighting faith we used to know. For the true pragmatist — for James and Dewey and all their tribe — intellectuals played a creative role in history. Ideas were precious tools for attaining practical ends. Consequently, being "practical" meant continually and deliberately adapting existing institutions to changing problems. For Boorstin, however, thought does not guide behavior; behavior defines thought, or makes it unnecessary. To him, the practical is the traditional, but for Americans only. Experiment is our hallowed prejudice, our native American orthodoxy. It is our way of conforming to circumstances, and this way seems to Boorstin all the more agreeable because it does not, like European conservatism, enshrine an otiose set of principles. In this view, the pragmatic virtues lose what little consistency they once had and all connection with a larger universe of values. Instead of furnishing any sense of direction at all, they become fossilized exhibits in our national museum. Activity turns into possession, and our pragmatic habits supply a symbol of acquiescence to any circumstances that can be labeled as distinctively American.

How did this larcenous seizure of pragmatic attitudes for the sake of a conservative historiography come about? The author of *The Americans* did not always write with such affection for the expediential and such scorn for theories. In 1948 he published *The Lost World of Thomas Jefferson*, a searching examination of the structure and presumptions of Jeffersonian thought. In that book he took abstract principles very seriously indeed. There he explored the philosophical results of the American pragmatic temper — and found them dangerous. The main emphasis fell on Jefferson's undervaluing of the reflective side of human nature: "the desire to get things done predominated over the need to be at peace with God and oneself." This book maintained that Jefferson's distrust of metaphysics mired him in intellectual confusion, and that his materialistic premises led ultimately to the moral obtuseness of modern American thought. Now, through an extraordinary reversal, the vices imputed to Jefferson have become the virtues of America. With incredible virtuosity, Boorstin has furnished a new map of American history with each spin of his own intellectual compass.

To understand this about-face, it may help to note that both books have a deeply conservative character, though in different ways. *The Lost World* rests on a philosophical conservatism. It might almost have been written by a neo-Thomist, for essentially it accuses the liberal tradition, which stretches from Jefferson to Dewey, of lacking humility in the face of God and history. *The Americans*, on the other hand, grows out of an empirical conservatism, which rejects all ideologies in the name of long-established institutions. The earlier book implies that we need a conservative philosophy. The recent one tells us that we have something much better: a conservative way of life.

The shift from one position to the other reflects, I think, a change of fashion in conservative thinking. During the late 1940's and early 1950's a good many intellectuals with historical interests were trying to define a tradition of conservative thought in America. Historians had for so long canonized a succession of liberal heroes that the first reaction to the new postwar mood was to create a competing pantheon of conservative luminaries. Books by Russell Kirk, Clinton Rossiter,[3] and other intellectual historians revealed that a number of American thinkers had respected original sin and had opposed the official cult of progress. Boorstin's *Lost World* fell in with this effort, though it contributed negatively by exposing the alleged failure of the liberal tradition.

Before long, however, the attempt to establish the value of a European type of conservatism in the American environment petered out; we hear very little of it today. The campaign had too obviously polemical a flavor and too unreal a taste: a tempest in an academic teapot. Great faith was required to believe that men like George Fitzhugh, Orestes Brownson, and Irving Babbitt ever had much profundity or any considerable impact. The really massive conservatism of American businessmen, politicians, and even most intellectuals, as we were discovering, spoke in the common language of the Enlightenment. Liberals and conservatives no longer seemed clearly distinguishable. As the ideological gap between them appeared to shrink, and as a mood of acquiescence spread in all quarters, the need to vindicate a conservative intellectual tradition disappeared. When the liberal ideology lost its cutting edge, conservatives ceased to require an ideological shield.

At this point a historiography that was conservative, without passing as such, won out. Instead of upholding the role of the right in America, it merges the left with the right. It argues that America has ordinarily fused a conservative temper with a liberal state of mind. It displays, therefore, the homogeneity and the continuity of American culture. Writing sympathetically about the intellectual conservatism of today, Eric McKitrick has recently pointed out that it stresses the power of institutions; it has no ideological case to make — except, one might add, a case against ideologies. Boorstin, in his last two books, has joined this school, and, in a sense, has taken the lead.

The advantages of this point of view for American historians have not been slight. It has enabled them to cut through the too easy dualisms of progressive historiography. It is inspiring them to do important and original work in understanding American institutions. They should continue to do so. The conservative frame of reference, however, creates a paralyzing incapacity to deal with the elements of spontaneity, effervescence, and violence in American history. Richard Chase, one of the few literary critics who has successfully defied the current mood, has recently called attention to the wildness and extravagance that characterized the outstanding American novels. Similar qualities have shaken our society, from the Great Awakening of the 18th century to the Great Red Scares of the 20th, in spite of its sturdy institutional structure. They deserve more than patronizing attention.

Moreover, contemporary conservatism has a deadening effect on the his-

---

[3] Russell Kirk, *The Conservative Mind, from Burke to Santayana* (1953); Clinton Rossiter, *Conservatism in America* (1955).

torian's ability to take a conflict of ideas seriously. Either he disbelieves in the conflict itself (Americans having been pretty much of one mind), or he trivializes it into a set of psychological adjustments to institutional change. In either case, the current fog of complacency, flecked with anxiety, spreads backward over the American past.

It is not likely in the near future that many critical scholars will emphasize the polarities that fascinated the great progressive historians, nor is it desirable that they should. Certainly no one contends today that the debate between Jefferson and Hamilton, or between human rights and property rights, frames our intellectual history. But to stand Parrington and Beard on their heads does not solve the problem. American thought has had other dialectical patterns, which the present cult of consensus hides. Above all, perhaps, that cult neutralizes some moral issues that have played a not entirely petty or ignoble part in the history of the United States. To rediscover their grandeur and urgency, historians do not need the categories of Beard and Parrington, and can probably do without their now debased pragmatic philosophy. But we pay a cruel price in dispensing with their deeper values: an appreciation of the crusading spirit, a responsiveness to indignation, a sense of injustice.

31

THE HISTORIAN AS "RADICAL"

In the preceding essay, written in 1959, John Higham complained that in the historical studies of the 1950's, "classes have turned into myths, sections have lost their solidarity, ideologies have vaporized into climates of opinion." He called for a return to "an appreciation of the crusading spirit, a responsiveness to indignation, a sense of injustice," that had characterized the historiography of the past. As the next article by Irwin Unger demonstrates, the decade of the 1960's was to see Higham's wish fulfilled (though not in the way he envisioned or called for). An increasing number of younger historians manifested a deep sense of impatience with and indignation toward the work that Higham branded with the term "consensus" history. Unfortunately, they have not yet even begun to displace that historiography with a coherent body of their own work.

Whatever their faults, the historians of the 1950's (who of course continued to write throughout the 1960's as well) asked new questions, established categories of their own, and borrowed rather heavily at times from the work of social scientists. This has been far less true of the historians of whom Unger writes. Revisionism in history, as in other disciplines, is a natural and healthy process. Without it there would be no progress and no change. But revisionism to be healthy must be natural; it must flow naturally from the historian's own research and not become an end in itself. When a scholar rubs too hard and too consciously against the theses of his predecessors, he risks the danger of becoming enmeshed in them. This, as Lee Benson has shown, was what happened for a long time to the critics of Charles Beard. In their zeal to revise Beard's arguments, they became trapped by his questions, his categories, his type of evidence. (See Lee Benson, *Turner and Beard: American Historical Writing Reconsidered* [1960].)

To an unfortunate degree, this is what has happened to many of the historians Unger writes of. They have been too consciously revisionist and in the process have been trapped too easily by the historical categories of the past; they have asked too few questions that are really new and conducive to the opening up of doors that have remained closed because no one has been able to see them; they have not yet utilized with any degree of imagination or insight the vast body of knowledge about human nature and human action that scholars in other disciplines have made available to historians. As Unger notes, thus far their work has been a work of rebuttal; insofar as they constitute a historical "school" at all it has been one defined by their dislikes and their indignation rather than by any innovative theses or methodology. Most striking in this respect is the general failure of these historians to follow up their insistent demands for more history of "the powerless, the inarticulate, the poor," with any solid work of their own. They have identified a vacuum and angrily blamed their elders for creating it, but, with such notable exceptions as Stephan Thernstrom, they have done little themselves to fill it.

For all its sensitivity and insight, Unger's analysis does contain some weaknesses. First of all, as Unger himself admits, he tends to use the rubric "New Left" a bit loosely. A number of the historians he names hardly fit the basic contours of his analysis. More importantly, although Unger does state in the subtitle of his article that he is discussing only "Some Recent Trends in United States Historiography," he does not emphasize this forcefully enough in the body of the article itself. It should be stressed, then, that the historians he discusses have by no means set the tone of the historiography of the 1960's. Throughout that decade the work of the majority of younger historians (including Unger himself) was not dominated by the need to disprove the historical writing of the 1950's or the desire to create a "usable" past. In the final analysis, this is perhaps the saddest thing of all about the work of those historians who do fit into Unger's category: in their preoccupation with the work of their predecessors and in their anger at what they call the historical "establishment," they have often overlooked the very important work of those of their contemporaries who, without making a great deal of noise about what needs to be done, have busied themselves doing it.

Irwin Unger is Professor of History at New York University.

The "New Left" and American History: Some Recent Trends in United States Historiography

Irwin Unger

It is impossible not to notice that there is a new political Left in America. The struggle for civil rights, while endorsed by liberals and "moderates," is largely led by young people of radical commitment. The student protests on university campuses derive their fire from young men and women who reject much of American life in the 1960's. Rent strikers, peace

Reprinted by permission of the author from the *American Historical Review*, 72 (July 1967), 1237–63.

marchers, and Vietnam protectors — all are deeply skeptical of the affluent society. Almost everywhere throughout the country, but especially where masses of young people are thrown together — most notably, of course, at the universities — new organizations, new journals, new movements are emerging, dedicated to restoring a radical voice to the contention of ideas in the United States.[1]

The average newspaper reader knows the New Left for its activism. But it is not surprising that a movement that enlists so many college students, and particularly graduate students in the humanities and social sciences, should also have a reflective side. While consistently pragmatic in their day-to-day activities, the various New Left groups have begun to feel the need for theory and analysis. Their experience has already given birth to a New Left sociology, economics, and political science.[2] They are now beginning to create a new, radical history, particularly a new, radical American history.

To understand this development, one must recall what has happened in American historical writing in the last two decades. As described by John Higham in his important article, "The Cult of the 'American Consensus,'" which appeared in 1959,[3] certain trends were already clear. Snce the 1940's something striking and significant had happened to the intellectual climate that surrounded the historians of America. They had abandoned the notion of struggle as the central theme of our past. Until the postwar years historians had acknowledged and indeed had emphasized the existence of social strife in the United States. The American past, like the past of other nations, seemed a series of confrontations between antagonistic and competing economic and class interest groups. American colonial history disclosed a sharp battle of yeoman and provincial nabob. The Revolution was both a

---

[1] By now descriptions of the New Left have become so numerous that it would be a formidable task to supply a reasonably complete list. The following, however, are among the best: Richard Armstrong, "The Explosive Revival of the Far Left," *Saturday Evening Post*, May 8, 1965, 27–39; various authors, *Partisan Review*, XXXII (Spring, Summer, Fall 1965), 183–205, 341–72, 526–42; *Dissent*, IX (Spring 1962), 129 ff.; Irving Howe, "New Styles in 'Leftism,'" *ibid.*, XII (Summer 1965), 295–323; Staughton Lynd, "The New Radicals and 'Participatory Democracy,'" *ibid.*, 324–33. The recent book by Philip A. Luce, as the author admits, is not a discussion of the broad spectrum New Left but rather of its Trotskyite and Communist extreme as represented by such groups as the Progressive Labor party and the DuBois Clubs. (See Luce, *The New Left* [New York, 1966].) A recent anthology of New Left writings, Paul Jacobs and Saul Landau, *The New Radicals: A Report with Documents* (New York, 1966), begins with a long and useful introduction by the editors. Finally, see Jack Newfield, *A Prophetic Minority* (New York, 1966).

[2] The outstanding New Left sociologist is, of course, C. Wright Mills. Robert Theobald and Ben Seligman may be said to represent a New Left mood in economics. For a sign of a New Left political science highly critical of the predominant "abstracted empiricists" or "behavioralists" of the discipline, see the review by Walter Batya of Frederick Barghoorn's *The Soviet Cultural Offensive* in *Studies on the Left*, II (1961), 90 ff.; and the article by James Peters, "Ideology and United States Political Scientists," *Science and Society*, XXIX (Spring 1965), 192–216.

[3] John Higham, "The Cult of the 'American Consensus,'" *Commentary*, XXVII (Feb. 1959), 93–100.

struggle over "home rule" and over "who should rule at home." The Constitution was a class document. Battles between Hamiltonians and Jeffersonians, Whigs and Jacksonians, were struggles between the privileged orders and the commonalty. The Civil War was a collision of an industrial North and an agrarian South. And so it went: through the age of the robber barons, the war with Spain, Progressivism, the Great Depression, the New Deal. The binding theme of our history was class conflict, or at least an American version of it.[4] The United States, then, was not "exceptional." The fine details of our history were different, perhaps, but at heart the American past was similar to the European past. The one plausible alternative to the class conflict view of American history — Frederick Jackson Turner's frontier thesis — by the 1930's had been thoroughly demolished, it seemed, by the combined attack of Marxists and "progressives." [5]

As described by Higham, the new history of Louis Hartz, Richard Hofstadter, Samuel Hays, David Potter, and Daniel Boorstin seemed to assert either that there had been no struggle in our past or that the struggle had been generated not by some real but by some imagined injustice. Rather than cataclysmic change, abrupt, angry, cacophonous, American history had been almost sedate. Americans had disagreed with one another, of course, but not irreconcilably or over the basic issues of property and political democracy. The experience of transplanted Europeans with a "new country" of abundant, unexploited resources had been fused with Lockean liberalism, engendering a mood of pragmatic moderation in all but a few American souls. The postwar generation of American historians had concluded, Higham wrote, that continuity, contentment, and "consensus" characterized the history of the nation; all else was either the illusion of the historian or that of his protagonists.[6]

---

[4] For the best brief description of the "progressive" school of American historical writing that flourished from about 1910 to shortly after World War II, see John Higham *et al.*, *History* (Englewood Cliffs, N.J., 1965), pt. III, Chap. 111.

[5] For the attack of the Marxists, who preferred a class struggle interpretation of the American past, see Louis Hacker, "Sections or Classes," *Nation*, CXXXVII (July 26, 1933). For a parallel assault by old-line progressives who, like the Marxists, found a class conflict view of our history congenial, see Fred A. Shannon, "The Homestead Act and the Labor Surplus," *American Historical Review*, XLI (July 1936), 637–51; Charles A. Beard, "The Frontier in American History," *New Republic*, XCVII (Feb. 1939), 359–62; Carter Goodrich and Sol Davidson, "The Wage-Earner and the Westward Movement," *Political Science Quarterly*, L (June 1935), 161–85, LI (Mar. 1936), 61–116. For a good brief review of the changing fortunes of the Turner thesis, see Gene M. Gressley, "The Turner Thesis: A Problem in Historiography," *Agricultural History*, XXXII (Oct. 1958), 227–49. For the attack of the 1930's, see esp. 232 ff.

[6] Higham, "Cult of the 'American Consensus,'" *passim*. See also Robin Brooks, "Class Distinction, Then and Now," a review of Staughton Lynd's *Anti-Federalism in Dutchess County, New York*, in *Studies on the Left*, IV (Winter 1964), 74–75. Higham does not mention Oscar Handlin who, it is now clear, has been immensely influential, both through his own work and his students', in developing the post-Beardian canon. For a mature expression of Handlin's views, see his volume *The Americans: A New History of the People of the United States* (Boston, 1963).

Since 1959 the list of "consensus" historians has lengthened considerably. For the colonial era one might cite Clarence Ver Steeg's *The Formative Years*. For the period of the Confederation we not only have Robert E. Brown's *Middle-Class Democracy and the Revolution in Massachusetts* and *Charles Beard and the Constitution* but also Forrest MacDonald's *We the People* and *E Pluribus Unum*. For the early national period there are the books of Paul Goodman and Noble Cunningham. For the Jackson era we have had, since 1959, the work of Lee Benson, Bray Hammond, Walter E. Hugins. For the Civil War period there are David Donald, Eric McKitrick, Stanley Elkins, and Stanley Coben. For the late nineteenth and early twentieth centuries we have Robert Wiebe's *Businessmen and Reform*, and, most recently, David J. Rothman's *Politics and Power*.[7]

Such an assemblage of authors immediately suggests the inadequacy of Higham's description. With a larger sample before us, we can now see that while the new postwar historians include consensusites pure and simple, they also include those who, in rejecting the dualisms of their predecessors, prefer to replace them with a pluralistic view of the American past. Instead of a simple dialogue the historical stage presents a complex and tumultuous crowd scene. It is also clearer now that social psychology and the other social sciences have profoundly influenced this complex view of the past. Higham believed in 1959 that the behavioral approach enabled the new generation of historians to obscure conflict in America by "psychologizing" it. Men thought they were exploited and victimized when they really were just emotionally disturbed. While it is true, as Higham noted, that the postwar historians are impressed by the stability of American society and by our broad agreement over fundamentals, we now know that many of them take social conflict quite seriously. But they define conflict more broadly than did the

---

[7] The full citations for these works are as follows: Clarence Ver Steeg, *The Formative Years, 1607–1763* (New York, 1964); Robert E. Brown, *Middle-Class Democracy and the Revolution in Massachusetts, 1691–1780* (Ithaca, N.Y., 1955), and *Charles Beard and the Constitution: A Critical Analysis of "An Economic Interpretation of the Constitution"* (Princeton, N.J., 1956); Forrest MacDonald, *We the People: The Economic Origins of the Constitution* (Chicago, 1958), and *E Pluribus Unum: The Formation of the American Republic, 1776–1790* (Boston, 1965); Paul Goodman, *The Democratic-Republicans of Massachusetts: Politics in a Young Republic* (Cambridge, Mass., 1964); Noble Cunningham, *The Jeffersonian Republicans: The Formation of Party Organization, 1789–1801* (Chapel Hill, N.C., 1957); Lee Benson, *The Concept of Jacksonian Democracy: New York as a Test Case* (Princeton, N.J., 1961); Bray Hammond, *Banks and Politics in America from the Revolution to the Civil War* (Princeton, N.J., 1957); Walter E. Hugins, *Jacksonian Democracy and the Working Class: A Study of the New York Workingmen's Movement, 1829–1837* (Stanford, Calif., 1960); David Donald, *Charles Sumner and the Coming of the Civil War* (New York, 1960); Eric McKitrick, *Andrew Johnson and Reconstruction* (Chicago, 1960); Stanley Elkins, *Slavery: A Problem in American Institutional and Intellectual Life* (Chicago, 1959); Stanley Coben, "Northeastern Business and Radical Reconstruction: A Re-examination," *Mississippi Valley Historical Review*, XLVI (June 1959); Robert H. Wiebe, *Businessmen and Reform: A Study of the Progressive Movement* (Cambridge, Mass., 1962); and David J. Rothman, *Politics and Power: The United States Senate, 1869–1901* (Cambridge, Mass., 1966). Needless to say, this list is not complete.

"progressive" historians of the previous generation. Besides the traditional haves versus have-nots in their many separate guises, we now have Catholic versus Protestant, dry versus wet, rural versus urban, white versus black, old versus young, ins versus outs. These are real conflicts, but they are psychologically or socially defined and open to the imputation that they are merely sick phantoms in the mind. We take seriously the man who finds himself in an economic vise; we tend to despise or pity the man who suffers from status anxieties. Somehow *Angst* seems less real than hunger.

It is easy to see why this shift in the analysis of conflict reduces the emotional charge of past historical movements. Not only does it suggest that all the discontented are mere malingerers, but it is also difficult to identify heroes and villains. If nothing else, both the guilty and the injured in a pluralistic society often turn out to be but a small part of some larger group. Businessmen can no longer be condemned as a whole. They disagree among themselves and can scarcely be held responsible for anything collectively. Farmers are no longer just farmers. They are north-eastern truck gardeners, or Wisconsin dairy farmers, or Kansas wheat-growers, or southern cotton planters, and they do not all suffer the same fate at the same time.

These ambiguities inevitably encourage a kind of neutrality and detachment that are congenial to the use of new statistical techniques borrowed from the sister social sciences. No longer intent on proving a case for "the people," historians can subject all the old conclusions to the dispassionate test of social statistics. There is no inherent reason why radicals cannot employ the same tools, but so far, with an occasional exception, the fascination with numbers has been the province of the postwar, "middle generation." Perhaps the young men of the Left fear that the figures will not bear them out. Certainly in American economic history the work of the new "cliometricians" has given comfort to "conservative" interpretations of such diverse issues as the origins of the American Revolution, the plight of the late nineteenth-century farmer, and the culpability of the robber barons.[8]

It would be a serious mistake to insist that there is absolute unanimity in either approach or conclusions among the postwar generation of historians. To some degree they are all "post-Beardians" since they are all trying to escape the Beardian matrix which imprisoned American history in the first four decades of this century. But they go beyond Beard in a number of dis-

---

[8] On the Revolution, see Robert P. Thomas, "A Quantitative Approach to the Study of the Effects of British Imperial Policy upon Colonial Welfare: Some Preliminary Findings," *Journal of Economic History*, XXV (Dec. 1965), 615–38; on the post–Civil War farmer, see Allan Bogue, *Money at Interest: The Farm Mortgage on the Middle Border* (Ithaca, N.Y., 1955); Leslie E. Decker, *Railroad Lands and Politics: The Taxation of Railroad Land Grants, 1865–1897* (Providence, R.I., 1964); on at least one group of robber barons, see Robert W. Fogel, *The Union Pacific Railroad: A Case Study in Premature Enterprise* (Baltimore, Md., 1960); for an overview of the whole "cliometric" literature, see Douglass North, *Growth and Welfare in the American Past: A New Economic History* (Englewood Cliffs, N.J., 1966).

tinct ways, and the label is at best only moderately useful as a descriptive term. Nevertheless, despite the difficulties of definition, Higham in 1959 clearly detected the beginnings of an important and substantial change in the writing of American history, and it is this change that is now beginning to generate a reaction among the young men of the Left.

It may now seem clearer what there is about the postwar history that antagonizes the new radicals. They are not primarily offended by the rejection of "historical materialism," the keystone of traditional Marxist historiography. A few Marxian "Old Leftists" like Herbert Aptheker, Philip Foner, and Harvey O'Connor are still writing history. But the New Left historians are not the captives of an official ideology.[9] We must "*Americanize the radical program* by bringing historically native radicalism up to date," writes Harold Cruse in *Studies on the Left*, a major forum of the New Left history.

> We do this by accepting what we need from the "Marxist method" insofar as the method applies to American social history. . . . While we allow that historical laws are universally applicable, these laws operate according to the dictates of different social ingredients in different places. We accept the fact that the Marxian revolution *could have happened* at a certain time given the proper leadership and impetus.[10]

When, as in the case of William Appleman Williams, the New Left historians make much of Marx, it is more often the early "soft" Marx, who speaks of "alienation," than the "hard" Marx of *Das Kapital*, with its class struggle and progressive "immiserization of the proletariat." [11]

Beard is a different case. The New Left has joined an older group of historians to perpetuate the Beardian vision.[12] In direct proportion as he has become a false prophet of the new postwar history, Beard has become the Moses of the New Left.[13] Williams, a man who actually owes little to Beard — except, perhaps, on recent American foreign policy — feels compelled to announce in his bellicose style, "it . . . seems appropriate, in view of all the bigoted and career building attacks, acts of purification in the form of mis-

---

[9] Indeed, they are sometimes embarrassed by the excesses of doctrinaire party-liners like Aptheker. See, e.g., Joseph A. Ernst, "Historians and the Colonial Era," *Studies on the Left*, I (Winter 1960), 79–84.

[10] Harold Cruse, "Americanizing the Radical Program," *ibid.*, III (Winter 1963), 69.

[11] Cf. Eugene Genovese, "William Appleman Williams on Marx and America," *ibid.*, VI (Jan.–Feb. 1966), 76.

[12] As, e.g., C. Vann Woodward, Matthew Josephson, and Jackson T. Main.

[13] Other gurus of the New Left include Paul Goodman, the social thinker and novelist, Herbert Marcuse, and Barrington Moore, Jr. All these men have helped form the New Left's vision of recent America, but none — except perhaps Moore — seem as yet to have had much effect on the way the New Left writes history.

representation, and even smart-alec criticism by supposed aristocrats, to acknowledge formally my respect for and debt to Charles Austin Beard." [14] Yet much of the homage is ceremonial. At their best, the New Left historians feel free to diverge from both masters. When they do, the results are often interesting.

It is not, then, uncritical loyalty to a particular master that makes the New Left bridle at the postwar history. It is rather what they perceive as the tone, commitment, and power of the post-Beardian historians that annoys and angers the young radicals. The most obvious of these characteristics is, of course, the imputed political conservatism of their elders. The new history is, so it seems to the young Leftists, history at the service of an elitist and aristocratic definition of society, and the "American Celebration." Until recently, notes Arnold Rogow, the American intellectual's "view of the common man was essentially Jeffersonian." Now the common man is being "muckraked," and the older liberal tradition is being repudiated as the intellectuals adopt the New Conservatism.[15] To Norman Pollack the new history represents the "treason of the intellectuals." Frightened by Joseph McCarthy's witch-hunts, they cravenly retreated from the exposed Left to a safe Right.[16]

Equally irritating to the New Left, though less widely advertised, are the supposed institutional power and influence of the post-Beardians. Intellectually complacent, often supercilious, they are, we are told, firmly implanted in the prestigious eastern private universities, where they form an academic establishment capable of using its professional power to proscribe dissent and encourage conformity.[17] Indeed, there is among the young radical academicians a sense of persecution that, since it is largely anticipatory, seems excessive. Convinced that they are struggling against a pernicious power elite, they see in their professional lives what they are convinced obtains in the flow of American history itself. The conspiracies against the people by the interests find a parallel in the efforts of the historical establishment to suppress the radical voice.

But perhaps the worst offense of the postwar history is its failure to provide the New Left with a "usable past." The charge like the term is

---

14 William Appleman Williams, *The Contours of American History* (Cleveland, 1961), 490.

15 Arnold A. Rogow, "The Revolt against Social Equality," *Dissent*, IV (Autumn 1957), 369–70. For a complaint from an older Populistic liberal and Beardian, see C. Vann Woodward, "The Populist Heritage and the Intellectuals," *American Scholar*, XXIX (Winter 1959–60), 55–72.

16 Norman Pollack, "Fear of Man: Populism, Authoritarianism and the Historian," *Agricultural History*, XXXIX (Apr. 1965), 59–67.

17 See the remarks of Richard Drinnon in an interview by Peter Loewenberg in *Studies on the Left*, II (No. 1, 1961), 79 ff. For an attack on the academic "establishment" which transcends the discipline of history, see the prospectus, "The Radicalism of Disclosure," *ibid.*, I (Fall 1959), 2–4.

ambiguous. "Usable past" implies in the first place a concern for historical guidelines, an interest that the New Left surely shares with much of mankind. At this point it would be well to recall that the New Left is programmatic and activist; it is the product not of a great book or a great prophet but of the social maladjustments of our day. Many of the young scholars who have joined the recent attack against the historiographic trends of the past decade have been men living and working very much in a radical and dissenting present. As historians and radicals it is natural that they should seek wisdom in the past. Staughton Lynd, a talented New Left historian, has been quite explicit about the need for a usable radical past to provide direction for the new radical community, which otherwise appears doomed, he declares, to rehash problems its predecessors have already settled.[18]

But the concept of a usable past also suggests that history may serve as a political weapon. To the young Leftists the most obvious partisan use of history is to domesticate radicalism in America. In all fairness, it must be said that this is largely a counterattack. The Right has always insisted that radicalism is un-American, a foreign import embraced only by those who have no roots in the native culture or who have lost contact with those roots. But until quite recently the conservative claim has not been academically respectable, for from about 1910 until the late 1940's the giants of the profession devoted their scholarly energies to exhibiting the long and honorable record of insurgency and dissent on the frontier, on the farms, in the mining camps and factory towns. Now, some of the leading scholars of the nation have apparently given the old charge intellectual sanction of an impressive order. There is no native American radicalism, they say — not one that any balanced man would wish to acknowledge. Radicalism has always been an exotic import, ill-suited to American circumstances, and hence deserving of the isolation and failure it has always suffered. The challenge is clearly fundamental. If there has been no true dissent in America; if a general consensus over capitalism, race relations, and expansionism has prevailed in the United States; if such dissent as has existed has been crankish and sour, the product not of a maladjusted society but of maladjusted men — then American history may well be monumentally irrelevant for contemporary radicalism. As scholars and social critics, simultaneously, the young New Left historians of course find this conclusion impossible to accept.

Having dismissed the new postwar history, what do the young men of the Left hope to put in its place? It is not possible to say in a simple, categorical way. The young radicals know what they reject, and in fact

---

[18] Staughton Lynd, "Socialism, the Forbidden Word," *ibid.*, III (Summer 1963), 14 ff. At the same time, however, Lynd was agreeing with N. Gordon Levin, Jr., that there was little if any native American radicalism. See Lynd's reply to Levin's letter in *Commentary*, XXXV (Jan. 1963), 74–75. For what Lynd does see as radical in the American past, see below, pp. 732–33.

their dislikes are often what most satisfactorily defines them.[19] They are not, however, as clear about what they accept. Dissensions within the New Left history are as general and intense as disagreements among the socialists, anarchists, pacifists, existentialists, and Neo-Populists who compose the New Left movement. It is a panorama as complex as the pluralistic history the young radicals would refute.

There is indeed an ambitious attempt at a general synthesis of America's past by a New Left historian of good credentials,[20] *The Contours of American History* by Professor William A. Williams of the University of Wisconsin, but unfortunately this interesting book fails as a chart to the emerging radical history. The major theme of *The Contours* is the persistent tension in America between the two world views of commonwealth and individualism. The first, identified with "mercantilism," is the very womb out of which the American nation emerged. As used by Williams, "mercantilism" must not be confused with the selfish, retrograde economic doctrine of the standard textbook discussions. It means a benevolent paternalism displayed by an enlightened class of gentlemen — the "gentry" — who placed the interest of the whole community above that of any single group including themselves. While not without its serious limitations, most notably its recourse to foreign expansion to solve domestic problems, mercantilism represents the benign side of the American tradition. Opposing it, and virtually without redeeming qualities, is "laissez-nous faire," and, what is its essential synonym, "individualism." To Williams this world view is socially corrosive, fostering competition rather than cooperation, anomy rather than community, profits rather than justice.

This may seem to be predictable Leftist dualism and may suggest at first glance the basis for a reconstructed radical history. Actually it gives aid and comfort to the enemy. Williams offers little to the New Left. It is quite clear from *The Contours* that few Americans ever questioned the sacrosanct nature of private property or ever could see much beyond more property or more geographic expansion as the solution for internal problems. Elements of American society did indeed differ in the depth of their social insight and the degree of their humane sympathies, but except for the small and impotent groups of socialists at the end of the nineteenth century, they

[19] This negative quality of almost all the New Left intellectuals has been noted by Michael Walzer, a young Leftist historian of English Puritanism. (See Walzer, "The Young Radicals: A Symposium," *Dissent*, IX [Spring 1962], 129 ff.)

[20] What constitutes "good credentials" for the New Left is exceedingly hard to say. Members of the New Left do not carry party cards; nor do they always acknowledge their affiliations. In selecting my New Left historians I have used a combination of personal knowledge, self-identification, internal evidence, and a sort of historical dead reckoning. The system, I am certain, is fallible. Some of those I have included among the Left will, perhaps, object to being so labeled. On the other hand others, surely, will be chagrined at being left out. Nevertheless I do not believe my imperfect definitions vitiate my conclusions.

all suffered from the same fatal weakness of social imagination. In a word, though Williams can scarcely intend it, we are back at consensus! [21]

In fact *The Contours* proves a constant embarrassment to the younger radical scholars. Williams not only accepts the broad theme of an American consensus; he also accepts a surprising number of the specific judgments of the post-Beardian history. He agrees with Brown and MacDonald that support for the Revolution and the Constitution transcended class lines.[22] He accepts the thesis of Hammond and Hofstadter that the Jacksonians were aggressive capitalist enterprisers.[23] He agrees that the abolitionists were often difficult and unreasonable men who failed to understand the complexities of race adjustment.[24] He acknowledges the dark side of Populism, although he is critical of what he considers the supercilious tone of its recent detractors.[25] To Williams, Franklin Roosevelt is a man who cherished power for its own sake; Hoover, a true progressive in the mercantilist tradition.[26] The book, moreover, is saturated with old-fashioned philosophical idealism. Ideas, not interests, are what count in history, for mercantilism, at least, is no mere rationalization of individual or class advantage. Derived from Biblical moralism, it is tough and autonomous with the power to blunt and tame the acquisitive instincts.[27] This is scarcely the stuff out of which to construct a new radical history, and with regret several of the young Leftist historians have conceded as much.[28]

If we stopped at this point, it would be difficult to see in what way it is possible to consider Williams a radical historian at all. His credentials derive, I think, from two major themes of *The Contours*. The first is his radical indictment of individualism and his extravagant praise of the proto-collectivism of the "gentry." In the absence of a viable socialist tradition the "mercantilism" of the gentry must satisfy Williams' yearning to discover virtue in the American past. The second is Williams' treatment of American foreign policy. Here the young Leftists find strong support for their conviction of America's total depravity. From the very outset, according to Wil-

---

[21] This implicit acceptance of consensus in *Contours* has been noticed by Higham, among others. See Higham's review of the book in *Studies on the Left*, II (No. 2, 1961), 73–76. Michael Wreszin, another young radical historian, observes the same phenomenon in Richard Drinnon's biography of Emma Goldman (*Rebel in Paradise: A Biography of Emma Goldman* [Chicago, 1961]). Drinnon's saving grace, Wreszin notes, is that unlike the conservative historians, while noting the consensus, he deplores it. (See Wreszin, "Heresy in Paradise: A Partisan for Emma," *Studies on the Left*, IV [Winter 1964], 80.)

[22] Williams, *Contours*, 105 ff., 138 ff.

[23] *Ibid.*, 222 ff. Indeed, Jackson's victory in 1828 is viewed as something of a national disaster.

[24] *Ibid.*, 250–55. He even defends the Old South from abolitionist attack! (*Ibid.*, 281–82).

[25] *Ibid.*, 333–38.

[26] *Ibid.*, 440, 445.

[27] *Ibid.*, 32 ff.

[28] See, e.g., Staughton Lynd's review of Williams' *Contours* in *Science and Society*, XXVII (Spring 1963), 227 ff.

liams, the United States has been an expansionist nation, preying on its weaker neighbors, whether the precivilized Indian tribes or the weaker national states and decrepit empires on its borders. This expansionism is a strangely persuasive mirror image of Turner's frontier thesis. Rather than a succession of new opportunities, each American frontier was a new evasion. It was not democracy that renewed itself in each new "West"; it was capitalism, and American foreign policy was merely the instrument of this evasive westward thrust.[29]

But neither mercantilism nor expansionism provides a historical framework for the New Left equal to class struggle for the old. In the end *The Contours* is too personal and idiosyncratic. Williams is an angry dissenter who, despite his announced faith in a cooperative society, is beholden to no man for his historical vision, or, one is sometimes tempted to say, for his historical facts. But still the radical scholars listen to Williams. He may supply little they can use for understanding America's domestic affairs, but he most emphatically speaks to them on the history of American foreign policy. *The Contours* and Williams' specific works in diplomatic history [30] have had a powerful impact on a group of young diplomatic historians, many of whom have worked with him or under him at the University of Wisconsin.

The most successful of these younger scholars is Walter LaFeber,[31] whose book, *The New Empire*, won the Albert J. Beveridge Award in 1962.[32] LaFeber is a sophisticated and urbane historian. Yet he is willing to make his radical philosophical stand quite explicit. In a 1962 book review he praises the tradition of Beard and Arthur B. Darling in American diplomatic history and assails those historians who "since 1945 . . . have been preoccupied with knifing Beard with one hand and using the other hand to pen caricatures of a unique unblemished Republic which became a world empire with little conscious human intervention." [33] The thesis of *The New Empire* is that America's venture into imperialism in the 1890's was neither

29 This point, implied in *Contours*, is made explicitly in Williams' latest book, *The Great Evasion: An Essay on the Contemporary Relevance of Karl Marx and on the Wisdom of Admitting the Heretic into the Dialogue about America's Future* (Chicago, 1964), esp. the introduction.

30 E.g., William Appleman Williams, *American-Russian Relations, 1781–1947* (New York, 1952), *The Tragedy of American Diplomacy* (Cleveland, 1959), *The United States, Cuba and Castro* (New York, 1962).

31 LaFeber was actually a student of Professor Fred Harvey Harrington at Wisconsin, although he acknowledges that he is deeply indebted to Williams for instruction. (See Walter LaFeber, *The New Empire: An Interpretation of American Expansion, 1860–1898* [Ithaca, N.Y., 1963], 428.)

32 That it should win this prestigious award casts some doubt either on the hostility of the establishment toward the New Left or on their academic influence.

33 Walter LaFeber, "The Conscious Creation of a 'World Wide Empire,'" a review of Richard Warner Van Alstyne's *The Rising American Empire*, in *Studies on the Left*, II (No. 3, 1962), 103 ff.

a historical accident nor a new departure. It was the culmination of a process dating at least to the 1850's or 1860's, the roots of which were primarily economic. Post–Civil War American imperialism sprang from the need of manufacturers for raw materials and markets. It was not absent-mindedness that led to the war with Spain and the annexation of Hawaii, the Philippines, and Puerto Rico; it was the demands of businessmen.

LaFeber does not approve of American expansionism, but he is not a crude polemicist. His imperialist businessmen and policy makers are "responsible, conscientious men who accepted the economic and social realities of their day . . . and . . . were unafraid to strike out on new and uncharted paths in order to create what they sincerely hoped would be a better nation and a better world." [34] Several other members of the Wisconsin school of diplomatic history are both less temperate and less convincing than LaFeber. John W. Rollins, in an essay on the anti-imperialists and American foreign policy in the twentieth century, reaches the tortured conclusion that even most of those who balked at overt American colonialism in the years since the Spanish-American War have been expansionists and imperialists. They may not have endorsed American occupation and control, but they have endorsed American economic penetration, and this is the same thing. Free trade, foreign investment, Point Four aid — all, presumably, have been tools of American hegemony.[35] Lloyd Gardner examines the foreign policy of the New Deal and concludes that following the disastrous economic setback of 1937–1938, "the New Deal forsook viable domestic remedies and readied itself for the pursuit of . . . world frontiers . . . as its solution to the crisis of the 1930's." In the end Gardner comes very close to attributing America's entrance into World War II, once cheered by the Left as the defense of democracy and freedom, to the reluctance of the Axis Powers to accept American demands for "liberal trade and the Open Door." [36] New Left revisionism could not be better designed to antagonize the generation that waged the crusade against fascism!

There is, in the New Left diplomatic history, an interesting rehabilitation, explicit or implied, of isolationism. Williams himself seems to be its source. By denying the serious practice of isolation by the United States he makes

[34] LaFeber, New Empire, ix.

[35] John W. Rollins, "The Anti-Imperialists and Twentieth Century American Foreign Policy," Studies on the Left, III (No. 1, 1962), 9 ff. This paper was the subject of a symposium and is followed by comments by Harold Baron and Thomas J. McCormick, who seem to function as a cheering section rather than as critics.

[36] It is obvious that part of the New Left attack on Roosevelt's foreign policy derives from Charles Beard's influential work, President Roosevelt and the Coming of the War, 1941: A Study in Appearances and Realities (New York, 1948). Gardner refuses, however, to accept the most extreme of Beard's charges, that Roosevelt engineered United States entrance into World War II for party purposes. (See Lloyd Gardner, "From New Deal to New Frontier, 1937–1941," Studies on the Left, I [Fall 1959], 29 ff.). In Gardner's recent book, Economic Aspects of New Deal Diplomacy (Madison, Wis., 1964), the polemical tone is still more muted.

the few sincere advocates of minding our own business into rare, heroic souls.[37] Beard's obscure 1934 attack on American intervention in European affairs, *The Open Door at Home*, has become an object of veneration among the Wisconsin school.[38] They give isolationist Progressives like William Borah credit for rare prescience in foretelling the dangers of the "garrison state, the weight of military costs, the penetration of American economic power into almost every sphere upon the globe, and the loss of liberty at home and abroad."[39]

The message in all this is clear. America's recent aggressive and provocative foreign policy is not the response of the moment; our reaction to world problems after 1945 was merely the latest term of an American tradition of aggrandizement that commenced with John Smith. From first to last, cupidity has been the governing principle of our relations with strangers, and we must not expect more of our acquisitive, capitalist society.

In its strictures on America's earlier foreign affairs the New Left is obviously projecting onto history its present cold war fears and frustrations. The pattern of present-mindedness persists in its view of America's domestic past. Just as they would transform the country's relations to the non-Western world, the young radicals are committed to reorienting American society itself, and nothing fascinates them more than their radical predecessors and the movements they inspired and led.[40]

As we have seen, the radical attempt to recover America's "progressive" past seems to serve a number of purposes simultaneously. It satisfies a natural curiosity about radical antecedents and represents an understandable quest for direction. But more important, and less disinterested, the New Left's concern with the nation's reformist past is an attempt to establish its own legitimacy.

This search for a historical sanction is the main concern of Pollack, although at times it might appear that his real purpose is to dethrone the leading representatives of the "establishment." Leaving aside this strong acerbic aspect of Pollack's work, we find that his main point is that there has indeed been a viable radical tradition native to America, a tradition associated with agrarian insurgency, which reached its apogee during the Populist revolt. Far from fleeing the industrial realities of the day, as has been suggested by Oscar Handlin, Hofstadter, and others, the Populists

37 Williams, *Tragedy of American Diplomacy*, esp. Chap. iv.
38 See, e.g., Gardner, "From New Deal to New Frontier," 30.
39 Orde S. Pinckney, "William E. Borah: Critic of American Foreign Policy," *Studies on the Left*, I (No. 3, 1960), 48 ff., esp. 61.
40 Only this intense preoccupation will explain the recent publication of Sidney Lens's *Radicalism in America* (New York, 1966). This book is an unimaginative narration of liberal-radical activities in America by an editor of the New Left journal *Liberation*. It might have been written by Vernon Parrington in the 1920's, though it is endorsed by Lynd and is clearly intended to teach the young Left something of their predecessors.

realistically diagnosed the problems of emerging industrialism and realistically prescribed for them. Neither rural xenophobes nor ignorant paranoids but perceptive radical humanitarians, they produced a critique of capitalist society still valid today. Indeed their analysis of American industrial capitalism closely paralleled Marx's dissection of early European industrial society, which suggests to Pollack the "extremely exciting prospect" that the "Populist experience might well challenge a basic proposition in historical writing — the uniqueness of America." True, contemporary American Marxists opposed the Populists, but only because the Marxists were excessively sectarian and poorly attuned to the needs of the American environment.[41]

Pollack's defense of the Populists from some of their more intemperate critics, largely sociologists and political scientists, has been useful. He has, I think, at least made us realize that Populism had a humane and progressive side as well as a retrograde, nativist one. He has not, however, made many converts to his major thesis — the viability of the Populist tradition — even among the New Left. Despite his impassioned pleading, Populism appears too *petit bourgeois* and too intellectually ambiguous to serve as part of our radical past.[42] His chief allies appear to be men identified with the old liberal Left who have retained their sympathy for insurgent rural America.[43] More congenial as ancestors for the New Leftists than the provincial dissenters of the 1890's are the certified urban radicals, the Socialists and anarchists. Williams, after — in *The Contours* — dismissing the Socialists of this era as impotent, later converts them into seers "who made between 1890 and 1917 the most relevant and mature adaptation to the end of

[41] Pollack's major statement of his position will be found in *The Populist Response to Industrial America* (Cambridge, Mass., 1962), but see also the following articles: "Hofstadter on Populism: A Critique of 'The Age of Reform,'" *Journal of Southern History*, XXVI (Nov. 1960), 478–500, "The Myth of Populist Anti-Semitism," *American Historical Review*, LXVIII (Oct. 1962), 76–80, "Handlin on Anti-Semitism: A Critique of 'American Views of the Jew,'" *Journal of American History*, LI (Dec. 1964), 391–403, and "Fear of Man." The words quoted are from *Populist Response*, 82–83.

[42] Pollack has not been totally rejected by the New Left, but it seems to me that, if only by their silence, they suggest that they find his work unconvincing. For an outright attack on Pollack by a member of the Left, see Ann Lane's review of *Populist Response* in *Science and Society*, XXVIII (Summer 1964), 326 ff. It is interesting that the plausible forerunners of the Populists, the Jeffersonians and Jacksonians, have been virtually ignored by the New Left, Williams again excepted. The only suggestion of a new radical position on either of these movements that I have found is contained in two reviews of Benson's *Concept of Jacksonian Democracy*. In both cases the reviewers disapproved of Benson's attempt to place Jacksonian Democracy within the broad consensus framework. (See Lynd's review in *Commentary*, XXXIII [Apr. 1962], 366–68; Michael Lebowitz, "The Significance of Claptrap in American History," *Studies on the Left*, III [Winter 1963], 79 ff.)

[43] Writers like Walter T. K. Nugent, Robert F. Durden, Paul Holbo, and C. Vann Woodward, who have recently championed the agrarian insurgency of the 1890's, are in the last analysis to be seen rather as men of rural background defending a rural Neo-Populist tradition against an urban attack than as members of the New Left seeking to legitimate radicalism in America. (See Irwin Unger, "Critique of Norman Pollack," *Agricultural History*, XXXIX [Apr. 1965], 17–22.)

the frontier." [44] James Weinstein, editor of *Studies on the Left*, has made that journal virtually into an instrument for pulling Socialism into the mainstream of American history.

In this endeavor Weinstein is battling the prevailing view that Socialism failed in the United States because of its own inner inadequacies. On the contrary, he asserts, American Socialism did not fall; it was knocked down. After riding a great popular wave during World War I, Socialism was smashed by the patriotic suppressions perpetrated by the Wilson administration.[45] Socialism is America's "hidden heritage," which has been maligned and abused as much by the historians as by the Attorney General. The historians "have provided little that is usable to the newly emerging American left." "But not all generations," he concludes, in a manifesto, "have an equal stake in obscuring the past. Hopefully the new historians of American radicalism will be more disposed to learn from it, and less inclined to bend it, however subconsciously, to their more narrow and immediate purpose." [46]

Weinstein's concern is with the mainstream Socialism of Eugene Debs. But part of the New Left prefers anarchism to Socialism and has sought to recover an antiauthoritarian radical past for the United States. Richard Drinnon, a self-declared radical, has written a sympathetic biography of anarchist Emma Goldman that turns that eccentric but truly interesting woman not only into a "courageous, compassionate, intelligent human being" but into a prophetess of dangerous totalitarian tendencies within the Left.[47] Henry David Thoreau is another radical who appeals to the anarchist Left. When Lynd recently questioned Thoreau's pacifist and anarchist credentials, the resulting furor amply confirmed his claim that the author of *Civil Disobedience* had "become the patron saint of the new radicals and of all unadjusted Americans." [48]

The young men of the Left find it possible to identify with the political failures, and outcasts. Urban middle-class reform, on the other hand, earns their contempt. Gabriel Kolko considers the progressive movement a fraud.

[44] In a symposium on Socialism published in *New Politics*, I (Spring 1962), 40.

[45] See James Weinstein, "Anti-War Sentiment and the Socialist Party, 1917–1918," *Political Science Quarterly*, LXXIV (June 1959), *passim*, and "Socialism's Hidden Heritage: Scholarship Reinforces Political Mythology," *Studies on the Left*, III (Fall 1963), *passim*; see also Weinstein's exchange with Gerald Friedberg, *ibid.*, IV (Summer 1964), 79–97.

[46] Weinstein, "Socialism's Hidden Heritage," 108. Weinstein is not an unbalanced doctrinaire. In defending American Socialism against Friedberg's charge of inner failure he concedes that "a tradition of political democracy, relative social mobility, and a generally increasing standard of living made possible by the expansion of American capitalism from the end of the Civil War to the middle 1920's" kept Socialism in America from becoming "a majority political movement." (See the exchange with Friedberg [p. 90], cited in note 45, above.)

[47] Drinnon, *Rebel in Paradise*, vii *et passim*.

[48] Staughton Lynd, "Henry Thoreau: The Admirable Radical," *Liberation*, VII (Feb. 1963), 21 ff.; for the response to Lynd's article, see *ibid.*, VIII (Apr. 1963), 22 ff.

The mass of early twentieth-century legislation ostensibly designed to regulate business in the interest of the common good was really engineered by businessmen themselves, anxious to prevent destructive competition.[49] The combination of glittering promise and empty performance in progressivism in the end headed off "the radical potential of mass grievances and aspirations of genuine progressivism," or, in other words, of true social reconstruction.[50] Martin J. Sklar tells us that Progressivism was a movement

> led by and consisting of large corporate interests and political and intellectual leaders affirming the large corporate industrial capital system, and convinced of the necessity of institutionalizing reforms, legal and otherwise, to accommodate the nation's law and habits and the people's thinking, to the new corporate business structure and its requirements, domestic and foreign.[51]

While Sklar, unlike Kolko, concedes that what emerged was reform and not mere sham, it is as difficult to recognize in his Progressivism as in Kolko's anything of the humanitarianism, the self-criticism, and the social imagination that historians have generally found in the liberal political movements of the early twentieth century.

The New Left treatment of the New Deal so far has been skimpy. But it is fairly clear, from some interesting fragments, what it will look like when it fully emerges. In a sharply critical review of Arthur Schlesinger, Jr.'s, *The Age of Roosevelt*, Jacob Cohen declares the "New Deal marks the last act . . . by which American politics accommodated itself to the problems of economic justice raised by the system of countervailing powers." He denies to Roosevelt and his associates the honorable label of "pragmatists." Pragmatism possesses a vision of society out of which true social experimentalism can emerge. The New Deal was goalless and aimless, without either moral or practical purposes.[52] "In the long run what *did* the New Deal do?" asks Marc Schleifer.

> Are there other, more flourishing offspring of the corporate and progressive income tax than Madison Avenue expense-account culture,

[49] In this insistence on the competitive nature of late nineteenth- and early twentieth-century business enterprise, Kolko is at serious odds with the old Left and the traditional Marxist thesis of the growing monopolization of the American economy. He also disagrees, of course, with the Populist-progressive view of economic trends during the period.

[50] Gabriel Kolko, *The Triumph of Conservatism: A Reinterpretation of American History, 1900–1916* (New York, 1963), *passim*, esp. 285. The same theme in a narrower compass may be found in Kolko's volume on railroad legislation during the progressive period. (See *id., Railroads and Regulation, 1877–1916* [Princeton, N.J., 1965].)

[51] Martin J. Sklar, "Woodrow Wilson and the Political Economy of Modern United States Liberalism," *Studies on the Left*, I (No. 3, 1960), 17 ff., esp. 40.

[52] Jacob Cohen, "Schlesinger and the New Deal," *Dissent*, VIII (Autumn 1961), 461 ff. It is interesting to compare this long review of *The Age of Roosevelt* with another by an orthodox Marxist. The latter, written under the pseudonym "George Brand," is far more sympathetic. (See George Brand, "Toward a History of the New Deal," *Monthly Review*, XII [May 1960], 28 ff.)

and the Pentagon? With the exception of Jimmy Hoffa and a few remnant leftist unions, what significance and militant honor is there now in a "strong" trade union movement? Who can better remember Pearl Harbor than the hundreds of thousands of dead Chinese, Koreans, Vietnamese, Laotians, Filipinos, etc., we have killed since the end of the Second World War? [53]

The New Left's harsh judgment of twentieth-century reform is not, I suggest, the inevitable conclusion imposed by the facts. It is dictated, in the first place, by ideological predispositions. Young Left historians like Kolko cannot endorse any political movement that did not aim at a cooperative society. Progressivism also gets bad marks, one suspects, because it was so eminently respectable. Kolko characteristically attacks the muckrakers as men "with commonplace talents and middle class values." [54] The assault on the New Deal, on the other hand, is a more complex matter. For some of the New Leftists it is an adolescent blow for independence. The New Deal was the political faith of their parents in a quite literal way. In rejecting it they are rejecting their fathers and their fathers' faith.[55] For others, as Schleifer's polemic suggests, the New Deal is the immediate source of the liberal welfare state, and they despise it as much as they do the flaccid, self-satisfied society that they hold is its direct descendant.

Each of these reform movements poses a problem of identification for the New Left. Whether they pass muster is not self-evident. To each must first be put a series of questions: Was it truly radical? Was it proletarian? What were its relations to the existing establishment? Each of the young men is asking himself: would I have supported it? For past reform movements there is, then, as yet no prescribed New Left canon of historical virtue, and the young Leftists are at this point groping for appropriate attitudes and responses. There is one exception to this uncertainty. There is no doubt how the young radicals would have responded to the movement for racial equality in America, and there is no ambiguity in their attitudes toward the historical champions of the Negro.

Without a doubt the struggle for Negro equality during the last century and a half has received more attention from the New Left than any other single "progressive" movement of our past. There is no need to belabor the present-mindedness of this concern. It flows from the intense immersion of the Left today in the problems of civil rights. What could be more obvious

[53] Marc Schleifer, "A Socialist Plea for Black Nationalism," *ibid.*, XV (Sept. 1963), 225 ff.

[54] Kolko, *Triumph of Conservatism*, 161.

[55] What else can we make of the following: "The more I came to think of it the more I came to hate my brainwashed childhood's beloved memory of Franklin Delano Roosevelt. Everybody's liberal Jewish middle-class parents will cry like mine if they ever read this. ('After all, didn't he save the Jews and take us out of the depression?') Because I am a Socialist, and not a liberal, I know the answer." (Schleifer, "Socialist Plea," 225–26.)

to even the most superficial student of history than that the battles of Little Rock, Selma, and Birmingham are the lineal descendants of those fought by the abolitionists and later by the Radical Republicans? To the New Left the label "New Abolitionists" for modern civil rights militants is more than a metaphor.[56]

In some sense, of course, the New Left history of abolitionism writes itself. There is no question about when to cheer and when to hiss; the problem is in identifying the historiographic, not the historical, heroes and villians. Up to this point, as we have seen, the New Left historians have been able to write history as rebuttal — rebuttal of some position of their professional elders. With the history of the American Negro, and the struggle over his lot and future, difficulties arise. The trouble is that the academic establishment already occupies the high ground. Even in the bad old days of the 1940's and 1950's the historiography of the race question in America was becoming radicalized. Paradoxically, at the very moment American historians were allegedly turning to the Right, they had adopted an egalitarian view of the Negro, and to a lesser extent were becoming more sympathetic to his friends. It was not Williams or Lynd who rehabilitated the abolitionists; it was Dwight Dumond and Gilbert Hobbs Barnes. It was not W. E. B. Du Bois or James Allen alone who were re-evaluating the accomplishments of black Reconstruction; Francis B. Simkins, Robert Woody, and Vernon Wharton were doing it equally well.[57] As far back as 1949 Arthur Schlesinger, Jr., who epitomizes for the New Left the academic as well as the political establishment, was insisting that the Civil War, however deplorable and destructive, did justify itself by destroying slavery.[58]

The New Left has compensated for this lack of a historiographic enemy, I believe, by singling out one of the few prominent middle generation historians who appears to be critical of the abolitionists. There may be legitimate grounds on which to quarrel with David Donald's work, but the

[56] Howard Zinn, SNCC: The New Abolitionists (Boston, 1964); see also Lynd's assertion that "the search for an American radical tradition should begin with the Abolitionists," since only they "punctured with the contempt it deserves, the white liberal hypocrisy that America is and has always been a democratic country without a feudal past. . . ." (Letter in Commentary, XXXV [Jan. 1963], 74.)

[57] The works referred to are: Dwight L. Dumond, Antislavery Origins of the Civil War in the United States (Ann Arbor, Mich., 1939); Gilbert Hobbs Barnes, The Anti-Slavery Impulse, 1830–1844 (New York, 1933); W. E. B. Du Bois, Black Reconstruction in America, 1860–1880 (New York, 1935); James Allen, Reconstruction, Battle for Democracy, 1865–1876 (New York, 1937); Francis B. Simkins and Robert Woody, South Carolina during Reconstruction (Chapel Hill, N.C., 1932); Vernon Wharton, The Negro in Mississippi, 1865–1890 (Chapel Hill, N.C., 1947). It would of course be a mistake to equate these older "liberals" with the New Left radicals. Their sympathies for the Negro and his friends did not run as deep, nor were they as unequivocal, as those of the young Leftists of today. Still, the advent of the Whartons and the Dumonds in the 1930's and 1940's represents a distinctly liberal shift in the historical treatment of race in America.

[58] Arthur Schlesinger, Jr., "The Causes of the Civil War: A Note on Historical Sentimentalism," Partisan Review, XVI (Oct. 1949), 969–81.

Left, I believe, chiefly dislikes his reluctance to accept the abolitionists at their own estimate. When, in 1956, in a composite social portrait of the abolitionists, and later in his *Charles Sumner and the Coming of the Civil War*, Donald suggested that antislavery men were not exempt from the ego drives, the neurotic compulsions, the personal failings, and the capacity for self-deception that afflict other men, he called down on his head the wrath of the neoabolitionists. Louis Ruchames charges Donald with "insensitivity to the evils of slavery." His biography of Sumner is "the subversion of the character of a founding father of American civil equality. . . ." [59] Fawn Brodie accuses Donald of performing a deft "surgical operation" on Sumner, not for the purpose of analyzing the man but to malign and discredit the cause he fought for.[60] Aileen Kraditor detects in Donald's essay, "Toward a Reconsideration of Abolitionists," as well as in Hofstadter's portrait of Wendell Phillips in *The American Political Tradition*, a "contempt for reform movements in general." [61]

It is not enough, I submit, for the New Left to make sentimental gestures. It is too bad that in their defense of the abolitionists they have not tackled the hard question Donald raises: why did so few out of so many Americans respond to the evil of slavery in such a way as to risk wealth, reputation, and even personal safety? A truly radical answer might be that America was so thoroughly and universally corrupt in its racial attitudes that only men who were virtually at war with their environment could really appreciate the evil of slavery and take an active and risky part in its destruction. Indeed, at least in part, this seems to be the implication of one New Left author, Leon Litwack, who notes that racist bigotry in ante bellum America pervaded every sector of society, including abolitionism itself.[62] Instead of such a bold assault on American values, however, the New Left

---

[59] Louis Ruchames, "The Pulitzer Prize Treatment of Charles Sumner," *Massachusetts Review*, II (Summer 1961), 761, 749.

[60] Fawn Brodie, "Who Defends the Abolitionist?" in *The Antislavery Vanguard: New Essays on the Abolitionists*, ed. Martin Duberman (Princeton, N.J., 1965), 52–67. This essay has been reprinted in *Dissent*, XII (Summer 1965), 348–59. The Duberman volume is a mine of New Left opinion on the antislavery movement. See particularly the essays by Lynd, Howard Zinn, and Duberman himself, in addition to Brodie's article. The essay by Silvan Tomkins, "The Psychology of Commitment: The Constructive Role of Violence and Suffering for the Individual and for His Society," suggests that the New Left has not been entirely willing to abandon social psychology to the older generation. The attempt to utilize psychology to reveal new things about the abolitionists, while at the same time avoiding the pitfall of behavioralism, is not successful, however. Tomkins merely clothes in psychological jargon the position of the Left that the evil of slavery was enough by itself to explain the abolitionist reaction to it.

[61] See Aileen Kraditor's review article, "The Abolitionist Rehabilitated," *Studies on the Left*, V (Spring 1965), 101. Actually the most "conservative" of Donald's writings is his essay, "An Excess of Democracy," reprinted in the paperback version of *Lincoln Reconsidered: Essays on the Civil War Era* (2d ed., New York, 1956), 208–35. This piece has not yet been noticed by the New Left, however.

[62] Leon Litwack, *North of Slavery: The Negro in the Free States, 1790–1860* (Chicago, 1961).

seldom does more than reiterate the evil of slavery — a fact no one seriously disputes — as sufficient explanation for the abolitionist impulse. In their anxiety to protect the civil rights movement, they have failed to face the obvious historical problem.

The abolitionists are a New Left "hero class." [63] To Pollack, at least, the Populists are another. Strangely, the wage earners of America do not seem to constitute a third. As a group, the "common people" receive little attention from the young radicals. Kolko and Michael Harrington, both young men of the Left, have "rediscovered" poverty in the United States after the liberals declared it extinct.[64] But although the continued presence of the poor in an ostensibly rich nation suggests still larger contrasts of wealth and condition in the past, neither work is, properly speaking, historical.

More satisfactory is Stephan Thernstrom's *Poverty and Progress*, a work that suggests how truly useful it can be to examine American mythology with the skeptical eye of the Left. Basically Thernstrom seeks to discover whether nineteenth-century America was really a land of opportunity for the laboring man. Unlike many of the new radicals, who, with Mills, confuse computers with conservatism, he is not afraid to use statistics or the insights of social psychology, and the resulting marriage of radical skepticism, and post-Beardian technique produces a lively offspring.

In his study of Newburyport in the mid-nineteenth century, Thernstrom puts the notion of America as a working-class paradise to the test. Whatever may have been true of the contemporary West, wages for common labor in the Massachusetts town between 1850 and 1880 were not high, he says, and the ubiquity of child and female labor demonstrates the inability of working men to support their families unaided. The community was not classless. Industrialism heightened social antagonism and aroused serious fears among the middle class, which sought to smother social unrest under the rhetoric of "the self-made man." The function, or at least the result, of this mythologizing was to turn class frustration into class guilt and reduce the danger of social upheaval by directing working-class discontent inward against the discontented themselves.[65]

Thus far it is easy to recognize the New Left tone. But the rest of the study is a first-rate piece of social analysis that transcends any special ideology. Was the myth of the self-made man valid, Thernstrom asks. In part. Ingeniously squeezing convincing conclusions out of the manuscript census returns, Thernstrom demonstrates that while few unskilled wage earners,

---

[63] The term is Rogow's in "Revolt against Social Equality," 370.

[64] Gabriel Kolko, *Wealth and Power in America: An Analysis of Social Class and Income Distribution* (New York, 1962); Michael Harrington, *The Other America: Poverty in the United States* (New York, 1964).

[65] Stephan Thernstrom, *Poverty and Progress: Social Mobility in a Nineteenth Century City* (Cambridge, Mass., 1964), Chaps. I–III.

native or immigrant, left the blue-collar class, their sons often did move up to semiskilled status, and, more interesting, it was possible for a working-class family, by exploiting every able-bodied member, and by "ruthless under consumption" to acquire some property, usually the family home.[66] In a word, mobility did exist in America, or at least in Newburyport, but it was limited and did not preclude class antagonisms and much human misery.

Thernstrom's book clearly opens up impressive possibilities for writing working-class history. Yet he has few followers or imitators among the New Left. The fact demands an explanation, for in the 1930's and 1940's, radical historians wrote passionate, engaged studies of the labor movement.[67] The answer, of course, is that the radical intellectuals no longer regard the laboring man in the same approving way. To the old Left the workingman was an object of both solicitude and hope. Time has made a mockery of both these sentiments. Industrial unionism has triumphed, but it is clear to the Left that it has only succeeded in creating another self-centered privileged class. As a social being the American wage earner has succumbed to the mindless distractions of consumerism; as a political being he and his leaders are among the chief supporters of the "Warfare State." The disillusion is profound, and, among some of the New Leftists, the working class has been replaced by the radical students and intellectuals themselves as the anticipated agents of progressive change.

If the New Left refuses to worship the wage earner, it more unexpectedly refuses to curse the businessmen. Kolko, at least obliquely, attacks the "revisionist" business historians for their uncritical appraisal of the robber barons,[68] and, in his studies of the progressive era and of railroad regulation, he pictures businessmen as operating covertly off stage in a way scarcely designed to win our approval.[69] Allen Solganick explicitly calls his recent article in *Science and Society* a "rebuttal" of the entrepreneurial school of business history.[70] But these two essays do not amount to much of an indictment, and we must place alongside such mild strictures of businessmen and their academic champions the rather favorable press provided by scholars like Williams, LaFeber, and Lynd.

While the New Left may not exalt workers at the expense of businessmen, surely, one assumes, they must reject a major premise of the new postwar history: the relative classlessness of America and the absence here of

---

[66] *Ibid.*, 80–137.

[67] E.g., Philip Foner, *History of the Labor Movement in the United States* (4 vols., New York, 1947–65); Leo Huberman, *The Labor Spy Racket* (New York, 1937).

[68] Gabriel Kolko, "The Premises of Business Revisionism," *Business History Review*, XXXIII (Autumn 1959), 335 ff.

[69] See esp. Kolko's *Railroads and Regulation, passim*.

[70] Allen Solganick, "The Robber Baron Concept and Its Revisionists," *Science and Society*, XXIX (Summer 1965), 257–69.

serious class conflict. No one really insists that revolution was endemic in the United States, but in at least two instances, surely, in the 1770's and again in the 1860's, Americans killed one another on American soil for reasons that appeared to them fundamental. Until recently most American historians — both Marxists and liberal progressives — were prepared to agree that on these two occasions something like a class conflict did occur in the United States. Then came the challenge. To the post–World War II historians the American Revolution was not a social cataclysm; it was a nationalist struggle for independence. Its sequel, the Constitution, was not a Thermidorian reaction but a popular document supported by all classes. The Civil War was not a struggle between industrial capitalism and agrarianism. It was generated by the failure of the political system, or the growth of rival sectional ideologies and mythologies, or the weakness of institutional bonds in America, or the mistakes and misdeeds of leaders and followers. There is indeed conflict in all this, but it is the conflict of the post-Beardian history: it is pluralistic rather than dualistic, psychic rather than material.

Now the challengers have themselves been challenged. Staughton Lynd of Yale University, chief New Left historian of the Revolution and the Confederation period, accepts a modified version of the class conflict motif. In an interesting brief study of Federalism in Dutchess County, New York, in the 1780's, Lynd concludes that the Beardian political dichotomy between Federalist magnates and Antifederalist yeomen is generally valid. The struggle over the Constitution, in the Hudson Valley at least, does have many of the elements of a dualistic class struggle. On the other hand he acknowledges serious flaws in the Beard-Becker interpretation. The adoption struggle was not one between former Tory Federalists and former patriot Antifederalists but between large magnates and landlords on one side and the yeomanry led by the lesser gentry on the other.[71] In an article in the Marxist journal *Science and Society*, Lynd gives us a still more muted Beardianism. If the New York experience is any guide, he tells us, the Constitution in its genesis was neither an antidemocratic weapon of an elite, nor a timeless, neutral distillation of political wisdom. Admittedly the Federalist leaders in New York were social conservatives. Yet they were also "deeply public-spirited men, critical of any tendency in each other to put private concerns before devotion to country and firmly committed to republican government." As for the party rank and file, they were often the city artisans who feared the foreign manufactures that the weak government under the Articles of Confederation could not exclude. Together these groups, the one fearful of the leveling spirit that had arisen during the war among the yeomanry and their leaders, the other anxious to pro-

---

[71] Staughton Lynd, *Anti-Federalism in Dutchess County, New York* (Chicago, 1962), *passim*. A more emphatic assertion of the theme of class struggle may be found in Lynd's article, "Who Should Rule at Home? Dutchess County, New York, in the American Revolution," *William and Mary Quarterly*, XVIII (July 1961), esp. 330–32.

tect its livelihood, succeeded in getting adopted a document that "established the most democratic government in any major nation of the world at that day." [72] This may be Beardian, but it is Beard in a highly sophisticated version and without the intrusive polemical tone.

Lynd's work on the Confederation period like Thernstrom's in social history reveals some of the possibilities of the New Left history. When used with imagination and flexibility it can tell us important things about complex historical events. In any case the questions the Left asks are still apt to be the interesting ones. Unfortunately that second great national crisis, the Civil War, has not received an equally perceptive treatment, although the work of Beard, Howard K. Beale, William B. Hesseltine, Du Bois, and others suggests the plausibility of a class conflict analysis.

The relative poverty of results arises, I think, from an intellectual and emotional dilemma that confronts the New Left historians when they contemplate the Civil War. On the one hand the war was a heroic battle for freedom, as the successful abolition of slavery attests. Was it also, as Beard and the Marxists would insist, a sectionalized struggle of classes with the North representing middle-class industrialism and the South aristocratic feudalism? If the latter, the New Left, with their jaundiced view of middle-class capitalist America, can at best be ambivalent about Union victory. If the former, where is class struggle? If both, how does one account for the selfish ruling class performing an act of such colossal generosity as emancipating the slaves? The old Left handled the problem in either of two ways. For Beard it scarcely existed; *The Rise of American Civilization* reveals him as relatively insensitive to the evils of slavery and harshly critical of the abolitionists. [73] There is, then, no crusade for freedom to embarrass him in his belief that the war was at heart an act of aggression by capitalists against agrarians. [74] A Marxist like James Allen, a man obviously alive to the moral issue of slavery, solves the problem by supposing the Radical Republicans, the agents of emancipation, to be also the political wing of a *progressive* industrial capitalist class. The war that freed the slaves also established the social preconditions for the eventual revolution. Both events in a word, were historically necessary and historically progressive. [75]

Neither of these solutions would seem possible for the New Left. One

<hr/>

[72] *Id.*, "Capitalism, Democracy and the United States Constitution: The Case of New York," *Science and Society*, XXVII (Fall 1963), 385–413.

[73] At least for the period before the rise of the Cotton Kingdom, Beard treats slavery as a benevolent institution, while he attacks the abolitionists for the "depths of their abuse and scurrility." As for the Radical Republicans, the particular postwar friends of the Negro, they are largely driven by a simple craving for power. (See Charles and Mary Beard, *The Rise of American Civilization* [2 vols., New York, 1933], I, 655, 698; II, 116.)

[74] Socialists like Irving Howe misread Beard, I think, when they claim him for the North in the Civil War. Unlike the Marxists, Beard never approved of the victory for industrial America, remaining sympathetic to the end to the agrarian society that the war presumably overthrew.

[75] Allen, *Reconstruction*, 17–28.

way to solve the difficulty is by acknowledging a sort of ambiguity in human affairs, which, in the last analysis, is fundamentally uncongenial to the New Left style. Irving Howe, who represents a bridge between the old and the New Left, notes that the war contained "a double truth." The conflict, he writes in a review of Edmund Wilson's *Patriotic Gore*, "did mark the victory of modern capitalism and did let loose those tendencies toward a centralized state which Wilson deplores, but also the Civil War brought to an end the system by which one man could own another and therefore . . . it represents a major turning in the moral development of the United States." [76] Similarly Howard Zinn, attempting to absolve the abolitionists from the grave charge of starting a bloody conflict, believes that, while the war was fought over slavery, it was not the result of the antislavery agitation. Paralleling the antipathy between abolitionist and slaveholder was a more potent conflict between "antitariff, antibank, anticapitalist [and] antinationalist" southern agrarians on the one side and the "natural political leaders and controllers of the national economy" on the other. It was the second group of antagonists who caused the war, for only they possessed sufficient power. But once the war had started, these powerless abolitionists transformed it into an irresistible attack on slavery! [77]

The other escape from the dilemma is to ignore, like Beard, the whole moral side of the great conflict. This is the course of Eugene Genovese of Sir George Williams University, one of the few confirmed Marxists among the young radical historians. Genovese redraws the economic lines between North and South and restores the struggle of material interests to the center of the stage. Slavery, at least by implication, caused the war, not because it aroused the moral indignation of the Western world, but because it isolated the South from the progressive economic currents of the day. Wedded to its slave system the South became increasingly feudal and backward. Ultimately "the South's slave civilization could not . . . coexist with an increasingly hostile, powerful and aggressive Northern Capitalism." [78]

[76] Irving Howe, "Edmund Wilson and the Sea Slugs," *Dissent*, X (Winter 1963), 70 ff.

[77] Howard Zinn, "The Tactics of Agitation," in *Antislavery Vanguard*, ed. Duberman, 445.

[78] Eugene Genovese, "The Slave South: An Interpretation," *Science and Society*, XXV (Dec. 1961), 320 ff. I do not mean to say that Genovese is a crude economic determinist: quite the contrary. In arguing, as he does, that slavery was an economic blight on the South, he introduces, quite properly, I believe, considerations of social values, the South's self-image, and other factors not usually encountered in a strict Marxist interpretation. For an extended treatment of his view on slavery, see his book, *The Political Economy of Slavery* (New York, 1965). Another example of a relatively "hard line" class conflict analysis of the Civil War is the chapter, "The American Civil War: The Last Capitalist Revolution," in Barrington Moore, Jr.'s, recent book, *Social Origins of Dictatorship and Democracy: Lord and Peasant in the Making of the Modern World* (Boston, 1966), 111–55. Moore's estimate of the war, "reached after much uncertainty," is that the struggle "was the last revolutionary offensive on the part of what one may legitimately call urban or bourgeois capitalism." (See page 112.) Moore is not,

The new Left counterattack on the historiographic trends of the last twenty years is still in its early stages. We see at present only the tip of the iceberg. Beneath the surface still lies the main mass of young radical scholars just now completing their training at the major cosmopolitan graduate schools. In the next few years these young men will be joining in the attempt to reconstruct a coherent Leftist view of the American past,[79] and in a period when the American intelligentsia has become fascinated by the radical student movement, these young historians will receive, I predict, an unusual amount of attention and display.[80] If for no other reason, then, than their impact on the literate public, they will have to be reckoned with by their professional elders. But they must also be listened to for the health of the historical profession. No discipline should be without a dialogue, least of all one that represents a difficult and problematical marriage of the humanities and the social sciences. Unanimity is fine in science; unanimity over the nature of man's past suggests either an official line or a disturbing poverty of imagination. Neither circumstance can be applauded by an honest scholar no matter what his ideological allegiance.

But prudential motives aside, does the New Left history deserve the attention of the senior men? I think it does. True, there has yet been no young radical scholar of arresting style or impressive technique. But, of course, great historians, unlike great mathematicians, are made, not born. For a group composed almost entirely of men and women in their thirties, the young radicals have done work that deserves respect. They cannot compete in craftsmanship with the men they have chosen to oppose, but surely we ought to extend to them the same courtesy of judging them against their peers that we extend to the more conventional younger scholars.

Ultimately, of course, their reception must depend not on their craft

---

of course, of the same generation as the New Leftists, but as noted above (note 13) the young radicals turn to him for inspiration.

[79] By now it is clear that this is becoming a conscious and organized goal of the Students for a Democratic Society, the largest of the New Left groups. The SDS has established within the last year the Radical Education Project, which has assumed as one of its tasks the writing of "radical history," for the purpose, as one REP letter puts it, of equipping "outrage with precision." The REP has already published its first Occasional Paper on American History, "Towards a Democratic History," by Professor Jesse Lemisch of the University of Chicago. This is both a brief review of what has been done and a call to further effort. For additional details, see "American Radical History: A Progress Report," *New Left Notes*, Jan. 13, 1967, 2. Mr. John Roberts of NYU called the REP and its plans to my attention.

[80] This fascination has already been exhibited in the extraordinary attention given Christopher Lasch's book, *The New Radicalism in America, 1889–1963: The Intellectual as a Social Type* (New York, 1965). This work, a series of lively and perceptive vignettes of various cultural radicals, is held together by an opaque and confusing thesis that actually defies all categories of Left or Right. Despite the ambiguities, Lasch has been lionized by the intellectual community, less I believe for his very real merits than for the fact that he writes in a literate way about two subjects irresistible to the intellectuals: the Left and themselves.

but on their content. Do they have anything to say that is worth listening to for its own sake? At their best I believe they do. As a historian personally convinced that Americans encountered a narrower range of cultural and political experience than did Europeans, I do not take seriously the reassertion of class war of some of the more militant radical scholars. But the work of Thernstrom, LaFeber, and even Williams is a useful antidote to the self-congratulatory note that may be found among some of the post–World War II historians. America may not exhibit as grim a record of exploitation and brutality as Romanov Russia or Bourbon Spain or Regency England, but it had its agonies and its injustices. More important, it had its evasions and its "unfinished revolutions." American "exceptionalism" did not include total exemption from the ills that societies are heir to; it most emphatically did not exclude failure.

But there is also a debit side of the ledger. The New Left has frequently confused intellectual disagreement with the battle of generations and has often failed to play the scholarly game by the most elementary rules of fair play. The young radicals are often bad tempered. In their civic concerns they are angry dissenters from the nation's current foreign and domestic policies, and they sometimes allow the tone and rhetoric of the picket line and the handbill to invade their professional work. The historical "establishment" is not the political establishment in Washington, and the young men of the Left must not treat scholarship as an opportunity for a political harangue.

But beyond these matters of taste there are weaknesses in the emerging class conflict history that threaten to stultify the whole New Left historical enterprise. The young radicals' rejection of the historical currents since 1945 has all too often implied a denial not only of "consensus" conclusions but also of the social sciences and the new statistical methodology. Admittedly both of these new methods can be abused, but by rejecting these analytical tools the young radical historians are, in effect, disarming themselves and perhaps, ultimately, are consigning their efforts to sterility. Their response is all the more surprising when we recall the old Left's respect for science and for "scientific" history.

But most disturbing of all is the New Left's exaggerated present-mindedness. It suggests a contempt for pure history, history that has not enlisted in the good fight. The young radicals' efforts are generally governed not by the natural dialogue of the discipline but by the concerns of the outside cultural and political world. Clio at their behest has donned a uniform and does battle for social virtue. It is true that a number of the middle generation have themselves been influenced by a conservative political bias; more common among them, as we have seen, is a political neutrality which, however inadequate for citizenship, is surely useful for scholarship.

It would be a pity if their social consciousness uncritically committed the emerging generation of American scholars to any prescribed reading of the American past. It would mean the loss of much youthful talent for history. It would also be a loss for the American political Left. If history has any programmatic value, surely it must be history that is allowed to speak for itself. Let the New Left ask its own questions of the past, but let the past then say its piece. America may well be "exceptional." Knowing it may be ultimately more useful for the Left than denying it. And in the end there is no need to confuse the truths of the past with the needs of the present and future. The complexities and perplexities of the next few decades may well justify the cooperative commonwealth without the need to play tricks on the dead.